Number 58599   Friday 1 February 2008   http://www.london-gazette.co.uk   1

Registered as a newspaper
Published by Authority
Established 1665

The London Gazette

of Thursday 31 January 2008
Supplement No. 2

List of Statutory Publications 2006

Contents

Preliminary Information	2
UK Legislation	**4**
Public general acts	4
Public general acts - explanatory notes	9
Local acts	11
Measures of the General Synod	11
Other statutory publications	12
Statutory Instruments, by subject heading	12
Statutory Instruments, by number	294
Subsidiary Numbers	331
Scottish Legislation	**338**
Other Scottish statutory publications	338
Acts of the Scottish Parliament	338
Acts of the Scottish Parliament - Explanatory notes	340
Scottish Statutory Instruments, by subject heading	340
Scottish Statutory Instruments, by number	396
Northern Ireland Legislation	**404**
Other Northern Ireland statutory publications	404
Statutory Rules of Northern Ireland, by subject heading	404
Statutory Rules of Northern Ireland, by number	446
Alphabetical Index	**453**

Preface

Content and Layout

This list contains details of the statutory publications and accompanying Explanatory Notes published during the month. It is arranged in three main sections that group the primary and delegated legislation of the United Kingdom, Scotland and Northern Ireland (Statutory Instruments made by the National Assembly for Wales are included within the UK section). Within each section the publications are listed in the same order:

- Acts and their Explanatory Notes;
- Statutory Instruments or Statutory Rules, arranged under subject headings. (Each entry includes, where available or appropriate: the enabling power; the date when the instrument was issued, made and laid and comes into force; a short note of any effect; territorial extent and classification; a note of the relevant EU legislation; pagination; ISBN and price);
- A numerical listing of the instruments, with their subject heading. This list also includes any subsidiary numbers in the series: C for commencement orders; L for instruments relating to court fees or procedure in England and Wales; NI for Orders in Council relating only to Northern Ireland; W for instruments made by the National Assembly for Wales;

There is a single alphabetical, subject index, which includes both subject headings and descriptive terms from the title. The index is cumulated throughout the year

Unpublished Statutory Instruments

Although the majority of Statutory Instruments are formally published, some SIs of limited, local application are unpublished. These are listed in this publication when they have been received and processed by the TSO Bibliographic Department, not necessarily in the month they are issued. This causes some discontinuity in the number sequence, which is resolved in the annual listing, which lists the complete number sequences.

Access to Documents

The full text of all legislation and delegated legislation (Statutory Instruments) is available from the OPSI website on the day of publication. The website contaians legislation dating back to 1998 for Acts and 1987 for Statuttory Instruments.

The relevant web addresses:

UK Acts and Statutory Instruments
www.opsi.gov.uk/legislation/uk.htm

Scottish Acts and Statutory Instruments
www.opsi.gov.uk/legislation/scotland/about.htm

Northern Ireland Acts and Statutory Rules
www.opsi.gov.uk/legislation/northernireland/ni_legislation.htm

Welsh Statutory Instruments
www.opsi.gov.uk/legislation/wales/wales_legislation.htm

The full text of the general statutory instruments and statutory rules are also published in the respective annual editions of: *Statutory Instruments, Scottish Statutory Instruments, Statutory Instruments made by the National Assembly for Wales* and *Statutory Rules of Northern Ireland.*

Copies of legislation and published delegated legislation can be purchased from the addresses on the back cover. Copies of local instruments unobtainable from The Stationery Office may be obtained at prevailing prices from:

- Her Majesty's Stationery Office, Statutory Publications Unit, Admiralty Arch, North Entrance, the Mall, London, SW1A 2WH (from 1922 onwards – except for the years 1942, 1950, 1951 and up to SI no. 940 of 1952)
- Reader Information Services Department, The National Archives, Kew, Richmond, Surrey TW9 4DU (as before, up to 1960)
- British Library, Official Publications and Social Sciences Service, 96 Euston Road, London, NW1 2DB (as before, up to 1980)

Standing Orders

Standing orders can be set up to ensure the receipt of all statutory publications in a particular subject area, without the need to continually scan lists of new publications or place individual orders. The subject categories used can be either broad or very specific. For more information please contact the TSO Standing Orders department on 0870 600 5522, or fax 0870 600 5533.

Copyright

Most Stationery Office publications are Crown or Parliamentary copyright. Information about the licensing arrangements for Crown and Parliamentary copyright can be found on the Office of Public Sector Information's website at www.opsi.gov.uk. Alternatively, you can apply for a licence by contacting OPSI at the following address:

Office of Public Sector Information
Licensing Division
St Clements House
2-16 Colegate
Norwich NR3 1BQ
Telephone: 01603 621000 Fax 01603 723000
Web: *http://www.opsi.gov.uk/click-use/index.htm*

List of Abbreviations

accord.	accordance
art(s).	article(s)
c.	chapter
C.	Commencement
CI.	Channel Islands
E.	England
EC	European Commission
EU	European Union
G.	Guernsey
GB.	Great Britain
GLA	Greater London Authority
IOM	Isle of Man
J.	Jersey
L.	Legal: fees or procedure in courts in E. & W.
NI.	Northern Ireland
para(s).	paragraph(s)
reg(s).	regulation(s)
s(s).	section(s)
S.	Scotland
sch(s).	schedule(s)
SI.	Statutory instrument(s)
SR.	Statutory rule(s) of Northern Ireland
SR & O.	Statutory rules and orders
SSI	Scottish Statutory Instrument
UK.	United Kingdom
W.	Wales

UK Legislation

Acts

Public General Acts 2006

Animal Welfare Act 2006: Elizabeth II. Chapter 45. - iii, 51p.: 30 cm. - Royal assent, 8th November 2006. An Act to make provision about animal welfare. Explanatory notes have been produced to assist in the understanding of this Act and are available separately (ISBN 9780105645061). - 978-0-10-544206-6 *£9.00*

Appropriation Act 2006: Elizabeth II. Chapter 6. - 30p.: 30 cm. - Royal assent, 30th March 2006. An Act to authorise the use of resources for the service of the years ending with 31st March 2005 and 31st March 2006 and to apply certain sums out of the Consolidated Fund to the service of the year ending with 31st March 2006; and to appropriate the supply authorised in this Session of Parliament for the service of the year ending with 31st March 2005 and the further supply authorised in this session of Parliament for the service of the year ending with 31st March 2006. - 978-0-10-540606-8 *£5.50*

Appropriation (No. 2) Act 2006: Elizabeth II. Chapter 24. - v, 72p.: 30 cm. - Royal assent, 19th July 2006. An Act to authorise the use of resources for the service of the year ending with 31st March 2007 and to apply certain sums out of the Consolidated Fund to the service of the year ending with 31st March 2007; to appropriate the supply authorised in this session of Parliament for the service of the year ending with 31st March 2007; to repeal certain Consolidated Fund and Appropriation Acts. - 978-0-10-542406-2 *£12.00*

Armed Forces Act 2006: Elizabeth II. Chapter 52. - xx, 323p.: 30 cm. - Royal assent, 8th November 2006. An Act to make provision with respect to the armed forces. Explanatory notes have been produced to assist in the understanding of this Act and are be available separately (ISBN 0105652067). - 978-0-10-544406-0 *£34.00*

Charities Act 2006: Elizabeth II. Chapter 50. - vi, 182p.: 30 cm. - An Act to provide for the establishment and functions of the Charity Commission for England and Wales and the Charity Tribunal; to make other amendments of the law about charities, including provision about charitable incorporated organisations; to make further provision about public charitable collections and other fund-raising carried on in connection with charities and other institutions; to make other provision about the funding of such institutions. Royal assent, 8th November 2006. Explanatory notes have been produced to assist in the understanding of this Act and are available separately (ISBN 0105650064). - 978-0-10-545006-1 *£26.00*

Childcare Act 2006: Elizabeth II. Chapter 21. - vi, 72p.: 30 cm. - Royal assent, 11th July 2006. An Act to make provision about the powers and duties of local authorities and other bodies in England in relation to the improvement of the well-being of young children; to make provision about the powers and duties of local authorities in England and Wales in relation to the provision of childcare and the provision of information to parents and other persons; to make provision about the regulation and inspection of childcare provision in England; to amend part 10A of the Children Act 1989 in relation to Wales. Explanatory notes have been produced to assist in the understanding of this Act and are available separately (ISBN 9780105631064). - 978-0-10-542106-1 *£12.00*

Children and Adoption Act 2006: Elizabeth II. Chapter 20. - ii, 27p.: 30 cm. - Royal assent, 21st June 2006. An Act to make provision as regards contact with children; to make provision as regards family assistance orders; to make provision about risk assessments; to make provision as regards adoptions with a foreign element. Explanatory notes have been produced to assist in the understanding of this Act and are available separately (ISBN 0105620068). - 978-0-10-542006-4 *£5.50*

Civil Aviation Act 2006: Elizabeth II. Chapter 34. - ii, 21p.: 30 cm. - Royal assent, 8th November 2006. An Act to make further provision about civil aviation, including provision about the funding of the Air Travel Trust. Explanatory notes have been produced to assist in the understanding of this Act and are available separately (ISBN 0105634069). - 978-0-10-543406-1 *£4.50*

Climate Change and Sustainable Energy Act 2006: Elizabeth II. Chapter 19. - ii, 21p.: 30 cm. - Royal assent, 21st June 2006. An Act to make provision about the reduction of emissions of greenhouse gases, the alleviation of fuel poverty, the promotion of microgeneration and the use of heat produced from renewable sources, compliance with building regulations relating to emissions of greenhouse gases and the use of fuel and power, the renewables obligation relating to the generation and supply of electricity and the adjustment of transmission charges for electricity. Explanatory notes to assist in the understanding of the Act are available separately (ISBN 010561906X). - 978-0-10-541906-8 *£4.50*

Commissioner for Older People (Wales) Act 2006: Elizabeth II. Chapter 30. - ii, 27p.: 30 cm. - Royal assent, 25th July 2006. An Act to establish and make provision about the office of Commissioner for Older People in Wales; to make provision about the functions of the Commissioner for Older People in Wales. Explanatory notes have been produced to assist in the understanding of this Act and are available separately (ISBN 0105630063). - 978-0-10-543006-3 *£5.50*

Commons Act 2006: Elizabeth II. Chapter 26. - iv, 51p.: 30 cm. - Royal assent, 19th July 2006. An Act to make provision about common land and town or village greens. Explanatory notes to the Act, prepared by the Department for Environment, Food and Rural Affairs, are available separately (ISBN 0105626066). - 978-0-10-542606-6 £9.00

Companies Act 2006: Elizabeth II. Chapter 46. - lix, 701p.: 30 cm. - An Act to reform company law and to restate the greater part of the enactments relating to companies; to make other provision relating to companies and other forms of business organisation; to make provision about directors' disqualification, business names, auditors and actuaries; to amend part 9 of the Enterprise Act 2002. Royal assent, 8th November 2006. Explanatory notes have been produced to assist in the understanding of this Act and are available separately (ISBN 9780105646068). A hardback version of the Act (ISBN 0108507076) and an accompanying document containing the table of origins and destinations to the Act are also available separately (ISBN 9780105659068). - 978-0-10-544606-4 £60.50

Companies Act 2006: [bound]: Elizabeth II. Chapter 46. - lix, 701p.: hdbk: 31 cm. - An Act to reform company law and to restate the greater part of the enactments relating to companies; to make other provision relating to companies and other forms of business organisation; to make provision about directors' disqualification, business names, auditors and actuaries; to amend part 9 of the Enterprise Act 2002. Royal assent, 8th November 2006. Explanatory notes have been produced to assist in the understanding of this Act and are available separately (ISBN 978010850783). A paperback version of the Act is also available separately (ISBN 9780105446064). An accompanying document containing the table of origins and destinations to the Act is also available (ISBN 9780105659068). - 978-0-10-850707-6 £100.00

Compensation Act 2006: Elizabeth II. Chapter 29. - ii, 17p.: 30 cm. - Royal assent, 25th July 2006. An Act to specify certain factors that may be taken into account by a court determining a claim in negligence or breach of statutory duty; to make provision about damages for mesothelioma; and to make provision for the regulation of claims management services. Explanatory notes have been produced to assist in the understanding of this Act and will be available separately. - 978-0-10-542906-7 £4.00

Consolidated Fund Act 2006: Elizabeth II. Chapter 54. - [8]p.: 30 cm. - Royal assent, 19 December 2006. An Act to authorise the use of resources for the service of the years ending with 31st March 2007 and 31st March 2008, and to apply certain sums out of the Consolidated Fund to the service of the years ending with 31st March 2007 and 31st March 2008. - 978-0-10-545406-9 £3.00

Consumer Credit Act 2006: Elizabeth II. Chapter 14. - iii, 71p.: 30 cm. - Royal assent, 30th March 2006. An Act to amend the Consumer Credit Act 1974; to extend the ombudsman scheme under the Financial Services and Markets Act 2000 to cover licensees under the Consumer Credit Act 1974. Explanatory notes have been produced to assist in the understanding of this Act and are available separately (ISBN 0105614068). - 978-0-10-541406-3 £9.00

Council Tax (New Valuation Lists for England) Act 2006: Elizabeth II. Chapter 7. - [8]p.: 30 cm. - Royal assent, 30th March 2006. An Act to make provision about the dates on which new valuation lists for the purposes of council tax must be compiled in relation to billing authorities in England. Explanatory notes have been produced to assist in the understanding of this Act and are available separately (ISBN 0105607061). - 978-0-10-540706-5 £3.00

Criminal Defence Service Act 2006: Elizabeth II. Chapter 9. - [12]p.: 30 cm. - Royal assent, 30th March 2006. An Act to make provision about representation funded as part of the Criminal Defence Service. Explanatory notes have been produced to assist in the understanding of this Act and are available separately (ISBN 0105609064). - 978-0-10-540906-9 £3.00

Education and Inspections Act 2006: Elizabeth II. Chapter 40. - x, 262p.: 30 cm. - Royal assent, 8th November 2006. Explanatory notes have been produced to assist in the understanding of this Act and are available separately (ISBN 9780105640066). An Act to make provision about primary, secondary and further education and about training; to make provision about food or drink provided on school premises or in connection with the provision of education or childcare; to provide for the establishment of an Office for Standards in Education, Children's Services and Skills and the appointment of Her Majesty's Chief Inspector of Education, Children's Services and Skills and make provision about the functions of that Office and that Chief Inspector; to provide for the amendment of references to local education authorities and children's services authorities; to amend section 29 of the Leasehold Reform Act 1967 in relation to university bodies- 978-0-10-544006-2 £31.00

Electoral Administration Act 2006: Elizabeth II. Chapter 22. - v, 146p.: 30 cm. - Royal assent, 11th July 2006. An Act to make provision in relation to the registration of electors and the keeping of electoral registration information; standing for election; the administration and conduct of elections and referendums; and the regulation of political parties. Explanatory notes have been produced to assist in the understanding of this Act and are available separately (ISBN 9780105622062). - 978-0-10-542206-8 £22.00

Emergency Workers (Obstruction) Act 2006: Elizabeth II. Chapter 39. - [2], 4p.: 30 cm. - Royal assent, 8th November 2006. An Act to make it an offence to obstruct or hinder persons who provide emergency services. - 978-0-10-543906-6 £3.00

Equality Act 2006: Elizabeth II. Chapter 3. - iv, 86p.: 30 cm. - An Act to make provision for the establishment of the Commission for Equality and Human Rights; to dissolve the Equal Opportunities Commission, the Commission for Racial Equality and the Disability Rights Commission; to make provision about discrimination on grounds of religion or belief; to enable provision to be made about discrimination on grounds of sexual orientation; to impose duties relating to sex discrimination on persons performing public functions; to amend the Disability Discrimination Act 1995. - Royal assent, 16th February 2006. Explanatory notes have been produced to assist in the understanding of this Act and are available separately (ISBN 0105603066). - 978-0-10-540306-7 £9.00

European Union (Accessions) Act 2006: Elizabeth II. Chapter 2. - [8]p.: 30 cm. - An Act to make provision consequential on the treaty concerning the accession of the Republic Bulgaria and Romania to the European Union, signed at Luxembourg on 25th April 2005; and to make provision in relation to the entitlement of nationals of those states to enter or reside in the United Kingdom as workers. - Royal assent, 16th February 2006. Explanatory notes have been produced to assist in the understanding of this Act and are available separately (ISBN 010560206X). - 978-0-10-540206-0 £3.00

Finance Act 2006: Elizabeth II. Chapter 25. - xi, 506p.: 30 cm. - Royal assent, 19th July 2006. An Act to grant certain duties, to alter other duties, and to amend the law relating to the National Debt and the Public Revenue, and to make further provision in connection with finance. - 978-0-10-542506-9 £45.00

Fraud Act 2006: Elizabeth II. Chapter 35. - [2], 16p.: 30 cm. - Royal assent, 8th November 2006. Explanatory note have been produced to assist in the understanding of this Act and are available separately (ISBN 9780105635062). An Act to make provision for, and in connection with, criminal liability for fraud and obtaining services dishonestly. - 978-0-10-543506-8 £3.50

Government of Wales Act 2006: Elizabeth II. Chapter 32. - vii, 203p.: 30 cm. - Royal assent, 25th July 2006. An Act to make provision about the government of Wales. Explanatory notes have been produced to assist in the understanding of this Act and are available separately (ISBN 0105632066). - 978-0-10-543206-7 £26.00

Health Act 2006: Elizabeth II. Chapter 28. - v, 91p.: 30 cm. - Royal assent, 19th July 2006. An Act to make provision for the prohibition of smoking in certain premises, places and vehicles and for amending the minimum age of persons to whom tobacco may be sold; to make provision in relation to the prevention and control of health care associated infections; to make provision in relation to the management and use of controlled drugs; to make provision in relation to the supervision of certain dealings with medicinal products and the running of pharmacy premises, and about orders under the Medicines Act 1968 and orders amending that Act under the Health Act 1999; to make further provision about the National Health Service in England and Wales, and about the recovery of National Health Service costs; to make provision for the establishment and functions of the Appointments Commission: to make further provision about the exercise of social care training functions. Explanatory notes, prepared by the Department of Health, have been produced to assist in the understanding of this Act and are available separately (ISBN 0105628069). - 978-0-10-542806-0 £13.50

Housing Corporation (Delegation) etc. Act 2006: Elizabeth II. Chapter 27. - [8]p.: 30 cm. - An Act to make provision about the delegation of functions by the Housing Corporation and Housing for Wales and about the validation of things done or evidenced by, and the authentication of the fixing of, their seals. - Royal assent, 19th July 2006. Explanatory notes have been produced to assist in the understanding of this Act and will be available separately. - 978-0-10-542706-3 £3.00

Identity Cards Act 2006: Elizabeth II. Chapter 15. - ii, 45p.: 30 cm. - Royal assent, 30th March 2006. An Act to make provision for a national scheme of registration of individuals and for the issue of cards capable of being used for identifying registered individuals; to make it an offence for a person to be in possession or control of an identity document to which he is not entitled, or of apparatus, articles or materials for making false identity documents; to amend the Consular Fees Act 1980; to make provision facilitating the verification of information provided with an application for a passport. Explanatory notes have been produced to assist in the understanding of this Act and are available separately (ISBN 0105615064). - 978-0-10-541506-0 £6.50

Immigration, Asylum and Nationality Act 2006: Elizabeth II. Chapter 13. - iii, 38p.: 30 cm. - Royal assent, 30th March 2006. An Act to make provision about immigration, asylum and nationality. Explanatory notes have been produced to assist in the understanding of this Act and are available separately (ISBN 0105613061). - 978-0-10-541306-6 £6.50

International Development (Reporting and Transparency) Act 2006: Elizabeth II. Chapter 31. - [12]p.: 30 cm. - Royal assent, 25th July 2006. An Act to require the Secretary of State to report annually on total expenditure on international aid and on the breakdown of such aid, and in particular on progress towards the target for expenditure on official development assistance to constitute 0.7 per cent of gross national income; to require such reports to contain information about expenditure by country, about the proportion of expenditure in low income countries and about the effectiveness of aid expenditure and the transparency of international aid. - 978-0-10-543106-0 £3.00

Investment Exchanges and Clearing Houses Act 2006: Elizabeth II. Chapter 55. - [12]p.: 30 cm. - Royal assent, 19 December 2006. An Act to confer power on the Financial Services Authority to disallow excessive regulatory provision by recognised investment exchanges and clearing houses. Explanatory notes have been produced to assist in the understanding of this Act and are available separately (ISBN 9780105655060). - 978-0-10-545506-6 £3.00

Legislative and Regulatory Reform Act 2006: Elizabeth II. Chapter 51. - ii, 23p.: 30 cm. - Royal assent, 8th November 2006. An Act to enable provision to be made for the purpose of removing or reducing burdens resulting from legislation and promoting regulatory principles; to make provision about the exercise of regulatory functions; to make provision about the interpretation of legislation relating to the European Communities and the European Economic Area; to make provision relating to section 2 (2) of the European Communities Act 1972. Explanatory notes have been produced to assist in the understanding of this Act and are available separately (ISBN 9780105651062). - 978-0-10-544306-3 £4.50

London Olympic Games and Paralympic Games Act 2006: Elizabeth II. Chapter 12. - ii, 51p.: 30 cm. - Royal assent, 30th March 2006. An Act to make provision in connection with the Olympic Games and Paralympic Games that are to take place in London in the year 2012; to amend the Olympic Symbol etc. (Protection) Act 1995. Explanatory notes have been produced to assist in the understanding of this Act and are available separately (ISBN 0105612065). - 978-0-10-541206-9 £7.50

Merchant Shipping (Pollution) Act 2006: Elizabeth II. Chapter 8. - [8]p.: 30 cm. - Royal assent, 30th March 2006. An Act to enable effect to be given to the Supplementary Fund Protocol 2003 and to future revisions of the international arrangements relating to compensation for oil pollution from ships; to enable effect to be given to Annex VI of the MARPOL Convention; and to amend section 178 (1) of the Merchant Shipping Act 1995. Explanatory notes have been produced to assist in the understanding of this Act and are available separately (ISBN 0105608068). - 978-0-10-540806-2 £3.00

National Health Service Act 2006: Elizabeth II. Chapter 41. - xiv, 258p.: 30 cm. - Royal assent, 8th November 2006. An Act to consolidate certain enactments relating to the health service. An accompanying document containing the table of origins to the Act is available separately (ISBN 9780105629054). - 978-0-10-545206-5 £31.00

National Health Service (Consequential Provisions) Act 2006: Elizabeth II. Chapter 43. - [2], 58p.: 30 cm. - Royal assent, 8th November 2006. An Act to make provision for repeals, revocations, consequential amendments, transitional and transitory modifications and savings in connection with the consolidation of enactments in the National Health Service Act 2006 and the National Health Service (Wales) Act 2006. A table of destinations relating to this Act is available separately (ISBN 9780105630050). - 978-0-10-545106-8 £9.00

National Health Service (Wales) Act 2006: Elizabeth II. Chapter 42. - xii, 183p.: 30 cm. - Royal assent, 8th November 2006. An Act to consolidate certain enactments relating to the health service. - 978-0-10-544506-7 £26.00

National Insurance Contributions Act 2006: Elizabeth II. Chapter 10. - 15p.: 30 cm. - Royal assent, 30th March 2006. An Act to make provision about national insurance contributions in cases where there is a retrospective change to the law relating to income tax and to enable related provision to be made for the purposes of contributory benefits, statutory payments and other matters; to make provision about the disclosure of information in relation to arrangements for the avoidance of national insurance contributions. Explanatory notes have been produced to assist in the understanding of this Act and will be available separately. - 978-0-10-541006-5 £3.50

National Lottery Act 2006: Elizabeth II. Chapter 23. - ii, 25p.: 30 cm. - Royal assent, 11th July 2006. An Act to make provision about the National Lottery. Explanatory notes to assist in the understanding of this Act are published separately (ISBN 0105623067). - 978-0-10-542306-5 £5.00

Natural Environment and Rural Communities Act 2006: Elizabeth II. Chapter 16. - vi, 107p.: 30 cm. - Royal assent, 30th March 2006. An Act to make provision about bodies concerned with the natural environment and rural communities; to make provision in connection with wildlife, sites of special scientific interest; National Parks and the Broads; to amend the law relating to rights of way; to make provision as to the Inland Waterways Amenity Advisory Council; to provide for flexible administrative arrangements in connection with functions relating to the environment and rural affairs and certain other functions. Explanatory notes have been produced to assist in the understanding of this Act and are available separately (ISBN 0105616060). - 978-0-10-541606-7 £10.50

NHS Redress Act 2006: Elizabeth II. Chapter 44. - [1], 12p.: 30 cm. - Royal assent, 8th November 2006. An Act to make provision about arrangements for redress in relation to liability in tort in connection with services provided as part of the health service in England or Wales. Explanatory notes have been produced and are available separately, see ISBN (0105644064). - 978-0-10-544106-9 £3.00

Northern Ireland Act 2006: Elizabeth II. Chapter 17. - [9]p.: 30 cm. - An Act to make provision for preparations for the restoration of devolved government in Northern Ireland and for the selection of persons to be Ministers on such restoration; to make provisions as to the consequences of selecting or not-selecting such persons. Royal assent, 8th May 2006. Explanatory notes have been produced to assist in the understanding of this Act and are available separately (ISBN 0105617067). - 978-0-10-541706-4 £3.00

Northern Ireland (Miscellaneous Provisions) Act 2006: Elizabeth II. Chapter 33. - iii, 41p.: 30 cm. - An Act to make provision about registration of electors and the Chief Electoral Officer for Northern Ireland; to amend the Northern Ireland Act 1998; to make provision about donations for political purposes; to extend the amnesty period for arms decommissioning in Northern Ireland; and to make miscellaneous amendments in the law relating to Northern Ireland. Royal assent, 25th July 2006. Explanatory notes have been produced to assist in the understanding of this Act and are available separately (ISBN 9780105633068). - 978-0-10-543306-4 £7.50

Northern Ireland (St Andrews Agreement) Act 2006: Elizabeth II. Chapter 53. - ii, 40p.: 30 cm. - Royal assent, 22nd November 2006. An Act to make provision for preparations for the restoration of devolved government in Northern Ireland in accordance with the St Andrews Agreement; to make provision as to the consequences of compliance, or non-compliance, with the St Andrews Agreement timetable; to amend the Northern Ireland Act 1998; to make provision about district policing partnerships; to amend the Education (Northern Ireland) Orders 1997 and 2006. Explanatory notes have been produced to assist in the understanding of this Act and are available separately (ISBN 0105653063). - 978-0-10-545306-2 £7.50

Northern Ireland (St Andrews Agreement) Act 2007: Elizabeth II. Chapter 4. - [8]p.: 30 cm. - Royal assent, 27th March 2007. An Act to modify the effect of the Northern Ireland (St Andrews Agreement) Act 2006. Explanatory notes have been produced to assist in the understanding of this Act and are available separately (ISBN 9780105604075). - 978-0-10-540407-1 £3.00

Parliamentary Costs Act 2006: Elizabeth II. Chapter 37. - ii, 11p.: 30 cm. - Royal assent, 8th November 2006. An Act to consolidate the House of Commons Costs Taxation Act 1847, the House of Lords Costs Taxation Act 1849, the Parliamentary Costs Act 1865, the Parliamentary Costs Act 1867, the Parliamentary Costs Act 1871 and the House of Commons Costs Taxation Act 1879, with amendments to give effect to recommendations of the Law Commission and the Scottish Law Commission. A table of origins and destinations relating to this Act is available separately (ISBN 0105633054). - 978-0-10-543706-2 £3.00

Police and Justice Act 2006: Elizabeth II. Chapter 48. - iv, 180p.: 30 cm. - Royal assent, 8th November 2006. An Act to establish a National Policing Improvement Agency; to make provision about police forces and police authorities and about police pensions; to make provision about police powers and about the powers and duties of community support officers, weights and measures inspectors and others; to make provision about the supply to the police and others of information contained in registers of death; to make further provision for combatting crime and disorder; to make further provision about certain inspectorates; to amend Part 12 of the Criminal Justice Act 2003; to amend the Computer Misuse Act 1990; to make provision about the forfeiture of indecent images of children; to provide for conferring of functions on the Independent Police Complaints Commission in relation to the exercise of enforcement functions by officials involved with immigration and asylum; to amend the Extradition Act 2003; to make further provision about the use of live links in criminal proceedings. Explanatory notes have been produced to assist in the understanding of this Act and are available separately (ISBN 010564806X). - 978-0-10-544806-8 £26.00

Racial and Religious Hatred Act 2006: Elizabeth II. Chapter 1. - [2], 8, [1]p.: 30 cm. - An Act to make provision about offences involving stirring up hatred against persons on racial or religious grounds. - Royal assent, 16th February 2006. - Explanatory notes have been produced to assist in the understanding of this Act and are available separately. - 978-0-10-540106-3 £3.00

Road Safety Act 2006: Elizabeth II. Chapter 49. - iii, 135p.: 30 cm. - Royal assent, 8th November 2006. An Act to make provision about road traffic, registration plates, vehicle and driver information, hackney carriages and private hire vehicles, and trunk road picnic areas. Explanatory notes have been produced to assist in the understanding of this Act and are available separately (ISBN 9780105649069). - 978-0-10-544906-5 £19.50

Safeguarding Vulnerable Groups Act 2006: Elizabeth II. Chapter 47. - iii, 88p.: 30 cm. - An Act to make provision in connection with the protection of children and vulnerable adults. Royal assent, 8th November 2006. Explanatory notes, prepared by the Department for Education and Skills, have been produced to assist in the understanding of this Act and are available separately (ISBN 9780105647065). - 978-0-10-544706-1 £13.50

Terrorism Act 2006: Elizabeth II. Chapter 11. - iii, 44p.: 30 cm. - Royal assent, 30th March 2006. An Act to make provision for and about offences relating to conduct carried out, or capable of being carried out, for purposes connected with Terrorism; to amend enactments relating to terrorism; to amend the Intelligence Services Act 1994 and the Regulation of Investigatory Powers Act 2000. Explanatory notes have been produced to assist in the understanding of this Act and are available separately (ISBN 9780105611066). - 978-0-10-541106-2 £6.50

Terrorism (Northern Ireland) Act 2006: Elizabeth II. Chapter 4. - [12]p.: 30 cm. - Royal assent, 16th February 2006. An Act to provide for Part 7 of the Terrorism Act 2000 to continue in force for a limited period after 18th February 2006 subject to modifications and to authorise the making of provision in connection with its ceasing to have effect. Explanatory notes have been produced to assist in the understanding of this Act are available separately (ISBN 0105604062). - 978-0-10-540406-4 £3.00

Transport (Wales) Act 2006: Elizabeth II. Chapter 5. - ii, 12p.: 30 cm. - An Act to make provision about transport to, from and within Wales. - Royal assent, 16th February 2006. Explanatory notes have been produced to assist in the understanding of this Act and are available separately (ISBN 0105605069). - 978-0-10-540506-1 £3.00

Violent Crime Reduction Act 2006: Elizabeth II. Chapter 38. - iv, 83p.: 30 cm. - Royal assent, 8th November 2006. An Act to make provision for reducing and dealing with the abuse of alcohol; to make provision about real and imitation firearms, about ammunition and about knives and other weapons; to amend the Football Spectators Act 1989 and the Football (Disorder) Act 2000; to amend the Sexual Offences Act 2003 and section 8 of the Crime and Disorder Act 1998; to amend section 23 of the Children and Young Persons Act 1969; to amend the Mobile Telephones (Reprogramming) Act 2002. Explanatory notes have been produced to assist in the understanding of this Act and are available separately (ISBN 0105638064). - 978-0-10-543806-9 £13.50

Wireless Telegraphy Act 2006: Elizabeth II. Chapter 36. - vi, 107p.: 30 cm. - Royal assent, 8th November 2006. An Act to consolidate enactments about wireless telegraphy. - 978-0-10-543606-5 £17.50

Work and Families Act 2006: Elizabeth II. Chapter 18. - ii, 23p.: 30 cm. - An Act to make provision about statutory rights to leave and pay in connection with the birth or adoption of children; to amend section 80F of the Employment Rights Act 1996; to make provision about workers' entitlement to annual leave; to provide for the increase in the sums specified in section 186 (1) and 227 (1) of that Act. - Royal assent, 21st June 2006. Explanatory notes have been produced to assist in the understanding of this Act and are available separately (ISBN 0105618063). - 978-0-10-541806-1 £5.00

Public General Acts - Explanatory Notes 2006

Animal Welfare Act 2006: chapter 45: explanatory notes. - 30p.: 30 cm. - These notes refer to the Animal Welfare Act 2006 (c. 45) (ISBN 9780105442066) which received Royal assent on 8 November 2006. - 978-0-10-564506-1 £5.50

Armed Forces Act 2006: chapter 52: explanatory notes. - 126p.: 30 cm. - These notes refer to the Armed Forces Act 2006 (c. 52) (ISBN 01054440651) which received Royal Assent on 8 November 2006. - 978-0-10-565206-9 £17.50

Charities Act 2006: chapter 50: explanatory notes. - 43p.: 30 cm. - These notes refer to the Charities Act 2006 (c. 50) (ISBN 0105450065) which received Royal assent on 8 November 2006. - 978-0-10-565006-5 £7.50

Childcare Act 2006: chapter 21: explanatory notes. - 29p.: 30 cm. - These notes refer to the Childcare Act 2006 (c. 21) (ISBN 0105421065) which received Royal assent on 11 July 2006. - 978-0-10-563106-4 £5.50

Children and Adoption Act 2006: chapter 20: explanatory notes. - 12p.: 30 cm. - These notes refer to the Children and Adoption Act 2006 (c. 20) (ISBN 0105420069) which received Royal Assent on 21 June 2006. - 978-0-10-562006-8 £3.00

Civil Aviation Act 2006: chapter 34: explanatory notes. - 12p.: 30 cm. - These notes refer to the Civil Aviation Act 2006 (c. 34) (ISBN 010543406X) which received Royal assent on 8 November 2006. - 978-0-10-563406-5 £3.00

Climate Change and Sustainable Energy Act 2006: chapter 19: explanatory notes. - 8p.: 30 cm. - These notes refer to the Climate Change and Sustainable Energy Act 2006 (c. 19) (ISBN 0105419060) which received Royal assent on 21 June 2006. - 978-0-10-561906-2 £3.00

Commissioner for Older People (Wales) Act 2006: chapter 30: explanatory notes. - 12p.: 30 cm. - These notes refer to the Commissioner for Older People (Wales) Act 2006 (c. 30) (ISBN 0105430064) which received Royal assent on 25 July 2006. - 978-0-10-563006-7 £3.00

Commons Act 2006: chapter 26: explanatory notes. - 53p.: 30 cm. - These notes refer to the Commons Act 2006 (c. 26) (ISBN 0105426067) which received Royal assent on 19 July 2006. - 978-0-10-562606-0 £9.00

Companies Act 2006: chapter 46: explanatory notes: [bound]. - 275p.: hdbk: 31 cm. - These notes refer to the Companies Act 2006 (c. 46) (ISBN 0108507076) (bound version) which received Royal Assent on 8th November 2006. Paperback versions of the Act (ISBN 0105446068) and the accompanying explanatory notes (ISBN 0105646067) are also available. - 978-0-10-850708-3 £80.00

Companies Act 2006: chapter 46: explanatory notes. - 275p.: 30 cm. - These notes refer to the Companies Act 2006 (c. 46) (ISBN 0105446068) which received Royal Assent on 8th November 2006. Hardback versions of the Act (ISBN 0108507076) and the accompanying explanatory notes (ISBN 0108507084) are also available- 978-0-10-564606-8 £31.00

Compensation Act 2006: chapter 29: explanatory notes. - 17p.: 30 cm. - These notes refer to the Compensation Act 2006 (c. 29) (ISBN 0105429066) which received Royal assent on 25 July 2006. - 978-0-10-562906-1 £3.50

Consumer Credit Act 2006: chapter 14: explanatory notes. - 32p.: 30 cm. - These notes refer to the Consumer Credit Act 2006 (c. 14) (ISBN 0105414069) which received Royal assent on 30th March 2006. - 978-0-10-561406-7 £5.50

Council Tax (New Valuation Lists for England) Act 2006: chapter 7: explanatory notes. - [8]p.: 30 cm. - These notes refer to the Council Tax (New Valuation Lists for England) Act 2006 (c. 7) (ISBN 0105407062) which received Royal assent on 30 March 2006. - 978-0-10-560706-9 £3.00

Criminal Defence Service Act 2006: chapter 9: explanatory notes. - 5p.: 30 cm. - These notes refer to the Criminal Defence Service Act 2006 (c. 9) (ISBN 0105609065) which received Royal assent on 30th March 2006. - 978-0-10-560906-3 £3.00

Education and Inspections Act 2006: chapter 40: explanatory notes. - 104p.: 30 cm. - These notes refer to the Education and Inspections Act 2006 (c. 40) (ISBN 010544006X) which received Royal assent on 8 November 2006. - 978-0-10-564006-6 £15.50

Electoral Administration Act 2006: chapter 22: explanatory notes. - 63p.: 30 cm. - These notes refer to the Electoral Administration Act 2006 (c. 22) (ISBN 0105422061) which received Royal assent on 11 July 2006. - 978-0-10-562206-2 £10.50

Equality Act 2006: chapter 3: explanatory notes. - 46p.: 30 cm. - These notes refer to the Equality Act 2006 (c. 3) (ISBN 0105403067) which received Royal assent on 16 February 2006. - 978-0-10-560306-1 £6.50

European Union (Accessions) Act 2006: chapter 2: explanatory notes. - [8]p.: 30 cm. - These notes refer to the European Union (Accessions) Act 2006 (c. 2) (ISBN 0105402060) which received Royal Assent on 16 February 2006. - 978-0-10-560206-4 £2.00

Fraud Act 2006: chapter 35: explanatory notes. - 14p.: 30 cm. - These notes refer to the Fraud Act 2006 (c. 35) (ISBN 0105435066) which received Royal assent on 8 November 2006. - 978-0-10-563506-2 £3.00

Government of Wales Act 2006: chapter 32: explanatory notes. - 126p.: 30 cm. - These notes refer to the Government of Wales Act 2006 (c. 32) (ISBN 0105432067) which received Royal assent on 25 July 2006. - 978-0-10-563206-1 £17.50

Health Act 2006: chapter 28: explanatory notes. - 49p.: 30 cm. - These notes refer to the Health Act 2006 (c. 28) (ISBN 010542806X) which received Royal assent on 19 July 2006. - 978-0-10-562806-4 £9.00

Identity Cards Act 2006: chapter 15: explanatory notes. - 30p.: 30 cm. - These notes refer to the Identity Cards Act 2006 (c. 15) (ISBN 0105415065) which received Royal Assent on 30 March 2006. - 978-0-10-561506-4 £5.50

Immigration, Asylum and Nationality Act 2006: chapter 13: explanatory notes. - 30p.: 30 cm. - These notes refer to the Immigration, Asylum and Nationality Act 2006 (c. 13) (ISBN 0105413062) which received Royal assent on 30th March 2006. - 978-0-10-561306-0 £5.50

Investment Exchanges and Clearing Houses Act 2006: chapter 55: explanatory notes. - [8]p.: 30 cm. - These notes refer to the Investment Exchanges and Clearing Houses Act 2006 (c. 55) (ISBN 0105455067) which received Royal assent on 19 December 2006. - 978-0-10-565506-0 £3.00

Legislative and Regulatory Reform Act 2006: chapter 51: explanatory notes. - 24p.: 30 cm. - These notes refer to the Legislative and Regulatory Reform Act 2006 (c. 51) (ISBN 0105443069) which received Royal assent on 8 November 2006. - 978-0-10-565106-2 £4.50

London Olympic Games and Paralympic Games Act 2006: chapter 12: explanatory notes. - 24p.: 30 cm. - These notes refer to the London Olympic Games and Paralympic Games Act 2006 (c. 12) (ISBN 0105412066) which received Royal assent on 30 March 2006. - 978-0-10-561206-3 £4.50

Merchant Shipping (Pollution) Act 2006: chapter 8: explanatory notes. - 8p.: 30 cm. - These notes refer to the Merchant Shipping (Pollution) Act 2006 (c. 8) (ISBN 0105408069) which received Royal assent on 30th March 2006. - 978-0-10-560806-6 £3.00

National Lottery Act 2006: chapter 23: explanatory notes. - 11p.: 30 cm. - These notes refer to the National Lottery Act 2006 (c. 23) (ISBN 0105423068) which received Royal assent on 11 July 2006. - 978-0-10-562306-9 £3.00

Natural Environment and Rural Communities Act 2006: chapter 16: explanatory notes. - 42p.: 30 cm. - These notes refer to the Natural Environment and Rural Communities Act 2006 (c.16) (ISBN 0105416061) which received Royal assent on 30 March 2006. With correction slip dated June 2006. - 978-0-10-561606-1 £6.50

Natural Environment and Rural Communities Act 2006: chapter 16: explanatory notes. - 1 sheet: 30 cm. - Correction slip dated June 2006 (to ISBN 0105616060). - 978-9-99-907089-8 *Free*

NHS Redress 2006: chapter 44: explanatory notes. - 12p.: 30 cm. - These notes refer to the NHS Redress 2006 (c. 44) (ISBN 0105441066) which received Royal assent on 8 November 2006. - 978-0-10-564406-4 £3.00

Northern Ireland Act 2006: chapter 17: explanatory notes. - 6p.: 30 cm. - These notes refer to the Northern Ireland Act 2006 (c. 17) (ISBN 0105417068) which received Royal Assent on 8th May 2006. - 978-0-10-561706-8 £3.00

Northern Ireland (Miscellaneous Provisions) Act 2006: chapter 33: explanatory notes. - 23p.: 30 cm. - These notes refer to the Northern Ireland (Miscellaneous Provisions) Act 2006 (c. 33) (ISBN 0105433063) which received Royal Assent on 25th July 2006. - 978-0-10-563306-8 £4.50

Northern Ireland (St Andrews Agreement) Act 2006: chapter 53: explanatory notes. - 22p.: 30 cm. - These notes refer to the Northern Ireland (St Andrews Agreement) Act 2006 (c. 53) (ISBN 0105453064) which received Royal Assent on 22 November 2006. - 978-0-10-565306-6 £4.50

Police and Justice Act 2006: chapter 48: explanatory notes. - 57p.: 30 cm. - These notes refer to the Police and Justice Act 2006 (c. 48) (ISBN 0105448060) which received Royal assent on 8 November 2006. - 978-0-10-564806-2 £9.00

Racial and Religious Hatred Act 2006: chapter 1: explanatory notes. - [4]p.: 30 cm. - These notes refer to the Racial and Religious Hatred Act 2006 (c. 1) (ISBN 0105401064) which received Royal Assent on 16th February 2006. - 978-0-10-560106-7 *£1.50*

Road Safety Act 2006: chapter 49: explanatory notes. - 30p.: 30 cm. - These notes refer to the Road Safety Act 2006 (c. 49) (ISBN 9780105449065) which received Royal assent on 8th November 2006. - 978-0-10-564906-9 *£5.50*

Safeguarding Vulnerable Groups Act 2006: chapter 47: explanatory notes. - 36p.: 30 cm. - These notes refer to the Safeguarding Vulnerable Groups Act 2006 (c. 47) (ISBN 0105447064) which received Royal assent on 8th November 2006. - 978-0-10-564706-5 *£5.50*

Terrorism Act 2006: chapter 11: explanatory notes. - 36p.: 30 cm. - These notes refer to the Terrorism Act 2006 (c. 11) (ISBN 010541106X) which received Royal Assent on 30 March 2006. - 978-0-10-561106-6 *£6.00*

Terrorism (Northern Ireland) Act 2006: chapter 4: explanatory notes. - [12]p.: 30 cm. - These notes refer to the Terrorism (Northern Ireland) Act 2006 (c. 4) (ISBN 0105404063) which received Royal Assent on 16th February 2006. - 978-0-10-560406-8 *£3.50*

Transport (Wales) Act 2006: chapter 5: explanatory notes. - [12]p.: 30 cm. - These notes refer to the Transport (Wales) Act 2006 (c. 5) (ISBN 010540506X) which received Royal assent on 16 February 2006. - 978-0-10-560506-5 *£2.50*

Violent Crime Reduction Act 2006: chapter 38: explanatory notes. - 43p.: 30 cm. - These notes refer to the Violent Crime Reduction Act 2006 (c. 38) (ISBN 0105438065) which received Royal assent on 8 November 2006. - 978-0-10-563806-3 *£7.50*

Work and Families Act 2006: chapter 18: explanatory notes. - 13p.: 30 cm. - These notes refer to the Work and Families Act 2006 (c. 18) (ISBN 0105418064) which received Royal assent on 21 June 2006. - 978-0-10-561806-5 *£3.00*

Local Acts 2006

HBOS Group Reorganisation Act 2006: Elizabeth II. Chapter i. - 2, 33p.: 30 cm. - Royal assent, 21st June 2006. - An Act to make new provision for the regulation and management of the Governor and Company of the Bank of Scotland upon its registration as a public company under the Companies Act 1985; to provide for the transfer of the undertakings of Capital Bank plc, Halifax plc and HBOS Treasury Services plc to the Governor and Company of the Bank of Scotland; to provide for the transfer of the assets of the Clerical, Medical and General Life Assurance Society to Clerical Medical Investment Group Limited. - 978-0-10-512106-0 *£6.00*

Leicester City Council Act 2006: Elizabeth II. Chapter ii. - 6p.: 30 cm. - Royal assent, 11th July 2006. - An Act to confer powers on Leicester City Council for the better control of street trading in the city of Leicester. - 978-0-10-512206-7 *£3.00*

Liverpool City Council Act 2006: Elizabeth II. Chapter iii. - 6p.: 30 cm. - Royal assent, 11th July 2006. - An Act to confer powers on Liverpool City Council for the better control of street trading in the city of Liverpool. - 978-0-10-512306-4 *£3.00*

Maidstone Borough Council Act 2006: Elizabeth II. Chapter iv. - 6p.: 30 cm. - Royal assent, 11th July 2006. - An Act to confer powers on Maidstone Borough Council for the better control of street trading in the borough of Maidstone. - 978-0-10-512406-1 *£3.00*

MEASURES OF THE GENERAL SYNOD

Measures of the General Synod 2006

1 **Church of England (Miscellaneous Provisions) Measure 2006**
- [2], 19, [1]p.: 30 cm. - Royal assent, 11th July 2006. A Measure passed by the General Synod of the Church of England to amend the Parsonages Measure 1938, the Church Commissioners Measure 1947, the Diocesan Stipends Funds Measure 1953; to amend section 2 of the Church Funds Investment Measure 1958; to amend section 7 of the Church Property (Miscellaneous Provisions) Measure 1960; to make new provision for the powers of the Church Commissioners relating to Farnham Castle; to amend the Ecclesiastical Jurisdiction Measure 1963; to amend Schedule 2 to the Synodical Government Measure 1969; to amend the Repair of Benefice Buildings Measure 1972, the Endowments and Glebe Measure 1976; to amend section 8 of the Church of England (Miscellaneous Provisions) Measure 1978; to amend the Pastoral Measure 1983, and to amend the National Institutions Measure 1998. - 978-0-10-530806-5 *£3.50*

2 **Pastoral (Amendment) Measure 2006**
- [8]p.: 30 cm. - Royal assent, 11th July 2006. A Measure passed by the General Synod of the Church of England to enable leases to be granted of parts of churches and land belonging or annexed to a church. - 978-0-10-530906-2 *£3.00*

Other statutory publications

Her Majesty's Stationery Office.

Chronological table of the statutes [1235-2005]. - 2v. (xii, 2606p.): hdbk: 25 cm. - 2 vols. not sold separately. Part 1: Covering the acts of the Parliaments of England, Great Britain and the United Kingdom from 1235 to the end of 1972; Part 2: Covering the acts of the Parliaments of the United Kingdom from 1973 to the end of 2005, the acts of the Parliaments of Scotland from 1424 to 1707, the acts of the Scottish Parliament from 1999 to the end of 2005, and the Church Assembly measures and General Synod measures from 1920 to the end of 2005. - 978-0-11-840427-3 £275.00 *per set*

The public general acts and General Synod measures 2003. - 1 sheet: 30 cm. - Correction slip to Part V, dated January 2006 (to ISBN 0118404156). - *Free*

The public general acts and General Synod measures 2005. - 4v. (a-h, 2905, dclxx, 113p.): hdbk: 31 cm. - 4 parts not sold separately. Contents: Part 1 Chapters 1-5; Part 2 Chapters 6-15; Part 3 Chapters 16-24 & Measures 1-3; Part 4 Tables and index. - 978-0-11-840434-1 £280.00 *per set*

The public general acts and General Synod measures 2005: tables and index. - a-h, dclxx, 113p.: 30 cm. - 978-0-11-840435-8 £65.00

Statutory instruments 2004

Part 3: Section 1 nos. 2246 to 2750; Section 2 nos. 2751 to 3316; Section 3 nos. 3317 to 3459. 1st September to 31st December 2004. - 3v. (xxi, p. 6807-10236): hdbk: 31 cm. - 3 vols. not sold separately. Contents: guide to the edition; general statutory instruments issued in the period; selected local instruments; selected instruments not registered as statutory instruments; classified list of local statutory instruments; tables of effect to legislation; numerical and issue list; and index to all parts. - 978-0-11-840420-4 £290.00 *per set*

Statutory instruments 2005

Part 1: Section 1 nos. 1 to 249; Section 2 nos. 250 to 449; Section 3 nos. 450 to 655; Section 4 nos. 656 to 894; Section 5 nos. 895 to 1263. 1st January to 30th April 2005. - 5v. (xxiii, p. 1-5450): hdbk: 31 cm. - 5 vols. not sold separately. Includes: Guide to the edition; General statutory instruments issued in the period; selected local instruments; selected instruments not registered as statutory instruments; and Index to part 1. - 978-0-11-840428-0 £540.00 *per set*

Part 2: Section 1 nos. 1265 to 1781; Section 2 nos. 1788 to 2039; Section 3 nos. 2040 to 2427. 1st May to 31st August 2005. - 3v. (xix, p. 5451-8868): hdbk: 31 cm. - 3 vols. not sold separately. Includes: Guide to the edition; General statutory instruments issued in the period; selected local instruments; selected instruments not registered as statutory instruments; and Index to part 1 and 2. - 978-0-11-840429-7 £290.00 *per set*

Part 3: Section 1 nos. 2446 to 2759; Section 2 nos. 2761 to 3103; Section 3 nos. 3104 to 3291; Section 4 nos. 3294 to 3491; Section 5 nos. 3492 to 3595. 1st September to 31st December 2005. - 5v. (xx, p. 8869-13720): hdbk: 31 cm. - 5 vols not sold separately. Includes: Guide to the edition; General statutory instruments issued in the period; selected local instruments; selected instruments not registered as statutory instruments; statutory instruments oitted from parts 1 and 2; classified list of local statutory instruments; tables of effect to legislation; numerical and issue list; and index to all parts. - 978-0-11-840430-3 £410.00 *per set*

Statutory instruments made by the National Assembly for Wales 2005. - 3v. (xxiii, 2683p.): hdbk: 31 cm. - 3 vols. not sold separately. Contents: Vol. 1: Nos. 35 to 1313, W. 2 to 95, 1 January to 10 May 2005; Vol. 2: Nos. 1314 to 2929, W. 96 to 214, 10 May to 19 October 2005; Vol. 3: Nos. 2984 to 3395, W. 218 to 271, 28 October to 31 December 2005, with Classified list of local statutory instruments registered during 2005, Tables of effects, Numerical and issue list 2005, and Index. - 978-0-11-840431-0 £275.00

Statutory Instruments
Arranged by Subject Headings

Acquisition of land, England: Compensation

The Home Loss Payments (Prescribed Amounts) (England) Regulations 2006 No. 2006/1658. - Enabling power: Land Compensation Act 1973, s. 30 (5). - Issued: 28.06.2006. Made: 21.06.2006. Laid: 28.06.2006. Coming into force: 01.09.2006. Effect: S.I. 2005/1635 revoked with saving. Territorial extent & classification: E. General. - 2p.: 30 cm. - 978-0-11-074739-2 £3.00

Acquisition of land, Wales

The Home Loss Payments (Prescribed Amounts) (Wales) Regulations 2006 No. 2006/1789 (W.185). - Enabling power: Land Compensation Act 1973, s. 30 (5). - Issued: 12.07.2006. Made: 04.07.2006. Coming into force: 01.09.2006. Effect: S.I. 2005/1808 (W. 13) revoked with savings. Territorial extent & classification: W. General. - In English and Welsh. Welsh title: Rheoliadau Taliadau Colli Cartref (Symiau Rhagnodedig) (Cymru) 2006. - 4p.: 30 cm. - 978-0-11-091378-0 £3.00

The National Assembly for Wales (The London to Fishguard Trunk Road (A40) (Llansantffraed, Talybont-on-Usk Junction Improvement) Compulsory Purchase Order 2006 No. 2006/1711 (W.173). - Enabling power: Highways Act 1980, ss. 239, 240, 246 and Acquisition of Land Act 1981, s. 2, sch. 2, part 1, paras 1 (1) (b) (3) (4). - Made: 20.06.2006. Coming into force: 29.06.2006. Effect: None. Territorial extent & classification: W. Local. - In English and Welsh
Unpublished

Agriculture

The Environmental Stewardship (England) and Organic Products (Amendment) Regulations 2006 No. 2006/2075. - Enabling power: Environment Act 1995, s. 98 & European Communities Act 1972, s. 2 (2). - Issued: 01.08.2006. Made: 25.07.2006. Laid: 28.07.2006. Coming into force: 04.09.2006. Effect: S.I. 2004/1604; 2005/621 amended & S.I. 2005/2003 revoked. Territorial extent & classification: E/W/S/NI [parts to E. only]. General. - 4p.: 30 cm. - 978-0-11-074953-2 £3.00

The Natural Environment and Rural Communities Act 2006 (Commencement No. 3 and Transitional Provisions) Order 2006 No. 2006/2541 (C.86). - Enabling power: Natural Environment and Rural Communities Act 2006, s. 107 (2) (6) (b) (7) (b) (8) (b) (c). Bringing into operation various provisions of the 2006 Act on 01.10.2006, in accord. with art. 2. - Issued: 28.09.2006. Made: 20.09.2006. Effect: None. Territorial extent & classification: UK [but parts E/W only]. General. - 8p.: 30 cm. - 978-0-11-075132-0 £3.00

Agriculture: Cereals marketing

The Home-Grown Cereals Authority (Rate of Levy) Order 2006 No. 2006/1357. - Enabling power: Cereals Marketing Act 1965, ss. 13 (3), 23 (1). - Issued: 24.05.2006. Made: 17.05.2006. Laid: 24.05.2006. Coming into force: 01.07.2006. Effect: None. Territorial extent & classification: E/W/S/NI. General. - 4p.: 30 cm. - 978-0-11-074595-4 £3.00

Agriculture, England

The Common Agricultural Policy Single Payment and Support Schemes (Amendment No. 2) Regulations 2006 No. 2006/301. - Enabling power: European Communities Act 1972, s. 2 (2). - Issued: 15.02.2006. Made: 09.02.2006. Laid: 13.02.2006. Coming into force: 14.02.2006. Effect: S.I. 2005/219 amended. Territorial extent & classification: E. General. - 2p.: 30 cm. - 978-0-11-074024-9 £3.00

The Common Agricultural Policy Single Payment and Support Schemes (Amendment) (No. 3) Regulations 2006 No. 2006/989. - Enabling power: European Communities Act 1972, s. 2 (2). - Issued: 05.04.2006. Made: 29.03.2006. Laid: 31.03.2006. Coming into force: 01.04.2006. Effect: S.I. 2005/219 amended. Territorial extent & classification: E. General. - 2p.: 30 cm. - 978-0-11-074436-0 £3.00

The Common Agricultural Policy Single Payment and Support Schemes (Amendment) Regulations 2006 No. 2006/239. - Enabling power: European Communities Act, s. 2 (2). - Issued: 09.02.2006. Made: 03.02.2006. Laid: 07.02.2006. Coming into force: 02.03.2006. Effect: S.I. 2005/219 amended in relation to England. Territorial extent & classification: E. General. - 4p.: 30 cm. - 978-0-11-074015-7 £3.00

The Common Agricultural Policy Single Payment and Support Schemes (Cross-compliance) (England) (Amendment) Regulations 2006 No. 2006/3254. - Enabling power: European Communities Act 1972, s. 2 (2). - Issued: 13.12.2006. Made: 05.12.2006. Laid: 08.12.2006. Coming into force: 01.01.2007. Effect: S.I. 2005/3459 amended. Territorial extent & classification: E. General. - EC note: Those Regulations make provision in England for the administration and enforcement of cross-compliance under Regulation (EC) No 1782/2003 and Commission Regulation (EC) No 796/2004 in relation to the system of income support schemes which came into force on 1st January 2005. - 8p.: 30 cm. - 978-0-11-075436-9 £3.00

The Common Agricultural Policy Single Payment and Support Schemes (Reductions from Payments) (England) Regulations 2006 No. 2006/169. - Enabling power: European Communities Act 1972, s. 2 (2). - Issued: 02.02.2006. Made: 26.01.2006. Laid: 31.01.2006. Coming into force: 26.02.2006. Effect: None. Territorial extent & classification: E. General. - EC note: These Regs, which apply in England only, are made in accordance with Article 3 of Commission Regulation (EC) No 1954/2005. They disapply Article 1 of the Commission Regulation with regard to payments to be made in respect of the year 2005 under the Single Payment Scheme and various other aid schemes established in Council Regulation (EC) No 1782/2003. - 2p.: 30 cm. - 978-0-11-073962-5 £3.00

The Common Agricultural Policy (Wine) (England and Northern Ireland) (Amendment) Regulations 2006 No. 2006/1499. - Enabling power: European Communities Act 1972, s. 2 (2). - Issued: 13.06.2006. Made: 05.06.2006. Laid: 09.06.2006. Coming into force: 01.07.2006. Effect: S.I. 2001/686 amended. Territorial extent & classification: E/NI. General. - 4p.: 30 cm. - 978-0-11-074664-7 £3.00

The England Rural Development Programme (Closure of Project-Based Schemes) Regulations 2006 No. 2006/2298. - Enabling power: European Communities Act 1972, s. 2 (2). - Issued: 31.08.2006. Made: 21.08.2006. Laid: 25.08.2006. Coming into force: 01.10.2006. Effect: None. Territorial extent & classification: E. General. - 2p.: 30 cm. - 978-0-11-075042-2 £3.00

The Environmental Impact Assessment (Agriculture) (England) (No.2) Regulations 2006 No. 2006/2522. - Enabling power: European Communities Act 1972, s. 2 (2). - Issued: 20.09.2006. Made: 13.09.2006. Laid: 15.09.2006. Coming into force: 30.09.2006 & 10.10.2006, in accord with reg. 1 (2). Effect: S.I. 2005/3459 amended & S.I. 2001/3966; 2005/1430 (10.10.2006); 2006/2362 (30.09.2006) revoked. Territorial extent & classification: E. General. - EC note: Implements Council Directives 85/337/EEC on the assessment of the effects of certain public and private projects on the environment (as last amended by Directive 2003/35/EC) (the 'EIA Directive') and 1992/43/EEC on the conservation of natural habitats and of wild flora and fauna (as last amended by the Act concerning the conditions of accession of the new Member States). - 32p.: 30 cm. - 978-0-11-075115-3 £5.50

The Environmental Impact Assessment (Agriculture) (England) Regulations 2006 No. 2006/2362. - Enabling power: European Communities Act 1972, s. 2 (2). - Issued: 12.09.2006. Made: 04.09.2006. Laid: 07.09.2006. Coming into force: 01.10.2006. Effect: S.I. 2005/3459 amended & S.I. 2001/3966; 2005/1430 revoked. Territorial extent & classification: E. General. - EC note: Implements Council Directive 85/337/EEC on the assessment of the effects of certain public and private projects on the environment (as last amended by Directive 2003/35/EC) and Council Directive 1992/43/EEC on the conservation of natural habitats and of wild flora and fauna (as last amended by the Act concerning the conditions of accession of the new Member States). - 32p.: 30 cm. - 978-0-11-075078-1 £5.50

The Environmental Stewardship (England) and Countryside Stewardship (Amendment) Regulations 2006 No. 2006/991. - Enabling power: Environment Act 1995, s. 98 & European Communities Act 1972, s. 2 (2). - Issued: 05.04.2006. Made: 21.03.2006. Laid: 31.03.2006. Coming into force: 30.04.2006. Effect: S.I. 2000/3048; 2005/621 amended. Territorial extent & classification: E. General. - 4p.: 30 cm. - 978-0-11-074439-1 £3.00

The Feeding Stuffs and the Feeding Stuffs (Sampling and Analysis) (Amendment) (England) Regulations 2006 No. 2006/113. - Enabling power: Agriculture Act 1970, ss. 66 (1), 74A, 77 (4), 78 (6), 84 & European Communities Act 1972, s. 2 (2). - Issued: 31.01.2006. Made: 23.01.2006. Laid: 26.01.2006. Coming into force: 16.02.2006. Effect: S.I. 1999/1663; 2005/3281 amended. Territorial extent & classification: E. General. - EC note: Implements the following EC legislation: Commission Directive 2005/6/EC amending Directive 71/250/EEC as regards reporting and interpretation of analytical results required under Directive 2002/32/EC; Commission Directive 2002/27/EC amending Directive 2002/70/EC establishing requirements for the determination of levels of dioxins and dioxin-like PCBs in feedingstuffs; Commission Directive 2002/8/EC amending Annex I to Directive 2002/32/EC of the European Parliament and the Council on undesirable substances in animal feed. Reg 2 of these Regulations implements Commission Directive 2005/8/EC by amending sch. 5 to 2005 Regs in respect of certain entries for lead, fluorine and mercury. - 4p.: 30 cm. - 978-0-11-073935-9 £3.00

The Feeding Stuffs (England) (Amendment) Regulations 2006 No. 2006/2808. - Enabling power: Agriculture Act 1970, ss. 66 (1), 68 (1), 69 (1), 74 (1), 74A. - Issued: 25.10.2006. Made: 19.10.2006. Laid: 25.10.2006. Coming into force: 17.11.2006. Effect: S.I. 2000/2481 in relation to England; 2003/1503; 2005/3281 amended. Territorial extent & classification: E. General. - 4p.: 30 cm. - 978-0-11-075210-5 £3.00

The Feed (Specified Undesirable Substances) (England) Regulations 2006 No. 2006/3120. - Enabling power: Agriculture Act 1970, ss. 66 (1), 68 (1), 69 (1), 74(1), 74A, 84. - Issued: 28.11.2006. Made: 22.11.2006. Laid: 28.11.2006. Coming into force: 26.12.2006. Effect: S.I. 2005/3280, 3281 amended. Territorial extent & classification: E. General. - EC note: Provide for the implementation of Directives 2005/86/EC, 2006/87/EC and 2006/13/EC, amending 2002/32/EC, on undesirable substances in animal feed; and also implement a provision in Directive 79/373/EC on the circulation of compound feedingstuffs. - 12p.: 30 cm. - 978-0-11-075364-5 £3.00

The Hill Farm Allowance (Amendment) Regulations 2006 No. 2006/518. - Enabling power: European Communities Act 1972, s. 2 (2). - Issued: 07.03.2006. Made: 27.02.2006. Laid: 03.03.2006. Coming into force: 28.03.2006. Effect: S.I. 2006/225 amended. Territorial extent & classification: E. General. - 2p.: 30 cm. - 978-0-11-074134-5 £3.00

The Hill Farm Allowance Regulations 2006 No. 2006/225. - Enabling power: European Communities Act 1972, s. 2 (2). - Issued: 09.02.2006. Made: 01.02.2006. Laid: 06.02.2006. Coming into force: 01.03.2006. Effect: S.I. 2000/3044 amended. Territorial extent & classification: E. General. - EC note: These Regs implement Council Reg (EC) no. 1257/1999 on support for rural development from the European Agricultural Guidance and Guarantee Fund (EAGGF) and amending and repealing certain Regulations, as amended by Council Reg (EC) no. 1783/2003, in so far as the Rural Development Regulation relates to less favoured areas. - 12p.: 30 cm. - 978-0-11-073998-4 £3.00

The Official Controls (Animals, Feed and Food) (England) Regulations 2006 No. 2006/3472. - Enabling power: European Communities Act 1972, s. 2 (2). - Issued: 09.01.2007. Made: 28.12.2006. Laid: 08.01.2007. Coming into force: 16.02.2007. Effect: S.I. 2006/15 amended. Territorial extent & classification: E. General. - EC note: These Regulations apply and enforce Regulation (EC) No. 882/2004 in England in relation to animal health and welfare rules, and feed and food law excluded from the Official Feed and Food Controls Regulations (England) 2006, which also apply and enforce Regulation 882/2004. - 12p.: 30 cm. - 978-0-11-075587-8 £3.00

The Official Feed and Food Controls (England) Regulations 2006 No. 2006/15. - Enabling power: European Communities Act 1972, s. 2 (2). - Issued: 31.01.2006. Made: 09.01.2006. Laid: 09.01.2006. Coming into force: 11.01.2006. Effect: S.I. 2005/3280 amended & S.I. 2005/2626 revoked. Territorial extent & classification: E. General- EC note: Relates to the execution and enforcement, in England, of Regulation (EC) No. 882/2004. They also impose prohibitions on the introduction of certain feed and food into England in the light of Article 11 of Regulation (EC) No. 178/2002 as last amended by Regulation (EC) No. 1642/2003. - 32p.: 30 cm. - 978-0-11-073889-5 £5.50

The Pig Carcase (Grading) (Amendment) (England) Regulations 2006 No. 2006/2192. - Enabling power: European Communities Act 1972, s. 2 (2). - Issued: 15.08.2006. Made: 07.08.2006. Laid: 11.08.2006. Coming into force: 05.09.2006. Effect: S.I. 1994/2155 amended in relation to England & S.I. 2003/2949; 2004/1505 revoked. Territorial extent & classification: E. General. - EC note: These Regulations amend the 1994 Regulations so as to take account of amendments made by Commission Decision (EC) No. 2006/374 to remove some of the rules specific to the UK. - 4p.: 30 cm. - 978-0-11-075005-7 £3.00

The Products of Animal Origin (Third Country Imports) (England) (No. 4) (Amendment) Regulations 2006 No. 2006/844. - Enabling power: European Communities Act 1972, s. 2 (2). - Issued: 31.03.2006. Made: 20.03.2006. Laid: 22.03.2006. Coming into force: 23.03.2006. Effect: S.I. 2004/3388 amended & S.I. 2005/3386 revoked. Territorial extent & classification: E. General. - Revoked by S.I. 2006/2841 (ISBN 0110752317). EC note: Implements for England Council Directive 97/78/EC laying down the principles governing the organisation of veterinary checks on products entering the Community from third countries. In particular, para. 3 of part VIII of sch. 1 gives effect to Commission Decision 2006/79/EC amending Decisions 2005/759/EC and 2005/760/EC. Para. 19 of part VIII of sch. 1 gives effect to the restrictions on the importation of untreated feathers from all third countries contained in Decision 2006/7/EC as amended by Decision 2006/183/EC. - 16p.: 30 cm. - 978-0-11-074377-6 £3.00

The Products of Animal Origin (Third Country Imports) (England) Regulations 2006 No. 2006/2841. - Enabling power: European Communities Act 1972, s. 2 (2) and Finance Act 1973, s. 56 (1) (2). - Issued: 03.11.2006. Made: 24.10.2006. Laid: 30.10.2006. Coming into force: 24.11.2006. Effect: S.I. 2004/3388; 2006/844 revoked. Territorial extent & classification: E. General. - EC note: These Regulations implement for England Council Directive 97/78/EC (laying down the principles governing the organisation of veterinary checks on products entering the Community from third countries). Commission Decision 2002/349/EC (laying down the list of products to be examined at border inspection posts under Council Directive 97/78/EC) specifies the products of animal origin to which the Directive applies - meat, fish (including shellfish), milk, and products made from these, together with egg products and a large number of animal by-products, including casings, skins, bones and blood - from third countries. - 56p.: 30 cm. - 978-0-11-075231-0 £9.00

The Rice Products (Restriction on First Placing on the Market) (England) Regulations 2006 No. 2006/2921. - Enabling power: European Communities Act 1972, s. 2 (2). - Issued: 13.11.2006. Made: 07.11.2006. Laid: 08.11.2006. Coming into force: 09.11.2006. Effect: None. Territorial extent & classification: E. General. - EC note: These Regulations implement in relation to England Commission Decision 2006/601/EC on emergency measures regarding the non-authorised genetically modified organism "LL RICE 601" in rice products as amended by Commission Decision 2006/754/EC. - 4p.: 30 cm. - 978-0-11-075275-4 £3.00

Agriculture, England and Wales

The EC Fertilisers (England and Wales) Regulations 2006 No. 2006/2486. - Enabling power: European Communities Act 1972, s. 2 (2). - Issued: 15.09.2006. Made: 06.09.2006. Laid: 14.09.2006. Coming into force: 11.10.2006. Effect: 1970 c. 40 Part IV and S.I. 1991/2197 (offence provisions); 1996/1342 (sampling and analysis provisions) disapplied. Territorial extent & classification: E/W. General. - EC note: These Regulations implement, in England and Wales, Regulation (EC) No. 2003/2003 relating to fertilisers- 12p.: 30 cm. - 978-0-11-075095-8 £3.00

The Pesticides (Maximum Residue Levels in Crops, Food and Feeding Stuffs) (England and Wales) (Amendment) (No. 2) Regulations 2006 No. 2006/1742. - Enabling power: European Communities Act 1972, s. 2 (2). - Issued: 07.07.2006. Made: 29.06.2006. Laid: 05.07.2006. Coming into force: 27.07.2006, except for reg. 3 which comes into force on 15.09.2006 in accord. with reg. 1 (3) (4). Effect: S.I. 2005/3286 amended. Territorial extent & classification: E/W. General. - EC note: The Regulations implement Commission Directives 2006/4/EC, 2006/9/EC and 2006/30/EC. - 12p., tables: 30 cm. - 978-0-11-074791-0 £3.00

The Pesticides (Maximum Residue Levels in Crops, Food and Feeding Stuffs) (England and Wales) (Amendment) (No. 3) Regulations 2006 No. 2006/2922. - Enabling power: European Communities Act 1972 , s. 2 (2). - Issued: 13.11.2006. Made: 06.11.2006. Laid: 10.11.2006. Coming into force: In accord. with reg. 1 (3) to (7). Effect: S.I. 2005/3286; 2006/985 amended. Territorial extent & classification: E/W. General. - EC note: The Regulations implement Commission Directives 2006/53/EC, 2006/59/EC, 2006/60/EC and 2006/61/EC. - 48p., tables: 30 cm. - 978-0-11-075279-2 £7.50

The Pesticides (Maximum Residue Levels In Crops, Food And Feeding Stuffs) (England and Wales) (Amendment) Regulations 2006 No. 2006/985. - Enabling power: European Communities Act 1972, s. 2 (2). - Issued: 17.05.2006. Made: 27.03.2006. Laid: 31.03.2006. Coming into force: 27.04.2006, 10.05.2006 & 21.04.2007 in accord. with reg. 1 (3) to (5). Effect: S.I. 2005/3286 amended. Territorial extent & classification: E/W. General. - EC note: Implements Commission Directives 2005/70/EC, 2005/74/EC and 2005/76/EC. - 24p., tables: 30 cm. - 978-0-11-074569-5 £4.00

Agriculture, Northern Ireland

The Common Agricultural Policy (Wine) (England and Northern Ireland) (Amendment) Regulations 2006 No. 2006/1499. - Enabling power: European Communities Act 1972, s. 2 (2). - Issued: 13.06.2006. Made: 05.06.2006. Laid: 09.06.2006. Coming into force: 01.07.2006. Effect: S.I. 2001/686 amended. Territorial extent & classification: E/NI. General. - 4p.: 30 cm. - 978-0-11-074664-7 £3.00

Agriculture, Wales

The Agricultural Subsidies and Grants Schemes (Appeals) (Wales) Regulations 2006 No. 2006/3342 (W.303). - Enabling power: European Communities Act 1972, s. 2 (2). - Issued: 08.01.2007. Made: 13.12.2006. Coming into force: 01.01.2007. Effect: S.I 1987/2026, 2027; 1993/1210, 1211; 1994/238, 239, 3099, 3100, 3101, 3102; 2001/2537 (W.212) amended & S.I. 1988/1291; 1992/905; 1997/829 amended in relation to Wales & S.I. 2004/2919 (W.258) revoked. Territorial extent & classification: W. General. - In English and Welsh. Welsh title: Rheoliadau Cynlluniau Cymorthdaliadau a Grantiau Amaethyddol (Apelau) (Cymru) 2006. - 8p.: 30 cm. - 978-0-11-091482-4 £3.00

The Common Agricultural Policy Single Payment and Support Schemes (Cross Compliance) (Wales) (Amendment) Regulations 2006 No. 2006/2831 (W.252). - Enabling power: European Communities Act 1972, s. 2 (2). - Issued: 03.11.2006. Made: 24.10.2006. Coming into force: 01.11.2006. Effect: S.I. 2004/3280 (W.284) amended. Territorial extent & classification: W. General. - In English and Welsh. Welsh title: Rheoliadau Cynllun Taliad Sengl a Chynlluniau Cymorth y Polisi Amaethyddol Cyffredin (Trawsgydymffurfio) (Cymru) 2006. - 8p.: 30 cm. - 978-0-11-091427-5 £3.00

The Common Agricultural Policy Single Payment and Support Schemes (Wales) (Amendment) Regulations 2006 No. 2006/357 (W.45). - Enabling power: European Communities Act 1972, s. 2 (2). - Issued: 22.02.2006. Made: 14.02.2006. Coming into force: 20.02.2006. Effect: S.I. 2005/360 (W.29) amended. Territorial extent & classification: W. General. - EC note: These Regs update references in the principal Regulations (SI 2005/360 (W.29)) to Commission Regulation 795/2004 and Commission Regulation 796/2004 to reflect the amendments that have been made to those regulations. They also substitute a new Reg 6 in the principal Regulations so as to authorise farmers to make use of the possibility, introduced by Commission Regulation (EC) no. 606/2005. - In English and Welsh. Welsh title: Rheoliadau Cynllun Taliad Sengl a Chynlluniau Cymorth y Polisi Amaethyddol Cyffredin (Cymru) (Diwygio) 2006. - 8p.: 30 cm. - 978-0-11-091274-5 £3.00

The Common Agricultural Policy Single Payment Scheme (Set-aside) (Wales) (Amendment) Regulations 2006 No. 2006/3101 (W.285). - Enabling power: European Communities Act 1972, s. 2 (2). - Issued: 30.11.2006. Made: 21.11.2006. Coming into force: 01.12.2006. Effect: S.I. 2005/45 (W.4) amended. Territorial extent & classification: W. General. - In English and Welsh. Welsh title: Rheoliadau Cynllun Taliad Sengl y Polisi Amaethyddol Cyffredin (Neilltir) (Cymru) (Diwygio) 2006. - 8p.: 30 cm. - 978-0-11-091454-1 £3.00

The Common Agricultural Policy (Wine) (Wales) (Amendment) Regulations 2006 No. 2006/1716 (W.178). - Enabling power: European Communities Act 1972, s. 2 (2). - Issued: 01.08.2006. Made: 28.06.2004. Coming into force: 01.07.2006. Effect: S.I. 2001/2193 (W.155) amended. Territorial extent & classification: W. General. - EC note: These Regs. update the references to EC legislation in the 2001 Regs. - In English and Welsh. Welsh title: Rheoliadau'r Polisi Amaethyddol Cyffredin (Gwin) (Cymru) (Diwygio) 2006. - 16p.: 30 cm. - 978-0-11-091392-6 £3.00

The Feeding Stuffs, the Feeding Stuffs (Sampling and Analysis) (Amendment) (Wales) Regulations 2006 No. 2006/617 (W.69). - Enabling power: Agriculture Act 1970, ss. 66 (1), 74A, 77 (4), 78 (6), 84. - Issued: 14.03.2006. Made: 07.03.2006. Coming into force: 10.03.2006. Effect: S.I. 2006/116 (W. 14) amended & S.I. 1999/1663 amended in relation to Wales. Territorial extent & classification: W. General. - EC note: These Regulations implement the following European Community legislation: Commission Directive 2005/6/EC amending Directive 71/250/EEC; Commission Directive 2002/7/EC amending Directive 2002/70/EC; Commission Directive 2002/8/EC amending Annex 1 to Directive 2002/32/EC; Reg. 2 of these Regulations implements Commission Directive 2005/8/EC. - In English and Welsh. Welsh title: Rheoliadau Bwydydd Anifeiliaid a Phorthiant (Samplu a Dadansoddi) (Diwygio) (Cymru) 2006. - 8p.: 30 cm. - 978-0-11-091296-7 £3.00

The Feeding Stuffs (Wales) (Amendment) Regulations 2006 No. 2006/2928 (W.263). - Enabling power: Agriculture Act 1970, ss. 66 (1), 68 (1), 69 (1), 74 (1), 74A. - Issued: 17.11.2006. Made: 08.11.2006. Coming into force: 17.11.2006. Effect: S.I. 2001/343 (W.15); 2003/1850 (W.200); 2006/116 (W.14) amended. Territorial extent & classification: W. General. - EC note: The 2001 Regs implemented in relation to Wales, art. 1.4 and art. 1.1(b) of Directive 2002/2/EC amending Council Directive 79/373/EEC on the circulation of compound feedingstuffs. The provisions were suspended (by the High Court) pending a referral to the European Court of Justice. During the suspension all of the 2001 Regs other than the suspended provisions were revoked and replaced by the 2006 Regs. The ECJ has now ruled that art. 1.4 is legally valid whereas art. 1.1(b) is not. - In English and Welsh. Welsh title: Rheoliadau Bwydydd Anifeiliaid (Cymru) (Diwygio) 2006. - 8p.: 30 cm. - 978-0-11-091433-6 £3.00

The Feeding Stuffs (Wales) Regulations 2006 No. 2006/116 (W.14). - Enabling power: Agriculture Act 1970, ss. 66 (1), 68 (1) (1A), 69 (1) (3), 70 (1), 71 (1), 74 (1), 74A, 77 (4), 78 (6) (10), 79 (1) (2) (9), 84 & European Communities Act 1972, s. 2 (2). - Issued: 03.02.2006. Made: 24.01.2006. Coming into force: 25.01.2006. Effect: 1970 c. 40 modified in relation to Wales & S.I. 1999/1663 amended in relation to Wales & S.I. 2001/343 (W.15) revoked with saving & S.I. 2001/3461 (W.280); 2002/1797 (W.172); 2003/989 (W.138), 1850 (W.200), 3119 (W.297); 2004/1749 (W.186), 3091 (W.265) revoked in so far as they amend the 2001 Regs. Territorial extent & classification: W. General. - With correction slip, dated April 2006. EC note: These Regs introduce new provisions to enforce and administer Regulation no. 1831/2003. They also provide for the implementation of the following: Directive 70/524/EEC as last amended by Regulation no. 1756/2002; Directive 79/373/EEC as last amended by Regulation no. 807/2003; Directive 82/471/EEC as last amended by Regulation no. 1831/2003; Directive 93/74/EEC as last amended by Regulation no. 806/2003; Directive 94/39/EC ; 96/25/EC as last amended by Regulation no. 806/2003; Directive 2002/32/EC as last amended by Directive 2003/100/EC. - In English and Welsh. Welsh title: Rheoliadau Bwydydd Anifeiliaid (Cymru) 2006. - 100p.: 30 cm. - 978-0-11-091257-8 £15.50

The Feed (Specified Undesirable Substances) (Wales) Regulations 2006 No. 2006/3256 (W.296). - Enabling power: Agriculture Act 1970, ss. 66 (1), 68 (1), 69 (1), 74A, 84. - Issued: 15.12.2006. Made: 05.12.2006. Coming into force: 26.12.2006. Effect: S.I. 2005/3368 (W.265); 2006/116 (W.14) amended. Territorial extent & classification: W. General. - EC note: These Regulations provide for the implementation of the following EC Directives: Commission Directive 2005/86/EC amending Annex I to Directive 2002/32/EC on undesirable substances in animal feed as regards camphechlor; Directive 2005/87/EC amending Annex I to Directive 2002/32/EC as regards lead, fluorine and cadmium; and Directive 2006/13/EC amending Annexes I and II to Directive 2002/32/EC as regards dioxins and dioxin-like PCBs. They also implement a provision contained in Council Directive 79/373/EEC on the circulation of compound feedingstuffs as last amended by Council Regulation (EC) No. 807/2003. This provision relates to the limits of variation for the declaration of the moisture content of compound pet foods. - In English and Welsh. Welsh title: Rheoliadau Bwyd Anifeiliaid (Sylweddau Annymunol Penodol) (Cymru) 2006. - 16p.: 30 cm. - 978-0-11-091469-5 £3.00

The Official Feed and Food Controls (Wales) Regulations 2006 No. 2006/590 (W.66). - Enabling power: Food Safety Act 1990, ss. 16 (1), 17 (2), 48 (1) & European Communities Act 1972, s. 2 (2). - Issued: 14.03.2006. Made: 07.03.2006. Coming into force: 08.03.2006. Effect: S.I. 2005/3368 (W. 265) amended & S.I. 2005/3254 (W. 247) revoked. Territorial extent & classification: W. General. - In English and Welsh. Welsh title: Rheoliadau Rheolaethau Swyddogol ar Fwyd Anifeiliaid a Bwyd (Cymru) 2006. - 56p.: 30 cm. - 978-0-11-091293-6 £9.00

Older Cattle (Disposal) (Wales) Regulations 2006 No. 2006/62 (W.11). - Enabling power: European Communities Act 1972, s. 2 (2). - Issued: 06.02.2006. Made: 18.01.2006. Coming into force: 23.01.2006. Effect: S.I. 1996/1193 revoked in relation to Wales. Territorial extent & classification: W. General. - EC note: These regs make provision for the enforcement of certain of the requirements of Commission Regulation 716/96 as amended by Commission Regulation 2109/2005. - In English and Welsh. Welsh title: Rheoliadau Gwartheg Hyn (Gwaredu) (Cymru) 2006. - With correction slip dated April 2006. - 12p.: 30 cm. - 978-0-11-091271-4 £3.00

The Paying Agency (National Assembly for Wales) (Amendment) Regulations 2006 No. 2006/2698 (W.230). - Enabling power: European Communities Act 1972, ss. 2 (2). - Issued: 18.10.2006. Made: 10.10.2006. Coming into force: 16.10.2006. Effect: S.I. 1999/2223 amended. Territorial extent & classification: W. General. - In English and Welsh. Welsh title: Rheoliadau Asiantaeth Dalu (Cynulliad Cenedlaethol Cymru) (Diwygio) 2006. - 4p.: 30 cm. - 978-0-11-091403-9 £3.00

The Products of Animal Origin (Third Country Imports) (Wales) (Amendment) (No. 2) Regulations 2006 No. 2006/1349 (W.135). - Enabling power: European Communities Act 1972, s. 2 (2). - Issued: 06.06.2006. Made: 16.05.2006. Coming into force: 31.05.2006. Effect: S.I. 2005/666 (W.56) amended. Territorial extent & classification: W. General. - EC note: Gives effect to the restrictions on the importation of products derived from birds contained in Commission Decision 2006/7/EC concerning certain protection measures in relation to the import of feathers from certain third countries, as amended by Commission Decision 2006/183/EC. - In English and Welsh. Welsh title: Rheoliadau Cynhyrchion sy'n Dod o Anifeiliaid (Mewnforion Trydydd Gwledydd) (Cymru) (Diwygio) (Rhif 2) 2006. - 4p.: 30 cm. - 978-0-11-091346-9 £3.00

The Products of Animal Origin (Third Country Imports) (Wales) (Amendment) Regulations 2006 No. 2006/767 (W.74). - Enabling power: European Communities Act 1972, s. 2 (2). - Issued: 10.04.2006. Made: 14.03.2006. Coming into force: 16.03.2006. Effect: S.I. 2005/666 (W.56) amended & S.I. 2005/3395 (W.271) revoked. Territorial extent & classification: W. General. - EC note: The 2005 Regulations are amended in order to give effect to the restrictions on the importation of products derived from birds contained in Commission Decision 2005/760/EC concerning certain protection measures in relation highly pathogenic avian influenza in certain third countries for the import of captive birds, as amended by Commission Decision 2005/862/EC. - In English and Welsh. Welsh title: Rheoliadau Cynhyrchion sy'n Dod o Anifeiliaid (Mewnforion Trydydd Gwledydd) (Cymru) (Diwygio) 2006. - 4p.: 30 cm. - 978-0-11-091313-1 £3.00

The Rural Development Programmes (Wales) Regulations 2006 No. 2006/3343 (W.304). - Enabling power: European Communities Act 1972, s. 2 (2). - Issued: 08.01.2007. Made: 13.12.2006. Coming into force: 01.01.2007. Effect: S.I. 1996/529; 1999/1176; 2001/424 (W.18), 496 (W.23), 1154 (W.61), 2446 (W.199), 3806 (W.314); 2006/41 (W.7) revoked with savings. Territorial extent & classification: W. General. - In English and Welsh. Welsh title: Rheoliadau Rhaglenni Datblygu Gwledig (Cymru) 2006. - 16p.: 30 cm. - 978-0-11-091483-1 £3.00

The Tir Cynnal (Wales) Regulations 2006 No. 2006/41 (W.7). - Enabling power: European Communities Act 1972, s. 2 (2). - Issued: 16.01.2006. Made: 10.01.2006. Coming into force: 13.01.2006. Effect: None. Territorial extent & classification: W. General. - EC note: These regs are made pursuant to Council Regulation 1257/1999 and the detailed framework for the implementation of that Council Regulation is contained in Commission Regulation 817/2004. - In English and Welsh. Welsh title: Rheoliadau Tir Cynnal (Cymru) 2006. - 24p.: 30 cm. - 978-0-11-091251-6 £4.00

The Tir Gofal (Wales) (Amendment) Regulations 2006 No. 2006/1717 (W.179). - Enabling power: European Communities Act 1972, s. 2 (2). - Issued: 10.07.2006. Made: 28.06.2006. Coming into force: 16.10.2006. Effect: S.I. 1999/1176 amended. Territorial extent & classification: W. General. - In English and Welsh. Welsh title: Rheoliadau Tir Gofal (Cymru) (Diwygio) 2006. - 8p.: 30 cm. - 978-0-11-091371-1 £3.00

Agriculture, Wales

Animals: Animal health

The Cattle Database (Amendment) Regulations 2006 No. 2006/1539. - Enabling power: European Communities Act 1972, s. 2 (2). - Issued: 20.06.2006. Made: 14.06.2006. Laid: 14.06.2006. Coming into force: 15.06.2006. Effect: S.I. 1998/1796 amended. Territorial extent & classification: E/W/S. General. - EC note: These Regulations amend the 1998 Regs to replace references to Council Regulation 820/97 with references to Council Regulation 1760/2000 and to replace references to Commission Regulation 2629/97 with references to Commission Regulation 911/2004. - 4p.: 30 cm. - 978-0-11-074701-9 £3.00

The Cattle Identification (Amendment) Regulations 2006 No. 2006/1538. - Enabling power: European Communities Act 1972, s. 2 (2). - Issued: 20.06.2006. Made: 14.06.2006. Laid: 14.06.2006. Coming into force: 15.06.2006. Effect: S.I. 1998/871 amended. Territorial extent & classification: E/W/S. General. - EC note: These Regulations amend the 1998 Regs to replace references to Council Regulation 820/97 with references to Council Regulation 1760/2000 and to replace references to Commission Regulation 2629/97 with references to Commission Regulation 911/2004. - 4p.: 30 cm. - 978-0-11-074700-2 £3.00

Animals, England

The Horses (Zootechnical Standards) (England) Regulations 2006 No. 2006/1757. - Enabling power: European Communities Act 1972, s. 2 (2). - Issued: 10.07.2006. Made: 03.07.2006. Laid: 07.07.2006. Coming into force: 28.07.2006. Effect: S.I. 1992/3045 revoked in relation to England. Territorial extent & classification: E. General. - EC note: These regs implement, for England, Commission Decision 92/353/EEC and Commission Decision 96/78/EC- 8p.: 30 cm. - 978-0-11-074801-6 £3.00

Animals, England: Animal health

The Animal Gatherings (England) Order 2006 No. 2006/2211. - Enabling power: Animal Health Act 1981, ss. 1, 7, 8, 83. - Issued: 16.08.2006. Made: 09.08.2006. Coming into force: 31.08.2006. Effect: S.I. 2004/1202 revoked. Territorial extent & classification: E. General. - 8p.: 30 cm. - 978-0-11-075010-1 £3.00

The Animals and Animal Products (Import and Export) (England) (Amendment) Regulations 2006 No. 2006/2126. - Enabling power: European Communities Act 1972, s. 2 (2). - Issued: 03.08.2006. Made: 28.07.2006. Laid: 31.07.2006. Coming into force: 01.08.2006 & 01.09.2006 in accord. with reg. 1 (2). Effect: S.I. 2006/1471 amended. Territorial extent & classification: E. General. - EC note: Gives effect to the extension of the European Union ban under Commission Decision 2005/760/EC, as amended by Commission Decision 2006/522/EC on the import of captive birds from third countries until 1st January 2007. - 2p.: 30 cm. - 978-0-11-074965-5 £3.00

The Animals and Animal Products (Import and Export) (England) Regulations 2006 No. 2006/1471. - Enabling power: European Communities Act 1972, s. 2 (2) & Finance Act 1973, s. 56 (1) (2). - Issued: 16.06.2006. Made: 06.06.2006. Laid: 08.06.2006. Coming into force: 29.06.2006. Effect: S.I. 2005/2002 revoked. Territorial extent & classification: E. General. - EC note: These Regs implement Council Directives 90/425/EEC (concerning veterinary and zootechnical checks applicable in intra-Community trade in certain live animals and products with a view to the completion of the internal market) and 91/496/EEC (laying down the principles governing the organisation of veterinary checks on animals entering the Community from third countries). - 56p.: 30 cm. - 978-0-11-074657-9 £9.00

The Avian Influenza and Influenza of Avian Origin in Mammals (England) (No.2) Order 2006 No. 2006/2702. - Enabling power: Animal Health Act 1981, ss. 1, 7 (1) (2), 8 (1), 11, 13, 15 (5), 17 (1), 23, 25, 28, 32 (2), 35 (1) (3), 38(1), 65A (3), 83 (2), 87(2) (5) (a), 88 (2). - Issued: 20.10.2006. Made: 11.10.2006. Coming into force: 13.11.2006. Effect: S.I. 1978/32 amended and S.I. 2006/1197 revoked with savings. Territorial extent & classification: E. General. - EC note: This Order continues to transpose Council Directive 2005/94/EC on Community measures for the control of avian influenza and repealing Directive 92/40/EC, other than Chapter IX. Also implements, in part, Commission Decision 2005/734/EC (as amended by Commission Decisions 2005/745/EC, 2005/855/EC and 2006/574/EC); Commission Decision 2006/474/EC and repealing Decision 2005/744/EC. - 52p.: 30 cm. - 978-0-11-075188-7 £9.00

The Avian Influenza and Influenza of Avian Origin in Mammals (England) Order 2006 No. 2006/1197. - Enabling power: Animal Health Act 1981, ss. 1, 7 (1) (2), 8 (1), 11, 13, 15 (5), 17 (1), 23, 25, 28, 32 (2), 35 (1) (3), 38(1), 65A (3), 83 (2), 87(2) (5) (a), 88 (4). - Issued: 05.05.2006. Made: 27.04.2006 at 4.30 pm. Coming into force: 27.04.2006 at 6.00 pm. Effect: S.I. 1978/32 (in relation to England); 2003/1078 amended. Territorial extent & classification: E. General. - Revoked by S.I. 2006/2702 (ISBN 0110751884) with savings. EC note: This Order transposes Council Directive 2005/94/EC on Community measures for the control of avian influenza and repealing Directive 92/40/EC, other than Chapter IX. Chapter IX of the Directive deals with vaccination and will be transposed by the Avian Influenza (Vaccination) (England) Regulations 2006. - 48p.: 30 cm. - 978-0-11-074540-4 £7.50

The Avian Influenza (H5N1 in Poultry) (England) Order 2006 No. 2006/3247. - Enabling power: Animal Health Act 1981, ss. 1, 7 (1) (2), 8(1), 11, 15 (5), 17 (1), 23, 25, 28, 35 (1) (3), 38 (1), 65 (A) (3), 83 (2). - Issued: 21.12.2006. Made: 05.12.2006. Coming into force: 30.12.2006. Effect: None. Territorial extent & classification: E. General. - EC note: This Order transposes: (a) Commission Decision 2006/415/EC repealing Decision 2006/135/EC, as amended by the Commission Decision amending Decisions 2006/415/EC, 2006/416/EC and 2006/563/EC; and (b) the Commission Decision establishing an alternative health mark pursuant to Directive 2002/99/EC. - 16p.: 30 cm. - 978-0-11-075426-0 £3.00

The Avian Influenza (H5N1 in Wild Birds) (England) Order 2006 No. 2006/3249. - Enabling power: Animal Health Act 1981, ss. 1, 7, 8 (1), 11, 15 (5), 17 (1), 23, 25, 28, 35 (1) (3), 38 (1), 65 (A) (3). - Issued: 22.12.2006. Made: 05.12.2006. Coming into force: 30.12.2006. Effect: None. Territorial extent & classification: E. General. - EC note: This Order implements (a) Commission Decision 2006/563/EC concerning certain protection measures in relation to highly pathogenic avian influenza in wild birds in the Community and repealing Decision 2006/115/EC, as amended by the Commission Decision amending Decisions 2006/415/EC, 2006/EC and 2006/563/EC as regards the health mark to be applied to fresh poultry meat adopted on 1st December 2006 (SANCO/10587/2006 Rev. 4) and (b) the Commission Decision establishing an alternative health mark pursuant to Directive 2002/99/EC, also adopted on 1st December 2006 (SANCO/10580/2006 Rev. 4). - 24p.: 30 cm. - 978-0-11-075428-4 £4.00

The Avian Influenza (Preventive Measures) (England) Regulations 2006 No. 2006/2701. - Enabling power: European Communities Act 1972, s. 2 (2). - Issued: 19.10.2006. Made: 10.10.2006. Laid: 16.10.2006. Coming into force: 13.11.2006. Effect: S.I. 2005/3394 revoked with savings. Territorial extent & classification: E. General. - EC note: These Regulations continue to give effect to paragraph 2 of Article 2a of Commission Decision 2005/734/EC laying down biosecurity measures to reduce the risk of transmission of highly pathogenic avian influenza caused by influenza A virus of subtype H5N1 from birds living in the wild to poultry and other captive birds and providing for an early detection system in areas at particular risk, as last amended by Commission Decision 2006/574/EC; give effect to Commission Decision 2006/474/EC concerning measures to prevent the spread of highly pathogenic avian influenza caused by influenza A virus of subtype H5N1 to birds kept in zoos and approved bodies, institutes and centres in the Member States and repealing Decision 2005/744/EC ; and implement provisions requiring or dependant on the identification of poultry premises under Council Directive 2005/94/EC on Community measures for the control of avian influenza and repealing Directive 92/40/EC. - 12p.: 30 cm. - 978-0-11-075187-0 £3.00

The Avian Influenza (Vaccination) (England) Regulations 2006 No. 2006/2703. - Enabling power: European Communities Act 1972, s. 2 (2). - Issued: 19.10.2006. Made: 11.10.2006. Laid: 17.10.2006. Coming into force: 14.11.2006. Effect: None. Territorial extent & classification: E. General. - EC note: These Regulations transpose, in relation to England, Council Directive 2005/94/EC on Community measures for the control of avian influenza repealing Directive 92/40/EEC insofar as it deals with vaccination against avian influenza. - 16p.: 30 cm. - 978-0-11-075190-0 £3.00

The Cattle Compensation (England) Order 2006 No. 2006/168. - Enabling power: Animal Health Act 1981, s. 32 (3). - Issued: 02.02.2006. Made: 26.01.2006. Laid: 31.01.2006. Coming into force: 01.02.2006. Effect: S.I. 2005/3434 amended & S.I. 1978/1483; 1980/80; 1981/1412; 1996/1352; 1998/2073 revoked in so far as they apply to England & S.I. 2005/3433 revoked. Territorial extent & classification: E. General. - 8p.: 30 cm. - 978-0-11-073961-8 £3.00

The Diseases of Animals (Approved Disinfectants) (Amendment) (England) Order 2006 No. 2006/1394. - Enabling power: Animal Health Act 1981, ss. 1, 7, 23 (f) (g). - Issued: 07.06.2006. Made: 20.05.2006. Coming into force: 16.06.2006. Effect: S.I. 1978/32 amended in relation to England & S.I. 2005/1908 revoked. Territorial extent & classification: E. General. - 8p.: 30 cm. - 978-0-11-074644-9 £3.00

The Equine Infectious Anaemia (Compensation) (England) Order 2006 No. 2006/2740. - Enabling power: Animal Health Act 1981, s. 32 (3). - Issued: 19.10.2006. Made: 12.10.2006. Laid: 16.10.2006. Coming into force: 06.11.2006. Effect: None. Territorial extent & classification: E. General. - 2p.: 30 cm. - 978-0-11-075189-4 £3.00

Animals, England: Animal health

The Foot-and-Mouth Disease (Control of Vaccination) (England) Regulations 2006 No. 2006/183. - Enabling power: European Communities Act 1972, s. 2 (2). - Issued: 08.02.2006. Made: 30.01.2006. Laid: 02.02.2006. Coming into force: 23.02.2006. Effect: S.I. 1972/1509; 2001/2375 revoked in relation to England. Territorial extent & classification: E. General. - EC note: These Regulations transpose for England Directive 2003/85/EC on Community measures for the control of foot-and-mouth disease insofar as it deals with vaccination against foot-and-mouth disease. - 32p.: 30 cm. - 978-0-11-073972-4 £5.50

The Foot-and-Mouth Disease (England) Order 2006 No. 2006/182. - Enabling power: Animal Health Act 1981, ss. 1, 2, 7 (1), 8 (1), 13, 15 (3) (4), 17 (1), 23, 25, 26 (1) (2), 28, 34 (7), 38 (1), 65A (3), 83 (2), 87 (2) (5). - Issued: 08.02.2006. Made: 30.01.2006. Coming into force: 23.02.2006. Effect: S.I. 1978/32; 2001/2734; 2003/1729 amended in relation to England & S.I. 1983/1950; 1993/3119 revoked in relation to England & S.I. 2001/571, 680, 974, 1078, 1241, 1407, 1514, 1862, 2238, 2735, 2814, 2994, 3140, 3722, 4029 revoked. Territorial extent & classification: E. General. - EC note: This Order partially transposes for England Directive 2003/85/EC on Community measures for the control of foot-and-mouth disease repealing Directive 85/511/EEC and Decisions 89/531/EEC and 91/665/EEC and amending Directive 92/46/EEC. - 60p.: 30 cm. - 978-0-11-073971-7 £9.00

The Salmonella in Broiler Flocks (Survey Powers) (England) Regulations 2006 No. 2006/864. - Enabling power: European Communities Act 1972, s. 2 (2). - Issued: 28.03.2006. Made: 20.03.2006. Laid: 22.03.2006. Coming into force: 12.04.2006. Effect: S.I. 2005/2927 revoked. Territorial extent & classification: E. General. - Revoked by S.I. 2006/2821 (ISBN 0110752244). EC note: These Regs provide a power of entry to inspectors (in relation to Salmonella spp. in flocks of broiler chickens) in accordance with provisions of Decision 2005/636/EC. This Statutory Instrument has been made in consequence of a defect in SI 2005/2927 and is being issued free of charge to all known recipients of that Statutory Instrument. - 4p.: 30 cm. - 978-0-11-074378-3 £3.00

The Salmonella in Turkey Flocks and Slaughter Pigs (Survey Powers) (England) Regulations 2006 No. 2006/2821. - Enabling power: European Communities Act 1972, s. 2 (2). - Issued: 30.10.2006. Made: 23.10.2006. Laid: 27.10.2006. Coming into force: 17.11.2006. Effect: S.I. 2005/359; 2006/864 revoked. Territorial extent & classification: E. General. - EC note: These Regs implement, in relation to England, Commission Decision 2006/668/EC and 2006/662/EC concerning a financial contribution from the Community towards a baseline survey on the prevalence of Salmonella in slaughter pigs and turkeys to be carried out in the Member States. - 8p.: 30 cm. - 978-0-11-075224-2 £3.00

The Sheep and Goats (Records, Identification and Movement) (England) (Amendment) Order 2006 No. 2006/2987. - Enabling power: Animal Health Act 1981, ss. 1, 8 (1), 83 (2). - Issued: 07.12.2006. Made: 14.11.2006. Coming into force: 11.12.2006. Effect: S.I. 2005/3100 amended. Territorial extent & classification: E. General. - 8p.: 30 cm. - 978-0-11-075408-6 £3.00

The Specified Animal Pathogens (Amendment) (England) Order 2006 No. 2006/1506. - Enabling power: Animal Health Act 1981, ss. 1, 88 (2) (4). - Issued: 27.06.2006. Made: 10.06.2006. Coming into force: 04.07.2006. Effect: S.I. 1998/463 amended. Territorial extent & classification: E. General. - 8p.: 30 cm. - 978-0-11-074738-5 £3.00

The Specified Diseases (Notification and Slaughter) Order 2006 No. 2006/2166. - Enabling power: Animal Health Act 1981, ss. 15 (4), 32 (2), 88 (2). - Issued: 11.08.2006. Made: 04.08.2006. Coming into force: 29.08.2006. Effect: S.I. 1992/3159; 1996/2628 amended. Territorial extent & classification: E. General. - 2p.: 30 cm. - 978-0-11-074987-7 £3.00

The Transmissible Spongiform Encephalopathies (No. 2) Regulations 2006 No. 2006/1228. - Enabling power: European Communities Act 1972, s. 2 (2). - Issued: 09.05.2006. Made: 02.05.2006. Laid: 02.05.2006. Coming into force: 03.05.2006. Effect: S.I. 1999/1103; 2005/404; 2006/68 revoked. Territorial extent & classification: E. General. - 44p.: 30 cm. - 978-0-11-074543-5 £6.50

The Transmissible Spongiform Encephalopathies Regulations 2006 No. 2006/68. - Enabling power: European Communities Act 1972, s. 2 (2). - Issued: 26.01.2006. Made: 17.01.2006. Laid: 20.01.2006. Coming into force: 01.03.2006. Effect: S.I. 1997/2964, 2965, 3062; 1998/2405, 2431; 1999/539; 2000/2672, 2726, 3234, 3377, 3381; 2001/447, 817, 2376, 2650; 2002/843, 1253, 2860; 2004/1518; 2005/556, 2633 revoked. Territorial extent & classification: E. General. - Revoked by S.I. 2006/1228 (ISBN 0110745434). EC note: These Regs revoke & remake the 2002 Regs, which give effect in England to the enforcement and administration of Regulation EC No. 999/2001 laying down rules for the prevention, control and eradication of certain transmissible spongiform encephalopathies. - 44p.: 30 cm. - 978-0-11-073920-5 £7.50

The Tuberculosis (England) (Amendment) Order 2006 No. 2006/140. - Enabling power: Animal Health Act 1981, ss. 1, 8 (1). - Issued: 31.01.2006. Made: 24.01.2006. Coming into force: 19.02.2006. Effect: SI 2005/3446 amended. Territorial extent & classification: E. General. - Revoked by S.I. 2006/394 (ISBN 0110740823). - 2p.: 30 cm. - 978-0-11-073954-0 £3.00

The Tuberculosis (England) Order 2006 No. 2006/394. - Enabling power: Animal Health Act 1981, ss. 1, 7 (1), 8 (1), 15 (4), 25, 32 (2), 87 (2), 88 (2). - Issued: 03.03.2006. Made: 17.02.2006. Coming into force: 18.02.2006 for art. 2 (1); 27.03.2006 for all other purposes. Effect: S.I. 1984/1943; 1990/1869 revoked in so far as they apply to England (27.03.2006); S.I. 2005/3446; 2006/140 revoked (18.02.2006). Territorial extent & classification: E. General. - 12p.: 30 cm. - 978-0-11-074082-9 £3.00

Animals, England: Animal health

The Welfare of Animals (Transport) (England) Order 2006 No. 2006/3260. - Enabling power: Animal Health Act 1981, ss. 1, 7, 8 (1), 37, 38 (1), 39, 83 (2), 87 (2) (3) (5) (a). - Issued: 13.12.2006. Made: 05.12.2006. Coming into force: 05.01.2007. Effect: S.I. 2003/1724 amended & S.I. 2000/646 revoked & S.I. 1975/1024; 1981/1051; 1997/1480; 1998/2537; 1999/1622 revoked in relation to England. Territorial extent & classification: E. General. - EC note: This Order makes provision in England for the administration and enforcement of Council Regulation (EC) No 1/2005 on the protection of animals during transport and related operations; and also provides for the administration and enforcement of Council Regulation 1255/97 concerning Community criteria for staging points. - 12p.: 30 cm. - 978-0-11-075437-6 £3.00

Animals, England: Prevention of cruelty

The Welfare of Animals (Slaughter or Killing) (Amendment) (England) Regulations 2006 No. 2006/1200. - Enabling power: European Communities Act 1972, s. 2 (2). - Issued: 05.05.2006. Made: 28.04.2006. Laid: 28.04.2006. Coming into force: 29.04.2006. Effect: S.I. 1995/731 amended in relation to England. Territorial extent & classification: E. General. - EC note: These regs amend the 1995 Regulations which give effect to Council Directive 93/119/EC on the protection of animals at the time of slaughter or killing, and permit ventilation shutdown as a method of killing birds for the purpose of disease control. - 2p.: 30 cm. - 978-0-11-074542-8 £3.00

Animals, England and Wales: Animal health

The Animal Health and Welfare (Scotland) Act 2006 (Consequential Provisions) (England and Wales) Order 2006 No. 2006/3407. - Enabling power: Scotland Act 1998, ss. 104, 112 (1), 113 (2) (3) (4) (5). - Issued: 29.12.2006. Made: 14.12.2006-. Coming into force: 15.12.2006. Effect: 1963 c.43; 1964 c.70; 1973 c. 60 amended. Territorial extent & classification: E/W. General. - Supersedes draft SI (ISBN 0110711300) issued 13.11.2006. - 8p.: 30 cm. - 978-0-11-071454-7 £3.00

Animals, Wales

The Horses (Zootechnical Standards) (Wales) Regulations 2006 No. 2006/2607 (W.220). - Enabling power: European Communities Act 1972, s. 2 (2). - Issued: 13.10.2006. Made: 26.09.2006. Coming into force: 30.09.2006. Effect: S.I. 1992/3045 revoked in relation to Wales. Territorial extent & classification: W. General. - EC note: These Regulations, which apply in relation to Wales, implement Commission Decision 92/353/EEC and 96/78/EC. - In English and Welsh. Welsh title: Rheoliadau Ceffylau (Safonau Sootechnegol) (Cymru) 2006. - 12p.: 30 cm. - 978-0-11-091401-5 £3.00

The Transmissible Spongiform Encephalopathies (Wales) Regulations 2006 No. 2006/1226 (W.117). - Enabling power: European Communities Act 1972, s. 2 (2). - Issued: 30.05.2006. Made: 02.05.2006. Coming into force: 03.05.2006. Effect: S.I. 2002/1416 (W.142) amended & S.I. 1997/2964, 2965, 3062; 1998/2405, 2431; 1999/539, 1103; 2000/2659, 2811, 3387 (W.224); 2001/1303 (W.80), 2732 (W.231), 2780 (W.233), 3546 (W.290); 2005/1392 (W.106), 1397 (W.111), 2902 (W.205) revoked (in relation to Wales where appropriate). Territorial extent & classification: W. General. - EC note: These Regulations revoke and remake with amendments the TSE (Wales) Regulations 2002, which enforced Regulation (EC) 999/2001. - In English & Welsh: Welsh title: Rheoliadau Enseffalopathïau Sbyngffurf Trosglwyddadwy (Cymru) 2006. - 64p.: 30 cm. - 978-0-11-091343-8 £10.50

Animals, Wales: Animal health

The Animal By-Products (Wales) Regulations 2006 No. 2006/1293 (W.127). - Enabling power: European Communities Act 1972, s. 2 (2). - Issued: 19.05.2006. Made: 10.05.2006. Coming into force: 12.05.2006. Effect: 1974 c. 3; 1906 c. 32 amended & S.I. 2001/1515; 2003/2756(W. 267) revoked. Territorial extent & classification: W. General. - EC note: These Regulations revoke and re-make the Animal By-Products Regulations 2003, which made provision in Wales for the administration and enforcement of Regulation (EC) No 1774/2002 laying down health rules concerning animal by-products not intended for human consumption. They enforce additional Community instruments: Commission Regulation (EC) 808/2003 , 811/2003, 813/2003, 668/2004, 878/2004, 79/2005, 92/2005/ 93/2005 & Decisions 2003/326/EC, 2004/407/EC. With correction slip dated September 2006(which replaced two earlier correction slips). - In English and Welsh. Welsh title: Rheoliadau Sgil-gynhyrchion Anifeiliaid (Cymru) 2006. - 52p.: 30 cm. - 978-0-11-091337-7 £9.00

The Animals and Animal Products (Import and Export) (Wales) (Amendment) (No. 2) Regulations 2006 No. 2006/3452 (W.313). - Enabling power: European Communities Act 1972, s. 2 (2). - Issued: 17.01.2007. Made: 21.12.2006. Coming into force: 31.12.2006. Effect: S.I. 2006/1536 (W.153) amended. Territorial extent & classification: W. General. - EC note: Gives effect to the extension of the European Union ban under Commission Decision 2005/760/EC as amended, on the import of captive birds from third countries until 31 March 2007. - In English and Welsh. Welsh title: Rheoliadau Anifeiliaid a Chynhyrchion Anifeiliaid (Mewnforio ac Allforio) (Cymru) (Diwygio) (Rhif 2) 2006. - 4p.: 30 cm. - 978-0-11-091484-8 £3.00

The Animals and Animal Products (Import and Export) (Wales) (Amendment) Regulations 2006 No. 2006/2128 (W.198). - Enabling power: European Communities Act 1972, s. 2 (2). - Issued: 22.08.2006. Made: 29.07.2006. Coming into force: 01.08.2006. Effect: S.I. 2006/1536 (W.153) amended. Territorial extent & classification: W. General. - EC note: These Regs amend the principal regulations (S.I. 2006/1536 (W.153) to give effect to the extension of the European Union ban under Commission Decision 2005/760/EC as amended by Commission Decision 2006/522/EC on the import of captive birds from third countries until 1 January 2007. - 4p.: 30 cm. - 978-0-11-091397-1 £3.00

The Animals and Animal Products (Import and Export) (Wales) Regulations 2006 No. 2006/1536 (W.153). - Enabling power: European Communities Act 1972, s. 2 (2) and Finance Act 1973, s. 56 (1) (2). - Issued: 26.07.2006. Made: 13.06.2006. Coming into force: 15.06.2006. Effect: S.I. 2005/1158 (W.75) revoked. Territorial extent & classification: W. General. - EC note: These Regulations revoke and re-make with changes S.I. 2005/1158 (W.75). They implement Council Directives 90/425/EEC and 91/496/EEC, and new provisions implement Commission Decision 2000/666/EC in relation to the import of captive birds. - 52p.: 30 cm. - 978-0-11-091391-9 £9.00

The Avian Influenza and Influenza of Avian Origin in Mammals (Wales) (No. 2) Order 2006 No. 2006/2927 (W.262). - Enabling power: Animal Health Act 1981, ss. 1, 7 (1) (2), 8 (1), 11, 13, 15 (5), 17 (1), 23, 25, 28, 32 (2), 35 (1) (3), 38 (1), 65A (3), 83 (2), 87 (2) (5) (a), 88 (2). - Issued: 28.11.2006. Made: 07.11.2006. Coming into force: 13.11.2006. Effect: S.I. 1978/32 amended in relation to Wales & S.I. 2006/1762 (W.184) revoked. Territorial extent & classification: W. General. - EC note: This Order revokes and replaces SI 2006/1762 (W.184). It continues to transpose Council Directive 2005/94/EC ("the Directive") on Community measures for the control of avian influenza, except for Chapter IX of the Directive. Chapter IX of the Directive deals with vaccination and will be transposed by the Avian Influenza (Vaccination) (Wales) Regulations 2006. The Directive repeals Council Directive 92/40/EEC. - 50p.: 30 cm. - 978-0-11-091446-6 £9.00

The Avian Influenza and Influenza of Avian Origin in Mammals (Wales) Order 2006 No. 2006/1762 (W.184). - Enabling power: Animal Health Act 1981, ss. 1, 7 (1) (2), 8 (1), 11, 13, 15 (5), 17 (1), 23, 25, 28, 32 (2), 35 (1) (3), 38 (1), 65A (3), 83 (2), 87 (2) (5) (a), 88 (4). - Issued: 07.08.2006. Made: 05.07.2006. Coming into force: 06.07.2006. Effect: S.I. 1978/32; 2003/1079 (W.148) amended. Territorial extent & classification: W. General. - Revoked by S.I. 2006/2927 (W.262) (ISBN 0110914465). EC note: This Order transposes Council Directive 2005/94/EC ("the Directive") on Community measures for the control of avian influenza, except for Chapter IX of the Directive. Chapter IX of the Directive deals with vaccination and will be transposed by the Avian Influenza (Vaccination) (Wales) Regulations 2006. The Directive repeals Council Directive 92/40/EEC. - 48p.: 30 cm. - 978-0-11-091395-7 £7.50

The Avian Influenza (H5N1 in Poultry) (Wales) Order 2006 No. 2006/3309 (W.299). - Enabling power: Animal Health Act 1981, ss. 1, 7 (1) (2), 8 (1), 11, 15 (5), 17 (1), 23, 25, 28, 35 (1) (3), 38 (1), 65 (A) (3), 83 (2). - Issued: 20.12.2006. Made: 12.12.2006. Coming into force: 13.12.2006. Effect: None. Territorial extent & classification: W. General. - EC note: This Order transposes Commission Decision 2006/415/EC concerning certain protection measures in relation to highly pathogenic avian influenza of subtype H5N1 in poultry in the Community and repealing Decision 2006/135/EC as amended by the Decision amending Decisions 2006/415/EC, 2006/416/EC and 2006/563/EC as regards the health mark to be applied to fresh poultry meat adopted on 1 December 2006 (SANCO/10587/2006 Rev.4). - 16p.: 30 cm. - 978-0-11-091472-5 £3.00

The Avian Influenza (H5N1 in Wild Birds) (Wales) Order 2006 No. 2006/3310 (W.300). - Enabling power: Animal Health Act 1981, ss. 1, 7 (1) (2), 8 (1), 11, 15 (5), 17 (1), 23, 25, 28, 35 (1) (3), 38 (1), 65 (A) (3). - Issued: 21.12.2006. Made: 12.12.2006. Coming into force: 13.12.2006. Effect: None. Territorial extent & classification: W. General. - EC note: These regulations implement in Wales Commission Decision 2006/563/EC, and repealing Decision 2006/115/EC, as amended by the Commission Decision amending Commission Decisions 2006/415/EC, 2006/416/EC and 2006/563/EC; and the Commission Decision establishing an alternative health mark pursuant to Directive 2002/99/EC. - 24p.: 30 cm. - 978-0-11-091475-6 £4.00

The Avian Influenza (Preventive Measures) (Wales) Regulations 2006 No. 2006/2803 (W.242). - Enabling power: European Communities Act 1972, s. 2 (2). - Issued: 30.10.2006. Made: 18.10.2006. Coming into force: 13.11.2006. Effect: S.I. 2005/3384 (W.268), 3385 (W.269) (with saving) revoked. Territorial extent & classification: W. General. - EC note: These regs continue to give effect to para. 2 of art. 2a of Commission Decision 2005/734/EC as last amended by Commission Decision 2006/574/EC. And give effect to Commission Decision 2006/474/EC and repealing Decision 2005/744/EC. Also implement provisions requiring or dependant on the identification of poultry premises under Council Directive 2005/94/EC and repealing Directive 92/40/EC. - In English and Welsh. Welsh title: Rheoliadau Ffliw Adar (Mesurau Atal) (Cymru) 2006. - 16p.: 30 cm. - 978-0-11-091416-9 £3.00

The Avian Influenza (Vaccination) (Wales) (No. 2) Regulations 2006 No. 2006/2932 (W.265). - Enabling power: European Communities Act 1972, s. 2 (2). - Issued: 27.11.2006. Made: 07.11.2006. Coming into force: 14.11.2006. Effect: S.I. 2006/1761 (W.183) revoked. Territorial extent & classification: W. General. - With correction slip dated February 2007. EC note: These Regulations transpose in relation to Wales, Council Directive 2005/94/EC on Community measures for the control of avian influenza repealing Directive 92/40/EEC insofar as it deals with vaccination against avian influenza. - In English and Welsh. Welsh title: Rheoliadau Ffliw Adar (Brechu) (Cymru) (Rhif 2) 2006. - 24p.: 30 cm. - 978-0-11-091437-4 £4.00

The Avian Influenza (Vaccination) (Wales) Regulations 2006 No. 2006/1761 (W.183). - Enabling power: European Communities Act 1972, s. 2 (2). - Issued: 08.08.2006. Made: 05.07.2006. Coming into force: 06.07.2006. Effect: None. Territorial extent & classification: W. General. - Revoked by S.I. 2006/2932 (W.265) (ISBN 0110914376). EC note: These Regulations transpose for Wales Council Directive 2005/94/EC on Community measures for the control of avian influenza repealing Directive 92/40/EEC insofar as it deals with vaccination against avian influenza. - In English and Welsh. Welsh title: Rheoliadau Ffliw Adar (Brechu) (Cymru) 2006. - 20p.: 30 cm. - 978-0-11-091396-4 *£4.00*

The Bovine Spongiform Encephalopathy (BSE) Compensation (Wales) Regulations 2006 No. 2006/1512 (W.148). - Enabling power: European Communities Act 1972, s. 2 (2). - Issued: 23.06.2006. Made: 13.06.2006. Coming into force: 14.06.2006. Effect: S.I. 2002/1416 partially revoked. Territorial extent & classification: W. General. - In English and Welsh. Welsh title: Rheoliadau Iawndal Enseffalopathi Sbyngffurf Buchol (BSE) (Cymru) 2006. - 8p.: 30 cm. - 978-0-11-091356-8 *£3.00*

The Brucellosis (Wales) Order 2006 No. 2006/866 (W.78). - Enabling power: Animal Health Act 1981, ss. 1, 6, 7 (1), 15 (4), 28, 32 (2), 34 (7), 35 (3), 87 (2). - Issued: 18.04.2006. Made: 21.03.2006. Coming into force: 31.03.2006. Effect: S.I. 1997/758 revoked in relation to Wales. Territorial extent & classification: W. General. - EC note: The Order implements the provisions relating to milk of Council Directive 64/432/EEC, as amended and Council Directive 77/391 EEC, as amended. These Directives require the operation of a monitoring and testing programme to maintain the officially brucellosis-free status of Great Britain under Council Directive 64/432/EEC. - In English and Welsh. Welsh title: Gorchymyn Brwselosis (Cymru) 2006. - 16p.: 30 cm. - 978-0-11-091321-6 *£3.00*

The Diseases of Animals (Approved Disinfectants) (Amendment) (Wales) Order 2006 No. 2006/3166 (W.291). - Enabling power: Animal Health Act 1981, ss. 1, 7, 23 (f) (g). - Issued: 06.12.2006. Made: 28.11.2006. Coming into force: 30.11.2006. Effect: S.I. 1978/32 amended in relation to Wales & S.I. 2005/583 (W.49) revoked. Territorial extent & classification: W. General. - In English and Welsh. Welsh title: Gorchymyn Clefydau Anifeiliaid (Diheintyddion a Gymeradwywyd) (Diwygio) (Cymru) 2006. - 20p.: 30 cm. - 978-0-11-091463-3 *£3.50*

The Enzootic Bovine Leukosis (Wales) Order 2006 No. 2006/867 (W.79). - Enabling power: Animal Health Act 1981, ss. 1,6, 7 (1), 15 (4), 28, 32 (2), 34 (7), 35 (3), 87 (2), 88 (2). - Issued: 28.03.2006. Made: 21.03.2006. Coming into force: 31.03.2006. Effect: S.I. 1997/757 revoked in relation to Wales. Territorial extent & classification: W. General. - EC note: The Order implements the provisions relating to milk of Council Directive 64/432/EEC, as amended and Council Directive 77/391 EEC, as amended. - In English and Welsh. Welsh title: Gorchymyn Lewcosis Buchol Ensootig (Cymru) 2006. - 12p.: 30 cm. - 978-0-11-091301-8 *£3.00*

The Foot-and-Mouth Disease (Control of Vaccination) (Wales) Regulations 2006 No. 2006/180 (W.31). - Enabling power: European Communities Act 1972, s. 2 (2). - Issued: 08.03.2006. Made: 31.01.2006. Coming into force: 01.02.2006. Effect: S.I. 2001/2374 (W.198) revoked & S.I. 1972/1509 revoked in relation to Wales. Territorial extent & classification: W. General. - EC note: These Regulations transpose for Wales Directive 2003/85/EC on Community measures for the control of foot-and-mouth disease insofar as it deals with vaccination against foot-and-mouth disease. - In English and Welsh. Welsh title: Rheoliadau Clwy'r Traed a'r Genau (Rheoli Brechu) (Cymru) 2006. - 44p.: 30 cm. - 978-0-11-091288-2 *£7.50*

The Foot-and-Mouth Disease (Wales) Order 2006 No. 2006/179 (W.30). - Enabling power: Animal Health Act 1981, ss. 1, 2, 7 (1), 8 (1), 13, 15 (3) (4), 17 (1), 23, 25, 26 (1) (2), 28, 34 (7), 38 (1), 65A (3), 83 (2), 87 (2) (5). - Issued: 09.03.2006. Made: 31.01.2006. Coming into force: 01.02.2006. Effect: S.I. 1978/32 amended in relation to Wales & S.I. 2001/2771 (W.232); 2003/1966 (W.211) amended & 1983/1950; 1993/3119 revoked in relation to Wales & S.I. 2001/572 (W.26), 658 (W.33), 968 (W.46), 1033 (W.47), 1234 (W.67), 1406/W.93), 1509 (W.106), 1874 (W.134), 2236 (W.162), 2813 (W.242), 2981 (W.248), 3145 (W.260), 3706 (W.303), 4009 (W.335) revoked. Territorial extent & classification: W. General. - EC note: This Order transposes, in part, Council Directive 2003/85/EC on Community measures for the control of foot and mouth disease. - 56p.: 30 cm. - 978-0-11-091292-9 *£9.00*

The Salmonella in Broiler Flocks (Survey Powers) (Wales) Regulations 2006 No. 2006/1511 (W.147). - Enabling power: European Communities Act 1972, s. 2 (2). - Issued: 21.06.2006. Made: 13.06.2006. Coming into force: 14.06.2006. Effect: None. Territorial extent & classification: W. General. - EC note: These Regulations, which apply to Wales only, provide a power of entry to inspectors to undertake the survey sampling required by Commission Decision 2005/636/EC in relation to salmonella prevalence in broiler chickens. - In English and Welsh. Welsh title: Rheoliadau Salmonela mewn Heidiau o Frwyliaid (Pwerau Arolygu) (Cymru) 2006. - 8p.: 30 cm. - 978-0-11-091355-1 *£3.00*

The Sheep and Goats (Records, Identification and Movement) (Wales) (Amendment) Order 2006 No. 2006/2926 (W.261). - Enabling power: Animal Health Act 1981, ss. 1, 8 (1), 83 (2). - Issued: 17.11.2006. Made: 07.11.2006. Coming into force: 01.01.2007. Effect: S.I. 2006/1036 (W.106) amended. Territorial extent & classification: W. General. - EC note: Amends the Principal Order (SI 2006/1036 (W.106)) to substitute sch. 3 which prescribes the form for recording animal movements. The new form contains a field to record the expected duration of the journey, this is a requirement of art. 4 of Council Regulation No. 1/2005. - In English and Welsh. Welsh title: Gorchymyn Defaid a Geifr (Cofnodion, Adnabod a Symud) (Cymru) (Diwygio) 2006. - 16p.: 30 cm. - 978-0-11-091435-0 *£3.00*

Animals, Wales: Animal health

The Sheep and Goats (Records, Identification and Movement) (Wales) Order 2006 No. 2006/1036 (W.106). - Enabling power: Animal Health Act 1981, ss. 1, 8 (1), 72. - Issued: 26.04.2006. Made: 04.04.2006. Coming into force: 05.04.2006. Effect: S.I. 2003/1966 (W.211) amended & S.I. 2002/2302 (W.227) (with savings); 2003/167 (W.27), 946 (W.127) revoked. Territorial extent & classification: W. General. - EC note: This Order makes provision for the administration and enforcement in Wales of Council Regulation (EC) no. 21/2004 (establishing a system for the identification and registration of ovine and caprine animals and amending Regulation (EC) 1782/2003 and Directives 92/102/EEC and 64/432/EEC). - In English and Welsh. Welsh title: Gorchymyn Defaid a Geifr (Cofnodion, Adnabod a Symod) (Cymru) 2006. - 44p.: 30 cm. - 978-0-11-091329-2 £7.50

The Sheep and Goats Transmissible Spongiform Encephalopathies (TSE) Compensation (Wales) Regulations 2006 No. 2006/1513 (W.149). - Enabling power: European Communities Act 1972, s. 2 (2). - Issued: 23.06.2006. Made: 13.06.2006. Coming into force: 14.06.2006. Effect: S.I. 2002/1416 partially revoked. Territorial extent & classification: W. General. - In English & Welsh: Welsh title: Rheoliadau Iawndal Enseffalopathi Sbyngffurf Trosglwyddadwy (TSE) Defaid a Geifr (Cymru) 2006. - 8p.: 30 cm. - 978-0-11-091357-5 £3.00

The Specified Animal Pathogens (Wales) Order 2006 No. 2006/2981 (W.272). - Enabling power: Animal Health Act 1981, ss. 1, 88 (2) (4). - Issued: 23.11.2006. Made: 14.11.2006. Coming into force: 24.11.2006. Effect: S.I. 1998/463 amended, in relation to Wales. Territorial extent & classification: W. General. - In English and Welsh. Welsh title: Gorchymyn Pathogenau Anifeiliaid Penodedig (Diwygio) (Cymru) 2006. - 8p.: 30 cm. - 978-0-11-091444-2 £3.00

The Specified Diseases (Notification and Slaughter) (Wales) Order 2006 No. 2006/2237 (W.199). - Enabling power: Animal Health Act 1981, ss. 15 (4), 32 (2), 88 (2). - Issued: 04.10.2006. Made: 16.08.2006. Coming into force: 29.08.2006. Effect: S.I. 1992/3159; 1996/2628 amended. Territorial extent & classification: W. General. - 4p.: 30 cm. - 978-0-11-091399-5 £3.00

The Tuberculosis (Wales) Order 2006 No. 2006/1053 (W.109). - Enabling power: Animal Health Act 1981, ss. 1, 7 (1), 8 (1), 15 (4), 25, 32 (2), 83 (2), 87 (2), 88 (2). - Issued: 18.04.2006. Made: 04.04.2006. Coming into force: 02.05.2006. Effect: S.I. 1984/1943; 1990/1869 revoked in relation to Wales. Territorial extent & classification: W. General. - In English and Welsh. Welsh title: Gorchymyn Twbercwlosis (Cymru) 2006. - 20p.: 30 cm. - 978-0-11-091323-0 £3.50

Atomic energy and radioactive substances

The Nuclear Industries Security (Amendment) Regulations 2006 No. 2006/2815. - Enabling power: Anti-terrorism, Crime and Security Act 2001, s: 77 (1) (a) to (f) (2) (g). - Issued: 30.10.2006. Made: 19.10.2006. Laid: 24.10.2006. Coming into force: 25.11.2006. Effect: S.I. 2003/403 amended. Territorial extent & classification: E/W/S/NI [except for reg. 8 which is GB only]. General. - 8p.: 30 cm. - 978-0-11-075215-0 £3.00

Atomic energy and radioactive substances, England and Wales

The Radioactive Substances (Emergency Exemption) (England and Wales) Order 2006 No. 2006/3169. - Enabling power: Radioactive Substances Act 1993, s. 15 (2). - Issued: 04.12.2006. Made: 28.11.2006. Laid: 29.11.2006. Coming into force: 30.11.2006. Effect: None. Territorial extent & classification: E/W. General. - Under this Order radioactive waste relating to the death of Alexander Litvinenko is excluded from the provisions of sections 13 and 14 of the Radioactive Substances Act 1993 (c.12). Those sections require a person to obtain an authorisation from the Environment Agency concerning the disposal and accumulation of radioactive waste. - 2p.: 30 cm. - 978-0-11-075391-1 £3.00

The Radioactive Substances (Testing Instruments) (England and Wales) Exemption Order 2006 No. 2006/1500. - Enabling power: Radioactive Substances Act 1993, ss. 8 (6) (7), 11 (1) (2), 15 (2). - Issued: 13.06.2006. Made: 05.06.2006. Laid: 09.06.2006. Coming into force: 06.10.2006. Effect: S.I. 1985/1049 revoked insofar as it extends to England & Wales. Territorial extent & classification: E/W. General. - 8p.: 30 cm. - 978-0-11-074666-1 £3.00

Bee diseases, England

The Bee Diseases and Pests Control (England) Order 2006 No. 2006/342. - Enabling power: Bees Act 1980, s. 1. - Issued: 20.02.2006. Made: 11.02.2006. Laid: 15.02.2006. Coming into force: 17.03.2006. Effect: S.I. 1982/107; 1997/310 revoked in relation to England. Territorial extent & classification: E. General. - EC note: Art. 11 implements for England the provisions of Commission Decision 2003/881/EC as amended by Commission Decision 2005/60/EC that apply to bees after they have been imported into England from a third country. - 8p.: 30 cm. - 978-0-11-074039-3 £3.00

Bee diseases, Wales

The Bee Diseases and Pests Control (Wales) Order 2006 No. 2006/1710 (W.172). - Enabling power: Bees Act 1980, s. 1. - Issued: 07.07.2006. Made: 27.06.2006. Coming into force: 01.07.2006. Effect: S.I. 1982/107; 1997/310 revoked in relation to Wales. Territorial extent & classification: W. General. - EC note: Implements for Wales the provisions of Commission Decision 2003/881/EC as amended by Decision 2005/60/EC that apply to bees after they have been imported into the UK from a third country. - In English and Welsh. Welsh title: Gorchymyn Rheoli Clefydau a Phlâu Gwenyn (Cymru) 2006. - 16p.: 30 cm. - 978-0-11-091376-6 £3.00

Betting, gaming and lotteries

The Gambling Act 2005 (Commencement No.3) Order 2006 No. 2006/631 (C. 14). - Enabling power: Gambling Act 2005, ss. 358 (1) (2). Bringing into operation various provisions of the 2005 Act on 31.03.2005, in accord. with reg. 2. - Issued:17.03.2006. Made: 05.03.2006. Effect: None. Territorial extent & classification: E/W/S. General. - 4p.: 30 cm. - 978-0-11-074204-5 £3.00

The Gambling Act 2005 (Commencement No. 4) Order 2006 No. 2006/2964 (C.103). - Enabling power: Gambling Act 2005, s. 358(1) (2). Bringing into operation various provisions of the 2005 Act on 13.11.2006. - Issued: 16.11.2006. Made: 12.11.2006. Effect: None. Territorial extent & classification: E/W/S. General. - 4p.: 30 cm. - 978-0-11-075304-1 £3.00

The Gambling Act 2005 (Commencement No. 5) Order 2006 No. 2006/3220 (C.115). - Enabling power: Gambling Act 2005, s. 358(1) (2). Bringing into operation various provisions of the 2005 Act on 05.12.2006. - Issued: 08.12.2006. Made: 04.12.2006. Effect: None. Territorial extent & classification: E/W/S. General. - With correction slip dated March 2007. - 2p.: 30 cm. - 978-0-11-075418-5 £3.00

The Gambling Act 2005 (Commencement No. 6 and Transitional Provisions) (Amendment) Order 2006 No. 2006/3361 (C.122). - Enabling power: Gambling Act 2005, s. 355 (1), 358 (1) (2), sch. 18, paras 2 to 11. Bringing into operation various provisions of the 2005 Act on 01.01.2007; 30.04.2007; 01.06.2007; 01.09.2007 (with transitional provisions in connection with the commencements). - Issued: 21.12.2006. Made: 14.12.2006. Effect: S.I. 2006/3272 (C.119) amended. Territorial extent & classification: E/W/S. General. - This Statutory Instrument has been made in consequence of defects in S.I. 2006/3272 and is made available free of charge to all known recipients of that Statutory Instrument. - 2p.: 30 cm. - 978-0-11-075509-0 £3.00

The Gambling Act 2005 (Commencement No. 6 and Transitional Provisions) Order 2006 No. 2006/3272 (C.119). - Enabling power: Gambling Act 2005, s. 355 (1), 358 (1) (2), sch. 18, paras 2 to 11. Bringing into operation various provisions of the 2005 Act on 01.01.2007; 30.04.2007; 01.06.2007; 01.09.2007 (with transitional provisions in connection with the commencements). - Issued: 18.12.2006. Made: 06.12.2006. Laid: 07.12.2006. Effect: None. Territorial extent & classification: E/W/S. General. - With correction slip dated March 2007. - 92p.: 30 cm. - 978-0-11-075452-9 £13.50

The Gambling Act 2005 (Definition of Small-scale Operator) Regulations 2006 No. 2006/3266. - Enabling power: Gambling Act 2005, s. 129 (2). - Issued: 14.12.2006. Made: 06.12.2006. Laid: 07.12.2006. Coming into force: 01.01.2007. Effect: None. Territorial extent & classification: E/W/S. General. - 4p.: 30 cm. - 978-0-11-075450-5 £3.00

The Gambling Act 2005 (Licensing Authority Policy Statement) (First Appointed Day) Order 2006 No. 2006/637. - Enabling power: Gambling Act 2005, s. 349 (6). - Issued: 15.03.2006. Made: 05.03.2006. Laid: 09.03.2006. Coming into force: 31.03.2006. Effect: None. Territorial extent & classification: E/W/S. General. - 2p.: 30 cm. - 978-0-11-074214-4 £3.00

The Gambling Act 2005 (Relevant Offences) (Amendment) Order 2006 No. 2006/3391. - Enabling power: Gambling Act 2005, sch. 7, para. 23. - Issued: 22.12.2006. Made: 16.12.2006. Laid: 18.12.2006. Coming into force: 08.01.2007. Effect: 2005 c.19 amended. Territorial extent & classification: E/W/S. General. - 4p.: 30 cm. - 978-0-11-075541-0 £3.00

The Gambling Act 2005 (Transitional Provisions) (No.2) Order 2006 No. 2006/1758. - Enabling power: Gambling Act 2005, s. 355 (1), sch. 18, paras 8, 11. - Issued: 10.07.2006. Made: 04.07.2006. Laid: 05.07.2006. Coming into force: 01.08.2006. Effect: None. Territorial extent & classification: E/W/S. General. - 8p.: 30 cm. - 978-0-11-074802-3 £3.00

The Gambling Act 2005 (Transitional Provisions) Order 2006 No. 2006/1038. - Enabling power: Gambling Act 2005, ss. 355 (1), sch. 18, paras 8, 11. - Issued: 10.04.2006. Made: 03.04.2006. Laid: 04.04.2006. Coming into force: 29.04.2006. Effect: 1968 c. 65 modified. Territorial extent & classification: E/W/S. General. - 4p.: 30 cm. - 978-0-11-074466-7 £3.00

The Gambling Appeals Tribunal Fees Regulations 2006 No. 2006/3287. - Enabling power: Gambling Act 2005, ss. 147, 355 (5). - Issued: 14.12.2006. Made: 08.12.2006. Laid: 11.12.2006. Coming into force: 01.01.2007. Effect: None. Territorial extent & classification: E/W/S. General. - 4p.: 30 cm. - 978-0-11-075473-4 £3.00

The Gambling Appeals Tribunal Rules 2006 No. 2006/3293. - Enabling power: Gambling Act 2005, ss. 146, 355 (5), sch. 8, paras. 9, 14. - Issued: 14.12.2006. Made: 08.12.2006. Laid: 11.12.2006. Coming into force: 01.01.2007. Effect: None. Territorial extent & classification: E/W/S. General. - 24p.: 30 cm. - 978-0-11-075474-1 £4.00

The Gambling (Operating Licence and Single-Machine Permit Fees) Regulations 2006 No. 2006/3284. - Enabling power: Gambling Act 2005, ss. 69 (2) (g) (5), 100 (2) (3), 103 (2), 104 (3) (4), 107 (2) (a), 250 (3) (e) (8), 355 (1). - Issued: 18.12.2006. Made: 10.12.2006. Laid: 11.12.2006. Coming into force: 01.01.2007 except for reg. 27; 01.09.2007 for reg. 27. Effect: None. Territorial extent & classification: E/W/S. General. - 28p.: 30 cm. - 978-0-11-075466-6 *£4.50*

The Gambling (Personal Licence Fees) Regulations 2006 No. 2006/3285. - Enabling power: Gambling Act 2005, ss. 69 (2) (g) (5), 104 (3) (4), 107 (2) (a), 128, 132 (2) (3), 355 (1). - Issued: 15.12.2006. Made: 10.12.2006. Laid: 11.12.2006. Coming into force: 01.01.2007. Effect: None. Territorial extent & classification: E/W/S. General. - 4p.: 30 cm. - 978-0-11-075467-3 *£3.00*

The Gambling (Personal Licences) (Modification of Part 5 of the Gambling Act 2005) Regulations 2006 No. 2006/3267. - Enabling power: Gambling Act 2005, s. 128 (1) (b). - Issued: 14.12.2006. Made: 06.12.2006. Laid: 07.12.2006. Coming into force: 01.01.2007. Effect: 2005 c.19 modified. Territorial extent & classification: E/W/S. General. - 8p.: 30 cm. - 978-0-11-075451-2 *£3.00*

The Gaming Act 1968 (Variation of Fees) Order 2006 No. 2006/541. - Enabling power: Gaming Act 1968, ss. 48 (5), 51 (4). - Issued: 08.03.2006. Made: 01.03.2006. Laid: 02.03.2006. Coming into force: 01.04.2006. Effect: 1968 c .65 amended & S.I. 2004/531; 2005/567 revoked. Territorial extent & classification: E/W/S. General. - 4p.: 30 cm. - 978-0-11-074146-8 *£3.00*

The Gaming Act 1968 (Variation of Monetary Limits) Order 2006 No. 2006/2663. - Enabling power: Gaming Act 1968, ss. 31 (3), 34 (9), 51 (3) (4). - Issued: 11.10.2006. Made: 03.10.2006. Laid: 05.10.2006. Coming into force: 27.10.2006. Effect: 1968 c .65 amended & S.I. 1997/2079 amended & S.I. 2001/3971; 2005/2776 revoked. Territorial extent & classification: E/W/S. General. - 4p.: 30 cm. - 978-0-11-075156-6 *£3.00*

The Lotteries (Gambling Commission Fees) Order 2006 No. 2006/542. - Enabling power: Lotteries and Amusements Act 1976, ss. 18 (1) (e) (eee) (2), 24 (2), sch. 1A, para. 6 (1) (a), sch. 2, para. 7 (1) (b). - Issued: 08.03.2006. Made: 01.03.2006. Laid: 02.03.2006. Coming into force: 01.04.2006. Effect: S.I. 2005/568 revoked. Territorial extent & classification: E/W/S. General. - 4p.: 30 cm. - 978-0-11-074147-5 *£3.00*

The Olympic Lotteries (Payments out of Fund) Regulations 2006 No. 2006/655. - Enabling power: Horserace Betting and Olympic Lottery Act 2004, ss. 26 (2) (a) (b) (f) (3). - Issued: 16.03.2006. Made: 08.03.2006. Laid: 10.03.06. Coming into force: 31.03.2006. Effect: None. Territorial extent & classification: E/W/S/NI. General. - 4p.: 30 cm. - 978-0-11-074237-3 *£3.00*

Betting, gaming and lotteries, England and Wales

The Gaming Act 1968 (Variation of Fees) (England and Wales) Order 2006 No. 2006/543. - Enabling power: Gaming Act 1968, ss. 48 (5), 51 (4). - Issued: 08.03.2006. Made: 01.03.2006. Laid: 02.03.2006. Coming into force: 01.04.2006. Effect: 1968 c.65 amended & S.I. 2005/566 amended. Territorial extent & classification: E/W. General. - 4p.: 30 cm. - 978-0-11-074148-2 *£3.00*

The Gambling Act 2005 (Licensing Authority Policy Statement) (England and Wales) Regulations 2006 No. 2006/636. - Enabling power: Gambling Act 2005, s. 349 (4). - Issued: 15.03.2006. Made: 05.03.2006. Laid: 09.03.2006. Coming into force: 31.03.2006. Effect: None. Territorial extent & classification: E/W. General. - 4p.: 30 cm. - 978-0-11-074203-8 *£3.00*

British nationality

The British Citizenship (Designated Service) Order 2006 No. 2006/1390. - Enabling power: British Nationality Act 1981, s. 2 (3). - Issued: 02.06.2006. Made: 23.05.2006. Laid: 25.05.2006. Coming into force: 16.06.2006. Effect: S.I. 1982/1004, 1709; 1984/1766; 1987/611; 1990/28; 1994/556; 1995/552 revoked. Territorial extent & classification: E/W/S/NI. General. - With correction slip dated July 2006. - 4p.: 30 cm. - 978-0-11-074610-4 *£3.00*

The British Nationality (Proof of Paternity) Regulations 2006 No. 2006/1496. - Enabling power: British Nationality Act 1981, s. 50 (9A) (9B). - Issued: 12.06.2006. Made: 05.06.2006. Laid: 09.06.2006. Coming into force: 01.07.2006. Effect: None. Territorial extent & classification: E/W/S/NI. General. - 2p.: 30 cm. - 978-0-11-074662-3 *£3.00*

Broadcasting

The Broadcasting Digital Terrestrial Sound (Technical Service) Order 2006 No. 2006/2793. - Enabling power: Broadcasting Act 1996, s. 63 (3) (b). - Issued: 25.10.2006. Made: 18.10.2006. Laid: 19.10.2006. Coming into force: 13.11.2006. Effect: S.I. 1998/685 amended. Territorial extent & classification: E/W/S/NI/Jersey/Guernsey. General. - 2p.: 30 cm. - 978-0-11-075201-3 *£3.00*

The Communications (Television Licensing) (Amendment) Regulations 2006 No. 2006/619. - Enabling power: Wireless Telegraphy Act 1967, s. 6 (1) & Communications Act 2003, ss. 365 (1) (4), 402 (3). - Issued: 14.03.2006. Made: 07.03.2006. Laid: 08.03.2006. Coming into force: 01.04.2006. Effect: S.I. 2004/692 amended. Territorial extent & classification: UK. General. - 12p.: 30 cm. - 978-0-11-074194-9 *£3.00*

The Gaelic Language (Scotland) Act 2005 (Consequential Modifications) Order 2006 No. 2006/241 (S.1). - Enabling power: Scotland Act 1998, ss. 104, 112 (1), 113. - Issued: 21.02.2006. Made: 14.02.2006. Coming into force: 31.03.2006. Effect: 1990 c. 42 amended. Territorial extent & classification: E/W/S/NI. General. - With correction slip dated April 2006, correcting the 'Made' date. - 4p.: 30 cm. - 978-0-11-069932-5 *£3.00*

The Radio Multiplex Services (Required Percentage of Digital Capacity) Order 2006 No. 2006/2130. - Enabling power: Broadcasting Act 1996, s. 54 (3). - Issued: 08.08.2006. Made: 24.07.2006. Coming into force: 25.07.2006. Effect: 1996 c. 55 modified. Territorial extent & classification: E/W/S/NI/Jersey/Guernsey. General. - 2p.: 30 cm. - 978-0-11-074979-2 *£3.00*

The Television Licensable Content Services Order 2006 No. 2006/2131. - Enabling power: Broadcasting Act 1996, s. 1 (5) and Communications Act 2003, ss. 234, 402 (3). - Issued: 08.08.2006. Made: 24.07.2006. Coming into force: 25.07.2006. Effect: 1996 c. 55; 2003 c. 21 amended. Territorial extent & classification: E/W/S/NI/Jersey/Guernsey. General. - 4p.: 30 cm. - 978-0-11-074980-8 *£3.00*

The Wireless Telegraphy (Guernsey) Order 2006 No. 2006/3325. - Enabling power: Wireless Telegraphy Act 1967, s. 15 (6); Broadcasting Act 1990, s. 204 (6); Intelligence Services Act 1994, s. 12 (4), Broadcasting Act 1996, s. 150 (4); Communications Act 2003, s. 411 (6) and Wireless Telegraphy Act 2006, ss. 118 (3) (6), 119 (3), sch. 8, para. 24. - Issued: 21.12.2006. Made: 14.12.2006. Coming into force: 08.02.2007. Effect: 2006 c.36 modified; S.I. 1994/1064; 2003/3195 modified and S.I. 1952/1900; 1967/1279; 1997/284 revoked as they relate to Guernsey; S.I. 1967/1274; 1998/1511 revoked. Territorial extent & classification: Guernsey. General. - 12p.: 30 cm. - 978-0-11-075520-5 *£3.00*

The Wireless Telegraphy (Jersey) Order 2006 No. 2006/3324. - Enabling power: Wireless Telegraphy Act 1967, s. 15 (6); Broadcasting Act 1990, s. 204 (6); Intelligence Services Act 1994, s. 12 (4), Broadcasting Act 1996, s. 150 (4); Communications Act 2003, s. 411 (6) and Wireless Telegraphy Act 2006, ss. 118 (3) (6), 119 (3), sch. 8, para. 24. - Issued: 21.12.2006. Made: 14.12.2006. Coming into force: 08.02.2007. Effect: 2006 c.36 modified; S.I. 2003/3197; 2004/308 amended and S.I. 1952/1900; 1967/1279; 1997/284 revoked as they relate to Jersey; S.I. 1967/1275; 1998/1512; 2003/3196 revoked. Territorial extent & classification: Jersey. General. - 16p.: 30 cm. - 978-0-11-075516-8 *£3.00*

Building and buildings, England and Wales

The Building and Approved Inspectors (Amendment) (No. 2) Regulations 2006 No. 2006/3318. - Enabling power: Building Act 1984, ss. 1 (1), 35, 47 (4), sch. 1, paras 1, 4, 7, 8, 10. - Issued: 18.12.2006. Made: 13.12.2006. Laid: 18.12.2006. Coming into force: 15.01.2007 & 06.04.2007 in accord. with reg. 1. Effect: S.I. 2000/2531, 2532 amended. Territorial extent & classification: E/W. General. - 8p.: 30 cm. - 978-0-11-075493-2 *£3.00*

The Building and Approved Inspectors (Amendment) Regulations 2006 No. 2006/652. - Enabling power: European Communities Act 1972, s. 2 (2) & Building Act 1984, ss. 1 (1), 2A, 3 (1), 8 (6), 35, 47, sch. 1, paras 1, 2, 4, 4A, 7, 8, 10. - Issued: 15.03.2006. Made: 09.03.2006. Laid: 15.03.2006. Coming into force: In accord. with reg. 1. Effect: S.I. 2000/2531, 2532 amended. Territorial extent & classification: E/W. General. - EC note: These Regs implement arts 3 to 6 of the Energy Performance of Buildings Directive 2002/91/EC by amending the Building Regs 2000 and Building (Approved Inspectors etc) Regs 2000. - 24p.: 30 cm. - 978-0-11-074239-7 *£4.00*

The Sustainable and Secure Buildings Act 2004 (Commencement No. 1) Order 2006 No. 2006/224 (C.4). - Enabling power: Sustainable and Secure Buildings Act 2004, s. 11 (3). Bringing into operation various provisions of the 2004 Act on 01.02.2006. - Issued: 08.02.2006. Made: 31.01.2006. Effect: None. Territorial extent & classification: E/W. General. - 2p.: 30 cm. - 978-0-11-074012-6 *£3.00*

Canals and inland waterways, England and Wales

The Transport and Works (Applications and Objections Procedure) (England and Wales) Rules 2006 No. 2006/1466. - Enabling power: Transport and Works Act 1992, ss. 6, 6A, 7 (3) (b) (c) (4), 10. - Issued: 14.06.2006. Made: 03.06.2006. Laid: 08.06.2006. Coming into force: 11.09.2006. Effect: S.I. 2000/2190 revoked with savings. Territorial extent & classification: E/W. General. - With correction slip dated July 2006. - 48p.: 30 cm. - 978-0-11-074665-4 *£7.50*

Capital gains tax

The Authorised Investment Funds (Tax) Regulations 2006 No. 2006/964. - Enabling power: Finance Act 1995, s. 152 & Finance (No. 2) Act 2005, ss. 17 (3), 18. - Issued: 06.04.2006. Made: 29.03.2006. Coming into force: 01.04.2006. Effect: 1970 c. 9; 1988 c. 1; 1992 c. 12; 1996 c. 8; 2005 c. 5, c. 7 amended & S.I. 1997/1154, 1715; 2002/1973; 2003/1831 revoked. Territorial extent & classification: E/W/S/NI. General. - Approved by the House of Commons. Supersedes draft SI (ISBN 0110740300) issued 17.02.2006. - 48p.: 30 cm. - 978-0-11-074427-8 *£7.50*

The Capital Gains Tax (Annual Exempt Amount) Order 2006 No. 2006/871. - Enabling power: Taxation of Chargeable Gains Act 1992, s. 3 (4). - Issued: 28.03.2006. Made: 22.03.2006. Coming into force: 22.03.2006. Effect: None. Territorial extent & classification: E/W/S/NI. General. - 2p.: 30 cm. - 978-0-11-074386-8 £3.00

The Capital Gains Tax (Definition of Permanent Interest Bearing Share) Regulations 2006 No. 2006/3291. - Enabling power: Taxation of Chargeable Gains Act 1992, s. 117 (12). - Issued: 14.12.2006. Made: 11.12.2006. Laid: 11.12.2006. Coming into force: 01.01.2007. Effect: 1992 c. 12 amended. Territorial extent & classification: E/W/S/NI. General. - 2p.: 30 cm. - 978-0-11-075475-8 £3.00

The Double Taxation Relief (Taxes on Income) (Botswana) Order 2006 No. 2006/1925. - Enabling power: Income and Corporation Taxes Act 1988, s. 788. - Issued: 26.07.2006. Made: 19.07.2006. Coming into force: 19.07.2006. Effect: None. Territorial extent & classification: E/W/S/NI. General. - Supersedes draft S.I. (ISBN 0110745159) issued 03.05.2006. - 20p.: 30 cm. - 978-0-11-074890-0 £3.50

The Double Taxation Relief (Taxes on Income) (Japan) Order 2006 No. 2006/1924. - Enabling power: Income and Corporation Taxes Act 1988, s. 788. - Issued: 26.07.2006. Made: 19.07.2006. Coming into force: 19.07.2006. Effect: None. Territorial extent & classification: E/W/S/NI. General. - Supersedes draft S.I. (ISBN 0110745124) issued 03.05.2006. - 28p.: 30 cm. - 978-0-11-074891-7 £4.50

The Double Taxation Relief (Taxes on Income) (Poland) Order 2006 No. 2006/3323. - Enabling power: Income and Corporation Taxes Act 1988, s. 788 & Finance Act 2006, s. 173 (1) to (3)- Issued: 04.01.2007. Made: 14.12.2006. Coming into force: 14.12.2006. Effect: None. Territorial extent & classification: E/W/S/NI. General. - Supersedes the draft S.I. (ISBN 0110752279) issued on 31.10.2006. - 20p.: 30 cm. - 978-0-11-075523-6 £3.50

The Pension Protection Fund (Tax) Regulations 2006 No. 2006/575. - Enabling power: Finance Act 2005, s. 102. - Issued: 14.03.2006. Made: 09.03.2006. Laid: 10.03.2006. Coming into force: 06.04.2006. Effect: None. Territorial extent & classification: E/W/S/NI. General. - 14p.: 30 cm. - 978-0-11-074218-2 £3.00

The Reporting of Savings Income Information (Amendment) Regulations 2006 No. 2006/3286. - Enabling power: Finance Act 2003, s. 199. - Issued: 14.12.2006. Made: 11.12.2006. Laid: 11.12.2006. Coming into force: 01.01.2007. Effect: S.I. 2003/3297 amended. Territorial extent & classification: E/W/S/NI. General. - With correction slip dated January 2007. EC note: These Regs amend the 2003 Regulations which implemented part of Council Directive 2003/48/EC on the taxation of savings income in the form of interest payments. The 2003 Directive has been amended by Council Directive 2006/98/EC adapting certain Directives in the field of taxation by reason of the accession of Bulgaria and Romania. - 4p.: 30 cm. - 978-0-11-075468-0 £3.00

The Taxation of Chargeable Gains (Gilt-edged Securities) (No.2) Order 2006 No. 2006/3170. - Enabling power: Taxation of Chargeable Gains Act 1992, sch. 9, para. 1. - Issued: 01.12.2006. Made: 28.11.2006. Coming into force: 28.11.2006. Effect: None. Territorial extent & classification: E/W/S/NI. General. - 2p.: 30 cm. - 978-0-11-075389-8 £3.00

The Taxation of Chargeable Gains (Gilt-edged Securities) Order 2006 No. 2006/184. - Enabling power: Taxation of Chargeable Gains Act 1992, sch. 9, para. 1. - Issued: 03.02.2006. Made: 30.01.2006. Coming into force: 30.01.2006. Effect: None. Territorial extent & classification: E/W/S/NI. General. - 2p.: 30 cm. - 978-0-11-073965-6 £3.00

The Tax Avoidance Schemes (Information) (Amendment) Regulations 2006 No. 2006/1544. - Enabling power: Finance Act 2004, ss. 308 (1) (3), 309 (1), 310, 313 (1), 317 (2), 318 (1). - Issued: 20.06.2006. Made: 15.06.2006. Laid: 15.06.2006. Coming into force: 01.08.2006. Effect: S.I. 2004/1864 amended. Territorial extent & classification: E/W/S/NI. General. - 4p.: 30 cm. - 978-0-11-074707-1 £3.00

The Tax Avoidance Schemes (Prescribed Descriptions of Arrangements) Regulations 2006 No. 2006/1543. - Enabling power: Finance Act 2004, s. 306 (1) (a) (b). - Issued: 20.06.2006. Made: 15.06.2006. Laid: 15.06.2006. Coming into force: 01.08.2006. Effect: S.I. 2004/1863, 2429 revoked. Territorial extent & classification: E/W/S/NI. General. - 12p.: 30 cm. - 978-0-11-074706-4 £3.00

Caribbean and North Atlantic territories

The Turks and Caicos Islands Constitution Order 2006 No. 2006/1913. - Enabling power: West Indies Act 1962, ss. 5, 7. - Issued: 26.07.2006. Made: 19.07.2006. Laid: 20.07.2006. Coming into force: In accordance with s. 1 (2). Effect: S.I. 1988/247; 1993/1248; 2002/2637 revoked. Territorial extent & classification: Turks & Caicos Is. General. - 52p.: 30 cm. - 978-0-11-074883-2 £9.00

Channel Tunnel

The Channel Tunnel (International Arrangements) (Amendment) Order 2006 No. 2006/2626. - Enabling power: Channel Tunnel Act 1987, s. 11. - Issued: 05.10.2006. Made: 29.09.2006. Laid: 05.10.2006. Coming into force: 26.10.2006. Effect: S.I. 1993/1813 amended. Territorial extent & classification: E/W/S/NI. General. - 2p.: 30 cm. - 978-0-11-075144-3 £3.00

The Channel Tunnel (Miscellaneous Provisions) (Amendment) Order 2006 No. 2006/2627. - Enabling power: Channel Tunnel Act 1987, s. 11. - Issued: 05.10.2006. Made: 29.09.2006. Laid: 05.10.2006. Coming into force: 26.10.2006. Effect: S.I. 1994/1405 amended. Territorial extent & classification: E/W/S/NI. General. - 2p.: 30 cm. - 978-0-11-075143-6 £3.00

Charities

The Charities and Trustee Investment (Scotland) Act 2005 (Consequential Provisions and Modifications) Order 2006 No. 2006/242 (S.2). - Enabling power: Scotland Act 1998, ss. 104, 112 (1), 113. - Issued: 21.02.2006. Made: 14.02.2006. Coming into force: In accords. with art. 1, 03.02.2006, 01.04.2006. Effect: 1974 c. 39; 1975 c. 24; 1985 c. 6; 1989 c. 40; 1990 c. 40; 1993 c. 10; 2000 c. 8; 2004 c. 27; S.I. 1997/2436; 1999/678; 2001/1201; 2005/1788 amended. Territorial extent & classification: E/W/S/NI. General. - With correction slip dated April 2006, correcting the 'Made' date. - 8p.: 30 cm. - 978-0-11-069931-8 £3.00

The Exempt Charities Order 2006 No. 2006/1452. - Enabling power: Charities Act 1993, sch. 2, para. (c). - Issued: 13.06.2006. Made: 07.06.2006. Coming into force: 08.06.2006. Effect: None. Territorial extent & classification: E/W/S/NI. General. - With correction slip dated June 2006. - 2p.: 30 cm. - 978-0-11-074677-7 £3.00

Charities, England and Wales

The Charities (Cheadle Royal Hospital, Manchester) Order 2006 No. 2006/921. - Enabling power: Charities Act 1993, s. 17 (2). - Issued: 31.03.2006. Made: 26.03.2006. Coming into force: 09.04.2006. Effect: Act 5 Victoria session 2 cap. i varied. Territorial extent & classification: E/W. General. - Supersedes draft SI (ISBN 0110739515) issued 02.02.2006. - 8p.: 30 cm. - 978-0-11-074399-8 £3.00

Children and young persons

The Child Abduction and Custody Act 1985 (Jersey) Order 2006 No. 2006/1917. - Enabling power: Child Abduction and Custody Act 1985, s. 28 (2). - Issued: 31.07.2006. Made: 19.07.2006. Laid: 31.07.2006. Coming into force: 21.08.2006. Effect: 1985 c. 60 modified. Territorial extent & classification: E/W/S/NI. General. - 2p.: 30 cm. - 978-0-11-074886-3 £3.00

The Family Law Act 1986 (Dependent Territories) (Amendment) Order 2006 No. 2006/1456. - Enabling power: Family Law Act 1986, s. 43. - Issued: 19.06.2006. Made: 07.06.2006. Laid: 19.06.2006. Coming into force: 10.07.2006. Effect: S.I. 1991/1723 amended. Territorial extent & classification: E/W/S/NI. General. - 4p.: 30 cm. - 978-0-11-074671-5 £3.00

Children and young persons, England

The Childcare Act 2006 (Commencement No. 1) Order 2006 No. 2006/3360 (C.121). - Enabling power: Childcare Act 2006, s. 109 (2). Bringing into operation various provisions of the 2006 Act on 20.12.2006. - Issued: 21.12.2006. Made: 14.12.2006. Effect: None. Territorial extent & classification: E. General. - 2p.: 30 cm. - 978-0-11-075507-6 £3.00

The Children Act 1989 Representations Procedure (England) Regulations 2006 No. 2006/1738. - Enabling power: Children Act 1989, 24D (1A) (2), 26 (3A) (3B) (3C) (4A) (5) (5A) (6), 26A (3) (b), 59 (4) (5) (6), 104 (4), sch. 7, para. 6 (2). - Issued: 07.07.2006. Made: 29.06.2006. Laid: 07.07.2006. Coming into force: 01.09.2006. Effect: S.I. 2001/2874, 3967; 2002/57, 546; 2004/719; 2005/3482 amended & S.I. 1991/894 revoked with saving. Territorial extent & classification: E. General. - 12p.: 30 cm. - 978-0-11-074787-3 £3.00

The Children Act 2004 (Commencement No. 8) Order 2006 No. 2006/927 (C.24). - Enabling power: Children Act 2004, s. 67 (2). Bringing into operation various provisions of the 2004 Act on 01.04.2006. - Issued: 03.04.2006. Made: 25.03.2006. Effect: None. Territorial extent & classification: E. General. - 4p.: 30 cm. - 978-0-11-074404-9 £3.00

The Commission for Social Care Inspection (Fees and Frequency of Inspections) (Amendment) Regulations 2006 No. 2006/517. - Enabling power: Care Standards Act 2000, ss. 12 (2), 15 (3), 16 (3), 31 (7), 45 (4), 118 (5) (6) & Children Act 1989, s. 87D (2). - Issued: 03.03.2006. Made: 28.02.2006. Laid: 03.03.2006. Coming into force: 01.04.2006. Effect: S.I. 2004/662 amended & S.I. 2005/575 revoked. Territorial extent & classification: E. General. - 4p.: 30 cm. - 978-0-11-074133-8 £3.00

The Day Care and Child Minding (Registration Fees) (England) (Amendment) Regulations 2006 No. 2006/2081. - Enabling power: Children Act 1989, ss. 79E (2) (c), 104 (4), sch. 9A, para. 7. - Issued: 04.08.2006. Made: 27.07.2006. Laid: 04.08.2006. Coming into force: 02.10.2006. Effect: S.I. 2005/2301 amended. Territorial extent & classification: E. General. - 2p.: 30 cm. - 978-0-11-074960-0 £3.00

The Education and Inspections Act 2006 (Commencement No. 1 and Saving Provisions) Order 2006 No. 2006/2990 (C.105). - Enabling power: Education and Inspections Act 2006, ss. 181, 188 (3). Bringing into operation various provisions of the 2006 Act on 12.12.2006. - Issued: 22.11.2006. Made: 15.11.2006. Effect: None. Territorial extent & classification: E. General. - 4p.: 30 cm. - 978-0-11-075330-0 £3.00

The Information Sharing Index (England) Regulations 2006 No. 2006/983. - Enabling power: Children Act 2004, ss. 12 (4) (f) (h) (5) (6) (11), 66 (1). - Issued: 06.04.2006. Made: 30.03.2006. Coming into force: 06.04.2006 in accord. with reg. 1 (1). Effect: None. Territorial extent & classification: E. General. - Supersedes draft SI (ISBN 0110741498) issued 09.03.2006. - 4p.: 30 cm. - 978-0-11-074433-9 £3.00

The Local Safeguarding Children Boards Regulations 2006 No. 2006/90. - Enabling power: Children Act 2004, ss. 13 (2), 14 (2) (3), 16 (1), 66 (1). - Issued: 26.01.2006. Made: 16.01.2006. Laid: 26.01.2006. Coming into force: 01.04.2006. Effect: None. Territorial extent & classification: E. General. - 4p.: 30 cm. - 978-0-11-073921-2 £3.00

The National Care Standards Commission (Commission for Social Care Inspection) (Fees) (Adoption Agencies, Adoption Support Agencies and Local Authority Fostering Functions) (Amendment) Regulations 2006 No. 2006/578. - Enabling power: Care Standards Act 2000, ss. 12 (2), 15 (3), 16 (3), 118 (5) (6) & Health and Social Care (Community Health and Standards Act) 2003, s. 86 (1). - Issued: 10.03.2006. Made: 06.03.2006. Laid: 10.03.2006. Coming into force: 01.04.2006. Effect: S.I. 2003/368 amended. Territorial extent & classification: E. General. - 4p.: 30 cm. - 978-0-11-074172-7 £3.00

The Office for Standards in Education, Children's Services and Skills (Transitional Provisions) Regulations 2006 No. 2006/2991. - Enabling power: Education and Inspections Act 2006, ss. 181 (2) (c), 183 (1) (2), sch. 15, para. 7 (1). - Issued: 22.11.2006. Made: 15.11.2006. Laid: 21.11.2006. Coming into force: 12.12.2006. Effect: None. Territorial extent & classification: E. General. - 4p.: 30 cm. - 978-0-11-075331-7 £3.00

Children and young persons, England and Wales

The Children (Prescribed Orders - Northern Ireland, Guernsey and Isle of Man) Amendment Regulations 2006 No. 2006/837. - Enabling power: Children Act 1989, s. 101. - Issued: 27.03.2006. Made: 20.03.2006. Laid: 22.03.2006. Coming into force: 12.04.2006. Effect: S.I. 1991/2032 amended. Territorial extent & classification: E/W. General. - 4p.: 30 cm. - 978-0-11-074368-4 £3.00

The Protection of Children and Vulnerable Adults and Care Standards Tribunal (Amendment) Regulations 2006 No. 2006/1930. - Enabling power: Protection of Children Act 1999, s. 9 (2) (3) (b) (d) (3B). - Issued: 24.07.2006. Made: 13.07.2006. Laid: 24.07.2006. Coming into force: 01.10.2006. Effect: S.I. 2002/816 amended. Territorial extent & classification: E/W. General. - 4p.: 30 cm. - 978-0-11-074863-4 £3.00

The Protection of Children and Vulnerable Adults and Care Standards Tribunal (Review of Disqualification Orders) Regulations 2006 No. 2006/1929. - Enabling power: Protection of Children Act 1999, s. 9 (2) (e) (3) (3B). - Issued: 24.07.2006. Made: 13.07.2006. Laid: 24.07.2006. Coming into force: 15.08.2006. Effect: None. Territorial extent & classification: E/W. General. - 12p.: 30 cm. - 978-0-11-074860-3 £3.00

Children and young persons, Wales

The Care Standards Act 2000 and the Children Act 1989 (Abolition of Fees) (Wales) Regulations 2006 No. 2006/878 (W.83). - Enabling power: Care Standards Act 2000, ss. 12 (2), 15 (3), 16 (3), 22 (7), 118 (5) to (7) & Children Act 1989, ss. 79F, 87D, 104 (4), sch. 9A, para. 7 & Health and Social Care (Community Health and Standards) Act 2003, s. 94 (6). - Issued: 29.03.2006. Made: 21.03.2006. Coming into force: 01.04.2006. Effect: S.I. 2002/919 (W.107), 2935 (W.277), 3161 (W.296); 2003/237 (W.35), 781 (W.92), 2527 (W. 242); 2004/219 (W.23), 1756 (W.188) amended & S.I. 2002/921 (W.109) revoked. Territorial extent & classification: W. General. - In English and Welsh. Welsh title: Rheoliadau Deddf Safonau Gofal 2000 a Deddf Plant 1989 (Dileu Ffioedd) (Cymru) 2006. - 4p.: 30 cm. - 978-0-11-091304-9 £3.00

The Care Standards Act 2000 and the Children Act 1989 (Regulatory Reform and Complaints) (Wales) Regulations 2006 No. 2006/3251 (W.295). - Enabling power: Children Act 1989, ss. 23 (2) (a) (9), 59 (2), 79C, 104 (4), sch. 2, para. 12; Care Standards Act 2000, ss. 14 (1) (d), 16, 22, 25, 33, 42 (1), 48 (1), 50, 118 (1) (5) to (7) and Adoption and Children Act 2002, ss. 2 (6) (b), 9(1) (3), 10, 140 (1). - Issued: 14.12.2006. Made: 05.12.2006. Coming into force: 01.01.2007. Effect: S.I. 2002/324 (W.37), 327 (W.40), 812 (W.92), 919 (W.107); 2003/237 (W.35), 781 (W.92), 2527 (W.242); 2004/219 (W.23), 1756 (W.188); 2005/1514 (W.118) amended. Territorial extent & classification: W. General. - In English and Welsh. Welsh title: Rheoliadau Deddf Safonau Gofal 2000 a Deddf Plant 1989 (Diwygio Rheoleiddiol a Chwynion) (Cymru) 2006. - 48p.: 30 cm. - 978-0-11-091467-1 £7.50

The Children Act 2004 (Commencement No. 6) (Wales) Order 2006 No. 2006/885 (W.85)(C.23). - Enabling power: Children Act 2004, s. 67 (3) (7) (a) (c) (e) (i), sch. 5. Bringing into operation various provisions of the 2004 Act in accord. with art 1. - Issued: 28.03.2006. Made: 21.03.2006. Effect: None. Territorial extent & classification: W. General. - In English and Welsh. Welsh title: Gorchymyn Deddf Plant 2004 (Cychwyn Rhif 6) (Cymru) 2006. - 8p.: 30 cm. - 978-0-11-091302-5 £3.00

The Children Act 2004 (Commencement No. 7) (Wales) Order 2006 No. 2006/870 (W.80)(C.20). - Enabling power: Children Act 2004, s. 67 (3) (4). Bringing into operation various provisions of the 2004 Act on 01.09.2006 & 01.10.2006 in accord. with art 2. - Issued: 10.04.2006. Made: 21.03.2006. Effect: None. Territorial extent & classification: W. General. - With correction slip dated May 2006. - In English and Welsh. Welsh title: Gorchymyn Deddf Plant 2004 (Cychwyn Rhif 7) (Cymru) 2006. - 8p.: 30 cm. - 978-0-11-091318-6 £3.00

The Children (Private Arrangements for Fostering) (Wales) Regulations 2006 No. 2006/940 (W.89). - Enabling power: Children Act 1989 ss. 67 (2) (2A) (6), 104 (4), sch. 8, para. 7. - Issued: 05.04.2006. Made: 28.03.2006. Coming into force: 01.04.2006. Effect: S.I. 1991/2050 revoked with savings in relation to Wales. Territorial extent & classification: W. General. - In English and Welsh. Welsh title: Rheoliadau Plant (Trefniadau Preifat ar gyfer Maethu) (Cymru) 2006. - 16p.: 30 cm. - 978-0-11-091308-7 *£3.00*

The Independent Review of Determinations (Adoption) (Wales) Regulations 2006 No. 2006/3100 (W.284). - Enabling power: Adoption and Children Act 2002, ss. 9, 12. - Issued: 05.12.2006. Made: 21.11.2006. Coming into force: 31.12.2006. Effect: S.I. 2005/2689 (W. 189) amended & S.I. 2005/1819 (W.147) revoked. Territorial extent & classification: W. General. - In English and Welsh. Welsh title: Rheoliadau Adolygu Penderfyniadau'n Annibynnol (Mabwysiadu) (Cymru) 2006. - 16p.: 30 cm. - 978-0-11-091450-3 *£3.00*

The Local Safeguarding Children Boards (Wales) Regulations 2006 No. 2006/1705 (W.167). - Enabling power: Children Act 2004, ss. 31 (2) (4) (5), 32 (2) (3), 34 (1), 66 (1). - Issued: 14.07.2006. Made: 27.06.2006. Coming into force: 01.10.2006. Effect: None. Territorial extent & classification: W. General. - With correction slip dated July 2006. - In English and Welsh. Welsh title: Rheoliadau Byrddau Lleol ar gyfer Diogelu Plant (Cymru) 2006. - 12p.: 30 cm. - 978-0-11-091377-3 *£3.00*

Child trust funds

The Child Trust Funds (Amendment No. 2) Regulations 2006 No. 2006/2684. - Enabling power: Child Trust Funds Act 2004, ss. 3 (5) (10), 16, 28 (1) to (4). - Issued: 13.10.2006. Made: 09.10.2006. Laid: 10.10.2006. Coming into force: 31.10.2006. Effect: S.I. 2004/1450 amended. Territorial extent & classification: E/W/S/NI. General. - 4p.: 30 cm. - 978-0-11-075165-8 *£3.00*

The Child Trust Funds (Amendment No. 3) Regulations 2006 No. 2006/3195. - Enabling power: Child Trust Funds Act 2004, ss. 13, 28 (1) to (4). - Issued: 05.12.2006. Made: 30.11.2006. Laid: 01.12.2006. Coming into force: 01.01.2007. Effect: S.I. 2004/1450 amended. Territorial extent & classification: E/W/S/NI. General. - 2p.: 30 cm. - 978-0-11-075404-8 *£3.00*

The Child Trust Funds (Amendment) Regulations 2006 No. 2006/199. - Enabling power: Child Trust Funds Act 2004, ss. 3, 5 (1) (4) (5), 8 (1), 28 (1) to (4). - Issued: 06.02.2006. Made: 31.01.2006. Laid: 31.01.2006. Coming into force: 07.02.2006. Effect: S.I. 2004/1450 amended. Territorial extent & classification: E/W/S/NI. General. - 2p.: 30 cm. - 978-0-11-073967-0 *£3.00*

Chiropractors

The General Chiropractic Council (Professional Conduct Committee and Health Committee) Amendment Rules Order of Council 2006 No. 2006/1630. - Enabling power: Chiropractors Act 1994, ss. 26, 35 (2), sch. 1, para. 21. - Issued: 30.06.2006. Made: 16.06.2006. Coming into force: 30.06.2006. Effect: S.I. 2000/3290, 3291 amended. Territorial extent & classification: E/W/S/NI. General. - 4p.: 30 cm. - 978-0-11-074730-9 *£3.00*

Cinemas and film

The European Convention on Cinematographic Co-production Order 2006 No. 2006/2656. - Enabling power: Films Act 1985, sch. 1, para. 4 (5). - Issued: 16.10.2006. Made: 10.10.2006. Coming into force: 11.10.2006. Effect: 24 S.I.s revoked in accord. with the schedule. Territorial extent & classification: E/W/S/NI. General. - 4p.: 30 cm. - 978-0-11-075174-0 *£3.00*

The Films Co-Production Agreements (Amendment) Order 2006 No. 2006/1921. - Enabling power: Films Act 1985, sch. 1, para. 4 (5). - Issued: 26.07.2006. Made: 19.07.2006. Coming into force: 20.07.2006. Effect: S.I. 1985/960 amended & S.I. 1985/2001; 1990/1513; 1991/1725; 1993/1805; 1994/3222; 2000/740 revoked. Territorial extent & classification: E/W/S/NI. General. - 2p.: 30 cm. - 978-0-11-074896-2 *£3.00*

The Films (Certification) (Amendment) Regulations 2006 No. 2006/642. - Enabling power: Films Act 1985, sch. 1, para. 10. - Issued: 16.03.2006. Made: 07.03.2006. Laid: 10.03.06. Coming into force: 01.04.2006 in accord. with reg. 1. Effect: S.I. 1985/994 amended. Territorial extent & classification: E/W/S/NI. General. - 4p.: 30 cm. - 978-0-11-074238-0 *£3.00*

The Films (Certification) Regulations 2006 No. 2006/3281. - Enabling power: Films Act 1985, sch. 1, para. 10 (1). - Issued: 15.12.2006. Made: 07.12.2006. Laid: 11.12.2006. Coming into force: In accord. with reg. 1. Effect: None. Territorial extent & classification: E/W/S/NI. General. - 8p.: 30 cm. - 978-0-11-075462-8 *£3.00*

The Films (Definition of "British Film") (No. 2) Order 2006 No. 2006/3430. - Enabling power: Films Act 1985, sch. 1, para. 10 (2). - Issued: 29.12.2006. Made: 18.12.2006. Coming into force: 01.01.2007. Effect: 1985 c. 21 amended. Territorial extent & classification: E/W/S/NI. General. - Supersedes draft SI (ISBN 0110753631) issued 01.12.2006. - 8p.: 30 cm. - 978-0-11-075571-7 *£3.00*

The Films (Definition of "British Film") Order 2006 No. 2006/643. - Enabling power: Films Act 1985, sch. 1, para. 10 (2). - Issued: 07.04.2006. Made: 31.03.2006. Coming into force: 01.04.2006. Effect: 1985 c. 21 amended. Territorial extent & classification: E/W/S/NI. General. - 8p.: 30 cm. - 978-0-11-074459-9 *£3.00*

Civil aviation

The Air Navigation (Amendment) Order 2006 No. 2006/2316. - Enabling power: Civil Aviation Act 1982, ss. 60 (1) (2) (b) (3) (h) (4), 61 (1) (a), 102 (2) (b), sch. 13, part 3, para. 2. - Issued: 11.09.2006. Made: 05.09.2006. Laid: 07.09.2006. Coming into force: 30.09.2006. Effect: S.I. 2005/1970 amended. Territorial extent & classification: E/W/S/NI. General. - 4p.: 30 cm. - 978-0-11-075080-4 £3.00

The Air Navigation (Dangerous Goods) (Amendment) Regulations 2006 No. 2006/1092. - Enabling power: S.I. 2005/1970, art. 70 (1). - Issued: 19.04.2006. Made: 10.04.2006. Coming into force: 21.04.2006. Effect: S.I. 2002/2786 amended. Territorial extent & classification: E/W/S/NI. General. - 2p.: 30 cm. - 978-0-11-074491-9 £3.00

The Air Navigation (General) Regulations 2006 No. 2006/601. - Enabling power: S.I. 2005/1970, arts. 16 (7) (a), 20 (2) (4), 42 (1) (c) (ii), 43 (5), 44 (5) (6), 45 (1), 56 (1), 57 (1), 58 (b), 131 (1), 142 (6), 143 (2), 155 (1), sch. 5, paras 4, 5 (1). - Issued: 15.03.2006. Made: 06.03.2006. Coming into force: 30.03.2006. Effect: S.I. 2005/1980 revoked. Territorial extent & classification: E/W/S/NI. General. - This Statutory Instrument has been made principally to remedy defects in S.I.2005/1980 and is being issued free of charge to all known recipients of that Statutory Instrument. - 36p.: 30 cm. - 978-0-11-074192-5 £6.50

The Air Navigation (Overseas Territories) (Amendment) Order 2006 No. 2006/1911. - Enabling power: Civil Aviation Act 1949, ss. 8, 41, 57, 58, 59, 61 & Civil Aviation Act 1982, s. 61. - Issued: 31.07.2006. Made: 19.07.2006. Laid: 31.07.2006. Coming into force: 21.08.2006. Effect: S.I. 2001/2128 amended. Territorial extent & classification: Anguilla, Bermuda, British Antarctic Territory, British Indian Ocean Territory, Cayman/Falkland Isles., Montserrat, Pitcairn, Henderson, Ducie & Oeno Is, St Helena & Dependencies (Tristan da Cunha/Ascension Is.), South Georgia & South Sandwich Is, Sovereign Base Areas of Akrotiri & Dhekelia, Turks & Caicos Is., Virgin Is. General. - 8p.: 30 cm. - 978-0-11-074885-6 £3.00

The Air Navigation (Restriction of Flying) (Abergele) Regulations 2006 No. 2006/101. - Enabling power: S.I. 2005/1970, art. 96. - Made: 08.01.2006. Coming into force: Forthwith. Effect: None. Territorial extent & classification: E. Local. - Revoked by S.I. 2006/102 (Unpublished) *Unpublished*

The Air Navigation (Restriction of Flying) (Abergele) (Revocation) Regulations 2006 No. 2006/102. - Enabling power: S.I. 2005/1970, art. 96. - Made: 08.01.2006. Coming into force: Forthwith. Effect: S.I. 2006/101 revoked. Territorial extent & classification: E. Local *Unpublished*

The Air Navigation (Restriction of Flying) (Arsingworth) Regulations 2006 No. 2006/1234. - Enabling power: S.I. 2005/1970, art. 96. - Made: 26.04.2006. Coming into force: Forthwith. Effect: None. Territorial extent & classification: E. Local. - Revoked by S.I. 2006/1235 (Unpublished) *Unpublished*

The Air Navigation (Restriction of Flying) (Arsingworth) (Revocation) Regulations 2006 No. 2006/1235. - Enabling power: S.I. 2005/1970, art. 96. - Made: 26.04.2006. Coming into force: Forthwith. Effect: S.I. 2006/1234 revoked. Territorial extent & classification: E. Local *Unpublished*

The Air Navigation (Restriction of Flying) (Beating the Retreat Ceremony) Regulations 2006 No. 2006/791. - Enabling power: S.I. 2005/1970, art. 96. - Made: 21.02.2006. Coming into force: 07.06.2006. Effect: None. Territorial extent & classification: E. Local *Unpublished*

The Air Navigation (Restriction of Flying) (Biggin Hill) Regulations 2006 No. 2006/109. - Enabling power: S.I. 2005/1970, art. 96. - Made: 17.01.2006. Coming into force: 03.06.2006. Effect: None. Territorial extent & classification: E. Local *Unpublished*

The Air Navigation (Restriction of Flying) (Blackburn) Regulations 2006 No. 2006/1350. - Enabling power: S.I. 2005/1970, art. 96. - Made: 20.03.2006. Coming into force: 31.03.2006. Effect: None. Territorial extent & classification: E. Local *Unpublished*

The Air Navigation (Restriction of Flying) (Bournemouth) Regulations 2006 No. 2006/2087. - Enabling power: S.I. 2005/1970, art. 96. - Made: 20.07.2006. Coming into force: 30.09.2006. Effect: None. Territorial extent & classification: E. Local *Unpublished*

The Air Navigation (Restriction of Flying) (Burnham Overy Staithe) Regulations 2006 No. 2006/1232. - Enabling power: S.I. 2005/1970, art. 96. - Made: 24.02.2006. Coming into force: 24.02.2006. Effect: None. Territorial extent & classification: E. Local. - Revoked by S.I. 2006/1233 *Unpublished*

The Air Navigation (Restriction of Flying) (Burnham Overy Staithe) (Revocation) Regulations 2006 No. 2006/1233. - Enabling power: S.I. 2005/1970, art. 96. - Made: 24.04.2006. Coming into force: Forthwith. Effect: S.I. 2006/1232 revoked. Territorial extent & classification: E. Local *Unpublished*

The Air Navigation (Restriction of Flying) (Christchurch) Regulations 2006 No. 2006/1397. - Enabling power: S.I. 2005/1970, art. 96. - Made: 19.05.2006. Coming into force: 19.05.2006. Effect: None. Territorial extent & classification: E. Local. - Revoked by S.I. 2006/1400 *Unpublished*

The Air Navigation (Restriction of Flying) (Christchurch) (Revocation) Regulations 2006 No. 2006/1400. - Enabling power: S.I. 2005/1970, art. 96. - Made: 21.05.2006. Coming into force: 21.05.2006. Effect: S.I. 2006/1397 revoked. Territorial extent & classification: E. Local *Unpublished*

The Air Navigation (Restriction of Flying) (Dover and the English channel) (Amendment) Regulations 2006 No. 2006/1168. - Enabling power: S.I. 2005/1970, art. 96. - Made: 07.04.2006. Coming into force: 16.06.2006. Effect: S.I. 2006/917 amended. Territorial extent & classification: E. Local *Unpublished*

The Air Navigation (Restriction of Flying) (Dover and the English Channel) Regulations 2006 No. 2006/917. - Enabling power: S.I. 2005/1970, art. 96. - Made: 17.03.2006. Coming into force: 16.06.2006. Effect: None. Territorial extent & classification: E. Local *Unpublished*

The Air Navigation (Restriction of Flying) (Dunsfold) Regulations 2006 No. 2006/1302. - Enabling power: S.I. 2005/1970, art. 96. - Made: 08.05.2006. Coming into force: 27.07.2006. Effect: None. Territorial extent & classification: E. Local *Unpublished*

The Air Navigation (Restriction of Flying) (Duxford) (No. 2) Regulations 2006 No. 2006/1303. - Enabling power: S.I. 2005/1970, art. 96. - Made: 08.05.2006. Coming into force: 08.07.2006. Effect: None. Territorial extent & classification: E. Local *Unpublished*

The Air Navigation (Restriction of Flying) (Duxford) (No. 3) Regulations 2006 No. 2006/1304. - Enabling power: S.I. 2005/1970, art. 96. - Made: 08.05.2006. Coming into force: 22.07.2006. Effect: None. Territorial extent & classification: E. Local *Unpublished*

The Air Navigation (Restriction of Flying) (Duxford) (No. 4) Regulations 2006 No. 2006/2086. - Enabling power: S.I. 2005/1970, art. 96. - Made: 20.07.2006. Coming into force: 02.09.2006. Effect: None. Territorial extent & classification: E. Local *Unpublished*

The Air Navigation (Restriction of Flying) (Duxford) (No. 5) Regulations 2006 No. 2006/2500. - Enabling power: S.I. 2005/1970, art. 96. - Made: 08.09.2006. Coming into force: 08.10.2006. Effect: None. Territorial extent & classification: E. Local *Unpublished*

The Air Navigation (Restriction of Flying) (Duxford) Regulations 2006 No. 2006/104. - Enabling power: S.I. 2005/1970, art. 96. - Made: 13.01.2006. Coming into force: 21.05.2006. Effect: None. Territorial extent & classification: E. Local *Unpublished*

The Air Navigation (Restriction of Flying) (Eastbourne) Regulations 2006 No. 2006/1088. - Enabling power: S.I. 2005/1970, art. 96. - Made: 29.03.2006. Coming into force: 17.08.2006. Effect: None. Territorial extent & classification: E. Local *Unpublished*

The Air Navigation (Restriction of Flying) (Elvington) Regulations 2006 No. 2006/1300. - Enabling power: S.I. 2005/1970, art. 96. - Made: 08.05.2006. Coming into force: 19.08.2006. Effect: None. Territorial extent & classification: E. Local *Unpublished*

The Air Navigation (Restriction of Flying) (Farnborough) (Amendment) Regulations 2006 No. 2006/1684. - Enabling power: S.I. 2005/1970, art. 96. - Made: 19.06.2006. Coming into force: 10.07.2006. Effect: S.I. 2006/916 amended. Territorial extent & classification: E. Local *Unpublished*

The Air Navigation (Restriction of Flying) (Farnborough) Regulations 2006 No. 2006/916. - Enabling power: S.I. 2005/1970, art. 96. - Made: 17.02.2006. Coming into force: 10.07.2006. Effect: None. Territorial extent & classification: E. Local *Unpublished*

The Air Navigation (Restriction of Flying) (Happisburth) Regulations 2006 No. 2006/1528. - Enabling power: S.I. 2005/1970, art. 96. - Made: 31.05.2006. Coming into force: Forthwith. Effect: None. Territorial extent & classification: E. Local. - Revoked by S.I. 2006/1529 *Unpublished*

The Air Navigation (Restriction of Flying) (Happisburth) (Revocation) Regulations 2006 No. 2006/1529. - Enabling power: S.I. 2005/1970, art. 96. - Made: 01.06.2006. Coming into force: Forthwith. Effect: S.I. 2006/1528 revoked. Territorial extent & classification: E. Local *Unpublished*

The Air Navigation (Restriction of Flying) (Hawick) Regulations 2006 No. 2006/2322. - Enabling power: S.I. 2005/1970, art. 96. - Made: 24.08.2006. Coming into force: Forthwith. Effect: None. Territorial extent & classification: E. Local. - Revoked by S.I. 2006/2502 (Unpublished) *Unpublished*

The Air Navigation (Restriction of Flying) (Hawick) (Revocation) Regulations 2006 No. 2006/2502. - Enabling power: S.I. 2005/1970, art. 96. - Made: 11.09.2006. Coming into force: Forthwith. Effect: S.I. 2006/2322 revoked. Territorial extent & classification: E. Local *Unpublished*

The Air Navigation (Restriction of Flying) (Hendon) Regulations 2006 No. 2006/2091. - Enabling power: S.I. 2005/1970, art. 96. - Made: 19.07.2006. Coming into force: Forthwith. Effect: S.I. 2006/2090 revoked. Territorial extent & classification: E. Local *Unpublished*

The Air Navigation (Restriction of Flying) (Hendon) Regulations 2006 No. 2006/2090. - Enabling power: S.I. 2005/1970, art. 96. - Made: 12.07.2006. Coming into force: Forthwith. Effect: None. Territorial extent & classification: E. Local *Unpublished*

The Air Navigation (Restriction of Flying) (Her Majesty the Queen's 80th Birthday Flypast) (Amendment) Regulations 2006 No. 2006/1236. - Enabling power: S.I. 2005/1970, art. 96. - Made: 25.04.2006. Coming into force: 12.06.2006. Effect: S.I. 2006/1167 amended. Territorial extent & classification: E. Local *Unpublished*

The Air Navigation (Restriction of Flying) (Her Majesty The Queen's 80th Birthday Flypast) Regulations 2006 No. 2006/1167. - Enabling power: S.I. 2005/1970, art. 96. - Made: 07.04.2006. Coming into force: 12.06.2006. Effect: None. Territorial extent & classification: E. Local *Unpublished*

The Air Navigation (Restriction of Flying) (High Wycombe) (Amendment) Regulations 2006 No. 2006/2302. - Enabling power: S.I. 2005/1970, art. 96. - Made: 10.08.2006. Coming into force: Forthwith. Effect: S.I. 2006/2301 amended. Territorial extent & classification: E. Local. - Revoked by S.I. 2006/2303 (Unpublished) *Unpublished*

Civil aviation

The Air Navigation (Restriction of Flying) (High Wycombe) Regulations 2006 No. 2006/2301. - Enabling power: S.I. 2005/1970, art. 96. - Made: 10.08.2006. Coming into force: Forthwith. Effect: None. Territorial extent & classification: E. Local. - Revoked by S.I. 2006/2303 (Unpublished) *Unpublished*

The Air Navigation (Restriction of Flying) (High Wycombe) (Revocation) Regulations 2006 No. 2006/2303. - Enabling power: S.I. 2005/1970, art. 96. - Made: 10.08.2006. Coming into force: Forthwith. Effect: S.I. 2006/2301, 2302 revoked. Territorial extent & classification: E. Local *Unpublished*

The Air Navigation (Restriction of Flying) (HMP Channings Wood) Regulations 2006 No. 2006/1841. - Enabling power: S.I. 2005/1970, art. 96. - Made: 03.07.2006. Coming into force: 03.07.2006. Effect: None. Territorial extent & classification: E. Local. - Revoked by S.I. 2006/1842 *Unpublished*

The Air Navigation (Restriction of Flying) (HMP Channings Wood) (Revocation) Regulations 2006 No. 2006/1842. - Enabling power: S.I. 2005/1970, art. 96. - Made: 04.07.2006. Coming into force: 04.07.2006. Effect: S.I. 2006/1841 revoked. Territorial extent & classification: E. Local *Unpublished*

The Air Navigation (Restriction of Flying) (Hullavington) Regulations 2006 No. 2006/1169. - Enabling power: S.I. 2005/1970, art. 96. - Made: 07.04.2006. Coming into force: 09.09.2006. Effect: None. Territorial extent & classification: E. Local *Unpublished*

The Air Navigation (Restriction of Flying) (Inverkeithing) Regulations 2006 No. 2006/108. - Enabling power: S.I. 2005/1970, art. 96. - Made: 16.01.2006. Coming into force: Forthwith. Effect: None. Territorial extent & classification: E. Local. - Revoked by S.I. 2006/110 (Unpublished) *Unpublished*

The Air Navigation (Restriction of Flying) (Inverkeithing) (Revocation) Regulations 2006 No. 2006/110. - Enabling power: S.I. 2005/1970, art. 96. - Made: 17.01.2006. Coming into force: Forthwith. Effect: S.I. 2006/108 revoked. Territorial extent & classification: E. Local *Unpublished*

The Air Navigation (Restriction of Flying) (Isle of Wight) Regulations 2006 No. 2006/1122. - Enabling power: S.I. 2005/1970, art. 96. - Made: 06.04.2006. Coming into force: 06.04.2006. Effect: None. Territorial extent & classification: E. Local. - Revoked by S.I. 2006/1123 *Unpublished*

The Air Navigation (Restriction of Flying) (Isle of Wight) (Revocation) Regulations 2006 No. 2006/1123. - Enabling power: S.I. 2005/1970, art. 96. - Made: 06.04.2006. Coming into force: 06.04.2006. Effect: S.I. 2006/1122 revoked. Territorial extent & classification: E. Local *Unpublished*

The Air Navigation (Restriction of Flying) (Jet Formation Display Teams) (Amendment) Regulations 2006 No. 2006/800. - Enabling power: S.I. 2005/1970, art. 96. - Made: 21.02.2006. Coming into force: 27.02.2006. Effect: S.I. 2006/117 amended. Territorial extent & classification: E. Local *Unpublished*

The Air Navigation (Restriction of Flying) (Jet Formation Display Teams) (No. 2) (Amendment) Regulations 2006 No. 2006/1297. - Enabling power: S.I. 2005/1970, art. 96. - Made: 04.05.2006. Coming into force: 11.06.2006. Effect: S.I. 2006/1170 amended. Territorial extent & classification: E. Local *Unpublished*

The Air Navigation (Restriction of Flying) (Jet Formation Display Teams) (No. 2) Regulations 2006 No. 2006/1170. - Enabling power: S.I. 2005/1970, art. 96. - Made: 07.04.2006. Coming into force: 11.06.2006. Effect: None. Territorial extent & classification: E. Local *Unpublished*

The Air Navigation (Restriction of Flying) (Jet Formation Display Teams) (No. 2) (Second Amendment) Regulations 2006 No. 2006/1845. - Enabling power: S.I. 2005/1970, art. 96. - Made: 07.07.2006. Coming into force: 07.07.2006. Effect: S.I. 2006/1170 amended. Territorial extent & classification: E. Local *Unpublished*

The Air Navigation (Restriction of Flying) (Jet Formation Display Teams) (No. 3) Regulations 2006 No. 2006/1525. - Enabling power: S.I. 2005/1970, art. 96. - Made: 01.06.2006. Coming into force: 11.08.2006. Effect: None. Territorial extent & classification: E. Local *Unpublished*

The Air Navigation (Restriction of Flying) (Jet Formation Display Teams) Regulations 2006 No. 2006/117. - Enabling power: S.I. 2005/1970, art. 96. - Made: 25.01.2006. Coming into force: 27.02.2006. Effect: None. Territorial extent & classification: E. Local *Unpublished*

The Air Navigation (Restriction of Flying) (Keevil) Regulations 2006 No. 2006/105. - Enabling power: S.I. 2005/1970, art. 96. - Made: 13.01.2006. Coming into force: 27.05.2006. Effect: None. Territorial extent & classification: E. Local *Unpublished*

The Air Navigation (Restriction of Flying) (Kemble) Regulations 2006 No. 2006/858. - Enabling power: S.I. 2005/1970, art. 96. - Made: 27.02.2006. Coming into force: 18.06.2006. Effect: None. Territorial extent & classification: E. Local *Unpublished*

The Air Navigation (Restriction of Flying) (Kesgrave) Regulations 2006 No. 2006/1086. - Enabling power: S.I. 2005/1970, art. 96. - Made: 01.04.2006. Coming into force: 01.04.2006. Effect: None. Territorial extent & classification: E. Local. - Revoked by S.I. 2006/1087 *Unpublished*

The Air Navigation (Restriction of Flying) (Kesgrave) (Revocation) Regulations 2006 No. 2006/1087. - Enabling power: S.I. 2005/1970, art. 96. - Made: 02.04.2006. Coming into force: 02.04.2006. Effect: S.I. 2006/1086 revoked. Territorial extent & classification: E. Local *Unpublished*

The Air Navigation (Restriction of Flying) (Kew Palace) Regulations 2006 No. 2006/1171. - Enabling power: S.I. 2005/1970, art. 96. - Made: 07.04.2006. Coming into force: 21.04.2006. Effect: None. Territorial extent & classification: E. Local *Unpublished*

Civil aviation

The Air Navigation (Restriction of Flying) (Llangeitho) Regulations 2006 No. 2006/3498. - Enabling power: S.I. 2005/1970, art. 96. - Made: 20.12.2006. Coming into force: Forthwith. Effect: None. Territorial extent & classification: E. Local. - Revoked by S.I. 2006/3499 *Unpublished*

The Air Navigation (Restriction of Flying) (Llangeitho) (Revocation) Regulations 2006 No. 2006/3499. - Enabling power: S.I. 2005/1970, art. 96. - Made: 21.12.2006. Coming into force: Forthwith. Effect: S.I. 2006/3498 revoked. Territorial extent & classification: E. Local *Unpublished*

The Air Navigation (Restriction of Flying) (Lowestoft) Regulations 2006 No. 2006/1165. - Enabling power: S.I. 2005/1970, art. 96. - Made: 07.04.2006. Coming into force: 27.07.2006. Effect: None. Territorial extent & classification: E. Local *Unpublished*

The Air Navigation (Restriction of Flying) (Manchester) Regulations 2006 No. 2006/2085. - Enabling power: S.I. 2005/1970, art. 96. - Made: 20.07.2006. Coming into force: 22.09.2006. Effect: None. Territorial extent & classification: E. Local *Unpublished*

The Air Navigation (Restriction of Flying) (Margate) Regulations 2006 No. 2006/794. - Enabling power: S.I. 2005/1970, art. 96. - Made: 21.02.2006. Coming into force: 17.06.2006. Effect: None. Territorial extent & classification: E. Local *Unpublished*

The Air Navigation (Restriction of Flying) (Mark Cross, East Sussex) Regulations 2006 No. 2006/2501. - Enabling power: S.I. 2005/1970, art. 96. - Made: 02.09.2006. Coming into force: Forthwith. Effect: None. Territorial extent & classification: E. Local. - Revoked by S.I. 2006/2622 (Unpublished) *Unpublished*

The Air Navigation (Restriction of Flying) (Mark Cross, East Sussex) (Revocation) Regulations 2006 No. 2006/2622. - Enabling power: S.I. 2005/1970, art. 96. - Made: 25.09.2006. Coming into force: Forthwith. Effect: S.I. 2006/2501 revoked. Territorial extent & classification: E. Local *Unpublished*

The Air Navigation (Restriction of Flying) (Morecombe Bay) Regulations 2006 No. 2006/3495. - Enabling power: S.I. 2005/1970, art. 96. - Made: 27.12.2006. Coming into force: Forthwith. Effect: None. Territorial extent & classification: E. Local. - Revoked by S.I. 2006/3496 *Unpublished*

The Air Navigation (Restriction of Flying) (Morecombe Bay) (Revocation) Regulations 2006 No. 2006/3496. - Enabling power: S.I. 2005/1970, art. 96. - Made: 28.12.2006. Coming into force: Forthwith. Effect: S.I. 2006/3495 revoked. Territorial extent & classification: E. Local *Unpublished*

The Air Navigation (Restriction of Flying) (Muston) Regulations 2006 No. 2006/796. - Enabling power: S.I. 2005/1970, art. 96. - Made: 14.02.2006. Coming into force: Forthwith. Effect: None. Territorial extent & classification: E. Local. - Revoked by SI 2006/797 (unpublished) *Unpublished*

The Air Navigation (Restriction of Flying) (Muston) (Revocation) Regulations 2006 No. 2006/797. - Enabling power: S.I. 2005/1970, art. 96. - Made: 15.02.2006. Coming into force: Forthwith. Effect: S.I. 2006/796 revoked. Territorial extent & classification: E. Local *Unpublished*

The Air Navigation (Restriction of Flying) (Nacton) (Amendment No. 2) Regulations 2006 No. 2006/3352. - Enabling power: S.I. 2005/1970, art. 96. - Made: 13.12.2006. Coming into force: Forthwith. Effect: S.I. 2006/3348 amended. Territorial extent & classification: E. Local *Unpublished*

The Air Navigation (Restriction of Flying) (Nacton) (Amendment) Regulations 2006 No. 2006/3349. - Enabling power: S.I. 2005/1970, art. 96. - Made: 12.12.2006. Coming into force: Forthwith. Effect: S.I. 2006/3348 amended. Territorial extent & classification: E. Local *Unpublished*

The Air Navigation (Restriction of Flying) (Nacton No. 2) (Revocation) Regulations 2006 No. 2006/3497. - Enabling power: S.I. 2005/1970, art. 96. - Made: 22.12.2006. Coming into force: Forthwith. Effect: S.I. 2006/2252 revoked. Territorial extent & classification: E. Local *Unpublished*

The Air Navigation (Restriction of Flying) (Nacton) Regulations 2006 No. 2006/3348. - Enabling power: S.I. 2005/1970, art. 96. - Made: 11.12.2006. Coming into force: Forthwith. Effect: None. Territorial extent & classification: E. Local *Unpublished*

The Air Navigation (Restriction of Flying) (North East London) Regulations 2006 No. 2006/2300. - Enabling power: S.I. 2005/1970, art. 96. - Made: 10.08.2006. Coming into force: With immediate effect. Effect: None. Territorial extent & classification: E. Local *Unpublished*

The Air Navigation (Restriction of Flying) (Northern North Sea) (Amendment) Regulations 2006 No. 2006/1840. - Enabling power: S.I. 2005/1970, art. 96. - Made: 03.07.2006. Coming into force: 10.09.2006. Effect: S.I. 2006/1526 amended. Territorial extent & classification: E. Local *Unpublished*

The Air Navigation (Restriction of Flying) (Northern North Sea) Regulations 2006 No. 2006/1526. - Enabling power: S.I. 2005/1970, art. 96. - Made: 01.06.2006. Coming into force: 10.09.2006. Effect: None. Territorial extent & classification: E. Local *Unpublished*

The Air Navigation (Restriction of Flying) (Orford Ness) Regulations 2006 No. 2006/1090. - Enabling power: S.I. 2005/1970, art. 96. - Made: 02.04.2006. Coming into force: 02.04.2006. Effect: None. Territorial extent & classification: E. Local. - Revoked by S.I. 2006/1091 *Unpublished*

The Air Navigation (Restriction of Flying) (Orford Ness) (Revocation) Regulations 2006 No. 2006/1091. - Enabling power: S.I. 2005/1970, art. 96. - Made: 02.04.2006. Coming into force: 02.04.2006. Effect: S.I. 2006/1090 revoked. Territorial extent & classification: E. Local *Unpublished*

Civil aviation

The Air Navigation (Restriction of Flying) (Peterborough) Regulations 2006 No. 2006/1328. - Enabling power: S.I. 2005/1970, art. 96. - Made: 10.05.2006. Coming into force: 10.05.2006. Effect: None. Territorial extent & classification: E. Local. - Revoked by S.I. 2006/1329 *Unpublished*

The Air Navigation (Restriction of Flying) (Peterborough) (Revocation) Regulations 2006 No. 2006/1329. - Enabling power: S.I. 2005/1970, art. 96. - Made: 10.05.2006. Coming into force: 10.05.2006. Effect: S.I. 2006/1328 revoked. Territorial extent & classification: E. Local *Unpublished*

The Air Navigation (Restriction of Flying) (Plymouth) Regulations 2006 No. 2006/1299. - Enabling power: S.I. 2005/1970, art. 96. - Made: 04.05.2006. Coming into force: 24.08.2006. Effect: None. Territorial extent & classification: E. Local *Unpublished*

The Air Navigation (Restriction of Flying) (Popular Flying Association Rally) Regulations 2006 No. 2006/918. - Enabling power: S.I. 2005/1970, art. 96. - Made: 17.03.2006. Coming into force: 18.08.2006. Effect: None. Territorial extent & classification: E. Local *Unpublished*

The Air Navigation (Restriction of Flying) (RAF Brize Norton) Regulations 2006 No. 2006/1305. - Enabling power: S.I. 2005/1970, art. 96. - Made: 16.05.2006. Coming into force: 14.07.2006. Effect: None. Territorial extent & classification: E. Local. - Revoked by S.I. 2006/1687 (Unpublished) *Unpublished*

The Air Navigation (Restriction of Flying) (RAF Brize Norton) (Revocation) Regulations 2006 No. 2006/1687. - Enabling power: S.I. 2005/1970, art. 96. - Made: 13.06.2006. Coming into force: With immediate effect. Effect: S.I. 2006/1305 revoked. Territorial extent & classification: E. Local *Unpublished*

The Air Navigation (Restriction of Flying) (RAF Fairford) Regulations 2006 No. 2006/1166. - Enabling power: S.I. 2005/1970, art. 96. - Made: 07.04.2006. Coming into force: 12.07.2006. Effect: None. Territorial extent & classification: E. Local *Unpublished*

The Air Navigation (Restriction of Flying) (Remembrance Sunday) Regulations 2006 No. 2006/2765. - Enabling power: S.I. 2005/1970, art. 96. - Made: 05.10.2006. Coming into force: 12.11.2006. Effect: None. Territorial extent & classification: E. Local *Unpublished*

The Air Navigation (Restriction of Flying) (Rough Tower) (Amendment) Regulations 2006 No. 2006/1844. - Enabling power: S.I. 2005/1970, art. 96. - Made: 23.06.2006. Coming into force: 23.06.2006. Effect: S.I. 2006/1843 amended. Territorial extent & classification: E. Local *Unpublished*

The Air Navigation (Restriction of Flying) (Rough Tower) Regulations 2006 No. 2006/1843. - Enabling power: S.I. 2005/1970, art. 96. - Made: 23.06.2006. Coming into force: 23.06.2006. Effect: None. Territorial extent & classification: E. Local *Unpublished*

The Air Navigation (Restriction of Flying) (Royal Air Force Leuchars) Regulations 2006 No. 2006/1296. - Enabling power: S.I. 2005/1970, art. 96. - Made: 04.05.2006. Coming into force: 08.09.2006. Effect: None. Territorial extent & classification: E. Local *Unpublished*

The Air Navigation (Restriction of Flying) (Royal Air Force Waddington) Regulations 2006 No. 2006/377. - Enabling power: S.I. 2005/1970, art. 96. - Made: 06.02.2006. Coming into force: 29.06.2006. Effect: None. Territorial extent & classification: E. Local *Unpublished*

The Air Navigation (Restriction of Flying) (Royal Albert Hall) Regulations 2006 No. 2006/2764. - Enabling power: S.I. 2005/1970, art. 96. - Made: 05.10.2006. Coming into force: 11.11.2006. Effect: None. Territorial extent & classification: E. Local *Unpublished*

The Air Navigation (Restriction of Flying) (Sandhurst) (No. 2) Regulations 2006 No. 2006/3351. - Enabling power: S.I. 2005/1970, art. 96. - Made: 08.12.2006. Coming into force: 15.12.2006. Effect: None. Territorial extent & classification: E. Local *Unpublished*

The Air Navigation (Restriction of Flying) (Sandhurst) Regulations 2006 No. 2006/1173. - Enabling power: S.I. 2005/1970, art. 96. - Made: 10.04.2006. Coming into force: 12.04.2006. Effect: None. Territorial extent & classification: E. Local *Unpublished*

The Air Navigation (Restriction of Flying) (Silverstone and Turweston) Regulations 2006 No. 2006/376. - Enabling power: S.I. 2005/1970, art. 96. - Made: 06.02.2006. Coming into force: 10.06.2006. Effect: None. Territorial extent & classification: E. Local *Unpublished*

The Air Navigation (Restriction of Flying) (Smailholm) Regulations 2006 No. 2006/2962. - Enabling power: S.I. 2005/1970, art. 96. - Made: 30.10.2006. Coming into force: Forthwith. Effect: None. Territorial extent & classification: E. Local *Unpublished*

The Air Navigation (Restriction of Flying) (Smailholm) (Revocation) Regulations 2006 No. 2006/2963. - Enabling power: S.I. 2005/1970, art. 96. - Made: 06.11.2006. Coming into force: Forthwith. Effect: S.I. 2006/2962 revoked. Territorial extent & classification: E. Local *Unpublished*

The Air Navigation (Restriction of Flying) (Southampton Water) (Amendment) Regulations 2006 No. 2006/790. - Enabling power: S.I. 2005/1970, art. 96. - Made: 22.02.2006. Coming into force: Forthwith. Effect: S.I. 2006/789 amended. Territorial extent & classification: E. Local *Unpublished*

The Air Navigation (Restriction of Flying) (Southampton Water) Regulations 2006 No. 2006/789. - Enabling power: S.I. 2005/1970, art. 96. - Made: 22.02.2006. Coming into force: Forthwith. Effect: None. Territorial extent & classification: E. Local *Unpublished*

The Air Navigation (Restriction of Flying) Southampton Water (Revocation) Regulations 2006 No. 2006/859. - Enabling power: S.I. 2005/1970, art. 96. - Made: 22.02.2006. Coming into force: Forthwith. Effect: S.I. 2006/789 revoked. Territorial extent & classification: E. Local *Unpublished*

The Air Navigation (Restriction of Flying) (Southend) Regulations 2006 No. 2006/106. - Enabling power: S.I. 2005/1970, art. 96. - Made: 13.01.2006. Coming into force: 28.05.2006. Effect: None. Territorial extent & classification: E. Local *Unpublished*

The Air Navigation (Restriction of Flying) (Southern North Sea) Regulations 2006 No. 2006/107. - Enabling power: S.I. 2005/1970, art. 96. - Made: 13.01.2006. Coming into force: 01.04.2006. Effect: None. Territorial extent & classification: E. Local. - Revoked by S.I. 2006/1688 (Unpublished) *Unpublished*

The Air Navigation (Restriction of Flying) (Southern North Sea) (Revocation) Regulations 2006 No. 2006/1688. - Enabling power: S.I. 2005/1970, art. 96. - Made: 20.06.2006. Coming into force: 20.06.2006. Effect: S.I. 2006/107 revoked. Territorial extent & classification: E. Local *Unpublished*

The Air Navigation (Restriction of Flying) (Southport) Regulations 2006 No. 2006/1527. - Enabling power: S.I. 2005/1970, art. 96. - Made: 01.06.2006. Coming into force: 02.09.2006. Effect: None. Territorial extent & classification: E. Local *Unpublished*

The Air Navigation (Restriction of Flying) (St Andrews) Regulations 2006 No. 2006/2767. - Enabling power: S.I. 2005/1970, art. 96. - Made: 02.10.2006. Coming into force: 11.10.2006. Effect: None. Territorial extent & classification: E. Local *Unpublished*

The Air Navigation (Restriction of Flying) (Stapleford)) Regulations 2006 No. 2006/854. - Enabling power: S.I. 2005/1970, art. 96. - Made: 02.03.2006. Coming into force: Forthwith. Effect: None. Territorial extent & classification: E. Local. - Revoked by S.I. 2006/855 *Unpublished*

The Air Navigation (Restriction of Flying) (Stapleford) (Revocation) Regulations 2006 No. 2006/855. - Enabling power: S.I. 2005/1970, art. 96. - Made: 03.03.2006. Coming into force: Forthwith. Effect: S.I. 2006/854 revoked. Territorial extent & classification: E. Local *Unpublished*

The Air Navigation (Restriction of Flying) (Staplehurst) Regulations 2006 No. 2006/856. - Enabling power: S.I. 2005/1970, art. 96. - Made: 03.03.2006. Coming into force: Forthwith. Effect: None. Territorial extent & classification: E. Local. - Revoked by S.I. 2006/857 *Unpublished*

The Air Navigation (Restriction of Flying) (Staplehurst) (Revocation) Regulations 2006 No. 2006/857. - Enabling power: S.I. 2005/1970, art. 96. - Made: 07.03.2006. Coming into force: Forthwith. Effect: S.I. 2006/856 revoked. Territorial extent & classification: E. Local *Unpublished*

The Air Navigation (Restriction of Flying) (State Opening of Parliament) Regulations 2006 No. 2006/2766. - Enabling power: S.I. 2005/1970, art. 96. - Made: 05.10.2006. Coming into force: 15.11.2006. Effect: None. Territorial extent & classification: E. Local *Unpublished*

The Air Navigation (Restriction of Flying) (St Austell) Regulations 2006 No. 2006/1396. - Enabling power: S.I. 2005/1970, art. 96. - Made: 19.05.2006. Coming into force: 01.06.2006. Effect: None. Territorial extent & classification: E. Local *Unpublished*

The Air Navigation (Restriction of Flying) (Stonehenge) Regulations 2006 No. 2006/793. - Enabling power: S.I. 2005/1970, art. 96. - Made: 21.02.2006. Coming into force: 20.06.2006. Effect: None. Territorial extent & classification: E. Local *Unpublished*

The Air Navigation (Restriction of Flying) (Stratford) (No. 2) Regulations 2006 No. 2006/1524. - Enabling power: S.I. 2005/1970, art. 96. - Made: 02.06.2006. Coming into force: Forthwith. Effect: S.I. 2006/1522 revoked. Territorial extent & classification: E. Local. - Revoked by S.I. 2006/1685 (Unpublished) *Unpublished*

The Air Navigation (Restriction of Flying) (Stratford No. 2) (Revocation) Regulations 2006 No. 2006/1685. - Enabling power: S.I. 2005/1970, art. 96. - Made: 09.06.2006. Coming into force: In accord.with reg. 1. Effect: S.I. 2006/1524 revoked. Territorial extent & classification: E. Local *Unpublished*

The Air Navigation (Restriction of Flying) (Stratford) Regulations 2006 No. 2006/1522. - Enabling power: S.I. 2005/1970, art. 96. - Made: 02.06.2006. Coming into force: 02.06.2006. Effect: None. Territorial extent & classification: E. Local. - Revoked by S.I. 2006/1523 and S.I. 2006/1524 *Unpublished*

The Air Navigation (Restriction of Flying) (Stratford) (Revocation) Regulations 2006 No. 2006/1523. - Enabling power: S.I. 2005/1970, art. 96. - Made: 02.06.2006. Coming into force: Forthwith. Effect: S.I. 2006/1522 revoked. Territorial extent & classification: E. Local *Unpublished*

The Air Navigation (Restriction of Flying) (Sunderland) Regulations 2006 No. 2006/1089. - Enabling power: S.I. 2005/1970, art. 96. - Made: 03.04.2006. Coming into force: 29.07.2006. Effect: None. Territorial extent & classification: E. Local *Unpublished*

The Air Navigation (Restriction of Flying) (Thursley) Regulations 2006 No. 2006/2088. - Enabling power: S.I. 2005/1970, art. 96. - Made: 15.07.2006. Coming into force: Forthwith. Effect: None. Territorial extent & classification: E. Local *Unpublished*

The Air Navigation (Restriction of Flying) (Thursley) (Revocation) Regulations 2006 No. 2006/2089. - Enabling power: S.I. 2005/1970, art. 96. - Made: 16.07.2006. Coming into force: Forthwith. Effect: S.I. 2006/2088 revoked. Territorial extent & classification: E. Local *Unpublished*

The Air Navigation (Restriction of Flying) (Tower of London) Regulations 2006 No. 2006/853. - Enabling power: S.I. 2005/1970, art. 96. - Made: 09.03.2006. Coming into force: 20.05.2006. Effect: None. Territorial extent & classification: E. Local *Unpublished*

Civil aviation

The Air Navigation (Restriction of Flying) (Trooping of the Colour Ceremony) Regulations 2006 No. 2006/792. - Enabling power: S.I. 2005/1970, art. 96. - Made: 21.02.2006. Coming into force: 03.06.2006. Effect: None. Territorial extent & classification: E. Local *Unpublished*

The Air Navigation (Restriction of Flying) (Wales and Southern England) Regulations 2006 No. 2006/1395. - Enabling power: S.I. 2005/1970, art. 96. - Made: 16.05.2006. Coming into force: 12.07.2006. Effect: None. Territorial extent & classification: E. Local. - Revoked by S.I. 2006/1686 *Unpublished*

The Air Navigation (Restriction of Flying) (Wales and Southern England) (Revocation) Regulations 2006 No. 2006/1686. - Enabling power: S.I. 2005/1970, art. 96. - Made: 13.06.2006. Coming into force: With immediate effect. Effect: S.I. 2006/1395 revoked. Territorial extent & classification: E. Local *Unpublished*

The Air Navigation (Restriction of Flying) (Warwickshire) Regulations 2006 No. 2006/2763. - Enabling power: S.I. 2005/1970, art. 96. - Made: 12.10.2006. Coming into force: 25.10.2006. Effect: None. Territorial extent & classification: E. Local *Unpublished*

The Air Navigation (Restriction of Flying) (Weston Park) Regulations 2006 No. 2006/1298. - Enabling power: S.I. 2005/1970, art. 96. - Made: 08.05.2006. Coming into force: 18.08.2006. Effect: None. Territorial extent & classification: E. Local *Unpublished*

The Air Navigation (Restriction of Flying) (Weston-Super-Mare) Regulations 2006 No. 2006/1301. - Enabling power: S.I. 2005/1970, art. 96. - Made: 08.05.2006. Coming into force: 26.07.2006. Effect: None. Territorial extent & classification: E. Local *Unpublished*

The Air Navigation (Restriction of Flying) (West Wales Airport) (No. 2) Regulations 2006 No. 2006/1174. - Enabling power: S.I. 2005/1970, art. 96. - Made: 20.04.2006. Coming into force: 08.07.2006. Effect: None. Territorial extent & classification: E. Local *Unpublished*

The Air Navigation (Restriction of Flying) (West Wales Airport) (No. 3) Regulations 2006 No. 2006/3350. - Enabling power: S.I. 2005/1970, art. 96. - Made: 11.12.2006. Coming into force: 01.03.2007. Effect: None. Territorial extent & classification: E. Local *Unpublished*

The Air Navigation (Restriction of Flying) (West Wales Airport) Regulations 2006 No. 2006/103. - Enabling power: S.I. 2005/1970, art. 96. - Made: 13.01.2006. Coming into force: 10.04.2006. Effect: None. Territorial extent & classification: E. Local *Unpublished*

The Air Navigation (Restriction of Flying) (Whittlesea) Regulations 2006 No. 2006/1398. - Enabling power: S.I. 2005/1970, art. 96. - Made: 18.05.2006. Coming into force: 18.05.2006. Effect: None. Territorial extent & classification: E. Local. - Revoked by S.I. 2006/1399 *Unpublished*

The Air Navigation (Restriction of Flying) (Whittlesea) Regulations 2006 No. 2006/1230. - Enabling power: S.I. 2005/1970, art. 96. - Made: 22.04.2006. Coming into force: 22.04.2006. Effect: None. Territorial extent & classification: E. Local. - Revoked by S.I. 2006/1231 *Unpublished*

The Air Navigation (Restriction of Flying) (Whittlesea) (Revocation) Regulations 2006 No. 2006/1231. - Enabling power: S.I. 2005/1970, art. 96. - Made: 22.04.2006. Coming into force: 22.04.2006. Effect: S.I. 2006/1230 revoked. Territorial extent & classification: E. Local *Unpublished*

The Air Navigation (Restriction of Flying) (Whittlesea) (Revocation) Regulations 2006 No. 2006/1399. - Enabling power: S.I. 2005/1970, art. 96. - Made: 18.05.2006. Coming into force: 18.05.2006. Effect: S.I. 2006/1398 revoked. Territorial extent & classification: E. Local *Unpublished*

The Air Navigation (Restriction of Flying) (Wycombe Air Park) Regulations 2006 No. 2006/1175. - Enabling power: S.I. 2005/1970, art. 96. - Made: 18.04.2006. Coming into force: 23.06.2006. Effect: None. Territorial extent & classification: E. Local *Unpublished*

The Airports Slot Allocation Regulations 2006 No. 2006/2665. - Enabling power: European Communities Act 1972, s. 2 (2). - Issued: 13.10.2006. Made: 05.10.2006. Laid: 11.10.2006. Coming into force: 01.01.2007. Effect: S.I. 2004/1256 amended & S.I. 1993/1067, 3042; 1994/1736 revoked. Territorial extent & classification: E/W/S/NI. General. - With correction slip dated January 2007. EC note: These Regs replace S.I. 1993/1067 which requires extensive amendment in consequence of the changes made to Council Reg. 95/93/EEC by Council Reg. 793/2004/EC. - 16p.: 30 cm. - 978-0-11-075159-7 £3.00

The Airports Slot Allocation Regulations 2006 (correction slip) No. 2006/2665 Cor.. - Correction slip (to ISBN 0110751590) dated January 2007. - 1 sheet: 30 cm. *Free*

The Civil Aviation (Provision of Information to Passengers) Regulations 2006 No. 2006/3303. - Enabling power: European Communities Act 1972, s. 2 (2). - Issued: 19.12.2006. Made: 12.12.2006. Laid: 14.12.2006. Coming into force: 16.01.2007. Effect: None. Territorial extent & classification: E/W/S/NI. General. - EC note: These Regulations create offences for the purpose of enforcing the obligations set out in Chapter III of Council Regulation (EC) No. 2111/2005 which require that air passengers be informed of the identity of the operating air carrier or carriers and offered a right of reimbursement or re-routing if the air carrier is subject to an operating ban. - 4p.: 30 cm. - 978-0-11-075480-2 £3.00

The Civil Aviation (Safety of Third-Country Aircraft) Regulations 2006 No. 2006/1384. - Enabling power: European Communities Act 1972, s. 2 (2). - Issued: 31.05.2006. Made: 23.05.2006. Laid: 26.05.2006. Coming into force: 30.06.2006. Effect: S.I. 2005/1970 amended. Territorial extent & classification: E/W/S/NI. General. - EC note: These Regs make provision to comply with Directive 2004/36/EC on the safety of aircraft from outside the Community using Community airports. - 8p.: 30 cm. - 978-0-11-074613-5 £3.00

The Single European Sky (Functions of the National Supervisory Authority) Regulations 2006 No. 2006/3104. - Enabling power: European Communities Act 1972, s. 2 (2). - Issued: 29.11.2006. Made: 21.11.2006. Laid: 24.11.2006. Coming into force: 21.12.2006. Effect: None. Territorial extent & classification: E/W/S/NI. General. - 4p.: 30 cm. - 978-0-11-075354-6 £3.00

Civil aviation, Scotland

The Transport Act 2000 (Consequential Amendment) (Scotland) Order 2006 No. 2006/1157 (S.11). - Enabling power: Transport Act 2000, s. 277 (1). - Issued: 28.04.2006. Made: 20.04.2006. Coming into force: 21.04.2006. Effect: 1997 c.8 & S.I. 1984/467; 1992/223 amended in relation to Scotland. Territorial extent & classification: S. General. - Supersedes draft SI (ISBN 0110739957) issued on 13.02.2006. - 4p.: 30 cm. - 978-0-11-074522-0 £3.00

Civil partnership

The Civil Partnership Act 2004 (Relationships Arising Through Civil Partnership) Order 2006 No. 2006/1121. - Enabling power: Civil Partnership Act 2004, s. 247 (2) (b). - Issued: 25.04.2006. Made: 19.04.2006. Laid: 20.04.2006. Coming into force: 11.05.2006. Effect: None. Territorial extent & classification: E/W/S. General. - This statutory instrument has been printed to correct an omission in S.I. 2005/3137 (ISBN 0110736141) and is being issued free of charge to all known recipients of that instrument. - 2p.: 30 cm. - 978-0-11-074513-8 £3.00

Civil partnership, England and Wales

The Civil Partnership Act 2004 (Commencement No. 3) Order 2006 No. 2006/639 (C.15). - Enabling power: Civil Partnership Act 2004, s. 263. Bringing into operation various provisions of the 2004 Act on 06.04.2006, in accord. with art. 2. - Issued: 15.03.2006. Made: 06.03.2006. Effect: None. Territorial extent & classification: E/W. General. - 8p.: 30 cm. - 978-0-11-074207-6 £3.00

The Dissolution etc. (Pension Protection Fund) Regulations 2006 No. 2006/1934. - Enabling power: Civil Partnership Act 2004, sch. 5, paras, 32, 35, 36. - Issued: 26.07.2006. Made: 17.07.2006. Laid: 18.07.2006. Coming into force: 08.08.2006. Effect: 2004 c. 33 modified; S.I. 2005/2920 amended. Territorial extent & classification: E/W. General. - 4p.: 30 cm. - 978-0-11-074866-5 £3.00

Civil partnership, Northern Ireland

The Civil Partnership Act 2004 (Commencement No. 4) (Northern Ireland) Order 2006 No. 2006/928 (C. 25). - Enabling power: Civil Partnership Act 2004, s. 263. Bringing into operation various provisions of the 2004 Act on 06.04.2006. - Issued: 12.04.2006. Made: 27.03.2006. Effect: None. Territorial extent & classification: NI. General- 8p.: 30 cm. - 978-0-11-080031-8 £3.00

Clean air, England

The Smoke Control Areas (Authorised Fuels) (England) (Amendment) Regulations 2006 No. 2006/1869. - Enabling power: Clean Air Act 1993, ss. 20 (6), 63 (1). - Issued: 18.07.2006. Made: 12.07.2006. Laid: 17.07.2006. Coming into force: 14.08.2006. Effect: S.I. 2001/3745 amended. Territorial extent & classification: E. General. - 2p.: 30 cm. - 978-0-11-074838-2 £3.00

The Smoke Control Areas (Exempted Fireplaces) (England) (No. 2) Order 2006 No. 2006/2704. - Enabling power: Clean Air Act 1993, s. 21. - Issued: 18.10.2006. Made: 11.10.2006. Laid: 17.10.2006. Coming into force: 10.11.2006. Effect: S. I. 2005/2304; 2006/1152 revoked. Territorial extent & classification: E. General. - 8p.: 30 cm. - 978-0-11-075186-3 £3.00

The Smoke Control Areas (Exempted Fireplaces) (England) Order 2006 No. 2006/1152. - Enabling power: Clean Air Act 1993, s. 21. - Issued: 28.04.2006. Made: 21.04.2006. Laid: 24.04.2006. Coming into force: 15.05.2006. Effect: None. Territorial extent & classification: E. General. - Revoked by S.I. 2006/2704 (ISBN 0110751868). - 4p.: 30 cm. - 978-0-11-074516-9 £3.00

Clean air, Wales

The Smoke Control Areas (Authorised Fuels) (Wales) Regulations 2006 No. 2006/2979 (W.270). - Enabling power: Clean Air Act 1993, ss. 20 (6), 63 (1). - Issued: 27.11.2006. Made: 14.11.2006. Coming into force: 24.11.2006. Effect: S.I. 2001/3762 (W.311), 3996 (W.327); 2002/3160 (W.295) revoked. Territorial extent & classification: W. General. - In English and Welsh. Welsh title: Rheoliadau Ardaloedd Rheoli Mwg (Tanwyddau Awdurdodedig) (Cymru) 2006. - 20p.: 30 cm. - 978-0-11-091438-1 £3.50

The Smoke Control Areas (Exempted Fireplaces) (Wales) Order 2006 No. 2006/2980 (W.271). - Enabling power: Clean Air Act 1993, s. 21. - Issued: 23.11.2006. Made: 14.11.2006. Coming into force: 24.11.2006. Effect: None. Territorial extent & classification: W. General. - With correction slip dated February 2007. - In English and Welsh. Welsh title: Gorchymyn Ardaloedd Rheoli Mwg (Lleoedd Tân Esempt) (Cymru) 2006. - 12p.: 30 cm. - 978-0-11-091439-8 £3.00

Climate change levy

The Climate Change Agreements (Eligible Facilities) (Amendment) Regulations 2006 No. 2006/1931. - Enabling power: Finance Act 2000, sch. 6, paras. 50 (3) (4), 146 (7). - Issued: 21.07.2006. Made: 14.07.2006. Laid: 19.07.2006. Coming into force: 15.08.2006. Effect: S.I. 2006/60 amended. Territorial extent & classification: E/W/S/NI. General. - 4p.: 30 cm. - 978-0-11-074862-7 *£3.00*

The Climate Change Agreements (Eligible Facilities) Regulations 2006 No. 2006/60. - Enabling power: Finance Act 2000, sch. 6, paras. 50 (3) (4), 146 (7). - Issued: 25.01.2006. Made: 18.01.2006. Laid: 20.01.2006. Coming into force: 21.01.2006. Effect: None. Territorial extent & classification: E/W/S/NI. General. - 4p.: 30 cm. - 978-0-11-073919-9 *£3.00*

The Climate Change Agreements (Energy-intensive Installations) Regulations 2006 No. 2006/59. - Enabling power: Finance Act 2000, s. 30, sch. 6, paras 52 (1) (2) (a), 146 (7). - Issued: 24.01.2006. Made: 18.01.2006. Coming into force: 21.01.2006 in accord. with reg. 1. Effect: None. Territorial extent & classification: E/W/S/NI. General. - Supersedes draft SI (ISBN0110737342) issued 12.12.2005. - 4p.: 30 cm. - 978-0-11-073917-5 *£3.00*

The Climate Change Agreements (Miscellaneous Amendments) Regulations 2006 No. 2006/1848. - Enabling power: Finance Act 2000, sch. 6, para. 52. - Issued: 17.07.2006. Made: 11.07.2006. Coming into force: 12.07.2006 in accord. with reg. 1. Effect: 2000 c. 17; S.I. 2006/59 amended. Territorial extent & classification: E/W/S/NI. General. - Supersedes draft SI (ISBN 011074683X) issued 15.06.2006. - 4p.: 30 cm. - 978-0-11-074837-5 *£3.00*

The Climate Change Levy (General) (Amendment) Regulations 2006 No. 2006/954. - Enabling power: Finance Act 2000, s. 30, sch. 6, paras 22 (1), 43 (4) (5), 146 (2), 146 (7), 147. - Issued: 03.04.2006. Made: 29.03.2006. Laid: 29.03.2006. Coming into force: 01.04.2006. Effect: S.I. 2001/838 amended. Territorial extent & classification: E/W/S/NI. General. - 4p.: 30 cm. - 978-0-11-074420-9 *£3.00*

Commercial property

The Olympics and Paralympics Association Rights (Appointment of Proprietors) Order 2006 No. 2006/1119. - Enabling power: Olympic Symbol etc. (Protection) Act 1995, ss. 1 (2) (2A) (3), 5A (2). - Issued: 25.04.2006. Made: 19.04.2006. Laid: 19.04.2006. Coming into force: 12.05.2006. Effect: S.I. 1995/2473 revoked. Territorial extent & classification: E/W/S/NI. General. - 8p.: 30 cm. - 978-0-11-074509-1 *£3.00*

The Paralympics Association Right (Paralympic Symbol) Order 2006 No. 2006/1120. - Enabling power: Olympic Symbol etc. (Protection) Act 1995, s. 18 (1). - Issued: 25.04.2006. Made: 19.04.2006. Laid: 19.04.2006. Coming into force: 12.05.2006. Effect: None. Territorial extent & classification: E/W/S/NI. General. - 4p., ill.: 30 cm. - 978-0-11-074510-7 *£3.00*

Commissioner for Older People, Wales

The Commissioner for Older People (Wales) Act 2006 (Commencement) Order 2006 No. 2006/2699 (W.231) (C.92). - Enabling power: Commissioner for Older People (Wales) Act 2006, s. 23. Bringing into operation various provisions of the 2006 Act on 14.10.2006 in accord. with art. 2. - Issued: 18.10.2006. Made: 10.10.2006. Effect: None. Territorial extent & classification: W. General. - In English and Welsh. Welsh title: Gorchmyn Deddf Comisiynydd Pobl Hyn (Cymru) 2006 (Cychwyn) 2006. - 4p.: 30 cm. - 978-0-11-091402-2 *£3.00*

Commons, England

The Commons Act 2006 (Commencement No. 1, Transitional Provisions and Savings) (England) Order 2006 No. 2006/2504 (C.84). - Enabling power: Commons Act 2006, ss. 56 (1), 59 (1). Bringing into operation various provisions of the 2006 on 01.10.2006. - Issued: 19.09.2006. Made: 11.09.2006. Effect: None. Territorial extent & classification: E. General. - 4p.: 30 cm. - 978-0-11-075108-5 *£3.00*

The Commons (Severance of Rights) (England) Order 2006 No. 2006/2145. - Enabling power: Commons Act 2006, ss. 9 (2) (7), 59 (1), 61 (1), sch. 1, para. 2 (1) (a). - Issued: 09.08.2006. Made: 03.08.2006. Laid: 07.08.2006. Coming into force: 09.09.2006. Effect: None. Territorial extent & classification: E. General. - 2p.: 30 cm. - 978-0-11-074983-9 *£3.00*

Companies

The Companies Act 1985 (Small Companies' Accounts and Audit) Regulations 2006 No. 2006/2782. - Enabling power: Companies Act 1985, s. 257. - Issued: 20.10.2006. Made: 16.10.2006. Laid: 16.10.2006. Coming into force: 08.11.2006. Effect: 1985 c. 6 amended & S.I. 2001/1090 amended. Territorial extent & classification: E/W/S. General. - 8p.: 30 cm. - 978-0-11-075192-4 *£3.00*

The Companies Act 2006 (Commencement No. 1, Transitional Provisions and Savings) Order 2006 No. 2006/3428 (C.132). - Enabling power: Companies Act 2006, ss. 1296 (1) (2), 1300 (2). Bringing into operation various provisions of the 2006 Act on 01.01.2007, 20.01.2007, 06.04.2007 in accord. with art. 1(3) (4) (5). - Issued: 03.01.2007. Made: 20.12.2006. Laid: 21.12.2006. Effect: None. Territorial extent & classification: E/W/S/NI. General. - 20p.: 30 cm. - 978-0-11-075568-7 *£3.00*

The Companies (Disclosure of Information) (Designated Authorities) Order 2006 No. 2006/1644. - Enabling power: Companies Act 1985, s. 449 (3) & Companies Act 1989, s. 87 (5). - Issued: 30.06.2006. Made: 20.06.2006. Laid: 23.06.2006. Coming into force: 01.10.2006. Effect: 1985. c. 6; 1989 c. 40 amended. Territorial extent & classification: E/W/S. General. - 4p.: 30 cm. - 978-0-11-074736-1 *£3.00*

The Companies (Registrar, Languages and Trading Disclosures) Regulations 2006 No. 2006/3429. - Enabling power: European Communities Act 1972, s. 2 (2); Companies Act 2006, ss. 1091 (4), 1105 (2) (d), 1106 (2) and Limited Liability Partnerships Act 2000, ss. 15, 17. - Issued: 29.12.2006. Made: 20.12.2006. Laid: 21.12.2006. Coming into force: 01.01.2007. Effect: 1985 c.6; 1986 c.45; S.I. 1985/854; 1986/1032 (NI.6); 1989/2405 (NI. 19); S.R. 1986/287 amended. Territorial extent & classification: E/W/S/NI. General. - EC note: These Regulations implement provisions of Directive 2003/58/EC amending Directive 68/151/EEC, as regards disclosure requirements in respect of certain types of companies. They do so by amending the Companies Act 1985 and the Companies (Northern Ireland) Order 1986 so far as not yet repealed by the Companies Act 2006, and by supplementing provisions of the Companies Act 2006 brought into force on the same date as these Regulations. - 8p.: 30 cm. - 978-0-11-075577-9 *£3.00*

The Takeovers Directive (Interim Implementation) Regulations 2006 No. 2006/1183. - Enabling power: European Communities Act 1972, s. 2 (2). - Issued: 05.05.2006. Made: 25.04.2006. Laid: 27.04.2006. Coming into force: 20.05.2006. Effect: 2000 c. 8 amended. Territorial extent & classification: E/W/S/NI. General. - EC note: Implement Directive 2004/25/EC of the European Parliament and of the Council on takeover bids- 36p.: 30 cm. - 978-0-11-074536-7 *£6.50*

Compensation

The Compensation Act 2006 (Contribution for Mesothelioma Claims) Regulations 2006 No. 2006/3259. - Enabling power: Compensation Act 2006, s. 3 (7) (8) (11). - Issued: 12.12.2006. Made:06.12.2006. Coming into force: In accord. with reg. 1 (1), 07.12.2006, Effect: 2000 c.8 modified & S.I. 2001/2967 amended. Territorial extent & classification: E/W/S/NI. General. - Supersedes the draft S.I. (ISBN 0110752538) published on 06.11.2006. - 4p.: 30 cm. - 978-0-11-075445-1 *£3.00*

Competition

The Competition Act 1998 (Public Policy Exclusion) Order 2006 No. 2006/605. - Enabling power: Competition Act 1998, sch. 3, para. 7 (1) (2). - Issued: 15.03.2006. Made: 06.03.2006. Laid: 09.03.2006. Coming into force: 03.04.2006. Effect: None. Territorial extent & classification: E/W/S/NI. General. - With correction slip dated April 2006. - 4p.: 30 cm. - 978-0-11-074196-3 *£3.00*

The Enterprise Act 2002 (Enforcement Undertakings and Orders) Order 2006 No. 2006/355. - Enabling power: Enterprise Act 2002, s. 277 (1) (2), sch. 24, paras 15 (1) to (3), 16 (1), 17 (1). - Issued: 23.02.2006. Made: 13.02.2006. Laid: 16.02.2006. Coming into force: 10.03.2006. Effect: S.I. 1998/1271; 2000/2088, 2110; 2005/37, 2751 amended. Territorial extent & classification: E/W/S/NI. General. - 8p.: 30 cm. - 978-0-11-074056-0 *£3.00*

The Enterprise Act 2002 (Enforcement Undertakings) (No.2) Order 2006 No. 2006/3095. - Enabling power: Enterprise Act 2002, s. 277 (1) (2), sch. 24, paras 15 (1) (3), 16 (1). - Issued: 29.11.2006. Made: 20.11.2006. Laid: 23.11.2006. Coming into force: 20.12.2006. Effect: None. Territorial extent & classification: E/W/S/NI. General. - 4p.: 30 cm. - 978-0-11-075351-5 *£3.00*

The Enterprise Act 2002 (Enforcement Undertakings) Order 2006 No. 2006/354. - Enabling power: Enterprise Act 2002, s. 277 (1) (2), sch. 24, paras 15 (1), 16 (1). - Issued: 23.02.2006. Made: 14.02.2006. Laid: 16.02.2006. Coming into force: 10.03.2006. Effect: None. Territorial extent & classification: E/W/S/NI. General. - 4p.: 30 cm. - 978-0-11-074060-7 *£3.00*

The Enterprise Act 2002 (Part 9 Restrictions on Disclosure of Information) (Amendment) Order 2006 No. 2006/2909. - Enabling power: Enterprise Act 2002, s. 241 (6). - Issued: 13.11.2006. Made: 02.11.2006. Laid: 07.11.2006. Coming into force: 01.12.2006. Effect: 2002 c. 40 amended. Territorial extent & classification: E/W/S/NI. General. - 2p.: 30 cm. - 978-0-11-075261-7 *£3.00*

The Enterprise Act 2002 (Water Services Regulation Authority) Order 2006 No. 2006/522. - Enabling power: Enterprise Act 2002, s. 205, 213. - Issued: 07.03.2006. Made: 01.03.2006. Laid: 03.03.2006. Coming into force: 01.04.2006. Effect: S.I. 2003/1368, 1399 amended. Territorial extent & classification: UK. General. - 4p.: 30 cm. - 978-0-11-074135-2 *£3.00*

Constitutional law

The Animal Health and Welfare (Scotland) Act 2006 (Consequential Provisions) (England and Wales) Order 2006 No. 2006/3407. - Enabling power: Scotland Act 1998, ss. 104, 112 (1), 113 (2) (3) (4) (5). - Issued: 29.12.2006. Made: 14.12.2006-. Coming into force: 15.12.2006. Effect: 1963 c.43; 1964 c.70; 1973 c. 60 amended. Territorial extent & classification: E/W. General. - Supersedes draft SI (ISBN 0110711300) issued 13.11.2006. - 8p.: 30 cm. - 978-0-11-071454-7 *£3.00*

The Charities and Trustee Investment (Scotland) Act 2005 (Consequential Provisions and Modifications) Order 2006 No. 2006/242 (S.2). - Enabling power: Scotland Act 1998, ss. 104, 112 (1), 113. - Issued: 21.02.2006. Made: 14.02.2006. Coming into force: In accords. with art. 1, 03.02.2006, 01.04.2006. Effect: 1974 c. 39; 1975 c. 24; 1985 c. 6; 1989 c. 40; 1990 c. 40; 1993 c. 10; 2000 c. 8; 2004 c. 27; S.I. 1997/2436; 1999/678; 2001/1201; 2005/1788 amended. Territorial extent & classification: E/W/S/NI. General. - With correction slip dated April 2006, correcting the 'Made' date. - 8p.: 30 cm. - 978-0-11-069931-8 *£3.00*

The Gaelic Language (Scotland) Act 2005 (Consequential Modifications) Order 2006 No. 2006/241 (S.1). - Enabling power: Scotland Act 1998, ss. 104, 112 (1), 113. - Issued: 21.02.2006. Made: 14.02.2006. Coming into force: 31.03.2006. Effect: 1990 c. 42 amended. Territorial extent & classification: E/W/S/NI. General. - With correction slip dated April 2006, correcting the 'Made' date. - 4p.: 30 cm. - 978-0-11-069932-5 *£3.00*

The Gaelic Language (Scotland) Act 2005 (Consequential Modifications) Order 2006 No. 2006/241 (S.1) Cor.. - Correction slip (to ISBN 0110699327) dated April 2006, changing made date to 14.02.2006. - 1 sheet: 30 cm. *Free*

The Management of Offenders etc. (Scotland) Act 2005 (Consequential Modifications) Order 2006 No. 2006/1055. - Enabling power: Scotland Act 1998, ss. 104, 112 (1), 113. - Issued: 19.04.2006. Made: 31.03.2006. Coming into force: 01.04.2006. Effect: 1975 c.24; 1997 c.43 amended & 2005 asp 14 modified. Territorial extent & classification: E/W/S/NI. General. - 4p.: 30 cm. - 978-0-11-070257-5 *£3.00*

The National Assembly for Wales (Disqualification) Order 2006 No. 2006/3335. - Enabling power: Government of Wales Act 1998, s. 12 (1) (b) (5). - Issued: 22.12.2006. Made: 14.12.2006. Coming into force: 10.01.2007. Effect: S.I. 2003/437 revoked. Territorial extent & classification: W. General. - 8p.: 30 cm. - 978-0-11-075550-2 *£3.00*

The National Assembly for Wales (Representation of the People) (Amendment) Order 2006 No. 2006/884. - Enabling power: Government of Wales Act 1998, s. 11. - Issued: 26.04.2006. Made: 22.03.2006. Coming into force: 23.04.2006 in accord. with art. 1 (1). Effect: S.I. 2003/284 amended. Territorial extent & classification: W. General. - This statutory instrument has been printed in substitution of the SI of the same number (and ISBN, issued on 21.04.2006) and is being issued free of charge to all known recipients of the original version. - 8p.: 30 cm. - 978-0-11-074384-4 *£3.00*

The National Assembly for Wales (Transfer of Functions) (No.2) Order 2006 No. 2006/3334. - Enabling power: Government of Wales Act 1998, ss. 22, 24 (1), sch. 3, paras 1, 3. - Issued: 28.12.2006. Made: 14.12.2006. Coming into force: 15.12.2006. Effect: S.I. 1999/672 amended. Territorial extent & classification: E/W. General. - 4p.: 30 cm. - 978-0-11-075517-5 *£3.00*

The National Assembly for Wales (Transfer of Functions) Order 2006 No. 2006/1458. - Enabling power: Government of Wales Act 1998, ss. 22, 24 (1), sch. 3, para. 1. - Issued: 14.06.2006. Made: 07.06.2006. Coming into force: 08.06.2006. Effect: None. Territorial extent & classification: E/W. General. - 4p.: 30 cm. - 978-0-11-074673-9 *£3.00*

The Northern Ireland Act 2000 (Modification) (No. 2) Order 2006 No. 2006/2132. - Enabling power: Northern Ireland Act 2000, sch., para. 1 (4). - Issued: 04.08.2006. Made: 28.07.2006. Coming into force: 29.07.2006. Effect: 2000 c.1 modified. Territorial extent & classification: NI. General. - Supersedes draft S.I. (ISBN 0110746074) issued 25.05.2006. - 2p.: 30 cm. - 978-0-11-074967-9 *£3.00*

The Northern Ireland Act 2000 (Modification) Order 2006 No. 2006/1012. - Enabling power: Northern Ireland Act 2000, sch., para. 1 (4). - Issued: 06.04.2006. Made: 30.03.2006. Coming into force: 31.3.2006. Effect: 2000 c.1 modified. Territorial extent & classification: NI. General. - Supersedes draft instrument (ISBN 0110741226) issued 03.03.2006. - 2p.: 30 cm. - 978-0-11-074454-4 *£3.00*

The Scotland Act 1998 (Agency Arrangements) (Specification) (No. 2) Order 2006 No. 2006/3248. - Enabling power: Scotland Act 1998, ss. 93 (3), 113 (2) (4). - Issued: 22.12.2006. Made: 14.12.2006. Laid: 08.01.2007. Laid before the Scottish Parliament: 08.01.2007. Coming into force: 29.01.2007. Effect: S.I. 1999/1512 modified. Territorial extent & classification: E/W/S/NI. General. - 4p.: 30 cm. - 978-0-11-071432-5 *£3.00*

The Scotland Act 1998 (Agency Arrangements) (Specification) (No. 3) Order 2006 No. 2006/3338. - Enabling power: Scotland Act 1998, ss. 93 (3), 113 (2) (3) (4). - Issued: 22.12.2006. Made: 14.12.2006. Laid: 22.12.2006. Laid before the Scottish Parliament: 22.12.2006. Coming into force: 29.01.2007. Effect: None. Territorial extent & classification: E/W/S. General. - 8p.: 30 cm. - 978-0-11-071418-9 *£3.00*

The Scotland Act 1998 (Agency Arrangements) (Specification) Order 2006 No. 2006/1251. - Enabling power: Scotland Act 1998, ss. 93 (3), 113. - Issued: 19.05.2006. Made: 09.05.2006. Laid: 19.05.2006. Coming into force: 10.06.2006. Effect: None. Territorial extent & classification: E/W/S/NI. General. - 4p.: 30 cm. - 978-0-11-070451-7 *£3.00*

The Scotland Act 1998 (Modifications of Schedule 5) Order 2006 No. 2006/609. - Enabling power: Scotland Act 1998, s. 30 (2). - Issued: 20.03.2006. Made: 08.03.2006. Coming into force: 01.05.2006. Effect: 1998 c.46 amended. Territorial extent & classification: E/W/S/NI. General. - 2p.: 30 cm. - 978-0-11-074246-5 *£3.00*

Constitutional law

The Scotland Act 1998 (River Tweed) Order 2006 No. 2006/2913. - Enabling power: Scotland Act 1998, ss. 111, 112 (1), 113. - Issued: 21.11.2006. Made: 14.11.2006. Coming into force: 15.11.2006. Effect: 1607 c.6; 1965 c.13; 1967 c.84; 1974 c.40; 1975 c.51; 1976 c.86; 1981 c.29; 1984 c.26; 1989 c.15; 1995 c.40; 1998 c.46; S.I. 1999/1746 amended; 1986 c.62 revoked except for s. 31 & 1857 c.cxlviii; 1859 c.lxx; 1868 c.123; 1902 c.29; 1933 c.35; 1951 c.26; 1969 c.xxiv; 1976 c.22; 2001 asp 3; S.I. 1996/1211 revoked. Territorial extent & classification: E/W/S. General. - Supersedes Draft SI (ISBN 0110705548) issued 02.06.2006. - 48p.: 30 cm. - 978-0-11-075329-4 £7.50

The Scotland Act 1998 (Transfer of Functions to the Scottish Ministers etc.) (No. 2) Order 2006 No. 2006/1040. - Enabling power: Scotland Act 1998, ss. 30 (3), 63, 113, 124 (2). - Issued: 18.04.2006. Made: 11.04.2006. Coming into force: In accord. with art. 1. Effect: S.I. 1999/1750 modified. Territorial extent & classification: E/W/S/NI. General. - Supersedes draft S.I. (ISBN 011074151X) issued on 08.03.2006. - 4p.: 30 cm. - 978-0-11-074495-7 £3.00

The Scotland Act 1998 (Transfer of Functions to the Scottish Ministers etc.) (No. 3) Order 2006 No. 2006/3258. - Enabling power: Scotland Act 1998, ss. 63, 113 (2) (3) (4), 124 (2). - Issued: 22.12.2006. Made: 14.12.2006. Coming into force: 15.12.2006; 16.12.2006 in accord. with art. 1. Effect: S.I. 1999/1750; 2000/3253; 2001/3504; 2005/849 amended. Territorial extent & classification: S. General. - 8p.: 30 cm. - 978-0-11-071417-2 £3.00

The Scotland Act 1998 (Transfer of Functions to the Scottish Ministers etc.) Order 2006 No. 2006/304 (S.3). - Enabling power: Scotland Act 1998, ss. 63, 113, 124 (2). - Issued: 23.02.2006. Made: 14.02.2006. Coming into force: 15.02.2006 in accord. with art. 1 (1). Effect: 1947 c. 41; 1970 c. 40 modified. Territorial extent & classification: E/W/S/NI. General. - Supersedes draft SI (ISBN 0110698649) issued on 15.12.2005. - 8p.: 30 cm. - 978-0-11-069962-2 £3.00

The Smoking, Health and Social Care (Scotland) Act 2005 and the Prohibition of Smoking in Certain Premises (Scotland) Regulations 2006 (Consequential Provisions) (Scotland) Order 2006 No. 2006/1115. - Enabling power: Scotland Act 1998, ss. 104, 112 (1), 113. - Issued: 21.04.2006. Made: 18.04.2006. Laid: 21.04.2006. Coming into force: 15.05.2006. Effect: None. Territorial extent & classification: E/W/S/NI. General. - 4p.: 30 cm. - 978-0-11-074503-9 £3.00

The Smoking, Health and Social Care (Scotland) Act 2005 (Consequential Modifications) (England, Wales and Northern Ireland) Order 2006 No. 2006/1056. - Enabling power: Scotland Act 1998, ss. 104, 112 (1), 113. - Issued: 12.04.2006. Made: 31.03.2006. Coming into force: In accord with art 1 (2). Effect: 1968 c.46; 1977 c.37, c.49; 1988 c.48; 1990 c.19; 1992 c.52; 1996 c.18 modified & S.I. 1992/662; 2001/1358 (W.86); 2004/1765; 2005/641 amended. Territorial extent & classification: E/W/NI. General. - 8p.: 30 cm. - 978-0-11-070258-2 £3.00

The Water Environment and Water Services (Scotland) Act 2003 (Consequential Provisions and Modifications) Order 2006 No. 2006/1054 (S.10). - Enabling power: Scotland Act 1998, ss. 104, 112 (1), 113. - Issued: 12.04.2006. Made: 31.03.2006. Coming into force: 01.04.2006. Effect: 1989 c. 29; 1996 c. 8 & S.I. 1996/1527 amended. Territorial extent & classification: S. General. - Supersedes draft SI (ISBN 0110699726) issued 03.03.2006. - 8p.: 30 cm. - 978-0-11-070249-0 £3.00

The Water Environment (Controlled Activities) (Scotland) Regulations 2005 (Notices in the Interests of National Security) Order 2006 No. 2006/661 (S.5). - Enabling power: Scotland Act 1998, ss. 104, 112 (1), 113. - Issued: 16.03.2006. Made: 09.03.2006. Laid: 15.03.2006. Coming into force: 05.04.2006. Effect: None. Territorial extent & classification: S. General. - 4p.: 30 cm. - 978-0-11-074257-1 £3.00

Consumer credit

The Consumer Credit Act 2006 (Commencement No. 1) Order 2006 No. 2006/1508 (C. 52). - Enabling power: Consumer Credit Act 2006, s. 71 (2). Bringing into operation various provisions of the 2006 Act on 16.06.2006 & 01.10.2006, in accord. with art. 3. - Issued: 16.06.2006. Made: 10.06.2006. Effect: None. Territorial extent & classification: E/W/S/NI. General. - 4p.: 30 cm. - 978-0-11-074684-5 £3.00

The Consumer Credit (Enforcement, Default and Termination Notices) (Amendment) Regulations 2006 No. 2006/3094. - Enabling power: Consumer Credit Act 1974, ss. 88 (1), 182 (2). - Issued: 29.11.2006. Made: 18.11.2006. Laid: 23.11.2006. Coming into force: 19.12.2006. Effect: S.I. 1983/1561 amended. Territorial extent & classification: E/W/S/NI. General. - 2p.: 30 cm. - 978-0-11-075350-8 £3.00

The Consumer Credit (Exempt Agreements) (Amendment) Order 2006 No. 2006/1273. - Enabling power: Consumer Credit Act 1974, ss. 16 (5), 182 (2) (4). - Issued: 17.05.2006. Made: 09.05.2006. Laid: 10.05.2006. Coming into force: 01.06.2006. Effect: S.I. 1989/869 amended. Territorial extent & classification: E/W/S/NI. General. - 2p.: 30 cm. - 978-0-11-074561-9 £3.00

Consumer protection

The Cosmetic Products (Safety) (Amendment) (No. 2) Regulations 2006 No. 2006/2231. - Enabling power: Consumer Protection Act 1987, s. 11. - Issued: 24.08.2006. Made: 15.08.2006. Laid: 17.08.2006. Coming into force: 01.09.2006. Effect: S.I. 2004/2152 amended. Territorial extent & classification: E/W/S/NI. General. - These Regulations amend the Cosmetic Products (Safety) Regulations 2004 ("the Principal Regulations") to give effect to Commission Directive 2006/65/EC which amends Council Directive 76/768/EEC. The Directive has been implemented by the Principal Regulations. - 4p.: 30 cm. - 978-0-11-075024-8 £3.00

The Cosmetic Products (Safety) (Amendment) (No. 3) Regulations 2006 No. 2006/2907. - Enabling power: Consumer Protection Act 1987, s. 11. - Issued: 13.11.2006. Made: 06.11.2006. Laid: 07.11.2006. Coming into force: 29.11.2006. Effect: S.I. 2004/2152 amended. Territorial extent & classification: E/W/S/NI. General. - This Statutory Instrument has been made in consequence of an error in SI 2006/2231 (ISBN 0110750241) and is being issued free of charge to all known recipients of that Statutory Instrument. - 2p.: 30 cm. - 978-0-11-075260-0 *£3.00*

The Cosmetic Products (Safety) (Amendment) Regulations 2006 No. 2006/1198. - Enabling power: European Communities Act 1972, s. 2 & Consumer Protection Act 1987, s. 11. - Issued: 08.05.2006. Made: 27.04.2006. Laid: 28.04.2006. Coming into force: 22.05.2006. Effect: S.I. 2004/2152 amended. Territorial extent & classification: E/W/S/NI. General. - These Regulations amend the Cosmetic Products (Safety) Regulations 2004 ("the Principal Regulations") to give effect to Commission Directive 2005/80/EC which amends Council Directive 76/768/EEC. The Directive has been implemented by the Principal Regulations. - 4p.: 30 cm. - 978-0-11-074539-8 *£3.00*

The Dangerous Substances and Preparations (Safety) Regulations 2006 No. 2006/2916. - Enabling power: Consumer Protection Act 1987, s. 11. - Issued: 15.11.2006. Made: 06.11.2006. Laid: 07.11.2006. Coming into force: 04.12.2006 except for regs 5, 11, 12; 16.01.2007 for reg 11; 15.06.2007 for reg 12; 24.08.2007 for reg 5. Effect: S.I. 1994/2844; 1996/2635; 2000/2897; 2002/1689 amended and S.I. 1999/2084 (04.12.2006); 2002/1770 (04.12.2006); 2002/3010 (24.08.2007); 2004/1417 (24.08.2007) revoked. Territorial extent & classification: E/W/S/NI. General. - EC note: Implements Directive 2005/59/EC (so far as it relates to toluene); Directive 2005/84/EC (phthalates in toys and childcare articles); and Directive 2005/90/EC (amendments to the list of substances classified as carcinogenic, mutagenic or toxic to reproduction). - 134p.: 30 cm. - 978-0-11-075268-6 *£19.50*

The Enterprise Act 2002 (Amendment) Regulations 2006 No. 2006/3363. - Enabling power: European Communities Act 1972, s. 2 (2). - Issued: 29.12.2006. Made: 14.12.2006. Laid: 15.12.2006. Coming into force: 08.01.2007. Effect: 1998 c.29; 2001 c.16; 2002 c.40 amended. Territorial extent & classification: E/W/S/NI. General. - EC note: These Regulations implement Articles 4(6) and 13(4) of Regulation (EC) No. 2006/2004 on cooperation between national authorities responsible for the enforcement of consumer protection laws, as amended by Directive 2005/29/EC of the European Parliament and of the Council of 11 May 2005 concerning unfair business-to-consumer commercial practices in the internal market. - 12p.: 30 cm. - 978-0-11-075522-9 *£3.00*

The Enterprise Act 2002 (Part 8 Community Infringements Specified UK Laws) Order 2006 No. 2006/3372. - Enabling power: Enterprise Act 2002, s. 212 (3) (6). - Issued: 22.12.2006. Made: 15.12.2006. Laid: 18.12.2006. Coming into force: 08.01.2007. Effect: None. Territorial extent & classification: E/W/S/NI. General. - EC note: This Order specifies, for the purposes of section 212 of the Enterprise Act 2002 the UK law which gives effect to the two directives and the regulation referred to in the Schedule (the "EC legislation"). Directive 97/55/EC amending Directive 84/450/EEC concerning misleading advertising so as to include comparative advertising. Directive 98/6/EC on consumer protection in the indication of prices of products offered to consumers. Regulation 261/2004 establishing common rules on compensation and assistance to air passengers in the event of denied boarding and of cancellation or long delay of flights. - 4p.: 30 cm. - 978-0-11-075534-2 *£3.00*

The Enterprise Act 2002 (Part 8 Notice to OFT of Intended Prosecution Specified Enactments) Order 2006 No. 2006/3371. - Enabling power: Enterprise Act 2002, s. 230 (1) (7). - Issued: 22.12.2006. Made: 15.12.2006. Laid: 18.12.2006. Coming into force: 08.01.2007. Effect: None. Territorial extent & classification: E/W/S/NI. General. - 2p.: 30 cm. - 978-0-11-075533-5 *£3.00*

The Enterprise Act 2002 (Part 9 Restrictions on Disclosure of Information) (Amendment) Order 2006 No. 2006/2909. - Enabling power: Enterprise Act 2002, s. 241 (6). - Issued: 13.11.2006. Made: 02.11.2006. Laid: 07.11.2006. Coming into force: 01.12.2006. Effect: 2002 c. 40 amended. Territorial extent & classification: E/W/S/NI. General. - 2p.: 30 cm. - 978-0-11-075261-7 *£3.00*

The Enterprise Act 2002 (Water Services Regulation Authority) Order 2006 No. 2006/522. - Enabling power: Enterprise Act 2002, s. 205, 213. - Issued: 07.03.2006. Made: 01.03.2006. Laid: 03.03.2006. Coming into force: 01.04.2006. Effect: S.I. 2003/1368, 1399 amended. Territorial extent & classification: UK. General. - 4p.: 30 cm. - 978-0-11-074135-2 *£3.00*

Tobacco Advertising and Promotion Act 2002 etc. (Amendment) Regulations 2006 No. 2006/2369. - Enabling power: European Communities Act 1972, s. 2 (2). - Issued: 07.09.2006. Made: 24.08.2006. Laid: 07.09.2006. Coming into force: 28.09.2006. Effect: 2002 c.36 amended & S.I. 2003/115 amended. Territorial extent & classification: E/W/S/NI. General. - EC note: Gives effect to Directive 2003/33/EC on the approximation of the laws, regulations and administrative provisions of the Member States relating to the advertising and sponsorship of tobacco products. - 8p.: 30 cm. - 978-0-11-075067-5 *£3.00*

The Unfair Terms in Consumer Contracts (Amendment) and Water Act 2003 (Transitional Provision) Regulations 2006 No. 2006/523. - Enabling power: European Communities Act 1972, s. 2 (2) & Water Act 2003, s. 103 (1) (b) (2) (b). - Issued: 07.03.2006. Made: 01.03.2006. Laid: 03.03.2006. Coming into force: 01.04.2006. Effect: S.I. 1999/2083 amended. Territorial extent & classification: UK, except for reg. 3 which extends only to E/W. General. - 4p.: 30 cm. - 978-0-11-074137-6 *£3.00*

Consumer protection, England and Wales

The Compensation Act 2006 (Commencement No. 1) Order 2006 No. 2006/3005 (C.107). - Enabling power: Compensation Act 2006, s. 16 (1). Bringing into operation various provisions of the 2006 Act on 01.12.2006. - Issued: 22.11.2006. Made: 09.11.2006. Effect: None. Territorial extent & classification: E/W. General. - 2p.: 30 cm. - 978-0-11-075333-1 *£3.00*

The Compensation (Claims Management Services) Regulations 2006 No. 2006/3322. - Enabling power: Compensation Act 2006, ss. 8 (8), 9, 15, sch. - Issued: 20.12.2006. Made: 12.12.2006. Coming into force: 13.12.2006. Effect: None. Territorial extent & classification: E/W. General. - Supersedes draft (ISBN 0110753267) issued 20.11.2006. - 24p.: 30 cm. - 978-0-11-075497-0 *£4.00*

The Compensation (Regulated Claims Management Services) Order 2006 No. 2006/3319. - Enabling power: Compensation Act 2006, ss. 4 (2) (e), 15 (1). - Issued: 19.12.2006. Made: 12.12.2006. Coming into force: 13.12.2006. Effect: None. Territorial extent & classification: E/W. General. - Supersedes draft (ISBN 0110753240) issued 20.11.2006. - 4p.: 30 cm. - 978-0-11-075495-6 *£3.00*

The Compensation (Specification of Benefits) Order 2006 No. 2006/3321. - Enabling power: Compensation Act 2006, s. 4 (5). - Issued: 18.12.2006. Made: 12.12.2006. Coming into force: 13.12.2006. Effect: None. Territorial extent & classification: E/W. General. - Supersedes draft (ISBN 0110753259) issued 21.11.2006. - 4p.: 30 cm. - 978-0-11-075496-3 *£3.00*

The Tobacco Advertising and Promotion Act 2002 (Commencement No. 9) Order 2006 No. 2006/2372 (C.81). - Enabling power: Tobacco Advertising and Promotion Act 2002, s. 22 (1). Bringing into operation various provisions of the 2002 Act on 26.09.2006 in accord. with art. 2. - Issued: 07.09.2006. Made: 24.08.2006. Effect: None. Territorial extent & classification: E/W/NI. General. - 4p.: 30 cm. - 978-0-11-075068-2 *£3.00*

Consumer protection, Northern Ireland

The Tobacco Advertising and Promotion Act 2002 (Commencement No. 9) Order 2006 No. 2006/2372 (C.81). - Enabling power: Tobacco Advertising and Promotion Act 2002, s. 22 (1). Bringing into operation various provisions of the 2002 Act on 26.09.2006 in accord. with art. 2. - Issued: 07.09.2006. Made: 24.08.2006. Effect: None. Territorial extent & classification: E/W/NI. General. - 4p.: 30 cm. - 978-0-11-075068-2 *£3.00*

Contracting out: Child support

The Contracting Out (Functions Relating to Child Support) Order 2006 No. 2006/1692. - Enabling power: Deregulation and Contracting Out Act 1994, s. 69. - Issued: 30.06.2006. Made: 27.06.2006. Coming into force: 03.07.2006. Effect: None. Territorial extent & classification: E/W/S. General. - Supersedes draft SI (ISBN 0110745841) issued 22.05.2006. - 2p.: 30 cm. - 978-0-11-074766-8 *£3.00*

Contracting out, England

The Transport for London (Best Value) (Contracting Out of Investment and Highway Functions) Order 2006 No. 2006/91. - Enabling power: Deregulation and Contracting Out Act 1994, s. 70. - Issued: 25.01.2006. Made: 19.01.2006. Coming into force: 20.01.2006. Effect: None. Territorial extent & classification: E. General. - 4p.: 30 cm. - 978-0-11-073925-0 *£3.00*

Cooperative societies

The European Cooperative Society Regulations 2006 No. 2006/2078. - Enabling power: European Communities Act 1972, s. 2 (2). - Issued: 01.08.2006. Made: 25.07.2006. Laid: 27.07.2006. Coming into force: 18.08.2006. Effect: 1986 c.45 amended. Territorial extent & classification: E/W/S/NI. General. - EC note: This instrument gives effect to Council Regulation (EC) No. 1435/2003 of 22nd July 2003 (on the Statute for a European Cooperative Society (SCE) in the United Kingdom. - 20p.: 30 cm. - 978-0-11-074954-9 *£3.50*

Copyright

The Copyright and Performances (Application to Other Countries) Order 2006 No. 2006/316. - Enabling power: Copyright, Designs and Patents Act 1988, ss. 159, 208 & European Communities Act 1972, s. 2 (2). - Issued: 03.03.2006. Made: 14.02.2006. Laid: 24.02.2006. Coming into force: 06.04.2006. Effect: S.I. 2005/852 revoked. Territorial extent & classification: E/W/S/NI. General. - 16p.: 30 cm. - 978-0-11-074059-1 *£3.00*

The Copyright (Certification of Licensing Scheme for Educational Recording of Broadcasts and Cable Programmes) (Educational Recording Agency Limited) (Revocation) Order 2006 No. 2006/35. - Enabling power: Copyright, Designs and Patents Act 1988, s. 143. - Issued: 17.01.2006. Made: 09.01.2006. Coming into force: 09.01.2006. Effect: S.I. 1990/879; 1992/211; 1993/193; 1994/247; 1996/191; 1998/203; 1999/3452; 2003/188 revoked. Territorial extent & classification: E/W/S/NI. General. - 4p.: 30 cm. - 978-0-11-073894-9 *£3.00*

The Performances (Moral Rights, etc.) Regulations 2006 No. 2006/18. - Enabling power: European Communities Act 1972, s. 2 (2). - Issued: 27.01.2006. Made: 09.01.2006. Laid: 11.01.2006. Coming into force: 01.02.2006. Effect: 1988 c. 48 amended. Territorial extent & classification: E/W/S/NI. General. - EC note: These Regulations amend the 1988 Act to enable the UK to ratify the WIPO Performers and Phonograms Treaty (1997, Cm. 3728), which has been specified as a Community treaty. - 12p.: 30 cm. - 978-0-11-073931-1 *£3.00*

Copyright, Gibraltar

The Copyright (Gibraltar) Revocation Order 2006 No. 2006/1039. - Enabling power: Copyright, Designs and Patents Act 1988, s. 157 (2). - Issued: 18.04.2006. Made: 11.04.2006. Coming into force: In acc.with art. 1. Effect: S.I. 2005/853 revoked. Territorial extent & classification: Gibraltar. General. - 2p.: 30 cm. - 978-0-11-074492-6 *£3.00*

Coroners, England

The Gloucestershire (Coroners' Districts) Order 2006 No. 2006/544. - Enabling power: Coroners' Act 1988, s. 4 (2). - Issued: 06.03.2006. Made: 16.02.2006. Laid: 06.03.2006. Coming into force: 01.04.2006. Effect: S.I. 1974/368 revoked. Territorial extent & classification: E. General. - 2p.: 30 cm. - 978-0-11-074144-4 *£3.00*

The Suffolk (Coroners' Districts) Order 2006 No. 2006/1747. - Enabling power: Coroners Act 1988, s. 4 (2). - Issued: 07.07.2006. Made: 30.06.2006. Laid: 04.07.2006. Coming into force: 01.08.2006. Effect: S.I. 2001/1220 revoked. Territorial extent & classification: E. General. - With correction slip dated August 2006. - 2p.: 30 cm. - 978-0-11-074795-8 *£3.00*

Coroners, England and Wales

The Discipline of Coroners (Designation) Order 2006 No. 2006/677. - Enabling power: Constitutional Reform Act 2005, s. 118 (2). - Issued: 17.03.2006. Made: 09.03.2006. Laid: 13.03.2006. Coming into force: 03.04.2006. Effect: None. Territorial extent & classification: E/W. General. - 2p.: 30 cm. - 978-0-11-074274-8 *£3.00*

Corporation tax

The Authorised Investment Funds (Tax) (Amendment) Regulations 2006 No. 2006/3239. - Enabling power: Finance (No. 2) Act 2005, ss. 17 (3), 18. - Issued: 11.12.2006. Made: 06.12.2006. Laid: 06.12.2006. Coming into force: 07.12.2006. Effect: S.I. 2006/964 amended. Territorial extent & classification: E/W/S/NI. General. - 4p.: 30 cm. - 978-0-11-075430-7 *£3.00*

The Authorised Investment Funds (Tax) Regulations 2006 No. 2006/964. - Enabling power: Finance Act 1995, s. 152 & Finance (No. 2) Act 2005, ss. 17 (3), 18. - Issued: 06.04.2006. Made: 29.03.2006. Coming into force: 01.04.2006. Effect: 1970 c. 9; 1988 c. 1; 1992 c. 12; 1996 c. 8; 2005 c. 5, c. 7 amended & S.I. 1997/1154, 1715; 2002/1973; 2003/1831 revoked. Territorial extent & classification: E/W/S/NI. General. - Approved by the House of Commons. Supersedes draft SI (ISBN 0110740300) issued 17.02.2006. - 48p.: 30 cm. - 978-0-11-074427-8 *£7.50*

The Capital Allowances (Energy-saving Plant and Machinery) (Amendment) Order 2006 No. 2006/2233. - Enabling power: Capital Allowances Act 2001, ss. 45A (3) (4), 45B (1), 45C (2) (b) (3) (b), 180A (2). - Issued: 21.08.2006. Made: 16.08.2006. Laid: 17.08.2006. Coming into force: 07.09.2006. Effect: S.I. 2001/2541 amended. Territorial extent & classification: E/W/S/NI. General. - 2p.: 30 cm. - 978-0-11-075026-2 *£3.00*

The Capital Allowances (Environmentally Beneficial Plant and Machinery) (Amendment) Order 2006 No. 2006/2235. - Enabling power: Capital Allowances Act 2001, ss. 45H (3) (4), 45J (3) (b). - Issued: 21.08.2006. Made: 16.08.2006. Laid: 17.08.2006. Coming into force: 07.09.2006. Effect: S.I. 2003/2076 amended. Territorial extent & classification: E/W/S/NI. General. - 2p.: 30 cm. - 978-0-11-075027-9 *£3.00*

The Double Taxation Relief (Taxes on Income) (Botswana) Order 2006 No. 2006/1925. - Enabling power: Income and Corporation Taxes Act 1988, s. 788. - Issued: 26.07.2006. Made: 19.07.2006. Coming into force: 19.07.2006. Effect: None. Territorial extent & classification: E/W/S/NI. General. - Supersedes draft S.I. (ISBN 0110745159) issued 03.05.2006. - 20p.: 30 cm. - 978-0-11-074890-0 *£3.50*

The Double Taxation Relief (Taxes on Income) (Japan) Order 2006 No. 2006/1924. - Enabling power: Income and Corporation Taxes Act 1988, s. 788. - Issued: 26.07.2006. Made: 19.07.2006. Coming into force: 19.07.2006. Effect: None. Territorial extent & classification: E/W/S/NI. General. - Supersedes draft S.I. (ISBN 0110745124) issued 03.05.2006. - 28p.: 30 cm. - 978-0-11-074891-7 *£4.50*

The Double Taxation Relief (Taxes on Income) (Poland) Order 2006 No. 2006/3323. - Enabling power: Income and Corporation Taxes Act 1988, s. 788 & Finance Act 2006, s. 173 (1) to (3)- Issued: 04.01.2007. Made: 14.12.2006. Coming into force: 14.12.2006. Effect: None. Territorial extent & classification: E/W/S/NI. General. - Supersedes the draft S.I. (ISBN 0110752279) issued on 31.10.2006. - 20p.: 30 cm. - 978-0-11-075523-6 *£3.50*

The Finance Act 2002, Schedule 26, (Parts 2 and 9) (Amendment) Order 2006 No. 2006/3269. - Enabling power: Finance Act 2002, sch. 26, para. 13 and Finance Act 2005, sch. 4, para. 52- Issued: 14.12.2006. Made: 07.12.2006. Laid: 08.12.2006. Coming into force: 30.12.2006. Effect: 2002 c. 23 amended. Territorial extent & classification: E/W/S/NI. General. - With correction slip dated February 2007. - 20p.: 30 cm. - 978-0-11-075455-0 *£3.50*

The Finance Act 2006, Section 53 (1) (Films and Sound Recordings) (Appointed Day) Order 2006 No. 2006/3399 (C.126). - Enabling power: Finance Act 2006, s. 53 (1). Bringing into force various provisions of the 2006 Act on 01.01.2007 in accord. with art. 2. - Issued: 22.12.2006. Made: 18.12.2006. Effect: None. Territorial extent & classification: E/W/S/NI. General. - 2p.: 30 cm. - 978-0-11-075551-9 *£3.00*

The Finance Act 2006, Section 53(2) (Films and Sound Recordings: Power to alter Dates) Order 2006 No. 2006/3265. - Enabling power: Finance Act 2006, s. 53 (2). - Issued: 12.12.2006. Made: 07.12.2006. Laid: 08.12.2006. Coming into force: 29.12.2006. Effect: 2006 c. 25 amended. Territorial extent & classification: E/W/S/NI. General. - With correction slip, dated January 2007. - 4p.: 30 cm. - 978-0-11-075444-4 *£3.00*

The Finance (No. 2) Act 2005, Section 17(1), (Appointed Day) Order 2006 No. 2006/982 (C.29). - Enabling power: Finance (No. 2) Act 2005, s. 19 (1). Bringing into operation various provisions of the 2005 Act on 01.04.2006; 06.04.2006. - Issued: 04.04.2006. Made: 30.03.2006. Effect: None. Territorial extent & classification: E/W/S/NI. General. - 2p.: 30 cm. - 978-0-11-074432-2 *£3.00*

The Group Relief for Overseas Losses (Modification of the Corporation Tax Acts for Non-resident Insurance Companies) (No. 2) Regulations 2006 No. 2006/3389. - Enabling power: Income and Corporation Taxes Act 1988, sch. 18A, para. 16 (2) to (5). - Issued: 22.12.2006. Made: 18.12.2006. Laid: 18.12.2006. Coming into force: 08.01.2007. Effect: 1988 c.1; 1989 c. 26 modified & S.I. 1996/2991; 2001/1757 modified & S.I. 2006/3218 revoked. Territorial extent & classification: E/W/S/NI. General. - This Statutory Instrument has been made in consequence of a defect in S.I. 2006/3218 (ISBN 0110754174) and is being issued free of charge to all known recipients of that Statutory Instrument. - 8p.: 30 cm. - 978-0-11-075540-3 *£3.00*

The Group Relief for Overseas Losses (Modification of the Corporation Tax Acts for Non-resident Insurance Companies) Regulations 2006 No. 2006/3218. - Enabling power: Finance Act 2006, sch. 1, paras 16 (2) to (5). - Issued: 08.12.2006. Made: 04.12.2006. Laid: 05.12.2006. Coming into force: 26.12.2006. Effect: 1988 c.1; 1989 c. 26; S.I. 1996/2991; 2001/1757 modified. Territorial extent & classification: E/W/S/NI General. - This SI contained a technical error and has been revoked by SI 2006/3389 (ISBN 0110755405) which is being issued free of charge to all known recipients of 2006/3218. - 8p.: 30 cm. - 978-0-11-075417-8 *£3.00*

The Income Tax (Trading and Other Income) Act 2005 (Consequential Amendments) Order 2006 No. 2006/959. - Enabling power: Income Tax (Trading and Other Income) Act 2005, s. 882 (2) to (5). - Issued: 04.04.2006. Made: 29.03.2006. Laid: 29.03.2006. Coming into force: 30.03.2006. Effect: 1988 c. 1; 1992 c. 12, c.48; 2002 c. 23 amended. Territorial extent & classification: E/W/S/NI. General. - 4p.: 30 cm. - 978-0-11-074424-7 *£3.00*

The Insurance Companies (Corporation Tax Acts) (Amendment No. 2) Order 2006 No. 2006/3387. - Enabling power: Income and Corporation Taxes Act 1988, s. 431A (1) (2) (7). - Issued: 22.12.2006. Made: 18.12.2006. Laid: 18.12.2006. Coming into force: 08.01.2007. Effect: 1988 c.1; 1989 c. 26 amended. Territorial extent & classification: E/W/S/NI. General. - 4p.: 30 cm. - 978-0-11-075539-7 *£3.00*

The Insurance Companies (Corporation Tax Acts) (Amendment) Order 2006 No. 2006/1358. - Enabling power: Income and Corporation Taxes Act 1988, s. 431A (3) (6). - Issued: 24.05.2006. Made: 18.05.2006. Laid: 19.05.2006. Coming into force: 09.06.2006. Effect: 1988 c.1 amended. Territorial extent & classification: E/W/S/NI. General. - With correction slip dated May 2006. - 8p.: 30 cm. - 978-0-11-074597-8 *£3.00*

The Insurance Companies (Corporation Tax Acts) (Miscellaneous Amendments) Order 2006 No. 2006/3270. - Enabling power: Income and Corporation Taxes Act 1988, s. 431A (1) (3). - Issued: 13.12.2006. Made: 07.12.2006. Laid: 08.12.2006. Coming into force: 31.12.2006. Effect: 1988 c. 1; 1989 c. 26; 1998 c. 36; 2002 c. 23 amended. Territorial extent & classification: E/W/S/NI. General. - 4p.: 30 cm. - 978-0-11-075456-7 *£3.00*

The Investment Trusts and Venture Capital Trusts (Definition of Capital Profits, Gains or Losses) Order 2006 No. 2006/1182. - Enabling power: Finance Act 1996, sch. 10, paras. 1A (2) (b), 1B (2) (b), 9 (1) & Finance Act 2002, sch. 26, paras. 38 (2) (b), 38A (2) (b). - Issued: 03.05.2006. Made: 26.04.2006. Laid: 27.04.2006. Coming into force: 18.05.2006. Effect: None. Territorial extent & classification: E/W/S/NI. General. - 4p.: 30 cm. - 978-0-11-074537-4 *£3.00*

The Lloyd's Sourcebook (Finance Act 1993 and Finance Act 1994) (Amendment) Order 2006 No. 2006/3273. - Enabling power: Financial Services and Markets Act 2000, ss. 417 (1), 426 (1). - Issued: 13.12.2006. Made: 07.12.2006. Laid: 08.12.2006. Coming into force: 31.12.2006. Effect: 1993 c. 34; 1994 c. 9 amended and S.I. 2005/1538 revoked. Territorial extent & classification: E/W/S/NI. General. - 2p.: 30 cm. - 978-0-11-075454-3 *£3.00*

The Lloyd's Underwriters (Conversion to Limited Liability Underwriting) (Tax) Regulations 2006 No. 2006/112. - Enabling power: Finance Act 1993, s. 182 (1) (b). - Issued: 27.01.2006. Made: 23.01.2006. Laid: 24.01.2006. Coming into force: 14.02.2006. Effect: 1993 c. 34 amended. Territorial extent & classification: E/W/S/NI. General. - 2p.: 30 cm. - 978-0-11-073934-2 *£3.00*

The Lloyd's Underwriters (Double Taxation Relief) (Corporate Members) Regulations 2006 No. 2006/3262. - Enabling power: Finance Act 1994, s. 229. - Issued: 13.12.2006. Made: 06.12.2006. Laid: 07.12.2006. Coming into force: 31.12.2006. Effect: None. Territorial extent & classification: E/W/S/NI. General. - 8p.: 30 cm. - 978-0-11-075442-0 £3.00

The Lloyd's Underwriters (Scottish Limited Partnerships) (Tax) (Amendment) Regulations 2006 No. 2006/111. - Enabling power: Finance Act 1993, s. 182 (1) and Finance Act 1994, s. 229. - Issued: 27.01.2006. Made: 23.01.2006. Laid: 24.01.2006. Coming into force: 14.02.2006. Effect: S.I. 1997/2681 amended. Territorial extent & classification: E/W/S/NI. General. - 4p.: 30 cm. - 978-0-11-073933-5 £3.00

The Loan Relationships and Derivative Contracts (Change of Accounting Practice) (Amendment) Regulations 2006 No. 2006/3238. - Enabling power: Finance Act 1996, s. 85B (3) (5), sch. 9, para. 19B & Finance Act 2002, sch. 26, para. 17C. - Issued: 11.12.2006. Made: 06.12.2006. Laid: 06.12.2006. Coming into force: 27.12.2006. Effect: S.I. 2004/3271 amended. Territorial extent & classification: E/W/S/NI. General. - 4p.: 30 cm. - 978-0-11-075429-1 £3.00

The Loan Relationships and Derivative Contracts (Disregard and Bringing into Account of Profits and Losses) (Amendment) Regulations 2006 No. 2006/3236. - Enabling power: Finance Act 1996, ss. 84A (3A), 85B (3) (a) (5) (b) & Finance Act 2002, sch. 26, paras 16 (3A), 17C (1) (3) (b) & Finance Act 2005, sch. 4, para. 52. - Issued: 11.12.2006. Made: 06.12.2006. Laid: 06.12.2006. Coming into force: 27.12.2006. Effect: S.I. 2004/3256 amended. Territorial extent & classification: E/W/S/NI. General. - 8p.: 30 cm. - 978-0-11-075431-4 £3.00

The Loan Relationships and Derivative Contracts (Disregard and Bringing into Account of Profits and Losses) (Amendment) Regulations 2006 No. 2006/936. - Enabling power: Finance Act 2002, sch. 26, paras. 17C (1), 54 (2A). - Issued: 31.03.2006. Made: 28.03.2006. Laid: 28.03.2006. Coming into force: 29.03.2006. Effect: S.I. 2006/843 amended. Territorial extent & classification: E/W/S/NI. General. - 2p.: 30 cm. - 978-0-11-074411-7 £3.00

The Loan Relationships and Derivative Contracts (Disregard and Bringing into Account of Profits and Losses) Regulations 2006 No. 2006/843. - Enabling power: Finance Act 1996, s. 84A (3A) & Finance Act 2002, sch. 26, paras 16 (3A), 17C (1). - Issued: 24.03.2006. Made: 21.03.2006. Laid: 21.03.2006. Coming into force: 22.03.2006. Effect: None. Territorial extent & classification: E/W/S/NI. General. - 4p.: 30 cm. - 978-0-11-074376-9 £3.00

The Oil Taxation (Market Value of Oil) Regulations 2006 No. 2006/3313. - Enabling power: Oil Taxation Act 1975, s. 21 (2), sch. 3, paras 2 (1B) (1C) (2E) (2F) & Finance Act 2006, s. 147 (4) (7). - Issued: 18.12.2006. Made: 13.12.2006. Coming into force: 14.12.2006. Effect: None. Territorial extent & classification: E/W/S/NI. General. - Supersedes draft SI (ISBN 0110753453) issued 01.12.2006. - 12p.: 30 cm. - 978-0-11-075490-1 £3.00

The Overseas Life Insurance Companies Regulations 2006 No. 2006/3271. - Enabling power: Finance Act 2003, s. 156. - Issued: 13.12.2006. Made: 07.12.2006. Laid: 08.12.2006. Coming into force: 31.12.2006. Effect: 1988 c. 1; 1989 c. 26; 1992 c. 12, 48; 1993 c. 34; 1995 c.4; 1996 c. 8; 1997 c. 16, 58; 2000 c. 17; 2001 c. 2; 2002 c. 23; S.I. 1995/3237; 1997/993; 1999/498; 2000/2075, 2188; 2001/3629; 2004/2310 amended & S.I. 2004/2200; 2005/3375 revoked. Territorial extent & classification: E/W/S/NI. General. - 16p.: 30 cm. - 978-0-11-075446-8 £3.00

The Pension Protection Fund (Tax) Regulations 2006 No. 2006/575. - Enabling power: Finance Act 2005, s. 102. - Issued: 14.03.2006. Made: 09.03.2006. Laid: 10.03.2006. Coming into force: 06.04.2006. Effect: None. Territorial extent & classification: E/W/S/NI. General. - 14p.: 30 cm. - 978-0-11-074218-2 £3.00

The Petroleum Revenue Tax (Nomination Scheme for Disposals and Appropriations) (Amendment) Regulations 2006 No. 2006/3089. - Enabling power: Finance Act 1987, s. 61 (8), sch. 10, paras 1 (1), 4 (1B) (a) (3), 5 (1) (h), 5A (1) (h), 7 (3), 12 & Finance Act 1999, s. 133 (1) & Finance Act 2006, s. 150 (15). - Issued: 24.11.2006. Made: 20.11.2006. Laid: 21.11.2006. Coming into force: 12.12.2006. Effect: S.I. 1987/1338 amended. Territorial extent & classification:E/W/S/NI. General. - 4p.: 30 cm. - 978-0-11-075348-5 £3.00

The Real Estate Investment Trusts (Assessment and Recovery of Tax) (Amendment) Regulations 2006 No. 2006/3222. - Enabling power: Finance Act 2006, s. 122, sch. 17, paras 4, 19. - Issued: 18.12.2006. Made: 04.12.2006. Laid: 05.12.2006. Coming into force: 26.12.2006. Effect: S.I. 2006/2867 amended. Territorial extent & classification: E/W/S/NI. General. - This Statutory Instrument has been made in consequence of an error in S.I. 2006/2867 (ISBN 0110752473) and is being issued free of charge to all known recipients of that Statutory Instrument. This correcting SI was initially published with an incorrect header (under ISBN 0110754204) and it is now republishing with a new ISBN. - 2p.: 30 cm. - 978-0-11-075500-7 £3.00

The Real Estate Investment Trusts (Assessment and Recovery of Tax) (Amendment) Regulations 2006 No. 2006/3222. - Enabling power: Finance Act 2006, s. 122, sch. 17, paras 4, 19. - Issued: 12.12.2006. Made: 04.12.2006. Laid: 05.12.2006. Coming into force: 26.12.2006. Effect: S.I. 2006/2867 amended. Territorial extent & classification: E/W/S/NI. General. - This Statutory Instrument has been replaced by a corrected version (ISBN 0110755006). - 2p.: 30 cm. - 978-0-11-075420-8 £3.00

The Real Estate Investment Trusts (Assessment and Recovery of Tax) Regulations 2006 No. 2006/2867. - Enabling power: Finance Act 2006, s. 122, sch. 17, paras 4, 19. - Issued: 06.11.2006. Made: 01.11.2006. Laid: 01.11.2006. Coming into force: 01.01.2007. Effect: None. Territorial extent & classification: E/W/S/NI. General. - 8p.: 30 cm. - 978-0-11-075247-1 £3.00

The Real Estate Investment Trusts (Breach of Conditions) Regulations 2006 No. 2006/2864. - Enabling power: Finance Act 2006, ss. 114 to 116, 122, 129 (2) (a) (b), 134 (1), 144. - Issued: 13.11.2006. Made: 01.11.2006. Laid: 01.11.2006. Coming into force: 01.01.2007. Effect: None. Territorial extent & classification: E/W/S/NI. General. - 8p.: 30 cm. - 978-0-11-075249-5 £3.00

The Real Estate Investment Trusts (Financial Statements of Group Real Estate Investment Trusts) Regulations 2006 No. 2006/2865. - Enabling power: Finance Act 2006, s. 144, sch. 17, para. 31 (7). - Issued: 10.11.2006. Made: 01.11.2006. Laid: 01.11.2006. Coming into force: 01.01.2007. Effect: None. Territorial extent & classification: E/W/S/NI. General. - 8p.: 30 cm. - 978-0-11-075248-8 £3.00

The Real Estate Investment Trusts (Joint Ventures) Regulations 2006 No. 2006/2866. - Enabling power: Finance Act 2006, s. 138. - Issued: 06.11.2006. Made: 01.11.2006. Laid: 01.11.2006. Coming into force: 01.01.2007. Effect: None. Territorial extent & classification: E/W/S/NI. General. - 12p.: 30 cm. - 978-0-11-075250-1 £3.00

The Reporting of Savings Income Information (Amendment) Regulations 2006 No. 2006/3286. - Enabling power: Finance Act 2003, s. 199. - Issued: 14.12.2006. Made: 11.12.2006. Laid: 11.12.2006. Coming into force: 01.01.2007. Effect: S.I. 2003/3297 amended. Territorial extent & classification: E/W/S/NI. General. - With correction slip dated January 2007. EC note: These Regs amend the 2003 Regulations which implemented part of Council Directive 2003/48/EC on the taxation of savings income in the form of interest payments. The 2003 Directive has been amended by Council Directive 2006/98/EC adapting certain Directives in the field of taxation by reason of the accession of Bulgaria and Romania. - 4p.: 30 cm. - 978-0-11-075468-0 £3.00

The Taxation of Chargeable Gains (Gilt-edged Securities) (No.2) Order 2006 No. 2006/3170. - Enabling power: Taxation of Chargeable Gains Act 1992, sch. 9, para. 1. - Issued: 01.12.2006. Made: 28.11.2006. Coming into force: 28.11.2006. Effect: None. Territorial extent & classification: E/W/S/NI. General. - 2p.: 30 cm. - 978-0-11-075389-8 £3.00

The Taxation of Chargeable Gains (Gilt-edged Securities) Order 2006 No. 2006/184. - Enabling power: Taxation of Chargeable Gains Act 1992, sch. 9, para. 1. - Issued: 03.02.2006. Made: 30.01.2006. Coming into force: 30.01.2006. Effect: None. Territorial extent & classification: E/W/S/NI. General. - 2p.: 30 cm. - 978-0-11-073965-6 £3.00

The Taxation of Securitisation Companies Regulations 2006 No. 2006/3296. - Enabling power: Finance Act 2005, s. 84. - Issued: 15.12.2006. Made: 11.12.2006. Coming into force: 12.12.2006. Effect: 1988 c. 1 modified. Territorial extent & classification: E/W/S/NI. General. - Supersedes the draft S.I. (ISBN 0110753275) issued on 21.11.2006. - 12p.: 30 cm. - 978-0-11-075476-5 £3.00

The Tax Avoidance Schemes (Information) (Amendment) Regulations 2006 No. 2006/1544. - Enabling power: Finance Act 2004, ss. 308 (1) (3), 309 (1), 310, 313 (1), 317 (2), 318 (1). - Issued: 20.06.2006. Made: 15.06.2006. Laid: 15.06.2006. Coming into force: 01.08.2006. Effect: S.I. 2004/1864 amended. Territorial extent & classification: E/W/S/NI. General. - 4p.: 30 cm. - 978-0-11-074707-1 £3.00

The Tax Avoidance Schemes (Prescribed Descriptions of Arrangements) Regulations 2006 No. 2006/1543. - Enabling power: Finance Act 2004, s. 306 (1) (a) (b). - Issued: 20.06.2006. Made: 15.06.2006. Laid: 15.06.2006. Coming into force: 01.08.2006. Effect: S.I. 2004/1863, 2429 revoked. Territorial extent & classification: E/W/S/NI. General. - 12p.: 30 cm. - 978-0-11-074706-4 £3.00

The Tonnage Tax (Exception of Financial Year 2006) Order 2006 No. 2006/333. - Enabling power: Finance Act 2000, sch. 22, paras 22B (2), 22C. - Issued: 17.02.2006. Made: 13.02.2006. Coming into force: 01.04.2006. Effect: None. Territorial extent & classification: E/W/S/NI. General. - 2p.: 30 cm. - 978-0-11-074033-1 £3.00

The Unit Trust Schemes and Offshore Funds (Non-qualifying Investments Test) Order 2006 No. 2006/981. - Enabling power: Finance Act 1996, sch. 10, paras. 8 (8), 9. - Issued: 04.04.2006. Made: 30.03.2006. Laid: 30.03.2006. Coming into force: 20.04.2006. Effect: 1996 c. 8 amended. Territorial extent & classification: E/W/S/NI. General. - 4p.: 30 cm. - 978-0-11-074431-5 £3.00

Council tax, England

The Council Tax and Non-Domestic Rating (Amendment) (England) Regulations 2006 No. 2006/3395. - Enabling power: Local Government Finance Act 1988, s. 143 (1) (2), sch. 9, paras. 1, 2 (2) (ga), 3 (2) & Local Government Finance Act 1992, ss. 24 (7) (a), 41 (3), sch. 1, para. 9, sch. 2, paras 2 (4) (e) (j), 21 (3), sch. 4, paras 5 (2) (e), 7 (2) (b), 8 (2) (b). - Issued: 21.12.2006. Made: 18.12.2006. Laid: 21.12.2006. Coming into force: 31.01.2007. Effect: S.I. 1989/1058; 1992/552, 613, 3239; 1993/290; 2003/2613 amended. Territorial extent & classification: E. General. - With correction slip dated January 2007. - 12p.: 30 cm. - 978-0-11-075542-7 £3.00

The Council Tax (Discount Disregards) (Amendment) (England) Order 2006 No. 2006/3396. - Enabling power: Local Government Finance Act 1992, sch. 1, paras. 4, 5. - Issued: 21.12.2006. Made: 18.12.2006. Laid: 21.12.2006. Coming into force: 31.01.2007. Effect: S.I. 1992/548 amended in relation to England. Territorial extent & classification: E General. - With correction slip dated January 2007. - 4p.: 30 cm. - 978-0-11-075543-4 £3.00

The Council Tax (Exempt Dwellings) (Amendment) (England) Order 2006 No. 2006/2318. - Enabling power: Local Government Finance Act 1992, s. 4. - Issued: 06.09.2006. Made: 25.08.2006. Laid: 06.09.2006. Coming into force: 01.04.2007. Effect: S.I. 1992/558 amended. Territorial extent & classification: E. General. - 4p.: 30 cm. - 978-0-11-075053-8 £3.00

The Non-Domestic Rating and Council Tax (Electronic Communications) (England) Order 2006 No. 2006/237. - Enabling power: Electronic Communications Act 2000, s. 8. - Issued: 08.02.2006. Made: 01.02.2006. Laid: 08.02.2006. Coming into force: 01.03.2006. Effect: S.I. 1989/1058, 2260; 1992/613 amended in relation to England. Territorial extent & classification: E. General. - 4p.: 30 cm. - 978-0-11-074019-5 *£3.00*

Council tax, Wales

The Local Authorities (Alteration of Requisite Calculations) (Wales) Regulations 2006 No. 2006/344 (W.41). - Enabling power: Local Government Finance Act 1992, ss. 32 (9), 33 (4), 43 (7), 44 (4), 113 (2). - Issued: 24.02.2006. Made: 14.02.2006. Coming into force: 15.02.2006. Effect: 1992 c. 14 modified in accord. with arts. 2 to 5. Territorial extent & classification: W. General. - In English & Welsh. Welsh title: Rheoliadau Awdurdodau Lleol (Addasu Cyfrifiadau Angenrheidiol) (Cymru) 2006. - With correction slip dated May 2006. - 8p.: 30 cm. - 978-0-11-091278-3 *£3.00*

Countryside, England

The Access to the Countryside (Exclusions and Restrictions) (England) (Amendment) Regulations 2006 No. 2006/990. - Enabling power: Countryside and Rights of Way Act 2000, ss. 32, 44 (2), 45 (1). - Issued: 05.04.2006. Made: 29.03.2006. Laid: 31.03.2006. Coming into force: 24.04.2006. Effect: S.I. 2003/2713 amended. Territorial extent & classification: E. General. - This Statutory Instrument has been made in consequence of defects in S.I. 2003/2713 (ISBN 0110480880) and is being issued free of charge to all known recipients of that S.I. - 2p.: 30 cm. - 978-0-11-074438-4 *£3.00*

The Environmental Stewardship (England) and Countryside Stewardship (Amendment) Regulations 2006 No. 2006/991. - Enabling power: Environment Act 1995, s. 98 & European Communities Act 1972, s. 2 (2). - Issued: 05.04.2006. Made: 21.03.2006. Laid: 31.03.2006. Coming into force: 30.04.2006. Effect: S.I. 2000/3048; 2005/621 amended. Territorial extent & classification: E. General. - 4p.: 30 cm. - 978-0-11-074439-1 *£3.00*

The Environmental Stewardship (England) and Organic Products (Amendment) Regulations 2006 No. 2006/2075. - Enabling power: Environment Act 1995, s. 98 & European Communities Act 1972, s. 2 (2). - Issued: 01.08.2006. Made: 25.07.2006. Laid: 28.07.2006. Coming into force: 04.09.2006. Effect: S.I. 2004/1604; 2005/621 amended & S.I. 2005/2003 revoked. Territorial extent & classification: E/W/S/NI [parts to E. only]. General. - 4p.: 30 cm. - 978-0-11-074953-2 *£3.00*

The National Park Authorities (England) Order 2006 No. 2006/3165. - Enabling power: Environment Act 1995, ss. 63 (1) (5), 75 (3) (4), sch. 7, paras 1 (2) to (6), 2 (1) to (3). - Issued: 04.12.2006. Made: 27.11.2006. Laid: 01.12.2006. Coming into force: 08.05.2007. Effect: S.I. 1996/1243; 2005/421 amended. Territorial extent & classification: E. General. - 4p.: 30 cm. - 978-0-11-075388-1 *£3.00*

Countryside, Wales

The Countryside and Rights of Way Act 2000 (Commencement No.9 and Saving) (Wales) Order 2006 No. 2006/3257 (W.297) (C.117). - Enabling power: Countryside and Rights of Way Act 2000, s. 103 (3) (4) (5). Bringing into operation various provisions of the 2006 on 06.12.2006; 01.04.2007. - Issued: 13.12.2006. Made: 05.12.2006. Effect: None. Territorial extent & classification: W. General. - In English and Welsh. Welsh title: Gorchymyn Deddf Cefn Gwlad a Hawliau Tramwy 2000 (Cychwyn Rhif 9 ac Arbediad) (Cymru) 2006. - 12p.: 30 cm. - 978-0-11-091466-4 *£3.00*

County courts, England and Wales

The Civil Courts (Amendment No.2) Order 2006 No. 2006/2920. - Enabling power: County Courts Act 1984, s. 2 (1). - Issued: 13.11.2006. Made: 07.11.2006. Laid: 08.11.2006. Coming into force: 30.11.2006. In accord. with art. 1. Effect: S.I. 1983/713 amended. Territorial extent & classification: E/W. General. - 2p.: 30 cm. - 978-0-11-075274-7 *£3.00*

The Civil Courts (Amendment) Order 2006 No. 2006/1542. - Enabling power: Race Relations Act 1976, s. 67 (1) (2) & County Courts Act 1984, s. 2 (1) & Matrimonial and Family Proceedings Act 1984, s. 33 (1) & Insolvency Act 1986, ss. 117, 374. - Issued: 19.06.2006. Made: 13.06.2006. Laid: 15.06.2006. Coming into force: 06.07.2006. Effect: S.I. 1983/713 amended. Territorial extent & classification: E/W. General. - 4p.: 30 cm. - 978-0-11-074703-3 *£3.00*

The Civil Procedure Act 1997 (Amendment) Order 2006 No. 2006/1847 (L.7). - Enabling power: Civil Procedure Act 1997, s. 2A (1). - Issued: 17.07.2006. Made: 10.07.2006. Laid: 12.07.2006. Coming into force: 01.09.2006. Effect: 1997 c. 12 amended. Territorial extent & classification: E/W. General. - 2p.: 30 cm. - 978-0-11-074836-8 *£3.00*

The Civil Procedure (Amendment No.2) Rules 2006 No. 2006/3132 (L.13). - Enabling power: Civil Procedure Act 1997, s. 2. - Issued: 29.11.2006. Made: 23.11.2006. Laid: 27.11.2006. Coming into force: 18.12.2006. Effect: S.I. 1998/3132 amended. Territorial extent & classification: E/W. General. - 4p.: 30 cm. - 978-0-11-075374-4 *£3.00*

The Civil Procedure (Amendment No.3) Rules 2006 No. 2006/3435 (L.15). - Enabling power: Civil Procedure Act 1997, s. 2. - Issued: 03.01.2007. Made: 19.12.2006. Laid: 21.12.2006. Coming into force: 06.04.2007. Effect: S.I. 1998/3132 amended. Territorial extent & classification: E/W. General. - 16p.: 30 cm. - 978-0-11-075578-6 *£3.00*

The Civil Procedure (Amendment) Rules 2006 No. 2006/1689 (L.6). - Enabling power: Civil Procedure Act 1997, s. 2. - Issued: 03.07.2006. Made: 26.06.2006. Laid: 27.06.2006. Coming into force: 02.10.2006. Effect: S.I. 1998/3132 amended. Territorial extent & classification: E/W. General. - 8p.: 30 cm. - 978-0-11-074765-1 *£3.00*

The Civil Proceedings Fees (Amendment) Order 2006 No. 2006/719 (L.4). - Enabling power: Courts Act 2003, s. 92 & Insolvency Act 1986, ss. 414, 415. - Issued: 20.03.2006. Made: 09.03.2006. Laid: 16.03.2006. Coming into force: 06.04.2006. Effect: S.I. 2004/3121 amended. Territorial extent & classification: E/W. General. - 4p.: 30 cm. - 978-0-11-074278-6 *£3.00*

The Courts Act 2003 (Consequential Amendment) Order 2006 No. 2006/1001. - Enabling power: Courts Act 2003, ss. 109 (4) (a) (5) (b). - Issued: 04.04.2006. Made: 29.03.2006. Coming into force: 06.04.2006. Effect: 1991 c.48 amended. Territorial extent & classification: E/W. General. - Supersedes draft. - 2p.: 30 cm. - 978-0-11-074447-6 *£3.00*

The Family Proceedings (Amendment) (No. 2) Rules 2006 No. 2006/2080 (L.8). - Enabling power: Matrimonial and Family Proceedings Act 1984, s. 40 (1). - Issued: 01.08.2006. Made: 25.07.2006. Laid: 27.07.2006. Coming into force: 21.08.2006. Effect: S.I. 1991/1247 amended. Territorial extent & classification: E/W. General. - 4p.: 30 cm. - 978-0-11-074957-0 *£3.00*

The Family Proceedings (Amendment) Rules 2006 No. 2006/352 (L.1). - Enabling power: Matrimonial and Family Proceedings Act 1984, s. 40 (1). - Issued: 21.02.2006. Made: 10.02.2006. Laid: 15.02.2006. Coming into force: 03.04.2006. Effect: S.I.1991/1247 amended. Territorial extent & classification: E/W. General. - 12p.: 30 cm. - 978-0-11-074057-7 *£3.00*

The Family Proceedings Fees (Amendment) Order 2006 No. 2006/739 (L.5). - Enabling power: Courts Act 2003, s. 92. - Issued: 20.03.2006. Made: 07.03.2006. Laid: 16.03.2006. Coming into force: 06.04.2006. Effect: S.I. 2004/3114 amended. Territorial extent & classification: E/W. General. - 2p.: 30 cm. - 978-0-11-074306-6 *£3.00*

Cremation, England and Wales

The Cremation (Amendment) Regulations 2006 No. 2006/92. - Enabling power: Cremation Act 1902, s. 7. - Issued: 26.01.2006. Made: 18.01.2006. Laid: 23.01.2006. Coming into force: 14.02.2006. Effect: S.R. & O. 1930/1016 amended. Territorial extent & classification: E/W. General. - 4p.: 30 cm. - 978-0-11-073929-8 *£3.00*

Criminal law

The Crime (International Co-operation) Act 2003 (Commencement No. 3) Order 2006 No. 2006/2811 (C.94). - Enabling power: Crime (International Co-operation) Act 2003, s. 94. Bringing into operation various provisions of the 2003 Act on 01.11.2006 in accord. with arts. 2 & 3. - Issued: 26.10.2006. Made: 19.10.2006. Effect: None. Territorial extent & classification: E/W/S/NI. General. - 2p.: 30 cm. - 978-0-11-075212-9 *£3.00*

The Domestic Violence, Crime and Victims Act 2004 (Victims' Code of Practice) Order 2006 No. 2006/629. - Enabling power: Domestic Violence, Crime and Victims Act 2004, ss. 33 (7). - Issued: 14.03.2006. Made: 06.03.2006. Laid: 13.03.2006. Coming into force: 03.04.2006. Effect: None. Territorial extent & classification: E/W/S/NI. General. - 2p.: 30 cm. - 978-0-11-074202-1 *£3.00*

The Fraud Act 2006 (Commencement) Order 2006 No. 2006/3200 (C.112). - Enabling power: Fraud Act 2006 s. 15. Bringing into operation various provisions of the 2006 Act on 15.01.2007. - Issued: 06.12.2006. Made: 29.11.2006. Effect: None. Territorial extent & classification: E/W/NI. General. - 2p.: 30 cm. - 978-0-11-075407-9 *£3.00*

The Management of Offenders etc. (Scotland) Act 2005 (Consequential Modifications) Order 2006 No. 2006/1055. - Enabling power: Scotland Act 1998, ss. 104, 112 (1), 113. - Issued: 19.04.2006. Made: 31.03.2006. Coming into force: 01.04.2006. Effect: 1975 c.24; 1997 c.43 amended & 2005 asp 14 modified. Territorial extent & classification: E/W/S/NI. General. - 4p.: 30 cm. - 978-0-11-070257-5 *£3.00*

Criminal law, England and Wales

The Anti-Social Behaviour Act 2003 (Commencement No.4) (Amendment) Order 2006 No. 2006/835. - Enabling power: Anti-social Behaviour Act 2003, ss 93, 94 (2). - Issued: 23.03.2006. Made: 20.03.2006. Coming into force: 31.03.2006. Effect: S.I. 2004/2168 amended. Territorial extent & classification: E/W. General. - 2p.: 30 cm. - 978-0-11-074371-4 *£3.00*

The Community Order (Review by Specified Courts in Liverpool and Salford) Order 2006 No. 2006/1006. - Enabling power: Criminal Justice Act 2003, ss. 178 (1), 330 (3) (a). - Issued: 05.04.2006. Made: 30.03.2006. Coming into force: 31.03.2006. Effect: None. Territorial extent & classification: E/W. General. - Supersedes the draft S.I. (ISBN 0110739094) issued 19.01.2006. - 4p.: 30 cm. - 978-0-11-074441-4 *£3.00*

The Crime and Disorder Act 1998 (Intervention Orders) Order 2006 No. 2006/2138. - Enabling power: Crime and Disorder Act 1998, s. 1G (1) (c) (9) to (11). - Issued: 07.08.2006. Made: 01.08.2006. Laid: 03.08.2006. Coming into force: 01.10.2006. Effect: None. Territorial extent & classification: E/W. General. - With correction slip dated August 2006. - 2p.: 30 cm. - 978-0-11-074975-4 £3.00

The Crime and Disorder Act 1998 (Relevant Authorities and Relevant Persons) Order 2006 No. 2006/2137. - Enabling power: Crime and Disorder Act 1998, s. 1A (2). - Issued: 07.08.2006. Made: 01.08.2006. Laid: 03.08.2006. Coming into force: 01.09.2006. Effect: None. Territorial extent & classification: E/W. General. - 2p.: 30 cm. - 978-0-11-074971-6 £3.00

The Criminal Justice Act 1988 (Reviews of Sentencing) Order 2006 No. 2006/1116. - Enabling power: Criminal Justice Act 1988, s. 35 (4). - Issued: 21.04.2006. Made: 18.04.2006. Laid: 21.04.2006. Coming into force: 16.05.2006. Effect: S.I. 1994/119; 1995/10; 2000/1924; 2003/2267 revoked. Territorial extent & classification: E/W/NI. General. - With correction slip dated June 2006. - With correction slip dated June 2006. - 4p.: 30 cm. - 978-0-11-074508-4 £3.00

The Criminal Justice Act 2003 (Commencement No.13 and Transitional Provision) Order 2006 No. 2006/1835 (C.61). - Enabling power: Criminal Justice Act 2003, ss. 330 (3) (b), 336 (3). Bringing into operation various provisions of the 2003 Act on 24.07.2006. - Issued: 17.07.2006. Made: 10.07.2006. Effect: None. Territorial extent & classification: E/W/NI. General. - 8p.: 30 cm. - 978-0-11-074828-3 £3.00

The Criminal Justice Act 2003 (Commencement No.14 and Transitional Provision) Order 2006 No. 2006/3217 (C.114). - Enabling power: Criminal Justice Act 2003, ss. 330 (3) (4), 336 (3). Bringing into operation various provisions of the 2003 Act on 01.01.2007. - Issued: 08.12.2006. Made: 04.12.2006. Effect: None. Territorial extent & classification: E/W. General. - 8p.: 30 cm. - 978-0-11-075416-1 £3.00

The Domestic Violence, Crime and Victims Act 2004 (Commencement No. 6) Order 2006 No. 2006/2662 (C.90). - Enabling power: Domestic Violence, Crime and Victims Act 2004, ss. 60, 61. Bringing into operation various provisions of the 2004 Act on 04.10.2006. - Issued: 11.10.2006. Made: 03.10.2006. Effect: None. Territorial extent & classification: E/W. General. - 2p.: 30 cm. - 978-0-11-075154-2 £3.00

The Domestic Violence, Crime and Victims Act 2004 (Commencement No. 7 and Transitional Provision) Order 2006 No. 2006/3423 (C.131). - Enabling power: Domestic Violence, Crime and Victims Act 2004, ss. 60, 61 (1). Bringing into operation various provisions of the 2004 Act on 08.01.2007. - Issued: 29.12.2006. Made: 19.12.2006. Effect: None. Territorial extent & classification: E/W/NI. General. - 4p.: 30 cm. - 978-0-11-075567-0 £3.00

The Police and Justice Act 2006 (Commencement No. 1, Transitional and Saving Provisions) Order 2006 No. 2006/3364 (C.123). - Enabling power: Police and Justice Act 2006, ss. 49 (3) (c), 53 (1). Bringing into operation various provisions of the 2006 Act on 15.01.2007 in accordance with art. 2. - Issued: 21.12.2006. Made: 14.12.2006. Effect: None. Territorial extent & classification: E/W. General. - This SI has been amended by SI 2007/29 (C.1) (ISBN 9780110756455) which is being issued free of charge to all known recipients of SI 2006/3364. - 4p.: 30 cm. - 978-0-11-075513-7 £3.00

The Serious Organised Crime and Police Act 2005 (Amendment of Section 61 (1)) Order 2006 No. 2006/1629. - Enabling power: Serious Organised Crime and Police Act 2005, s. 61 (4). - Issued: 22.06.2006. Made: 19.06.2006. Coming into force: 20.06.2006. Effect: 2005 c. 15 amended. Territorial extent & classification: E/W. General. - Supersedes draft SI (ISBN 0110745345) issued 03.05.2006. - 2p.: 30 cm. - 978-0-11-074716-3 £3.00

The Serious Organised Crime and Police Act 2005 (Appeals under Section 74) Order 2006 No. 2006/2135. - Enabling power: Serious Organised Crime and Police Act 2005, s. 74 (12). - Issued: 07.08.2006. Made: 31.07.2006. Laid: 03.08.2006. Coming into force: 28.08.2006. Effect: None. Territorial extent & classification: E/W/NI. General. - 16p.: 30 cm. - 978-0-11-074972-3 £3.00

The Serious Organised Crime and Police Act 2005 (Commencement No. 5 and Transitional and Transitory Provisions and Savings) Order 2006 No. 2006/378 (C.9). - Enabling power: Serious Organised Crime and Police Act 2005, s. 178 (8) (9) (10). Bringing into operation various provisions of the 2005 Act in accord. with arts. 2, 3, 4, 5, 6, 7. - Issued: 22.02.2006. Made: 15.02.2006. Effect: None. Territorial extent & classification: E/W/NI [parts to E/W or NI only].. General. - 12p.: 30 cm. - 978-0-11-074072-0 £3.00

The Serious Organised Crime and Police Act 2005 (Commencement) (No. 8) Order 2006 No. 2006/1871 (C.62). - Enabling power: Serious Organised Crime and Police Act 2005, s. 178 (8) (9). Bringing into operation various provisions of the 2005 Act on 20.07.2006. - Issued: 20.07.2006. Made: 12.07.2006. Effect: None. Territorial extent & classification: E/W. General. - Title originally printed as 'Commencment 7'. Amended by S.I. 2006/2182 (C.74) to read 'Commencement 8'. - 4p.: 30 cm. - 978-0-11-074840-5 £3.00

Criminal law, Northern Ireland

The Criminal Justice Act 1988 (Reviews of Sentencing) Order 2006 No. 2006/1116. - Enabling power: Criminal Justice Act 1988, s. 35 (4). - Issued: 21.04.2006. Made: 18.04.2006. Laid: 21.04.2006. Coming into force: 16.05.2006. Effect: S.I. 1994/119; 1995/10; 2000/1924; 2003/2267 revoked. Territorial extent & classification: E/W/NI. General. - With correction slip dated June 2006. - 4p.: 30 cm. - 978-0-11-074508-4 £3.00

The Criminal Justice Act 2003 (Commencement No.13 and Transitional Provision) Order 2006 No. 2006/1835 (C.61). - Enabling power: Criminal Justice Act 2003, ss. 330 (3) (b), 336 (3). Bringing into operation various provisions of the 2003 Act on 24.07.2006. - Issued: 17.07.2006. Made: 10.07.2006. Effect: None. Territorial extent & classification: E/W/NI. General. - 8p.: 30 cm. - 978-0-11-074828-3 £3.00

The Criminal Justice Act 2003 (Commencement No.15) Order 2006 No. 2006/3422 (C. 130). - Enabling power: Criminal Justice Act 2003, s. 336 (3) (4). Bringing into operation various provisions of the 2003 Act on 08.01.2007. - Issued: 29.12.2006. Made: 19.12.2006. Effect: None. Territorial extent & classification: NI. General. - 8p.: 30 cm. - 978-0-11-075566-3 £3.00

The Domestic Violence, Crime and Victims Act 2004 (Commencement No. 7 and Transitional Provision) Order 2006 No. 2006/3423 (C.131). - Enabling power: Domestic Violence, Crime and Victims Act 2004, ss. 60, 61 (1). Bringing into operation various provisions of the 2004 Act on 08.01.2007. - Issued: 29.12.2006. Made: 19.12.2006. Effect: None. Territorial extent & classification: E/W/NI. General. - 4p.: 30 cm. - 978-0-11-075567-0 £3.00

The Northern Ireland (Miscellaneous Provisions) Act 2006 (Commencement No.2) Order 2006 No. 2006/2966 (C.104). - Enabling power: Northern Ireland (Miscellaneous Provisions) Act 2006, s. 31 (3). Bringing into operation various provisions of the 2005 Act on 01.12.2006 & 31.03.2007. - Issued: 20.11.2006. Made: 13.11.2006. Effect: None. Territorial extent & classification: NI. General. - 2p.: 30 cm. - 978-0-11-075306-5 £3.00

The Serious Organised Crime and Police Act 2005 (Appeals under Section 74) Order 2006 No. 2006/2135. - Enabling power: Serious Organised Crime and Police Act 2005, s. 74 (12). - Issued: 07.08.2006. Made: 31.07.2006. Laid: 03.08.2006. Coming into force: 28.08.2006. Effect: None. Territorial extent & classification: E/W/NI. General. - 16p.: 30 cm. - 978-0-11-074972-3 £3.00

The Serious Organised Crime and Police Act 2005 (Commencement No. 5 and Transitional and Transitory Provisions and Savings) Order 2006 No. 2006/378 (C.9). - Enabling power: Serious Organised Crime and Police Act 2005, s. 178 (8) (9) (10). Bringing into operation various provisions of the 2005 Act in accord. with arts. 2, 3, 4, 5, 6, 7. - Issued: 22.02.2006. Made: 15.02.2006. Effect: None. Territorial extent & classification: E/W/S/NI [parts to E/W or NI only]. General. - 12p.: 30 cm. - 978-0-11-074072-0 £3.00

Customs

The Burma (Sale, Supply, Export, Technical Assistance, Financing and Financial Assistance) (Penalties and Licences) Regulations 2006 No. 2006/2682. - Enabling power: European Communities Act 1972, s. 2 (2). - Issued: 17.10.2006. Made: 09.10.2006. Laid: 10.10.2006. Coming into force: 11.10.2006. Effect: S.I. 2004/1315 revoked. Territorial extent & classification: UK. General. - EC note: These Regulations make provision in respect of Burma for offences, penalties and enforcement in respect of Council Regulation (EC) No. 817/2006 which repeals and replaces Council Regulation (EC) No.798/2004. - 4p.: 30 cm. - 978-0-11-075164-1 £3.00

The Customs and Excise Duties (Travellers' Allowances and Personal Reliefs) (New Member States) (Amendment) Order 2006 No. 2006/3157. - Enabling power: Customs and Excise Duties (General Reliefs) Act 1979, s. 13 (1) (3). - Issued: 01.12.2006. Made: 28.11.2006. Laid: 29.11.2006. Coming into force: 01.01.2007. Effect: S.I. 2004/1002 amended. Territorial extent & classification: E/W/S/NI. General. - Order made by the Commissioners for Her Majesty's Revenue and Customs, laid before the House of Commons for approval by that House within twenty-eight days. Superseded by S.I. of same no. (ISBN 0110755014). - 4p.: 30 cm. - 978-0-11-075386-7 £3.00

The Customs and Excise Duties (Travellers' Allowances and Personal Reliefs) (New Member States) (Amendment) Order 2006 No. 2006/3157. - Enabling power: Customs and Excise Duties (General Reliefs) Act 1979, s. 13 (1) (3). - Issued: 19.12.2006. Made: 28.11.2006. Laid: 29.11.2006. Coming into force: 01.01.2007. Effect: S.I. 2004/1002 amended. Territorial extent & classification: E/W/S/NI. General. - Supersedes SI of same no. (ISBN 0110753860) issued 01.12.2006. - 4p.: 30 cm. - 978-0-11-075501-4 £3.00

The Export Control (Amendment) Order 2006 No. 2006/2271. - Enabling power: Export Control Act 2002, ss. 1, 2, 3, 4, 5, 7. - Issued: 29.08.2006. Made: 19.08.2006. Laid: 22.08.2006. Coming into force: 23.08.2006. Effect: S.I. 2003/2764, 2765 amended. Territorial extent & classification: E/W/S/NI. General. - This Statutory Instrument has been made in consequence of defects in SI 2006/1696 (ISBN 0110747771) and is being issued free of charge to all known recipients of that Statutory Instrument. - 2p.: 30 cm. - 978-0-11-075034-7 £3.00

The Export Control (Bosnia and Herzegovina) Order 2006 No. 2006/300. - Enabling power: Export Control Act 2002, ss. 1, 4, 5, 7. - Issued: 17.02.2006. Made: 07.02.2006. Laid: 10.02.2006. Coming into force: 06.03.2006. Effect: S.I. 2003/2764, 2004/318 amended. Territorial extent & classification: E/W/S/NI. General. - 2p.: 30 cm. - 978-0-11-074025-6 £3.00

The Export Control (Lebanon, etc.) Order 2006 No. 2006/2683. - Enabling power: Export Control Act 2002, ss. 1, 4, 5, 7. - Issued: 17.10.2006. Made: 09.10.2006. Laid: 10.10.2006. Coming into force: 11.10.2006. Effect: S.I. 2003/2764; 2004/318 amended. Territorial extent & classification: E/W/S/NI. General. - 2p.: 30 cm. - 978-0-11-075162-7 £3.00

The Export Control (Liberia) Order 2006 No. 2006/2065. - Enabling power: Export Control Act 2002, ss. 3, 4, 5, 7. - Issued: 02.08.2006. Made: 25.07.2006. Laid: 26.07.2006. Coming into force: 27.07.2006. Effect: S.I. 2004/432 revoked. Territorial extent & classification: E/W/S/NI. General. - EC note: This Order makes provision in respect of Liberia in consequence of Council Regulation 234/2004 ("the 2004 Regulation") and Council Regulation 1126/2006 which amends the 2004 Regulation. - 4p.: 30 cm. - 978-0-11-074947-1 £3.00

The Export Control Order 2006 No. 2006/1331. - Enabling power: Export Control Act 2002, ss. 1, 2, 3, 4, 5, 7. - Issued: 22.05.2006. Made: 09.05.2006. Laid: 15.05.2006. Coming into force: 06.06.2006. Effect: S.I. 2003/2764, 2765; 2004/318 amended. Territorial extent & classification: E/W/S/NI. General. - 20p.: 30 cm. - 978-0-11-074591-6 £3.50

The Export Control (Security and Para-military Goods) Order 2006 No. 2006/1696. - Enabling power: Export Control Act 2002, ss. 1, 2, 3, 4, 5, 7. - Issued: 07.07.2006. Made: 29.06.2006. Laid: 30.06.2006. Coming into force: 30.07.2006. Effect: S.I. 2003/2764, 2765; 2004/318 amended. Territorial extent & classification: E/W/S/NI. General. - With second correction slip dated September 2006 which supersedes/incorporates the previous correction dated August 2006. This SI contained defects in the effects on other legislation, and those defects have been corrected by SI 2006/2271 (ISBN 0110750349) which is being issued free of charge to all known recipients of SI 2006/1696. - 8p.: 30 cm. - 978-0-11-074777-4 £3.00

The Export of Radioactive Sources (Control) Order 2006 No. 2006/1846. - Enabling power: Export Control Act 2002, ss. 1, 5, 7. - Issued: 14.07.2006. Made: 07.07.2006. Laid: 12.07.2006. Coming into force: 01.10.2006. Effect: None. Territorial extent & classification: E/W/S/NI. General. - 8p.: 30 cm. - 978-0-11-074835-1 £3.00

The Free Zone Designations (Amendments) Order 2006 No. 2006/1834. - Enabling power: Customs and Excise Management Act 1979, ss. 100A (1), 100A (3), 100A (4) (b). - Issued: 14.07.2006. Made: 10.07.2006. Coming into force: 01.08.2006. Effect: S.I. 2001/2880, 2881, 2882; 2002/1418; 2004/2742 amended. Territorial extent & classification: E/W/S/NI. Local. - 2p.: 30 cm. - 978-0-11-074827-6 £3.00

The Lebanon (Technical Assistance, Financing and Financial Assistance) (Penalties and Licences) Regulations 2006 No. 2006/2681. - Enabling power: European Communities Act 1972, s. 2 (2). - Issued: 17.10.2006. Made: 09.10.2006. Laid: 10.10.2006. Coming into force: 11.10.2006. Effect: None. Territorial extent & classification: UK. General. - EC note: These Regulations make provision in respect of Lebanon for penalties and enforcement in respect of Council Regulation (EC) No. 1412/2006. - 4p.: 30 cm. - 978-0-11-075163-4 £3.00

The Relief for Legacies Imported from Third Countries (Application) Order 2006 No. 2006/3158. - Enabling power: Customs and Excise Duties (General Reliefs) Act 1979, s. 7. - Issued: 01.12.2006. Made: 28.11.2006. Laid: 29.11.2006. Coming into force: 01.01.2007. Effect: S.I. 1992/3193 updated in respect of a reference to Directive 73/388/EC. Territorial extent & classification: E/W/S/NI. General. - 2p.: 30 cm. - 978-0-11-075385-0 £3.00

The Technical Assistance Control Regulations 2006 No. 2006/1719. - Enabling power: European Communities Act 1972, s. 2 (2). - Issued: 07.07.2006. Made: 29.06.2006. Laid: 30.06.2006. Coming into force: 30.07.2006. Effect: None. Territorial extent & classification: UK. General. - EC note: These Regulations make provision for penalties and enforcement in respect of Council Regulation (EC) No 1236/ 2005 of 27 June 2005 concerning trade in certain goods which could be used for capital punishment, torture or other cruel, inhuman or degrading treatment or punishment. - 4p.: 30 cm. - 978-0-11-074778-1 £3.00

Dangerous drugs

The Misuse of Drugs Act 1971 (Amendment) Order 2006 No. 2006/3331. - Enabling power: Misuse of Drugs Act 1971, s. 2 (2). - Issued: 21.12.2006. Made: 14.12.2006. Coming into force: 18.01.2007. Effect: 1971 c. 38 amended. Territorial extent & classification: E/W/S/NI. General. - Supersedes draft S.I. (ISBN 0110751515) issued 12.10.2006. - 2p.: 30 cm. - 978-0-11-075511-3 £3.00

The Misuse of Drugs (Amendment No. 2) Regulations 2006 No. 2006/1450. - Enabling power: Misuse of Drugs Act 1971, ss. 7, 10, 22, 31. - Issued: 09.06.2006. Made: 27.05.2006. Laid: 09.06.2006. Coming into force: In accord. with reg. 2 on 07.07.2006 & 01.01.2007. Effect: S.I. 2001/3998 amended. Territorial extent & classification: E/W/S. General. - 8p.: 30 cm. - 978-0-11-074641-8 £3.00

The Misuse of Drugs (Amendment No. 3) Regulations 2006 No. 2006/2178. - Enabling power: Misuse of Drugs Act 1971, ss. 7, 10, 31. - Issued: 11.08.2006. Made: 03.08.2006. Laid: 11.08.2006. Coming into force: 01.09.2006, except for reg. 4 which will come into force in Wales on 01.01.2007. Effect: S.I. 2001/3998; 2006/1450 amended. Territorial extent & classification: E/W/S. General. - This statutory instrument has been made in consequence of defects in SI 2006/1450 (ISBN 0110746414) and is being issued free of charge to all known recipients of that statutory instrument. With correction slip dated January 2007. - 2p.: 30 cm. - 978-0-11-074993-8 £3.00

**The Misuse of Drugs (Amendment) Regulations 2006
No. 2006/986**. - Enabling power: Misuse of Drugs Act 1971, ss. 7 (1) (2), 10, 22, 31 (1). - Issued: 05.04.2006. Made: 29.03.2006. Laid: 03.04.2006. Coming into force: 01.05.2006. Effect: S.I. 2001/3998 amended. Territorial extent & classification: E/W/S/NI. General. - 4p.: 30 cm. - 978-0-11-074440-7 *£3.00*

Dangerous drugs, England

The Controlled Drugs (Supervision of Management and Use) Regulations 2006 No. 2006/3148. - Enabling power: Health Act 2006, ss. 17, 18, 20 (3) (7), 79 (3). - Issued: 30.11.2006. Made: 21.11.2006. Laid: 30.11.2006. Coming into force: 01.01.2007 as they apply to England; 01.03.2007 as they apply to Scotland. Effect: None. Territorial extent & classification: E/S. General. - 24p.: 30 cm. - 978-0-11-075379-9 *£4.00*

The Health Act 2006 (Commencement No.2) Order 2006 No. 2006/3125 (C.108). - Enabling power: Health Act 2006, s. 83 (7) (8). Bringing into operation various provisions of the 2006 Act on 01.01.2007; 29.01.2007; 28.02.2007; 01.03.2007 in accord. with arts 2 to 4. - Issued: 29.11.2006. Made: 21.11.2006. Effect: None. Territorial extent & classification: E/W/S [parts only to E/S; and parts only to E/W]. General. - 4p.: 30 cm. - 978-0-11-075372-0 *£3.00*

Dangerous drugs, England and Wales

The Drugs Act 2005 (Commencement No. 4) Order 2006 No. 2006/2136 (C.71). - Enabling power: Drugs Act 2005, s. 24 (3). Bringing into operation various provisions of the 2005 Act on 01.10.2006. - Issued: 07.08.2006. Made: 01.08.2006. Effect: None. Territorial extent & classification: E/W. General. - 2p.: 30 cm. - 978-0-11-074973-0 *£3.00*

Dangerous drugs, Scotland

The Controlled Drugs (Supervision of Management and Use) Regulations 2006 No. 2006/3148. - Enabling power: Health Act 2006, ss. 17, 18, 20 (3) (7), 79 (3). - Issued: 30.11.2006. Made: 21.11.2006. Laid: 30.11.2006. Coming into force: 01.01.2007 as they apply to England; 01.03.2007 as they apply to Scotland. Effect: None. Territorial extent & classification: E/S. General. - 24p.: 30 cm. - 978-0-11-075379-9 *£4.00*

The Health Act 2006 (Commencement No.2) Order 2006 No. 2006/3125 (C.108). - Enabling power: Health Act 2006, s. 83 (7) (8). Bringing into operation various provisions of the 2006 Act on 01.01.2007; 29.01.2007; 28.02.2007; 01.03.2007 in accord. with arts 2 to 4. - Issued: 29.11.2006. Made: 21.11.2006. Effect: None. Territorial extent & classification: E/W/S [parts only to E/S; and parts only to E/W]. General. - 4p.: 30 cm. - 978-0-11-075372-0 *£3.00*

Data protection

The Data Protection (Processing of Sensitive Personal Data) Order 2006 No. 2006/2068. - Enabling power: Data Protection Act 1998, s. 67 (2), sch. 3, para. 10. - Issued: 31.07.2006. Made: 25.07.2006. Coming into force: 26.07.2006 in accord. with art. 1 (1). Effect: None. Territorial extent & classification: E/W/S/NI. General. - Supersedes draft SI (ISBN 0110747127) issued 20.06.2006. - 4p.: 30 cm. - 978-0-11-074949-5 *£3.00*

Defence

The Armed Forces Act 2001 (Commencement No. 6) Order 2006 No. 2006/235 (C.6). - Enabling power: Armed Forces Act 2001, s. 39 (2). Bringing into operation various provisions of the 2001 Act on 03.02.2006. - Issued: 09.02.2006. Made: 01.02.2006. Effect: None. Territorial extent & classification: E/W/S/NI. General. - 2p.: 30 cm. - 978-0-11-073997-7 *£3.00*

The Armed Forces Act 2001 (Commencement No. 7) Order 2006 No. 2006/2309 (C.79). - Enabling power: Armed Forces Act 2001, s. 39 (2). Bringing into operation various provisions of the 2001 Act on 25.08.2006, in accord. with art. 2. - Issued: 31.08.2006. Made: 24.08.2006. Effect: None. Territorial extent & classification: E/W/S/NI. General. - 2p.: 30 cm. - 978-0-11-075046-0 *£3.00*

The Armed Forces (Entry, Search and Seizure) (Amendment) Order 2006 No. 2006/3244. - Enabling power: Armed Forces Act 2001, ss. 5 (10), 11 (2), 35 (1). - Issued: 12.12.2006. Made: 06.12.2006. Laid: 08.12.2006. Coming into force: 01.01.2007. Effect: S.I. 2003/2273 amended. Territorial extent & classification: E/W/S/NI. General. - 4p.: 30 cm. - 978-0-11-075425-3 *£3.00*

The Armed Forces (Entry, Search and Seizure) Order 2006 No. 2006/3243. - Enabling power: Armed Forces Act 2001, ss. 31(3), 35. - Issued: 12.12.2006. Made: 06.12.2006. Laid: 08.12.2006. Coming into force: 01.01.2007. Effect: None. Territorial extent & classification: E/W/S/NI. General. - With correction slip dated January 2007. - 16p.: 30 cm. - 978-0-11-075424-6 *£3.00*

The Army, Air Force and Naval Discipline Acts (Continuation) Order 2006 No. 2006/1910. - Enabling power: Armed Forces Act 2001, s. 1 (2). - Issued: 26.07.2006. Made: 19.07.2006. Coming into force: 19.07.2006. Effect: 1955 c.18, c.19; 1957 c. 53 shall continue in force until 31.12.2006. Territorial extent & classification: E/W/S/NI. General. - 2p.: 30 cm. - 978-0-11-074895-5 *£3.00*

The Courts-Martial (Prosecution Appeals) Order 2006 No. 2006/1786. - Enabling power: Armed Forces Act 2001, s. 31 (3). - Issued: 10.07.2006. Made: 05.07.2006. Coming into force: 05.07.2006. Effect: None. Territorial extent & classification: E/W/S/NI. General. - 8p.: 30 cm. - 978-0-11-074807-8 *£3.00*

The Courts-Martial (Prosecution Appeals) (Supplementary Provisions) Order 2006 No. 2006/1788. - Enabling power: Armed Forces Act 2001, s. 31. - Issued: 10.07.2006. Made: 05.07.2006. Laid: 10.07.2006. Coming into force: 01.08.2006. Effect: None. Territorial extent & classification: E/W/S/NI. General. - With correction slip dated January 2007. - 16p.: 30 cm. - 978-0-11-074811-5 *£3.00*

The Courts-Martial (Royal Navy, Army and Royal Air Force) (Evidence) Rules 2006 No. 2006/2889. - Enabling power: Army Act 1955, s. 103; Air Force Act 1955, s. 103; Naval Discipline Act 1957, s. 58 & Youth Justice and Criminal Evidence Act 1999, ss. 20 (6), 37 (5), 38 (6), 43 (3), 65 (1). - Issued: 08.11.2006. Made: 30.10.2006. Laid: 06.11.2006. Coming into force: 06.12.2006. Effect: S.I. 1997/169, 170, 171 amended. Territorial extent & classification: E/W/S/NI. General. - 28p.: 30 cm. - 978-0-11-075243-3 *£4.50*

The Criminal Justice Act 1988 (Application to Service Courts) (Evidence) Order 2006 No. 2006/2890. - Enabling power: Criminal Justice Act 1988, sch. 13, paras 8, 9, 10. - Issued: 07.11.2006. Made: 30.10.2006. Laid: 06.11.2006. Coming into force: 06.12.2006. Effect: 1988 c. 33 modified and S.I. 1996/2592 revoked. Territorial extent & classification: E/W/S/NI. General. - 4p.: 30 cm. - 978-0-11-075244-0 *£3.00*

The Criminal Justice and Public Order Act 1994 (Application to the Armed Forces) Order 2006 No. 2006/2326. - Enabling power: Criminal Justice and Public Order Act 1994, s. 39 (1). - Issued: 05.09.2006. Made: 24.08.2006. Laid: 04.09.2006. Coming into force: 26.09.2006. Effect: 1994 c. 33 modified & S.I. 1997/16 amended. Territorial extent & classification: E/W/S/NI. General. - 8p.: 30 cm. - 978-0-11-075061-3 *£3.00*

The Police and Criminal Evidence Act 1984 (Application to the Armed Forces) Order 2006 No. 2006/2015. - Enabling power: Police and Criminal Evidence Act 1984, s. 113 (1) & Armed Forces Act 2001, s. 31 (3). - Issued: 07.08.2006. Made: 24.07.2006. Laid: 27.07.2006. Coming into force: 31.12.2006. Effect: 1984 c.60 modified & S.I. 1997/15 revoked. Territorial extent & classification: E/W/S/NI. General. - With correction slip dated January 2007. - 32p.: 30 cm. - 978-0-11-074941-9 *£5.50*

The Protection of Military Remains Act 1986 (Designation of Vessels and Controlled Sites) Order 2006 No. 2006/2616. - Enabling power: Protection of Military Remains Act 1986, s. 1 (2). - Issued: 03.10.2006. Made: 21.09.2006. Coming into force: 01.11.2006. Effect: S.I. 2002/1761; 2003/405 revoked. Territorial extent & classification: E/W/S/NI. General. - 4p.: 30 cm. - 978-0-11-075138-2 *£3.00*

The Royal Marines Terms of Service Regulations 2006 No. 2006/2917. - Enabling power: Armed Forces Act 1966, s. 2. - Issued: 13.11.2006. Made: 03.11.2006. Laid: 09.11.2006. Coming into force: 01.12.2006. Effect: S.I. 1988/1395; 2000/1772; 2001/1520; 2002/201 revoked. Territorial extent & classification: E/W/S/NI. General. - 8p.: 30 cm. - 978-0-11-075270-9 *£3.00*

The Royal Navy Terms of Service (Ratings) Regulations 2006 No. 2006/2918. - Enabling power: Armed Forces Act 1966, s. 2. - Issued: 13.11.2006. Made: 03.11.2006. Laid: 09.11.2006. Coming into force: 01.12.2006. Effect: S.I. 1982/834; 1983/897; 1985/2003; 1986/2074; 2000/1771; 2001/1521 revoked. Territorial extent & classification: E/W/S/NI. General. - 8p.: 30 cm. - 978-0-11-075271-6 *£3.00*

The Standing Civilian Courts (Evidence) Rules 2006 No. 2006/2891. - Enabling power: Armed Forces Act 1976, sch. 3, para. 12 & Youth Justice and Criminal Evidence Act 1999, ss. 20 (6), 65 (1). - Issued: 08.11.2006. Made: 30.10.2006. Laid: 06.11.2006. Coming into force: 06.12.2006. Effect: S.I. 1997/172 amended. Territorial extent & classification: E/W/S/NI. General. - 20p.: 30 cm. - 978-0-11-075245-7 *£3.50*

The Youth Justice and Criminal Evidence Act 1999 (Application to Courts-Martial) Order 2006 No. 2006/2886. - Enabling power: Youth Justice and Criminal Evidence Act 1999, s. 61 (1) (2). - Issued: 07.11.2006. Made: 30.10.2006. Laid: 06.11.2006. Coming into force: 06.12.2006. Effect: 1999 c. 23 modified. Territorial extent & classification: E/W/S/NI. General. - 12p.: 30 cm. - 978-0-11-075246-4 *£3.00*

The Youth Justice and Criminal Evidence Act 1999 (Application to Standing Civilian Courts) Order 2006 No. 2006/2888. - Enabling power: Youth Justice and Criminal Evidence Act 1999, s. 61 (1) (2). - Issued: 07.11.2006. Made: 30.10.2006. Laid: 06.11.2006. Coming into force: 06.12.2006. Effect: 1999 c. 23 modified. Territorial extent & classification: E/W/S/NI. General. - 12p.: 30 cm. - 978-0-11-075241-9 *£3.00*

The Youth Justice and Criminal Evidence Act 1999 (Application to the Courts-Martial Appeal Court) Order 2006 No. 2006/2887. - Enabling power: Youth Justice and Criminal Evidence Act 1999, s. 61 (1). - Issued: 07.11.2006. Made: 30.10.2006. Laid: 06.11.2006. Coming into force: 06.12.2006. Effect: 1999 c. 23 modified. Territorial extent & classification: E/W/S/NI. General. - 8p.: 30 cm. - 978-0-11-075240-2 *£3.00*

The Youth Justice and Criminal Evidence Act 1999 (Commencement No. 12) Order 2006 No. 2006/2885 (C.99). - Enabling power: Youth Justice and Criminal Evidence Act 1999, ss. 64 (4), 68 (3). Bringing into operation various provisions of the 1999 Act on 06.12.2006, in accord. with art. 2. - Issued: 07.11.2006. Made: 30.10.2006. Effect: None. Territorial extent & classification: E/W/S/NI. General. - 4p.: 30 cm. - 978-0-11-075239-6 *£3.00*

Derelict land, England

The Derelict Land Clearance Area (Briar's Lane, Hatfield) Order 2006 No. 2006/1950. - Enabling power: Derelict Land Act 1982, s. 1 (7). - Issued: 25.07.2006. Made: 17.07.2006. Laid before the Parliament: 25.07.2006. Coming into force: 24.08.2006. Effect: None. Territorial extent & classification: E. General. - 4p.: 30 cm. - 978-0-11-074880-1 *£3.00*

Designs

The Design Right (Semiconductor Topographies) (Amendment) Regulations 2006 No. 2006/1833. - Enabling power: European Communities Act 1972, s. 2 (2). - Issued: 18.07.2006. Made: 10.07.2006. Laid: 10.07.2006. Coming into force: 01.08.2006. Effect: SI 1989/1100 amended & SI 1989/2147; 1990/1003; 1991/2237; 1992/400; 1993/2497 revoked. Territorial extent & classification: E/W/S/NI. General. - 8p.: 30 cm. - 978-0-11-074826-9 £3.00

The Designs (Convention Countries) Order 2006 No. 2006/317. - Enabling power: Registered Designs Act 1949, ss. 13 (1), 37 (5). - Issued: 03.03.2006. Made: 14.02.2006. Coming into force: 06.04.2006. Effect: S.I. 2004/3336 revoked. Territorial extent & classification: E/W/S/NI. General. - 8p.: 30 cm. - 978-0-11-074053-9 £3.00

The Registered Designs (Fees) (No. 2) Rules 2006 No. 2006/2617. - Enabling power: Registered Designs Act 1949, ss. 36, 40. - Issued: 03.10.2006. Made: 27.09.2006. Laid: 28.09.2006. Coming into force: 01.10.2006. Effect: S.I. 2006/2424 revoked. Territorial extent & classification: E/W/S/NI/IOM. General. - This Statutory Instrument has been made in consequence of a defect in SI 2006/2424 (ISBN 0110750942) and is being issued free of charge to all known recipients of that Statutory Instrument. - 8p.: 30 cm. - 978-0-11-075139-9 £3.00

The Registered Designs (Fees) Rules 2006 No. 2006/2424. - Enabling power: Registered Designs Act 1949, ss. 36, 40. - Issued: 14.09.2006. Made: 06.09.2006. Laid: 08.09.2006. Coming into force: 01.10.2006. Effect: SI 1998/1777; 2001/3951 revoked. Territorial extent & classification: E/W/S/NI/IOM. General. - Revoked by S.I. 2006/2617 (ISBN 0110751396). - 8p.: 30 cm. - 978-0-11-075094-1 £3.00

The Registered Designs Rules 2006 No. 2006/1975. - Enabling power: Registered Designs Act 1949, ss. 29 to 31, 36. - Issued: 04.08.2006. Made: 27.07.2006. Laid: 28.07.2006. Coming into force: 01.10.2006. Effect: S.I. 2006/760, 1029 amended & S.I. 1995/2912; 1999/3196; 2001/3950 revoked. Territorial extent & classification: E/W/S/NI/IoM. General. - 44p.: 30 cm. - 978-0-11-074963-1 £7.50

The Regulatory Reform (Registered Designs) Order 2006 No. 2006/1974. - Enabling power: Regulatory Reform Act 2001, s. 1. - Issued: 04.08.2006. Made: 26.07.2006. Coming into force: 01.10.2006. Effect: 1949 c. 88 amended. Territorial extent & classification: E/W/S/NI. General. - 8p.: 30 cm. - 978-0-11-074962-4 £3.00

Devolution, Scotland

The Animal Health and Welfare (Scotland) Act 2006 (Consequential Provisions) (England and Wales) Order 2006 No. 2006/3407. - Enabling power: Scotland Act 1998, ss. 104, 112 (1), 113 (2) (3) (4) (5). - Issued: 29.12.2006. Made: 14.12.2006-. Coming into force: 15.12.2006. Effect: 1963 c.43; 1964 c.70; 1973 c. 60 amended. Territorial extent & classification: E/W. General. - Supersedes draft SI (ISBN 0110711300) issued 13.11.2006. - 8p.: 30 cm. - 978-0-11-071454-7 £3.00

The Charities and Trustee Investment (Scotland) Act 2005 (Consequential Provisions and Modifications) Order 2006 No. 2006/242 (S.2). - Enabling power: Scotland Act 1998, ss. 104, 112 (1), 113. - Issued: 21.02.2006. Made: 14.02.2006. Coming into force: In accords. with art. 1, 03.02.2006, 01.04.2006. Effect: 1974 c. 39; 1975 c. 24; 1985 c. 6; 1989 c. 40; 1990 c. 40; 1993 c. 10; 2000 c. 8; 2004 c. 27; S.I. 1997/2436; 1999/678; 2001/1201; 2005/1788 amended. Territorial extent & classification: E/W/S/NI. General. - With correction slip dated April 2006, correcting the 'Made' date. - 8p.: 30 cm. - 978-0-11-069931-8 £3.00

The Gaelic Language (Scotland) Act 2005 (Consequential Modifications) Order 2006 No. 2006/241 (S.1). - Enabling power: Scotland Act 1998, ss. 104, 112 (1), 113. - Issued: 21.02.2006. Made: 14.02.2006. Coming into force: 31.03.2006. Effect: 1990 c. 42 amended. Territorial extent & classification: E/W/S/NI. General. - With correction slip dated April 2006, correcting the 'Made' date. - 4p.: 30 cm. - 978-0-11-069932-5 £3.00

The Management of Offenders etc. (Scotland) Act 2005 (Consequential Modifications) Order 2006 No. 2006/1055. - Enabling power: Scotland Act 1998, ss. 104, 112 (1), 113. - Issued: 19.04.2006. Made: 31.03.2006. Coming into force: 01.04.2006. Effect: 1975 c.24; 1997 c.43 amended & 2005 asp 14 modified. Territorial extent & classification: E/W/S/NI. General. - 4p.: 30 cm. - 978-0-11-070257-5 £3.00

The Scotland Act 1998 (Agency Arrangements) (Specification) (No. 2) Order 2006 No. 2006/3248. - Enabling power: Scotland Act 1998, ss. 93 (3), 113 (2) (4). - Issued: 22.12.2006. Made: 14.12.2006. Laid: 08.01.2007. Laid before the Scottish Parliament: 08.01.2007. Coming into force: 29.01.2007. Effect: S.I. 1999/1512 modified. Territorial extent & classification: E/W/S/NI. General. - 4p.: 30 cm. - 978-0-11-071432-5 £3.00

The Scotland Act 1998 (Agency Arrangements) (Specification) (No. 3) Order 2006 No. 2006/3338. - Enabling power: Scotland Act 1998, ss. 93 (3), 113 (2) (3) (4). - Issued: 22.12.2006. Made: 14.12.2006. Laid: 22.12.2006. Laid before the Scottish Parliament: 22.12.2006. Coming into force: 29.01.2007. Effect: None. Territorial extent & classification: E/W/S. General. - 8p.: 30 cm. - 978-0-11-071418-9 £3.00

The Scotland Act 1998 (Agency Arrangements) (Specification) Order 2006 No. 2006/1251. - Enabling power: Scotland Act 1998, ss. 93 (3), 113. - Issued: 19.05.2006. Made: 09.05.2006. Laid: 19.05.2006. Coming into force: 10.06.2006. Effect: None. Territorial extent & classification: E/W/S/NI. General. - 4p.: 30 cm. - 978-0-11-070451-7 £3.00

The Scotland Act 1998 (Modifications of Schedule 5) Order 2006 No. 2006/609. - Enabling power: Scotland Act 1998, s. 30 (2). - Issued: 20.03.2006. Made: 08.03.2006. Coming into force: 01.05.2006. Effect: 1998 c.46 amended. Territorial extent & classification: E/W/S/NI. General. - 2p.: 30 cm. - 978-0-11-074246-5 £3.00

The Scotland Act 1998 (River Tweed) Order 2006 No. 2006/2913. - Enabling power: Scotland Act 1998, ss. 111, 112 (1), 113. - Issued: 21.11.2006. Made: 14.11.2006. Coming into force: 15.11.2006. Effect: 1607 c.6; 1965 c.13; 1967 c.84; 1974 c.40; 1975 c.51; 1976 c.86; 1981 c.29; 1984 c.26; 1989 c.15; 1995 c.40; 1998 c.46; S.I. 1999/1746 amended; 1986 c.62 revoked except for s. 31 & 1857 c.cxlviii; 1859 c.lxx; 1868 c.123; 1902 c.29; 1933 c.35; 1951 c.26; 1969 c.xxiv; 1976 c.22; 2001 asp 3; S.I. 1996/1211 revoked. Territorial extent & classification: E/W/S. General. - Supersedes Draft SI (ISBN 0110705548) issued 02.06.2006. - 48p.: 30 cm. - 978-0-11-075329-4 £7.50

The Scotland Act 1998 (Transfer of Functions to the Scottish Ministers etc.) (No. 2) Order 2006 No. 2006/1040. - Enabling power: Scotland Act 1998, ss. 30 (3), 63, 113, 124 (2). - Issued: 18.04.2006. Made: 11.04.2006. Coming into force: In accord. with art. 1. Effect: S.I. 1999/1750 modified. Territorial extent & classification: E/W/S/NI. General. - Supersedes draft S.I. (ISBN 011074151X) issued on 08.03.2006. - 4p.: 30 cm. - 978-0-11-074495-7 £3.00

The Scotland Act 1998 (Transfer of Functions to the Scottish Ministers etc.) (No. 3) Order 2006 No. 2006/3258. - Enabling power: Scotland Act 1998, ss. 63, 113 (2) (3) (4), 124 (2). - Issued: 22.12.2006. Made: 14.12.2006. Coming into force: 15.12.2006; 16.12.2006 in accord. with art. 1. Effect: S.I. 1999/1750; 2000/3253; 2001/3504; 2005/849 amended. Territorial extent & classification: S. General. - 8p.: 30 cm. - 978-0-11-071417-2 £3.00

The Scotland Act 1998 (Transfer of Functions to the Scottish Ministers etc.) Order 2006 No. 2006/304 (S.3). - Enabling power: Scotland Act 1998, ss. 63, 113, 124 (2). - Issued: 23.02.2006. Made: 14.02.2006. Coming into force: 15.02.2006 in accord. with art. 1 (1). Effect: 1947 c. 41; 1970 c. 40 modified. Territorial extent & classification: E/W/S/NI. General. - Supersedes draft SI (ISBN 0110698649) issued on 15.12.2005. - 8p.: 30 cm. - 978-0-11-069962-2 £3.00

The Smoking, Health and Social Care (Scotland) Act 2005 and the Prohibition of Smoking in Certain Premises (Scotland) Regulations 2006 (Consequential Provisions) (Scotland) Order 2006 No. 2006/1115. - Enabling power: Scotland Act 1998, ss. 104, 112 (1), 113. - Issued: 21.04.2006. Made: 18.04.2006. Laid: 21.04.2006. Coming into force: 15.05.2006. Effect: None. Territorial extent & classification: E/W/S/NI. General. - 4p.: 30 cm. - 978-0-11-074503-9 £3.00

The Smoking, Health and Social Care (Scotland) Act 2005 (Consequential Modifications) (England, Wales and Northern Ireland) Order 2006 No. 2006/1056. - Enabling power: Scotland Act 1998, ss. 104, 112 (1), 113. - Issued: 12.04.2006. Made: 31.03.2006. Coming into force: In accord with art 1 (2). Effect: 1968 c.46; 1977 c.37, c.49; 1988 c.48; 1990 c.19; 1992 c.52; 1996 c.18 modified & S.I. 1992/662; 2001/1358 (W.86); 2004/1765; 2005/641 amended. Territorial extent & classification: E/W/NI. General. - 8p.: 30 cm. - 978-0-11-070258-2 £3.00

The Water Environment and Water Services (Scotland) Act 2003 (Consequential Provisions and Modifications) Order 2006 No. 2006/1054 (S.10). - Enabling power: Scotland Act 1998, ss. 104, 112 (1), 113. - Issued: 12.04.2006. Made: 31.03.2006. Coming into force: 01.04.2006. Effect: 1989 c. 29; 1996 c. 8 & S.I. 1996/1527 amended. Territorial extent & classification: S. General. - Supersedes draft SI (ISBN 0110699726) issued 03.03.2006. - 8p.: 30 cm. - 978-0-11-070249-0 £3.00

The Water Environment (Controlled Activities) (Scotland) Regulations 2005 (Notices in the Interests of National Security) Order 2006 No. 2006/661 (S.5). - Enabling power: Scotland Act 1998, ss. 104, 112 (1), 113. - Issued: 16.03.2006. Made: 09.03.2006. Laid: 15.03.2006. Coming into force: 05.04.2006. Effect: None. Territorial extent & classification: S. General. - 4p.: 30 cm. - 978-0-11-074257-1 £3.00

Devolution, Wales

The National Assembly for Wales (Representation of the People) (Amendment) Order 2006 No. 2006/884. - Enabling power: Government of Wales Act 1998, s. 11. - Issued: 26.04.2006. Made: 22.03.2006. Coming into force: 23.04.2006 in accord. with art. 1 (1). Effect: S.I. 2003/284 amended. Territorial extent & classification: W. General. - This statutory instrument has been printed in substitution of the SI of the same number (and ISBN, issued on 21.04.2006) and is being issued free of charge to all known recipients of the original version. - 8p.: 30 cm. - 978-0-11-074384-4 £3.00

The National Assembly for Wales (Transfer of Functions) (No.2) Order 2006 No. 2006/3334. - Enabling power: Government of Wales Act 1998, ss. 22, 24 (1), sch. 3, paras 1, 3. - Issued: 28.12.2006. Made: 14.12.2006. Coming into force: 15.12.2006. Effect: S.I. 1999/672 amended. Territorial extent & classification: E/W. General. - 4p.: 30 cm. - 978-0-11-075517-5 £3.00

The National Assembly for Wales (Transfer of Functions) Order 2006 No. 2006/1458. - Enabling power: Government of Wales Act 1998, ss. 22, 24 (1), sch. 3, para. 1. - Issued: 14.06.2006. Made: 07.06.2006. Coming into force: 08.06.2006. Effect: None. Territorial extent & classification: E/W. General. - 4p.: 30 cm. - 978-0-11-074673-9 £3.00

Diplomatic Service

The Consular Fees (Amendment) Order 2006 No. 2006/1912. - Enabling power: Consular Fees Act 1980, s. 1 (1). - Issued: 26.07.2006. Made: 19.07.2006. Coming into force: 05.10.2006. Effect: S.I. 2005/1465 amended. Territorial extent & classification: E/W/S/NI. General. - 2p.: 30 cm. - 978-0-11-074893-1 £3.00

Disabled persons

The Disability Discrimination Act 1995 (Amendment) (Further and Higher Education) Regulations 2006 No. 2006/1721. - Enabling power: European Communities Act 1972, s. 2 (2). - Issued: 10.07.2006. Made: 29.06.2006. Laid: 10.07.2006. Coming into force: 01.09.2006. Effect: 1995 c. 50; 2006 c.3 amended. Territorial extent & classification: E/W/S. General. - EC note: These Regulations implement (in Great Britain) the provisions of Council Directive 2000/78/EC, establishing a general framework for equal treatment in employment and occupation, so far as it relates to disability discrimination but only insofar as the Directive's obligations impact upon Chapter 2 of Part 4 of the Disability Discrimination Act 1995 (c. 50). The Disability Discrimination Act 1995 (Amendment) Regulations 2003 (S.I. 2003/1673), which came into force on 1st October 2004, implemented the Directive's obligations with respect to Parts 2 and 3 of the Act. - 16p.: 30 cm. - 978-0-11-074780-4 £3.00

The Disability Discrimination Code of Practice (Goods, Facilities, Services and Premises) (Revocation) Order 2006 No. 2006/1966. - Enabling power: Disability Discrimination Act 1995, ss. 53A (6) (c), 67 (3) (a). - Issued: 27.07.2006. Made: 20.07.2006. Laid before the Parliament: 24.07.2006. Coming into force: 04.12.2006. Effect: Disability Discrimination Act 1995 Code of Practice on Rights of Access Goods, Facilities, Services and Premises (ISBN 0117028606) is revoked, subject art. 3. Territorial extent & classification: E/W/S. General. - 2p.: 30 cm. - 978-0-11-074912-9 £3.00

The Disability Discrimination Code of Practice (Public Authorities) (Duty to Promote Equality, Scotland) (Appointed Day) Order 2006 No. 2006/219. - Enabling power: Disability Discrimination Act 1995, s. 53A (6) (a). Bringing the "The Duty to Promote Disability Equality: Statutory Code of Practice (Scotland)" (ISBN 0117036064) into effect on 01.02.2006. - Issued: 07.02.2006. Made: 31.01.2006. Effect: None. Territorial extent & classification: E/W/S. General. - 2p.: 30 cm. - 978-0-11-074002-7 £3.00

The Disability Discrimination Code of Practice (Services, Public Functions, Private Clubs and Premises) (Appointed Day) Order 2006 No. 2006/1967. - Enabling power: Disability Discrimination Act 1995, ss. 53A (6) (a), 67 (3) (a). Appoints 04.12.2006 for the coming into effect of the Disability Discrimination Act 1995 Code of Practice on Rights of Access: services to the public, public authority functions, private clubs and premises. - Issued: 27.07.2006. Made: 20.07.2006. Laid before the Parliament: -. Effect: None. Territorial extent & classification: E/W/S. General. - 4p.: 30 cm. - 978-0-11-074911-2 £3.00

The Disability Discrimination Code of Practice (Supplement to Part 3 Code of Practice) (Provision and Use of Transport Vehicles) (Appointed Day) Order 2006 No. 2006/1094. - Enabling power: Disability Discrimination Act 1995, s. 53A (6) (a). - Issued: 20.04.2006. Made: 12.04.2006. Coming into force: 18.04.2006, in accord.with art. 2. Effect: None. Territorial extent & classification: E/W/S/NI. General. - 2p.: 30 cm. - 978-0-11-074500-8 £3.00

The Disability Discrimination (Guidance on the Definition of Disability) Appointed Day Order 2006 No. 2006/1005. - Enabling power: Disability Discrimination Act 1995, ss. 3 (9), 67 (2) (3) (a). - Issued: 05.04.2006. Made: 30.03.2006. Coming into force: 01.05.2006. Effect: None. Territorial extent & classification: E/W/S. General. - Appoints 01.05.2006 as the day for the coming into force of the Guidance on matters to be taken into account in determining questions relating to the definition of disability issued by the Secretary of State on 29th March 2006 under section 3(8) of the Disability Discrimination Act 1995. - 4p.: 30 cm. - 978-0-11-074448-3 £3.00

The Disability Discrimination (Guidance on the Definition of Disability) Revocation Order 2006 No. 2006/1007. - Enabling power: Disability Discrimination Act 1995, ss. 3 (11) (b), 67 (2) (3) (a). - Issued: 06.04.2006. Made: 30.03.2006. Laid: 06.04.2006. Coming into force: 01.05.2006. Effect: Revokes (with saving) the Guidance on matters to be taken into account in determining questions relating to the definition of disability (ISBN 0-11-270955-9) referred to in S.I. 1996/1996 (C.52). Territorial extent & classification: E/W/S. General. - 2p.: 30 cm. - 978-0-11-074443-8 £3.00

The Disability Discrimination (Premises) Regulations 2006 No. 2006/887. - Enabling power: Disability Discrimination Act 1995, ss. 22 (3A), 22A (4), 24 (4A) (5), 24K (3), 24L (1) (2), 67 (3), 68 (1). - Issued: 28.03.2006. Made: 21.03.2006. Laid: 28.03.2006. Coming into force: 04.12.2006. Effect: S.I 1996/1836; 2002/1980 revoked. Territorial extent & classification: E/W/S. General. - 8p.: 30 cm. - 978-0-11-074365-3 £3.00

The Disability Rights Commission Act 1999 (Commencement No.3) Order 2006 No. 2006/3189 (C.110). - Enabling power: Disability Rights Commission Act 1999, s. 16 (2). Bringing into operation various provisions of the 1999 Act on 04.12.2006. - Issued: 05.12.2006. Made: 27.11.2006. Effect: None. Territorial extent & classification: E/W/S. General. - 2p.: 30 cm. - 978-0-11-075399-7 £3.00

The Rail Vehicle Accessibility (Gatwick Express Class 458 Vehicles) Exemption Order 2006 No. 2006/933. - Enabling power: Disability Discrimination Act 1995, s. 47 (1) (b) (1A) (a) (4). - Issued: 06.04.2006. Made: 28.03.2006. Coming into force: 06.04.2006. Effect: None. Territorial extent & classification: E/W/S. General. - 4p.: 30 cm. - 978-0-11-074410-0 £3.00

Disabled persons, England and Wales

The Disability Discrimination Act 1995 (Private Hire Vehicles) (Carriage of Guide Dogs, etc.) (England and Wales) (Amendment) Regulations 2006 No. 2006/1617. - Enabling power: Disability Discrimination Act 1995, ss. 37A (8) (b) (9), 67 (2). - Issued: 26.06.2006. Made: 16.06.2006. Laid: 22.06.2006. Coming into force: 17.07.2006. Effect: S.I. 2003/3122 amended. Territorial extent & classification: E/W. General. - This Statutory Instrument has been printed to correct errors in SI 2003/3122 (ISBN 0110482565) and is being issued free of charge to all known recipients of that Statutory Instrument. - 4p.: 30 cm. - 978-0-11-074718-7 £3.00

The Disability Discrimination Act 1995 (Taxis) (Carrying of Guide Dogs etc.) (England and Wales) (Amendment) Regulations 2006 No. 2006/1616. - Enabling power: Disability Discrimination Act 1995, ss. 37 (8) (b) (9), 67 (2). - Issued: 26.06.2006. Made: 16.06.2006. Laid: 22.06.2006. Coming into force: 17.07.2006. Effect: S.I. 2000/2990 amended. Territorial extent & classification: E/W. General. - This Statutory Instrument has been printed to correct errors in SI 2000/2990 (ISBN 0110187660) and is being issued free of charge to all known recipients of that Statutory Instrument. - 4p.: 30 cm. - 978-0-11-074717-0 £3.00

Disclosure of information

The Enterprise Act 2002 (Part 9 Restrictions on Disclosure of Information) (Amendment) Order 2006 No. 2006/2909. - Enabling power: Enterprise Act 2002, s. 241 (6). - Issued: 13.11.2006. Made: 02.11.2006. Laid: 07.11.2006. Coming into force: 01.12.2006. Effect: 2002 c. 40 amended. Territorial extent & classification: E/W/S/NI. General. - 2p.: 30 cm. - 978-0-11-075261-7 £3.00

Dogs, England: Control of dogs

The Controls on Dogs (Non-application to Designated Land) Order 2006 No. 2006/779. - Enabling power: Clean Neighbourhoods and Environment Act 2005, s. 57 (3). - Issued: 22.03.2006. Made: 10.03.2006. Laid: 16.03.2006. Coming into force: 06.04.2006. Effect: None. Territorial extent & classification: E. General. - 4p.: 30 cm. - 978-0-11-074351-6 £3.00

The Dog Control Orders (Prescribed Offences and Penalties, etc.) Regulations 2006 No. 2006/1059. - Enabling power: Clean Neighbourhoods and Environment Act 2005, ss. 55 (4) (5), 56 (1) (3), 67 (1). - Issued: 12.04.2006. Made: 05.04.2006. Coming into force: 06.04.2006. In accord. with reg. 1 (b). Effect: None. Territorial extent & classification: E. General. - Supersedes draft S.I. (ISBN 0110739590) issued on 28.02.2006. - 16p.: 30 cm. - 978-0-11-074480-3 £3.00

The Dog Control Orders (Procedures) Regulations 2006 No. 2006/798. - Enabling power: Clean Neighbourhoods and Environment Act 2005, s. 56 (4) (5). - Issued: 23.03.2006. Made: 10.03.2006. Laid: 16.03.2006. Coming into force: 06.04.2006. Effect: None. Territorial extent & classification: E. General. - 4p.: 30 cm. - 978-0-11-074354-7 £3.00

Ecclesiastical law, England

The Care of Cathedrals Rules 2006 No. 2006/1941. - Enabling power: Care of Churches and Ecclesiastical Jurisdiction Measure 1991, s. 26. - Issued: 01.08.2006. Made: 07.07.2006. Laid: 25.07.2006. Coming into force: In accord. with rule 1 (2) (3). Effect: S.I. 1990/2335 revoked. Territorial extent & classification: E. General. - 96p.: 30 cm. - 978-0-11-074876-4 £13.50

Ecclesiastical law, England: Fees

The Ecclesiastical Judges, Legal Officers and Others (Fees) Order 2006 No. 2006/1943. - Enabling power: Ecclesiastical Fees Measure 1986, s. 6. - Issued: 26.07.2006. Made: 07.07.2006. Laid: 25.07.2006. Coming into force: 01.01.2007. Effect: S.I. 2005/2020 revoked. Territorial extent & classification: E. General. - 12p.: 30 cm. - 978-0-11-074875-7 £3.00

The Legal Officers (Annual Fees) Order 2006 No. 2006/1940. - Enabling power: Ecclesiastical Fees Measure 1986, s. 4. - Issued: 25.07.2006. Made: 07.07.2006. Laid before the Parliament: 25.07.2006. Coming into force: 01.01.2007. Effect: S.I. 2005/2018 revoked. Territorial extent & classification: E. General. - 12p.: 30 cm. - 978-0-11-074873-3 £3.00

The Parochial Fees Order 2006 No. 2006/1942. - Enabling power: Ecclesiastical Fees Measure 1986, ss. 1, 2. - Issued: 25.07.2006. Made: 13.07.2006. Laid: 07.07.2006. Laid before the Parliament: 25.07.2006. Coming into force: 01.01.2007. Effect: S. I. 2005/2016 revoked. Territorial extent & classification: E. General. - 8p.: 30 cm. - 978-0-11-074874-0 £3.00

Ecclesiastical law, England: Legal aid

The Church of England (Legal Aid) (Amendment) Rules 2006 No. 2006/1939. - Enabling power: Church of England (Legal Aid) Measure 1994, s. 4. - Issued: 25.07.2006. Made: 15.06.2006. Approved by the General Synod: 07.07.2006. Laid before the Parliament: 25.07.2006. Coming into force: 01.08.2006. Effect: S.I. 1995/2034 amended. Territorial extent & classification: E. General. - 4p.: 30 cm. - 978-0-11-074872-6 £3.00

Ecclesiastical law, England and Wales

The Grants to the Churches Conservation Trust Order 2006 No. 2006/1008. - Enabling power: Redundant Churches and other Religious Buildings Act 1969, s. 1 (1) (2) (3). - Issued: 06.04.2006. Made: 30.03.2006. Coming into force: 31.03.2006. Effect: S.I. 2000/402; 2003/829 revoked. Territorial extent & classification: E/W. General. - 2p.: 30 cm. - 978-0-11-074451-3 £3.00

Education

The Education (Supply of Student Support Information to Governing Bodies) Regulations 2006 No. 2006/141. - Enabling power: Higher Education Act 2004, ss. 45, 47 (5). - Issued: 02.02.2006. Made: 25.01.2006. Laid: 02.01.2006. Coming into force: 01.03.2006. Effect: None. Territorial extent & classification: E/W/S/NI. General. - Incorrect subject heading "Education, England" printed on document. - 4p.: 30 cm. - 978-0-11-073956-4 £3.00

Education, England

The Amesbury Church of England Voluntary Controlled Primary School (Designation as having a Religious Character) Order 2006 No. 2006/1904. - Enabling power: School Standards and Framework Act 1998, s. 69 (3) (4). - Issued: 24.07.2006. Made: 12.07.2006. Coming into force: 12.07.2006. Effect: None. Territorial extent & classification: E. Local. - 2p.: 30 cm. - 978-0-11-074854-2 £3.00

The Archbishop Courtenay Primary School (Designation as having a Religious Character) Order 2006 No. 2006/838. - Enabling power: School Standards and Framework Act 1998, s. 69 (3) (4). - Issued: 27.03.2006. Made: 15.03.2006. Coming into force: 15.03.2006. Effect: None. Territorial extent & classification: E. Local. - 2p.: 30 cm. - 978-0-11-074369-1 £3.00

The Belford St Mary's Church of England Voluntary Aided Middle School (Designation as having a Religious Character) Order 2006 No. 2006/1905. - Enabling power: School Standards and Framework Act 1998, s. 69 (3) (4). - Issued: 24.07.2006. Made: 12.07.2006. Coming into force: 12.07.2006. Effect: None. Territorial extent & classification: E. Local. - 2p.: 30 cm. - 978-0-11-074855-9 £3.00

The Bidston Church of England Primary School (Designation as having a Religious Character) Order 2006 No. 2006/1903. - Enabling power: School Standards and Framework Act 1998, s. 69 (3) (4). - Issued: 24.07.2006. Made: 12.07.2006. Coming into force: 12.07.2006. Effect: None. Territorial extent & classification: E. Local. - 2p.: 30 cm. - 978-0-11-074853-5 £3.00

The Blessed Trinity RC College (Designation as having a Religious Character) Order 2006 No. 2006/1900. - Enabling power: School Standards and Framework Act 1998, s. 69 (3) (4). - Issued: 24.07.2006. Made: 12.07.2006. Coming into force: 12.07.2006. Effect: None. Territorial extent & classification: E. Local. - 2p.: 30 cm. - 978-0-11-074851-1 £3.00

The Bradford Cathedral Community College (Designation as having a Religious Character) Order 2006 No. 2006/2938. - Enabling power: School Standards and Framework Act 1998, s. 69 (3) (4). - Issued: 17.11.2006. Made: 09.11.2006. Coming into force: 09.11.2006. Effect: None. Territorial extent & classification: E. Local. - 2p.: 30 cm. - 978-0-11-075288-4 £3.00

The Cadishead Primary School (Change to School Session Times) Order 2006 No. 2006/2370. - Enabling power: Education Act 2002, s. 2 (1). - Issued: 08.09.2006. Made: 27.08.2006. Laid: 08.09.2006. Coming into force: 30.09.2006. Effect: None. Territorial extent & classification: E. General. - 2p.: 30 cm. - 978-0-11-075066-8 £3.00

The Central Leeds Learning Federation (Change to School Session Times) Order 2006 No. 2006/2005. - Enabling power: Education Act 2002, s. 2 (1). - Issued: 28.07.2006. Made: 20.07.2006. Laid: 28.07.2006. Coming into force: 01.09.2006. Effect: None. Territorial extent & classification: E. General. - Revoked by S.I. 2006/2142 (ISBN 0110749812). - 2p.: 30 cm. - 978-0-11-074929-7 £3.00

The Central Leeds Learning Federation (Change to School Session Times) (Revocation) Order 2006 No. 2006/2142. - Enabling power: Education Act 2002, s. 3 (1) (b). - Issued: 09.08.2006. Made: 02.08.2006. Laid: 09.08.2006. Coming into force: 01.09.2006. Effect: S.I. 2006/2005 revoked. Territorial extent & classification: E. General. - 2p.: 30 cm. - 978-0-11-074981-5 £3.00

The Christ College, Cheltenham (Designation as having a Religious Character) Order 2006 No. 2006/2939. - Enabling power: School Standards and Framework Act 1998, s. 69 (3) (4). - Issued: 17.11.2006. Made: 09.11.2006. Coming into force: 09.11.2006. Effect: None. Territorial extent & classification: E. Local. - 2p.: 30 cm. - 978-0-11-075289-1 £3.00

The Churchfields, The Village School (Designation as having a Religious Character) Order 2006 No. 2006/1901. - Enabling power: School Standards and Framework Act 1998, s. 69 (3) (4). - Issued: 24.07.2006. Made: 12.07.2006. Coming into force: 12.07.2006. Effect: None. Territorial extent & classification: E. Local. - 2p.: 30 cm. - 978-0-11-074850-4 £3.00

The Consistent Financial Reporting (England) (Amendment) Regulations 2006 No. 2006/437. - Enabling power: Education Act 2002, s. 44. - Issued: 02.03.2006. Made: 22.02.2006. Laid: 02.03.2006. Coming into force: 01.04.2006. Effect: S.I. 2003/373 amended. Territorial extent & classification: E. General. - 2p.: 30 cm. - 978-0-11-074099-7 £3.00

The Crawley Down Village CE School (Designation as having a Religious Character) Order 2006 No. 2006/2940. - Enabling power: School Standards and Framework Act 1998, s. 69 (3) (4). - Issued: 17.11.2006. Made: 09.11.2006. Coming into force: 09.11.2006. Effect: None. Territorial extent & classification: E. Local. - 2p.: 30 cm. - 978-0-11-075290-7 £3.00

The Designation of Schools Having a Religious Character (Independent Schools) (England) Order 2006 No. 2006/1533. - Enabling power: School Standards and Framework Act 1998, s. 69 (3). - Issued: 21.06.2006. Made: 13.06.2006. Coming into force: 13.06.2006. Effect: None. Territorial extent & classification: E. General. - 4p.: 30 cm. - 978-0-11-074698-2 £3.00

The Diocese of Bradford (Educational Endowments) Order 2006 No. 2006/1504. - Enabling power: Education Act 1996, ss. 554, 556 & Reverter of Sites Act 1987, s. 5. - Made: 08.06.2006. Coming into force: 30.06.2006. Effect: None. Territorial extent & classification: E. Local
Unpublished

The Diocese of Bradford (Educational Endowments) Order 2006 No. 2006/2542. - Enabling power: Education Act 1996, ss. 554, 556 & Reverter of Sites Act 1987, s. 5. - Made: 22.09.2006. Coming into force: 15.10.2006. Effect: None. Territorial extent & classification: E. Local
Unpublished

The Diocese of Lincoln (Educational Endowments) Order 2006 No. 2006/2079. - Enabling power: Education Act 1996, ss. 554, 556 & Reverter of Sites Act 1987, s. 5. - Made: 26.07.2006. Coming into force: 16.08.2006. Effect: None. Territorial extent & classification: E. Local
Unpublished

The Diocese of Manchester (Educational Endowments) Order 2006 No. 2006/2976. - Enabling power: Education Act 1996, ss. 554, 556 & Reverter of Sites Act 1987, s. 5. - Made: 14.11.2006. Coming into force: 06.12.2006. Effect: None. Territorial extent & classification: E. Local
Unpublished

The Diocese of York Whorlton Parochial School (Educational Endowments) Order 2006 No. 2006/1673. - Enabling power: Education Act 1996, ss. 554, 556. - Made: 23.06.2006. Coming into force: 17.07.2006. Effect: None. Territorial extent & classification: E. Local
Unpublished

The Education Act 2002 (Commencement No. 9 and Savings) Order 2006 No. 2006/2895 (C.100). - Enabling power: Education Act 2002, s. 216 (4) (5). Bringing into operation various provisions of the 2002 Act on 06.11.2006 in accord. with art. 2. - Issued: 08.11.2006. Made: 31.10.2006. Effect: None. Territorial extent & classification: E. General. - 12p.: 30 cm. - 978-0-11-075251-8 £3.00

The Education (Admission of Looked After Children) (England) Regulations 2006 No. 2006/128. - Enabling power: School Standards and Framework Act 1998, ss. 89 (1A), 138 (7). - Issued: 31.01.2006. Made: 25.01.2006. Laid: 31.01.2006. Coming into force: 21.02.2006. Effect: None. Territorial extent & classification: E. General. - 4p.: 30 cm. - 978-0-11-073940-3 £3.00

The Education and Inspections Act 2006 (Commencement No. 1 and Saving Provisions) Order 2006 No. 2006/2990 (C.105). - Enabling power: Education and Inspections Act 2006, ss. 181, 188 (3). Bringing into operation various provisions of the 2006 Act on 12.12.2006. - Issued: 22.11.2006. Made: 15.11.2006. Effect: None. Territorial extent & classification: E. General. - 4p.: 30 cm. - 978-0-11-075330-0 £3.00

The Education and Inspections Act 2006 (Commencement No. 2) Order 2006 No. 2006/3400 (C. 127). - Enabling power: Education and Inspections Act 2006, ss. 181, 188 (3). Bringing into operation various provisions of the 2006 Act on 08.01.2007; 08.02.2007; 27.02.2007 in relation to England. - Issued: 28.11.2006. Made: 16.12.2006. Effect: None. Territorial extent & classification: E. General. - 4p.: 30 cm. - 978-0-11-075546-5 £3.00

The Education (Aptitude for Particular Subjects) (Amendment) (England) Regulations 2006 No. 2006/3408. - Enabling power: School Standards and Framework Act 1998, ss. 102 (1), 138 (7). - Issued: 29.11.2006. Made: 16.12.2006. Laid: 29.12.2006. Coming into force: 27.02.2007. Effect: S.I. 1999/258 amended. Territorial extent & classification: E. General. - 2p.: 30 cm. - 978-0-11-075554-0 £3.00

The Education (Assisted Places) (Amendment) (England) Regulations 2006 No. 2006/1812. - Enabling power: Education (Schools) Act 1997, s. 3 (1) (2). - Issued: 17.07.2006. Made: 06.07.2006. Laid: 17.07.2006. Coming into force: 01.09.2006. Effect: S.I. 1997/1968 amended. Territorial extent & classification: E. General. - 2p.: 30 cm. - 978-0-11-074821-4 £3.00

The Education (Assisted Places) (Incidental Expenses) (Amendment) (England) Regulations 2006 No. 2006/1813. - Enabling power: Education (Schools) Act 1997, s. 3 (1) (3) (4). - Issued: 17.07.2006. Made: 06.07.2006. Laid: 17.07.2006. Coming into force: 01.09.2006. Effect: S.I. 1997/1969 amended. Territorial extent & classification: E. General. - With correction slip dated January 2007. - 2p.: 30 cm. - 978-0-11-074822-1 £3.00

The Education (Budget Statements) (England) Regulations 2006 No. 2006/511. - Enabling power: School Standards and Framework Act 1998, ss. 52 (1) (1A) (3) (4), 138 (7). - Issued: 06.03.2006. Made: 27.02.2006. Laid: 06.03.2006. Coming into force: 27.03.2006. Effect: None. Territorial extent & classification: E. General. - 36p.: 30 cm. - 978-0-11-074125-3 £6.50

The Education (Change of Category of Maintained Schools) (Amendment) (England) Regulations 2006 No. 2006/1164. - Enabling power: School Standards and Framework Act 1998, ss. 138 (7), sch. 8, para. 2 (2). - Issued: 04.05.2006. Made: 24.04.2006. Laid: 04.05.2006. Coming into force: 31.05.2006. Effect: S.I. 2000/2195; 2005/1731 amended. Territorial extent & classification: E. General. - This Statutory Instrument has been made in consequence of a defect in SI 2005/1731 (ISBN 0110730305) and is being issued free of charge to all known recipients of that Statutory Instrument. - 4p.: 30 cm. - 978-0-11-074526-8 £3.00

The Education (Change of Category of Maintained Schools) (Amendment) (No.2) (England) Regulations 2006 No. 2006/1507. - Enabling power: School Standards and Framework Act 1998, ss. 138 (7), sch. 8, para. 2 (2). - Issued: 23.06.2006. Made: 09.06.2006. Laid: 23.06.2006. Coming into force: 01.08.2006. Effect: S.I. 2000/2195 amended. Territorial extent & classification: E. General. - 2p.: 30 cm. - 978-0-11-074682-1 £3.00

The Education (Chief Inspector of Schools in England) Order 2006 No. 2006/1460. - Enabling power: Education Act 2005, s. 1 (1) (4). - Issued: 14.06.2006. Made: 07.06.2006. Coming into force: 08.06.2006 in accord. with art. 1. Effect: S.I. 2005/3505 revoked. Territorial extent & classification: E. General. - 2p.: 30 cm. - 978-0-11-074676-0 £3.00

The Education (Designated Institutions in Further Education) (Amendment) Order 2006 No. 2006/408. - Enabling power: Further and Higher Education Act 1992, ss. 28, 29 (1) (b). - Issued: 03.03.2006. Made: 23.02.2006. Laid: 03.03.2006. Coming into force: 31.03.2006. Effect: S.I. 1993/435 amended. Territorial extent & classification: E. General. - 2p.: 30 cm. - 978-0-11-074102-4 £3.00

The Education (Designated Institutions) (No. 2) Order 2006 No. 2006/1744. - Enabling power: Education Reform Act 1988, s. 129 (1). - Issued: 11.07.2006. Made: 01.07.2006. Laid: 11.07.2006. Coming into force: 01.08.2006. Effect: None. Territorial extent & classification: E. General. - 2p.: 30 cm. - 978-0-11-074792-7 £3.00

The Education (Designated Institutions) Order 2006 No. 2006/1674. - Enabling power: Education Reform Act 1988, s. 129(1). - Issued: 30.06.2006. Made: 22.06.2006. Laid: 30.06.2006. Coming into force: 01.08.2006. Effect: None. Territorial extent & classification: E. General. - 2p.: 30 cm. - 978-0-11-074748-4 £3.00

The Education (Disqualification Provisions: Bankruptcy and Mental Health) (England) Regulations 2006 No. 2006/2198. - Enabling power: School Standards and Framework Act 1998, s. 21 (5) & Education Act 2002, ss. 12, 19 (1) (3), 34 (5), 210 (7). - Issued: 15.08.2006. Made: 08.08.2006. Laid: 15.08.2006. Coming into force: 08.09.2006. Effect: S.I. 2000/2872; 2002/2978, 3177; 2003/348, 1558 amended. Territorial extent & classification: E. General. - 4p.: 30 cm. - 978-0-11-075008-8 £3.00

The Education (Individual Pupil Information) (Prescribed Persons) (Amendment) Regulations 2006 No. 2006/1505. - Enabling power: Education Act 1996, ss. 537A (4) (5) (6), 569 (4). - Issued: 19.06.2006. Made: 08.06.2006. Laid: 19.06.2006. Coming into force: 10.07.2006. Effect: S.I. 1999/903 amended. Territorial extent & classification: E. General. - 4p.: 30 cm. - 978-0-11-074679-1 £3.00

The Education (Infant Class Sizes) (England) (Amendment) Regulations 2006 No. 2006/3409. - Enabling power: School Standards and Framework Act 1998, ss. 1, 138 (7). - Issued: 29.11.2006. Made: 16.12.2006. Laid: 29.12.2006. Coming into force: 27.02.2007. Effect: SI 1998/1973 amended. Territorial extent & classification: E. General. - 2p.: 30 cm. - 978-0-11-075555-7 £3.00

The Education (Information About Individual Pupils) (England) Regulations 2006 No. 2006/2601. - Enabling power: Education Act 1996, ss. 537A (1) (2), 569(4) and Education Act 2002, s. 214. - Issued: 03.10.2006. Made: 21.09.2006. Laid: 03.10.2006. Coming into force: 31.10.2006. Effect: S.I. 2003/689 amended and S.I. 2001/4020; 2002/3112; 2003/3277; 2005/3101 revoked. Territorial extent & classification: E. General. - 12p.: 30 cm. - 978-0-11-075134-4 £3.00

The Education (Information as to Provision of Education) (England) (Amendment) Regulations 2006 No. 2006/1033. - Enabling power: Education Act 1996, ss. 29 (3), 569 (4). - Issued: 07.04.2006. Made: 31.03.2006. Laid: 07.04.2006. Coming into force: 30.04.2006. Effect: S.I. 1999/1066 amended. Territorial extent & classification: E. General. - 2p.: 30 cm. - 978-0-11-074462-9 £3.00

The Education (Inspectors of Schools in England) (No.2) Order 2006 No. 2006/1920. - Enabling power: Education Act 2005, s. 1 (2). - Issued: 26.07.2006. Made: 19.07.2006. Coming into force: 04.09.2006. Effect: None. Territorial extent & classification: E. General. - 2p.: 30 cm. - 978-0-11-074887-0 £3.00

The Education (Inspectors of Schools in England) (No.3) Order 2006 No. 2006/2317. - Enabling power: Education Act 2005, s. 1 (2). - Issued: 13.09.2006. Made: 05.09.2006. Coming into force: 06.09.2006. Effect: None. Territorial extent & classification: E. General. - 2p.: 30 cm. - 978-0-11-075081-1 £3.00

The Education (Inspectors of Schools in England) (No.4) Order 2006 No. 2006/2658. - Enabling power: Education Act 2005, s. 1 (2). - Issued: 16.10.2006. Made: 10.10.2006. Coming into force: 01.11.2006. Effect: None. Territorial extent & classification: E. General. - 2p.: 30 cm. - 978-0-11-075175-7 £3.00

The Education (Inspectors of Schools in England) Order 2006 No. 2006/306. - Enabling power: Education Act 2005, s. 1 (2)- Issued: 21.02.2006. Made: 14.02.2006. Coming into force: 14.02.2006. Effect: None. Territorial extent & classification: E. General. - 2p.: 30 cm. - 978-0-11-074061-4 £3.00

Education, England

The Education (Local Education Authority Performance Targets) (England) (Amendment) Regulations 2006 No. 2006/3150. - Enabling power: Education Act 1996, ss. 29 (3), 569 (4) & Education Act 2005, ss. 102, 120 (1). - Issued: 06.12.2006. Made: 28.11.2006. Laid: 06.12.2006. Coming into force: 28.12.2006. Effect: S.I. 2005/2450 amended. Territorial extent & classification: E. General. - 4p.: 30 cm. - 978-0-11-075400-0 £3.00

The Education (National Curriculum) (Exceptions at Key Stage 4) (Revocation and Savings) (England) Regulations 2006 No. 2006/2495. - Enabling power: Education Act 2002, ss. 91, 96, 210. - Issued: 15.09.2006. Made: 06.09.2006. Laid: 15.09.2006. Coming into force: 09.10.2006. Effect: S.I. 2003/252 (with savings); 2004/264 revoked. Territorial extent & classification: E. General. - 4p.: 30 cm. - 978-0-11-075106-1 £3.00

The Education (New Secondary School Proposals) (England) Regulations 2006 No. 2006/2139. - Enabling power: School Standards and Framework Act 1998, ss. 28A (4) (6) (8), 138, sch. 4, para. 5 & Education Act 2005, ss. 66, 120, 124, sch. 10, paras 3, 4, 5, 7, 8, 9, 10. - Issued: 10.08.2006. Made: 02.08.2006. Laid: 10.08.2006. Coming into force: 01.09.2006. Effect: S.I. 1999/2213 amended & S.I. 2003/1200, 1421 revoked with savings. Territorial extent & classification: E. General. - 24p.: 30 cm. - 978-0-11-074976-1 £4.00

The Education (Nutritional Standards for School Lunches) (England) Regulations 2006 No. 2006/2381. - Enabling power: School Standards and Framework Act 1998, ss. 114 (1) (4), 138 (7) (8). - Issued: 11.09.2006. Made: 04.09.2006. Laid: 08.09.2006. Coming into force: 11.09.2006. Effect: S.I. 2000/1777 amended. Territorial extent & classification: E. General. - 4p.: 30 cm. - 978-0-11-075077-4 £3.00

The Education (Outturn Statements) (England) Regulations 2006 No. 2006/1760. - Enabling power: School Standards and Framework Act 1998, ss. 52 (2) (2B) (3), 138 (7). - Issued: 13.07.2006. Made: 04.07.2006. Laid: 07.07.2006. Coming into force: 28.07.2006. Effect: S.I. 2005/1386 revoked with saving. Territorial extent & classification: E. General. - 24p.: 30 cm. - 978-0-11-074806-1 £4.00

The Education (Pupil Exclusions and Appeals) (Miscellaneous Amendments) (England) Regulations 2006 No. 2006/2189. - Enabling power: Education Act 2002, ss. 52, 210. - Issued: 15.08.2006. Made: 08.08.2006. Laid: 15.08.2006. Coming into force: 06.09.2006. Effect: S.I. 2002/3178, 3179 amended. Territorial extent & classification: E. General. - 8p.: 30 cm. - 978-0-11-075003-3 £3.00

The Education (Pupil Referral Units) (Application of Enactments) (England) (Amendment) (No. 2) Regulations 2006 No. 2006/3226. - Enabling power: Education Act 1996, s. 569 (4), sch. 1, para. 3. - Issued: 11.12.2006. Made: 04.12.2006. Laid: 11.12.2006. Coming into force: 01.01.2007. Effect: S.I. 2005/2039 amended. Territorial extent & classification: E. General. - 4p.: 30 cm. - 978-0-11-075421-5 £3.00

The Education (Pupil Referral Units) (Application of Enactments) (England) (Amendment) Regulations 2006 No. 2006/1068. - Enabling power: Education Act 1996, s. 569 (4) (5), sch. 1, para. 3. - Issued: 20.04.2006. Made: 08.04.2006. Laid: 20.04.2006. Coming into force: 12.05.2006. Effect: S.I. 2005/2039 amended. Territorial extent & classification: E. General. - 2p.: 30 cm. - 978-0-11-074486-5 £3.00

The Education (Pupil Registration) (England) Regulations 2006 No. 2006/1751. - Enabling power: Education Act 1996, ss. 434 (1) (3) (4), 551 (1), 569. - Issued: 12.07.2006. Made: 01.07.2006. Laid: 12.07.2006. Coming into force: 01.09.2006. Effect: S.I. 1995/2089; 1997/2624 revoked in relation to England and S.I. 2001/2802 revoked. Territorial extent & classification: E. General. - With correction slip, dated August 2006 (which supersedes the correction slip issued in July 2006). The correction slip changes the Laid date to read 12th July 2006 and makes another amendment. - 12p.: 30 cm. - 978-0-11-074798-9 £3.00

The Education (Recognised Awards) (Richmond The American International University in London) Order 2006 No. 2006/3121. - Enabling power: Education Reform Act 1988, s. 214 (2) (c) (3). - Issued: 30.11.2006. Made: 23.11.2006. Coming into force: 31.12.2006. Effect: S.I. 1996/2564 revoked. Territorial extent & classification: E. General. - 2p.: 30 cm. - 978-0-11-075366-9 £3.00

The Education (School Performance Information) (England) (Amendment) Regulations 2006 No. 2006/2896. - Enabling power: Education Act 1996, ss. 29 (3), 408, 537, 537A (1) (2), 569 (4) (5). - Issued: 09.11.2006. Made: 01.11.2006. Laid: 09.11.2006. Coming into force: 30.11.2006. Effect: S.I. 2001/3446 amended. Territorial extent & classification: E. General. - 8p.: 30 cm. - 978-0-11-075252-5 £3.00

The Education (School Performance Targets) (England) (Amendment) Regulations 2006 No. 2006/3151. - Enabling power: Education Act 1997, ss. 19, 54 (3). - Issued: 11.12.2006. Made: 30.11.2006. Laid: 06.12.2006. Coming into force: 28.12.2006. Effect: S.I. 2004/2858 amended. Territorial extent & classification: E. General. - With correction slip dated January 2007, amending coming into force date. - 4p.: 30 cm. - 978-0-11-075412-3 £3.00

The Education (School Teacher Performance Management) (England) Regulations 2006 No. 2006/2661. - Enabling power: Education Act 2000, ss. 21, 131, 210. - Issued: 13.10.2006. Made: 04.10.2006. Laid: 09.10.2006. Coming into force: 01.09.2007. Effect: S.I. 2000/2122 amended & S.I. 2001/2855 revoked with saving. Territorial extent & classification: E. General. - With correction slip, dated November 2006. - 20p.: 30 cm. - 978-0-11-075152-8 £3.50

The Education (Special Educational Needs) (England) (Consolidation) (Amendment) Regulations 2006 No. 2006/3346. - Enabling power: Education Act 1996, ss. 322 (4), 324 (2), 326A (4) (6) (a), 328 (3B) (6), 336A (1) (2) (a), 569 (1) (2) (4), 579 (1), sch. 26, paras 3 (1) (3) (4); sch. 27, paras 2B (3) 5 (3), 7 (1) (2) (5) and School Standards and Framework Act 1998, ss. 71 (7), 98 (5), 138 (7), 144 (1). - Issued: 21.12.2006. Made: 14.12.2006. Laid: 21.12.2006. Coming into force: 01.03.2007. Effect: S.I. 1999/2212; 2001/3455 amended. Territorial extent & classification: E. General. - 12p.: 30 cm. - 978-0-11-075503-8 £3.00

The Education (Student Support) (Amendment) (No. 2) Regulations 2006 No. 2006/1745. - Enabling power: Teaching and Higher Education Act 1998, ss. 22, 42 (6), 43 (1). - Issued: 11.07.2006. Made: 01.07.2006. Laid: 11.07.2006. Coming into force: 01.08.2006. Effect: S.I. 2006/119 amended. Territorial extent & classification: E. General. - 2p.: 30 cm. - 978-0-11-074793-4 £3.00

The Education (Student Support) (European Institutions) (Amendment) Regulations 2006 No. 2006/1785. - Enabling power: Teaching and Higher Education Act 1998, ss. 22, 42 (6), 43 (1). - Issued: 14.07.2006. Made: 01.07.2006. Laid: 14.07.2006. Coming into force: 11.08.2006. Effect: S.I. 2006/953 amended. Territorial extent & classification: E. General. - With correction slip dated January 2007. - 2p.: 30 cm. - 978-0-11-074808-5 £3.00

The Education (Student Support) (European Institutions) (No. 2) Regulations 2006 No. 2006/3156. - Enabling power: Teaching and Higher Education Act 1998, ss. 22, 42 (6), 43 (1). - Issued: 07.12.2006. Made: 24.11.2006. Laid: 07.12.2006. Coming into force: 31.12.2006. Effect: S.I. 2006/953, 1785 revoked with savings in relation to England. Territorial extent & classification: E. General. - With correction slip dated January 2007. - 28p.: 30 cm. - 978-0-11-075383-6 £4.50

The Education (Student Support) (European Institutions) Regulations 2006 No. 2006/953. - Enabling power: Teaching and Higher Education Act 1998, ss. 22, 42 (6), 43 (1). - Issued: 06.04.2006. Made: 28.03.2006. Laid: 06.04.2006. Coming into force: 30.04.2006. Effect: S.I. 2000/2197 (with savings); 2001/563, 2892 revoked in relation to England. Territorial extent & classification: E. General. - EC note: These Regulations implement the provisions of Directive 2004/38/EC of the European Parliament and of the Council of 29th April 2004 on the rights of citizens of the Union and their family members to move and reside freely in the territory of the member states so far as the Directive relates to student support. - 32p.: 30 cm. - 978-0-11-074416-2 £5.50

The Farnsfield St Michael's Church of England Primary (Voluntary Aided) School (Designation as having a Religious Character) Order 2006 No. 2006/2941. - Enabling power: School Standards and Framework Act 1998, s. 69 (3) (4). - Issued: 17.11.2006. Made: 09.11.2006. Coming into force: 09.11.2006. Effect: None. Territorial extent & classification: E. Local. - 2p.: 30 cm. - 978-0-11-075291-4 £3.00

The Five Lanes CofE VC Primary School (Designation as having a Religious Character) Order 2006 No. 2006/2942. - Enabling power: School Standards and Framework Act 1998, s. 69 (3) (4). - Issued: 17.11.2006. Made: 09.11.2006. Coming into force: 09.11.2006. Effect: None. Territorial extent & classification: E. Local. - 2p.: 30 cm. - 978-0-11-075292-1 £3.00

The Further Education (Providers of Education) (England) Regulations 2006 No. 2006/3199. - Enabling power: Education Act 2002, ss. 136 (c), 210 (7), 214. - Issued: 08.12.2006. Made: 30.11.2006. Laid: 08.12.2006. Coming into force: 01.01.2007. Effect: None. Territorial extent & classification: E. General. - 8p.: 30 cm. - 978-0-11-075406-2 £3.00

The Great and Little Preston Voluntary Controlled Church of England Primary School (Designation as having a Religious Character) Order 2006 No. 2006/1899. - Enabling power: School Standards and Framework Act 1998, s. 69 (3) (4). - Issued: 24.07.2006. Made: 12.07.2006. Coming into force: 12.07.2006. Effect: None. Territorial extent & classification: E. Local. - 2p.: 30 cm. - 978-0-11-074849-8 £3.00

The Hadley Learning Community (School Governance) Order 2006 No. 2006/2212. - Enabling power: Education Act 2002, s. 2 (1). - Issued: 16.08.2006. Made: 09.08.2006. Laid: 16.08.2006. Coming into force: 08.09.2006. Effect: None. Territorial extent & classification: E. General. - 2p.: 30 cm. - 978-0-11-075011-8 £3.00

The Holy Trinity Rosehill (VA) CE Primary School (Designation as having a Religious Character) Order 2006 No. 2006/1898. - Enabling power: School Standards and Framework Act 1998, s. 69 (3) (4). - Issued: 24.07.2006. Made: 12.07.2006. Coming into force: 12.07.2006. Effect: None. Territorial extent & classification: E. Local. - 2p.: 30 cm. - 978-0-11-074857-3 £3.00

The Hope Hamilton CE Primary School (Designation as having a Religious Character) Order 2006 No. 2006/2943. - Enabling power: School Standards and Framework Act 1998, s. 69 (3) (4). - Issued: 17.11.2006. Made: 09.11.2006. Coming into force: 09.11.2006. Effect: None. Territorial extent & classification: E. Local. - 2p.: 30 cm. - 978-0-11-075293-8 £3.00

The Hucknall National Church of England (VA) Primary School (Designation as having a Religious Character) Order 2006 No. 2006/1896. - Enabling power: School Standards and Framework Act 1998, s. 69 (3) (4). - Issued: 24.07.2006. Made: 12.07.2006. Coming into force: 12.07.2006. Effect: None. Territorial extent & classification: E. Local. - 2p.: 30 cm. - 978-0-11-074847-4 £3.00

The Immanuel CofE Community College (Designation as having a Religious Character) Order 2006 No. 2006/2944. - Enabling power: School Standards and Framework Act 1998, s. 69 (3) (4). - Issued: 17.11.2006. Made: 09.11.2006. Coming into force: 09.11.2006. Effect: None. Territorial extent & classification: E. Local. - 2p.: 30 cm. - 978-0-11-075294-5 £3.00

The Isle College (Dissolution) Order 2006 No. 2006/555.
- Enabling power: Further and Higher Education Act 1992,
s. 27. - Issued: 10.03.2006. Made: 02.03.2006. Laid:
10.03.2006. Coming into force: 01.04.2006. Effect: None.
Territorial extent & classification: E. General. - 2p.: 30 cm.
- 978-0-11-074156-7 £3.00

The Josiah Mason Sixth Form College, Erdington, Birmingham (Dissolution) Order 2006 No. 2006/1754. -
Enabling power: Further and Higher Education Act 1992,
s. 27. - Issued: 10.07.2006. Made: 03.07.2006. Laid:
10.07.2006. Coming into force: 01.08.2006. Effect: None.
Territorial extent & classification: E. General. - 2p.: 30 cm.
- 978-0-11-074799-6 £3.00

The Leatherhead Trinity Primary School (Designation as having a Religious Character) Order 2006 No. 2006/2945. - Enabling power: School Standards and
Framework Act 1998, s. 69 (3) (4). - Issued: 17.11.2006.
Made: 09.11.2006. Coming into force: 09.11.2006. Effect:
None. Territorial extent & classification: E. Local. - 2p.: 30
cm. - 978-0-11-075295-2 £3.00

The Lowick Church of England Voluntary Controlled First School (Designation as having a Religious Character) Order 2006 No. 2006/1894. - Enabling
power: School Standards and Framework Act 1998, s. 69
(3) (4). - Issued: 24.07.2006. Made: 12.07.2006. Coming
into force: 12.07.2006. Effect: None. Territorial extent &
classification: E. Local. - 2p.: 30 cm. - 978-0-11-074845-0
£3.00

The Monkseaton Community High School (Governing Body Procedures) Order 2006 No. 2006/1078. - Enabling
power: Education Act 2002, s. 2 (1). - Issued: 18.04.2006.
Made: 05.04.2006. Laid: 18.04.2006. Coming into force:
12.05.2006. Effect: None. Territorial extent &
classification: E. General. - 2p.: 30 cm. -
978-0-11-074485-8 £3.00

The Newark and Sherwood College (Dissolution) Order 2006 No. 2006/3160. - Enabling power: Further and
Higher Education Act 1992, s. 27. - Issued: 06.12.2006.
Made: 24.11.2006. Laid: 06.12.2006. Coming into force:
01.01.2007. Effect: None. Territorial extent &
classification: E. General. - 2p.: 30 cm. -
978-0-11-075384-3 £3.00

The Newfield School (Change to School Session Times) Order 2006 No. 2006/3147. - Enabling power: Education
Act 2002, s. 2 (1). - Issued: 04.12.2006. Made: 25.11.2006.
Laid: 04.12.2006. Coming into force: 27.12.2006. Effect:
None. Territorial extent & classification: E. General. - 2p.:
30 cm. - 978-0-11-075381-2 £3.00

The Nobel School (Change to School Session Times) Order 2006 No. 2006/1072. - Enabling power: Education
Act 2002, s. 2 (1). - Issued: 18.04.2006. Made: 05.04.2006.
Laid: 18.04.2006. Coming into force: 12.05.2006. Effect:
None. Territorial extent & classification: E. General. - 2p.:
30 cm. - 978-0-11-074478-0 £3.00

The Office for Standards in Education, Children's Services and Skills (Transitional Provisions) Regulations 2006 No. 2006/2991. - Enabling power:
Education and Inspections Act 2006, ss. 181 (2) (c), 183
(1) (2), sch. 15, para. 7 (1). - Issued: 22.11.2006. Made:
15.11.2006. Laid: 21.11.2006. Coming into force:
12.12.2006. Effect: None. Territorial extent &
classification: E. General. - 4p.: 30 cm. -
978-0-11-075331-7 £3.00

The Orchard Primary School (Designation as having a Religious Character) Order 2006 No. 2006/2946. -
Enabling power: School Standards and Framework Act
1998, s. 69 (3) (4). - Issued: 17.11.2006. Made:
09.11.2006. Coming into force: 09.11.2006. Effect: None.
Territorial extent & classification: E. Local. - 2p.: 30 cm. -
978-0-11-075296-9 £3.00

The Our Lady of Walsingham Catholic Primary School (Designation as having a Religious Character) Order 2006 No. 2006/2947. - Enabling power: School Standards
and Framework Act 1998, s. 69 (3) (4). - Issued:
17.11.2006. Made: 09.11.2006. Coming into force:
09.11.2006. Effect: None. Territorial extent &
classification: E. Local. - 2p.: 30 cm. - 978-0-11-075297-6
£3.00

The People's College, Nottingham (Dissolution) Order 2006 No. 2006/1184. - Enabling power: Further and
Higher Education Act 1992, s. 27. - Issued: 05.05.2006.
Made: 27.04.2006. Laid: 05.05.2006. Coming into force:
01.06.2006. Effect: None. Territorial extent &
classification: E. General. - 2p.: 30 cm. -
978-0-11-074533-6 £3.00

The Sacred Heart RC Primary School (Designation as having a Religious Character) Order 2006 No. 2006/2948. - Enabling power: School Standards and
Framework Act 1998, s. 69 (3) (4). - Issued: 17.11.2006.
Made: 09.11.2006. Coming into force: 09.11.2006. Effect:
None. Territorial extent & classification: E. Local. - 2p.: 30
cm. - 978-0-11-075298-3 £3.00

The Saint Cecilia's, Wandsworth Church of England School (Designation as having a Religious Character) Order 2006 No. 2006/1902. - Enabling power: School
Standards and Framework Act 1998, s. 69 (3) (4). - Issued:
24.07.2006. Made: 12.07.2006. Coming into force:
12.07.2006. Effect: None. Territorial extent &
classification: E. Local. - 2p.: 30 cm. - 978-0-11-074852-8
£3.00

The School Finance (England) Regulations 2006 No. 2006/468. - Enabling power: School Standards and
Framework Act 1998, ss. 45A, 45AA, 47, 48 (1) (2), 138
(7), sch. 14, para. 1 (7) (b). - Issued: 06.03.2006. Made:
23.02.2006. Coming into force: 25.02.2006. In acc.with
reg. 1 (1). Effect: S.I. 2003/3247; 2004/3131; 2005/526
revoked (01.04.2006). Territorial extent & classification:
E. General. - Supersedes draft S.I. (ISBN 0110738985)
issued on 20.01.2006. - 32p.: 30 cm. - 978-0-11-074107-9
£5.50

Education, England

The School Staffing (England) (Amendment) (No.2) Regulations 2006 No. 2006/3197. - Enabling power: School Standards and Framework Act 1998, ss. 72, 138 (7) & Education Act 2002, ss. 35 (4) (5), 36 (4) (5), 210 (7). - Issued: 04.01.2007. Made: 29.11.2006. Laid: 08.12.2006. Coming into force: 01.01.2007. Effect: S.I. 2003/1963 amended. Territorial extent & classification: E. General. - This Statutory Instrument has been printed in substitution of the SI of the same number and ISBN (published 08.12.2006) and is being issued free of charge to all known recipients of the original version. - 8p.: 30 cm. - 978-0-11-075405-5 *£3.00*

The School Staffing (England) (Amendment) Regulations 2006 No. 2006/1067. - Enabling power: School Standards and Framework Act 1998, ss. 72, 138 (7) & Education Act 2002, ss. 35 (4) (5), 36 (4) (5), 210 (7). - Issued: 20.04.2006. Made: 08.04.2006. Laid: 20.04.2006. Coming into force: 12.05.2006. Effect: S.I. 2003/1963 amended. Territorial extent & classification: E. General. - 4p.: 30 cm. - 978-0-11-074488-9 *£3.00*

The Shire Oak CofE Primary School (Designation as having a Religious Character) Order 2006 No. 2006/2971. - Enabling power: School Standards and Framework Act 1998, s. 69 (3) (4). - Issued: 21.11.2006. Made: 09.11.2006. Coming into force: 09.11.2006. Effect: None. Territorial extent & classification: E. Local. - 2p.: 30 cm. - 978-0-11-075315-7 *£3.00*

The St Anne's RC Primary School (Designation as having a Religious Character) Order 2006 No. 2006/2956. - Enabling power: School Standards and Framework Act 1998, s. 69 (3) (4). - Issued: 17.11.2006. Made: 09.11.2006. Coming into force: 09.11.2006. Effect: None. Territorial extent & classification: E. Local. - 2p.: 30 cm. - 978-0-11-075302-7 *£3.00*

The St Benedict's Catholic Primary School (Designation as having a Religious Character) Order 2006 No. 2006/2949. - Enabling power: School Standards and Framework Act 1998, s. 69 (3) (4). - Issued: 17.11.2006. Made: 09.11.2006. Coming into force: 09.11.2006. Effect: None. Territorial extent & classification: E. Local. - 2p.: 30 cm. - 978-0-11-075301-0 *£3.00*

The St Georges VA Church Primary School (Designation as having a Religious Character) Order 2006 No. 2006/1895. - Enabling power: School Standards and Framework Act 1998, s. 69 (3) (4). - Issued: 24.07.2006. Made: 12.07.2006. Coming into force: 12.07.2006. Effect: None. Territorial extent & classification: E. Local. - 2p.: 30 cm. - 978-0-11-074846-7 *£3.00*

The St John the Baptist Roman Catholic Primary School (Designation as having a Religious Character) Order 2006 No. 2006/1893. - Enabling power: School Standards and Framework Act 1998, s. 69 (3) (4). - Issued: 24.07.2006. Made: 12.07.2006. Coming into force: 12.07.2006. Effect: None. Territorial extent & classification: E. Local. - 2p.: 30 cm. - 978-0-11-074844-3 *£3.00*

The St Peter's Church of England Junior and Infant School (Designation as having a Religious Character) Order 2006 No. 2006/2960. - Enabling power: School Standards and Framework Act 1998, s. 69 (3) (4). - Issued: 24.11.2006. Made: 09.11.2006. Coming into force: 09.11.2006. Effect: None. Territorial extent & classification: E. Local. - This Statutory Instrument has been printed in substitution of the SI incorrectly published with the same number and ISBN (entitled The St Theresa ..) and is being issued free of charge to all known recipients of that statutory instrument. - 2p.: 30 cm. - 978-0-11-075303-4 *£3.00*

The St Teresa of Lisieux Catholic Infant School (Designation as having a Religious Character) Order 2006 No. 2006/2977. - Enabling power: School Standards and Framework Act 1998, s. 69 (3) (4). - Issued: 22.11.2006. Made: 09.11.2006. Coming into force: 09.11.2006. Effect: None. Territorial extent & classification: E. Local. - 2p.: 30 cm. - With correction slip correcting the spelling of the name of the school from 'Liseaux' to 'Lisieux'. - 978-0-11-075321-8 *£3.00*

The Student Fees (Amounts) (England) (Amendment) Regulations 2006 No. 2006/2382. - Enabling power: Higher Education Act 2004, ss. 24 (6), 47. - Issued: 12.09.2006. Made: 04.09.2006. Laid: 12.09.2006. Coming into force: 01.09.2007. Effect: S.I. 2004/1932 amended. Territorial extent & classification: E. General. - 2p.: 30 cm. - 978-0-11-075079-8 *£3.00*

The Student Fees (Inflation Index) Regulations 2006 No. 2006/507. - Enabling power: Higher Education Act 2004, ss. 26 (3), 47. - Issued: 07.03.2006. Made: 27.02.2006. Laid: 07.03.2006. Coming into force: 31.03.2006. Effect: None. Territorial extent & classification: E. General. - 2p.: 30 cm. - 978-0-11-074123-9 *£3.00*

The Student Fees (Qualifying Courses and Persons) Regulations 2006 No. 2006/482. - Enabling power: Higher Education Act 2004, ss. 24 (6), 47. - Issued: 07.03.2006. Made: 26.02.2006. Laid: 07.03.2006. Coming into force: 31.03.2006. Effect: S.I. 1999/603 to the extent not already revoked. Territorial extent & classification: E. General. - 4p.: 30 cm. - 978-0-11-074110-9 *£3.00*

The Tauheedul Islam Girls High School (Designation as having a Religious Character) Order 2006 No. 2006/1906. - Enabling power: School Standards and Framework Act 1998, s. 69 (3) (4). - Issued: 24.07.2006. Made: 12.07.2006. Coming into force: 12.07.2006. Effect: None. Territorial extent & classification: E. Local. - 2p.: 30 cm. - 978-0-11-074856-6 *£3.00*

The Trinity CoE VC Primary School (Designation as having a Religious Character) Order 2006 No. 2006/841. - Enabling power: School Standards and Framework Act 1998, s. 69 (3) (4). - Issued: 27.03.2006. Made: 15.03.2006. Coming into force: 15.03.2006. Effect: None. Territorial extent & classification: E. Local. - 2p.: 30 cm. - 978-0-11-074374-5 *£3.00*

The Unity College (Designation as having a Religious Character) Order 2006 No. 2006/840. - Enabling power: School Standards and Framework Act 1998, s. 69 (3) (4). - Issued: 27.03.2006. Made: 15.03.2006. Coming into force: 15.03.2006. Effect: None. Territorial extent & classification: E. Local. - 2p.: 30 cm. - 978-0-11-074373-8 £3.00

The Westminster Church of England Primary School (Designation as having a Religious Character) Order 2006 No. 2006/839. - Enabling power: School Standards and Framework Act 1998, s. 69 (3) (4). - Issued: 27.03.2006. Made: 15.03.2006. Coming into force: 15.03.2006. Effect: None. Territorial extent & classification: E. Local. - 2p.: 30 cm. - 978-0-11-074367-7 £3.00

The Widnes and Runcorn Sixth Form College (Dissolution) Order 2006 No. 2006/1739. - Enabling power: Further and Higher Education Act 1992, s. 27. - Issued: 10.07.2006. Made: 01.07.2006. Laid: 10.07.2006. Coming into force: 01.08.2006. Effect: None. Territorial extent & classification: E. General. - 2p.: 30 cm. - 978-0-11-074788-0 £3.00

The Wimbledon School of Art Higher Education Corporation (Dissolution) Order 2006 No. 2006/1746. - Enabling power: Education Reform Act 1988, s. 128. - Issued: 10.07.2006. Made: 01.07.2006. Laid: 10.07.2006. Coming into force: 01.08.2006. Effect: None. Territorial extent & classification: E. General. - 2p.: 30 cm. - 978-0-11-074794-1 £3.00

The Workers' Educational Association (Designated Institution in Further Education) Order 2006 No. 2006/409. - Enabling power: Further and Higher Education Act 1992, s. 28. - Issued: 03.03.2006. Made: 23.02.2006. Laid: 03.03.2006. Coming into force: 31.03.2006. Effect: None. Territorial extent & classification: E. General. - 2p.: 30 cm. - 978-0-11-074103-1 £3.00

Education, England and Wales

The Education Act 2005 (Commencement No. 2 and Transitional Provisions and Savings) Order 2006 No. 2006/2129 (C.70). - Enabling power: Education Act 2005, ss. 120 (2), 125 (4). Bringing into operation various provisions of the 2005 Act on 01.08.2006 & 01.09.2006. - Issued: 07.08.2006. Made: 31.07.2006. Effect: None. Territorial extent & classification: E/W. General. - 8p.: 30 cm. - 978-0-11-074970-9 £3.00

The Education (Fees and Awards) (Amendment) Regulations 2006 No. 2006/483. - Enabling power: Education (Fees and Awards) Act 1983, ss. 1, 2. - Issued: 07.03.2006. Made: 26.02.2006. Laid: 07.03.2006. Coming into force: 31.03.2006. Effect: S.I. 1997/1972 amended. Territorial extent & classification: E/W. General. - With correction slip dated April 2006. EC note: These regs implement the provisions of Directive 2004/38/EC on the rights of citizens of the Union and their family members to move and reside freely in the territory of the member states. So far as the Directive relates to the charging of fees the Schedule implements the provisions in relation to England and Wales. So far as the Directive relates to discretionary awards the Schedule implements the provisions only in relation to England. - 12p.: 30 cm. - 978-0-11-074111-6 £3.00

The Education (Mandatory Awards) (Amendment) Regulations 2006 No. 2006/930. - Enabling power: Education Act 1962, ss. 1, 4 (2) & Education Act 1973, s. 3 (1) (2). - Issued: 05.04.2006. Made: 27.03.2006. Laid: 05.04.2006. Coming into force: 30.04.2006; 01.09.2006 in accord. with reg. 2. Effect: S.I. 2003/1994; 2005/2083 amended. Territorial extent & classification: E/W. General. - EC note: Implements Directive 2004/38/EC on the rights of citizens of the Union and their family members to move and reside freely in the territory of the member states so far as the Directive relates to mandatory awards. - 12p.: 30 cm. - 978-0-11-074407-0 £3.00

The Education (School Teachers' Pay and Conditions) (No. 2) (Amendment) Order 2006 No. 2006/3171. - Enabling power: Education Act 2002, ss. 122 (1), 123, 124, 210 (7). - Issued: 08.12.2006. Made: 28.11.2006. Laid: 08.12.2006. Coming into force: 01.01.2007. Effect: S.I. 2006/2133 amended. Territorial extent & classification: E/W. General. - Please note that this Statutory Instrument should have contained the following heading: 'This Statutory Instrument has been printed to correct errors and omissions in S.I. 2006/2133 (ISBN 0110749685) and is being issued free of charge to all known recipients of that S.I.'. - 4p.: 30 cm. - 978-0-11-075390-4 £3.00

The Education (School Teachers' Pay and Conditions) (No. 2) Order 2006 No. 2006/2133. - Enabling power: Education Act 2002, ss. 122 (1), 123, 124, 210 (7). - Issued: 07.08.2006. Made: 01.08.2006. Laid: 07.08.2006. Coming into force: 01.09.2006. Effect: S.I. 2005/2212, 3479; 2006/1274 revoked. Territorial extent & classification: E/W. General. - 2p.: 30 cm. - 978-0-11-074968-6 £3.00

The Education (School Teachers' Pay and Conditions) Order 2006 No. 2006/1274. - Enabling power: Education Act 2002, ss. 122 (1), 123, 124, 210 (7). - Issued: 16.05.2006. Made: 09.05.2006. Laid: 11.05.2006. Coming into force: 01.06.2006. Effect: School Teachers' Pay and Conditions Document 2005 (ISBN 0 112711804 which was given legal effect by (S.I. 2005/2212)) amended. Territorial extent & classification: E/W. General. - Revoked by S.I. 2006/2133 (ISBN 0110749685). - 4p.: 30 cm. - 978-0-11-074560-2 £3.00

The Education (Student Loans) (Amendment) (England and Wales) Regulations 2006 No. 2006/929. - Enabling power: Education (Student Loans) Act 1990, s. 1 (1) (2) (7), sch. 1, para. 1 (1). - Issued: 05.04.2006. Made: 27.03.2006. Laid: 05.04.2006. Coming into force: 30.04.2006; 01.08.2006 in accord. with reg. 2. Effect: S.I. 1998/211; 2005/1718; 2006/2119 amended. Territorial extent & classification: E/W. General. - EC note: Implements Directive 2004/38/EC on the rights of citizens of the Union and their family members to move and reside freely in the territory of the member states so far as the Directive relates to student loans. - 12p.: 30 cm. - 978-0-11-074406-3 *£3.00*

The Education (Student Loans) (Repayment) (Amendment) Regulations 2006 No. 2006/2009. - Enabling power: Teaching and Higher Education Act 1998, ss. 22, 42. - Issued: 31.07.2006. Made: 22.07.2006. Laid: 31.07.2006. Coming into force: 01.09.2006. Effect: S.I. 2000/944 amended. Territorial extent & classification: E/W. General. - 8p.: 30 cm. - 978-0-11-074937-2 *£3.00*

The Education (Student Support) (Amendment) Regulations 2006 No. 2006/955. - Enabling power: Teaching and Higher Education Act 1998, ss. 22, 42 (6), 43 (1). - Issued: 06.04.2006. Made: 28.03.2006. Laid: 06.04.2006. Coming into force: 30.04.2006. Effect: S.I. 2005/52; 2006/119 amended. Territorial extent & classification: E/W. General. - EC note: Amends S.I. 2005/52 in order to implement the provisions of Directive 2004/38/EC of the European Parliament and of the Council on the rights of citizens of the Union and their family members to move and reside freely in the territory of the member states so far as the Directive relates to student support. - 20p.: 30 cm. - 978-0-11-074418-6 *£3.50*

The Education (Student Support) Regulations 2006 No. 2006/119. - Enabling power: Teaching and Higher Education Act 1998, ss. 22, 42 (6), 43 (1). - Issued: 07.02.2006. Made: 23.01.2006. Laid: 07.02.2006. Coming into force: 01.03.2006. Effect: S.I. 2005/52, 1341, 2084 revoked with saving (on 01.09.2006). Territorial extent & classification: E/W/NI. General. - EC note: These regs implement the provisions of Directive 2004/38/EC on the rights of citizens of the Union and their family members to move and reside freely in the territory of the member states so far as the Directive relates to student support. - 94p.: 30 cm. - 978-0-11-073936-6 *£13.50*

The Higher Education Act 2004 (Commencement No. 4) Order 2006 No. 2006/51 (C.1). - Enabling power: Higher Education Act 2004, s. 52 (2) (6). Bringing into operation various provisions of the 2004 Act on 14.01.2006, in accord. with art. 2. - Issued: 17.01.2006. Made: 11.01.2006. Effect: None. Territorial extent & classification: E/W. General. - 4p.: 30 cm. - 978-0-11-073900-7 *£3.00*

The Teachers (Compensation for Redundancy and Premature Retirement) (Amendment) Regulations 2006 No. 2006/2216. - Enabling power: Superannuation Act 1972, s. 24, sch. 3, para. 13. - Issued: 21.08.2006. Made: 09.08.2006. Laid: 21.08.2006. Coming into force: 01.10.2006. Effect: S.I. 1997/311 amended. Territorial extent & classification: E/W. General. - 2p.: 30 cm. - 978-0-11-075013-2 *£3.00*

The Teachers' Pensions etc. (Reform Amendments) Regulations 2006 No. 2006/3122. - Enabling power: Superannuation Act 1972, ss. 9, 12, 24, sch. 3. - Issued: 07.12.2006. Made: 22.11.2006. Laid: 07.12.2006. Coming into force: 01.01.2007. Effect: S.I.1994/2924; 1997/311, 3001 amended. Territorial extent & classification: E/W. General. - With correction slip dated January 2007. - 56p.: 30 cm. - 978-0-11-075365-2 *£9.00*

The Teachers' Pensions (Miscellaneous Amendments) (No. 2) Regulations 2006 No. 2006/2214. - Enabling power: Superannuation Act 1972, ss. 9, 12, sch. 3. - Issued: 21.08.2006. Made: 09.08.2006. Laid: 21.08.2006. Coming into force: 01.10.2006. Effect: S.I. 1994/2924; 1997/3001 amended. Territorial extent & classification: E/W. General. - 8p.: 30 cm. - 978-0-11-075014-9 *£3.00*

The Teachers' Pensions (Miscellaneous Amendments) Regulations 2006 No. 2006/736. - Enabling power: Superannuation Act 1972, ss. 9, 12, sch. 3. - Issued: 21.03.2006. Made: 13.03.2006. Laid: 16.03.2006. Coming into force: 06.04.2006. Effect: S.I. 1994/2924; 1997/3001 amended. Territorial extent & classification: E/W. General. - 8p.: 30 cm. - 978-0-11-074305-9 *£3.00*

Education, Northern Ireland

The Education (Student Support) Regulations 2006 No. 2006/119. - Enabling power: Teaching and Higher Education Act 1998, ss. 22, 42 (6), 43 (1). - Issued: 07.02.2006. Made: 23.01.2006. Laid: 07.02.2006. Coming into force: 01.03.2006. Effect: S.I. 2005/52, 1341, 2084 revoked with saving (on 01.09.2006). Territorial extent & classification: E/W/NI. General. - EC note: These regs implement the provisions of Directive 2004/38/EC on the rights of citizens of the Union and their family members to move and reside freely in the territory of the member states so far as the Directive relates to student support. - 94p.: 30 cm. - 978-0-11-073936-6 *£13.50*

Education, Wales

The Anti-social Behaviour Act 2003 (Commencement No. 5) (Wales) Order 2006 No. 2006/1278 (W.123) (C.41). - Enabling power: Anti-social Behaviour Act 2003, s. 93 (2) (b). Bringing into operation various provisions of the 2003 Act on 11.05.2006 in accord. with art. 2. - Issued: 17.05.2006. Made: 10.05.2006. Effect: None. Territorial extent & classification: W. General. - In English and Welsh. Welsh title: Gorchymyn Deddf Ymddygiad Gwrthgymdeithasol 2003 (Cychwyn Rhif 5) (Cymru) 2006. - 8p.: 30 cm. - 978-0-11-091334-6 *£3.00*

The Assembly Learning Grants and Loans (Higher Education) (Wales) (Amendment) Regulations 2006 No. 2006/1863 (W.196). - Enabling power: Teaching and Higher Education Act 1998, ss. 22, 42 (6), 43 (1). - Issued: 19.07.2006. Made: 12.07.2006. Coming into force: 14.07.2006. Effect: S.I. 2006/126 (W.19) amended. Territorial extent & classification: W. General. - In English and Welsh. Welsh title: Rheoliadau Grantiau a Benthyciadau Dysgu y Cynulliad (Addysg Uwch) (Cymru) (Diwygio) 2006. - 28p.: 30 cm. - 978-0-11-091388-9 £4.50

The Assembly Learning Grants and Loans (Higher Education) (Wales) Regulations 2006 No. 2006/126 (W.19). - Enabling power: Teaching and Higher Education Act 1998, ss. 22, 42 (6), 43 (1). - Issued: 02.02.2006. Made: 24.01.2006. Coming into force: 01.03.2006. Effect: S.I. 2005/52, 1341, 2084 amended in relation to Wales. Territorial extent & classification: W. General. - In English and Welsh. Welsh title: Rheoliadau Grantiau a Benthyciadau Dysgu y Cynulliad (Addysg Uwch) (Cymru) 2006. - 109p.: 30 cm. - 978-0-11-091256-1 £15.50

The Assembly Learning Grants (European Institutions) (Wales) Regulations 2006 No. 2006/1794 (W.189). - Enabling power: Teaching and Higher Education Act 1998, ss. 22, 42 (6), 43 (1). - Issued: 13.07.2006. Made: 05.07.2006. Coming into force: 07.07.2006. Effect: S.I. 2000/2197; 2001/563, 2892 revoked in relation to Wales. Territorial extent & classification: W. General. - In English and Welsh. Welsh title: Rheoliadua Grantiau Dysgu y Cynulliad (Sefydliadau Ewropeaidd) (Cymru) 2006. - 52p.: 30 cm. - 978-0-11-091384-1 £9.00

The Education Act 2002 (Commencement No. 8) (Wales) Order 2006 No. 2006/172 (W.23) (C.2). - Enabling power: Education Act 2002, s. 216 (4) (b) (5). Bringing into force various provisions of the 2002 Act on 01.02.2006. & 01.09.2006. - Issued: 06.02.2006. Made: 31.01.2006. Effect: None. Territorial extent & classification: W. General. - With two correction slips. - In English and Welsh. Welsh title: Gorchymyn Deddf Addysg 2002 (Cychwyn Rhif 8) (Cymru) 2006. - 12p.: 30 cm. - 978-0-11-091268-4 £3.00

The Education Act 2002 (Commencement No. 9 and Transitional Provisions) (Wales) Order 2006 No. 2006/879 (W.84)(C.21). - Enabling power: Education Act 2002, s. 216 (4) (b) (5). Bringing into force various provisions of the 2002 Act on 01.04.2006. - Issued: 29.03.2006. Made: 21.03.2006. Effect: None. Territorial extent & classification: W. General. - In English and Welsh. Welsh title: Gorchymyn Deddf Addysg 2002 (Cychwyn Rhif 9 a Darpariaethau Trosianol) (Cymru) 2006. - 16p.: 30 cm. - 978-0-11-091303-2 £3.00

The Education Act 2002 (Commencement No. 10 and Transitional Provisions) (Wales) Order 2006 No. 2006/1336 (W.129) (C.44). - Enabling power: Education Act 2002, s. 216 (4) (b) (5). Bringing into force various provisions of the 2002 Act on 31.05.2006. - Issued: 09.06.2006. Made: 16.05.2006. Effect: None. Territorial extent & classification: W. General. - In English and Welsh. Welsh title: Gorchymyn Deddf Addysg 2002 (Cychwyn Rhif 10 a Darpariaethau Trosiannol) (Cymru) 2006. - 12p.: 30 cm. - 978-0-11-091347-6 £3.00

The Education Act 2002 (Transitional Provisions and Consequential Amendments) (Wales) Regulations 2006 No. 2006/173 (W.24). - Enabling power: Education Act 2002, s. 214. - Issued: 06.02.2006 Made: 31.01.2006. Coming into force: 01.02.2006. Effect: 1998 c. 31 amended in relation to Wales & S.I. 1999/1671; 2001/2678 (W.219); 2004/1576 amended & 1999/1064 revoked in relation to Wales. Territorial extent & classification: W. General. - With correction slip, dated April 2006. - In English and Welsh. Welsh title: Rheoliadau Deddf Addysg 2002 (Darpariaethau Trosiannol a Diwygiadau Canlyniadol) (Cymru) 2006. - 8p.: 30 cm. - 978-0-11-091266-0 £3.00

The Education Act 2005 (Commencement No. 1 and Transitional Provisions) (Wales) Order 2006 No. 2006/1338 (W.130) (C.45). - Enabling power: Education Act 2005, ss. 120 (2), 125 (4). Bringing into force various provisions of the 2005 Act on 01.09.2006 for Wales only and 01.04.2007 for England and Wales in accord. with regs. 3 to 5. - Issued: 23.05.2006. Made: 16.05.2006. Effect: None. Territorial extent & classification: W [For technical reasons those listed in Schedules 2 and 3 are brought into force in relation to England and Wales, although, for practical purposes, they have no application in England]. General. - In English and Welsh. Welsh title: Gorchymyn Deddf Addysg 2005 (Cychwyn Rhif 1 a Darpariaethau Trosiannol) (Cymru) 2006. - 16p.: 30 cm. - 978-0-11-091338-4 £3.00

The Education (Assisted Places) (Amendment) (Wales) Regulations 2006 No. 2006/3097 (W.281). - Enabling power: Education (Schools) Act 1997, s. 3 (1) (2) (5) (9). - Issued: 04.12.2006. Made: 21.11.2006. Coming into force: 23.11.2006. Effect: S.I. 1997/1968 (in relation to Wales); 2005/2838 (W. 202) amended. Territorial extent & classification: W. General. - In English and Welsh. Welsh title: Rheoliadau Addysg (Lleoedd a Gynorthwyir) (Diwygio) (Cymru) 2006. - 8p.: 30 cm. - 978-0-11-091462-6 £3.00

The Education (Assisted Places) (Incidental Expenses) (Amendment) (Wales) Regulations 2006 No. 2006/3098 (W.282). - Enabling power: Education (Schools) Act 1997, s. 3 (1) (3) (4) (5) (9). - Issued: 04.12.2006. Made: 21.11.2006. Coming into force: 23.11.2006. Effect: S.I. 1997/1969 (in relation to Wales); 2005/2837 (W. 201) amended. Territorial extent & classification: W. General. - In English and Welsh. Welsh title: Rheoliadau Addysg (Lleoedd a Gynorthwyir) (Mân Dreuliau) (Diwygio) (Cymru) 2006. - 8p.: 30 cm. - 978-0-11-091461-9 £3.00

The Education (Determination of Admission Arrangements) (Wales) Regulations 2006 No. 2006/174 (W.25). - Enabling power: School Standards and Framework Act 1998, ss. 89 (2) (2A) (8) (8A), 89A (3), 138 (7), 144 (1). - Issued: 06.02.2006. Made: 31.01.2006. Coming into force: 01.02.2006. Effect: S.I. 1999/126 revoked in relation to Wales. Territorial extent & classification. W. General. - With correction slip, dated April 2006. - In English and Welsh. Welsh title: Rheoliadau Addysg (Penderfynu Trefniadau Derbyn) (Cymru) 2006. - 12p.: 30 cm. - 978-0-11-091265-3 £3.00

The Education (Fees and Awards) (Amendment) (Wales) Regulations 2006 No. 2006/1795 (W.190). - Enabling power: Education (Fees and Awards) Act 1983, s. 2. - Issued: 17.07.2006. Made: 05.07.2006. Coming into force: 07.07.2006. Effect: S.I. 1997/1972 amended in relation to Wales. Territorial extent & classification: W. General. - In English and Welsh. Welsh title: Rheoliadau Addysg (Ffioedd a Dyfarniadau) (Diwygio) (Cymru) 2006. - 8p.: 30 cm. - 978-0-11-091383-4 £3.00

The Education (Information About Individual Pupils) (Wales) (Amendment) Regulations 2006 No. 2006/30 (W.4). - Enabling power: Education Act 1996, ss. 537A (1) (2) (4), 569 (4) (5). - Issued: 13.01.2006. Made: 10.01.2006. Coming into force: 11.01.2006. Effect: S.I. 2003/3237 (W.137) amended. Territorial extent & classification: W. General. - In English and Welsh. Welsh title: Rheoliadau Addysg (Gwybodaeth am Ddisgyblion Unigol) (Cymru) (Diwygio) 2006. - 4p.: 30 cm. - 978-0-11-091252-3 £3.00

The Education (Inspectors of Education and Training in Wales) Order 2006 No. 2006/2660. - Enabling power: Education Act 2005, s. 19 (2). - Issued: 16.10.2006. Made: 10.10.2006. Coming into force: 11.10.2006. Effect: None. Territorial extent & classification: W. General. - 4p.: 30 cm. - 978-0-11-075173-3 £3.00

The Education (Modification of Enactments Relating to Employment) (Wales) Order 2006 No. 2006/1073. - Enabling power: School Standards and Framework Act 1998, ss. 81 (1), 138 (7). - Issued: 18.04.2006. Made: 05.04.2006. Laid: 18.04.2006. Coming into force: 12.05.2006. Effect: 1975 c. 65; 1976 c. 74; 1992 c. 52; 1995 c. 50; 1996 c. 18; 2002 c.22 modified in relation to Wales & S.I. 1999/2256 revoked in relation to Wales. Territorial extent & classification: W. General. - With correction slip dated April 2006. - 8p.: 30 cm. - 978-0-11-074479-7 £3.00

The Education (National Curriculum for Wales) (Disapplication of Science at Key Stage 4) Regulations 2006 No. 2006/1335 (W.128). - Enabling power: Education Act 2002, ss. 112, 210 (7). - Issued: 23.05.2006. Made: 16.05.2006. Coming into force: 01.08.2006. Effect: None. Territorial extent & classification: W. General. - In English and Welsh. Welsh title: Rheoliadau Addysg (Cwricwlwm Cenedlaethol Cymru) (Datgymhwyso Gwyddoniaeth yng Nghyfnod Allweddol 4) 2006. - 4p.: 30 cm. - 978-0-11-091341-4 £3.00

The Education (Objections to Admission Arrangements) (Wales) Regulations 2006 No. 2006/176 (W.27). - Enabling power: School Standards and Framework Act 1998, ss. 90, 138 (7). - Issued: 06.02.2006. Made: 31.01.2006. Coming into force: 01.02.2006. Effect: S.I. 1999/125 revoked in relation to Wales. Territorial extent & classification. W. General. - In English and Welsh. Welsh title: Rheoliadau Addysg (Gwrthwynebiadau i Drefniadau Derbyn) (Cymru) 2006. - 12p.: 30 cm. - 978-0-11-091263-9 £3.00

The Education (Parenting Orders) (Wales) Regulations 2006 No. 2006/1277 (W.122). - Enabling power: Anti-social Behaviour Act 2003, ss. 20 (1), 21 (4), 94 (2). - Issued: 17.05.2006. Made: 10.05.2006. Coming into force: 11.05.2006. Effect: None. Territorial extent & classification: W. General. - In English and Welsh. Welsh title: Rheoliadau Addysg (Gorchmynion Rhianta) (Cymru) 2006. - 4p.: 30 cm. - 978-0-11-091336-0 £3.00

The Education (School Day and School Year) (Wales) (Amendment) Regulations 2006 No. 2006/1262 (W.119). - Enabling power: Education Act 1996, ss. 551, 569 (4) (5). - Issued: 09.05.2006. Made: 03.05.2006. Coming into force: 01.08.2006. Effect: S.I. 2003/3231 (W.311) amended. Territorial extent & classification: W. General. - In English and Welsh. Welsh title: Rheoliadau Addysg (Y Diwrnod Ysgol a'r Flwyddyn Ysgol) (Cymru) (Diwygio) 2006. - 4p.: 30 cm. - 978-0-11-091332-2 £3.00

The Education (School Inspection) (Wales) Regulations 2006 No. 2006/1714 (W.176). - Enabling power: Education Act 2005, ss. 25 (3) (b), 28 (1) (8), 36 (2), 38 (4), 39 (2) (3) (5) (7) (b), 40 (3), 41 (4), 42 (2) (a) (3) (c) (4) (5), 50 (2) (4) (8), 52 (5) (b), 120 (2), 124 (1) (3), sch. 4, para. 6, sch. 6, para. 2 (1) (2) (4), 3 (1) (2) (3). - Issued: 07.07.2006. Made: 27.06.2006. Coming into force: 01.09.2006. Effect: S.I. 2005/2911 (W.208) amended & S.I. 1998/1866; 1999/1440; 2004/784 (W.81) revoked & S.I. 1992/2025 revoked in relation to Wales. Territorial extent & classification. W. General. - In English and Welsh. Welsh title: Rheoliadau Addysg (Arolygu Ysgolion) (Cymru) 2006. - 16p.: 30 cm. - 978-0-11-091375-9 £3.00

The Education (School Performance and Unauthorised Absence Targets) (Wales) Amendment Regulations 2006 No. 2006/125 (W.18). - Enabling power: School Standards and Framework Act 1998, ss. 63, 138 (7) (8). - Issued: 31.01.2006. Made: 24.01.2006. Coming into force: 01.02.2006. Effect: S.I. 1999/1811 amended. Territorial extent & classification: W. General. - In English & Welsh. Welsh title: Rheoliadau Addysg (Perfformiad Ysgol a Thargedau Absenolddeb heb Awdurdod) (Cymru) (Diwygio) 2006. - 4p.: 30 cm. - 978-0-11-091258-5 £3.00

The Education (Variation of Admission Arrangements) (Wales) Regulations 2006 No. 2006/177 (W.28). - Enabling power: School Standards and Framework Act 1998, ss. 89 (8) (e) (f), 138 (7). - Issued: 06.02.2006. Made: 31.01.2006. Coming into force: 01.02.2006. Effect: None. Territorial extent & classification. W. General. - With correction slip, dated April 2006. - In English and Welsh. Welsh title: Rheoliadau Addysg (Amrywio Trefniadau Derbyn) (Cymru) 2006. - 4p.: 30 cm. - 978-0-11-091267-7 £3.00

The General Teaching Council for Wales (Additional Functions) (Amendment) Order 2006 No. 2006/1341 (W.132). - Enabling power: Teaching and Higher Education Act 1998, ss. 7 (1) (4), 42 (6) (7). - Issued: 09.06.2006. Made: 16.05.2006. Coming into force: 31.05.2006. Effect: S.I. 2000/1941 (W.139) amended. Territorial extent & classification: W. General. - In English and Welsh. Welsh title: Gorchymyn Cyngor Addysgu Cyffredinol Cymru (Swyddogaethau Ychwanegol) (Diwygio) 2006. - 4p.: 30 cm. - 978-0-11-091348-3 £3.00

The General Teaching Council for Wales (Functions) (Amendment) Regulations 2006 No. 2006/1343 (W.133). - Enabling power: Teaching and Higher Education Act 1998, ss. 3 (3D), 4 (2) (ba) (d), 4A, 14 (3), 42 (6) (7). - Issued: 19.06.2006. Made: 16.05.2006. Coming into force: 31.05.2006. Effect: S.I. 2000/1979 (W.140) amended. Territorial extent & classification: W. General. - In English and Welsh. Welsh title: Rheoliadau Cyngor Addysgu Cyffredinol Cymru (Swyddogaethau) (Diwygio) 2006. - 8p.: 30 cm. - 978-0-11-091350-6 £3.00

The Government of Further Education Corporations (Revocation) (Wales) Regulations 2006 No. 2006/621 (W.70). - Enabling power: Further and Higher Education Act 1992, ss. 21 (1). - Issued: 14.03.2006. Made: 07.03.2006. Coming into force: 06.03.2006. Effect: S.I. 1994/1450 revoked & S.I. 1992/1957, 1963 revoked in relation to Wales. Territorial extent & classification: W. General. - In English and Welsh. - Welsh title: Rheoliadau Llywodraethu Corfforaethau Addysg Bellach (Dirymu) (Cymru) 2006. - 4p.: 30 cm. - 978-0-11-091294-3 £3.00

The Higher Education Act 2004 (Commencement No. 2 and Transitional Provision) (Wales) (Amendment) Order 2006 No. 2006/1660 (W.159) (C.56). - Enabling power: Higher Education Act 2004, ss. 47 (5), 52 (3) (4) (6). - Issued: 30.06.2006. Made: 21.06.2006. Coming into force: 21.06.2006. Effect: S.I. 2005/1833 (W.149) (C.79) amended. Territorial extent & classification: W. General. - In English and Welsh. Welsh title: Gorchymyn Deddf Addysg Uwch 2004 (Cychwyn Rhif 2 a Darpariaeth Drosiannol) (Cymru) (Diwygio) 2006. - 4p.: 30 cm. - 978-0-11-091361-2 £3.00

The Inspection of the Careers and Related Services (Wales) Regulations 2006 No. 2006/3103 (W.286). - Enabling power: Education Act 2005, ss. 55 (4), 56 (3), 57 (7) (9) (10), 120 (2). - Issued: 30.11.2006. Made: 21.11.2006. Coming into force: 01.04.2007. Effect: None. Territorial extent & classification: W. General. - In English and Welsh. Welsh title: Rheoliadau Arolygu'r Gwasanaeth Gyrfaoedd a Gwasanaethau Cysylltiedig (Cymru) 2006. - 8p.: 30 cm. - 978-0-11-091456-5 £3.00

The Merthyr Tydfil College (Dissolution) Order 2006 No. 2006/1420 (W.141). - Enabling power: Further and Higher Education Act 1992, s. 27. - Made: 17.05.2006. Coming into force: 18.05.2006. Effect: None. Territorial extent & classification: W. Local. - In English and Welsh *Unpublished*

The New School (Admissions) (Wales) Regulations 2006 No. 2006/175 (W.26). - Enabling power: School Standards and Framework Act 1998, ss. 72, 138 (7). - Issued: 06.02.2006. Made: 31.01.2006. Coming into force: 01.02.2006. Effect: S.I. 1999/2800 (W.14) revoked with saving. Territorial extent & classification. W. General. - In English and Welsh. Welsh title: Rheoliadau Ysgolion Newydd (Derbyniadau) (Cymru) 2006. - 12p.: 30 cm. - 978-0-11-091264-6 £3.00

The Single Education Plan (Wales) Regulations 2006 No. 2006/877 (W.82). - Enabling power: Education Act 1996, ss. 29 (3) (5), 569 & Children Act 2004, ss. 26, 66 (1). - Issued: 30.03.2006. Made: 21.03.2006. Coming into force: 01.04.2006. Effect: S.I. 2003/893 (W.113) amended & S.I. 1998/644; 2001/606 (W.29); 2002/1187 (W.135); 2003/1732 (W.190); 2005/434 (W.45) revoked. Territorial extent & classification: W. General. - In English and Welsh. Welsh title: Rheoliadau'r Cynllun Addysg Sengl (Cymru) 2006. - 20p.: 30 cm. - 978-0-11-091305-6 £3.50

The Staffing of Maintained Schools (Wales) Regulations 2006 No. 2006/873 (W.81). - Enabling power: School Standards and Framework Act 1998, ss. 72, 138 (7) & Education Act 2002, ss. 19 (3), 34 (5), 35 (4) (5), 36 (4) (5), 210 (7). - Issued: 31.03.2006. Made: 21.03.2006. Coming into force: In accord. with reg. 1 (1). Effect: S.I. 1999/2243 (W. 3), 2817 (W. 18); 2005/2914 (W. 211) amended & S.I. 1999/2802 (W. 15) revoked in relation to Wales (01.04.2006). Territorial extent & classification: W. General. - With correction slip dated May 2006. - In English and Welsh. Welsh title: Rheoliadau Staffio Ysgolion a Gynhelir (Cymru) 2006. - 32p.: 30 cm. - 978-0-11-091306-3 £5.50

The Supply of Student Support Information to Governing Bodies (Wales) Regulations 2006 No. 2006/2828 (W.250). - Enabling power: Higher Education Act 2004, ss. 45, 47 (5). - Issued: 01.11.2006. Made: 24.10.2006. Coming into force: 27.10.2006. Effect: None. Territorial extent & classification: W. General. - In English and Welsh. Welsh title: Rheoliadau Cyflenwi Gwybodaeth Ar Gyfer Cymorth I Fyfyrwyr I Gyrff Llywodraethu (Cymru) 2006. - 8p.: 30 cm. - 978-0-11-091418-3 £3.00

The Transition from Primary to Secondary School (Wales) Regulations 2006 No. 2006/520 (W.64). - Enabling power: Education Act 2002, ss. 198 (3), 210 (7). - Issued: 09.03.2006 Made: 28.02.2006. Coming into force: 01.09.2006. Effect: None. Territorial extent & classification: W. General. - In English and Welsh. Welsh title: Rheoliadau Pontio Rhwng yr Ysgol Gynradd a'r Ysgol Uwchradd) (Cymru) 2006. - 12p.: 30 cm. - 978-0-11-091290-5 £3.00

The Youth and Community Work Education and Training (Inspection) Wales Regulations 2006 No. 2006/2804 (W.243). - Enabling power: Learning and Skills Act 2000, ss. 75 (1) (e), 152 (5). - Issued: 26.10.2006. Made: 17.10.2006. Coming into force: 23.10.2006. Effect: None. Territorial extent & classification: W. General. - In English and Welsh. Welsh title: Rheoliadau Addysg a Hyfforddiant mewn Gwaith Ieuenctid a Chymunedol (Arolygu) Cymru 2006. - 4p.: 30 cm. - 978-0-11-091409-1 £3.00

Electoral Commission

The Electoral Administration Act 2006 (Commencement No. 1 and Transitional Provisions) (Amendment) Order 2006 No. 2006/2268 (C.77). - Enabling power: Electoral Administration Act 2006, s. 77 (2) (3) (4). - Issued: 25.08.2006. Made: 17.08.2006. Coming into force: 25.08.2006. Effect: S.I. 2006/1972 (C.67) amended. Territorial extent & classification: E/W/S. General. - This Statutory Instrument has been made in consequence of a defect in SI 2006/1972 (C. 67) (ISBN 0110749065) and is being issued free of charge to all known recipients of that Statutory Instrument. - 2p.: 30 cm. - 978-0-11-075033-0 £3.00

The Electoral Administration Act 2006 (Commencement No. 1 and Transitional Provisions) Order 2006 No. 2006/1972 (C.67). - Enabling power: Electoral Administration Act 2006, s. 77 (2) (3) (4). Bringing into operation various provisions of the 2006 Act on 11.09.2006, subject to transitional provisions in sch. 2. - Issued: 26.07.2006. Made: 20.07.2006. Effect: None. Territorial extent & classification: E/W/S. General. - 8p.: 30 cm. - 978-0-11-074906-8 £3.00

Electricity

The Electricity Act 1989 (Exemption from the Requirement for an Interconnector Licence) Order 2006 No. 2006/2002. - Enabling power: Electricity Act 1989, s. 5. - Issued: 31.07.2006. Made: 21.07.2006. Laid: 24.07.2006. Coming into force: 14.08.2006. Effect: None. Territorial extent & classification: E/W/S. General. - 4p.: 30 cm. - 978-0-11-074930-3 £3.00

The Electricity and Gas Appeals (Modification of Time Limits) Order 2006 No. 2006/1519. - Enabling power: Energy Act 2004, sch. 22, para. 14. - Issued: 22.06.2006. Made: 12.06.2006. Laid: 15.06.2006. Coming into force: 27.06.2006. Effect: 2004 c.20 amended. Territorial extent & classification: E/W/S. General. - 2p.: 30 cm. - 978-0-11-074689-0 £3.00

The Electricity (Prepayment Meter) Regulations 2006 No. 2006/2010. - Enabling power: Electricity Act 1989, s. 60, sch. 7, para. 12. - Issued: 01.08.2006. Made: 23.07.2006. Coming into force: 01.09.2006. Effect: None. Territorial extent & classification: E/W/S. General. - 4p.: 30 cm. - 978-0-11-074934-1 £3.00

The Electricity Safety, Quality and Continuity (Amendment) Regulations 2006 No. 2006/1521. - Enabling power: Electricity Act 1989, ss. 29, 30 (3) (3A), 60. - Issued: 16.06.2006. Made: 13.06.2006. Laid: 15.06.2006. Coming into force: 01.10.2006. Effect: S.I. 2002/2665 amended. Territorial extent & classification: E/W/S. General. - 4p.: 30 cm. - 978-0-11-074691-3 £3.00

The Energy Act 2004 (Commencement No. 7) Order 2006 No. 2006/1964 (C.66). - Enabling power: Energy Act 2004, s. 198 (2). Bringing into operation various provisions of the 2004 Act on 14.08.2006. - Issued: 28.07.2006. Made: 21.07.2006. Effect: None. Territorial extent & classification: E/W/S. General. - 4p.: 30 cm. - 978-0-11-074914-3 £3.00

Electricity, England and Wales

The Electricity Act 1989 (Exemption from the Requirement for a Generation Licence) (England and Wales) Order 2006 No. 2006/2978. - Enabling power: Electricity Act 1989, s. 5. - Issued: 21.11.2006. Made: 14.11.2006. Laid: 16.11.2006. Coming into force: 08.12.2006. Effect: None. Territorial extent & classification: E/W. General. - 4p.: 30 cm. - 978-0-11-075322-5 £3.00

The Electricity from Non-Fossil Fuel Sources Arrangements (England and Wales) Order 2006 No. 2006/2388. - Enabling power: Utilities Act 2000, s. 67 (1) (c). - Issued: 14.09.2006. Made: 05.09.2006. Laid: 08.09.2006. Coming into force: 01.10.2006. Effect: None. Territorial extent & classification: E/W. General. - 4p.: 30 cm. - 978-0-11-075086-6 £3.00

The Electricity (Offshore Generating Stations) (Applications for Consent) Regulations 2006 No. 2006/2064. - Enabling power: Electricity Act 1989, ss. 36 (8), 60 (3), sch. 8, paras 1 (3), 2 (3), 3 (1), 7A & Energy Act 2004, s. 188. - Issued: 03.08.2006. Made: 23.07.2006. Laid: 27.07.2006. Coming into force: 01.10.2006. Effect: S.I. 1990/455 disapplied. Territorial extent & classification: E/W. General. - 8p.: 30 cm. - 978-0-11-074945-7 £3.00

The Renewables Obligation Order 2006 No. 2006/1004. - Enabling power: Electricity Act 1989, ss. 32 to 32C. - Issued: 07.04.2006. Made: 30.03.2006. Coming into force: 01.04.2006. Effect: S.I. 2005/926 revoked (with savings). Territorial extent & classification: E/W. General. - 40p.: 30 cm. - 978-0-11-074449-0 £6.50

Electromagnetic compatibility

The Electromagnetic Compatibility (Amendment) Regulations 2006 No. 2006/1449. - Enabling power: European Communities Act 1972, s. 2 (2). - Issued: 14.06.2006. Made: 26.05.2006. Laid: 05.06.2006. Coming into force: 28.06.2006. Effect: S.I. 2005/281 amended. Territorial extent & classification: E/W/S/NI. General. - This Statutory Instrument has been made in consequence of a defect in S.I. 2005/281 (ISBN 0110722477) and is being issued free of charge to all known recipients of that statutory instrument. EC note: In these Regs, Reg. 2 amends Reg. 29 of the 2005 Regulations to provide that only radio equipment and telecommunications terminal equipment covered by Directive 1995/5/EC on radio equipment and telecommunications terminal equipment and the mutual recognition of their conformity is excluded from the application of the 2005 Regulations. - 4p.: 30 cm. - 978-0-11-074638-8 £3.00

The Electromagnetic Compatibility Regulations 2006 No. 2006/3418. - Enabling power: European Communities Act 1972, s. 2 (2). - Issued: 28.12.2006. Made: 18.12.2006. Laid: 20.12.2006. Coming into force: 20.01.2007 for regs 1, 3, 24, 25, sch. 5; 20.07.2007 for remaining purposes. Effect: S.I. 1952/2023; 1963/1895; 1971/1675; 1978/1267, 1268; 1982/635 cease to have effect in relation to the extent that they impose electromagnetic compatibility requirements & S.I. 2004/693 amended & S.I. 2005/281 revoked (20.07.2007). Territorial extent & classification: E/W/S/NI. General. - EC note: These Regulations implement Directive 2004/108/EC on the approximation of the laws of member States relating to electromagnetic compatibility and repealing Directive 89/336/EEC. - 36p.: 30 cm. - 978-0-11-075564-9 £6.50

Electronic communications

The Broadcasting Digital Terrestrial Sound (Technical Service) Order 2006 No. 2006/2793. - Enabling power: Broadcasting Act 1996, s. 63 (3) (b). - Issued: 25.10.2006. Made: 18.10.2006. Laid: 19.10.2006. Coming into force: 13.11.2006. Effect: S.I. 1998/685 amended. Territorial extent & classification: E/W/S/NI/Jersey/Guernsey. General. - 2p.: 30 cm. - 978-0-11-075201-3 £3.00

The Communications Act 2003 (Maximum Penalty for Persistent Misuse of Network or Service) Order 2006 No. 2006/1032. - Enabling power: Communications Act 2003, s. 130 (9). - Issued: 10.04.2006. Made: 02.04.2006. Coming into force: 06.04.2006. Effect: 2003 c. 21 amended. Territorial extent & classification: E/W/S/NI. General. - Supersedes draft S.I. (ISBN 0110741676) issued on 10.03.2006. - 2p.: 30 cm. - 978-0-11-074461-2 £3.00

The Communications (Television Licensing) (Amendment) Regulations 2006 No. 2006/619. - Enabling power: Wireless Telegraphy Act 1967, s. 6 (1) & Communications Act 2003, ss. 365 (1) (4), 402 (3). - Issued: 14.03.2006. Made: 07.03.2006. Laid: 08.03.2006. Coming into force: 01.04.2006. Effect: S.I. 2004/692 amended. Territorial extent & classification: UK. General. - 12p.: 30 cm. - 978-0-11-074194-9 £3.00

The Housing Benefit and Council Tax Benefit (Electronic Communications) Order 2006 No. 2006/2968. - Enabling power: Electronic Communications Act 2000, ss. 8, 9. - Issued: 20.11.2006. Made: 14.11.2006. Laid: 20.11.2006. Coming into force: 20.12.2006. Effect: S.I. 2006/213, 214, 215, 216 amended. Territorial extent & classification: E/W/S. General. - 8p.: 30 cm. - 978-0-11-075308-9 £3.00

The Television Licensable Content Services Order 2006 No. 2006/2131. - Enabling power: Broadcasting Act 1996, s. 1 (5) and Communications Act 2003, ss. 234, 402 (3). - Issued: 08.08.2006. Made: 24.07.2006. Coming into force: 25.07.2006. Effect: 1996 c. 55; 2003 c. 21 amended. Territorial extent & classification: E/W/S/NI/Jersey/Guernsey. General. - 4p.: 30 cm. - 978-0-11-074980-8 £3.00

Tobacco Advertising and Promotion Act 2002 etc. (Amendment) Regulations 2006 No. 2006/2369. - Enabling power: European Communities Act 1972, s. 2 (2). - Issued: 07.09.2006. Made: 24.08.2006. Laid: 07.09.2006. Coming into force: 28.09.2006. Effect: 2002 c.36 amended & S.I. 2003/115 amended. Territorial extent & classification: E/W/S/NI. General. - EC note: Gives effect to Directive 2003/33/EC on the approximation of the laws, regulations and administrative provisions of the Member States relating to the advertising and sponsorship of tobacco products. - 8p.: 30 cm. - 978-0-11-075067-5 £3.00

The Wireless Telegraphy (Exemption) (Amendment) Regulations 2006 No. 2006/2994. - Enabling power: Wireless Telegraphy Act 1949, s. 1 (1). - Issued: 24.11.2006. Made: 16.11.2006. Coming into force: 08.12.2006. Effect: S.I. 2003/74 amended. Territorial extent & classification: E/W/S/NI/IoM/CI. General. - 8p.: 30 cm. - 978-0-11-075332-4 £3.00

The Wireless Telegraphy (Guernsey) Order 2006 No. 2006/3325. - Enabling power: Wireless Telegraphy Act 1967, s. 15 (6); Broadcasting Act 1990, s. 204 (6); Intelligence Services Act 1994, s. 12 (4), Broadcasting Act 1996, s. 150 (4); Communications Act 2003, s. 411 (6) and Wireless Telegraphy Act 2006, ss. 118 (3) (6), 119 (3), sch. 8, para. 24. - Issued: 21.12.2006. Made: 14.12.2006. Coming into force: 08.02.2007. Effect: 2006 c.36 modified; S.I. 1994/1064; 2003/3195 modified and S.I. 1952/1900; 1967/1279; 1997/284 revoked as they relate to Guernsey; S.I. 1967/1274; 1998/1511 revoked. Territorial extent & classification: Guernsey. General. - 12p.: 30 cm. - 978-0-11-075520-5 £3.00

The Wireless Telegraphy (Jersey) Order 2006 No. 2006/3324. - Enabling power: Wireless Telegraphy Act 1967, s. 15 (6); Broadcasting Act 1990, s. 204 (6); Intelligence Services Act 1994, s. 12 (4), Broadcasting Act 1996, s. 150 (4); Communications Act 2003, s. 411 (6) and Wireless Telegraphy Act 2006, ss. 118 (3) (6), 119 (3), sch. 8, para. 24. - Issued: 21.12.2006. Made: 14.12.2006. Coming into force: 08.02.2007. Effect: 2006 c.36 modified; S.I. 2003/3197; 2004/308 amended and S.I. 1952/1900; 1967/1279; 1997/284 revoked as they relate to Jersey; S.I. 1967/1275; 1998/1512; 2003/3196 revoked. Territorial extent & classification: Jersey. General. - 16p.: 30 cm. - 978-0-11-075516-8 £3.00

The Wireless Telegraphy (Licence Award) (No. 2) Regulations 2006 No. 2006/1806. - Enabling power: Wireless Telegraphy Act 1998, s. 3 (1) (3) (4) (5B) & Communications Act 2003, s. 403 (7). - Issued: 14.07.2006. Made: 07.07.2006. Coming into force: 07.08.2006. Effect: None. Territorial extent & classification: E/W/S/NI (but not Channel Islands and Isle of Man). General. - 24p.: 30 cm. - 978-0-11-074818-4 £4.00

The Wireless Telegraphy (Licence Award) Regulations 2006 No. 2006/338. - Enabling power: Wireless Telegraphy Act 1998, s. 3 (1) (3) (4) (5B) & Communications Act 2003, s. 403 (7). - Issued: 21.02.2006. Made: 14.02.2006. Coming into force: 10.03.2006. Effect: None. Territorial extent & classification: E/W/S/NI [not CI/IoM]. General. - 20p.: 30 cm. - 978-0-11-074040-9 £3.50

The Wireless Telegraphy (Licence Charges) (Amendment) Regulations 2006 No. 2006/2894. - Enabling power: Wireless Telegraphy Act 1998, ss. 1, 2 (2) & Communications Act 2003, s. 403 (7). - Issued: 08.11.2006. Made: 01.11.2006. Coming into force: 01.12.2006. Effect: S.I. 2005/1378 amended. Territorial extent & classification: E/W/S/NI/IoM/CI. General. - 4p.: 30 cm. - 978-0-11-075242-6 £3.00

The Wireless Telegraphy (Licensing Procedures) Regulations 2006 No. 2006/2785. - Enabling power: Wireless Telegraphy Act 1949, s. 1D (3). - Issued: 26.10.2006. Made: 16.10.2006. Coming into force: 16.11.2006. Effect: None. Territorial extent & classification: E/W/S/NI (but not Channel Is. or Isle of Man). General. - 8p.: 30 cm. - 978-0-11-075194-8 £3.00

The Wireless Telegraphy (Limitation of Number of Concurrent Spectrum Access Licences) Order 2006 No. 2006/341. - Enabling power: Communications Act 2003, s. 164 (1) to (3). - Issued: 21.02.2006. Made: 14.02.2006. Coming into force: 10.03.2006. Effect: None. Territorial extent & classification: E/W/S/NI [not CI/IoM]. General. - 2p.: 30 cm. - 978-0-11-074043-0 £3.00

The Wireless Telegraphy (Limitation of Number of Licences) (Amendment) Order 2006 No. 2006/2786. - Enabling power: Communications Act 2003, s. 164 (1) to (3). - Issued: 26.10.2006. Made: 16.10.2006. Coming into force: 16.11.2006. Effect: S.I. 2003/1902 amended. Territorial extent & classification: E/W/S/NI (but not Channel Is. or Isle of Man). General. - 16p.: 30 cm. - 978-0-11-075195-5 £3.00

The Wireless Telegraphy (Limitation of Number of Spectrum Access Licences) Order 2006 No. 2006/1809. - Enabling power: Communications Act 2003, s. 164 (1) to (3). - Issued: 14.07.2006. Made: 07.07.2006. Coming into force: 07.08.2006. Effect: None. Territorial extent & classification: E/W/S/NI (but not Channel Islands or the Isle of Man). General. - 2p.: 30 cm. - 978-0-11-074820-7 £3.00

The Wireless Telegraphy (Pre-Consolidation Amendments) Order 2006 No. 2006/1391. - Enabling power: Communications Act 2003, s. 407. - Issued: 31.05.2006. Made: 23.05.2006. Coming into force: In accord. with art. 1. Effect: 1949 c. 56; 1984 c. 12; 1998 c. 6 amended & 1989 c. 15; 1991 c. 56, c. 57; 1993 c. 43; 1999 c. 29; 2000 c. 26, c. 27, c. 38; 2002 c. 40 & S.I. 2003/419 (N.I. 6) modified. Territorial extent & classification: E/W/S/NI. General. - Supersedes draft S.I. (ISBN 0110745388) issued on 05.05.2006. - 8p.: 30 cm. - 978-0-11-074611-1 £3.00

The Wireless Telegraphy (Register) (Amendment) (No. 2) Regulations 2006 No. 2006/1808. - Enabling power: Communications Act 2003, s. 170 (1) (2), 403 (7). - Issued: 14.07.2006. Made: 07.07.2006. Coming into force: 07.08.2006. Effect: S.I. 2004/3155 amended. Territorial extent & classification: E/W/S/NI. General. - 2p.: 30 cm. - 978-0-11-074829-0 £3.00

The Wireless Telegraphy (Register) (Amendment) Regulations 2006 No. 2006/340. - Enabling power: Communications Act 2003, ss. 170(1) (2), 403 (7). - Issued: 22.02.2006. Made: 14.02.2006. Coming into force: 10.03.2006. Effect: S.I. 2004/3155 amended. Territorial extent & classification: E/W/S/NI [not CI/IoM]. General. - 2p.: 30 cm. - 978-0-11-074044-7 £3.00

The Wireless Telegraphy (Spectrum Trading) (Amendment) (No. 2) Regulations 2006 No. 2006/1807. - Enabling power: Communications Act 2003, ss. 168 (1) (3), 403 (7). - Issued: 14.07.2006. Made: 07.07.2006. Coming into force: 07.08.2006. Effect: S.I. 2004/3154 amended. Territorial extent & classification: E/W/S/NI. General. - 2p.: 30 cm. - 978-0-11-074817-7 £3.00

The Wireless Telegraphy (Spectrum Trading) (Amendment) Regulations 2006 No. 2006/339. - Enabling power: Communications Act 2003, ss. 168 (1) (3), 403 (7). - Issued: 21.02.2006. Made: 14.02.2006. Coming into force: 10.03.2006. Effect: S.I. 2004/3154 amended. Territorial extent & classification: E/W/S/NI [not CI/IoM]. General. - 4p.: 30 cm. - 978-0-11-074041-6 £3.00

Employment

The Gangmasters (Appeals) Regulations 2006 No. 2006/662. - Enabling power: Gangmasters (Licensing) Act 2004, ss. 10, 25 (2). - Issued: 16.03.2006. Made: 08.03.2006. Laid: 13.03.06. Coming into force: 06.04.2006. Effect: None. Territorial extent & classification: E/W/S. General. - 12p.: 30 cm. - 978-0-11-074234-2 £3.00

The Gangmasters (Licensing) Act 2004 (Commencement No.3) Order 2006 No. 2006/2406 (C.85). - Enabling power: Gangmasters (Licensing) Act 2004, s. 29 (1) (2). Bringing various provisions of the 2004 Act into operation on 01.10.2006. - Issued: 18.09.2006. Made: 06.09.2006. Effect: None. Territorial extent & classification: E/W/S/NI. General. - This Statutory Instrument has been printed to replace the SI of the same number and ISBN (but incorrectly numbered C.81) published on 13.09.2006, and is being issued free of charge to all known recipients of the original version. - 2p.: 30 cm. - 978-0-11-075091-0 £3.00

The Gangmasters (Licensing) Act 2004 (Commencement No. 4) Order 2006 No. 2006/2906 (C.101). - Enabling power: Gangmasters (Licensing) Act 2004, s. 29 (1) (2). Bringing into operation various provisions of the 2004 Act on 01.12.2006. - Issued: 10.11.2006. Made: 03.11.2006. Effect: None. Territorial extent & classification: E/W/S/NI. General. - 2p.: 30 cm. - 978-0-11-075262-4 £3.00

The Gangmasters (Licensing Conditions) (No.2) Rules 2006 No. 2006/2373. - Enabling power: Gangmasters (Licensing) Act 2004, s. 8. - Issued: 08.09.2006. Made: 05.09.2006. Laid: 07.09.2006. Coming into force: 01.10.2006. Effect: S.I. 2006/660 revoked. Territorial extent & classification: E/W/S/NI. General. - 16p.: 30 cm. - 978-0-11-075069-9 *£3.00*

The Gangmasters (Licensing Conditions) Rules 2006 No. 2006/660. - Enabling power: Gangmasters (Licensing) Act 2004, s. 8 (3). - Issued: 16.03.2006. Made: 08.03.2006. Laid: 13.03.06. Coming into force: 06.04.2006. Effect: None. Territorial extent & classification: E/W/S/NI. General. - Revoked by S.I. 2006/2373 (ISBN 0110750691). - 16p.: 30 cm. - 978-0-11-074230-4 *£3.00*

The Gangmasters Licensing (Exclusions) Regulations 2006 No. 2006/658. - Enabling power: Gangmasters (Licensing) Act 2004, s. 6 (2). - Issued: 16.03.2006. Made: 08.03.2006. Laid: 13.03.06. Coming into force: 06.04.2006. Effect: None. Territorial extent & classification: E/W/S. General. - 4p.: 30 cm. - 978-0-11-074233-5 *£3.00*

Employment and training

The Industrial Training Levy (Construction Board) Order 2006 No. 2006/334. - Enabling power: Industrial Training Act 1982, ss. 11 (2), 12 (3) (4). - Issued: 20.02.2006. Made: 12.02.2006. Coming into force: 19.02.2006. Effect: None. Territorial extent & classification: E/W/S. General. - Supersedes draft SI (ISBN 0110738748) issued on 09.01.2006. - 8p.: 30 cm. - 978-0-11-074034-8 *£3.00*

The Industrial Training Levy (Engineering Construction Board) Order 2006 No. 2006/335. - Enabling power: Industrial Training Act 1982, ss. 11 (2), 12 (3) (4). - Issued: 20.02.2006. Made: 12.02.2006. Coming into force: 19.02.2006. Effect: None. Territorial extent & classification: E/W/S. General. - Supersedes draft SI (ISBN 0110738764) issued on 09.01.2006. - 8p.: 30 cm. - 978-0-11-074035-5 *£3.00*

Employment and training: Age discrimination

The Employment Equality (Age) (Amendment No. 2) Regulations 2006 No. 2006/2931. - Enabling power: European Communities Act 1972, s. 2 (2). - Issued: 16.11.2006. Made: 09.11.2006. Laid: 10.11.2006. Coming into force: 01.12.2006. Effect: S.I. 2006/1031 amended. Territorial extent & classification: E/W/S. General. - EC note: These Regs and the Age Regulations implement in GB Council Directive 2000/78/EC establishing a general framework for equal treatment in employment so far as it relates to discrimination on grounds of age. These Regulations deal with provisions relating to pensions. - 16p.: 30 cm. - 978-0-11-075284-6 *£3.00*

The Employment Equality (Age) (Amendment) Regulations 2006 No. 2006/2408. - Enabling power: European Communities Act 1972, s. 2 (2). - Issued: 12.09.2006. Made: 06.09.2006. Laid: 08.09.2006. Coming into force: 30.09.2006. Effect: S.I. 2006/1031 amended. Territorial extent & classification: E/W/S. General. - EC note: These Regs amend the 2006 Regs by postponing until 1st December 2006, the date in which certain provisions come into force. The 2006 Regs implemented Council Directive 2000/78/EC by establishing a general framework for equal treatment in employment and occupation- 4p.: 30 cm. - 978-0-11-075090-3 *£3.00*

The Employment Equality (Age) Regulations 2006 No. 2006/1031. - Enabling power: European Communities Act 1972, s. 2 (2). - Issued: 28.04.2006. Made: 03.04.2006. Coming into force: 01.10.2006. Effect: 16 acts, 18 statutory instruments and 2 Scottish Acts are amended see schs 8, 9. Territorial extent & classification: E/W/S. General. - Supersedes draft SI (ISBN 0110742664). - EC note: These Regs implement Council Directive 2000/78/EC, establishing a general framework for equal treatment in employment. - 68p.: 30 cm. - 978-0-11-074460-5 *£10.50*

Energy conservation

The Boiler (Efficiency) (Amendment) Regulations 2006 No. 2006/170. - Enabling power: European Communities Act 1972, s. 2 (2). - Issued: 02.02.2006. Made: 26.01.2006. Laid: 31.01.2006. Coming into force: 21.02.2006. Effect: S.I. 1993/3083 amended. Territorial extent & classification: E/W/S/NI. General. - EC note: These Regs implement article 16 of Directive 2004/8/EC on the promotion of cogeneration based on a useful heat demand in the internal energy market and amending Directive 92/42/EEC. - 2p.: 30 cm. - 978-0-11-073964-9 *£3.00*

Energy conservation, England

The Home Energy Efficiency Scheme (England) (Amendment) Regulations 2006 No. 2006/1953. - Enabling power: Social Security Act 1990, s. 15. - Issued: 25.07.2006. Made: 18.07.2006. Laid: 20.07.2006. Coming into force: 10.08.2006. Effect: S.I.2005/1530 amended. Territorial extent & classification: E. General. - 4p.: 30 cm. - 978-0-11-074882-5 *£3.00*

Environmental protection

The Agricultural or Forestry Tractors (Emission of Gaseous and Particulate Pollutants) (Amendment) Regulations 2006 No. 2006/2393. - Enabling power: European Communities Act 1972, s. 2 (2). - Issued: 14.09.2006. Made: 05.09.2006. Laid: 11.09.2006. Coming into force: 12.10.2006. Effect: S.I. 2002/1891 amended. Territorial extent & classification: E/W/S/NI. General. - With correction slip dated October 2006. EC note: These Regs amend the Agricultural or Forestry Tractors (Emission of Gaseous and Particulate Pollutants) Regulations 2002, in order to implement EC Directive 2005/13/EC, as far as it relates to the entry into service of tractors and tractor engines. - 12p.: 30 cm. - 978-0-11-075089-7 *£3.00*

The Controls on Dangerous Substances and Preparations Regulations 2006 No. 2006/3311. - Enabling power: European Communities Act 1972, s. 2 (2). - Issued: 18.12.2006. Made: 11.12.2006. Laid: 15.12.2006. Coming into force: 07.01.2007. Effect: S.I. 1987/783; 1992/31 (with savings), 1583; 1993/1, 1643; 2001/3141; 2003/3274; 2004/1816, 3278 & S.R. 1994/223 (with savings), 224; 2003/105, 106, 165, 548; 2004/302, 509 revoked. Territorial extent & classification: E/W/S/NI. General. - EC note: These Regulations give effect to restrictions on the marketing and use of certain of the dangerous substances and preparations set out in Council Directive 76/769/EEC on the approximation of the laws, regulations and administrative provisions of the Member States relating to restrictions on the marketing and use of certain dangerous substances and preparations as amended. With correction slip dated February 2007. - 32p.: 30 cm. - 978-0-11-075485-7 *£5.50*

The Greenhouse Gas Emissions Trading Scheme (Amendment) Regulations 2006 No. 2006/737. - Enabling power: European Communities Act 1972, s. 2 (2) & Pollution Prevention and Control Act 1999, s. 2 (1). - Issued: 20.03.2006. Made: 12.03.2006. Laid: 16.03.2006. Coming into force: 06.04.2006. Effect: S.I. 2005/925 amended. Territorial extent & classification: E/W/S/NI. General. - EC note: These Regulations amend the Greenhouse Gas Emissions Trading Scheme Regulations 2005 which provide a framework for a greenhouse gas emissions trading scheme and implement Directive 2003/87/EC establishing a scheme for greenhouse gas emission allowance trading within the Community and amending Council Directive 96/61/EC- 16p.: 30 cm. - 978-0-11-074304-2 *£3.00*

The Non-Road Mobile Machinery (Emission of Gaseous and Particulate Pollutants) (Amendment) Regulations 2006 No. 2006/29. - Enabling power: European Communities Act 1972, s. 2 (2). - Issued: 19.01.2006. Made: 09.01.2006. Laid: 13.01.2006. Coming into force: 17.02.2006. Effect: S.I. 1999/1053 amended. Territorial extent & classification: E/W/S/NI. General. - EC note: These regs implement the provisions of Directive 2004/26/EC which amends Directive 1997/68/EC on the approximation of the laws of the member States relating to measures against the emission of gaseous and particulate pollutants from internal combustion engines to be installed in non-road mobile machinery, so as to impose new emissions limits on certain types of engine already covered by Directive 1997/68/EC and to extend that Directive's scope to include engines installed in inland waterway vessels, locomotives and railcars. - 20p.: 30 cm. - 978-0-11-073897-0 *£3.50*

The Ozone Depleting Substances (Qualifications) Regulations 2006 No. 2006/1510. - Enabling power: European Communities Act 1972, s. 2 (2). - Issued: 16.06.2006. Made: 08.06.2006. Laid: 16.06.2006. Coming into force: 10.07.2006. Effect: S.I. 2002/528 amended. Territorial extent & classification: E/W/S. General. - EC note: Gives effect, in relation to England, Wales and Scotland, to the provisions in Arts. 16.5 and 17.1, first paragraph, of Regulation 2037/2000 on substances that deplete the ozone layer (as amended by Regulations 2038/2000, 2039/2000 and 1804/2003, and Council Decisions 2003/160/EC and 2004/232/EC). - 8p.: 30 cm. - 978-0-11-074687-6 *£3.00*

The Packaging (Essential Requirements) (Amendment) Regulations 2006 No. 2006/1492. - Enabling power: European Communities Act 1972, s. 2 (2). - Issued: 14.06.2006. Made: 02.06.2006. Laid: 07.06.2006. Coming into force: 01.07.2006. Effect: S.I. 2003/1941 amended. Territorial extent & classification: E/W/S/NI. General. - 2p.: 30 cm. - 978-0-11-074659-3 *£3.00*

The Restriction of the Use of Certain Hazardous Substances in Electrical and Electronic Equipment Regulations 2006 No. 2006/1463. - Enabling power: European Communities Act 1972, s. 2 (2). - Issued: 13.06.2006. Made: 25.05.2006. Laid: 06.06.2006. Coming into force: 01.07.2006. Effect: S.I. 2004/693 amended & S.I. 2005/2748 revoked. Territorial extent & classification: E/W/S/NI. General. - EC note: These Regs implement the European Parliament and Council Directive 2002/95/EC on the Restriction of the Use of Certain Hazardous Substances in Electrical and Electronic Equipment ("the Directive"), as amended by Decision 2005/618/EC establishing maximum concentration values for certain hazardous substances in electrical and electronic equipment. They incorporate the further amendments to the Annex of Directive 2002/95/EC by Commission Decision 2005/717/EC, Commission Decision 2005/747/EC and Commission Decision 2006/310/EC. These Decisions amend the list of exempt applications set out in the Annex. - 12p.: 30 cm. - 978-0-11-074648-7 *£3.00*

The Waste Electrical and Electronic Equipment Regulations 2006 No. 2006/3289. - Enabling power: European Communities Act 1972, s. 2 (2). - Issued: 14.12.2006. Made: 11.12.2006. Laid: 12.12.2006. Coming into force: In accord. with reg. 1 (2) to (4). Effect: 1995 c.25 amended. Territorial extent & classification: E/W/S/NI (but regs 4, 45 and 51 do not apply to NI) General. - EC note: These Regulations transpose the main provisions of Council Directive 2002/96/EC on waste electrical and electronic equipment as amended by Council Directive 2003/108/EC. - 68p.: 30 cm. - 978-0-11-075479-6 £10.50

Environmental protection, England

The Anti-social Behaviour Act 2003 (Commencement No. 6) (England) Order 2006 No. 2006/393 (C.11). - Enabling power: Anti-social Behaviour Act 2003, s. 93 (2) (a). Bringing into operation various provisions of the 2003 on 06.04.2006. - Issued: 23.02.2006. Made: 16.02.2006. Effect: None. Territorial extent & classification: E. General. - 4p.: 30 cm. - 978-0-11-074083-6 £3.00

The Clean Neighbourhoods and Environment Act 2005 (Commencement No.1, Transitional and Savings Provisions) (England) Order 2006 No. 2006/795 (C. 19). - Enabling power: Clean Neighbourhoods and Environment Act 2005, s. 108(1)(a), (3)(h), (i) (j) (5). Bringing into operation various provisions of the 2005 Act on 14.03.2006; 01.04.2006; 06.04.2006, in accord. with art. 2. - Issued: 23.03.2006. Made: 09.03.2006. Effect: None. Territorial extent & classification: E. General. - 8p.: 30 cm. - 978-0-11-074357-8 £3.00

The Clean Neighbourhoods and Environment Act 2005 (Commencement No. 2) (England) Order 2006 No. 2006/1361 (C.46). - Enabling power: Clean Neighbourhoods and Environment Act 2005, s. 108 (1) (a) (2) (r). Bringing into operation various provisions of the 2005 on 04.08.2006, in accord. with art. 2. - Issued: 25.05.2006. Made: 17.05.2006. Effect: None. Territorial extent & classification: E. General. - 4p.: 30 cm. - 978-0-11-074596-1 £3.00

The Clean Neighbourhoods and Environment Act 2005 (Commencement No. 3) (England) Order 2006 No. 2006/2006 (C.69). - Enabling power: Clean Neighbourhoods and Environment Act 2005, s. 108 (1) (a). Bringing into operation various provisions of the 2005 Act on 01.10.2006. - Issued: 25.08.2006. Made: 23.07.2006. Effect: None. Territorial extent & classification: E. General. - 4p.: 30 cm. - 978-0-11-074932-7 £3.00

The Contaminated Land (England) Regulations 2006 No. 2006/1380. - Enabling power: Environmental Protection Act 1990, ss. 78A (9), 78C (8) to (10), 78E (1) (6), 78G (5) (6), 78L (4) (5), 78R (1) (2) (8). - Issued: 14.06.2006. Made: 17.05.2006. Laid: 23.05.2006. Coming into force: 04.08.2006. Effect: S.I. 2000/227; 2001/663 revoked. Territorial extent & classification: E. General. - This Statutory Instrument has been printed in substitution of the SI of the same number and ISBN, issued on 26.05.2006, and is being issued free of charge to all known recipients of the original version. With correction slip July 2006. - 16p.: 30 cm. - 978-0-11-074602-9 £3.00

The Environmental Noise (England) Regulations 2006 No. 2006/2238. - Enabling power: European Communities Act 1972, s. 2 (2). - Issued: 07.09.2006. Made: 08.08.2006. Laid: 07.09.2006. Coming into force: 01.10.2006. Effect: None. Territorial extent & classification: E. General. - EC note: These Regulations implement Directive 2002/49/EC relating to the assessment and management of environmental noise. - 20p.: 30 cm. - 978-0-11-075029-3 £3.50

The Environmental Offences (Fixed Penalties) (Miscellaneous Provisions) Regulations 2006 No. 2006/783. - Enabling power: Refuse Disposal (Amenity) Act 1978, ss. 2A (11), 2C (2) (d) (3); Control of Pollution (Amendment) Act 1989, ss. 5B (12), 5C (3) (b) (4); Environmental Protection Act 1990, ss. 34A (12), 47ZB (4) (5), 73A (2) (b) (3), 88 (11), 97A (1) (2) (4); Noise Act 1996, ss. 8A (4) (5), 9 (4A) (b) (4B); Anti-social Behaviour Act 2003, ss. 43A (4) (5), 47 (4) & Clean Neighbourhoods and Environment Act 2005, ss. 6 (11), 8 (2) (d) (3), 59 (12), 60 (4) (5), 74 (4) (5), 75 (2) (d) (3). - Issued: 22.03.2006. Made: 10.03.2006. Laid: 16.03.2006. Coming into force: 06.04.2006. Effect: None. Territorial extent & classification: E. General. - 8p.: 30 cm. - 978-0-11-074353-0 £3.00

The Environmental Offences (Use of Fixed Penalty Receipts) Regulations 2006 No. 2006/1334. - Enabling power: Clean Neighbourhoods and Environment Act 2005, ss. 96 (4) (d) (5), 97 (1) (2) (a) (b) (c) (3), 98 (2). - Issued: 24.05.2006. Made: 05.04.2006. Coming into force: 06.04.2006 In accord.with reg. 1 (b). Effect: None. Territorial extent & classification: E. General. - 4p.: 30 cm. - 978-0-11-074585-5 £3.00

The Environmental Protection Act 1990 (Isles of Scilly) Order 2006 No. 2006/1381. - Enabling power: Environmental Protection Act 1990, s. 78Y(2) & Environment Act 1995, s. 117 (2) (3). - Issued: 13.06.2006. Made: 17.05.2006. Laid: 23.05.2006. Coming into force: 04.08.2006. Effect: None. Territorial extent & classification: E. General. - EC note: Transposes arts 48 and 53 of Council Directive 1996/29/Euratom laying down basic safety standards for the protection of the health of workers and the general public against the dangers arising from ionizing radiation in relation to the Isles of Scilly. - This Statutory Instrument has been printed in substitution of the SI of the same number and ISBN, issued on 26.05.2006, and is being issued free of charge to all known recipients of the original version. - With correction slip dated July 2006. - 2p.: 30 cm. - 978-0-11-074603-6 £3.00

The Environmental Protection (Waste Recycling Payments) Regulations 2006 No. 2006/743. - Enabling power: Environmental Protection Act 1990, s. 52 (1) (a) (3) (a). - Issued: 31.03.2006. Made: 12.03.2006. Laid: 16.03.2006. Coming into force: 06.04.2006. Effect: S.I. 2004/639; 2005/415 revoked. Territorial extent & classification: E. General. - 4p.: 30 cm. - 978-0-11-074310-3 £3.00

The Highways Act 1980 (Gating Orders) (England) Regulations 2006 No. 2006/537. - Enabling power: Highways Act 1980, ss. 129C, 129E, 129F. - Issued: 08.03.2006. Made: 01.03.2006. Laid: 08.03.2006. Coming into force: 01.04.2006. Effect: None. Territorial extent & classification: E. General. - 8p.: 30 cm. - 978-0-11-074141-3 £3.00

The Joint Waste Disposal Authorities (Recycling Payments) (Disapplication) (England) Order 2006 No. 2006/651. - Enabling power: Environmental Protection Act 1990, s. 52 (1A). - Issued: 16.03.2006. Made: 07.03.2006. Laid: 10.03.06. Coming into force: 01.04.2006. Effect: None. Territorial extent & classification: E. General. - 2p.: 30 cm. - 978-0-11-074235-9 £3.00

The Pollution Prevention and Control (England and Wales) (Amendment) (England) Regulations 2006 No. 2006/2311. - Enabling power: Pollution Prevention and Control Act 1999, s. 2. - Issued: 01.09.2006. Made: 23.08.2006. Laid: 29.08.2006. Coming into force: 01.10.2006. Effect: S.I. 2000/1973 amended. Territorial extent & classification: E. General. - EC note: These Regulations amend the 2000 Regulations to exempt certain operators from the permit requirements of Directive 1999/13/EC (the Solvent Emissions Directive) and to meet a UK obligation arising from the UNECE Protocol to the 1979 Convention on Long-Range Transboundary Air Pollution Concerning the Control of Emissions of Volatile Organic Compounds or their Transboundary Fluxes. - 4p.: 30 cm. - 978-0-11-075048-4 £3.00

The Radioactive Contaminated Land (Modification of Enactments) (England) Regulations 2006 No. 2006/1379. - Enabling power: Environmental Protection Act 1990, ss. 78A (9), 78YC. - Issued: 10.07.2006. Made: 17.05.2006. Laid: 23.05.2006. Coming into force: 04.08.2006. Effect: 1990 c. 43; 1995 c. 25 modified. Territorial extent & classification: E. General. - This Statutory Instrument has been printed in substitution of the SI of the same number (ISBN 0110746015, published 26.05.2006) and is being issued free of charge to all known recipients of that Statutory Instrument. - EC note: Transposes arts 48 and 53 of Council Directive 1996/29/Euratom laying down basic safety standards for the protection of the health of workers and the general public against the dangers arising from ionizing radiation. - 12p.: 30 cm. - 978-0-11-074813-9 £3.00

The Radioactive Contaminated Land (Modification of Enactments) (England) Regulations 2006 No. 2006/1379. - Enabling power: Environmental Protection Act 1990, ss. 78A (9), 78YC. - Issued: 26.05.2006. Made: 17.05.2006. Laid: 23.05.2006. Coming into force: 04.08.2006. Effect: 1990 c. 43; 1995 c. 25 amended. Territorial extent & classification: E. General. - EC note: Transposes arts 48 and 53 of Council Directive 1996/29/Euratom laying down basic safety standards for the protection of the health of workers and the general public against the dangers arising from ionizing radiation. - Superseded by SI of same number (ISBN 0110748131) published on 10.07.2006. - 12p.: 30 cm. - 978-0-11-074601-2 £3.00

The Statutory Nuisance (Appeals) (Amendment) (England) Regulations 2006 No. 2006/771. - Enabling power: Environmental Protection Act 1990, sch. 3, para. 1 (4). - Issued: 21.03.2006. Made: 10.03.2006. Laid: 16.03.2006. Coming into force: 06.04.2006. Effect: S.I. 1995/2644 amended. Territorial extent & classification: E. General. - 4p.: 30 cm. - 978-0-11-074335-6 £3.00

Environmental protection, England: Statutory nuisances and clean air

The Statutory Nuisances (Artificial Lighting) (Designation of Relevant Sports) (England) Order 2006 No. 2006/781. - Enabling power: Environmental Protection Act 1990, s. 80 (8B). - Issued: 22.03.2006. Made: 10.03.2006. Laid: 16.03.2006. Coming into force: 06.04.2006. Effect: None. Territorial extent & classification: E. General. - 4p.: 30 cm. - 978-0-11-074352-3 £3.00

The Statutory Nuisances (Insects) Regulations 2006 No. 2006/770. - Enabling power: Environmental Protection Act 1990, s. 79 (7C) (d). - Issued: 21.03.2006. Made: 10.03.2006. Laid: 16.03.2006. Coming into force: 06.03.2006. Effect: None. Territorial extent & classification: E. General. - 4p.: 30 cm. - 978-0-11-074334-9 £3.00

Environmental protection, England and Wales

The Clean Neighbourhoods and Environment Act 2005 (Commencement No.2, Transitional Provisions and Savings) (England and Wales) (Amendment) Order 2006 No. 2006/1002 (C.31). - Enabling power: Clean Neighbourhoods and Environment Act 2005, s. 108 (5). - Issued: 05.04.2006. Made: 30.03.2006. Coming into force: 01.04.2006. Effect: S.I. 2005/2896 amended. Territorial extent & classification: E/W. General. - 2p.: 30 cm. - 978-0-11-074442-1 £3.00

The Clean Neighbourhoods and Environment Act 2005 (Commencement No. 4) Order 2006 No. 2006/656 (C.16). - Enabling power: Clean Neighbourhoods and Environment Act 2005, s. 108 (3) (d). Bringing into operation various provisions of the 2005 Act on 07.03.2006; 06.04.2006. - Issued: 16.03.2006. Made: 06.03.2006. Effect: None. Territorial extent & classification: E/W. General. - 2p.: 30 cm. - 978-0-11-074232-8 £3.00

The Environment Act 1995 (Commencement No. 23) (England and Wales) Order 2006 No. 2006/934 (C.27). - Enabling power: Environment Act 1995, s. 125 (3). Bringing into operation various provisions of the 1995 Act on 15.05.2006. - Issued: 03.04.2006. Made: 27.03.2006. Effect: None. Territorial extent & classification: E/W. General. - EC note: These Regulations amend the 1990 Act so that the definition of "waste" is the same as that in Council Directive 75/442/EEC. Para 95 inserts a new sch.2B to the 1990 Act in relation to s. 75 of that Act. That schedule transposes Annex 1 of Council Directive 75/442/EEC. - 8p.: 30 cm. - 978-0-11-074414-8 £3.00

The Financial Assistance for Environmental Purposes Order 2006 No. 2006/1735. - Enabling power: Environmental Protection Act 1990, s. 153 (4). - Issued: 06.07.2006. Made: 29.06.2006. Laid: 03.07.2006. Coming into force: 31.07.2006. Effect: 1990 c.43 amended. Territorial extent & classification: E/W/NI, except for Art. 2(b) which extends only to E/W. General. - 2p.: 30 cm. - 978-0-11-074784-2 £3.00

The Waste Electrical and Electronic Equipment (Waste Management Licensing) (England and Wales) Regulations 2006 No. 2006/3315. - Enabling power: European Communities Act 1972, s. 2 (2) and Environmental Protection Act 1990, ss. 33 (3), 34 (5), 35 (6). - Issued: 19.12.2006. Made: 12.12.2006. Laid: 15.12.2006. Coming into force: 05.01.2007. Effect: S.I. 1994/1056 amended. Territorial extent & classification: E/W. General. - EC note: These Regulations transpose the permit requirements of Article 6 and Annexes II and III of Council Directive 2002/96/EC on waste electrical and electronic equipment as amended by Council Directive 2003/108/EC. - 12p.: 30 cm. - 978-0-11-075494-9 £3.00

The Waste Management (England and Wales) Regulations 2006 No. 2006/937. - Enabling power: European Communities Act 1972, s. 2 (2) & Control of Pollution (Amendment) Act 1989, s. 1 (3) (a) & Environmental Protection Act 1990, ss. 33 (3), 75 (8), 156. - Issued: 04.04.2006. Made: 28.03.2006. Laid: 30.03.2006. Coming into force: 15.05.2006. Effect: 1990 c.43; 1995 c.25; S.I. 1991/1624; 1992/588; 1994/1056; 1996/634; 1998/2746; 2002/1559; 2005/894, 1806 (W.138), 1728 amended. Territorial extent & classification: E/W. General. - EC note: These Regulations implement (in part), in relation to England and Wales, Council Directive 75/442/EEC on waste ("the Waste Framework Directive") and Council Directive 1999/31/EC on the landfill of waste ("the Landfill Directive"). - 16p.: 30 cm. - 978-0-11-074412-4 £3.00

Environmental protection, Northern Ireland

The Financial Assistance for Environmental Purposes Order 2006 No. 2006/1735. - Enabling power: Environmental Protection Act 1990, s. 153 (4). - Issued: 06.07.2006. Made: 29.06.2006. Laid: 03.07.2006. Coming into force: 31.07.2006. Effect: 1990 c.43 amended. Territorial extent & classification: E/W/NI, except for Art. 2(b) which extends only to E/W. General. - 2p.: 30 cm. - 978-0-11-074784-2 £3.00

Environmental protection, Scotland

The Water Environment (Controlled Activities) (Scotland) Regulations 2005 (Notices in the Interests of National Security) Order 2006 No. 2006/661 (S.5). - Enabling power: Scotland Act 1998, ss. 104, 112 (1), 113. - Issued: 16.03.2006. Made: 09.03.2006. Laid: 15.03.2006. Coming into force: 05.04.2006. Effect: None. Territorial extent & classification: S. General. - 4p.: 30 cm. - 978-0-11-074257-1 £3.00

Environmental protection, Wales

The Clean Neighbourhoods and Environment Act 2005 (Commencement No.1 and Savings) (Wales) Order 2006 No. 2006/768 (W.75)(C.18). - Enabling power: Clean Neighbourhoods and Environment Act 2005, s. 108(1) (b) (2) (5). Bringing into operation various provisions of the 2005 Act on 16.03.2006 and another date in accord. with art. 4. - Issued: 24.03.2006. Made: 15.03.2006. Effect: None. Territorial extent & classification: W. General. - With correction slip dated May 2006. - In English and Welsh. Welsh title: Gorchymyn Deddf Cymdogaethau Glân a'r Amgylchedd 2005 (Cychwyn Rhif 1 ac Arbedion) (Cymru) 2006. - 8p.: 30 cm. - 978-0-11-091300-1 £3.00

The Clean Neighbourhoods and Environment Act 2005 (Commencement No.2, Transitional Provisions and Savings) (Wales) Order 2006 No. 2006/2797 (W.236)(C.93). - Enabling power: Clean Neighbourhoods and Environment Act 2005, s. 108(1) (b) (2) (5). Bringing into operation various provisions of the 2005 Act in accord. with arts. 2 to 7. - Issued: 25.10.2006. Made: 17.10.2006. Effect: S.I. 2006/768 (W.75) (C.18) amended. Territorial extent & classification: W. General. - In English and Welsh. Welsh title: Gorchymyn Deddf Cymdogaethau Glân a'r Amgylchedd 2005 (Cychwyn Rhif 2, Darpariaethau Trosiannol ac Arbedion) (Cymru) 2006. - 16p.: 30 cm. - 978-0-11-091406-0 £3.00

The Contaminated Land (Wales) Regulations 2006 No. 2006/2989 (W.278). - Enabling power: Environmental Protection Act 1990, ss. 78A (9), 78C (8) to (10), 78E (1) (6), 78G (5) (6), 78L (4) (5), 78R (1) (2) (8). - Issued: 23.11.2006. Made: 15.11.2006. Coming into force: 10.12.2006. Effect: S.I. 2001/2197 (W.157) revoked. Territorial extent & classification: W. General. - In English and Welsh. Welsh title: Rheoliadau Tir Halogedig (Cymru) 2006. - 28p.: 30 cm. - 978-0-11-091442-8 £4.50

The Environmental Noise (Wales) Regulations 2006 No. 2006/2629 (W.225). - Enabling power: European Communities Act 1972, s. 2 (2). - Issued: 13.10.2006. Made: 03.10.2006. Coming into force: 04.10.2006. Effect: None. Territorial extent & classification: W. General. - EC note: These Regs implement Directive 2002/49/EC relating to the assessment and management of environmental noise. - In English and Welsh. Welsh title: Rheoliadau Swn Amgylcheddol (Cymru) 2006. - With correction dated November 2006. - 32p.: 30 cm. - 978-0-11-091400-8 £5.50

The Pollution Prevention and Control (England and Wales) (Amendment) (Wales) Regulations 2006 No. 2006/2802 (W.241). - Enabling power: Pollution Prevention and Control Act 1999, s. 2 (4). - Issued: 26.10.2006. Made: 17.10.2006. Coming into force: 25.10.2006. Effect: S.I. 2000/1973 amended. Territorial extent & classification: W. General. - In English and Welsh. Welsh title: Rheoliadau Atal a Rheoli Llygredd (Cymru a Lloegr) (Diwygio) (Cymru) 2006. - 8p.: 30 cm. - 978-0-11-091408-4 £3.00

The Radioactive Contaminated Land (Modification of Enactments) (Wales) Regulations 2006 No. 2006/2988 (W.277). - Enabling power: Environmental Protection Act 1990, ss. 78A (9), 78YC. - Issued: 23.11.2006. Made: 15.11.2006. Coming into force: In accord. with reg. 1 (2). Effect: 1990 c.43; 1995 c.25 modified. Territorial extent & classification: W. General. - In English and Welsh. Welsh title: Rheoliadau Tir a Halogwyd yn Ymbelydrol (Addasu Deddfiadau) (Cymru) 2006. - 16p.: 30 cm. - 978-0-11-091443-5 £3.00

The Waste (Household Waste Duty of Care) (Wales) Regulations 2006 No. 2006/123 (W.16). - Enabling power: European Communities Act 1972, s. 2 (2). - Issued: 31.01.2006. Made: 24.01.2006. Coming into force: 26.01.2006. Effect: 1990 c.43; S.I. 1992/588 amended. Territorial extent & classification: W. General. - EC note: These Regs implement, in relation to Wales, art. 8 of Council Directive 75/442/EEC on waste as respects an occupier of domestic property in relation to the household waste produced on the property. - In English and Welsh. Welsh title: Rheoliadau Gwastraff (Dyletswydd Gofal o ran Gwastraff Cartref (Cymru) 2006. - 4p.: 30 cm. - 978-0-11-091259-2 £3.00

Equal opportunities and human rights

The Equality Act 2006 (Commencement No. 1) Order 2006 No. 2006/1082 (C.36). - Enabling power: Equality Act 2006, s. 93. Bringing into operation various provisions of the 2006 Act in accord.with arts. 2, 3, 4. - Issued: 19.04.2006. Made: 07.04.2006. Effect: None. Territorial extent & classification: E/W/S/NI. General. - 2p.: 30 cm. - 978-0-11-074494-0 £3.00

European Communities

The European Communities (Definition of Treaties) (Cooperation Agreement between the European Community and its Member States and the Swiss Confederation to Combat Fraud) Order 2006 No. 2006/307. - Enabling power: European Communities Act 1972, s. 1 (3). - Issued: 21.02.2006. Made: 14.02.2006. Coming into force: In accord. with art. 1. Effect: None. Territorial extent & classification: E/W/S/NI. General. - 2p.: 30 cm. - 978-0-11-074058-4 £3.00

The European Communities (Designation) (Amendment) Order 2006 No. 2006/3329. - Enabling power: European Communities Act 1972, s. 2 (2) and Government of Wales Act 1998, s. 29 (1). - Issued: 21.12.2006. Made: 14.12.2006. Laid: 21.12.2006. Coming into force: 11.01.2007. Effect: S.I. 2000/2812; 2004/706; 2005/850, 2766 amended. Territorial extent & classification: E/W/S/NI. General. - 2p.: 30 cm. - 978-0-11-075506-9 £3.00

The European Communities (Designation) (No. 2) Order 2006 No. 2006/1461. - Enabling power: European Communities Act 1972, s. 2 (2). - Issued: 13.06.2006. Made: 07.06.2006. Laid: 08.06.2006. Coming into force: 29.06.2006. Effect: None. Territorial extent & classification: E/W/S/NI. General. - 4p.: 30 cm. - 978-0-11-074668-5 £3.00

The European Communities (Designation) Order 2006 No. 2006/608. - Enabling power: European Communities Act 1972, s. 2 (2). - Issued: 15.03.2006. Made: 08.03.2006. Laid: 09.03.2006. Coming into force: 30.03.2006. Effect: S.I. 1992/1711; 2005/2766 amended. Territorial extent & classification: E/W/S/NI. General. - 4p.: 30 cm. - 978-0-11-074213-7 £3.00

The Nuclear Reactors (Environmental Impact Assessment for Decommissioning) (Amendment) Regulations 2006 No. 2006/657. - Enabling power: European Communities Act 1972, s. 2 (2). - Issued: 16.03.2006. Made: 08.03.2006. Laid: 16.03.06. Coming into force: 06.04.2006. Effect: S.I. 1999/2892 amended. Territorial extent & classification: E/W/S. General. - EC note: Regulation 2(2), (3), (5)-(7), and (9) implement Council Directive 2003/35/EC providing for public participation in respect of the drawing up of certain plans and programmes relating to the environment and amending with regard to public participation and access to justice Council Directives 85/337/EEC and 96/61/EC- 4p.: 30 cm. - 978-0-11-074242-7 £3.00

European Communities, Wales

The Structural Funds (National Assembly for Wales) Regulations 2006 No. 2006/3282. - Enabling power: European Communities Act 1972, s. 2 (2). - Issued: 18.12.2006. Made: 07.12.2006. Laid: 11.12.2006. Coming into force: 01.01.2007. Effect: None. Territorial extent & classification: W. General. - EC note: These Regulations enable the National Assembly for Wales ("the Assembly") to exercise in relation to Wales certain functions under Council Regulation 1083/2006 and repealing Regulation 1260/1999 ("the 2006 Structural Funds Regulation"). Additionally, these Regulations enable the Assembly to exercise in relation to Wales certain functions under Regulation 1080/2006 and repealing Regulation 1783/1999 ("the 2006 Regional Development Fund Regulation"). - 8p.: 30 cm. - 978-0-11-075464-2 £3.00

Excise

The Air Passenger Duty (Rate) (Qualifying Territories) Order 2006 No. 2006/2693. - Enabling power: Finance Act 1994, s. 30 (9B). - Issued: 16.10.2006. Made: 10.10.2006. Laid: 11.10.2006. Coming into force: 01.11.2006. Effect: 1994 c.9 amended. Territorial extent & classification: E/W/S/NI. General. - 2p.: 30 cm. - 978-0-11-075181-8 £3.00

The Beer, Cider and Perry, Spirits, and Wine and Made-wine (Amendment) Regulations 2006 No. 2006/1058. - Enabling power: Alcoholic Liquor Duties Act 1979, ss. 2 (3) (4), 13 (1) (1A), 15 (6), 19 (1), 49 (1) (a) (g) (2), 55A (2), 56 (1), 62 (5). - Issued: 10.04.2006. Made: 05.04.2006. Laid: 06.04.2006. Coming into force: 01.05.2006. Effect: S.I. 1989/1355, 1356; 1991/2564; 1993/1228; 2002/1265 amended & S.I. 1978/1786; 1979/1146; 1989/916; 1992/3157 revoked. Territorial extent & classification: E/W/S/NI. General. - 8p.: 30 cm. - 978-0-11-074470-4 £3.00

The Customs and Excise Duties (Travellers' Allowances and Personal Reliefs) (New Member States) (Amendment) Order 2006 No. 2006/3157. - Enabling power: Customs and Excise Duties (General Reliefs) Act 1979, s. 13 (1) (3). - Issued: 01.12.2006. Made: 28.11.2006. Laid: 29.11.2006. Coming into force: 01.01.2007. Effect: S.I. 2004/1002 amended. Territorial extent & classification: E/W/S/NI. General. - Order made by the Commissioners for Her Majesty's Revenue and Customs, laid before the House of Commons for approval by that House within twenty-eight days. Superseded by S.I. of same no. (ISBN 0110755014). - 4p.: 30 cm. - 978-0-11-075386-7 £3.00

The Customs and Excise Duties (Travellers' Allowances and Personal Reliefs) (New Member States) (Amendment) Order 2006 No. 2006/3157. - Enabling power: Customs and Excise Duties (General Reliefs) Act 1979, s. 13 (1) (3). - Issued: 19.12.2006. Made: 28.11.2006. Laid: 29.11.2006. Coming into force: 01.01.2007. Effect: S.I. 2004/1002 amended. Territorial extent & classification: E/W/S/NI. General. - Supersedes SI of same no. (ISBN 0110753860) issued 01.12.2006. - 4p.: 30 cm. - 978-0-11-075501-4 £3.00

The Duty Stamps (Amendment of paragraph 1(3) of Schedule 2A to the Alcoholic Liquor Duties Act 1979) Order 2006 No. 2006/144. - Enabling power: Alcoholic Liquor Duties Act 1979, sch. 2A, para. 2 (2). - Issued: 01.02.2006. Made: 25.01.2006. Coming into force: 01.02.2006. Effect: 1979 c. 4 amended. Territorial extent & classification: E/W/S/NI. General. - 2p.: 30 cm. - 978-0-11-073957-1 £3.00

The Duty Stamps Regulations 2006 No. 2006/202. - Enabling power: Customs and Excise Management Act 1979, ss. 93 (2) (fa), 118A (1) (2), 127A & Alcoholic Liquor Duties Act 1979, sch. 2A, paras 1, 3, 4, 5. - Issued: 07.02.2006. Made: 01.02.2006. Laid: 01.02.2006. Coming into force: 22.02.2006. Effect: S.I. 1988/809 amended. Territorial extent & classification: E/W/S/NI. General. - 24p.: 30 cm. - 978-0-11-073974-8 £4.00

The Excise Duties (Road Fuel Gas) (Reliefs) Regulations 2006 No. 2006/1980. - Enabling power: Hydrocarbon Oil Duties Act 1979, s. 20AA (1) (a) (2) (a) (b) (c) (h) (i). - Issued: 27.07.2006. Made: 21.07.2006. Laid: 24.07.2006. Coming into force: 01.09.2006. Effect: None. Territorial extent & classification: E/W/S/NI. General. - 2p.: 30 cm. - 978-0-11-074919-8 £3.00

The Excise Duties (Road Fuel Gas) (Reliefs) (Revocation) Regulations 2006 No. 2006/3234. - Enabling power: Hydrocarbon Oil Duties Act 1979, ss. 20AA (1) (a) (2) (a) (b) (c) (h) (i). - Issued: 12.12.2006. Made: 06.12.2006. Laid: 06.12.2006. Coming into force: 07.12.2006. Effect: S.I. 2006/1980 revoked. Territorial extent & classification: E/W/S/NI. General. - 2p.: 30 cm. - 978-0-11-075427-7 £3.00

The Excise Duties (Surcharges or Rebates) (Hydrocarbon Oils etc.) Order 2006 No. 2006/1979. - Enabling power: Excise Duties (Surcharges or Rebates) Act 1979, ss. 1 (2), 2 (3). - Issued: 28.07.2006. Made: 24.07.2006. Laid: 24.07.2006. Coming into force: 01.09.2006. Effect: None. Territorial extent & classification: E/W/S/NI. General. - 4p.: 30 cm. - 978-0-11-074931-0 £3.00

The Excise Duties (Surcharges or Rebates) (Hydrocarbon Oils etc.) (Revocation) Order 2006 No. 2006/3235. - Enabling power: Excise Duties (Surcharges or Rebates) Act 1979, ss. 1 (2), 2 (3). - Issued: 12.12.2006. Made: 06.12.2006. Laid: 06.12.2006. Coming into force: 07.12.2006. Effect: S.I. 2006/1979 revoked. Territorial extent & classification: E/W/S/NI. General. - For approval by resolution of that House within twenty-eight days, beginning with the day on which the Order was made, subject to extension for periods of dissolution, prorogation or adjournment for more than four days. Superseded by the S.I. of the same number (ISBN 9780110756097). - 4p.: 30 cm. - 978-0-11-075434-5 *£3.00*

The Excise Duties (Surcharges or Rebates) (Hydrocarbon Oils etc.) (Revocation) Order 2006 No. 2006/3235. - Enabling power: Excise Duties (Surcharges or Rebates) Act 1979, ss. 1 (2), 2 (3). - Issued: 25.01.2007. Made: 06.12.2006. Laid: 06.12.2006. Coming into force: 07.12.2006. Effect: S.I. 2006/1979 revoked. Territorial extent & classification: E/W/S/NI. General. - Supersedes the S.I. of the same number and title (ISBN 9780110754345). - 2p.: 30 cm. - 978-0-11-075609-7 *£3.00*

The Excise Duty Points (Etc.) (New Member States) (Amendment) Regulations 2006 No. 2006/3159. - Enabling power: Customs and Excise Management Act 1979, ss. 93 (1) (2) (a) (fa) (fb) (3), 100G, 100H & Tobacco Products Duty Act 1979, s. 7 (1) (a) (1A) (b) & Finance (No. 2) Act 1992, ss. 1, 2. - Issued: 01.12.2006. Made: 28.11.2006. Laid: 29.11.2006. Coming into force: 01.01.2007. Effect: S.I. 2004/1003 amended. Territorial extent & classification: E/W/S/NI. General. - 4p.: 30 cm. - 978-0-11-075387-4 *£3.00*

The Finance Act 2004 (Duty Stamps) (Appointed Day) Order 2006 No. 2006/201 (C.3). - Enabling power: Finance Act 2004, s. 4 (5) (6). Bringing into operation various provisions of the 2004 Act on 22.02.2006. - Issued: 07.02.2006. Made: 01.02.2006. Effect: None. Territorial extent & classification: E/W/S/NI. General. - 2p.: 30 cm. - 978-0-11-073973-1 *£3.00*

The Finance Act 2006 (Tobacco Products Duty: Evasion) (Appointed Day) Order 2006 No. 2006/2367 (C.80). - Enabling power: Finance Act 2006, s. 2 (3). Bringing into operation various provisions of the 2006 Act on 01.10.2006. - Issued: 11.09.2006. Made: 06.09.2006. Effect: None. Territorial extent & classification: E/W/S/NI. General. - 2p.: 30 cm. - 978-0-11-075083-5 *£3.00*

The Fuel-testing Pilot Projects (Biogas Project) Regulations 2006 No. 2006/1348. - Enabling power: Hydrocarbon Oil Duties Act 1979, s. 20AB (1) to (3) (5) (12). - Issued: 22.05.2006. Made: 17.05.2006. Laid: 18.05.2006. Coming into force: 10.06.2006. Effect: None. Territorial extent & classification: E/W/S/NI. General. - 4p.: 30 cm. - 978-0-11-074589-3 *£3.00*

The Gaming Duty (Amendment) Regulations 2006 No. 2006/1999. - Enabling power: Finance Act 1997, ss. 12 (4), 14 (1). - Issued: 28.07.2006. Made: 20.07.2006. Laid: 24.07.2006. Coming into force: 01.10.2006. Effect: S.I. 1997/2196 amended & S.I. 2004/2243 revoked. Territorial extent & classification: E/W/S/NI. General. - 4p.: 30 cm. - 978-0-11-074922-8 *£3.00*

The Hydrocarbon Oil Duties (Sulphur-free Diesel) (Hydrogenation of Biomass) (Reliefs) Regulations 2006 No. 2006/3426. - Enabling power: Hydrocarbon Oil Duties Act 1979, s. 20AA (1) (a) (2) (a) (b) (c) (e) (h) (i). - Issued: 02.01.2007. Made: 20.12.2006. Laid: 21.12.2006. Coming into force: 12.01.2007. Effect: None. Territorial extent & classification: E/W/S/NI. General. - These regulations shall cease to have effect on 12th January 2009. With correction slip dated February 2007. - 4p.: 30 cm. - 978-0-11-075575-5 *£3.00*

The Mutual Assistance Provisions Order 2006 No. 2006/3283. - Enabling power: Finance Act 2003, s. 197 (5). - Issued: 14.12.2006. Made: 11.12.2006. Laid: 11.12.2006. Coming into force: 01.01.2007. Effect: 2003 c.14 amended. Territorial extent & classification: E/W/S/NI. General. - With correction slip dated January 2007. - 2p.: 30 cm. - 978-0-11-075465-9 *£3.00*

The Relief for Legacies Imported from Third Countries (Application) Order 2006 No. 2006/3158. - Enabling power: Customs and Excise Duties (General Reliefs) Act 1979, s. 7. - Issued: 01.12.2006. Made: 28.11.2006. Laid: 29.11.2006. Coming into force: 01.01.2007. Effect: S.I. 1992/3193 updated in respect of a reference to Directive 73/388/EC. Territorial extent & classification: E/W/S/NI. General. - 2p.: 30 cm. - 978-0-11-075385-0 *£3.00*

The Tobacco Products (Amendment) Regulations 2006 No. 2006/2368. - Enabling power: Tobacco Products Duty Act 1979, ss. 7A (7), 9 (2). - Issued: 11.09.2006. Made: 05.09.2006. Laid: 07.09.2006. Coming into force: 01.10.2006. Effect: S.I. 2001/1712 amended. Territorial extent & classification: E/W/S/NI. General. - 4p.: 30 cm. - 978-0-11-075084-2 *£3.00*

The Tobacco Products and Excise Goods (Amendment) Regulations 2006 No. 2006/1787. - Enabling power: Tobacco Products Duty Act 1979, ss. 2 (2), 7 (1) (1A) & Finance (No.2) Act 1992, s. 1. - Issued: 10.07.2006. Made: 05.07.2006. Laid: 06.07.2006. Coming into force: 01.08.2006. Effect: S.I. 1992/3135; 2001/1712 amended. Territorial extent & classification: E/W/S/NI. General. - 4p.: 30 cm. - 978-0-11-074810-8 *£3.00*

The Warehousekeepers and Owners of Warehoused Goods (Amendment) Regulations 2006 No. 2006/577. - Enabling power: Customs and Excise Management Act 1979, s. 100H (1) (k). - Issued: 10.03.2006. Made: 06.03.2006. Laid: 07.03.2006. Coming into force: 01.04.2006. Effect: S.I. 1999/1278 amended. Territorial extent & classification: E/W/S/NI. General. - 2p.: 30 cm. - 978-0-11-074171-0 *£3.00*

Extradition

The Extradition Act 2003 (Amendment to Designations) Order 2006 No. 2006/3451. - Enabling power: Extradition Act 2003, ss. 1, 69 (1), 71 (4), 73 (5), 84 (7), 86 (7). - Issued: 29.12.2006. Made: 21.12.2006. Coming into force: 22.12.2006 for arts 1, and 2; 01.01.2007 for art. 3. Effect: S.I. 2003/3333, 3334 amended. Territorial extent & classification: E/W/S/NI. General- 2p.: 30 cm. - 978-0-11-075583-0 *£3.00*

The Police and Justice Act 2006 (Commencement No. 1, Transitional and Saving Provisions) Order 2006 No. 2006/3364 (C.123). - Enabling power: Police and Justice Act 2006, ss. 49 (3) (c), 53 (1). Bringing into operation various provisions of the 2006 Act on 15.01.2007 in accordance with art. 2. - Issued: 21.12.2006. Made: 14.12.2006. Effect: None. Territorial extent & classification: E/W. General. - This SI has been amended by SI 2007/29 (C.1) (ISBN 9780110756455) which is being issued free of charge to all known recipients of SI 2006/3364. - 4p.: 30 cm. - 978-0-11-075513-7 £3.00

Family law: Child support

The Child Support (Miscellaneous Amendments) Regulations 2006 No. 2006/1520. - Enabling power: Child Support Act 1991, ss. 14 (1), 16 (4), 29 (2) (3), 32, 34, 40B (3), 52 (4), 54, sch. 1, part 2, para. 11. - Issued: 16.06.2006. Made: 13.06.2006. Laid: 16.06.2006. Coming into force: 12.07.2006 in accord with art. 1 (1) (2). Effect: S.I. 1992/1812, 1989; 1999/991; 2001/157, 162 amended. Territorial extent & classification: E/W/S. General. - 4p.: 30 cm. - 978-0-11-074690-6 £3.00

Family law, England and Wales

The Dissolution etc. (Pension Protection Fund) Regulations 2006 No. 2006/1934. - Enabling power: Civil Partnership Act 2004, sch. 5, paras, 32, 35, 36. - Issued: 26.07.2006. Made: 17.07.2006. Laid: 18.07.2006. Coming into force: 08.08.2006. Effect: 2004 c. 33 modified; S.I. 2005/2920 amended. Territorial extent & classification: E/W. General. - 4p.: 30 cm. - 978-0-11-074866-5 £3.00

The Divorce etc. (Pension Protection Fund) Regulations 2006 No. 2006/1932. - Enabling power: Matrimonial Causes Act 1973, ss. 25E (5) (8) (9). - Issued: 25.07.2006. Made: 17.07.2006. Laid: 18.07.2006. Coming into force: 08.08.2006. Effect: 1973 c. 18 modified. Territorial extent & classification: E/W. General. - 4p.: 30 cm. - 978-0-11-074864-1 £3.00

Family proceedings, England and Wales

The Children (Allocation of Proceedings) (Amendment) Order 2006 No. 2006/1541. - Enabling power: Children Act 1989, sch. 11, part 1. - Issued: 19.06.2006. Made: 13.06.2006. Laid: 15.06.2006. Coming into force: 06.07.2006. Effect: S.I. 1991/1677 amended. Territorial extent & classification: E/W. General. - 2p.: 30 cm. - 978-0-11-074704-0 £3.00

The Family Proceedings (Amendment) (No. 2) Rules 2006 No. 2006/2080 (L.8). - Enabling power: Matrimonial and Family Proceedings Act 1984, s. 40 (1). - Issued: 01.08.2006. Made: 25.07.2006. Laid: 27.07.2006. Coming into force: 21.08.2006. Effect: S.I. 1991/1247 amended. Territorial extent & classification: E/W. General. - 4p.: 30 cm. - 978-0-11-074957-0 £3.00

The Family Proceedings (Amendment) Rules 2006 No. 2006/352 (L.1). - Enabling power: Matrimonial and Family Proceedings Act 1984, s. 40 (1). - Issued: 21.02.2006. Made: 10.02.2006. Laid: 15.02.2006. Coming into force: 03.04.2006. Effect: S.1.1991/1247 amended. Territorial extent & classification: E/W. General. - 12p.: 30 cm. - 978-0-11-074057-7 £3.00

The Family Proceedings Fees (Amendment) Order 2006 No. 2006/739 (L.5). - Enabling power: Courts Act 2003, s. 92. - Issued: 20.03.2006. Made: 07.03.2006. Laid: 16.03.2006. Coming into force: 06.04.2006. Effect: S.I. 2004/3114 amended. Territorial extent & classification: E/W. General. - 2p.: 30 cm. - 978-0-11-074306-6 £3.00

Fees and charges

The Measuring Instruments (EEC Requirements) (Fees) (Amendment No. 2) Regulations 2006 No. 2006/2679. - Enabling power: Finance Act 1973, s. 56 (1) (2). - Issued: 16.10.2006. Made: 09.10.2006. Laid: 09.10.2006. Coming into force: 30.10.2006. Effect: S.I. 2004/1300 amended. Territorial extent & classification: E/W/S/NI. General. - 4p.: 30 cm. - 978-0-11-075160-3 £3.00

The Measuring Instruments (EEC Requirements) (Fees) (Amendment) Regulations 2006 No. 2006/604. - Enabling power: Finance Act 1973, s. 56 (1) (2). - Issued: 16.03.2006. Made: 06.03.2006. Laid: 08.03.2006. Coming into force: 01.04.2006. Effect: S.I. 2004/1300 amended. Territorial extent & classification: E/W/S/NI. General. - 4p.: 30 cm. - 978-0-11-074197-0 £3.00

The Medicines for Human Use and Medical Devices (Fees Amendments) Regulations 2006 No. 2006/494. - Enabling power: European Communities Act 1972, s. 2 (2) & Finance Act 1973, s. 56 (1) (2) & Medicines Act 1971, s. 1 (1) (2). - Issued: 03.03.2006. Made: 27.02.2006. Laid: 03.03.2006. Coming into force: 01.04.2006. Effect: S.I. 1994/105; 1995/449, 1116 amended. Territorial extent & classification: E/W/S/NI. General. - 12p.: 30 cm. - 978-0-11-074114-7 £3.00

The Medicines for Human Use (Fees Amendments) Regulations 2006 No. 2006/2125. - Enabling power: Medicines Act 1971, s. 1 (1) (2). - Issued: 01.08.2006. Made: 26.07.2006. Laid: 01.08.2006. Coming into force: 01.09.2006. Effect: S.I. 1994/105; 1995/1116 amended. Territorial extent & classification: E/W/S/NI. General. - 8p.: 30 cm. - 978-0-11-074964-8 £3.00

Financial services

The Financial Markets and Insolvency (Settlement Finality) (Amendment) Regulations 2006 No. 2006/50. - Enabling power: European Communities Act 1972, s. 2 (2). - Issued: 23.01.2006. Made: 11.01.2006. Laid: 12.01.2006. Coming into force: 02.02.2006. Effect: S.I. 1999/2979 amended. Territorial extent & classification: E/W/S/NI. General. - EC note: These regulations extend coverage of the Financial Markets and Insolvency (Settlement Finality) Regulations 1999 to Northern Ireland and thus the implementation of Directive 98/26/EC to Northern Ireland. - 4p.: 30 cm. - 978-0-11-073899-4 £3.00

The Proceeds of Crime Act 2002 and Money Laundering Regulations 2003 (Amendment) Order 2006 No. 2006/308. - Enabling power: European Communities Act 1972, s. 2 (2). - Issued: 23.02.2006. Made: 14.02.2006. Coming into force: 21.02.2006. Effect: 2002 c.29; S.I. 2003/3075 amended. Territorial extent & classification: E/W/S/NI. General. - 4p.: 30 cm. - 978-0-11-074049-2 £3.00

Financial services and markets

The Capital Requirements Regulations 2006 No. 2006/3221. - Enabling power: European Communities Act 1972, s. 2 (2). - Issued: 11.12.2006. Made: 04.12.2006. Laid: 05.12.2006. Coming into force: 01.01.2007. Effect: 8 Acts & 19 SIs amended. Territorial extent & classification: E/W/S/NI. General. - EC note: These Regulations implement, in part, Directive 2006/48/EC relating to the taking up and pursuit of the business of credit institutions and Directive 2006/49/EC on the capital adequacy of investment firms and credit institutions. These two Directives recast and replace Directives 2000/12/EC and 93/6/EEC. - 24p.: 30 cm. - 978-0-11-075419-2 £4.00

The Financial Services and Markets Act 2000 (Appointed Representatives) (Amendment) Regulations 2006 No. 2006/3414. - Enabling power: Financial Services and Markets Act 2000, ss. 39(1), 417 (1), 428 (3). - Issued: 28.12.2006. Made: 19.12.2006. Laid: 19.12.2006. Coming into force: 01.11.2007. Effect: S.I. 2001/1217 amended. Territorial extent & classification: E/W/S/NI. General. - EC note: These regulations implement in part Directive 2004/39/EC on markets in financial instruments. With correction dated February 2007. - 4p.: 30 cm. - 978-0-11-075561-8 £3.00

The Financial Services and Markets Act 2000 (Designated Professional Bodies) (Amendment) Order 2006 No. 2006/58. - Enabling power: Financial Services and Markets Act 2000, s. 326. - Issued: 20.01.2006. Made: 16.01.2006. Laid: 17.01.2006. Coming into force: 10.02.2006. Effect: S.I. 2001/1226 amended. Territorial extent & classification: E/W/S/NI. General. - 2p.: 30 cm. - 978-0-11-073913-7 £3.00

The Financial Services and Markets Act 2000 (Disclosure of Confidential Information) (Amendment) Regulations 2006 No. 2006/3413. - Enabling power: Financial Services and Markets Act 2000, ss. 349 (1) (2) (3), 417 (1), 428 (3). - Issued: 28.12.2006. Made: 19.12.2006. Laid: 19.12.2006. Coming into force: 20.01.2007 for regs 3 (a) (ii) (b) (c), 8 and 9; 01.11.2007 for all other purposes. Effect: S.I. 2001/2188 amended. Territorial extent & classification: E/W/S/NI. General. - EC note: These regulations implement in part Directive 2004/39/EC markets in financial instruments. These Regs also take into account amendments made to Directive2001/34/EC by Directive 2003/71/EC & Directive 2004/109/EC. - With correction slip dated February 2007. - 8p.: 30 cm. - 978-0-11-075560-1 £3.00

The Financial Services and Markets Act 2000 (EEA Passport Rights) (Amendment) Regulations 2006 No. 2006/3385. - Enabling power: Financial Services and Markets Act 2000, s. 428 (3), sch. 3, paras 13 (1) (b) (iii), 14 (1) (b), 17 (b), 22. - Issued: 22.12.2006. Made: 18.12.2006. Laid: 18.12.2006. Coming into force: 01.04.2007; 01.11.2007 in accord. with art. 1 (2). Effect: S.I. 2001/2511 amended. Territorial extent & classification: E/W/S/NI. General. - EC note: These Regulations implement in part Directive 2004/39/EC on markets in financial instruments. - With correction slip dated February 2007. - 8p.: 30 cm. - 978-0-11-075536-6 £3.00

The Financial Services and Markets Act 2000 (Gibraltar) (Amendment) Order 2006 No. 2006/1805. - Enabling power: Financial Services and Markets Act 2000, s. 409 (1). - Issued: 12.07.2006. Made: 06.07.2006. Laid: 07.07.2006. Coming into force: 31.07.2005. Effect: S.I. 2001/3084 amended. Territorial extent & classification: E/W/S/NI. General. - 2p.: 30 cm. - 978-0-11-074816-0 £3.00

The Financial Services and Markets Act 2000 (Markets in Financial Instruments) (Modification of Powers) Regulations 2006 No. 2006/2975. - Enabling power: European Communities Act 1972, s. 2 (2). - Issued: 20.11.2006. Made: 15.11.2006. Laid: 15.11.2006. Coming into force: 06.12.2006. Effect: 2000 c. 8 amended. Territorial extent & classification: E/W/S/NI. General. - EC note: These Regulations implement, in part, Directive 2004/39/EC on markets in financial instruments- 8p.: 30 cm. - 978-0-11-075319-5 £3.00

The Financial Services and Markets Act 2000 (Recognition Requirements for Investment Exchanges and Clearing Houses) (Amendment) Regulations 2006 No. 2006/3386. - Enabling power: Financial Services and Markets Act 2000, ss. 286 (1) (4A) (4B) (4C) (4D), 292 (3) (a), 428 (3). - Issued: 22.12.2006. Made: 18.12.2006. Laid: 18.12.2006. Coming into force: 01.11.2007. Effect: S.I. 2001/995 amended. Territorial extent & classification: E/W/S/NI. General. - EC note: These Regulations implement in part Directive 2004/39/EC on markets in financial instruments. With correction slip dated February 2007. - 12p.: 30 cm. - 978-0-11-075537-3 £3.00

The Financial Services and Markets Act 2000 (Regulated Activities) (Amendment) (No.2) Order 2006 No. 2006/2383. - Enabling power: Financial Services and Markets Act 2000, ss. 22 (1) (5), 426, 427, 428 (3), sch. 2, para. 25. - Issued: 18.09.2006. Made: 12.09.2006. Laid: 13.09.2006. Coming into force: 06.11.2006 & 06.04.2007 in accord. with art. 1 (2). Effect: 1974 c.39; 1985 c.6; 1989 c.34; 2000 c.8 & S.I. 2001/544, 1177, 1201, 1217, 1227; 2003/3075; 2004/1484; 2005/1529 amended. Territorial extent & classification: E/W/S/NI. General. - For approval by a resolution of each House of Parliament within a period of twenty-eight days. - 28p.: 30 cm. - 978-0-11-075103-0 £4.50

The Financial Services and Markets Act 2000 (Regulated Activities) (Amendment) (No.2) Order 2006 No. 2006/2383. - Enabling power: Financial Services and Markets Act 2000, ss. 22 (1) (5), 426, 427, 428 (3), sch. 2, para. 25. - Issued: 31.10.2006. Made: 12.09.2006. Laid: 13.09.2006. Coming into force: 06.11.2006 & 06.04.2007 in accord. with art. 1 (2). Effect: 1974 c.39; 1985 c.6; 1989 c.34; 2000 c.8 & S.I. 2001/544, 1177, 1201, 1217, 1227; 2003/3075; 2004/1484; 2005/1529 amended. Territorial extent & classification: E/W/S/NI. General. - Approved by both Houses of Parliament. - 28p.: 30 cm. - 978-0-11-075223-5 £4.50

The Financial Services and Markets Act 2000 (Regulated Activities) (Amendment No. 3) Order 2006 No. 2006/3384. - Enabling power: Financial Services and Markets Act 2000, ss. 22 (1) (5), 428 (3), sch. 2, para. 25. - Issued: 22.12.2006. Made: 18.12.2006. Laid: 18.12.2006. Coming into force: 01.04.2007; 01.11.2007 in accord. with art. 1 (2). Effect: 1973 c.41; 1989 c.40; 2000 c. 11 & S.I. 1987/2117; 1990/1504 (N.I. 10); 2001/544, 1062, 1177, 2509; 2003/3075; 2005/1529 amended. Territorial extent & classification: E/W/S/NI. General. - Superseded by the S.I. of the same number and title issued on 31.01.2007 (ISBN 9780110756103). EC note: This Order implements in part Directive 2004/39/EC on markets in financial instruments. For approval by a resolution of each House of Parliament within a period of twenty-eight days. - 20p.: 30 cm. - 978-0-11-075535-9 £3.50

The Financial Services and Markets Act 2000 (Regulated Activities) (Amendment No. 3) Order 2006 No. 2006/3384. - Enabling power: Financial Services and Markets Act 2000, ss. 22 (1) (5), 428 (3), sch. 2, para. 25. - Issued: 31.01.2007. Made: 18.12.2006. Laid: 18.12.2006. Coming into force: 01.04.2007; 01.11.2007 in accord. with art. 1 (2). Effect: 1973 c.41; 1989 c.40; 2000 c. 11 & S.I. 1987/2117; 1990/1504 (N.I. 10); 2001/544, 1062, 1177, 2509; 2003/3075; 2005/1529 amended. Territorial extent & classification: E/W/S/NI. General. - Supersedes the S.I. of the same number and title issued on 22.12.2006 (ISBN 9780110755359) following approval by Parliament. EC note: This Order implements in part Directive 2004/39/EC on markets in financial instruments. - 20p.: 30 cm. - 978-0-11-075610-3 £3.50

The Financial Services and Markets Act 2000 (Regulated Activities) (Amendment) Order 2006 No. 2006/1969. - Enabling power: Financial Services and Markets Act 2000, ss. 22 (1) (5), 426, 427, 428 (3), sch. 2, para. 25. - Issued: 01.08.2006. Made: 28.06.2006. Laid: 29.06.2006. Coming into force: In accord. with art. 1 (2) (3), 01.10.2006, 06.04.2007. Effect: 2000 c. 8 modified & S.I. 2001/544, 1062, 1177, 1201, 1227, 2005/1529 amended. Territorial extent & classification: E/W/S/NI. General. - Approved by both Houses of Parliament. Supersedes SI of same number (ISBN 0110747690) published on 03.07.2006. - 8p.: 30 cm. - 978-0-11-074946-4 £3.00

The Financial Services and Markets Act 2000 (Regulated Activities) (Amendment) Order 2006 No. 2006/1969. - Enabling power: Financial Services and Markets Act 2000, ss. 22 (1) (5), 426, 427, 428 (3), sch. 2, para. 25. - Issued: 03.07.2006. Made: 28.06.2006. Laid: 29.06.2006. Coming into force: In accord. with art. 1 (2) (3). Effect: S.I. 2001/544, 1062, 1177, 1201, 1227, 2005/1529 amended. Territorial extent & classification: E/W/S/NI. General. - 8p.: 30 cm. - 978-0-11-074769-9 £3.00

Fire and rescue services

The Scotland Act 1998 (Agency Arrangements) (Specification) Order 2006 No. 2006/1251. - Enabling power: Scotland Act 1998, ss. 93 (3), 113. - Issued: 19.05.2006. Made: 09.05.2006. Laid: 19.05.2006. Coming into force: 10.06.2006. Effect: None. Territorial extent & classification: E/W/S/NI. General. - 4p.: 30 cm. - 978-0-11-070451-7 £3.00

Fire and rescue services, England

The Devon and Somerset Fire and Rescue Authority (Combination Scheme) Order 2006 No. 2006/2790. - Enabling power: Fire and Rescue Services Act 2004, ss. 2 to 4, 60. - Issued: 23.10.2006. Made: 16.10.2006. Laid: 23.10.2006. Coming into force: 20.11.2006 for arts 1 & 2 and 01.04.2007 for art. 3, in accord. with art. 1. Effect: S.I. 1997/2698 revoked (01.04.2007). Territorial extent & classification: E. General. - 8p.: 30 cm. - 978-0-11-075200-6 £3.00

The Fire and Rescue Services (National Framework) (England) Order 2006 No. 2006/1084. - Enabling power: Fire and Rescue Services Act 2004, s. 21 (6). - Issued: 19.04.2006. Made: 10.04.2006. Laid: 19.04.2006. Coming into force: 10.05.2006. Effect: None. Territorial extent & classification: E. General. - The Fire and Rescue National Framework 2006/08, published by the Office of the Deputy Prime Minister on 6 April 2006, shall have effect as a revision of the Fire and Rescue National Framework 2005/06 (Given effect by virtue of S.I. 2004/3217). - 2p.: 30 cm. - 978-0-11-074498-8 £3.00

The Firefighters' Compensation Scheme (England) (Amendment) Order 2006 No. 2006/3434. - Enabling power: Fire and Rescue Services Act 2004, ss. 34, 60. - Issued: 04.01.2007. Made: 19.12.2006. Laid: 04.01.2007. Coming into force: 25.01.2007. Effect: S.I. 2006/1811 amended. Territorial extent & classification: E. General. - 16p.: 30 cm. - 978-0-11-075572-4 *£3.00*

The Firefighters' Compensation Scheme (England) Order 2006 No. 2006/1811. - Enabling power: Fire and Rescue Services Act 2004, ss. 34, 60. - Issued: 17.07.2006. Made: 10.07.2006. Laid: 17.07.2006. Coming into force: 07.08.2006. Effect: S.I. 1992/129 amended in relation to England. Territorial extent & classification: E. General. - 40p.: 30 cm. - 978-0-11-074833-7 *£6.50*

The Firefighters' Pension Scheme (Amendment) (England) Order 2006 No. 2006/1810. - Enabling power: Fire Services Act 1947, s. 26 (1) to (5) & Superannuation Act 1972, s. 12. - Issued: 17.07.2006. Made: 10.07.2006. Laid: 17.07.2006. Coming into force: 07.08.2006. Effect: S.I. 1992/129 amended in relation to England. Territorial extent & classification: E. General. - 28p.: 30 cm. - 978-0-11-074832-0 *£4.50*

The Firefighters' Pension Scheme (Amendment) (No.2) (England) Order 2006 No. 2006/3433. - Enabling power: Fire Services Act 1947, s. 26 (1) to (5) & Superannuation Act 1972, s. 12. - Issued: 04.01.2007. Made: 19.12.2006. Laid: 04.01.2007. Coming into force: 25.01.2007. Effect: S.I. 1992/129 amended in relation to England, with effect 06.04.2006. Territorial extent & classification: E. General. - 8p.: 30 cm. - 978-0-11-075573-1 *£3.00*

The Firefighters' Pension Scheme (England) Order 2006 No. 2006/3432. - Enabling power: Fire and Rescue Services Act 2004, ss. 34, 60. - Issued: 23.03.2007. Made: 19.12.2006. Laid: 04.01.2007. Coming into force: 25.01.2007. Effect: 1992 scheme (S.I. 1992/129) ceasing to have effect in England, with savings, (paras. (2) & (3)). Territorial extent & classification: E. General. - This Statutory Instrument has been printed in substitution of the SI of the same number and is being issued free of charge to all known recipients of that SI. - 72p.: 30 cm. - 978-0-11-075574-8 *£10.50*

Fire and rescue services, Wales

The Fire and Rescue Services (Charging) (Wales) Order 2006 No. 2006/1852 (W.195). - Enabling power: Fire and Rescue Services Act 2004, ss. 19, 60, 62. - Issued: 04.08.2006. Made: 11.07.2006. Coming into force: 13.07.2006. Effect: None. Territorial extent & classification: W. General. - With correction slip dated August 2006 amending the coming into force date to 13.07.2006. - In English and Welsh. Welsh title: Gorchymyn y Gwasanaethau Tân ac Achub (Codi Taliadau) (Cymru) 2006 (Cymru) 2006. - 8p.: 30 cm. - 978-0-11-091393-3 *£3.00*

The Firefighters' Pension (Wales) Scheme (Amendment) Order 2006 No. 2006/1672 (W.160). - Enabling power: Fire Services Act 1947, s. 26 & Superannuation Act 1972, s. 12 & Fire and Rescue Services Act 2004, ss. 36, 53, 60, 62 & Civil Partnership Act 2004, s. 259 (1) (2) (c) (4) (b). - Issued: 30.06.2006. Made: 21.06.2006. Coming into force: 23.06.2006. Effect: S.I. 1992/129 amended in relation to Wales. Territorial extent & classification: W. General. - In English and Welsh. Welsh title: Gorchymyn Cynllun Pensiwn Dynion Tân (Cymru) (Diwygio) 2006. - 44p.: 30 cm. - 978-0-11-091363-6 *£7.50*

Food

The Animals and Animal Products (Examination for Residues and Maximum Residue Limits) (Amendment) Regulations 2006 No. 2006/755. - Enabling power: European Communities Act 1972, s. 2 (2) & Food Safety Act 1990, ss. 6 (4), 16 (1) (a) (b) (f), 16 (3), 17 (1) (2), 26 (1) (2) (a) (3), 30 (9), 31 (1), 48 (1), sch. 1, para. 7. - Issued: 21.03.2006. Made: 10.03.2006. Laid: 16.03.2006. Coming into force: 06.04.2006. Effect: S.I. 1997/1729 amended. Territorial extent & classification: E/W/S. General. - EC note: These Regulations amend provisions of the (S.I. 1997/1729) that give effect to Council Directive 96/22/EC concerning the prohibition on the use in stockfarming of certain substances having a hormonal or thyrostatic action and of beta-agonists, and repealing Directives 81/602/EEC, 88/146/EEC and 88/299/EEC. Paragraph (10) transposes Commission Decision 2002/657 implementing Council Directive 96/23/EC concerning the performance of analytical methods and the interpretation of results by amending regulation 20. - 8p.: 30 cm. - 978-0-11-074317-2 *£3.00*

The Ceramic Articles in Contact with Food (England) Regulations 2006 No. 2006/1179. - Enabling power: Food Safety Act 1990, ss. 16 (2), 17 (1), 26 (1) (a) (2) (a) (3), 48 (1) & Consumer Protection Act 1987, s. 11. - Issued: 05.05.2006. Made: 24.04.2006. Laid: 27.04.2006. Coming into force: 20.05.2006 except for regs 3 (3) (a) (b), 4; 20.05.2007 for regs 3 (3) (a) (b), 4. Effect: S.I. 1988/1647 revoked except in their application to Scotland. Territorial extent & classification: E. (except for paragraphs 1 (1) and (2)). General. - EC note: These Regs implement Council Directive 84/500/EEC on the approximation of the laws of the Member States relating to ceramic articles intended to come into contact with foodstuffs as amended by Commission Directive 2005/31/EC regarding a declaration of compliance and performance criteria of the analytical method for ceramic articles intended to come into contact with foodstuffs. The former Directive was previously implemented by the Ceramic Ware (Safety) Regulations 1988 (S.I. 1988/1647) which these Regulations revoke in respect of England, Wales and Northern Ireland. - 8p.: 30 cm. - 978-0-11-074531-2 *£3.00*

The Charges for Inspections and Controls (Amendment) Regulations 2006 No. 2006/756. - Enabling power: Food Safety Act 1990, ss. 45, 48 (1) (b) (c). - Issued: 21.03.2006. Made: 12.03.2006. Laid: 16.03.2006. Coming into force: 06.04.2006. Effect: S.I. 1997/2893 amended. Territorial extent & classification: E/W/S. General. - Revoked by S.I. 2006/2285 (ISBN 011075039X). - 4p.: 30 cm. - 978-0-11-074315-8 £3.00

The Charges for Residues Surveillance Regulations 2006 No. 2006/2285. - Enabling power: Food Safety Act 1990, ss. 6 (4), 45, 48 (1) (b) (c). - Issued: 30.08.2006. Made: 22.08.2006. Laid: 25.08.2006. Coming into force: 01.10.2006. Effect: S.I. 1997/2893; 1998/2880; 2004/1871; 2005/12, 2715; 2006/756 revoked. Territorial extent & classification: E/W/S. General. - EC note: Gives effect, until 1st January 2007, to art. 2 of Council Directive 85/73/EEC on the financing of veterinary inspections and controls covered by Directives 89/662/EEC, 90/425/EEC, 90/675/EEC and 91/496/EEC ('the old rules'), which was last amended by Council Directive 97/79/EC. From 1st January 2007, these Regs give effect (except for honey) to art. 27, as read with Annex IV section A of Regulation (EC) no. 882/2004 on official controls performed to ensure the verification of compliance with feed and food law, animal health and animal welfare rules instead of the old rules. - 8p.: 30 cm. - 978-0-11-075039-2 £3.00

The Dairy Produce Quotas (Amendment) Regulations 2006 No. 2006/120. - Enabling power: European Communities Act 1972, s. 2 (2). - Issued: 03.02.2006. Made: 24.01.2006. Laid: 26.01.2006. Coming into force: 31.03.2006. Effect: S.I. 2005/465 amended. Territorial extent & classification: E/W/S/NI. General. - This is a corrected reprint of the S.I. of the same number and ISBN (originally published on 30.01.2006) which omitted the following note: This Statutory Instrument has been printed to correct errors in S.I. 2005/465 and is being issued free of charge to all known recipients of that Statutory Instrument. - 4p.: 30 cm. - 978-0-11-073937-3 £3.00

The Healthy Start Scheme and Welfare Food (Amendment No. 2) Regulations 2006 No. 2006/2818. - Enabling power: Social Security Act 1988, s. 13 & Social Security Contributions and Benefits Act 1992, s. 175 (2) to (5). - Issued: 27.10.2006. Made: 23.10.2006. Laid: 27.10.2006. Coming into force: 27.11.2006 Effect: S.I. 1996/1434; 2005/3262 amended. Territorial extent & classification: E/W/S. General. - 8p.: 30 cm. - 978-0-11-075218-1 £3.00

The Healthy Start Scheme and Welfare Food (Amendment) Regulations 2006 No. 2006/589. - Enabling power: Social Security Act 1988, s. 13 & Social Security Contributions and Benefits Act 1992, s. 175 (2) to (5). - Issued: 10.03.2006. Made: 06.03.2006. Laid: 10.03.2006. Coming into force: 06.04.2006. Effect: S.I. 1996/1434; 2005/3262 amended. Territorial extent & classification: E/W/S. General. - 4p.: 30 cm. - 978-0-11-074179-6 £3.00

The Olive Oil (Marketing Standards) (Amendment) Regulations 2006 No. 2006/3367. - Enabling power: European Communities Act 1972, s. 2 (2). - Issued: 21.12.2006. Made: 13.12.2006. Laid: 19.12.2006. Coming into force: 10.01.2007. Effect: S.I. 2003/2577 amended. Territorial extent & classification: E/W/S. General. - 2p.: 30 cm. - 978-0-11-075524-3 £3.00

The Scotland Act 1998 (Agency Arrangements) (Specification) (No. 2) Order 2006 No. 2006/3248. - Enabling power: Scotland Act 1998, ss. 93 (3), 113 (2) (4). - Issued: 22.12.2006. Made: 14.12.2006. Laid: 08.01.2007. Laid before the Scottish Parliament: 08.01.2007. Coming into force: 29.01.2007. Effect: S.I. 1999/1512 modified. Territorial extent & classification: E/W/S/NI. General. - 4p.: 30 cm. - 978-0-11-071432-5 £3.00

Food, England

The Contaminants in Food (England) Regulations 2006 No. 2006/1464. - Enabling power: Food Safety Act 1990, ss. 16 (1) (a) (e) (f), 17(2), 26 (1) (a) (2) (e) (3), 48 (1). - Issued: 09.06.2006. Made: 05.06.2006. Laid: 09.06.2006. Coming into force: 01.07.2006. Effect: 1990 c. 16 modified in relation to England & S.I. 1990/2463 amended in relation to England & S.I. 2005/3251 revoked. Territorial extent & classification: E. General. - EC note: These Regs make provision for the execution and enforcement of Commission Regulation (EC) No. 466/2001 setting maximum levels for contaminants in foodstuffs as corrected and amended. - 8p.: 30 cm. - 978-0-11-074649-4 £3.00

The Curd Cheese (Restriction on Placing on the Market) (England) Regulations 2006 No. 2006/2787. - Enabling power: European Communities Act 1972, s. 2 (2). - Issued: 20.10.2006. Made: 16.10.2006. Laid: 17.10.2006. Coming into force: 18.10.2006. Effect: None. Territorial extent & classification: E. General. - EC note: These Regs implement, in relation to England, Commission Decision 2006/694/EC prohibiting placing on the market of curd cheese manufactured in a dairy establishment in the UK. - 8p.: 30 cm. - 978-0-11-075193-1 £3.00

The Fishery Products (Official Controls Charges) (England) Regulations 2006 No. 2006/2904. - Enabling power: European Communities Act 1972, s. 2 (2). - Issued: 15.11.2006. Made: 03.11.2006. Laid: 15.11.2006. Coming into force: 01.01.2007. Effect: S.I. 2005/2991 revoked. Territorial extent & classification: E. General. - EC note: These Regs provide for the execution and enforcement in relation to England of arts. 26 & 27 of Reg (EC) no. 882/2004, on official controls performed to ensure the verification of compliance with feed and food law, animal health and animal welfare rules. - 12p.: 30 cm. - 978-0-11-075256-3 £3.00

The Fish Labelling (Amendment) (England) Regulations 2006 No. 2006/506. - Enabling power: Food Safety Act 1990, ss. 16 (1) (e) (f), 17 (2), 26 (3), 48 (1). - Issued: 09.03.2006. Made: 27.02.2006. Laid: 09.03.2006. Coming into force: 06.04.2006. Effect: S.I. 2003/461 amended. Territorial extent & classification: E. General. - 12p.: 30 cm. - 978-0-11-074121-5 *£3.00*

The Food (Emergency Control) (Revocation) (England) Regulations 2006 No. 2006/2289. - Enabling power: European Communities Act 1972, s. 2 (2). - Issued: 29.08.2006. Made: 22.08.2006. Laid: 29.08.2006. Coming into force: 01.10.2006. Effect: S.I. 2002/2350, 2351; 2003/1722, 1956, 2074 revoked. Territorial extent & classification: E. General. - 2p.: 30 cm. - 978-0-11-075040-8 *£3.00*

The Food for Particular Nutritional Uses (Addition of Substances for Specific Nutritional Purposes) (England) (Amendment) Regulations 2006 No. 2006/3116. - Enabling power: Food Safety Act 1990, ss. 16 (1) (f), 17 (1), 26 (3), 48 (1). - Issued: 28.11.2006. Made: 20.11.2006. Laid: 28.11.2006. Coming into force: 31.12.2006. Effect: S.I. 2002/333 (in relation to England), 1817 amended. Territorial extent & classification: E. General. - EC note: These Regs. which apply to England, implement Commission Directive 2006/34/EC amending the Annex to Directive 2001/15/EC as regards the inclusion of certain substances. - 4p.: 30 cm. - 978-0-11-075362-1 *£3.00*

The Food Hygiene (England) Regulations 2006 No. 2006/14. - Enabling power: European Communities Act 1972, s. 2 (2). - Issued: 13.01.2006. Made: 09.01.2006. Laid: 09.01.2006. Coming into force: 11.01.2006. Effect: S.I. 1995/614, 3124; 1996/1499; 1997/2959, 2003/1596 amended in relation to England & S.I. 2005/2059 revoked. Territorial extent & classification: E. General. - EC note: These Regulations provide for the execution and enforcement, in England, of Regulations (EC) Nos. 852/2004, 853/2004, 854/2004, 2073/2005, 2075/2005. - 39p.: 30 cm. - 978-0-11-073888-8 *£6.50*

The Meat (Official Controls Charges) (England) Regulations 2006 No. 2006/2705. - Enabling power: European Communities Act 1972, s. 2 (2). - Issued: 18.10.2006. Made: 11.10.2006. Laid: 18.10.2006. Coming into force: 01.01.2007. Effect: S.I. 2005/2983 revoked. Territorial extent & classification: E. General. - EC note: These Regulations provide for the execution and enforcement in relation to England of arts 26 and 27 of Regulation (EC) No. 882/2004 on official controls performed to ensure the verification of compliance with feed and food law, animal health and animal welfare rules, and to verify compliance with the animal welfare rules set out in Council Directive 93/119/EC in so far as they apply in relation to animals slaughtered for human consumption at slaughterhouses. - 12p.: 30 cm. - 978-0-11-075185-6 *£3.00*

The Official Controls (Animals, Feed and Food) (England) Regulations 2006 No. 2006/3472. - Enabling power: European Communities Act 1972, s. 2 (2). - Issued: 09.01.2007. Made: 28.12.2006. Laid: 08.01.2007. Coming into force: 16.02.2007. Effect: S.I. 2006/15 amended. Territorial extent & classification: E. General. - EC note: These Regulations apply and enforce Regulation (EC) No. 882/2004 in England in relation to animal health and welfare rules, and feed and food law excluded from the Official Feed and Food Controls Regulations (England) 2006, which also apply and enforce Regulation 882/2004. - 12p.: 30 cm. - 978-0-11-075587-8 *£3.00*

The Official Feed and Food Controls (England) Regulations 2006 No. 2006/15. - Enabling power: European Communities Act 1972, s. 2 (2). - Issued: 31.01.2006. Made: 09.01.2006. Laid: 09.01.2006. Coming into force: 11.01.2006. Effect: S.I. 2005/3280 amended & S.I. 2005/2626 revoked. Territorial extent & classification: E. General- EC note: Relates to the execution and enforcement, in England, of Regulation (EC) No. 882/2004. They also impose prohibitions on the introduction of certain feed and food into England in the light of Article 11 of Regulation (EC) No. 178/2002 as last amended by Regulation (EC) No. 1642/2003. - 32p.: 30 cm. - 978-0-11-073889-5 *£5.50*

The Plastic Materials and Articles in Contact with Food (England) (No.2) Regulations 2006 No. 2006/2687. - Enabling power: Food Safety Act 1990, ss. 16 (2), 17 (1) (2), 26 (1) (a) (3), 31, 48 (1). - Issued: 17.10.2006. Made: 09.10.2006. Laid: 17.10.2006. Coming into force: 19.11.2006. Effect: S.I. 1990/2463; 2005/898 amended & S.I. 2006/1401 revoked. Territorial extent & classification: E. General. - EC note: These Regs include the amendments made to Commission Directive 2002/72/EC by Commission Directive 2005/79/EC. The principal Directives implemented by these Regulations are: (a) Council Directive 82/711/EEC as amended by Commission Directives 93/8/EEC and 97/48/EC; (b) Council Directive 85/572/EEC; (c) Commission Directive 2002/72/EC as amended by Commission Directives 2004/1/EC, 2004/19/EC, and 2005/79/EC. - 36p.: 30 cm. - 978-0-11-075168-9 *£6.50*

The Plastic Materials and Articles in Contact with Food (England) Regulations 2006 No. 2006/1401. - Enabling power: Food Safety Act 1990, ss. 16 (2), 17 (1) (2), 26 (1) (a) (3), 31, 48 (1). - Issued: 02.06.2006. Made: 23.05.2006. Laid: 02.06.2006. Coming into force: 30.06.2006. Effect: S.I. 1990/2463; 2005/898 amended & S.I. 1998/1376 revoked in relation to England; S.I. 2000/3162; 2002/2364, 3008; 2004/3113; 2005/325 revoked. Territorial extent & classification: E. General. - Revoked by S.I. 2006/2687 (ISBN 011075168X). EC note: These Regs continue to implement, in England, Council Directives 82/711/EEC (as amended by Commission Directives 93/8/EEC and 97/48/EEC) and 85/572/EEC; and Commission Directive 2002/72/EC (as amended by Commission Directives 2004/1/EC and 2004/19/EC). They also provide for the execution and enforcement of Commission Regulation no. 1895/2005 on the restriction of use of certain epoxy derivatives in materials and articles intended to come into contact with food. - 76p.: 30 cm. - 978-0-11-074615-9 *£12.00*

The Rice Products (Restriction on First Placing on the Market) (England) Regulations 2006 No. 2006/2921. - Enabling power: European Communities Act 1972, s. 2 (2). - Issued: 13.11.2006. Made: 07.11.2006. Laid: 08.11.2006. Coming into force: 09.11.2006. Effect: None. Territorial extent & classification: E. General. - EC note: These Regulations implement in relation to England Commission Decision 2006/601/EC on emergency measures regarding the non-authorised genetically modified organism "LL RICE 601" in rice products as amended by Commission Decision 2006/754/EC. - 4p.: 30 cm. - 978-0-11-075275-4 *£3.00*

Food, England and Wales

The Eggs (Marketing Standards) (Amendment) (England and Wales) Regulations 2006 No. 2006/1540. - Enabling power: European Communities Act 1972, s. 2 (2). - Issued: 20.06.2006. Made: 14.06.2006. Laid: 14.06.2006. Coming into force: 15.06.2006. Effect: S.I. 1995/1544 amended. Territorial extent & classification: E/W. General. - EC note: The 1995 Regulations provide for the enforcement and execution of certain provisions of EC Regulations. Since the 1995 Regulations were last amended Commission Regulation (EEC) No. 1274/91 has been repealed and replaced by Commission Regulation (EC) No. 2295/2003. This has itself since been amended. Council Regulation (EEC) No. 1907/90, Council Regulation (EEC) No. 2782/75 and Commission Regulation (EEC) No. 1868/77 have also been amended. - 4p.: 30 cm. - 978-0-11-074702-6 *£3.00*

The Health and Social Care (Community Health and Standards) Act 2003 (Commencement) (No. 10) Order 2006 No. 2006/2817 (C.96). - Enabling power: Health and Social Care (Community Health and Standards) Act 2003, s. 199 (1). Bringing into operation various provisions of the 2003 Act on 27.10.2006 in accord. with art. 2. - Issued: 26.10.2006. Made: 23.10.2006. Effect: None. Territorial extent & classification: E/W. General. - 8p.: 30 cm. - 978-0-11-075217-4 *£3.00*

Food, Wales

The Ceramic Articles in Contact with Food (Wales) Regulations 2006 No. 2006/1704 (W.166). - Enabling power: Food Safety Act 1990, ss. 16 (2), 17 (1), 26 (2) (a) (3), 48 (1). - Issued: 18.07.2006. Made: 27.06.2006. Coming into force: 30.06.2006. Effect: S.I. 2006/590 (W.66) amended. Territorial extent & classification: W. General. - EC note: These Regs implement Council Directive 84/500/EEC on the approximation of the laws of the Member States relating to ceramic articles intended to come into contact with foodstuffs as amended by Commission Directive 2005/31/EC. - In English and Welsh. Welsh title: Rheoliadau Eitemau Ceramig mewn Cyffyrddiad â Bwyd (Cymru) 2006. - 12p.: 30 cm. - 978-0-11-091386-5 *£3.00*

The Contaminants in Food (Wales) (No. 2) Regulations 2006 No. 2006/1850 (W.193). - Enabling power: Food Safety Act 1990, ss. 16 (1) (a) (e) (f), 17 (2), 26 (1) (a) (2) (e) (3), 48 (1). - Issued: 19.07.2006. Made: 11.07.2006. Coming into force: 13.07.2006. Effect: S.I. 1990/2463 amended in relation to Wales & S.I. 2006/485 (W.55) revoked. Territorial extent & classification: W. General. - EC note: To make provision for the execution and enforcement of Commission Regulation (EC) no. 466/2001. - In English and Welsh. Welsh title: Rheoliadau Halogion mewn Bwyd (Cymru) (Rhif 2) 2006. - 12p.: 30 cm. - 978-0-11-091389-6 *£3.00*

The Contaminants in Food (Wales) Regulations 2006 No. 2006/485 (W.55). - Enabling power: Food Safety Act 1990, ss. 16 (1) (a) (e) (f), 17 (1) (2), 26 (1) (a) (2) (e) (3), 31 (1) (2) (b) (c) (f), 48 (1) (c). - Issued: 07.03.2006. Made: 28.02.2006. Coming into force: 01.03.2006. Effect: S.I. 1990/2463 amended & S.I. 2005/364 (W.31); 2005/1629 (W.123) revoked. Territorial extent & classification: W. General. - Revoked by S.I. 2006/1850 (W.193) (ISBN 0110913892). EC note: To make provision for the execution and enforcement of Commission Regulation (EC) no. 466/2001. These Regs implement Commission Directive 98/53/EC; 2001/22/EC; 2002/26/EC; 2002/69/EC; 2003/78/EC; 2004/16/EC; 2005/10/EC. - In English and Welsh. Welsh title: Rheoliadau Halogion mewn Bwyd (Cymru) 2006. - 20p.: 30 cm. - 978-0-11-091282-0 *£3.50*

The Curd Cheese (Restriction on Placing on the Market) (Wales) Regulations 2006 No. 2006/2792 (W.233). - Enabling power: European Communities Act 1972, s. 2 (2). - Issued: 30.10.2006. Made: 17.10.2006. Coming into force: 18.10.2006. Effect: None. Territorial extent & classification: W. General. - EC note: These Regs implement, in relation to Wales, Commission Decision 2006/694/EC prohibiting placing on the market of curd cheese manufactured in a dairy establishment in the UK. - 8p.: 30 cm. - 978-0-11-091417-6 *£3.00*

The Dairy Produce Quotas (Wales) (Amendment) Regulations 2006 No. 2006/762 (W.72). - Enabling power: European Communities Act 1972, s. 2 (2). - Issued: 20.03.2006. Made: 14.03.2006. Coming into force: 31.03.2006. Effect: S.I. 2005/537 (W. 47) amended. Territorial extent & classification: W. General. - In English and Welsh. Welsh title: Rheoliadau Cwotâu Cynnyrch Llaeth (Cymru) (Diwygio) 2006. - 8p.: 30 cm. - 978-0-11-091297-4 *£3.00*

The Fishery Products (Official Controls Charges) (Wales) Regulations 2006 No. 2006/3344 (W.305). - Enabling power: European Communities Act 1972, s. 2 (2). - Issued: 24.01.2007. Made: 13.12.2006. Coming into force: 01.01.2007. Effect: S.I. 2005/3297 (W.255) revoked. Territorial extent & classification: W. General. - EC note: These Regulations provide for the execution and enforcement in relation to Wales of Art. 26 and 27 of Regulation (EC) No. 882/2004 on official controls performed to ensure the verification of compliance with feed and food law, animal health and animal welfare rules (the revised text of Regulation (EC) No. 882/2004 is now set out in a Corrigendum) so far as those provisions require fees to be collected to cover the costs occasioned by official controls performed on fishery products under Annex III to Regulation (EC) No. 854/2004 laying down specific rules for the organisation of official controls on products of animal origin intended for human consumption (the revised text of Regulation (EC) No. 854/2004 is now set out in a Corrigendum). - In English and Welsh. Welsh title: Rheoliadau Cynhyrchion Pysgodfeydd (Taliadau Rheolaethau Swyddogol) (Cymru) 2006. - 20p.: 30 cm. - 978-0-11-091485-5 *£3.50*

The Fish Labelling (Wales) (Amendment) Regulations 2006 No. 2006/1339 (W.131). - Enabling power: Food Safety Act 1990, ss. 16 (1) (e) (f), 17 (2), 26 (3), 48 (1). - Issued: 25.05.2006. Made: 16.05.2006. Coming into force: 24.05.2006. Effect: S.I. 2003/1635 (W.177) amended. Territorial extent & classification: W. General. - In English and Welsh. Welsh title: Rheoliadau Labelu Pysgod (Cymru) (Diwygio) 2006. - 20p.: 30 cm. - 978-0-11-091342-1 *£3.50*

The Food (Emergency Control) (Revocation) (Wales) Regulations 2006 No. 2006/2830 (W.251). - Enabling power: European Communities Act 1972, s. 2 (2). - Issued: 01.11.2006. Made: 24.10.2006. Coming into force: 27.10.2006. Effect: S.I. 2002/1726 (W.161), 2295 (W.224), 2296 (W.225); 2003/2254 (W.224), 2288 (W.227), 2292 (W.228), 2299 (W.229),2003/2910 (W.276); 2005/257 (W.23) revoked. Territorial extent & classification: W. General. - EC note: These Regs, which apply in relation to Wales, provide for the revocation of specified instruments which implemented Commission Decisions imposing conditions on the import of specific products that could be contaminated with excessive levels of aflatoxins. - In English and Welsh. Welsh title: Rheoliadau Bwyd (Rheolaeth Frys) (Dirymu) (Cymru) 2006. - 8p.: 30 cm. - 978-0-11-091419-0 *£3.00*

The Food Hygiene (Wales) (Amendment) Regulations 2006 No. 2006/1534 (W.151). - Enabling power: European Communities Act 1972, s. 2 (2). - Issued: 27.06.2006. Made: 13.06.2006. Coming into force: 15.06.2006. Effect: S.I. 2006/31 (W.5) amended. Territorial extent & classification: W. General. - In English and Welsh. Welsh title: Rheoliadau Hylendid Bwyd (Cymru) (Diwygio) 2006. - 4p.: 30 cm. - 978-0-11-091358-2 *£3.00*

The Food Hygiene (Wales) Regulations 2006 No. 2006/31 (W.5). - Enabling power: European Communities Act 1972, s. 2 (2) & Food Safety Act 1990, s. 16 (1) (e). - Issued: 15.02.2006. Made: 10.01.2006. Coming into force: 11.01.2006. Effect: S.I. 2005/3292 (W.252) revoked & S.I. 1995/614, 3124; 1996/1499; 1997/2959 amended in relation to Wales. Territorial extent & classification: W. General. - EC note: These Regs provide for the execution and enforcement in relation to Wales of the following Community Instruments: Reg (EC) nos. 852/2004, 853/2004, 854/2004 & Commission Reg nos. 2073/2005, 2075/2005. - In English and Welsh. Welsh title: Rheoliadau Hylendid Bwyd (Cymru) 2006. - 60p.: 30 cm. - 978-0-11-091273-8 *£9.00*

The Kava-kava in Food (Wales) Regulations 2006 No. 2006/1851 (W.194). - Enabling power: Food Safety Act 1990, ss. 16 (1) (a) (e) (f), 18 (1) (c), 26 (1) (3), 48 (1). - Issued: 21.07.2006. Made: 11.07.2006. Coming into force: 14.07.2006. Effect: None. Territorial extent & classification: W. General. - In English and Welsh. Welsh title: Rheoliadau Cafa-cafa mewn Bwyd (Cymru) 2006. - 8p.: 30 cm. - 978-0-11-091390-2 *£3.00*

The Meat (Official Controls Charges) (Wales) Regulations 2006 No. 2006/3245 (W.293). - Enabling power: European Communities 1972, s. 2 (2). - Issued: 15.12.2006. Made: 05.12.2006. Coming into force: 01.01.2007. Effect: S.I. 2005/3370 (W.267) revoked. Territorial extent & classification: W. General. - EC note: These Regulations provide for the execution and enforcement in relation to Wales of Articles 26 and 27 of Regulation (EC) No. 882/2004 on official controls performed to ensure the verification of compliance with feed and food law, animal health and animal welfare rules, in so far as those provisions require fees to be collected to cover the costs occasioned by official controls performed. - In English and Welsh. Welsh title: Rheoliadau Cig (Ffioedd Rheolaethau Swyddogol) (Cymru) 2006. - 20p.: 30 cm. - 978-0-11-091470-1 *£3.50*

The Official Feed and Food Controls (Wales) Regulations 2006 No. 2006/590 (W.66). - Enabling power: Food Safety Act 1990, ss. 16 (1), 17 (2), 48 (1) & European Communities Act 1972, s. 2 (2). - Issued: 14.03.2006. Made: 07.03.2006. Coming into force: 08.03.2006. Effect: S.I. 2005/3368 (W. 265) amended & S.I. 2005/3254 (W. 247) revoked. Territorial extent & classification: W. General. - In English and Welsh. Welsh title: Rheoliadau Rheolaethau Swyddogol ar Fwyd Anifeiliaid a Bwyd (Cymru) 2006. - 56p.: 30 cm. - 978-0-11-091293-6 *£9.00*

The Plastic Materials and Articles in Contact with Food (Wales) Regulations 2006 No. 2006/2982 (W.273). - Enabling power: Food Safety Act 1990, ss. 16 (2), 17 (1) (2), 26 (1) (a) (3), 31, 48 (1). - Issued: 01.12.2006. Made: 14.11.2006. Coming into force: 19.11.2006. Effect: S.I. 1990/2463 (in relation to Wales); 1998/1376 (in relation to Wales); 2005/1647 (W.128) amended & S.I. 2001/1263 (W.70); 2002/2834 (W.272); 2003/302 (W.44); 2005/182 (W.15), 1649 (W.130) revoked. Territorial extent & classification: W. General. - With correction slip dated February 2007. EC note: These Regulations revoke and re-enact SI 1998/1376 in so far as they apply to Wales. They also provide for the execution and enforcement Regulation (EC) 1895/2005 on the restriction of use of certain epoxy derivatives in materials and articles intended to come into contact with food. - In English and Welsh. Welsh title: Rheoliadau Deunyddiau ac Eitemau Plastig mewn Cysylltiad â Bwyd (Cymru) 2006. - 41p.: 30 cm. - 978-0-11-091457-2 £7.50

The Rice Products (Restriction on First Placing on the Market) (Wales) (Amendment) Regulations 2006 No. 2006/2969 (W.268). - Enabling power: European Communities Act 1972, s. 2 (2). - Issued: 04.12.2006. Made: 14.11.2006. Coming into force: 15.11.2006. Effect: S.I. 2006/2923 (W.260) amended. Territorial extent & classification: W. General. - 4p.: 30 cm. - 978-0-11-091459-6 £3.00

The Rice Products (Restriction on First Placing on the Market) (Wales) Regulations 2006 No. 2006/2923 (W.260). - Enabling power: European Communities Act 1972, s. 2 (2). - Issued: 28.11.2006. Made: 08.11.2006. Coming into force: 09.11.2006. Effect: None. Territorial extent & classification: W. General. - EC note: These Regulations implement in Wales Decision 2006/601/EC on emergency measures regarding the non-authorised genetically modified organism "LL RICE 601" in rice products, as amended by 2006/754/EC. - 8p.: 30 cm. - 978-0-11-091451-0 £3.00

Forestry

The Regulatory Reform (Forestry) Order 2006 No. 2006/780. - Enabling power: Regulatory Reform Act 2001, s. 1. - Issued: 23.03.2006. Made: 15.03.2006. Coming into force: 16.03.2006 in accord. with art. 1. Effect: 1967 c.10; 1968 c.41 amended. Territorial extent & classification: E/W/S. General. - 8p.: 30 cm. - 978-0-11-074358-5 £3.00

Forestry, England and Wales

The Environmental Impact Assessment (Forestry) (England and Wales) (Amendment) Regulations 2006 No. 2006/3106. - Enabling power: European Communities Act 1972, s. 2 (2). - Issued: 28.11.2006. Made: 22.11.2006. Laid: 27.11.2006. Coming into force: 31.12.2006. Effect: S.I. 1999/2228 amended. Territorial extent & classification: E/W. General. - EC note: Implement amendments made to Directive 85/337/EEC by 2003/35/EC. - 4p.: 30 cm. - 978-0-11-075356-0 £3.00

Gas

The Electricity and Gas Appeals (Modification of Time Limits) Order 2006 No. 2006/1519. - Enabling power: Energy Act 2004, sch. 22, para. 14. - Issued: 22.06.2006. Made: 12.06.2006. Laid: 15.06.2006. Coming into force: 27.06.2006. Effect: 2004 c.20 amended. Territorial extent & classification: E/W/S. General. - 2p.: 30 cm. - 978-0-11-074689-0 £3.00

The Energy Act 2004 (Commencement No. 7) Order 2006 No. 2006/1964 (C.66). - Enabling power: Energy Act 2004, s. 198 (2). Bringing into operation various provisions of the 2004 Act on 14.08.2006. - Issued: 28.07.2006. Made: 21.07.2006. Effect: None. Territorial extent & classification: E/W/S. General. - 4p.: 30 cm. - 978-0-11-074914-3 £3.00

The Gas Act 1986 (Exemption from the Requirement for an Interconnector Licence) Order 2006 No. 2006/2000. - Enabling power: Gas Act 1986, s. 6A (1). - Issued: 31.07.2006. Made: 21.07.2006. Laid: 24.07.2006. Coming into force: 14.08.2006. Effect: None. Territorial extent & classification: E/W/S. General. - 2p.: 30 cm. - 978-0-11-074926-6 £3.00

The Gas (Prepayment Meter) Regulations 2006 No. 2006/2011. - Enabling power: Gas Act 1986, s. 47, sch. 2B, para. 6A. - Issued: 31.07.2006. Made: 23.07.2006. Coming into force: 01.09.2006. Effect: None. Territorial extent & classification: E/W/S. General. - 4p.: 30 cm. - 978-0-11-074933-4 £3.00

Gender recognition

The Gender Recognition (Application Fees) Order 2006 No. 2006/758. - Enabling power: Gender Recognition Act 2004, s. 7 (2). - Issued: 20.03.2006. Made: 09.03.2006. Laid: 16.03.2006. Coming into force: 06.04.2006. Effect: S.I. 2005/638 revoked with saving. Territorial extent & classification: E/W/S/NI. General. - 4p.: 30 cm. - 978-0-11-074318-9 £3.00

Government resources and accounts

The Special Health Authorities (Audit) Order 2006 No. 2006/960. - Enabling power: Government Resources and Accounts Act 2000, s. 25 (6) (7). - Issued: 04.04.2006. Made: 29.03.2006. Coming into force: 30.03.2006. Effect: 1977 c.49; 1998 c.18 amended. Territorial extent & classification: E/W/S/NI. General. - 4p.: 30 cm. - 978-0-11-074426-1 £3.00

The Special Health Authorities (Summarised Accounts) Order 2006 No. 2006/250. - Enabling power: Government Resources and Accounts Act 2000, s. 14. - Issued: 13.02.2006. Made: 07.02.2006. Laid: 08.02.2006. Coming into force: 24.03.2006. Effect: None. Territorial extent & classification: E/W/S/NI. General. - 4p.: 30 cm. - 978-0-11-073987-8 £3.00

Government trading funds

The Driving Standards Agency Trading Fund (Maximum Borrowing) Order 2006 No. 2006/623. - Enabling power: Government Trading Funds Act 1973, ss. 1, 2C. - Issued: 15.03.2006. Made: 07.03.2006. Laid: 10.03.2006. Coming into force: 01.04.2006. Effect: S.I. 1997/873 amended. Territorial extent & classification: E/W/S. General. - 2p.: 30 cm. - 978-0-11-074206-9 £3.00

The Ordnance Survey Trading Fund (Maximum Borrowing) Order 2006 No. 2006/2835. - Enabling power: Government Trading Funds Act 1973, ss. 1, 2C. - Issued: 01.11.2006. Made: 24.10.2006. Laid: 01.11.2006. Coming into force: 15.12.2006 Effect: S.I. 1999/965 amended. Territorial extent & classification: E/W/S. General. - 2p.: 30 cm. - 978-0-11-075228-0 £3.00

Harbours, docks, piers and ferries

The Associated British Ports (Hull) Harbour Revision Order 2006 No. 2006/1135. - Enabling power: Harbours Act 1964, s. 14. - Issued: 28.04.2006. Made: 13.04.2006. Coming into force: 25.04.2006. Effect: 1907 c.lxvii amended. Territorial extent & classification: E. Local. - 12p.: 30 cm. - 978-0-11-074517-6 £3.00

The Dover Harbour Revision Order 2006 No. 2006/2167. - Enabling power: Harbours Act 1964, s. 14 (7). - Issued: 19.09.2006. Made: 02.08.2006. Coming into force: 16.08.2006. Effect: 1954 c. 2; 1963 c. xxix; S.I. 1969/1578; 1978/1069 amended & S.I. 1977/2082 revoked. Territorial extent & classification: E. Local. - 16p., col. map: 30 cm. - 978-0-11-074994-5 £4.00

The Humber Sea Terminal (Phase III) Harbour Revision Order 2006 No. 2006/2604. - Enabling power: Harbours Act 1964, s. 14 (7). - Issued: 03.10.2006. Made: 21.09.2006. Coming into force: 12.10.2006. Effect: None. Territorial extent & classification: E. Local. - 16p.: 30 cm. - 978-0-11-075135-1 £3.00

The Port of Ipswich Harbour Revision Order 2006 No. 2006/554. - Enabling power: Harbours Act 1964, s. 14 (7). - Issued: 05.04.2006. Made: 21.02.2006. Coming into force: 07.03.2006. Effect: None. Territorial extent & classification: E/W/S/NI. General. - This Statutory Instrument has been printed in substitution of the SI of the same number and isbn, issued 10.3.2006 and is being issued free of charge to all known recipients of that Statutory Instrument. - 12p., col. map: 30 cm. - 978-0-11-074155-0 £7.20

Health

The Smoking, Health and Social Care (Scotland) Act 2005 and the Prohibition of Smoking in Certain Premises (Scotland) Regulations 2006 (Consequential Provisions) (Scotland) Order 2006 No. 2006/1115. - Enabling power: Scotland Act 1998, ss. 104, 112 (1), 113. - Issued: 21.04.2006. Made: 18.04.2006. Laid: 21.04.2006. Coming into force: 15.05.2006. Effect: None. Territorial extent & classification: E/W/S/NI. General. - 4p.: 30 cm. - 978-0-11-074503-9 £3.00

Health and safety

The Blood Safety and Quality (Amendment) Regulations 2006 No. 2006/2013. - Enabling power: European Communities Act 1972, s. 2 (2) & Finance Act 1973, s. 56 (1) (2). - Issued: 31.07.2006. Made: 24.07.2006. Laid: 25.07.2006. Coming into force: 31.08.2006. Effect: S.I. 2005/50 amended. Territorial extent & classification: E/W/S/NI. General. - 16p.: 30 cm. - 978-0-11-074943-3 £3.00

The Control of Asbestos Regulations 2006 No. 2006/2739. - Enabling power: Health and Safety at Work etc. Act 1974, ss. 15 (1) (2) (3) (4) (5) (6) (b) (9), 18 (2), 80 (1), 82 (3), sch. 3, paras 1 (1) to (4), 2, 3 (2), 4, 6, 8 to 11, 13 (1) (3), 14, 15 (1), 16, 20 & European Communities Act 1972, s. 2 (2). - Issued: 20.10.2006. Made: 12.10.2006. Laid: 20.10.2006. Coming into force: 13.11.2006 & 06.04.2007 in accord. with reg. 1. Effect: 10 S.Is and 1 S.S.I. amended & S.I. 1983/1649; 1992/3067; 1998/3233; 1999/2373, 2977; 2002/2675; 2003/1889 revoked (13.11.2006). Territorial extent & classification: E/W/S. General. - EC note: They implement, in relation to Britain, Directive 76/769/EEC (as amended by Directives 83/478/EEC and 85/467/EEC), and Commission Directives 91/659/EEC and 1999/43/EC; Directive 83/477/EEC (as amended by 91/382/EEC and 2003/18/EC); Directives 90/394/EEC and 98/24/EC. - 28p.: 30 cm. - 978-0-11-075191-7 £4.50

The Health and Safety (Enforcing Authority for Railways and Other Guided Transport Systems) Regulations 2006 No. 2006/557. - Enabling power: Health and Safety at Work etc. Act 1974, ss. 15 (1) (2) (3) (a) (c) (4) (a) (5) (b), 82 (3) (a), sch. 3, paras 1 (1) (a) (c), 3 (1), 6 (2), 7, 8 (1), 14, 15 (1), 20 & European Communities Act 1972, s. 2 (2) & Railways and Transport Safety Act 2003, ss. 7 (1), 9, 11 (1). - Issued: 09.03.2006. Made: 02.03.2006. Laid: 09.03.2006. Coming into force: 01.04.2006. Effect: 1992 c.42; S.I. 1994/157, 299, 3140; 1997/553; 1998/494, 1833; 1999/2244; 2000/2688; 2001/2975; 2002/2677; 2004/568; 2005/1093, 1643, 1992 amended. Territorial extent & classification: E/W/S [except for para. 15 of the schedule which applies to the whole of the UK]. General. - 20p.: 30 cm. - 978-0-11-074157-4 £3.50

The Health and Safety (Fees) Regulations 2006 No. 2006/336. - Enabling power: European Communities Act 1972, s. 2 (2) & Health and Safety at Work etc. Act 1974, ss. 43 (2) (4) (5) (6), 82 (3) (a). - Issued: 16.02.2006. Made: 13.02.2006. Laid: 16.02.2006. Coming into force: 06.04.2006. Effect: S.I. 2005/2466, 3117 amended & S.I. 2005/676 revoked. Territorial extent & classification: E/W/S. General. - 52p.: 30 cm. - 978-0-11-074037-9 £9.00

The Ionising Radiation (Medical Exposure) (Amendment) Regulations 2006 No. 2006/2523. - Enabling power: European Communities Act 1972, s. 2 (2). - Issued: 21.09.2006. Made: 13.09.2006. Laid: 21.09.2006. Coming into force: 01.11.2006. Effect: S.I. 2000/1059 amended. Territorial extent & classification: E/W/S. General. - EC note: Relates to the partial implementation as respects Great Britain of Directive 97/43/Euratom. - 4p.: 30 cm. - 978-0-11-075114-6 £3.00

The Management of Health and Safety at Work (Amendment) Regulations 2006 No. 2006/438. - Enabling power: European Communities Act 1972, s. 2 (2) & Health and Safety at Work etc. Act 1974, ss. 15 (1) (2), 47 (2). - Issued: 28.02.2006. Made: 23.02.2006. Laid: 28.02.2006. Coming into force: 06.04.2006. Effect: S.I. 1999/3242 amended. Territorial extent & classification: E/W/S. General. - 2p.: 30 cm. - 978-0-11-074098-0 £3.00

The Railway Safety Levy Regulations 2006 No. 2006/1010. - Enabling power: Health and Safety at Work etc. Act 1974, ss. 43A (1) (5) to (8), 82 (3) (a). - Issued: 07.04.2006. Made: 30.03.2006. Coming into force: 01.04.2006 in accord. with reg. 1. Effect: None. Territorial extent & classification: E/W/S. General. - Supersedes draft (ISBN 0110740734) published on 24.02.2006. - 8p.: 30 cm. - 978-0-11-074452-0 £3.00

The Railways and Other Guided Transport Systems (Safety) (Amendment) Regulations 2006 No. 2006/1057. - Enabling power: Health and Safety at Work etc. Act 1974, ss. 15 (1), 80. - Issued: 10.04.2006. Made: 04.04.2006. Laid: 07.04.2006. Coming into force: 10.04.2006 except for reg. 2 (3); 01.10.2006 for reg. 2 (3). Effect: S.I. 2006/599 amended. Territorial extent & classification: E/W/S. General. - This Statutory Instrument has been printed to correct an error in SI 2006/599 (ISBN 0110743075) and is being issued free of charge to all known recipients of that Statutory Instrument. - 2p.: 30 cm. - 978-0-11-074469-8 £3.00

The Railways and Other Guided Transport Systems (Safety) Regulations 2006 No. 2006/599. - Enabling power: Health and Safety at Work etc. Act 1974, ss. 15 (1) (2) (3) (a) (c) (4) (5) (6), 18 (2), 43 (2) to (6), 47 (2), 80, 82 (3) (a), sch. 3, paras 1 (1) (a) (c) (2), 4 (1), 6, 7, 8 (1), 9, 14, 15 (1), 16, 18 (a), 20. - Issued: 21.03.2006. Made: 09.03.2006. Laid: 17.03.2006. Coming into force: 10.04.2006 except for regs 19, 23 to 26, 29 and 34; 01.10.2006 for regs 19, 23 to 26, 29 and 34. Effect: S.I. 1995/3163; 1997/553; 1999/2244; 2001/3291; 2003/1400; 2004/129 amended & S.I. 1994/157, 299; 2000/2688; 2003/579 revoked. Territorial extent & classification: E/W/S. General. - EC note: These Regs implement, insofar as they apply to the mainline railway, in relation to Great Britain, Directive 2004/49/EC on safety on the Community's railways and amending Council Directive 95/18/EC on the licensing of transport undertakings and Directive 2001/14/EC on the allocation of infrastructure capacity and the levying of charges for use of infrastructure and safety certification. - With correction slip dated April 2007. - This Statutory Instrument has been corrected by SI 2006/1057 (ISBN 0110744691) which is being issued free of charge to all known recipients of SI 2006/599. - 40p.: 30 cm. - 978-0-11-074307-3 £6.50

Healthcare and associated professions

The General Optical Council (Continuing Education and Training) (Amendment No. 2) Rules Order of Council 2006 No. 2006/2901. - Enabling power: Opticians Act 1989, ss. 11A, 11B, 31A. - Issued: 15.11.2006. Made: 30.10.2006. Laid: 09.11.2006. Coming into force: 01.01.2007. Effect: S.I. 2005/1473 amended & The General Optical Council (Continuing Education and Training) (Amendment) Rules 2006 revoked. Territorial extent & classification: E/W/S/NI. General. - 8p.: 30 cm. - 978-0-11-075258-7 £3.00

The Nurses and Midwives (Parts of and Entries in the Register) Amendment Order of Council 2006 No. 2006/1015. - Enabling power: S.I. 2002/253, art. 6. - Issued: 07.04.2006. Made: 03.04.2006. Laid: 04.04.2006. Coming into force: 01.05.2006. Effect: S.I. 2004/1765 amended. Territorial extent & classification: E/W/S/NI. General. - 2p.: 30 cm. - 978-0-11-074455-1 £3.00

The Nursing and Midwifery Council (Practice Committees) (Constitution) Rules Order of Council 2006 No. 2006/1199. - Enabling power: S.I. 2002/253, arts. 47 (2), sch. 1, para. 17. - Issued: 17.05.2006. Made: 19.04.2006. Laid: 02.05.2006. Coming into force: 31.07.2006. Effect: S.I. 2003/1738 revoked. Territorial extent & classification: E/W/S/NI. General. - 8p.: 30 cm. - 978-0-11-074541-1 £3.00

Healthcare and associated professions: Dentists

The Dentists Act 1984 (Amendment) Order 2005 Transitional Provisions Order of Council 2006 No. 2006/1671. - Enabling power: S.I. 2005/2011, art. 50 (2). - Issued: 29.06.2006. Made: 23.06.2006. Laid: 29.06.2006. Coming into force: 31.07.2006. Effect: None. Territorial extent & classification: E/W/S/NI. General. - 8p.: 30 cm. - 978-0-11-074749-1 £3.00

The General Dental Council (Appointments Committee and Appointment of Members of Committees) Rules Order of Council 2006 No. 2006/1664. - Enabling power: Dentists Act 1984, s. 50C (5) (6), sch. 1, para 8 (1) (b) (c). - Issued: 29.06.2006. Made: 23.06.2006. Coming into force: 31.07.2006. Effect: General Dental Council (Appointment of Members of Committees) Rules 2003; General Dental Council (Appointments Committee) Rules 2003 revoked with saving. Territorial extent & classification: E/W/S/NI. General. - 8p.: 30 cm. - 978-0-11-074757-6 £3.00

The General Dental Council (Constitution) Order of Council 2006 No. 2006/1666. - Enabling power: Dentists Act 1984, s. 1 (2A) (2B). - Issued: 29.06.2006. Made: 23.06.2006. Laid: 29.06.2006. Coming into force: 31.07.2006. Effect: None. Territorial extent & classification: E/W/S/NI. General. - 4p.: 30 cm. - 978-0-11-074750-7 £3.00

The General Dental Council (Fitness to Practise) Rules Order of Council 2006 No. 2006/1663. - Enabling power: Dentists Act 1984, s. 50C (5) (6), sch. 3, paras. 2, 3, 7, sch. 4B, paras. 2, 3, 7, sch. 4C, paras. 1, 2, 3. - Issued: 29.06.2006. Made: 23.06.2006. Laid: 29.06.2006. Coming into force: 31.07.2006. Effect: None. Territorial extent & classification: E/W/S/NI. General. - 24p.: 30 cm. - 978-0-11-074751-4 £4.00

The General Dental Council (Registration Appeals) Rules Order of Council 2006 No. 2006/1668. - Enabling power: Dentists Act 1984, s. 50C (5) (6), sch. 3, paras. 2, 3, sch. 4B, paras. 2, 3. - Issued: 29.06.2006. Made: 23.06.2006. Laid: 29.06.2006. Coming into force: 31.07.2006. Effect: None. Territorial extent & classification: E/W/S/NI. General. - With correction slip dated October 2006. - 8p.: 30 cm. - 978-0-11-074752-1 £3.00

Healthcare and associated professions: Doctors

The Medical Act 1983 (Amendment) and Miscellaneous Amendments Order 2006 No. 2006/1914. - Enabling power: Health Act 1999, ss. 60, 62 (4). - Issued: 26.07.2006. Made: 19.07.2006. Coming into force: In accord. with art. 1 (2) (3). Effect: 1983 c.54; 1989 c.44; 1994 c.23; S.I. 1989/1796; 1996/1591; 2002/253, 3135; 2004/585, 957, 1020, 3038; 2005/2250; S.S.I. 2004/114 amended. Territorial extent & classification: E/W/S/NI. General. - With correction slip dated August 2006. - 40p.: 30 cm. - 978-0-11-074898-6 £6.50

The Postgraduate Medical Education and Training Board (Fees) Rules Order 2006 No. 2006/515. - Enabling power: S.I. 2003/1250, arts. 24, 25 (1). - Issued: 03.03.2006. Made: 28.02.2006. Laid: 03.03.2006. Coming into force: 01.04.2006. Effect: S.I. 2005/1872 revoked. Territorial extent & classification: E/W/S/NI. General. - 8p.: 30 cm. - 978-0-11-074131-4 £3.00

Healthcare and associated professions: Health professions

The Health Professions (Parts of and Entries in the Register) (Amendment) Order of Council 2006 No. 2006/1996. - Enabling power: S.I. 2002/254, art. 6 (3) (a). - Issued: 31.07.2006. Made: 19.07.2006. Laid: 31.07.2006. Coming into force: 21.08.2006. Effect: S.I. 2003/1571 amended. Territorial extent & classification: E/WS/NI. General. - 2p.: 30 cm. - 978-0-11-074916-7 £3.00

Healthcare and associated professions: Nurses and midwives

The Nursing and Midwifery Order 2001 (Transitional Provisions) (Amendment) Order of Council 2006 No. 2006/1441. - Enabling power: S.I. 2002/253, art. 54 (2). - Issued: 07.06.2006. Made: 24.05.2006. Coming into force: 01.06.2006. Effect: S.I. 2004/1762 amended. Territorial extent & classification: E/W/S/NI. General. - 2p.: 30 cm. - 978-0-11-074634-0 £3.00

Healthcare and associated professions: Osteopaths

The General Osteopathic Council (Continuing Professional Development) Rules Order of Council 2006 No. 2006/3511. - Enabling power: Osteopaths Act 1993, ss. 6 (2) (3), 17, 35 (2). - Issued: 22.01.2007. Made: 18.12.2006. Laid: 19.01.2007. Coming into force: 01.03.2007. Effect: None. Territorial extent & classification: UK. General. - 8p.: 30 cm. - 978-0-11-075608-0 £3.00

Healthcare and associated professions: Professions complementary to dentistry

The Dentists Act 1984 (Amendment) Order 2005 Transitional Provisions Order of Council 2006 No. 2006/1671. - Enabling power: S.I. 2005/2011, art. 50 (2). - Issued: 29.06.2006. Made: 23.06.2006. Laid: 29.06.2006. Coming into force: 31.07.2006. Effect: None. Territorial extent & classification: E/W/S/NI. General. - 8p.: 30 cm. - 978-0-11-074749-1 £3.00

The European Qualifications (Professions Complementary to Dentistry) Regulations 2006 No. 2006/1718. - Enabling power: European Communities Act 1972, s. 2 (2). - Issued: 05.07.2006. Made: 28.06.2006. Laid: 05.07.2006. Coming into force: 28.07.2006. Effect: 1984 c.24; S.I. 2002/2934 amended. Territorial extent & classification: E/W/S/NI. General. - EC note: These Regs apply the requirements of Council Directive 92/51/EEC on a second general system for the regulation of professional education and training, as amended, to the professions of clinical dental technician, dental nurse, dental technician and orthodontic therapist. - 4p.: 30 cm. - 978-0-11-074779-8 £3.00

The General Dental Council (Appointments Committee and Appointment of Members of Committees) Rules Order of Council 2006 No. 2006/1664. - Enabling power: Dentists Act 1984, s. 50C (5) (6), sch. 1, para 8 (1) (b) (c). - Issued: 29.06.2006. Made: 23.06.2006. Coming into force: 31.07.2006. Effect: General Dental Council (Appointment of Members of Committees) Rules 2003; General Dental Council (Appointments Committee) Rules 2003 revoked with saving. Territorial extent & classification: E/W/S/NI. General. - 8p.: 30 cm. - 978-0-11-074757-6 £3.00

The General Dental Council (Constitution of Committees) Order of Council 2006 No. 2006/1665. - Enabling power: Dentists Act 1984, s. 2 (6) (7). - Issued: 29.06.2006. Made: 23.06.2006. Coming into force: 31.07.2006. Effect: S.I. 2003/1081 revoked with saving; 2004/67 revoked. Territorial extent & classification: E/W/S/NI. General. - 2p.: 30 cm. - 978-0-11-074758-3 £3.00

The General Dental Council (Constitution) Order of Council 2006 No. 2006/1666. - Enabling power: Dentists Act 1984, s. 1 (2A) (2B). - Issued: 29.06.2006. Made: 23.06.2006. Laid: 29.06.2006. Coming into force: 31.07.2006. Effect: None. Territorial extent & classification: E/W/S/NI. General. - 4p.: 30 cm. - 978-0-11-074750-7 £3.00

The General Dental Council (Fitness to Practise) Rules Order of Council 2006 No. 2006/1663. - Enabling power: Dentists Act 1984, s. 50C (5) (6), sch. 3, paras. 2, 3, 7, sch. 4B, paras. 2, 3, 7, sch. 4C, paras. 1, 2, 3. - Issued: 29.06.2006. Made: 23.06.2006. Laid: 29.06.2006. Coming into force: 31.07.2006. Effect: None. Territorial extent & classification: E/W/S/NI. General. - 24p.: 30 cm. - 978-0-11-074751-4 £4.00

The General Dental Council (Professions Complementary to Dentistry) (Business of Dentistry) Rules Order of Council 2006 No. 2006/1670. - Enabling power: Dentists Act 1984, s. 41 (1) (3). - Issued: 29.06.2006. Made: 23.06.2006. Laid: 29.06.2006. Coming into force: 31.07.2006. Effect: None. Territorial extent & classification: E/W/S/NI. General. - 2p.: 30 cm. - 978-0-11-074755-2 £3.00

The General Dental Council (Professions Complementary to Dentistry) (Dental Hygienists and Dental Therapists) Regulations Order of Council 2006 No. 2006/1667. - Enabling power: Dentists Act 1984, s. 36A (2) (3). - Issued: 29.06.2006. Made: 23.06.2006. Laid: 29.06.2006. Coming into force: 31.07.2006. Effect: None. Territorial extent & classification: E/W/S/NI. General. - 4p.: 30 cm. - 978-0-11-074753-8 £3.00

The General Dental Council (Professions Complementary to Dentistry) (Qualifications and Supervision of Dental Work) Rules Order of Council 2006 No. 2006/1669. - Enabling power: Dentists Act 1984, ss. 36D (5), 37 (2) (b), 50C (6). - Issued: 29.06.2006. Made: 23.06.2006. Coming into force: 31.07.2006. Effect: None. Territorial extent & classification: E/W/S/NI. General. - 4p.: 30 cm. - 978-0-11-074756-9 £3.00

The General Dental Council (Professions Complementary to Dentistry) Regulations Order of Council 2006 No. 2006/1440. - Enabling power: Dentists Act 1984, ss. 36A (2) (3), 52 (1A) (1B). - Issued: 07.06.2006. Made: 31.05.2006. Laid: 02.06.2006. Laid before the Scottish Parliament: 06.06.2006. Coming into force: 31.07.2006. Effect: None. Territorial extent & classification: E/W/S/NI. General. - 8p.: 30 cm. - 978-0-11-074631-9 £3.00

The General Dental Council (Registration Appeals) Rules Order of Council 2006 No. 2006/1668. - Enabling power: Dentists Act 1984, s. 50C (5) (6), sch. 3, paras. 2, 3, sch. 4B, paras. 2, 3. - Issued: 29.06.2006. Made: 23.06.2006. Laid: 29.06.2006. Coming into force: 31.07.2006. Effect: None. Territorial extent & classification: E/W/S/NI. General. - With correction slip dated October 2006. - 8p.: 30 cm. - 978-0-11-074752-1 £3.00

Healthcare and associated professions, England and Wales

The Health Act 2006 (Commencement No. 1 and Transitional Provisions) Order 2006 No. 2006/2603 (C.88). - Enabling power: Health Act 2006, ss. 79 (3), 83 (3) (7) (8). Bringing into operation various provisions of the 2006 Act on 28.09.2006 and 01.10.2006. - Issued: 29.09.2006. Made: 22.09.2006. Effect: None. Territorial extent & classification: E/W. General. - 8p.: 30 cm. - 978-0-11-075136-8 £3.00

Healthcare and associated professions, Wales

The Health Professions Wales Abolition Order 2006 No. 2006/978 (W.101). - Enabling power: Health (Wales) Act 2003, s. 5. - Issued: 10.04.2006. Made: 29.03.2006. Coming into force: 01.04.2006. Effect: S.I. 2004/550 (W.54), 551 (W.55) revoked. Territorial extent & classification: W. General. - In English and Welsh. Welsh title: Gorchymyn Diddymu Proffesiynau Iechyd Cymru 2006. - 8p.: 30 cm. - 978-0-11-091315-5 *£3.00*

Highways, England

The A1 (A57 and A614 Junction Improvement Apleyhead) Trunk Road Order 2006 No. 2006/1697. - Enabling power: Highways Act 1980, ss. 10, 41. - Issued: 04.07.2006. Made: 22.06.2006. Coming into force: 07.07.2006. Effect: None. Territorial extent & classification: E/W. Local. - 4p.: 30 cm. - 978-0-11-074774-3 *£3.00*

The A1 Motorway (Bramham Crossroads to Kirk Deighton Junction and Connecting Roads) Scheme 2006 No. 2006/3301. - Enabling power: Highways Act 1980, ss. 16, 17, 19. - Issued: 19.12.2006. Made: 08.12.2006. Coming into force: 04.01.2007. Effect: None. Territorial extent & classification: E. Local. - 2p.: 30 cm. - 978-0-11-075486-4 *£3.00*

The A1 Trunk Road (A1(M)), A614 and B6045 Junction Improvement (Blyth) (Detrunking) Order 2006 No. 2006/1419. - Enabling power: Highways Act 1980, ss. 10, 12. - Issued: 02.06.2006. Made: 22.05.2006. Coming into force: 02.06.2006. Effect: None. Territorial extent & classification: E. Local. - 2p.: 30 cm. - 978-0-11-074625-8 *£3.00*

The A1 Trunk Road (A1(M)), A614 and B6045 Junction Improvement (Blyth) Order 2006 No. 2006/1417. - Enabling power: Highways Act 1980, ss. 10, 41. - Issued: 02.06.2006. Made: 22.05.2006. Coming into force: 02.06.2006. Effect: None. Territorial extent & classification: E. Local. - 2p.: 30 cm. - 978-0-11-074624-1 *£3.00*

The A1 Trunk Road (A57, A638 and B1164 Junction Improvement Markham Moor) (Detrunking) Order 2006 No. 2006/2862. - Enabling power: Highways Act 1980, ss. 10, 12. - Issued: 03.11.2006. Made: 16.10.2006. Coming into force: 03.11.2006. Effect: None. Territorial extent & classification: E/W. Local. - 2p.: 30 cm. - 978-0-11-075236-5 *£3.00*

The A1 Trunk Road (A57, A638 and B1164 Junction Improvement Markham Moor) Order 2006 No. 2006/2861. - Enabling power: Highways Act 1980, ss. 10, 41. - Issued: 03.11.2006. Made: 16.10.2006. Coming into force: 03.11.2006. Effect: None. Territorial extent & classification: E/W. Local. - 2p.: 30 cm. - 978-0-11-075235-8 *£3.00*

The A1 Trunk Road (A57 and A614 Junction Improvement Apleyhead) (Detrunking) Order 2006 No. 2006/1698. - Enabling power: Highways Act 1980, ss. 10, 12. - Issued: 04.07.2006. Made: 22.06.2006. Coming into force: 07.07.2006. Effect: None. Territorial extent & classification: E/W. Local. - 2p.: 30 cm. - 978-0-11-074775-0 *£3.00*

The A1 Trunk Road (B1081 Junction Improvement Carpenter's Lodge) (Detrunking) Order 2006 No. 2006/3164. - Enabling power: Highways Act 1980, ss. 10, 12. - Issued: 04.12.2006. Made: 02.11.2006. Coming into force: 01.12.2006. Effect: None. Territorial extent & classification: E. Local. - 2p.: 30 cm. - 978-0-11-075395-9 *£3.00*

The A1 Trunk Road (B1081 Junction Improvement Carpenter's Lodge) Order 2006 No. 2006/3163. - Enabling power: Highways Act 1980, ss. 10, 12. - Issued: 04.12.2006. Made: 02.11.2006. Coming into force: 01.12.2006. Effect: None. Territorial extent & classification: E. Local. - 2p.: 30 cm. - 978-0-11-075394-2 *£3.00*

The A1 Trunk Road (B1174 Junction Improvement Gonerby Moor) (Detrunking) Order 2006 No. 2006/2172. - Enabling power: Highways Act 1980, ss. 10, 12. - Issued: 11.08.2006. Made: 03.08.2006. Coming into force: 18.08.2006. Effect: None. Territorial extent & classification: E/W. Local. - With correction slip dated August 2006. - 2p.: 30 cm. - 978-0-11-074995-2 *£3.00*

The A1 Trunk Road (B1174 Junction Improvement Gonerby Moor) Order 2006 No. 2006/2173. - Enabling power: Highways Act 1980, ss. 10, 41. - Issued: 11.08.2006. Made: 03.08.2006. Coming into force: 18.08.2006. Effect: None. Territorial extent & classification: E/W. Local. - 4p.: 30 cm. - 978-0-11-074996-9 *£3.00*

The A1 Trunk Road (Bramham to Wetherby Upgrading) (Detrunking) Order 2006 No. 2006/3302. - Enabling power: Highways Act 1980, ss. 10, 12. - Issued: 19.12.2006. Made: 08.12.2006. Coming into force: 04.01.2007. Effect: None. Territorial extent & classification: E. Local. - 2p.: 30 cm. - 978-0-11-075487-1 *£3.00*

The A1 Trunk Road (Bramham to Wetherby Upgrading) (River Wharfe Bridge) Order 2006 No. 2006/3300. - Enabling power: Highways Act 1980, ss. 10, 41. - Issued: 19.12.2006. Made: 08.12.2006. Coming into force: 04.01.2007. Effect: None. Territorial extent & classification: E. Local. - 2p.: 30 cm. - 978-0-11-075488-8 *£3.00*

The A1 Trunk Road (Long Bennington Southbound Access Slip Road) (Detrunking) Order 2006 No. 2006/2040. - Enabling power: Highways Act 1980, ss. 10, 12. - Made: 19.07.2006. Coming into force: 11.09.2006. Effect: None. Territorial extent & classification: E. Local *Unpublished*

The A3 Trunk Road (Hindhead) Detrunking Order 2006 No. 2006/3078. - Enabling power: Highways Act 1980, ss. 10, 12. - Issued: 07.12.2006. Made: 02.11.2006. Coming into force: 13.11.2006. Effect: None. Territorial extent & classification: E. Local. - 2p.: 30 cm. - 978-0-11-075341-6 *£3.00*

The A3 Trunk Road (Hindhead) Order 2006 No. 2006/3076. - Enabling power: Highways Act 1980, ss. 10, 41. - Issued: 07.12.2006. Made: 02.11.2006. Coming into force: 13.11.2006. Effect: None. Territorial extent & classification: E. Local. - 2p.: 30 cm. - 978-0-11-075339-3 *£3.00*

The A3 Trunk Road (Hindhead) Slip Roads Order 2006 No. 2006/3077. - Enabling power: Highways Act 1980, ss. 10, 41. - Issued: 07.12.2006. Made: 02.11.2006. Coming into force: 13.11.2006. Effect: None. Territorial extent & classification: E. Local. - 2p.: 30 cm. - 978-0-11-075340-9 *£3.00*

The A27 Trunk Road (Southerham to Beddingham Improvements) Order 2006 No. 2006/2230. - Enabling power: Highways Act 1980, s. 10. - Issued: 17.08.2006. Made: 10.08.2006. Coming into force: 21.08.2006. Effect: None. Territorial extent & classification: E. Local. - 2p.: 30 cm. - 978-0-11-075022-4 *£3.00*

The A38 Trunk Road (Dobwalls Bypass) (Detrunking) Order 2006 No. 2006/2270. - Enabling power: Highways Act 1980, ss. 10, 12. - Issued: 19.09.2006. Made: 25.08.2006. Coming into force: 01.09.2006. Effect: None. Territorial extent & classification: E. Local. - 4p.: 30 cm. - 978-0-11-075113-9 *£3.00*

The A38 Trunk Road (Dobwalls Bypass) Order 2006 No. 2006/2269. - Enabling power: Highways Act 1980, ss. 10, 41. - Issued: 19.09.2006. Made: 25.08.2006. Coming into force: 01.09.2006. Effect: None. Territorial extent & classification: E. Local. - 4p.: 30 cm. - 978-0-11-075112-2 *£3.00*

The A63 Trunk Road (East of Peckfield Bar to Boot & Shoe) (Detrunking) Order 2006 No. 2006/1285. - Enabling power: Highways Act 1980, ss. 10, 12. - Issued: 15.05.2006. Made: 25.04.2006. Coming into force: 25.05.2006. Effect: None. Territorial extent & classification: E. Local. - 2p.: 30 cm. - 978-0-11-074572-5 *£3.00*

The A65 Trunk Road (Gargrave Bypass) Order 1990, as varied by the A65 Trunk Road (Gargrave Bypass) Order 1990 Amendment and New Trunk Road Order 1993 (Revocation) Order 2006 No. 2006/3465. - Enabling power: Highways Act 1980, ss. 10, 41. - Issued: 08.01.2007. Made: 18.12.2006. Coming into force: 12.01.2007. Effect: The A65 Trunk Road (Gargrave Bypass) Order 1990, as varied by the A65 Trunk Road (Gargrave Bypass) Order 1990 Amendment & New Trunk Road Order 1993 revoked. Territorial extent & classification: E. Local. - 2p.: 30 cm. - 978-0-11-075585-4 *£3.00*

The A65 Trunk Road (Hellifield and Long Preston Bypass and Slip Roads) Order 1993 (Revocation) Order 2006 No. 2006/3466. - Enabling power: Highways Act 1980, ss. 10, 41. - Issued: 08.01.2007. Made: 18.12.2006. Coming into force: 12.01.2007. Effect: S.I. 1993/631 revoked. Territorial extent & classification: E. Local. - 2p.: 30 cm. - 978-0-11-075586-1 *£3.00*

The A69 Carlisle to Newcastle Trunk Road (Haydon Bridge Bypass) (Detrunking) Order 2006 No. 2006/2784. - Enabling power: Highways Act 1980, ss. 10, 12. - Issued: 19.10.2006. Made: 27.09.2006. Coming into force: 20.10.2006. Effect: None. Territorial extent & classification: E/W. Local. - 2p.: 30 cm. - 978-0-11-075199-3 *£3.00*

The A69 Carlisle to Newcastle Trunk Road (Haydon Bridge Bypass) Order 2006 No. 2006/2783. - Enabling power: Highways Act 1980, ss. 10, 41, 106. - Issued: 19.10.2006. Made: 27.09.2006. Coming into force: 20.10.2006. Effect: None. Territorial extent & classification: E/W. Local. - 2p.: 30 cm. - 978-0-11-075198-6 *£3.00*

The A74 Trunk Road (Carlisle to Guards Mill Section) (Detrunking) Order 2006 No. 2006/1096. - Enabling power: Highways Act 1980, ss. 10, 12. - Issued: 21.04.2006. Made: 05.04.2006. Coming into force: 21.04.2006. Effect: None. Territorial extent & classification: E/W. Local. - 2p.: 30 cm. - 978-0-11-074502-2 *£3.00*

The A168 Trunk Road (Blakey Lane) (Detrunking) Order 2006 No. 2006/1238. - Enabling power: Highways Act 1980, ss. 10, 12. - Made: 28.04.2006. Coming into force: 02.05.2006. Effect: None. Territorial extent & classification: E. Local *Unpublished*

The A419 Trunk Road (Blunsdon Bypass and Slip Roads) (Detrunking) Order 2006 No. 2006/1546. - Enabling power: Highways Act 1980, ss. 10, 12. - Issued: 28.06.2006. Made: 13.06.2006. Coming into force: 29.06.2006. Effect: None. Territorial extent & classification: E. Local. - 2p.: 30 cm. - 978-0-11-074744-6 *£3.00*

The A419 Trunk Road (Blunsdon Bypass and Slip Roads) Order 2006 No. 2006/1545. - Enabling power: Highways Act 1980, ss. 10, 41. - Issued: 28.06.2006. Made: 13.06.2006. Coming into force: 29.06.2006. Effect: None. Territorial extent & classification: E. Local. - 4p.: 30 cm. - 978-0-11-074743-9 *£3.00*

The A449 and A456 Trunk Roads (Kidderminster, Blakedown and Hagley Bypass and Slip Roads) Order 1996 (Revocation) Order 2006 No. 2006/3126. - Enabling power: Highways Act 1980, ss. 10, 41. - Issued: 28.11.2006. Made: 01.11.2006. Coming into force: 06.12.2006. Effect: S.I. 1996/1937 revoked. Territorial extent & classification: E. Local. - 2p.: 30 cm. - 978-0-11-075369-0 *£3.00*

The A550 and A5117 Trunk Roads (Improvement Between M56 & A548) and Connecting Roads Order 2006 No. 2006/1451. - Enabling power: Highways Act 1980, ss. 10, 41. - Issued: 07.06.2006. Made: 25.05.2006. Coming into force: 09.06.2006. Effect: None. Territorial extent & classification: E. Local. - 4p.: 30 cm. - 978-0-11-074645-6 *£3.00*

The A550 Trunk Road (Improvement between Deeside Park and Ledsham) (Detrunking) Order 1994 (Revocation) Order 2006 No. 2006/2261. - Enabling power: Highways Act 1980, ss. 10, 12, 326. - Issued: 24.08.2006. Made: 09.08.2006. Coming into force: 01.09.2006. Effect: S.I. 1994/2406 revoked. Territorial extent & classification: E. Local. - 2p.: 30 cm. - 978-0-11-075032-3 *£3.00*

The A595 Grizebeck to Chapel Brow Trunk Road (Parton to Lillyhall Improvement) (Detrunking) Order 2006 No. 2006/2180. - Enabling power: Highways Act 1980, ss. 10, 12. - Issued: 14.08.2006. Made: 03.08.2006. Coming into force: 18.08.2006. Effect: None. Territorial extent & classification: E/W. Local. - 2p.: 30 cm. - 978-0-11-075002-6 *£3.00*

The A595 Grizebeck to Chapel Brow Trunk Road (Parton to Lillyhall Improvement) Order 2006 No. 2006/2179. - Enabling power: Highways Act 1980, ss. 10, 41, 106. - Issued: 14.08.2006. Made: 03.08.2006. Coming into force: 18.08.2006. Effect: None. Territorial extent & classification: E/W. Local. - 2p.: 30 cm. - 978-0-11-075001-9 *£3.00*

The A595 Trunk Road (Calder Bridge to A5092 at Grizebeck) (Detrunking) Order 2006 No. 2006/923. - Enabling power: Highways Act 1980, ss. 10, 12. - Issued: 29.03.2006. Made: 07.03.2006. Coming into force: 01.10.2006. Effect: None. Territorial extent & classification: E. Local. - 2p.: 30 cm. - 978-0-11-074401-8 *£3.00*

The A5092 Trunk Road (Between A595 and A590) (Detrunking) Order 2006 No. 2006/922. - Enabling power: Highways Act 1980, ss. 10, 12. - Issued: 29.03.2006. Made: 07.03.2006. Coming into force: 01.10.2006. Effect: None. Territorial extent & classification: E. Local. - 2p.: 30 cm. - 978-0-11-074400-1 *£3.00*

The Bournemouth-Swanage Motor Road and Ferry (Revision of Charges and Traffic Classifications) Order 2006 No. 2006/1723. - Enabling power: Transport Charges etc. (Miscellaneous Provisions) Act 1954, s. 6. - Made: 27.06.2006. Coming into force: 07.07.2006. Effect: S.I. 2004/1139 revoked. Territorial extent & classification: E. Local *Unpublished*

The Cambridgeshire County Council (Construction of Cambridge Riverside Foot/Cycle Bridge) Scheme 2006 Confirmation Instrument 2006 No. 2006/2531. - Enabling power: Highways Act 1980, s. 106 (3). - Issued: 22.09.2006. Made: 13.09.2006. Coming into force: In accord. with art. 1. Effect: None. Territorial extent & classification: E. Local. - 4p., plans: 30 cm. - 978-0-11-075123-8 *£3.00*

The Clifton Suspension Bridge Tolls (Revision) Order 2006 No. 2006/3375. - Enabling power: Transport Charges &c. (Miscellaneous Provisions Act 1954, s. 6. - Made: 14.12.2006. Coming into force: 01.01.2007. Effect: S.I. 1981/1798; 2003/820 revoked. Territorial extent & classification: E. Local *Unpublished*

The Crime Prevention (Designated Areas) Order 2006 No. 2006/302. - Enabling power: Highways Act 1980, s.118B (1) (a). - Issued: 15.02.2006. Made: 09.02.2006. Laid: 14.02.2006. Coming into force: 17.03.2006. Effect: None. Territorial extent & classification: E. General. - 2p.: 30 cm. - 978-0-11-074027-0 *£3.00*

The Dartford - Thurrock Crossing (Amendment) Regulations 2006 No. 2006/585. - Enabling power: Dartford - Thurrock Crossing Act 1988, s. 25 (1) (b). - Issued: 15.03.2006. Made: 01.03.2006. Laid: 15.03.2006. Coming into force: 12.04.2006. Effect: S.I. 1998/1908 amended. Territorial extent & classification: E. General. - 2p.: 30 cm. - 978-0-11-074183-3 *£3.00*

The Doncaster By-Pass Special Road Scheme 1957 (Variation) Scheme 2006 No. 2006/1418. - Enabling power: Highways Act 1980, ss. 16, 17, 19, 326. - Issued: 02.06.2006. Made: 22.05.2006. Coming into force: 02.06.2006. Effect: S.I. 1957/1024 amended. Territorial extent & classification: E. Local. - 2p.: 30 cm. - 978-0-11-074626-5 *£3.00*

The Greater Manchester City Council (Carrington, Spur, Trafford) (Special Road) Scheme 1984 Revocation Scheme 2005 Confirmation Instrument 2006 No. 2006/399. - Enabling power: Highways Act 1980, ss. 16, 326. - Issued: 28.02.2006. Made: 16.02.2006. Coming into force: In accord. with art. 1. Effect: None. Territorial extent & classification: E. Local. - 2p.: 30 cm. - 978-0-11-074096-6 *£3.00*

The Humber Bridge (Revision of Tolls and Vehicle Classifications) Order 2005 No. 2006/939. - Enabling power: Humber Bridge Act 1971, s. 10. - Made: 27.03.2006. Coming into force: 01.04.2006. Effect: S.I. 2002/786 revoked. Territorial extent & classification: E. Local *Unpublished*

The Lincolnshire County Council Car Dyke Crossing Bridge Scheme 2004 Confirmation Instrument 2006 No. 2006/2936. - Enabling power: Highways Act 1980, s. 106 (3). - Issued: 21.11.2006. Made: 31.10.2006. Coming into force: In accord. with art. 1. Effect: None. Territorial extent & classification: E. Local. - 4p.: 30 cm. - 978-0-11-075320-1 *£3.00*

The M4 Motorway (Theale to Winnersh Section) Connecting Roads Scheme 1968 (Variation) Scheme 2006 No. 2006/2496. - Enabling power: Highways Act 1980, ss. 16, 17, 19, 326. - Issued: 19.09.2006. Made: 31.08.2006. Coming into force: 22.09.2006. Effect: S.I. 1968/1486 varied. Territorial extent & classification: E. Local. - 2p.: 30 cm. - 978-0-11-075109-2 *£3.00*

The M6 Motorway (Carlisle to Guards Mill Section) and Connecting Roads Scheme 2006 No. 2006/1095. - Enabling power: Highways Act 1980, ss. 16, 17, 19. - Issued: 21.04.2006. Made: 05.04.2006. Coming into force: 21.04.2006. Effect: None. Territorial extent & classification: E/W. Local. - 2p.: 30 cm. - 978-0-11-074501-5 £3.00

The M56 Motorway (Hapsford to Lea-by-Backford Section) and Connecting Roads Scheme 1976 (Partial Revocation) Scheme 2006 No. 2006/2262. - Enabling power: Highways Act 1980, ss. 16, 17, 19, 326. - Issued: 24.08.2006. Made: 09.08.2006. Coming into force: 01.09.2006. Effect: S.I. 1976/4 partially revoked. Territorial extent & classification: E. Local. - 2p.: 30 cm. - 978-0-11-075031-6 £3.00

The Manchester City Council (Mancunian Way) Special Road Scheme 1968 Variation Scheme 2005 Confirmation Instrument 2006 No. 2006/398. - Enabling power: Highways Act 1980, ss. 16, 326. - Issued: 28.02.2006. Made: 16.02.2006. Coming into force: In accord. with art. 1. Effect: None. Territorial extent & classification: E. Local. - 4p., map: 30 cm. - 978-0-11-074095-9 £3.00

The North of Edgware Bury-Aldenham Special Roads Scheme (Variation) Order 2006 No. 2006/2200. - Enabling power: Highways Act 1980, ss. 16, 17, 19, 326. - Made: 18.05.2006. Coming into force: 18.05.2006. Effect: S.I. 1962/2255 varied. Territorial extent & classification: E. Local *Unpublished*

The River Tyne (Tunnels) (Revisoin of Tolls) Order 2006 No. 2006/3213. - Enabling power: Tyne and Wear Act 1976, s. 13 and S.I. 2005/2222, sch. 14. - Made: 04.12.2006. Coming into force: 01.01.2007. Effect: None. Territorial extent & classification: E. Local *Unpublished*

The Severn Bridges Tolls Order 2006 No. 2006/3246. - Enabling power: Severn Bridges Act 1992, s. 9 (1) (2) (b) (3) (b) (4) (6). - Issued: 12.1.2006. Made: 05.12.2006. Coming into force: 01.01.2007. Effect: S.I. 2005/3461 revoked. Territorial extent & classification: E. Local. - 2p.: 30 cm. - 978-0-11-075439-0 £3.00

The Stockton-on-Tees Borough Council North Shore Development (North Shore Footbridge) Scheme 2006 Confirmation Instrument 2006 No. 2006/2503. - Enabling power: Highways Act 1980, s. 106 (3). - Issued: 20.09.2006. Made: 07.09.2006. Coming into force: In accord. with art. 1. Effect: None. Territorial extent & classification: E. Local. - 8p., plans: 30 cm. - 978-0-11-075110-8 £3.00

The Traffic Management Act 2004 (Commencement No.3) (England) Order 2006 No. 2006/1736 (C.60). - Enabling power: Traffic Management Act 2004, s. 99. Bringing into operation various provisions of the 2004 Act on 29.09.2006 in accord. with art. 2. - Issued: 07.07.2006. Made: 29.06.2006. Effect: None. Territorial extent & classification: E. General. - With correction slip, dated November 2006, amending the commencement number from 1 to 3. - 2p.: 30 cm. - 978-0-11-074785-9 £3.00

Highways, England and Wales

The Restricted Byways (Application and Consequential Amendment of Provisions) Regulations 2006 No. 2006/1177. - Enabling power: Countryside and Rights of Way Act 2000, s. 52 (1) (a) (b). - Issued: 02.05.2006. Made: 20.04.2006. Coming into force: In accord. with reg. 1. Effect: 1842 c. 94, 1964 c. 40; 1968 c. 41; 1970 c. 44; 1972 c. 70; 1980 c. 66; 1981 c. 69; 1984 c. 12, 27; 1988 c. 52; 1990 c. 8; 1991 c. 56, 57; 1992 c. 42; S.I. 1969/414; 1987/2004; 1992/1215; 1993/9, 10, 11, 12, 407; 1997/1160; 1999/221; 2000/2190, 2853 amended. Territorial extent & classification: E/W. General. - Supersedes draft SI (ISBN 0110740696) issued 23.02.2006. - 20p.: 30 cm. - 978-0-11-074529-9 £3.50

Highways, Wales

The M4 Motorway (Junction 30 (Pentwyn) Slip Roads) (Trunking) Scheme 2006 No. 2006/3383 (W.309). - Enabling power: Highways Act 1980, ss. 16, 19. - Issued: 22.12.2006. Made: 18.12.2006. Coming into force: 21.12.2006. Effect: None. Territorial extent & classification: W. General. - In English and Welsh. Welsh title: Cynllun Traffordd yr M4 Slipffyrdd Cyffordd 30 (Pentwyn)) (Peri bod Ffordd yn dod yn Gefnffordd) 2006. - 4p.: 30 cm. - 978-0-11-091480-0 £3.00

The National Assembly for Wales (The London to Fishguard Trunk Road (A40) (Llansantffraed, Talybont-on-Usk Junction Improvement) Compulsory Purchase Order 2006 No. 2006/1711 (W.173). - Enabling power: Highways Act 1980, ss. 239, 240, 246 and Acquisition of Land Act 1981, s. 2, sch. 2, part 1, paras 1 (1) (b) (3) (4). - Made: 20.06.2006. Coming into force: 29.06.2006. Effect: None. Territorial extent & classification: W. Local. - In English and Welsh *Unpublished*

The Public Rights of Way (Registers) (Wales) Regulations 2006 No. 2006/42 (W.8). - Enabling power: Highways Act 1980, ss. 31A, 121B & Wildlife and Countryside Act 1981, s. 53B. - Issued: 13.01.2006. Made: 10.01.2006. Coming into force: 15.01.2006. Effect: None. Territorial extent & classification: W. General. - In English and Welsh. Welsh title: Rheoliadau Hawliau Tramwy Cyhoeddus (Cofrestrau) (Cymru) 2006. - 8p.: 30 cm. - 978-0-11-091250-9 £3.00

The Street Works (Inspection Fees) (Wales) Regulations 2006 No. 2006/1532 (W.150). - Enabling power: New Roads and Street Works Act 1991, ss. 75, 104 (1). - Issued: 21.06.2006. Made: 13.06.2006. Coming into force: 02.10.2006. Effect: S.I. 1992/1688 revoked in relation to Wales and S.I. 2001/2681 (W.222); 2002/3181 (W.297); 2004/1809 (W.196) revoked. Territorial extent & classification: W. General. - In English and Welsh. Welsh title: Rheoliadau Gwaith Stryd (Ffioedd Arolygu) (Cymru) 2006. - 8p.: 30 cm. - 978-0-11-091354-4 £3.00

The Street Works (Reinstatement) (Amendment) (Wales) Regulations 2006 No. 2006/2934 (W.266). - Enabling power: New Roads and Street Works Act 1991, ss. 71, 104 (3). - Issued: 30.11.2006. Made: 07.11.2006. Coming into force: 24.01.2007. Effect: S.I. 1992/1689 amended in relation to Wales. Territorial extent & classification: W. General. - This Statutory Instrument has been printed in substitution of the SI of the same title (ISBN 0110914341) issued on 17.11.2006, which was incorrectly published as S.I. 2006/2932 (W.265), and it is being issued free of charge to all known recipients of that Statutory Instrument. - In English and Welsh. Welsh title: Rheoliadau Gwaith Stryd (Adfer) (Diwygio) (Cymru) 2006. - 4p.: 30 cm. - 978-0-11-091452-7 *£3.00*

The Street Works (Reinstatement) (Amendment) (Wales) Regulations 2006 No. 2006/2932 (W.265). - Enabling power: New Roads and Street Works Act 1991, ss. 71, 104 (3). - Issued: 17.11.2006. Made: 07.11.2006. Coming into force: 24.01.2007. Effect: S.I. 1992/1689 amended in relation to Wales. Territorial extent & classification: W. General. - This Statutory Instrument was incorrectly published as SI 2006/2932 (W.265) and it has been superseded by the SI of the same title but numbered SI 2006/2934 (W.266) issued on 30.11.2006 (ISBN 011091452X). - In English and Welsh. Welsh title: Rheoliadau Gwaith Stryd (Adfer) (Diwygio) (Cymru) 2006. - 4p.: 30 cm. - 978-0-11-091434-3 *£3.00*

Housing

The Persons Subject to Immigration Control (Housing Authority Accommodation and Homelessness) Order 2006 No. 2006/2521. - Enabling power: Immigration and Asylum Act 1999, ss. 118, 119, 166 (3). - Issued: 19.09.2006. Made: 13.09.2006. Laid: 18.09.2006. Coming into force: 09.10.2006. Effect: S.I. 2000/706 amended. Territorial extent & classification: E/W/S/NI. General. - 2p.: 30 cm. - 978-0-11-075111-5 *£3.00*

Housing, England

The Allocation of Housing and Homelessness (Amendment) (England) Regulations 2006 No. 2006/1093. - Enabling power: Housing Act 1996, ss. 160A (3), 172 (4), 185 (2), 215 (2). - Issued: 18.04.2006. Made: 11.04.2006. Laid: 18.04.2006. Coming into force: 20.04.2006. Effect: S.I. 2000/701; 2002/3264 amended. Territorial extent & classification: E. General. - Revoked by S.I. 2006/1294 (ISBN 0110745701). - 2p.: 30 cm. - 978-0-11-074497-1 *£3.00*

The Allocation of Housing and Homelessness (Eligibility) (England) (Amendment) (No.2) Regulations 2006 No. 2006/3340. - Enabling power: Housing Act 1996, ss. 160A (5), 172 (4), 185 (3), 215 (2). - Issued: 19.12.2006. Made: 14.12.2006. Laid: 15.12.2006. Coming into force: 01.01.2007. Effect: S.I. 2006/1294 amended. Territorial extent & classification: E. General. - 4p.: 30 cm. - 978-0-11-075502-1 *£3.00*

The Allocation of Housing and Homelessness (Eligibility) (England) (Amendment) Regulations 2006 No. 2006/2007. - Enabling power: Housing Act 1996, ss. 160A (5), 172 (4), 185 (3). - Issued: 31.07.2006. Made: 24.07.2006. Laid: 25.07.2006. Coming into force: 25.07.2006 at 4.00 p.m. Effect: S.I. 2006/1294 amended. Territorial extent & classification: E. General. - 4p.: 30 cm. - 978-0-11-074938-9 *£3.00*

The Allocation of Housing and Homelessness (Eligibility) (England) Regulations 2006 No. 2006/1294. - Enabling power: Housing Act 1996, ss. 160A (3) (5), 172 (4), 185 (2) (3), 215 (2). - Issued: 18.05.2006. Made: 11.05.2006. Laid: 11.05.2006. Coming into force: 01.06.2006. Effect: S.I. 2002/3264 amended & S.I. 2000/701; 2004/1235; 2006/1093 revoked. Territorial extent & classification: E. General. - With correction slip dated June 2006. - 8p.: 30 cm. - 978-0-11-074570-1 *£3.00*

The Allocation of Housing and Homelessness (Miscellaneous Provisions) (England) Regulations 2006 No. 2006/2527. - Enabling power: Housing Act 1996, ss. 160A (3), 172 (4), 185 (2), 198 (4), 215 (4). - Issued: 21.09.2006. Made: 14.09.2006. Laid: 18.09.2006. Coming into force: 09.10.2006. Effect: S.I. 2006/1294 amended. Territorial extent & classification: E. General. - With correction slip dated October 2006. - 2p.: 30 cm. - 978-0-11-075119-1 *£3.00*

The Houses in Multiple Occupation (Specified Educational Establishments) (England) (No. 2) Regulations 2006 No. 2006/2280. - Enabling power: Housing Act 2004, sch. 14, para. 4 (2). - Issued: 30.08.2006. Made: 22.08.2006. Laid: 30.08.2006. Coming into force: 01.10.2006. Effect: S.I. 2006/647 revoked. Territorial extent & classification: E. General. - 8p.: 30 cm. - 978-0-11-075038-5 *£3.00*

The Houses in Multiple Occupation (Specified Educational Establishments) (England) Regulations 2006 No. 2006/647. - Enabling power: Housing Act 2004, sch. 14, para. 4 (2). - Issued: 16.03.2006. Made: 09.03.2006. Laid: 16.03.2006. Coming into force: 06.04.2006. Effect: None. Territorial extent & classification: E. General. - Revoked by S.I. 2006/2280 (ISBN 0110750381). - 8p.: 30 cm. - 978-0-11-074267-0 *£3.00*

The Housing Act 2004 (Commencement No. 5 and Transitional Provisions and Savings) (England) Order 2006 No. 2006/1060 (C.34). - Enabling power: Housing Act 2004, ss. 76 (6), 250 (2), 270 (4) (5) (9). Bringing into operation various provisions of the 2004 Act in accord with art. 2. - Issued: 10.04.2006. Made: 04.04.2006. Effect: None. Territorial extent & classification: E. General. - 16p.: 30 cm. - 978-0-11-074468-1 *£3.00*

The Housing Act 2004 (Commencement No. 6) (England) Order 2006 No. 2006/3191 (C. 111). - Enabling power: Housing Act 2004, s. 270 (4) (5) (c). Bringing into operation various provisions of the 2004 on 02.01.2007. - Issued: 05.12.2006. Made: 27.11.2006. Effect: None. Territorial extent & classification: E. General. - 4p.: 30 cm. - 978-0-11-075397-3 *£3.00*

The Housing (Approval of Codes of Management Practice) (Student Accommodation) (England) Order 2006 No. 2006/646. - Enabling power: Housing Act 2004, ss. 233 (1) (4) (9). - Issued: 16.03.2006. Made: 09.03.2006. Laid: 16.03.2006. Coming into force: 06.04.2006. Effect: None. Territorial extent & classification: E. General. - 2p.: 30 cm. - 978-0-11-074241-0 *£3.00*

The Housing (Assessment of Accommodation Needs) (Meaning of Gypsies and Travellers) (England) Regulations 2006 No. 2006/3190. - Enabling power: Housing Act 2004, s. 225 (5) (a). - Issued: 05.12.2006. Made: 27.11.2006. Laid: 05.12.2006. Coming into force: 02.01.2007. Effect: None. Territorial extent & classification: E. General. - 2p.: 30 cm. - 978-0-11-075398-0 *£3.00*

The Housing (Empty Dwelling Management Orders) (Prescribed Exceptions and Requirements) (England) Order 2006 No. 2006/367. - Enabling power: Housing Act 2004, s. 134 (5) (a) (c) (6). - Issued: 22.02.2006. Made: 15.02.2006. Laid: 22.02.2006. Coming into force: 06.04.2006. Effect: None. Territorial extent & classification: E. General. - 4p.: 30 cm. - 978-0-11-074071-3 *£3.00*

The Housing (Interim Management Orders) (Prescribed Circumstances) (England) Order 2006 No. 2006/369. - Enabling power: Housing Act 2004, s. 103 (5) (a) (6). - Issued: 22.02.2006. Made: 15.02.2006. Laid: 22.02.2006. Coming into force: 06.04.2006. Effect: None. Territorial extent & classification: E. General. - 2p.: 30 cm. - 978-0-11-074077-5 *£3.00*

The Housing (Management Orders and Empty Dwelling Management Orders) (Supplemental Provisions) (England) Regulations 2006 No. 2006/368. - Enabling power: Housing Act 2004, s. 145. - Issued: 22.02.2006. Made: 15.02.2006. Laid: 22.02.2006. Coming into force: 06.04.2006. Effect: None. Territorial extent & classification: E. General. - 4p.: 30 cm. - 978-0-11-074070-6 *£3.00*

The Housing (Right to Buy) (Designated Rural Areas and Designated Region) (England) Order 2006 No. 2006/1948. - Enabling power: Housing Act 1985, s. 157 (1) (c) (3). - Issued: 24.07.2006. Made: 17.07.2006. Laid before the Parliament: 24.07.2006. Coming into force: 24.08.2006. Effect: None. Territorial extent & classification: E. General. - 4p.: 30 cm. - 978-0-11-074877-1 *£3.00*

The Housing (Right to Buy) (Priority of Charges) (England) (No.2) Order 2006 No. 2006/2563. - Enabling power: Housing Act 1985, s. 156 (4). - Issued: 27.09.2006. Made: 19.09.2006. Coming into force: 10.10.2006. Effect: None. Territorial extent & classification: E. General. - 2p.: 30 cm. - 978-0-11-075131-3 *£3.00*

The Housing (Right to Buy) (Priority of Charges) (England) (No.3) Order 2006 No. 2006/3242. - Enabling power: Housing Act 1985, s. 156 (4). - Issued: 12.12.2006. Made: 05.12.2006. Coming into force: 26.12.2006. Effect: None. Territorial extent & classification: E. General. - 2p.: 30 cm. - 978-0-11-075423-9 *£3.00*

The Housing (Right to Buy) (Priority of Charges) (England) Order 2006 No. 2006/1263. - Enabling power: Housing Act 1985, s. 156 (4). - Issued: 11.05.2006. Made: 02.05.2006. Coming into force: 26.05.2006. Effect: None. Territorial extent & classification: E. General. - 2p.: 30 cm. - 978-0-11-074551-0 *£3.00*

The Introductory Tenancies (Review of Decisions to Extend a Trial Period) (England) Regulations 2006 No. 2006/1077. - Enabling power: Housing Act 1996, s. 125B (3) (4). - Issued: 11.04.2006. Made: 05.04.2006. Laid: 11.04.2006. Coming into force: 03.05.2006. Effect: None. Territorial extent & classification: E. General. - 4p.: 30 cm. - 978-0-11-074484-1 *£3.00*

The Licensing and Management of Houses in Multiple Occupation and Other Houses (Miscellaneous Provisions) (England) Regulations 2006 No. 2006/373. - Enabling power: Housing Act 2004, ss. 59 (2) (3) (4), 60 (6), 63 (5) (6), 65 (3) (4), 83 (2) (4), 84 (6), 87 (5) (6), 232 (3) (7), 250 (2), 258 (2) (b) (5) (6) 259 (2) (c), sch. 14, paras 3, 6 (1) (c). - Issued: 22.02.2006. Made: 15.02.2006. Laid: 22.02.2006. Coming into force: 06.04.2006. Effect: None. Territorial extent & classification: E. General. - 16p.: 30 cm. - 978-0-11-074080-5 *£3.00*

The Licensing of Houses in Multiple Occupation (Prescribed Descriptions) (England) Order 2006 No. 2006/371. - Enabling power: Housing Act 2004, s. 55 (3). - Issued: 22.02.2006. Made: 15.02.2006. Laid: 22.02.2006. Coming into force: 06.04.2006. Effect: None. Territorial extent & classification: E. General. - 4p.: 30 cm. - 978-0-11-074075-1 *£3.00*

The Management of Houses in Multiple Occupation (England) Regulations 2006 No. 2006/372. - Enabling power: Housing Act 2004, s. 234. - Issued: 22.02.2006. Made: 15.02.2006. Laid: 22.02.2006. Coming into force: 06.04.2006. Effect: None. Territorial extent & classification: E. General. - 8p.: 30 cm. - 978-0-11-074074-4 *£3.00*

The Residential Property Tribunal (Fees) (England) Regulations 2006 No. 2006/830. - Enabling power: Housing Act 2004, sch. 13, paras. 1, 11. - Issued: 23.03.2006. Made: 17.03.2006. Laid: 23.03.2006. Coming into force: 13.04.2006. Effect: None. Territorial extent & classification: E. General. - 8p.: 30 cm. - 978-0-11-074370-7 *£3.00*

The Residential Property Tribunal Procedure (England) Regulations 2006 No. 2006/831. - Enabling power: Housing Act 2004, s. 250 (2) (a), sch. 13. - Issued: 23.03.2006. Made: 17.03.2006. Laid: 23.03.2006. Coming into force: 13.04.2006. Effect: None. Territorial extent & classification: E. General. - 32p.: 30 cm. - 978-0-11-074372-1 *£5.50*

The Selective Licensing of Houses (Specified Exemptions) (England) Order 2006 No. 2006/370. - Enabling power: Housing Act 2004, s. 79 (4). - Issued: 22.02.2006. Made: 15.02.2006. Laid: 22.02.2006. Coming into force: 06.04.2006. Effect: None. Territorial extent & classification: E. General. - 4p.: 30 cm. - 978-0-11-074076-8 *£3.00*

The Social Housing (Grants to Bodies other than Registered Social Landlords) (Additional Purposes) (England) Order 2006 No. 2006/583. - Enabling power: Housing Act 1996, s. 27A (3) (4) (d). - Issued: 13.03.2006. Made: 03.03.2006. Laid: 13.03.2006. Coming into force: 06.04.2006. Effect: None. Territorial extent & classification: E. General. - 4p.: 30 cm. - 978-0-11-074176-5 £3.00

The Social Landlords (Permissible Additional Purposes) (England) Order 2006 No. 2006/1968. - Enabling power: Housing Act 1996, s. 2 (7). - Issued: 26.07.2006. Made: 19.07.2006. Laid: 26.07.2006. Coming into force: 24.08.2006. Effect: None. Territorial extent & classification: E. General. - With correction slip dated August 2006. - 4p.: 30 cm. - 978-0-11-074908-2 £3.00

Housing, England and Wales

The Home Information Pack Regulations 2006 No. 2006/1503. - Enabling power: Housing Act 2004, ss. 161, 163, 164, 250 (2), sch. 8, paras 2, 11 (b). - Issued: 14.06.2006. Made: 09.06.2006. Laid: 14.06.2006. Coming into force: 06.07.2006 for part 7; 01.06.2007 for all other purposes. Effect: None. Territorial extent & classification: E/W. General. - 56p.: 30 cm. - 978-0-11-074678-4 £9.00

Housing, Wales

The Allocation of Housing (Wales) (Amendment) Regulations 2006 No. 2006/2645 (W.226). - Enabling power: Housing Act 1996, ss. 160A (3), 172 (4). - Issued: 23.10.2006. Made: 03.10.2006. Coming into force: 09.10.2006. Effect: S.I. 2003/239 (W.36) amended. Territorial extent & classification: W. General. - In English and Welsh. Welsh title: Rheoliadau Dyrannu Tai (Cymru) (Diwygio) 2006. - 4p.: 30 cm. - 978-0-11-091404-6 £3.00

The Approval of Codes of Management Practice (Residential Property) (Wales) Order 2006 No. 2006/178 (W.29). - Enabling power: Leasehold Reform, Housing and Urban Development Act 1993, ss. 87, 100. - Issued: 06.02.2006. Made: 31.01.2006. Coming into force: 01.02.2006. Effect: None. Territorial extent & classification: W. General. - With correction slip, dated April 2006. - In English and Welsh. Welsh title: Gorchymym Cymeradwyo Codau Ymarfer ar gyfer Rheoli (Eiddo Preswyl) (Cymru) 2006. - 4p.: 30 cm. - 978-0-11-091261-5 £3.00

The Homelessness (Suitability of Accommodation) (Wales) Regulations 2006 No. 2006/650 (W.71). - Enabling power: Housing Act 1996, ss. 210 (2), 215 (2). - Issued: 20.03.2006. Made: 08.03.2006. Coming into force: 03.04.2006, 02.04.2007 & 07.04.2008, in accord. with art.1. Effect: None. Territorial extent & classification: W. General. - In English and Welsh. Welsh title: Gorchymyn Digartrefedd (Addasrwydd Llety) (Cymru) 2006. - 16p.: 30 cm. - 978-0-11-091298-1 £3.00

Homelessness (Wales) Regulations 2006 No. 2006/2646 (W.227). - Enabling power: Housing Act 1996, s. 185 (2) (3). - Issued: 23.10.2006. Made: 03.10.2006. Coming into force: 09.10.2006. Effect: S.I. 2000/1079 (W.72) revoked. Territorial extent & classification: W. General. - In English and Welsh. Welsh title: Rheoliadau Digartrefedd (Cymru) 2006. - 12p.: 30 cm. - 978-0-11-091405-3 £3.00

The Houses in Multiple Occupation (Specific Educational Establishment) (Wales) Regulations 2006 No. 2006/1707 (W.169). - Enabling power: Housing Act 2004, sch. 14, para. 4 (2). - Issued: 10.07.2006. Made: 27.06.2006. Coming into force: 07.07.2006. Effect: None. Territorial extent & classification: W. General. - In English and Welsh. Welsh title: Rheoliadau Tai Amlfeddiannaeth (Sefydliadau Addysgol Penodedig) (Cymru) 2006. - 8p.: 30 cm. - 978-0-11-091374-2 £3.00

The Housing Act 2004 (Commencement No. 3 and Transitional Provisions and Savings) (Wales) Order 2006 No. 2006/1535 (W.152) (C.54). - Enabling power: Housing Act 2004, ss. 76 (6), 250 (2), 270 (4) (5) (10). Bringing into operation in Wales various provisions of the 2004 Act on 16.06.2006. - Issued: 10.07.2006. Made: 13.06.2006. Effect: None. Territorial extent & classification: W. General. - In English and Welsh. Welsh title: Gorchymyn Deddf Tai 2004 (Cychwyn Rhif 3 a Darpariaethau Trosiannol ac Arbedion) (Cymru) 2006. - 20p.: 30 cm. - 978-0-11-091367-4 £3.50

The Housing (Approval of Codes of Management Practice) (Student Accommodation) (Wales) Order 2006 No. 2006/1709 (W.171). - Enabling power: Housing Act 2004, s. 233 (1) (4). - Issued: 07.07.2006. Made: 27.06.2006. Coming into force: 07.07.2006. Effect: None. Territorial extent & classification: W. General. - In English and Welsh. Welsh title: Gorchymyn Tai (Cymeradwyo Codau Ymarfer Rheoli) (Llety Myfyrwyr) (Cymru) 2006. - 4p.: 30 cm. - 978-0-11-091372-8 £3.00

The Housing (Empty Dwelling Management Orders) (Prescribed Exceptions and Requirements) (Wales) Order 2006 No. 2006/2823 (W.246). - Enabling power: Housing Act 2004, s. 134 (5) (a) (c) (6). - Issued: 01.11.2006. Made: 25.10.2006. Coming into force: 26.10.2006. Effect: None. Territorial extent & classification: W. General. - In English and Welsh. Welsh title: Gorchymyn Tai (Gorchmynion Rheoli Anheddau Gwag) (Eithriadau a Gofynion Rhagnodedig) (Cymru) 2006. - 8p.: 30 cm. - 978-0-11-091425-1 £3.00

The Housing Health and Safety Rating System (Wales) Regulations 2006 No. 2006/1702 (W.164). - Enabling power: Housing Act 2004, ss. 2, 4, 250 (2) (a). - Issued: 06.07.2006. Made: 27.06.2006. Coming into force: 30.06.2006. Effect: None. Territorial extent & classification: W. General. - In English and Welsh. Welsh title: Rheoliadau System Mesur Iechyd a Diogelwch ar gyfer Tai (Cymru) 2006. - 16p.: 30 cm. - 978-0-11-091366-7 £3.00

The Housing (Interim Management Orders) (Prescribed Circumstances) (Wales) Order 2006 No. 2006/1706 (W.168). - Enabling power: Housing Act 2004, s. 103 (5) (a) (6). - Issued: 07.07.2006. Made: 27.06.2006. Coming into force: 30.06.2006. Effect: None. Territorial extent & classification: W. General. - In English and Welsh. Welsh title: Gorchymyn Tai (Gorchmynion Rheoli Dros Dro) (Amgylchiadau Rhagnodedig) (Cymru) 2006. - 4p.: 30 cm. - 978-0-11-091370-4 £3.00

Housing (Management Orders and Empty Dwelling Management Orders) (Supplemental Provisions) (Wales) Regulations 2006 No. 2006/2822 (W.245). - Enabling power: Housing Act 2004, s. 145. - Issued: 01.11.2006. Made: 25.10.2006. Coming into force: 26.10.2006. Effect: None. Territorial extent & classification: W. General. - In English and Welsh. Welsh title: Rheoliadau Tai (Gorchmynion Rheoli a Gorchmynion Rheoli Anheddau Gwag) (Darpariaethau Atodol) (Cymru) 2006. - 8p.: 30 cm. - 978-0-11-091424-4 £3.00

The Housing Renewal Grants (Amendment) (Wales) Regulations 2006 No. 2006/2801 (W.240). - Enabling power: Housing Grants, Construction and Regeneration Act 1996, ss. 30, 146 (1) (2). - Issued: 26.10.2006. Made: 17.10.2006. Coming into force: 20.10.2006. Effect: S.I. 1996/2890 amended in relation to Wales & S.I. 2005/2605 (W.180) revoked. Territorial extent & classification: W. General. - In English and Welsh. Welsh title: Rheoliadau Grantiau Adnewyddu Tai (Diwygio) (Cymru) 2006. - 20p.: 30 cm. - 978-0-11-091410-7 £3.50

The Housing Renewal Grants (Prescribed Form and Particulars) (Amendment) (Wales) Regulations 2006 No. 2006/2800 (W.239). - Enabling power: Housing Grants, Construction and Regeneration Act 1996, ss. 2 (2) (4), 146 (1) (2). - Issued: 26.10.2006. Made: 17.10.2006. Coming into force: 20.10.2006. Effect: S.I. 1996/2891 amended in relation to Wales. Territorial extent & classification: W. General. - In English and Welsh. Welsh title: Rheoliadau Grantiau Adnewyddu Tai (Ffurflen a Manylion Rhagnodedig) (Diwygio) (Cymru) 2006. - 4p.: 30 cm. - 978-0-11-091411-4 £3.00

The Housing (Right to Buy) (Priority of Charges) (Wales) Order 2006 No. 2006/950 (W.99). - Enabling power: Housing Act 1985, s. 156 (4). - Issued: 07.04.2006. Made: 28.03.2006. Coming into force: 31.03.2006. Effect: None. Territorial extent & classification: W. General. - In English and Welsh. Welsh title: Gorchymyn Tai (Hawl i Brynu) (Blaenoriaeth Arwystlon) (Cymru) 2006. - 4p.: 30 cm. - 978-0-11-091312-4 £3.00

The Introductory Tenancies (Review of Decisions to Extend a Trial Period) (Wales) Regulations 2006 No. 2006/2983 (W.274). - Enabling power: Housing Act 1996, s. 125B (3) (4). - Issued: 08.12.2006. Made: 14.11.2006. Coming into force: 17.11.2006. Effect: None. Territorial extent & classification: W. General. - In English and Welsh. Welsh title: Rheoliadau Tenantiaethau Rhagarweiniol (Adolygu Penderfyniadau i Estyn Cyfnod Treialu) (Cymru) 2006. - 8p.: 30 cm. - 978-0-11-091464-0 £3.00

The Licensing and Management of Houses in Multiple Occupation and other Houses (Miscellaneous Provisions) (Wales) Regulations 2006 No. 2006/1715 (W.177). - Enabling power: Housing Act 2004, ss. 59 (2) (3) (4), 60 (6), 63 (5) (6), 65 (3) (4), 83 (2) (3) (4), 84 (6), 87 (5) (6), 232 (3) (7), 250 (2), 258 (2) (b) (5) (6), 259 (2) (c), sch. 14, paras 3, 6 (1) (c). - Issued: 10.07.2006. Made: 27.06.2006. Coming into force: 30.06.2006. Effect: None. Territorial extent & classification: W. General. - In English and Welsh. Welsh title: Rheoliadau Trwyddedu a Rheoli Tai Amlfeddiannaeth a Thai Eraill (Darpariaethau Amrywiol) (Cymru) 2006. - 24p.: 30 cm. - 978-0-11-091369-8 £4.00

The Licensing of Houses in Multiple Occupation (Prescribed Descriptions) (Wales) Regulations 2006 No. 2006/1712 (W.174). - Enabling power: Housing Act 2004, s. 55 (3). - Issued: 10.07.2006. Made: 27.06.2006. Coming into force: 30.06.2006. Effect: None. Territorial extent & classification: W. General. - In English and Welsh. Welsh title: Gorchymyn Trwyddedu Tai Amlfeddiannaeth (Disgrifiadau Rhagnodedig) (Cymru) 2006. - 4p.: 30 cm. - 978-0-11-091373-5 £3.00

The Management of Houses in Multiple Occupation (Wales) Regulations 2006 No. 2006/1713 (W.175). - Enabling power: Housing Act 2004, s. 234 (1). - Issued: 07.07.2006. Made: 27.06.2006. Coming into force: 30.06.2006. Effect: None. Territorial extent & classification: W. General. - In English and Welsh. Welsh title: Rheoliadau Rheoli Tai Amlfeddiannaeth (Cymru) 2006. - 12p.: 30 cm. - 978-0-11-091368-1 £3.00

The Residential Property Tribunal (Fees) (Wales) Regulations 2006 No. 2006/1642 (W.157). - Enabling power: Housing Act 2004, sch. 13, paras. 1, 11. - Issued: 30.06.2006. Made: 20.06.2006. Coming into force: 23.06.2006. Effect: None. Territorial extent & classification: W. General. - In English and Welsh. Welsh title: Rheoliadau Tribiwynlys Eiddo Preswyl (Ffioedd) (Cymru) 2006. - 8p.: 30 cm. - 978-0-11-091360-5 £3.00

The Residential Property Tribunal Procedure (Wales) Regulations 2006 No. 2006/1641 (W.156). - Enabling power: Housing Act 2004, sch. 13, s. 250 (2) (a). - Issued: 03.07.2006. Made: 20.06.2006. Coming into force: 23.06.2006. Effect: None. Territorial extent & classification: W. General. - In English and Welsh. Welsh title: Rheoliadau Gweithdrefn Tribiwnlys Eiddo Preswyl (Cymru) 2006. - 48p.: 30 cm. - 978-0-11-091362-9 £7.50

The Selective Licensing of Houses (Additional Conditions) (Wales) Order 2006 No. 2006/2825 (W.248). - Enabling power: Housing Act 2004, s. 80 (7). - Issued: 01.11.2006. Made: 25.10.2006. Coming into force: 26.10.2006. Effect: None. Territorial extent & classification: W. General. - In English and Welsh. Welsh title: Gorchymyn Trwyddedu Dethol Tai (Amodau Ychwanegol) (Cymru) 2006. - 4p.: 30 cm. - 978-0-11-091422-0 £3.00

The Selective Licensing of Houses (Specified Exemptions) (Wales) Order 2006 No. 2006/2824 (W.247). - Enabling power: Housing Act 2004, s. 79 (4). - Issued: 01.11.2006. Made: 25.10.2006. Coming into force: 26.10.2006. Effect: None. Territorial extent & classification: W. General. - In English and Welsh. Welsh title: Gorchymyn Trwyddedu Dethol Tai (Esemptiadau Penodedig) (Cymru) 2006. - 8p.: 30 cm. - 978-0-11-091423-7 £3.00

Hovercraft

The Hovercraft (Fees) (Amendment) Regulations 2006 No. 2006/2053. - Enabling power: S.I. 1972/674, art. 35. - Issued: 03.08.2006. Made: 24.07.2006. Coming into force: 11.09.2006. Effect: S.I. 1997/320 amended. Territorial extent & classification: E/W/S/NI. General. - 4p.: 30 cm. - 978-0-11-074959-4 £3.00

Human rights

The Proscribed Organisations Appeal Commission (Human Rights Act 1998 Proceedings) Rules 2006 No. 2006/2290. - Enabling power: Human Rights Act 1998, s. 7 (9) (a) (b). - Issued: 29.08.2006. Made: 22.08.2006. Laid: 25.08.2006. Coming into force: 20.09.2006. Effect: S.I. 2001/127 revoked. Territorial extent & classification: E/W/S/NI. General. - 2p.: 30 cm. - 978-0-11-075041-5 £3.00

Human tissue

The Human Tissue Act 2004 (Persons who Lack Capacity to Consent and Transplants) Regulations 2006 No. 2006/1659. - Enabling power: Human Tissue Act 2004, ss. 6, 33 (3) (7), 52 (1), sch. 4, para. 12 (2). - Issued: 28.06.2006. Made: 22.06.2006. Coming into force: 01.09.2006. Effect: None. Territorial extent & classification: E/W/S/NI. General. - Supersedes the draft SI (ISBN 0110746082) issued on 26.05.2006. - 12p.: 30 cm. - 978-0-11-074742-2 £3.00

Human tissue, England and Wales

The Human Tissue Act 2004 (Commencement No. 4 and Transitional Provisions) Order 2006 No. 2006/404 (C.12). - Enabling power: Human Tissue Act 2004, ss. 58 (3), 60 (2). Bringing into operation various provisions of the 2004 Act on 01.03.2006, 07.04.2006. - Issued: 27.02.2006. Made: 19.02.2006. Effect: None. Territorial extent & classification: E/W/NI. General. - With correction slip dated January 2007. - 8p.: 30 cm. - 978-0-11-074090-4 £3.00

The Human Tissue Act 2004 (Commencement No.5 and Transitional Provisions) (Amendment) Order 2006 No. 2006/2169. - Enabling power: Human Tissue Act 2004, s. 58 (3) (4). - Issued: 11.08.2006. Made: 05.08.2006. Coming into force: 11.08.2006. Effect: S.I. 2006/1997 (C.68) amended. Territorial extent & classification: E/W/NI. General. - This Order has been made in consequence of a defect in SI 2006/1997 (C.68) (ISBN 0110749154) and is being issued free of charge to all known recipients of that Order. With correction slip dated January 2007. - 4p.: 30 cm. - 978-0-11-074990-7 £3.00

The Human Tissue Act 2004 (Commencement No. 5 and Transitional Provisions) Order 2006 No. 2006/1997 (C.68). - Enabling power: Human Tissue Act 2004, ss. 58 (3) (4), 60 (2). Bringing into operation various provisions of the 2004 Act on 31.07.1006, 01.09.2006, 01.12.2006. - Issued: 26.07.2006. Made: 20.07.2006. Effect: None. Territorial extent & classification: E/W/NI. General. - With correction slip dated January 2007. - 8p.: 30 cm. - 978-0-11-074915-0 £3.00

The Human Tissue Act 2004 (Ethical Approval, Exceptions from Licensing and Supply of Information about Transplants) Regulations 2006 No. 2006/1260. - Enabling power: Human Tissue Act 2004, ss. 1 (9), 16 (3), 34 (1), 52 (1), sch. 4, para. 10 (b), sch. 5, para. 4 (5). - Issued: 10.05.2006. Made: 25.04.2006. Laid: 10.05.2006. Coming into force: 01.09.2006. Effect: None. Territorial extent & classification: E/W/NI. General. - With correction slip dated August 2006. - 8p.: 30 cm. - 978-0-11-074552-7 £3.00

The Human Tissue Act 2004 (Powers of Entry and Search: Supply of Information) Regulations 2006 No. 2006/538. - Enabling power: Human Tissue Act 2004, s. 52 (1), sch. 5, para. 4 (5). - Issued: 10.03.2006. Made: 01.03.2006. Laid: 10.03.2006. Coming into force: 07.04.2006. Effect: None. Territorial extent & classification: E/W/NI. General. - 4p.: 30 cm. - 978-0-11-074142-0 £3.00

Human tissue, Northern Ireland

The Human Tissue Act 2004 (Commencement No. 4 and Transitional Provisions) Order 2006 No. 2006/404 (C.12). - Enabling power: Human Tissue Act 2004, ss. 58 (3), 60 (2). Bringing into operation various provisions of the 2004 Act on 01.03.2006, 07.04.2006. - Issued: 27.02.2006. Made: 19.02.2006. Effect: None. Territorial extent & classification: E/W/NI. General. - With correction slip dated January 2007. - 8p.: 30 cm. - 978-0-11-074090-4 £3.00

The Human Tissue Act 2004 (Commencement No.5 and Transitional Provisions) (Amendment) Order 2006 No. 2006/2169. - Enabling power: Human Tissue Act 2004, s. 58 (3) (4). - Issued: 11.08.2006. Made: 05.08.2006. Coming into force: 11.08.2006. Effect: S.I. 2006/1997 (C.68) amended. Territorial extent & classification: E/W/NI. General. - This Order has been made in consequence of a defect in SI 2006/1997 (C.68) (ISBN 0110749154) and is being issued free of charge to all known recipients of that Order. With correction slip dated January 2007. - 4p.: 30 cm. - 978-0-11-074990-7 *£3.00*

The Human Tissue Act 2004 (Commencement No. 5 and Transitional Provisions) Order 2006 No. 2006/1997 (C.68). - Enabling power: Human Tissue Act 2004, ss. 58 (3) (4), 60 (2). Bringing into operation various provisions of the 2004 Act on 31.07.1006, 01.09.2006, 01.12.2006. - Issued: 26.07.2006. Made: 20.07.2006. Effect: None. Territorial extent & classification: E/W/NI. General. - With correction slip dated January 2007. - 8p.: 30 cm. - 978-0-11-074915-0 *£3.00*

The Human Tissue Act 2004 (Ethical Approval, Exceptions from Licensing and Supply of Information about Transplants) Regulations 2006 No. 2006/1260. - Enabling power: Human Tissue Act 2004, ss. 1 (9), 16 (3), 34 (1), 52 (1), sch. 4, para. 10 (b), sch. 5, para. 4 (5). - Issued: 10.05.2006. Made: 25.04.2006. Laid: 10.05.2006. Coming into force: 01.09.2006. Effect: None. Territorial extent & classification: E/W/NI. General. - With correction slip dated August 2006. - 8p.: 30 cm. - 978-0-11-074552-7 *£3.00*

The Human Tissue Act 2004 (Powers of Entry and Search: Supply of Information) Regulations 2006 No. 2006/538. - Enabling power: Human Tissue Act 2004, s. 52 (1), sch. 5, para. 4 (5). - Issued: 10.03.2006. Made: 01.03.2006. Laid: 10.03.2006. Coming into force: 07.04.2006. Effect: None. Territorial extent & classification: E/W/NI. General. - 4p.: 30 cm. - 978-0-11-074142-0 *£3.00*

Identity cards

The Identity Cards Act 2006 (Commencement No.1) Order 2006 No. 2006/1439 (C.49). - Enabling power: Identity Cards Act 2006, s. 44 (3). Bringing into operation various provisions of the 2006 Act on 07.06.2006. - Issued: 05.06.2006. Made: 31.05.2006. Effect: None. Territorial extent & classification: E/W/S/NI. General. - 2p.: 30 cm. - 978-0-11-074632-6 *£3.00*

The Identity Cards Act 2006 (Commencement No.2) Order 2006 No. 2006/2602 (C.87). - Enabling power: Identity Cards Act 2006, s. 44 (3). Bringing into operation various provisions of the 2006 Act on 30.09.2006. - Issued: 29.09.2006. Made: 23.09.2006. Effect: None. Territorial extent & classification: E/W/S/NI. General. - 2p.: 30 cm. - 978-0-11-075137-5 *£3.00*

Immigration

The Accession (Immigration and Worker Authorisation) Regulations 2006 No. 2006/3317. - Enabling power: European Communities Act 1972, s. 2 (2) & European Union (Accessions) Act 2006, s. 2. - Issued: 19.12.2006. Made: 13.12.2006. Coming into force: 01.01.2007. Effect: None. Territorial extent & classification: E/W/S/NI. General. - Supersedes draft S.I. (ISBN) issued on 22.11.2006. - 20p.: 30 cm. - 978-0-11-075499-4 *£3.50*

The Asylum and Immigration (Treatment of Claimants, etc.) Act 2004 (Commencement No. 6) Order 2006 No. 2006/1517 (C.53). - Enabling power: Asylum and Immigration (Treatment of Claimants, etc.) Act 2004, s. 48 (3). Bringing various provisions of the 2004 Act into operation on 29.06.2006, in accord. with art. 2. - Issued: 16.06.2006. Made: 13.06.2006. Effect: None. Territorial extent & classification: E/W/S/NI. General. - 4p.: 30 cm. - 978-0-11-074688-3 *£3.00*

The Asylum and Immigration Tribunal (Fast Track Procedure) (Amendment No. 2) Rules 2006 No. 2006/2898 (L.12). - Enabling power: Nationality, Immigration and Asylum Act 2002, ss. 106 (1) to (3), 112 (3) and British Nationality Act 1981, s. 40A (3). - Issued: 21.11.2006. Made: 02.11.2006. Laid: 03.11.2006. Coming into force: 27.11.2006. Effect: S.I. 2006/2789 amended. Territorial extent & classification: E/W/S/NI. General. - This Statutory Instrument has been made in consequence of a defect in SI 2006/2789 and is being issued free of charge to all known recipients of that Statutory Instrument. - 2p.: 30 cm. - 978-0-11-075335-5 *£3.00*

The Asylum and Immigration Tribunal (Fast Track Procedure) (Amendment) Rules 2006 No. 2006/2789 (L.11). - Enabling power: Nationality, Immigration and Asylum Act 2002, ss. 106 (1) to (3), 112 (3) & British Nationality Act 1981, s. 40A (3). - Issued: 23.10.2006. Made: 13.10.2006. Laid: 17.10.2006. Coming into force: 13.11.2006. Effect: S.I. 2005/560 amended. Territorial extent & classification: E/W/S/NI. General. - 2p.: 30 cm. - 978-0-11-075197-9 *£3.00*

The Asylum and Immigration Tribunal (Procedure) (Amendment) Rules 2006 No. 2006/2788 (L.10). - Enabling power: Nationality, Immigration and Asylum Act 2002, ss. 106 (1) to (3), 112 (3) & British Nationality Act 1981, s. 40A (3). - Issued: 23.10.2006. Made: 13.10.2006. Laid: 17.10.2006. Coming into force: In accord. with rule 1. Effect: S.I. 2005/230 amended. Territorial extent & classification: E/W/S/NI. General. - 8p.: 30 cm. - 978-0-11-075196-2 *£3.00*

The Asylum (Designated States) (Amendment) (No. 2) Order 2006 No. 2006/3275. - Enabling power: Nationality, Immigration and Asylum Act 2002, s. 94 (6). - Issued: 13.12.2006. Made: 07.12.2006. Laid: 12.12.2006. Coming into force: 13.12.2006. Effect: 2002 c.41 amended. Territorial extent & classification: E/W/S/NI. General. - 2p.: 30 cm. - 978-0-11-075460-4 *£3.00*

The Asylum (Designated States) (Amendment) Order 2006 No. 2006/3215. - Enabling power: Nationality, Immigration and Asylum Act 2002, s. 94 (6). - Issued: 08.12.2006. Made: 30.11.2006. Laid: 06.12.2006. Coming into force: 01.01.2007. Effect: 2002 c.41 amended. Territorial extent & classification: E/W/S/NI. General. - 2p.: 30 cm. - 978-0-11-075403-1 *£3.00*

The Asylum (First List of Safe Countries) (Amendment) Order 2006 No. 2006/3393. - Enabling power: Asylum and Immigration (Treatment of Claimants, etc.) Act 2004, sch. 3, para. 20 (1). - Issued: 22.12.2006. Made: 18.12.2006. Coming into force: 01.01.2007. Effect: 2004 c.19 amended. Territorial extent & classification: E/W/S/NI. General. - Supersedes the draft S.I. (ISBN 0110753003) issued on 17.11.2006. - 2p.: 30 cm. - 978-0-11-075544-1 *£3.00*

The Asylum Support (Amendment) Regulations 2006 No. 2006/733. - Enabling power: Immigration and Asylum Act 1999, ss. 166 (3), sch. 8, paras 1, 3 (a). - Issued: 17.03.2006. Made: 13.03.2006. Laid: 17.03.2006. Coming into force: 10.04.2006. Effect: S.I. 2000/704 amended & S.I. 2005/738 revoked. Territorial extent & classification: E/W/S/NI. General. - 2p.: 30 cm. - 978-0-11-074279-3 *£3.00*

The Immigration, Asylum and Nationality Act 2006 (Commencement No. 1) Order 2006 No. 2006/1497 (C.50). - Enabling power: Immigration, Asylum and Nationality Act 2006, s. 62. Bringing into operation various provisions of the 2006 Act on 16.06.2006 & 30.06.2006. - Issued: 12.06.2006. Made: 02.06.2006. Effect: None. Territorial extent & classification: E/W/S/NI. General. - 4p.: 30 cm. - 978-0-11-074661-6 *£3.00*

The Immigration, Asylum and Nationality Act 2006 (Commencement No. 2) Order 2006 No. 2006/2226 (C.75). - Enabling power: Immigration, Asylum and Nationality Act 2006, s. 62. Bringing into operation various provisions of the 2006 Act on 31.08.2006 in accord. with art. 3. - Issued: 17.08.2006. Made: 13.08.2006. Effect: None. Territorial extent & classification: E/W/S/NI. General. - 4p.: 30 cm. - 978-0-11-075017-0 *£3.00*

The Immigration, Asylum and Nationality Act 2006 (Commencement No. 3) Order 2006 No. 2006/2838 (C.98). - Enabling power: Immigration, Asylum and Nationality Act 2006, s. 62. Bringing into operation various provisions of the 2006 Act on 13.11.2006 & 04.12.2006. - Issued: 30.10.2006. Made: 25.10.2006. Effect: None. Territorial extent & classification: E/W/S/NI. General. - 4p.: 30 cm. - 978-0-11-075229-7 *£3.00*

The Immigration (Certificate of Entitlement to Right of Abode in the United Kingdom) Regulations 2006 No. 2006/3145. - Enabling power: Nationality, Immigration and Asylum Act 2002, s. 10 (1). - Issued: 30.11.2006. Made: 23.11.2006. Laid: 29.11.2006. Coming into force: 21.12.2006. Effect: None. Territorial extent & classification: E/W/S/NI. General. - 8p.: 30 cm. - 978-0-11-075378-2 *£3.00*

The Immigration (Continuation of Leave) (Notices) Regulations 2006 No. 2006/2170. - Enabling power: Immigration Act 1971, s. 3C (6). - Issued: 10.08.2006. Made: 04.08.2006. Laid: 10.08.2006. Coming into force: 31.08.2006. Effect: None. Territorial extent & classification: E/W/S/NI. General. - 2p.: 30 cm. - 978-0-11-074989-1 *£3.00*

The Immigration (Designation of Travel Bans) (Amendment) Order 2006 No. 2006/3277. - Enabling power: Immigration Act 1971, 8B (5). - Issued: 13.12.2006. Made: 07.12.2006. Laid: 12.12.2006. Coming into force: 13.12.2006. Effect: S.I. 2000/2724 amended and S.I. 2005/3310 revoked. Territorial extent & classification: E/W/S/NI. General. - 8p.: 30 cm. - 978-0-11-075459-8 *£3.00*

The Immigration (European Economic Area) Regulations 2006 No. 2006/1003. - Enabling power: European Communities Act 1972, s. 2 (2) & Nationality, Immigration and Asylum Act 2002, s. 109. - Issued: 06.04.2006. Made: 30.03.2006. Laid: 04.04.2006. Coming into force: 30.04.2006. Effect: S.I. 1993/1813; 2002/313; 2003/658, 2818, 3214; 2004/755, 1219, 1236; 2005/230 amended & S.I. 2000/2326; 2001/865; 2002/1241; 2003/549, 3188; 2005/47, 671 revoked (with savings). Territorial extent & classification: E/W/S/NI. General. - EC note: These Regulations implement Directive 2004/38/EC on the right of citizens of the Union and their family members to move and reside freely within the territory of the Member States amending Regulation (EEC) No 1612/68 and repealing Directives 64/221/EEC, 68/360/EEC, 72/194/EEC, 73/148/EEC, 75/35/EEC, 90/364/EEC, 90/365/EEC and 93/96/EEC. - 32p.: 30 cm. - 978-0-11-074465-0 *£5.50*

The Immigration (Leave to Remain) (Prescribed Forms and Procedures) (Amendment No.2) Regulations 2006 No. 2006/2899. - Enabling power: Immigration Act 1971, s. 31A. - Issued: 15.11.2006. Made: 31.10.2006. Laid: 07.11.2006. Coming into force: 08.11.2006. Effect: S.I. 2006/1421 amended. Territorial extent & classification: E/W/S/NI. General. - 32p.: 30 cm. - 978-0-11-075283-9 *£5.50*

The Immigration (Leave to Remain) (Prescribed Forms and Procedures) (Amendment) Regulations 2006 No. 2006/1548. - Enabling power: Immigration Act 1971, s. 31A. - Issued: 10.07.2006. Made: 14.06.2006. Laid: 19.06.2006. Coming into force: 22.06.2006. Effect: S.I. 2006/1421 amended. Territorial extent & classification: E/W/S/NI. General. - This Statutory Instrument has been made in consequence of a defect in S.I. 2006/1421 (ISBN 0110747119) and is being issued free of charge to all known recipients of that Statutory Instrument. - 52p.: 30 cm. - 978-0-11-074809-2 *£9.00*

The Immigration (Leave to Remain) (Prescribed Forms and Procedures) Regulations 2006 No. 2006/1421. - Enabling power: Immigration Act 1971, s. 31A. - Issued: 21.06.2006. Made: 25.05.2006. Laid: 01.06.2006. Coming into force: 22.06.2006. Effect: S.I. 2005/2358 revoked. Territorial extent & classification: E/W/S/NI. General. - 112p.: 30 cm. - 978-0-11-074711-8 *£15.50*

The Immigration (Notices) (Amendment) Regulations 2006 No. 2006/2168. - Enabling power: Nationality, Immigration and Asylum Act 2002, ss. 105, 112 (1) to (3). - Issued: 10.08.2006. Made: 03.08.2006. Laid: 10.08.2006. Coming into force: 31.08.2006. Effect: S.I. 2003/658 amended. Territorial extent & classification: E/W/S/NI. General. - 2p.: 30 cm. - 978-0-11-074988-4 £3.00

The Immigration (Passenger Transit Visa) (Amendment) Order 2006 No. 2006/493. - Enabling power: Immigration and Asylum Act 1999, s. 41. - Issued: 02.03.2006. Made: 27.02.2006. Laid: 01.03.2006. Coming into force: 02.03.2006. Effect: S.I. 2003/1185 amended. Territorial extent & classification: E/W/S/NI. General. - 2p.: 30 cm. - 978-0-11-074117-8 £3.00

The Immigration (Provision of Physical Data) Regulations 2006 No. 2006/1743. - Enabling power: Nationality, Immigration and Asylum Act 2002, s. 126 (1). - Issued: 07.07.2006. Made: 03.07.2006. Coming into force: 04.07.2006. Effect: S.I. 2003/1875; 2004/474, 1834; 2005/3127 revoked. Territorial extent & classification: E/W/S/NI. General. - 8p.: 30 cm. - 978-0-11-074790-3 £3.00

The Immigration Services Commissioner (Designated Professional Body) (Fees) Order 2006 No. 2006/400. - Enabling power: Immigration and Asylum Act 1999, s. 86 (10) (12). - Issued: 24.02.2006. Made: 20.02.2006. Laid: 23.02.2006. Coming into force: 16.03.2006. Effect: None. Territorial extent & classification: E/W/S/NI. General. - 2p.: 30 cm. - 978-0-11-074088-1 £3.00

The Nationality, Immigration and Asylum Act 2002 (Commencement No. 11) Order 2006 No. 2006/1498 (C.51). - Enabling power: Nationality, Immigration and Asylum Act 2002, s. 162 (1) (5). Bringing into operation various provisions of the 2002 Act in accord. with art. 2. - Issued: 12.06.2006. Made: 05.06.2006. Effect: None. Territorial extent & classification: E/W/S/NI. General. - 8p.: 30 cm. - 978-0-11-074663-0 £3.00

The Nationality, Immigration and Asylum Act 2002 (Commencement No. 12) Order 2006 No. 2006/3144 (C. 109). - Enabling power: Nationality, Immigration and Asylum Act 2002, s. 162 (1). Bringing into operation various provisions of the 2002 Act on 21.12.2006. - Issued: 30.11.2006. Made: 23.11.2006. Effect: None. Territorial extent & classification: E/W/S/NI. General. - 4p.: 30 cm. - 978-0-11-075375-1 £3.00

The Nationality, Immigration and Asylum Act 2002 (Juxtaposed Controls) (Amendment) Order 2006 No. 2006/2908. - Enabling power: Nationality, Immigration and Asylum Act 2002, s. 141. - Issued: 10.11.2006. Made: 04.11.2006. Coming into force: 18.11.2006. Effect: S.I. 2003/2818 amended. Territorial extent & classification: E/W/S/NI. General. - Supersedes draft SI (ISBN 0110751450) published on 18.10.2006. - 2p.: 30 cm. - 978-0-11-075259-4 £3.00

The Persons Subject to Immigration Control (Housing Authority Accommodation and Homelessness) Order 2006 No. 2006/2521. - Enabling power: Immigration and Asylum Act 1999, ss. 118, 119, 166 (3). - Issued: 19.09.2006. Made: 13.09.2006. Laid: 18.09.2006. Coming into force: 09.10.2006. Effect: S.I. 2000/706 amended. Territorial extent & classification: E/W/S/NI. General. - 2p.: 30 cm. - 978-0-11-075111-5 £3.00

The Refugee or Person in Need of International Protection (Qualification) Regulations 2006 No. 2006/2525. - Enabling power: European Communities Act 1972, s. 2 (2). - Issued: 19.09.2006. Made: 11.09.2006. Laid: 18.09.2006. Coming into force: 09.10.2006. Effect: None. Territorial extent & classification: E/W/S/NI. General. - EC note: These Regulations together with amendments to the Immigration Rules (HC 395) in part implement Council Directive 2004/83/EC on minimum standards for the qualification and status of third country nationals or stateless persons as refugees or as persons who otherwise need international protection and the content of the protection granted- 4p.: 30 cm. - 978-0-11-075117-7 £3.00

Income tax

The Armed Forces and Reserve Forces (Compensation Scheme) (Excluded Benefits for Tax Purposes) Regulations 2006 No. 2006/132. - Enabling power: Income Tax (Earnings and Pensions) Act 2003, s. 393B. - Issued: 31.01.2006. Made: 25.01.2006. Laid: 26.01.2006. Coming into force: 06.04.2006. Effect: None. Territorial extent & classification: E/W/S/NI. General. - 2p.: 30 cm. - 978-0-11-073944-1 £3.00

The Authorised Investment Funds (Tax) Regulations 2006 No. 2006/964. - Enabling power: Finance Act 1995, s. 152 & Finance (No. 2) Act 2005, ss. 17 (3), 18. - Issued: 06.04.2006. Made: 29.03.2006. Coming into force: 01.04.2006. Effect: 1970 c. 9; 1988 c. 1; 1992 c. 12; 1996 c. 8; 2005 c. 5, c. 7 amended & S.I. 1997/1154, 1715; 2002/1973; 2003/1831 revoked. Territorial extent & classification: E/W/S/NI. General. - Approved by the House of Commons. Supersedes draft SI (ISBN 0110740300) issued 17.02.2006. - 48p.: 30 cm. - 978-0-11-074427-8 £7.50

The Capital Allowances (Energy-saving Plant and Machinery) (Amendment) Order 2006 No. 2006/2233. - Enabling power: Capital Allowances Act 2001, ss. 45A (3) (4), 45B (1), 45C (2) (b) (3) (b), 180A (2). - Issued: 21.08.2006. Made: 16.08.2006. Laid: 17.08.2006. Coming into force: 07.09.2006. Effect: S.I. 2001/2541 amended. Territorial extent & classification: E/W/S/NI. General. - 2p.: 30 cm. - 978-0-11-075026-2 £3.00

The Capital Allowances (Environmentally Beneficial Plant and Machinery) (Amendment) Order 2006 No. 2006/2235. - Enabling power: Capital Allowances Act 2001, ss. 45H (3) (4), 45J (3) (b). - Issued: 21.08.2006. Made: 16.08.2006. Laid: 17.08.2006. Coming into force: 07.09.2006. Effect: S.I. 2003/2076 amended. Territorial extent & classification: E/W/S/NI. General. - 2p.: 30 cm. - 978-0-11-075027-9 £3.00

The Double Taxation Relief (Taxes on Income) (Botswana) Order 2006 No. 2006/1925. - Enabling power: Income and Corporation Taxes Act 1988, s. 788. - Issued: 26.07.2006. Made: 19.07.2006. Coming into force: 19.07.2006. Effect: None. Territorial extent & classification: E/W/S/NI. General. - Supersedes draft S.I. (ISBN 0110745159) issued 03.05.2006. - 20p.: 30 cm. - 978-0-11-074890-0 £3.50

The Double Taxation Relief (Taxes on Income) (Japan) Order 2006 No. 2006/1924. - Enabling power: Income and Corporation Taxes Act 1988, s. 788. - Issued: 26.07.2006. Made: 19.07.2006. Coming into force: 19.07.2006. Effect: None. Territorial extent & classification: E/W/S/NI. General. - Supersedes draft S.I. (ISBN 0110745124) issued 03.05.2006. - 28p.: 30 cm. - 978-0-11-074891-7 £4.50

The Double Taxation Relief (Taxes on Income) (Poland) Order 2006 No. 2006/3323. - Enabling power: Income and Corporation Taxes Act 1988, s. 788 & Finance Act 2006, s. 173 (1) to (3)- Issued: 04.01.2007. Made: 14.12.2006. Coming into force: 14.12.2006. Effect: None. Territorial extent & classification: E/W/S/NI. General. - Supersedes the draft S.I. (ISBN 0110752279) issued on 31.10.2006. - 20p.: 30 cm. - 978-0-11-075523-6 £3.50

The Employer-Financed Retirement Benefits (Excluded Benefits for Tax Purposes) Regulations 2006 No. 2006/210. - Enabling power: Income Tax (Earnings and Pensions) Act 2003, s. 393B (3) (d). - Issued: 07.02.2006. Made: 01.02.2006. Laid: 02.02.2006. Coming into force: 06.04.2006. Effect: None. Territorial extent & classification: E/W/S/NI. General. - With correction slip, dated April 2006. - 2p.: 30 cm. - 978-0-11-073979-3 £3.00

The Energy-Saving Items Regulations 2006 No. 2006/912. - Enabling power: Income Tax (Trading and Other Income) Act 2005, s. 312 (5) (c). - Issued: 29.03.2006. Made: 23.03.2006. Laid: 24.03.2006. Coming into force: 06.04.2006. Effect: None. Territorial extent & classification: E/W/S/NI. General. - 2p.: 30 cm. - 978-0-11-074395-0 £3.00

The Exemption from Income Tax for Certain Interest and Royalty Payments (Amendment of Section 757 (2) of the Income Tax (Trading and Other Income) Act 2005) Order 2006 No. 2006/3288. - Enabling power: Income Tax (Trading and Other Income) Act 2005, s. 767 (1). - Issued: 14.12.2006. Made: 11.12.2006. Laid: 11.12.2006. Coming into force: 01.01.2007. Effect: 2005 c. 5 amended. Territorial extent & classification: E/W/S/NI. General. - With correction slip dated February 2007. - 2p.: 30 cm. - 978-0-11-075469-7 £3.00

The Finance Act 2004, Section 77 (1) and (7), (Appointed Day) Order 2006 No. 2006/3240 (C.116). - Enabling power: Finance Act 2004, s. 77 (1) (7). Bringing into operation various provisions of the 2004 Act on 06.04.2007. - Issued: 15.12.2006. Made: 06.12.2006. Effect: None. Territorial extent & classification: E/W/S/NI. General. - 2p.: 30 cm. - 978-0-11-075498-7 £3.00

The Finance Act 2006, Section 53 (1) (Films and Sound Recordings) (Appointed Day) Order 2006 No. 2006/3399 (C.126). - Enabling power: Finance Act 2006, s. 53 (1). Bringing into force various provisions of the 2006 Act on 01.01.2007 in accord. with art. 2. - Issued: 22.12.2006. Made: 18.12.2006. Effect: None. Territorial extent & classification: E/W/S/NI. General. - 2p.: 30 cm. - 978-0-11-075551-9 £3.00

The Finance Act 2006, Section 53(2) (Films and Sound Recordings: Power to alter Dates) Order 2006 No. 2006/3265. - Enabling power: Finance Act 2006, s. 53 (2). - Issued: 12.12.2006. Made: 07.12.2006. Laid: 08.12.2006. Coming into force: 29.12.2006. Effect: 2006 c. 25 amended. Territorial extent & classification: E/W/S/NI. General. - With correction slip, dated January 2007. - 4p.: 30 cm. - 978-0-11-075444-4 £3.00

The Finance (No. 2) Act 2005, Section 17(1), (Appointed Day) Order 2006 No. 2006/982 (C.29). - Enabling power: Finance (No. 2) Act 2005, s. 19 (1). Bringing into operation various provisions of the 2005 Act on 01.04.2006; 06.04.2006. - Issued: 04.04.2006. Made: 30.03.2006. Effect: None. Territorial extent & classification: E/W/S/NI. General. - 2p.: 30 cm. - 978-0-11-074432-2 £3.00

The Income Tax (Exempt Amounts for Childcare Vouchers and for Employer Contracted Childcare) Order 2006 No. 2006/882. - Enabling power: Income Tax (Earnings and Pensions) Act 2003, ss. 270A (11), 318D (1). - Issued: 28.03.2006. Made: 22.03.2006. Laid: 22.03.2006. Coming into force: 06.04.2006. Effect: 2003 c. 1 amended. Territorial extent & classification: E/W/S/NI. General. - 2p.: 30 cm. - 978-0-11-074392-9 £3.00

The Income Tax (Indexation) (No. 2) Order 2006 No. 2006/3241. - Enabling power: Income and Corporation Taxes Act 1988, s. 257C (3). - Issued: 11.12.2006. Made: 06.12.2006. Coming into force: 06.12.2006. Effect: None. Territorial extent & classification: E/W/S/NI. General. - 4p.: 30 cm. - 978-0-11-075433-8 £3.00

The Income Tax (Indexation) Order 2006 No. 2006/872. - Enabling power: Income and Corporation Act 1988, s. 1 (6). - Issued: 28.03.2006. Made: 22.03.2006. Coming into force: 22.03.2006. Effect: None. Territorial extent & classification: E/W/S/NI. General. - 2p.: 30 cm. - 978-0-11-074387-5 £3.00

The Income Tax (Pay As You Earn) (Amendment) Regulations 2006 No. 2006/243. - Enabling power: Income Tax (Earnings and Pensions) Act 2003, s. 684. - Issued: 09.02.2006. Made: 02.02.2006. Laid: 06.02.2006. Coming into force: 06.04.2006. Effect: S.I. 2003/2682 amended. Territorial extent & classification: E/W/S/NI. General. - 4p.: 30 cm. - 978-0-11-073996-0 £3.00

The Income Tax (Pay As You Earn, etc.), (Amendment) Regulations 2006 No. 2006/777. - Enabling power: Income Tax (Earnings and Pensions) Act 2003, s. 684 & Finance Act 2000, s. 143 (1), sch. 38. - Issued: 21.03.2006. Made: 15.03.2006. Laid: 16.03.2006. Coming into force: 06.04.2006. Effect: S.I. 2003/2682, 2495 amended. Territorial extent & classification: E/W/S/NI. General. - 2p.: 30 cm. - 978-0-11-074325-7 £3.00

The Income Tax (Pension Funds Pooling Schemes) (Amendment) Regulations 2006 No. 2006/1162. - Enabling power: Income and Corporation Taxes Act 1988, s. 469 (7) (8). - Issued: 27.04.2006. Made: 24.04.2006. Laid: 25.04.2006. Coming into force: 16.05.2006. Effect: S.I. 1996/1585 amended. Territorial extent & classification: E/W/S/NI. General. - 2p.: 30 cm. - 978-0-11-074519-0 £3.00

The Income Tax (Trading and Other Income) Act 2005 (Consequential Amendments) Order 2006 No. 2006/959. - Enabling power: Income Tax (Trading and Other Income) Act 2005, s. 882 (2) to (5). - Issued: 04.04.2006. Made: 29.03.2006. Laid: 29.03.2006. Coming into force: 30.03.2006. Effect: 1988 c. 1; 1992 c. 12, c.48; 2002 c. 23 amended. Territorial extent & classification: E/W/S/NI. General. - 4p.: 30 cm. - 978-0-11-074424-7 £3.00

The Individual Savings Account (Amendment) Regulations 2006 No. 2006/3194. - Enabling power: Income Tax (Trading and Other Income) Act 2005, ss. 694 (1) (3) (5), 701 (1) & Taxation of Chargeable Gains Act 1992, s. 151. - Issued: 05.12.2006. Made: 30.11.2006. Laid: 01.12.2006. Coming into force: 01.01.2007. Effect: S.I. 1998/1870 amended. Territorial extent & classification: E/W/S/NI. General. - 2p.: 30 cm. - 978-0-11-075402-4 £3.00

The Investment-regulated Pension Schemes (Exception of Tangible Moveable Property) Order 2006 No. 2006/1959. - Enabling power: Finance Act 2004, sch. 29A, para. 11. - Issued: 26.07.2006. Made: 20.07.2006. Laid: 21.07.2006. Coming into force: 11.08.2006 and shall have effect from 06.4.2006. Effect: None. Territorial extent & classification: E/W/S/NI. General. - 2p.: 30 cm. - 978-0-11-074903-7 £3.00

The Lloyd's Underwriters (Conversion to Limited Liability Underwriting) (Tax) Regulations 2006 No. 2006/112. - Enabling power: Finance Act 1993, s. 182 (1) (b). - Issued: 27.01.2006. Made: 23.01.2006. Laid: 24.01.2006. Coming into force: 14.02.2006. Effect: 1993 c. 34 amended. Territorial extent & classification: E/W/S/NI. General. - 2p.: 30 cm. - 978-0-11-073934-2 £3.00

The Lloyd's Underwriters (Scottish Limited Partnerships) (Tax) (Amendment) Regulations 2006 No. 2006/111. - Enabling power: Finance Act 1993, s. 182 (1) and Finance Act 1994, s. 229. - Issued: 27.01.2006. Made: 23.01.2006. Laid: 24.01.2006. Coming into force: 14.02.2006. Effect: S.I. 1997/2681 amended. Territorial extent & classification: E/W/S/NI. General. - 4p.: 30 cm. - 978-0-11-073933-5 £3.00

The Partnerships (Restrictions on Contributions to a Trade) Regulations 2006 No. 2006/1639. - Enabling power: Finance Act 2004, s. 122A (2) to (4). - Issued: 26.06.2006. Made: 21.06.2006. Coming into force: 22.06.2006. Effect: None. Territorial extent & classification: E/W/S/NI. General. - 4p.: 30 cm. - 978-0-11-074734-7 £3.00

The Pension Benefits (Insurance Company Liable as Scheme Administrator) Regulations 2006 No. 2006/136. - Enabling power: Finance Act 2004, s. 273A (1) (2). - Issued: 31.01.2006. Made: 25.01.2006. Laid: 26.01.2006. Coming into force: 06.04.2006. Effect: None. Territorial extent & classification: E/W/S/NI. General. - 2p.: 30 cm. - 978-0-11-073948-9 £3.00

The Pension Protection Fund (Tax) Regulations 2006 No. 2006/575. - Enabling power: Finance Act 2005, s. 102. - Issued: 14.03.2006. Made: 09.03.2006. Laid: 10.03.2006. Coming into force: 06.04.2006. Effect: None. Territorial extent & classification: E/W/S/NI. General. - 14p.: 30 cm. - 978-0-11-074218-2 £3.00

The Pension Schemes (Categories of Country and Requirements for Overseas Pension Schemes and Recognised Overseas Pension Schemes) Regulations 2006 No. 2006/206. - Enabling power: Finance Act 2004, s. 150 (7) (8). - Issued: 07.02.2006. Made: 01.02.2006. Laid: 02.02.2006. Coming into force: 06.04.2006. Effect: None. Territorial extent & classification: E/W/S/NI. General. - 4p.: 30 cm. - 978-0-11-073975-5 £3.00

The Pension Schemes (Information Requirements - Qualifying Overseas Pension Schemes, Qualifying Recognised Overseas Pensions Schemes and Corresponding Relief) Regulations 2006 No. 2006/208. - Enabling power: Finance Act 2004, s. 169, sch. 33, para. 5 (2), sch. 36, para. 51 (4). - Issued: 07.02.2006. Made: 01.02.2006. Laid: 02.02.2006. Coming into force: 06.04.2006. Effect: None. Territorial extent & classification: E/W/S/NI. General. - 4p.: 30 cm. - 978-0-11-073977-9 £3.00

The Pension Schemes (Reduction in Pension Rates) Regulations 2006 No. 2006/138. - Enabling power: Finance Act 2004, sch. 28, para. 2 (4) (e) (h). - Issued: 31.01.2006. Made: 25.01.2006. Laid: 26.01.2006. Coming into force: 06.04.2006. Effect: None. Territorial extent & classification: E/W/S/NI. General. - 4p.: 30 cm. - 978-0-11-073950-2 £3.00

The Pension Schemes (Relevant Migrant Members) Regulations 2006 No. 2006/212. - Enabling power: Finance Act 2004, sch. 33, para. 4 (c). - Issued: 07.02.2006. Made: 01.02.2006. Laid: 02.02.2006. Coming into force: 06.04.2006. Effect: None. Territorial extent & classification: E/W/S/NI. General. - 2p.: 30 cm. - 978-0-11-074000-3 £3.00

The Pension Schemes (Transfers, Reorganisations and Winding Up) (Transitional Provisions) Order 2006 No. 2006/573. - Enabling power: Finance Act 2004, s. 283 (2). - Issued: 14.03.2006. Made: 09.03.2006. Laid: 10.03.2006. Coming into force: 06.04.2006. Effect: None. Territorial extent & classification: E/W/S/NI. General. - 8p.: 30 cm. - 978-0-11-074219-9 £3.00

The Pensions Schemes (Application of UK Provisions to Relevant Non-UK Schemes) (Amendment) Regulations 2006 No. 2006/1960. - Enabling power: Finance Act 2004, sch. 34, paras. 4 (2) (4), 7, 7A. - Issued: 26.07.2006. Made: 20.07.2006. Laid: 21.07.2006. Coming into force: 11.08.2006 and shall have effect from 06.04.2006. Effect: S.I. 2006/207 amended. Territorial extent & classification: E/W/S/NI. General. - 8p.: 30 cm. - 978-0-11-074904-4 £3.00

The Pensions Schemes (Application of UK Provisions to Relevant Non-UK Schemes) Regulations 2006 No. 2006/207. - Enabling power: Finance Act 2004, sch. 34, paras 3 (2) (5) (6), 4 (2) (4), 7, 12, 19. - Issued: 07.02.2006. Made: 01.02.2006. Laid: 02.02.2006. Coming into force: 06.04.2006. Effect: 2004 c. 12 modified. Territorial extent & classification: E/W/S/NI. General. - 12p.: 30 cm. - 978-0-11-073976-2 £3.00

The Pensions Schemes (Taxable Property Provisions) Regulations 2006 No. 2006/1958. - Enabling power: Finance Act 2004, s. 273ZA, sch. 29A, paras 33 (4), 34 (4), 36, 37. - Issued: 26.07.2006. Made: 20.07.2006. Laid: 21.07.2006. Coming into force: 11.08.2006 and shall have effect from 06.04.2006. Effect: 2003 c.14; 2004 c. 12 modified. Territorial extent & classification: E/W/S/NI. General. - 8p.: 30 cm. - 978-0-11-074905-1 £3.00

The Registered Pension Schemes and Overseas Pension Schemes (Electronic Communication of Returns and Information) Regulations 2006 No. 2006/570. - Enabling power: Finance Act 1999, ss. 132, 133 (2) & Finance Act 2002, ss. 135, 136. - Issued: 15.03.2006. Made: 09.03.2006. Laid: 10.03.2006. Coming into force: In accord. with reg. 1. Effect: None. Territorial extent & classification: E/W/S/NI. General. - 8p.: 30 cm. - 978-0-11-074250-2 £3.00

The Registered Pension Schemes (Authorised Member Payments) (No. 2) Regulations 2006 No. 2006/571. - Enabling power: Finance Act 2004, s. 164 (f). - Issued: 14.03.2006. Made: 09.03.2006. Laid: 10.03.06. Coming into force: 06.04.2006. Effect: None. Territorial extent & classification: E/W/S/NI. General. - With correction slip, dated April 2006. - 2p.: 30 cm. - 978-0-11-074223-6 £3.00

The Registered Pension Schemes (Authorised Member Payments) Regulations 2006 No. 2006/137. - Enabling power: Finance Act 2004, s. 164 (f). - Issued: 31.01.2006. Made: 25.01.2006. Laid: 26.01.2006. Coming into force: 06.04.2006. Effect: None. Territorial extent & classification: E/W/S/NI. General. - 4p.: 30 cm. - 978-0-11-073949-6 £3.00

The Registered Pension Schemes (Authorised Payments - Arrears of Pension) Regulations 2006 No. 2006/614. - Enabling power: Finance Act 2004, s. 164 (f). - Issued: 15.03.2006. Made: 09.03.2006. Laid: 10.03.2006. Coming into force: 06.04.2006. Effect: None. Territorial extent & classification: E/W/S/NI. General. - 2p.: 30 cm. - 978-0-11-074225-0 £3.00

The Registered Pension Schemes (Authorised Payments) Regulations 2006 No. 2006/209. - Enabling power: Finance Act 2004, s. 164 (f). - Issued: 07.02.2006. Made: 01.02.2006. Laid: 02.02.2006. Coming into force: 06.04.2006. Effect: None. Territorial extent & classification: E/W/S/NI. General. - 4p.: 30 cm. - 978-0-11-073978-6 £3.00

The Registered Pension Schemes (Authorised Payments) (Transfers to the Pension Protection Fund) Regulations 2006 No. 2006/134. - Enabling power: Finance Act 2004, s. 164 (f). - Issued: 31.01.2006. Made: 25.01.2006. Laid: 26.01.2006. Coming into force: 06.04.2006. Effect: None. Territorial extent & classification: E/W/S/NI. General. - 2p.: 30 cm. - 978-0-11-073947-2 £3.00

The Registered Pension Schemes (Authorised Reductions) Regulations 2006 No. 2006/1465. - Enabling power: Finance Act 2004, sch. 28, para. 2 (4) (h) (4A) (8)- Issued: 09.06.2006. Made: 06.06.2006. Laid: 06.06.2006. Coming into force: 27.06.2006. Effect: None. Territorial extent & classification: E/W/S/NI. General. - 2p.: 30 cm. - 978-0-11-074650-0 £3.00

The Registered Pension Schemes (Authorised Surplus Payments) Regulations 2006 No. 2006/574. - Enabling power: Finance Act 2004, s. 177. - Issued: 15.03.2006. Made: 09.03.2006. Laid: 10.03.2006. Coming into force: 06.04.2006. Effect: None. Territorial extent & classification: E/W/S/NI. General. - 4p.: 30 cm. - 978-0-11-074224-3 £3.00

The Registered Pension Schemes (Block Transfers) (Permitted Membership Period) Regulations 2006 No. 2006/498. - Enabling power: Finance Act 2004, sch. 36, para. 22 (6) (b). - Issued: 06.03.2006. Made: 28.02.2006. Laid: 01.03.2006. Coming into force: 06.04.2006. Effect: None. Territorial extent & classification: E/W/S/NI. General. - 2p.: 30 cm. - 978-0-11-074126-0 £3.00

The Registered Pension Schemes (Co-ownership of Living Accommodation) Regulations 2006 No. 2006/133. - Enabling power: Finance Act 2004, s. 173 (8) (a). - Issued: 31.01.2006. Made: 25.01.2006. Laid: 26.01.2006. Coming into force: 06.04.2006. Effect: None. Territorial extent & classification: E/W/S/NI. General. - 4p.: 30 cm. - 978-0-11-073945-8 £3.00

The Registered Pension Schemes (Enhanced Lifetime Allowance) (Amendment) Regulations 2006 No. 2006/3261. - Enabling power: Finance Act 2004, ss. 220 (5), 221 (6), 224 (9), 251 (1) (6), 256, sch. 36, paras 7 (1) (b), 11A (1) (c), 12 (1), 15A (1) (b), 18 (6), & Taxes Management Act 1970, s. 113 (1). - Issued: 12.12.2006. Made: 06.12.2006. Laid: 07.12.2006. Coming into force: 28.12.2006. Effect: S.I. 2006/131 amended. Territorial extent & classification: E/W/S/NI. General. - 8p.: 30 cm. - 978-0-11-075441-3 £3.00

Income tax

The Registered Pension Schemes (Enhanced Lifetime Allowance) Regulations 2006 No. 2006/131. - Enabling power: Finance Act 2004, ss. 220 (5), 221 (6), 224 (9), 251 (1) (6), 256, sch. 36, paras 7 (1) (b), 12 (1), 18 (6) and Taxes Management Act 1970, s. 113 (1). - Issued: 01.02.2006. Made: 25.01.2006. Laid: 26.01.2006. Coming into force: 06.04.2006. Effect: None. Territorial extent & classification: E/W/S/NI. General. - 16p.: 30 cm. - 978-0-11-073942-7 £3.00

The Registered Pension Schemes (Extension of Migrant Member Relief) Regulations 2006 No. 2006/1957. - Enabling power: Finance Act 2004, sch. 33, para. 4 (2) (3). - Issued: 26.07.2006. Made: 20.07.2006. Laid: 21.07.2006. Coming into force: 11.08.2006 and shall have effect in relation to all times on or after 06.04.2006. Effect: None. Territorial extent & classification: E/W/S/NI. General. - 4p.: 30 cm. - 978-0-11-074907-5 £3.00

The Registered Pension Schemes (Meaning of Pension Commencement Lump Sum) Regulations 2006 No. 2006/135. - Enabling power: Finance Act 2004, sch. 29, para. 1 (6). - Issued: 31.01.2006. Made: 25.01.2006. Laid: 26.01.2006. Coming into force: 06.04.2006. Effect: None. Territorial extent & classification: E/W/S/NI. General. - 4p.: 30 cm. - 978-0-11-073946-5 £3.00

The Registered Pension Schemes (Modification of the Rules of Existing Schemes) Regulations 2006 No. 2006/364. - Enabling power: Finance Act 2004, sch. 36, para. 3. - Issued: 22.02.2006. Made: 16.02.2006. Laid: 17.02.2006. Coming into force: 06.04.2006. Effect: None. Territorial extent & classification: E/W/S/NI. General. - 8p.: 30 cm. - 978-0-11-074067-6 £3.00

The Registered Pension Schemes (Prescribed Manner of Determining Amount of Annuities) Regulations 2006 No. 2006/568. - Enabling power: Finance Act 2004, sch. 28, paras. 3 (1) (d), 6 (1) (e), 17 (1) (c), 20 (1) (e). - Issued: 15.03.2006. Made: 09.03.2006. Laid: 10.03.2006. Coming into force: 06.04.2006. Effect: None. Territorial extent & classification: E/W/S/NI. General. - 4p.: 30 cm. - 978-0-11-074255-7 £3.00

The Registered Pension Schemes (Provision of Information) (Amendment) Regulations 2006 No. 2006/1961. - Enabling power: Finance Act 2004, ss. 169, 251 (1) (a) (b) (4) (a) (b) (5) (6), sch. 36, para. 51 (4). - Issued: 26.07.2006. Made: 20.07.2006. Laid: 21.07.2006. Coming into force: 11.08.2006. Effect: S.I. 2006/208, 567 amended. Territorial extent & classification: E/W/S/NI. General. - 4p.: 30 cm. - 978-0-11-074901-3 £3.00

The Registered Pension Schemes (Provision of Information) Regulations 2006 No. 2006/567. - Enabling power: Finance Act 2004, ss. 220 (5), 221 (6), 224 (9), 251 (1) (a) (b) (4)(a) (b) (5) (6), 256, sch. 36, paras 7 (1) (b), 12 (1), 18 (6). - Issued: 15.03.2006. Made: 09.03.2006. Laid: 10.03.2006. Coming into force: 06.04.2006. Effect: None. Territorial extent & classification: E/W/S/NI. General. - 16p.: 30 cm. - 978-0-11-074221-2 £3.00

The Registered Pension Schemes (Relevant Annuities) Regulations 2006 No. 2006/129. - Enabling power: Finance Act 2004, sch. 28, para. 14. - Issued: 31.01.2006. Made: 25.01.2006. Laid: 26.01.2006. Coming into force: 06.04.2006. Effect: None. Territorial extent & classification: E/W/S/NI. General. - 4p.: 30 cm. - 978-0-11-073941-0 £3.00

The Registered Pension Schemes (Splitting of Schemes) Regulations 2006 No. 2006/569. - Enabling power: Finance Act 2004, s. 274A. - Issued: 15.03.2006. Made: 09.03.2006. Laid: 10.03.2006. Coming into force: 06.04.2006. Effect: 2004 c. 12 amended. Territorial extent & classification: E/W/S/NI. General. - 12p.: 30 cm. - 978-0-11-074226-7 £3.00

The Registered Pension Schemes (Surrender of Relevant Excess) Regulations 2006 No. 2006/211. - Enabling power: Finance Act 2004, s. 172A (5) (f), sch. 36, paras 3 (1), 12 (5). - Issued: 07.02.2006. Made: 01.02.2006. Laid: 02.02.2006. Coming into force: 06.04.2006. Effect: None. Territorial extent & classification: E/W/S/NI. General. - 4p.: 30 cm. - 978-0-11-073999-1 £3.00

The Registered Pension Schemes (Transfer of Sums and Assets) Regulations 2006 No. 2006/499. - Enabling power: Finance Act 2004, s. 169 (1B) (1C) (1D) (1E), sch. 28, paras 2 (4) (h) (6A), 3 (2B) (2C), 6 (1B) (1C), 16 (2A) (2B), 17 (3) (4), 20 (1B) (1C). - Issued: 06.03.2006. Made: 28.02.2006. Laid: 01.03.2006. Coming into force: 06.04.2006. Effect: None. Territorial extent & classification: E/W/S/NI. General. - 8p.: 30 cm. - 978-0-11-074127-7 £3.00

The Registered Pension Schemes (Unauthorised Payments by Existing Schemes) Regulations 2006 No. 2006/365. - Enabling power: Finance Act 2004, s. 241 (2) (e). - Issued: 22.02.2006. Made: 16.02.2006. Laid: 17.02.2006. Coming into force: 06.04.2006. Effect: None. Territorial extent & classification: E/W/S/NI. General. - 4p.: 30 cm. - 978-0-11-074068-3 £3.00

The Registered Pension Schemes (Uprating Percentages for Defined Benefits Arrangements and Enhanced Protection Limits) Regulations 2006 No. 2006/130. - Enabling power: Finance Act 2004, s. 235 (3) (c), sch. 36, paras 15 (5) (b), 16 (5A) (b), 17 (6) (b). - Issued: 31.01.2006. Made: 25.01.2006. Laid: 26.01.2006. Coming into force: 06.04.2006. Effect: None. Territorial extent & classification: E/W/S/NI. General. - 4p.: 30 cm. - 978-0-11-073943-4 £3.00

The Reporting of Savings Income Information (Amendment) Regulations 2006 No. 2006/3286. - Enabling power: Finance Act 2003, s. 199. - Issued: 14.12.2006. Made: 11.12.2006. Laid: 11.12.2006. Coming into force: 01.01.2007. Effect: S.I. 2003/3297 amended. Territorial extent & classification: E/W/S/NI. General. - With correction slip dated January 2007. EC note: These Regs amend the 2003 Regulations which implemented part of Council Directive 2003/48/EC on the taxation of savings income in the form of interest payments. The 2003 Directive has been amended by Council Directive 2006/98/EC adapting certain Directives in the field of taxation by reason of the accession of Bulgaria and Romania. - 4p.: 30 cm. - 978-0-11-075468-0 £3.00

The Taxation of Judicial Pensions (Consequential Provisions) Order 2006 No. 2006/497. - Enabling power: Finance Act 2004, s. 281 (2) (3). - Issued: 06.03.2006. Made: 28.02.2006. Laid: 01.03.2006. Coming into force: 06.04.2006. Effect: 1959 c. 25; 1960 c. 2; 1981 c. 20; 1993 c. 8 amended. Territorial extent & classification: E/W/S/NI. General. - 8p.: 30 cm. - 978-0-11-074128-4 £3.00

The Taxation of Pension Schemes (Consequential Amendments) (No. 2) Order 2006 No. 2006/1963. - Enabling power: Finance Act 2004, s. 281 (2) (4). - Issued: 26.07.2006. Made: 20.07.2006. Laid before the Parliament: 21.07.2006. Coming into force: 11.08.2006. Effect: 1988 c. 1; 1995 c. 4; 2003 c. 1 amended. Territorial extent & classification: E/W/S/NI. General. - 2p.: 30 cm. - 978-0-11-074902-0 £3.00

The Taxation of Pension Schemes (Consequential Amendments) Order 2006 No. 2006/745. - Enabling power: Finance Act 2004, s. 281 (2). - Issued: 03.04.2006. Made: 14.03.2006. Laid: 15.03.2006. Coming into force: 06.04.2006. Effect: 1984 c.12; 1989 c.29; 1992 c.4, c.7; 1993 c.43, c.48, c.49; 1994 c.21; 1995 c.18, c.26; 1999 c.29, c.30; 2000 c.8; 2004 c.35 & S.I. 1990/2231; 1995/2705 (N.I. 15), 3036; 3213 (N.I. 22); 1996/1537, 1585; 1999/3147 (N.I. 11); 2000/944; 2002/2006; 2003/2682; 2005/255 (N.I. 1) & S.R. 1997/56 amended. Territorial extent & classification: E/W/S/NI. General. - 16p.: 30 cm. - 978-0-11-074327-1 £3.00

The Taxation of Pension Schemes (Transitional Provisions) (Amendment No. 2) Order 2006 No. 2006/2004. - Enabling power: Finance Act 2004, s. 283 (2). - Issued: 28.07.2006. Made: 24.07.2006. Laid: 24.07.2006. Coming into force: 25.07.2006. Effect: S.I. 2006/572 amended. Territorial extent & classification: E/W/S/NI. General. - 8p.: 30 cm. - 978-0-11-074927-3 £3.00

The Taxation of Pension Schemes (Transitional Provisions) (Amendment) Order 2006 No. 2006/1962. - Enabling power: Finance Act 2004, s. 283(2) (3A) (3B) (3C). - Issued: 26.07.2006. Made: 20.07.2006. Laid: 21.07.2006. Coming into force: 11.08.2006 and shall effect in certain respects from 06.04.2006. Effect: S.I. 2006/572 amended. Territorial extent & classification: E/W/S/NI. General. - 4p.: 30 cm. - 978-0-11-074900-6 £3.00

The Taxation of Pension Schemes (Transitional Provisions) Order 2006 No. 2006/572. - Enabling power: Finance Act 2004, s. 283 (2). - Issued: 15.03.2006. Made: 09.03.2006. Laid: 10.03.2006. Coming into force: 06.04.2006. Effect: 2004 c. 12 modified. Territorial extent & classification: E/W/S/NI. General. - 32p.: 30 cm. - 978-0-11-074222-9 £5.50

The Tax Avoidance Schemes (Information) (Amendment) Regulations 2006 No. 2006/1544. - Enabling power: Finance Act 2004, ss. 308 (1) (3), 309 (1), 310, 313 (1), 317 (2), 318 (1). - Issued: 20.06.2006. Made: 15.06.2006. Laid: 15.06.2006. Coming into force: 01.08.2006. Effect: S.I. 2004/1864 amended. Territorial extent & classification: E/W/S/NI. General. - 4p.: 30 cm. - 978-0-11-074707-1 £3.00

The Tax Avoidance Schemes (Prescribed Descriptions of Arrangements) Regulations 2006 No. 2006/1543. - Enabling power: Finance Act 2004, s. 306 (1) (a) (b). - Issued: 20.06.2006. Made: 15.06.2006. Laid: 15.06.2006. Coming into force: 01.08.2006. Effect: S.I. 2004/1863, 2429 revoked. Territorial extent & classification: E/W/S/NI. General. - 12p.: 30 cm. - 978-0-11-074706-4 £3.00

The Tax Information Exchange Agreement (Taxes on Income) (Gibraltar) Order 2006 No. 2006/1453. - Enabling power: Income and Corporation Taxes Act 1988, s. 815C. - Issued: 14.06.2006. Made: 07.06.2006. Coming into force: 07.06.2006. Effect: None. Territorial extent & classification: E/W/S/NI. General. - Supersedes draft SI (ISBN 0110745140) issued 03.05.2006. - 20p.: 30 cm. - 978-0-11-074669-2 £3.50

The Unit Trust Schemes and Offshore Funds (Non-qualifying Investments Test) Order 2006 No. 2006/981. - Enabling power: Finance Act 1996, sch. 10, paras. 8 (8), 9. - Issued: 04.04.2006. Made: 30.03.2006. Laid: 30.03.2006. Coming into force: 20.04.2006. Effect: 1996 c. 8 amended. Territorial extent & classification: E/W/S/NI. General. - 4p.: 30 cm. - 978-0-11-074431-5 £3.00

Industrial and provident societies

The Community Benefit Societies (Restriction on Use of Assets) Regulations 2006 No. 2006/264. - Enabling power: Co-operatives and Community Benefit Societies Act 2003, s. 1. - Issued: 14.02.2006. Made: 07.02.2006. Coming into force: 06.04.2006. Effect: 1965 c. 12 modified. Territorial extent & classification: E/W/S/NI. General. - Supersedes draft SI (ISBN 0110737865) issued 16.12.2005. - 12p.: 30 cm. - 978-0-11-073982-3 £3.00

The Credit Unions (Maximum Interest Rate on Loans) Order 2006 No. 2006/1276. - Enabling power: Credit Unions Act 1979, s. 11 (7). - Issued: 16.05.2006. Made: 10.05.2006. Laid: 10.05.2006. Coming into force: 01.06.2006. Effect: None. Territorial extent & classification: E/W/S/NI. General. - 2p.: 30 cm. - 978-0-11-074567-1 £3.00

The Friendly and Industrial and Provident Societies Act 1968 (Audit Exemption) (Amendment) Order 2006 No. 2006/265. - Enabling power: Industrial and Provident Societies Act 2002, s. 2. - Issued: 14.02.2006. Made: 07.02.2006. Coming into force: 06.04.2006. Effect: 1968 c. 55 amended. Territorial extent & classification: E/W/S/NI. General. - Supersedes draft SI (ISBN 0110737857) issued 16.12.2005. - 4p.: 30 cm. - 978-0-11-073983-0 *£3.00*

Inheritance tax

The Inheritance Tax (Delivery of Accounts) (Excepted Estates) (Amendment) Regulations 2006 No. 2006/2141. - Enabling power: Inheritance Tax Act 1984, s. 256 (1), (1A) (3). - Issued: 07.08.2006. Made: 02.08.2006. Laid: 03.08.2006. Coming into force: 01.09.2006. Effect: S.I. 2004/2543 amended. Territorial extent & classification: E/W/S/NI. General. - 4p.: 30 cm. - 978-0-11-074978-5 *£3.00*

The Pension Protection Fund (Tax) Regulations 2006 No. 2006/575. - Enabling power: Finance Act 2005, s. 102. - Issued: 14.03.2006. Made: 09.03.2006. Laid: 10.03.2006. Coming into force: 06.04.2006. Effect: None. Territorial extent & classification: E/W/S/NI. General. - 14p.: 30 cm. - 978-0-11-074218-2 *£3.00*

Inquiries

The Inquiry Rules 2006 No. 2006/1838. - Enabling power: Inquiries Act 2005, s. 41. - Issued: 17.07.2006. Made: 11.07.2006. Laid: 11.07.2006. Coming into force: 01.08.2006. Effect: None. Territorial extent & classification: E/W/S/NI. General. - With correction slip dated November 2006. - 12p.: 30 cm. - 978-0-11-074831-3 *£3.00*

Insolvency: Companies

The Banks (Former Authorised Institutions) (Insolvency) Order 2006 No. 2006/3107. - Enabling power: Insolvency Act 1986, s. 422. - Issued: 29.11.2006. Made: 20.11.2006. Laid: 23.11.2006. Coming into force: 15.12.2006. Effect: 1986 c.45 amended & S.I. 1989/1276 revoked with savings. Territorial extent & classification: E/W/S. General. - 4p.: 30 cm. - 978-0-11-075357-7 *£3.00*

The Cross-border Insolvency Regulations 2006 No. 2006/1030. - Enabling power: Insolvency Act 2000, s. 14. - Issued: 10.04.2006. Made: 03.04.2006. Coming into force: 04.04.2006. In accord. with art. 1 (1). Effect: 1986 c.45, section 338 disapplied. Territorial extent & classification: E/W/S. General. - Supersedes draft S.I. (ISBN 0110741587) issued on 09.03.2006. - 60p.: 30 cm. - 978-0-11-074473-5 *£9.00*

Insolvency: Individuals

The Cross-border Insolvency Regulations 2006 No. 2006/1030. - Enabling power: Insolvency Act 2000, s. 14. - Issued: 10.04.2006. Made: 03.04.2006. Coming into force: 04.04.2006. In accord. with art. 1 (1). Effect: 1986 c.45, section 338 disapplied. Territorial extent & classification: E/W/S. General. - Supersedes draft S.I. (ISBN 0110741587) issued on 09.03.2006. - 60p.: 30 cm. - 978-0-11-074473-5 *£9.00*

The Enterprise Act 2002 (Disqualification from Office: General) Order 2006 No. 2006/1722. - Enabling power: Enterprise Act 2002, s. 268. - Issued: 06.07.2006. Made: 28.06.2006. Coming into force: 29.06.2006, in accord. with art. 1 (1). Effect: 1902 c.41; 1975 c.68; 1977 c.3; 1981 c.56; 1991 c.59; 1993 c.10; 1995 c.26; 1999 c.29; S.I. 1950/1326; 1968/2049; 1989/469; 1990/2024; 1994/1738; 1995/2801; 1996/707; 1998/1870; 2000/89, 2872; 2001/715, 794, 1742, 1744; 2002/2376 amended. Territorial extent & classification: E/W/S/NI. General. - 8p.: 30 cm. - 978-0-11-074781-1 *£3.00*

Insolvency, England and Wales

The Insolvent Partnerships (Amendment) Order 2006 No. 2006/622. - Enabling power: Insolvency Act 1986, s. 420. - Issued: 23.03.2006. Made: 07.03.2006. Laid: 08.03.2006. Coming into force: 06.04.2006. Effect: S.I. 1994/2421 amended. Territorial extent & classification: E/W. General. - This Statutory Instrument has been made in consequence of defects in S.I. 2005/1516 and is being issued free of charge to all known recipients of that Statutory Instrument. - 12p.: 30 cm. - 978-0-11-074363-9 *£3.00*

Insolvency, England and Wales: Companies

The Insolvency (Amendment) Rules 2006 No. 2006/1272. - Enabling power: Insolvency Act 1986, s. 411. - Issued: 17.05.2006. Made: 09.05.2006. Laid: 10.05.2006. Coming into force: 01.06.2006. Effect: S.I. 1986/1925 amended. Territorial extent & classification: E/W. General. - 4p.: 30 cm. - 978-0-11-074562-6 *£3.00*

Insolvency, England and Wales: Fees

The Insolvency Proceedings (Fees) (Amendment) Order 2006 No. 2006/561. - Enabling power: Insolvency Act 1986, ss. 414, 415 & Companies Act 1985, s. 663 (4) & Bankruptcy Act 1914, s. 133. - Issued: 13.03.2006. Made: 02.03.2006. Laid: 06.03.2006. Coming into force: 01.04.2006. Effect: S.I. 1984/880; 1985/1784; 2004/593 amended. Territorial extent & classification: E/W. General. - 4p.: 30 cm. - 978-0-11-074166-6 *£3.00*

Insolvency, Scotland: Companies

The Energy Administration (Scotland) Rules 2006 No. 2006/772 (S. 8). - Enabling power: Insolvency Act 1986, s. 411 & Energy Act 2004, s. 159 (3). - Issued: 27.03.2006. Made: 13.03.2006. Laid before the Scottish Parliament: 15.03.2006. Coming into force: 06.04.2006. Effect: None. Territorial extent & classification: S. General. - 80p.: 30 cm. - 978-0-11-070130-1 £12.00

The Insolvency (Scotland) Amendment Order 2006 No. 2006/735 (S.7). - Enabling power: Enterprise Act 2002, s. 277 (1). - Issued: 21.03.2006. Made: 13.03.2006. Laid: 14.03.2006. Coming into force: 06.04.2006. Effect: S.I. 1986/1915 amended. Territorial extent & classification: S. General. - 4p.: 30 cm. - 978-0-11-070122-6 £3.00

The Insolvency (Scotland) Amendment Rules 2006 No. 2006/734 (S.6). - Enabling power: Insolvency Act 1986, s. 411. - Issued: 21.03.2006. Made: 13.03.2006. Laid: 14.03.2006. Coming into force: 06.04.2006. Effect: S.I. 1986/1915 amended. Territorial extent & classification: S. General. - With correction slip dated April 2006. - 28p.: 30 cm. - 978-0-11-070121-9 £4.50

Insurance premium tax

The Insurance Premium Tax (Amendment) Regulations 2006 No. 2006/2700. - Enabling power: Finance Act 1994, ss. 53 (6), 53AA (8). - Issued: 18.10.2006. Made: 10.10.2006. Laid: 12.10.2006. Coming into force: 01.12.2006. Effect: S.I. 1994/1774 amended. Territorial extent & classification: E/W/S/NI. General. - 8p.: 30 cm. - 978-0-11-075184-9 £3.00

The Mutual Assistance Provisions Order 2006 No. 2006/3283. - Enabling power: Finance Act 2003, s. 197 (5). - Issued: 14.12.2006. Made: 11.12.2006. Laid: 11.12.2006. Coming into force: 01.01.2007. Effect: 2003 c.14 amended. Territorial extent & classification: E/W/S/NI. General. - With correction slip dated January 2007. - 2p.: 30 cm. - 978-0-11-075465-9 £3.00

Intellectual property

The Intellectual Property (Enforcement, etc.) Regulations 2006 No. 2006/1028. - Enabling power: European Communities Act 1972, s. 2 (2). - Issued: 13.04.2006. Made: 05.04.2006. Laid: 06.04.2006. Coming into force: 29.04.2006. Effect: 1949 c.88; 1977 c. 37; 1988 c. 48; 1994 c. 26 & S.I. 1995/3297; 1996/2967; 1997/3032; 2005/2339 amended. Territorial extent & classification: E/W/S/NI. General. - EC note: This Instrument implements or further implements the following Community instruments: (a) Directive 2004/48/EC on the enforcement of intellectual property rights; (b) Agreement establishing the World Trade Organisation (including the Agreement on Trade-related Aspects of Intellectual Property Rights (Cm. 3044-6, 3080, 3263-4, 3268-9, 3271, 3275-7 and 3282) which was specified as a Community treaty by SI 1995/265; (c) Directive 98/71/EC on the legal protection of designs; (d) Council Regulation EC no. 6 of 2002 on Community designs; and (e) European Economic Area Agreement. - 20p.: 30 cm. - 978-0-11-074474-2 £3.50

The Patents, Trade Marks and Designs (Address for Service and Time Limits, ,etc.) Rules 2006 No. 2006/760. - Enabling power: Patents Act 1977, s. 123 & Trade Marks Act 1994, s. 78 & Registered Designs Act 1949, s. 36 & Copyright, Designs and Patents Act 1988, s. 250. - Issued: 22.03.2006. Made: 14.03.2006. Laid: 15.03.2006. Coming into force: 06.04.2006. Effect: S.I. 1989/1130; 1995/2093 , 2912; 2000/136 amended. Territorial extent & classification: UK. General. - 8p.: 30 cm. - 978-0-11-074329-5 £3.00

The Registered Designs Act 1949 and Patents Act 1977 (Electronic Communications) Order 2006 No. 2006/1229. - Enabling power: Electronic Communications Act 2000, ss. 8, 9. - Issued: 10.05.2006. Made: 26.04.2006. Laid: 03.05.2006. Coming into force: 01.10.2006. Effect: 1949 c. 88; 1977 c. 37 amended. Territorial extent & classification: UK. General. - 4p.: 30 cm. - 978-0-11-074544-2 £3.00

The Trade Marks and Designs (Address For Service) (Amendment) Rules 2006 No. 2006/1029. - Enabling power: Trade Marks Act 1994, s. 78 & Registered Designs Act 1949, s. 36. - Issued: 11.04.2006. Made: 03.04.2006. Laid: 04.04.2006. Coming into force: 06.04.2006. Effect: S.I. 1995/2912; 2000/136 amended. Territorial extent & classification: E/W/S/NI. General. - This Statutory Instrument has been printed to correct errors in SI 1995/2912 and SI 2000/136 caused by amendments made to those Statutory Instruments by SI 2006/760. This Statutory Instrument is being issued free of charge to all known recipients of SI 2006/760. - 2p.: 30 cm. - 978-0-11-074458-2 £3.00

Intellectual property: Artists

The Artist's Resale Right Regulations 2006 No. 2006/346. - Enabling power: European Communities Act 1972, s. 2 (2). - Issued: 20.02.2006. Made: 13.02.2006. Coming into force: 14.02.2006 in accord. with reg. 1 (1). Effect: None. Territorial extent & classification: E/W/S/NI. General. - EC note: These Regs implement Directive 2001/84/EC on the resale right for the benefit of the author of an original work of art. The Regs also amount to the implementation by the UK of the option given by art. 14 of the Berne Copyright Convention (Cmnd. 5002). Supersedes draft SI (ISBN 0110738209) issued on 15.12.2005. - 12p.: 30 cm. - 978-0-11-074042-3 £3.00

International development

The African Development Bank (Tenth Replenishment of the African Development Fund) Order 2006 No. 2006/2327. - Enabling power: International Development Act 2002, s. 11. - Issued: 04.09.2006. Made: 06.07.2006. Coming into force: 06.07.2006. Effect: None. Territorial extent & classification: E/W/S/NI. General. - Supersedes draft instrument (ISBN 0110742613) issued 15.03.2006. - 4p.: 30 cm. - 978-0-11-075060-6 £3.00

African Development Fund (Multilateral Debt Relief Initiative) Order 2006 No. 2006/2321. - Enabling power: International Development Act 2002, s. 11. - Issued: 04.09.2006. Made: 06.07.2006. Coming into force: 06.07.2006. Effect: None. Territorial extent & classification: E/W/S/NI. General. - Supersedes draft instrument (ISBN 0110746228) issued 31.05.2006. - 4p.: 30 cm. - 978-0-11-075056-9 £3.00

The Asian Development Bank (Eighth Replenishment of the Asian Development Fund) Order 2006 No. 2006/2324. - Enabling power: International Development Act 2002, s. 11. - Issued: 04.09.2006. Made: 06.07.2006. Coming into force: 06.07.2006. Effect: None. Territorial extent & classification: E/W/S/NI. General. - Supersedes draft instrument (ISBN 0110742478) issued 15.03.2006. - 4p.: 30 cm. - 978-0-11-075059-0 £3.00

The Caribbean Development Bank (Sixth Replenishment of the Unified Special Development Fund) Order 2006 No. 2006/2325. - Enabling power: International Development Act 2002, s. 11. - Issued: 04.09.2006. Made: 06.07.2006. Coming into force: 06.07.2006. Effect: None. Territorial extent & classification: E/W/S/NI. General. - Supersedes draft instrument (ISBN 0110742486) issued 15.03.2006. - 4p.: 30 cm. - 978-0-11-075058-3 £3.00

The International Development Association (Fourteenth Replenishment) Order 2006 No. 2006/1071. - Enabling power: International Development Act 2002, s. 11. - Issued: 11.04.2006. Made: 15.03.2006. Coming into force: 15.03.2006. Effect: None. Territorial extent & classification: UK. General. - 4p.: 30 cm. - 978-0-11-074477-3 £3.00

The International Development Association (Multilateral Debt Relief Initiative) Order 2006 No. 2006/2323. - Enabling power: International Development Act 2002, s. 11. - Issued: 04.09.2006. Made: 14.06.2006. Coming into force: 14.06.2006. Effect: None. Territorial extent & classification: E/W/S/NI. General. - Supersedes draft instrument (ISBN 0110745353) issued 04.05.2006. - 4p.: 30 cm. - 978-0-11-075057-6 £3.00

International immunities and privileges

The Commonwealth Countries and Ireland (Immunities and Privileges) (Amendment) Order 2006 No. 2006/309. - Enabling power: Consular Relations Act 1968, s. 12 (1). - Issued: 21.02.2006. Made: 14.02.2006. Laid: 24.02.2006. Coming into force: 01.04.2006. Effect: S.I. 1985/1983 amended. Territorial extent & classification: E/W/S/NI. General. - 2p.: 30 cm. - 978-0-11-074051-5 £3.00

The European Organization for Nuclear Research (Privileges and Immunities) Order 2006 No. 2006/1922. - Enabling power: International Organisations Act 1968, s. 1. - Issued: 26.07.2006. Made: 19.07.2006. Coming into force: In accord. with art. 1. Effect: None. Territorial extent & classification: E/W/S/NI. General. - Supersedes draft S.I. (ISBN 0110746333) issued 06.06.2006. - 8p.: 30 cm. - 978-0-11-074894-8 £3.00

The International Criminal Court (Immunities and Privileges) (No. 1) Order 2006 No. 2006/1907. - Enabling power: International Criminal Court Act 2001, sch. 1, para. 1. - Issued: 26.07.2006. Made: 19.07.2006. Coming into force: In accord. with art. 1. Effect: None. Territorial extent & classification: E/W/S/NI. General. - 12p.: 30 cm. - 978-0-11-074897-9 £3.00

The International Criminal Court (Immunities and Privileges) (No. 2) Order 2006 No. 2006/1908. - Enabling power: International Criminal Court Act 2001, sch. 1, para. 1. - Issued: 27.07.2006. Made: 19.07.2006. Coming into force: In accord. with art. 1. Effect: None. Territorial extent & classification: E/W/S/NI. General. - Supersedes draft SI (ISBN 0110705416) issued 3.05.2006. - 4p.: 30 cm. - 978-0-11-074921-1 £3.00

The International Organisations (Immunities and Privileges) Miscellaneous Provisions Order 2006 No. 2006/1075. - Enabling power: International Organisations Act 1968, ss. 1 (7), 10 (3). - Issued: 21.04.2006. Made: 11.04.2006. Coming into force: 12.04.2006. Effect: S.I. 1974/1253, 1256, 1258, 1260, 1261; 1995/266; 2000/1815, 1817; 2001/3921; 2004/1282 amended. Territorial extent & classification: E/W/S/NI. General. - Supersedes draft S.I. (ISBN 0110741188) issued on 10.03.2006. - 4p.: 30 cm. - 978-0-11-074496-4 £3.00

Investigatory powers

The Regulation of Investigatory Powers (Communications Data) (Additional Functions and Amendment) Order 2006 No. 2006/1878. - Enabling power: Regulation of Investigatory Powers Act 2000, ss. 22 (2) (h), 25 (1) (g), (2) (3). - Issued: 18.07.2006. Made: 12.07.2006. Coming into force: 26.07.2006. Effect: S.I. 2003/3172 amended. Territorial extent & classification: E/W/S/NI. General. - Supersedes draft SI (ISBN 0110746473) issued on 08.06.2006. - 8p.: 30 cm. - 978-0-11-074839-9 £3.00

The Regulation of Investigatory Powers (Directed Surveillance and Covert Human Intelligence Sources) (Amendment) Order 2006 No. 2006/1874. - Enabling power: Regulation of Investigatory Powers Act 2000, s. 30 (1) (3) (5) (6). - Issued: 18.07.2006. Made: 12.07.2006. Coming into force: 26.07.2006. Effect: 2000 c.23; S.I. 2003/3171 amended. Territorial extent & classification: E/W/NI. General. - Supersedes draft SI (ISBN 0110746465) issued 09.06.2006. - 8p.: 30 cm. - 978-0-11-074841-2 £3.00

Judicial appointments and discipline

The Constitutional Reform Act 2005 (Commencement No. 5) Order 2006 No. 2006/1014 (C.33). - Enabling power: Constitutional Reform Act 2005, s. 148. Bringing into operation various provisions of the 2005 Act on 03.04.2006, 02.10.2006 & 02.04.2007. - Issued: 06.04.2006. Made: 02.04.2006. Effect: None. Territorial extent & classification: E/W/S/NI. General. - 8p.: 30 cm. - 978-0-11-074457-5 £3.00

The Judicial Appointments and Discipline (Modification of Offices) (No.2) Order 2006 No. 2006/1551. - Enabling power: Constitutional Reform Act 2005, s. 85 (3). - Issued: 20.06.2006. Made: 11.06.2006. Laid: 16.06.2006. Coming into force: 10.07.2006. Effect: 2005 c. 4 amended. Territorial extent & classification: E/W/S. General. - 2p.: 30 cm. - 978-0-11-074709-5 £3.00

The Judicial Appointments and Discipline (Modification of Offices) Order 2006 No. 2006/678. - Enabling power: Constitutional Reform Act 2005, s. 85 (3). - Issued: 17.03.2006. Made: 10.03.2006. Laid: 13.03.06. Coming into force: 03.04.2006. Effect: 2005 c.4 amended. Territorial extent & classification: E/W/S/NI. General. - 4p.: 30 cm. - 978-0-11-074264-9 £3.00

The Judicial Discipline (Prescribed Procedures) Regulations 2006 No. 2006/676. - Enabling power: Constitutional Reform Act 2005, ss. 115, 120, 121. - Issued: 20.03.2006. Made: 10.03.2006. Laid: 13.03.2006. Coming into force: 03.04.2006. Effect: None. Territorial extent & classification: E/W/S/NI. General. - 20p.: 30 cm. - 978-0-11-074272-4 £3.50

The Permitted Persons (Designation) Order 2006 No. 2006/679. - Enabling power: Constitutional Reform Act 2005, s. 107 (6). - Issued: 17.03.2006. Made: 09.03.2006. Laid: 13.03.2006. Coming into force: 03.04.2006. Effect: None. Territorial extent & classification: E/W/S/NI. General. - 4p.: 30 cm. - 978-0-11-074273-1 £3.00

Judicial appointments and removals, Northern Ireland

The Constitutional Reform Act 2005 (Commencement No. 5) Order 2006 No. 2006/1014 (C.33). - Enabling power: Constitutional Reform Act 2005, s. 148. Bringing into operation various provisions of the 2005 Act on 03.04.2006, 02.10.2006 & 02.04.2007. - Issued: 06.04.2006. Made: 02.04.2006. Effect: None. Territorial extent & classification: E/W/S/NI. General. - 8p.: 30 cm. - 978-0-11-074457-5 £3.00

The Constitutional Reform Act 2005 (Commencement No. 6) Order 2006 No. 2006/1537 (C.55). - Enabling power: Constitutional Reform Act 2005, s. 148. Bringing into operation various provisions of the 2005 Act on 15.06.2006 & 25.09.2006 in accord. with arts 2 & 3. - Issued: 19.06.2006. Made: 13.06.2006. Effect: None. Territorial extent & classification: NI. General. - 4p.: 30 cm. - 978-0-11-074699-9 £3.00

Justices of the Peace, England and Wales

The Local Justice Areas (No. 1) Order 2006 No. 2006/1839. - Enabling power: Courts Act 2003, ss. 8 (4), 108 (6). - Issued: 17.07.2006. Made: 11.07.2006. Laid: 12.07.2006. Coming into force: 02.08.2006 for sch. part 1; 01.01.2007 for all other purposes. Effect: S.I. 2005/554 amended. Territorial extent & classification: E/W. General. - 8p.: 30 cm. - 978-0-11-074834-4 £3.00

The Local Justice Areas (No. 2) Order 2006 No. 2006/2315. - Enabling power: Courts Act 2003, ss. 8 (4), 108 (6). - Issued: 01.09.2006. Made: 23.08.2006. Laid: 29.08.2006. Coming into force: 22.09.2006 (not 2003 as printed in document) for sch., part 1; 01.01.2007 for all other purposes. Effect: S.I. 2005/554 amended. Territorial extent & classification: E/W. General. - With correction slip dated September 2006, amending the coming into force date to 22.09.2006. - 8p.: 30 cm. - 978-0-11-075052-1 £3.00

Land charges, England

The Constitutional Reform Act 2005 (Supplementary Provisions) Order 2006 No. 2006/1693. - Enabling power: Constitutional Reform Act 2005, s. 143. - Issued: 03.07.2006. Made: 27.06.2006. Laid: 28.06.2006. Coming into force: 28.06.2006 in accord. with art. 1. Effect: None. Territorial extent & classification: E. General. - 4p.: 30 cm. - 978-0-11-074768-2 £3.00

Land drainage, England

The Broads (2006) Internal Drainage Board Order 2006 No. 2006/773. - Enabling power: Land Drainage Act 1991, s. 3 (5) (7), sch. 3, para. 3 (2). - Issued: 30.03.2006. Made: 18.01.2006. Coming into force: In accord with art. 1. Effect: None. Territorial extent & classification: E. Local. - 8p.: 30 cm. - 978-0-11-074336-3 *£3.00*

The General Drainage Charges (Anglian Region) Order 2006 No. 2006/826. - Enabling power: Water Resources Act 1991, s. 135 (2) (3) (4). - Issued: 23.03.2006. Made: 16.03.2006. Laid: 20.03.2006. Coming into force: 10.04.2006. Effect: S.I. 2004/388 revoked. Territorial extent & classification: E. General. - 4p.: 30 cm. - 978-0-11-074361-5 *£3.00*

The North West Regional Flood Defence Committee Order 2006 No. 2006/804. - Enabling power: Environment Act 1995, s. 16 (5) (b) (8). - Issued: 23.03.2006. Made: 16.03.2006. Coming into force: 01.04.2006. Effect: S.I. 1998/1637 revoked. Territorial extent & classification: E. General. - 4p.: 30 cm. - 978-0-11-074356-1 *£3.00*

The Severn-Trent Regional Flood Defence Committee Order 2006 No. 2006/803. - Enabling power: Environment Act 1995, s. 16 (5) (b) (8). - Issued: 23.03.2006. Made: 16.03.2006. Coming into force: 01.04.2006. Effect: S.I. 1998/1638 revoked. Territorial extent & classification: E. General. - 4p.: 30 cm. - 978-0-11-074355-4 *£3.00*

The Waveney, Lower Yare, and Lothingland Internal Drainage Board Order 2006 No. 2006/2140. - Enabling power: Land Drainage Act 1991, s. 3 (5) (7). - Issued: 08.08.2006. Made: 09.06.2006. Coming into force: In accord with art. 1. Effect: None. Territorial extent & classification: E. Local. - 12p.: 30 cm. - 978-0-11-074977-8 *£3.00*

The Witham Third District Internal Drainage District (Alteration of Boundaries) Order 2006 No. 2006/774. - Enabling power: Land Drainage Act 1991, s. 3 (5) (7), sch. 3, para. 3 (2). - Issued: 31.03.2006. Made: 18.01.2006. Coming into force: In accord with art. 1. Effect: None. Territorial extent & classification: E. Local. - 8p.: 30 cm. - 978-0-11-074333-2 *£3.00*

Land drainage, England and Wales

The Environmental Impact Assessment (Land Drainage Improvement Works) (Amendment) Regulations 2006 No. 2006/618. - Enabling power: European Communities Act 1972, s. 2 (2). - Issued: 14.03.2006. Made: 07.03.2006. Laid: 09.03.2006. Coming into force: 30.03.2006. Effect: S.I. 1999/1783 amended. Territorial extent & classification: E/W. General. - This Statutory Instrument has been made in consequence of a defect in S.I. 2005/1399 and is being issued free of charge to all known recipients of that Statutory Instrument. - 4p.: 30 cm. - 978-0-11-074193-2 *£3.00*

Land drainage, Wales

The Welsh Regional Flood Defence Committee (Composition) Order 2006 No. 2006/980 (W.103). - Enabling power: Environment Act 1995, s. 16A. - Issued: 10.04.2006. Made: 29.03.2006. Coming into force: 01.04.2006 in acc.with art. 1 (1). Effect: S.I. 1996/538 revoked. Territorial extent & classification: W. General. - In English and Welsh. Welsh title: Gorchymyn Pwyllgor Rhanbarthol Amddiffyn Rhag Llifogydd (Cyfansoddiad) 2006. - 8p.: 30 cm. - 978-0-11-091316-2 *£3.00*

Landfill tax

The Landfill Tax (Amendment) Regulations 2006 No. 2006/865. - Enabling power: Finance Act 1996, ss. 51 (1), 53 (1) (4). - Issued: 28.03.2006. Made: 22.03.2006. Laid: 22.03.2006. Coming into force: 01.04.2006. Effect: S.I. 1996/1527 amended. Territorial extent & classification: E/W/S/NI. General. - 2p.: 30 cm. - 978-0-11-074391-2 *£3.00*

Landlord and tenant, England

The Agricultural Holdings (Units of Production) (England) Order 2006 No. 2006/2628. - Enabling power: Agricultural Holdings Act 1986, sch. 6, para. 4. - Issued: 09.10.2006. Made: 02.10.2006. Laid: 05.10.2006. Coming into force: 07.11.2006. Effect: S.I. 2005/2867 revoked. Territorial extent & classification: E. General. - 8p.: 30 cm. - 978-0-11-075146-7 *£3.00*

Landlord and tenant, England and Wales

The Regulatory Reform (Agricultural Tenancies) (England and Wales) Order 2006 No. 2006/2805. - Enabling power: Regulatory Reform Act 2001, s. 1. - Issued: 26.10.2006. Made: 18.10.2006. Coming into force: 19.10.2006 in accord. with art. 1 (1). Effect: 1986 c.5, c.49; 1992 c.53; 1993 c.8; 1995 c.8, c.42; 1996 c.23; 2005 c.4; S.I. 1986/1611; 1987/710, 908; 1996/337; 1998/3132; 2005/465, 537 amended & S.I. 1990/1472 revoked. Territorial extent & classification: E/W. General. - 16p.: 30 cm. - 978-0-11-075207-5 *£3.00*

Landlord and tenant, Wales

The Agricultural Holdings (Units of Production) (Wales) Order 2006 No. 2006/2796 (W.235). - Enabling power: Agricultural Holdings Act 1986, sch. 6, para. 4. - Issued: 30.10.2006. Made: 17.10.2006. Coming into force: 27.10.2006. Effect: S.I. 2004/1218 (W.133) revoked. Territorial extent & classification: W. General. - In English and Welsh: Welsh title: Gorchymyn Daliadau Amaethyddol (Unedau Cynhyrchu) (Cymru) 2006. - 28p.: 30 cm. - 978-0-11-091413-8 *£4.50*

Land registration, England and Wales

The Land Registration Fee Order 2006 No. 2006/1332. - Enabling power: Land Registration Act 2002, ss. 102, 128 (1). - Issued: 18.08.2006. Made: 15.05.2006. Laid: 15.05.2006. Coming into force: 07.08.2006. Effect: S.I. 2004/595, 1833 revoked. Territorial extent & classification: E/W. General. - 16p.: 30 cm. - 978-0-11-074581-7 *£3.00*

Lands tribunal, England and Wales

The Lands Tribunal (Amendment) Rules 2006 No. 2006/880. - Enabling power: Lands Tribunal Act 1949, s. 3 (6). - Issued: 28.03.2006. Made: 20.03.2006. Coming into force: In accord. with rule 1 (1). Effect: S.I. 1996/1022 amended. Territorial extent & classification: E/W. General. - 4p.: 30 cm. - 978-0-11-074382-0 *£3.00*

Legal Services Commission, England and Wales

The Community Legal Service (Financial) (Amendment No. 2) Regulations 2006 No. 2006/2363. - Enabling power: Access to Justice Act 1999, ss. 7, 10. - Issued: 07.09.2006. Made: 28.08.2006. Laid: 01.09.2006. Coming into force: 02.10.2006. Effect: S.I. 2000/516 amended. Territorial extent & classification: E/W. General. - 4p.: 30 cm. - 978-0-11-075063-7 *£3.00*

The Community Legal Service (Financial) (Amendment) Regulations 2006 No. 2006/713. - Enabling power: Access to Justice Act 1999, ss. 7, 10. - Issued: 20.03.2006. Made: 09.03.2006. Laid: 16.03.2006. Coming into force: 10.04.2006. Effect: S.I. 2000/516 amended. Territorial extent & classification: E/W. General. - 4p.: 30 cm. - 978-0-11-074254-0 *£3.00*

The Community Legal Service (Funding) (Amendment) Order 2006 No. 2006/2366. - Enabling power: Access to Justice Act 1999, s. 6 (4). - Issued: 07.09.2006. Made: 28.08.2006. Laid: 01.09.2006. Coming into force: 02.10.2006. Effect: S.I. 2000/627 amended. Territorial extent & classification: E/W. General. - 4p.: 30 cm. - 978-0-11-075064-4 *£3.00*

The Community Legal Service (Funding) (Counsel in Family Proceedings) (Amendment) Order 2006 No. 2006/2364. - Enabling power: Access to Justice Act 1999, s. 6 (4). - Issued: 07.09.2006. Made: 28.08.2006. Laid: 01.09.2006. Coming into force: 02.10.2006. Effect: S.I. 2001/1077 amended. Territorial extent & classification: E/W. General. - 4p.: 30 cm. - 978-0-11-075065-1 *£3.00*

The Criminal Defence Service Act 2006 (Commencement) Order 2006 No. 2006/2491 (C.83). - Enabling power: Criminal Defence Service Act 2006, s. 5 (2). Bringing into operation various provisions of the 2006 Act on 02.10.2006. - Issued: 18.09.2006. Made: 11.09.2006. Coming into effect: -. Effect: None. Territorial extent & classification: E/W. General. - 2p.: 30 cm. - 978-0-11-075100-9 *£3.00*

The Criminal Defence Service (Financial Eligibility) Regulations 2006 No. 2006/2492. - Enabling power: Access to Justice Act 1999, s. 26, sch. 3, para. 3B. - Issued: 22.09.2006. Made: 11.09.2006. Coming into force: 02.10.2006. Effect: None. Territorial extent & classification: E/W. General. - Supersedes the draft S.I. (ISBN 0110747372) issued on 27.06.2006. - 8p.: 30 cm. - 978-0-11-075104-7 *£3.00*

The Criminal Defence Service (Funding) (Amendment) Order 2006 No. 2006/389. - Enabling power: Access to Justice Act 1999, s. 14 (3). - Issued: 22.02.2006. Made: 16.02.2006. Laid: 20.02.2006. Coming into force: 13.03.2006. Effect: S.I.2001/855 amended. Territorial extent & classification: E/W. General. - 2p.: 30 cm. - 978-0-11-074079-9 *£3.00*

The Criminal Defence Service (General) (No. 2) (Amendment) Regulations 2006 No. 2006/2490. - Enabling power: Access to Justice Act 1999, ss. 13 (1), 15 (2), 26, sch. 3, paras 2 (1) (4) (5), 3. - Issued: 22.09.2006. Made: 11.09.2006. Laid: 11.09.2006. Coming into force: 02.10.2006. Effect: S.I. 2001/1437 amended. Territorial extent & classification: E/W. General. - 4p.: 30 cm. - 978-0-11-075097-2 *£3.00*

The Criminal Defence Service (Representation Orders and Consequential Amendments) Regulations 2006 No. 2006/2493. - Enabling power: Access to Justice Act 1999, s. 26, sch. 3, para. 2A, 3A (2). - Issued: 19.09.2006. Made: 11.09.2006. Coming into force: 02.10.2006. Effect: 1980 c. 43; 1998 c. 37; 1999 c. 22; S.I. 2005/545 amended. Territorial extent & classification: E/W. General. - Supersedes the draft S.I. (ISBN 0110747402) issued on 27.06.2006. - 4p.: 30 cm. - 978-0-11-075107-8 *£3.00*

The Criminal Defence Service (Representation Orders: Appeals etc.) Regulations 2006 No. 2006/2494. - Enabling power: Access to Justice Act 1999, s. 26, sch. 3, para. 4. - Issued: 18.09.2006. Made: 11.09.2006. Coming into force: 02.10.2006. Effect: S.I. 2001/1168 revoked. Territorial extent & classification: E/W. General. - Supersedes the draft S.I. 2006/2494 (ISBN 0110747410) issued on 27.06.2006. - 4p.: 30 cm. - 978-0-11-075105-4 *£3.00*

Legal services, England and Wales

The Association of Law Costs Draftsmen Order 2006 No. 2006/3333. - Enabling power: Courts and Legal Services Act 1990, ss. 27 (9) (c), 28 (5) (b). - Issued: 21.12.2006. Made: 14.12.2006. Coming into force: 01.01.2007. Effect: None. Territorial extent & classification: E/W. General. - Supersedes the draft S.I. (ISBN 0110752066) issued 25.10.2006. - 2p.: 30 cm. - 978-0-11-075519-9 *£3.00*

The Legal Services Ombudsman (Jurisdiction) (Amendment) Order 2006 No. 2006/3362. - Enabling power: Courts and Legal Services Act 1990, s. 22 (11) (b). - Issued: 21.12.2006. Made: 15.12.2006. Laid: 15.12.2006. Coming into force: 05.01.2007. Effect: S.I. 1990/2485 amended. Territorial extent & classification: E/W. General. - 2p.: 30 cm. - 978-0-11-075521-2 *£3.00*

Libraries

The Public Lending Right Scheme 1982 (Commencement of Variation) Order 2006 No. 2006/3294. - Enabling power: Public Lending Right Act 1979, s. 3 (7). - Issued: 15.12.2006. Made: 07.12.2006. Laid: 12.12.2006. Coming into force: 02.01.2007. Effect: None. Territorial extent & classification: E/W/S/NI. General. - 2p.: 30 cm. - 978-0-11-075470-3 £3.00

Licences and licensing, England

The Licensing Act 2003 (Consequential Amendment) (Non-Domestic Rating) (Public Houses in England) Order 2006 No. 2006/591. - Enabling power: Licensing Act 2003, ss. 197 (2), 198 (2). - Issued: 13.03.2006. Made: 07.03.2006. Laid: 07.03.2006. Coming into force: 31.03.2006. Effect: S.I. 2001/1345 amended. Territorial extent & classification: E. General. - 4p.: 30 cm. - 978-0-11-074184-0 £3.00

Local government

The Transport for London (Sloane Square House) Order 2006 No. 2006/2188. - Enabling power: Greater London Authority Act 1999, s. 163. - Issued: 16.08.2006. Made: 08.08.2006. Laid: 15.08.2006. Coming into force: 06.09.2006. Effect: None. Territorial extent & classification: E/W/S/NI. General. - 4p., map: 30 cm. - 978-0-11-075009-5 £3.00

Local government, England

The Accounts and Audit (Amendment) (England) Regulations 2006 No. 2006/564. - Enabling power: Audit Commission Act 1998, s. 27 & Greater London Authority Act 1999, s. 134 (6). - Issued: 10.03.2006. Made: 03.03.2006. Laid: 10.03.2006. Coming into force: 01.04.2006. Effect: S.I. 2003/533 amended & S.I. 1983/1849 revoked. Territorial extent & classification: E. General. - With correction slip dated May 2006. - 12p.: 30 cm. - 978-0-11-074169-7 £3.00

The Borough of Corby (Electoral Changes) Order 2006 No. 2006/1404. - Enabling power: Local Government Act 1992, ss. 17, 26. - Issued: 01.06.2006. Made: 25.05.2006. Coming into force: In accord. with art. 1 (2). Effect: S.I. 1998/2506 revoked. Territorial extent & classification: E. Local. - 4p.: 30 cm. - 978-0-11-074616-6 £3.00

The Borough of Eastbourne (Whole Council Elections) Order 2006 No. 2006/1753. - Enabling power: Local Government Act 1972, s. 7 (6), 17 (4). - Issued: 11.07.2006. Made: 03.07.2006. Coming into force: 02.08.2006. Effect: S.I. 2001/4057 amended. Territorial extent & classification: E. Local. - 2p.: 30 cm. - 978-0-11-074804-7 £3.00

The Borough of Kettering (Electoral Changes) Order 2006 No. 2006/3109. - Enabling power: Local Government Act 1992, ss. 17, 26. - Issued: 29.11.2006. Made: 23.11.2006. Coming into force: In accord. with art. 1 (2). Effect: S.I. 2001/3356 amended & S.I. 1998/2508 revoked save for art. 5. Territorial extent & classification: E. Local. - 8p.: 30 cm. - 978-0-11-075361-4 £3.00

The Borough of Tunbridge Wells (Electoral Changes) (Amendment) Order 2006 No. 2006/2619. - Enabling power: Local Government Act 1992, ss. 17, 26. - Issued: 04.10.2006. Made: 28.09.2006. Coming into force: In accord. with art. 1 (2). Effect: S.I. 2001/3559 amended. Territorial extent & classification: E. Local. - 2p.: 30 cm. - 978-0-11-075141-2 £3.00

The Borough of Waverley (Electoral Changes) (Amendment) Order 2006 No. 2006/2620. - Enabling power: Local Government Act 1992, ss. 17, 26. - Issued: 04.10.2006. Made: 28.09.2006. Coming into force: 29.09.2006 in accord. with art. 1 (2). Effect: S.I. 2000/3366 amended. Territorial extent & classification: E. Local. - 2p.: 30 cm. - 978-0-11-075140-5 £3.00

The Bradford (Parish Electoral Arrangements) Order 2006 No. 2006/508. - Enabling power: Local Government and Rating Act 1997, ss. 14, 23. - Made: 27.02.2006. Coming into force: In accordance with art. 1 (2). Effect: S.I. 2004/122 amended. Territorial extent & classification: E. Local *Unpublished*

The Bradford (Parishes) (No. 2) Order 2006 No. 2006/3417. - Enabling power: Local Government and Rating Act 1997, ss. 14, 23. - Made: 18.12.2006. Coming into force: In accord. with art. 1 (2). Effect: None. Territorial extent & classification: E. Local *Unpublished*

The Bradford (Parishes) Order 2005 No. 2006/505. - Enabling power: Local Government and Rating Act 1997, ss. 14, 23. - Made: 24.02.2006. Coming into force: In accord. with art. 1 (2). Effect: None. Territorial extent & classification: E. Local *Unpublished*

The Bus Lane Contraventions (Approved Local Authorities) (England) (Amendment) (No. 2) Order 2006 No. 2006/1447. - Enabling power: Transport Act 2000, s. 144 (3) (b) (14). - Issued: 07.06.2006. Made: 31.05.2006. Laid: 06.06.2006. Coming into force: 04.07.2006. Effect: S.I. 2005/2755 amended. Territorial extent & classification: E. General. - With correction slip dated August 2006. - 4p.: 30 cm. - 978-0-11-074643-2 £3.00

The Bus Lane Contraventions (Approved Local Authorities) (England) (Amendment) (No. 3) Order 2006 No. 2006/1516. - Enabling power: Transport Act 2000, s. 144 (3) (b) (14). - Issued: 23.06.2006. Made: 13.06.2006. Laid: 16.06.2006. Coming into force: 11.07.2006. Effect: S.I. 2005/2755 amended. Territorial extent & classification: E. General. - With correction slip dated August 2006. - 4p.: 30 cm. - 978-0-11-074705-7 £3.00

The Bus Lane Contraventions (Approved Local Authorities) (England) (Amendment) (No. 4) Order 2006 No. 2006/2632. - Enabling power: Transport Act 2000, s. 144 (3) (b) (14). - Issued: 12.10.2006. Made: 04.10.2006. Laid: 06.10.2006. Coming into force: 02.11.2006. Effect: S.I. 2005/2755 amended. Territorial extent & classification: E. General. - 4p.: 30 cm. - 978-0-11-075158-0 £3.00

The Bus Lane Contraventions (Approved Local Authorities) (England) (Amendment) (No. 5) Order 2006 No. 2006/2820. - Enabling power: Transport Act 2000, s. 144 (3) (b) (14). - Issued: 03.11.2006. Made: 24.10.2006. Laid: 27.10.2006. Coming into force: 28.11.2006. Effect: S.I. 2005/2755 amended. Territorial extent & classification: E. General. - 4p.: 30 cm. - 978-0-11-075221-1 £3.00

The Bus Lane Contraventions (Approved Local Authorities) (England) (Amendment) (No. 6) Order 2006 No. 2006/3212. - Enabling power: Transport Act 2000, s. 144 (3) (b) (14). - Issued: 11.12.2006. Made: 01.12.2006. Laid: 06.12.2006. Coming into force: 03.01.2007. Effect: S.I. 2005/2755 amended. Territorial extent & classification: E. General. - 2p.: 30 cm. - 978-0-11-075414-7 £3.00

The Bus Lane Contraventions (Approved Local Authorities) (England) (Amendment) (No. 7) Order 2006 No. 2006/3425. - Enabling power: Transport Act 2000, ss. 144 (3) (b) (14). - Issued: 29.12.2006. Made: 20.12.2006. Laid: 21.12.2006. Coming into force: 02.02.2007. Effect: S.I. 2005/2755 amended. Territorial extent & classification: E. General. - 2p.: 30 cm. - 978-0-11-075582-3 £3.00

The Bus Lane Contraventions (Approved Local Authorities) (England) (Amendment) (No. 8) Order 2006 No. 2006/3419. - Enabling power: Transport Act 2000, ss. 144 (3) (b) (14). - Issued: 29.12.2006. Made: 19.12.2006. Laid: 21.12.2006. Coming into force: 06.02.2007. Effect: S.I. 2005/2755 amended. Territorial extent & classification: E. General. - 2p.: 30 cm. - 978-0-11-075580-9 £3.00

The Bus Lane Contraventions (Approved Local Authorities) (England) (Amendment) Order 2006 No. 2006/593. - Enabling power: Transport Act 2000, ss. 144 (3) (b) (14). - Issued: 14.03.2006. Made: 07.03.2006. Laid: 10.03.2006. Coming into force: 04.04.2006. Effect: S.I. 2005/2755 amended. Territorial extent & classification: E. General. - With correction slip dated August 2006. - 4p.: 30 cm. - 978-0-11-074191-8 £3.00

The Castle Point (Parish) Order 2006 No. 2006/3467. - Enabling power: Local Government and Rating Act 1997, ss. 14, 23. - Made: 22.12.2006. Coming into force: In accord. with art. 1 (2). Effect: None. Territorial extent & classification: E. Local *Unpublished*

The City of Lincoln (Electoral Changes) Order 2006 No. 2006/3110. - Enabling power: Local Government Act 1992, ss. 17, 26. - Issued: 29.11.2006. Made: 23.11.2006. Coming into force: In accord. with art. 1 (2). Effect: S.I. 1998/2334 revoked save for art. 3 (7). Territorial extent & classification: E. Local. - 8p.: 30 cm. - 978-0-11-075358-4 £3.00

The District of Broadland (Whole Council Elections) Order 2006 No. 2006/245. - Enabling power: Local Government Act 1972, s. 7 (6) & Local Government Act 1992, ss. 17 (3) (4), 26. - Issued: 13.02.2006. Made: 06.02.2006. Coming into force: 17.02.2006. Effect: S.I. 1977/1390; 2003/157 amended. Territorial extent & classification: E. Local. - 4p.: 30 cm. - 978-0-11-073993-9 £3.00

The District of North Hertfordshire (Electoral Changes) Order 2006 No. 2006/3112. - Enabling power: Local Government Act 1992, ss. 17, 26. - Issued: 29.11.2006. Made: 23.11.2006. Coming into force: In accord. with art. 1 (2) (3) (4). Effect: S.I. 1998/2555 partially revoked. Territorial extent & classification: E. Local. - 8p.: 30 cm. - 978-0-11-075359-1 £3.00

The District of North Kesteven (Electoral Changes) Order 2006 No. 2006/1405. - Enabling power: Local Government Act 1992, ss. 17, 26. - Issued: 01.06.2006. Made: 25.05.2006. Coming into force: In accord. with art. 1 (2). Effect: S.I. 1998/2338 partially revoked. Territorial extent & classification: E. Local. - 8p.: 30 cm. - 978-0-11-074617-3 £3.00

The District of North Shropshire (Electoral Changes) (Amendment) Order 2006 No. 2006/2618. - Enabling power: Local Government Act 1992, ss. 17, 26. - Issued: 04.10.2006. Made: 28.09.2006. Coming into force: 29.09.2006 in accord. with art. 1 (2). Effect: S.I. 2000/1419 amended. Territorial extent & classification: E. Local. - 2p.: 30 cm. - 978-0-11-075142-9 £3.00

The District of South Northamptonshire (Electoral Changes) Order 2006 No. 2006/3111. - Enabling power: Local Government Act 1992, ss. 17, 26. - Issued: 29.11.2006. Made: 23.11.2006. Coming into force: In accord. with art. 1 (2). Effect: S.I. 2001/3044 amended & S.I. 1998/2509 revoked. Territorial extent & classification: E. Local. - 8p.: 30 cm. - 978-0-11-075360-7 £3.00

The East Lindsey (Parish Electoral Arrangements) Order 2006 No. 2006/3113. - Enabling power: Local Government and Rating Act 1997, ss. 14, 23. - Made: 23.11.2006. Coming into force: In accordance with art. 1 (2). Effect: None. Territorial extent & classification: E. Local *Unpublished*

The Gateshead (Parish) Order 2005 No. 2006/716. - Enabling power: Local Government and Rating Act 1997, ss. 14, 23. - Made: 10.03.2006. Coming into force: 01.04.2006. Effect: None. Territorial extent & classification: E. Local *Unpublished*

The Hinckley and Bosworth (Parish) Order 2006 No. 2006/3469. - Enabling power: Local Government and Rating Act 1997, ss. 14, 23. - Made: 19.12.2006. Coming into force: In accord. with art. 1 (2). Effect: None. Territorial extent & classification: E. Local *Unpublished*

The Isle of Wight (Parish Electoral Arrangements) Order 2006 No. 2006/510. - Enabling power: Local Government and Rating Act 1997, ss. 14, 23. - Made: 27.02.2006. Coming into force: In accordance with art. 1 (2). Effect: None. Territorial extent & classification: E. Local *Unpublished*

The Isle of Wight (Parishes) Order 2005 No. 2006/503. - Enabling power: Local Government and Rating Act 1997, ss. 14, 23. - Made: 24.02.2006. Coming into force: In accord. with art. 1 (2). Effect: None. Territorial extent & classification: E. Local *Unpublished*

The Kettering (Parishes) Order 2005 No. 2006/504. - Enabling power: Local Government and Rating Act 1997, ss. 14, 23. - Made: 24.02.2006. Coming into force: In accord. with art. 1 (2). Effect: None. Territorial extent & classification: E. Local *Unpublished*

The King's Lynn and West Norfolk (Parishes) Order 2006 No. 2006/3450. - Enabling power: Local Government and Rating Act 1997, ss. 14, 23. - Made: 18.12.2006. Coming into force: In accord. with art. 1 (2). Effect: None. Territorial extent & classification: E. Local *Unpublished*

The Local Authorities (Armorial Bearings) Order 2006 No. 2006/3330. - Enabling power: Local Government Act 1972, s. 247. - Issued: 21.12.2006. Made: 14.12.2006. Coming into force: 15.12.2006. Effect: None. Territorial extent & classification: E. General. - 2p.: 30 cm. - 978-0-11-075508-3 £3.00

The Local Authorities (Capital Finance and Accounting) (Amendment) (England) Regulations 2006 No. 2006/521. - Enabling power: Local Government Act 2003, ss. 9 (3), 11, 21(1), 123 (1) (2). - Issued: 08.03.2006. Made: 01.03.2006. Laid: 08.03.2006. Coming into force: 31.03.2006 for regs. 1 & 15; 01.04.2006 for all other purposes. Effect: S.I. 2003/3146 amended. Territorial extent & classification: E. General. - 12p.: 30 cm. - 978-0-11-074136-9 £3.00

The Local Authorities (Categorisation) (England) Order 2006 No. 2006/3096. - Enabling power: Local Government Act 2003, s. 99 (4). - Issued: 24.11.2006. Made: 17.11.2006. Laid: 24.11.2006. Coming into force: 15.12.2006. Effect: S.I. 2005/2416 revoked. Territorial extent & classification: E. General. - 16p.: 30 cm. - 978-0-11-075352-2 £3.00

The Local Authorities (Executive Arrangements) (Access to Information) (Amendment) (England) Regulations 2006 No. 2006/69. - Enabling power: Local Government Act 2000, ss. 22, 105. - Issued: 26.01.2006. Made: 18.01.2006. Laid: 26.01.2006. Coming into force: 01.03.2006. Effect: S.I. 2000/3272 amended. Territorial extent and classification: E. General. - 4p.: 30 cm. - 978-0-11-073918-2 £3.00

The Local Authorities (Functions and Responsibilities) (Amendment) (England) Regulations 2006 No. 2006/886. - Enabling power: Local Government Act 2000, ss. 13, 105. - Issued: 29.03.2006. Made: 22.03.2006. Laid: 29.03.2006. Coming into force: 21.04.2006. Effect: S.I. 2000/2853 amended. Territorial extent & classification: E. General. - 4p.: 30 cm. - 978-0-11-074381-3 £3.00

The Local Government (Assistants for Political Groups) (Remuneration) (England) Order 2006 No. 2006/1509. - Enabling power: Local Government and Housing Act 1989, s. 9 (4). - Issued: 16.06.2006. Made: 12.06.2006. Laid: 16.06.2006. Coming into force: 04.07.2006. Effect: S.I. 1995/2456 revoked in relation to England. Territorial extent & classification: E. General. - 2p.: 30 cm. - 978-0-11-074685-2 £3.00

The Local Government (Best Value Authorities) (Power to Trade) (Amendment) (England) Order 2006 No. 2006/3102. - Enabling power: Local Government Act 2003, s. 95. - Issued: 24.11.2006. Made: 17.11.2006. Laid: 24.11.2006. Coming into force: 15.12.2006. Effect: S.I. 2004/1705 amended. Territorial extent & classification: E. General. - 2p.: 30 cm. - 978-0-11-075353-9 £3.00

The Local Government (Best Value) Performance Indicators and Performance Standards (Amendment) (England) Order 2006 No. 2006/553. - Enabling power: Local Government Act 1999, ss. 4 (1) (2), 28 (1) (b). - Issued: 10.03.2006. Made: 02.03.2006. Laid: 10.03.2006. Coming into force: 01.04.2006. Effect: S.I. 2005/598 amended. Territorial extent & classification: E. General. - 8p.: 30 cm. - 978-0-11-074154-3 £3.00

The Rugby (Parishes) Order 2006 No. 2006/3470. - Enabling power: Local Government and Rating Act 1997, ss. 14, 23. - Made: 19.12.2006. Coming into force: In accord. with art. 1 (2). Effect: None. Territorial extent & classification: E. Local *Unpublished*

The Stratford-on-Avon (Parishes) (Amendment) Order 2006 No. 2006/61. - Enabling power: Local Government and Rating Act 1997, ss. 14, 23. - Made: 12.01.2006. Coming into force: 12.01.2006 in accordance with art. 1. Effect: None. Territorial extent & classification: E. Local *Unpublished*

The Stratford-on-Avon (Parishes) Order 2005 No. 2006/526. - Enabling power: Local Government and Rating Act 1997, ss. 14, 23. - Made: 28.02.2006. Coming into force: In accord. with art. 1 (2). Effect: None. Territorial extent & classification: E. Local *Unpublished*

The Tandridge (Parishes) Order 2006 No. 2006/2499. - Enabling power: Local Government and Rating Act 1997, ss. 14, 23. - Made: 25.08.2006. Coming into force: 01.04.2007. Effect: None. Territorial extent & classification: E. Local *Unpublished*

The Torbay (Parishes) Order 2006 No. 2006/3280. - Enabling power: Local Government and Rating Act 1997, ss. 14, 23. - Made: 04.12.2006. Coming into force: In accord. with art. 1 (2). Effect: None. Territorial extent & classification: E. Local *Unpublished*

The Uttlesford (Parish Electoral Arrangements) Order 2006 No. 2006/3114. - Enabling power: Local Government and Rating Act 1997, ss. 14, 23. - Made: 23.11.2006. Coming into force: In accordance with art. 1 (2). Effect: S.I. 2001/2434 amended. Territorial extent & classification: E. Local *Unpublished*

The Wealdon (Parishes) Order 2006 No. 2006/3468. - Enabling power: Local Government and Rating Act 1997, ss. 14, 23. - Made: 19.12.2006. Coming into force: In accord. with art. 1 (2). Effect: None. Territorial extent & classification: E. Local *Unpublished*

The Wear Valley (Parishes) Order 2006 No. 2006/3279. - Enabling power: Local Government and Rating Act 1997, ss. 14, 23. - Made: 04.12.2006. Coming into force: In accord. with art. 1 (2). Effect: None. Territorial extent & classification: E. Local *Unpublished*

The Wormley Recreation Ground (Revocation of Parish Council Byelaws) Order 2006 No. 2006/1462. - Enabling power: Local Government Act 1972, s. 262 (8) (d). - Issued: 12.06.2006. Made: 05.06.2006. Laid: 12.06.2006. Coming into force: 03.07.2006. Effect: Revokes byelaws made by Wormley Parish Council on 21st July 1924 with respect to the Wormley Recreation Ground revoked. Territorial extent & classification: E. Local. - 2p.: 30 cm. - 978-0-11-074651-7 *£3.00*

Local government, England: Finance

The Joint Waste Disposal Authorities (Levies) (England) Regulations 2006 No. 2006/248. - Enabling power: Local Government Finance Act 1988, ss. 74, 143 (1) (2). - Issued: 13.02.2006. Made: 06.02.2006. Laid: 08.02.2006. Coming into force: 01.03.2006. Effect: None. Territorial extent & classification: E. General. - 8p.: 30 cm. - 978-0-11-073990-8 *£3.00*

The Local Authorities (Alteration of Requisite Calculations) (England) Regulations 2006 No. 2006/247. - Enabling power: Local Government Finance Act 1992, ss. 32 (9), 33 (4), 43 (7), 44 (4), 113 (2) & Greater London Authority Act 1999, ss. 86 (5), 88 (8), 89 (9), 420 (1). - Issued: 10.02.2006. Made: 06.02.2006. Laid: 07.02.2006. Coming into force: 08.02.2006. Effect: 1992 c. 14; 1999 c. 29 modified in relation to England. Territorial extent & classification: E. General. - 8p.: 30 cm. - 978-0-11-073991-5 *£3.00*

Local government, England and Wales

The Local Government (Access to Information) (Variation) Order 2006 No. 2006/88. - Enabling power: Local Government Act 1972, ss. 100F (3), 100I (2), 254. - Issued: 26.01.2006. Made: 18.01.2006. Laid: 26.01.2006. Coming into force: 01.03.2006. Effect: 1972 c. 70 amended. Territorial extent & classification: E/W. General. - 12p.: 30 cm. - 978-0-11-073923-6 *£3.00*

The Relevant Authorities (Standards Committee) (Amendment) Regulations 2006 No. 2006/87. - Enabling power: Local Government Act 2000, ss. 53 (6) (12), 55 (8), 105. - Issued: 26.01.2006. Made: 18.01.2006. Laid: 26.01.2006. Coming into force: 01.03.2006. Effect: S.I. 2001/2812 amended. Territorial extent & classification: E/W. General. - 4p.: 30 cm. - 978-0-11-073924-3 *£3.00*

The Representation of the People (England and Wales) (Amendment) Regulations 2006 No. 2006/752. - Enabling power: Representation of the People Act 1983, ss. 4 (4), 9 (2), 10A (1) (9), 13 (3), 13A (1) (2) (6), 13B (3), 36 (3C), 53, 201 (1) (3), sch. 1, rule 24, 45 (1B), sch. 2, paras. 3A, 5A (2) (3), 10A, 10B, 11, 12, 13 (1A) & Representation of the People Act 1985, s. 15 (5) & Representation of the People Act 2000, sch. 4, paras. 3 (1) (b) (2) (c), 4 (1) (b) (2) (c) (4) (a), 6 (7) (8), 7 (5) (c) (7) & Local Government Act 2000, ss. 44, 45, 105. - Issued: 20.03.2006. Made: 09.03.2006. Coming into force: 23.03.2006 in accord. with reg. 1. Effect: S.I. 2001/341, 1298; 2002/185 amended. Territorial extent & classification: E/W. General. - 20p.: 30 cm. - 978-0-11-074311-0 *£3.50*

Local government, Wales

The Bridgend (Brackla and Coity Higher) Order 2006 No. 2006/1064 (W.110). - Enabling power: Local Government Act 1972, ss. 58 (2). - Issued: 04.05.2006. Made: 26.03.2006. Coming into force: In accord. with art. 1(2). Effect: S.I. 1976/246 amended. Territorial extent & classification: W. General. - In English and Welsh. Welsh title: Gorchymyn Pen-y-bont ar Ogwr (Bracla a Choety Uchaf) 2006. - [8]p., maps: 30 cm. - 978-0-11-091330-8 *£3.00*

The Local Authorities (Capital Finance and Accounting) (Wales) (Amendment) Regulations 2006 No. 2006/944 (W.93) . - Enabling power: Local Government Act 2003, ss. 9 (3), 10, 11, 16 (2), 21, 23 (1) (2), 24, 123 (1) (2), 124. - Issued: 07.04.2006. Made: 28.03.2006. Coming into force: 01.04.2006. Effect: S.I. 2003/3239 (W.319) amended. Territorial extent & classification: W. General. - In English and Welsh. Welsh title: Rheoliadau Awdurdodau Lleol (Cyllid Cyfalaf a Chyfrifyddu) (Cymru) (Diwygio) 2006. - 8p.: 30 cm. - 978-0-11-091310-0 *£3.00*

The Local Authorities (Indemnities for Members and Officers) (Wales) Order 2006 No. 2006/249 (W.37). - Enabling power: Local Government Act 2000, ss. 101, 105. - Issued: 15.02.2006. Made: 07.02.2006. Coming into force: 08.02.2006. Effect: None. Territorial extent & classification: W. General. - In English and Welsh. Welsh title: Gorchymyn Awdurdodau Lleol (Indemniadau ar gyfer Aelodau a Swyddogion) Cymru 2006. - 12p.: 30 cm. - 978-0-11-091272-1 *£3.00*

The Local Authorities (Standing Orders) (Wales) Regulations 2006 No. 2006/1275 (W.121). - Enabling power: Local Government and Housing Act 1989, ss. 8, 20, 190. - Issued: 23.05.2006. Made: 09.05.2006. Coming into force: 03.07.2006. Effect: S.I. 1993/202 revoked with savings in relation to Wales. Territorial extent & classification: W. General. - In English and Welsh. Welsh title: Rheoliadau Awdurdodau Lleol (Rheolau Sedyflog) (Cymru) 2006. - 24p.: 30 cm. - 978-0-11-091340-7 *£4.00*

The Local Government Act 2003 (Commencement No. 1 and Savings) (Wales) Order 2006 No. 2006/3339 (W.302) (C.120). - Enabling power: Local Government Act 2003, s. 128 (4) (9). Bringing into operation various provisions of the 2003 on 01.04.2007. - Issued: 20.12.2006. Made: 12.12.2006. Effect: None. Territorial extent & classification: W. General. - In English and Welsh. Welsh title: Gorchymyn Deddf Llywodraeth Leol 2003 (Cychwyn Rhif 1 ac Arbedion) (Cymru) 2006. - 4p.: 30 cm. - 978-0-11-091473-2 *£3.00*

The Local Government (Best Value Authorities) (Power to Trade) (Wales) Order 2006 No. 2006/979 (W.102). - Enabling power: Local Government Act 2003, ss. 95, 96, 123. - Issued: 10.04.2006. Made: 29.03.2006. Coming into force: 01.04.2006. Effect: None. Territorial extent & classification: W. General. - In English and Welsh. Welsh title: Gorchymyn Llywodraeth Leol (Awdurdodau Gwerth Gorau) (Pwwer i Fasnachu) (Cymru) 2006. - 4p.: 30 cm. - 978-0-11-091314-8 *£3.00*

The Local Government (Improved Plans) (Wales) Order 2006 No. 2006/615 (W.68). - Enabling power: Local Government Act 1999, ss. 5 (2), 6 (3), 7 (6), 29 (1). - Issued: 14.03.2006. Made: 07.03.2006. Coming into force: 01.04.2006. Effect: S.I. 2002/886 (W. 101); 2004/1575 (W. 161) revoked. Territorial extent & classification: W. General. - In English and Welsh. Welsh title: Gorchymyn Lywodraeth Leol (Cynlluniau Gwella) (Cymru) 2006. - 4p.: 30 cm. - 978-0-11-091295-0 *£3.00*

The Public Services Ombudsman for Wales (Standards Investigations) Order 2006 No. 2006/949 (W.98). - Enabling power: Local Government Act 2000, s. 70 (1) (2). - Issued: 10.04.2006. Made: 28.03.2006. Coming into force: 01.04.2006. Effect: S.I. 2001/2286 (W.174) revoked. Territorial extent & classification: W. General. - In English and Welsh. Welsh title: Gorchymyn Ombwdsmon Gwasanaethau Cyhoeddus Cymru (Ymchwiliadau Safonau) 2006. - 12p.: 30 cm. - 978-0-11-091317-9 *£3.00*

The Revenue Support Grant (Specified Bodies) (Wales) (Amendment) Regulations 2006 No. 2006/764 (W.73). - Enabling power: Local Government Finance Act 1988, ss. 76 (4), 140 (4). - Issued: 21.03.2006. Made: 14.03.2006. Coming into force: 20.03.2006. Effect: S.I. 2000/718 (W.25) amended. Territorial extent & classification: W. General. - In English & Welsh. Welsh title: Rheoliadau Grant Cynnal Refeniw (Cyrff Penodedig) (Cymru) (Diwygio) 2006. - 4p.: 30 cm. - 978-0-11-091299-8 *£3.00*

The Standards Committees (Wales) (Amendment) Regulations 2006 No. 2006/1849 (W.192). - Enabling power: Local Government Act 2000, ss. 53 (11), 54A (a), 56 (5). - Issued: 19.07.2006. Made: 11.07.2006. Coming into force: 14.07.2006. Effect: S.I. 2001/2283 (W.172) amended. Territorial extent & classification: W. General. - In English and Welsh. Welsh title: Rheoliadau Pwyllgorau Safonau (Cymru) (Diwygio) 2006. - 8p.: 30 cm. - 978-0-11-091387-2 *£3.00*

London government

The Greater London Authority (Allocation of Grants for Precept Calculations) Regulations 2006 No. 2006/351. - Enabling power: Greater London Authority Act 1999, ss. 88 (3) (b), 89 (5) (b). - Issued: 17.02.2006. Made: 14.02.2006. Laid: 15.02.2006. Coming into force: 16.02.2006. Effect: None. Territorial extent & classification: E. General. - 2p.: 30 cm. - 978-0-11-074047-8 *£3.00*

The Transport for London (Best Value) (Contracting Out of Investment and Highway Functions) Order 2006 No. 2006/91. - Enabling power: Deregulation and Contracting Out Act 1994, s. 70. - Issued: 25.01.2006. Made: 19.01.2006. Coming into force: 20.01.2006. Effect: None. Territorial extent & classification: E. General. - 4p.: 30 cm. - 978-0-11-073925-0 *£3.00*

Lord Chancellor

The Constitutional Reform Act 2005 (Commencement No. 5) Order 2006 No. 2006/1014 (C.33). - Enabling power: Constitutional Reform Act 2005, s. 148. Bringing into operation various provisions of the 2005 Act on 03.04.2006, 02.10.2006 & 02.04.2007. - Issued: 06.04.2006. Made: 02.04.2006. Effect: None. Territorial extent & classification: E/W/S/NI. General. - 8p.: 30 cm. - 978-0-11-074457-5 *£3.00*

The Discipline of Coroners (Designation) Order 2006 No. 2006/677. - Enabling power: Constitutional Reform Act 2005, s. 118 (2). - Issued: 17.03.2006. Made: 09.03.2006. Laid: 13.03.2006. Coming into force: 03.04.2006. Effect: None. Territorial extent & classification: E/W. General. - 2p.: 30 cm. - 978-0-11-074274-8 *£3.00*

The Lord Chancellor (Transfer of Functions and Supplementary Provisions) (No.2) Order 2006 No. 2006/1016. - Enabling power: Constitutional Reform Act 2005, ss. 19, 143. - Issued: 06.04.2006. Made: 02.04.2006. Coming into force: 03.04.2006. Effect: 1876 c. 59; 1887 c. 70; 1984 c. 42; 1988 c. 48; 2002 c. 41; 2004 c. 7, c. 18, c. 33, c. 35; 2005 c. 2, c. 9, c. 18, c. 19; S.I. 1953/1849; 1962/2834; 2003/284; 2004/1193 amended. Territorial extent & classification: E/W/S/NI. General. - 12p.: 30 cm. - 978-0-11-074456-8 *£3.00*

The Lord Chancellor (Transfer of Functions and Supplementary Provisions) (No. 3) Order 2006 No. 2006/1640. - Enabling power: Constitutional Reform Act 2005, ss. 19, 140 (4) (b), 143. - Issued: 26.06.2006. Made: 21.06.2006. Coming into force: In accord. with art. 1. Effect: 1972 c. 48; 1975 c. 27; 1987 c. 45; 1991 c. 5; 2004 c. 36 & Church Commissioners Measure 1947 No. 2 & S.I. 1948/1 amended. Territorial extent & classification: E/W/S/NI. General. - Supersedes draft SI (ISBN 0110745906) issued 22.05.2006. - 8p.: 30 cm. - 978-0-11-074735-4 *£3.00*

The Lord Chancellor (Transfer of Functions and Supplementary Provisions) Order 2006 No. 2006/680. - Enabling power: Constitutional Reform Act 2005, ss. 19, 143. - Issued: 17.03.2006. Made: 10.03.2006. Laid: 13.03.06. Coming into force: 03.04.2006. Effect: 58 instruments amended. Territorial extent & classification: E/W/S/NI. General. - 20p.: 30 cm. - 978-0-11-074265-6 £3.00

Lord Chief Justice

The Constitutional Reform Act 2005 (Commencement No. 5) Order 2006 No. 2006/1014 (C.33). - Enabling power: Constitutional Reform Act 2005, s. 148. Bringing into operation various provisions of the 2005 Act on 03.04.2006, 02.10.2006 & 02.04.2007. - Issued: 06.04.2006. Made: 02.04.2006. Effect: None. Territorial extent & classification: E/W/S/NI. General. - 8p.: 30 cm. - 978-0-11-074457-5 £3.00

The Discipline of Coroners (Designation) Order 2006 No. 2006/677. - Enabling power: Constitutional Reform Act 2005, s. 118 (2). - Issued: 17.03.2006. Made: 09.03.2006. Laid: 13.03.2006. Coming into force: 03.04.2006. Effect: None. Territorial extent & classification: E/W. General. - 2p.: 30 cm. - 978-0-11-074274-8 £3.00

The Judicial Discipline (Prescribed Procedures) Regulations 2006 No. 2006/676. - Enabling power: Constitutional Reform Act 2005, ss. 115, 120, 121. - Issued: 20.03.2006. Made: 10.03.2006. Laid: 13.03.2006. Coming into force: 03.04.2006. Effect: None. Territorial extent & classification: E/W/S/NI. General. - 20p.: 30 cm. - 978-0-11-074272-4 £3.50

The Lord Chancellor (Transfer of Functions and Supplementary Provisions) (No.2) Order 2006 No. 2006/1016. - Enabling power: Constitutional Reform Act 2005, ss. 19, 143. - Issued: 06.04.2006. Made: 02.04.2006. Coming into force: 03.04.2006. Effect: 1876 c. 59; 1887 c. 70; 1984 c. 42; 1988 c. 48; 2002 c. 41; 2004 c. 7, c. 18, c. 33, c. 35; 2005 c. 2, c. 9, c. 18, c. 19; S.I. 1953/1849; 1962/2834; 2003/284; 2004/1193 amended. Territorial extent & classification: E/W/S/NI. General. - 12p.: 30 cm. - 978-0-11-074456-8 £3.00

The Lord Chancellor (Transfer of Functions and Supplementary Provisions) Order 2006 No. 2006/680. - Enabling power: Constitutional Reform Act 2005, ss. 19, 143. - Issued: 17.03.2006. Made: 10.03.2006. Laid: 13.03.06. Coming into force: 03.04.2006. Effect: 58 instruments amended. Territorial extent & classification: E/W/S/NI. General. - 20p.: 30 cm. - 978-0-11-074265-6 £3.00

Magistrates' courts, England and Wales

The Assistants to Justices' Clerks Regulations 2006 No. 2006/3405 (L.14). - Enabling power: Courts Act 2003, s. 27 (6). - Issued: 28.12.2006. Made: 18.12.2006. Laid: 19.12.2006. Coming into force: 09.01.2007. Effect: S.I. 1979/570; 1998/3107; 1999/2814; 2001/2269 revoked. Territorial extent & classification: E/W. General. - 4p.: 30 cm. - 978-0-11-075557-1 £3.00

The Collection of Fines (Final Scheme) Order 2006 No. 2006/1737. - Enabling power: Courts Act 2003, ss. 97 (7) (9), 108 (6), 109 (4) (5). - Issued: 07.07.2006. Made: 29.06.2006. Coming into force: 03.07.2006. Effect: 1971 c.32; 1980 c.43; 2003 c.39; 2004 c. 28 amended. Territorial extent & classification: E/W. General. - Supersedes draft S.I. (ISBN 0110745051) issued 24.04.2006. - 16p.: 30 cm. - 978-0-11-074786-6 £3.00

The Collection of Fines (Pilot Scheme) and Discharge of Fines by Unpaid Work (Pilot Schemes) (Amendment) Order 2006 No. 2006/502. - Enabling power: Courts Act 2003, ss. 97 (5) (6), 108 (6). - Issued: 10.03.2006. Made: 06.03.2006. Laid: 06.03.2006. Coming into force: 27.03.2006 except for art. 2; 30.03.2006 for art. 2. Effect: 1971 c. 32; 1980 c. 43; 2003 c.39 modified & S.I. 2004/2198 amended & S.I. 2004/175, 1406; 2005/487, 642, 2410, 3166 revoked (27.03.2006). Territorial extent & classification: E/W. General. - This Order, with the exception of article 2, shall cease to have effect on 02.07.2006. - 12p.: 30 cm. - 978-0-11-074164-2 £3.00

The Courts Act 2003 (Consequential Amendment) Order 2006 No. 2006/1001. - Enabling power: Courts Act 2003, ss. 109 (4) (a) (5) (b). - Issued: 04.04.2006. Made: 29.03.2006. Coming into force: 06.04.2006. Effect: 1991 c.48 amended. Territorial extent & classification: E/W. General. - Supersedes draft. - 2p.: 30 cm. - 978-0-11-074447-6 £3.00

The Criminal Procedure (Amendment No. 2) Rules 2006 No. 2006/2636 (L.9). - Enabling power: Courts Act 2003, s. 69. - Issued: 11.10.2006. Made: 03.10.2006. Laid: 04.10.2006. Coming into force: 06.11.2006. Effect: S.I. 2005/384 (L.4) amended. Territorial extent and classification: E/W. General. - 12p.: 30 cm. - 978-0-11-075153-5 £3.00

The Criminal Procedure (Amendment) Rules 2006 No. 2006/353 (L.2). - Enabling power: Courts Act 2003, s. 69 & Juries Act 1974, ss. 9 (3), 9A (3). - Issued: 21.02.2006. Made: 09.02.2006. Laid: 15.02.2006. Coming into force: 03.04.2006. Effect: S.I. 2005/384 (L. 4) amended. Territorial extent and classification: E/W. General. - 16p.: 30 cm. - 978-0-11-074065-2 £3.00

The Fines Collection Regulations 2006 No. 2006/501. - Enabling power: Courts Act 2003, ss. 108 (6), sch. 5, paras 38 (2) (b), 41, 42 (3), 42A (4), 43, 44, 45, 46. - Issued: 10.03.2006. Made: 06.03.2006. Laid: 06.03.2006. Coming into force: 27.03.2006. Effect: S.I. 1971/809; 1992/2182 modified & S.I. 2004/176, 1407; 2005/484 revoked. Territorial extent & classification: E/W. General. - 20p.: 30 cm. - 978-0-11-074165-9 £3.00

The Magistrates' Courts Fees (Amendment) Order 2006 No. 2006/715 (L.3). - Enabling power: Courts Act 2003, s. 92. - Issued: 20.03.2006. Made: 09.03.2006. Laid: 16.03.2006. Coming into force: 06.04.2006. Effect: S.I. 2005/3444 amended. Territorial extent & classification: E/W. General. - 8p.: 30 cm. - 978-0-11-074271-7 £3.00

Marine pollution

The Merchant Shipping (Prevention of Air Pollution from Ships) Order 2006 No. 2006/1248. - Enabling power: Merchant Shipping Act 1995, s. 128 (1) (da) (3) (4). - Issued: 19.05.2006. Made: 09.05.2006. Laid: 19.05.2006. Coming into force: 12.06.2006. Effect: None. Territorial extent & classification: E/W/S/NI. General. - 2p.: 30 cm. - 978-0-11-074565-7 £3.00

The Merchant Shipping (Prevention of Pollution by Sewage and Garbage) Order 2006 No. 2006/2950. - Enabling power: Merchant Shipping Act 1995, s. 128 (1) (a) (3) (4). - Issued: 21.11.2006. Made: 14.11.2006. Laid: 21.11.2006. Coming into force: 12.12.2006. Effect: S.I. 1997/2569; 1998/254 amended & S.I. 1988/2252; 1993/1581 revoked. Territorial extent & classification: E/W/S/NI. General. - 4p.: 30 cm. - 978-0-11-075317-1 £3.00

Medicines

The Medicines (Administration of Radioactive Substances) Amendment Regulations 2006 No. 2006/2806. - Enabling power: Medicines Act 1968, ss. 60 (2), 129 (5) & European Communities Act 1972, s. 2 (2). - Issued: 26.10.2006. Made: 19.10.2006. Laid: 26.10.2006. Coming into force: 17.11.2006. Effect: S.I. 1978/1006 amended. Territorial extent & classification: E/W/S/NI. General. - 4p.: 30 cm. - 978-0-11-075208-2 £3.00

The Medicines (Advisory Board on the Registration of Homoeopathic Products) Amendment Order 2006 No. 2006/2386. - Enabling power: Medicines Act 1968, ss. 4, 129 (4). - Issued: 11.09.2006. Made: 29.08.2006. Coming into force: 01.09.2006. Effect: S.I. 1995/309 amended. Territorial extent & classification: E/W/S/NI. General. - 4p.: 30 cm. - 978-0-11-075082-8 £3.00

The Medicines for Human Use (Administration and Sale or Supply) (Miscellaneous Amendments) Order 2006 No. 2006/2807. - Enabling power: Medicines Act 1968, ss. 57 (1) (2), 58 (4) (5), 129 (4). - Issued: 26.10.2006. Made: 19.10.2006. Laid: 26.10.2006. Coming into force: 17.11.2006. Effect: S.I. 1997/1830; 1980/1924 amended. Territorial extent & classification: E/W/S/NI. General. - 8p.: 30 cm. - 978-0-11-075209-9 £3.00

The Medicines for Human Use and Medical Devices (Fees Amendments) Regulations 2006 No. 2006/494. - Enabling power: European Communities Act 1972, s. 2 (2) & Finance Act 1973, s. 56 (1) (2) & Medicines Act 1971, s. 1 (1) (2). - Issued: 03.03.2006. Made: 27.02.2006. Laid: 03.03.2006. Coming into force: 01.04.2006. Effect: S.I. 1994/105; 1995/449, 1116 amended. Territorial extent & classification: E/W/S/NI. General. - 12p.: 30 cm. - 978-0-11-074114-7 £3.00

The Medicines for Human Use (Clinical Trials) Amendment (No. 2) Regulations 2006 No. 2006/2984. - Enabling power: European Communities Act 1972, s. 2 (2). - Issued: 21.11.2006. Made: 15.11.2006. Laid: 21.11.2006. Coming into force: 12.12.2006. Effect: S.I. 2004/1031 amended. Territorial extent & classification: E/W/S/NI. General. - EC note: These Regulations amend the Medicines for Human Use (Clinical Trials) Regulations 2004 which implement Directive 2001/20/EC on the approximation of the laws, regulations and administrative provisions of the Member States relating to the implementation of good clinical practice in the conduct of clinical trials on medicinal products in human use. - 4p.: 30 cm. - 978-0-11-075328-7 £3.00

The Medicines for Human Use (Clinical Trials) Amendment Regulations 2006 No. 2006/1928. - Enabling power: European Communities Act 1972, s. 2 (2). - Issued: 20.07.2006. Made: 13.07.2006. Laid: 20.07.2006. Coming into force: 29.08.2006. Effect: S.I. 2004/1031 amended. Territorial extent & classification: E/W/S/NI. General. - EC note: These Regulations amend the Medicines for Human Use (Clinical Trials) Regulations 2004 which implement Directive 2001/20/EC on the approximation of the laws, regulations and administrative provisions of the Member States relating to the implementation of good clinical practice in the conduct of clinical trials on medicinal products in human use. In particular, they implement Commission Directive 2005/28/EC laying down principles and detailed guidelines for good clinical practice as regards investigational medicinal products for human use, as well as the requirements for authorisation of the manufacturing or importation of such products (the GCP Directive) and make other miscellaneous amendments. - 12p.: 30 cm. - 978-0-11-074861-0 £3.00

The Medicines for Human Use (Fees Amendments) Regulations 2006 No. 2006/2125. - Enabling power: Medicines Act 1971, s. 1 (1) (2). - Issued: 01.08.2006. Made: 26.07.2006. Laid: 01.08.2006. Coming into force: 01.09.2006. Effect: S.I. 1994/105; 1995/1116 amended. Territorial extent & classification: E/W/S/NI. General. - 8p.: 30 cm. - 978-0-11-074964-8 £3.00

The Medicines for Human Use (National Rules for Homoeopathic Products) Regulations 2006 No. 2006/1952. - Enabling power: European Communities Act 1972, s. 2 (2). - Issued: 21.07.2006. Made: 19.07.2006. Laid: 21.07.2006. Coming into force: 01.09.2006. Effect: S.I. 1994/3144 amended. Territorial extent & classification: E/W/S/NI. General. - 8p.: 30 cm. - 978-0-11-074879-5 £3.00

The Medicines for Human Use (Prescribing) (Miscellaneous Amendments) Order 2006 No. 2006/915. - Enabling power: Medicines Act 1968, ss. 57 (1) (2), 58 (1) (1A) (4) (4A) (4B) (5), 129 (4). - Issued: 03.04.2006. Made: 23.03.2006. Laid: 03.04.2006. Coming into force: 01.05.2006. Effect: S.I. 1980/1924; 1997/1830 amended. Territorial extent & classification: E/W/S/NI. General. - 12p.: 30 cm. - 978-0-11-074398-1 *£3.00*

The Medicines (Pharmacies) (Applications for Registration and Fees) Amendment Regulations 2006 No. 2006/3264. - Enabling power: Medicines Act 1968, ss. 75 (1), 76 (1) (2), 129 (1) (5). - Issued: 12.12.2006. Made: 06.12.2006. Laid: 12.12.2006. Coming into force: 01.01.2007. Effect: S.I. 1973/1822 amended & S.I. 2005/3259 revoked. Territorial extent & classification: E/W/S/NI. General. - 4p.: 30 cm. - 978-0-11-075447-5 *£3.00*

The Medicines (Sale or Supply) (Miscellaneous Amendments) Regulations 2006 No. 2006/914. - Enabling power: Medicines Act 1968, ss. 66 (1), 87 (1), 91 (2), 129 (5) & European Communities Act 1972, s. 2 (2). - Issued: 03.04.2006. Made: 23.03.2006. Laid: 03.04.2006. Coming into force: 01.05.2006. Effect: S.I. 1980/1923; 1994/3144; 2003/2317; 2005/2750 amended. Territorial extent & classification: E/W/S/NI. General. - 8p.: 30 cm. - 978-0-11-074397-4 *£3.00*

The Medicines (Traditional Herbal Medicinal Products for Human Use) (Consequential Amendment) Regulations 2006 No. 2006/395. - Enabling power: European Communities Act 1972, s. 2 (2). - Issued: 24.02.2006. Made: 14.02.2006. Laid: 24.02.2006. Coming into force: 01.04.2006. Effect: S.I. 1977/2130 amended. Territorial extent & classification: E/W/S/NI. General. - This Statutory Instrument has been made to correct an error in SI 2005/2750 and is being issued free of charge to all known recipients of that Statutory Instrument. - 2p.: 30 cm. - 978-0-11-074086-7 *£3.00*

The Veterinary Medicines Regulations 2006 No. 2006/2407. - Enabling power: European Communities Act 1972, s. 2 (2) & Finance Act 1973, s. 56 (1). - Issued: 18.09.2006. Made: 05.09.2006. Laid: 08.09.2006. Coming into force: 01.10.2006. Effect: 1954 c. 61; 1968 c. 29, 67; 1971 c. 69; 1972 c. 66; 1977 c. xv; 1985 c. 57; 1986 c. 14; 1987 c. 43; 1990 c. 43; 1994 c. 20, 23; 1995 c. 39; 1999 c. 28; 2003 c. 17 amended & S.I. 1971/1267; 1976/968; 1978/1004, 1006; 1980/1212; 1982/234; 1984/187; 1986/1761; 1991/472; 1992/605; 1994/105, 1932, 1933, 3144; 1996/3124; 2003/1076; 2005/2754, 2791 amended & S.I. 1976/31; 1985/273; 1994/3143; 2005/2745 revoked. Territorial extent & classification: E/W/S/NI. General. - EC note: These Regs implement Directive 2001/82/EC on the Community Code relating to veterinary medicinal products, as amended by Directive 2004/28/EC. They also identify the competent authority for, and provide for enforcement of, relevant provisions of Regulations (EC) 178/2002, 1831/2003, 882/2004, and 183/2005; and they also implement Directive 90/167 so far as they are not rendered spent by Regulation (EC) 183/2005. - 96p., col. ill.: 30 cm. - 978-0-11-075096-5 *£14.00*

Mental capacity, England

The Mental Capacity Act 2005 (Appropriate Body) (England) (Amendment) Regulations 2006 No. 2006/3474. - Enabling power: Mental Capacity Act 2005, s. 30 (4) (6) (a). - Issued: 09.01.2007. Made: 19.12.2006. Laid: 09.01.2007. Coming into force: 31.01.2007. Effect: S.I. 2006/2810 amended. Territorial extent & classification: E. General. - Will be superseded by the S.I. of the same number (ISBN 9780110756493) issued on 16.01.2007. - 2p.: 30 cm. - 978-0-11-075589-2 *£3.00*

The Mental Capacity Act 2005 (Appropriate Body) (England) (Amendment) Regulations 2006 No. 2006/3474. - Enabling power: Mental Capacity Act 2005, ss. 30 (4) (6) (a). - Issued: 16.01.2007. Made: 19.12.2006. Laid: 11.01.2007. Coming into force: 31.01.2007. Effect: S.I. 2006/2810 amended. Territorial extent & classification: E. General- This Statutory Instrument has been printed in substitution of the SI of the same number (ISBN 9780110755892 published 09.01.2007) and is being issued free of charge to all known recipients of that Statutory Instrument. - 2p.: 30 cm. - 978-0-11-075649-3 *£3.00*

The Mental Capacity Act 2005 (Appropriate Body) (England) Regulations 2006 No. 2006/2810. - Enabling power: Mental Capacity Act 2005, s. 30 (4) (6) (a). - Issued: 27.10.2006. Made: 21.10.2006. Laid: 27.10.2006. Coming into force: 01.02.2007 for the purpose mentioned in reg. 1 (1) (a); & 01.04.2007 for all other purposes, in accord. with reg. 1 (1). Effect: None. Territorial extent & classification: E. General. - 2p.: 30 cm. - 978-0-11-075219-8 *£3.00*

The Mental Capacity Act 2005 (Commencement No.1) (Amendment) Order 2006 No. 2006/3473 (C.133). - Enabling power: Mental Capacity Act 2005, s. 68 (2) (a) (3). Bringing into operation various provisions of the 2005 Act on 01.07.2007; 01.10.2007; 01.10.2008 in accord. with art 2. - Issued: 09.01.2007. Made: 19.12.2006. Effect: None. Territorial extent & classification: E. General. - 2p.: 30 cm. - 978-0-11-075588-5 *£3.00*

The Mental Capacity Act 2005 (Commencement No.1) Order 2006 No. 2006/2814 (C.95). - Enabling power: Mental Capacity Act 2005, s. 68 (2) (a) (3). Bringing into operation various provisions of the 2005 Act on 01.11.2006, 01.02.2007, 01.04.2007 & 01.04.2008 in accord. with arts 2 to 5. - Issued: 26.10.2006. Made: 20.10.2006. Effect: None. Territorial extent & classification: E. General. - 2p.: 30 cm. - 978-0-11-075214-3 *£3.00*

The Mental Capacity Act 2005 (Independent Mental Capacity Advocates) (Expansion of Role) Regulations 2006 No. 2006/2883. - Enabling power: Mental Capacity Act 2005, ss. 41 (1) (2), 64 (1), 65 (1). - Issued: 01.11.2006. Made: 30.10.2006. Coming into force: 01.11.2006 & 01.04.2007, in accord. with reg. 1 (2). Effect: None. Territorial extent & classification: E. General. - Supersedes draft S.I. (ISBN 0110748255) issued 13.07.2006. - 8p.: 30 cm. - 978-0-11-075234-1 *£3.00*

The Mental Capacity Act 2005 (Independent Mental Capacity Advocates) (General) Regulations 2006 No. 2006/1832. - Enabling power: Mental Capacity Act 2005, ss. 35 (2) (3), 36, 37 (6) (7), 38 (8), 64 (1), 65 (1). - Issued: 13.07.2006. Made: 07.07.2006. Laid: 13.07.2006. Coming into force: In accord. with reg. 1 (2). Effect: None. Territorial extent & classification: E. General. - 4p.: 30 cm. - 978-0-11-074824-5 £3.00

Mental health, England and Wales

The Court of Protection (Amendment) Rules 2006 No. 2006/653. - Enabling power: Mental Health Act 1983, ss. 106, 108. - Issued: 16.03.2006. Made: 09.03.2006. Laid: 10.03.06. Coming into force: 01.04.2006. Effect: S.I. 2001/824 amended. Territorial extent & classification: E/W. General. - 8p.: 30 cm. - 978-0-11-074220-5 £3.00

Merchant shipping

The General Lighthouse Authorities (Beacons: Automatic Identification System) Order 2006 No. 2006/1977. - Enabling power: Merchant Shipping Act 1995, s. 223 (3). - Issued: 31.07.2006. Made: 19.07.2006. Coming into force: 20.07.2006. Effect: None. Territorial extent & classification: E/W/S/NI. General. - 2p.: 30 cm. - 978-0-11-074913-6 £3.00

The Merchant Shipping and Fishing Vessels (Lifting Operations and Lifting Equipment) Regulations 2006 No. 2006/2184. - Enabling power: European Communities Act 1972, s. 2 (2) & Merchant Shipping Act 1995, ss. 85 (1) (a) (b) (3) (7), 86 (1). - Issued: 18.08.2006. Made: 08.08.2006. Laid: 15.08.2006. Coming into force: 24.11.2006. Effect: S.I. 1988/1636 revoked. Territorial extent & classification: E/W/S/NI. General. - EC note: Implements in part Council Directive 89/655/EEC, as amended by Directive 95/63/EC the minimum safety and health requirements for the use of work equipment. - 16p.: 30 cm. - 978-0-11-075018-7 £3.00

The Merchant Shipping and Fishing Vessels (Provision and Use of Work Equipment) Regulations 2006 No. 2006/2183. - Enabling power: European Communities Act 1972, s. 2 (2) & Merchant Shipping Act 1995, ss. 85 (1) (a) (b) (3) (7), 86 (1). - Issued: 18.08.2006. Made: 08.08.2006. Laid: 15.08.2006. Coming into force: 24.11.2006. Effect: S.I. 1988/1641, 2274 amended & S.I. 1988/1636 revoked. Territorial extent & classification: E/W/S/NI. General. - EC note: Implements Council Directive 89/655/EEC, as amended by Directive 95/63/EC, the minimum safety and health requirements for the use of work equipment. - 20p.: 30 cm. - 978-0-11-075016-3 £3.50

The Merchant Shipping (Fees) (Amendment) Regulations 2006 No. 2006/3225. - Enabling power: Merchant Shipping Act 1995, s. 302 (1). - Issued: 13.12.2006. Made: 04.12.2006. Laid: 07.12.2006. Coming into force: 01.01.2007. Effect: S.I. 2006/2055 amended. Territorial extent & classification: E/W/S/NI. General. - 4p.: 30 cm. - 978-0-11-075453-6 £3.00

The Merchant Shipping (Fees) Regulations 2006 No. 2006/2055. - Enabling power: Merchant Shipping Act 1995, s. 302. - Issued: 03.08.2006. Made: 24.07.2006. Laid: 27.07.2006. Coming into force: 11.09.2006. Effect: S.I. 1997/1820; 1998/1609; 2004/302 amended & S.I. 1996/3243; 1998/531; 1999/1063, 1923; 2000/1683; 2001/3340, 3628; 2003/788; 2004/1977; 2005/580 revoked. Territorial extent & classification: E/W/S/NI. General. - 24p.: 30 cm. - 978-0-11-074958-7 £4.00

The Merchant Shipping (Light Dues) (Amendment) Regulations 2006 No. 2006/649. - Enabling power: Merchant Shipping Act 1995, s. 205 (5). - Issued: 20.03.2006. Made: 08.03.2006. Laid: 10.03.2006. Coming into force: 01.04.2006. Effect: S.I. 1997/562 amended. Territorial extent & classification: E/W/S/NI. General. - 2p.: 30 cm. - 978-0-11-074229-8 £3.00

The Merchant Shipping (Local Passenger Vessels) (Crew) Regulations 2006 No. 2006/3224. - Enabling power: Merchant Shipping Act 1995, ss. 85 (1) (3) (5) (7), 86 (1) (2). - Issued: 13.12.2006. Made: 05.12.2006. Laid: 07.12.2006. Coming into force: 01.01.2007. Effect: S.I. 1993/1213 revoked. Territorial extent & classification: E/W/S/NI. General. - 8p.: 30 cm. - 978-0-11-075448-2 £3.00

The Merchant Shipping (Oil Pollution) (Bunkers Convention) Regulations 2006 No. 2006/1244. - Enabling power: European Communities Act 1972, s. 2 (2). - Issued: 11.05.2006. Made: 02.05.2006. Laid: 04.05.2006. Coming into force: In acord. with reg. 1 (2) to (4). Effect: 1995 c. 21 amended. Territorial extent & classification: E/W/S/NI. General. - EC note: These Regulations amend Chapter 3 of Part 6 of the Merchant Shipping Act 1995 in order to implement Council Decision 2002/762/EC authorising the Member States, in the interests of the Community, to sign, ratify or accede to the International Convention on Civil Liability for Bunker Oil Pollution Damage 2001. - 12p.: 30 cm. - 978-0-11-074545-9 £3.00

The Merchant Shipping (Oil Pollution) (Supplementary Fund Protocol) Order 2006 No. 2006/1265. - Enabling power: Merchant Shipping (Pollution) Act 2006, s. 1 (2) (a) (4) to (6). - Issued: 19.05.2006. Made: 09.05.2006. Laid: 19.05.2006. Coming into force: In accord. with art. 1 (2). Effect: 1981 c. 54; 1995 c. 21 amended. Territorial extent & classification: E/W/S/NI. General. - With correction slip dated July 2006. - 8p.: 30 cm. - 978-0-11-074566-4 £3.00

Merchant shipping: Masters and seamen

The Merchant Shipping (Training and Certification and Minimum Standards of Safety Communications) (Amendment) Regulations 2006 No. 2006/89. - Enabling power: European Communities Act 1972, s. 2 (2) & Merchant Shipping Act 1995, ss. 47 (1) (3) (4), 85 (1) (3) (5). - Issued: 30.01.2006. Made: 18.01.2006. Laid: 24.01.2006. Coming into force: 20.02.2006. Effect: S.I. 1997/348, 529 amended. Territorial extent & classification: E/W/S/NI. General. - EC note: These Regs give effect to Council Directive 2003/103/EC amending Directive 2001/25/EC as amended by Directive 2002/84/EC on the minimum level of training for seafarers. - 8p.: 30 cm. - 978-0-11-073922-9 £3.00

Merchant shipping: Safety

The Merchant Shipping (Inland Waterway and Limited Coastal Operations) (Boatmasters' Qualifications and Hours of Work) Regulations 2006 No. 2006/3223. - Enabling power: European Communities Act 1972, s. 2 (2) and Merchant Shipping Act 1995, ss. 47 (1) to (4), 85 (1) (3) (6) (7), 86 (1) (2), 302 (1), 307 (1). - Issued: 13.12.2006. Made: 04.12.2006. Laid: 07.12.2006. Coming into force: for reg. 33 on 22.12.2006; for all other purposes on 01.01.2007. Effect: S.I. 1993/1213; 2002/2125; 2003/3049 amended. Territorial extent & classification: E/W/S/NI. General. - With correction slip dated January 2007. EC note: Implements, as far as it is necessary to do so for the UK, Council Directive 96/50/EC on the harmonisation of the conditions for obtaining national boatmasters' certificates for the carriage of goods and passengers by inland waterway, as amended by Regulation (EC) 1882/2003. - 48p.: 30 cm. - 978-0-11-075449-9 £7.50

Metropolitan and city districts: Private hire vehicles

The Private Hire Vehicles (London) (Transitional and Saving Provisions) (Amendment) Regulations 2006 No. 2006/584. - Enabling power: Private Hire Vehicles (London) Act 1998, s. 37 (1) (2). - Issued: 14.03.2006. Made: 06.03.2006. Laid: 13.03.2006. Coming into force: 04.04.2006. Effect: S.I. 2003/655 amended. Territorial extent & classification: E/W (has no implications outside London). General. - 2p.: 30 cm. - 978-0-11-074182-6 £3.00

Ministers of the Crown

The Secretary of State for Communities and Local Government Order 2006 No. 2006/1926. - Enabling power: Ministers of the Crown Act 1975, ss. 1, 2. - Issued: 31.07.2006. Made: 19.07.2006. Laid: 31.07.2006. Coming into force: 21.08.2006. Effect: 1962 c.46; 1967 c.13; 1990 c.8, c.9, c.10; 1992 c.42; 2000 c.23; 2004 c.28 & S.I. 2005/2966 amended. Territorial extent & classification: E/W/S/NI. General. - Copies are supplied by TSO's On-demand publishing service. - 8p.: 30 cm. - 978-0-11-074888-7 £3.00

The Transfer of Functions (Office of Her Majesty's Paymaster General) Order 2006 No. 2006/607. - Enabling power: Ministers of the Crown Act 1975, s. 1. - Issued: 14.03.2006. Made: 08.03.2006. Laid: 09.03.2006. Coming into force: 03.04.2006. Effect: None. Territorial extent & classification: E/W/S/NI. General. - 4p.: 30 cm. - 978-0-11-074209-0 £3.00

The Transfer of Functions (Statutory Instruments) Order 2006 No. 2006/1927. - Enabling power: Ministers of the Crown Act 1975, s. 1. - Issued: 31.07.2006. Made: 19.07.2006. Laid: 31.07.2006. Coming into force: 31.10.2006. Effect: 1946 c.36 & S.I. 1948/1 amended. Territorial extent & classification: E/W/S/NI. General. - 4p.: 30 cm. - 978-0-11-074889-4 £3.00

The Transfer of Functions (Third Sector, Communities and Equality) Order 2006 No. 2006/2951. - Enabling power: Ministers of the Crown Act 1975, ss. 1, 2. - Issued: 21.11.2006. Made: 14.11.2006. Laid: 21.11.2006. Coming into force: 13.12.2006. Effect: 1916 c. 31; 1939 c. 44; 1992 c. 41; 1993 c. 10 amended. Territorial extent & classification: E/W/S/NI. General. - 8p.: 30 cm. - 978-0-11-075316-4 £3.00

Mobile homes, England

The Mobile Homes Act 1983 (Amendment of Schedule 1) (England) Order 2006 No. 2006/1755. - Enabling power: Mobile Homes Act 1983, s. 2A. - Issued: 11.07.2006. Made: 04.07.2006. Coming into force: 01.10.2006. Effect: 1983 c.34 amended. Territorial extent & classification: E. General. - 12p.: 30 cm. - 978-0-11-074805-4 £3.00

The Mobile Homes (Written Statement) (England) Regulations 2006 No. 2006/2275. - Enabling power: Mobile Homes Act 1983, s. 1 (2) (e). - Issued: 29.08.2006. Made: 22.08.2006. Laid: 29.08.2006. Coming into force: 01.10.2006. Effect: S.I. 1983/749 revoked in relation to England. Territorial extent & classification: E. General. - 16p.: 30 cm. - 978-0-11-075035-4 £3.00

Museums and galleries

The Natural History Museum (Authorised Repositories) Order 2006 No. 2006/1547. - Enabling power: British Museum Act 1963, s. 10 (2). - Issued: 21.06.2006. Made: 15.06.2006. Laid: 16.06.2006. Coming into force: 10.07.2006. Effect: 1963 c.24 amended. Territorial extent & classification: E/W/S/NI. General. - 2p.: 30 cm. - 978-0-11-074708-8 £3.00

National assistance services, England

The National Assistance (Sums for Personal Requirements and Assessment of Resources) (Amendment) (England) Regulations 2006 No. 2006/674. - Enabling power: National Assistance Act 1948, s. 22 (4). - Issued: 15.03.2006. Made: 09.03.2006. Laid: 15.03.2006. Coming into force: 10.04.2006. Effect: S.I. 1992/2977; 2003/628 amended. Territorial extent & classification: E. General. - 4p.: 30 cm. - 978-0-11-074256-4 £3.00

National assistance services, Wales

The National Assistance (Assessment of Resources and Sums for Personal Requirements) (Amendment) (Wales) Regulations 2006 No. 2006/1051 (W.107). - Enabling power: National Assistance Act 1948, s. 22 (4) (5). - Issued: 12.04.2006. Made: 04.04.2006. Coming into force: 10.04.2006. Effect: S.I. 1992/2977 amended in relation to Wales & S.I. 2005/663 (W.53) revoked. Territorial extent & classification: W. General. - In English & Welsh. Welsh title: Rheoliadau Cymorth Gwladol (Asesu Adnoddau a Symiau at Anghenion Personol) (Diwygio) (Cymru) 2006. - 4p.: 30 cm. - 978-0-11-091320-9 £3.00

National election expenditure

The Electoral Administration Act 2006 (Commencement No. 1 and Transitional Provisions) (Amendment) Order 2006 No. 2006/2268 (C.77). - Enabling power: Electoral Administration Act 2006, s. 77 (2) (3) (4). - Issued: 25.08.2006. Made: 17.08.2006. Coming into force: 25.08.2006. Effect: S.I. 2006/1972 (C.67) amended. Territorial extent & classification: E/W/S. General. - This Statutory Instrument has been made in consequence of a defect in SI 2006/1972 (C. 67) (ISBN 0110749065) and is being issued free of charge to all known recipients of that Statutory Instrument. - 2p.: 30 cm. - 978-0-11-075033-0 £3.00

The Electoral Administration Act 2006 (Commencement No. 1 and Transitional Provisions) Order 2006 No. 2006/1972 (C.67). - Enabling power: Electoral Administration Act 2006, s. 77 (2) (3) (4). Bringing into operation various provisions of the 2006 Act on 11.09.2006, subject to transitional provisions in sch. 2. - Issued: 26.07.2006. Made: 20.07.2006. Effect: None. Territorial extent & classification: E/W/S. General. - 8p.: 30 cm. - 978-0-11-074906-8 £3.00

The Political Parties, Elections and Referendums Act 2000 (Commencement No. 3 and Transitional Provisions) Order 2006 No. 2006/3416 (C.129). - Enabling power: Election Publications Act 2001, s. 2. Bringing into operation various provisions of the Political Parties, Elections and Referendums Act 2000, c. 41, on 01.01.2007. - Issued: 28.12.2006. Made: 18.12.2006. Effect: 2001 c. 5 modified. Territorial extent & classification: E/W/S. General. - 4p.: 30 cm. - 978-0-11-075565-6 £3.00

National Health Service

The Scotland Act 1998 (Agency Arrangements) (Specification) (No. 3) Order 2006 No. 2006/3338. - Enabling power: Scotland Act 1998, ss. 93 (3), 113 (2) (3) (4). - Issued: 22.12.2006. Made: 14.12.2006. Laid: 22.12.2006. Laid before the Scottish Parliament: 22.12.2006. Coming into force: 29.01.2007. Effect: None. Territorial extent & classification: E/W/S. General. - 8p.: 30 cm. - 978-0-11-071418-9 £3.00

National Health Service, England

The Appointments Commission Regulations 2006 No. 2006/2380. - Enabling power: Health Act 2006, ss. 65, 79 (3), sch. 4, paras 2 (b) (d), 3 (3) (b), 7 (1) (2), 10 (3) (c) (5) (6), 18 (2) (b). - Issued: 11.09.2006. Made: 04.09.2006. Laid: 05.09.2006. Coming into force: 01.10.2006. Effect: S.I. 2001/794 revoked. Territorial extent & classification: E/W/S/NI [parts E. only]. General. - 12p.: 30 cm. - 978-0-11-075076-7 £3.00

The Birmingham Children's Hospital National Health Service Trust (Establishment) Amendment Order 2006 No. 2006/366. - Enabling power: National Health Service Act 1977, s. 126 (3) & National Health Service and Community Care Act 1990, s. 5 (1), sch. 2, paras. 3 (1) (b) (c). - Issued: 21.02.2006. Made: 15.02.2006. Coming into force: 25.02.2006. Effect: S.I. 1994/3182 amended. Territorial extent & classification: E. General. - 2p.: 30 cm. - 978-0-11-074066-9 £3.00

The Buckinghamshire Mental Health National Health Service Trust (Dissolution) Order 2006 No. 2006/785. - Enabling power: National Health Service Act 1977, s. 126 (3) & National Health Service and Community Care Act 1990, sch. 2, para. 29 (1). - Issued: 21.03.2006. Made: 14.03.2006. Coming into force: 01.04.2006. Effect: S.I. 2001/333 revoked. Territorial extent & classification: E. General. - 2p.: 30 cm. - 978-0-11-074343-1 £3.00

The City and Hackney Primary Care Trust (Establishment) Amendment Order 2006 No. 2006/2076. - Enabling power: National Health Service Act 1977, ss. 16A (1) (2) (3), 126 (3) (4). - Issued: 31.07.2006. Made: 24.07.2006. Coming into force: 05.08.2006. Effect: S.I. 2001/272 amended. Territorial extent & classification: E. General. - 2p.: 30 cm. - 978-0-11-074956-3 *£3.00*

The Commission for Patient and Public Involvement in Health (Membership and Procedure) (Amendment) Regulations 2006 No. 2006/486. - Enabling power: National Health Service Reform and Health Care Professions Act 2002, s. 38 (7), sch. 6, para. 5. - Issued: 03.03.2006. Made: 24.02.2006. Laid: 03.03.2006. Coming into force: 01.04.2006. Effect: S.I. 2002/3038 amended. Territorial extent & classification: E. General. - 2p.: 30 cm. - 978-0-11-074115-4 *£3.00*

The Coventry and Warwickshire Partnership National Health Service Trust (Establishment) Regulations 2006 No. 2006/2524. - Enabling power: National Health Service and Community Care Act 1990, s. 5 (1), sch. 2, para 3. - Issued: 19.09.2006. Made: 14.09.2006. Coming into force: 01.10.2006. Effect: None. Territorial extent & classification: E. General. - 2p.: 30 cm. - 978-0-11-075116-0 *£3.00*

The Doncaster and South Humberside Healthcare National Health Service Trust (Transfer of Trust Property) Order 2006 No. 2006/200. - Enabling power: National Health Service Act 1977, ss. 92 (1), 96 (1), 126 (4)- Issued: 08.02.2006. Made: 25.01.2006. Laid: 08.02.2006. Coming into force: 15.03.2006. Effect: None. Territorial extent & classification: E. General. - 2p.: 30 cm. - 978-0-11-073968-7 *£3.00*

The East Midlands Ambulance Service National Health Service Trust (Establishment) Order 2006 No. 2006/1620. - Enabling power: National Health Service and Community Care Act 1990, s. 5 (1), sch. 2, paras 1, 3. - Issued: 22.06.2006. Made: 15.06.2006. Coming into force: 01.07.2006. Effect: None. Territorial extent & classification: E. General. - 2p.: 30 cm. - 978-0-11-074725-5 *£3.00*

The East of England Ambulance Service National Health Service Trust (Establishment) Order 2006 No. 2006/1619. - Enabling power: National Health Service and Community Care Act 1990, s. 5 (1), sch. 2, paras 1, 3. - Issued: 22.06.2006. Made: 15.06.2006. Coming into force: 01.07.2006. Effect: None. Territorial extent & classification: E. General. - 2p.: 30 cm. - 978-0-11-074724-8 *£3.00*

The Functions of Primary Care Trusts and Strategic Health Authorities and the NHS Business Services Authority (Awdurdod Gwasanaethau Busnes y GIG) (Primary Dental Services) (England) Regulations 2006 No. 2006/596. - Enabling power: National Health Service Act 1977, ss. 16, 16B, 18 (3), 126 (4). - Issued: 10.03.2006. Made: 03.03.2006. Laid: 10.03.2006. Coming into force: 01.04.2006. Effect: None. Territorial extent & classification: E. General. - 20p.: 30 cm. - 978-0-11-074185-7 *£3.50*

The Functions of Primary Care Trusts (Dental Public Health) (England) Regulations 2006 No. 2006/185. - Enabling power: National Health Service Act 1977, s. 16CB (1). - Issued: 06.02.2006. Made: 26.01.2006. Laid: 06.02.2006. Coming into force: 01.04.2006. Effect: None. Territorial extent & classification: E. General. - 2p.: 30 cm. - 978-0-11-073966-3 *£3.00*

The Great Western Ambulance Service National Health Service Trust (Establishment) and the Avon Ambulance Service National Health Service Trust, the Gloucestershire Ambulance Service National Health Service Trust and the Wiltshire Ambulance Service National Health Service Trust (Dissolution) Order 2006 No. 2006/788. - Enabling power: National Health Service Act 1977, s. 126 (3) & National Health Service and Community Care Act 1990, s. 5 (1), sch. 2, paras 3, 29 (1). - Issued: 21.03.2006. Made: 14.03.2006. Coming into force: 01.04.2006. Effect: S.I. 1991/2320, 2352; 1992/2503 revoked. Territorial extent & classification: E. General. - 4p.: 30 cm. - 978-0-11-074346-2 *£3.00*

The Health and Social Care Act 2001 (Commencement No. 14) (England) Order 2006 No. 2006/481 (C.12). - Enabling power: Health and Social Care Act 2001, ss. 64 (6), 70. Bringing into operation various provisions of the 2001 Act on 28.02.2006; 01.04.2006 in accord. with art. 2. - Issued: 01.03.2006. Made: 26.02.2006. Effect: None. Territorial extent & classification: E. General. - With correction slip dated April 2006. - 4p.: 30 cm. - 978-0-11-074108-6 *£3.00*

The Health Authorities (Membership and Procedure) Amendment (England) Regulations 2006 No. 2006/1393. - Enabling power: National Health Service Act 1977, s. 126 (4), sch. 5, paras 2, 12. - Issued: 02.06.2006. Made: 24.05.2006. Laid: 02.06.2006. Coming into force: 01.07.2006. Effect: S.I. 1996/707 amended in relation to England. Territorial extent & classification: E. General. - 2p.: 30 cm. - 978-0-11-074621-0 *£3.00*

The Health Service Commissioner for England (Special Health Authorities) (Revocation) Order 2006 No. 2006/3332. - Enabling power: Health Service Commissioners Act 1993, s. 2 (5) (b) (6). - Issued: 22.12.2006. Made: 14.12.2006. Laid: 22.12.2006. Coming into force: 22.01.2007. Effect: S.I. 1983/1115; 1994/2954; 2004/1119 revoked. Territorial extent & classification: E. General. - 2p.: 30 cm. - 978-0-11-075510-6 *£3.00*

The Isle of Wight National Health Service Primary Care Trust (Establishment) and Isle of Wight Healthcare National Health Service Trust and Isle of Wight Primary Care Trust (Dissolution) Order 2006 No. 2006/2537. - Enabling power: National Health Service Act 1977, ss. 16A (1) (2) (3), 126 (3) (4), sch. 5A, para. 1 & National Health Service and Community Care Act 1990, sch. 2, para. 29 (1). - Issued: 26.09.2006. Made: 20.09.2006. Coming into force: 01.10.2006. Effect: S.I. 1996/2768; 2002/2982 revoked. Territorial extent & classification: E. General. - 4p.: 30 cm. - 978-0-11-075127-6 *£3.00*

The Kent and Medway National Health Service and Social Care Partnership Trust (Establishment) and the West Kent National Health Service and Social Care Trust and the East Kent National Health Service and Social Care Partnership Trust (Dissolution) Order 2006 No. 2006/825. - Enabling power: National Health Service Act 1977, s. 126 (3) & National Health Service and Community Care Act 1990, s. 5 (1), sch. 2, paras 3, 29 (1). - Issued: 21.03.2006. Made: 14.03.2006. Coming into force: 01.04.2006. Effect: S.I. 1992/2529; 1998/845; 2002/1337; 2003/1496 revoked. Territorial extent & classification: E. General. - 4p.: 30 cm. - 978-0-11-074359-2 £3.00

The London Ambulance Service National Health Service Trust (Establishment) Amendment Order 2006 No. 2006/1628. - Enabling power: National Health Service Act 1977, s. 126 (3) & National Health Service and Community Care Act 1990, s. 5 (1), sch. 2, paras 1, 3. - Issued: 22.06.2006. Made: 15.06.2006. Coming into force: 01.07.2006. Effect: S.I. 1996/90 amended. Territorial extent & classification: E. General. - 2p.: 30 cm. - 978-0-11-074727-9 £3.00

The Medway Primary Care Trust (Establishment) Amendment (Consequential Amendments on Variation of Area) Order 2006 No. 2006/2538. - Enabling power: National Health Service Act 1977, ss. 16A (1) (2) (3), 126 (3) (4). - Issued: 26.09.2006. Made: 20.09.2006. Coming into force: 01.10.2006. Effect: S.I. 2006/2073 amended. Territorial extent & classification: E. General. - With correction slip dated February 2007. - 8p.: 30 cm. - 978-0-11-075128-3 £3.00

The Medway Primary Care Trust (Establishment) Amendment Order 2006 No. 2006/2073. - Enabling power: National Health Service Act 1977, ss. 16A (1) (2) (3), 126 (3) (4). - Issued: 31.07.2006. Made: 24.07.2006. Coming into force: 01.10.2006. Effect: S.I. 2002/960 amended. Territorial extent & classification: E. General. - With correction slip dated February 2007. - 2p.: 30 cm. - 978-0-11-074951-8 £3.00

The Middlesbrough Primary Care Trust (Establishment) Amendment (Consequential Amendments on Variation of Area) Order 2006 No. 2006/2539. - Enabling power: National Health Service Act 1977, ss. 16A (1) (2) (3), 126 (3) (4). - Issued: 26.09.2006. Made: 20.09.2006. Coming into force: 01.10.2006. Effect: S.I. 2006/2074 amended. Territorial extent & classification: E. General. - 8p.: 30 cm. - 978-0-11-075129-0 £3.00

The Middlesbrough Primary Care Trust (Establishment) Amendment Order 2006 No. 2006/2074. - Enabling power: National Health Service Act 1977, ss. 16A (1) (2) (3), 126 (3) (4). - Issued: 31.07.2006. Made: 24.07.2006. Coming into force: 01.10.2006. Effect: S.I. 2002/138 amended. Territorial extent & classification: E. General. - 2p.: 30 cm. - 978-0-11-074952-5 £3.00

The National Health Service (Charges for Drugs and Appliances) and (Travel Expenses and Remission of Charges) Amendment Regulations 2006 No. 2006/675. - Enabling power: National Health Service Act 1977, ss. 77, 83A, 126 (4). - Issued: 14.03.2006. Made: 10.03.2006. Laid: 10.03.2006. Coming into force: 01.04.2006. Effect: S.I. 1987/1967; 2000/620; 2003/2382 amended. Territorial extent & classification: E. General. - 4p.: 30 cm. - 978-0-11-074259-5 £3.00

The National Health Service (Charges to Overseas Visitors) (Amendment) Regulations 2006 No. 2006/3306. - Enabling power: National Health Service Act 1977, ss. 121, 126 (4). - Issued: 19.12.2006. Made: 11.12.2006. Laid: 18.12.2006. Coming into force: 15.01.2007. Effect: S.I.1989/306 amended. Territorial extent & classification: E. General. - 2p.: 30 cm. - 978-0-11-075481-9 £3.00

The National Health Service (Clinical Negligence Scheme) Amendment (No. 2) Regulations 2006 No. 2006/3087. - Enabling power: National Health Service Act 1977, s. 126 (4) & National Health Service and Community Care Act 1990, s. 21. - Issued: 24.11.2006. Made: 20.11.2006. Laid: 20.11.2006. Coming into force: 22.11.2006. Effect: S.I. 1996/251 amended & S.I. 2006/2390 revoked. Territorial extent & classification: E. General. - This statutory instrument has been made in consequence of a defect in S.I. 2006/2390 (ISBN 0110750888) and is being issued free of charge to all known recipients of that Statutory Instrument. - 4p.: 30 cm. - 978-0-11-075343-0 £3.00

The National Health Service (Clinical Negligence Scheme) (Amendment) Regulations 2006 No. 2006/2390. - Enabling power: National Health Service Act 1977, s. 126 (4) & National Health Service and Community Care Act 1990, s. 21. - Issued: 12.09.2006. Made: 06.09.2006. Laid: 08.09.2006. Coming into force: 01.10.2006. Effect: S.I. 1996/251 amended. Territorial extent & classification: E. General. - Revoked by S.I. 2006/3087 (ISBN 0110753437). - 4p.: 30 cm. - 978-0-11-075088-0 £3.00

The National Health Service (Complaints) Amendment Regulations 2006 No. 2006/2084. - Enabling power: Health and Social Care (Community Health and Standards) Act 2003, ss. 113 (1) (3) (4), 115 (1) (2) (5) (6), 195 (1). - Issued: 01.08.2006. Made: 27.07.2006. Laid: 01.08.2006. Coming into force: 01.09.2006. Effect: S.I. 2004/1768 amended. Territorial extent & classification: E. General. - 8p.: 30 cm. - 978-0-11-074961-7 £3.00

The National Health Service (Dental Charges) Amendment Regulations 2006 No. 2006/1837. - Enabling power: National Health Service Act 1977, ss. 79, 126 (4). - Issued: 13.07.2006. Made: 11.07.2006. Laid: 13.07.2006. Coming into force: 10.08.2006. Effect: S.I. 2005/3477 amended. Territorial extent & classification: E. General. - This Statutory Instrument has been printed to correct an error in S.I. 2005/3477 and is being issued free of charge to all known recipients of that Statutory Instrument. - 2p.: 30 cm. - 978-0-11-074830-6 £3.00

The National Health Service (Functions of Strategic Health Authorities and Primary Care Trusts and Administration Arrangements) (England) (Amendment) Regulations 2006 No. 2006/359. - Enabling power: National Health Service Act 1977, ss. 16D, 17, 18, 126 (3) (4). - Issued: 24.02.2006. Made: 14.02.2006. Laid: 24.02.2006. Coming into force: 01.04.2006. Effect: S.I. 2002/2375 amended. Territorial extent & classification: E. General. - 4p.: 30 cm. - 978-0-11-074064-5 £3.00

The National Health Service (General Dental Services Contracts and Personal Dental Services Agreements) Amendment Regulations 2006 No. 2006/563. - Enabling power: National Health Service Act 1977, ss. 28E, 28O, 126 (4). - Issued: 10.03.2006. Made: 03.03.2006. Laid: 10.03.2006. Coming into force: 01.04.2006. Effect: S.I. 2005/3361, 3373 amended. Territorial extent & classification: E. General. - This Statutory Instrument has been printed to correct errors in Statutory Instruments 2005/3361 and 3373 and is being issued free of charge to all known recipients of those Statutory Instruments. - 4p.: 30 cm. - 978-0-11-074168-0 £3.00

The National Health Service (General Ophthalmic Services etc.) Amendment Regulations 2006 No. 2006/1550. - Enabling power: National Health Service Act 1977, ss. 38, 39, 43D, 49I, 126 (4). - Issued: 21.06.2006. Made: 14.06.2006. Laid: 21.06.2006. Coming into force: 19.07.2006. Effect: S.I. 1986/975; 2005/480 amended. Territorial extent & classification: E. General. - 8p.: 30 cm. - 978-0-11-074710-1 £3.00

The National Health Service (Local Pharmaceutical Services etc.) Regulations 2006 No. 2006/552. - Enabling power: National Health Service Act 1977, ss. 42 (2A), 126 (4), sch. 8A, paras 1 (3), 2 (1), 3, 4 & Health and Social Care Act 2001, ss. 30, 34, 37 (b), 41, 65 (1) (2), sch. 2, para. 1 (2) (b). - Issued: 08.03.2006. Made: 02.03.2006. Laid: 08.03.2006. Coming into force: 01.04.2006. Effect: 1977 c.49; 1993 c.46; S.I. 1990/2024; 1995/2801; 2000/89, 620, 1763; 2001/3798; 2002/888, 2016; 2003/2277; 2004/1768; 2005/641 amended. Territorial extent & classification: E. General. - 44p.: 30 cm. - 978-0-11-074153-6 £7.50

The National Health Service (Miscellaneous Amendments Relating to Independent Prescribing) Regulations 2006 No. 2006/913. - Enabling power: National Health Service Act 1977, ss. 41, 42, 77, 83A, 126(4), sch. 8A, para. 3. - Issued: 03.04.2006. Made: 23.03.2006. Laid: 03.04.2006. Coming into force: 01.05.2006. Effect: S.I. 2000/620; 2005/641; 2006/552 amended. Territorial extent & classification: E. General. - 8p.: 30 cm. - 978-0-11-074396-7 £3.00

The National Health Service (Optical Charges and Payments) Amendment (No.2) Regulations 2006 No. 2006/3123. - Enabling power: National Health Service Act 1977, ss. 38, 78 (1), 126 (4), sch. 12, paras 2, 2A. - Issued: 04.12.2006. Made: 22.11.2006. Laid: 29.11.2006. Coming into force: 20.12.2006. Effect: S.I. 1997/818 amended. Territorial extent & classification: E. General. - 2p.: 30 cm. - 978-0-11-075373-7 £3.00

The National Health Service (Optical Charges and Payments) Amendment Regulations 2006 No. 2006/479. - Enabling power: National Health Service Act 1977, s. 126 (4), sch. 12, para. 2A. - Issued: 13.03.2006. Made: 23.02.2006. Laid: 02.03.2006. Coming into force: 01.04.2006. Effect: S.I. 1997/818 amended. Territorial extent & classification: E. General. - 4p.: 30 cm. - 978-0-11-074101-7 £3.00

The National Health Service (Performers Lists) Amendment Regulations 2006 No. 2006/1385. - Enabling power: National Health Service Act 1977, ss. 28X, 126 (4). - Issued: 02.06.2006. Made: 23.05.2006. Laid: 02.06.2006. Coming into force: 03.07.2006. Effect: S.I. 2004/585 amended. Territorial extent & classification: E. General. - 2p.: 30 cm. - 978-0-11-074609-8 £3.00

The National Health Service (Pharmaceutical Services) (Amendment) Regulations 2006 No. 2006/3373. - Enabling power: National Health Service Act 1977, ss. 41, 42, 43, 126 (4), sch. 8A, para.3. - Issued: 20.12.2006. Made: 13.12.2006. Laid: 18.12.2006. Coming into force: 19.01.2007. Effect: S.I. 2005/641; 2006/552 amended. Territorial extent & classification: E. General. - 12p.: 30 cm. - 978-0-11-075530-4 £3.00

The National Health Service (Primary Medical Services and Pharmaceutical Services) (Miscellaneous Amendments) Regulations 2006 No. 2006/1501. - Enabling power: National Health Service Act 1977, ss. 28E, 28V, 42, 43, 126 (4). - Issued: 16.06.2006. Made: 05.06.2006. Laid: 16.06.2006. Coming into force: 24.07.2006. Effect: S.I. 2004/291, 627; 2005/641 amended. Territorial extent & classification: E. General. - 8p.: 30 cm. - 978-0-11-074675-3 £3.00

The National Health Service (Travel Expenses and Remission of Charges) Amendment (No.2) Regulations 2006 No. 2006/2171. - Enabling power: National Health Service Act 1977, ss. 83A, 126 (4). - Issued: 11.08.2006. Made: 05.08.2006. Laid: 11.08.2006. Coming into force: 01.09.2006. Effect: S.I. 2003/2382 amended. Territorial extent & classification: E. General. - 4p.: 30 cm. - 978-0-11-074991-4 £3.00

The National Health Service (Travel Expenses and Remission of Charges) Amendment Regulations 2006 No. 2006/1065. - Enabling power: National Health Service Act 1977, ss. 83A, 126 (4). - Issued: 10.04.2006. Made: 05.04.2006. Laid: 10.04.2006. Coming into force: 01.05.2006. Effect: S.I. 2003/2382 amended. Territorial extent & classification: E. General. - 2p.: 30 cm. - 978-0-11-074471-1 £3.00

The National Health Service Trusts (Dissolution) Order 2006 No. 2006/1618. - Enabling power: National Health Service Act 1977, s. 126 (3) (4) & National Health Service and Community Care Act 1990, s. 5 (1), sch. 2, paras 1, 29 (1). - Issued: 22.06.2006. Made: 15.06.2006. Coming into force: 01.07.2006. Effect: 25 SIs revoked. Territorial extent & classification: E. General. - 4p.: 30 cm. - 978-0-11-074723-1 £3.00

The North East Ambulance Service National Health Service Trust (Establishment) Order 2006 No. 2006/1621. - Enabling power: National Health Service and Community Care Act 1990, s. 5 (1), sch. 2, paras 1, 3. - Issued: 22.06.2006. Made: 15.06.2006. Coming into force: 01.07.2006. Effect: None. Territorial extent & classification: E. General. - 2p.: 30 cm. - 978-0-11-074726-2 £3.00

The Northumberland, Tyne and Wear National Health Service Trust (Establishment) and the South of Tyne and Wearside Mental Health National Health Service Trust, the Northgate and Prudhoe National Health Service Trust and the Newcastle, North Tyneside and Northumberland Mental Health National Health Service Trust (Dissolution) Order 2006 No. 2006/828. - Enabling power: National Health Service Act 1977, s. 126 (3) & National Health Service and Community Care Act 1990, s. 5 (1), sch. 2, paras 3, 29 (1). - Issued: 22.03.2006. Made: 16.03.2006. Coming into force: 01.04.2006. Effect: S.I. 1994/198; 2001/213; 2002/1324 revoked. Territorial extent & classification: E. General. - 4p.: 30 cm. - 978-0-11-074362-2 £3.00

The North West Ambulance Service National Health Service Trust (Establishment) Order 2006 No. 2006/1622. - Enabling power: National Health Service and Community Care Act 1990, s. 5 (1), sch. 2, paras 1, 3. - Issued: 22.06.2006. Made: 15.06.2006. Coming into force: 01.07.2006. Effect: None. Territorial extent & classification: E. General. - 2p.: 30 cm. - 978-0-11-074720-0 £3.00

The Nottingham University Hospitals National Health Service Trust (Establishment) and the Nottingham City Hospital National Health Service Trust and the Queen's Medical Centre, Nottingham, University Hospital National Health Service Trust (Dissolution) Order 2006 No. 2006/782. - Enabling power: National Health Service Act 1977, s. 126 (3) & National Health Service and Community Care Act 1990, s. 5 (1), sch. 2, paras 3, 29 (1). - Issued: 21.03.2006. Made: 15.03.2006. Coming into force: 01.04.2006. Effect: S.I. 1991/2380; 1992/2478; 1998/2947 revoked. Territorial extent & classification: E. General. - 4p.: 30 cm. - 978-0-11-074344-8 £3.00

The Nottingham University Hospitals National Health Service Trust (Transfer of Trust Property) Order 2006 No. 2006/2690. - Enabling power: National Health Service and Community Care Act 1990, s. 11 (3) & National Health Service Act 1977, s. 126 (4). - Issued: 16.10.2006. Made: 11.10.2006. Coming into force: 06.11.2006. Effect: None. Territorial extent & classification: E. General. - 2p.: 30 cm. - 978-0-11-075176-4 £3.00

The Nottingham University Hospitals National Health Service Trust (Trust Funds: Appointment of Trustees) Order 2006 No. 2006/1741. - Enabling power: National Health Service and Community Care Act 1990, s. 11 (1) (2)- Issued: 07.07.2006. Made: 01.07.2006. Coming into force: 20.07.2006. Effect: None. Territorial extent & classification: E. General. - 2p.: 30 cm. - 978-0-11-074789-7 £3.00

The Oxfordshire Mental Healthcare National Health Service Trust (Change of Name) (Establishment) Amendment Order 2006 No. 2006/787. - Enabling power: National Health Service Act 1977, s. 126 (3) (4) & National Health Service and Community Care Act 1990, s. 5 (1), sch. 2, paras 3 (1) (a) to (c). - Issued: 21.03.2006. Made: 14.03.2006. Coming into force: 01.04.2006. Effect: S.I. 1993/2566 amended. Territorial extent & classification: E. General. - 4p.: 30 cm. - 978-0-11-074342-4 £3.00

The Primary Care Trusts (Establishment and Dissolution) (England) Order 2006 No. 2006/2072. - Enabling power: National Health Service Act 1977, ss. 16A (1) (2) (3), 126 (3) (4), sch. 5A, para. 1. - Issued: 31.07.2006. Made: 24.07.2006. Coming into force: 01.10.2006. Effect: 245 SIs revoked. Territorial extent & classification: E. General. - 36p.: 30 cm. - 978-0-11-074950-1 £6.50

The Primary Care Trusts Establishment Orders (Amendment) (England) Order 2006 No. 2006/2077. - Enabling power: National Health Service Act 1977, ss. 16A (1) (2) (3), 126 (3) (4), sch. 5A, para. 1. - Issued: 31.07.2006. Made: 24.07.2006. Coming into force: 01.10.2006. Effect: 26 SIs amended & S.I. 2002/729 revoked. Territorial extent & classification: E. General. - 8p.: 30 cm. - 978-0-11-074955-6 £3.00

The Solihull Primary Care Trust (Change of Name) (Establishment) Amendment Order 2006 No. 2006/2526. - Enabling power: National Health Service Act 1977, ss. 16A (1) (2), 126 (3) (4), sch. 5A, para. 1 & Health and Social Care Act 2001. s. 45. - Issued: 20.09.2006. Made: 13.09.2006. Coming into force: 01.10.2006. Effect: S.I. 2001/211 amended. Territorial extent & classification: E. General. - 4p.: 30 cm. - 978-0-11-075118-4 £3.00

The South Central Ambulance Service National Health Service Trust (Establishment) Order 2006 No. 2006/1624. - Enabling power: National Health Service and Community Care Act 1990, s. 5 (1), sch. 2, paras 1, 3. - Issued: 22.06.2006. Made: 15.06.2006. Coming into force: 01.07.2006. Effect: None. Territorial extent & classification: E. General. - 2p.: 30 cm. - 978-0-11-074722-4 £3.00

The South East Coast Ambulance Service National Health Service Trust (Establishment) Order 2006 No. 2006/1623. - Enabling power: National Health Service and Community Care Act 1990, s. 5 (1), sch. 2, paras 1, 3. - Issued: 22.06.2006. Made: 15.06.2006. Coming into force: 01.07.2006. Effect: None. Territorial extent & classification: E. General. - 2p.: 30 cm. - 978-0-11-074721-7 £3.00

The South Western Ambulance Service National Health Service Trust (Establishment) Order 2006 No. 2006/1625. - Enabling power: National Health Service and Community Care Act 1990, s. 5 (1), sch. 2, paras 1, 3. - Issued: 22.06.2006. Made: 15.06.2006. Coming into force: 01.07.2006. Effect: None. Territorial extent & classification: E. General. - 2p.: 30 cm. - 978-0-11-074729-3 £3.00

The Special Trustees for the Queen's Medical Centre, Nottingham University Hospital National Health Service Trust (Transfer of Trust Property) Order 2006 No. 2006/2691. - Enabling power: National Health Service Act 1977, ss. 92 (6), 126 (4). - Issued: 16.10.2006. Made: 11.10.2006. Laid: 16.10.2006. Coming into force: 06.11.2006. Effect: None. Territorial extent & classification: E. General. - 4p.: 30 cm. - 978-0-11-075177-1 *£3.00*

The Strategic Health Authorities (Establishment and Abolition) (England) Amendment Order 2006 No. 2006/1448. - Enabling power: National Health Service Act 1977, ss. 8 (4), 126 (3) (4). - Issued: 07.06.2006. Made: 31.05.2006. Laid: 07.06.2006. Coming into force: 30.06.2006. Effect: S.I. 2006/1408 amended. Territorial extent & classification: E. General. - This Statutory Instrument has been made in consequence of a defect in SI 2006/1408 (ISBN 0110746236) and is being issued free of charge to all known recipients of that Statutory Instrument. - 2p.: 30 cm. - 978-0-11-074636-4 *£3.00*

The Strategic Health Authorities (Establishment and Abolition) (England) Order 2006 No. 2006/1408. - Enabling power: National Health Service Act 1977, ss. 8 (1), (2), (3), (4), (7) (8), 126 (3) (4). - Issued: 02.06.2006. Made: 25.05.2006. Laid: 02.06.2006. Coming into force: 01.07.2006. Effect: S.I. 2002/553; 2004/37 revoked. Territorial extent & classification: E. General. - This Statutory Instrument has been amended, due to a defect, by SI 2006/1448 (ISBN 0110746368) which is being issued free of charge to all known recipients of SI 2006/1408. - 8p.: 30 cm. - 978-0-11-074623-4 *£3.00*

The Surrey and Borders Partnership National Health Service Trust (Originating Capital) Order 2006 No. 2006/775. - Enabling power: National Health Service and Community Care Act 1990, s. 9 (1). - Issued: 21.03.2006. Made: 14.03.2006. Coming into force: 31.03.2006. Effect: None. Territorial extent & classification: E. General. - 2p.: 30 cm. - 978-0-11-074331-8 *£3.00*

The Sussex Partnership National Health Service Trust (Establishment) and the East Sussex County Healthcare National Health Service Trust and the West Sussex Health and Social Care National Health Service Trust (Dissolution) Order 2006 No. 2006/786. - Enabling power: National Health Service Act 1977, s. 126 (3) & National Health Service and Community Care Act 1990, s. 5 (1), sch. 2, paras 3, 29 (1). - Issued: 21.03.2006. Made: 14.03.2006. Coming into force: 01.04.2006. Effect: S.I. 1992/2534; 2002/1362, 2397 revoked. Territorial extent & classification: E. General. - 4p.: 30 cm. - 978-0-11-074345-5 *£3.00*

The Tees, Esk and Wear Valleys National Health Service Trust (Establishment) and the County Durham and Darlington Priority Services National Health Service Trust and the Tees and North East Yorkshire National Health Service Trust (Dissolution) Order 2006 No. 2006/827. - Enabling power: National Health Service Act 1977, s. 126 (3) & National Health Service and Community Care Act 1990, s. 5 (1), sch. 2, paras 3, 29 (1). - Issued: 22.03.2006. Made: 16.03.2006. Coming into force: 01.04.2006. Effect: S.I. 1998/829; 1999/60, 847 revoked. Territorial extent & classification: E. General. - 4p.: 30 cm. - 978-0-11-074364-6 *£3.00*

The West Midlands Ambulance Service National Health Service Trust (Establishment) Order 2006 No. 2006/1626. - Enabling power: National Health Service and Community Care Act 1990, s. 5 (1), sch. 2, paras 1, 3. - Issued: 22.06.2006. Made: 15.06.2006. Coming into force: 01.07.2006. Effect: None. Territorial extent & classification: E. General. - 2p.: 30 cm. - 978-0-11-074719-4 *£3.00*

The Yorkshire Ambulance Service National Health Service Trust (Establishment) Order 2006 No. 2006/1627. - Enabling power: National Health Service and Community Care Act 1990, s. 5 (1), sch. 2, paras 1, 3. - Issued: 22.06.2006. Made: 15.06.2006. Coming into force: 01.07.2006. Effect: None. Territorial extent & classification: E. General. - 2p.: 30 cm. - 978-0-11-074728-6 *£3.00*

National Health Service, England and Wales

The General Dental Services, Personal Dental Services and Abolition of the Dental Practice Board Transitional and Consequential Provisions Order 2006 No. 2006/562. - Enabling power: Health and Social Care (Community Health and Standards) Act 2003, ss. 173, 195, 200, 201. - Issued: 10.03.2006. Made: 03.03.2006. Laid: 10.03.2006. Coming into force: 01.04.2006. Effect: S.I. 1980/1924; 1990/2024; 1992/664; 1994/3144; 1996/707, 709; 1997/1830; 1999/2337; 2000/89, 620; 2001/3750; 2002/1920, 2375, 2469, 3048; 2003/1324, 2124, 2277, 2382, 2863; 2004/696, 865, 905, 1031, 1768; 2005/502, 641, 2435 amended & S.I. 1990/1638; 1991/580; 1992/655, 661, 1509; 1993/2209, 3172; 1995/3092; 1996/704, 2051; 1997/2289, 2929; 1998/3, 646, 1330, 1648, 2222, 2223, 2224; 2000/2459; 2001/289, 705, 1677, 1678, 1746, 2421, 3741, 3963; 2002/558; 2003/250, 1702 revoked. Territorial extent & classification: E/W. General. - 36p.: 30 cm. - 978-0-11-074174-1 *£6.50*

The Health Act 2006 (Commencement No. 1 and Transitional Provisions) Order 2006 No. 2006/2603 (C.88). - Enabling power: Health Act 2006, ss. 79 (3), 83 (3) (7) (8). Bringing into operation various provisions of the 2006 Act on 28.09.2006 and 01.10.2006. - Issued: 29.09.2006. Made: 22.09.2006. Effect: None. Territorial extent & classification: E/W. General. - 8p.: 30 cm. - 978-0-11-075136-8 *£3.00*

The Health Act 2006 (Commencement No.2) Order 2006 No. 2006/3125 (C.108). - Enabling power: Health Act 2006, s. 83 (7) (8). Bringing into operation various provisions of the 2006 Act on 01.01.2007; 29.01.2007; 28.02.2007; 01.03.2007 in accord. with arts 2 to 4. - Issued: 29.11.2006. Made: 21.11.2006. Effect: None. Territorial extent & classification: E/W/S [parts only to E/S; and parts only to E/W]. General. - 4p.: 30 cm. - 978-0-11-075372-0 £3.00

The Health and Social Care (Community Health and Standards) Act 2003 Commencement (No.3 and No.8) (Amendment) Order 2006 No. 2006/836 (C.22). - Enabling power: Health and Social Care (Community Health and Standards) Act 2003, s. 199 (1) (3). Bringing into operation various provisions of the 2003 Act on 01.04.2006; 01.04.2007 & 01.04.2008. - Issued: 27.03.2006. Made: 20.03.2006. Effect: S.I. 2004/759; 2005/2925 amended. Territorial extent & classification: E/W. General. - 4p.: 30 cm. - 978-0-11-074380-6 £3.00

The Health and Social Care (Community Health and Standards) Act 2003 Commencement (No. 9) Order 2006 No. 2006/1680 (C.57). - Enabling power: Health and Social Care (Community Health and Standards) Act 2003, ss. 195 (1), 199 (1). Bringing into operation various provisions of the 2003 Act on 27.06.2006; 01.09.2006. - Issued: 30.06.2006. Made: 26.06.2006. Effect: None. Territorial extent & classification: E/W. Applies in relation the England only apart from article 2 (2) which applies in relation to England and Wales. General. - 8p.: 30 cm. - 978-0-11-074762-0 £3.00

The Health and Social Care (Community Health and Standards) Act 2003 (Commencement) (No. 10) Order 2006 No. 2006/2817 (C.96). - Enabling power: Health and Social Care (Community Health and Standards) Act 2003, s. 199 (1). Bringing into operation various provisions of the 2003 Act on 27.10.2006 in accord. with art. 2. - Issued: 26.10.2006. Made: 23.10.2006. Effect: None. Territorial extent & classification: E/W. General. - 8p.: 30 cm. - 978-0-11-075217-4 £3.00

The Health and Social Care (Community Health and Standards) Act 2003 (Commencement) (No. 11) Order 2006 No. 2006/3397 (C.125). - Enabling power: Health and Social Care (Community Health and Standards) Act 2003, ss. 195 (1), 199 (1). Bringing into operation various provisions of the 2003 Act in accord. with art. 2, 3, 4, 5. - Issued: 21.12.2006. Made: 12.12.2006. Effect: None. Territorial extent & classification: E/W. General. - 8p.: 30 cm. - 978-0-11-075547-2 £3.00

The Health Service Commissioner for England (Special Health Authorities) Order 2006 No. 2006/305. - Enabling power: Health Service Commissioners Act 1993, s. 2 (5) (b) (6) (b). - Issued: 24.02.2006. Made: 14.02.2006. Laid: 24.02.2006. Coming into force: 01.04.2006. Effect: None. Territorial extent & classification: E. General (although this S.I. does bring a body that may carry out some functions in Wales within the jurisdiction of the Health Service Commissioner for England). - 2p.: 30 cm. - 978-0-11-074055-3 £3.00

The National Health Service (Pension Scheme and Compensation for Premature Retirement) Amendment Regulations 2006 No. 2006/2919. - Enabling power: Superannuation Act 1972, ss. 10 (1) (2), 12 (1) (2), 24 (1) (3) (4), sch. 3. - Issued: 13.11.2006. Made: 06.11.2006. Laid: 07.11.2006. Coming into force: 01.12.2006. Effect: S.I. 1995/300; 2002/1311 amended. Territorial extent & classification: E/W. General. - 8p.: 30 cm. - 978-0-11-075272-3 £3.00

The National Health Service (Pension Scheme, Injury Benefits and Additional Voluntary Contributions) Amendment Regulations 2006 No. 2006/600. - Enabling power: Superannuation Act 1972, ss. 10 (1) (2), 12 (1) (2) (3), sch. 3. - Issued: 10.03.2006. Made: 07.03.2006. Laid: 10.03.2006. Coming into force: 01.04.2006 & 06.04.2006 in accord. with reg. 1 (2). Effect: S.I. 1995/300, 866; 2000/619 amended. Territorial extent & classification: E/W. General. - 24p.: 30 cm. - 978-0-11-074187-1 £4.00

The National Health Service (Pre-consolidation Amendments) Order 2006 No. 2006/1407. - Enabling power: National Health Service Reform and Health Care Professions Act 2002, ss. 36, 38. - Issued: 31.05.2006. Made: 25.05.2006. Coming into force: In accord. with art. 1 (1). Effect: 1977 c.49 & 17 other Acts & 6 SIs amended & 1919 c. 21 repealed & S.I. 1999/2795 revoked. Territorial extent & classification: E/W. General. - Supersedes draft S.I. (ISBN 0110745183) issued on 26.04.2006. - 16p.: 30 cm. - 978-0-11-074620-3 £3.00

The NHS Blood and Transplant (Gwaed a Thrawsblaniadau'r GIG) (Amendment) Regulations 2006 No. 2006/640. - Enabling power: National Health Service Act 1977, ss. 126 (4), sch. 5, para 12. - Issued: 14.03.2006. Made: 09.03.2006. Laid: 10.03.2006. Coming into force: 01.04.2006. Effect: S.I. 2005/2531 amended. Territorial extent & classification: E/W. General. - 4p.: 30 cm. - 978-0-11-074211-3 £3.00

The NHS Business Services Authority (Awdurdod Gwasanaethau Busnes y GIG) (Amendment) Regulations 2006 No. 2006/633. - Enabling power: National Health Service Act 1977, s. 126 (4), sch. 5, para 12. - Issued: 14.03.2006. Made: 08.03.2006. Laid: 10.03.2006. Coming into force: 01.04.2006. Effect: S.I. 2005/2415 amended. Territorial extent & classification: E/W. General. - 4p.: 30 cm. - 978-0-11-074216-8 £3.00

The NHS Business Services Authority (Awdurdod Gwasanaethau Busnes y GIG) (Establishment and Constitution) (Amendment) Order 2006 No. 2006/632. - Enabling power: National Health Service Act 1977, ss. 11 (1) (2) (4), 126 (3) (4). - Issued: 15.03.2006. Made: 08.03.2006. Laid: 10.03.2006. Coming into force: 01.04.2006. Effect: S.I. 2005/2414 amended. Territorial extent & classification: E/W. General. - 4p.: 30 cm. - 978-0-11-074263-2 £3.00

The NHS Pensions Agency (Asiantaeth Pensiynau'r GIG) Abolition Order 2006 No. 2006/634. - Enabling power: National Health Service Act 1977, ss. 11 (1) (2) (4), 126 (3) (4). - Issued: 15.03.2006. Made: 08.03.2006. Laid: 10.03.2006. Coming into force: 01.04.2006. Effect: S.I. 2004/1714; 2005/251 amended & S.I. 2004/667, 668 revoked. Territorial extent & classification: E/W. General. - With correction slip dated April 2006. - 4p.: 30 cm. - 978-0-11-074245-8 £3.00

The Personal Injuries (NHS Charges) (General) and Road Traffic (NHS Charges) (Amendment) Regulations 2006 No. 2006/3388. - Enabling power: Road Traffic (NHS Charges) Act 1999, s. 16 (2) & Health and Social Care (Community Health and Standards) Act 2003, ss. 151 (8) (9), 153 (10) (11), 160 (1) to (3), 162 (3), 163, 164 (4), 195 (1) (2), sch. 10, para. 8. - Issued: 21.12.2006. Made: 12.12.2006. Laid: 19.12.2006. Coming into force: 29.01.2007. Effect: S.I. 2005/475 amended. Territorial extent & classification: E/W. General. - 8p.: 30 cm. - 978-0-11-075548-9 £3.00

The Personal Injuries (NHS Charges) (Reviews and Appeals) and Road Traffic (NHS Charges) (Reviews and Appeals) (Amendment) Regulations 2006 No. 2006/3398. - Enabling power: Road Traffic (NHS Charges) Act 1999, ss. 7 (4), 16 (2) and Health and Social Care (Community Health and Standards) Act 2003, ss. 153 (2) (5) (7) (8), 163 (1), 195 (1) (2). - Issued: 21.12.2006. Made: 12.12.2006. Laid: 19.12.2006. Coming into force: 29.01.2007. Effect: S.I. 1999/786 amended. Territorial extent & classification: E/W. General. - 12p.: 30 cm. - 978-0-11-075549-6 £3.00

The Public Benefit Corporation (Register of Members) Amendment Regulations 2006 No. 2006/361. - Enabling power: Health and Social Care (Community Health and Standards) Act 2003, s. 195 (2), sch. 1, para. 22 (3). - Issued: 22.02.2006. Made: 15.02.2006. Laid: 22.02.2006. Coming into force: 23.03.2006. Effect: S.I. 2004/539 amended. Territorial extent & classification: E/W. General. - 2p.: 30 cm. - 978-0-11-074063-8 £3.00

The Road Traffic (NHS Charges) Amendment Regulations 2006 No. 2006/401. - Enabling power: Road Traffic (NHS Charges) Act 1999, ss. 3 (2) (4), 16 (2), 17. - Issued: 28.02.2006. Made: 19.02.2006. Laid: 28.02.2006. Coming into force: 01.04.2006. Effect: S.I. 1999/785 amended. Territorial extent & classification: E/W. General. - 2p.: 30 cm. - 978-0-11-074089-8 £3.00

The Special Health Authorities Abolition Order 2006 No. 2006/635. - Enabling power: National Health Service Act 1977, ss. 11 (1) (2) (4), 126 (3) (4). - Issued: 15.03.2006. Made: 08.03.2006. Laid: 10.03.2006. Coming into force: 01.04.2006. Effect: 23 instruments amended in accord. with schedule 2 & S.I. 1990/1718, 1719; 1991/2001, 2002; 1993/2210, 2211; 1995/2457; 2000/603; 2002/3039, 3040 revoked. Territorial extent & classification: E/W. General. - 12p.: 30 cm. - 978-0-11-074243-4 £3.00

National Health Service, Scotland

The Smoking, Health and Social Care (Scotland) Act 2005 (Consequential Modifications) (England, Wales and Northern Ireland) Order 2006 No. 2006/1056. - Enabling power: Scotland Act 1998, ss. 104, 112 (1), 113. - Issued: 12.04.2006. Made: 31.03.2006. Coming into force: In accord with art 1 (2). Effect: 1968 c.46; 1977 c.37, c.49; 1988 c.48; 1990 c.19; 1992 c.52; 1996 c.18 modified & S.I. 1992/662; 2001/1358 (W.86); 2004/1765; 2005/641 amended. Territorial extent & classification: E/W/NI [the modifications have the same extent as the legislation modified, but exclude Scotland in each case]. General. - 8p.: 30 cm. - 978-0-11-070258-2 £3.00

National Health Service, Wales

The Community Health Council (Establishment of Carmarthenshire Community Health Council, Transfer of Functions and Abolition of Llanelli/Dinefwr and Carmarthen/Dinefwr Community Health Councils) Order 2006 No. 2006/942 (W.91). - Enabling power: National Health Service Act 1977, ss. 16BB (4), 20A (2), 126 (4), sch. 7A, para. 2. - Issued: 07.04.2006. Made: 28.03.2006. Coming into force: 01.04.2006. Effect: None. Territorial extent & classification: W. General. - In English & Welsh. Welsh title: Gorchymyn Cyngor Iechyd Cymuned (Sefydlu Cyngor Iechyd Cymuned Sir Gaerfyrddin, Trosglwyddo Swyddogaethau a Diddymu Cynghorau Iechyd Cymuned Llanelli/Dinefwr a Chaerfyrddin/Dinefwr) 2006. - 8p.: 30 cm. - 978-0-11-091311-7 £3.00

The Functions of Local Health Boards and the NHS Business Services Authority (Awdurdod Gwasanaethau Busnes y GIG) (Primary Dental Services) (Wales) Regulations 2006 No. 2006/941 (W.90). - Enabling power: National Health Service Act 1977, ss. 16BB, 16BC, 18 (3), 126 (4). - Issued: 25.04.2006. Made: 28.03.2006. Coming into force: 01.04.2006. Effect: None. Territorial extent & classification: W. General. - 20p.: 30 cm. - 978-0-11-091326-1 £3.50

The Functions of Local Health Boards (Dental Public Health) (Wales) Regulations 2006 No. 2006/487 (W.56). - Enabling power: National Health Service Act 1977, ss. 16CB (2), 126. - Issued: 07.03.2006. Made: 28.02.2006. Coming into force: 01.03.2006. Effect: None. Territorial extent & classification: W. General. - 4p.: 30 cm. - 978-0-11-091285-1 £3.00

The General Dental Services and Personal Dental Services Transitional and Consequential Provisions (Wales) Order 2006 No. 2006/946 (W.95). - Enabling power: Health and Social Care (Community Health and Standards) Act 2003, ss. 173, 195, 200, 201. - Issued: 18.04.2006. Made: 28.03.2006. Coming into force: 01.04.2006. Effect: S.I. 2006/488 (W.57) & S.I. 1990/2024; 1992/662, 664; 1996/707; 2001/1358, 3750 amended in relation to Wales & 25 SI's revoked. Territorial extent & classification: W. General. - 28p.: 30 cm. - 978-0-11-091325-4 £4.50

The General Dental Services and Personal Dental Services Transitional Provisions) (Wales) Order 2006 No. 2006/488 (W.57). - Enabling power: Health and Social Care (Community Health and Standards) Act 2003, ss. 173, 195, 200, 201. - Issued: 07.03.2006. Made: 28.02.2006. Coming into force: 03.03.2006. Effect: S.I. 1992/661 amended in relation to Wales. Territorial extent & classification: W. General. - 20p.: 30 cm. - 978-0-11-091284-4 £3.50

The General Medical Services Transitional and Consequential Provisions (Wales) (Amendment) Order 2006 No. 2006/360 (W.47) . - Enabling power: Health and Social Care (Community Health and Standards) Act 2003, s. 200. - Issued: 28.02.2006. Made: 14.02.2006. Coming into force: 01.03.2006. Effect: S.I. 2004/1016 (W.113) amended. Territorial extent & classification: W. General. - In English and Welsh. Welsh title: Gorchymyn Darpariaethau Trosiannol a Chanlyniadol y Gwasanaethau Meddygol Cyffredinol (Cymru) (Diywygio) 2006. - 4p.: 30 cm. - 978-0-11-091281-3 £3.00

The Health and Social Care (Community Health and Standards) Act 2003 Commencement (Wales) (No. 4) Order 2006 No. 2006/345 (W.42) (C.8). - Enabling power: Health and Social Care (Community Health and Standards) Act 2003, ss. 195 (1), 199 (1). Bringing into operation certain provisions of the 2003 Act on 15.02.2006 & 01.04.2006, in accord. with arts. 2 to 7. - Issued: 28.02.2006. Made: 14.02.2006. Effect: S.I. 2004/480 (W.49) amended. Territorial extent & classification: W. General. - 12p.: 30 cm. - 978-0-11-091280-6 £3.00

The Healthy Start Scheme (Description of Healthy Start Food) (Wales) Regulations 2006 No. 2006/3108 (W.287). - Enabling power: Social Security Act 1988, s. 13 (1) (6). - Issued: 30.11.2006. Made: 22.11.2006. Coming into force: 27.11.2006. Effect: None. Territorial extent & classification: W. General. - In English and Welsh. Welsh title: Rheoliadau'r Cynllun Cychwyn Iach (Disgrifio Bwyd Cychwyn Iach) (Cymru) 2006. - 4p.: 30 cm. - 978-0-11-091455-8 £3.00

The Local Health Boards (Establishment) (Wales) (Amendment) Order 2006 No. 2006/1790 (W.186). - Enabling power: National Health Service Act 1977, ss. 16BA (1) (2) (3), 126 (4), sch. 5B, para. 1. - Issued: 12.07.2006. Made: 04.07.2006. Coming into force: 06.07.2006. Effect: S.I. 2003/148 (W. 18) amended. Territorial extent & classification: W. General. - Welsh title: Gorchymyn Byrddau Iechyd Lleol (Sefydlu) (Cymru) (Diwygio) 2006. - In English and Welsh. - 4p.: 30 cm. - 978-0-11-091380-3 £3.00

The National Health Service (Charges for Drugs and Appliances) (Wales) (Amendment) (No. 2) Regulations 2006 No. 2006/1792 (W.188). - Enabling power: National Health Service Act 1977, ss. 77, 83, 83A, 126 (4), sch. 12, para. 1. - Issued: 14.07.2006. Made: 04.07.2006. Coming into force: 01.08.2006. Effect: S.I. 2001/1358 (W.86) amended. Territorial extent & classification: W. General. - In English & WelshWelsh title: Rheoliadau'r Gwasanaeth Iechyd Gwladol (Ffioedd am Gyffuriau a Chyfarpar) (Cymru) (Diwygio) (Rhif 2) 2006. - 8p.: 30 cm. - 978-0-11-091385-8 £3.00

The National Health Service (Charges for Drugs and Appliances) (Wales) (Amendment) Regulations 2006 No. 2006/943 (W.92). - Enabling power: National Health Service Act 1977, ss. 77, 83, 83A, 126 (4). - Issued: 05.04.2006. Made: 28.03.2006. Coming into force: 01.04.2006. Effect: S.I. 2001/1358 (W.86) amended. Territorial extent & classification: W. General. - In English & WelshWelsh title: Rheoliadau'r Gwasanaeth Iechyd Gwladol (Ffioedd am Gyffuriau a Chyfarpar) (Cymru) (Diwygio) 2006. - 8p.: 30 cm. - 978-0-11-091309-4 £3.00

The National Health Service (Dental Charges) (Wales) (Amendment) Regulations 2006 No. 2006/3366 (W.308). - Enabling power: National Health Service Act 1977, ss. 79, 126 (4). - Issued: 22.12.2006. Made: 13.12.2006. Coming into force: 15.12.2006. Effect: S.I. 2006/491 (W.60) amended. Territorial extent & classification: W. General. - In English and Welsh. Welsh title: Rheoliadau'r Gwasanaeth Iechyd Gwladol (Ffioedd Deintyddol) (Cymru) (Diwygio) 2006. - 4p.: 30 cm. - 978-0-11-091481-7 £3.00

The National Health Service (Dental Charges) (Wales) Regulations 2006 No. 2006/491 (W.60). - Enabling power: National Health Service Act 1977, ss. 79, 83A, 126 (4), sch. 12ZA. - Issued: 07.03.2006. Made: 28.02.2006. Coming into force: 01.04.2006. Effect: S.I. 1989/394; 1993/419; 1998/2221; 2000/977; 2001/1359 (W. 87); 2003/138 (W.10) revoked. Territorial extent & classification: W. General. - 16p.: 30 cm. - 978-0-11-091283-7 £3.00

The National Health Service (General Dental Services Contracts and Personal Dental Services Agreements) (Amendment) (Wales) Regulations 2006 No. 2006/947 (W.96). - Enabling power: National Health Service Act 1977, ss. 28E, 28O, 126 (4). - Issued: 25.04.2006. Made: 29.03.2006. Coming into force: 01.04.2006. Effect: S.I. 2006/489 (W.58), 490 (W.59) amended. Territorial extent & classification: W. General. - 4p.: 30 cm. - 978-0-11-091327-8 £3.00

The National Health Service (General Dental Services Contracts) (Wales) Regulations 2006 No. 2006/490 (W.59). - Enabling power: National Health Service Act 1977, ss. 28L, 28M, 28O, 28P, 126 (4) & National Health Service and Community Care Act 1990, s. 4 (5). - Issued: 08.03.2006. Made: 28.02.2006. Coming into force: 01.03.2006. Effect: None. Territorial extent & classification: W. General. - 60p.: 30 cm. - 978-0-11-091286-8 £9.00

The National Health Service (General Ophthalmic Services Supplementary List) and (General Ophthalmic Services) (Amendment and Consequential Amendment) (Wales) Regulations 2006 No. 2006/181 (W.32). - Enabling power: National Health Service Act 1977, ss. 38, 39, 43ZA, 43D, 49F, 49I, 49M, 49N, 49O, 49P, 49Q, 49R, 126 (4) & Health and Social Care Act 2001, s. 65. - Issued: 24.02.2006. Made: 31.01.2006. Coming into force: 01.02.2006 & 01.08.2006 in accord. with art. 1 (1) (2). Effect: S.I. 1986/975; 1997/818 amended in relation to Wales. Territorial extent & classification: W. General. - In English and Welsh. Welsh title: Rheoliadau'r Gwasanaeth Iechyd Gwladol (Rhestr Atodol Gwasanaethau Offthalmig Cyffredinol) a (Gwasanaethau Offthalmig Cyffredinol) (Diwygio a Diwygiad Canlyniadol) (Cymru) 2006. - 76p.: 30 cm. - 978-0-11-091279-0 *£12.00*

The National Health Service (Optical Charges and Payments) (Amendment) (Wales) Regulations 2006 No. 2006/1749 (W.181). - Enabling power: National Health Service Act 1977, s. 126 (4), sch. 12, para. 2A. - Issued: 12.07.2006. Made: 04.07.2006. Coming into force: 05.07.2006. Effect: S.I. 1997/818 amended in relation to Wales. Territorial extent & classification: W. General. - In English and Welsh. Welsh title: Rheoliadau'r Gwasanaeth Iechyd Gwladol (Ffioedd a Thaliadau Optegol) (Diwygio) (Cymru) 2006. - 8p.: 30 cm. - 978-0-11-091379-7 *£3.00*

The National Health Service (Performers Lists) (Wales) (Amendment) Regulations 2006 No. 2006/945 (W.94). - Enabling power: National Health Service Act 1977, ss. 28X, 126 (4). - Issued: 05.04.2006. Made: 28.03.2006. Coming into force: 01.04.2006. Effect: S.I. 1986/975; 2004/478 (W.48), 668, 1020 (W.117); 2005/2415, 2531; 2006/181 (W.32) amended. Territorial extent & classification: W. General. - 16p.: 30 cm. - 978-0-11-091307-0 *£3.00*

The National Health Service (Personal Dental Services Agreements) (Wales) Regulations 2006 No. 2006/489 (W.58). - Enabling power: National Health Service Act 1977, ss. 28D, 28E, 126 (4) & National Health Service and Community Care Act 1990, s. 4 (5). - Issued: 08.03.2006. Made: 28.02.2006. Coming into force: 01.03.2006. Effect: None. Territorial extent & classification: W. General. - 56p.: 30 cm. - 978-0-11-091289-9 *£9.00*

National Health Service (Pharmaceutical Services) (Amendment) (Wales) Regulations 2006 No. 2006/2985 (W.275). - Enabling power: National Health Service Act 1977, ss. 42, 43, 126 (4). - Issued: 27.11.2006. Made: 15.11.2006. Coming into force: 16.11.2006. Effect: S.I. 1992/662 amended in relation to Wales. Territorial extent & classification: W. General. - In English and Welsh. Welsh title: Rheoliadau'r Gwasanaeth Iechyd Gwladol (Gwasanaethau Fferyllol) (Diwygio) (Cymru) 2006. - 4p.: 30 cm. - 978-0-11-091447-3 *£3.00*

The National Health Service (Primary Medical Services) (Miscellaneous Amendments) (Wales) Regulations 2006 No. 2006/358 (W.46). - Enabling power: National Health Service Act 1977, ss. 28R, 28S, 28V, 28W, 28X, 126 (4) & National Health Service and Community Care Act 1990, s. 4 (5). - Issued: 24.02.2006. Made: 14.02.2006. Coming into force: 01.03.2006. Effect: S.I. 2004/478 (W.48), 1020 (W.117) amended. Territorial extent & classification: W. General. - In English and Welsh. Welsh title: Rheoliadau'r Gwasanaeth Iechyd Gwladol (Gwasanaeth Meddygol Sylfaenol) (Diwygiadau Amrywiol) (Cymru) 2006. - 24p.: 30 cm. - 978-0-11-091277-6 *£4.00*

The National Health Service (Travelling Expenses and Remission of Charges) (Amendment) (No. 2) (Wales) Regulations 2006 No. 2006/2791 (W.232). - Enabling power: National Health Service Act 1977, ss. 83A, 126 (4). - Issued: 25.10.2006. Made: 17.10.2006. Coming into force: 18.10.2006. Effect: S.I. 1988/551 amended in relation to Wales. Territorial extent & classification: W. General. - In English and Welsh. Welsh title: Rheoliadau'r Gwasanaeth Iechyd Gwladol (Treuliau Teithio a Pheidio â Chodi Tâl) (Diwygio) (Rhif 2) (Cymru) 2006. - 8p.: 30 cm. - 978-0-11-091407-7 *£3.00*

The National Health Service (Travelling Expenses and Remission of Charges) (Amendment) (Wales) Regulations 2006 No. 2006/1389 (W.139). - Enabling power: National Health Service Act 1977, ss. 83A, 126 (4), 128 (1). - Issued: 01.06.2006. Made: 23.05.2006. Coming into force: 24.06.2006. Effect: S.I. 1988/551 amended in relation to Wales. Territorial extent & classification: W. General. - In English and Welsh. Welsh title: Rheoliadau'r Gwasanaeth Iechyd Gwladol (Treuliau Teithio a Pheidio â Chodi Tâl) (Diwygio) (Cymru) 2006. - 4p.: 30 cm. - 978-0-11-091345-2 *£3.00*

National lottery

The Big Lottery Fund (Prescribed Expenditure) Order 2006 No. 2006/3202. - Enabling power: National Lottery etc. Act 1993, ss. 22 (3A) (3B), 36B (3) (4). - Issued: 07.12.2006. Made: 30.11.2006. Coming into force: In accord. with art. 1 (1). Effect: None. Territorial extent & classification: E/W/S/NI. General. - Supersedes draft SI (ISBN 0110751795) issued 17.10.2006. - 4p.: 30 cm. - 978-0-11-075410-9 *£3.00*

The National Endowment for Science, Technology and the Arts (Increase of Endowment) Order 2006 No. 2006/396. - Enabling power: National Lottery Act 1998, s. 19 (2). - Issued: 23.02.2006. Made: 16.02.2006. Coming into force: 17.02.2006. Effect: None. Territorial extent & classification: E/W/S/NI. General. - Supersedes draft (ISBN 011073887X) issued 12,01.2006. - 2p.: 30 cm. - 978-0-11-074085-0 *£3.00*

The National Lottery Act 2006 (Commencement No. 1) Order 2006 No. 2006/2177 (C.73). - Enabling power: National Lottery Act 2006, s. 22. Bringing into operation various provisions of the 2006 Act on 01.08.2006. - Issued: 11.08.2006. Made: 31.07.2006. Effect: None. Territorial extent & classification: E/W/S/NI. General. - 2p.: 30 cm. - 978-0-11-074992-1 £3.00

The National Lottery Act 2006 (Commencement No. 2 and Transitional Provisions) Order 2006 No. 2006/2630 (C.89). - Enabling power: National Lottery Act 2006, s. 22. Bringing into operation various provisions of the 2006 Act on 01.10.2006. - Issued: 09.10.2006. Made: 23.09.2006. Effect: None. Territorial extent & classification: E/W/S/NI. General. - 4p.: 30 cm. - 978-0-11-075148-1 £3.00

The National Lottery Act 2006 (Commencement No. 3) Order 2006 No. 2006/3201 (C.113). - Enabling power: National Lottery Act 2006, s. 22. Bringing into operation various provisions of the 2006 Act on 01.12.2006. - Issued: 07.12.2006. Made: 30.11.2006. Effect: None. Territorial extent & classification: E/W/S/NI. General. - 4p.: 30 cm. - 978-0-11-075409-3 £3.00

The National Lottery Distributors Dissolution Order 2006 No. 2006/2915. - Enabling power: National Lottery etc. Act 1993, s. 43B, sch. 5, para. 1, sch. 6, para. 2, sch. 6A, para. 1 & National Lottery Act 2006, s. 16. - Issued: 10.11.2006. Made: 05.11.2006. Laid: 07.11.2006. Coming into force: In accord. with art. 1. Effect: S.I. 1999/1878; 2000/3355; 2003/2869, 3033; 2005/1102, 2470, 3235 revoked. Territorial extent & classification: E/W/S/NI. General. - 4p.: 30 cm. - 978-0-11-075265-5 £3.00

The National Lottery etc. Act 1993 (Amendment of Section 23) Order 2006 No. 2006/654. - Enabling power: National Lottery etc. Act 1993, ss. 29 (1) (d) (4), 60 (5). - Issued: 16.03.2006. Made: 08.03.2006. Laid: 10.03.06. Coming into force: 01.04.06. Effect: 1993 c. 39 amended. Territorial extent & classification: E/W/S/NI. General. - 2p.: 30 cm. - 978-0-11-074236-6 £3.00

National lottery, England

The Awards for All (England) Joint Scheme (Authorisation) Order 2006 No. 2006/565. - Enabling power: National Lottery etc. Act 1993, sch. 3A, paras 2 (1), 3, 6 (1). - Issued: 10.03.2006. Made: 04.03.2006. Laid: 06.03.2006. Coming into force: 01.04.2006. Effect: S.I. 2005/374 revoked. Territorial extent & classification: E. General. - 4p.: 30 cm. - 978-0-11-074170-3 £3.00

The Transformational Grants Joint Scheme (Revocation) Order 2006 No. 2006/3146. - Enabling power: National Lottery etc. Act 1993, sch. 3A, para. 2 (1). - Issued: 01.12.2006. Made: 22.11.2006. Laid: 27.11.2006. Coming into force: 01.12.2006. Effect: S.I. 2005/608 revoked. Territorial extent & classification: E. General. - 2p.: 30 cm. - 978-0-11-075380-5 £3.00

Natural environment, England and Wales

The Natural Environment and Rural Communities Act 2006 (Commencement No.1) Order 2006 No. 2006/1176 (C.40). - Enabling power: Natural Environment and Rural Communities Act 2006, s. 107. Bringing into operation various provisions of the 2006 Act on 02.05.2006. - Issued: 02.05.2006. Made: 18.04.2006. Effect: None. Territorial extent & classification: E/W/NI (art. 4 to E/W; art. 5 to E/W/NI; art. 6 to E only). General. - 4p.: 30 cm. - 978-0-11-074528-2 £3.00

The Natural Environment and Rural Communities Act 2006 (Commencement No. 2) Order 2006 No. 2006/1382 (C.47). - Enabling power: Natural Environment and Rural Communities Act 2006, s. 107. Bringing into operation various provisions of the 2006 Act on 31.05.2006. - Issued: 26.05.2006. Made: 19.05.2006. Effect: None. Territorial extent & classification: E/W. General. - 2p.: 30 cm. - 978-0-11-074604-3 £3.00

The Natural Environment and Rural Communities Act 2006 (Commencement No. 3 and Transitional Provisions) Order 2006 No. 2006/2541 (C.86). - Enabling power: Natural Environment and Rural Communities Act 2006, s. 107 (2) (6) (b) (7) (b) (8) (b) (c). Bringing into operation various provisions of the 2006 Act on 01.10.2006, in accord. with art. 2. - Issued: 28.09.2006. Made: 20.09.2006. Effect: None. Territorial extent & classification: UK [but parts E/W only]. General. - 8p.: 30 cm. - 978-0-11-075132-0 £3.00

Natural environment, Northern Ireland

The Natural Environment and Rural Communities Act 2006 (Commencement No.1) Order 2006 No. 2006/1176 (C.40). - Enabling power: Natural Environment and Rural Communities Act 2006, s. 107. Bringing into operation various provisions of the 2006 Act on 02.05.2006. - Issued: 02.05.2006. Made: 18.04.2006. Effect: None. Territorial extent & classification: E/W/NI (art. 4 to E/W; art. 5 to E/W/NI; art. 6 to E only). General. - 4p.: 30 cm. - 978-0-11-074528-2 £3.00

Nature conservation

The Natural Environment and Rural Communities Act 2006 (Commencement No. 3 and Transitional Provisions) Order 2006 No. 2006/2541 (C.86). - Enabling power: Natural Environment and Rural Communities Act 2006, s. 107 (2) (6) (b) (7) (b) (8) (b) (c). Bringing into operation various provisions of the 2006 Act on 01.10.2006, in accord. with art. 2. - Issued: 28.09.2006. Made: 20.09.2006. Effect: None. Territorial extent & classification: UK [but parts E/W only]. General. - 8p.: 30 cm. - 978-0-11-075132-0 £3.00

Nature conservation, England and Wales

The Natural Environment and Rural Communities Act 2006 (Commencement No. 2) Order 2006 No. 2006/1382 (C.47). - Enabling power: Natural Environment and Rural Communities Act 2006, s. 107. Bringing into operation various provisions of the 2006 Act on 31.05.2006. - Issued: 26.05.2006. Made: 19.05.2006. Effect: None. Territorial extent & classification: E/W. General. - 2p.: 30 cm. - 978-0-11-074604-3 *£3.00*

Northern Ireland

The Budget (No. 2) (Northern Ireland) Order 2006 No. 2006/1916 (N.I.12). - Enabling power: Northern Ireland Act 2000, sch., para. 1 (1). - Issued: 26.07.2006. Made: 19.07.2006. Coming into force: In accord. with art. 1. Effect: S.I. 2003/429 (N.I.7), 1885 (N.I.14) repealed. Territorial extent & classification: NI. General- An explanatory memorandum is available separately (ISBN 033796596X). - 24p.: 30 cm. - 978-0-11-080043-1 *£4.00*

The Budget (Northern Ireland) Order 2006 No. 2006/613 (N.I.6). - Enabling power: Northern Ireland Act 2000, sch. para. 1 (1). - Issued: 16.03.2006. Made: 08.03.2006. Coming into operation: In accord. with art. 1. Effect: None. Territorial extent & classification: NI. General. - 36p.: 30 cm. - 978-0-11-080026-4 *£6.00*

The Disability Discrimination (Northern Ireland) Order 2006 No. 2006/312 (N.I.1). - Enabling power: Northern Ireland Act 2000, sch. 1, para 1 (1). - Issued: 22.02.2006. Made: 14.02.2006. Coming into force: In accord. with art. 1 (2). Effect: 1995 c. 50 amended. Territorial extent & classification: NI. General- With correction slip, dated August 2006. An explanatory memorandum, produced by the Office of the First Minister and Deputy First Minister, is available separately (ISBN 0337963592). For approval by resolution of each House of Parliament. - 60p.: 30 cm. - 978-0-11-080020-2 *£8.50*

The Education (Northern Ireland) Order 2006 No. 2006/1915 (NI.11). - Enabling power: Northern Ireland Act 2000, sch., para. 1 (1). - Issued: 28.07.2006. Made: 19.07.2006. Coming into operation: In accord. with art. 1 (2) to (7). Effect: 1949 c. 2 & S.I. 1986/594 (N.I.3); 1989/2406 (N.I.20); 1993/2810 (N.I.12); 1996/274 (N.I.1); 1997/866 (N.I.5), 1772 (N.I.15); 1998/1759 (N.I.13); 2003/424 (N.I.12); 2005/147 (N.I.6) amended. Territorial extent & classification: NI. General. - Supersedes draft SI (ISBN 0110800419) issued 28.06.2006. An explanatory memorandum is available separately (ISBN 0337965951). - iv, 44p.: 30 cm. - 978-0-11-080048-6 *£7.00*

The Electricity Consents (Planning) (Northern Ireland) Order 2006 No. 2006/2955 (N.I. 19). - Enabling power: Northern Ireland Act 2000, sch., para. 1 (1). - Issued: 21.11.2006. Made: 14.11.2006. Coming into operation: In accord. with art. 1 (2). Effect: S.I. 1992/231 (N.I. 1) amended. Territorial extent & classification: NI. General. - Explanatory memorandum is also available (ISBN 0337967210). Supersedes draft SI (ISBN 0110800516) issued 10.10.2006. - 8p.: 30 cm. - 978-0-11-080056-1 *£3.00*

The Fire and Rescue Services (Northern Ireland) Order 2006 No. 2006/1254 (N.I.9). - Enabling power: Northern Ireland Act 2000, sch. para. 1 (1). - Issued: 17.05.2006. Made: 09.05.2006. Coming into force: In accord.with art. 1. Effect: 12 Acts & 15 S.I.s amended & S.I. 1984/1821 (N.I. 11); 1993/1578 (N.I. 7); 1998/1549 (N.I. 11) revoked. Territorial extent & classification: NI. General- An explanatory memorandum, produced by the Department of Health, Social Services and Public Safety, is available separately (ISBN 0337965013). Superseded by the SI of same number (ISBN 0110800370) issued on 02.06.2006. - 52p.: 30 cm. - 978-0-11-080035-6 *£7.00*

The Fire and Rescue Services (Northern Ireland) Order 2006 No. 2006/1254 (N.I.9). - Enabling power: Northern Ireland Act 2000, sch. para. 1 (1). - Issued: 02.06.2006. Made: 24.05.2006. Coming into force: In accord.with art. 1 (2) (3). Effect: 12 Acts & 15 S.I.s amended & S.I. 1984/1821 (N.I. 11); 1993/1578 (N.I. 7); 1998/1549 (N.I. 11) revoked. Territorial extent & classification: NI. General. - EC note: Makes provision for implementing in part Council Directives 89/391/EEC, 89/654/EEC, 91/383/EEC, 94/33/EC, 98/24/EC and 99/92/EC. An explanatory memorandum, produced by the Department of Health, Social Services and Public Safety, is available separately (ISBN 0337965013). This Statutory Instrument has been printed in substitution of the SI of the same number (issued on 17.05.2006 as ISBN 0110800354) and is being issued free of charge to all known recipients of that Statutory Instrument. - iv, 48p.: 30 cm. - 978-0-11-080037-0 *£7.00*

The Housing (Amendment) (Northern Ireland) Order 2006 No. 2006/3337 (N.I. 22). - Enabling power: Northern Ireland Act 2000, sch., para. 1 (1). - Issued: 20.12.2006. Made: -. Coming into operation: In accord. with art. 1 (2) (3). Effect: 2000 c.17; 2003 c.14; S.I. 1992/1725 (N.I. 15) amended. Territorial extent & classification: NI. General. - Supersedes draft S.I. (ISBN 0110800540) issued on 21.11.2006. - 8p.: 30 cm. - 978-0-11-080064-6 *£3.00*

The Industrial and Provident Societies (Northern Ireland) Order 2006 No. 2006/314 (N.I.3). - Enabling power: Northern Ireland Act 2000, sch. 1, para 1 (1). - Issued: 22.02.2006. Made: 14.02.2006. Coming into force: In accord. with art. 1 (2) (3). Effect: 1969 c. 24; S.I. 1986/1035 (NI.9); S.I. 2002/3150 (NI.14) amended. Territorial extent & classification: NI. General- 16p.: 30 cm. - 978-0-11-080022-6 *£3.00*

The Law Reform (Miscellaneous Provisions) (Northern Ireland) Order 2006 No. 2006/1945 (N.I.14). - Enabling power: Northern Ireland Act 2000, sch. para. 1 (1). - Issued: 27.07.2006. Made: 19.07.2006. Coming into force: In accord. with art. 1 (3). Effect: 1968 c.34; 2004 c. 7, 33; S.I. 1984/1984 (NI. 14); 1993/1576 (NI.6) amended. Territorial extent & classification: NI. General- Supersedes draft SI (ISBN 0110800397) issued 13.06.2006. An explanatory memorandum is available separately (ISBN 0337965943). - 8p.: 30 cm. - 978-0-11-080046-2 £3.00

The Local Government (Boundaries) (Northern Ireland) Order 2006 No. 2006/1253 (N.I.8). - Enabling power: Northern Ireland Act 2000, sch. para. 1 (1). - Issued: 15.05.2006. Made: 09.05.2006. Coming into force: In accord. with art. 1 (2) to (4). Effect: 1972 c. 9 amended & S.I. 1992/810 (NI.6) amended & 1971 c.9 repealed & S.I. 1990/2149 revoked. Territorial extent & classification: NI. General. - An explanatory memorandum, produced by the Department of the Environment, is available separately (ISBN 033796503X). - 16p.: 30 cm. - 978-0-11-080033-2 £3.00

The Northern Ireland Act 1998 (Modification) Order 2006 No. 2006/2659. - Enabling power: Northern Ireland Act 1998, s. 87 (7). - Issued: 24.10.2006. Made: 10.10.2006. Laid: 24.10.2006. Coming into force: 15.11.2006. Effect: 1998 c.47 modified. Territorial extent & classification: E/W/S/NI. General. - 4p.: 30 cm. - 978-0-11-075172-6 £3.00

The Northern Ireland Act 2000 (Modification) (No. 2) Order 2006 No. 2006/2132. - Enabling power: Northern Ireland Act 2000, sch., para. 1 (4). - Issued: 04.08.2006. Made: 28.07.2006. Coming into force: 29.07.2006. Effect: 2000 c.1 modified. Territorial extent & classification: NI. General. - Supersedes draft S.I. (ISBN 0110746074) issued 25.05.2006. - 2p.: 30 cm. - 978-0-11-074967-9 £3.00

The Northern Ireland Act 2000 (Modification) Order 2006 No. 2006/1012. - Enabling power: Northern Ireland Act 2000, sch., para. 1 (4). - Issued: 06.04.2006. Made: 30.03.2006. Coming into force: 31.3.2006. Effect: 2000 c.1 modified. Territorial extent & classification: NI. General. - Supersedes draft instrument (ISBN 0110741226) issued 03.03.2006. - 2p.: 30 cm. - 978-0-11-074454-4 £3.00

Northern Ireland Arms Decommissioning Act 1997 (Amnesty Period) Order 2006 No. 2006/480. - Enabling power: Northern Ireland Arms Decommissioning Act 1997, s. 2 (2) (b). - Issued: 03.03.2006. Made: 23.02.2006. Coming into force: 24.02.2006. Effect: S.I. 2005/418 revoked. Territorial extent & classification: NI. General. - 2p.: 30 cm. - 978-0-11-074106-2 £3.00

The Northern Ireland (Miscellaneous Provisions) Act 2006 (Commencement No. 1) Order 2006 No. 2006/2688 (C.91). - Enabling power: Northern Ireland (Miscellaneous Provisions) Act 2006, s. 31 (3). Bringing operation various provisions of the 2006 Act on 16.10.2006 & 01.12.2006 in accord. with arts. 2 & 3. - Issued: 13.10.2006. Made: 09.10.2006. Effect: None. Territorial extent & classification: NI. General. - 2p.: 30 cm. - 978-0-11-075169-6 £3.00

The Northern Ireland (Miscellaneous Provisions) Act 2006 (Commencement No. 3) Order 2006 No. 2006/3263 (C. 118). - Enabling power: Northern Ireland (Miscellaneous Provisions) Act 2006, s. 31 (3). Bringing into operation various provisions of the 2005 Act on 10.12.2006, in accord. with art. 2. - Issued: 12.12.2006. Made: 07.12.2006. Effect: None. Territorial extent & classification: NI. General. - 2p.: 30 cm. - 978-0-11-075443-7 £3.00

The Planning Reform (Northern Ireland) Order 2006 No. 2006/1252 (N.I. 7). - Enabling power: Northern Ireland Act 2000, sch. para. 1 (1). - Issued: 17.05.2006. Made: 09.05.2006. Coming into force: In accord. with art. 1 (2) to (5). Effect: 1969 c. 35 (NI) amended & S.I. 1991/1220 (N.I. 11); 1997/1772 (N.I. 15); 2003/430 (N.I. 8) amended. Territorial extent & classification: NI. General- An explanatory memorandum, produced by the Department of the Environment, is available separately (ISBN 0337965021). - 60p.: 30 cm. - 978-0-11-080034-9 £8.50

The Police and Criminal Evidence (Northern Ireland) Order 1989 (Codes of Practice) (Temporary Modification to Code D) Order 2006 No. 2006/1081. - Enabling power: S.I. 1989/1341 (N.I. 12), art. 66 (6A). - Issued: 18.04.2006. Made: 07.04.2006. Laid: 12.04.2006. Coming into force: 12.05.2006. Effect: The code of practice for the identification of persons by police officers ("Code D"), issued under S.I. 1989/1341 (N.I. 12), art. 65, modified. Territorial extent & classification: NI. General. - 20p.: 30 cm. - 978-0-11-074489-6 £3.50

The Private Tenancies (Northern Ireland) Order 2006 No. 2006/1459 (N.I.10). - Enabling power: Northern Ireland Act 2000, sch. para. 1 (1). - Issued: 15.06.2006. Made: 07.06.2006. Coming into force: In accord. with art. 1 (2) (3). Effect: 1970 c.18; 1992 c.9; 2001 c.10; 2004 c.33 & S.I. 1978/1050 (N.I. 20); 1981/156 (N.I. 3); 1983/1118 (N.I. 15); 1986/1301 (N.I. 13); 1992/1725 (N.I. 15); 1996/1298 (N.I. 8); 1998/1071 (N.I. 6); 2003/412 (N.I. 2) amended. Territorial extent & classification: NI. General- An explanatory memorandum, prepared by the Department for Social Development, is available separately (ISBN 0337965498). - 40p.: 30 cm. - 978-0-11-080040-0 £6.00

The Rates (Amendment) (Northern Ireland) Order 2006 No. 2006/2954 (N.I. 18). - Enabling power: Northern Ireland Act 2000, sch., para. 1 (1). - Issued: 22.11.2006. Made: 14.11.2006. Coming into operation: In accordance with art. 1. Effect: 1975 c.25 amended & S.I. 1977/2157 (N.I.28); 1978/1050 (N.I.20); 1979/297 (N.I.4); 1981/437 (N.I.13); 1982/338 (N.I.6); 1983/421 (N.I.7); 1996/3162 (N.I.25); 2004/703 (N.I.4); 2006/611 (N.I.4) amended. Territorial extent & classification: NI. General. - Explanatory memorandum is also available (ISBN 0337967229). Supersedes the draft S.I. (ISBN 0110800524) issued on 10.10.2006. - 56p.: 30 cm. - 978-0-11-080058-5 £9.00

The Rates (Capital Values, etc.) (Northern Ireland) Order 2006 No. 2006/611 (N.I.4). - Enabling power: Northern Ireland Act 2000, sch. para. 1 (1). - Issued: 16.03.2006. Made: 08.03.2006. Coming into operation: In accord. with art. 1 (2) (3). Effect: S.I. 1977/2157 (N.I. 28); 1979/297 (N.I. 4); 1994/1987 (N.I. 11) amended. Territorial extent & classification: NI. General. - 16p.: 30 cm. - 978-0-11-080027-1 £3.00

The Recovery of Health Services Charges (Northern Ireland) Order 2006 No. 2006/1944 (N.I.13). - Enabling power: Northern Ireland Act 2000, sch. para. 1 (1). - Issued: 27.07.2006. Made: 19.07.2006. Coming into force: In accord. with art. 1 (2) (3). Effect: 2001 c.3; S.I. 1981/154 (NI. 1) amended. Territorial extent & classification: NI. General- Supersedes draft SI (ISBN 0110800362) issued 24.05.2006. An explanatory memorandum is available separately (ISBN 0337965978). - 24p.: 30 cm. - 978-0-11-080047-9 £4.00

The Safety of Sports Grounds (Northern Ireland) Order 2006 No. 2006/313 (N.I.2). - Enabling power: Northern Ireland Act 2000, sch. 1, para 1 (1). - Issued: 22.02.2006. Made: 14.02.2006. Coming into force: In accord. with art. 1 (2)(3). Effect: None. Territorial extent & classification: NI. General- An explanatory memorandum, produced by the Department of Culture, Arts and Leisure, is available separately (ISBN 0337963606). For approval by resolution of each House of Parliament. - 24p.: 30 cm. - 978-0-11-080021-9 £4.00

The Smoking (Northern Ireland) Order 2006 No. 2006/2957 (N.I. 20). - Enabling power: Northern Ireland Act 2000, sch. para. 1 (1). - Issued: 21.11.2006. Made: 14.11.2006. Coming into operation: In accord. with art. 1 (2) (3). Effect: 1967 c. 37 amended. Territorial extent & classification: NI. General. - Supersedes draft SI (ISBN 0110800427) issued 04.07.2006. - 16p.: 30 cm. - 978-0-11-080057-8 £3.00

The Stormont Estate (Northern Ireland) Order 2006 No. 2006/612 (N.I. 5). - Enabling power: Northern Ireland Act 2000, sch. para. 1 (1). - Issued: 16.03.2006. Made: 08.03.2006. Coming into operation: 09.02.2006 in accord. with art. 1 (2). Effect: None. Territorial extent & classification: NI. General. - 8p.: 30 cm. - 978-0-11-080028-8 £3.00

The Terrorism Act 2000 (Revised Code of Practice for the Identification of Persons by Police Officers) (Northern Ireland) Order 2006 No. 2006/1330. - Enabling power: Terrorism Act 2000, s. 101 (4). - Issued: 19.05.2006. Made: 11.05.2006. Coming into force: 12.05.2006. Effect: None. Territorial extent & classification: NI. General. - Supersedes draft S.I. (ISBN 011074280X) issued 17.03.2006. - 2p.: 30 cm. - 978-0-11-074579-4 £3.00

The Victims and Survivors (Northern Ireland) Order 2006 No. 2006/2953 (N.I. 17). - Enabling power: Northern Ireland Act 2000, sch., para. 1 (1). - Issued: 21.11.2006. Made: 14.11.2006. Coming into operation: In accord. with art. 1 (2) to (4). Effect: 1975 c. 25; 2000 c. 36 & S.I. 1996/1297 (N.I.7) amended. Territorial extent & classification: NI. General. - Supersedes Draft SI (ISBN 0110800508) issued 10.10.2006. - 12p.: 30 cm. - 978-0-11-080055-4 £3.00

The Water and Sewerage Services (Miscellaneous Provisions) (Northern Ireland) Order 2006 No. 2006/1946 (N.I.15). - Enabling power: Northern Ireland Act 2000, sch. para. 1 (1). - Issued: 28.07.2006. Made: 19.07.2006. Coming into operation: 01.08.2006. Effect: S.I. 1999/662 (N.I.6) amended. Territorial extent & classification: NI. General. - Supersedes draft SI (ISBN 0110800389) issued 07.06.2006. An explanatory memorandum, prepared jointly by the Department for Regional Development and the Department of the Environment, is available separately (ISBN 0337966028). - 12p.: 30 cm. - 978-0-11-080045-5 £3.00

The Water and Sewerage Services (Northern Ireland) Order 2006 No. 2006/3336 (N.I.21). - Enabling power: Northern Ireland Act 2000, sch. para. 1 (1). - Issued: 28.12.2006. Made: 14.12.2006. Coming into operation: In accord. with art. 1 (2) to (4). Effect: 66 Acts & S.I.s amended & 1966 c.31 repealed & S.I. 1973/70 (N.I.2); 1985/756 (N.I.7); 1987 (N.I.21); 1993/3165 (N.I.16) revoked. Territorial extent & classification: NI. General. - Supersedes draft SI (ISBN 0110800494) issued 10.10.2006. - 316p.: 30 cm. - 978-0-11-080065-3 £32.00

The Work and Families (Northern Ireland) Order 2006 No. 2006/1947 (N.I.16). - Enabling power: Northern Ireland Act 2000, sch., para. 1 (1). - Issued: 26.07.2006. Made: 19.07.2006. Laid: 26.07.2006. Coming into force: In accord. with art. 1 (2) (3). Effect: 1992 c.7; 2002 c.10; S.I. 1989/1342 (N.I.13); 1996/1919 (N.I.16); 2002/2836 (N.I.2) amended. Territorial extent & classification: NI. General. - An explanatory memorandum, prepared by the Department for Employment and Learning, is available (ISBN 0337965935). - 24p.: 30 cm. - 978-0-11-080044-8 £4.00

Nurses and midwives

The Nurses and Midwives (Parts of and Entries in the Register) Amendment Order of Council 2006 No. 2006/1015. - Enabling power: S.I. 2002/253, art. 6. - Issued: 07.04.2006. Made: 03.04.2006. Laid: 04.04.2006. Coming into force: 01.05.2006. Effect: S.I. 2004/1765 amended. Territorial extent & classification: E/W/S/NI. General. - 2p.: 30 cm. - 978-0-11-074455-1 £3.00

The Nursing and Midwifery Council (Practice Committees) (Constitution) Rules Order of Council 2006 No. 2006/1199. - Enabling power: S.I. 2002/253, arts. 47 (2), sch. 1, para. 17. - Issued: 17.05.2006. Made: 19.04.2006. Laid: 02.05.2006. Coming into force: 31.07.2006. Effect: S.I. 2003/1738 revoked. Territorial extent & classification: E/W/S/NI. General. - 8p.: 30 cm. - 978-0-11-074541-1 £3.00

Offshore installations

The Offshore Installations (Safety Zones) (No.2) Order 2006 No. 2006/952. - Enabling power: Petroleum Act 1987, s. 22 (1) (2). - Issued: 04.04.2006. Made: 29.03.2006. Coming into force: 19.04.2006. Effect: None. Territorial extent & classification: E/W/S. General. - 2p.: 30 cm. - 978-0-11-074415-5 £3.00

The Offshore Installations (Safety Zones) (No.3) Order 2006 No. 2006/1949. - Enabling power: Petroleum Act 1987, s. 22 (1) (2). - Issued: 24.07.2006. Made: 18.07.2006. Laid before the Parliament: -. Coming into force: 08.08.2006. Effect: None. Territorial extent & classification: E/W/S. General. - 2p.: 30 cm. - 978-0-11-074878-8 £3.00

The Offshore Installations (Safety Zones) (No.4) Order 2006 No. 2006/2794. - Enabling power: Petroleum Act 1987, s. 22 (1) (2). - Issued: 25.10.2006. Made: 18.10.2006. Coming into force: 08.08.2006. Effect: None. Territorial extent & classification: E/W/S. General. - 2p.: 30 cm. - 978-0-11-075202-0 £3.00

The Offshore Installations (Safety Zones) Order 2006 No. 2006/356. - Enabling power: Petroleum Act 1987, s. 22 (1) (2). - Issued: 20.02.2006. Made: 15.02.2006. Coming into force: 08.03.2006. Effect: None. Territorial extent & classification: E/W/S. General. - 2p.: 30 cm. - 978-0-11-074062-1 £3.00

Olympic Games and Paralympic Games

The London Olympic Games and Paralympic Games Act 2006 (Commencement No. 1) Order 2006 No. 2006/1118 (C.38). - Enabling power: London Olympic Games and Paralympic Games Act 2006, s. 40 (2) to (4) (9). Bringing into operation certain provisions of the 2006 Act on 30.05.2006. - Issued: 25.04.2006. Made: 19.04.2006. Effect: None. Territorial extent & classification: E/W/S/NI. General. - 4p.: 30 cm. - 978-0-11-074507-7 £3.00

Opticians

The General Optical Council (Continuing Education and Training) (Amendment No. 2) Rules Order of Council 2006 No. 2006/2901. - Enabling power: Opticians Act 1989, ss. 11A, 11B, 31A. - Issued: 15.11.2006. Made: 30.10.2006. Laid: 09.11.2006. Coming into force: 01.01.2007. Effect: S.I. 2005/1473 amended & The General Optical Council (Continuing Education and Training) (Amendment) Rules 2006 revoked. Territorial extent & classification: E/W/S/NI. General. - 8p.: 30 cm. - 978-0-11-075258-7 £3.00

Outer space

The Outer Space Act 1986 (Bermuda) Order 2006 No. 2006/2959. - Enabling power: Outer Space Act 1986, s. 15 (6). - Issued: 20.11.2006. Made: 14.11.2006. Coming into force: 14.12.2006. Effect: 1986 c. 38 modified. Territorial extent & classification: Bermuda. General. - 4p.: 30 cm. - 978-0-11-075318-8 £3.00

Overseas territories

The Belarus (Restrictive Measures) (Overseas Territories) Order 2006 No. 2006/1909. - Enabling power: Saint Helena Act 1833, s. 112 & British Settlements Acts 1887 & 1945. - Issued: 25.07.2006. Made: 19.07.2006. Laid: 20.07.2006. Coming into force: 21.07.2006. Effect: None. Territorial extent & classification: Anguilla, British Antarctic Territory, British Indian Ocean Territory, Cayman Is., Falkland Is., Montserrat, Pitcairn, Henderson, Ducie & Oeno Is., St Helena & Dependencies, South Georgia & South Sandwich Is., the Sovereign Base Areas of Akrotiri & Dhekelia (Cyprus), Turks & Caicos Is., Virgin Is. General. - EC note: These regs give effect in the overseas territories to Council Common Position 2006/276/CFSP as amended by Council Common Position 2006/362/CFSP, which were given effect in the European Union by Council Regulation (EC) No 765/2006. They prohibit making available funds, financial assets or economic resources to listed persons and the freezing of their funds, financial assets or economic resources. - 12p.: 30 cm. - 978-0-11-074884-9 £3.00

The Ivory Coast (Restrictive Measures) (Overseas Territories) (Amendment) Order 2006 No. 2006/610. - Enabling power: Saint Helena Act 1833, s. 112 & British Settlements Acts 1887 & 1945. - Issued: 14.03.2006. Made: 08.03.2006. Laid: 09.03.2006. Coming into force: 10.03.2006. Effect: S.I. 2005/242 amended. Territorial extent & classification: Anguilla; British Antarctic Territory; British Indian Ocean Territory; Cayman Is.; Falkland Is.; Montserrat; Pitcairn, Henderson, Ducie & Oeno Is.; St Helena & Dependencies; South Georgia & South Sandwich Is.; the Sovereign Base Areas of Akrotiri & Dhekelia; Turks & Caicos Is.; Virgin Is. General. - 4p.: 30 cm. - 978-0-11-074210-6 £3.00

The Uzbekistan (Restrictive Measures) (Overseas Territories) Order 2006 No. 2006/310. - Enabling power: Saint Helena Act 1833, s. 112 & British Settlements Acts 1887 & 1945. - Issued: 20.02.2006. Made: 14.02.2006. Laid: 15.02.2006. Coming into force: 16.02.2006. Effect: None. Territorial extent & classification: Anguilla, British Antarctic Territory, British Indian Ocean Territory, Cayman Is., Falkland Is., Montserrat, Pitcairn, Henderson, Ducie & Oeno Is., St Helena & Dependencies, South Georgia & South Sandwich Is., the Sovereign Base Areas of Akrotiri & Dhekelia (Cyprus), Turks & Caicos Is., Virgin Is. General. - EC note: These regs give effect in the overseas territories to Council Common Position 2005/792/CFSP which prohibits (a) the delivery or supply of arms and related material to Uzbekistan, from Members States' territories, by their nationals, or using their flagged vessels and aircraft; (b) the provision of technical assistance, brokering services and other services related to military activities and to the provision, manufacture, maintenance and use of arms and related material to any person, entity or body in, or for use in Uzbekistan; and (c) the provision of financing or financial assistance related to military activities to any person, entity or body, in or for use in, Uzbekistan. - 16p.: 30 cm. - 978-0-11-074048-5 £3.00

Parliament

The Parliamentary Corporate Bodies (Crown Immunities etc.) (Amendment) Order 2006 No. 2006/1457. - Enabling power: Parliamentary Corporate Bodies Act 1992, ss. 1 (6), 2 (6). - Issued: 19.06.2006. Made: 07.06.2006. Laid: 19.06.2006. Coming into force: 10.07.2006. Effect: S.I. 1992/1732 amended. Territorial extent & classification: E. General. - 2p.: 30 cm. - 978-0-11-074672-2 £3.00

Parliamentary Commissioner

The Parliamentary Commissioner Order 2006 No. 2006/3328. - Enabling power: Parliamentary Commissioner Act 1967, ss. 4 (2), 5 (9). - Issued: 22.12.2006. Made: 14.12.2006. Laid: 22.12.2006. Coming into force: 22.01.2007. Effect: 1967 c.13 amended & S.I. 1968/1859; 1970/1535; 1972/1716; 1975/1033; 1977/816; 1978/616; 1979/915, 1705; 1981/1537; 1986/1889; 1988/585, 1985; 1995/1615; 1996/1914, 2601; 1999/277, 2028; 2000/739; 2003/2921; 2004/2670 revoked. Territorial extent & classification: E/W/S/NI. General. - 4p.: 30 cm. - 978-0-11-075512-0 £3.00

Patents

The Patents (Convention Countries) Order 2006 No. 2006/315. - Enabling power: Patents Act 1977, ss. 90 (1), 124 (3). - Issued: 03.03.2006. Made: 14.02.2006. Laid: 24.02.2006. Coming into force: 06.04.2006. Effect: S.I. 2004/3335 revoked. Territorial extent & classification: E/W/S/NI. General. - 8p.: 30 cm. - 978-0-11-074054-6 £3.00

Pensions

The Armed Forces and Reserve Forces (Compensation Scheme) (Amendment) Order 2006 No. 2006/1438. - Enabling power: Armed Forces (Pensions and Compensation) Act 2004, ss. 1 (2), 10 (2) (3). - Issued: 08.06.2006. Made: 31.05.2006. Laid: 05.06.2006. Coming into force: 30.06.2006 except for art. 8; 26.07.2006 for art. 8. Effect: S.I. 2005/439 amended. Territorial extent & classification: E/W/S/NI. General. - 24p.: 30 cm. - 978-0-11-074630-2 £4.00

The Armed Forces Pension Scheme etc. (Amendment) Order 2006 No. 2006/717. - Enabling power: Armed Forces (Pensions and Compensation) Act 2004, ss. 1 (1) (3), 10 (2) (3). - Issued: 17.03.2006. Made: 13.03.2006. Laid: 15.03.2006. Coming into force: 06.04.2006. Effect: S.I. 2005/437, 438 amended. Territorial extent & classification: E/W/S/NI. General. - 12p.: 30 cm. - 978-0-11-074275-5 £3.00

The Armed Forces Redundancy Scheme Order 2006 No. 2006/55. - Enabling power: Armed Forces (Pensions and Compensation) Act 2004, ss. 1 (1) (a), 10 (2). - Issued: 20.01.2006. Made: 12.01.2006. Laid: 19.01.2006. Coming into force: 06.04.2006. Effect: None. Territorial extent & classification: E/W/S/NI. General. - 8p.: 30 cm. - 978-0-11-073908-3 £3.00

The European Parliamentary (United Kingdom Representatives) Pensions (Amendment) Order 2006 No. 2006/919. - Enabling power: European Parliament (Pay and Pensions) Act 1979, s. 4 (1) (2) (3). - Issued: 29.03.2006. Made: 23.03.2006. Laid: 29.03.2006. Coming into force: 06.04.2006. Effect: S.I. 1994/1662; 1995/739 amended. Territorial extent & classification: E/W/S/NI. General. - 28p.: 30 cm. - 978-0-11-074402-5 £4.50

The Financial Assistance Scheme (Miscellaneous Amendments) Regulations 2006 No. 2006/3370. - Enabling power: Pensions Act 2004, ss. 286, 315 (2) (4), 318 (1) (4) (a). - Issued: 22.12.2006. Made: 15.12.2006. Coming into force: In accord. with reg. 1 (1). Effect: S.I. 2005/1986, 1994, 3273 amended. Territorial extent & classification: E/W/S/NI. General. - Supersedes draft S.I. (ISBN 0110752996) issued on 15.11.2006. - 12p.: 30 cm. - 978-0-11-075528-1 £3.00

The Guaranteed Minimum Pensions Increase Order 2006 No. 2006/673. - Enabling power: Pension Schemes Act 1993, s. 109 (4). - Issued: 16.03.2006. Made: 08.03.2006. Coming into force: 06.04.2006. Effect: None. Territorial extent & classification: E/W/S. General. - 2p.: 30 cm. - 978-0-11-074252-6 £3.00

The Judicial Pensions (Additional Voluntary Contributions) (Amendment) Regulations 2006 No. 2006/747. - Enabling power: Judicial Pensions Act 1981, s. 33A & Judicial Pensions and Retirement Act 1993, ss. 10, 29 (3) (4). - Issued: 20.03.2006. Made: 13.03.2006. Laid: 16.03.2006. Coming into force: 06.04.2006. Effect: S.I. 1995/639 amended. Territorial extent & classification: E/W/S/NI. General. - 8p.: 30 cm. - 978-0-11-074324-0 £3.00

The Judicial Pensions and Retirement Act 1993 (Addition of Qualifying Judicial Offices) Order 2006 No. 2006/391. - Enabling power: Judicial Pensions and Retirement Act 1993, ss. 1 (8), 26 (9) (a). - Issued: 27.02.2006. Made: 16.02.2006. Laid: 20.02.2006. Coming into force: 03.04.2006. Effect: 1993 c. 8 amended. Territorial extent & classification: UK. General. - 2p.: 30 cm. - 978-0-11-080023-3 £3.00

The Judicial Pensions (Contributions) (Amendment) Regulations 2006 No. 2006/749. - Enabling power: Judicial Pensions Act 1981, s. 23 & Judicial Pensions and Retirement Act 1993, s. 9. - Issued: 20.03.2006. Made: 13.03.2006. Laid: 16.03.2006. Coming into force: 06.04.2006. Effect: S.I. 1987/375; 1991/2731; 1998/1219 amended. Territorial extent & classification: E/W/S/NI. General. - 4p.: 30 cm. - 978-0-11-074312-7 £3.00

The Naval, Military and Air Forces Etc. (Disablement and Death) Service Pensions (Amendment) (No. 2) Order 2006 No. 2006/1455. - Enabling power: Social Security (Miscellaneous Provisions) Act 1977, ss. 12 (1), 24 (3). - Issued: 19.06.2006. Made: 07.06.2006. Laid: 19.06.2006. Coming into force: 21.06.2006. Effect: S.I. 2006/606 amended. Territorial extent & classification: E/W/S/NI. General. - This statutory instrument has been printed to correct errors in S.I. 2006/606 (ISBN 0110742281) and is being issued free of charge to all known recipients of that statutory instrument. - 2p.: 30 cm. - 978-0-11-074670-8 £3.00

The Naval, Military and Air Forces Etc. (Disablement and Death) Service Pensions (Amendment) Order 2006 No. 2006/303. - Enabling power: Naval and Marine Pay and Pensions Act 1865, s. 3; Pensions and Yeomanry Pay Act 1884, s. 2 (1); Air Force (Constitution) Act 1917, s. 2 (1) & Social Security (Miscellaneous Provisions) Act 1977, ss. 12 (1), 24 (3). - Issued: 24.02.2006. Made: 14.02.2006. Laid: 24.02.2006. Coming into force: 13.03.2006. Effect: S.I. 1983/883 amended. Territorial extent & classification: E/W/S/NI General. - This Statutory Instrument has been made in consequence of defects in Statutory Instrument 2005/851 and is being issued free of charge to all known recipients of that Statutory Instrument. - 2p.: 30 cm. - 978-0-11-074052-2 £3.00

The Naval, Military and Air Forces Etc. (Disablement and Death) Service Pensions Order 2006 No. 2006/606. - Enabling power: Social Security (Miscellaneous Provisions) Act 1977, ss. 12 (1), 24 (3). - Issued: 16.03.2006. Made: 08.03.2006. Laid: 20.03.06. Coming into force: 10.04.2006. Effect: 34 instruments revoked in accord. with sch. 5. Territorial extent & classification: E/W/S/NI. General. - 84p.: 30 cm. - 978-0-11-074228-1 £12.00

The Occupational and Personal Pension Schemes (Consultation by Employers and Miscellaneous Amendment) Regulations 2006 No. 2006/349. - Enabling power: Pensions Act 2004, ss. 10 (5) (a), 259 (1) (2), 260 (1), 261 (2) (4), 286 (1) (3) (g), 315 (2) (3) (5), 318 (1) (4) (a) (5). - Issued: 22.02.2006. Made: 15.02.2006. Coming into force: 06.04.2006 except for reg. 22; 16.02.2006 for reg. 22. Effect: 1996 c.18; S.I. 2005/1994 amended. Territorial extent & classification: E/W/S (with the exception of the amendment to the 2005 Regulations, which extends to Northern Ireland). General. - 20p.: 30 cm. - 978-0-11-074081-2 £3.50

The Occupational and Personal Pension Schemes (Miscellaneous Amendments) Regulations 2006 No. 2006/778. - Enabling power: Pension Schemes Act 1993, ss. 55 (2B), 101C (2), 113 (1) (d), 181 (1), 182 (2) (3) & Pension Schemes (Northern Ireland) Act 1993, ss. 51 (2B) (2ZA) & Pensions Act 1995, ss. 35 (3) (4), 40 (2), 41 (1), 47 (5) (6), 49 (1) (2) (4) (9) (b), 87 (1), 88 (1), 91 (5), 124 (1), 174 (2) (3) & Pensions Act 2004, ss. 259 (1), 260 (1), 315 (2), 318 (1). - Issued: 21.03.2006. Made: 14.03.2006. Laid: 16.03.2006. Coming into force: In accord. with reg. 1 (1). Effect: S.R. 1996/493; S.I. 1996/1172, 1715, 1975; 1997/785; 2000/1054, 2692; 2005/3378; 2006/349 amended. Territorial extent & classification: E/W/S/NI General. - 8p.: 30 cm. - 978-0-11-074337-0 £3.00

The Occupational Pension Schemes (Consultation by Employers) (Modification for Multi-employer Schemes) Regulations 2006 No. 2006/16. - Enabling power: Pensions Act 2004, ss. 307 (1), 315 (2) (3) (5), 318 (1). - Issued: 12.01.2006. Made: 09.01.2006. Laid: 12.01.2006. Coming into force: 02.02.2006. Effect: 2004 c. 35 modified. Territorial extent & classification: E/W/S. General. - 2p.: 30 cm. - 978-0-11-073892-5 £3.00

The Occupational Pension Schemes (Contracting-out) (Amendment) Regulations 2006 No. 2006/1337. - Enabling power: Pension Schemes Act 1993, ss. 21 (1), 181 (1), 182 (2) (3). - Issued: 24.05.2006. Made: 16.05.2006. Laid: 23.05.2006. Coming into force: 14.06.2006. Effect: S.I. 1996/1172 amended. Territorial extent & classification: E/W/S. General. - 2p.: 30 cm. - 978-0-11-074586-2 £3.00

The Occupational Pension Schemes (Cross-border Activities) (Amendment) Regulations 2006 No. 2006/925. - Enabling power: Pensions Act 2004, ss. 288 (1), 289 (1), 315 (2), 318 (1). - Issued: 31.03.2006. Made: 27.03.2006. Laid: 27.03.2006. Coming into force: 28.03.2006. Effect: S.I. 2005/3381 amended. Territorial extent & classification: E/W/S. General. - 2p.: 30 cm. - 978-0-11-074405-6 £3.00

The Occupational Pension Schemes (Early Leavers: Cash Transfer Sums and Contribution Refunds) Regulations 2006 No. 2006/33. - Enabling power: Pension Schemes Act 1993, ss. 101AC (2) (a), 101AE (2), 101AF, 113A, 181 (1), 182 (2), 183. - Issued: 12.01.2006. Made: 09.01.2006. Laid: 12.01.2006. Coming into force: 06.04.2006. Effect: None. Territorial extent & classification: E/W/S. General. - 8p.: 30 cm. - 978-0-11-073896-3 £3.00

The Occupational Pension Schemes (Fraud Compensation Levy) Regulations 2006 No. 2006/558. - Enabling power: Pensions Act 1995, ss. 10 (3), 75 (10), 89 (2), 124 (1) & Pensions Act 2004, ss. 189 (1) (4) (6) (11), 315 (2) (5), 318 (1). - Issued: 08.03.2006. Made: 01.03.2006. Laid: 08.03.2006. Coming into force: 01.04.2006. Effect: S.I. 2005/678 amended. Territorial extent & classification: E/W/S. General. - 8p.: 30 cm. - 978-0-11-074159-8 £3.00

The Occupational Pension Schemes (Levies) (Amendment) Regulations 2006 No. 2006/935. - Enabling power: Pensions Act 2004, ss. 117 (1) (3), 126 (1) (b), 181 (8) (a), 209 (7) (8), 315 (2), 318 (1). - Issued: 31.03.2006. Made: 28.03.2006. Coming into force: 01.04.2006. Effect: S.I. 2005/842 amended. Territorial extent & classification: E/W/S. General. - 4p.: 30 cm. - 978-0-11-074413-1 £3.00

The Occupational Pension Schemes (Levy Ceiling - Earnings Percentage Increase) Order 2006 No. 2006/3105. - Enabling power: Pensions Act 2004, s. 178 (6). - Issued: 27.11.2006. Made: 21.11.2006. Laid: 27.11.2006. Coming into force: 18.12.2006. Effect: None. Territorial extent & classification: E/W/S. General. - 2p.: 30 cm. - 978-0-11-075355-3 £3.00

The Occupational Pension Schemes (Levy Ceiling) Order 2006 No. 2006/742. - Enabling power: Pensions Act 2004, ss. 178 (1), 315 (2). - Issued: 20.03.2006. Made: 13.03.2006. Coming into force: 14.03.2006 in accord. with art. 1. Effect: None. Territorial extent & classification: E/W/S. General. - Supersedes the draft S.I. (ISBN 0110740092) issued 08.02.2006. - 2p.: 30 cm. - 978-0-11-074314-1 £3.00

The Occupational Pension Schemes (Member-nominated Trustees and Directors) Regulations 2006 No. 2006/714. - Enabling power: Pensions Act 2004, ss. 241 (8) (c), 242 (10), 243 (2), 315 (2) (4) (5), 318 (1). - Issued: 16.03.2006. Made: 13.03.2006. Laid: 16.03.2006. Coming into force: 06.04.2006 in accord. with reg. 1 (1). Effect: 2004 c.35 modified; S.I. 1997/786; 1999/3198; 2000/1403; 2001/3649 amended & S.I. 1996/1216; 2002/3227 revoked. Territorial extent & classification: E/W/S. General. - 8p.: 30 cm. - 978-0-11-074281-6 £3.00

The Occupational Pension Schemes (Modification of Schemes) Regulations 2006 No. 2006/759. - Enabling power: Pensions Act 1995, ss. 67 (1) (b) (3) (b), 67C (7) (a) (ii), 67D (4) (5), 68 (2) (e) (6), 124 (1), 174 (2) (3). - Issued: 24.03.2006. Made: 14.03.2006. Laid: 16.03.2006. Coming into force: 30.03.2006 for regs. 6 & 7; 06.04.2006 for remainder. Effect: S.I. 1997/786; 1999/3198; 2002/681; 2005/2050, 2877 amended & S.I. 1996/2517 revoked Territorial extent & classification: E/W/S. General. - 8p.: 30 cm. - 978-0-11-074321-9 £3.00

The Occupational Pension Schemes (Payments to Employer) Regulations 2006 No. 2006/802. - Enabling power: Pensions Act 1995, ss. 37 (3) (a) (b) (g) (4) (5) (8), 76 (2) (3) (d) (8), 124 (1), 125 (3), 174 (2) (3) & Pensions Act 2004, ss. 251 (6) (a), 318 (1). - Issued: 22.03.2006. Made: 16.03.2006. Laid: 16.03.2006. Coming into force: 06.04.2006. Effect: S.I. 1997/786; 2005/706 amended & S.I. 1996/2156; 1997/2559 revoked. Territorial extent & classification: E/W/S. General. - 16p.: 30 cm. - 978-0-11-074349-3 £3.00

The Occupational Pension Schemes (Pension Protection Levies) (Transitional Period and Modification for Multi-employer Schemes) Regulations 2006 No. 2006/566. - Enabling power: Pensions Act 2004, ss. 180 (1) (a) (3), 315 (2) (4) (5), 318 (1). - Issued: 09.03.2006. Made: 06.03.2006. Laid: 09.03.2006. Coming into force: 30.03.2006. Effect: 2004 c. 35 modified. Territorial extent & classification: E/W/S. General- 8p.: 30 cm. - 978-0-11-074173-4 £3.00

The Occupational Pension Schemes (Republic of Ireland Schemes Exemption (Revocation) and Tax Exempt Schemes (Miscellaneous Amendments)) Regulations 2006 No. 2006/467. - Enabling power: Pension Schemes Act 1993, ss. 113, 168 (1) (4), 175, 181 (1) (4), 182 (2) (4) & Pensions Act 1995, ss. 10 (3), 27, 37 (10), 38 (3) (b), 40 (1) (2), 41 (1) (6), 47 (5), 49 (2) (3), 50 (7), 68 (2) (e) (6), 69 (6), 73 (2) (b), 75 (1) (b) (5) (6D) (b) (i) (10), 75A (1) to (4), 76 (8), 87 (1), 89 (2), 118 (1) (2), 119, 124 (1), 125 (3), 174 (2) (3) & Pensions Act 2004, ss. 38 (1) (b), 52 (1) (b) (7) (a), 59 (2), 288, 289 (1), 315 (2) (4) (5), 318 (1). - Issued: 27.02.2006. Made: 23.02.2006. Laid: 27.02.2006. Coming into force: In accord. with reg. 1 (1) to (3). Effect: S.I. 1996/1655, 1715, 1975, 3126; 2005/597, 626, 678, 706, 931, 3381 amended & S.I. 2000/3198 revoked (20.03.2006). Territorial extent & classification: E/W/S and NI (reg. 4). General. - 8p.: 30 cm. - 978-0-11-074100-0 £3.00

The Occupational Pension Schemes (Transfer Values etc.) (Coal Staff and Mineworkers' Schemes) (Amendment) Regulations 2006 No. 2006/34. - Enabling power: Pension Schemes Act 1993, ss. 97 (1), 101I, 181 (1), 182 (2) (3), 183 (3) & Welfare Reform and Pensions Act 1999, ss. 30, 83 (4) (6). - Issued: 16.01.2006. Made: 10.01.2006. Laid: 16.01.2006. Coming into force: 06.02.2006. Effect: S.I. 1996/1847; 2000/1052, 1054 amended. Territorial extent & classification: E/W/S. General- 4p.: 30 cm. - 978-0-11-073895-6 £3.00

The Occupational Pension Schemes (Trustees' Knowledge and Understanding) Regulations 2006 No. 2006/686. - Enabling power: Pensions Act 2004, ss. 249 (2) (a), 318 (1). - Issued: 16.03.2006. Made: 09.03.2006. Laid: 16.03.2006. Coming into force: 06.04.2006. Effect: None. Territorial extent & classification: E/W/S. General. - 4p.: 30 cm. - 978-0-11-074268-7 £3.00

The Occupational Pension Schemes (Winding up Procedure Requirement) Regulations 2006 No. 2006/1733. - Enabling power: European Communities Act 1972, s. 2 (2) & Pension Schemes Act 1993, ss. 113 (1), 181 (1), 182 (2) (3) & Pensions Act 2004, ss. 60 (2) (h), 69 (2) (a), 315 (2) (5), 318 (1). - Issued: 06.07.2006. Made: 29.06.2006. Laid: 03.07.2006. Coming into force: 24.07.2006. Effect: 2004 c. 35; S.I. 1996/1655; 2005/597, 3377 amended. Territorial extent & classification: E/W/S. General. - 4p.: 30 cm. - 978-0-11-074782-8 £3.00

The Occupational Pensions (Revaluation) Order 2006 No. 2006/3086. - Enabling power: Pension Schemes Act 1993, sch. 3, para. 2 (1). - Issued: 24.11.2006. Made: 20.11.2006. Laid: 24.11.2006. Coming into force: 01.01.2007. Effect: None. Territorial extent & classification: E/W/S. General. - 2p.: 30 cm. - 978-0-11-075342-3 £3.00

The Parliamentary Pensions (Amendment) (No. 2) Regulations 2006 No. 2006/1965. - Enabling power: Parliamentary and other Pensions Act 1987, ss. 2 (1) (2) (4). - Issued: 24.07.2006. Made: 19.07.2006. Laid before the Parliament: 24.07.2006. Coming into force: 18.08.2006 (Reg. 2 has effect from 05.07.2006). Effect: S.I. 1993/3253 amended. Territorial extent & classification: E/W/S/NI. General. - 2p.: 30 cm. - 978-0-11-074899-3 £3.00

The Parliamentary Pensions (Amendment) Regulations 2006 No. 2006/920. - Enabling power: Parliamentary and other Pensions Act 1987, s. 2 (1) (2) (4). - Issued: 29.03.2006. Made: 23.03.2006. Laid: 29.03.2006. Coming into force: In accord. with reg. 1 (2) to (4). Effect: S.I. 1993/3252, 3253 amended. Territorial extent & classification: E/W/S/NI. General. - With correction slip dated August 2006. - 36p.: 30 cm. - 978-0-11-074403-2 £5.50

The Pension Protection Fund (General and Miscellaneous Amendments) Regulations 2006 No. 2006/580. - Enabling power: Pensions Act 2004, ss. 126 (1) (b), 151 (9) (b), 161 (6) (7), 163 (3) (4) (a) (ii) (b) (ii) (6) (a), 166 (5), 168 (1) (2) (a) (b) (c) (e) (f), 170 (2) (3), 171 (4), 179 (3), 181 (5) (8) (a), 315 (2) (4) (5), 318 (1), sch. 7, para. 24 (1) (2). - Issued: 10.03.2006. Made: 06.03.2006. Laid: 10.03.2006. Coming into force: 01.04.2006 for regs. 19, 20, 23; 06.04.2006 for all other purposes. Effect: S.I. 2005/590, 670, 672 amended. Territorial extent & classification: E/W/S. General. - 16p.: 30 cm. - 978-0-11-074175-8 £3.00

The Pension Protection Fund (Levy Ceiling) Regulations 2006 No. 2006/2692. - Enabling power: Pensions Act 2004, ss. 177 (4), 178 (4) (7) (9), 315 (2) (4), 318 (1). - Issued: 16.10.2006. Made: 10.10.2006. Laid: 16.10.2006. Coming into force: 06.11.2006. Effect: None. Territorial extent & classification: E/W/S. General. - 4p.: 30 cm. - 978-0-11-075178-8 £3.00

The Pension Protection Fund (Pension Compensation Cap) Order 2006 No. 2006/347. - Enabling power: Pensions Act 2004, sch. 7, paras 26 (7), 27 (2) (3). - Issued: 20.02.2006. Made: 13.02.2006. Coming into force: 01.04.2006. Effect: S.I. 2005/825 revoked. Territorial extent & classification: E/W/S. General. - Supersedes draft SI (ISBN 0110738845) issued on 11.01.2006. - 2p.: 30 cm. - 978-0-11-074045-4 £3.00

The Pension Protection Fund (Pension Sharing) Regulations 2006 No. 2006/1690. - Enabling power: Pensions Act 2004, ss. 220, 315 (2) (4) (5), 318 (1). - Issued: 30.06.2006. Made: 25.06.2006. Laid: 30.06.2006. Coming into force: 01.08.2006. Effect: 1999 c. 30; 2004 c. 35 modified. Territorial extent & classification: E/W/S. General. - 4p.: 30 cm. - 978-0-11-074763-7 £3.00

The Pension Protection Fund (Provision of Information) (Amendment) Regulations 2006 No. 2006/595. - Enabling power: Pensions Act 2004, ss. 190, 203 (1), 315 (2) (4) (5), 318 (1). - Issued: 13.03.2006. Made: 07.03.2006. Laid: 13.03.2006. Coming into force: 06.04.2006. Effect: S.I. 2005/674 amended. Territorial extent & classification: E/W/S. General. - 4p.: 30 cm. - 978-0-11-074189-5 £3.00

The Pension Protection Fund (Reviewable Matters and Review and Reconsideration of Reviewable Matters) (Amendment) Regulations 2006 No. 2006/685. - Enabling power: Pensions Act 2004, ss. 206 (2) (a) (4) (a), 207 (2) (5) (a), 315 (2), 318 (1). - Issued: 20.03.2006. Made: 09.03.2006. Laid: 16.03.2006. Coming into force: 06.04.2006. Effect: 2004 c.35 amended. Territorial extent & classification: E/W/S. General. - 4p.: 30 cm. - 978-0-11-074262-5 £3.00

The Pension Protection Fund (Risk-based Pension Protection Levy) Regulations 2006 No. 2006/672. - Enabling power: Pensions Act 2004, ss. 175 (3) (b), 315 (2) (4), 318 (1). - Issued: 16.03.2006. Made: 08.03.2006. Coming into force: 09.03.2006. Effect: None. Territorial extent & classification: E/W/S. General. - 2p.: 30 cm. - 978-0-11-074227-4 £3.00

The Pension Protection Fund (Valuation of the Assets and Liabilities of the Pension Protection Fund) Regulations 2006 No. 2006/597. - Enabling power: Pensions Act 2004, ss. 315 (2) (4) (5), 318 (1), sch. 5, para. 22 (4). - Issued: 10.03.2006. Made: 07.03.2006. Laid: 10.03.2006. Coming into force: 01.04.2006. Effect: None. Territorial extent & classification: E/W/S/NI. General. - 4p.: 30 cm. - 978-0-11-074186-4 £3.00

The Pensions Act 2004 (Codes of Practice) (Early Leavers, Late Payment of Contributions and Trustee Knowledge and Understanding) Appointed Day Order 2006 No. 2006/1383. - Enabling power: Pensions Act 2004, s. 91 (9). Appoints 30.05.2006 as the date for the coming into effect of the Pensions Regulator Code of Practice nos 4, 5, 6 and 7. - Issued: 21.07.2006. Made: 22.05.2006. Effect: None. Territorial extent & classification: E/W/S. General. - This Statutory Instrument has been printed to correct an error in the SI of the same number and is being issued free of charge to all known recipients of that SI. - 2p.: 30 cm. - 978-0-11-074606-7 £3.00

The Pensions Act 2004 (Codes of Practice) (Member-nominated Trustees and Directors and Internal Controls) Appointed Day Order 2006 No. 2006/3079. - Enabling power: Pensions Act 2004, s. 91 (9). Bringing into operation various provisions of the 2004 Act on 22.11.2006. - Issued: 24.11.2006. Made: 17.11.2006. Effect: None. Territorial extent & classification: E/W/S. General. - 2p.: 30 cm. - 978-0-11-075338-6 £3.00

The Pensions Act 2004 (Commencement No. 9) Order 2006 No. 2006/560 (C.13). - Enabling power: Pension Act 2004, ss. 315 (2), 322 (1). Bringing into operation various provisions of the 2004 Act on 09.03.2006, 01.04.2006, 06.04.2006. - Issued: 09.03.2006. Made: 02.03.2006. Effect: None. Territorial extent & classification: E/W/S. General. - 16p.: 30 cm. - 978-0-11-074161-1 £3.00

The Pensions Act 2004 (Commencement No. 10 and Saving Provision) Order 2006 No. 2006/2272 (C.78). - Enabling power: Pension Act 2004, ss. 315 (2) (5), 322 (1) (5) (b). Bringing into operation various provisions of the 2004 Act in accord. with art. 2. - Issued: 29.08.2006. Made: 19.08.2006. Effect: None. Territorial extent & classification: E/W/S. General. - 16p.: 30 cm. - 978-0-11-075036-1 £3.00

The Pensions Act 2004 (Disclosure of Restricted Information) (Amendment of Specified Persons) Order 2006 No. 2006/2937. - Enabling power: Pensions Act 2004, ss. 86 (2) (a) (i) (ii), 200 (2) (a) (i) (ii). - Issued: 16.11.2006. Made: 09.11.2006. Laid: 16.11.2006. Coming into force: 07.12.2006. Effect: 2004 c. 35 amended. Territorial extent & classification: E/W/S. General. - 4p.: 30 cm. - 978-0-11-075287-7 £3.00

The Pensions Act 2004 (Funding Defined Benefits) Appointed Day Order 2006 No. 2006/337. - Enabling power: Pensions Act 2004, s. 91 (9). Appoints 15.02.2006 as the date for the coming into effect of the Pensions Regulator Code of Practice No. 03: Funding defined benefits. - Issued: 17.02.2006. Made: 13.02.2006. Effect: None. Territorial extent & classification: E/W/S. General. - 2p.: 30 cm. - 978-0-11-074036-2 £3.00

The Pensions Act 2004 (PPF Payments and FAS Payments) (Consequential Provisions) Order 2006 No. 2006/343. - Enabling power: Pensions Act 2004, ss. 315 (5), 319 (2) (a). - Issued: 20.02.2006. Made: 13.02.2006. Coming into force: 14.02.2006 in accord. with art. 1 (1). Effect: 1992 c.4; 1995 c.18; 2002 c.16 amended. Territorial extent & classification: E/W/S/NI. General. - Supersedes draft SI (ISBN 0110738829) issued on 09.01.2006. - 8p.: 30 cm. - 978-0-11-074038-6 £3.00

The Pensions Appeal Tribunals (Additional Rights of Appeal) (Amendment) Regulations 2006 No. 2006/2893. - Enabling power: Pensions Appeal Tribunals Act 1943, s. 5A (2). - Issued: 07.11.2006. Made: 30.10.2006. Coming into force: In accord. with reg. 1 (1), 31.10.2006. Effect: S.I. 2001/1031 amended. Territorial extent & classification: E/W/S/NI. General. - 4p.: 30 cm. - 978-0-11-075238-9 £3.00

The Pensions Appeal Tribunals (Armed Forces and Reserve Forces Compensation Scheme) (Rights of Appeal) Amendment Regulations 2006 No. 2006/2892. - Enabling power: Pensions Appeal Tribunals Act 1943, s. 5A (2). - Issued: 06.11.2006. Made: 30.10.2006. Coming into force: In accord. with reg. 1 (1). Effect: S.I. 2005/1029 amended. Territorial extent & classification: E/W/S/NI. General. - Supersedes draft S.I. (ISBN 0110746406) issued on 07.06.2006. - 4p.: 30 cm. - 978-0-11-075237-2 £3.00

The Pensions Increase (Armed Forces Pension Schemes and Conservation Board) Regulations 2006 No. 2006/801. - Enabling power: Pensions (Increase) Act 1971, s. 5 (2). - Issued: 21.03.2006. Made: 16.03.2006. Laid: 17.03.2006. Coming into force: 07.04.2006. Effect: None. Territorial extent & classification: E/W/S/NI. General. - 2p.: 30 cm. - 978-0-11-074347-9 £3.00

The Pensions Increase (Review) Order 2006 No. 2006/741. - Enabling power: Social Security Pensions Act 1975, s. 59 (1) (2) (5) (5ZA). - Issued: 20.03.2006. Made: 14.03.2006. Laid: 15.03.2006. Coming into force: 10.04.2006. Effect: None. Territorial extent & classification: E/W/S/NI. General. - 8p.: 30 cm. - 978-0-11-074308-0 £3.00

The Personal Injuries (Civilian) (Amendment) Scheme 2006 No. 2006/765. - Enabling power: Personal Injuries (Emergency Provisions) Act 1939, ss. 1, 2. - Issued: 21.03.2006. Made: 14.03.2006. Laid: 17.03.2006. Coming into force: 10.04.2006. Effect: S.I. 1983/686 amended. Territorial extent & classification: E/W/S/NI. General. - 12p.: 30 cm. - 978-0-11-074332-5 £3.00

The Personal Pension Schemes (Appropriate Schemes) (Amendment) Regulations 2006 No. 2006/147. - Enabling power: Pension Schemes Act 1993, ss. 9 (5) (a), 181 (1), 182 (3). - Issued: 01.02.2006. Made: 26.01.2006. Laid: 01.02.2006. Coming into force: 06.04.2006. Effect: S.I. 1997/470 amended. Territorial extent & classification: E/W/S. General. - 4p.: 30 cm. - 978-0-11-073960-1 £3.00

The Social Security (Reduced Rates of Class 1 Contributions, Rebates and Minimum Contributions) Order 2006 No. 2006/1009. - Enabling power: Pension Schemes Act 1993, ss. 42, 42B, 45A, 182 (2) & Pension Schemes (Northern Ireland) Act 1993, ss. 38(1), 38B, 41A. - Issued: 05.04.2006. Made: 30.03.2006. Coming into force: 06.04.2007. Effect: 1993 c. 48, c.49 amended. Territorial extent & classification: E/W/S/NI. General. - Supersedes draft S.I. (ISBN 0110741609) issued on 15.03.2006. - 20p.: 30 cm. - 978-0-11-074450-6 £3.50

The Superannuation (Admission to Schedule 1 to the Superannuation Act 1972) Order 2006 No. 2006/3374. - Enabling power: Superannuation Act 1972, s. 1 (5) (7) (8) (a) (c). - Issued: 20.12.2006. Made: 14.12.2006. Laid: 18.12.2006. Coming into force: 02.02.2007. Effect: 1972 c.11; S.I. 2005/3171 amended. Territorial extent & classification: E/W/S/NI. General. - 4p.: 30 cm. - 978-0-11-075532-8 £3.00

The War Pensions Committees (Amendment) Regulations 2006 No. 2006/3152. - Enabling power: Social Security Act 1989, ss. 25, 29 & Social Security Contributions and Benefits Act 1992, s. 175 (2) to (5). - Issued: 01.12.2006. Made: 27.11.2006. Laid: 01.12.2006. Coming into force: 01.01.2007. Effect: S.I. 2000/3032 amended. Territorial extent & classification: E/W/S/NI. General. - 4p.: 30 cm. - 978-0-11-075382-9 £3.00

Pensions, England

The Firefighters' Compensation Scheme (England) (Amendment) Order 2006 No. 2006/3434. - Enabling power: Fire and Rescue Services Act 2004, ss. 34, 60. - Issued: 04.01.2007. Made: 19.12.2006. Laid: 04.01.2007. Coming into force: 25.01.2007. Effect: S.I. 2006/1811 amended. Territorial extent & classification: E. General. - 16p.: 30 cm. - 978-0-11-075572-4 £3.00

The Firefighters' Compensation Scheme (England) Order 2006 No. 2006/1811. - Enabling power: Fire and Rescue Services Act 2004, ss. 34, 60. - Issued: 17.07.2006. Made: 10.07.2006. Laid: 17.07.2006. Coming into force: 07.08.2006. Effect: S.I. 1992/129 amended in relation to England. Territorial extent & classification: E. General. - 40p.: 30 cm. - 978-0-11-074833-7 £6.50

The Firefighters' Pension Scheme (Amendment) (England) Order 2006 No. 2006/1810. - Enabling power: Fire Services Act 1947, s. 26 (1) to (5) & Superannuation Act 1972, s. 12. - Issued: 17.07.2006. Made: 10.07.2006. Laid: 17.07.2006. Coming into force: 07.08.2006. Effect: S.I. 1992/129 amended in relation to England. Territorial extent & classification: E. General. - 28p.: 30 cm. - 978-0-11-074832-0 £4.50

The Firefighters' Pension Scheme (Amendment) (No.2) (England) Order 2006 No. 2006/3433. - Enabling power: Fire Services Act 1947, s. 26 (1) to (5) & Superannuation Act 1972, s. 12. - Issued: 04.01.2007. Made: 19.12.2006. Laid: 04.01.2007. Coming into force: 25.01.2007. Effect: S.I. 1992/129 amended in relation to England, with effect 06.04.2006. Territorial extent & classification: E. General. - 8p.: 30 cm. - 978-0-11-075573-1 £3.00

The Firefighters' Pension Scheme (England) Order 2006 No. 2006/3432. - Enabling power: Fire and Rescue Services Act 2004, ss. 34, 60. - Issued: 23.03.2007. Made: 19.12.2006. Laid: 04.01.2007. Coming into force: 25.01.2007. Effect: 1992 scheme (S.I. 1992/129) ceasing to have effect in England, with savings, (paras. (2) & (3)). Territorial extent & classification: E. General. - This Statutory Instrument has been printed in substitution of the SI of the same number and is being issued free of charge to all known recipients of that SI. - 72p.: 30 cm. - 978-0-11-075574-8 £10.50

Pensions, England and Wales

The Dissolution etc. (Pension Protection Fund) Regulations 2006 No. 2006/1934. - Enabling power: Civil Partnership Act 2004, sch. 5, paras, 32, 35, 36. - Issued: 26.07.2006. Made: 17.07.2006. Laid: 18.07.2006. Coming into force: 08.08.2006. Effect: 2004 c. 33 modified; S.I. 2005/2920 amended. Territorial extent & classification: E/W. General. - 4p.: 30 cm. - 978-0-11-074866-5 £3.00

The Divorce etc. (Pension Protection Fund) Regulations 2006 No. 2006/1932. - Enabling power: Matrimonial Causes Act 1973, ss. 25E (5) (8) (9). - Issued: 25.07.2006. Made: 17.07.2006. Laid: 18.07.2006. Coming into force: 08.08.2006. Effect: 1973 c. 18 modified. Territorial extent & classification: E/W. General. - 4p.: 30 cm. - 978-0-11-074864-1 £3.00

The Local Government (Early Termination of Employment) (Discretionary Compensation) (England and Wales) Regulations 2006 No. 2006/2914. - Enabling power: Superannuation Act 1972, s. 24. - Issued: 10.11.2006. Made: 06.11.2006. Laid: 07.11.2006. Coming into force: 29.11.2006. Effect: S.I. 1995/2837; 1996/330; 2001/3649; 2003/533, 1022, 3239; 2005/3069 amended & S.I. 2000/1410; 2002/769; revoked with savings. Territorial extent & classification: E/W. General. - 8p.: 30 cm. - 978-0-11-075278-5 £3.00

The Local Government Pension Scheme (Amendment) (No. 2) Regulations 2006 No. 2006/2008. - Enabling power: Superannuation Act 1972, ss. 7, 12. - Issued: 01.08.2006. Made: 24.07.2006. Laid: 25.07.2006. Coming into force: 01.10.2006. Effect: S.I.1997/1612; 2006/966 amended. Territorial extent & classification: E/W. General. - 8p.: 30 cm. - 978-0-11-074939-6 £3.00

The Local Government Pension Scheme (Amendment) Regulations 2006 No. 2006/966. - Enabling power: Superannuation Act 1972, s. 7. - Issued: 03.04.2006. Made: 29.03.2006. Laid: 30.03.2006. Coming into force: In accord. with reg. 1. Effect: S.I. 1997/1612 amended. Territorial extent & classification: E/W. General. - 12p.: 30 cm. - 978-0-11-074429-2 £3.00

The Police Pensions (Amendment) Regulations 2006 No. 2006/740. - Enabling power: Police Pensions Act 1976, s. 1. - Issued: 20.03.2006. Made: 14.03.2006. Laid: 15.03.2006. Coming into force: 05.04.2006. Effect: S.I. 1987/257; 1991/1304 amended. Territorial extent & classification: E/W. General. - 12p.: 30 cm. - 978-0-11-074309-7 £3.00

The Police Pensions Regulations 2006 No. 2006/3415. - Enabling power: Police Pensions Act 1976, ss. 1 to 7. - Issued: 29.12.2006. Made: 19.12.2006. Laid: 21.12.2006. Coming into force: 01.02.2007 though have effect from 06.04.2007 except for 13(3)(b), 78(7) which have effect from 01.02.2007. Effect: S.I. 2006/932 amended. Territorial extent & classification: E/W. General. - 76p.: 30 cm. - 978-0-11-075562-5 £12.00

Pensions, Wales

The Firefighters' Pension (Wales) Scheme (Amendment) Order 2006 No. 2006/1672 (W.160). - Enabling power: Fire Services Act 1947, s. 26 & Superannuation Act 1972, s. 12 & Fire and Rescue Services Act 2004, ss. 36, 53, 60, 62 & Civil Partnership Act 2004, s. 259 (1) (2) (c) (4) (b). - Issued: 30.06.2006. Made: 21.06.2006. Coming into force: 23.06.2006. Effect: S.I. 1992/129 amended in relation to Wales. Territorial extent & classification: W. General. - In English and Welsh. Welsh title: Gorchymyn Cynllun Pensiwn Dynion Tân (Cymru) (Diwygio) 2006. - 44p.: 30 cm. - 978-0-11-091363-6 £7.50

Pesticides, England and Wales

The Pesticides (Maximum Residue Levels in Crops, Food and Feeding Stuffs) (England and Wales) (Amendment) (No. 2) Regulations 2006 No. 2006/1742. - Enabling power: European Communities Act 1972, s. 2 (2). - Issued: 07.07.2006. Made: 29.06.2006. Laid: 05.07.2006. Coming into force: 27.07.2006, except for reg. 3 which comes into force on 15.09.2006 in accord. with reg. 1 (3) (4). Effect: S.I. 2005/3286 amended. Territorial extent & classification: E/W. General. - EC note: The Regulations implement Commission Directives 2006/4/EC, 2006/9/EC and 2006/30/EC. - 12p., tables: 30 cm. - 978-0-11-074791-0 £3.00

The Pesticides (Maximum Residue Levels in Crops, Food and Feeding Stuffs) (England and Wales) (Amendment) (No. 3) Regulations 2006 No. 2006/2922. - Enabling power: European Communities Act 1972 , s. 2 (2). - Issued: 13.11.2006. Made: 06.11.2006. Laid: 10.11.2006. Coming into force: In accord. with reg. 1 (3) to (7). Effect: S.I. 2005/3286; 2006/985 amended. Territorial extent & classification: E/W. General. - EC note: The Regulations implement Commission Directives 2006/53/EC, 2006/59/EC, 2006/60/EC and 2006/61/EC. - 48p., tables: 30 cm. - 978-0-11-075279-2 £7.50

The Pesticides (Maximum Residue Levels In Crops, Food And Feeding Stuffs) (England and Wales) (Amendment) Regulations 2006 No. 2006/985. - Enabling power: European Communities Act 1972, s. 2 (2). - Issued: 17.05.2006. Made: 27.03.2006. Laid: 31.03.2006. Coming into force: 27.04.2006, 10.05.2006 & 21.04.2007 in accord. with reg. 1 (3) to (5). Effect: S.I. 2005/3286 amended. Territorial extent & classification: E/W. General. - EC note: Implements Commission Directives 2005/70/EC, 2005/74/EC and 2005/76/EC. - 24p., tables: 30 cm. - 978-0-11-074569-5 £4.00

The Plant Protection Products (Amendment) (No.2) Regulations 2006 No. 2006/2933. - Enabling power: European Communities Act 1972, s. 2(2). - Issued: 15.11.2006. Made: 08.11.2006. Laid: 13.11.2006. Coming into force: 06.12.2006 except for reg 2 (3); 01.02.2007 for reg 2 (3). Effect: S.I. 2005/1435 amended. Territorial extent & classification: E/W. General. - 4p.: 30 cm. - 978-0-11-075285-3 £3.00

The Plant Protection Products (Amendment) Regulations 2006 No. 2006/1295. - Enabling power: European Communities Act 1972, s. 2 (2). - Issued: 17.05.2006. Made: 10.05.2006. Laid: 11.05.2006. Coming into force: In accord. with reg. 1 (3) to (9). Effect: S.I. 2005/1435 amended. Territorial extent & classification: E/W. General. - EC note: These Regs amend S.I. 2005/1435 which implemented in England and Wales Council Directive 91/414/EEC concerning the placing of plant protection products on the market. - 8p.: 30 cm. - 978-0-11-074571-8 £3.00

Petroleum

The Petroleum Licensing (Exploration and Production) (Seaward and Landward Areas) (Amendment) Regulations 2006 No. 2006/784. - Enabling power: Petroleum Act 1998, s. 4. - Issued: 23.03.2006. Made: 15.03.2006. Laid: 16.03.2006. Coming into force: 13.04.2006. Effect: S.I. 2004/352 amended. Territorial extent & classification: E/W/S/NI. General. - 4p.: 30 cm. - 978-0-11-074340-0 £3.00

Petroleum revenue tax

The Oil Taxation (Market Value of Oil) Regulations 2006 No. 2006/3313. - Enabling power: Oil Taxation Act 1975, s. 21 (2), sch. 3, paras 2 (1B) (1C) (2E) (2F) & Finance Act 2006, s. 147 (4) (7). - Issued: 18.12.2006. Made: 13.12.2006. Coming into force: 14.12.2006. Effect: None. Territorial extent & classification: E/W/S/NI. General. - Supersedes draft SI (ISBN 0110753453) issued 01.12.2006. - 12p.: 30 cm. - 978-0-11-075490-1 £3.00

The Petroleum Revenue Tax (Attribution of Blended Crude Oil) Regulations 2006 No. 2006/3312. - Enabling power: Oil Taxation Act 1975, s. 2 (5B) to (5D) & Finance Act 2006, s. 148 (3). - Issued: 18.12.2006. Made: 13.12.2006. Coming into force: 14.12.2006. Effect: None. Territorial extent & classification: E/W/S/NI. General. - Supersedes the draft SI (ISBN 0110753445) issued 24.11.2006. - 8p.: 30 cm. - 978-0-11-075489-5 £3.00

The Petroleum Revenue Tax (Nomination Scheme for Disposals and Appropriations) (Amendment) Regulations 2006 No. 2006/3089. - Enabling power: Finance Act 1987, s. 61 (8), sch. 10, paras 1 (1), 4 (1B) (a) (3), 5 (1) (h), 5A (1) (h), 7 (3), 12 & Finance Act 1999, s. 133 (1) & Finance Act 2006, s. 150 (15). - Issued: 24.11.2006. Made: 20.11.2006. Laid: 21.11.2006. Coming into force: 12.12.2006. Effect: S.I. 1987/1338 amended. Territorial extent & classification:E/W/S/NI. General. - 4p.: 30 cm. - 978-0-11-075348-5 £3.00

Plant breeders' rights

The Plant Breeders' Rights (Naming and Fees) Regulations 2006 No. 2006/648. - Enabling power: Plant Varieties Act 1997, ss. 18 (1) (2), 28, 29, 48 (1) (b). - Issued: 16.03.2006. Made: 07.03.2006. Laid: 10.03.2006. Coming into force: 31.03.2006. Effect: S.I. 1998/1027 amended & S.I. 1978/294; 1998/1021; 2002/1677 revoked. Territorial extent & classification: E/W/S/NI. General. - 8p.: 30 cm. - 978-0-11-074231-1 £3.00

Plant breeders' rights, Wales

The Plant Breeders' Rights (Discontinuation of Prior Use Exemption) (Wales) Order 2006 No. 2006/1261 (W.118). - Enabling power: Plant Varieties Act 1997, s. 9 (6). - Issued: 09.05.2006. Made: 03.05.2006. Coming into force: 12.05.2006. Effect: 1997 c. 66 amended. Territorial extent & classification: W. General. - In English & Welsh. Welsh title: Gorchymyn Hawliau Bridwyr Planhigion (Dirwyn i Ben Esemptiad o Ddefnydd Blaenorol) (Cymru) 2006. - 4p.: 30 cm. - 978-0-11-091333-9 £3.00

Plant health

The Plant Health (Fees) (Forestry) Regulations 2006 No. 2006/2697. - Enabling power: European Communities Act 1972, s. 2 (2). - Issued: 18.10.2006. Made: 10.10.2006. Laid: 13.10.2006. Coming into force: 06.11.2006. Effect: S.I. 1996/2291; 1997/655; 1999/783 revoked. Territorial extent & classification: E/W/S. General. - EC note: Implements Article 13d of Council Directive 2000/29/EC on protective measures against the introduction into the Community of organisms harmful to plants or plant products and against their spread within the Community. - 8p.: 30 cm. - 978-0-11-075183-2 £3.00

The Plant Health (Forestry) (Amendment) Order 2006 No. 2006/2696. - Enabling power: Plant Health Act 1967, ss. 2, 3 (1). - Issued: 18.10.2006. Made: 10.10.2006. Laid: 13.10.2006. Coming into force: 06.11.2006. Effect: S.I. 2005/2517 amended. Territorial extent & classification: E/W/S. General. - 4p.: 30 cm. - 978-0-11-075182-5 £3.00

The Plant Health (Wood Packaging Material Marking) (Forestry) Order 2006 No. 2006/2695. - Enabling power: Plant Health Act 1967, ss. 3 (1) (4), 4A. - Issued: 17.10.2006. Made: 09.10.2006. Laid: 13.10.2006. Coming into force: 06.11.2006. Effect: None. Territorial extent & classification: E/W/S. General. - UN note: This Order implements International Standard for Phytosanitary Measures No. 15 (March 2002) on Guidelines for regulating wood packaging material in international trade, prepared by the Secretariat of the International Plant Protection Convention (IPPC) established by the FAO. - 12p.: 30 cm. - 978-0-11-075180-1 £3.00

Plant health, England

The Plant Health (England) (Amendment) Order 2006 No. 2006/2307. - Enabling power: Plant Health Act 1967, ss. 2, 3 (1) (4). - Issued: 31.08.2006. Made: 23.08.2006. Laid: 25.08.2006. Coming into force: 01.10.2006. Effect: S.I. 2005/2530 amended. Territorial extent & classification: E. General. - EC note: This Order amends the Plant Health (England) Order 2005 (SI 2005/2530) ("the principal Order") so as to implement Commission Directive 2005/77/EC amending Annex V to Council Directive 2000/29/EC on protective measures against the introduction into the Community of organisms harmful to plants or plant products and against their spread in the Community. Commission Decision 2005/870/EC recognising Bulgaria as being free from Clavibacter michiganensis (Smith) Davis et al. Commission Directive 2006/35/EC amending Annexes I to IV to Council Directive 2000/29/EC. Commission Decision 2006/473/EC recognising certain third countries and areas as being free from Xanthomonas campestris (all strains pathogenic to Citrus). Commission Decision 2006/464/EC on provisional emergency measures to prevent the introduction into and the spread within the Community of Dryocosmus kuriphilus Yasumatsu- 8p.: 30 cm. - 978-0-11-075045-3 £3.00

The Plant Health (Import Inspection Fees) (England) Regulations 2006 No. 2006/1879. - Enabling power: Finance Act 1973, s. 56 (1). - Issued: 19.07.2006. Made: 12.07.2006. Laid: 14.07.2006. Coming into force: 04.08.2006. Effect: S.I. 2005/906 revoked. Territorial extent & classification: E. General. - 12p.: 30 cm. - 978-0-11-074842-9 £3.00

Plant health, Wales

The Plant Health (Export Certification) (Wales) Order 2006 No. 2006/1701 (W.163). - Enabling power: Plant Health Act 1967, ss. 3 (1) (4), 4A. - Issued: 06.07.2006. Made: 27.06.2006. Coming into force: 30.06.2006. Effect: None. Territorial extent & classification: W. General. - Welsh title: Gorchymyn Iechyd Planhigion (Tystysgrifau Allforio) (Cymru) 2006. - In English and Welsh. - 12p.: 30 cm. - 978-0-11-091365-0 £3.00

The Plant Health (Import Inspection Fees) (Wales) (No. 2) Regulations 2006 No. 2006/2832 (W.253). - Enabling power: Finance Act 1973, s. 56 (1) & Government of Wales Act 1998, s. 29 (4). - Issued: 01.11.2006. Made: 24.10.2006. Coming into force: 31.10.2006. Effect: S.I. 2006/171 (W.22) revoked. Territorial extent & classification: W. General. - In English & Welsh. Welsh title: Rheoliadau Iechyd Planhigion (Ffioedd Arolygu Mewnforio) (Cymru) (Rhif 2) 2006. - 16p.: 30 cm. - 978-0-11-091420-6 £3.00

The Plant Health (Import Inspection Fees) (Wales) Regulations 2006 No. 2006/171 (W.22). - Enabling power: Finance Act 1973, s. 56 (1) & Government of Wales Act 1998, s. 29 (4). - Issued: 07.02.2006. Made: 31.01.2006. Coming into force: 01.02.2006. Effect: None. Territorial extent & classification: W. General. - Revoked by S.I. 2006/2832 (W.253) (ISBN 0110914201). With correction slip dated April 2006. - EC note: These Regulations give effect in Wales to article 13D of Council Directive 2000/29/EC. - In English & Welsh. Welsh title: Rheoliadau Iechyd Planhigion (Ffioedd Arolygu Mewnforio) (Cymru) 2006. - 16p.: 30 cm. - 978-0-11-091269-1 *£3.00*

The Plant Health (Phytophthora ramorum) (Wales) Order 2006 No. 2006/1344 (W.134). - Enabling power: Plant Health Act 1967, ss. 2, 3 (1) (2) (b) (4), 4 (1). - Issued: 23.05.2006. Made: 16.05.2006. Coming into force: 24.05.2006. Effect: S.I. 2002/2762 (W.263) revoked. Territorial extent & classification: W. General. - In English and Welsh. Welsh title: Gorchymyn Iechyd Planhigion (Phytopthora ramoram) (Cymru) 2006. - 20p.: 30 cm. - 978-0-11-091339-1 *£3.50*

The Plant Health (Wales) Order 2006 No. 2006/1643 (W.158). - Enabling power: Plant Health Act 1967, ss. 2, 3 (1) to (4), 4 (1). - Issued: 03.07.2006. Made: 20.06.2006. Coming into force: 27.06.2006. Effect: S.I. 1993/1320, 3213; 1995/1358, 2929; 1996/25, 1165, 3242; 1997/1145, 2907; 1998/349, 1121, 2245; 1999/2641; 2001/2500, 3761; 2002/1805; 2003/1851; 2005/70 revoked. Territorial extent & classification: W. General. - EC note: Implements, in relation to Wales, Council Directive 2002/89/EC amending Directive 2000/29/EC, and Commission Directives 2004/103, 2004/105/EC, 2005/16/EC, 2005/17/EC, 2005/77, 2005/260/EC, 2005/870/EC and 2006/35/EC. - 108p.: 30 cm. - 978-0-11-091359-9 *£15.50*

Police

The Serious Organised Crime and Police Act 2005 (Consequential and Supplementary Amendments to Secondary Legislation) Order 2006 No. 2006/594. - Enabling power: Serious Organised Crime and Police Act 2005, s. 173 (1). - Issued: 10.03.2006. Made: 06.03.2006. Laid: 09.03.2006. Coming into force: 01.04.2006. Effect: 44 instruments amended & S.I. 2002/1298 revoked. Territorial extent & classification: E/W/S/NI. General. - 16p.: 30 cm. - 978-0-11-074188-8 *£3.00*

Police, England and Wales

The Criminal Justice Act 2003 (Commencement No.12) Order 2006 No. 2006/751 (C.17). - Enabling power: Criminal Justice Act 2003, s. 336 (3). Bringing into operation various provisions of the 2003 Act on 06.04.2006. - Issued: 20.03.2006. Made: 14.03.2006. Effect: None. Territorial extent & classification: E/W. General. - 8p.: 30 cm. - 978-0-11-074319-6 *£3.00*

The NCIS and NCS (Abolition) Order 2006 No. 2006/540. - Enabling power: Serious Organised Crime and Police Act 2005, s. 1 (3). - Issued: 07.03.2006. Made: 01.03.2006. Coming into force: 01.04.2006. Effect: None. Territorial extent & classification: E/W. General. - 2p.: 30 cm. - 978-0-11-074152-9 *£3.00*

The Police Act 1996 (Local Policing Summaries) Order 2006 No. 2006/122. - Enabling power: Police Act 1996, s. 8A (3). - Issued: 27.01.2006. Made: 23.01.2006. Laid: 27.01.2006. Coming into force: 01.04.2006. Effect: None. Territorial extent & classification: E/W. General. - 2p.: 30 cm. - 978-0-11-073938-0 *£3.00*

The Police Act 1997 (Criminal Records) (Amendment No.2) Regulations 2006 No. 2006/2181. - Enabling power: Police Act 1997, ss. 113B (2) (b) (9), 113D (4) (d), 124 (6) (e) (f), 125. - Issued: 14.08.2006. Made: 08.08.2006. Laid: 10.08.2006. Coming into force: 01.09.2006 except for reg. 2 (g) and 25.09.2006 for reg. 2 (g). Effect: S.I. 2002/233 amended. Territorial extent & classification: E/W. General. - 4p.: 30 cm. - 978-0-11-074997-6 *£3.00*

The Police Act 1997 (Criminal Records) (Amendment) Regulations 2006 No. 2006/748. - Enabling power: Police Act 1997, ss. 113A (1) (b), 113B (1) (b) (2) (b) (9), 113E (3) (c), 114 (1) (b), 116 (1) (b), 125. - Issued: 20.03.2006. Made: 14.03.2006. Laid: 16.03.2006. Coming into force: 06.04.2006. Effect: S.I. 2002/233 amended. Territorial extent & classification: E/W. General. - 8p.: 30 cm. - 978-0-11-074328-8 *£3.00*

The Police Act 1997 (Criminal Records) (Registration) Regulations 2006 No. 2006/750. - Enabling power: Police Act 1997, s. 120ZA, 120AA, 125 (1) (5). - Issued: 20.03.2006. Made: 14.03.2006. Laid: 16.03.2006. Coming into force: 06.04.2006. Effect: S.I. 2001/1194, 2498 revoked. Territorial extent & classification: E/W. General. - 8p.: 30 cm. - 978-0-11-074338-7 *£3.00*

The Police (Amendment) (No. 2) Regulations 2006 No. 2006/3449. - Enabling power: Police Act 1996, s. 50. - Issued: 29.12.2006. Made: 21.12.2006. Laid: 22.12.2006. Coming into force: 01.02.2007 but regs 6, 8. 9 take retrospective effect from 16.04.2003, 24.07.2003, 01.04.2004 respectively. Effect: S.I. 2003/527 amended. Territorial extent & classification: E/W. General- 4p.: 30 cm. - 978-0-11-075579-3 *£3.00*

The Police (Amendment) Regulations 2006 No. 2006/1467. - Enabling power: Police Act 1996, s. 50. - Issued: 09.06.2006. Made: 05.06.2006. Laid: 08.06.2006. Coming into force: 01.07.2006. Effect: S.I. 2003/527 amended. Territorial extent & classification: E/W. General. - 2p.: 30 cm. - 978-0-11-074654-8 *£3.00*

The Police and Criminal Evidence Act 1984 (Code of Practice C and Code of Practice H) Order 2006 No. 2006/1938. - Enabling power: Police and Criminal Evidence Act 1984, s. 67 (5) (7D). - Issued: 21.07.2006. Made: 17.07.2006. Coming into force: 25.07.2006. Effect: None. Territorial extent & classification: E/W. General. - 2p.: 30 cm. - 978-0-11-074871-9 *£3.00*

The Police and Criminal Evidence Act 1984 (Codes of Practice) (Revisions to Code A) Order 2006 No. 2006/2165. - Enabling power: Police and Criminal Evidence Act 1984, s. 67 (5). - Issued: 10.08.2006. Made: 03.08.2006. Laid: 10.08.2006. Coming into force: 31.08.2007. Effect: None. Territorial extent & classification: E/W. General. - 2p.: 30 cm. - 978-0-11-074986-0 £3.00

The Police and Justice Act 2006 (Commencement No. 1, Transitional and Saving Provisions) Order 2006 No. 2006/3364 (C.123). - Enabling power: Police and Justice Act 2006, ss. 49 (3) (c), 53 (1). Bringing into operation various provisions of the 2006 Act on 15.01.2007 in accordance with art. 2. - Issued: 21.12.2006. Made: 14.12.2006. Effect: None. Territorial extent & classification: E/W. General. - This SI has been amended by SI 2007/29 (C.1) (ISBN 9780110756455) which is being issued free of charge to all known recipients of SI 2006/3364. - 4p.: 30 cm. - 978-0-11-075513-7 £3.00

The Police and Justice Act 2006 (Supplementary and Transitional Provisions) Order 2006 No. 2006/3365. - Enabling power: Police and Justice Act 2006, s. 51. - Issued: 21.12.2006. Made: 14.12.2006. Laid: 18.12.2006. Coming into force: 15.01.2007. Effect: None. Territorial extent & classification: E/W. General. - 4p.: 30 cm. - 978-0-11-075518-2 £3.00

The Police Authorities (Best Value) Performance Indicators (Amendment) Order 2006 No. 2006/620. - Enabling power: Local Government Act 1999, s. 4 (1) (a). - Issued: 13.03.2006. Made: 08.03.2006. Laid: 10.03.2006. Coming into force: 01.04.2006. Effect: S.I. 2005/470 amended. Territorial extent & classification: E/W. General. - 2p.: 30 cm. - 978-0-11-074195-6 £3.00

The Police (Complaints and Misconduct) (Amendment) Regulations 2006 No. 2006/1406. - Enabling power: Police Reform Act 2002, ss. 13, 20 (5), 21 (10), 23, sch. 3, paras 4 (4), 13 (4), 14C (2), 17, 21. - Issued: 02.06.2006. Made: 24.05.2006. Laid: 26.05.2006. Coming into force: 22.06.2006. Effect: S.I. 2004/643 amended. Territorial extent & classification: E/W. General. - 4p.: 30 cm. - 978-0-11-074618-0 £3.00

The Police (Injury Benefit) Regulations 2006 No. 2006/932. - Enabling power: Police Pensions Act 1976, ss. 1, 6, 7, 8. - Issued: 06.04.2006. Made: 27.03.2006. Laid: 30.03.2006. Coming into force: 20.04.2006. Effect: S.I. 1987/256, 257; 2005/1439 amended & S.I. 1987/156 revoked. Territorial extent & classification: E/W. General. - 40p.: 30 cm. - 978-0-11-074409-4 £6.50

The Police (Minimum Age for Appointment) Regulations 2006 No. 2006/2278. - Enabling power: Police Act 1996, ss. 50, 51. - Issued: 29.08.2006. Made: 22.08.2006. Laid: 29.08.2006. Coming into force: 19.09.2006. Effect: S.I. 1965/536; 2003/527 amended. Territorial extent & classification: E/W. General. - 2p.: 30 cm. - 978-0-11-075037-8 £3.00

The Police Pensions (Amendment) Regulations 2006 No. 2006/740. - Enabling power: Police Pensions Act 1976, s. 1. - Issued: 20.03.2006. Made: 14.03.2006. Laid: 15.03.2006. Coming into force: 05.04.2006. Effect: S.I. 1987/257; 1991/1304 amended. Territorial extent & classification: E/W. General. - 12p.: 30 cm. - 978-0-11-074309-7 £3.00

The Police Pensions Regulations 2006 No. 2006/3415. - Enabling power: Police Pensions Act 1976, ss. 1 to 7. - Issued: 29.12.2006. Made: 19.12.2006. Laid: 21.12.2006. Coming into force: 01.02.2007 though have effect from 06.04.2007 except for 13(3)(b), 78(7) which have effect from 01.02.2007. Effect: S.I. 2006/932 amended. Territorial extent & classification: E/W. General. - 76p.: 30 cm. - 978-0-11-075562-5 £12.00

The Police (Promotion)(Amendment) Regulations 2006 No. 2006/1442. - Enabling power: Police Act 1996, s. 50. - Issued: 06.06.2006. Made: 31.05.2006. Laid: 02.06.2006. Coming into force: 01.07.2006. Effect: S.I. 1996/1685 amended. Territorial extent & classification: E/W. General. - This Statutory Instrument has been made in consequence of a defect in S.I. 2005/178 and is being issued free of charge to all known recipients of that Statutory Instrument. - 2p.: 30 cm. - 978-0-11-074635-7 £3.00

The Serious Organised Crime and Police Act 2005 (Commencement No. 5 and Transitional and Transitory Provisions and Savings) Order 2006 No. 2006/378 (C.9). - Enabling power: Serious Organised Crime and Police Act 2005, s. 178 (8) (9) (10). Bringing into operation various provisions of the 2005 Act in accord. with arts. 2, 3, 4, 5, 6, 7. - Issued: 22.02.2006. Made: 15.02.2006. Effect: None. Territorial extent & classification: E/W/S/NI [parts to E/W or NI only]. General. - 12p.: 30 cm. - 978-0-11-074072-0 £3.00

The Serious Organised Crime and Police Act 2005 (Commencement No. 6 and Appointed Day) Order 2006 No. 2006/1085 (C.37). - Enabling power: Serious Organised Crime and Police Act 2005, ss. 161 (4), 178 (8). Bringing into operation various provisions of the 2005 Act on 08.05.2006; 15.05.2006. - Issued: 19.04.2006. Made: 06.04.2006. Effect: None. Territorial extent & classification: Art. 3 applies to E/W/S/NI; art. 2 to E/W. General. - 8p.: 30 cm. - 978-0-11-074490-2 £3.00

The Serious Organised Crime and Police Act 2005 (Commencement No.9 and Amendment) Order 2006 No. 2006/2182 (C.74). - Enabling power: Serious Organised Crime and Police Act 2005, s. 178 (8) (9). Bringing into operation various provisions of the 2005 Act on 25.09.2006. - Issued: 14.08.2006. Made: 08.08.2006. Coming into force: 15.08.2006. Effect: S.I. 2006/1871 (C.62) amended. Territorial extent & classification: E/W. General. - 4p.: 30 cm. - 978-0-11-074998-3 £3.00

Police, Northern Ireland

The Police and Criminal Evidence (Northern Ireland) Order 1989 (Codes of Practice) (Temporary Modification to Code D) Order 2006 No. 2006/1081. - Enabling power: S.I. 1989/1341 (N.I. 12), art. 66 (6A). - Issued: 18.04.2006. Made: 07.04.2006. Laid: 12.04.2006. Coming into force: 12.05.2006. Effect: The code of practice for the identification of persons by police officers ("Code D"), issued under S.I. 1989/1341 (N.I. 12), art. 65, modified. Territorial extent & classification: NI. General. - 20p.: 30 cm. - 978-0-11-074489-6 £3.50

Political parties

The Electoral Administration Act 2006 (Commencement No. 1 and Transitional Provisions) (Amendment) Order 2006 No. 2006/2268 (C.77). - Enabling power: Electoral Administration Act 2006, s. 77 (2) (3) (4). - Issued: 25.08.2006. Made: 17.08.2006. Coming into force: 25.08.2006. Effect: S.I. 2006/1972 (C.67) amended. Territorial extent & classification: E/W/S. General. - This Statutory Instrument has been made in consequence of a defect in SI 2006/1972 (C. 67) (ISBN 0110749065) and is being issued free of charge to all known recipients of that Statutory Instrument. - 2p.: 30 cm. - 978-0-11-075033-0 £3.00

The Electoral Administration Act 2006 (Commencement No. 1 and Transitional Provisions) Order 2006 No. 2006/1972 (C.67). - Enabling power: Electoral Administration Act 2006, s. 77 (2) (3) (4). Bringing into operation various provisions of the 2006 Act on 11.09.2006, subject to transitional provisions in sch. 2. - Issued: 26.07.2006. Made: 20.07.2006. Effect: None. Territorial extent & classification: E/W/S. General. - 8p.: 30 cm. - 978-0-11-074906-8 £3.00

The Political Parties, Elections and Referendums Act 2000 (Commencement No. 3 and Transitional Provisions) Order 2006 No. 2006/3416 (C.129). - Enabling power: Election Publications Act 2001, s. 2. Bringing into operation various provisions of the Political Parties, Elections and Referendums Act 2000, c. 41, on 01.01.2007. - Issued: 28.12.2006. Made: 18.12.2006. Effect: 2001 c. 5 modified. Territorial extent & classification: E/W/S. General. - 4p.: 30 cm. - 978-0-11-075565-6 £3.00

Political parties, England and Wales: Donations

The Political Donations and Regulated Transactions (Anonymous Electors) (England and Wales) Regulations 2006 No. 2006/2974. - Enabling power: Political Parties, Elections and Referendums Act 2000, s. 65(2A), sch. 6, paras 2 (3B) (3C), 3 (2) (3), sch. 6A, para. 2 (3), sch. 7, para. 10 (4A), sch. 11, para. 10 (4), sch. 15, para. 10 (4). - Issued: 20.11.2006. Made: 10.11.2006. Laid: 16.11.2006. Coming into force: 01.01.2007. Effect: None. Territorial extent & classification: E/W. General. - 2p.: 30 cm. - 978-0-11-075312-6 £3.00

Post Office

The Postal Services (Jersey) Order 2006 No. 2006/1918. - Enabling power: Post Office Act 1969, s. 87. - Issued: 31.07.2006. Made: 19.07.2006. Coming into force: 20.07.2006. Effect: S.I. 1969/1366 revoked & S.I. 1969/1368; 1973/960 revoked in relation to Jersey. Territorial extent & classification: E/W/S/NI. General. - 2p.: 30 cm. - 978-0-11-074920-4 £3.00

Prevention and suppression of terrorism

The Prevention of Terrorism Act 2005 (Continuance in force of sections 1 to 9) Order 2006 No. 2006/512. - Enabling power: Prevention of Terrorism Act 2005, s. 13 (2) (c). - Issued: 03.03.2006. Made: 25.02.2006. Coming into force: 11.03.2006. Effect: None. Territorial extent & classification: E/W/S/NI. General. - Supersedes draft S.I. (ISBN 0110739698) issued 08.02.2006. - 2p.: 30 cm. - 978-0-11-074124-6 £3.00

The Proscribed Organisations (Applications for Deproscription etc.) Regulations 2006 No. 2006/2299. - Enabling power: Terrorism Act 2000, s. 4 (3). - Issued: 29.08.2006. Made: 22.08.2006. Laid: 25.08.2006. Coming into force: 20.09.2006. Effect: S.I. 2001/107 revoked. Territorial extent & classification: E/W/S/NI. General. - 4p.: 30 cm. - 978-0-11-075043-9 £3.00

The Proscribed Organisations (Name Changes) Order 2006 No. 2006/1919. - Enabling power: Terrorism Act 2000, s. 3 (6). - Issued: 20.07.2006. Made: 14.07.2006. Laid: 17.07.2006. Coming into force: 14.08.2006. Effect: None. Territorial extent & classification: E/W/S/NI. General. - 2p.: 30 cm. - 978-0-11-074858-0 £3.00

The Terrorism Act 2000 (Business in the Regulated Sector) Order 2006 No. 2006/2384. - Enabling power: Terrorism Act 2000, sch. 3A, para. 5. - Issued: 15.09.2006. Made: 12.09.2006. Laid: 13.09.2006. Coming into force: 06.04.2007. Effect: 2000 c. 11 amended. Territorial extent & classification: E/W/S/NI. General. - 2p.: 30 cm. - 978-0-11-075102-3 £3.00

The Terrorism Act 2000 (Proscribed Organisations) (Amendment) Order 2006 No. 2006/2016. - Enabling power: Terrorism Act 2000, s. 3 (3) (a). - Issued: 28.07.2006. Made: 25.07.2006. Coming into force: 26.07.2006. Effect: 2000 c. 11 amended. Territorial extent & classification: E/W/S/NI. General. - Superseded draft SI (ISBN 011074859X) issued on 20.07.2006. - 2p.: 30 cm. - 978-0-11-074942-6 *£3.00*

The Terrorism Act 2000 (Revised Code of Practice for the Identification of Persons by Police Officers) (Northern Ireland) Order 2006 No. 2006/1330. - Enabling power: Terrorism Act 2000, s. 101 (4). - Issued: 19.05.2006. Made: 11.05.2006. Coming into force: 12.05.2006. Effect: None. Territorial extent & classification: NI. General. - Supersedes draft S.I. (ISBN 011074280X) issued 17.03.2006. - 2p.: 30 cm. - 978-0-11-074579-4 *£3.00*

The Terrorism Act 2006 (Commencement No. 1) Order 2006 No. 2006/1013 (C.32). - Enabling power: Terrorism Act 2006, s. 39 (2). Bringing into operation various provisions of the 2006 Act on 13.04.2006. - Issued: 06.04.2006. Made: 30.03.2006. Effect: None. Territorial extent & classification: E/W/S/NI. General. - 2p.: 30 cm. - 978-0-11-074453-7 *£3.00*

The Terrorism Act 2006 (Commencement No. 2) Order 2006 No. 2006/1936 (C.64). - Enabling power: Terrorism Act 2006, s. 39 (2). Bringing into operation various provisions of the 2006 Act on 25.07.2006. - Issued: 21.07.2006. Made: 17.07.2006. Effect: None. Territorial extent & classification: E/W/S/NI. General. - 2p.: 30 cm. - 978-0-11-074870-2 *£3.00*

Probation, England and Wales

The Local Probation Boards (Appointment and Miscellaneous Provisions) (Amendment) Regulations 2006 No. 2006/2664. - Enabling power: Criminal Justice and Court Services Act 2000, sch. 1, paras. 2 (4) (6), 3 (4) (6). - Issued: 11.10.2006. Made: 04.10.2006. Laid: 10.10.2006. Coming into force: 01.11.2006. Effect: S.I. 2000/3342; 2001/786 amended. Territorial extent & classification: E/W. General. - 2p.: 30 cm. - 978-0-11-075155-9 *£3.00*

Proceeds of crime

The Proceeds of Crime Act 2002 and Money Laundering Regulations 2003 (Amendment) Order 2006 No. 2006/308. - Enabling power: European Communities Act 1972, s. 2 (2). - Issued: 23.02.2006. Made: 14.02.2006. Coming into force: 21.02.2006. Effect: 2002 c.29; S.I. 2003/3075 amended. Territorial extent & classification: E/W/S/NI. General. - 4p.: 30 cm. - 978-0-11-074049-2 *£3.00*

The Proceeds of Crime Act 2002 (Business in the Regulated Sector) Order 2006 No. 2006/2385. - Enabling power: Proceeds of Crime Act 2002, sch. 9, para. 5. - Issued: 15.09.2006. Made: 12.09.2006. Laid: 13.09.2006. Coming into force: 06.04.2007. Effect: 2002 c. 29 amended. Territorial extent & classification: E/W/S/NI. General. - 2p.: 30 cm. - 978-0-11-075101-6 *£3.00*

The Proceeds of Crime Act 2002 (Money Laundering: Exceptions to Overseas Conduct Defence) Order 2006 No. 2006/1070. - Enabling power: Proceeds of Crime Act 2002, ss. 327 (2A) (b) (ii), 328 (3) (b) (ii), 329 (2A) (b) (ii). - Issued: 12.04.2006. Made: 05.04.2006. Laid: 12.04.2006. Coming into force: 15.05.2006. Effect: None. Territorial extent & classification: E/W/S/NI. General. - 2p.: 30 cm. - 978-0-11-074476-6 *£3.00*

The Proceeds of Crime Act 2002 (Recovery of Cash in Summary Proceedings: Minimum Amount) Order 2006 No. 2006/1699. - Enabling power: Proceeds of Crime Act 2002, s. 303. - Issued: 04.07.2006. Made: 28.06.2006. Laid: 04.07.2006. Coming into force: 31.07.2006. Effect: S.I. 2004/420 revoked. Territorial extent & classification: E/W/S/NI. General. - 2p.: 30 cm. - 978-0-11-074776-7 *£3.00*

The Serious Organised Crime and Police Act 2005 (Commencement No. 6 and Appointed Day) Order 2006 No. 2006/1085 (C.37). - Enabling power: Serious Organised Crime and Police Act 2005, ss. 161 (4), 178 (8). Bringing into operation various provisions of the 2005 Act on 08.05.2006; 15.05.2006. - Issued: 19.04.2006. Made: 06.04.2006. Effect: None. Territorial extent & classification: Art. 3 applies to E/W/S/NI; art. 2 to E/W. General. - 8p.: 30 cm. - 978-0-11-074490-2 *£3.00*

Proceeds of crime, England and Wales

The Proceeds of Crime Act 2002 (References to Financial Investigators) (Amendment) Order 2006 No. 2006/57. - Enabling power: Proceeds of Crime Act 2002, ss. 453, 459 (2). - Issued: 23.01.2006. Made: 14.01.2006. Laid: 23.01.2006. Coming into force: 01.03.2006. Effect: S.I. 2003/172 amended. Territorial extent & classification: E/W/NI. General. - 4p.: 30 cm. - 978-0-11-073912-0 *£3.00*

Proceeds of crime, Northern Ireland

The Proceeds of Crime Act 2002 (References to Financial Investigators) (Amendment) Order 2006 No. 2006/57. - Enabling power: Proceeds of Crime Act 2002, ss. 453, 459 (2). - Issued: 23.01.2006. Made: 14.01.2006. Laid: 23.01.2006. Coming into force: 01.03.2006. Effect: S.I. 2003/172 amended. Territorial extent & classification: E/W/NI. General. - 4p.: 30 cm. - 978-0-11-073912-0 *£3.00*

Professional qualifications

The European Communities (Recognition of Professional Qualifications) (Second General System) (Amendment) Regulations 2006 No. 2006/3214. - Enabling power: European Communities Act 1972, s. 2 (2). - Issued: 11.12.2006. Made: 04.12.2006. Laid: 11.12.2006. Coming into force: 01.01.2007. Effect: S.I. 2002/2934 amended. Territorial extent & classification: E/W/S/NI. General. - EC note: These Regulations give effect in the United Kingdom to Council Directive 2006/100/EC adapting certain directives in the field of freedom of movement of persons, by reason of the accession of the Republics of Bulgaria and Romania, which amends Annex C to Council Directive 92/51/EEC. - 4p.: 30 cm. - 978-0-11-075413-0 *£3.00*

The European Communities (Recognition of Qualifications and Experience) (Third General System) (Amendment) Regulations 2006 No. 2006/2228. - Enabling power: European Communities Act 1972, s. 2 (2). - Issued: 23.08.2006. Made: 09.08.2006. Laid: 23.08.2006. Coming into force: 02.10.2006. Effect: S.I. 2002/1597 amended. Territorial extent & classification: E/W/S/NI. General. - With correction slip dated January 2007. EC note: These Regulations amend the 2002 Regulations, which implemented Directive 99/42, in order to provide for mutual recognition in the Member States of qualifications in respect of certain activities. - 2p.: 30 cm. - 978-0-11-075020-0 *£3.00*

Protection of wrecks, England

The Protection of Wrecks (Designation) (England) (No.1) Order 2006 No. 2006/1178. - Enabling power: Protection of Wrecks Act 1973, ss. 1 (1) (2), 3 (2). - Issued: 02.05.2006. Made: 26.04.2006. Laid: 26.04.2006. Coming into force: 17.05.2006. Effect: S.I. 1980/1456; 1983/128 revoked. Territorial extent & classification: E. General. - 2p.: 30 cm. - 978-0-11-074530-5 *£3.00*

The Protection of Wrecks (Designation) (England) (No.2) Order 2006 No. 2006/1340. - Enabling power: Protection of Wrecks Act 1973, ss. 1 (1) (2), 3 (2). - Issued: 26.05.2006. Made: 16.05.2006. Laid: 17.05.2006. Coming into force: 07.06.2006. Effect: S.I. 1989/2294 revoked. Territorial extent & classification: E. General. - 2p.: 30 cm. - 978-0-11-074587-9 *£3.00*

The Protection of Wrecks (Designation) (England) (No.3) Order 2006 No. 2006/1342. - Enabling power: Protection of Wrecks Act 1973, ss. 1 (1) (2), 3 (2). - Issued: 23.05.2006. Made: 17.05.2006. Laid: 17.05.2006. Coming into force: 07.06.2006. Effect: S.I. 1993/2526 revoked. Territorial extent & classification: E. General. - 2p.: 30 cm. - 978-0-11-074588-6 *£3.00*

The Protection of Wrecks (Designation) (England) (No.4) Order 2006 No. 2006/1392. - Enabling power: Protection of Wrecks Act 1973, s. 1 (1) (2). - Issued: 31.05.2006. Made: 23.05.2006. Laid: 24.05.2006. Coming into force: 14.06.2006. Effect: None. Territorial extent & classification: E. General. - 2p.: 30 cm. - 978-0-11-074612-8 *£3.00*

The Protection of Wrecks (Designation) (England) (No.5) Order 2006 No. 2006/1468. - Enabling power: Protection of Wrecks Act 1973, ss. 1 (1) (2), 3 (2). - Issued: 12.06.2006. Made: 06.06.2006. Laid: 06.06.2006. Coming into force: 07.06.2006. Effect: S.I. 1989/2294; 2006/1340 revoked. Territorial extent & classification: E. General. - 2p.: 30 cm. - 978-0-11-074653-1 *£3.00*

The Protection of Wrecks (Designation) (England) (No.6) Order 2006 No. 2006/1470. - Enabling power: Protection of Wrecks Act 1973, ss. 1 (1) (2), 3 (2). - Issued: 12.06.2006. Made: 06.06.2006. Laid: 06.06.2006. Coming into force: 07.06.2006. Effect: S.I. 1993/2526; 2006/1342 revoked. Territorial extent & classification: E. General. - 2p.: 30 cm. - 978-0-11-074656-2 *£3.00*

The Protection of Wrecks (Designation) (England) (No.7) Order 2006 No. 2006/2535. - Enabling power: Protection of Wrecks Act 1973, ss. 1, 3. - Issued: 27.09.2006. Made: 20.09.2006. Laid: 21.09.2006. Coming into force: 21.09.2006 in accord. with art. 1. Effect: S.I. 1982/47 amended. Territorial extent & classification: E. General. - 2p.: 30 cm. - 978-0-11-075125-2 *£3.00*

Public bodies, Wales

The Ancient Monuments Board for Wales (Abolition) Order 2006 No. 2006/64 (W.13). - Enabling power: Government of Wales Act 1998, s. 28, sch. 4, part 1. - Issued: 24.01.2006. Made: 18.01.2006. Coming into force: 01.04.2006. Effect: 1976 c. 74; 1979 c. 46; 1998 c. 38; 2000 c. 36; S.I. 2001/3458; 2002/2812 amended in relation to Wales. Territorial extent & classification: W. General. - In English and Welsh. Welsh title: Gorchymyn (Diddymu) Bwrdd Henebion Cymru 2006. - 8p.: 30 cm. - 978-0-11-091255-4 *£3.00*

The Historic Buildings Council for Wales (Abolition) Order 2006 No. 2006/63 (W.12). - Enabling power: Government of Wales Act 1998, s. 28, sch. 4, part 1. - Issued: 24.01.2006. Made: 18.01.2006. Coming into force: 01.04.2006. Effect: 1953 c.49; 1976 c. 74; 1989 c. 29; 1990 c. 9; 1998 c. 38; 2000 c. 36; S.I. 1992/31; 2001/3458; 2002/2812 amended in relation to Wales. Territorial extent & classification: W. General. - In English and Welsh. Welsh title: Gorchymyn (Diddymu) Cyngor Adeiladau Hanesyddol Cymru 2006. - 8p.: 30 cm. - 978-0-11-091254-7 *£3.00*

Public health

The Appointments Commission Regulations 2006 No. 2006/2380. - Enabling power: Health Act 2006, ss. 65, 79 (3), sch. 4, paras 2 (b) (d), 3 (3) (b), 7 (1) (2), 10 (3) (c) (5) (6), 18 (2) (b). - Issued: 11.09.2006. Made: 04.09.2006. Laid: 05.09.2006. Coming into force: 01.10.2006. Effect: S.I. 2001/794 revoked. Territorial extent & classification: E/W/S/NI. General. - 12p.: 30 cm. - 978-0-11-075076-7 £3.00

The Vaccine Damage Payments (Specified Disease) Order 2006 No. 2006/2066. - Enabling power: Vaccine Damage Payments Act 1979, ss. 1 (2) (i). - Issued: 01.08.2006. Made: 25.07.2006. Laid: 01.08.2006. Coming into force: 04.09.2006. Effect: 1979 c. 17 modified. Territorial extent & classification: E/W/S/NI/IoM. General- 2p.: 30 cm. - 978-0-11-074948-8 £3.00

Public health, England

The Private and Voluntary Health Care (England) (Amendment No. 2) Regulations 2006 No. 2006/1734. - Enabling power: Care Standards Act 2000, ss. 16 (3), 118 (6). - Issued: 05.07.2006. Made: 28.06.2006. Laid: 05.07.2006. Coming into force: 01.08.2006. Effect: S.I. 2001/3968 amended & S.I. 2004/661; 2005/647 revoked. Territorial extent & classification: E. General. - 4p.: 30 cm. - 978-0-11-074783-5 £3.00

The Private and Voluntary Health Care (England) (Amendment) Regulations 2006 No. 2006/539. - Enabling power: Care Standards Act 2000, ss. 31 (7), 118 (6). - Issued: 07.03.2006. Made: 01.03.2006. Laid: 07.03.2006. Coming into force: 01.04.2006. Effect: S.I. 2001/3968; 2004/661 amended. Territorial extent & classification: E. General. - 2p.: 30 cm. - 978-0-11-074143-7 £3.00

The Smoke-free (Premises and Enforcement) Regulations 2006 No. 2006/3368. - Enabling power: Health Act 2006, ss. 2 (5), 10 (1) (2), 79 (3). - Issued: 20.12.2006. Made: 13.12.2006. Laid: 18.12.2006. Coming into force: 01.07.2007. Effect: None. Territorial extent & classification: E. General. - 4p.: 30 cm. - 978-0-11-075529-8 £3.00

Public health, England and Wales

The Health Act 2006 (Commencement No. 1 and Transitional Provisions) Order 2006 No. 2006/2603 (C.88). - Enabling power: Health Act 2006, ss. 79 (3), 83 (3) (7) (8). Bringing into operation various provisions of the 2006 Act on 28.09.2006 and 01.10.2006. - Issued: 29.09.2006. Made: 22.09.2006. Effect: None. Territorial extent & classification: E/W. General. - 8p.: 30 cm. - 978-0-11-075136-8 £3.00

Public health, Wales

The Care Standards Act 2000 and the Children Act 1989 (Abolition of Fees) (Wales) Regulations 2006 No. 2006/878 (W.83). - Enabling power: Care Standards Act 2000, ss. 12 (2), 15 (3), 16 (3), 22 (7), 118 (5) to (7) & Children Act 1989, ss. 79F, 87D, 104 (4), sch. 9A, para. 7 & Health and Social Care (Community Health and Standards) Act 2003, s. 94 (6). - Issued: 29.03.2006. Made: 21.03.2006. Coming into force: 01.04.2006. Effect: S.I. 2002/919 (W.107), 2935 (W.277), 3161 (W.296); 2003/237 (W.35), 781 (W.92), 2527 (W. 242); 2004/219 (W.23), 1756 (W.188) amended & S.I. 2002/921 (W.109) revoked. Territorial extent & classification: W. General. - In English and Welsh. Welsh title: Rheoliadau Deddf Safonau Gofal 2000 a Deddf Plant 1989 (Dileu Ffioedd) (Cymru) 2006. - 4p.: 30 cm. - 978-0-11-091304-9 £3.00

The Private and Voluntary Health Care and Miscellaneous (Wales) (Amendment) Regulations 2006 No. 2006/1703 (W.165). - Enabling power: Care Standards Act 2000, ss. 2 (4) (7) (f) (8), 12 (2), 14 (1) (d), 15 (3), 16 (1) (3), 22 (1) (2) (a) to (d), (f) to (j), (5) (a) (7) (a) to (h), (j) (k), 25 (1), 34 (1), 35, 118 (5) to (7). - Issued: 06.07.2006. Made: 27.06.2006. Coming into force: 06.07.2006. Effect: S.I. 2002/325 (W.38), 919 (W.107) amended. Territorial extent & classification: W. General. - In English & Welsh. Welsh title: Rheoliadau Gofal Iechyd Preifat a Gwirfoddol ac Amrywiol (Cymru) (Diwygio) 2006. - With correction slip dated September 2006. - 8p.: 30 cm. - 978-0-11-091364-3 £3.00

Public passenger transport

The Transport Act 2000 (Commencement No. 12) Order 2006 No. 2006/1933 (C.63). - Enabling power: Transport Act 2000, s. 275 (1). Bringing into operation various provisions of the 2000 Act on 01.10.2006 in accord. with art. 2. - Issued: 25.07.2006. Made: 17.07.2006. Effect: None. Territorial extent & classification: E/W/S/NI. General. - 8p.: 30 cm. - 978-0-11-074865-8 £3.00

Public procurement, England and Wales

The Public Contracts Regulations 2006 No. 2006/5. - Enabling power: European Communities Act 1972, s. 2 (2). - Issued: 25.01.2006. Made: 09.01.2006. Laid: 09.01.2006. Coming into force: 31.01.2006. Effect: 1993 c. 51; 1999 c. 29 & S.I. 1996/974; 1997/1744; 1999/506, 1042, 1820; 2000/1553; 2001/1149; 2002/881, 2114; 2003/1615, 1987, 2909; 2004/684; 3168; 2005/2929 amended & S.I. 1991/2680; 1993/3228; 1995/201; 2000/2009; 2003/46 revoked with savings in relation to England, Wales and Northern Ireland. Territorial extent & classification: E/W/NI. General. - EC note: These Regulations implement, for England, Wales and Northern Ireland, Directive 2004/18/EC on the co-ordination of procedures for the award of public works contracts, public supply contracts and public services contracts. They also provide remedies for breaches of these Regulations in order to implement Council Directive 89/665/EEC. - 88p.: 30 cm. - 978-0-11-073885-7 £13.50

The Utilities Contracts Regulations 2006 No. 2006/6. - Enabling power: European Communities Act 1972, s. 2 (2). - Issued: 25.01.2006. Made: 09.01.2006. Laid: 09.01.2006. Coming into force: 31.01.2006. Effect: S.I. 1996/2911; 2001/2418 revoked with savings in relation to England, Wales and Northern Ireland. Territorial extent & classification: E/W/NI. General. - EC note: These Regulations implement, for England, Wales and Northern Ireland, Directive 2004/17/EC coordinating the procurement procedures of entities operating in the water, energy, transport and postal services sectors. They also provide remedies for breaches of these Regulations, in order to implement Council Directive 92/13/EEC. - 64p.: 30 cm. - 978-0-11-073886-4 £10.50

Public procurement, Northern Ireland

The Public Contracts Regulations 2006 No. 2006/5. - Enabling power: European Communities Act 1972, s. 2 (2). - Issued: 25.01.2006. Made: 09.01.2006. Laid: 09.01.2006. Coming into force: 31.01.2006. Effect: 1993 c. 51; 1999 c. 29 & S.I. 1996/974; 1997/1744; 1999/506, 1042, 1820; 2000/1553; 2001/1149; 2002/881, 2114; 2003/1615, 1987, 2909; 2004/684; 3168; 2005/2929 amended & S.I. 1991/2680; 1993/3228; 1995/201; 2000/2009; 2003/46 revoked with savings in relation to England, Wales and Northern Ireland. Territorial extent & classification: E/W/NI. General. - EC note: These Regulations implement, for England, Wales and Northern Ireland, Directive 2004/18/EC on the co-ordination of procedures for the award of public works contracts, public supply contracts and public services contracts. They also provide remedies for breaches of these Regulations in order to implement Council Directive 89/665/EEC. - 88p.: 30 cm. - 978-0-11-073885-7 £13.50

The Utilities Contracts Regulations 2006 No. 2006/6. - Enabling power: European Communities Act 1972, s. 2 (2). - Issued: 25.01.2006. Made: 09.01.2006. Laid: 09.01.2006. Coming into force: 31.01.2006. Effect: S.I. 1996/2911; 2001/2418 revoked with savings in relation to England, Wales and Northern Ireland. Territorial extent & classification: E/W/NI. General. - EC note: These Regulations implement, for England, Wales and Northern Ireland, Directive 2004/17/EC coordinating the procurement procedures of entities operating in the water, energy, transport and postal services sectors. They also provide remedies for breaches of these Regulations, in order to implement Council Directive 92/13/EEC. - 64p.: 30 cm. - 978-0-11-073886-4 £10.50

Race relations

The Race Relations Act 1976 (General Statutory Duty) Order 2006 No. 2006/2470. - Enabling power: Race Relations Act 1976, s. 71 (5). - Issued: 15.09.2006. Made: 11.09.2006. Laid: 12.09.2006. Coming into force: 03.10.2006. Effect: 1976 c. 74 amended. Territorial extent & classification: E/W/S. General. - 4p.: 30 cm. - 978-0-11-075098-9 £3.00

The Race Relations Act 1976 (Statutory Duties) Order 2006 No. 2006/2471. - Enabling power: Race Relations Act 1976, s. 71 (2) (3). - Issued: 15.09.2006. Made: 11.09.2006. Laid: 12.09.2006. Coming into force: 03.10.2006. Effect: S.I. 2003/3006 amended. Territorial extent & classification: E/W/S. General. - 4p.: 30 cm. - 978-0-11-075099-6 £3.00

The Race Relations Code of Practice (Housing) (Appointed Day) Order 2006 No. 2006/2239. - Enabling power: Race Relations Act 1976, s. 47 (7) (8) (9). - Issued: 24.08.2006. Made: 17.08.2006. Laid: 24.08.2006. Coming into force: 01.10.2006. Effect: S.I. 1991/227; 1992/619 revoked. Territorial extent & classification: E/W/S. General. - 4p.: 30 cm. - 978-0-11-075030-9 £3.00

The Race Relations Code of Practice relating to Employment (Appointed Day) Order 2006 No. 2006/630. - Enabling power: Race Relations Act 1976, s. 47 (7) (8). - Issued: 15.03.2006. Made: 06.03.2006. Laid: 15.03.2006. Coming into force: 06.04.2006. Effect: S.I. 1983/1081 revoked. Territorial extent & classification: E/W/S. General. - 2p.: 30 cm. - 978-0-11-074201-4 £3.00

Rating and valuation, England

The Central Rating List (Amendment) (England) Regulations 2006 No. 2006/495. - Enabling power: Local Government Finance Act 1988, ss. 53 (1) (2) (4) (4A) (5), 64 (3), 65 (4), 143 (1) (2). - Issued: 06.03.2006. Made: 27.02.2006. Laid: 06.03.2006. Coming into force: 01.04.2006. Effect: S.I. 2005/551 amended. Territorial extent & classification: E. General. - 2p.: 30 cm. - 978-0-11-074112-3 £3.00

The Council Tax and Non-Domestic Rating (Amendment) (England) Regulations 2006 No. 2006/3395. - Enabling power: Local Government Finance Act 1988, s. 143 (1) (2), sch. 9, paras. 1, 2 (2) (ga), 3 (2) & Local Government Finance Act 1992, ss. 24 (7) (a), 41 (3), sch. 1, para. 9, sch. 2, paras 2 (4) (e) (j), 21 (3), sch. 4, paras 5 (2) (e), 7 (2) (b), 8 (2) (b). - Issued: 21.12.2006. Made: 18.12.2006. Laid: 21.12.2006. Coming into force: 31.01.2007. Effect: S.I. 1989/1058; 1992/552, 613, 3239; 1993/290; 2003/2613 amended. Territorial extent & classification: E. General. - With correction slip dated January 2007. - 12p.: 30 cm. - 978-0-11-075542-7 *£3.00*

The Council Tax and Non-Domestic Rating (Demand Notices) (Amendment) (England) Regulations 2006 No. 2006/492. - Enabling power: Local Government Finance Act 1988, s. 143 (1) (2), sch. 9. paras. 1, 2 (2) (ga). - Issued: 06.03.2006. Made: 27.02.2006. Laid: 06.03.2006. Coming into force: 31.03.2006. Effect: S.I. 2003/2613 amended. Territorial extent & classification: E. General. - 4p.: 30 cm. - 978-0-11-074116-1 *£3.00*

The Licensing Act 2003 (Consequential Amendment) (Non-Domestic Rating) (Public Houses in England) Order 2006 No. 2006/591. - Enabling power: Licensing Act 2003, ss. 197 (2), 198 (2). - Issued: 13.03.2006. Made: 07.03.2006. Laid: 07.03.2006. Coming into force: 31.03.2006. Effect: S.I. 2001/1345 amended. Territorial extent & classification: E. General. - 4p.: 30 cm. - 978-0-11-074184-0 *£3.00*

The Non-Domestic Rating (Alteration of Lists and Appeals) (England) (Amendment) Regulations 2006 No. 2006/2312. - Enabling power: Local Government Finance Act 1988, ss. 55 (2) (4) to (6), 143 (1) (2), sch. 11, para. 8. - Issued: 01.09.2006. Made: 23.08.2006. Laid: 01.09.2006. Coming into force: 01.10.2006. Effect: S.I. 2005/659 amended. Territorial extent & classification: E. General. - 8p.: 30 cm. - 978-0-11-075047-7 *£3.00*

The Non-Domestic Rating and Council Tax (Electronic Communications) (England) Order 2006 No. 2006/237. - Enabling power: Electronic Communications Act 2000, s. 8. - Issued: 08.02.2006. Made: 01.02.2006. Laid: 08.02.2006. Coming into force: 01.03.2006. Effect: S.I. 1989/1058, 2260; 1992/613 amended in relation to England. Territorial extent & classification: E. General. - 4p.: 30 cm. - 978-0-11-074019-5 *£3.00*

The Non-Domestic Rating (Chargeable Amounts) (Amendment) (England) Regulations 2006 No. 2006/3394. - Enabling power: Local Government Finance Act 1988, ss. 57A, 140 (4), 143 (1) (2), 146 (6). - Issued: 22.12.2006. Made: 13.12.2006. Coming into force: 14.12.2006. Effect: S.I. 2004/3387 amended. Territorial extent & classification: E. General. - Supersedes the draft S.I. (ISBN 0110748697) issued on 24.07.2006. - For approval by resolution of each House of Parliament. - 2p.: 30 cm. - 978-0-11-075545-8 *£3.00*

The Non-Domestic Rating Contributions (Amendment) (England) Regulations 2006 No. 2006/3167. - Enabling power: Local Government Finance Act 1988, ss. 143 (1) (2), sch. 8, paras 4, 6. - Issued: 04.12.2006. Made: 28.11.2006. Laid: 04.12.2006. Coming into force: 31.12.2006. Effect: S.I. 1992/3082 amended. Territorial extent & classification: E. General. - 2p.: 30 cm. - 978-0-11-075392-8 *£3.00*

The Non-Domestic Rating (Small Business Rate Relief) (Amendment) (England) Order 2006 No. 2006/2313. - Enabling power: Local Government Finance Act 1988, ss. 43 (4B) (a) (ii) (iii) (4C), 143 (1) (2). - Issued: 01.09.2006. Made: 23.08.2006. Laid: 01.09.2006. Coming into force: 01.10.2006. Effect: S.I. 2004/3315 amended. Territorial extent & classification: E. General. - 8p.: 30 cm. - 978-0-11-075049-1 *£3.00*

Rating and valuation, Wales

The Non-Domestic Rating (Alteration of Lists and Appeals) (Wales) (Amendment) Regulations 2006 No. 2006/1035 (W.105). - Enabling power: Local Government Finance Act 1988, ss. 55 (2) to (6) (7A), 143 (1) (2), sch. 7A, para. 12, sch. 11, paras 1, 8. - Issued: 18.04.2006. Made: 04.04.2006. Coming into force: 05.04.2006. Effect: S.I. 2005/758 (W.63) amended. Territorial extent & classification: W. General. - In English and Welsh. Welsh title: Rhwoliadau Ardrethu Annomestig (Newid Rhestri ac Apelau) (Cymru) (Diwygio) 2006. - 4p.: 30 cm. - 978-0-11-091324-7 *£3.00*

The Non-Domestic Rating Contributions (Wales) (Amendment) Regulations 2006 No. 2006/3347 (W.307). - Enabling power: Local Government Finance Act 1988, ss. 60, 140 (4), 143 (1) (2), sch. 8, paras 4, 6. - Issued: 21.12.2006. Made: 12.12.2006. Coming into force: 31.12.2006. Effect: S.I. 1992/3238 amended. Territorial extent & classification: W. General. - In English and Welsh: Welsh title: Rheoliadau Cyfraniadau Ardredthu Annomestig (Cymru) (Diwygio) 2006. - 4p.: 30 cm. - 978-0-11-091476-3 *£3.00*

The Non-Domestic Rating (Demand Notices and Discretionary Relief) (Wales) (Amendment) Regulations 2006 No. 2006/3392 (W.311). - Enabling power: Local Government Finance Act 1988, ss. 47 (8), 62, sch. 9, paras 1, 2 (2). - Issued: 22.12.2006. Made: 12.12.2006. Coming into force: 01.04.2007. Effect: S.I. 1989/1059 amended in relation to Wales & 1993/252 amended. Territorial extent & classification: W. General. - In English and Welsh. Welsh title: Rheoliadau Ardrethu Annomestig (Hysbysiadau Galw am Dalu a Rhyddhad yn ôl Disgresiwn) (Cymru) (Diwygio) 2006. - 8p.: 30 cm. - 978-0-11-091478-7 *£3.00*

The Non-Domestic Rating (Small Business Relief) (Wales) Order 2006 No. 2006/3345 (W.306). - Enabling power: Local Government Finance Act 1988, ss. 43 (4B) (b), 44 (9), 143 (1) (2). - Issued: 21.12.2006. Made: 12.12.2006. Coming into force: 01.04.2007. Effect: S.I. 1998/2963; 2002/331 (W.44) revoked with savings. Territorial extent & classification: W. General. - In English and Welsh: Welsh title: Gorchymyn Ardredthu Annomestig (Rhyddhad Ardrethi i Fusnesau Bach) (Cymru) 2006. - 8p.: 30 cm. - 978-0-11-091477-0 £3.00

Recovery of taxes

The Mutual Assistance Provisions Order 2006 No. 2006/3283. - Enabling power: Finance Act 2003, s. 197 (5). - Issued: 14.12.2006. Made: 11.12.2006. Laid: 11.12.2006. Coming into force: 01.01.2007. Effect: 2003 c.14 amended. Territorial extent & classification: E/W/S/NI. General. - With correction slip dated January 2007. - 2p.: 30 cm. - 978-0-11-075465-9 £3.00

Referendums

The Electoral Administration Act 2006 (Commencement No. 1 and Transitional Provisions) (Amendment) Order 2006 No. 2006/2268 (C.77). - Enabling power: Electoral Administration Act 2006, s. 77 (2) (3) (4). - Issued: 25.08.2006. Made: 17.08.2006. Coming into force: 25.08.2006. Effect: S.I. 2006/1972 (C.67) amended. Territorial extent & classification: E/W/S. General. - This Statutory Instrument has been made in consequence of a defect in SI 2006/1972 (C. 67) (ISBN 0110749065) and is being issued free of charge to all known recipients of that Statutory Instrument. - 2p.: 30 cm. - 978-0-11-075033-0 £3.00

The Electoral Administration Act 2006 (Commencement No. 1 and Transitional Provisions) Order 2006 No. 2006/1972 (C.67). - Enabling power: Electoral Administration Act 2006, s. 77 (2) (3) (4). Bringing into operation various provisions of the 2006 Act on 11.09.2006, subject to transitional provisions in sch. 2. - Issued: 26.07.2006. Made: 20.07.2006. Effect: None. Territorial extent & classification: E/W/S. General. - 8p.: 30 cm. - 978-0-11-074906-8 £3.00

Registration of births, deaths and marriages, etc., England and Wales

The Registration of Births and Deaths (Amendment) Regulations 2006 No. 2006/2827. - Enabling power: Births and Deaths Registration Act 1953, ss. 1, 5, 7, 9, 15, 20, 23 (2) (b), 23 (3), 29, 39, 41 (as extended by s. 26 (3) of the Welsh Language Act 1993) & Registration Service Act 1953, ss. 20, 21 (1). - Issued: 30.10.2006. Made: 25.10.2006. Coming into force: 13.11.2006. Effect: S.I. 1987/2088, 2089 amended. Territorial extent & classification: E/W. General. - 12p.: 30 cm. - 978-0-11-075225-9 £3.00

The Registration of Births and Deaths (Electronic Communications and Electronic Storage) Order 2006 No. 2006/2809. - Enabling power: Electronic Communications Act 2000, ss. 8, 9. - Issued: 25.10.2006. Made: 20.10.2006. Laid: 23.10.2006. Coming into force: 13.11.2006. Effect: 1953 c.20 modified. Territorial extent & classification: E/W. General. - 4p.: 30 cm. - 978-0-11-075211-2 £3.00

Registration of political parties

The Electoral Administration Act 2006 (Commencement No. 1 and Transitional Provisions) (Amendment) Order 2006 No. 2006/2268 (C.77). - Enabling power: Electoral Administration Act 2006, s. 77 (2) (3) (4). - Issued: 25.08.2006. Made: 17.08.2006. Coming into force: 25.08.2006. Effect: S.I. 2006/1972 (C.67) amended. Territorial extent & classification: E/W/S. General. - This Statutory Instrument has been made in consequence of a defect in SI 2006/1972 (C. 67) (ISBN 0110749065) and is being issued free of charge to all known recipients of that Statutory Instrument. - 2p.: 30 cm. - 978-0-11-075033-0 £3.00

The Electoral Administration Act 2006 (Commencement No. 1 and Transitional Provisions) Order 2006 No. 2006/1972 (C.67). - Enabling power: Electoral Administration Act 2006, s. 77 (2) (3) (4). Bringing into operation various provisions of the 2006 Act on 11.09.2006, subject to transitional provisions in sch. 2. - Issued: 26.07.2006. Made: 20.07.2006. Effect: None. Territorial extent & classification: E/W/S. General. - 8p.: 30 cm. - 978-0-11-074906-8 £3.00

The Registration of Political Parties (Prohibited Words and Expressions) (Amendment) Order 2006 No. 2006/3252. - Enabling power: Political Parties, Elections and Referendums Act 2000, s. 28A (2) (g). - Issued: 11.12.2006. Made: 06.12.2006. Laid: 07.12.2006. Coming into force: 01.01.2007. Effect: S.I. 2001/82 amended. Territorial extent & classification: E/W/S/NI & Gibraltar. General. - 4p.: 30 cm. - 978-0-11-075438-3 £3.00

Regulatory reform

The Regulatory Reform (Forestry) Order 2006 No. 2006/780. - Enabling power: Regulatory Reform Act 2001, s. 1. - Issued: 23.03.2006. Made: 15.03.2006. Coming into force: 16.03.2006 in accord. with art. 1. Effect: 1967 c.10; 1968 c.41 amended. Territorial extent & classification: E/W/S. General. - 8p.: 30 cm. - 978-0-11-074358-5 £3.00

The Regulatory Reform (Registered Designs) Order 2006 No. 2006/1974. - Enabling power: Regulatory Reform Act 2001, s. 1. - Issued: 04.08.2006. Made: 26.07.2006. Coming into force: 01.10.2006. Effect: 1949 c. 88 amended. Territorial extent & classification: E/W/S/NI. General. - 8p.: 30 cm. - 978-0-11-074962-4 £3.00

Regulatory reform, England and Wales

The Regulatory Reform (Agricultural Tenancies) (England and Wales) Order 2006 No. 2006/2805. - Enabling power: Regulatory Reform Act 2001, s. 1. - Issued: 26.10.2006. Made: 18.10.2006. Coming into force: 19.10.2006 in accord. with art. 1 (1). Effect: 1986 c.5, c.49; 1992 c.53; 1993 c.8; 1995 c.8, c.42; 1996 c.23; 2005 c.4; S.I. 1986/1611; 1987/710, 908; 1996/337; 1998/3132; 2005/465, 537 amended & S.I. 1990/1472 revoked. Territorial extent & classification: E/W. General. - 16p.: 30 cm. - 978-0-11-075207-5 £3.00

The Regulatory Reform (Fire Safety) Subordinate Provisions Order 2006 No. 2006/484. - Enabling power: Regulatory Reform Act 2001, s. 1. - Issued: 06.03.2006. Made: 23.02.2006. Laid: 06.03.2006. Coming into force: 31.03.2006. Effect: S.I. 2005/1541 modified in relation to England & Wales. Territorial extent & classification: E/W. General. - 2p.: 30 cm. - 978-0-11-074113-0 £3.00

Rehabilitation of offenders, England and Wales

The Rehabilitation of Offenders Act 1974 (Exceptions) (Amendment) (England and Wales) Order 2006 No. 2006/2143. - Enabling power: Rehabilitation of Offenders Act 1974, ss. 4 (4), 7 (4), 10 (1). - Issued: 08.08.2006. Made: 25.07.2006. Coming into force: 26.07.2006. Effect: S.I. 1975/1023 amended. Territorial extent & classification: E/W. General. - 8p.: 30 cm. - 978-0-11-074982-2 £3.00

The Rehabilitation of Offenders Act 1974 (Exceptions) (Amendment No. 2) (England and Wales) Order 2006 No. 2006/3290. - Enabling power: Rehabilitation of Offenders Act 1974, ss. 4 (4), 7 (4), 10(1). - Issued: 15.12.2006. Made: 06.12.2006. Coming into force: 07.12.2006. Effect: S.I. 1975/1023 amended. Territorial extent & classification: E/W. General. - 2p.: 30 cm. - 978-0-11-075472-7 £3.00

Representation of the people

The Elections (Policy Development Grants Scheme) Order 2006 No. 2006/602. - Enabling power: Political Parties, Elections and Referendums Act 2000, s.12. - Issued: 13.03.2006. Made: 07.03.2006. Laid: 09.03.2006. Coming into force: 01.04.2006. Effect: S.I. 2002/224 revoked. Territorial extent & classification: E/W/S/NI. General. - 8p.: 30 cm. - 978-0-11-074190-1 £3.00

The Electoral Administration Act 2006 (Commencement No. 1 and Transitional Provisions) (Amendment) Order 2006 No. 2006/2268 (C.77). - Enabling power: Electoral Administration Act 2006, s. 77 (2) (3) (4). - Issued: 25.08.2006. Made: 17.08.2006. Coming into force: 25.08.2006. Effect: S.I. 2006/1972 (C.67) amended. Territorial extent & classification: E/W/S. General. - This Statutory Instrument has been made in consequence of a defect in SI 2006/1972 (C. 67) (ISBN 0110749065) and is being issued free of charge to all known recipients of that Statutory Instrument. - 2p.: 30 cm. - 978-0-11-075033-0 £3.00

The Electoral Administration Act 2006 (Commencement No. 1 and Transitional Provisions) Order 2006 No. 2006/1972 (C.67). - Enabling power: Electoral Administration Act 2006, s. 77 (2) (3) (4). Bringing into operation various provisions of the 2006 Act on 11.09.2006, subject to transitional provisions in sch. 2. - Issued: 26.07.2006. Made: 20.07.2006. Effect: None. Territorial extent & classification: E/W/S. General. - 8p.: 30 cm. - 978-0-11-074906-8 £3.00

The Electoral Administration Act 2006 (Commencement No. 2, Transitional and Savings Provisions) Order 2006 No. 2006/3412 (C.128). - Enabling power: Electoral Administration Act 2006, s. 77. Bringing into operation various provisions of the 2006 Act on 01.01.2007, 31.01.2007. - Issued: 28.12.2006. Made: 18.12.2006. Effect: None. Territorial extent & classification: E/W/S/NI. General. - 8p.: 30 cm. - 978-0-11-075559-5 £3.00

The Political Parties, Elections and Referendums Act 2000 (Commencement No. 3 and Transitional Provisions) Order 2006 No. 2006/3416 (C.129). - Enabling power: Election Publications Act 2001, s. 2. Bringing into operation various provisions of the Political Parties, Elections and Referendums Act 2000, c. 41, on 01.01.2007. - Issued: 28.12.2006. Made: 18.12.2006. Effect: 2001 c. 5 modified. Territorial extent & classification: E/W/S. General. - 4p.: 30 cm. - 978-0-11-075565-6 £3.00

The Review of Polling Districts and Polling Places (Parliamentary Elections) Regulations 2006 No. 2006/2965. - Enabling power: Representation of the People Act 1983, s. 18C, sch. A1, paras 3 (3), 7. - Issued: 17.11.2006. Made: 10.11.2006. Coming into force: 01.01.2007. Effect: None. Territorial extent & classification: E/W/S. General. - Supersedes the draft SI (ISBN 011075204X) issued 25.10.2006. - 4p.: 30 cm. - 978-0-11-075305-8 £3.00

The Service Voters' Registration Period Order 2006 No. 2006/3406. - Enabling power: Representation of the People Act 1983, s. 15 (9) (10). - Issued: 28.12.2006. Made: 18.12.2006. Coming into force: In accord. with art. 1 (2). Effect: S.I. 2001/341, 497(S.2) amended. Territorial extent & classification: E/W/S. General. - Supersedes the draft S.I. (ISBN 0110752058) issued on 25.10.2006. - 4p.: 30 cm. - 978-0-11-075556-4 £3.00

Representation of the people, England and Wales

The Absent Voting (Transitional Provisions) (England and Wales) Regulations 2006 No. 2006/2973. - Enabling power: Electoral Administration Act 2006, s. 14 (5) (7). - Issued: 20.11.2006. Made: 10.11.2006. Laid: 16.11.2006. Coming into force: 01.01.2007. Effect: None. Territorial extent & classification: E/W. General. - 4p.: 30 cm. - 978-0-11-075310-2 £3.00

The Encouraging Electoral Participation (Reimbursement of Expenses) (England and Wales) Regulations 2006 No. 2006/2972. - Enabling power: Electoral Administration Act 2006, s. 69 (5) (6). - Issued: 20.11.2006. Made: 10.11.2006. Laid: 16.11.2006. Coming into force: 01.04.2007. Effect: None. Territorial extent & classification: E/W. General. - 2p.: 30 cm. - 978-0-11-075311-9 £3.00

The Local Elections (Parishes and Communities) (England and Wales) Rules 2006 No. 2006/3305. - Enabling power: Representation of the People Act 1983, s. 36 (2). - Issued: 28.12.2006. Made: 12.12.2006. Laid: 12.12.2006. Coming into force: In accord. with rule 1 (2). Effect: 1983 c. 2 modified & S.I. 1986/2215; 1987/260; 1990/157; 1998/585; 1999/395; 2001/80; 2004/224, 1040; 2006/390 revoked (02.01.2007). Territorial extent & classification: E/W. General. - 100p.: 30 cm. - 978-0-11-075526-7 £15.50

The Local Elections (Principal Areas and Parishes and Communities) (Amendment) (England and Wales) Rules 2006 No. 2006/390. - Enabling power: Representation of the People Act 1983, s. 36 (2). - Issued: 02.03.2006. Made: 16.02.2006. Laid: 22.02.2006. Coming into force: 24.03.2006. Effect: S.I. 1986/2214, 2215 amended. Territorial extent & classification: E/W. General. - 4p.: 30 cm. - 978-0-11-074078-2 £3.00

The Local Elections (Principal Areas) (England and Wales) Rules 2006 No. 2006/3304. - Enabling power: Representation of the People Act 1983, s. 36 (2). - Issued: 28.12.2006. Made: 12.12.2006. Laid: 12.12.2006. Coming into force: In accord. with rule 1 (2). Effect: S.I. 2002/185; 2005/2114 amended & S.I. 1986/2214; 1987/261; 1990/158; 1998/578; 1999/394; 2001/81; 2004/223, 1041; 2006/390 (except for rule 3) revoked (02.01.2007). Territorial extent & classification: E/W. General. - 100p.: 30 cm. - 978-0-11-075525-0 £15.50

The Representation of the People (Combination of Polls) (England and Wales) (Amendment) Regulations 2006 No. 2006/3278. - Enabling power: Representation of the People Act 1983, s. 36 (3C) & Representation of the People Act 1985, s. 15 (5) & Local Government Act 2000, ss. 44, 45. - Issued: 18.12.2006. Made: 12.12.2006. Coming into force: In accord. with reg. 1. Effect: S.I. 2004/294 amended. Territorial extent & classification: E/W. General. - Supersedes the draft S.I. (ISBN 0110752732) issued on 13.11.2006. - 8p.: 30 cm. - 978-0-11-075478-9 £3.00

The Representation of the People (England and Wales) (Amendment) (No. 2) Regulations 2006 No. 2006/2910. - Enabling power: Representation of the People Act 1983, ss. 7 (3) (aa), 7A (3) (aa), 7C (2) (aa), 10A (1) (a) (3) (5) (b), 13A (1) (a), 13B, 15 (2) (aa), 36 (3C), 53, 57, sch. 1, rules 19A, 24, 28 (3), 31A, 45 (1B), 57, sch. 2, paras 1 (4), 2A, 2B, 3A, 5A, 8A, 10, 12, 13 (1A), sch. 2A, para. 10 (2) & Representation of the People Act 1985, ss. 2 (2) (aa), 15 (5) & Local Government Act 2000, ss. 44, 45 & Representation of the People Act 2000, sch. 4, paras 3 (1) (b), (2) (c), (9) (10), 4 (1) (b), (2) (c), (4) (a) (7), 6 (7) (8), 7 (5) (c) (13), 7B, 7D & Electoral Administration Act 2006, s. 42. - Issued: 28.12.2006. Made: 10.11.2006. Coming into force: In accord. with reg. 1 (1) to (4). Effect: S.I. 2001/341 amended. Territorial extent & classification: E/W. General. - 64p.: 30 cm. - 978-0-11-075538-0 £10.50

The Representation of the People (England and Wales) (Amendment) Regulations 2006 No. 2006/752. - Enabling power: Representation of the People Act 1983, ss. 4 (4), 9 (2), 10A (1) (9), 13 (3), 13A (1) (2) (6), 13B (3), 36 (3C), 53, 201 (1) (3), sch. 1, rule 24, 45 (1B), sch. 2, paras. 3A, 5A (2) (3), 10A, 10B, 11, 12, 13 (1A) & Representation of the People Act 1985, s. 15 (5) & Representation of the People Act 2000, sch. 4, paras. 3 (1) (b) (2) (c), 4 (1) (b) (2) (c) (4) (a), 6 (7) (8), 7 (5) (c) (7) & Local Government Act 2000, ss. 44, 45, 105. - Issued: 20.03.2006. Made: 09.03.2006. Coming into force: 23.03.2006 in accord. with reg. 1. Effect: S.I. 2001/341, 1298; 2002/185 amended. Territorial extent & classification: E/W. General. - 20p.: 30 cm. - 978-0-11-074311-0 £3.50

The Representation of the People (Form of Canvass) (England and Wales) Regulations 2006 No. 2006/1694. - Enabling power: Representation of the People Act 1983, ss. 10 (4), 53, 201 (1) (3), sch. 2, para. 10 (2). - Issued: 30.06.2006. Made: 27.06.2006. Coming into force: 11.07.2006. Effect: S.I. 2001/341 amended & S.I. 2004/1848 revoked. Territorial extent & classification: E/W. General. - Supersedes draft SI (ISBN 0110746198) issued 02.06.2006. - 8p.: 30 cm. - 978-0-11-074767-5 £3.00

Representation of the people, Northern Ireland

The Northern Ireland (Miscellaneous Provisions) Act 2006 (Commencement No. 1) Order 2006 No. 2006/2688 (C.91). - Enabling power: Northern Ireland (Miscellaneous Provisions) Act 2006, s. 31 (3). Bringing operation various provisions of the 2006 Act on 16.10.2006 & 01.12.2006 in accord. with arts. 2 & 3. - Issued: 13.10.2006. Made: 09.10.2006. Effect: None. Territorial extent & classification: NI. General. - 2p.: 30 cm. - 978-0-11-075169-6 £3.00

Representation of the people, Scotland

The Representation of the People (Form of Canvass) (Scotland) Regulations 2006 No. 2006/1836 (S.12). - Enabling power: Representation of the People Act 1983, ss. 10 (4), 53, 201 (1) (3), 202 (1), sch. 2, para. 10 (2). - Issued: 18.07.2006. Made: 06.07.2006. Coming into force: 20.07.2006. Effect: S.I. 2001/497 amended & S.I. 2004/1960 revoked. Territorial extent & classification: S. General. - 8p.: 30 cm. - 978-0-11-070870-6 £3.00

The Representation of the People (Scotland) (Amendment) Regulations 2006 No. 2006/834 (S. 9). - Enabling power: Representation of the People Act 1983, ss. 4 (4), 9 (2), 10A (1) (9), 13 (3), 13A (1) (2) (6), 13B (3), 53, 201 (1) (3), sch. 1, rules 24, 45 (1B), sch. 2, paras 3A, 5A (2) (3), 10A, 10B, 11, 12, 13 (1A) & Representation of the People Act 2000, sch. 4, paras 3 (1) (b) (2) (c), 4 (1) (b) (2) (c) (4) (a), 6 (7) (8), 7 (5) (c) (7). - Issued: 05.04.2006. Made: 09.03.2006. Coming into force: 23.03.2006. Effect: S.I. 2001/497 amended. Territorial extent & classification: S. General. - Supersedes the draft S.I. (ISBN 0110699394) issued on 15.02.2006. - 16p.: 30 cm. - 978-0-11-070225-4 £3.00

Representation of the people, Wales

The National Assembly for Wales (Representation of the People) (Amendment) Order 2006 No. 2006/884. - Enabling power: Government of Wales Act 1998, s. 11. - Issued: 26.04.2006. Made: 22.03.2006. Coming into force: 23.04.2006 in accord. with art. 1 (1). Effect: S.I. 2003/284 amended. Territorial extent & classification: W. General. - This statutory instrument has been printed in substitution of the SI of the same number (and ISBN, issued on 21.04.2006) and is being issued free of charge to all known recipients of the original version. - 8p.: 30 cm. - 978-0-11-074384-4 £3.00

The National Assembly for Wales (Returning Officers' Charges) Order 2006 No. 2006/3268 (W.298). - Enabling power: S.I. 2003/284, art 21 (1) (2). - Issued: 15.12.2006. Made: 06.12.2006. Coming into force: 08.12.2006. Effect: S.I. 2002/3053 (W.288); 2003/3117 (W. 295) revoked. Territorial extent & classification: W. General. - In English and Welsh. Welsh title: Gorchymyn Cynulliad Cenedlaethol Cymru (Taliadau Swyddogion Canlyniadau) 2006. - 16p.: 30 cm. - 978-0-11-091468-8 £3.00

Representation of the people, Wales: Redistribution of seats

The Parliamentary Constituencies and Assembly Electoral Regions (Wales) Order 2006 No. 2006/1041. - Enabling power: Parliamentary Constituencies Act 1986, s. 4. - Issued: 24.04.2006. Made: 11.04.2006. Coming into force: In accord. with art. 1 (2). Effect: S.I. 1995/1036 revoked. Territorial extent & classification: W. General. - Supersedes draft S.I. (ISBN 0110738454) issued on 28.12.2005. - 32p.: 30 cm. - 978-0-11-074493-3 £5.50

Revenue and customs, England and Wales

The Revenue and Customs (Complaints and Misconduct) (Amendment) Regulations 2006 No. 2006/1748. - Enabling power: Commissioners for Revenue and Customs Act 2005, s. 28 (1) (2) (a). - Issued: 07.07.2006. Made: 03.07.2006. Laid: 04.07.2006. Coming into force: 27.07.2006. Effect: S.I. 2005/3311 amended. Territorial extent & classification: E/W. General. - This Statutory Instrument has been made to correct an error in S.I. 2005/3311 and is being issued free of charge to all known recipients of that Statutory Instrument. - 4p.: 30 cm. - 978-0-11-074796-5 £3.00

Rights in performances

The Copyright and Performances (Application to Other Countries) Order 2006 No. 2006/316. - Enabling power: Copyright, Designs and Patents Act 1988, ss. 159, 208 & European Communities Act 1972, s. 2 (2). - Issued: 03.03.2006. Made: 14.02.2006. Laid: 24.02.2006. Coming into force: 06.04.2006. Effect: S.I. 2005/852 revoked. Territorial extent & classification: E/W/S/NI. General. - 16p.: 30 cm. - 978-0-11-074059-1 £3.00

The Performances (Moral Rights, etc.) Regulations 2006 No. 2006/18. - Enabling power: European Communities Act 1972, s. 2 (2). - Issued: 27.01.2006. Made: 09.01.2006. Laid: 11.01.2006. Coming into force: 01.02.2006. Effect: 1988 c. 48 amended. Territorial extent & classification: E/W/S/NI. General. - EC note: These Regulations amend the 1988 Act to enable the UK to ratify the WIPO Performers and Phonograms Treaty (1997, Cm. 3728), which has been specified as a Community treaty. - 12p.: 30 cm. - 978-0-11-073931-1 £3.00

Rights of way, England

The Countryside and Rights of Way Act 2000 (Commencement No.11 and Savings) Order 2006 No. 2006/1172 (C.39). - Enabling power: Countryside and Rights of Way Act 2000, s. 103 (3) (4) (5). Bringing into operation various provisions of the 2000 Act on 02.05.2006, in accord. with art. 2. - Issued: 02.05.2006. Made: 18.04.2006. Effect: None. Territorial extent & classification: E. General. - 4p.: 30 cm. - 978-0-11-074527-5 £3.00

The Natural Environment and Rural Communities Act 2006 (Commencement No.1) Order 2006 No. 2006/1176 (C.40). - Enabling power: Natural Environment and Rural Communities Act 2006, s. 107. Bringing into operation various provisions of the 2006 Act on 02.05.2006. - Issued: 02.05.2006. Made: 18.04.2006. Effect: None. Territorial extent & classification: E/W/NI (art. 4 to E/W; art. 5 to E/W/NI; art. 6 to E only). General. - 4p.: 30 cm. - 978-0-11-074528-2 £3.00

Rights of way, Wales

The Countryside and Rights of Way Act 2000 (Commencement No. 8 and Transitional Provisions) (Wales) Order 2006 No. 2006/1279 (W.124) (C.42). - Enabling power: Countryside and Rights of Way Act 2000, s. 103 (3) (4) (5). Bringing into operation various provisions of the 2000 Act on 11.05.2006 in accord. with art. 2. - Issued: 17.05.2006. Made: 10.05.2006. Effect: None. Territorial extent & classification: W. General. - In English and Welsh. Welsh title: Gorchymyn Deddf Cefn Gwlad a Hawliau Tramwy 2000 (Cychwyn Rhif 8 a Darpariaethau Trosiannol) (Cymru) 2006. - 12p.: 30 cm. - 978-0-11-091335-3 £3.00

The Countryside and Rights of Way Act 2000 (Commencement No.9 and Saving) (Wales) Order 2006 No. 2006/3257 (W.297) (C.117). - Enabling power: Countryside and Rights of Way Act 2000, s. 103 (3) (4) (5). Bringing into operation various provisions of the 2006 on 06.12.2006; 01.04.2007. - Issued: 13.12.2006. Made: 05.12.2006. Effect: None. Territorial extent & classification: W. General. - In English and Welsh. Welsh title: Gorchymyn Deddf Cefn Gwlad a Hawliau Tramwy 2000 (Cychwyn Rhif 9 ac Arbediad) (Cymru) 2006. - 12p.: 30 cm. - 978-0-11-091466-4 £3.00

The Natural Environment and Rural Communities Act 2006 (Commencement) (Wales) Order 2006 No. 2006/2992 (W.279) (C.106). - Enabling power: Natural Environment and Rural Communities Act 2006, s. 107 (4) (b). Bringing into operation various provisions of the 2006 Act on 16.11.2006. - Issued: 23.11.2006. Made: 15.11.2006. Effect: None. Territorial extent & classification: W. General. - In English and Welsh. Welsh title: Gorchymyn Deddf yr Angylchedd Naturiol a Chymunedau Gwledig 2006 (Cychwyn) (Cymru) 2006. - 4p.: 30 cm. - 978-0-11-091445-9 £3.00

River, England and Wales

The Scotland Act 1998 (River Tweed) Order 2006 No. 2006/2913. - Enabling power: Scotland Act 1998, ss. 111, 112 (1), 113. - Issued: 21.11.2006. Made: 14.11.2006. Coming into force: 15.11.2006. Effect: 1607 c.6; 1965 c.13; 1967 c.84; 1974 c.40; 1975 c.51; 1976 c.86; 1981 c.29; 1984 c.26; 1989 c.15; 1995 c.40; 1998 c.46; S.I. 1999/1746 amended; 1986 c.62 revoked except for s. 31 & 1857 c.cxlviii; 1859 c.lxx; 1868 c.123; 1902 c.29; 1933 c.35; 1951 c.26; 1969 c.xxiv; 1976 c.22; 2001 asp 3; S.I. 1996/1211 revoked. Territorial extent & classification: E/W/S. General. - Supersedes Draft SI (ISBN 0110705548) issued 02.06.2006. - 48p.: 30 cm. - 978-0-11-075329-4 £7.50

River, Scotland

The Scotland Act 1998 (River Tweed) Order 2006 No. 2006/2913. - Enabling power: Scotland Act 1998, ss. 111, 112 (1), 113. - Issued: 21.11.2006. Made: 14.11.2006. Coming into force: 15.11.2006. Effect: 1607 c.6; 1965 c.13; 1967 c.84; 1974 c.40; 1975 c.51; 1976 c.86; 1981 c.29; 1984 c.26; 1989 c.15; 1995 c.40; 1998 c.46; S.I. 1999/1746 amended; 1986 c.62 revoked except for s. 31 & 1857 c.cxlviii; 1859 c.lxx; 1868 c.123; 1902 c.29; 1933 c.35; 1951 c.26; 1969 c.xxiv; 1976 c.22; 2001 asp 3; S.I. 1996/1211 revoked. Territorial extent & classification: E/W/S. General. - Supersedes Draft SI (ISBN 0110705548) issued 02.06.2006. - 48p.: 30 cm. - 978-0-11-075329-4 £7.50

Road traffic

The Community Drivers' Hours and Working Time (Road Tankers) (Temporary Exception) (Amendment) Regulations 2006 No. 2006/244. - Enabling power: European Communities Act 1972, s. 2 (2). - Issued: 14.02.2006. Made: 04.02.2006. Laid: 07.02.2006. Coming into force: 11.02.2006. Effect: S.I. 2006/17 amended. Territorial extent & classification: E/W/S. General. - EC note: These regulations extend the expiry date of the exceptions provided for in S.I. 2006/17 until 12.03.2006 while awaiting the Commission's response to the request for an exception in accordance with art 13 (2) of regulation 3820/85. - 2p.: 30 cm. - 978-0-11-073994-6 £3.00

The Community Drivers' Hours and Working Time (Road Tankers) (Temporary Exception) Regulations 2006 No. 2006/17. - Enabling power: European Communities Act 1972, s. 2 (2). - Issued: 18.01.2006. Made: 09.01.2006. Laid: 11.01.2006. Coming into force: 12.01.2006. Effect: S.I. 2005/639 modified in accord. with art 4. Territorial extent & classification: E/W/S. General. - These Regs provide for the operation of road tankers which transport petroleum products in the exceptional circumstances arising from the fire at Buncefield fuel depot. They modify arts 6 (1) (2) and 8 (3) of Council Regulation (EEC) no. 3820/85 in relation to maximum working and rest periods permitted. - 4p.: 30 cm. - 978-0-11-073893-2 £3.00

The Motor Cars (Driving Instruction) (Amendment) Regulations 2006 No. 2006/525. - Enabling power: Road Traffic Act 1988, ss. 132 (1) (2) (c), 141. - Issued: 09.03.2006. Made: 27.02.2006. Laid: 09.03.2006. Coming into force: 01.04.2006. Effect: S.I. 2005/1902 amended. Territorial extent & classification: E/W/S. General. - 2p.: 30 cm. - 978-0-11-074139-0 £3.00

The Motor Cycles Etc. (EC Type Approval) (Amendment) Regulations 2006 No. 2006/2935. - Enabling power: European Communities Act 1972, s. 2 (2). - Issued: 15.11.2006. Made: 09.11.2006. Laid: 15.11.2006. Coming into force: 11.12.2006. Effect: S.I. 1999/2920 amended. Territorial extent & classification: E/W/S/NI. General. - EC note: Implement Commission Directive 2005/30/EC, amending, for the purposes of their adaptation to technical progress, Directives 97/24/EC and 2002/24/EC, relating to the type-approval of two or three-wheel motor vehicles. - 2p.: 30 cm. - 978-0-11-075286-0 £3.00

The Motor Vehicles (Driving Licences) (Amendment) Regulations 2006 No. 2006/524. - Enabling power: Road Traffic Act 1988, ss. 89 (3) (4), 97 (3), 105 (1) (3). - Issued: 09.03.2006. Made: 27.02.2006. Laid: 09.03.2006. Coming into force: 01.04.2006 except for reg 9 (3); 01.07.2007 for reg 9 (3). Effect: S.I. 1999/2864 amended. Territorial extent & classification: E/W/S. General. - With correction slip dated May 2006. - 8p.: 30 cm. - 978-0-11-074138-3 £3.00

The Motor Vehicles (EC Type Approval) (Amendment No. 2) Regulations 2006 No. 2006/1695. - Enabling power: European Communities Act 1972, s. 2 (2). - Issued: 05.07.2006. Made: 27.06.2006. Laid: 30.06.2006. Coming into force: 30.07.2006. Effect: S.I. 1998/2051 amended. Territorial extent & classification: E/W/S/NI. General. - EC note: Amends the definition of the 'Framework Directive; in the 1998 Regs so that it encompasses the further amendments made to Council Directive 70/156/EEC by Commission Directives 2005/49/EC and 2006/28/EC. - 4p.: 30 cm. - 978-0-11-074770-5 £3.00

The Motor Vehicles (EC Type Approval) (Amendment No. 3) Regulations 2006 No. 2006/2409. - Enabling power: European Communities Act 1972, s. 2 (2). - Issued: 14.09.2006. Made: 05.09.2006. Laid: 11.09.2006. Coming into force: 13.10.2006. Effect: S.I. 1998/2051 amended. Territorial extent & classification: E/W/S/NI. General. - EC note: These regs amend the definition of "the Framework Directive" in regulation 3(1) of S.I. 1998/2051 so that it encompasses the further amendments made to Council Directive 70/156/EEC, by Directive 2005/66/EC. - With correction slip dated September 2006. - 4p.: 30 cm. - 978-0-11-075092-7 £3.00

The Motor Vehicles (EC Type Approval) (Amendment No. 4) Regulations 2006 No. 2006/2816. - Enabling power: European Communities Act 1972, s. 2 (2). - Issued: 30.10.2006. Made: 21.10.2006. Laid: 26.10.2006. Coming into force: 30.11.2006. Effect: S.I. 1998/2051 amended. Territorial extent & classification: E/W/S/NI. General. - EC note: These Regulations implement for the purposes of the type approval of light passenger vehicles, Directives 2005/55/EC, 2005/78/EC and 2006/51/EC. These measures repeal and recast Directive 88/77/EEC and its amending Directives. - 4p.: 30 cm. - 978-0-11-075216-7 £3.00

The Motor Vehicles (EC Type Approval) (Amendment) Regulations 2006 No. 2006/142. - Enabling power: European Communities Act 1972, s. 2 (2). - Issued: 06.02.2006. Made: 26.01.2006. Laid: 01.02.2006. Coming into force: 21.04.2006. Effect: S.I. 1998/2051 amended. Territorial extent & classification: E/W/S/NI. General. - 4p.: 30 cm. - 978-0-11-073963-2 £3.00

The Motor Vehicles (Tests) (Amendment) (No. 2) Regulations 2006 No. 2006/2680. - Enabling power: Road Traffic Act 1988, ss. 45, 46. - Issued: 16.10.2006. Made: 07.10.2006. Laid: 11.10.2006. Coming into force: 07.11.2006. Effect: S.I. 1981/1694 amended. Territorial extent & classification: E/W/S. General. - 4p.: 30 cm. - 978-0-11-075161-0 £3.00

The Motor Vehicles (Tests) (Amendment) Regulations 2006 No. 2006/1998. - Enabling power: Road Traffic Act 1988, ss. 45, 46. - Issued: 28.07.2006. Made: 20.07.2006. Laid: 25.07.2006. Coming into force: 08.09.2006. Effect: S.I. 1981/1694 amended. Territorial extent & classification: E/W/S. General. - 4p.: 30 cm. - 978-0-11-074917-4 £3.00

The Motor Vehicles (Type Approval and Approval Marks) (Fees) (Amendment) Regulations 2006 No. 2006/1638. - Enabling power: Road Traffic Act 1988, s. 61 (1) (2) & Finance Act 1973, s. 56 (1) (2) & Finance Act 1990, s. 128 & S.I. 1988/643, sch. 1. - Issued: 28.06.2006. Made: 19.06.2006. Laid: 23.06.2006. Coming into force: 09.08.2006. Effect: S.I. 1999/2149 amended. Territorial extent & classification: E/W/S. General. - EC note: Amends the 1999 Regs so as to take account of new or amended Community instruments or ECE Regulations (as defined in reg. 3 (2) of the 1999 Regs). - 12p.: 30 cm. - 978-0-11-074731-6 £3.00

The Motor Vehicles (Wearing of Seat Belts) (Amendment) Regulations 2006 No. 2006/1892. - Enabling power: European Communites Act 1972, s. 2 (2) & Road Traffic Act 1988, ss. 14 (1) (2), 15 (3) (5). - Issued: 21.07.2006. Made: 13.07.2006. Coming into force: 18.09.2006. Effect: 1988 c. 52, c.53 & S.I. 1993/176 amended. Territorial extent & classification: E/W/S. General. - EC note: These Regs implement requirements of Council Directive 2003/20/EC. - 12p.: 30 cm. - 978-0-11-074843-6 £3.00

The Motor Vehicles (Wearing of Seat Belts by Children in Front Seats) (Amendment) Regulations 2006 No. 2006/2213. - Enabling power: Road Traffic Act 1988, s. 15 (1) (5) (5A) (6). - Issued: 21.08.2006. Made: 09.08.2006. Laid: 16.08.2006. Coming into force: 18.09.2006. Effect: S.I. 1993/31 amended. Territorial extent & classification: E/W/S. General. - EC note: These Regs implement requirements of Council Directive 2003/20/EC. - 4p.: 30 cm. - 978-0-11-075012-5 £3.00

The Passenger and Goods Vehicles (Community Recording Equipment Regulation) Regulations 2006 No. 2006/3276. - Enabling power: European Communities Act 1972, s. 2 (2). - Issued: 15.12.2006. Made: 06.12.2006. Laid: 11.12.2006. Coming into force: 03.01.2007. Effect: 1968 c. 73; 1988 c. 52; S.I. 1979/1746, 1984/144; 1986/1456; 2005/1140, 1904; 2006/1937 amended & S.I. 1996/941 revoked. Territorial extent & classification: E/W/S. General. - EC note: These regs take into account of the amendments to Council Regulation (EEC) No.3821/85 made by Commission Regulations (EC) Nos.1056/97, 1360/2002 and 432/2004, by Council Regulation (EC) No.2135/98 and by Regulations (EC) No.1882/2003 and 561/2006. - 4p.: 30 cm. - 978-0-11-075457-4 £3.00

The Passenger and Goods Vehicles (Recording Equipment) (Fitting Date) Regulations 2006 No. 2006/1117. - Enabling power: European Communities Act 1972, s. 2 (2). - Issued: 24.04.2006. Made: 18.04.2006. Laid: 20.04.2006. Coming into force: 01.05.2006. Effect: 1968 c. 73 amended. Territorial extent & classification: E/W/S/NI. General. - EC note: Amends section 97 of the Transport Act 1968 to set the date from which the new digital tachograph must be fitted to a new vehicle which requires a tachograph. The digital tachograph is provided for by Council Regulation 2135/98 which amended Regulation 3821/85 on recording equipment in road transport. - 2p.: 30 cm. - 978-0-11-074506-0 £3.00

The Passenger and Goods Vehicles (Recording Equipment) (Tachograph Card) Regulations 2006 No. 2006/1937. - Enabling power: European Communities Act 1972, s. 2 (2). - Issued: 25.07.2006. Made: 18.07.2006. Laid: 20.07.2006. Coming into force: 21.08.2007. Effect: None. Territorial extent & classification: E/W/S. General. - EC note: These Regs make provision in relation to the cards (company cards, control cards, driver cards and workshop cards) used with digital tachographs, which are tachographs complying with Annex IB to Regulation (EEC) 3821/85. - 8p.: 30 cm. - 978-0-11-074868-9 £3.00

The Road Vehicles (Construction and Use) (Amendment) Regulations 2006 No. 2006/1756. - Enabling power: Road Traffic Act 1988, s. 41 (1) (2) (5). - Issued: 10.07.2006. Made: 04.07.2006. Laid: 07.07.2006. Coming into force: 01.08.2006. Effect: S.I. 1986/1078 amended. Territorial extent & classification: E/W/S. General. - 2p.: 30 cm. - 978-0-11-074800-9 £3.00

The Road Vehicles (Construction and Use) and Motor Vehicles (Type Approval for Goods Vehicles) (Great Britain) (Amendment) Regulations 2006 No. 2006/2565. - Enabling power: Road Traffic Act 1988, ss. 41 (1) (2) (5), 54 (1), 61 (1). - Issued: 02.10.2006. Made: 21.09.2006. Laid: 27.09.2006. Coming into force: 20.10.2006 except for regs 4 (5), 6 (10) (13) & 09.11.2006 for regs 4 (5), 6 (10) (13). Effect: S.I. 1982/1271; 1986/1078 amended. Territorial extent & classification: E/W/S. General. - EC note: These Regs amend the 1986 Regs (Construction and Use Regulations) to incorporate the requirements of Directives 2005/55/EC and 2005/78/EC, as amended by Directive 2006/51/EC. They also amend the provisions relating to emissions requirements for end-of-series vehicles to ensure that European law is fully implemented. Finally, they align the calculation of the maximum number of vehicles that may enter into service under the emissions end-of-series provisions, both in the Construction and Use Regulations and under the 1982 Regs ("the Type Approval for Goods Vehicles Regulations"), with that used in European law and in particular Directive 70/156/EEC. - 8p.: 30 cm. - 978-0-11-075133-7 £3.00

The Road Vehicles (Registration and Licensing) (Amendment) Regulations 2006 No. 2006/2320. - Enabling power: Vehicle Excise and Registration Act 1994, ss. 57 (1) (2), 61B. - Issued: 07.09.2006. Made: 30.08.2006. Laid: 01.09.2006. Coming into force: 01.10.2006. Effect: S.I. 2002/2742 amended. Territorial extent & classification: E/W/S/NI. General. - 4p.: 30 cm. - 978-0-11-075055-2 £3.00

The Tractor etc (EC Type-Approval) (Amendment) Regulations 2006 No. 2006/2533. - Enabling power: European Communities Act 1972, s. 2 (2). - Issued: 27.09.2006. Made: 19.09.2006. Laid: 22.09.2006. Coming into force: 18.10.2006. Effect: S.I. 2005/390 amended & S.I. 1988/1567; 1989/2275; 1990/2336; 1992/80; 2000/828; 2001/1710; 2002/1890 revoked. Territorial extent & classification: E/W/S/NI. General. - EC note: These Regs transpose Directives 2005/13/EC, 2005/67/EC and 2006/26/EC in so far as they relate to the EC Type-Approval scheme for tractors. - 4p.: 30 cm. - 978-0-11-075124-5 £3.00

The Traffic Signs (Amendment) Regulations 2006 No. 2006/2083. - Enabling power: Road Traffic Regulation Act 1984, s. 64 (1) (2) (3). - Issued: 07.08.2006. Made: 26.07.2006. Laid: 31.07.2006. Coming into force: 21.08.2006. Effect: S.I. 2002/3113 amended. Territorial extent & classification: E/W/S. General. - 4p., col. ill.: 30 cm. - 978-0-11-074974-7 £3.00

Road traffic: Speed limits

The A1 and A14 Trunk Roads (Brampton Hut Interchange, Cambrdigeshire) (40 Miles Per Hour Speed Limit) Order 2006 No. 2006/2881. - Enabling power: Road Traffic Regulation Act 1984, ss. 84 (1) (2) (a), sch. 9, para. 27 (1). - Made: 20.10.2006. Coming into force: 03.11.2006. Effect: Any Derestriction Order made under the Road Traffic Regulation Act 1984 or any enactment replaced by that Act derestricting the lengths of the trunk roads mentioned in the Schedule revoked. Territorial extent & classification: E. Local *Unpublished*

The A1 Trunk Road (Great North Road, Bedfordshire to Cambridgeshire) (Variable Speed Limit) Order 2004 Revocation Order 2006 No. 2006/1880. - Enabling power: Road Traffic Regulation Act 1984, s. 84 (1) (a) (2), sch. 9, para. 27 (1). - Made: 06.07.2006. Coming into force: 20.07.2006. Effect: S.I. 2004/2602 revoked. Territorial extent & classification: E. Local *Unpublished*

The A3 Trunk Road (Esher Bypass, Northbound Carriageway) (50 Miles Per Hour Speed Limit) Order 2006 No. 2006/3136. - Enabling power: Road Traffic Regulation Act 1984, s. 84 (1) (a) (2). - Made: 20.11.2006. Coming into force: 11.12.2006. Effect: None. Territorial extent & classification: E. Local *Unpublished*

The A11 and A47 Trunk Roads (Cringleford/Thickthorn Interchange, Norfolk) (40 Miles Per Hour Speed Limit) Order 2006 No. 2006/417. - Enabling power: Road Traffic Regulation Act 1984, s. 84 (1) (a) (2), sch. 9, para. 27 (1). - Made: 14.02.2006. Coming into force: 28.02.2006. Effect: S.I. 1990/22 varied. Territorial extent & classification: E. Local *Unpublished*

The A12 Trunk Road (Ingatestone Bypass) (De-Restriction) Order 2006 No. 2006/328. - Enabling power: Road Traffic Regulation Act 1984, ss. 82 (2), 83 (1). - Made: 03.02.2006. Coming into force: 17.02.2006. Effect: None. Territorial extent & classification: E. Local *Unpublished*

The A12 Trunk Road (Stanway to Spring Lane, Essex) (Derestriction) Order 2006 No. 2006/1598. - Enabling power: Road Traffic Regulation Act 1984, ss. 82 (2), 83 (1). - Made: 06.06.2006. Coming into force: 20.06.2006. Effect: None. Territorial extent & classification: E. Local *Unpublished*

The A14 Trunk Road (Cambridgeshire - Northamptonshire) (Variable Speed Limit) Order 2005 Revocation Order 2006 No. 2006/2995. - Enabling power: Road Traffic Regulation Act 1984, s. 84 (1) (a) (2), sch. 9, para 27 (1). - Made: 27.10.2006. Coming into force: 17.11.2006. Effect: S.I. 2005/1679 revoked. Territorial extent & classification: E. Local *Unpublished*

The A14 Trunk Road (Cambridgeshire - Suffolk) (Variable Speed Limit) Order 2005 Revocation Order 2006 No. 2006/2997. - Enabling power: Road Traffic Regulation Act 1984, s. 84 (1) (a) (2), sch. 9, para 27 (1). - Made: 30.10.2006. Coming into force: 13.11.2006. Effect: S.I. 2005/1690 revoked. Territorial extent & classification: E. Local *Unpublished*

The A14 Trunk Road (Copdock Interchange to Felixstowe Dock Gate No. 1 Roundabout, Suffolk) (Temporary 30 Miles Per Hour Speed Restriction) Order 2006 No. 2006/2850. - Enabling power: Road Traffic Regulation Act 1984, ss. 88 (1) (2) (3). - Made: 09.10.2006. Coming into force: 16.10.2006. Effect: None. Territorial extent & classification: E. Local *Unpublished*

The A14 Trunk Road (Spittals Interchange, Huntingdon, Cambridgeshire) (40 Miles Per Hour Speed Limit) Order 2006 No. 2006/161. - Enabling power: Road Traffic Regulation Act 1984, ss. 84 (1) (a) (2), sch. 9, para. 27 (1). - Made: 19.01.2006. Coming into force: 02.02.2006. Effect: None. Territorial extent & classification: E. Local *Unpublished*

The A36 Trunk Road (Wilton to Salisbury) (50mph Speed Limit) Order 2006 No. 2006/2623. - Enabling power: Road Traffic Regulation Act 1984, s. 84 (1) (a) (2), sch. 9, para. 27 (1). - Made: 30.05.2006. Coming into force: 10.06.2006. Effect: S.I. 2004/3072 revoked. Territorial extent & classification: E. Local *Unpublished*

The A38 Trunk Road (A50 to A61, Derbyshire) and the A516 Trunk Road (40 Miles Speed Limit and Derestriction) Order 2006 No. 2006/2707. - Enabling power: Road Traffic Regulation Act 1984, ss. 82 (2), 83 (1), 84 (1) (a) (2), sch. 9, para. 27 (1). - Made: 21.09.2006. Coming into force: 05.10.2006. Effect: Any previous Order made under the Road Traffic Regulation Act 1984 or any enactment replaced by that Act which imposed a speed limit of 40 miles per hour on the A38 Trunk Road is amended by excluding any reference to the lengths of trunk road specified in schedule 1. Any Order made under the Road Traffic Regulation Act 1984 or any enactment replaced by that Act which provided that the ltrunk road or any part thereof should cease to be a restricted road is amended by excluding any reference to the lengths of trunk road specified in schedule 2. Territorial extent & classification: E. Local *Unpublished*

The A38 Trunk Road (Holbrook, Derbyshire) (Link Roads) (50 Miles Speed Limit and Derestriction) Order 2006 No. 2006/2708. - Enabling power: Road Traffic Regulation Act 1984, ss. 82 (2), 83 (1), 84 (1) (a) (2), sch. 9, para. 27 (1). - Made: 21.09.2006. Coming into force: 05.10.2006. Effect: Any previous Order made under the Road Traffic Regulation Act 1984 or any enactment replaced by that Act which imposed a speed limit of 50 miles per hour on the lengths of the link roads specified in schedule 1, or any part thereof, is amended by excluding any reference to those lengths of link roads. Any previous Order made under the Road Traffic Regulation Act 1984 or any enactment replaced by that Act which provided that the link roads or any part thereof should cease to be a restricted road is amended by excluding any reference to the lengths of the link roads in schedule 2. Territorial extent & classification: E. Local *Unpublished*

The A43 Trunk Road (Northamptonshire - Oxfordshire) (Variable Speed Limit) Order 2005 Revocation Order 2006 No. 2006/2842. - Enabling power: Road Traffic Regulation Act 1984, ss. 84 (1) (a) (2), sch. 9, para. 27 (1). - Made: 09.10.2006. Coming into force: 23.10.2006. Effect: S.I. 2005/1680 revoked. Territorial extent & classification: E. Local *Unpublished*

The A45 Trunk Road (Northamptonshire) (Variable Speed Limit) Order 2005 Revocation Order 2006 No. 2006/2879. - Enabling power: Road Traffic Regulation Act 1984, ss. 84 (1) (a) (2), sch. 9, para. 27 (1). - Made: 23.10.2006. Coming into force: 06.11.2006. Effect: S.I. 2005/1678 revoked. Territorial extent & classification: E. Local *Unpublished*

The A45 Trunk Road (Ryton on Dunsmore, Warwickshire) (50 Miles Per Hour Speed Limit) Order 2001 Variation Order 2006 No. 2006/3016. - Enabling power: Road Traffic Regulation Act 1984, ss. 84 (1) (a) (2), sch. 9, para. 27 (1). - Made: 21.09.2006. Coming into force: 05.10.2006. Effect: S.I. 2001/1007 varied. Territorial extent & classification: E. Local *Unpublished*

The A47 Trunk Road (Little Fransham, Norfolk) (40 Miles Per Hour Speed Limit) Order 2006 No. 2006/419. - Enabling power: Road Traffic Regulation Act 1984, s. 84 (1) (a) (2), sch. 9, para. 27 (1). - Made: 16.02.2006. Coming into force: 03.03.2006. Effect: None. Territorial extent & classification: E. Local *Unpublished*

The A50 Trunk Road and A38 Trunk Road (A50/A38 Interchange, Derbyshire) (Restriction and 40 Miles Per Hour Speed Limit) Order 2006 No. 2006/2158. - Enabling power: Road Traffic Regulation Act 1984, ss. 82 (2), 83 (1), 84 (1) (a) (2), sch. 9, para. 27 (1). - Made: 17.07.2006. Coming into force: 31.07.2006. Effect: S.I. 1998/378 varied. Territorial extent & classification: E. Local *Unpublished*

The A63 Trunk Road (Cliffe and Hemingbrough) (40 Miles Per Hour Speed Limit) Order 2006 No. 2006/1351. - Enabling power: Road Traffic Regulation Act 1984, s. 84 (1) (a) (2), sch. 9, para. 27 (1). - Made: 04.05.2006. Coming into force: 10.05.2006. Effect: None. Territorial extent & classification: E. Local *Unpublished*

The A65 Trunk Road (Ingleton) (Continuation of 40 Miles Per Hour Speed Limit) Order 2006 No. 2006/1371. - Enabling power: Road Traffic Regulation Act 1984, s. 84 (1) (2), sch. 9, para. 27 (1). - Made: 18.04.2006. Coming into force: 29.04.2006. Effect: None. Territorial extent & classification: E. Local *Unpublished*

The A65 Trunk Road (Kirkby Lonsdale) (40 Miles Per Hour Speed Limit) Order 2006 No. 2006/1206. - Enabling power: Road Traffic Regulation Act 1984, s. 84 (1) (2), sch. 9, para. 27 (1). - Made: 18.04.2006. Coming into force: 29.04.2006. Effect: None. Territorial extent & classification: E. Local *Unpublished*

The A167 Trunk Road (Blind Lane Interchange Roundabout) (40 Miles Per Hour Speed Limit) Order 2006 No. 2006/2265. - Enabling power: Road Traffic Regulation Act 1984, s. 84 (1) (a) (2), sch. 9, para. 27 (1). - Made: 09.08.2006. Coming into force: 21.08.2006. Effect: None. Territorial extent & classification: E. Local *Unpublished*

The A421 Trunk Road (Bedfordshire) (Variable Speed Limit) Order 2005 Revocation Order 2006 No. 2006/3034. - Enabling power: Road Traffic Regulation Act 1984, s. 84 (1) (a) (2), sch. 9, para 27 (1). - Made: 30.10.2006. Coming into force: 13.11.2006. Effect: S.I. 2005/1315 revoked. Territorial extent & classification: E. Local *Unpublished*

The A421 Trunk Road (Great Barford Bypass, Bedfordshire) (Derestriction) Order 2006 No. 2006/2430. - Enabling power: Road Traffic Regulation Act 1984, ss. 82 (1), 83 (1). - Made: 17.08.2006. Coming into force: 24.08.2006. Effect: None. Territorial extent & classification: E. Local *Unpublished*

The A428 Trunk Road (Cambridgeshire and Bedfordshire) (Variable Speed Limit) Order 2005 Revocation Order 2006 No. 2006/2852. - Enabling power: Road Traffic Regulation Act 1984, s. 84 (1) (a) (2), sch. 9, para. 27 (1). - Made: 16.10.2006. Coming into force: 30.10.2006. Effect: S.I. 2005/1843 revoked. Territorial extent & classification: E. Local *Unpublished*

The A449 Trunk Road (Wall Heath) (40 Miles Per Hour Speed Limit) Order 2006 No. 2006/1110. - Enabling power: Road Traffic Regulation Act 1984, s. 84 (1) (a) (2). - Made: 06.04.2006. Coming into force: 20.04.2006. Effect: None. Territorial extent & classification: E. Local *Unpublished*

The A453 Trunk Road and the A52 Trunk Road (Nottingham) (40 Miles Per Hour and 50 Miles Per Hour Speed Limit) Order 2006 No. 2006/1632. - Enabling power: Road Traffic Regulation Act 1984, s. 84 (1) (a) (2), sch. 9, para, 27 (1). - Made: 30.05.2006. Coming into force: 12.06.2006. Effect: S.I. 1985/1406 varied & S.I. 1995/108 revoked. Territorial extent & classification: E. Local *Unpublished*

Road traffic: Traffic regulation

The A1 and A46 Trunk Roads (Newark-on-Trent, Nottinghamshire) (Temporary Prohibition of Traffic) Order 2006 No. 2006/2755. - Enabling power: Road Traffic Regulation Act 1984, s. 14 (1) (a). - Made: 06.10.2006. Coming into force: 13.10.2006. Effect: None. Territorial extent & classification: E. Local *Unpublished*

The A1 and A47 Trunk Roads (Brampton Hut Interchange, Huntingdon, Cambridgeshire) (Temporary Restriction and Prohibition of Traffic) Order 2006 No. 2006/2127. - Enabling power: Road Traffic Regulation Act 1984, s. 14 (1) (a). - Made: 17.07.2006. Coming into force: 24.07.2006. Effect: None. Territorial extent & classification: E. Local *Unpublished*

The A1 and A47 Trunk Roads (Wansford, Peterborough) (Temporary Restriction and Prohibition of Traffic) Order 2006 No. 2006/1196. - Enabling power: Road Traffic Regulation Act 1984, s. 14 (1) (a). - Made: 19.04.2006. Coming into force: 26.04.2006. Effect: None. Territorial extent & classification: E. Local *Unpublished*

The A1(M) and A14(M) Motorways (Junctions 14 to 17) Slip Roads (Cambridgeshire) (Temporary Prohibition of Traffic) Order 2006 No. 2006/2119. - Enabling power: Road Traffic Regulation Act 1984, s. 14 (1) (a). - Made: 24.07.2006. Coming into force: 31.07.2006. Effect: None. Territorial extent & classification: E. Local *Unpublished*

The A1(M) and the A1 Trunk Road (Blyth, Nottinghamshire) (Temporary 30 and 50 Miles Per Hour Restriction) Order 2006 No. 2006/2518. - Enabling power: Road Traffic Regulation Act 1984, s. 14 (1) (a). - Made: 04.09.2006. Coming into force: 11.09.2006. Effect: None. Territorial extent & classification: E. Local. - Revoked by S.I. 2006/3017 (Unpublished) *Unpublished*

The A1(M) and the A1 Trunk Road (Blyth, Nottinghamshire) (Temporary 30 and 50 Miles Per Hour Speed Restriction) (No. 2) Order 2006 No. 2006/3017. - Enabling power: Road Traffic Regulation Act 1984, s. 14 (1) (a), sch. 9, para. 27 (1). - Made: 03.11.2006. Coming into force: 10.11.2006. Effect: S.I. 2006/2518 revoked. Territorial extent & classification: E. Local *Unpublished*

The A1(M) and the A1 Trunk Road (Chesterton, Cambridgeshire) (Temporary Restriction and Prohibition of Traffic) Order 2006 No. 2006/2401. - Enabling power: Road Traffic Regulation Act 1984, s. 14 (1) (a). - Made: 21.08.2006. Coming into force: 28.08.2006. Effect: None. Territorial extent & classification: E. Local *Unpublished*

The A1(M) and the A1 Trunk Road (Stamford to Peterborough) (Temporary Restriction and Prohibition of Traffic) Order 2006 No. 2006/3026. - Enabling power: Road Traffic Regulation Act 1984, s. 14 (1) (a). - Made: 10.11.2006. Coming into force: 17.11.2006. Effect: None. Territorial extent & classification: E. Local *Unpublished*

The A1(M) Motorway and the A1 Trunk Road (Biggleswade North Roundabout, Bedfordshire) (Temporary Restriction and Prohibition of Traffic) Order 2006 No. 2006/459. - Enabling power: Road Traffic Regulation Act 1984, s. 14 (1) (a). - Made: 20.02.2006. Coming into force: 27.02.2006. Effect: None. Territorial extent & classification: E. Local *Unpublished*

The A1(M) Motorway and the A1 Trunk Road (Clow Beck Accommodation to the A1231 Overbridge) (Temporary 50 Miles Per Hour Speed Restriction) Order 2006 No. 2006/697. - Enabling power: Road Traffic Regulation Act 1984, s. 14 (1) (b). - Made: 02.03.2006. Coming into force: 13.03.2006. Effect: None. Territorial extent & classification: E. Local *Unpublished*

The A1(M) Motorway and the M18 Motorway (Wadworth Interchange) (Temporary Prohibition of Traffic) Order 2006 No. 2006/2751. - Enabling power: Road Traffic Regulation Act 1984, s. 14 (1) (a). - Made: 11.10.2006. Coming into force: 22.10.2006. Effect: None. Territorial extent & classification: E. Local *Unpublished*

The A1(M) Motorway (Bramham Crossroads) (Temporary Prohibition of Traffic) Order 2006 No. 2006/1568. - Enabling power: Road Traffic Regulation Act 1984, s. 14 (1) (a). - Made: 02.06.2006. Coming into force: 14.06.2006. Effect: None. Territorial extent & classification: E. Local *Unpublished*

The A1(M) Motorway (Hatfield Tunnel) (Temporary Prohibition of Traffic) Order 2006 No. 2006/3232. - Enabling power: Road Traffic Regulation Act 1984, s. 14 (1) (a). - Made: 04.12.2006. Coming into force: 01.01.2007. Effect: None. Territorial extent & classification: E. Local *Unpublished*

The A1(M) Motorway (Junction 1, South Mimms) (Temporary Prohibition of Traffic) Order 2006 No. 2006/79. - Enabling power: Road Traffic Regulation Act 1984, s. 14 (1) (a). - Made: 16.01.2006. Coming into force: 24.01.2006. Effect: None. Territorial extent & classification: E. Local. - Revoked by S.I. 2006/2778 (Unpublished) *Unpublished*

The A1(M) Motorway (Junction 2, Slip Roads) (Temporary Prohibition of Traffic) Order 2006 No. 2006/908. - Enabling power: Road Traffic Regulation Act 1984, s. 14 (1) (a). - Made: 20.03.2006. Coming into force: 01.04.2006. Effect: None. Territorial extent & classification: E. Local. - Revoked by S.I. 2006/2778 (Unpublished) *Unpublished*

The A1(M) Motorway (Junction 4, Southbound Entry Slip Road) (Temporary Prohibition of Traffic) Order 2006 No. 2006/2174. - Enabling power: Road Traffic Regulation Act 1984, s. 14 (1) (a). - Made: 17.07.2006. Coming into force: 22.07.2006. Effect: None. Territorial extent & classification: E. Local *Unpublished*

The A1(M) Motorway (Junction 6, Welwyn, Hertfordshire) (Temporary Restriction and Prohibition of Traffic) Order 2006 No. 2006/3381. - Enabling power: Road Traffic Regulation Act 1984, s. 14 (1) (a). - Made: 11.12.2006. Coming into force: 18.12.2006. Effect: None. Territorial extent & classification: E. Local *Unpublished*

The A1(M) Motorway (Junction 7, Hertfordshire) (Temporary Prohibition of Traffic) Order 2006 No. 2006/3018. - Enabling power: Road Traffic Regulation Act 1984, s. 14 (1) (a). - Made: 08.11.2006. Coming into force: 15.11.2006. Effect: None. Territorial extent & classification: E. Local *Unpublished*

The A1(M) Motorway (Junction 8 - Junction 9) (Milksy Lane Underbridge, Hertfordshire) (Temporary 50 Miles Per Hour Speed Restriction) Order 2006 No. 2006/3128. - Enabling power: Road Traffic Regulation Act 1984, s. 14 (1) (a). - Made: 17.11.2006. Coming into force: 24.11.2006. Effect: None. Territorial extent & classification: E. Local *Unpublished*

The A1(M) Motorway (Junction 9, Hertfordshire) Northbound Exit Slip Road (Temporary Prohibition of Traffic) Order 2006 No. 2006/2162. - Enabling power: Road Traffic Regulation Act 1984, s. 14 (1) (a). - Made: 31.07.2006. Coming into force: 07.08.2006. Effect: None. Territorial extent & classification: E. Local *Unpublished*

The A1(M) Motorway (Junction 9, Hertfordshire) (Temporary Prohibition of Traffic) Order 2006 No. 2006/2637. - Enabling power: Road Traffic Regulation Act 1984, s. 14 (1) (a). - Made: 26.09.2006. Coming into force: 03.10.2006. Effect: None. Territorial extent & classification: E. Local *Unpublished*

The A1(M) Motorway (Junction 9, Letchworth Gate, Hertfordshire) (Temporary Prohibition of Traffic) Order 2006 No. 2006/2454. - Enabling power: Road Traffic Regulation Act 1984, s. 14 (1) (a). - Made: 29.08.2006. Coming into force: 01.09.2006. Effect: None. Territorial extent & classification: E. Local *Unpublished*

The A1(M) Motorway (Junction 9) (Temporary 40 Miles Per Hour Speed Restriction) Order 2006 No. 2006/1489. - Enabling power: Road Traffic Regulation Act 1984, s. 14 (1) (a). - Made: 31.05.2006. Coming into force: 09.06.2006. Effect: None. Territorial extent & classification: E. Local *Unpublished*

The A1(M) Motorway (Junction 16 (Stilton) to Junction 17 (Haddon)) (Temporary Prohibition of Traffic) Order 2006 No. 2006/2243. - Enabling power: Road Traffic Regulation Act 1984, s. 14 (1) (a). - Made: 07.08.2006. Coming into force: 14.08.2006. Effect: None. Territorial extent & classification: E. Local *Unpublished*

The A1(M) Motorway (Junction 38 to Junction 37) (Temporary Prohibition of Traffic) Order 2006 No. 2006/3179. - Enabling power: Road Traffic Regulation Act 1984, s. 14 (1) (a). - Made: 24.11.2006. Coming into force: 03.12.2006. Effect: None. Territorial extent & classification: E. Local *Unpublished*

The A1(M) Motorway (Junction 57 to Junction 56), and the A1 Trunk Road (Temporary 50 Miles Per Hour Speed Restriction) (No. 2) Order 2006 No. 2006/846. - Enabling power: Road Traffic Regulation Act 1984, s. 14 (1) (a). - Made: 10.03.2006. Coming into force: 23.03.2006. Effect: None. Territorial extent & classification: E. Local *Unpublished*

The A1(M) Motorway (Junction 57 to Junction 56), and the A1 Trunk Road (Temporary 50 Miles Per Hour Speed Restriction) Order 2006 No. 2006/258. - Enabling power: Road Traffic Regulation Act 1984, s. 14 (1) (a). - Made: 01.02.2006. Coming into force: 05.02.2006. Effect: None. Territorial extent & classification: E. Local *Unpublished*

The A1(M) Motorway (Junction 58, Burtree) (Temporary Prohibition of Traffic) Order 2006 No. 2006/2748. - Enabling power: Road Traffic Regulation Act 1984, s. 14 (1) (a). - Made: 10.10.2006. Coming into force: 22.10.2006. Effect: None. Territorial extent & classification: E. Local *Unpublished*

The A1(M) Motorway (Junction 58 to Junction 57) (Temporary Restriction and Prohibition of Traffic) Order 2006 No. 2006/3004. - Enabling power: Road Traffic Regulation Act 1984, s. 14 (1) (a) (7). - Made: 02.11.2006. Coming into force: 19.11.2006. Effect: None. Territorial extent & classification: E. Local *Unpublished*

The A1(M) Motorway (Junction 58 to Junction 59) (Temporary 50 Miles Per Hour Speed Restriction) Order 2006 No. 2006/899. - Enabling power: Road Traffic Regulation Act 1984, s. 14 (1) (a). - Made: 17.03.2006. Coming into force: 31.03.2006. Effect: None. Territorial extent & classification: E. Local *Unpublished*

The A1(M) Motorway (Junction 59 to Junction 60) (Temporary Restriction and Prohibition of Traffic) Order 2006 No. 2006/3027. - Enabling power: Road Traffic Regulation Act 1984, s. 14 (1) (a) (7). - Made: 24.10.2006. Coming into force: 05.11.2006. Effect: None. Territorial extent & classification: E. Local *Unpublished*

The A1(M) Motorway (Junction 61, Bowburn) (Temporary Prohibition of Traffic) Order 2006 No. 2006/2422. - Enabling power: Road Traffic Regulation Act 1984, s. 14 (1) (a). - Made: 21.08.2006. Coming into force: 28.08.2006. Effect: None. Territorial extent & classification: E. Local *Unpublished*

The A1(M) Motorway (Junction 61 to Junction 60) (Temporary 50 Miles Per Hour Speed Restriction) Order 2006 No. 2006/257. - Enabling power: Road Traffic Regulation Act 1984, s. 14 (1) (a). - Made: 01.02.2006. Coming into force: 05.02.2006. Effect: None. Territorial extent & classification: E. Local *Unpublished*

The A1(M) Motorway (Junction 63, Blind Lane Interchange) (Temporary 50 Miles Per Hour Speed Restriction) Order 2006 No. 2006/463. - Enabling power: Road Traffic Regulation Act 1984, s. 14 (1) (a). - Made: 21.02.2006. Coming into force: 05.03.2006. Effect: None. Territorial extent & classification: E. Local *Unpublished*

The A1(M) Motorway (Junctions 1 - 2) (Temporary Restriction and Prohibition of Traffic) Order 2006 No. 2006/2197. - Enabling power: Road Traffic Regulation Act 1984, s. 14 (1) (a) (7). - Made: 07.08.2006. Coming into force: 12.08.2006. Effect: None. Territorial extent & classification: E. Local *Unpublished*

The A1(M) Motorway (Junctions 3, 4, and 6) (Temporary Prohibition of Traffic) Order 2006 No. 2006/1046. - Enabling power: Road Traffic Regulation Act 1984, s. 14 (1) (a). - Made: 03.04.2006. Coming into force: 13.04.2006. Effect: None. Territorial extent & classification: E. Local. - Revoked by S.I. 2006/2778 (Unpublished) *Unpublished*

The A1(M) Motorway (Junctions 3 - 6) (Temporary Restriction and Prohibition of Traffic) Order 2006 No. 2006/1770. - Enabling power: Road Traffic Regulation Act 1984, s. 14 (1) (a) (7). - Made: 26.06.2006. Coming into force: 01.07.2006. Effect: None. Territorial extent & classification: E. Local *Unpublished*

The A1(M) Motorway (Junctions 4 - 6, Northbound) (Temporary Restriction and Prohibition of Traffic) Order 2006 No. 2006/3062. - Enabling power: Road Traffic Regulation Act 1984, s. 14 (1) (a) (7). - Made: 30.10.2006. Coming into force: 04.11.2006. Effect: None. Territorial extent & classification: E. Local *Unpublished*

The A1(M) Motorway (Junctions 6 - 4, Southbound Carriageway) (Temporary Restriction of Traffic) Order 2006 No. 2006/969. - Enabling power: Road Traffic Regulation Act 1984, s. 14 (1) (a) (7). - Made: 27.03.2006. Coming into force: 01.04.2006. Effect: None. Territorial extent & classification: E. Local *Unpublished*

The A1(M) Motorway (Junctions 8 - 9) (Hertfordshire) (Temporary Restriction and Prohibition of Traffic) Order 2006 No. 2006/3510. - Enabling power: Road Traffic Regulation Act 1984, s. 14 (1) (a) (7). - Made: 29.12.2006. Coming into force: 05.01.2007. Effect: None. Territorial extent & classification: E. Local *Unpublished*

The A1(M) Motorway (Knebworth, Hertfordshire) (Temporary Restriction and Prohibition of Traffic) Order 2006 No. 2006/1776. - Enabling power: Road Traffic Regulation Act 1984, s. 14 (1) (a). - Made: 19.06.2006. Coming into force: 26.06.2006. Effect: None. Territorial extent & classification: E. Local *Unpublished*

The A1(M) Motorway (Staindrop Road Bridge) (Temporary Restriction of Traffic) Order 2006 No. 2006/2590. - Enabling power: Road Traffic Regulation Act 1984, s. 14 (1) (a) (7). - Made: 11.09.2006. Coming into force: 17.09.2006. Effect: None. Territorial extent & classification: E. Local *Unpublished*

The A1(M) Trunk Road (Junctions 10 - 9, Hertfordshire) (Temporary 50 Miles Per Hour Speed Restriction) Order 2006 No. 2006/3209. - Enabling power: Road Traffic Regulation Act 1984, s. 14 (1) (a). - Made: 24.11.2006. Coming into force: 01.12.2006. Effect: None. Territorial extent & classification: E. Local *Unpublished*

The A1 Trunk Road (A5135 Junction, Northbound Entry Slip Road) (Temporary Prohibition of Traffic) 2006 No. 2006/252. - Enabling power: Road Traffic Regulation Act 1984, s. 14 (1) (a). - Made: 30.01.2006. Coming into force: 06.02.2006. Effect: None. Territorial extent & classification: E. Local. - Revoked by S.I. 2006/2778 (Unpublished) *Unpublished*

The A1 Trunk Road (Alnwick Bypass) (Temporary Restriction and Prohibition of Traffic) Order 2006 No. 2006/1317. - Enabling power: Road Traffic Regulation Act 1984, s. 14 (1) (b). - Made: 02.05.2006. Coming into force: 15.05.2006. Effect: None. Territorial extent & classification: E. Local *Unpublished*

The A1 Trunk Road (Alnwick South Junction) (Temporary Prohibition of Traffic) (No. 2) Order 2006 No. 2006/2579. - Enabling power: Road Traffic Regulation Act 1984, s. 14 (1) (a). - Made: 19.09.2006. Coming into force: 01.10.2006. Effect: None. Territorial extent & classification: E. Local *Unpublished*

The A1 Trunk Road (Alnwick South Junction) (Temporary Prohibition of Traffic) Order 2006 No. 2006/1429. - Enabling power: Road Traffic Regulation Act 1984, s. 14 (1) (a). - Made: 23.05.2006. Coming into force: 04.06.2006. Effect: None. Territorial extent & classification: E. Local *Unpublished*

The A1 Trunk Road and the A1(M) Motorway (A5135 Junction - Junction 6) (Temporary Prohibition of Traffic) Order 2006 No. 2006/2778. - Enabling power: Road Traffic Regulation Act 1984, s. 14 (1) (a), sch. 9, para. 27 (1). - Made: 09.10.2006. Coming into force: 14.10.2006. Effect: S.I. 2005/3007, 3413; 2006/79, 252, 908, 1046 revoked. Territorial extent & classification: E. Local *Unpublished*

The A1 Trunk Road and the A1(M) Motorway (Dishforth Interchange to Baldersby Interchange) and the A168 Trunk Road (Dishforth) (Temporary Restriction and Prohibition of Traffic) Order 2006 No. 2006/2423. - Enabling power: Road Traffic Regulation Act 1984, s. 14 (1) (a) (7). - Made: 21.08.2006. Coming into force: 04.09.2006. Effect: None. Territorial extent & classification: E. Local *Unpublished*

The A1 Trunk Road and the A1(M) Motorway (Junction 46) (Temporary Prohibition of Traffic) Order 2006 No. 2006/1203. - Enabling power: Road Traffic Regulation Act 1984, s. 14 (1) (a). - Made: 21.04.2006. Coming into force: 03.05.2006. Effect: None. Territorial extent & classification: E. Local *Unpublished*

The A1 Trunk Road and the A1(M) Motorway (Redhouse Interchange to Holmfield Interchange), and the A162 Trunk Road (Temporary Prohibition of Traffic) Order 2006 No. 2006/1870. - Enabling power: Road Traffic Regulation Act 1984, s. 14 (1) (a). - Made: 07.07.2006. Coming into force: 21.07.2006. Effect: None. Territorial extent & classification: E. Local *Unpublished*

The A1 Trunk Road and the A52 Trunk Road (Near Barrowby, Lincolnshire) (LInk Road) (Temporary Prohibition of Traffic) Order 2006 No. 2006/2505. - Enabling power: Road Traffic Regulation Act 1984, s. 14 (1) (a). - Made: 01.09.2006. Coming into force: 08.09.2006. Effect: None. Territorial extent & classification: E. Local *Unpublished*

The A1 Trunk Road and the A66 Trunk Road (Scotch Corner Interchange) (Temporary Restriction and Prohibition of Traffic) Order 2006 No. 2006/465. - Enabling power: Road Traffic Regulation Act 1984, s. 14 (1) (a). - Made: 21.02.2006. Coming into force: 05.03.2006. Effect: None. Territorial extent & classification: E. Local *Unpublished*

The A1 Trunk Road and the A696 Trunk Road (Kenton Bar Interchange) (Temporary Restriction and Prohibition of Traffic) Order 2006 No. 2006/700. - Enabling power: Road Traffic Regulation Act 1984, s. 14 (1) (a). - Made: 28.02.2006. Coming into force: 12.03.2006. Effect: None. Territorial extent & classification: E. Local *Unpublished*

The A1 Trunk Road (Apley Head to South of Elkesley, Nottinghamshire) (Temporary Prohibition of Traffic) Order 2006 No. 2006/665. - Enabling power: Road Traffic Regulation Act 1984, s. 14 (1) (a). - Made: 20.02.2006. Coming into force: 27.02.2006. Effect: None. Territorial extent & classification: E. Local *Unpublished*

The A1 Trunk Road (B6267, Sinderby Junction) (Temporary 50 Miles Per Hour Speed Restriction) Order 2006 No. 2006/457. - Enabling power: Road Traffic Regulation Act 1984, s. 14 (1) (a). - Made: 17.02.2006. Coming into force: 28.02.2006. Effect: None. Territorial extent & classification: E. Local *Unpublished*

The A1 Trunk Road (B6353, Fenwick Junction) (Temporary Restriction and Prohibition of Traffic) Order 2006 No. 2006/2749. - Enabling power: Road Traffic Regulation Act 1984, s. 14 (1) (a). - Made: 09.10.2006. Coming into force: 22.10.2006. Effect: None. Territorial extent & classification: E. Local *Unpublished*

The A1 Trunk Road (Belford Bypass) (Temporary Prohibition and Restriction of Traffic) Order 2006 No. 2006/3030. - Enabling power: Road Traffic Regulation Act 1984, s. 14 (1) (a). - Made: 20.10.2006. Coming into force: 07.11.2006. Effect: None. Territorial extent & classification: E. Local *Unpublished*

The A1 Trunk Road (Belford) (Temporary Restriction and Prohibition of Traffic) Order 2006 No. 2006/1427. - Enabling power: Road Traffic Regulation Act 1984, s. 14 (1) (a) (7). - Made: 22.05.2006. Coming into force: 02.06.2006. Effect: None. Territorial extent & classification: E. Local *Unpublished*

The A1 Trunk Road (Black Cat Roundabout to Tempsford Bridge, Bedfordshire) (Temporary 50 Miles Per Hour speed Restriction) Order 2006 No. 2006/2446. - Enabling power: Road Traffic Regulation Act 1984, s. 14 (1) (a). - Made: 29.08.2006. Coming into force: 05.09.2006. Effect: None. Territorial extent & classification: E. Local *Unpublished*

The A1 Trunk Road (Blaydon Interchange to Kenton Bar Interchange) (Temporary Restriction and Prohibition of Traffic) Order 2006 No. 2006/2855. - Enabling power: Road Traffic Regulation Act 1984, s. 14 (1) (a). - Made: 17.10.2006. Coming into force: 29.10.2006. Effect: None. Territorial extent & classification: E. Local *Unpublished*

The A1 Trunk Road (Bramham Crossroads) (Temporary Prohibition of Traffic) Order 2006 No. 2006/1049. - Enabling power: Road Traffic Regulation Act 1984, s. 14 (1) (a). - Made: 31.03.2006. Coming into force: 18.04.2006. Effect: None. Territorial extent & classification: E. Local *Unpublished*

The A1 Trunk Road (Brampton Hut and Alconbury Interchanges, Cambridgeshire) (Temporary Restriction and Prohibition of Traffic) Order 2006 No. 2006/2880. - Enabling power: Road Traffic Regulation Act 1984, s. 14 (1) (a). - Made: 23.10.2006. Coming into force: 06.11.2006. Effect: None. Territorial extent & classification: E. Local *Unpublished*

The A1 Trunk Road (Bridge Mill to Cheswick) (Temporary Restriction and Prohibition of Traffic) Order 2006 No. 2006/849. - Enabling power: Road Traffic Regulation Act 1984, s. 14 (1) (a). - Made: 07.03.2006. Coming into force: 19.03.2006. Effect: None. Territorial extent & classification: E. Local *Unpublished*

The A1 Trunk Road (Carlton-on-Trent) (Temporary Prohibition and Restriction of Traffic) 2006 No. 2006/196. - Enabling power: Road Traffic Regulation Act 1984, s. 14 (1) (a). - Made: 23.01.2006. Coming into force: 30.01.2006. Effect: None. Territorial extent & classification: E. Local *Unpublished*

The A1 Trunk Road (Carpenters Lodge Roundabout, Peterborough) (Temporary Restriction of Traffic) Order 2006 No. 2006/1772. - Enabling power: Road Traffic Regulation Act 1984, s. 14 (1) (a). - Made: 23.06.2006. Coming into force: 30.06.2006. Effect: None. Territorial extent & classification: E. Local *Unpublished*

The A1 Trunk Road (Cawledge Layby, Heckley House Layby and Browneside Layby) (Temporary Prohibition of Traffic) Order 2006 No. 2006/115. - Enabling power: Road Traffic Regulation Act 1984, s. 14 (1) (a). - Made: 19.01.2006. Coming into force: 29.01.2006. Effect: None. Territorial extent & classification: E. Local *Unpublished*

The A1 Trunk Road (Colsterworth - Great Ponton, Lincolnshire) (Temporary 40 Miles Per Hour Speed Restriction) Order 2006 No. 2006/992. - Enabling power: Road Traffic Regulation Act 1984, s. 14 (1) (a). - Made: 20.03.2006. Coming into force: 27.03.2006. Effect: None. Territorial extent & classification: E. Local *Unpublished*

The A1 Trunk Road (Cromwell, Nottinghamshire) (Temporary Prohibition of Traffic) Order 2006 No. 2006/291. - Enabling power: Road Traffic Regulation Act 1984, s. 14 (1) (a). - Made: 03.02.2006. Coming into force: 10.02.2006. Effect: None. Territorial extent & classification: E. Local *Unpublished*

The A1 Trunk Road (Denwick Interchange) (Temporary Restriction and Prohibition of Traffic) Order 2006 No. 2006/38. - Enabling power: Road Traffic Regulation Act 1984, s. 14 (1) (a). - Made: 03.01.2006. Coming into force: 15.01.2006. Effect: None. Territorial extent & classification: E. Local *Unpublished*

The A1 Trunk Road (Elkesley, Nottinghamshire) (Temporary Prohibition of Traffic) Order 2006 No. 2006/3478. - Enabling power: Road Traffic Regulation Act 1984, s. 14 (1) (b). - Made: 22.12.2006. Coming into force: 29.12.2006. Effect: None. Territorial extent & classification: E. Local *Unpublished*

The A1 Trunk Road (Elkesley, Nottinghamshire) (Temporary Restriction and Prohibition of Traffic) Order 2006 No. 2006/1018. - Enabling power: Road Traffic Regulation Act 1984, s. 14 (1) (a). - Made: 24.03.2006. Coming into force: 31.03.2006. Effect: None. Territorial extent & classification: E. Local *Unpublished*

Road traffic: Traffic regulation

The A1 Trunk Road (Fenwick Stead to Fenwick Granary Junction) (Temporary 10 Miles Per Hour and 40 Miles Per Hour Speed Restriction) (No. 2) Order 2006 No. 2006/1428. - Enabling power: Road Traffic Regulation Act 1984, s. 14 (1) (a). - Made: 23.05.2006. Coming into force: 04.06.2006. Effect: None. Territorial extent & classification: E. Local *Unpublished*

The A1 Trunk Road (Fenwick Stead to Fenwick Granary Junction) (Temporary 10 Miles Per Hour and 40 Miles Per Hour Speed Restriction) Order 2006 No. 2006/699. - Enabling power: Road Traffic Regulation Act 1984, s. 14 (1) (a). - Made: 28.02.2006. Coming into force: 12.03.2006. Effect: None. Territorial extent & classification: E. Local *Unpublished*

The A1 Trunk Road (Five Lanes End to Ranby, Nottinghamshire) (Temporary Prohibition of Traffic) Order 2006 No. 2006/1873. - Enabling power: Road Traffic Regulation Act 1984, s. 14 (1) (a). - Made: 30.06.2006. Coming into force: 07.07.2006. Effect: None. Territorial extent & classification: E. Local *Unpublished*

The A1 Trunk Road (Gonerby Moor to Long Bennington) (Temporary Restriction and Prohibition of Traffic) Order 2006 No. 2006/1653. - Enabling power: Road Traffic Regulation Act 1984, s. 14 (1) (a). - Made: 12.06.2006. Coming into force: 19.06.2006. Effect: None. Territorial extent & classification: E. Local *Unpublished*

The A1 Trunk Road (Grantham to Stretton) (Temporary Restriction and Prohibition of Traffic) Order 2006 No. 2006/1415. - Enabling power: Road Traffic Regulation Act 1984, s. 14 (1) (a). - Made: 22.05.2006. Coming into force: 29.05.2006. Effect: None. Territorial extent & classification: E. Local *Unpublished*

The A1 Trunk Road (Great North Road, Bedfordshire to Cambridgeshire) (Temporary Variable Speed Limit) Order 2006 No. 2006/1488. - Enabling power: Road Traffic Regulation Act 1984, ss. 14, 15. - Made: 30.05.2006. Coming into force: 06.06.2006. Effect: None. Territorial extent & classification: E. Local *Unpublished*

The A1 Trunk Road (Haggerston) (Temporary Restriction and Prohibition of Traffic) Order 2006 No. 2006/723. - Enabling power: Road Traffic Regulation Act 1984, s. 14 (1) (a). - Made: 07.03.2006. Coming into force: 20.03.2006. Effect: None. Territorial extent & classification: E. Local *Unpublished*

The A1 Trunk Road (Haggerston to West Mains Junction) (Temporary Restriction and Prohibition of Traffic) Order 2006 No. 2006/2425. - Enabling power: Road Traffic Regulation Act 1984, s. 14 (1) (a). - Made: 22.08.2006. Coming into force: 03.09.2006. Effect: None. Territorial extent & classification: E. Local *Unpublished*

The A1 Trunk Road (Highfields to Scottish Border) (Temporary Restriction and Prohibition of Traffic) Order 2006 No. 2006/464. - Enabling power: Road Traffic Regulation Act 1984, s. 14 (1) (a). - Made: 21.02.2006. Coming into force: 05.03.2006. Effect: None. Territorial extent & classification: E. Local *Unpublished*

The A1 Trunk Road (Hollinside Road Interchange) (Temporary Restriction and Prohibition of Traffic) Order 2006 No. 2006/845. - Enabling power: Road Traffic Regulation Act 1984, s. 14 (1) (a). - Made: 13.03.2006. Coming into force: 23.03.2006. Effect: None. Territorial extent & classification: E. Local *Unpublished*

The A1 Trunk Road (Holtby Grange to Leases Hall Bridge) (Temporary Restriction and Prohibition of Traffic) Order 2006 No. 2006/1586. - Enabling power: Road Traffic Regulation Act 1984, s. 14 (1) (a). - Made: 02.06.2006. Coming into force: 15.06.2006. Effect: None. Territorial extent & classification: E. Local *Unpublished*

The A1 Trunk Road (Junction 1, Northbound Exit Slip Road) (Temporary Prohibition of Traffic) Order 2006 No. 2006/1047. - Enabling power: Road Traffic Regulation Act 1984, s. 14 (1) (a). - Made: 03.04.2006. Coming into force: 08.04.2006. Effect: None. Territorial extent & classification: E. Local *Unpublished*

The A1 Trunk Road (Ladywood Lane Overbridge, Nottinghamshire) (Temporary Restriction and Prohibition of Traffic) 2006 No. 2006/197. - Enabling power: Road Traffic Regulation Act 1984, s. 14 (1) (a). - Made: 23.01.2006. Coming into force: 30.01.2006. Effect: None. Territorial extent & classification: E. Local *Unpublished*

The A1 Trunk Road (Markham Moor to Carlton on Trent, Nottinghamshire) (Temporary Prohibition of Traffic) Order 2006 No. 2006/2575. - Enabling power: Road Traffic Regulation Act 1984, s. 14 (1) (a). - Made: 15.09.2006. Coming into force: 22.09.2006. Effect: None. Territorial extent & classification: E. Local *Unpublished*

The A1 Trunk Road (Morpeth Bypass) (Temporary Restriction and Prohibition of Traffic) (No. 2) Order 2006 No. 2006/1224. - Enabling power: Road Traffic Regulation Act 1984, s. 14 (1) (a) (7). - Made: 25.04.2006. Coming into force: 07.05.2006. Effect: None. Territorial extent & classification: E. Local *Unpublished*

The A1 Trunk Road (Morpeth Bypass) (Temporary Restriction and Prohibition of Traffic) (No. 3) Order 2006 No. 2006/2426. - Enabling power: Road Traffic Regulation Act 1984, s. 14 (1) (a) (7). - Made: 22.08.2006. Coming into force: 03.09.2006. Effect: None. Territorial extent & classification: E. Local *Unpublished*

The A1 Trunk Road (Morpeth Bypass) (Temporary Restriction and Prohibition of Traffic) Order 2006 No. 2006/722. - Enabling power: Road Traffic Regulation Act 1984, s. 14 (1) (a). - Made: 07.03.2006. Coming into force: 19.03.2006. Effect: None. Territorial extent & classification: E. Local *Unpublished*

The A1 Trunk Road (Newark on Trent to Grantham) (Temporary Restriction and Prohibition of Traffic) Order 2006 No. 2006/3012. - Enabling power: Road Traffic Regulation Act 1984, s. 14 (1) (a). - Made: 03.11.2006. Coming into force: 10.11.2006. Effect: None. Territorial extent & classification: E. Local *Unpublished*

Road traffic: Traffic regulation

The A1 Trunk Road (Newton on the Moor Layby) (Temporary Prohibition of Traffic) Order 2006 No. 2006/698. - Enabling power: Road Traffic Regulation Act 1984, s. 14 (1) (a). - Made: 28.02.2006. Coming into force: 12.03.2006. Effect: None. Territorial extent & classification: E. Local *Unpublished*

The A1 Trunk Road (Newton on the Moor South Junction) (Temporary Restriction of Traffic) Order 2006 No. 2006/3476. - Enabling power: Road Traffic Regulation Act 1984, s. 14 (1) (a). - Made: 21.12.2006. Coming into force: 07.01.2007. Effect: None. Territorial extent & classification: E. Local *Unpublished*

The A1 Trunk Road (Ranby, Nottinghamshire) (Slip Roads) (Temporary Prohibition of Traffic) Order 2006 No. 2006/3230. - Enabling power: Road Traffic Regulation Act 1984, s. 14 (1) (a). - Made: 01.12.2006. Coming into force: 08.12.2006. Effect: None. Territorial extent & classification: E. Local *Unpublished*

The A1 Trunk Road (Sandy Roundabout, Bedfordshire) (Temporary Restriction and Prohibition of Traffic) Order 2006 No. 2006/2452. - Enabling power: Road Traffic Regulation Act 1984, s. 14 (1) (a). - Made: 04.09.2006. Coming into force: 11.09.2006. Effect: None. Territorial extent & classification: E. Local *Unpublished*

The A1 Trunk Road (Scotch Corner Interchange) (Temporary Restriction and Prohibition of Traffic) Order 2006 No. 2006/3178. - Enabling power: Road Traffic Regulation Act 1984, s. 14 (1) (a). - Made: 24.11.2006. Coming into force: 06.12.2006. Effect: None. Territorial extent & classification: E. Local *Unpublished*

The A1 Trunk Road (Scotswood Interchange) (Temporary Prohibition of Traffic) Order 2006 No. 2006/1318. - Enabling power: Road Traffic Regulation Act 1984, s. 14 (1) (a). - Made: 28.04.2006. Coming into force: 10.05.2006. Effect: None. Territorial extent & classification: E. Local *Unpublished*

The A1 Trunk Road (Scottish Border Layby) (Temporary Prohibition of Traffic) Order 2006 No. 2006/452. - Enabling power: Road Traffic Regulation Act 1984, s. 14 (1) (a). - Made: 14.02.2006. Coming into force: 26.02.2006. Effect: None. Territorial extent & classification: E. Local *Unpublished*

The A1 Trunk Road (Scremerston Roundabout to East Ord Roundabout) (Temporary Restriction and Prohibition of Traffic) 2006 No. 2006/255. - Enabling power: Road Traffic Regulation Act 1984, s. 14 (1) (a). - Made: 24.01.2006. Coming into force: 05.02.2006. Effect: None. Territorial extent & classification: E. Local *Unpublished*

The A1 Trunk Road (Seaton Burn to Stannington) and the A19 Trunk Road (Seaton Burn) (Temporary Restriction and Prohibition of Traffic) Order 2006 No. 2006/2649. - Enabling power: Road Traffic Regulation Act 1984, s. 14 (1) (a) (7). - Made: 26.09.2006. Coming into force: 08.10.2006. Effect: None. Territorial extent & classification: E. Local *Unpublished*

The A1 Trunk Road (Southoe Bends to Buckden Roundabout, Huntingdon, Cambrdigeshire) (Temporary 40 Miles Per Hour Speed Restriction) Order 2006 No. 2006/2436. - Enabling power: Road Traffic Regulation Act 1984, s. 14 (1) (a). - Made: 22.08.2006. Coming into force: 29.08.2006. Effect: None. Territorial extent & classification: E. Local *Unpublished*

The A1 Trunk Road (South of Grantham, Lincolnshire) (Temporary Restriction and Prohibition of Traffic) Order 2006 No. 2006/2671. - Enabling power: Road Traffic Regulation Act 1984, s. 14 (1) (a). - Made: 22.09.2006. Coming into force: 29.09.2006. Effect: None. Territorial extent & classification: E. Local *Unpublished*

The A1 Trunk Road (Stamford to Long Bennington) (Temporary Restriction and Prohibition of Traffic) Order 2006 No. 2006/451. - Enabling power: Road Traffic Regulation Act 1984, s. 14 (1) (a). - Made: 13.02.2006. Coming into force: 20.02.2006. Effect: None. Territorial extent & classification: E. Local *Unpublished*

The A1 Trunk Road (Stamford to South Witham) (Temporary Restriction and Prohibition of Traffic) (No. 3) Order 2006 No. 2006/2249. - Enabling power: Road Traffic Regulation Act 1984, s. 14 (1) (a). - Made: 11.08.2006. Coming into force: 18.08.2006. Effect: None. Territorial extent & classification: E. Local *Unpublished*

The A1 Trunk Road (Stannington) (Temporary Prohibition of Traffic) Order 2006 No. 2006/2427. - Enabling power: Road Traffic Regulation Act 1984, s. 14 (1) (a). - Made: 21.08.2006. Coming into force: 29.08.2006. Effect: None. Territorial extent & classification: E. Local *Unpublished*

The A1 Trunk Road (Tuxford to Markham Moor) (Temporary Prohibition of Traffic) Order 2006 No. 2006/1020. - Enabling power: Road Traffic Regulation Act 1984, s. 14 (1) (a). - Made: 24.03.2006. Coming into force: 31.03.2006. Effect: None. Territorial extent & classification: E. Local *Unpublished*

The A1 Trunk Road (Tweed Bridge to Duns Road Junction) (Temporary Restriction and Prohibition of Traffic) Order 2006 No. 2006/2102. - Enabling power: Road Traffic Regulation Act 1984, s. 14 (1) (a) (7). - Made: 25.07.2006. Coming into force: 06.08.2006. Effect: None. Territorial extent & classification: E. Local *Unpublished*

The A1 Trunk Road (Wansford, Peterborough) (Temporary Prohibition of Traffic) Order 2006 No. 2006/3229. - Enabling power: Road Traffic Regulation Act 1984, s. 14 (1) (a). - Made: 04.12.2006. Coming into force: 11.12.2006. Effect: None. Territorial extent & classification: E. Local *Unpublished*

The A1 Trunk Road (Wansford, Peterborough) (Temporary Restriction and Prohibition of Traffic) Order 2006 No. 2006/3175. - Enabling power: Road Traffic Regulation Act 1984, s. 14 (1) (a). - Made: 27.11.2006. Coming into force: 04.12.2006. Effect: None. Territorial extent & classification: E. Local *Unpublished*

The A1 Trunk Road (Winthorpe, Newark-on-Trent, Nottinghamshire) (Temporary 40 Miles Per Hour Speed Restriction) Order 2006 No. 2006/1611. - Enabling power: Road Traffic Regulation Act 1984, s. 14 (1) (a). - Made: 19.05.2006. Coming into force: 26.05.2006. Effect: None. Territorial extent & classification: E. Local *Unpublished*

The A1 Trunk Road (Winthorpe, Newark-on-Trent, Nottinghamshire) (Temporary Prohibition of Traffic) Order 2006 No. 2006/1866. - Enabling power: Road Traffic Regulation Act 1984, s. 14 (1) (a). - Made: 03.07.2006. Coming into force: 10.07.2006. Effect: None. Territorial extent & classification: E. Local *Unpublished*

The A1 Trunk Road (Winthorpe, Nottinghamshire) (Temporary Prohibition of Traffic) Order 2006 No. 2006/448. - Enabling power: Road Traffic Regulation Act 1984, s. 14 (1) (a). - Made: 14.02.2006. Coming into force: 21.02.2006. Effect: None. Territorial extent & classification: E. Local *Unpublished*

The A1 Trunk Road (Winthorpe to Barrowby) (Temporary Restriction and Prohibition of Traffic) Order 2006 No. 2006/444. - Enabling power: Road Traffic Regulation Act 1984, s. 14 (1) (a). - Made: 10.02.2006. Coming into force: 17.02.2006. Effect: None. Territorial extent & classification: E. Local *Unpublished*

The A1 Trunk Road (Winthorpe to Dry Doddington) (Temporary Prohibition of Traffic) Order 2006 No. 2006/3048. - Enabling power: Road Traffic Regulation Act 1984, s. 14 (1) (a). - Made: 13.10.2006. Coming into force: 20.10.2006. Effect: None. Territorial extent & classification: E. Local *Unpublished*

The A1 Trunk Road (Winthorpe to South of Balderton, Nottinghamshire) (Temporary Prohibition of Traffic) Order 2006 No. 2006/2117. - Enabling power: Road Traffic Regulation Act 1984, s. 14 (1) (a). - Made: 21.07.2006. Coming into force: 28.07.2006. Effect: None. Territorial extent & classification: E. Local *Unpublished*

The A1 Trunk Road (Wothorpe to Wittering) (Temporary Prohibition of Traffic) Order 2006 No. 2006/478. - Enabling power: Road Traffic Regulation Act 1984, s. 14 (1) (a). - Made: 17.02.2006. Coming into force: 24.02.2006. Effect: None. Territorial extent & classification: E. Local *Unpublished*

The A2 and A282 Trunk Roads and the M25 Motorway (Dartford) (Temporary Restriction and Prohibition of Traffic) Order 2006 No. 2006/1601. - Enabling power: Road Traffic Regulation Act 1984, ss. 14 (1) (a) (7), 15 (2). - Made: 12.06.2006. Coming into force: 19.06.2006. Effect: None. Territorial extent & classification: E. Local *Unpublished*

The A2 Trunk Road (A2018 Junction - Bexley Brough Boundary) (Temporary Prohibition of Traffic) Order 2006 No. 2006/2070. - Enabling power: Road Traffic Regulation Act 1984, s. 14 (1) (a). - Made: 24.07.2006. Coming into force: 31.07.2006. Effect: None. Territorial extent & classification: E. Local *Unpublished*

The A2 Trunk Road (A2050 Junction, Near Bridge) (Temporary Prohibition of Traffic) Order 2006 No. 2006/1768. - Enabling power: Road Traffic Regulation Act 1984, s. 14 (1) (a). - Made: 26.06.2006. Coming into force: 01.07.2006. Effect: None. Territorial extent & classification: E. Local *Unpublished*

The A2 Trunk Road (A2050 Junction, Near Bridge) (Temporary Restriction and Prohibition of Traffic) Order 2006 No. 2006/157. - Enabling power: Road Traffic Regulation Act 1984, s. 14 (1) (a). - Made: 23.01.2006. Coming into force: 28.01.2006. Effect: None. Territorial extent & classification: E. Local *Unpublished*

The A2 Trunk Road (A2050 Junction, Near Bridge) (Temporary Restriction and Prohibition of Traffic) Order 2006 No. 2006/531. - Enabling power: Road Traffic Regulation Act 1984, s. 14 (1) (a). - Made: 27.02.2006. Coming into force: 04.03.2006. Effect: None. Territorial extent & classification: E. Local *Unpublished*

The A2 Trunk Road (Bean - Cobham) (Temporary Restriction and Prohibition of Traffic) Order 2006 No. 2006/3442. - Enabling power: Road Traffic Regulation Act 1984, ss. 14 (1) (a), 15 (2). - Made: 18.12.2006. Coming into force: 13.01.2007. Effect: None. Territorial extent & classification: E. Local *Unpublished*

The A2 Trunk Road (Canterbury Bypass) (Temporary Restriction and Prohibition of Traffic) Order 2006 No. 2006/1882. - Enabling power: Road Traffic Regulation Act 1984, s. 14 (1) (a). - Made: 10.07.2006. Coming into force: 15.07.2006. Effect: None. Territorial extent & classification: E. Local *Unpublished*

The A2 Trunk Road (Dunkirk, Londonbound Exit Slip Road) (Temporary Prohibition of Traffic) Order 2006 No. 2006/446. - Enabling power: Road Traffic Regulation Act 1984, s. 14 (1) (a). - Made: 20.02.2006. Coming into force: 25.02.2006. Effect: None. Territorial extent & classification: E. Local *Unpublished*

The A2 Trunk Road (Jubilee Way, Coastbound Carriageway) (Temporary Prohibition of Traffic) Order 2006 No. 2006/2641. - Enabling power: Road Traffic Regulation Act 1984, s. 14 (1) (a). - Made: 25.09.2006. Coming into force: 01.10.2006. Effect: None. Territorial extent & classification: E. Local *Unpublished*

The A2 Trunk Road (Lydden) (Temporary 40 Miles Per Hour Speed Restriction) Order 2006 No. 2006/3299. - Enabling power: Road Traffic Regulation Act 1984, s. 14 (1) (a). - Made: 11.12.2006. Coming into force: 16.12.2006. Effect: None. Territorial extent & classification: E. Local *Unpublished*

The A2 Trunk Road (M25 Junction 2 - A227 Junction) (Temporary Restriction and Prohibition of Traffic) Order 2002 Revocation Order 2006 No. 2006/439. - Enabling power: Road Traffic Regulation Act 1984, ss. 14 (1) (a), 15 (2), sch. 9, para. 27 (1). - Made: 13.02.2006. Coming into force: 20.02.2006. Effect: S.I. 2002/1631 revoked. Territorial extent & classification: E. Local *Unpublished*

The A2 Trunk Road (M25 Junction 2, Entry Slip Roads) (Temporary Prohibition of Traffic) Order 2006 No. 2006/924. - Enabling power: Road Traffic Regulation Act 1984, s. 14 (1) (a). - Made: 13.03.2006. Coming into force: 22.03.2006. Effect: None. Territorial extent & classification: E. Local *Unpublished*

The A2 Trunk Road (Pepper Hill - Singlewell) (Temporary Restriction and Prohibition of Traffic) Order 2006 No. 2006/2848. - Enabling power: Road Traffic Regulation Act 1984, s. 14 (1) (a). - Made: 16.10.2006. Coming into force: 17.10.2006. Effect: None. Territorial extent & classification: E. Local *Unpublished*

The A2 Trunk Road (Upper Harbledown - Bridge) (Temporary Restriction and Prohibition of Traffic) Order 2006 No. 2006/2587. - Enabling power: Road Traffic Regulation Act 1984, s. 14 (1) (a). - Made: 11.09.2006. Coming into force: 16.09.2006. Effect: None. Territorial extent & classification: E. Local *Unpublished*

The A2 Trunk Road (Upper Harbledown, Coastbound) (Temporary Prohibition of Traffic) Order 2006 No. 2006/1985. - Enabling power: Road Traffic Regulation Act 1984, s. 14 (1) (a). - Made: 17.07.2006. Coming into force: 22.07.2006. Effect: None. Territorial extent & classification: E. Local *Unpublished*

The A3 and A27 Trunk Roads and the A3 (M) and M27 Motorways (Havant/Portsmouth) (Temporary Restriction and Prohibition of Traffic) Order 2006 No. 2006/3440. - Enabling power: Road Traffic Regulation Act 1984, s. 14 (1) (a) (7). - Made: 18.12.2006. Coming into force: 02.01.2007. Effect: None. Territorial extent & classification: E. Local *Unpublished*

The A3(M) Motorway (Junction 2, Southbound Entry Slip Road) (Temporary Prohibition of Traffic) Order 2006 No. 2006/1983. - Enabling power: Road Traffic Regulation Act 1984, s. 14 (1) (a). - Made: 17.07.2006. Coming into force: 22.07.2006. Effect: None. Territorial extent & classification: E. Local *Unpublished*

The A3(M) Motorway (Junction 3, Southbound Slip Roads) (Temporary Prohibition of Traffic) Order 2006 No. 2006/973. - Enabling power: Road Traffic Regulation Act 1984, s. 14 (1) (a). - Made: 27.03.2006. Coming into force: 01.04.2006. Effect: None. Territorial extent & classification: E. Local *Unpublished*

The A3(M) Motorway (Junctions 3 and 4, Slip Roads) (Temporary Prohibition of Traffic) Order 2006 No. 2006/48. - Enabling power: Road Traffic Regulation Act 1984, s. 14 (1) (a). - Made: 09.01.2006. Coming into force: 14.01.2006. Effect: None. Territorial extent & classification: E. Local *Unpublished*

The A3 Trunk Road (A31 Hogs Back Interchange) (Temporary Prohibition of Traffic) Order 2006 No. 2006/47. - Enabling power: Road Traffic Regulation Act 1984, s. 14 (1) (a). - Made: 09.01.2006. Coming into force: 14.01.2006. Effect: None. Territorial extent & classification: E. Local *Unpublished*

The A3 Trunk Road and the A3(M) Motorway (Junctions 2 - 1, Northbound) (Temporary Restriction and Prohibition of Traffic) Order 2006 No. 2006/1431. - Enabling power: Road Traffic Regulation Act 1984, s. 14 (1) (a). - Made: 22.05.2006. Coming into force: 27.05.2006. Effect: S.I. 2005/3009 revoked. Territorial extent & classification: E. Local *Unpublished*

The A3 Trunk Road (Bramshott Chase - Hindhead) (Temporary 10 Miles Per Hour Speed Restriction) Order 2006 No. 2006/406. - Enabling power: Road Traffic Regulation Act 1984, s. 14 (1) (a). - Made: 20.02.2006. Coming into force: 25.02.2006. Effect: None. Territorial extent & classification: E. Local *Unpublished*

The A3 Trunk Road (Clanfield, Slip Roads) (Temporary Prohibition of Traffic) Order 2006 No. 2006/2727. - Enabling power: Road Traffic Regulation Act 1984, s. 14 (1) (a). - Made: 02.10.2006. Coming into force: 07.10.2006. Effect: None. Territorial extent & classification: E. Local *Unpublished*

The A3 Trunk Road (Esher Bypass) (Temporary 40 MPH Speed Restriction) Order 2006 No. 2006/3445. - Enabling power: Road Traffic Regulation Act 1984, s. 14 (1) (a). - Made: 18.12.2006. Coming into force: 23.12.2006. Effect: None. Territorial extent & classification: E. Local *Unpublished*

The A3 Trunk Road (Gravel Hill, Near Clanfield) (Temporary Restriction and Prohibition of Traffic) Order 2006 No. 2006/3043. - Enabling power: Road Traffic Regulation Act 1984, s. 14 (1) (a). - Made: 06.11.2006. Coming into force: 11.11.2006. Effect: None. Territorial extent & classification: E. Local *Unpublished*

The A3 Trunk Road (Guildford Bypass) (Temporary Restriction and Prohibition of Traffic) Order 2006 No. 2006/1432. - Enabling power: Road Traffic Regulation Act 1984, s. 14 (1) (a). - Made: 22.05.2006. Coming into force: 27.05.2006. Effect: None. Territorial extent & classification: E. Local *Unpublished*

The A3 Trunk Road (Guildford Bypass) (Temporary Restriction of Traffic) Order 2006 No. 2006/150. - Enabling power: Road Traffic Regulation Act 1984, s. 14 (1) (a). - Made: 23.01.2006. Coming into force: 28.01.2006. Effect: None. Territorial extent & classification: E. Local *Unpublished*

The A3 Trunk Road (Hindhead - Liphook) (Temporary Speed Restrictions) Order 2006 No. 2006/1646. - Enabling power: Road Traffic Regulation Act 1984, s. 14 (1) (a). - Made: 19.06.2006. Coming into force: 24.06.2006. Effect: None. Territorial extent & classification: E. Local *Unpublished*

The A3 Trunk Road (Hog's Back Junction - Compton) (Temporary Prohibition of Traffic) Order 2006 No. 2006/2724. - Enabling power: Road Traffic Regulation Act 1984, s. 14 (1) (a). - Made: 02.10.2006. Coming into force: 07.10.2006. Effect: None. Territorial extent & classification: E. Local *Unpublished*

Road traffic: Traffic regulation

The A3 Trunk Road (Hurtmore Interchange) (Temporary Restriction and Prohibition of Traffic) Order 2006 No. 2006/2329. - Enabling power: Road Traffic Regulation Act 1984, s. 14 (1) (a). - Made: 21.08.2006. Coming into force: 26.08.2006. Effect: None. Territorial extent & classification: E. Local *Unpublished*

The A3 Trunk Road (Ladymead Bridges) (Temporary Restriction and Prohibition of Traffic) Order 2006 No. 2006/2203. - Enabling power: Road Traffic Regulation Act 1984, s. 14 (1) (a). - Made: 07.08.2006. Coming into force: 12.08.2006. Effect: None. Territorial extent & classification: E. Local *Unpublished*

The A3 Trunk Road (Longmoor - Flexcombe) (Temporary Restriction and Prohibition of Traffic) Order 2006 No. 2006/2774. - Enabling power: Road Traffic Regulation Act 1984, s. 14 (1) (a). - Made: 09.10.2006. Coming into force: 14.10.2006. Effect: None. Territorial extent & classification: E. Local *Unpublished*

The A3 Trunk Road (M25 Junction 10, Hook) (Temporary Prohibition of Traffic) Order 2006 No. 2006/1982. - Enabling power: Road Traffic Regulation Act 1984, s. 14 (1) (a). - Made: 17.07.2006. Coming into force: 22.07.2006. Effect: None. Territorial extent & classification: E. Local *Unpublished*

The A3 Trunk Road (M25 Junction 10, Wisley Interchange) (Temporary Prohibition of Traffic) Order 2006 No. 2006/1978. - Enabling power: Road Traffic Regulation Act 1984, s. 14 (1) (a). - Made: 17.07.2006. Coming into force: 22.07.2006. Effect: None. Territorial extent & classification: E. Local *Unpublished*

The A3 Trunk Road (Milford Interchange - Compton Interchange) (Temporary Speed Restrictions) Order 2006 No. 2006/2332. - Enabling power: Road Traffic Regulation Act 1984, s. 14 (1) (a). - Made: 21.08.2006. Coming into force: 26.08.2006. Effect: None. Territorial extent & classification: E. Local *Unpublished*

The A3 Trunk Road (Ockham, Northbound Entry Slip Road) (Temporary Prohibition of Traffic) Order 2006 No. 2006/1853. - Enabling power: Road Traffic Regulation Act 1984, s. 14 (1) (a). - Made: 03.07.2006. Coming into force: 12.07.2006. Effect: None. Territorial extent & classification: E. Local. - Revoked by S.I. 2007/35 (Unpublished) *Unpublished*

The A3 Trunk Road (Wisley Lane and Wisley Lay-by) (Temporary Prohibition of Traffic) Order 2006 No. 2006/1603. - Enabling power: Road Traffic Regulation Act 1984, s. 14 (1) (a). - Made: 12.06.2006. Coming into force: 17.06.2006. Effect: None. Territorial extent & classification: E. Local *Unpublished*

The A4 Trunk Road and A46 Trunk Road (Bailbrook Underpass, Bath) (Temporary Prohibition of Traffic) Order 2006 No. 2006/1477. - Enabling power: Road Traffic Regulation Act 1984, s. 14 (1) (a). - Made: 30.05.2006. Coming into force: 02.06.2006. Effect: None. Territorial extent & classification: E. Local *Unpublished*

The A4 Trunk Road (Saltford, Between Bristol and Bath) (Temporary Prohibition and Restriction of Traffic) Order 2006 No. 2006/2032. - Enabling power: Road Traffic Regulation Act 1984, s. 14 (1) (a). - Made: 11.07.2006. Coming into force: 14.07.2006. Effect: None. Territorial extent & classification: E. Local *Unpublished*

The A5 and A458 Trunk Roads (Montford Bridge to Woodcote, Shropshire) (Temporary Prohibition of Traffic) Order 2006 No. 2006/1654. - Enabling power: Road Traffic Regulation Act 1984, s. 14 (1) (a). - Made: 12.06.2006. Coming into force: 19.06.2006. Effect: None. Territorial extent & classification: E. Local *Unpublished*

The A5 and A483 Trunk Roads (Mile End Roundabout, Shropshire) (Temporary 10 Miles Per Hour Speed Restriction) Order 2006 No. 2006/3355. - Enabling power: Road Traffic Regulation Act 1984, s. 14 (1) (a). - Made: 01.12.2006. Coming into force: 08.12.2006. Effect: None. Territorial extent & classification: E. Local *Unpublished*

The A5 Trunk Road (Atherstone, Warwickshire) (Temporary Restriction and Prohibition of Traffic) Order 2006 No. 2006/3477. - Enabling power: Road Traffic Regulation Act 1984, s. 14 (1) (a). - Made: 20.12.2006. Coming into force: 27.12.2006. Effect: None. Territorial extent & classification: E. Local *Unpublished*

The A5 Trunk Road (Atherstone, Warwickshire) (Temporary Restriction and Prohibition of Traffic) Order 2006 No. 2006/73. - Enabling power: Road Traffic Regulation Act 1984, s. 14 (1) (a). - Made: 09.01.2006. Coming into force: 16.01.2006. Effect: None. Territorial extent & classification: E. Local *Unpublished*

The A5 Trunk Road (Cuttle Mill, Northamptonshire) (Temporary Prohibition of Traffic) Order 2006 No. 2006/2049. - Enabling power: Road Traffic Regulation Act 1984, s. 14 (1) (a). - Made: 10.07.2006. Coming into force: 17.07.2006. Effect: None. Territorial extent & classification: E. Local *Unpublished*

The A5 Trunk Road (Dordon, Warwickshire) (Temporary Prohibition and Restriction of Traffic) Order 2006 No. 2006/1571. - Enabling power: Road Traffic Regulation Act 1984, s. 14 (1) (a). - Made: 22.05.2006. Coming into force: 29.05.2006. Effect: None. Territorial extent & classification: E. Local *Unpublished*

The A5 Trunk Road (Gibbet Hill to Catthorpe, Warwickshire) (Slip Road) (Temporary Restriction and Prohibition of Traffic) Order 2006 No. 2006/3053. - Enabling power: Road Traffic Regulation Act 1984, s. 14 (1) (a). - Made: 20.10.2006. Coming into force: 27.10.2006. Effect: None. Territorial extent & classification: E. Local *Unpublished*

The A5 Trunk Road (High Cross to Gibbet Hill) (Temporary Restriction and Prohibition of Traffic) Order 2006 No. 2006/1727. - Enabling power: Road Traffic Regulation Act 1984, s. 14 (1) (a). - Made: 26.06.2006. Coming into force: 03.07.2006. Effect: None. Territorial extent & classification: E. Local *Unpublished*

The A5 Trunk Road (Hinckley, Leicestershire) and the M69 Motorway (Junction 1) (Temporary Restriction and Prohibition of Traffic) Order 2006 No. 2006/2034. - Enabling power: Road Traffic Regulation Act 1984, s. 14 (1) (a). - Made: 07.07.2006. Coming into force: 14.07.2006. Effect: None. Territorial extent & classification: E. Local *Unpublished*

The A5 Trunk Road (Little Brickhill Roundabout, Milton Keynes) (Temporary Prohibition of Traffic) Order 2006 No. 2006/3138. - Enabling power: Road Traffic Regulation Act 1984, s. 14 (1) (a). - Made: 13.11.2006. Coming into force: 20.11.2006. Effect: None. Territorial extent & classification: E. Local *Unpublished*

The A5 Trunk Road (London Road, Dunstable, Bedfordshire) (Temporary Prohibition of Traffic) Order 2006 No. 2006/809. - Enabling power: Road Traffic Regulation Act 1984, s. 14 (1) (a). - Made: 13.03.2006. Coming into force: 20.03.2006. Effect: None. Territorial extent & classification: E. Local *Unpublished*

The A5 Trunk Road (London Road, Dunstable) (Restriction of Waiting) Order 2006 No. 2006/1597. - Enabling power: Road Traffic Regulation Act 1984, ss. 1 (1), 2 (1) (2), 4 (1) (2). - Made: 06.06.2006. Coming into force: 20.06.2006. Effect: None. Territorial extent & classification: E. Local *Unpublished*

The A5 Trunk Road (M1 Motorway, Junction 9, Hertfordshire) (Temporary Restriction and Prohibition of Traffic) Order 2006 No. 2006/2596. - Enabling power: Road Traffic Regulation Act 1984, s. 14 (1) (a). - Made: 11.09.2006. Coming into force: 18.09.2006. Effect: None. Territorial extent & classification: E. Local *Unpublished*

The A5 Trunk Road (Milton Keynes Bypass, Buckinghamshire) (Temporary Prohibition of Traffic) Order 2006 No. 2006/1476. - Enabling power: Road Traffic Regulation Act 1984, s. 14 (1) (a). - Made: 30.05.2006. Coming into force: 09.06.2006. Effect: None. Territorial extent & classification: E. Local *Unpublished*

The A5 Trunk Road (Milton Keynes) (Temporary Restriction and Prohibition of Traffic) Order 2006 No. 2006/3488. - Enabling power: Road Traffic Regulation Act 1984, s. 14 (1) (a). - Made: 20.12.2006. Coming into force: 27.12.2006. Effect: None. Territorial extent & classification: E. Local *Unpublished*

The A5 Trunk Road (Near Higham on the Hill) (Warwickshire) (Temporary Restriction and Prohibition of Traffic) Order 2006 No. 2006/3131. - Enabling power: Road Traffic Regulation Act 1984, s. 14 (1) (a). - Made: 20.10.2006. Coming into force: 27.10.2006. Effect: None. Territorial extent & classification: E. Local *Unpublished*

The A5 Trunk Road (Old Stratford Roundabout, Northamptonshire) (Temporary Prohibition of Traffic) Order 2006 No. 2006/2435. - Enabling power: Road Traffic Regulation Act 1984, s. 14 (1) (a). - Made: 22.08.2006. Coming into force: 29.08.2006. Effect: None. Territorial extent & classification: E. Local *Unpublished*

The A5 Trunk Road (Portway Interchange, Milton Keynes) (Temporary Prohibition of Traffic) Order 2006 No. 2006/96. - Enabling power: Road Traffic Regulation Act 1984, s. 14 (1) (a). - Made: 16.01.2006. Coming into force: 23.01.2006. Effect: None. Territorial extent & classification: E. Local *Unpublished*

The A5 Trunk Road (Portway, Milton Keynes) (Temporary 50 Miles Per Hour Speed Restriction) Order 2006 No. 2006/2060. - Enabling power: Road Traffic Regulation Act 1984, s. 14 (1) (a). - Made: 17.07.2006. Coming into force: 24.07.2006. Effect: None. Territorial extent & classification: E. Local *Unpublished*

The A5 Trunk Road (Redmoor Roundabout, Milton Keynes) (Temporary Prohibition of Traffic) Order 2006 No. 2006/3505. - Enabling power: Road Traffic Regulation Act 1984, s. 14 (1) (a). - Made: 29.12.2006. Coming into force: 05.01.2007. Effect: None. Territorial extent & classification: E. Local *Unpublished*

The A5 Trunk Road (Shrewsbury Bypass, Shropshire) (Temporary Restriction and Prohibition of Traffic) Order 2006 No. 2006/706. - Enabling power: Road Traffic Regulation Act 1984, s. 14 (1) (a). - Made: 24.02.2006. Coming into force: 03.03.2006. Effect: None. Territorial extent & classification: E. Local *Unpublished*

The A5 Trunk Road (Tamworth Bypass, Staffordshire) (Temporary Restriction and Prohibition of Traffic) Order 2006 No. 2006/2037. - Enabling power: Road Traffic Regulation Act 1984, s. 14 (1) (a). - Made: 10.07.2006. Coming into force: 17.07.2006. Effect: None. Territorial extent & classification: E. Local *Unpublished*

The A5 Trunk Road (Tamworth, Staffordshire) (Slip Roads) (Temporary Prohibition of Traffic) Order 2006 No. 2006/3206. - Enabling power: Road Traffic Regulation Act 1984, s. 14 (1) (a). - Made: 27.11.2006. Coming into force: 04.12.2006. Effect: None. Territorial extent & classification: E. Local *Unpublished*

The A5 Trunk Road (Tamworth, Staffordshire) (Temporary Restriction and Prohibition of Traffic) Order 2006 No. 2006/2670. - Enabling power: Road Traffic Regulation Act 1984, s. 14 (1) (a). - Made: 18.09.2006. Coming into force: 25.09.2006. Effect: None. Territorial extent & classification: E. Local *Unpublished*

The A5 Trunk Road (Thorn, South Bedfordshire) (Temporary Restriction and Prohibition of Traffic) Order 2006 No. 2006/2284. - Enabling power: Road Traffic Regulation Act 1984, s. 14 (1) (a). - Made: 15.08.2006. Coming into force: 22.08.2006. Effect: None. Territorial extent & classification: E. Local *Unpublished*

The A5 Trunk Road (Wall, Staffordshire) (Temporary Restriction and Prohibition of Traffic) Order 2006 No. 2006/3457. - Enabling power: Road Traffic Regulation Act 1984, s. 14 (1) (a). - Made: 20.12.2006. Coming into force: 27.12.2006. Effect: None. Territorial extent & classification: E. Local *Unpublished*

Road traffic: Traffic regulation

The A5 Trunk Road (Watford Locks Underbridge, Northamptonshire) (Temporary Restriction and Prohibition of Traffic) Order 2006 No. 2006/43. - Enabling power: Road Traffic Regulation Act 1984, s. 14 (1) (a). - Made: 03.01.2006. Coming into force: 16.01.2006. Effect: None. Territorial extent & classification: E. Local *Unpublished*

The A5 Trunk Road (Weedon, Northamptonshire) (Temporary 10 Miles Per Hour and 30 Miles Per Hour Speed Restriction) Order 2006 No. 2006/2120. - Enabling power: Road Traffic Regulation Act 1984, s. 14 (1) (a). - Made: 24.07.2006. Coming into force: 31.07.2006. Effect: None. Territorial extent & classification: E. Local *Unpublished*

The A5 Trunk Road (Weeford to Gailey, Staffordshire) (Temporary 40 Miles Per Hour Speed Restriction) Order 2006 No. 2006/1555. - Enabling power: Road Traffic Regulation Act 1984, s. 14 (1) (a). - Made: 30.05.2006. Coming into force: 06.06.2006. Effect: None. Territorial extent & classification: E. Local *Unpublished*

The A5 Trunk Road (Wolfshead Roundabout to Shotatton, Shropshire) (Temporary Prohibition of Traffic) Order 2006 No. 2006/2220. - Enabling power: Road Traffic Regulation Act 1984, s. 14 (1) (a). - Made: 28.07.2006. Coming into force: 04.08.2006. Effect: None. Territorial extent & classification: E. Local *Unpublished*

The A10 Trunk Road (Cheshunt, Hertfordshire) (Temporary Prohibition of Traffic) Order 2006 No. 2006/2608. - Enabling power: Road Traffic Regulation Act 1984, s. 14 (1) (a). - Made: 18.09.2006. Coming into force: 25.09.2006. Effect: None. Territorial extent & classification: E. Local *Unpublished*

The A10 Trunk Road (Chipping, Hertfordshire) (Temporary 10 Miles Per Hour and 40 Miles Per Hour Speed Restriction) Order 2006 No. 2006/1858. - Enabling power: Road Traffic Regulation Act 1984, s. 14 (1) (a). - Made: 03.07.2006. Coming into force: 10.07.2006. Effect: None. Territorial extent & classification: E. Local *Unpublished*

The A10 Trunk Road (Great Cambridge Road, Cheshunt, Hertfordshire) (Temporary Restriction and Prohibition of Traffic) Order 2006 No. 2006/433. - Enabling power: Road Traffic Regulation Act 1984, s. 14 (1) (a). - Made: 13.02.2006. Coming into force: 20.02.2006. Effect: None. Territorial extent & classification: E. Local *Unpublished*

The A10 Trunk Road (Half Hide Lane, Turnford, Hertfordshire) (Temporary 10 Miles Per Hour Speed Restriction) Order 2006 No. 2006/2286. - Enabling power: Road Traffic Regulation Act 1984, s. 14 (1) (a). - Made: 15.08.2006. Coming into force: 22.08.2006. Effect: None. Territorial extent & classification: E. Local *Unpublished*

The A10 Trunk Road (Hoddesdon and Ware, Hertfordshire) (Temporary Restriction and Prohibition of Traffic) Order 2006 No. 2006/1856. - Enabling power: Road Traffic Regulation Act 1984, s. 14 (1) (a). - Made: 03.07.2006. Coming into force: 10.07.2006. Effect: None. Territorial extent & classification: E. Local *Unpublished*

The A10 Trunk Road (Hoddesdon Interchange, Broxbourne, Hertfordshire) (Temporary Restriction of Traffic) Order 2006 No. 2006/2292. - Enabling power: Road Traffic Regulation Act 1984, s. 14 (1) (a). - Made: 17.08.2006. Coming into force: 24.08.2006. Effect: None. Territorial extent & classification: E. Local *Unpublished*

The A10 Trunk Road (Rush Green Interchange, Hertfordshire) (Temporary Prohibition of Traffic) Order 2006 No. 2006/45. - Enabling power: Road Traffic Regulation Act 1984, s. 14 (1) (a). - Made: 09.01.2006. Coming into force: 16.01.2006. Effect: None. Territorial extent & classification: E. Local *Unpublished*

The A10 Trunk Road (Turnford Interchange, Broxbourne, Hertfordshire) (Temporary Restriction of Traffic) Order 2006 No. 2006/2599. - Enabling power: Road Traffic Regulation Act 1984, s. 14 (1) (a). - Made: 11.09.2006. Coming into force: 18.09.2006. Effect: None. Territorial extent & classification: E. Local *Unpublished*

The A10 Trunk Road (Turnford Interchange, Hertfordshire) (Temporary 40 Miles Per Hour Speed Restriction) Order 2006 No. 2006/968. - Enabling power: Road Traffic Regulation Act 1984, s. 14 (1) (a). - Made: 24.03.2006. Coming into force: 31.03.2006. Effect: None. Territorial extent & classification: E. Local *Unpublished*

The A11 and A14 Trunk Roads (Nine Mile Hill Interchange, Cambridgeshire and Suffolk) (Temporary Restriction and Prohibition of Traffic) Order 2006 No. 2006/2480. - Enabling power: Road Traffic Regulation Act 1984, s. 14 (1) (a). - Made: 04.09.2006. Coming into force: 11.09.2006. Effect: None. Territorial extent & classification: E. Local *Unpublished*

The A11 Trunk Road (A505, Icknield Bridge, Cambridgeshire) (Temporary Restriction and Prohibition of Traffic) Order 2006 No. 2006/2651. - Enabling power: Road Traffic Regulation Act 1984, ss. 14, 15. - Made: 18.09.2006. Coming into force: 24.09.2006. Effect: None. Territorial extent & classification: E. Local *Unpublished*

The A11 Trunk Road (Attleborough, Norfolk) (Temporary Prohibition of Traffic) Order 2006 No. 2006/2472. - Enabling power: Road Traffic Regulation Act 1984, s. 14 (1) (a). - Made: 30.08.2006. Coming into force: 11.09.2006. Effect: None. Territorial extent & classification: E. Local *Unpublished*

The A11 Trunk Road (Attleborough, Norfolk) (Temporary Prohibition of Traffic) Order 2006 No. 2006/3055. - Enabling power: Road Traffic Regulation Act 1984, s. 14 (1) (a). - Made: 19.10.2006. Coming into force: 23.10.2006. Effect: None. Territorial extent & classification: E. Local *Unpublished*

The A11 Trunk Road (Barton Mills, Suffolk) (Temporary 40 Miles Per Hour Speed Restriction) Order 2006 No. 2006/294. - Enabling power: Road Traffic Regulation Act 1984, s. 14 (1). - Made: 06.02.2006. Coming into force: 13.02.2006. Effect: None. Territorial extent & classification: E. Local *Unpublished*

Road traffic: Traffic regulation

The A11 Trunk Road (Bridgham Heath Breckland, Norfolk) (Temporary Restriction and Prohibition of Traffic) Order 2006 No. 2006/2349. - Enabling power: Road Traffic Regulation Act 1984, s. 14 (1) (a). - Made: 18.08.2006. Coming into force: 25.08.2006. Effect: None. Territorial extent & classification: E. Local *Unpublished*

The A11 Trunk Road (Chalk Hill Layby, Barton Mills, Suffolk) (Temporary Prohibition of Traffic) Order 2006 No. 2006/2849. - Enabling power: Road Traffic Regulation Act 1984, s. 14 (1) (a). - Made: 16.10.2006. Coming into force: 23.10.2006. Effect: None. Territorial extent & classification: E. Local *Unpublished*

The A11 Trunk Road (London Road Roundabout t0 Brandon Road Roundabout, Thetford, Norfolk) (Temporary 10 Miles Per Hour and 40 Miles Per Hour Speed Restriction) Order 2006 No. 2006/2509. - Enabling power: Road Traffic Regulation Act 1984, s. 14 (1) (a). - Made: 06.09.2006. Coming into force: 13.09.2006. Effect: None. Territorial extent & classification: E. Local *Unpublished*

The A11 Trunk Road (Near Newmarket, Suffolk) (Temporary 40 Miles Per Hour Speed Restriction) Order 2006 No. 2006/1888. - Enabling power: Road Traffic Regulation Act 1984, s. 14 (1) (b). - Made: 05.07.2006. Coming into force: 12.07.2006. Effect: None. Territorial extent & classification: E. Local *Unpublished*

The A11 Trunk Road (Northbound Exit Slip Road, Chippenham, Cambridgeshire) (Temporary 10 Miles Per Hour and 40 Miles Per Hour Speed Restriction) Order 2006 No. 2006/687. - Enabling power: Road Traffic Regulation Act 1984, s. 14 (1) (a). - Made: 04.03.2006. Coming into force: 11.03.2006. Effect: None. Territorial extent & classification: E. Local *Unpublished*

The A11 Trunk Road (Red Lodge Interchange, Forest Heath, Suffolk) (Temporary Restriction and Prohibition of Traffic) Order 2006 No. 2006/2476. - Enabling power: Road Traffic Regulation Act 1984, s. 14 (1) (a). - Made: 04.09.2006. Coming into force: 11.09.2006. Effect: None. Territorial extent & classification: E. Local *Unpublished*

The A11 Trunk Road (Six Mile Bottom, Cambridgeshire) (Temporary Prohibition of Traffic) Order 2006 No. 2006/2287. - Enabling power: Road Traffic Regulation Act 1984, s. 14 (1) (a). - Made: 15.08.2006. Coming into force: 22.08.2006. Effect: None. Territorial extent & classification: E. Local *Unpublished*

The A11 Trunk Road (Six Mile Bottom - Swaffham Heath, Cambridgeshire) (Temporary Restriction and Prohibition of Traffic) Order 2006 No. 2006/2348. - Enabling power: Road Traffic Regulation Act 1984, s. 14 (1) (a). - Made: 18.08.2006. Coming into force: 25.08.2006. Effect: None. Territorial extent & classification: E. Local *Unpublished*

The A11 Trunk Road (Waterhall Bridge, Cambridgeshire) (Temporary Restriction of Traffic) Order 2006 No. 2006/2710. - Enabling power: Road Traffic Regulation Act 1984, s. 14 (1) (a). - Made: 02.10.2006. Coming into force: 09.10.2006. Effect: None. Territorial extent & classification: E. Local *Unpublished*

The A11 Trunk Road (Wymondham Bypass, Norfolk) (Temporary Restriction and Prohibition of Traffic) Order 2006 No. 2006/3376. - Enabling power: Road Traffic Regulation Act 1984, s. 14 (1) (a). - Made: 11.12.2006. Coming into force: 18.12.2006. Effect: None. Territorial extent & classification: E. Local *Unpublished*

The A12 and A14 Trunk Roads (Copdock Interchange, Babergh, Suffolk) (Temporary Restriction and Prohibition of Traffic) Order 2006 No. 2006/2610. - Enabling power: Road Traffic Regulation Act 1984, s. 14 (1) (a). - Made: 18.09.2006. Coming into force: 25.09.2006. Effect: None. Territorial extent & classification: E. Local *Unpublished*

The A12 and A120 Trunk Roads (Birchwood Interchange to Marks Tey Interchange Colchester, Essex) (Temporary Restriction and Prohibition of Traffic) Order 2006 No. 2006/905. - Enabling power: Road Traffic Regulation Act 1984, s. 14 (1) (a). - Made: 20.03.2006. Coming into force: 27.03.2006. Effect: None. Territorial extent & classification: E. Local *Unpublished*

The A12 and A120 Trunk Roads (Braiswick, Colchester, Essex) (Temporary Restriction and Prohibition of Traffic) Order 2006 No. 2006/2860. - Enabling power: Road Traffic Regulation Act 1984, s. 14 (1) (a). - Made: 18.10.2006. Coming into force: 25.10.2006. Effect: None. Territorial extent & classification: E. Local *Unpublished*

The A12 and A120 Trunk Roads (Colchestser Bypass) (Temporary Prohibition of Traffic) Order 2006 No. 2006/2600. - Enabling power: Road Traffic Regulation Act 1984, s. 14 (1) (a). - Made: 11.09.2006. Coming into force: 18.09.2006. Effect: None. Territorial extent & classification: E. Local *Unpublished*

The A12 and A120 Trunk Roads (Marks Tey Interchange - Ardleigh Crown Interchange, Essex) (Temporary Restriction and Prohibition of Traffic) Order 2006 No. 2006/114. - Enabling power: Road Traffic Regulation Act 1984, s. 14 (1) (a). - Made: 19.01.2006. Coming into force: 26.01.2006. Effect: None. Territorial extent & classification: E. Local *Unpublished*

The A12 and A120 Trunk Roads (Marks Tey Roundabout, Colchestser, Essex) (Temporary Restriction and Prohibition of Traffic) Order 2006 No. 2006/814. - Enabling power: Road Traffic Regulation Act 1984, s. 14 (1) (a). - Made: 13.03.2006. Coming into force: 20.03.2006. Effect: None. Territorial extent & classification: E. Local *Unpublished*

The A12 Trunk Road (A1117 Bentley Drive Roundabout - St Peters Street/Jubilee Way Roundabout, Oulton, Suffolk) (Temporary Restriction of Traffic) Order 2006 No. 2006/904. - Enabling power: Road Traffic Regulation Act 1984, s. 14 (1). - Made: 20.03.2006. Coming into force: 27.03.2006. Effect: None. Territorial extent & classification: E. Local *Unpublished*

The A12 Trunk Road (Bascule Bridge, Lowestoft, Suffolk) (Temporary Prohibition of Traffic) Order 2006 No. 2006/461. - Enabling power: Road Traffic Regulation Act 1984, s. 14 (1) (a). - Made: 20.02.2006. Coming into force: 27.02.2006. Effect: None. Territorial extent & classification: E. Local *Unpublished*

The A12 Trunk Road (Bascule Bridge, Lowestoft, Suffolk) (Temporary Prohibition of Traffic) Order 2006 No. 2006/1413. - Enabling power: Road Traffic Regulation Act 1984, s. 14 (1) (a). - Made: 16.05.2006. Coming into force: 23.05.2006. Effect: None. Territorial extent & classification: E. Local *Unpublished*

The A12 Trunk Road (Brentwood, Essex) (Temporary Prohibition of Traffic) 2006 No. 2006/460. - Enabling power: Road Traffic Regulation Act 1984, s. 14 (1) (a). - Made: 20.02.2006. Coming into force: 27.02.2006. Effect: None. Territorial extent & classification: E. Local *Unpublished*

The A12 Trunk Road (Breydon Bridge, Great Yarmouth, North Norfolk) (Temporary Prohibition of Traffic) Order 2006 No. 2006/548. - Enabling power: Road Traffic Regulation Act 1984, s. 14 (1) (a) (7). - Made: 27.02.2006. Coming into force: 06.03.2006. Effect: None. Territorial extent & classification: E. Local *Unpublished*

The A12 Trunk Road (Chelmsford Bypass, Junction 18 - Junction 19 and Howe Green Interchange, Junction 17, Chelmsford, Essex) (Temporary Prohibition of Traffic) Order 2006 No. 2006/1324. - Enabling power: Road Traffic Regulation Act 1984, s. 14 (1) (a). - Made: 02.05.2006. Coming into force: 08.05.2006. Effect: None. Territorial extent & classification: E. Local *Unpublished*

The A12 Trunk Road (Corton Lane, Suffolk) (Temporary Restriction and Prohibition of Traffic) Order 2006 No. 2006/2713. - Enabling power: Road Traffic Regulation Act 1984, s. 14 (1) (a). - Made: 02.10.2006. Coming into force: 09.10.2006. Effect: None. Territorial extent & classification: E. Local *Unpublished*

The A12 Trunk Road (Denmark Road, Lowestoft, Suffolk) (Temporary Prohibition of Traffic) Order 2006 No. 2006/1025. - Enabling power: Road Traffic Regulation Act 1984, s. 14 (1) (a). - Made: 27.03.2006. Coming into force: 03.04.2006. Effect: None. Territorial extent & classification: E. Local *Unpublished*

The A12 Trunk Road (Eight Ash Green Interchange to Marks Tey, Colchester, Essex) (Temporary Restriction and Prohibition of Traffic) Order 2006 No. 2006/3379. - Enabling power: Road Traffic Regulation Act 1984, s. 14 (1) (a). - Made: 11.12.2006. Coming into force: 18.12.2006. Effect: None. Territorial extent & classification: E. Local *Unpublished*

The A12 Trunk Road (Harfrey's Roundabout, Great Yarmouth, Norfolk) (Temporary 40 Miles Per Hour Speed Restriction) Order 2006 No. 2006/2652. - Enabling power: Road Traffic Regulation Act 1984, s. 14 (1) (a). - Made: 22.09.2006. Coming into force: 29.09.2006. Effect: None. Territorial extent & classification: E. Local *Unpublished*

The A12 Trunk Road (Hopton To Gorleston, Norfolk) (Closure of Gaps in the Central Reservation) Order 2006 No. 2006/898. - Enabling power: Road Traffic Regulation Act 1984, ss. 1 (1), 2 (1) (2). - Made: 17.03.2006. Coming into force: 31.03.2006. Effect: None. Territorial extent & classification: E. Local *Unpublished*

The A12 Trunk Road (Hopton to Gorleston, Norfolk) (Temporary 40 Miles Per Hour Speed Restriction) Order 2006 No. 2006/296. - Enabling power: Road Traffic Regulation Act 1984, s. 14 (1) (a). - Made: 06.02.2006. Coming into force: 13.02.2006. Effect: None. Territorial extent & classification: E. Local *Unpublished*

The A12 Trunk Road (Kelvedon Bypass, Braintree, Essex) (Temporary Restriction and Prohibition of Traffic) (No. 2) Order 2006 No. 2006/3162. - Enabling power: Road Traffic Regulation Act 1984, ss. 14, 15. - Made: 13.11.2006. Coming into force: 20.11.2006. Effect: None. Territorial extent & classification: E. Local *Unpublished*

The A12 Trunk Road (Kelvedon Bypass, Essex) (Temporary Restriction and Prohibition of Traffic) Order 2006 No. 2006/2122. - Enabling power: Road Traffic Regulation Act 1984, s. 14 (1) (a). - Made: 24.07.2006. Coming into force: 31.07.2006. Effect: None. Territorial extent & classification: E. Local *Unpublished*

The A12 Trunk Road (M25 Brook Street Interchange, Junction 11, Brentwood Bypass, Essex) (Temporary Prohibition of Traffic) Order 2006 No. 2006/1074. - Enabling power: Road Traffic Regulation Act 1984, s. 14 (1). - Made: 03.04.2006. Coming into force: 10.04.2006. Effect: None. Territorial extent & classification: E. Local *Unpublished*

The A12 Trunk Road (Marks Tey, Colchester, Essex) (Temporary Restriction and Prohibition of Traffic) Order 2006 No. 2006/86. - Enabling power: Road Traffic Regulation Act 1984, s. 14 (1) (a). - Made: 16.01.2006. Coming into force: 23.01.2006. Effect: None. Territorial extent & classification: E. Local *Unpublished*

The A12 Trunk Road (Marks Tey Interchange, Essex) (Temporary Prohibition of Traffic) Order 2006 No. 2006/2613. - Enabling power: Road Traffic Regulation Act 1984, s. 14 (1) (a). - Made: 13.09.2006. Coming into force: 20.09.2006. Effect: None. Territorial extent & classification: E. Local *Unpublished*

The A12 Trunk Road (Spring Lane Interchange, Colchester, Essex) (Temporary Prohibition of Traffic) Order 2006 No. 2006/3129. - Enabling power: Road Traffic Regulation Act 1984, s. 14 (1) (a). - Made: 20.10.2006. Coming into force: 27.11.2006. Effect: None. Territorial extent & classification: E. Local *Unpublished*

The A12 Trunk Road (Webbs Farm Interchange, Essex) (Temporary Prohibition of Traffic) Order 2006 No. 2006/2597. - Enabling power: Road Traffic Regulation Act 1984, s. 14 (1) (a). - Made: 11.09.2006. Coming into force: 18.09.2006. Effect: None. Territorial extent & classification: E. Local *Unpublished*

The A13 and A282 Trunk Roads (Wennington - A1089) (Temporary Restriction and Prohibition of Traffic) Order 2006 No. 2006/2256. - Enabling power: Road Traffic Regulation Act 1984, s. 14 (1) (a). - Made: 14.08.2006. Coming into force: 19.08.2006. Effect: None. Territorial extent & classification: E. Local *Unpublished*

The A13 and A1089 Trunk Roads (Mardyke Interchange - Marshfoot Interchange) (Temporary Prohibition of Traffic) Order 2006 No. 2006/3038. - Enabling power: Road Traffic Regulation Act 1984, s. 14 (1) (a). - Made: 06.11.2006. Coming into force: 14.11.2006. Effect: None. Territorial extent & classification: E. Local *Unpublished*

The A13 and the A1089 Trunk Roads (Near Grays) (Temporary Restriction and Prohibition of Traffic) Order 2006 No. 2006/3173. - Enabling power: Road Traffic Regulation Act 1984, s. 14 (1) (a). - Made: 30.10.2006. Coming into force: 04.11.2006. Effect: None. Territorial extent & classification: E. Local *Unpublished*

The A13 Trunk Road (A1012 and A1089 Junctions, Slip Roads) (Temporary Prohibition of Traffic) Order 2006 No. 2006/158. - Enabling power: Road Traffic Regulation Act 1984, s. 14 (1) (a). - Made: 23.01.2006. Coming into force: 04.02.2006. Effect: None. Territorial extent & classification: E. Local *Unpublished*

The A13 Trunk Road (A1012 Junction, Slip Roads) (Temporary Prohibition of Traffic) Order 2006 No. 2006/277. - Enabling power: Road Traffic Regulation Act 1984, s. 14 (1) (a). - Made: 30.01.2006. Coming into force: 04.02.2006. Effect: None. Territorial extent & classification: E. Local *Unpublished*

The A14 Trunk Road and M11 Motorway (Spittals Interchange - Girton Interchange, Cambridgeshire) (Temporary Restriction and Prohibition of Traffic) Order 2006 No. 2006/3380. - Enabling power: Road Traffic Regulation Act 1984, s. 14 (1) (a). - Made: 11.12.2006. Coming into force: 18.12.2006. Effect: None. Territorial extent & classification: E. Local *Unpublished*

The A14 Trunk Road (Barham - Levington, Suffolk) (Temporary 40 Miles Per Hour Speed Restriction) Order 2006 No. 2006/2431. - Enabling power: Road Traffic Regulation Act 1984, s. 14 (1) (a). - Made: 22.08.2006. Coming into force: 29.08.2006. Effect: None. Territorial extent & classification: E. Local *Unpublished*

The A14 Trunk Road (Bar Hill Eastbound Exit Slip Road) (Temporary Prohibition of Traffic) Order 2006 No. 2006/163. - Enabling power: Road Traffic Regulation Act 1984, s. 14 (1). - Made: 23.01.2006. Coming into force: 30.01.2006. Effect: None. Territorial extent & classification: E. Local *Unpublished*

The A14 Trunk Road (Beacon Hill Interchange, Suffok) (Temporary Restriction and Prohibition of Traffic) Order 2006 No. 2006/3011. - Enabling power: Road Traffic Regulation Act 1984, s. 14 (1) (a). - Made: 07.11.2006. Coming into force: 14.11.2006. Effect: None. Territorial extent & classification: E. Local *Unpublished*

The A14 Trunk Road (Beacon Hill Interchange to Cedars Interchange, Suffolk) (Temporary Restriction and Prohibition of Traffic) Order 2006 No. 2006/810. - Enabling power: Road Traffic Regulation Act 1984, s. 14 (1) (a). - Made: 13.03.2006. Coming into force: 20.03.2006. Effect: None. Territorial extent & classification: E. Local *Unpublished*

The A14 Trunk Road (Beyton, Suffolk) (Temporary Restriction and Prohibition of Traffic) Order 2006 No. 2006/97. - Enabling power: Road Traffic Regulation Act 1984, s. 14 (1) (a). - Made: 17.01.2006. Coming into force: 24.01.2006. Effect: None. Territorial extent & classification: E. Local *Unpublished*

The A14 Trunk Road (Blackbridge Footbridge, Barton, Seagrave, Northamptonshire) (Temporary Restriction and Prohibition of Traffic) Order 2006 No. 2006/1316. - Enabling power: Road Traffic Regulation Act 1984, s. 14 (1) (a). - Made: 02.05.2006. Coming into force: 09.05.2006. Effect: None. Territorial extent & classification: E. Local *Unpublished*

The A14 Trunk Road (Bury St Edmunds, Suffolk) (Temporary Restriction and Prohibition of Traffic) Order 2006 No. 2006/2595. - Enabling power: Road Traffic Regulation Act 1984, s. 14 (1) (a). - Made: 08.09.2006. Coming into force: 15.09.2006. Effect: None. Territorial extent & classification: E. Local *Unpublished*

The A14 Trunk Road (Cambridge Northern Bypass, Milton, Cambridgeshire) (Temporary 40 Miles Per Hour Speed Restriction) Order 2006 No. 2006/416. - Enabling power: Road Traffic Regulation Act 1984, s. 14 (1) (a). - Made: 15.02.2006. Coming into force: 22.02.2006. Effect: None. Territorial extent & classification: E. Local *Unpublished*

The A14 Trunk Road (Cambridgeshire and Northamptonshire) (Temporary Variable Speed Limit) Order 2006 No. 2006/3080. - Enabling power: Road Traffic Regulation Act 1984, ss. 14, 15. - Made: 10.11.2006. Coming into force: 17.11.2006. Effect: None. Territorial extent & classification: E. Local *Unpublished*

The A14 Trunk Road (Claydon Interchange, Suffolk) (Temporary Restriction and Prohibition of Traffic) 2006 No. 2006/267. - Enabling power: Road Traffic Regulation Act 1984, s. 14 (1) (a). - Made: 27.01.2006. Coming into force: 03.02.2006. Effect: None. Territorial extent & classification: E. Local *Unpublished*

The A14 Trunk Road (Copdock Mill Interchange - Sproughton Interchange, Suffolk) (Temporary Restriction and Prohibition of Traffic) Order 2006 No. 2006/1370. - Enabling power: Road Traffic Regulation Act 1984, s. 14 (1) (a) (7). - Made: 05.05.2006. Coming into force: 12.05.2006. Effect: None. Territorial extent & classification: E. Local *Unpublished*

The A14 Trunk Road (Exning Bypass, Newmarket, Suffolk) (Temporary Restriction and Prohibition of Traffic) Order 2006 No. 2006/1237. - Enabling power: Road Traffic Regulation Act 1984, s. 14 (1) (a). - Made: 25.04.2006. Coming into force: 02.05.2006. Effect: None. Territorial extent & classification: E. Local *Unpublished*

The A14 Trunk Road (Four Mile Stable to Girton Interchange, Cambridgeshire) (Temporary Restriction and Prohibition of Traffic) 2006 No. 2006/269. - Enabling power: Road Traffic Regulation Act 1984, s. 14 (1) (a). - Made: 30.01.2006. Coming into force: 06.02.2006. Effect: None. Territorial extent & classification: E. Local *Unpublished*

The A14 Trunk Road (Galley Hill Interchange, St. Ives, Cambridgeshire) (Temporary Prohibition of Traffic) Order 2006 No. 2006/1475. - Enabling power: Road Traffic Regulation Act 1984, s. 14 (1) (a). - Made: 16.05.2006. Coming into force: 23.05.2006. Effect: None. Territorial extent & classification: E. Local *Unpublished*

The A14 Trunk Road (Girton Interchange, Cambridgeshire - Felixstowe, Suffolk) (24 Hours Clearway) Order 2006 No. 2006/268. - Enabling power: Road Traffic Regulation Act 1984, ss. 1 (1), 2 (1) (2), 4 (1) (2), sch. 9, para. 27 (1). - Made: 30.01.2006. Coming into force: 13.02.2006. Effect: S.I. 1963/1172; 1985/665 varied & S.I. 1978/731; 1983/791, 832; 1986/2307 revoked. Territorial extent & classification: E. Local *Unpublished*

The A14 Trunk Road (Girton Interchange, Cambridgeshire) (Temporary Prohibition of Traffic) Order 2006 No. 2006/2453. - Enabling power: Road Traffic Regulation Act 1984, s. 14 (1) (a). - Made: 29.08.2006. Coming into force: 04.09.2006. Effect: None. Territorial extent & classification: E. Local *Unpublished*

The A14 Trunk Road (Godmanchester, Cambrdigeshire) (Temporary Prohibition of Traffic) Order 2006 No. 2006/711. - Enabling power: Road Traffic Regulation Act 1984, s. 14 (1) (a). - Made: 06.03.2006. Coming into force: 13.03.2006. Effect: None. Territorial extent & classification: E. Local *Unpublished*

The A14 Trunk Road (Godmanchester to Bar Hill, Cambridgeshire) (Temporary Prohibition of Traffic) Order 2006 No. 2006/1859. - Enabling power: Road Traffic Regulation Act 1984, s. 14 (1) (a). - Made: 03.07.2006. Coming into force: 10.07.2006. Effect: None. Territorial extent & classification: E. Local *Unpublished*

The A14 Trunk Road (Godmanchester to Bar Hill, Cambridgeshire) (Temporary Restriction and Prohibition of Traffic) Order 2006 No. 2006/162. - Enabling power: Road Traffic Regulation Act 1984, s. 14 (1) (a). - Made: 23.01.2006. Coming into force: 30.01.2006. Effect: None. Territorial extent & classification: E. Local *Unpublished*

The A14 Trunk Road (Haughley - Beyton, Suffolk) (Temporary 40 Miles Per Hour Speed Restriction) Order 2006 No. 2006/2433. - Enabling power: Road Traffic Regulation Act 1984, s. 14 (1) (a). - Made: 22.08.2006. Coming into force: 29.08.2006. Effect: None. Territorial extent & classification: E. Local *Unpublished*

The A14 Trunk Road (Haughley, Suffolk) (Temporary Restriction and Prohibition of Traffic) Order 2006 No. 2006/2456. - Enabling power: Road Traffic Regulation Act 1984, s. 14 (1) (a). - Made: 29.08.2006. Coming into force: 05.09.2006. Effect: None. Territorial extent & classification: E. Local *Unpublished*

The A14 Trunk Road (Higham, Suffolk) (Temporary Restriction and Prohibition of Traffic) Order 2006 No. 2006/2712. - Enabling power: Road Traffic Regulation Act 1984, s. 14 (1) (a). - Made: 02.10.2006. Coming into force: 09.10.2006. Effect: None. Territorial extent & classification: E. Local *Unpublished*

The A14 Trunk Road (Junction 32) Westbound Exit Slip Road (Histon Interchange Cambrdigeshire) (Temporary Prohibition of Traffic) Order 2006 No. 2006/1111. - Enabling power: Road Traffic Regulation Act 1984, s. 14 (1) (a). - Made: 10.04.2006. Coming into force: 21.04.2006. Effect: None. Territorial extent & classification: E. Local *Unpublished*

The A14 Trunk Road (Kelmarsh to Orton, Daventry, Northamptonshire) (Temporary Restriction and Prohibition of Traffic) Order 2006 No. 2006/3036. - Enabling power: Road Traffic Regulation Act 1984, s. 14 (1) (a). - Made: 06.11.2006. Coming into force: 13.11.2006. Effect: None. Territorial extent & classification: E. Local *Unpublished*

The A14 Trunk Road (Kentford Interchange to Waterhall Interchange, Suffolk) (Temporary Restriction and Prohibition of Traffic) Order 2006 No. 2006/812. - Enabling power: Road Traffic Regulation Act 1984, s. 14 (1) (a). - Made: 13.03.2006. Coming into force: 20.03.2006. Effect: None. Territorial extent & classification: E. Local *Unpublished*

The A14 Trunk Road (Kettering Southern Bypass, Northamptonshire) (Temporary Prohibition of Traffic) 2006 No. 2006/259. - Enabling power: Road Traffic Regulation Act 1984, s. 14 (1) (a). - Made: 30.01.2006. Coming into force: 06.02.2006. Effect: None. Territorial extent & classification: E. Local *Unpublished*

The A14 Trunk Road (M1 Junction 19) (Temporary Prohibition of Traffic) Order 2006 No. 2006/1240. - Enabling power: Road Traffic Regulation Act 1984, s. 14 (1) (a). - Made: 25.04.2006. Coming into force: 02.05.2006. Effect: None. Territorial extent & classification: E. Local *Unpublished*

The A14 Trunk Road (Milton Interchange - Girton Interchange, Cambridgeshire) (Temporary 40 Miles Per Hour Speed Restriction) Order 2006 No. 2006/2448. - Enabling power: Road Traffic Regulation Act 1984, s. 14 (1) (a). - Made: 22.08.2006. Coming into force: 29.08.2006. Effect: None. Territorial extent & classification: E. Local *Unpublished*

The A14 Trunk Road (Milton Interchange to Fen Ditton Interchange, Cambridgeshire) (Temporary Restriction and Prohibition of Traffic) Order 2006 No. 2006/2510. - Enabling power: Road Traffic Regulation Act 1984, s. 14 (1) (a). - Made: 04.09.2006. Coming into force: 11.09.2006. Effect: None. Territorial extent & classification: E. Local *Unpublished*

The A14 Trunk Road (Nacton Interchange, Suffolk) (Temporary Restriction and Prohibition of Traffic) Order 2006 No. 2006/2738. - Enabling power: Road Traffic Regulation Act 1984, s. 14 (1) (a). - Made: 02.10.2006. Coming into force: 09.10.2006. Effect: None. Territorial extent & classification: E. Local *Unpublished*

Road traffic: Traffic regulation

The A14 Trunk Road (Nene Viaduct, Thrapston, Northamptonshire) (Temporary Restriction and Prohibition of Traffic) Order 2006 No. 2006/2051. - Enabling power: Road Traffic Regulation Act 1984, s. 14 (1) (a). - Made: 10.07.2006. Coming into force: 17.07.2006. Effect: None. Territorial extent & classification: E. Local *Unpublished*

The A14 Trunk Road (Port of Felixstowe Road, Suffolk) (Temporary Prohibition of Traffic) Order 2006 No. 2006/98. - Enabling power: Road Traffic Regulation Act 1984, s. 14 (1) (a). - Made: 17.01.2006. Coming into force: 24.01.2006. Effect: None. Territorial extent & classification: E. Local *Unpublished*

The A14 Trunk Road (Risby - Higham Interchange, Suffolk) (Temporary Restriction and Prohibition of Traffic) Order 2006 No. 2006/2434. - Enabling power: Road Traffic Regulation Act 1984, s. 14 (1) (a). - Made: 22.08.2006. Coming into force: 29.08.2006. Effect: None. Territorial extent & classification: E. Local *Unpublished*

The A14 Trunk Road (Risby Interchange to Westley Interchange, Bury St Edmunds, Suffolk) (Temporary Prohibition of Traffic) Order 2006 No. 2006/95. - Enabling power: Road Traffic Regulation Act 1984, s. 14 (1) (a). - Made: 17.01.2006. Coming into force: 24.01.2006. Effect: None. Territorial extent & classification: E. Local *Unpublished*

The A14 Trunk Road (Risby, Suffolk) (Temporary Restriction and Prohibition of Traffic) Order 2006 No. 2006/2709. - Enabling power: Road Traffic Regulation Act 1984, s. 14 (1) (a). - Made: 02.10.2006. Coming into force: 09.10.2006. Effect: None. Territorial extent & classification: E. Local *Unpublished*

The A14 Trunk Road (Risby - Trimley St Martin, Suffolk) (Temporary Restriction and Prohibition of Traffic) Order 2006 No. 2006/430. - Enabling power: Road Traffic Regulation Act 1984, s. 14 (1) (a). - Made: 13.02.2006. Coming into force: 20.02.2006. Effect: None. Territorial extent & classification: E. Local *Unpublished*

The A14 Trunk Road (Seven Hills Interchange, Suffolk) (Temporary Restriction and Prohibition of Traffic) Order 2006 No. 2006/295. - Enabling power: Road Traffic Regulation Act 1984, s. 14 (1) (a). - Made: 06.02.2006. Coming into force: 13.02.2006. Effect: None. Territorial extent & classification: E. Local *Unpublished*

The A14 Trunk Road (Snailwell, Cambridgeshire) (Prohibition of Entry) Order 2006 No. 2006/967. - Enabling power: Road Traffic Regulation Act 1984, ss. 1 (1), 2 (1) (2). - Made: 24.03.2006. Coming into force: 07.04.2006. Effect: None. Territorial extent & classification: E. Local *Unpublished*

The A14 Trunk Road (Snailwell, Cambridgeshire) (Temporary Restriction and Prohibition of Traffic) Order 2006 No. 2006/93. - Enabling power: Road Traffic Regulation Act 1984, s. 14 (1) (a). - Made: 16.01.2006. Coming into force: 23.01.2006. Effect: None. Territorial extent & classification: E. Local *Unpublished*

The A14 Trunk Road (Spittals Interchange to Swavesey, Cambridgeshire) (Temporary 40 Miles Per Hour Speed Restriction) Order 2006 No. 2006/3007. - Enabling power: Road Traffic Regulation Act 1984, s. 14 (1) (a). - Made: 06.11.2006. Coming into force: 13.11.2006. Effect: None. Territorial extent & classification: E. Local *Unpublished*

The A14 Trunk Road (Stow-Cum-Quy, Cambridgeshire) (Temporary Restriction and Prohibition of Traffic) Order 2006 No. 2006/431. - Enabling power: Road Traffic Regulation Act 1984, s. 14 (1) (a). - Made: 13.02.2006. Coming into force: 20.02.2006. Effect: None. Territorial extent & classification: E. Local *Unpublished*

The A14 Trunk Road (Stowmarket, Suffolk) (Temporary Restriction and Prohibition of Traffic) Order 2006 No. 2006/3083. - Enabling power: Road Traffic Regulation Act 1984, ss. 14 (1) (a). - Made: 06.11.2006. Coming into force: 13.11.2006. Effect: None. Territorial extent & classification: E. Local *Unpublished*

The A14 Trunk Road (St Saviours Interchange, Bury St Edmunds, Suffolk) (Temporary Restriction and Prohibition of Traffic) Order 2006 No. 2006/2455. - Enabling power: Road Traffic Regulation Act 1984, s. 14 (1) (a). - Made: 29.08.2006. Coming into force: 05.09.2006. Effect: None. Territorial extent & classification: E. Local *Unpublished*

The A14 Trunk Road (Thrapston - Catworth, Northamptonshire and Cambridgeshire) (Temporary Restriction and Prohibition of Traffic and Pedestrians) Order 2006 No. 2006/2447. - Enabling power: Road Traffic Regulation Act 1984, s. 14 (1) (a). - Made: 22.08.2006. Coming into force: 29.08.2006. Effect: None. Territorial extent & classification: E. Local *Unpublished*

The A14 Trunk Road (Trimley St. Mary, Suffolk) (Temporary Prohibition of Traffic) Order 2006 No. 2006/2432. - Enabling power: Road Traffic Regulation Act 1984, s. 14 (1) (a). - Made: 22.08.2006. Coming into force: 29.08.2006. Effect: None. Territorial extent & classification: E. Local *Unpublished*

The A14 Trunk Road (Two Mile Spinney, Bury St Edmunds, Suffolk) (Temporary Restriction and Prohibition of Traffic) Order 2006 No. 2006/3071. - Enabling power: Road Traffic Regulation Act 1984, s. 14 (1) (a). - Made: 25.10.2006. Coming into force: 01.11.2006. Effect: None. Territorial extent & classification: E. Local *Unpublished*

The A19 Trunk Road and the A66 Trunk Road (Stockton Road Interchange) (Temporary Prohibition of Traffic) (No. 2) Order 2006 No. 2006/2612. - Enabling power: Road Traffic Regulation Act 1984, s. 14 (1) (a). - Made: 19.09.2006. Coming into force: 01.10.2006. Effect: None. Territorial extent & classification: E. Local *Unpublished*

Road traffic: Traffic regulation

The A19 Trunk Road and the A66 Trunk Road (Stockton Road Interchange) (Temporary Prohibition of Traffic) Order 2006 No. 2006/1227. - Enabling power: Road Traffic Regulation Act 1984, s. 14 (1) (a). - Made: 09.05.2006. Coming into force: 21.05.2006. Effect: None. Territorial extent & classification: E. Local *Unpublished*

The A19 Trunk Road and the A66 Trunk Road (Stockton Road Interchange to Portrack Interchange) (Temporary Prohibition of Traffic) Order 2006 No. 2006/2267. - Enabling power: Road Traffic Regulation Act 1984, s. 14 (1) (a). - Made: 15.08.2006. Coming into force: 28.08.2006. Effect: None. Territorial extent & classification: E. Local *Unpublished*

The A19 Trunk Road and the A168 Trunk Road (Thirsk Bypass) (Temporary Restriction and Prohibition of Traffic) Order 2006 No. 2006/40. - Enabling power: Road Traffic Regulation Act 1984, s. 14 (1) (a) (7). - Made: 03.01.2006. Coming into force: 15.01.2006. Effect: None. Territorial extent & classification: E. Local *Unpublished*

The A19 Trunk Road (Borrowby to Over Stilton) (Temporary Restriction and Prohibition of Traffic) Order 2006 No. 2006/2337. - Enabling power: Road Traffic Regulation Act 1984, s. 14 (1) (a) (7). - Made: 21.08.2006. Coming into force: 02.09.2006. Effect: None. Territorial extent & classification: E. Local *Unpublished*

The A19 Trunk Road (Chester Road and Herrington Interchanges) (Temporary Prohibition of Traffic) Order 2006 No. 2006/2394. - Enabling power: Road Traffic Regulation Act 1984, s. 14 (1) (a). - Made: 25.08.2006. Coming into force: 07.09.2006. Effect: None. Territorial extent & classification: E. Local *Unpublished*

The A19 Trunk Road (Chester Road Interchange) (Temporary Restriction and Prohibition of Traffic) Order 2006 No. 2006/1204. - Enabling power: Road Traffic Regulation Act 1984, s. 14 (1) (a). - Made: 21.04.2006. Coming into force: 04.05.2006. Effect: None. Territorial extent & classification: E. Local *Unpublished*

The A19 Trunk Road (Cold Hesledon) (Temporary Restriction and Prohibition of Traffic) Order 2006 No. 2006/2392. - Enabling power: Road Traffic Regulation Act 1984, s. 14 (1) (a). - Made: 24.08.2006. Coming into force: 03.09.2006. Effect: None. Territorial extent & classification: E. Local *Unpublished*

The A19 Trunk Road (Crathorne Interchange to Tontine Interchange) (Prohibition of Use of Gap in Central Reservation & U-Turns) Order 2006 No. 2006/65. - Enabling power: Road Traffic Regulation Act 1984, s. 1 (1), 2 (1) (2). - Made: 11.01.2006. Coming into force: 16.01.2006. Effect: S.I. 1984/1612 revoked. Territorial extent & classification: E. Local *Unpublished*

The A19 Trunk Road (Damsdykes Accommodation Bridge to Moor Farm Roundabout) (Temporary 10 Miles Per Hour and 40 Miles Per Hour Speed Restriction) Order 2006 No. 2006/332. - Enabling power: Road Traffic Regulation Act 1984, s. 14 (1) (a). - Made: 07.02.2006. Coming into force: 19.02.2006. Effect: None. Territorial extent & classification: E. Local *Unpublished*

The A19 Trunk Road (Hangman's Lane Overbridge) (Temporary Restriction and Prohibition of Traffic) Order 2006 No. 2006/143. - Enabling power: Road Traffic Regulation Act 1984, s. 14 (1) (a). - Made: 23.12.2005. Coming into force: 08.01.2006. Effect: None. Territorial extent & classification: E. Local *Unpublished*

The A19 Trunk Road (Howdon Interchange to Silverlink Interchange) (Temporary Restriction and Prohibition of Traffic) Order 2006 No. 2006/2027. - Enabling power: Road Traffic Regulation Act 1984, s. 14 (1) (a). - Made: 11.07.2006. Coming into force: 23.07.2006. Effect: None. Territorial extent & classification: E. Local *Unpublished*

The A19 Trunk Road (Hylton Bridge to Hylton Grange Interchange) (Temporary 50 Miles Per Hour Speed Restriction) Order 2006 No. 2006/2581. - Enabling power: Road Traffic Regulation Act 1984, s. 14 (1) (a). - Made: 18.09.2006. Coming into force: 24.09.2006. Effect: None. Territorial extent & classification: E. Local *Unpublished*

The A19 Trunk Road (Hylton Grange to Chester Road) (Temporary Restriction and Prohibition of Traffic) Order 2006 No. 2006/3180. - Enabling power: Road Traffic Regulation Act 1984, s. 14 (1) (a). - Made: 31.10.2006. Coming into force: 12.11.2006. Effect: None. Territorial extent & classification: E. Local *Unpublished*

The A19 Trunk Road (Killingworth Interchange to Moor Farm Roundabout) (Temporary Prohibition of Traffic) Order 2006 No. 2006/66. - Enabling power: Road Traffic Regulation Act 1984, s. 14 (1) (a). - Made: 10.01.2006. Coming into force: 22.01.2006. Effect: None. Territorial extent & classification: E. Local *Unpublished*

The A19 Trunk Road (Parkway Interchange to Portrack Interchange) and the A174 Trunk Road (Parkway Interchange to Blue Bell Interchange) (Temporary Restriction and Prohibition of Traffic) Order 2006 No. 2006/2030. - Enabling power: Road Traffic Regulation Act 1984, s. 14 (1) (a). - Made: 11.07.2006. Coming into force: 23.07.2006. Effect: None. Territorial extent & classification: E. Local *Unpublished*

The A19 Trunk Road (Parkway Interchange to Stockton Road Interchange) and the A66 Trunk Road (Stockton Road Interchange) (Temporary Restriction and Prohibition of Traffic) Order 2006 No. 2006/2338. - Enabling power: Road Traffic Regulation Act 1984, s. 14 (1) (a). - Made: 21.08.2006. Coming into force: 03.09.2006. Effect: None. Territorial extent & classification: E. Local *Unpublished*

The A19 Trunk Road (Sheraton Interchange) (Temporary 50 Miles Per Hour Speed Restriction) Order 2006 No. 2006/1109. - Enabling power: Road Traffic Regulation Act 1984, s. 14 (1) (a). - Made: 11.04.2006. Coming into force: 23.04.2006. Effect: None. Territorial extent & classification: E. Local *Unpublished*

The A19 Trunk Road (Three Tuns Overbridge, Knayton) (Temporary 50 Miles Per Hour Speed Restriction) Order 2006 No. 2006/3028. - Enabling power: Road Traffic Regulation Act 1984, s. 14 (1) (a). - Made: 01.11.2006. Coming into force: 06.11.2006. Effect: None. Territorial extent & classification: E. Local *Unpublished*

The A20 Trunk Road and the M20 and M25 Motorways (Swanley Interchange) (Temporary Restriction and Prohibition of Traffic) Order 2006 No. 2006/407. - Enabling power: Road Traffic Regulation Act 1984, s. 14 (1) (a). - Made: 20.02.2006. Coming into force: 25.02.2006. Effect: None. Territorial extent & classification: E. Local *Unpublished*

The A20 Trunk Road (Court Wood Junction) (Temporary Prohibition of Traffic) Order 2006 No. 2006/2093. - Enabling power: Road Traffic Regulation Act 1984, s. 14 (1) (a). - Made: 24.07.2006. Coming into force: 29.07.2006. Effect: None. Territorial extent & classification: E. Local *Unpublished*

The A20 Trunk Road (Folkestone - Dover) (Temporary Prohibition of Traffic) Order 2006 No. 2006/2557. - Enabling power: Road Traffic Regulation Act 1984, s. 14 (1) (a). - Made: 18.09.2006. Coming into force: 23.09.2006. Effect: None. Territorial extent & classification: E. Local *Unpublished*

The A20 Trunk Road (Limekiln Roundabout and the Viaduct) (Temporary Restriction of Traffic) Order 2006 No. 2006/2462. - Enabling power: Road Traffic Regulation Act 1984, s. 14 (1) (a). - Made: 04.09.2006. Coming into force: 09.09.2006. Effect: None. Territorial extent & classification: E. Local *Unpublished*

The A20 Trunk Road (Western Heights Roundabout - Prince of Wales Roundabout) (Temporary Speed Restrictions) Order 2006 No. 2006/1133. - Enabling power: Road Traffic Regulation Act 1984, s. 14 (1) (a). - Made: 18.04.2006. Coming into force: 24.04.2006. Effect: S.I. 2005/2616 revoked. Territorial extent & classification: E. Local *Unpublished*

The A21 Trunk Road (A268/B2087 Junctions, Flimwell) (Temporary Restriction and Prohibition of Traffic) Order 2006 No. 2006/1129. - Enabling power: Road Traffic Regulation Act 1984, s. 14 (1) (a). - Made: 18.04.2006. Coming into force: 22.04.2006. Effect: None. Territorial extent & classification: E. Local *Unpublished*

The A21 Trunk Road (A268 Junction, Flimwell) (Temporary Restriction and Prohibition of Traffic) Order 2006 No. 2006/443. - Enabling power: Road Traffic Regulation Act 1984, s. 14 (1) (a). - Made: 20.02.2006. Coming into force: 25.02.2006. Effect: None. Territorial extent & classification: E. Local *Unpublished*

The A21 Trunk Road (Beech House Lane - Northbridge Street) (Temporary Speed Restrictions) Order 2006 No. 2006/1984. - Enabling power: Road Traffic Regulation Act 1984, s. 14 (1) (a). - Made: 17.07.2006. Coming into force: 22.07.2006. Effect: None. Territorial extent & classification: E. Local *Unpublished*

The A21 Trunk Road (Northbridge Street Roundabout) (Temporary Prohibition of Traffic) Order 2006 No. 2006/3065. - Enabling power: Road Traffic Regulation Act 1984, s. 16A (2) (a). - Made: 30.10.2006. Coming into force: 04.11.2006. Effect: None. Territorial extent & classification: E. Local *Unpublished*

The A21 Trunk Road (Pierce Barn Overbridge - Rosemary Lane) (Temporary Speed Restrictions) Order 2006 No. 2006/970. - Enabling power: Road Traffic Regulation Act 1984, s. 14 (1) (a). - Made: 27.03.2006. Coming into force: 01.04.2006. Effect: None. Territorial extent & classification: E. Local. - Revoked by S.I. 2006/1883 *Unpublished*

The A21 Trunk Road (Pierce Barn Overbridge to Rosemary Lane and Cuckoo Lane to Forstal Farm Roundabout) (Temporary Restriction of Traffic) Order 2006 No. 2006/1883. - Enabling power: Road Traffic Regulation Act 1984, s. 14 (1) (a). - Made: 10.07.2006. Coming into force: 15.07.2006. Effect: S.I. 2006/970 revoked. Territorial extent & classification: E. Local *Unpublished*

The A21 Trunk Road (Robertsbridge/Vinehall Street) (Temporary Restriction and Prohibition of Traffic) Order 2006 No. 2006/2194. - Enabling power: Road Traffic Regulation Act 1984, s. 14 (1) (a). - Made: 07.08.2006. Coming into force: 12.08.2006. Effect: None. Territorial extent & classification: E. Local *Unpublished*

The A21 Trunk Road (Sevenoaks By-pass) (Temporary Restriction and Prohibition of Traffic) Order 2006 No. 2006/2418. - Enabling power: Road Traffic Regulation Act 1984, s. 14 (1) (a). - Made: 29.08.2006. Coming into force: 02.09.2006. Effect: None. Territorial extent & classification: E. Local *Unpublished*

The A21 Trunk Road (Tonbridge Bypass, Londonbound Exit Slip Road) (Temporary Prohibition of Traffic) Order 2006 No. 2006/435. - Enabling power: Road Traffic Regulation Act 1984, s. 14 (1) (a). - Made: 13.02.2006. Coming into force: 18.02.2006. Effect: None. Territorial extent & classification: E. Local *Unpublished*

The A21 Trunk Road (Tonbridge Bypass) (Temporary Restriction and Prohibition of Traffic) Order 2006 No. 2006/2334. - Enabling power: Road Traffic Regulation Act 1984, s. 14 (1) (a). - Made: 21.08.2006. Coming into force: 26.08.2006. Effect: None. Territorial extent & classification: E. Local *Unpublished*

The A21 Trunk Road (Tonbridge Bypass) (Temporary Restriction of Traffic) Order 2006 No. 2006/151. - Enabling power: Road Traffic Regulation Act 1984, s. 14 (1) (a). - Made: 23.01.2006. Coming into force: 28.01.2006. Effect: None. Territorial extent & classification: E. Local *Unpublished*

The A26 Trunk Road (Itford Farm) (Temporary Restriction and Prohibition of Traffic) Order 2006 No. 2006/436. - Enabling power: Road Traffic Regulation Act 1984, s. 14 (1) (a). - Made: 13.02.2006. Coming into force: 18.02.2006. Effect: None. Territorial extent & classification: E. Local *Unpublished*

The A26 Trunk Road (Three Ponds Caravan Park)
(Temporary Restriction and Prohibition of Traffic)
Order 2006 No. 2006/3358. - Enabling power: Road
Traffic Regulation Act 1984, s. 14 (1) (a). - Made:
11.12.2006. Coming into force: 16.12.2006. Effect: None.
Territorial extent & classification: E. Local *Unpublished*

The A27 and A26 Trunk Roads (Southerham -
Beddingham) (Temporary Restriction and Prohibition
of Traffic) Order 2006 No. 2006/2776. - Enabling power:
Road Traffic Regulation Act 1984, ss. 14 (1) (a), 15 (2). -
Made: 09.10.2006. Coming into force: 16.10.2006. Effect:
None. Territorial extent & classification: E. Local
Unpublished

The A27 Trunk Road (A280 Junction Near Selden and
Mill Road Junction Near Slindon) (Temporary
Prohibition of Traffic) Order 2006 No. 2006/823. -
Enabling power: Road Traffic Regulation Act 1984, s. 14
(1) (a). - Made: 13.03.2006. Coming into force:
18.03.2006. Effect: None. Territorial extent &
classification: E. Local *Unpublished*

The A27 Trunk Road (Beddingham - Polegate)
(Temporary 40 MPH Speed Restriction) Order 2006
No. 2006/3443. - Enabling power: Road Traffic Regulation
Act 1984, s. 14 (1) (a). - Made: 18.12.2006. Coming into
force: 23.12.2006. Effect: None. Territorial extent &
classification: E. Local *Unpublished*

The A27 Trunk Road (Beddingham Roundabout -
Southerham Roundabout) (Temporary Prohibition of
Traffic) Order 2006 No. 2006/1374. - Enabling power:
Road Traffic Regulation Act 1984, s. 14 (1) (a). - Made:
15.05.2006. Coming into force: 26.05.2006. Effect: None.
Territorial extent & classification: E. Local *Unpublished*

The A27 Trunk Road (Busticle Lane - Lancing Manor
Roundabout) (Temporary Restriction and Prohibition
of Traffic) Order 2006 No. 2006/2582. - Enabling power:
Road Traffic Regulation Act 1984, s. 14 (1) (a). - Made:
11.09.2006. Coming into force: 16.09.2006. Effect: None.
Territorial extent & classification: E. Local *Unpublished*

The A27 Trunk Road (Causeway Roundabout,
Arundel) (Temporary Restriction and Prohibition of
Traffic) Order 2006 No. 2006/78. - Enabling power: Road
Traffic Regulation Act 1984, s. 14 (1) (a). - Made:
16.01.2006. Coming into force: 21.01.2006. Effect: None.
Territorial extent & classification: E. Local *Unpublished*

The A27 Trunk Road (Causeway Roundabout - Binsted
Lane) (Temporary Speed Restrictions) Order 2006 No.
2006/2875. - Enabling power: Road Traffic Regulation Act
1984, s. 14 (1) (a). - Made: 23.10.2006. Coming into force:
28.10.2006. Effect: None. Territorial extent &
classification: E. Local *Unpublished*

The A27 Trunk Road (Drusilla's Roundabout, Near
Berwick) (Temporary Prohibition of Traffic) Order
2006 No. 2006/818. - Enabling power: Road Traffic
Regulation Act 1984, s. 14 (1) (a). - Made: 13.03.2006.
Coming into force: 18.03.2006. Effect: None. Territorial
extent & classification: E. Local *Unpublished*

The A27 Trunk Road (Hammerpot, Westbound)
(Temporary Prohibition of Traffic) Order 2006 No.
2006/2255. - Enabling power: Road Traffic Regulation Act
1984, s. 14 (1) (a). - Made: 14.08.2006. Coming into force:
19.08.2006. Effect: None. Territorial extent &
classification: E. Local *Unpublished*

The A27 Trunk Road (Harts Farm Interchange)
(Temporary Restriction and Prohibition of Traffic)
Order 2006 No. 2006/2108. - Enabling power: Road
Traffic Regulation Act 1984, s. 14 (1) (a). - Made:
24.07.2006. Coming into force: 29.07.2006. Effect: None.
Territorial extent & classification: E. Local *Unpublished*

The A27 Trunk Road (Hilsea, Eastbound Entry Slip
Road) (Temporary Prohibition of Traffic) Order 2006
No. 2006/2202. - Enabling power: Road Traffic Regulation
Act 1984, s. 14 (1) (a). - Made: 07.08.2006. Coming into
force: 12.08.2006. Effect: None. Territorial extent &
classification: E. Local *Unpublished*

The A27 Trunk Road (Holmbush Interchange to
Hangleton) (Temporary Prohibition of Traffic) Order
2006 No. 2006/892. - Enabling power: Road Traffic
Regulation Act 1984, s. 14 (1) (a). - Made: 20.03.2006.
Coming into force: 01.04.2006. Effect: None. Territorial
extent & classification: E. Local *Unpublished*

The A27 Trunk Road (New Barn Road - Mill Hill)
(Temporary 40 Miles Per Hour Speed Restriction)
Order 2006 No. 2006/1127. - Enabling power: Road
Traffic Regulation Act 1984, s. 14 (1) (a). - Made:
13.04.2006. Coming into force: 15.04.2006. Effect: None.
Territorial extent & classification: E. Local *Unpublished*

The A27 Trunk Road (Old Shoreham Road and
Shoreham Bypass) (Temporary Restriction Traffic)
Order 2006 No. 2006/2465. - Enabling power: Road
Traffic Regulation Act 1984, s. 14 (1) (b). - Made:
04.09.2006. Coming into force: 12.09.2006. Effect: None.
Territorial extent & classification: E. Local *Unpublished*

The A27 Trunk Road (Patcham) (Temporary
Restriction and Prohibition of Traffic) Order 2006 No.
2006/2550. - Enabling power: Road Traffic Regulation Act
1984, s. 14 (1) (a). - Made: 04.09.2006. Coming into force:
09.09.2006. Effect: None. Territorial extent &
classification: E. Local *Unpublished*

The A27 Trunk Road (Patcham, Westbound Exit Slip
Road) (Temporary Prohibition of Traffic) Order 2006
No. 2006/387. - Enabling power: Road Traffic Regulation
Act 1984, s. 14 (1) (a). - Made: 13.02.2006. Coming into
force: 18.02.2006. Effect: None. Territorial extent &
classification: E. Local *Unpublished*

The A27 Trunk Road (Pook Lane Footbridge)
(Temporary Restriction and Prohibition of Traffic)
Order 2006 No. 2006/2559. - Enabling power: Road
Traffic Regulation Act 1984, s. 14 (1) (a). - Made:
18.09.2006. Coming into force: 23.09.2006. Effect: None.
Territorial extent & classification: E. Local *Unpublished*

The A27 Trunk Road (Selmeston - Alciston)
(Temporary Restriction and Prohibition of Traffic)
Order 2006 No. 2006/2415. - Enabling power: Road
Traffic Regulation Act 1984, s. 14 (1) (a). - Made:
29.08.2006. Coming into force: 02.09.2006. Effect: None.
Territorial extent & classification: E. Local *Unpublished*

The A27 Trunk Road (Southerham Railway Bridge)
(Temporary Restriction of Traffic) Order 2006 No.
2006/1103. - Enabling power: Road Traffic Regulation Act
1984, s. 14 (1) (a). - Made: 10.04.2006. Coming into force:
15.04.2006. Effect: None. Territorial extent &
classification: E. Local *Unpublished*

The A27 Trunk Road (Tangmere Roundabout)
(Temporary 50 Miles Per Hour Speed Restriction)
Order 2006 No. 2006/817. - Enabling power: Road Traffic
Regulation Act 1984, s. 14 (1) (a). - Made: 13.03.2006.
Coming into force: 18.03.2006. Effect: None. Territorial
extent & classification: E. Local *Unpublished*

The A27 Trunk Road (West Firle - Alciston)
(Temporary 40 Miles Per Hour Speed Restriction)
Order 2006 No. 2006/3184. - Enabling power: Road
Traffic Regulation Act 1984, s. 14 (1) (a). - Made:
27.11.2006. Coming into force: 02.12.2006. Effect: None.
Territorial extent & classification: E. Local *Unpublished*

The A30 Trunk Road (Alphington Interchange, Near
Exter) (Temporary Restriction of Traffic) Order 2006
No. 2006/1765. - Enabling power: Road Traffic Regulation
Act 1984, s. 14 (1) (a). - Made: 27.06.2006. Coming into
force: 01.07.2006. Effect: None. Territorial extent &
classification: E. Local *Unpublished*

The A30 Trunk Road (Alphington Interchange to
Pearces Hill Interchange, Exeter) (Temporary
Prohibition of Traffic) Order 2006 No. 2006/3046. -
Enabling power: Road Traffic Regulation Act 1984, s. 14
(1) (a). - Made: 26.10.2006. Coming into force:
31.10.2006. Effect: None. Territorial extent &
classification: E. Local *Unpublished*

The A30 Trunk Road (Alphington Interchange to
Pearces Hill Interchange, South of Exeter) (Temporary
Prohibition of Traffic) Order 2006 No. 2006/415. -
Enabling power: Road Traffic Regulation Act 1984, s. 14
(1) (a). - Made: 20.02.2006. Coming into force:
25.02.2006. Effect: None. Territorial extent &
classification: E. Local *Unpublished*

The A30 Trunk Road (Blowing House Viaduct,
Redruth) (Temporary 10 Miles Per Hour and 40 Miles
Per Hour Speed Restriction) Order 2006 No. 2006/690.
- Enabling power: Road Traffic Regulation Act 1984, s. 14
(1) (a). - Made: 27.02.2006. Coming into force:
04.03.2006. Effect: None. Territorial extent &
classification: E. Local *Unpublished*

The A30 Trunk Road (Callestick Crossroads, near
Zelah) (Temporary Restriction of Traffic) Order 2006
No. 2006/1613. - Enabling power: Road Traffic Regulation
Act 1984, s. 14 (1) (a). - Made: 12.06.2006. Coming into
force: 17.06.2006. Effect: None. Territorial extent &
classification: E. Local *Unpublished*

The A30 Trunk Road (Dunheved Bridge, Launceston)
(Temporary Restriction and Prohibition of Traffic)
Order 2006 No. 2006/159. - Enabling power: Road Traffic
Regulation Act 1984, s. 14 (1) (a), 122A. - Made:
18.01.2006. Coming into force: 20.01.2006. Effect: None.
Territorial extent & classification: E. Local *Unpublished*

The A30 Trunk Road (Dunheved to Bulsworthy,
Launceston) (Temporary Prohibition and Restriction of
Traffic) Order 2006 No. 2006/2475. - Enabling power:
Road Traffic Regulation Act 1984, s. 14 (1) (a). - Made:
05.09.2006. Coming into force: 08.09.2006. Effect: None.
Territorial extent & classification: E. Local *Unpublished*

The A30 Trunk Road (Gilberts Coombe Viaduct,
Redruth) (Temporary 10 Miles Per Hour and 40 Miles
Per Hour Speed Restriction) Order 2006 No. 2006/689.
- Enabling power: Road Traffic Regulation Act 1984, s. 14
(1) (a). - Made: 06.03.2006. Coming into force:
11.03.2006. Effect: None. Territorial extent &
classification: E. Local *Unpublished*

The A30 Trunk Road (Highgate Interchange, Indian
Queens, Cornwall) (Temporary Prohibition of Traffic)
Order 2006 No. 2006/473. - Enabling power: Road Traffic
Regulation Act 1984, s. 14 (1) (a). - Made: 22.02.2006.
Coming into force: 27.02.2006. Effect: None. Territorial
extent & classification: E. Local *Unpublished*

The A30 Trunk Road (Indian Queens Contraflow)
(Temporary Prohibition and Restriction of Traffic)
Order 2006 No. 2006/2578. - Enabling power: Road
Traffic Regulation Act 1984, s. 14 (1) (a). - Made:
19.09.2006. Coming into force: 22.09.2006. Effect: None.
Territorial extent & classification: E. Local *Unpublished*

The A30 Trunk Road (Indian Queens to Lanivet)
(Temporary Restriction of Traffic) Order 2005
(Variation) Order 2006 No. 2006/2176. - Enabling
power: Road Traffic Regulation Act 1984, s. 14 (1) (a),
sch. 9, para. 27 (1). - Made: 31.07.2006. Coming into
force: 03.08.2006. Effect: S.I. 2005/3319 varied. Territorial
extent & classification: E. Local *Unpublished*

The A30 Trunk Road (Innis Downs Junction, Near
Bodmin) (Temporary Prohibition and Restriction of
Traffic) 2006 No. 2006/236. - Enabling power: Road
Traffic Regulation Act 1984, s. 14 (1) (a). - Made:
31.01.2006. Coming into force: 04.02.2006. Effect: None.
Territorial extent & classification: E. Local *Unpublished*

The A30 Trunk Road (Innis Downs Roundabout)
(Temporary Prohibition of Traffic) Order 2006 No.
2006/1474. - Enabling power: Road Traffic Regulation Act
1984, s. 14 (1) (b) (5) (b). - Made: 24.05.2006. Coming
into force: 26.05.2006. Effect: None. Territorial extent &
classification: E. Local *Unpublished*

The A30 Trunk Road (Innis Downs Roundabout)
(Temporary Prohibition of Traffic) Order 2006
(Variation) Order 2006 No. 2006/2153. - Enabling
power: Road Traffic Regulation Act 1984, s. 14 (1) (b),
sch. 9, para. 27 (1). - Made: 31.07.2006. Coming into
force: 03.08.2006. Effect: S.I. 2006/1474 varied. Territorial
extent & classification: E. Local *Unpublished*

Road traffic: Traffic regulation

The A30 Trunk Road (Loggans Moor Roundabout to Treswithian Interchange, Cornwall) (Temporary Prohibition of Traffic) 2006 No. 2006/455. - Enabling power: Road Traffic Regulation Act 1984, s. 14 (1) (a). - Made: 14.02.2006. Coming into force: 18.02.2006. Effect: None. Territorial extent & classification: E. Local *Unpublished*

The A30 Trunk Road (Menacrin Downs, Near Bodmin) (Temporary Prohibition and Restriction of Traffic) Order 2006 No. 2006/2737. - Enabling power: Road Traffic Regulation Act 1984, s. 14 (1) (a). - Made: 26.09.2006. Coming into force: 28.09.2006. Effect: None. Territorial extent & classification: E. Local *Unpublished*

The A30 Trunk Road (Menacrin Downs, Near Bodmin) (Temporary Prohibition and Restriction of Traffic) Order 2006 (Variation) Order 2006 No. 2006/3085. - Enabling power: Road Traffic Regulation Act 1984, s. 14 (1) (a), sch. 9, para. 27 (1). - Made: 15.11.2006. Coming into force: 17.11.2006. Effect: S.I. 2006/2737 varied. Territorial extent & classification: E. Local *Unpublished*

The A30 Trunk Road (Merrymeet Junction) (Temporary Prohibition and Restriction of Traffic) Order 2006 No. 2006/85. - Enabling power: Road Traffic Regulation Act 1984, s. 14 (1) (a). - Made: 17.01.2006. Coming into force: 21.01.2006. Effect: None. Territorial extent & classification: E. Local *Unpublished*

The A30 Trunk Road (Merrymeet Roundabout) (Temporary Prohibition of Traffic) Order 2006 No. 2006/998. - Enabling power: Road Traffic Regulation Act 1984, s. 14 (1) (a). - Made: 28.03.2006. Coming into force: 01.04.2006. Effect: None. Territorial extent & classification: E. Local *Unpublished*

The A30 Trunk Road (Merrymeet Roundabout to Coombe Head, Devon) (Temporary Prohibition of Traffic) Order 2006 No. 2006/2152. - Enabling power: Road Traffic Regulation Act 1984, s. 14 (1) (a). - Made: 31.07.2006. Coming into force: 05.08.2006. Effect: None. Territorial extent & classification: E. Local *Unpublished*

The A30 Trunk Road (Pounds Conce to Temple Fishery Junction, near Bodmin) (Temporary Restriction of Traffic) Order 2006 No. 2006/1645. - Enabling power: Road Traffic Regulation Act 1984, s. 14 (1) (a). - Made: 19.06.2006. Coming into force: 23.06.2006. Effect: None. Territorial extent & classification: E. Local *Unpublished*

The A30 Trunk Road (Tavistock Road to Liftondown, Dunheved Bridge, Launceston) (Temporary Prohibition of Traffic) Order 2006 No. 2006/1480. - Enabling power: Road Traffic Regulation Act 1984, s. 14 (1) (a). - Made: 30.05.2006. Coming into force: 03.06.2006. Effect: None. Territorial extent & classification: E. Local *Unpublished*

The A31 Trunk Road (Ashley Heath Junction, Westbound Exit Slip/Link Road) (Temporary Prohibition of Traffic) Order 2006 No. 2006/3233. - Enabling power: Road Traffic Regulation Act 1984, s. 14 (1) (a). - Made: 13.11.2006. Coming into force: 18.11.2006. Effect: None. Territorial extent & classification: E. Local *Unpublished*

The A31 Trunk Road (Ashley Heath Roundabout, Eastbound Exit Slip Road) (Temporary Prohibition of Traffic) Order 2006 No. 2006/2554. - Enabling power: Road Traffic Regulation Act 1984, s. 14 (1) (a). - Made: 18.09.2006. Coming into force: 23.09.2006. Effect: None. Territorial extent & classification: E. Local *Unpublished*

The A31 Trunk Road (Canford Bottom Roundabout) (Temporary Speed Restriction) Order 2006 No. 2006/3042. - Enabling power: Road Traffic Regulation Act 1984, s. 14 (1) (a). - Made: 06.11.2006. Coming into force: 11.11.2006. Effect: None. Territorial extent & classification: E. Local *Unpublished*

The A31 Trunk Road (Merley Roundabout - Ameysford Roundabout) (Temporary Restriction and Prohibition of Traffic) Order 2006 No. 2006/2466. - Enabling power: Road Traffic Regulation Act 1984, s. 14 (1) (a). - Made: 04.09.2006. Coming into force: 09.09.2006. Effect: None. Territorial extent & classification: E. Local *Unpublished*

The A31 Trunk Road (Ringwood - Ashley Heath) (Temporary Restriction and Prohibition of Traffic) Order 2006 No. 2006/1130. - Enabling power: Road Traffic Regulation Act 1984, s. 14 (1) (a). - Made: 18.04.2006. Coming into force: 22.04.2006. Effect: None. Territorial extent & classification: E. Local *Unpublished*

The A31 Trunk Road (Ringwood - Verwood Interchange) (Temporary Restriction and Prohibition of Traffic) Order 2006 No. 2006/3438. - Enabling power: Road Traffic Regulation Act 1984, s. 14 (1) (a). - Made: 18.12.2006. Coming into force: 30.12.2006. Effect: None. Territorial extent & classification: E. Local *Unpublished*

The A31 Trunk Road (Sturminster Marshall) (Temporary Speed Restrictions) Order 2006 No. 2006/1043. - Enabling power: Road Traffic Regulation Act 1984, s. 14 (1) (a). - Made: 03.04.2006. Coming into force: 08.04.2006. Effect: None. Territorial extent & classification: E. Local *Unpublished*

The A31 Trunk Road (Woolsbridge Roundabout - Boundary Lane Roundabout) (Temporary Speed Restrictions) Order 2006 No. 2006/1491. - Enabling power: Road Traffic Regulation Act 1984, s. 14 (1) (a). - Made: 30.05.2006. Coming into force: 03.06.2006. Effect: None. Territorial extent & classification: E. Local *Unpublished*

The A34 and A500 Trunk Roads (Talke, Staffordshire) (Temporary 40 Miles Per Hour Speed Restriction) Order 2006 No. 2006/2252. - Enabling power: Road Traffic Regulation Act 1984, s. 14 (1) (a). - Made: 07.08.2006. Coming into force: 14.08.2006. Effect: None. Territorial extent & classification: E. Local *Unpublished*

The A34 Trunk Road (A33 Junction - Bullington Cross) (Temporary Prohibition of Traffic) Order 2006 No. 2006/2585. - Enabling power: Road Traffic Regulation Act 1984, s. 14 (1) (a). - Made: 11.09.2006. Coming into force: 16.09.2006. Effect: None. Territorial extent & classification: E. Local *Unpublished*

Road traffic: Traffic regulation

The A34 Trunk Road (A420 Botley Interchange, Southbound) (Temporary Restriction and Prohibition of Traffic) Order 2006 No. 2006/2414. - Enabling power: Road Traffic Regulation Act 1984, s. 14 (1) (a). - Made: 29.08.2006. Coming into force: 02.09.2006. Effect: None. Territorial extent & classification: E. Local *Unpublished*

The A34 Trunk Road (B4027 Junction, Northbound Slip Roads) (Temporary Prohibition of Traffic) Order 2006 No. 2006/2071. - Enabling power: Road Traffic Regulation Act 1984, s. 14 (1) (a). - Made: 24.07.2006. Coming into force: 29.07.2006. Effect: None. Territorial extent & classification: E. Local *Unpublished*

The A34 Trunk Road (Beedon - Speen) (Temporary Restriction and Prohibition of Traffic) Order 2006 No. 2006/3357. - Enabling power: Road Traffic Regulation Act 1984, s. 14 (1) (a). - Made: 11.12.2006. Coming into force: 06.01.2007. Effect: None. Territorial extent & classification: E. Local *Unpublished*

The A34 Trunk Road (Bullington Cross - Whitchurch) (Temporary Restriction and Prohibition of Traffic) Order 2006 No. 2006/1484. - Enabling power: Road Traffic Regulation Act 1984, s. 14 (1) (a). - Made: 30.05.2006. Coming into force: 03.06.2006. Effect: None. Territorial extent & classification: E. Local *Unpublished*

The A34 Trunk Road (Litchfield, Northbound Carriageway) (Temporary Speed Restrictions) Order 2006 No. 2006/972. - Enabling power: Road Traffic Regulation Act 1984, s. 14 (1) (a). - Made: 27.03.2006. Coming into force: 01.04.2006. Effect: None. Territorial extent & classification: E. Local *Unpublished*

The A34 Trunk Road (M4 Junction 13) (Temporary Prohibition of Traffic) Order 2006 No. 2006/1483. - Enabling power: Road Traffic Regulation Act 1984, s. 14 (1) (a). - Made: 30.05.2006. Coming into force: 03.06.2006. Effect: None. Territorial extent & classification: E. Local *Unpublished*

The A34 Trunk Road (Marcham Interchange) (Temporary Restriction and Prohibition of Traffic) Order 2006 No. 2006/816. - Enabling power: Road Traffic Regulation Act 1984, s. 14 (1) (a). - Made: 13.03.2006. Coming into force: 18.03.2006. Effect: None. Territorial extent & classification: E. Local *Unpublished*

The A34 Trunk Road (Milton Interchange - Marcham Interchange) (Temporary Restriction and Prohibition of Traffic) Order 2006 No. 2006/1607. - Enabling power: Road Traffic Regulation Act 1984, s. 14 (1) (a). - Made: 12.06.2006. Coming into force: 17.06.2006. Effect: None. Territorial extent & classification: E. Local *Unpublished*

The A34 Trunk Road (Near Didcot) (Temporary Restriction of Traffic) Order 2006 No. 2006/533. - Enabling power: Road Traffic Regulation Act 1984, s. 14 (1) (a). - Made: 27.02.2006. Coming into force: 04.03.2006. Effect: None. Territorial extent & classification: E. Local *Unpublished*

The A34 Trunk Road (Speen, Northbound Exit Slip Road) (Temporary Prohibition of Traffic) Order 2006 No. 2006/2722. - Enabling power: Road Traffic Regulation Act 1984, s. 14 (1) (a). - Made: 02.10.2006. Coming into force: 07.10.2006. Effect: None. Territorial extent & classification: E. Local *Unpublished*

The A34 Trunk Road (Speen, Southbound Exit Slip Road) (Temporary Prohibition of Traffic) Order 2006 No. 2006/900. - Enabling power: Road Traffic Regulation Act 1984, s. 14 (1) (a). - Made: 20.03.2006. Coming into force: 25.03.2006. Effect: None. Territorial extent & classification: E. Local *Unpublished*

The A34 Trunk Road (Sutton Scotney - M3 Junction 9) (Temporary Restriction and Prohibition of Traffic) Order 2006 No. 2006/532. - Enabling power: Road Traffic Regulation Act 1984, s. 14 (1) (a). - Made: 27.02.2006. Coming into force: 04.03.2006. Effect: None. Territorial extent & classification: E. Local *Unpublished*

The A34 Trunk Road (Sutton Scotney - South Wonston) (Temporary Restriction and Prohibition of Traffic) Order 2006 No. 2006/1881. - Enabling power: Road Traffic Regulation Act 1984, s. 14 (1) (a). - Made: 10.07.2006. Coming into force: 15.07.2006. Effect: None. Territorial extent & classification: E. Local *Unpublished*

The A34 Trunk Road (Whitchurch Interchange, Southbound) (Temporary Restriction and Prohibition of Traffic) Order 2006 No. 2006/2195. - Enabling power: Road Traffic Regulation Act 1984, s. 14 (1) (a). - Made: 07.08.2006. Coming into force: 12.08.2006. Effect: None. Territorial extent & classification: E. Local *Unpublished*

The A35 Trunk Road (Melplash Show, Bridport, Dorset) (Temporary Prohibition of Traffic) Order 2006 No. 2006/2282. - Enabling power: Road Traffic Regulation Act 1984, s. 14 (1) (b). - Made: 17.08.2006. Coming into force: 22.08.2006. Effect: None. Territorial extent & classification: E. Local *Unpublished*

The A35 Trunk Road (Sea Road South Bridport, Dorset) (Prohibition of Right Turn) (Experimental) Order 2006 No. 2006/2294. - Enabling power: Road Traffic Regulation Act 1984, ss. 9 (1) to (3), 10 (1) (2). - Made: 16.08.2006. Coming into force: 01.09.2006. Effect: None. Territorial extent & classification: E. Local *Unpublished*

The A36 Trunk Road (Churchill Way North, Salisbury) (Temporary Prohibition of Pedestrians) Order 2006 No. 2006/379. - Enabling power: Road Traffic Regulation Act 1984, s. 14 (1) (a). - Made: 13.02.2006. Coming into force: 18.02.2006. Effect: None. Territorial extent & classification: E. Local *Unpublished*

The A36 Trunk Road (Claverton, Bath), A4 Trunk Road (Batheaston, Bath), A4 Trunk Road (The Globe Roundabout, Bath) and A46 Trunk Road (Upper Swainswick, Bath) (Temporary Traffic Restrictions and Prohibitions) Order 2006 No. 2006/3073. - Enabling power: Road Traffic Regulation Act 1984, s. 14 (1) (b). - Made: 26.10.2006. Coming into force: 28.10.2006. Effect: None. Territorial extent & classification: E. Local *Unpublished*

Road traffic: Traffic regulation

The A36 Trunk Road (Heytesbury to Stockton Bend, Wiltshire) (Temporary 30 Miles Per Hour Speed Restriction) Order 2006 No. 2006/1594. - Enabling power: Road Traffic Regulation Act 1984, s. 14 (1) (a). - Made: 06.06.2006. Coming into force: 12.06.2006. Effect: None. Territorial extent & classification: E. Local *Unpublished*

The A36 Trunk Road (Landford to Holwell Green, Near Salisbury) (Temporary Prohibition of Traffic) Order 2006 No. 2006/2459. - Enabling power: Road Traffic Regulation Act 1984, s. 14 (1) (a). - Made: 04.09.2006. Coming into force: 08.09.2006. Effect: None. Territorial extent & classification: E. Local *Unpublished*

The A36 Trunk Road (Monkton Combe to Limpley Stoke, Near Bath) (Temporary Prohibition of Traffic) Order 2006 No. 2006/1763. - Enabling power: Road Traffic Regulation Act 1984, s. 14 (1) (a). - Made: 26.06.2006. Coming into force: 01.07.2006. Effect: None. Territorial extent & classification: E. Local *Unpublished*

The A38 and A50 Trunk Roads (Toyota Intersection, Derbyshire) (Temporary Restriction and Prohibition of Traffic) Order 2006 No. 2006/1239. - Enabling power: Road Traffic Regulation Act 1984, s. 14 (1) (a). - Made: 24.04.2006. Coming into force: 01.05.2006. Effect: None. Territorial extent & classification: E. Local *Unpublished*

The A38 and A516 Trunk Roads (South of Derby) (Temporary Restriction and Prohibition of Traffic) Order 2006 No. 2006/320. - Enabling power: Road Traffic Regulation Act 1984, s. 14 (1) (a). - Made: 06.02.2006. Coming into force: 13.02.2006. Effect: None. Territorial extent & classification: E. Local *Unpublished*

The A38 Trunk Road (Alfreton, Derbyshire) (Temporary Prohibition of Traffic) Order 2006 No. 2006/2217. - Enabling power: Road Traffic Regulation Act 1984, s. 14 (1) (a). - Made: 01.08.2006. Coming into force: 08.08.2006. Effect: None. Territorial extent & classification: E. Local *Unpublished*

The A38 Trunk Road (Allestree, Derby) (Temporary 40 Miles Per Hour Speed Restriction) Order 2006 No. 2006/2674. - Enabling power: Road Traffic Regulation Act 1984, s. 14 (1) (a). - Made: 29.09.2006. Coming into force: 06.10.2006. Effect: None. Territorial extent & classification: E. Local *Unpublished*

The A38 Trunk Road (Alrewas to Barton-under-Needwood, Staffordshire) (Temporary Prohibition of Traffic) Order 2006 No. 2006/2036. - Enabling power: Road Traffic Regulation Act 1984, s. 14 (1) (a). - Made: 10.07.2006. Coming into force: 17.07.2006. Effect: None. Territorial extent & classification: E. Local *Unpublished*

The A38 Trunk Road (Alrewas to Barton-Under-Needwood) (Temporary Restriction and Prohibition of Traffic) Order 2006 No. 2006/3056. - Enabling power: Road Traffic Regulation Act 1984, s. 14 (1) (a). - Made: 13.10.2006. Coming into force: 20.10.2006. Effect: None. Territorial extent & classification: E. Local *Unpublished*

The A38 Trunk Road (Bassett's Pole Roundabout, Staffordshire) (Temporary Prohibition of Traffic) Order 2006 No. 2006/1592. - Enabling power: Road Traffic Regulation Act 1984, s. 14 (1) (a). - Made: 01.06.2006. Coming into force: 08.06.2006. Effect: None. Territorial extent & classification: E. Local *Unpublished*

The A38 Trunk Road (Belper, Derbyshire) (Temporary Restriction and Prohibition of Traffic) Order 2006 No. 2006/2400. - Enabling power: Road Traffic Regulation Act 1984, s. 14 (1) (a). - Made: 21.08.2006. Coming into force: 28.08.2006. Effect: None. Territorial extent & classification: E. Local *Unpublished*

The A38 Trunk Road (Between A50 Derby Southern Bypass and M1 Junction 28, Derbyshire) and the A516 Trunk Road (24 Hours Clearway) Order 2006 No. 2006/2706. - Enabling power: Road Traffic Regulation Act 1984, ss. 1 (1), 2 (1) (2), 4 (1), sch. 9, para. 27 (1). - Made: 21.09.2006. Coming into force: 02.10.2006. Effect: None. Territorial extent & classification: E. Local *Unpublished*

The A38 Trunk Road (Boley Park, Lichfield, Staffordshire) (Temporary Restriction and Prohibition of Traffic) Order 2006 No. 2006/1195. - Enabling power: Road Traffic Regulation Act 1984, s. 14 (1) (a). - Made: 18.04.2006. Coming into force: 25.04.2006. Effect: None. Territorial extent & classification: E. Local *Unpublished*

The A38 Trunk Road (Branston, Staffordshire) (Temporary Prohibition and Restriction of Traffic) Order 2006 No. 2006/1364. - Enabling power: Road Traffic Regulation Act 1984, s. 14 (1) (a). - Made: 15.05.2006. Coming into force: 22.05.2006. Effect: None. Territorial extent & classification: E. Local *Unpublished*

The A38 Trunk Road (Branston, Staffordshire) (Temporary Restriction and Prohibition of Traffic) Order 2006 No. 2006/1143. - Enabling power: Road Traffic Regulation Act 1984, s. 14 (1) (a). - Made: 11.04.2006. Coming into force: 18.04.2006. Effect: None. Territorial extent & classification: E. Local *Unpublished*

The A38 Trunk Road (Burton on Trent, Staffordshire) (Temporary Restriction and Prohibition of Traffic) Order 2006 No. 2006/70. - Enabling power: Road Traffic Regulation Act 1984, s. 14 (1) (a). - Made: 06.01.2006. Coming into force: 13.01.2006. Effect: None. Territorial extent & classification: E. Local *Unpublished*

The A38 Trunk Road (Chudleigh Station Bridge to Clay Lane Junction at Chudleigh Knighton, Near Newton Abbot) (Temporary Prohibition of Traffic) Order 2006 No. 2006/1855. - Enabling power: Road Traffic Regulation Act 1984, s. 14 (1) (a). - Made: 04.07.2006. Coming into force: 06.07.2006. Effect: None. Territorial extent & classification: E. Local *Unpublished*

The A38 Trunk Road (Clay Mills, Burton-on-Trent, Staffordshire) (Temporary Prohibition of Traffic) Order 2006 No. 2006/2869. - Enabling power: Road Traffic Regulation Act 1984, s. 14 (1) (b). - Made: 16.10.2006. Coming into force: 23.10.2006. Effect: None. Territorial extent & classification: E. Local *Unpublished*

Road traffic: Traffic regulation

The A38 Trunk Road (Clay Mills, Staffordshire) (Temporary Restriction and Prohibition of Traffic) Order 2006 No. 2006/2677. - Enabling power: Road Traffic Regulation Act 1984, s. 14 (1) (a). - Made: 22.09.2006. Coming into force: 29.09.2006. Effect: None. Territorial extent & classification: E. Local *Unpublished*

The A38 Trunk Road (Clay Mills to Willington) (Temporary Restriction and Prohibition of Traffic) Order 2006 No. 2006/2741. - Enabling power: Road Traffic Regulation Act 1984, s. 14 (1) (a). - Made: 09.10.2006. Coming into force: 16.10.2006. Effect: None. Territorial extent & classification: E. Local *Unpublished*

The A38 Trunk Road (Darnford, Near Lichfield, Staffordshire) (Temporary 40 Miles Per Hour Speed Restriction) Order 2006 No. 2006/3455. - Enabling power: Road Traffic Regulation Act 1984, s. 14 (1) (a). - Made: 20.12.2006. Coming into force: 27.12.2006. Effect: None. Territorial extent & classification: E. Local *Unpublished*

The A38 Trunk Road (Drumbridges Interchange to Goodstone Interchange, Near Newton Abbot) (Temporary Prohibition of Traffic) Order 2006 No. 2006/1764. - Enabling power: Road Traffic Regulation Act 1984, s. 14 (1) (a). - Made: 27.06.2006. Coming into force: 01.07.2006. Effect: None. Territorial extent & classification: E. Local *Unpublished*

The A38 Trunk Road (Eggington, Derbyshire) (Temporary Restriction and Prohibition of Traffic) Order 2006 No. 2006/3454. - Enabling power: Road Traffic Regulation Act 1984, s. 14 (1) (a). - Made: 20.12.2006. Coming into force: 27.12.2006. Effect: None. Territorial extent & classification: E. Local *Unpublished*

The A38 Trunk Road (Egginton Brook Bridge, Derbyshire) (Temporary Prohibition of Traffic) Order 2006 No. 2006/2743. - Enabling power: Road Traffic Regulation Act 1984, s. 14 (1) (a). - Made: 09.10.2006. Coming into force: 16.10.2006. Effect: None. Territorial extent & classification: E. Local *Unpublished*

The A38 Trunk Road (Findern Interchange to Markeaton Roundabout, Derby) and the A516 Trunk Road (Temporary Restriction and Prohibition of Traffic) Order 2006 No. 2006/1363. - Enabling power: Road Traffic Regulation Act 1984, s. 14 (1) (a). - Made: 08.05.2006. Coming into force: 15.05.2006. Effect: None. Territorial extent & classification: E. Local *Unpublished*

The A38 Trunk Road (Fradley to Hilliards Cross, Staffordshire) (Temporary Restriction and Prohibition of Traffic) Order 2006 No. 2006/1362. - Enabling power: Road Traffic Regulation Act 1984, s. 14 (1) (a). - Made: 08.05.2006. Coming into force: 15.05.2006. Effect: None. Territorial extent & classification: E. Local *Unpublished*

The A38 Trunk Road (Glynn Valley, Bodmin) (Temporary Prohibition of Traffic) Order 2006 No. 2006/3082. - Enabling power: Road Traffic Regulation Act 1984, ss. 14 (1) (a). - Made: 14.11.2006. Coming into force: 18.11.2006. Effect: None. Territorial extent & classification: E. Local *Unpublished*

The A38 Trunk Road (Glynn Valley) (Temporary Prohibition of Traffic) Order 2006 No. 2006/547. - Enabling power: Road Traffic Regulation Act 1984, s. 14 (1) (a). - Made: 27.02.2006. Coming into force: 04.03.2006. Effect: None. Territorial extent & classification: E. Local *Unpublished*

The A38 Trunk Road (Haldon Hill, South of Exeter) (Temporary Prohibition and Restriction of Traffic) Order 2006 No. 2006/3081. - Enabling power: Road Traffic Regulation Act 1984, ss. 14 (1) (a). - Made: 14.11.2006. Coming into force: 17.11.2006. Effect: None. Territorial extent & classification: E. Local *Unpublished*

The A38 Trunk Road (Junctions 15 - 16) (Temporary Restriction of Traffic) Order 2006 No. 2006/22. - Enabling power: Road Traffic Regulation Act 1984, s. 14 (1) (a) (7). - Made: 04.01.2006. Coming into force: 07.01.2006. Effect: None. Territorial extent & classification: E. Local *Unpublished*

The A38 Trunk Road (Junction with A6 to Junction with A61, Derbyshire) (Temporary Restriction and Prohibition of Traffic) Order 2006 No. 2006/1657. - Enabling power: Road Traffic Regulation Act 1984, s. 14 (1) (a). - Made: 12.06.2006. Coming into force: 19.06.2006. Effect: None. Territorial extent & classification: E. Local *Unpublished*

The A38 Trunk Road (Kingsway, Derby) (Temporary Prohibition of Pedestrians) Order 2006 No. 2006/3015. - Enabling power: Road Traffic Regulation Act 1984, s. 14 (1) (a). - Made: 06.11.2006. Coming into force: 13.11.2006. Effect: None. Territorial extent & classification: E. Local *Unpublished*

The A38 Trunk Road (Lichfield to Barton Under Needwood, Staffordshire) (Temporary Restriction and Prohibition of Traffic) Order 2006 No. 2006/821. - Enabling power: Road Traffic Regulation Act 1984, s. 14 (1) (a). - Made: 03.03.2006. Coming into force: 10.03.2006. Effect: None. Territorial extent & classification: E. Local *Unpublished*

The A38 Trunk Road (Liskeard to North Treviddo, Cornwall) (Temporary Prohibition and Restriction of Traffic) Order 2006 No. 2006/999. - Enabling power: Road Traffic Regulation Act 1984, s. 14 (1) (a). - Made: 28.03.2006. Coming into force: 01.04.2006. Effect: None. Territorial extent & classification: E. Local *Unpublished*

The A38 Trunk Road (Lower Clicker, Near Liskeard, Cornwall) (Temporary 10 Miles Per Hour and 40 Miles Per Hour Speed Restriction) Order 2006 No. 2006/684. - Enabling power: Road Traffic Regulation Act 1984, s. 14 (1) (a). - Made: 22.02.2006. Coming into force: 27.02.2006. Effect: None. Territorial extent & classification: E. Local *Unpublished*

The A38 Trunk Road (Manadon Interchange to Forder Valley Interchange, Plymouth) (Temporary Prohibition of Traffic) Order 2006 No. 2006/1767. - Enabling power: Road Traffic Regulation Act 1984, s. 14 (1) (a). - Made: 27.06.2006. Coming into force: 01.07.2006. Effect: None. Territorial extent & classification: E. Local *Unpublished*

The A38 Trunk Road (Minworth Roundabout, Sutton Coldfield) (Temporary 40 Miles Per Hour Speed Restriction) Order 2006 No. 2006/2023. - Enabling power: Road Traffic Regulation Act 1984, s. 14 (1) (a). - Made: 17.07.2006. Coming into force: 24.07.2006. Effect: None. Territorial extent & classification: E. Local *Unpublished*

The A38 Trunk Road (Notterbridge Junction, near Saltash) (Temporary Restriction of Traffic) Order 2006 No. 2006/1614. - Enabling power: Road Traffic Regulation Act 1984, s. 14 (1) (a). - Made: 12.06.2006. Coming into force: 17.06.2006. Effect: None. Territorial extent & classification: E. Local *Unpublished*

The A38 Trunk Road (Pearces Hill Interchange, Exeter) (Temporary Prohibition of Traffic) Order 2006 No. 2006/1579. - Enabling power: Road Traffic Regulation Act 1984, s. 14 (1) (a). - Made: 13.06.2006. Coming into force: 17.06.2006. Effect: None. Territorial extent & classification: E. Local *Unpublished*

The A38 Trunk Road (River Derwent Bridge, Derbyshire) (Temporary Prohibition of Traffic) Order 2006 No. 2006/3508. - Enabling power: Road Traffic Regulation Act 1984, s. 14 (1) (a). - Made: 29.12.2006. Coming into force: 05.01.2007. Effect: None. Territorial extent & classification: E. Local *Unpublished*

The A38 Trunk Road (Smithaleigh Overbridge, Near Ivybridge, Devon) (Temporary 10 Miles Per Hour and 40 Miles Per Hour Speed Restriction) Order 2006 No. 2006/471. - Enabling power: Road Traffic Regulation Act 1984, s. 14 (1) (a). - Made: 22.02.2006. Coming into force: 27.02.2006. Effect: None. Territorial extent & classification: E. Local *Unpublished*

The A38 Trunk Road (South of Weeford, Staffordshire) (Temporary 40 Miles Per Hour Speed Restriction) Order 2006 No. 2006/3459. - Enabling power: Road Traffic Regulation Act 1984, s. 14 (1) (a). - Made: 20.12.2006. Coming into force: 27.12.2006. Effect: None. Territorial extent & classification: E. Local *Unpublished*

The A38 Trunk Road (Splatford Interchange, Kennford) (Temporary Prohibition of Traffic) Order 2006 No. 2006/688. - Enabling power: Road Traffic Regulation Act 1984, s. 14 (1) (a). - Made: 24.02.2006. Coming into force: 03.03.2006. Effect: None. Territorial extent & classification: E. Local *Unpublished*

The A38 Trunk Road (Streethay to Alrewas, Staffordshire) (Temporary 40 Miles Per Hour Speed Restriction) Order 2006 No. 2006/1412. - Enabling power: Road Traffic Regulation Act 1984, s. 14 (1) (a). - Made: 19.05.2006. Coming into force: 26.05.2006. Effect: None. Territorial extent & classification: E. Local *Unpublished*

The A38 Trunk Road (Swinfen Roundabout, Staffordshire) (Temporary Restriction and Prohibition of Traffic) Order 2006 No. 2006/1243. - Enabling power: Road Traffic Regulation Act 1984, s. 14 (1) (a). - Made: 21.04.2006. Coming into force: 28.04.2006. Effect: None. Territorial extent & classification: E. Local *Unpublished*

The A38 Trunk Road (Tinkers Lane to Trerulefoot, Near Liskeard) (Temporary Restriction and Prohibition of Traffic) Order 2006 No. 2006/2642. - Enabling power: Road Traffic Regulation Act 1984, s. 14 (1) (a). - Made: 26.09.2006. Coming into force: 29.09.2006. Effect: None. Territorial extent & classification: E. Local *Unpublished*

The A38 Trunk Road (Torhill Underbridge, Bittaford, Devon) (Temporary 10 Miles Per Hour and 40 Miles Per Hour Speed Restriction) Order 2006 No. 2006/472. - Enabling power: Road Traffic Regulation Act 1984, s. 14 (1) (a). - Made: 22.02.2006. Coming into force: 27.02.2006. Effect: None. Territorial extent & classification: E. Local *Unpublished*

The A38 Trunk Road (Toyota Interchange to Kingsway Roundabout, Derbyshire) (Temporary Restriction and Prohibition of Traffic) Order 2006 No. 2006/1367. - Enabling power: Road Traffic Regulation Act 1984, s. 14 (1) (a). - Made: 05.05.2006. Coming into force: 12.05.2006. Effect: None. Territorial extent & classification: E. Local *Unpublished*

The A38 Trunk Road (Toyota Interchange to Mickleover, Derbyshire) (Temporary Prohibition of Traffic) Order 2006 No. 2006/3139. - Enabling power: Road Traffic Regulation Act 1984, s. 14 (1) (a). - Made: 17.11.2006. Coming into force: 24.11.2006. Effect: None. Territorial extent & classification: E. Local *Unpublished*

The A38 Trunk Road (Turfdown Crossroads, Bodmin) (Temporary Restriction of Traffic) Order 2006 No. 2006/23. - Enabling power: Road Traffic Regulation Act 1984, s. 14 (1) (a). - Made: 04.01.2006. Coming into force: 06.01.2006. Effect: None. Territorial extent & classification: E. Local *Unpublished*

The A38 Trunk Road (West Coast Railway Bridge, Lichfield, Staffordshire) (Temporary Restriction and Prohibition of Traffic) (No. 2) Order 2006 No. 2006/2669. - Enabling power: Road Traffic Regulation Act 1984, s. 14 (1) (a), sch. 9, para. 27 (1). - Made: 22.09.2006. Coming into force: 29.09.2006. Effect: S.I. 2006/2221 revoked. Territorial extent & classification: E. Local *Unpublished*

The A38 Trunk Road (West Coast Railway Bridge, Lichfield, Staffordshire) (Temporary Restriction and Prohibition of Traffic) Order 2006 No. 2006/2221. - Enabling power: Road Traffic Regulation Act 1984, s. 14 (1) (a). - Made: 28.07.2006. Coming into force: 04.08.2006. Effect: None. Territorial extent & classification: E. Local. - Revoked by S.I. 2006/2669 (Unpublished) *Unpublished*

The A40 and A449 Trunk Roads and the M50 Motorway (Ross-on-Wye, Herefordshire) (Temporary Restriction and Prohibition of Traffic) Order 2006 No. 2006/1987. - Enabling power: Road Traffic Regulation Act 1984, s. 14 (1) (a). - Made: 14.07.2006. Coming into force: 21.07.2006. Effect: None. Territorial extent & classification: E. Local *Unpublished*

The A40 Trunk Road (Denham Roundabout, Eastbound Slip Road) (Temporary Prohibition of Traffic) Order 2006 No. 2006/2254. - Enabling power: Road Traffic Regulation Act 1984, s. 14 (1) (a). - Made: 14.08.2006. Coming into force: 23.08.2006. Effect: None. Territorial extent & classification: E. Local *Unpublished*

The A40 Trunk Road (Huntley to Churcham, Gloucestershire) (Temporary Prohibition and Restriction of Traffic) Order 2006 No. 2006/454. - Enabling power: Road Traffic Regulation Act 1984, s. 14 (1) (a). - Made: 21.02.2006. Coming into force: 23.02.2006. Effect: None. Territorial extent & classification: E. Local *Unpublished*

The A40 Trunk Road (Longford Layby, Gloucester Northern Bypass) (Temporary Prohibition of Traffic) Order 2006 No. 2006/1610. - Enabling power: Road Traffic Regulation Act 1984, s. 14 (1) (a). - Made: 09.06.2006. Coming into force: 13.06.2006. Effect: None. Territorial extent & classification: E. Local *Unpublished*

The A40 Trunk Road (Over Roundabout to Elmbridge Roundabout, Gloucester) (Temporary Prohibition of Traffic) Order 2006 No. 2006/2457. - Enabling power: Road Traffic Regulation Act 1984, s. 14 (1) (a). - Made: 25.08.2006. Coming into force: 30.08.2006. Effect: None. Territorial extent & classification: E. Local *Unpublished*

The A40 Trunk Road (Wilton Roundabout to Overross Roundabout, Herefordshire) (Temporary Restriction and Prohibition of Traffic) Order 2006 No. 2006/13. - Enabling power: Road Traffic Regulation Act 1984, s. 14 (1) (a). - Made: 03.01.2006. Coming into force: 10.01.2006. Effect: None. Territorial extent & classification: E. Local *Unpublished*

The A42 Trunk Road (Ashby-de-la-Zouch) (Temporary Restriction and Prohibition of Traffic) Order 2006 No. 2006/2112. - Enabling power: Road Traffic Regulation Act 1984, s. 14 (1) (a). - Made: 24.07.2006. Coming into force: 31.07.2006. Effect: None. Territorial extent & classification: E. Local *Unpublished*

The A43 Trunk Road (Bandbrook, Near Whittlebury, Northamptonshire) (Temporary 40 Miles Per Hour Speed Restriction) Order 2006 No. 2006/2118. - Enabling power: Road Traffic Regulation Act 1984, s. 14 (1) (a). - Made: 24.07.2006. Coming into force: 31.07.2006. Effect: None. Territorial extent & classification: E. Local *Unpublished*

The A43 Trunk Road (Brackley and Evenley, Northamptonshire) (Temporary Restriction and Prohibition of Traffic) Order 2006 No. 2006/3486. - Enabling power: Road Traffic Regulation Act 1984, s. 14 (1) (a). - Made: 20.12.2006. Coming into force: 27.12.2006. Effect: None. Territorial extent & classification: E. Local *Unpublished*

The A43 Trunk Road (Brackley Hatch, Northamptonshire) (Prohibition of Waiting) Order 2006 No. 2006/327. - Enabling power: Road Traffic Regulation Act 1984, ss. 1 (1), 2 (1) (2), 4 (1) (2), sch. 9. - Made: 06.02.2006. Coming into force: 20.02.2006. Effect: None. Territorial extent & classification: E. Local *Unpublished*

The A43 Trunk Road (Buckingham Road Roundabout, Brackley, Northamptonshire) (Temporary Restriction and Prohibition of Traffic) Order 2006 No. 2006/2028. - Enabling power: Road Traffic Regulation Act 1984, s. 14 (1) (a). - Made: 07.07.2006. Coming into force: 14.07.2006. Effect: None. Territorial extent & classification: E. Local *Unpublished*

The A43 Trunk Road (Buckingham Road Roundabout - Whitfield Turn, Northamptonshire) (Temporary Restriction and Prohibition of Traffic) Order 2006 No. 2006/1825. - Enabling power: Road Traffic Regulation Act 1984, s. 14 (1) (a). - Made: 26.06.2006. Coming into force: 03.07.2006. Effect: None. Territorial extent & classification: E. Local *Unpublished*

The A43 Trunk Road (Evenley Roundabout, Brackley, Northamptonshire) (Temporary 50 Miles Per Hour Speed Restriction) Order 2006 No. 2006/2635. - Enabling power: Road Traffic Regulation Act 1984, s. 14 (1) (a). - Made: 26.09.2006. Coming into force: 03.10.2006. Effect: None. Territorial extent & classification: E. Local *Unpublished*

The A43 Trunk Road (Hazelborough, Northamptonshire) (Temporary Restriction and Prohibition of Traffic) Order 2006 No. 2006/2513. - Enabling power: Road Traffic Regulation Act 1984, s. 14 (1) (a). - Made: 05.09.2006. Coming into force: 12.09.2006. Effect: None. Territorial extent & classification: E. Local *Unpublished*

The A43 Trunk Road (M1 Motorway - Tove Roundabout, Northamptonshire) (Temporary Restriction and Prohibition of Traffic) Order 2006 No. 2006/2207. - Enabling power: Road Traffic Regulation Act 1984, s. 14 (1) (b). - Made: 04.08.2006. Coming into force: 11.08.2006. Effect: None. Territorial extent & classification: E. Local *Unpublished*

The A43 Trunk Road (Silverstone British Grand Prix, Brackley to Towcester, Northamptonshire) (Temporary Restriction and Prohibition of Traffic) Order 2006 No. 2006/1676. - Enabling power: Road Traffic Regulation Act 1984, s. 14 (1) (b). - Made: 26.05.2006. Coming into force: 02.06.2006. Effect: None. Territorial extent & classification: E. Local *Unpublished*

The A43 Trunk Road (Swan Valley Roundabout and Rothersthorpe Service Area, Northamptonshire) (Temporary Prohibition of Traffic) Order 2006 No. 2006/1138. - Enabling power: Road Traffic Regulation Act 1984, s. 14 (1) (a). - Made: 18.04.2006. Coming into force: 25.04.2006. Effect: None. Territorial extent & classification: E. Local *Unpublished*

The A43 Trunk Road (Tiffield and Blisworth Junctions, Northamptonshire) (Temporary Restriction and Prohibition of Traffic and Pedestrians) Order 2006 No. 2006/2512. - Enabling power: Road Traffic Regulation Act 1984, s. 14 (1) (a). - Made: 05.09.2006. Coming into force: 12.09.2006. Effect: None. Territorial extent & classification: E. Local *Unpublished*

Road traffic: Traffic regulation

The A43 Trunk Road (Towcester Bypass, Northamptonshire) (Temporary Restriction and Prohibition of Traffic) Order 2006 No. 2006/44. - Enabling power: Road Traffic Regulation Act 1984, s. 14 (1) (a). - Made: 09.01.2006. Coming into force: 16.01.2006. Effect: None. Territorial extent & classification: E. Local *Unpublished*

The A43 Trunk Road (Whitefield Layby, Northamptonshire) (Temporary Prohibition of Traffic) Order 2006 No. 2006/2057. - Enabling power: Road Traffic Regulation Act 1984, s. 14 (1) (a). - Made: 17.07.2006. Coming into force: 24.07.2006. Effect: None. Territorial extent & classification: E. Local *Unpublished*

The A43 Trunk Road (Whitfield Turn, Northamptonshire) (Temporary Restriction and Prohibition of Traffic) Order 2006 No. 2006/2288. - Enabling power: Road Traffic Regulation Act 1984, s. 14 (1) (a). - Made: 15.08.2006. Coming into force: 22.08.2006. Effect: None. Territorial extent & classification: E. Local *Unpublished*

The A43 Trunk Road (Whittlewood Bridge to Brackley Road Roundabout, Northamptonshire) (Temporary 40 Miles Per Hour Speed Restriction) Order 2006 No. 2006/2731. - Enabling power: Road Traffic Regulation Act 1984, ss. 14, 15. - Made: 27.09.2006. Coming into force: 04.10.2006. Effect: None. Territorial extent & classification: E. Local *Unpublished*

The A45 and A423 Trunk Roads (South of Coventry) (Temporary Restriction and Prohibition of Traffic) Order 2005 No. 2006/76. - Enabling power: Road Traffic Regulation Act 1984, s. 14 (1) (a). - Made: 06.01.2006. Coming into force: 13.01.2006. Effect: None. Territorial extent & classification: E. Local *Unpublished*

The A45 Trunk Road (Aggate Way Bridge, Earls Barton, Northamptonshire) (Temporary Restriction and Prohibition of Traffic) Order 2006 No. 2006/418. - Enabling power: Road Traffic Regulation Act 1984, s. 14 (1). - Made: 18.02.2006. Coming into force: 25.02.2006. Effect: None. Territorial extent & classification: E. Local *Unpublished*

The A45 Trunk Road (Barnes Meadow Interchange, Northamptonshire) Eastbound Entry Slip Road (Temporary Prohibition of Traffic) Order 2006 No. 2006/2507. - Enabling power: Road Traffic Regulation Act 1984, s. 14 (1) (a). - Made: 04.09.2006. Coming into force: 11.09.2006. Effect: None. Territorial extent & classification: E. Local *Unpublished*

The A45 Trunk Road (Brackmills Interchange to Queen Eleanor Interchange, Northamptonshire) (Temporary Prohibition of Traffic) Order 2006 No. 2006/432. - Enabling power: Road Traffic Regulation Act 1984, s. 14 (1) (a). - Made: 13.02.2006. Coming into force: 20.02.2006. Effect: None. Territorial extent & classification: E. Local *Unpublished*

The A45 Trunk Road (Brackmills to Queen Eleanor, Northamptonshire) (Temporary Restriction and Prohibition of Traffic) Order 2006 No. 2006/2056. - Enabling power: Road Traffic Regulation Act 1984, s. 14 (1) (a). - Made: 17.07.2006. Coming into force: 24.07.2006. Effect: None. Territorial extent & classification: E. Local *Unpublished*

The A45 Trunk Road (Ditchford Lane Bridge, Rushden, Northamptonshire) (Temporary Prohibition of Traffic) Order 2006 No. 2006/1829. - Enabling power: Road Traffic Regulation Act 1984, s. 14 (1) (a). - Made: 28.06.2006. Coming into force: 05.07.2006. Effect: None. Territorial extent & classification: E. Local *Unpublished*

The A45 Trunk Road (Festival Island, Coventry) (Temporary Prohibition of Traffic) Order 2006 No. 2006/2506. - Enabling power: Road Traffic Regulation Act 1984, s. 14 (1) (a). - Made: 01.09.2006. Coming into force: 08.09.2006. Effect: None. Territorial extent & classification: E. Local *Unpublished*

The A45 Trunk Road (Festival Island to Tollbar End, Coventry) (Temporary Restriction and Prohibition of Traffic) Order 2006 No. 2006/3010. - Enabling power: Road Traffic Regulation Act 1984, s. 14 (1) (a). - Made: 06.11.2006. Coming into force: 13.11.2006. Effect: None. Territorial extent & classification: E. Local *Unpublished*

The A45 Trunk Road (Festival Island to Tollbar End, Coventry) (Temporary Restriction and Prohibition of Traffic) Order 2006 No. 2006/1565. - Enabling power: Road Traffic Regulation Act 1984, s. 14 (1) (a). - Made: 22.05.2006. Coming into force: 29.05.2006. Effect: None. Territorial extent & classification: E. Local *Unpublished*

The A45 Trunk Road (Junction with the A452, Stonebridge) (Temporary Restriction and Prohibition of Traffic) Order 2006 No. 2006/1872. - Enabling power: Road Traffic Regulation Act 1984, s. 14 (1) (a). - Made: 30.06.2006. Coming into force: 07.07.2006. Effect: None. Territorial extent & classification: E. Local *Unpublished*

The A45 Trunk Road (Lumbertubs Interchange - Barnes Meadow Interchange, Northamptonshire) (Temporary Restriction and Prohibition of Traffic) Order 2006 No. 2006/1425. - Enabling power: Road Traffic Regulation Act 1984, s. 14 (1) (a). - Made: 23.05.2006. Coming into force: 30.05.2006. Effect: None. Territorial extent & classification: E. Local *Unpublished*

The A45 Trunk Road (M1 Junction 15 to Earls Barton, Northamptonshire) (Temporary Restriction and Prohibition of Traffic) Order 2006 No. 2006/3504. - Enabling power: Road Traffic Regulation Act 1984, s. 14 (1) (a). - Made: 29.12.2006. Coming into force: 05.01.2007. Effect: None. Territorial extent & classification: E. Local *Unpublished*

The A45 Trunk Road (M42 Junction 6) (Slip Road) (Temporary Prohibition of Traffic) Order 2006 No. 2006/1864. - Enabling power: Road Traffic Regulation Act 1984, s. 14 (1) (a). - Made: 30.07.2006. Coming into force: 07.07.2006. Effect: None. Territorial extent & classification: E. Local *Unpublished*

The A45 Trunk Road (Northamptonshire) (Temporary Variable Speed Limit) Order 2006 No. 2006/2996. - Enabling power: Road Traffic Regulation Act 1984, ss. 14, 15. - Made: 30.10.2006. Coming into force: 06.11.2006. Effect: None. Territorial extent & classification: E. Local *Unpublished*

The A45 Trunk Road (Queen Eleanor Interchange, Northamptonshire) (Temporary 40 Miles Per Hour Speed Restriction) Order 2006 No. 2006/167. - Enabling power: Road Traffic Regulation Act 1984, s. 14 (1) (a). - Made: 23.01.2006. Coming into force: 30.01.2006. Effect: None. Territorial extent & classification: E. Local *Unpublished*

The A45 Trunk Road (Raunds Roundabout to Stanwick Roundabout, Northamptonshire) (Temporary Restriction and Prohibition of Traffic) Order 2006 No. 2006/1636. - Enabling power: Road Traffic Regulation Act 1984, s. 14 (1) (a). - Made: 12.06.2006. Coming into force: 19.06.2006. Effect: None. Territorial extent & classification: E. Local *Unpublished*

The A45 Trunk Road (Ryton-on-Dunsmore, Warwickshire) (Temporary 40 Miles Per Hour Speed Restriction) Order 2006 No. 2006/2672. - Enabling power: Road Traffic Regulation Act 1984, s. 14 (1) (a). - Made: 22.09.2006. Coming into force: 29.09.2006. Effect: None. Territorial extent & classification: E. Local *Unpublished*

The A45 Trunk Road (Stretton-on-Dunsmore, Warwickshire) (Temporary Restriction and Prohibition of Traffic) Order 2006 No. 2006/1728. - Enabling power: Road Traffic Regulation Act 1984, s. 14 (1) (a). - Made: 26.06.2006. Coming into force: 03.07.2006. Effect: None. Territorial extent & classification: E. Local *Unpublished*

The A46 Trunk Road (A46/A607 Junction, Leicestershire) (Temporary Prohibition of Traffic) Order 2006 No. 2006/292. - Enabling power: Road Traffic Regulation Act 1984, s. 14 (1) (a). - Made: 03.02.2006. Coming into force: 10.02.2006. Effect: None. Territorial extent & classification: E. Local *Unpublished*

The A46 Trunk Road (Anstey, Leicestershire) (Slip Road) (Temporary Prohibition of Traffic) Order 2006 No. 2006/2514. - Enabling power: Road Traffic Regulation Act 1984, s. 14 (1) (a). - Made: 05.09.2006. Coming into force: 12.09.2006. Effect: None. Territorial extent & classification: E. Local *Unpublished*

The A46 Trunk Road (Anstey to M1 Junction 21A, Leicestershire) (Temporary Prohibition of Traffic) Order 2006 No. 2006/2576. - Enabling power: Road Traffic Regulation Act 1984, s. 14 (1) (a). - Made: 15.09.2006. Coming into force: 22.09.2006. Effect: None. Territorial extent & classification: E. Local *Unpublished*

The A46 Trunk Road (Between Broughton Lodge and Six Hills) (Temporary Prohibition of Traffic in Laybys) Order 2006 No. 2006/3192. - Enabling power: Road Traffic Regulation Act 1984, s. 14 (1) (a). - Made: 24.11.2006. Coming into force: 01.12.2006. Effect: None. Territorial extent & classification: E. Local *Unpublished*

The A46 Trunk Road (Car Colston, Nottinghamshire) (Temporary Restriction and Prohibition of Traffic) Order 2006 No. 2006/1651. - Enabling power: Road Traffic Regulation Act 1984, s. 14 (1) (a). - Made: 16.06.2006. Coming into force: 23.06.2006. Effect: None. Territorial extent & classification: E. Local *Unpublished*

The A46 Trunk Road (Carholme Roundabout, Lincolnshire) (Temporary Restriction of Traffic) Order 2006 No. 2006/2225. - Enabling power: Road Traffic Regulation Act 1984, s. 14 (1) (a). - Made: 31.07.2006. Coming into force: 07.08.2006. Effect: None. Territorial extent & classification: E. Local *Unpublished*

The A46 Trunk Road (Cold Ashton Roundabout, Near Bath) (Temporary Prohibition and Restriction of Traffic) Order 2006 No. 2006/2591. - Enabling power: Road Traffic Regulation Act 1984, s. 14 (1) (a). - Made: 12.09.2006. Coming into force: 15.09.2006. Effect: None. Territorial extent & classification: E. Local *Unpublished*

The A46 Trunk Road (Evesham Bypass, Worcestershire) (Temporary 10 Miles Per Hour and 40 Miles Per Hour Speed Restriction) (No. 2) Order 2006 No. 2006/666. - Enabling power: Road Traffic Regulation Act 1984, s. 14 (1) (a). - Made: 20.02.2006. Coming into force: 27.02.2006. Effect: None. Territorial extent & classification: E. Local *Unpublished*

The A46 Trunk Road (Evesham Bypass, Worcestershire) (Temporary 10 Miles Per Hour and 40 Miles Per Hour Speed Restriction) Order 2006 No. 2006/447. - Enabling power: Road Traffic Regulation Act 1984, s. 14 (1) (a). - Made: 15.02.2006. Coming into force: 22.02.2006. Effect: None. Territorial extent & classification: E. Local *Unpublished*

The A46 Trunk Road (Leicester Western Bypass) (Temporary Restriction and Prohibition of Traffic) Order 2006 No. 2006/725. - Enabling power: Road Traffic Regulation Act 1984, s. 14 (1) (a). - Made: 03.03.2006. Coming into force: 10.03.2006. Effect: None. Territorial extent & classification: E. Local *Unpublished*

The A46 Trunk Road (Marraway Roundabout, Northeast of Snitterfield, Warwickshire) (Temporary 10 Miles Per Hour and 40 Miles Per Hour Speed Restriction) Order 2006 No. 2006/671. - Enabling power: Road Traffic Regulation Act 1984, s. 14 (1) (a). - Made: 20.02.2006. Coming into force: 27.02.2006. Effect: None. Territorial extent & classification: E. Local *Unpublished*

The A46 Trunk Road (Near Swinderby, Lincolnshire) (Temporary Restriction and Prohibition of Traffic) Order 2006 No. 2006/2573. - Enabling power: Road Traffic Regulation Act 1984, s. 14 (1) (a). - Made: 15.09.2006. Coming into force: 22.09.2006. Effect: None. Territorial extent & classification: E. Local *Unpublished*

The A46 Trunk Road (Near Widmerpool, Nottinghamshire) (Temporary Restriction and Prohibition of Traffic) Order 2006 No. 2006/2038. - Enabling power: Road Traffic Regulation Act 1984, s. 14 (1) (a). - Made: 10.07.2006. Coming into force: 17.07.2006. Effect: None. Territorial extent & classification: E. Local *Unpublished*

The A46 Trunk Road (Newark-on-Trent, Nottinghamshire) (Temporary Restriction and Prohibition of Traffic) Order 2006 No. 2006/2398. - Enabling power: Road Traffic Regulation Act 1984, s. 14 (1) (a). - Made: 21.08.2006. Coming into force: 29.08.2006. Effect: None. Territorial extent & classification: E. Local *Unpublished*

The A46 Trunk Road (Pennsylvania) (Temporary Restriction of Traffic) Order 2006 No. 2006/456. - Enabling power: Road Traffic Regulation Act 1984, s. 14 (1) (a). - Made: 14.02.2006. Coming into force: 18.02.2006. Effect: None. Territorial extent & classification: E. Local *Unpublished*

The A46 Trunk Road (Pennsylvania to Nimlet, Near Cold Ashton) (Temporary Restriction of Traffic) Order 2006 No. 2006/2473. - Enabling power: Road Traffic Regulation Act 1984, s. 14 (1) (a). - Made: 05.09.2006. Coming into force: 08.09.2006. Effect: None. Territorial extent & classification: E. Local *Unpublished*

The A46 Trunk Road (Ratcliffe on the Wreake, Leicestershire) (Slip Road) (Temporary Prohibition of Traffic) Order 2006 No. 2006/1410. - Enabling power: Road Traffic Regulation Act 1984, s. 14 (1) (a). - Made: 17.05.2006. Coming into force: 24.05.2006. Effect: None. Territorial extent & classification: E. Local *Unpublished*

The A46 Trunk Road (Ratcliffe on the Wreake, Leicestershire) (Temporary Restriction and Prohibition of Traffic) Order 2006 No. 2006/2675. - Enabling power: Road Traffic Regulation Act 1984, s. 14 (1) (a). - Made: 22.09.2006. Coming into force: 29.09.2006. Effect: None. Territorial extent & classification: E. Local *Unpublished*

The A46 Trunk Road (Saxondale Roundabout to Widmerpool Roundabout, Nottinghamshire) (Temporary Prohibition of Traffic) Order 2006 No. 2006/3022. - Enabling power: Road Traffic Regulation Act 1984, s. 14 (1) (a). - Made: 10.11.2006. Coming into force: 17.11.2006. Effect: S.I. 2006/2843 amended. Territorial extent & classification: E. Local *Unpublished*

The A46 Trunk Road (Saxondale to Newark on Trent, Nottinghamshire) (Temporary Prohibition of Traffic) Order 2006 No. 2006/287. - Enabling power: Road Traffic Regulation Act 1984, s. 14 (1) (a). - Made: 03.02.2006. Coming into force: 10.02.2006. Effect: None. Territorial extent & classification: E. Local *Unpublished*

The A46 Trunk Road (Saxondale to Widmerpool, Nottinghamshire) (Temporary Prohibition of Traffic) Order 2006 No. 2006/724. - Enabling power: Road Traffic Regulation Act 1984, s. 14 (1) (a). - Made: 24.02.2006. Coming into force: 03.03.2006. Effect: None. Territorial extent & classification: E. Local *Unpublished*

The A46 Trunk Road (Six Hills, Charnwood, Leicestershire) (Closure of Gap in the Central Reservation) Order 2006 No. 2006/731. - Enabling power: Road Traffic Regulation Act 1984, ss. 1 (1), 2 (1) (2). - Made: 02.03.2006. Coming into force: 16.03.2006. Effect: None. Territorial extent & classification: E. Local *Unpublished*

The A46 Trunk Road (Six Hills to Widmerpool) (Temporary Restriction and Prohibition of Traffic) Order 2006 No. 2006/1140. - Enabling power: Road Traffic Regulation Act 1984, s. 14 (1) (a). - Made: 10.04.2006. Coming into force: 17.04.2006. Effect: None. Territorial extent & classification: E. Local *Unpublished*

The A46 Trunk Road (South West of Lincoln, Lincolnshire) (Temporary Restriction and Prohibition of Traffic) Order 2006 No. 2006/2571. - Enabling power: Road Traffic Regulation Act 1984, s. 14 (1) (a). - Made: 15.09.2006. Coming into force: 22.09.2006. Effect: None. Territorial extent & classification: E. Local *Unpublished*

The A46 Trunk Road (Stratford-upon-Avon Northern Bypass, Warwickshire) (Temporary Restriction and Prohibition of Traffic) Order 2006 No. 2006/71. - Enabling power: Road Traffic Regulation Act 1984, s. 14 (1) (a). - Made: 09.01.2006. Coming into force: 16.01.2006. Effect: None. Territorial extent & classification: E. Local *Unpublished*

The A46 Trunk Road (Temple Grafton, Warwickshire) (Temporary Prohibition and Restriction of Traffic) Order 2006 No. 2006/445. - Enabling power: Road Traffic Regulation Act 1984, s. 14 (1) (a). - Made: 15.02.2006. Coming into force: 22.02.2006. Effect: None. Territorial extent & classification: E. Local *Unpublished*

The A46 Trunk Road (Warwick Bypass) (Slip Road) (Temporary Prohibition of Traffic) Order 2006 No. 2006/3049. - Enabling power: Road Traffic Regulation Act 1984, s. 14 (1) (a). - Made: 23.10.2006. Coming into force: 30.10.2006. Effect: None. Territorial extent & classification: E. Local *Unpublished*

The A46 Trunk Road (Warwick Bypass, Warwickshire) (Temporary Restriction and Prohibition of Traffic) Order 2006 No. 2006/1142. - Enabling power: Road Traffic Regulation Act 1984, s. 14 (1) (a). - Made: 11.04.2006. Coming into force: 18.04.2006. Effect: None. Territorial extent & classification: E. Local *Unpublished*

The A46 Trunk Road (Willoughby-Widmerpool, Nottinghamshire) (Temporary Prohibition of Traffic) Order 2006 No. 2006/863. - Enabling power: Road Traffic Regulation Act 1984, s. 14 (1) (a). - Made: 17.03.2006. Coming into force: 24.03.2006. Effect: None. Territorial extent & classification: E. Local *Unpublished*

The A47 Trunk Road (Acle Straight, Norfolk) (Temporary Restriction and Prohibition of Traffic) Order 2006 No. 2006/2654. - Enabling power: Road Traffic Regulation Act 1984, s. 14 (1) (a). - Made: 25.09.2006. Coming into force: 02.10.2006. Effect: None. Territorial extent & classification: E. Local *Unpublished*

The A47 Trunk Road (Bretton Way Interchange - Paston Interchange, Soke Parkway, Peterborough) (Temporary Restriction and Prohibition of Traffic) Order 2006 No. 2006/2451. - Enabling power: Road Traffic Regulation Act 1984, s. 14 (1) (a). - Made: 29.09.2006. Coming into force: 05.09.2006. Effect: None. Territorial extent & classification: E. Local *Unpublished*

The A47 Trunk Road (City of Peterborough) (Temporary Restriction and Prohibition of Traffic) Order 2006 No. 2006/2163. - Enabling power: Road Traffic Regulation Act 1984, s. 14 (1) (a). - Made: 31.07.2006. Coming into force: 07.08.2006. Effect: None. Territorial extent & classification: E. Local *Unpublished*

The A47 Trunk Road (Elm, Wisbech, Cambridgeshire) (Temporary 10 Miles Per Hour and 40 Miles Per Hour Speed Restriction) Order 2006 No. 2006/2347. - Enabling power: Road Traffic Regulation Act 1984, s. 14 (1) (a). - Made: 16.08.2006. Coming into force: 23.08.2006. Effect: None. Territorial extent & classification: E. Local *Unpublished*

The A47 Trunk Road (Fulbridge Interchange to Dogsthorpe Interchange, Cambridge) (Temporary Restriction and Prohibition of Traffic) Order 2006 No. 2006/822. - Enabling power: Road Traffic Regulation Act 1984, s. 14 (1) (a). - Made: 10.03.2006. Coming into force: 17.03.2006. Effect: None. Territorial extent & classification: E. Local *Unpublished*

The A47 Trunk Road (Hardwick Roundabout, Kings Lynn Bypass, Norfolk) (Temporary Prohibition of Traffic) Order 2006 No. 2006/549. - Enabling power: Road Traffic Regulation Act 1984, s. 14 (1) (a). - Made: 27.02.2006. Coming into force: 08.03.2006. Effect: None. Territorial extent & classification: E. Local *Unpublished*

The A47 Trunk Road (Middleton Village, Kings Lynn, Norfolk) (Temporary Prohibition of Traffic) Order 2006 No. 2006/2482. - Enabling power: Road Traffic Regulation Act 1984, s. 14 (1) (a). - Made: 04.09.2006. Coming into force: 11.09.2006. Effect: None. Territorial extent & classification: E. Local *Unpublished*

The A47 Trunk Road (North Pickenham, Norfolk) (Temporary Restriction and Prohibition of Traffic) Order 2006 No. 2006/2868. - Enabling power: Road Traffic Regulation Act 1984, s. 14 (1) (a). - Made: 18.10.2006. Coming into force: 25.10.2006. Effect: None. Territorial extent & classification: E. Local *Unpublished*

The A47 Trunk Road (Norwich Southern Bypass, Norfolk) (Temporary Restriction and Prohibition of Traffic) Order 2006 No. 2006/83. - Enabling power: Road Traffic Regulation Act 1984, s. 14 (1) (a). - Made: 16.01.2006. Coming into force: 23.01.2006. Effect: None. Territorial extent & classification: E. Local *Unpublished*

The A47 Trunk Road (Peterborough, Cambridgeshire) (Temporary Restriction and Prohibition of Traffic) Order 2006 No. 2006/164. - Enabling power: Road Traffic Regulation Act 1984, s. 14 (1). - Made: 23.01.2006. Coming into force: 30.01.2006. Effect: None. Territorial extent & classification: E. Local *Unpublished*

The A47 Trunk Road (Saddlebow Interchange to Pullover Interchange, Kings Lynn, Norfolk) (Temporary Restriction and Prohibition of Traffic) Order 2006 No. 2006/166. - Enabling power: Road Traffic Regulation Act 1984, s. 14 (1) (a). - Made: 23.01.2006. Coming into force: 30.01.2006. Effect: None. Territorial extent & classification: E. Local *Unpublished*

The A47 Trunk Road (Swaffham, Norfolk) (Temporary Restriction and Prohibition of Traffic) Order 2006 No. 2006/2477. - Enabling power: Road Traffic Regulation Act 1984, s. 14 (1) (a). - Made: 04.09.2006. Coming into force: 11.09.2006. Effect: None. Territorial extent & classification: E. Local *Unpublished*

The A47 Trunk Road (Thorney Toll to Guyhirn, Cambridgeshire) (Temporary Restriction and Prohibition of Traffic) Order 2006 No. 2006/2449. - Enabling power: Road Traffic Regulation Act 1984, s. 14 (1) (a). - Made: 04.09.2006. Coming into force: 11.09.2006. Effect: None. Territorial extent & classification: E. Local *Unpublished*

The A47 Trunk Road (Wansford, City of Peterborough) (Temporary Prohibition of Traffic) Order 2006 No. 2006/2121. - Enabling power: Road Traffic Regulation Act 1984, s. 14 (1) (a). - Made: 24.07.2006. Coming into force: 31.07.2006. Effect: None. Territorial extent & classification: E. Local *Unpublished*

The A47 Trunk Road (Wisbech Level Crossing, Cambridgeshire) (Temporary Prohibition of Traffic) Order 2006 No. 2006/808. - Enabling power: Road Traffic Regulation Act 1984, s. 14 (1) (a). - Made: 13.03.2006. Coming into force: 20.03.2006. Effect: None. Territorial extent & classification: E. Local *Unpublished*

The A49 Trunk Road (Brimfield, Herefordshire) (Temporary Restriction and Prohibition of Traffic) Order 2006 No. 2006/2250. - Enabling power: Road Traffic Regulation Act 1984, s. 14 (1) (a). - Made: 04.08.2006. Coming into force: 11.08.2006. Effect: None. Territorial extent & classification: E. Local *Unpublished*

The A49 Trunk Road (Bromfield to Craven Arms, Shropshire) (Temporary Prohibition of Traffic) Order 2006 No. 2006/2039. - Enabling power: Road Traffic Regulation Act 1984, s. 14 (1) (a). - Made: 10.07.2006. Coming into force: 17.07.2006. Effect: None. Territorial extent & classification: E. Local *Unpublished*

The A49 Trunk Road (Greyfriars Bridge, Hereford) (Temporary Prohibition of Traffic) Order 2006 No. 2006/668. - Enabling power: Road Traffic Regulation Act 1984, s. 14 (1) (a). - Made: 20.02.2006. Coming into force: 27.02.2006. Effect: None. Territorial extent & classification: E. Local *Unpublished*

The A49 Trunk Road (Harewood End to Much Birch, Herefordshire) (Temporary 10 Miles Per Hour Speed Restriction) Order 2006 No. 2006/1307. - Enabling power: Road Traffic Regulation Act 1984, s. 14 (1) (a). - Made: 01.05.2006. Coming into force: 08.05.2006. Effect: None. Territorial extent & classification: E. Local *Unpublished*

The A49 Trunk Road (Hereford) (Temporary Prohibition of Right Turns) Order 2006 No. 2006/2253. - Enabling power: Road Traffic Regulation Act 1984, s. 14 (1) (a). - Made: 10.08.2006. Coming into force: 17.08.2006. Effect: None. Territorial extent & classification: E. Local *Unpublished*

The A49 Trunk Road (Hope under Dinmore to Hereford) (Temporary Prohibition of Traffic) Order 2006 No. 2006/2046. - Enabling power: Road Traffic Regulation Act 1984, s. 14 (1) (a). - Made: 10.07.2006. Coming into force: 17.07.2006. Effect: None. Territorial extent & classification: E. Local *Unpublished*

The A49 Trunk Road (Kings Thorn, Herefordshire) (Temporary 10 Miles Per Hour Speed Limit) (No. 2) Order 2006 No. 2006/1656. - Enabling power: Road Traffic Regulation Act 1984, s. 14 (1) (a). - Made: 12.06.2006. Coming into force: 19.06.2006. Effect: None. Territorial extent & classification: E. Local *Unpublished*

The A49 Trunk Road (Kings Thorn, Herefordshire) (Temporary 10 Miles Per Hour Speed Limit) Order 2006 No. 2006/10. - Enabling power: Road Traffic Regulation Act 1984, s. 14 (1) (a). - Made: 03.01.2006. Coming into force: 10.01.2006. Effect: None. Territorial extent & classification: E. Local *Unpublished*

The A49 Trunk Road (Leominster, Herefordshire) (Temporary Restriction and Prohibition of Traffic) Order 2006 No. 2006/2397. - Enabling power: Road Traffic Regulation Act 1984, s. 14 (1) (a). - Made: 14.08.2006. Coming into force: 21.08.2006. Effect: None. Territorial extent & classification: E. Local *Unpublished*

The A49 Trunk Road (Longnor, Shropshire) (Temporary 10 Miles Per Hour Speed Restriction) (No. 2) Order 2006 No. 2006/1781. - Enabling power: Road Traffic Regulation Act 1984, s. 14 (1) (a). - Made: 19.06.2006. Coming into force: 26.06.2006. Effect: None. Territorial extent & classification: E. Local *Unpublished*

The A49 Trunk Road (Longnor, Shropshire) (Temporary 10 Miles Per Hour Speed Restriction) Order 2006 No. 2006/528. - Enabling power: Road Traffic Regulation Act 1984, s. 14 (1) (a). - Made: 30.01.2006. Coming into force: 06.02.2006. Effect: None. Territorial extent & classification: E. Local *Unpublished*

The A49 Trunk Road (North of Ludlow, Shropshire) (Temporary 10 Miles Per Hour Speed Restriction) (No. 2) Order 2006 No. 2006/1773. - Enabling power: Road Traffic Regulation Act 1984, s. 14 (1) (a). - Made: 23.06.2006. Coming into force: 30.06.2006. Effect: None. Territorial extent & classification: E. Local *Unpublished*

The A49 Trunk Road (North of Ludlow, Shropshire) (Temporary 10 Miles Per Hour Speed Restriction) Order 2006 No. 2006/271. - Enabling power: Road Traffic Regulation Act 1984, s. 14 (1) (a). - Made: 23.01.2006. Coming into force: 30.01.2006. Effect: None. Territorial extent & classification: E. Local *Unpublished*

The A49 Trunk Road (Onibury Bridge, Shropshire) (Temporary Prohibition of Traffic) Order 2006 No. 2006/3003. - Enabling power: Road Traffic Regulation Act 1984, s. 14 (1) (a). - Made: 30.10.2006. Coming into force: 06.11.2006. Effect: None. Territorial extent & classification: E. Local *Unpublished*

The A49 Trunk Road (Poolmill - Bridstow, Herefordshire) (Temporary 10 Miles Per Hour Speed Limit) Order 2006 No. 2006/729. - Enabling power: Road Traffic Regulation Act 1984, s. 14 (1) (a). - Made: 07.03.2006. Coming into force: 14.03.2006. Effect: None. Territorial extent & classification: E. Local *Unpublished*

The A49 Trunk Road (Strefford, Shropshire) (Temporary 10 Miles Per Hour Speed Restriction) Order 2006 No. 2006/270. - Enabling power: Road Traffic Regulation Act 1984, s. 14 (1) (a). - Made: 23.01.2006. Coming into force: 30.01.2006. Effect: None. Territorial extent & classification: E. Local *Unpublished*

The A49 Trunk Road (Wellington to Moreton on Lugg, Herefordshire) (Temporary 10 Miles Per Hour Speed Restriction) Order 2006 No. 2006/1241. - Enabling power: Road Traffic Regulation Act 1984, s. 14 (1) (a). - Made: 24.04.2006. Coming into force: 01.05.2006. Effect: None. Territorial extent & classification: E. Local *Unpublished*

The A49 Trunk Road (Wistanstow, Shropshire) (Temporary 10 Miles Per Hour Speed Restriction) Order 2006 No. 2006/3489. - Enabling power: Road Traffic Regulation Act 1984, s. 14 (1) (a). - Made: 27.12.2006. Coming into force: 03.01.2007. Effect: None. Territorial extent & classification: E. Local *Unpublished*

The A49 Trunk Road (Wistanstow, Shropshire) (Temporary 10 Miles Per Hour Speed Restriction) Order 2006 No. 2006/273. - Enabling power: Road Traffic Regulation Act 1984, s. 14 (1) (a). - Made: 16.01.2006. Coming into force: 23.01.2006. Effect: None. Territorial extent & classification: E. Local *Unpublished*

The A49 Trunk Road (Woofferton, Shropshire) (Temporary 10 Miles Per Hour Speed Restriction) Order 2006 No. 2006/2020. - Enabling power: Road Traffic Regulation Act 1984, s. 14 (1) (a). - Made: 17.07.2006. Coming into force: 24.07.2006. Effect: None. Territorial extent & classification: E. Local *Unpublished*

The A50 Trunk Road (A6 Spur, Derbyshire) (Slip Roads) (Temporary Prohibition of Traffic) Order 2006 No. 2006/1022. - Enabling power: Road Traffic Regulation Act 1984, s. 14 (1) (a). - Made: 24.03.2006. Coming into force: 31.03.2006. Effect: None. Territorial extent & classification: E. Local *Unpublished*

The A50 Trunk Road (Blythe Bridge to Uttoxeter, Staffordshire) (Temporary 40 Miles Per Hour Speed Restriction) Order 2006 No. 2006/1867. - Enabling power: Road Traffic Regulation Act 1984, s. 14 (1) (a). - Made: 30.06.2006. Coming into force: 07.07.2006. Effect: None. Territorial extent & classification: E. Local *Unpublished*

The A50 Trunk Road (Chellaston, Derbyshire) (Slip Road) (Temporary Prohibition of Traffic) Order 2006 No. 2006/2511. - Enabling power: Road Traffic Regulation Act 1984, s. 14 (1) (a). - Made: 25.08.2006. Coming into force: 01.09.2006. Effect: None. Territorial extent & classification: E. Local *Unpublished*

The A50 Trunk Road (Church Street, Lockington, Leicestershire) (Prohibition of Traffic Movements) Order 2006 No. 2006/1144. - Enabling power: Road Traffic Regulation Act 1984, ss. 1 (1), 2 (1) (2), 122A. - Made: 10.04.2006. Coming into force: 24.04.2006. Effect: None. Territorial extent & classification: E. Local *Unpublished*

The A50 Trunk Road (Derbyshire) (Temporary Prohibition of Traffic in Laybys) Order 2006 No. 2006/2113. - Enabling power: Road Traffic Regulation Act 1984, s. 14 (1) (a). - Made: 21.07.2006. Coming into force: 28.07.2006. Effect: None. Territorial extent & classification: E. Local *Unpublished*

The A50 Trunk Road (Doveridge Bypass) (Temporary Prohibition of Traffic) Order 2006 No. 2006/3057. - Enabling power: Road Traffic Regulation Act 1984, s. 14 (1) (a). - Made: 13.10.2006. Coming into force: 20.10.2006. Effect: None. Territorial extent & classification: E. Local *Unpublished*

The A50 Trunk Road (Doveridge, Derbyshire) (Temporary Prohibition of Traffic) Order 2006 No. 2006/1368. - Enabling power: Road Traffic Regulation Act 1984, s. 14 (1) (a). - Made: 05.05.2006. Coming into force: 12.05.2006. Effect: None. Territorial extent & classification: E. Local *Unpublished*

The A50 Trunk Road (Etwall, Derbyshire) (Temporary Prohibition of Traffic) Order 2006 No. 2006/1561. - Enabling power: Road Traffic Regulation Act 1984, s. 14 (1) (a). - Made: 26.05.2006. Coming into force: 02.06.2006. Effect: None. Territorial extent & classification: E. Local *Unpublished*

The A50 Trunk Road (Etwall, Derbyshire) (Temporary Restriction and Prohibition of Traffic) Order 2006 No. 2006/3458. - Enabling power: Road Traffic Regulation Act 1984, s. 14 (1) (a). - Made: 20.12.2006. Coming into force: 27.12.2006. Effect: None. Territorial extent & classification: E. Local *Unpublished*

The A50 Trunk Road (Findern, Derbyshire) (Temporary Restriction and Prohibition of Traffic) Order 2006 No. 2006/3480. - Enabling power: Road Traffic Regulation Act 1984, s. 14 (1) (a). - Made: 22.12.2006. Coming into force: 29.12.2006. Effect: None. Territorial extent & classification: E. Local *Unpublished*

The A50 Trunk Road (Foston, Derbyshire) (Temporary Prohibition of Traffic) Order 2006 No. 2006/3008. - Enabling power: Road Traffic Regulation Act 1984, s. 14 (1) (a). - Made: 06.11.2006. Coming into force: 13.11.2006. Effect: None. Territorial extent & classification: E. Local *Unpublished*

The A50 Trunk Road (Grindley Lane Interchange, Staffordshire) (Temporary Prohibition and Restriction of Traffic) Order 2006 No. 2006/2746. - Enabling power: Road Traffic Regulation Act 1984, s. 14 (1) (a). - Made: 06.10.2006. Coming into force: 13.10.2006. Effect: None. Territorial extent & classification: E. Local *Unpublished*

The A50 Trunk Road (Junction with Blurton Road, Stoke on Trent) (Temporary Prohibition of Traffic) Order 2006 No. 2006/1726. - Enabling power: Road Traffic Regulation Act 1984, s. 14 (1) (a). - Made: 26.06.2006. Coming into force: 03.07.2006. Effect: None. Territorial extent & classification: E. Local *Unpublished*

The A50 Trunk Road (Junction with the A6, Aston-on-Trent) (Temporary Prohibition of Traffic) Order 2006 No. 2006/2114. - Enabling power: Road Traffic Regulation Act 1984, s. 14 (1) (a). - Made: 24.07.2006. Coming into force: 31.07.2006. Effect: None. Territorial extent & classification: E. Local *Unpublished*

The A50 Trunk Road (Junction with the A6, Near Chellaston) (Temporary Prohibition of Traffic) Order 2006 No. 2006/2871. - Enabling power: Road Traffic Regulation Act 1984, s. 14 (1) (a). - Made: 16.10.2006. Coming into force: 23.10.2006. Effect: None. Territorial extent & classification: E. Local *Unpublished*

The A50 Trunk Road (Lockington Roundabout, Leicestershire) (Temporary 40 Miles Per Hour Speed Restriction) Order 2006 No. 2006/2018. - Enabling power: Road Traffic Regulation Act 1984, s. 14 (1) (a). - Made: 17.07.2006. Coming into force: 24.07.2006. Effect: None. Territorial extent & classification: E. Local *Unpublished*

The A50 Trunk Road (Meir, Stoke-on-Trent) (Footway) (Temporary Prohibition of Traffic and Pedestrians) Order 2006 No. 2006/1556. - Enabling power: Road Traffic Regulation Act 1984, s. 14 (1) (a). - Made: 30.05.2006. Coming into force: 06.06.2006. Effect: None. Territorial extent & classification: E. Local *Unpublished*

The A50 Trunk Road (Meir Tunnel, Stoke-on-Trent) (Temporary Prohibition of Traffic) Order 2006 No. 2006/820. - Enabling power: Road Traffic Regulation Act 1984, s. 14 (1) (a). - Made: 03.03.2006. Coming into force: 10.03.2006. Effect: None. Territorial extent & classification: E. Local *Unpublished*

The A50 Trunk Road (Near Chellaston, Derbyshire) (Temporary Prohibition of Traffic) Order 2006 No. 2006/2111. - Enabling power: Road Traffic Regulation Act 1984, s. 14 (1) (a). - Made: 24.07.2006. Coming into force: 31.07.2006. Effect: None. Territorial extent & classification: E. Local *Unpublished*

The A50 Trunk Road (Sideway to Heron Cross, Stoke-on-Trent) (Temporary Prohibition of Traffic) Order 2006 No. 2006/1554. - Enabling power: Road Traffic Regulation Act 1984, s. 14 (1) (a). - Made: 22.05.2006. Coming into force: 29.05.2006. Effect: None. Territorial extent & classification: E. Local *Unpublished*

The A50 Trunk Road (Stoke on Trent) (Temporary Restriction and Prohibition of Traffic) Order 2006 No. 2006/2564. - Enabling power: Road Traffic Regulation Act 1984, s. 14 (1) (a). - Made: 18.09.2006. Coming into force: 25.09.2006. Effect: None. Territorial extent & classification: E. Local *Unpublished*

The A50 Trunk Road (Uttoxeter to Stoke-on-Trent, Staffordshire) (Temporary Prohibition of Traffic) Order 2006 No. 2006/2021. - Enabling power: Road Traffic Regulation Act 1984, s. 14 (1) (a). - Made: 18.07.2006. Coming into force: 25.07.2006. Effect: None. Territorial extent & classification: E. Local *Unpublished*

The A50 Trunk Road (West Broughton, Derbyshire) (Temporary Prohibition of Traffic) Order 2006 No. 2006/281. - Enabling power: Road Traffic Regulation Act 1984, s. 14 (1) (a). - Made: 30.01.2006. Coming into force: 06.02.2006. Effect: None. Territorial extent & classification: E. Local *Unpublished*

The A52 and A453 Trunk Roads (Clifton Lane, Nottingham) (Slip Roads) (Temporary Prohibition of Traffic) Order 2006 No. 2006/74. - Enabling power: Road Traffic Regulation Act 1984, s. 14 (1) (a). - Made: 09.01.2006. Coming into force: 16.01.2006. Effect: None. Territorial extent & classification: E. Local *Unpublished*

The A52 and A453 Trunk Roads (Silverdale Roundabout, Nottinghamshire) (Temporary Prohibition of Traffic) Order 2006 No. 2006/3231. - Enabling power: Road Traffic Regulation Act 1984, s. 14 (1) (a). - Made: 01.12.2006. Coming into force: 08.12.2006. Effect: None. Territorial extent & classification: E. Local *Unpublished*

The A52 Trunk Road (Bardills Roundabout, Stapleford, Nottinghamshire) (Temporary Prohibition of Traffic) Order 2006 No. 2006/3479. - Enabling power: Road Traffic Regulation Act 1984, s. 14 (1) (a). - Made: 22.12.2006. Coming into force: 29.12.2006. Effect: None. Territorial extent & classification: E. Local *Unpublished*

The A52 Trunk Road (Beeston, Nottinghamshire) (Temporary Restriction and Prohibition of Traffic) Order 2006 No. 2006/1771. - Enabling power: Road Traffic Regulation Act 1984, s. 14 (1) (a). - Made: 19.06.2006. Coming into force: 26.06.2006. Effect: None. Territorial extent & classification: E. Local *Unpublished*

The A52 Trunk Road (Bingham, Nottinghamshire) (Temporary Prohibition and Restriction of Traffic) Order 2006 No. 2006/3205. - Enabling power: Road Traffic Regulation Act 1984, s. 14 (1) (a). - Made: 27.11.2006. Coming into force: 04.12.2006. Effect: None. Territorial extent & classification: E. Local *Unpublished*

The A52 Trunk Road (Borrowash Bypass, Derbyshire) (Temporary 40 Miles Per Hour Speed Restriction) Order 2006 No. 2006/2520. - Enabling power: Road Traffic Regulation Act 1984, s. 14 (1) (a). - Made: 25.08.2006. Coming into force: 01.09.2006. Effect: None. Territorial extent & classification: E. Local *Unpublished*

The A52 Trunk Road (Bottesford Bypass) (Temporary Restriction of Traffic) Order 2006 No. 2006/1589. - Enabling power: Road Traffic Regulation Act 1984, s. 14 (1) (a). - Made: 05.06.2006. Coming into force: 12.06.2006. Effect: None. Territorial extent & classification: E. Local *Unpublished*

The A52 Trunk Road (Bottesford to Sedgebrook) (Temporary Prohibition of Traffic) 2006 No. 2006/195. - Enabling power: Road Traffic Regulation Act 1984, s. 14 (1) (a). - Made: 23.01.2006. Coming into force: 30.01.2006. Effect: None. Territorial extent & classification: E. Local *Unpublished*

The A52 Trunk Road (Bottesford to Sedgebrook) (Temporary Prohibition of Traffic) Order 2006 No. 2006/2577. - Enabling power: Road Traffic Regulation Act 1984, s. 14 (1) (a). - Made: 15.09.2006. Coming into force: 22.09.2006. Effect: None. Territorial extent & classification: E. Local *Unpublished*

The A52 Trunk Road (Bramcote Island, Nottinghamshire) (Temporary Restriction and Prohibition of Traffic) Order 2006 No. 2006/2116. - Enabling power: Road Traffic Regulation Act 1984, s. 14 (1) (a). - Made: 21.07.2006. Coming into force: 28.07.2006. Effect: None. Territorial extent & classification: E. Local *Unpublished*

The A52 Trunk Road (Derby Road, Nottingham) (Bus/Cycle Lane) (Temporary Suspension of Statutory Provisions) Order 2006 No. 2006/2403. - Enabling power: Road Traffic Regulation Act 1984, s. 14 (1) (a) (7). - Made: 22.08.2006. Coming into force: 29.08.2006. Effect: None. Territorial extent & classification: E. Local *Unpublished*

The A52 Trunk Road (Muston, Leicestershire) (Temporary 40 Miles Per Hour Speed Restriction) Order 2006 No. 2006/421. - Enabling power: Road Traffic Regulation Act 1984, s. 14 (1) (a). - Made: 13.02.2006. Coming into force: 20.02.2006. Effect: None. Territorial extent & classification: E. Local *Unpublished*

The A52 Trunk Road (Near Radcliffe-on-Trent, Nottinghamshire) (Temporary 50 Miles Per Hour Speed Restriction) Order 2006 No. 2006/3481. - Enabling power: Road Traffic Regulation Act 1984, s. 14 (1) (a). - Made: 22.12.2006. Coming into force: 29.12.2006. Effect: None. Territorial extent & classification: E. Local *Unpublished*

The A52 Trunk Road (Nottingham Knight Roundabout to Wheatcroft Roundabout, Nottinghamshire) (Temporary Restriction and Prohibition of Traffic) Order 2006 No. 2006/2744. - Enabling power: Road Traffic Regulation Act 1984, s. 14 (1) (a). - Made: 09.10.2006. Coming into force: 16.10.2006. Effect: None. Territorial extent & classification: E. Local *Unpublished*

The A52 Trunk Road (Queens Medical Centre Roundabout, Nottingham) (Temporary Prohibition of Traffic and Pedestrians) Order 2006 No. 2006/2222. - Enabling power: Road Traffic Regulation Act 1984, s. 14 (1) (a). - Made: 28.07.2006. Coming into force: 04.08.2006. Effect: None. Territorial extent & classification: E. Local *Unpublished*

The A52 Trunk Road (Risley, Derbyshire) (Temporary 40 Miles Per Hour Speed Restriction) Order 2006 No. 2006/2508. - Enabling power: Road Traffic Regulation Act 1984, s. 14 (1) (a). - Made: 01.09.2006. Coming into force: 08.09.2006. Effect: None. Territorial extent & classification: E. Local *Unpublished*

The A52 Trunk Road (Saxondale, Nottinghamshire) (Temporary 40 Miles Per Hour Speed Restriction) Order 2006 No. 2006/325. - Enabling power: Road Traffic Regulation Act 1984, s. 14 (1) (a). - Made: 06.02.2006. Coming into force: 13.02.2006. Effect: None. Territorial extent & classification: E. Local *Unpublished*

The A52 Trunk Road (Stapleford, Nottinghamshire) (Temporary Prohibition of Traffic) Order 2006 No. 2006/2872. - Enabling power: Road Traffic Regulation Act 1984, s. 14 (1) (a). - Made: 16.10.2006. Coming into force: 23.10.2006. Effect: None. Territorial extent & classification: E. Local *Unpublished*

The A52 Trunk Road (Stapleford) (Temporary Prohibition of Traffic) Order 2006 No. 2006/1017. - Enabling power: Road Traffic Regulation Act 1984, s. 14 (1) (a). - Made: 24.03.2006. Coming into force: 31.03.2006. Effect: None. Territorial extent & classification: E. Local *Unpublished*

The A55 Trunk Road (Junctions with A51 and A56 and Access Slip Road from A51) (Temporary Prohibition of Traffic) Order 2006 No. 2006/1675. - Enabling power: Road Traffic Regulation Act 1984, s. 14 (1) (a). - Made: 19.05.2006. Coming into force: 18.06.2006. Effect: None. Territorial extent & classification: E. Local *Unpublished*

The A55 Trunk Road (Northbound Entry Slip Road from the A51 at Vicars Cross) (Temporary Prohibition of Traffic) Order 2006 No. 2006/1150. - Enabling power: Road Traffic Regulation Act 1984, s. 14 (1) (a). - Made: 17.04.2006. Coming into force: 11.05.2006. Effect: None. Territorial extent & classification: E. Local *Unpublished*

The A55 Trunk Road (Southbound Entry Slip Road at Junction 12, M53) (Temporary Prohibition of Traffic) Order 2006 No. 2006/1437. - Enabling power: Road Traffic Regulation Act 1984, s. 14 (1) (a). - Made: 19.05.2006. Coming into force: 19.06.2006. Effect: None. Territorial extent & classification: E. Local *Unpublished*

The A56 Trunk Road (Northbound Exit Slip Road to the A679) (Temporary Prohibition of Traffic) Order 2006 No. 2006/2516. - Enabling power: Road Traffic Regulation Act 1984, s. 14 (1) (a). - Made: 04.09.2006. Coming into force: 28.09.2006. Effect: None. Territorial extent & classification: E. Local *Unpublished*

The A56 Trunk Road (Southbound Carriageway and Entry Slip Road from the A680) (Temporary Prohibition of Traffic) Order 2006 No. 2006/2736. - Enabling power: Road Traffic Regulation Act 1984, s. 14 (1) (a). - Made: 04.09.2006. Coming into force: 28.09.2006. Effect: None. Territorial extent & classification: E. Local *Unpublished*

The A57 Trunk Road (Market Street Junction, Mottram) (Temporary 10 Miles Per Hour Speed Restriction) Order 2006 No. 2006/850. - Enabling power: Road Traffic Regulation Act 1984, s. 14 (1) (a). - Made: 15.03.2006. Coming into force: 19.03.2006. Effect: None. Territorial extent & classification: E. Local *Unpublished*

The A59 and A5036 Trunk Roads (Switch Island) (Prohibition of Traffic, Clearway, Prohibition of Pedestrians and Unsegregated Footway/cycle Track) Order 2006 No. 2006/721. - Enabling power: Road Traffic Regulation Act 1984, ss. 1 (1), 2 (1) (2), 4 (1), 122A, sch. 9, para. 27 (1). - Made: 07.03.2006. Coming into force: 18.03.2006. Effect: None. Territorial extent & classification: E. Local *Unpublished*

The A61 Trunk Road (M1 Motorway to Westwood Roundabout) (Temporary Restriction and Prohibition of Traffic) Order 2006 No. 2006/1580. - Enabling power: Road Traffic Regulation Act 1984, s. 14 (1) (a). - Made: 13.06.2006. Coming into force: 25.06.2006. Effect: None. Territorial extent & classification: E. Local *Unpublished*

The A63 Trunk Road (Austhorpe Interchange Roundabout) (Temporary Prohibition of Traffic) Order 2006 No. 2006/2750. - Enabling power: Road Traffic Regulation Act 1984, s. 14 (1) (a). - Made: 09.10.2006. Coming into force: 22.10.2006. Effect: None. Territorial extent & classification: E. Local *Unpublished*

The A63 Trunk Road (Daltry Street Interchange to Mytongate Roundabout) (Temporary Prohibition of Traffic) Order 2006 No. 2006/2567. - Enabling power: Road Traffic Regulation Act 1984, s. 14 (1) (a). - Made: 15.09.2006. Coming into force: 24.09.2006. Effect: None. Territorial extent & classification: E. Local *Unpublished*

The A63 Trunk Road (Lowfield Lane Junction, Welton) (Temporary Prohibition of Traffic) Order 2006 No. 2006/938. - Enabling power: Road Traffic Regulation Act 1984, s. 14 (1) (b). - Made: 24.03.2006. Coming into force: 05.04.2006. Effect: None. Territorial extent & classification: E. Local *Unpublished*

The A63 Trunk Road (Lowfield Lane, Welton) (Prohibition of Use of Gap In Central Reservation) Order 2006 No. 2006/3001. - Enabling power: Road Traffic Regulation Act 1984, ss. 1 (1), 2 (1) (2). - Made: 01.11.2006. Coming into force: 06.11.2006. Effect: None. Territorial extent & classification: E. Local *Unpublished*

The A63 Trunk Road (Melton) (Prohibition of Use of Gaps in the Central Reservation) Order 2006 No. 2006/2193. - Enabling power: Road Traffic Regulation Act 1984, s. 1 (1), 2 (1) (2). - Made: 02.08.2006. Coming into force: 1408.2006. Effect: None. Territorial extent & classification: E. Local *Unpublished*

The A63 Trunk Road (Melton to North Ferriby) (Temporary 40 Miles Per Hour Speed Restriction) Order 2005 Amendment Order 2006 No. 2006/193. - Enabling power: Road Traffic Regulation Act 1984, s. 14 (1) (a). - Made: 11.01.2006. Coming into force: 26.01.2006. Effect: None. Territorial extent & classification: E. Local *Unpublished*

The A63 Trunk Road (Myton Bridge) (Temporary Prohibition of Traffic) Order 2006 No. 2006/1023. - Enabling power: Road Traffic Regulation Act 1984, s. 14 (1) (a). - Made: 28.03.2006. Coming into force: 08.04.2006. Effect: None. Territorial extent & classification: E. Local *Unpublished*

Road traffic: Traffic regulation

The A63 Trunk Road (North Cave Interchange, Westbound Exit Slip Road) (Temporary 40 Miles Per Hour Speed Restriction) Order 2006 No. 2006/2103. - Enabling power: Road Traffic Regulation Act 1984, s. 14 (1) (a). - Made: 25.07.2006. Coming into force: 06.08.2006. Effect: None. Territorial extent & classification: E. Local *Unpublished*

The A63 Trunk Road (Priory Way Junction) (Temporary Restriction and Prohibition of Traffic) Order 2006 No. 2006/3493. - Enabling power: Road Traffic Regulation Act 1984, s. 14 (1) (a). - Made: 29.12.2006. Coming into force: 07.01.2007. Effect: None. Territorial extent & classification: E. Local *Unpublished*

The A63 Trunk Road (Queen Street/Market Place Junction, Hull) (Temporary Prohibition of Traffic) Order 2006 No. 2006/2350. - Enabling power: Road Traffic Regulation Act 1984, s. 14 (1) (a). - Made: 22.08.2006. Coming into force: 03.09.2006. Effect: None. Territorial extent & classification: E. Local *Unpublished*

The A63 Trunk Road (Queen Street/Market Place Junction, Hull) (Temporary Prohibition of Traffic) Order 2006 (Amendment) Order 2006 No. 2006/2633. - Enabling power: Road Traffic Regulation Act 1984, s. 14 (1) (a). - Made: 26.09.2006. Coming into force: 07.10.2006. Effect: S.I. 2006/2350 amended. Territorial extent & classification: E. Local *Unpublished*

The A63 Trunk Road (Selby bypass) (Temporary Prohibition of Traffic) Order 2006 No. 2006/2353. - Enabling power: Road Traffic Regulation Act 1984, s. 14 (1) (a). - Made: 22.08.2006. Coming into force: 03.09.2006. Effect: None. Territorial extent & classification: E. Local *Unpublished*

The A63 Trunk Road (Selby Bypass, the A1041 to the A19) (Temporary Prohibition of Traffic) Order 2006 No. 2006/3090. - Enabling power: Road Traffic Regulation Act 1984, ss. 14 (1). - Made: 16.11.2006. Coming into force: 02.12.2006. Effect: None. Territorial extent & classification: E. Local *Unpublished*

The A64 Trunk Road (Askham Bryan to Bilbrough) (Temporary Restriction and Prohibition of Traffic) Order 2006 No. 2006/2718. - Enabling power: Road Traffic Regulation Act 1984, s. 14 (1) (a) (7). - Made: 02.10.2006. Coming into force: 13.10.2006. Effect: None. Territorial extent & classification: E. Local *Unpublished*

The A64 Trunk Road (Bilbrough to Copmanthorpe) (Temporary 40 Miles Per Hour Speed Restriction) 2006 No. 2006/1582. - Enabling power: Road Traffic Regulation Act 1984, s. 14 (1) (a). - Made: 16.05.2006. Coming into force: 30.05.2006. Effect: None. Territorial extent & classification: E. Local *Unpublished*

The A64 Trunk Road (Bond Hill Ash Junction) (Temporary Prohibition of Traffic) Order 2006 No. 2006/2352. - Enabling power: Road Traffic Regulation Act 1984, s. 14 (1) (a). - Made: 22.08.2006. Coming into force: 03.09.2006. Effect: None. Territorial extent & classification: E. Local *Unpublished*

The A64 Trunk Road (Calcaria (River Wharf) Bridge) (Temporary Restriction and Prohibition of Traffic) Order 2006 No. 2006/1108. - Enabling power: Road Traffic Regulation Act 1984, s. 14 (1) (a). - Made: 11.04.2006. Coming into force: 23.04.2006. Effect: None. Territorial extent & classification: E. Local *Unpublished*

The A64 Trunk Road (Chapel Close Junction, Staxton to Seamer Roundabout) (Temporary 40 Miles Per Hour Speed Restriction) 2006 No. 2006/1486. - Enabling power: Road Traffic Regulation Act 1984, s. 14 (1) (a). - Made: 02.05.2006. Coming into force: 14.05.2006. Effect: None. Territorial extent & classification: E. Local *Unpublished*

The A64 Trunk Road (Chestnut Avenue, Welburn) (Temporary 40 Miles Per Hour Speed Restriction) 2006 No. 2006/261. - Enabling power: Road Traffic Regulation Act 1984, s. 14 (1) (a). - Made: 31.01.2006. Coming into force: 12.02.2006. Effect: None. Territorial extent & classification: E. Local *Unpublished*

The A64 Trunk Road (Chestnut Avenue, Welburn to Malton) (Temporary 40 Miles Per Hour Speed Restriction) 2006 No. 2006/1581. - Enabling power: Road Traffic Regulation Act 1984, s. 14 (1) (a). - Made: 13.06.2006. Coming into force: 25.06.2006. Effect: None. Territorial extent & classification: E. Local *Unpublished*

The A64 Trunk Road (Ganton to Staxton) (Temporary 40 Miles Per Hour Speed Restriction) Order 2006 No. 2006/2719. - Enabling power: Road Traffic Regulation Act 1984, s. 14 (1) (a). - Made: 15.09.2006. Coming into force: 01.10.2006. Effect: None. Territorial extent & classification: E. Local *Unpublished*

The A64 Trunk Road (Jinnah Restaurant to Chestnut Avenue, Welburn) (Temporary 40 Miles Per Hour Speed Restriction) 2006 No. 2006/1583. - Enabling power: Road Traffic Regulation Act 1984, s. 14 (1) (a). - Made: 30.05.2006. Coming into force: 11.06.2006. Effect: None. Territorial extent & classification: E. Local *Unpublished*

The A64 Trunk Road (River Ouse Bridge) (Temporary Restriction and Prohibition of Traffic) Order 2006 No. 2006/94. - Enabling power: Road Traffic Regulation Act 1984, s. 14 (1) (a). - Made: 17.01.2006. Coming into force: 29.01.2006. Effect: None. Territorial extent & classification: E. Local *Unpublished*

The A64 Trunk Road (Seamer Roundabout to Eastfield Roundabout) (Temporary 40 Miles Per Hour Speed Restriction) Order 2006 No. 2006/1378. - Enabling power: Road Traffic Regulation Act 1984, s. 14 (1) (a). - Made: 09.05.2006. Coming into force: 21.05.2006. Effect: None. Territorial extent & classification: E. Local *Unpublished*

The A64 Trunk Road (Tadcaster Bar to Bilbrough) (Prohibition of Use of Gaps in Central Reservation) Order 2006 No. 2006/3431. - Enabling power: Road Traffic Regulation Act 1984, ss. 1 (1), 2 (1) (2). - Made: 14.12.2006. Coming into force: 22.12.2006. Effect: S.I. 1998/1251 varied. Territorial extent & classification: E. Local *Unpublished*

The A65 and A590 Trunk Roads (M6 Junction 36, Farleton Interchange) (Temporary Restriction and Prohibition of Traffic) Order 2006 No. 2006/1189. - Enabling power: Road Traffic Regulation Act 1984, s. 14 (1) (a). - Made: 17.04.2006. Coming into force: 14.05.2006. Effect: None. Territorial extent & classification: E. Local *Unpublished*

The A65 Trunk Road (Austwick) (Temporary Restriction and Prohibition of Traffic) Order 2006 No. 2006/2752. - Enabling power: Road Traffic Regulation Act 1984, s. 14 (1) (a). - Made: 10.10.2006. Coming into force: 05.11.2006. Effect: None. Territorial extent & classification: E. Local *Unpublished*

The A65 Trunk Road (Boothes Roundabout) (Temporary Restriction and Prohibition of Traffic) Order 2006 No. 2006/1608. - Enabling power: Road Traffic Regulation Act 1984, s. 14 (1) (a). - Made: 06.06.2006. Coming into force: 02.07.2006. Effect: None. Territorial extent & classification: E. Local *Unpublished*

The A65 Trunk Road (Far West Houses Patching Scheme) (Temporary Restriction of Traffic) Order 2006 No. 2006/1797. - Enabling power: Road Traffic Regulation Act 1984, s. 14 (1) (a). - Made: 13.06.2006. Coming into force: 10.07.2006. Effect: None. Territorial extent & classification: E. Local *Unpublished*

The A65 Trunk Road (Hornsbarrow Farm Patching Scheme) (Temporary Restriction of Traffic) Order 2006 No. 2006/1800. - Enabling power: Road Traffic Regulation Act 1984, s. 14 (1) (a). - Made: 27.06.2006. Coming into force: 10.07.2006. Effect: None. Territorial extent & classification: E. Local *Unpublished*

The A65 Trunk Road (Long Preston Renewal Scheme) (Temporary Restriction and Prohibition of Traffic) Order 2006 No. 2006/2283. - Enabling power: Road Traffic Regulation Act 1984, s. 14 (1) (a). - Made: 15.08.2006. Coming into force: 10.09.2006. Effect: None. Territorial extent & classification: E. Local *Unpublished*

The A65 Trunk Road (New Road, Ingleton) (Temporary Restriction and Prohibition of Traffic) Order 2006 No. 2006/530. - Enabling power: Road Traffic Regulation Act 1984, s. 14 (1) (a). - Made: 21.02.2006. Coming into force: 12.03.2006. Effect: None. Territorial extent & classification: E. Local *Unpublished*

The A65 Trunk Road (Rathmell) (Temporary Restriction and Prohibition of Traffic) Order 2006 No. 2006/2759. - Enabling power: Road Traffic Regulation Act 1984, s. 14 (1) (a). - Made: 03.10.2006. Coming into force: 31.10.2006. Effect: None. Territorial extent & classification: E. Local *Unpublished*

The A65 Trunk Road (Thorlby) (Temporary Restriction and Prohibition of Traffic) Order 2006 No. 2006/2762. - Enabling power: Road Traffic Regulation Act 1984, s. 14 (1) (a). - Made: 03.10.2006. Coming into force: 29.10.2006. Effect: None. Territorial extent & classification: E. Local *Unpublished*

The A66(M) Motorway (Blackwell Spur to Blackwell Roundabout) (Temporary Prohibition of Traffic) Order 2006 No. 2006/754. - Enabling power: Road Traffic Regulation Act 1984, s. 14 (1) (a). - Made: 10.03.2006. Coming into force: 23.03.2006. Effect: None. Territorial extent & classification: E. Local *Unpublished*

The A66 Trunk Road and the A1 Trunk Road (Scotch Corner Interchange) (Temporary Restriction and Prohibition of Traffic) Order 2006 No. 2006/2568. - Enabling power: Road Traffic Regulation Act 1984, s. 14 (1) (a). - Made: 15.09.2006. Coming into force: 28.09.2006. Effect: None. Territorial extent & classification: E. Local *Unpublished*

The A66 Trunk Road (Blackhill Farm, Winston Crossings) (Temporary Restriction and Prohibition of Traffic) Order 2006 No. 2006/386. - Enabling power: Road Traffic Regulation Act 1984, s. 14 (1) (a). - Made: 03.02.2006. Coming into force: 16.02.2006. Effect: None. Territorial extent & classification: E. Local *Unpublished*

The A66 Trunk Road (Bowes) (Temporary 50 Miles Per Hour Speed Restriction) Order 2006 No. 2006/462. - Enabling power: Road Traffic Regulation Act 1984, s. 14 (1) (a). - Made: 21.02.2006. Coming into force: 05.03.2006. Effect: None. Territorial extent & classification: E. Local *Unpublished*

The A66 Trunk Road (Briery Interchange) (Temporary Restriction of Traffic) Order 2006 No. 2006/276. - Enabling power: Road Traffic Regulation Act 1984, s. 14 (1) (a). - Made: 23.01.2006. Coming into force: 17.02.2006. Effect: None. Territorial extent & classification: E. Local *Unpublished*

The A66 Trunk Road (Cocker Bridge, Cockermouth) (Temporary Restriction of Traffic) Order 2006 No. 2006/49. - Enabling power: Road Traffic Regulation Act 1984, s. 14 (1) (a). - Made: 05.01.2006. Coming into force: 15.01.2006. Effect: None. Territorial extent & classification: E. Local *Unpublished*

The A66 Trunk Road (Coltsford Bridge, Brough) (Temporary Prohibition and Restriction of Traffic) Order 2006 No. 2006/3031. - Enabling power: Road Traffic Regulation Act 1984, s. 14 (1) (a). - Made: 07.11.2006. Coming into force: 01.12.2006. Effect: None. Territorial extent & classification: E. Local *Unpublished*

The A66 Trunk Road (Eaglescliffe Interchange to Little Burdon Roundabout) (Temporary Restriction and Prohibition of Traffic) Order 2006 No. 2006/1585. - Enabling power: Road Traffic Regulation Act 1984, ss. 14 (1) (a). - Made: 30.05.2006. Coming into force: 11.06.2006. Effect: None. Territorial extent & classification: E. Local *Unpublished*

The A66 Trunk Road (Flitholme Junction) (Temporary Restriction of Traffic) Order 2006 No. 2006/2761. - Enabling power: Road Traffic Regulation Act 1984, s. 14 (1) (a). - Made: 03.10.2006. Coming into force: 29.10.2006. Effect: None. Territorial extent & classification: E. Local *Unpublished*

The A66 Trunk Road (Greta Bridge to Threlkeld) (Temporary Restriction and Prohibition of Traffic) Order 2006 No. 2006/2266. - Enabling power: Road Traffic Regulation Act 1984, ss. 14 (1) (a). - Made: 14.08.2006. Coming into force: 10.09.2006. Effect: None. Territorial extent & classification: E. Local *Unpublished*

The A66 Trunk Road (Kemplay Bank to Brougham) (Temporary 10 Miles Per Hour and 40 Miles Per Hour Speed Restriction and Prohibition of Traffic) Order 2006 No. 2006/474. - Enabling power: Road Traffic Regulation Act 1984, s. 14 (1) (a). - Made: 20.02.2006. Coming into force: 19.03.2006. Effect: None. Territorial extent & classification: E. Local *Unpublished*

The A66 Trunk Road (Kentigern Bridge, Keswick) (Temporary Restriction of Traffic) Order 2006 No. 2006/3464. - Enabling power: Road Traffic Regulation Act 1984, s. 14 (1) (a). - Made: 21.12.2006. Coming into force: 07.01.2007. Effect: None. Territorial extent & classification: E. Local *Unpublished*

The A66 Trunk Road (Kirkby Thore) (Temporary Restriction of Traffic) Order 2006 No. 2006/191. - Enabling power: Road Traffic Regulation Act 1984, s. 14 (1) (a). - Made: 23.01.2006. Coming into force: 12.02.2006. Effect: None. Territorial extent & classification: E. Local *Unpublished*

The A66 Trunk Road (Little Burdon Roundabout to Elton Interchange) (Temporary Restriction and Prohibition of Traffic) Order 2006 No. 2006/1778. - Enabling power: Road Traffic Regulation Act 1984, s. 14 (1) (a). - Made: 20.06.2006. Coming into force: 02.07.2006. Effect: None. Territorial extent & classification: E. Local *Unpublished*

The A66 Trunk Road (Morton Palms Roundabout) (Temporary 30 Miles Per Hour Speed Restriction) Order 2006 No. 2006/3072. - Enabling power: Road Traffic Regulation Act 1984, s. 14 (1) (a). - Made: 26.10.2006. Coming into force: 28.10.2006. Effect: None. Territorial extent & classification: E. Local *Unpublished*

The A66 Trunk Road (Morton Palms Roundabout to Yarm Road Interchange) (Temporary Restriction and Prohibition of Traffic) Order 2006 No. 2006/2730. - Enabling power: Road Traffic Regulation Act 1984, s. 14 (1) (a). - Made: 29.09.2006. Coming into force: 10.10.2006. Effect: None. Territorial extent & classification: E. Local *Unpublished*

The A66 Trunk Road (Penrith to Workington) (Temporary 10 Miles Per Hour and 40 Miles Per Hour Speed Restriction) Order 2006 No. 2006/753. - Enabling power: Road Traffic Regulation Act 1984, s. 14 (1) (a). - Made: 08.03.2006. Coming into force: 12.03.2006. Effect: None. Territorial extent & classification: E. Local *Unpublished*

The A66 Trunk Road (Rokeby Junction to Thorpe Grange Junction) (Temporary 10 Miles Per Hour and 40 Miles Per Hour Speed Restriction) Order 2006 No. 2006/331. - Enabling power: Road Traffic Regulation Act 1984, s. 14 (1) (a). - Made: 07.02.2006. Coming into force: 19.02.2006. Effect: None. Territorial extent & classification: E. Local *Unpublished*

The A66 Trunk Road (Scotch Corner to Greta Bridge) (Temporary Restriction and Prohibition of Traffic) (No. 2) Order 2006 No. 2006/3172. - Enabling power: Road Traffic Regulation Act 1984, s. 14 (1) (a) (7). - Made: 23.10.2006. Coming into force: 05.11.2006. Effect: None. Territorial extent & classification: E. Local *Unpublished*

The A66 Trunk Road (Scotch Corner to Greta Bridge) (Temporary Restriction and Prohibition of Traffic) Order 2006 No. 2006/1290. - Enabling power: Road Traffic Regulation Act 1984, ss. 14 (1) (a). - Made: 05.05.2006. Coming into force: 17.05.2006. Effect: None. Territorial extent & classification: E. Local *Unpublished*

The A66 Trunk Road (Smallways Beck New Bridge) (Temporary Restriction and Prohibition of Traffic) Order 2006 No. 2006/39. - Enabling power: Road Traffic Regulation Act 1984, s. 14 (1) (a). - Made: 03.01.2006. Coming into force: 15.01.2006. Effect: None. Territorial extent & classification: E. Local *Unpublished*

The A66 Trunk Road (Stockton and Thornaby Bypass) (Temporary Restriction and Prohibition of Traffic) Order 2006 No. 2006/67. - Enabling power: Road Traffic Regulation Act 1984, ss. 14 (1) (a), 15 (2). - Made: 03.01.2006. Coming into force: 14.01.2006. Effect: None. Territorial extent & classification: E. Local *Unpublished*

The A66 Trunk Road (Stockton and Thornaby Bypass) (Temporary Restriction and Prohibition of Traffic) Order 2006 (Amendment) (No. 2) Order 2006 No. 2006/2650. - Enabling power: Road Traffic Regulation Act 1984, ss. 14 (1) (a), 15 (2). - Made: 25.09.2006. Coming into force: 25.09.2006. Effect: S.I. 2006/67 amended. Territorial extent & classification: E. Local *Unpublished*

The A66 Trunk Road (Stockton and Thornaby Bypass) (Temporary Restriction and Prohibition of Traffic) Order 2006 (Amendment) Order 2006 No. 2006/1097. - Enabling power: Road Traffic Regulation Act 1984, ss. 14 (1) (a), 15 (2). - Made: 04.04.2006. Coming into force: 15.04.2006. Effect: S.I. 2006/67 amended. Territorial extent & classification: E. Local *Unpublished*

The A66 Trunk Road (Temple Sowerby Bypass) (Temporary Restriction of Traffic) Order 2006 No. 2006/1319. - Enabling power: Road Traffic Regulation Act 1984, s. 14 (1) (a). - Made: 03.05.2006. Coming into force: 28.05.2006. Effect: None. Territorial extent & classification: E. Local *Unpublished*

The A66 Trunk Road (Westray Farm to Embleton) (Temporary Prohibition and Restriction of Traffic) Order 2006 No. 2006/3463. - Enabling power: Road Traffic Regulation Act 1984, s. 14 (1) (a). - Made: 12.12.2006. Coming into force: 07.01.2007. Effect: None. Territorial extent & classification: E. Local *Unpublished*

The A66 Trunk Road (Whinfell Park Resurfacing Scheme) (Temporary Restriction Traffic) Order 2006 No. 2006/2402. - Enabling power: Road Traffic Regulation Act 1984, s. 14 (1) (a). - Made: 22.08.2006. Coming into force: 17.09.2006. Effect: None. Territorial extent & classification: E. Local *Unpublished*

The A69 Trunk Road (Denton Burn Roundabout to West Denton Interchange) (Temporary Prohibition of Traffic) Order 2006 No. 2006/2396. - Enabling power: Road Traffic Regulation Act 1984, s. 14 (1) (a). - Made: 24.08.2006. Coming into force: 03.09.2006. Effect: None. Territorial extent & classification: E. Local *Unpublished*

The A69 Trunk Road (Denton Burn to Hexham) (Temporary 30 Miles Per Hour and 50 Milies Per Hour Speed Restriction) Order 2006 No. 2006/897. - Enabling power: Road Traffic Regulation Act 1984, s. 14 (1) (a). - Made: 17.03.2006. Coming into force: 31.03.2006. Effect: None. Territorial extent & classification: E. Local *Unpublished*

The A69 Trunk Road (Marsh Lane Overbridge to Throckley Interchange) (Temporary Restriction and Prohibition of Traffic) Order 2006 No. 2006/1487. - Enabling power: Road Traffic Regulation Act 1984, s. 14 (1) (a). - Made: 19.05.2006. Coming into force: 02.06.2006. Effect: None. Territorial extent & classification: E. Local *Unpublished*

The A69 Trunk Road (Rosehill Roundabout to Aglionby) (Temporary Restriction and Prohibition of Traffic) Order 2006 No. 2006/2428. - Enabling power: Road Traffic Regulation Act 1984, s. 14 (1) (a) (7). - Made: 24.08.2006. Coming into force: 03.09.2006. Effect: None. Territorial extent & classification: E. Local *Unpublished*

The A69 Trunk Road (Scarrow Hill to Low Row and Haltwhistle to Melkridge) (Temporary Restriction and Prohibition of Traffic) Order 2006 No. 2006/2395. - Enabling power: Road Traffic Regulation Act 1984, s. 14 (1) (a). - Made: 24.08.2006. Coming into force: 03.09.2006. Effect: None. Territorial extent & classification: E. Local *Unpublished*

The A69 Trunk Road (Warwick Bridge) (Temporary Restriction and Prohibition of Traffic) Order 2006 No. 2006/1205. - Enabling power: Road Traffic Regulation Act 1984, s. 14 (1) (a). - Made: 24.04.2006. Coming into force: 06.05.2006. Effect: None. Territorial extent & classification: E. Local *Unpublished*

The A74 Trunk Road and M6 Motorway (M6 Extension Project) (Carlisle to Guardsmill) (Temporary Restriction and Prohibition of Traffic) Order 2006 No. 2006/3401. - Enabling power: Road Traffic Regulation Act 1984, ss. 14 (1) (a), 15 (2). - Made: 11.12.2006. Coming into force: 31.12.2006. Effect: None. Territorial extent & classification: E. Local *Unpublished*

The A74 Trunk Road and M6 Motorway (M6 Extenstion Project) (Temporary Restriction and Prohibition of Traffic) Order 2006 No. 2006/2052. - Enabling power: Road Traffic Regulation Act 1984, ss. 14 (1) (a) (7), 15 (2). - Made: 11.07.2006. Coming into force: 16.07.2006. Effect: None. Territorial extent & classification: E. Local *Unpublished*

The A74 Trunk Road and the M6 Motorway (Harker Bridge) (Temporary Restriction and Prohibition of Traffic) Order 2006 No. 2006/1190. - Enabling power: Road Traffic Regulation Act 1984, s. 14 (1) (a). - Made: 18.04.2006. Coming into force: 14.05.2006. Effect: None. Territorial extent & classification: E. Local *Unpublished*

The A74 Trunk Road (Guardmill to Mossband Resurfacing) (Temporary Restriction and Prohibition of Traffic) Order 2006 No. 2006/2123. - Enabling power: Road Traffic Regulation Act 1984, s. 14 (1) (a). - Made: 18.07.2006. Coming into force: 13.08.2006. Effect: None. Territorial extent & classification: E. Local *Unpublished*

The A74 Trunk Road (Swaffham, Norfolk) (Temporary Restriction and Prohibition of Traffic) (No. 2) Order 2006 No. 2006/3402. - Enabling power: Road Traffic Regulation Act 1984, s. 14 (1) (a). - Made: 12.12.2006. Coming into force: 19.12.2006. Effect: None. Territorial extent & classification: E. Local *Unpublished*

The A74 Trunk Road (Todhills to Mossband, Layby Closures) (Temporary Restriction and Prohibition of Traffic) 2006 No. 2006/234. - Enabling power: Road Traffic Regulation Act 1984, s. 14 (1) (a) (b). - Made: 30.01.2006. Coming into force: 26.02.2006. Effect: None. Territorial extent & classification: E. Local *Unpublished*

The A120 and A12 Trunk Roads (Braintree - Marks Tey, Essex) (Temporary Restriction and Prohibition of Traffic) Order 2006 No. 2006/2450. - Enabling power: Road Traffic Regulation Act 1984, s. 14 (1) (a). - Made: 22.08.2006. Coming into force: 29.08.2006. Effect: None. Territorial extent & classification: E. Local *Unpublished*

The A120 and A133 Trunk Roads (Ardleigh - Hare Green, Colchester, Essex) (Temporary Restriction and Prohibition of Traffic) Order 2006 No. 2006/1076. - Enabling power: Road Traffic Regulation Act 1984, s. 14 (1) (a). - Made: 03.04.2006. Coming into force: 15.04.2006. Effect: None. Territorial extent & classification: E. Local *Unpublished*

The A120 Trunk Road (Braintree to Marks Tey, Essex) (Temporary Restriction of Traffic) Order 2006 No. 2006/1414. - Enabling power: Road Traffic Regulation Act 1984, s. 14 (1) (a). - Made: 08.05.2006. Coming into force: 15.05.2006. Effect: None. Territorial extent & classification: E. Local *Unpublished*

The A120 Trunk Road (Coggeshall Bypass, Braintree, Essex) (Temporary 40 Miles Per Hour Speed Restriction) Order 2006 No. 2006/1490. - Enabling power: Road Traffic Regulation Act 1984, s. 14 (1) (a). - Made: 01.06.2006. Coming into force: 12.06.2006. Effect: None. Territorial extent & classification: E. Local *Unpublished*

The A120 Trunk Road (Coggeshall Bypass, Braintree, Essex) (Temporary Restriction and Prohibition of Traffic) (No. 2) Order 2006 No. 2006/3382. - Enabling power: Road Traffic Regulation Act 1984, s. 14 (1) (a). - Made: 11.12.2006. Coming into force: 18.12.2006. Effect: None. Territorial extent & classification: E. Local *Unpublished*

The A120 Trunk Road (Colchester to Stansted, Braintree, Essex) (Temporary 10 Miles Per Hour and 40 Miles Per Hour Speed Restriction) Order 2006 No. 2006/813. - Enabling power: Road Traffic Regulation Act 1984, s. 14 (1) (a). - Made: 13.03.2006. Coming into force: 20.03.2006. Effect: None. Territorial extent & classification: E. Local *Unpublished*

The A120 Trunk Road (Great Notley, Braintree, Essex) (Temporary Prohibition of Traffic) Order 2006 No. 2006/3503. - Enabling power: Road Traffic Regulation Act 1984, s. 14 (1) (a). - Made: 29.12.2006. Coming into force: 05.01.2007. Effect: None. Territorial extent & classification: E. Local *Unpublished*

The A120 Trunk Road (Junction 6) Eastbound Entry Slip Road (Stansted Airport, Essex) (Temporary Prohibition of Traffic) Order 2006 No. 2006/326. - Enabling power: Road Traffic Regulation Act 1984, s. 14 (1) (a). - Made: 07.02.2006. Coming into force: 14.02.2006. Effect: None. Territorial extent & classification: E. Local *Unpublished*

The A160 Trunk Road and the A180 Trunk Road (Brocklesby Interchange) (Temporary Prohibition of Traffic) Order 2006 No. 2006/2041. - Enabling power: Road Traffic Regulation Act 1984, s. 14 (1) (a). - Made: 21.07.2006. Coming into force: 31.07.2006. Effect: None. Territorial extent & classification: E. Local *Unpublished*

The A160 Trunk Road (Ulceby Road to Top Road Roundabout) (Temporary Prohibition of Traffic) Order 2006 No. 2006/2293. - Enabling power: Road Traffic Regulation Act 1984, s. 14 (1) (a). - Made: 17.08.2006. Coming into force: 31.08.2006. Effect: None. Territorial extent & classification: E. Local *Unpublished*

The A162 Trunk Road (Darrington Overbridge to the A645, Knottingley Road) (Temporary Prohibition of Traffic) Order 2006 No. 2006/625. - Enabling power: Road Traffic Regulation Act 1984, s. 14 (1) (a). - Made: 03.03.2006. Coming into force: 17.03.2006. Effect: None. Territorial extent & classification: E. Local *Unpublished*

The A162 Trunk Road (Ferrybridge Interchange and the A645, Knottingley Road/Pontefract Road Junction) (Temporary Prohibition of Traffic) Order 2006 No. 2006/1820. - Enabling power: Road Traffic Regulation Act 1984, s. 14 (1) (a). - Made: 27.06.2006. Coming into force: 08.07.2006. Effect: None. Territorial extent & classification: E. Local *Unpublished*

The A162 Trunk Road, the A1246 Trunk Road and the A63 Trunk Road (Ferrybridge to Boot and Shoe Roundabout) (Temporary Restriction and Prohibition of Traffic) Order 2006 No. 2006/695. - Enabling power: Road Traffic Regulation Act 1984, s. 14 (1) (a) (7). - Made: 07.03.2006. Coming into force: 18.03.2006. Effect: None. Territorial extent & classification: E. Local *Unpublished*

The A180 Trunk Road (Barnetby Interchange to Brocklesby Interchange) (Temporary Prohibition of Traffic) Order 2006 No. 2006/2569. - Enabling power: Road Traffic Regulation Act 1984, s. 14 (1) (a). - Made: 15.09.2006. Coming into force: 24.09.2006. Effect: None. Territorial extent & classification: E. Local *Unpublished*

The A194(M) Motorway (Blackfell Bridge) (Temporary 50 Miles Per Hour Speed Restriction) Order 2006 No. 2006/279. - Enabling power: Road Traffic Regulation Act 1984, s. 14 (1) (b). - Made: 31.01.2006. Coming into force: 12.02.2006. Effect: None. Territorial extent & classification: E. Local *Unpublished*

The A194(M) Motorway (Havannah Interchange) (Temporary Restriction and Prohibition of Traffic) Order 2006 No. 2006/280. - Enabling power: Road Traffic Regulation Act 1984, s. 14 (1) (a) (7). - Made: 30.01.2006. Coming into force: 12.02.2006. Effect: None. Territorial extent & classification: E. Local *Unpublished*

The A194(M) Motorway (Springwell Bridge) (Temporary 50 Miles Per Hour Speed Restriction) Order 2005 No. 2006/37. - Enabling power: Road Traffic Regulation Act 1984, s. 14 (1) (a). - Made: 03.01.2006. Coming into force: 17.01.2006. Effect: None. Territorial extent & classification: E. Local *Unpublished*

The A249 Trunk Road (B2005 Junction - Kingsferry Roundabout) (Temporary 30 Miles Per Hour Speed Restriction) Order 2006 No. 2006/888. - Enabling power: Road Traffic Regulation Act 1984, s. 14 (1) (a). - Made: 20.03.2006. Coming into force: 01.04.2006. Effect: None. Territorial extent & classification: E. Local *Unpublished*

The A249 Trunk Road (Brielle Way, Sheerness) (Temporary Prohibition of Traffic) Order 2006 No. 2006/1217. - Enabling power: Road Traffic Regulation Act 1984, s. 14 (1) (a). - Made: 24.04.2006. Coming into force: 29.04.2006. Effect: None. Territorial extent & classification: E. Local *Unpublished*

The A249 Trunk Road (Kingsferry Roundabout - Cowstead Corner Roundabout) (Temporary Prohibition of Traffic) Order 2006 No. 2006/1602. - Enabling power: Road Traffic Regulation Act 1984, s. 14 (1) (a). - Made: 12.06.2006. Coming into force: 20.06.2006. Effect: None. Territorial extent & classification: E. Local *Unpublished*

The A249 Trunk Road (The Sheppey Crossing) (Temporary Prohibition of Traffic) Order 2006 No. 2006/1775. - Enabling power: Road Traffic Regulation Act 1984, ss. 16A (2) a) (10), 122A. - Made: 22.06.2006. Coming into force: 01.07.2006. Effect: None. Territorial extent & classification: E. Local *Unpublished*

The A259 and the A2070 Trunk Roads (Brenzett Roundabout) (Temporary Speed Restrictions) Order 2006 No. 2006/2723. - Enabling power: Road Traffic Regulation Act 1984, s. 14 (1) (a). - Made: 02.10.2006. Coming into force: 07.10.2006. Effect: None. Territorial extent & classification: E. Local *Unpublished*

The A259 Trunk Road (Belle Hill/King Offa Way, Bexhill) (Temporary Prohibition of Traffic) Order 2006 No. 2006/3041. - Enabling power: Road Traffic Regulation Act 1984, s. 14 (1) (a). - Made: 06.11.2006. Coming into force: 11.11.2006. Effect: None. Territorial extent & classification: E. Local *Unpublished*

The A259 Trunk Road (East Guldeford - Brookland) (Temporary Prohibition of Traffic) Order 2006 No. 2006/1209. - Enabling power: Road Traffic Regulation Act 1984, s. 14 (1) (a). - Made: 24.04.2006. Coming into force: 02.05.2006. Effect: None. Territorial extent & classification: E. Local *Unpublished*

The A259 Trunk Road (Little Common Road, Bexhill) (Temporary Prohibition of Traffic) Order 2006 No. 2006/3063. - Enabling power: Road Traffic Regulation Act 1984, s. 16A (2) (a). - Made: 30.10.2006. Coming into force: 06.11.2006. Effect: None. Territorial extent & classification: E. Local *Unpublished*

The A259 Trunk Road (Pevensey - Winchelsea) (Temporary 40 MPH Speed Restriction) Order 2006 No. 2006/3447. - Enabling power: Road Traffic Regulation Act 1984, s. 14 (1) (a). - Made: 18.12.2006. Coming into force: 23.12.2006. Effect: None. Territorial extent & classification: E. Local *Unpublished*

The A259 Trunk Road (Royal Military Road) (Temporary Speed Restrictions) Order 2006 No. 2006/2417. - Enabling power: Road Traffic Regulation Act 1984, s. 14 (1) (a). - Made: 29.08.2006. Coming into force: 02.09.2006. Effect: None. Territorial extent & classification: E. Local *Unpublished*

The A259 Trunk Road (Various Roads, Rye) (Temporary Prohibition of Traffic) Order 2006 No. 2006/1211. - Enabling power: Road Traffic Regulation Act 1984, s. 14 (1) (a). - Made: 24.04.2006. Coming into force: 29.04.2006. Effect: None. Territorial extent & classification: E. Local *Unpublished*

The A259 Trunk Road (Various Roads, Rye) (Temporary Restriction and Prohibition of Traffic) Order 2006 No. 2006/3064. - Enabling power: Road Traffic Regulation Act 1984, s. 16A (2) (a). - Made: 30.10.2006. Coming into force: 06.11.2006. Effect: None. Territorial extent & classification: E. Local *Unpublished*

The A259 Trunk Road (Winchelsea Road, Guestling Green) (Temporary 40 Miles Per Hour Speed Restriction) Order 2006 No. 2006/1854. - Enabling power: Road Traffic Regulation Act 1984, s. 14 (1) (a). - Made: 03.07.2006. Coming into force: 08.07.2006. Effect: None. Territorial extent & classification: E. Local *Unpublished*

The A282 Trunk Road (Junction 1A, Northbound Entry Slip Road) (Temporary Prohibition of Traffic) Order 2006 No. 2006/545. - Enabling power: Road Traffic Regulation Act 1984, s. 14 (1) (a). - Made: 20.02.2006. Coming into force: 25.02.2006. Effect: None. Territorial extent & classification: E. Local *Unpublished*

The A282 Trunk Road (Junction 1A) (Temporary Prohibition of Traffic) Order 2006 No. 2006/1435. - Enabling power: Road Traffic Regulation Act 1984, s. 14 (1) (a). - Made: 22.05.2006. Coming into force: 27.05.2006. Effect: None. Territorial extent & classification: E. Local *Unpublished*

The A282 Trunk Road (Junction 1B, Southbound Entry Slip Road) (Temporary Prohibition of Traffic) Order 2006 No. 2006/811. - Enabling power: Road Traffic Regulation Act 1984, s. 14 (1) (a). - Made: 13.03.2006. Coming into force: 22.03.2006. Effect: None. Territorial extent & classification: E. Local *Unpublished*

The A282 Trunk Road (M25 Junction 2 - Dartford Tunnels) (Temporary Restriction and Prohibition of Traffic) Order 2006 No. 2006/1482. - Enabling power: Road Traffic Regulation Act 1984, s. 14 (1) (b). - Made: 30.05.2006. Coming into force: 03.06.2006. Effect: None. Territorial extent & classification: E. Local *Unpublished*

The A303 Trunk Road (A343 Salisbury Road Junction) (Temporary Restriction and Prohibition of Traffic) (No. 2) Order 2006 No. 2006/2157. - Enabling power: Road Traffic Regulation Act 1984, s. 14 (1) (a) ,sch. 9, para. 27 (1). - Made: 31.07.2006. Coming into force: 07.08.2006. Effect: S.I. 2006/434 revoked. Territorial extent & classification: E. Local *Unpublished*

The A303 Trunk Road (A343 Salisbury Road Junction) (Temporary Restriction and Prohibition of Traffic) Order 2006 No. 2006/434. - Enabling power: Road Traffic Regulation Act 1984, s. 14 (1) (a). - Made: 13.02.2006. Coming into force: 18.02.2006. Effect: None. Territorial extent & classification: E. Local. - Revoked by S.I. 2006/2157 (Unpublished) *Unpublished*

The A303 Trunk Road (Amesbury to Berwick Down) (Temporary Restriction of Traffic) Order 2006 No. 2006/2391. - Enabling power: Road Traffic Regulation Act 1984, s. 14 (1) (b). - Made: 29.08.2006. Coming into force: 01.09.2006. Effect: None. Territorial extent & classification: E. Local *Unpublished*

The A303 Trunk Road (Bishopswood Junction to A30, Near Chard) (Temporary Prohibition of Traffic) Order 2006 No. 2006/2474. - Enabling power: Road Traffic Regulation Act 1984, s. 14 (1) (a). - Made: 05.09.2006. Coming into force: 08.09.2006. Effect: None. Territorial extent & classification: E. Local *Unpublished*

The A303 Trunk Road (Bullington Cross, Eastbound Slip Road) (Temporary Prohibition of Traffic) Order 2006 No. 2006/1648. - Enabling power: Road Traffic Regulation Act 1984, s. 14 (1) (a). - Made: 19.06.2006. Coming into force: 24.06.2006. Effect: None. Territorial extent & classification: E. Local *Unpublished*

The A303 Trunk Road (Hundred Acre Roundabout, Eastbound Entry Slip Road) (Temporary Prohibition of Traffic) Order 2006 No. 2006/703. - Enabling power: Road Traffic Regulation Act 1984, s. 14 (1) (a). - Made: 06.03.2006. Coming into force: 11.03.2006. Effect: None. Territorial extent & classification: E. Local *Unpublished*

The A303 Trunk Road (Mere to Junction with the A350) (Temporary Prohibition of Traffic) Order 2006 No. 2006/1995. - Enabling power: Road Traffic Regulation Act 1984, s. 14 (1) (a). - Made: 18.07.2006. Coming into force: 21.07.2006. Effect: None. Territorial extent & classification: E. Local *Unpublished*

Road traffic: Traffic regulation

The A303 Trunk Road (Micheldever Junction, Eastbound) (Temporary Restriction and Prohibition of Traffic) Order 2006 No. 2006/2847. - Enabling power: Road Traffic Regulation Act 1984, s. 14 (1) (a). - Made: 16.10.2006. Coming into force: 21.10.2006. Effect: None. Territorial extent & classification: E. Local *Unpublished*

The A303 Trunk Road (Picket Twenty Interchange) (Temporary Restriction and Prohibition of Traffic) Order 2006 No. 2006/3067. - Enabling power: Road Traffic Regulation Act 1984, s. 14 (1) (a). - Made: 30.10.2006. Coming into force: 04.11.2006. Effect: None. Territorial extent & classification: E. Local *Unpublished*

The A303 Trunk Road (Podimore Roundabout to Hazelgrove Roundabout) (Temporary Prohibition of Traffic) Order 2006 No. 2006/1766. - Enabling power: Road Traffic Regulation Act 1984, s. 14 (1) (a). - Made: 27.06.2006. Coming into force: 30.06.2006. Effect: None. Territorial extent & classification: E. Local *Unpublished*

The A303 Trunk Road (Podimore Roundabout to South Petherton) (Temporary Restriction of Traffic) Order 2006 No. 2006/2345. - Enabling power: Road Traffic Regulation Act 1984, s. 14 (1) (a). - Made: 22.08.2006. Coming into force: 25.08.2006. Effect: None. Territorial extent & classification: E. Local *Unpublished*

The A303 Trunk Road (Slip Road to A350, West of Chicklade) (Temporary Prohibition of Traffic) Order 2006 No. 2006/3210. - Enabling power: Road Traffic Regulation Act 1984, s. 14 (1) (a). - Made: 23.11.2006. Coming into force: 29.11.2006. Effect: None. Territorial extent & classification: E. Local *Unpublished*

The A303 Trunk Road (Thruxton Circuit Interchange, Eastbound Entry Slip Road) (Temporary Prohibition of Traffic) Order 2006 No. 2006/3068. - Enabling power: Road Traffic Regulation Act 1984, s. 14 (1) (a). - Made: 30.10.2006. Coming into force: 04.11.2006. Effect: None. Territorial extent & classification: E. Local *Unpublished*

The A303 Trunk Road (Thruxton Hill, Eastbound Carriageway) (Temporary Speed Restrictions) Order 2006 No. 2006/2640. - Enabling power: Road Traffic Regulation Act 1984, s. 14 (1) (a). - Made: 25.09.2006. Coming into force: 30.09.2006. Effect: None. Territorial extent & classification: E. Local *Unpublished*

The A303 Trunk Road (Tinkers Lane, Wincanton to Hazlegrove Roundabout, Sparkford) (Temporary Prohibition of Traffic) Order 2006 No. 2006/2717. - Enabling power: Road Traffic Regulation Act 1984, s. 14 (1) (a). - Made: 03.10.2006. Coming into force: 06.10.2006. Effect: None. Territorial extent & classification: E. Local *Unpublished*

The A303 Trunk Road (Tintinhull) (Temporary Prohibition of Traffic) Order 2006 No. 2006/1593. - Enabling power: Road Traffic Regulation Act 1984, s. 14 (1) (b). - Made: 06.06.2006. Coming into force: 08.06.2006. Effect: None. Territorial extent & classification: E. Local *Unpublished*

The A303 Trunk Road (Winchester Road Interchange, Eastbound Carriageway) (Temporary Speed Restrictions) Order 2006 No. 2006/46. - Enabling power: Road Traffic Regulation Act 1984, s. 14 (1) (a). - Made: 09.01.2006. Coming into force: 14.01.2006. Effect: None. Territorial extent & classification: E. Local *Unpublished*

The A404(M) Motorway and the A404 Trunk Road (Western Region Railway Bridge) (Temporary Speed Restriction) Order 2006 No. 2006/1291. - Enabling power: Road Traffic Regulation Act 1984, s. 14 (1) (a). - Made: 08.05.2006. Coming into force: 13.05.2006. Effect: None. Territorial extent & classification: E. Local *Unpublished*

The A404(M) Motorway (Junction 9A, Exit Slip Roads) (Temporary Prohibition of Traffic) Order 2006 No. 2006/2416. - Enabling power: Road Traffic Regulation Act 1984, s. 14 (1) (a). - Made: 29.08.2006. Coming into force: 02.09.2006. Effect: None. Territorial extent & classification: E. Local *Unpublished*

The A404 Trunk Road and the M40 Motorway (Handy Cross) (Temporary Restriction and Prohibition of Traffic) Order 2006 No. 2006/440. - Enabling power: Road Traffic Regulation Act 1984, s. 14 (1) (a). - Made: 13.02.2006. Coming into force: 18.02.2006. Effect: None. Territorial extent & classification: E. Local *Unpublished*

The A404 Trunk Road (Handy Cross - A4155 Junction) (Temporary Prohibition of Traffic) Order 2006 No. 2006/2196. - Enabling power: Road Traffic Regulation Act 1984, s. 14 (1) (a). - Made: 07.08.2006. Coming into force: 11.08.2006. Effect: None. Territorial extent & classification: E. Local *Unpublished*

The A405 Trunk Road (M1 Junction 6 - M25 Junction 21A) (Temporary Speed Restriction) Order 2006 No. 2006/3446. - Enabling power: Road Traffic Regulation Act 1984, s. 14 (1) (a). - Made: 18.12.2006. Coming into force: 23.12.2006. Effect: None. Territorial extent & classification: E. Local *Unpublished*

The A405 Trunk Road (M1 Junction 6) (Temporary Prohibition of Traffic) Order 2006 No. 2006/1214. - Enabling power: Road Traffic Regulation Act 1984, s. 14 (1) (a). - Made: 24.04.2006. Coming into force: 04.05.2006. Effect: None. Territorial extent & classification: E. Local *Unpublished*

The A417 Trunk Road (Cowley Roundabout to Churn Valley Viaduct, Cirencester) (Temporary Prohibition and Restriction of Traffic) Order 2006 No. 2006/2780. - Enabling power: Road Traffic Regulation Act 1984, s. 14 (1) (a). - Made: 10.10.2006. Coming into force: 13.10.2006. Effect: None. Territorial extent & classification: E. Local *Unpublished*

The A417 Trunk Road (Shurdington Road, Junction to the Air Balloon Roundabout, Crickley Hill, Cheltenham) (Temporary Prohibition of Traffic) Order 2006 No. 2006/2161. - Enabling power: Road Traffic Regulation Act 1984, s. 14 (1) (a). - Made: 02.08.2006. Coming into force: 07.08.2006. Effect: None. Territorial extent & classification: E. Local *Unpublished*

The A417 Trunk Road (Zoons Court Roundabout to Business Park Roundabout, Gloucester) and M5 Motorway (Junction 11A) (Temporary Prohibition of Traffic) Order 2006 No. 2006/2098. - Enabling power: Road Traffic Regulation Act 1984, s. 14 (1) (a). - Made: 25.07.2006. Coming into force: 28.07.2006. Effect: None. Territorial extent & classification: E. Local *Unpublished*

The A419 and A417 Trunk Roads (Cricklade, Wiltshire to Cirencester, Gloucestershire) (Temporary Prohibition of Traffic) Order 2006 No. 2006/2191. - Enabling power: Road Traffic Regulation Act 1984, s. 14 (1) (a). - Made: 07.08.2006. Coming into force: 11.08.2006. Effect: None. Territorial extent & classification: E. Local *Unpublished*

The A419 Trunk Road (A420 Junction to A361 Rat Trap Junction, Swindon) (Temporary Prohibition of Traffic) Order 2006 No. 2006/1631. - Enabling power: Road Traffic Regulation Act 1984, s. 14 (1) (a). - Made: 16.06.2006. Coming into force: 23.06.2006. Effect: None. Territorial extent & classification: E. Local *Unpublished*

The A419 Trunk Road (A420 Junctoin to Commonhead Roundabout, Swindon) (Temporary Prohibition of Traffic) Order 2006 No. 2006/1326. - Enabling power: Road Traffic Regulation Act 1984, s. 14 (1) (a). - Made: 08.05.2006. Coming into force: 15.05.2006. Effect: None. Territorial extent & classification: E. Local *Unpublished*

The A419 Trunk Road (Castle Eaton and Kingshill Junctions, Near Cricklade) (Temporary Prohibition of Traffic) Order 2006 No. 2006/1877. - Enabling power: Road Traffic Regulation Act 1984, s. 14 (1) (b). - Made: 05.07.2006. Coming into force: 13.07.2006. Effect: None. Territorial extent & classification: E. Local *Unpublished*

The A419 Trunk Road (Castle Eaton Junction to Calcutt Overbridge, Near Swindon) (Temporary 40 Miles Per Hour Speed Restriction) Order 2006 No. 2006/1100. - Enabling power: Road Traffic Regulation Act 1984, s. 14 (1) (a). - Made: 10.04.2006. Coming into force: 17.04.2006. Effect: None. Territorial extent & classification: E. Local *Unpublished*

The A419 Trunk Road (Commonhead Roundabout, Swindon) (Temporary Prohibition of Traffic) Order 2006 No. 2006/2223. - Enabling power: Road Traffic Regulation Act 1984, s. 14 (1) (a). - Made: 09.08.2006. Coming into force: 16.08.2006. Effect: None. Territorial extent & classification: E. Local *Unpublished*

The A421 Trunk Road (Bedfordshire) (Temporary Restriction of Traffic) Order 2006 No. 2006/2851. - Enabling power: Road Traffic Regulation Act 1984, s. 14 (1) (a). - Made: 16.10.2006. Coming into force: 23.10.2006. Effect: None. Territorial extent & classification: E. Local *Unpublished*

The A421 Trunk Road (Bedfordshire) (Temporary Variable Speed Limit) Order 2006 No. 2006/3084. - Enabling power: Road Traffic Regulation Act 1984, ss. 14, 15. - Made: 06.11.2006. Coming into force: 13.11.2006. Effect: None. Territorial extent & classification: E. Local *Unpublished*

The A421 Trunk Road (Great Barford Bypass, Bedfordshire) (24 Hour Clearway) Order 2006 No. 2006/2429. - Enabling power: Road Traffic Regulation Act 1984, s. 1 (1), 2 (1) (2), 4 (1). - Made: 17.08.2006. Coming into force: 24.08.2006. Effect: None. Territorial extent & classification: E. Local *Unpublished*

The A421 Trunk Road (Kempston Retail Park, Bedfordshire) (Temporary Prohibition of Traffic) Order 2006 No. 2006/1777. - Enabling power: Road Traffic Regulation Act 1984, s. 14 (1) (a). - Made: 12.06.2006. Coming into force: 19.06.2006. Effect: None. Territorial extent & classification: E. Local *Unpublished*

The A421 Trunk Road (Marsh Leys Roundabout, Kempstonbrogborough, Bedfordshire) (Temporary Restriction and Prohibition of Traffic) Order 2006 No. 2006/274. - Enabling power: Road Traffic Regulation Act 1984, s. 14 (1) (a). - Made: 23.01.2006. Coming into force: 30.01.2006. Effect: None. Territorial extent & classification: E. Local *Unpublished*

The A428 and A14 Trunk Roads and the M11 Motorway (Hardwick-Girton, Cambridgeshire) (Temporary Restriction and Prohibition of Traffic) Order 2006 No. 2006/709. - Enabling power: Road Traffic Regulation Act 1984, s. 14 (1) (a). - Made: 06.03.2006. Coming into force: 13.03.2006. Effect: None. Territorial extent & classification: E. Local *Unpublished*

The A428 Trunk Road (Cambourne Junction, Cambridgeshire) (Temporary Restriction and Prohibition of Traffic) (No. 2) Order 2006 No. 2006/2209. - Enabling power: Road Traffic Regulation Act 1984, s. 14 (1) (a), sch. 9, para. 27 (1). - Made: 01.08.2006. Coming into force: 08.08.2006. Effect: S.I. 2006/1436 revoked. Territorial extent & classification: E. Local *Unpublished*

The A428 Trunk Road (Cambourne Junction, Cambridgeshire) (Temporary Restriction and Prohibition of Traffic) Order 2006 No. 2006/1436. - Enabling power: Road Traffic Regulation Act 1984, s. 14 (1) (a). - Made: 15.05.2006. Coming into force: 23.05.2006. Effect: None. Territorial extent & classification: E. Local. - Revoked by S.I. 2006/2209 (Unpublished) *Unpublished*

The A428 Trunk Road (Cambourne to Hardwick Improvement) (Prohibition of Use of Gap in the Central Reservation) Order 2006 No. 2006/997. - Enabling power: Road Traffic Regulation Act 1984, ss. 1 (1), 2 (1) (2). - Made: 13.03.2006. Coming into force: 03.04.2006. Effect: None. Territorial extent & classification: E. Local *Unpublished*

The A428 Trunk Road (Cambridgeshire and Bedfordshire) (Temporary Variable Speed Limit) Order 2006 No. 2006/3127. - Enabling power: Road Traffic Regulation Act 1984, ss. 14, 15. - Made: 23.10.2006. Coming into force: 30.10.2006. Effect: None. Territorial extent & classification: E. Local *Unpublished*

Road traffic: Traffic regulation

The A428 Trunk Road (Caxton Common to Hardwick, Cambridgeshire) (Temporary Restriction and Prohibition of Traffic) Order 2006 No. 2006/1814. - Enabling power: Road Traffic Regulation Act 1984, s. 14 (1) (a). - Made: 26.06.2006. Coming into force: 03.07.2006. Effect: None. Territorial extent & classification: E. Local *Unpublished*

The A435 Trunk Road (Alcester to M42 Junction 3) (Temporary Restriction and Prohibition of Traffic) Order 2006 No. 2006/1552. - Enabling power: Road Traffic Regulation Act 1984, s. 14 (1) (a). - Made: 30.05.2006. Coming into force: 06.06.2006. Effect: None. Territorial extent & classification: E. Local *Unpublished*

The A435 Trunk Road (Branson's Cross, Worcestershire) (Temporary Restriction and Prohibition of Traffic) Order 2006 No. 2006/2745. - Enabling power: Road Traffic Regulation Act 1984, s. 14 (1) (a). - Made: 09.10.2006. Coming into force: 16.10.2006. Effect: None. Territorial extent & classification: E. Local *Unpublished*

The A435 Trunk Road (Coughton, North of Alcester, Warwickshire) (Temporary 10 Miles Per Hour and 40 Miles Per Hour Speed Restriction) Order 2006 No. 2006/670. - Enabling power: Road Traffic Regulation Act 1984, s. 14 (1) (a). - Made: 20.02.2006. Coming into force: 27.02.2006. Effect: None. Territorial extent & classification: E. Local *Unpublished*

The A435 Trunk Road (Gorcott Hill to Kings Coughton) (Temporary Restriction and Prohibition of Traffic) Order 2006 No. 2006/728. - Enabling power: Road Traffic Regulation Act 1984, s. 14 (1) (a). - Made: 24.02.2006. Coming into force: 03.03.2006. Effect: None. Territorial extent & classification: E. Local *Unpublished*

The A435 Trunk Road (Gorcott Hill to Kings Coughton) (Temporary Restriction of Traffic) Order 2006 No. 2006/8. - Enabling power: Road Traffic Regulation Act 1984, s. 14 (1) (a). - Made: 03.01.2006. Coming into force: 10.012006. Effect: None. Territorial extent & classification: E. Local *Unpublished*

The A435 Trunk Road (Gorcott Hill, Warwickshire) (Temporary Prohibition and Restriction of Traffic) Order 2006 No. 2006/2545. - Enabling power: Road Traffic Regulation Act 1984, s. 14 (1) (a). - Made: 15.09.2006. Coming into force: 22.09.2006. Effect: None. Territorial extent & classification: E. Local *Unpublished*

The A435 Trunk Road (Mappleborough Green to Studley, Warwickshire) (Temporary 10 Miles Per Hour and 40 Miles Per Hour Speed Restriction) Order 2006 No. 2006/664. - Enabling power: Road Traffic Regulation Act 1984, s. 14 (1) (a). - Made: 20.02.2006. Coming into force: 27.02.2006. Effect: None. Territorial extent & classification: E. Local *Unpublished*

The A446 Trunk Road (Coleshill to Hams Hall Roundabout, Warwickshire) (Temporary Prohibition of Traffic) Order 2006 No. 2006/819. - Enabling power: Road Traffic Regulation Act 1984, s. 14 (1) (a). - Made: 03.03.2006. Coming into force: 10.03.2006. Effect: None. Territorial extent & classification: E. Local *Unpublished*

The A446 Trunk Road (Little Packington) (Temporary Prohibition of Traffic) Order 2006 No. 2006/422. - Enabling power: Road Traffic Regulation Act 1984, s. 14 (1) (a). - Made: 13.02.2006. Coming into force: 20.02.2006. Effect: None. Territorial extent & classification: E. Local *Unpublished*

The A449 Trunk Road (Beggars Bush Lane, Wombourne, Staffordshire) (Prohibition of Right Turns) Order 2006 No. 2006/903. - Enabling power: Road Traffic Regulation Act 1984, ss. 1 (1), 2 (1) (2). - Made: 13.03.2006. Coming into force: 27.03.2006. Effect: None. Territorial extent & classification: E. Local *Unpublished*

The A449 Trunk Road (Caunsall, Worcestershire) (Temporary 10 Miles Per Hour and 40 Miles Per Hour Speed Restriction) Order 2006 No. 2006/1141. - Enabling power: Road Traffic Regulation Act 1984, s. 14 (1) (a). - Made: 10.04.2006. Coming into force: 17.04.2006. Effect: None. Territorial extent & classification: E. Local *Unpublished*

The A449 Trunk Road (Chester Road North, Kidderminster, Worcestershire) (Temporary 10 Miles Per Hour and 40 Miles Per Hour Speed Restriction) Order 2006 No. 2006/682. - Enabling power: Road Traffic Regulation Act 1984, s. 14 (1) (a). - Made: 20.02.2006. Coming into force: 27.02.2006. Effect: None. Territorial extent & classification: E. Local *Unpublished*

The A449 Trunk Road (Claines to Ombersley, Worcestershire) (Temporary 10 Miles Per Hour and 40 Miles Per Hour Speed Restriction) Order 2006 No. 2006/669. - Enabling power: Road Traffic Regulation Act 1984, s. 14 (1) (a). - Made: 20.02.2006. Coming into force: 27.02.2006. Effect: None. Territorial extent & classification: E. Local *Unpublished*

The A449 Trunk Road (Crossway Green, Worcestershire) (Temporary 10 Miles Per Hour and 40 Miiles Per Hour Speed Restriction) Order 2006 No. 2006/1862. - Enabling power: Road Traffic Regulation Act 1984, s. 14 (1) (a). - Made: 30.06.2006. Coming into force: 07.07.2006. Effect: None. Territorial extent & classification: E. Local *Unpublished*

The A449 Trunk Road (Gilbert Lane, Wombourne, Staffordshire) (Prohibition of Right Turns) Order 2006 No. 2006/550. - Enabling power: Road Traffic Regulation Act 1984, ss. 1 (1), 2 (1) (2). - Made: 20.02.2006. Coming into force: 06.03.2006. Effect: None. Territorial extent & classification: E. Local *Unpublished*

The A449 Trunk Road (Himley, Staffordshire) (Temporary 10 Miles Per Hour and 40 Miles Per Hour Speed Restriction) Order 2006 No. 2006/681. - Enabling power: Road Traffic Regulation Act 1984, s. 14 (1) (a). - Made: 20.02.2006. Coming into force: 27.02.2006. Effect: None. Territorial extent & classification: E. Local *Unpublished*

The A449 Trunk Road (Himley to Wombourne, Staffordshire) (Temporary Restriction of Traffic) Order 2006 No. 2006/272. - Enabling power: Road Traffic Regulation Act 1984, s. 14 (1) (a). - Made: 16.01.2006. Coming into force: 23.01.2006. Effect: None. Territorial extent & classification: E. Local *Unpublished*

The A449 Trunk Road (Hoobrook to Summerfield, Kidderminster) (Temporary 10 Miles Per Hour and 40 Miles Per Hour Speed Restriction) Order 2006 No. 2006/1861. - Enabling power: Road Traffic Regulation Act 1984, s. 14 (1) (a). - Made: 03.07.2006. Coming into force: 10.07.2006. Effect: None. Territorial extent & classification: E. Local *Unpublished*

The A449 Trunk Road (Kingswinford to Prestwood) (Temporary Restriction and Prohibition of Traffic) Order 2006 No. 2006/2251. - Enabling power: Road Traffic Regulation Act 1984, s. 14 (1) (a). - Made: 07.08.2006. Coming into force: 14.08.2006. Effect: None. Territorial extent & classification: E. Local *Unpublished*

The A449 Trunk Road (Lloyd Hill, Wolverhampton) (Temporary 10 Miles Per Hour and 40 Miles Per Hour Speed Restriction) Order 2006 No. 2006/683. - Enabling power: Road Traffic Regulation Act 1984, s. 14 (1) (a). - Made: 20.02.2006. Coming into force: 27.02.2006. Effect: None. Territorial extent & classification: E. Local *Unpublished*

The A449 Trunk Road (M5 Junction 6 to Ombersley, Worcestershire) (Temporary Restriction and Prohibition of Traffic) Order 2006 No. 2006/2498. - Enabling power: Road Traffic Regulation Act 1984, s. 14 (1) (a). - Made: 30.08.2006. Coming into force: 06.09.2006. Effect: None. Territorial extent & classification: E. Local *Unpublished*

The A449 Trunk Road (Mitre Oak Roundabout to Ombersley, Worcestershire) (Temporary Restriction and Prohibition of Traffic) Order 2006 No. 2006/1860. - Enabling power: Road Traffic Regulation Act 1984, s. 14 (1) (a). - Made: 03.07.2006. Coming into force: 10.07.2006. Effect: None. Territorial extent & classification: E. Local *Unpublished*

The A449 Trunk Road (North of Hartlebury, Worcestershire) (Temporary 10 Miles Per Hour and 40 Miles Per Hour Speed Restriction) Order 2006 No. 2006/1366. - Enabling power: Road Traffic Regulation Act 1984, s. 14 (1) (a). - Made: 08.05.2006. Coming into force: 15.05.2006. Effect: None. Territorial extent & classification: E. Local *Unpublished*

The A449 Trunk Road (Stourbridge Road, Wombourne) (Temporary Restriction and Prohibition of Traffic) Order 2006 No. 2006/726. - Enabling power: Road Traffic Regulation Act 1984, s. 14 (1) (a). - Made: 24.02.2006. Coming into force: 03.03.2006. Effect: None. Territorial extent & classification: E. Local *Unpublished*

The A449 Trunk Road (Wall Health, Dudley) (Temporary Prohibition of Traffic) Order 2006 No. 2006/3002. - Enabling power: Road Traffic Regulation Act 1984, s. 14 (1) (b). - Made: 30.10.2006. Coming into force: 06.11.2006. Effect: None. Territorial extent & classification: E. Local *Unpublished*

The A449 Trunk Road (Wall Heath) (Temporary 10 Miles Per Hour Speed Restriction) Order 2006 No. 2006/861. - Enabling power: Road Traffic Regulation Act 1984, s. 14 (1) (a). - Made: 13.03.2006. Coming into force: 20.03.2006. Effect: None. Territorial extent & classification: E. Local *Unpublished*

The A449 Trunk Road (Warndon to Claines, Worcestershire) (Temporary Restriction and Prohibition of Traffic) Order 2006 No. 2006/1308. - Enabling power: Road Traffic Regulation Act 1984, s. 14 (1) (a). - Made: 28.04.2006. Coming into force: 05.05.2006. Effect: None. Territorial extent & classification: E. Local *Unpublished*

The A449 Trunk Road (Wombourne to Lloyd Hill) (Temporary Restriction and Prohibition of Traffic) Order 2006 No. 2006/1567. - Enabling power: Road Traffic Regulation Act 1984, s. 14 (1) (a). - Made: 22.05.2006. Coming into force: 29.05.2006. Effect: None. Territorial extent & classification: E. Local *Unpublished*

The A453 and A52 Trunk Roads (Clifton Bridge, Nottingham) (Temporary Prohibition of Traffic) Order 2006 No. 2006/2146. - Enabling power: Road Traffic Regulation Act 1984, s. 14 (1) (a). - Made: 28.07.2006. Coming into force: 04.08.2006. Effect: None. Territorial extent & classification: E. Local *Unpublished*

The A453 and A52 Trunk Roads (Nottingham) (Temporary Restriction and Prohibition of Traffic) Order 2006 No. 2006/1193. - Enabling power: Road Traffic Regulation Act 1984, s. 14 (1) (a). - Made: 14.04.2006. Coming into force: 21.04.2006. Effect: None. Territorial extent & classification: E. Local *Unpublished*

The A453 Trunk Road (M1 Junction 24 to Barton in Fabis) (Temporary Restriction and Prohibition of Traffic) 2006 No. 2006/194. - Enabling power: Road Traffic Regulation Act 1984, s. 14 (1) (a). - Made: 23.01.2006. Coming into force: 30.01.2006. Effect: None. Territorial extent & classification: E. Local *Unpublished*

The A453 Trunk Road (M1 Junctions 23A - 24, Kegworth) (Temporary Restriction and Prohibition of Traffic) Order 2006 No. 2006/2404. - Enabling power: Road Traffic Regulation Act 1984, s. 14 (1) (a). - Made: 18.08.2006. Coming into force: 25.08.2006. Effect: None. Territorial extent & classification: E. Local *Unpublished*

The A456 Trunk Road (Hagley Causeway, Worcestershire) (Temporary 40 Miles Per Hour Speed Restriction) Order 2006 No. 2006/1114. - Enabling power: Road Traffic Regulation Act 1984, s. 14 (1) (a). - Made: 04.04.2006. Coming into force: 11.04.2006. Effect: None. Territorial extent & classification: E. Local *Unpublished*

The A456 Trunk Road (Hagley, Worcestershire) (Temporary Restriction and Prohibition of Traffic) Order 2006 No. 2006/3143. - Enabling power: Road Traffic Regulation Act 1984, s. 14 (1) (a). - Made: 17.11.2006. Coming into force: 24.11.2006. Effect: None. Territorial extent & classification: E. Local *Unpublished*

The A456 Trunk Road (Hayley Green, Dudley) (Temporary Restriction and Prohibition of Traffic) Order 2006 No. 2006/11. - Enabling power: Road Traffic Regulation Act 1984, s. 14 (1) (a). - Made: 03.01.2006. Coming into force: 10.01.2006. Effect: None. Territorial extent & classification: E. Local *Unpublished*

The A456 Trunk Road (Near Hagley, Worcestershire) (Temporary Prohibition of Traffic) Order 2006 No. 2006/2497. - Enabling power: Road Traffic Regulation Act 1984, s. 14 (1) (a). - Made: 29.08.2006. Coming into force: 05.09.2006. Effect: None. Territorial extent & classification: E. Local *Unpublished*

The A456 Trunk Road (West Hagley, Worcestershire) (Temporary Restriction and Prohibition of Traffic) Order 2006 No. 2006/708. - Enabling power: Road Traffic Regulation Act 1984, s. 14 (1) (a). - Made: 24.02.2006. Coming into force: 03.03.2006. Effect: None. Territorial extent & classification: E. Local *Unpublished*

The A458 Trunk Road (Cardeston, Shropshire) (Temporary Prohibition of Traffic) Order 2006 No. 2006/1587. - Enabling power: Road Traffic Regulation Act 1984, s. 14 (1) (a). - Made: 02.06.2006. Coming into force: 09.06.2006. Effect: None. Territorial extent & classification: E. Local *Unpublished*

The A465 Trunk Road (Allensmore, Herefordshire) (Temporary 10 Miles Per Hour Speed Limit) Order 2006 No. 2006/72. - Enabling power: Road Traffic Regulation Act 1984, s. 14 (1) (a). - Made: 09.01.2006. Coming into force: 16.01.2006. Effect: None. Territorial extent & classification: E. Local *Unpublished*

The A465 Trunk Road (Belmont Road, Herefordshire) (Temporary 10 Miles Per Hour Speed Restriction) Order 2006 No. 2006/3009. - Enabling power: Road Traffic Regulation Act 1984, s. 14 (1) (a). - Made: 06.11.2006. Coming into force: 13.11.2006. Effect: None. Territorial extent & classification: E. Local *Unpublished*

The A465 Trunk Road (Didley, Herefordshire) (Temporary 40 Miles Per Hour Speed Restriction) Order 2006 No. 2006/3506. - Enabling power: Road Traffic Regulation Act 1984, s. 14 (1) (a). - Made: 27.12.2006. Coming into force: 03.01.2007. Effect: None. Territorial extent & classification: E. Local *Unpublished*

The A465 Trunk Road (Hereford) (Footway) (Temporary Prohibition of Traffic) Order 2006 No. 2006/1566. - Enabling power: Road Traffic Regulation Act 1984, s. 14 (1) (a). - Made: 22.05.2006. Coming into force: 29.05.2006. Effect: None. Territorial extent & classification: E. Local *Unpublished*

The A483 Trunk Road (Llynclys, Shropshire) (Temporary 10 Miles Per Hour Speed Restriction) Order 2006 No. 2006/1242. - Enabling power: Road Traffic Regulation Act 1984, s. 14 (1) (a). - Made: 21.04.2006. Coming into force: 28.04.2006. Effect: None. Territorial extent & classification: E. Local *Unpublished*

The A500 Trunk Road (Audley, Staffordshire) (Temporary Restriction and Prohibition of Traffic) Order 2006 No. 2006/1192. - Enabling power: Road Traffic Regulation Act 1984, s. 14 (1) (a). - Made: 18.04.2006. Coming into force: 25.04.2006. Effect: None. Territorial extent & classification: E. Local *Unpublished*

The A500 Trunk Road (East of Barthomley Roundabout, Staffordshire) (Temporary Restriction and Prohibition of Traffic) Order 2006 No. 2006/2757. - Enabling power: Road Traffic Regulation Act 1984, s. 14 (1) (a). - Made: 11.09.2006. Coming into force: 18.09.2006. Effect: None. Territorial extent & classification: E. Local *Unpublished*

The A500 Trunk Road (Hanford to Sideway, Stoke-on-Trent) (Temporary Prohibition and Restriction of Traffic) Order 2006 No. 2006/2035. - Enabling power: Road Traffic Regulation Act 1984, s. 14 (1) (a). - Made: 10.07.2006. Coming into force: 17.07.2006. Effect: None. Territorial extent & classification: E. Local *Unpublished*

The A500 Trunk Road (Hanford to Sideway, Stoke on Trent) (Temporary Prohibition of Traffic) Order 2006 No. 2006/3491. - Enabling power: Road Traffic Regulation Act 1984, s. 14 (1) (a). - Made: 27.12.2006. Coming into force: 03.01.2007. Effect: None. Territorial extent & classification: E. Local *Unpublished*

The A500 Trunk Road (M6 Junction 16) (Temporary Restriction and Prohibition of Traffic) Order 2006 No. 2006/2742. - Enabling power: Road Traffic Regulation Act 1984, s. 14 (1) (a). - Made: 09.10.2006. Coming into force: 16.10.2006. Effect: None. Territorial extent & classification: E. Local *Unpublished*

The A500 Trunk Road (Near Bignall End, Staffordshire) (Temporary 40 Miles Per Hour Speed Restriction) Order 2006 No. 2006/3193. - Enabling power: Road Traffic Regulation Act 1984, s. 14 (1) (a). - Made: 27.11.2006. Coming into force: 04.12.2006. Effect: None. Territorial extent & classification: E. Local *Unpublished*

The A500 Trunk Road (Porthill Interchange, Stoke-on-Trent) (Temporary Prohibition of Traffic) Order 2006 No. 2006/862. - Enabling power: Road Traffic Regulation Act 1984, s. 14 (1) (a). - Made: 13.03.2006. Coming into force: 20.03.2006. Effect: None. Territorial extent & classification: E. Local *Unpublished*

The A500 Trunk Road (Porthill to Wolstanton, Newcastle-under-Lyme, Stoke-on-Trent) (Temporary Restriction and Prohibition of Traffic) Order 2006 No. 2006/2678. - Enabling power: Road Traffic Regulation Act 1984, s. 14 (1) (a). - Made: 22.09.2006. Coming into force: 29.09.2006. Effect: None. Territorial extent & classification: E. Local *Unpublished*

The A500 Trunk Road (Sideway, Stoke-on-Trent) (Temporary Restriction and Prohibition of Traffic) Order 2006 No. 2006/2676. - Enabling power: Road Traffic Regulation Act 1984, s. 14 (1) (a). - Made: 22.09.2006. Coming into force: 29.09.2006. Effect: None. Territorial extent & classification: E. Local *Unpublished*

The A500 Trunk Road (Southbound Exit slip Road to Whieldon Road) (Temporary Prohibition of Traffic) Order 2006 No. 2006/1105. - Enabling power: Road Traffic Regulation Act 1984, s. 14 (1) (a). - Made: 10.04.2006. Coming into force: 04.05.2006. Effect: None. Territorial extent & classification: E. Local *Unpublished*

The A500 Trunk Road (Stoke Pathfinder Project) (30 Miles Per Hour and Northern Surfacing) (Temporary Prohibition and Restriction of Traffic) 2006 No. 2006/1416. - Enabling power: Road Traffic Regulation Act 1984, s. 14 (1) (a). - Made: 16.05.2006. Coming into force: 11.06.2006. Effect: None. Territorial extent & classification: E. Local *Unpublished*

The A500 Trunk Road (Stoke Pathfinder Project) (50 Miles Per Hour and Clearway) (Temporary Prohibition and Restriction of Traffic) 2006 No. 2006/2643. - Enabling power: Road Traffic Regulation Act 1984, ss. 14 (1) (a), 122A. - Made: 21.09.2006. Coming into force: 23.09.2006. Effect: None. Territorial extent & classification: E. Local *Unpublished*

The A500 Trunk Road (Stoke Pathfinder Project) (Temporary Prohibition of Traffic) 2006 No. 2006/56. - Enabling power: Road Traffic Regulation Act 1984, s. 14 (1) (a). - Made: 09.01.2006. Coming into force: 03.02.2006. Effect: None. Territorial extent & classification: E. Local *Unpublished*

The A500 Trunk Road (Talke Pits, Staffordshire) (Temporary 30 Miles Per Hour Speed Restriction) Order 2006 No. 2006/290. - Enabling power: Road Traffic Regulation Act 1984, s. 14 (1) (a). - Made: 03.02.2006. Coming into force: 10.02.2006. Effect: None. Territorial extent & classification: E. Local *Unpublished*

The A500 Trunk Road (Talke, Staffordshire) (Temporary Prohibition and Restriction of Traffic) 2006 No. 2006/1560. - Enabling power: Road Traffic Regulation Act 1984, s. 14 (1) (a). - Made: 22.05.2006. Coming into force: 29.05.2006. Effect: None. Territorial extent & classification: E. Local *Unpublished*

The A500 Trunk Road (Wolstanton, Staffordshire) (Temporary Prohibition and Restriction of Traffic) Order 2006 No. 2006/1784. - Enabling power: Road Traffic Regulation Act 1984, s. 14 (1) (a). - Made: 16.06.2006. Coming into force: 23.06.2006. Effect: None. Territorial extent & classification: E. Local *Unpublished*

The A556 Trunk Road (M6 Motorway Junction 19 Tabley Roundabout) (Temporary Prohibition and Restriction of Traffic) Order 2006 No. 2006/2843. - Enabling power: Road Traffic Regulation Act 1984, s. 14 (1) (a). - Made: 06.10.2006. Coming into force: 05.11.2006. Effect: None. Territorial extent & classification: E. Local *Unpublished*

The A556 Trunk Road (M6 Motorway Junction 19 Tabley Roundabout) (Temporary Prohibition and Restriction of Traffic) Order 2006 Amendment Order 2006 No. 2006/3020. - Enabling power: Road Traffic Regulation Act 1984, s. 14 (1) (a). - Made: 09.11.2006. Coming into force: 06.12.2006. Effect: S.I. 2006/2843 amended. Territorial extent & classification: E. Local *Unpublished*

The A556 Trunk Road (M6 Motorway Junction 19 to Bucklow Hill) (Temporary Prohibition of Traffic) Order 2006 No. 2006/2715. - Enabling power: Road Traffic Regulation Act 1984, s. 14 (1) (a). - Made: 22.09.2006. Coming into force: 15.10.2006. Effect: None. Territorial extent & classification: E. Local *Unpublished*

The A556 Trunk Road (RHS Flower Show) (Temporary Prohibition of Right Turns) Order 2006 No. 2006/1827. - Enabling power: Road Traffic Regulation Act 1984, s. 14 (1) (b). - Made: 23.06.2006. Coming into force: 18.07.2006. Effect: None. Territorial extent & classification: E. Local *Unpublished*

The A570 Trunk Road (Scarth Hill to Stanley Gate) (Temporary Prohibition of Traffic) Order 2006 No. 2006/2555. - Enabling power: Road Traffic Regulation Act 1984, s. 14 (1) (a). - Made: 25.08.2006. Coming into force: 19.09.2006. Effect: None. Territorial extent & classification: E. Local *Unpublished*

The A585 Trunk Road (Dock Street, Fleetwood) (Prohibition of Right Turns and Prohibition of Waiting) 2006 No. 2006/380. - Enabling power: Road Traffic Regulation Act 1984, ss. 1 (1), 2 (1) (2), 122A. - Made: 06.02.2006. Coming into force: 17.02.2006. Effect: None. Territorial extent & classification: E. Local *Unpublished*

The A585 Trunk Road (Fleetwood Road, Greenhalgh) (Temporary Prohibition and Restriction of Traffic) Order 2006 No. 2006/3500. - Enabling power: Road Traffic Regulation Act 1984, s. 14 (1) (a). - Made: 27.12.2006. Coming into force: 21.01.2007. Effect: None. Territorial extent & classification: E. Local *Unpublished*

The A585 Trunk Road (Singleton Crossroads) (Temporary Restriction of Traffic) 2006 No. 2006/230. - Enabling power: Road Traffic Regulation Act 1984, s. 14 (1) (a). - Made: 02.02.2006. Coming into force: 26.02.2006. Effect: None. Territorial extent & classification: E. Local *Unpublished*

The A590 Trunk Road (A5092 Greenodd Junction) (Temporary Restriction and Prohibition of Traffic) 2006 No. 2006/231. - Enabling power: Road Traffic Regulation Act 1984, s. 14 (1) (a). - Made: 01.02.2006. Coming into force: 19.02.2006. Effect: None. Territorial extent & classification: E. Local *Unpublished*

The A590 Trunk Road (Ayside) High and Low Newton Bypass (Temporary Restriction of Traffic) Order 2006 No. 2006/3501. - Enabling power: Road Traffic Regulation Act 1984, s. 14 (1) (a). - Made: 27.12.2006. Coming into force: 04.01.2007. Effect: None. Territorial extent & classification: E. Local *Unpublished*

The A590 Trunk Road (Brettargh Holt Entry Slip Road) (Temporary Prohibition of Traffic) Order 2006 No. 2006/1188. - Enabling power: Road Traffic Regulation Act 1984, s. 14 (1) (a). - Made: 18.04.2006. Coming into force: 14.05.2006. Effect: None. Territorial extent & classification: E. Local *Unpublished*

Road traffic: Traffic regulation

The A590 Trunk Road (Green Lane) (Temporary Prohibition of Traffic) Order 2006 No. 2006/188. - Enabling power: Road Traffic Regulation Act 1984, s. 14 (1) (b). - Made: 23.12.2005. Coming into force: 14.02.2006. Effect: None. Territorial extent & classification: E. Local *Unpublished*

The A590 Trunk Road (Haverthwaite) (Temporary Prohibition and Restriction of Traffic) Order 2006 No. 2006/190. - Enabling power: Road Traffic Regulation Act 1984, s. 14 (1) (a). - Made: 17.01.2006. Coming into force: 05.02.2006. Effect: None. Territorial extent & classification: E. Local *Unpublished*

The A590 Trunk Road (High Newton to Ayside) (Temporary Restriction of Traffic) Order 2006 No. 2006/701. - Enabling power: Road Traffic Regulation Act 1984, s. 14 (1) (a). - Made: 28.02.2006. Coming into force: 26.03.2006. Effect: None. Territorial extent & classification: E. Local *Unpublished*

The A590 Trunk Road (Lindale Bypass) (Temporary Restriction of Traffic) Order 2006 No. 2006/2224. - Enabling power: Road Traffic Regulation Act 1984, s. 14 (1) (a). - Made: 01.08.2006. Coming into force: 13.08.2006. Effect: None. Territorial extent & classification: E. Local *Unpublished*

The A590 Trunk Road (Meathop Roundabout to Catcragg) (Temporary Prohibition and Restriction of Traffic) 2006 No. 2006/232. - Enabling power: Road Traffic Regulation Act 1984, s. 14 (1) (a). - Made: 31.02.2006. Coming into force: 27.02.2006. Effect: None. Territorial extent & classification: E. Local *Unpublished*

The A590 Trunk Road (Milton Layby - Near Millness) (Temporary Prohibition and Restriction of Traffic) Order 2006 No. 2006/2479. - Enabling power: Road Traffic Regulation Act 1984, s. 14 (1) (a). - Made: 05.09.2006. Coming into force: 14.10.2006. Effect: None. Territorial extent & classification: E. Local *Unpublished*

The A590 Trunk Road (Milton) (Temporary Restriction of Traffic) Order 2006 No. 2006/3092. - Enabling power: Road Traffic Regulation Act 1984, s. 14 (1) (a). - Made: 14.11.2006. Coming into force: 10.12.2006. Effect: None. Territorial extent & classification: E. Local *Unpublished*

The A590 Trunk Road (Newby Bridge Surfacing Scheme) (Temporary Prohibition and Restriction of Traffic) Order 2006 No. 2006/1220. - Enabling power: Road Traffic Regulation Act 1984, s. 14 (1) (a). - Made: 21.04.2006. Coming into force: 16.05.2006. Effect: None. Territorial extent & classification: E. Local *Unpublished*

The A590 Trunk Road (Witherslack to Meathop) (Temporary Prohibition and Restriction of Traffic) Order 2006 No. 2006/1187. - Enabling power: Road Traffic Regulation Act 1984, s. 14 (1) (a). - Made: 18.04.2006. Coming into force: 14.05.2006. Effect: None. Territorial extent & classification: E. Local *Unpublished*

The A595 Trunk Road (Broadgate Resurfacing Scheme) (Temporary Restriction of Traffic) Order 2006 No. 2006/2208. - Enabling power: Road Traffic Regulation Act 1984, s. 14 (1) (a). - Made: 04.08.2006. Coming into force: 28.08.2006. Effect: None. Territorial extent & classification: E. Local *Unpublished*

The A595 Trunk Road (Gosforth Drainage Renewal Scheme) (Temporary Restriction of Traffic) Order 2006 No. 2006/2210. - Enabling power: Road Traffic Regulation Act 1984, s. 14 (1) (a). - Made: 04.08.2006. Coming into force: 03.09.2006. Effect: None. Territorial extent & classification: E. Local *Unpublished*

The A595 Trunk Road (Lillyhall) (Temporary Prohibition and Restriction of Traffic) Order 2006 No. 2006/3404. - Enabling power: Road Traffic Regulation Act 1984, s. 14 (1) (a). - Made: 11.12.2006. Coming into force: 07.01.2007. Effect: None. Territorial extent & classification: E. Local *Unpublished*

The A595 Trunk Road (Lillyhall to Distington) (Temporary Prohibition and Restriction of Traffic) Order 2006 No. 2006/2469. - Enabling power: Road Traffic Regulation Act 1984, s. 14 (1) (a). - Made: 21.08.2006. Coming into force: 17.09.2006. Effect: None. Territorial extent & classification: E. Local *Unpublished*

The A595 Trunk Road (Saltcoats to Thornflatt) (Temporary Prohibition and Restriction of Traffic) Order 2006 No. 2006/1609. - Enabling power: Road Traffic Regulation Act 1984, s. 14 (1) (a). - Made: 06.06.2006. Coming into force: 02.07.2006. Effect: None. Territorial extent & classification: E. Local *Unpublished*

The A616 Trunk Road (Westwood Roundabout to Newton Chambers Roundabout) (Temporary Prohibition of Traffic) Order 2006 No. 2006/1099. - Enabling power: Road Traffic Regulation Act 1984, s. 14 (1) (a). - Made: 07.04.2006. Coming into force: 19.04.2006. Effect: None. Territorial extent & classification: E. Local *Unpublished*

The A616 Trunk Road (Wortley Junction to Westwood Roundabout) (Temporary Prohibition of Traffic) Order 2006 No. 2006/2281. - Enabling power: Road Traffic Regulation Act 1984, s. 14 (1) (a). - Made: 17.08.2006. Coming into force: 30.08.2006. Effect: None. Territorial extent & classification: E. Local *Unpublished*

The A628 Trunk Road (Crowden to Tintwistle) (Temporary 10 Miles Per Hour Speed Restriction) Order 2006 No. 2006/2264. - Enabling power: Road Traffic Regulation Act 1984, s. 14 (1) (a). - Made: 08.08.2006. Coming into force: 20.08.2006. Effect: None. Territorial extent & classification: E. Local *Unpublished*

The A628 Trunk Road (Crowden Youth Hostel) (Temporary 10 Miles Per Hour Speed Restriction) Order 2006 No. 2006/1577. - Enabling power: Road Traffic Regulation Act 1984, s. 14 (1) (a). - Made: 30.05.2006. Coming into force: 11.06.2006. Effect: None. Territorial extent & classification: E. Local *Unpublished*

The A628 Trunk Road (Five Arches Bridge to Salter's Brook Bridge) (Temporary 10 Miles Per Hour Speed Restriction) Order 2006 No. 2006/2354. - Enabling power: Road Traffic Regulation Act 1984, s. 14 (1) (a). - Made: 22.08.2006. Coming into force: 03.09.2006. Effect: None. Territorial extent & classification: E. Local *Unpublished*

The A628 Trunk Road (Five Arches Bridge, Woodhead Pass) (Temporary Restriction and Prohibition of Traffic) Order 2006 No. 2006/2570. - Enabling power: Road Traffic Regulation Act 1984, s. 14 (1) (a). - Made: 15.09.2006. Coming into force: 28.09.2006. Effect: None. Territorial extent & classification: E. Local *Unpublished*

The A628 Trunk Road (Woolley Lane (West)Junction to Honngworth Brook Bridge) (Temporary Restriction and Prohibition of Traffic) Order 2006 No. 2006/1890. - Enabling power: Road Traffic Regulation Act 1984, s. 14 (1) (a). - Made: 04.07.2006. Coming into force: 16.07.2006. Effect: None. Territorial extent & classification: E. Local *Unpublished*

The A629 Trunk Road (Cononley Crossroads) (Temporary Restriction and Prohibition of Traffic) Order 2006 No. 2006/2062. - Enabling power: Road Traffic Regulation Act 1984, s. 14 (1) (a). - Made: 18.07.2006. Coming into force: 30.07.2006. Effect: None. Territorial extent & classification: E. Local *Unpublished*

The A650 Trunk Road (Crossflatts Roundabout) (Temporary Restriction and Prohibition of Traffic) Order 2006 No. 2006/2720. - Enabling power: Road Traffic Regulation Act 1984, s. 14 (1) (a). - Made: 02.10.2006. Coming into force: 15.10.2006. Effect: None. Territorial extent & classification: E. Local *Unpublished*

The A1089 Trunk Road (ASDA Roundabout - Tilbury Docks) (Temporary Restriction and Prohibition of Traffic) Order 2006 No. 2006/2777. - Enabling power: Road Traffic Regulation Act 1984, s. 14 (1) (a). - Made: 09.10.2006. Coming into force: 14.10.2006. Effect: None. Territorial extent & classification: E. Local *Unpublished*

The A1089 Trunk Road (Marchfoot Interchange) (Temporary Prohibition of Traffic) Order 2006 No. 2006/1434. - Enabling power: Road Traffic Regulation Act 1984, s. 14 (1) (a). - Made: 22.05.2006. Coming into force: 01.06.2006. Effect: None. Territorial extent & classification: E. Local *Unpublished*

The A1089 Trunk Road (Orsett Heath, Southbound Carriageway) (Temporary Restriction and Prohibition of Traffic) Order 2006 No. 2006/1986. - Enabling power: Road Traffic Regulation Act 1984, s. 14 (1) (b). - Made: 17.07.2006. Coming into force: 22.07.2006. Effect: None. Territorial extent & classification: E. Local *Unpublished*

The A2070 Trunk Road (A2042 Junction - Brenzett) (Temporary Restriction and Prohibition of Traffic) Order 2006 No. 2006/2725. - Enabling power: Road Traffic Regulation Act 1984, s. 14 (1) (b). - Made: 02.10.2006. Coming into force: 07.10.2006. Effect: None. Territorial extent & classification: E. Local *Unpublished*

The A2070 Trunk Road (Badmunstereifel Road, Near Ashford) (Temporary Restriction and Prohibition of Traffic) Order 2006 No. 2006/3044. - Enabling power: Road Traffic Regulation Act 1984, s. 14 (1) (a). - Made: 03.11.2006. Coming into force: 04.11.2006. Effect: None. Territorial extent & classification: E. Local *Unpublished*

The A2070 Trunk Road (Bad Munstereifel Road, Sevington) (Temporary Restriction of Traffic) Order 2006 No. 2006/1134. - Enabling power: Road Traffic Regulation Act 1984, s. 14 (1) (a). - Made: 18.04.2006. Coming into force: 24.04.2006. Effect: S.I. 2005/3008 revoked. Territorial extent & classification: E. Local *Unpublished*

The A3113 Trunk Road (M25 Junction 14 - A3044) (Temporary 50 Miles Per Hour Speed Restriction) Order 2006 No. 2006/1433. - Enabling power: Road Traffic Regulation Act 1984, s. 14 (1) (b). - Made: 22.05.2006. Coming into force: 01.06.2006. Effect: None. Territorial extent & classification: E. Local *Unpublished*

The A4123 Trunk Road (Oldbury) (Temporary 10 Miles Per Hour Speed Restriction) Order 2006 No. 2006/2562. - Enabling power: Road Traffic Regulation Act 1984, s. 14 (1) (a). - Made: 18.09.2006. Coming into force: 25.09.2006. Effect: None. Territorial extent & classification: E. Local *Unpublished*

The A4123 Trunk Road (Wolverhampton Road) (Prohibition and Restriction of Waiting) Order 2006 No. 2006/84. - Enabling power: Road Traffic Regulation Act 1984, ss. 1 (1), 2 (1) (2), 4 (1) (2), sch. 9, para. 27 (1). - Made: 04.01.2006. Coming into force: 18.01.2006. Effect: S.I. 1991/2183 revoked. Territorial extent & classification: E. Local *Unpublished*

The A5036 Trunk Road (Church Road) (Temporary Prohibition of Traffic) Order 2006 No. 2006/2735. - Enabling power: Road Traffic Regulation Act 1984, s. 14 (1) (a). - Made: 18.09.2006. Coming into force: 15.10.2006. Effect: None. Territorial extent & classification: E. Local *Unpublished*

The A5036 Trunk Road Princess Way (Eastbound Carriageway Between the A567 (Bridge Road) Roundabout and the A5090 (Hawthorne Road)) (Temporary Prohibition of Traffic) Order 2006 No. 2006/2566. - Enabling power: Road Traffic Regulation Act 1984, s. 14 (1) (a). - Made: 21.08.2006. Coming into force: 17.09.2006. Effect: None. Territorial extent & classification: E. Local *Unpublished*

The A5036 Trunk Road (Westbound Between St Matthew's Avenue and Orrell Road) (Temporary Prohibition of Traffic and Pedestrians) Order 2006 No. 2006/1799. - Enabling power: Road Traffic Regulation Act 1984, s. 14 (1) (a). - Made: 26.06.2006. Coming into force: 23.07.2006. Effect: None. Territorial extent & classification: E. Local *Unpublished*

The A5103 Trunk Road (Southbound, Exit Slip Road to the A560 Altrincham Road) (Temporary Prohibition of Traffic) Order 2006 No. 2006/2358. - Enabling power: Road Traffic Regulation Act 1984, s. 14 (1) (a). - Made: 11.08.2006. Coming into force: 10.09.2006. Effect: None. Territorial extent & classification: E. Local *Unpublished*

Road traffic: Traffic regulation

The A5103 Trunk Road (Southbound, Exit Slip Road to the B5167 Palatine Road) (Temporary Prohibition of Traffic) Order 2006 No. 2006/2357. - Enabling power: Road Traffic Regulation Act 1984, s. 14 (1) (a). - Made: 11.08.2006. Coming into force: 10.09.2006. Effect: None. Territorial extent & classification: E. Local *Unpublished*

The A5111 Trunk Road (Link Road) (Raynesway, Derby) (Temporary Prohibition and Restriction of Traffic) Order 2006 No. 2006/324. - Enabling power: Road Traffic Regulation Act 1984, s. 14 (1) (a). - Made: 06.02.2006. Coming into force: 13.02.2006. Effect: None. Territorial extent & classification: E. Local *Unpublished*

The A5111 Trunk Road (Raynesway, Derby) (Link Roads) (Temporary Prohibition of Traffic) Order 2006 No. 2006/3176. - Enabling power: Road Traffic Regulation Act 1984, s. 14 (1) (a). - Made: 24.11.2006. Coming into force: 01.12.2006. Effect: None. Territorial extent & classification: E. Local *Unpublished*

The A5117 Trunk Road (Deeside Junction Improvement) (Temporary Restriction of Traffic) Order 2006 No. 2006/2758. - Enabling power: Road Traffic Regulation Act 1984, s. 14 (1) (a). - Made: 04.10.2006. Coming into force: 09.10.2006. Effect: None. Territorial extent & classification: E. Local *Unpublished*

The M1 and M42 Motorways and the A42 Trunk Road (M42 Junction 11 to M1 Junction 23A, Leicestershire) (Temporary Restriction and Prohibition of Traffic) Order 2006 No. 2006/2517. - Enabling power: Road Traffic Regulation Act 1984, s. 14 (1) (a). - Made: 01.09.2006. Coming into force: 08.09.2006. Effect: None. Territorial extent & classification: E. Local *Unpublished*

The M1and M69 Motorways (M1 Junction 21, Leicestershire) (Temporary 30 Miles Per Hour and 50 Miles Per Hour Speed Restriction) Order 2006 No. 2006/2029. - Enabling power: Road Traffic Regulation Act 1984, ss. 14 (1) (a), 15 (2), sch. 9, para. 27 (1). - Made: 17.07.2006. Coming into force: 24.07.2006. Effect: S.I. 2006/441 revoked. Territorial extent & classification: E. Local *Unpublished*

The M1 and M69 Motorways (M1 Junction 21, Leicestershire) (Temporary Prohibition of Traffic) Order 2006 No. 2006/2547. - Enabling power: Road Traffic Regulation Act 1984, s. 14 (1) (a). - Made: 15.09.2006. Coming into force: 22.09.2006. Effect: None. Territorial extent & classification: E. Local *Unpublished*

The M1 and M69 Motorways (M1 Junction 21, Leicestershire) (Temporary Prohibition of Traffic) Order 2006 No. 2006/1021. - Enabling power: Road Traffic Regulation Act 1984, s. 14 (1) (a). - Made: 24.03.2006. Coming into force: 31.03.2006. Effect: None. Territorial extent & classification: E. Local *Unpublished*

The M1 and M69 Motorways (M1 Junction 21, Leicestershire) (Temporary Restriction of Traffic) Order 2006 No. 2006/441. - Enabling power: Road Traffic Regulation Act 1984, s. 14 (1) (a). - Made: 10.02.2006. Coming into force: 17.02.2006. Effect: None. Territorial extent & classification: E. Local. - Revoked by S.I. 2006/2029 (Unpublished) *Unpublished*

The M1 Motorway and the M10 Motorway (Junctions 6 - 8 and M10 Junction 1) (Temporary Prohibition of Traffic) Order 2006 No. 2006/2107. - Enabling power: Road Traffic Regulation Act 1984, s. 14 (1) (a), sch. 9, para. 27 (1). - Made: 24.07.2006. Coming into force: 01.08.2006. Effect: S.I. 2005/2370, 3013; 2006/891, 894 revoked. Territorial extent & classification: E. Local *Unpublished*

The M1 Motorway and the M62 Motorway (Lofthouse Interchange) (Temporary Prohibition of Traffic) (No. 2) Order 2006 No. 2006/1823. - Enabling power: Road Traffic Regulation Act 1984, s. 14 (1) (a). - Made: 16.06.2006. Coming into force: 29.06.2006. Effect: None. Territorial extent & classification: E. Local *Unpublished*

The M1 Motorway and the M62 Motorway (Lofthouse Interchange) (Temporary Prohibition of Traffic) Order 2006 No. 2006/1576. - Enabling power: Road Traffic Regulation Act 1984, s. 14 (1) (a). - Made: 30.05.2006. Coming into force: 11.06.2006. Effect: None. Territorial extent & classification: E. Local *Unpublished*

The M1 Motorway and the M62 Motorway (Lofthouse Interchange) (Temporary Restriction and Prohibition of Traffic) Order 2006 No. 2006/3492. - Enabling power: Road Traffic Regulation Act 1984, s. 14 (1) (a). - Made: 29.12.2006. Coming into force: 07.01.2007. Effect: None. Territorial extent & classification: E. Local *Unpublished*

The M1 Motorway (Courteenhall - Quinton Road Bridge, Northamptonshire) (Temporary 50 Miles Per Hour Speed Restriction) Order 2006 No. 2006/1201. - Enabling power: Road Traffic Regulation Act 1984, s. 14 (1) (a). - Made: 24.04.2006. Coming into force: 01.05.2006. Effect: None. Territorial extent & classification: E. Local *Unpublished*

The M1 Motorway (Junction 1, Northbound Entry Slip Road) (Temporary Prohibition of Traffic) Order 2006 No. 2006/1575. - Enabling power: Road Traffic Regulation Act 1984, s. 14 (1) (a). - Made: 05.06.2006. Coming into force: 14.06.2006. Effect: None. Territorial extent & classification: E. Local *Unpublished*

The M1 Motorway (Junction 4, Northbound Entry Slip Road) (Temporary Prohibition of Traffic) Order 2006 No. 2006/3040. - Enabling power: Road Traffic Regulation Act 1984, s. 14 (1) (a). - Made: 06.11.2006. Coming into force: 13.11.2006. Effect: None. Territorial extent & classification: E. Local *Unpublished*

The M1 Motorway (Junction 6 - Junction 11), the M10 Motorway (M1 - Junction 1) and the A414 Trunk Road (Temporary Restriction and Prohibition of Traffic) (No. 2) Order 2006 No. 2006/1557. - Enabling power: Road Traffic Regulation Act 1984, ss. 14 (1) (a) (7), 15 (2), sch. 9, para. 27 (1). - Made: 22.05.2006. Coming into force: 29.05.2006. Effect: S.I. 2006/815 revoked. Territorial extent & classification: E. Local *Unpublished*

Road traffic: Traffic regulation

The M1 Motorway (Junction 6 - Junction 11), the M10 Motorway (M1 - Junction 1) and the A414 Trunk Road (Temporary Restriction and Prohibition of Traffic) Order 2006 No. 2006/815. - Enabling power: Road Traffic Regulation Act 1984, ss. 14 (1) (a) (7), 15 (2). - Made: 10.03.2006. Coming into force: 17.03.2006. Effect: None. Territorial extent & classification: E. Local. - Revoked by S.I. 2006/1557 *Unpublished*

The M1 Motorway (Junction 6, Slip Roads) (Temporary Prohibition of Traffic) Order 2006 No. 2006/891. - Enabling power: Road Traffic Regulation Act 1984, s. 14 (1) (a). - Made: 20.03.2006. Coming into force: 01.04.2006. Effect: None. Territorial extent & classification: E. Local. - Revoked by S.I. 2006/2107 (Unpublished) *Unpublished*

The M1 Motorway (Junction 8, Southbound Slip Roads) (Temporary Prohibition of Traffic) Order 2006 No. 2006/894. - Enabling power: Road Traffic Regulation Act 1984, s. 14 (1) (a). - Made: 20.03.2006. Coming into force: 01.04.2006. Effect: None. Territorial extent & classification: E. Local. - Revoked by S.I. 2006/2107 (Unpublished) *Unpublished*

The M1 Motorway (Junction 10) Southbound Exit Slip Road (Temporary Prohibition of Traffic) Order 2006 No. 2006/329. - Enabling power: Road Traffic Regulation Act 1984, s. 14 (1) (a). - Made: 06.02.2006. Coming into force: 13.02.2006. Effect: None. Territorial extent & classification: E. Local *Unpublished*

The M1 Motorway (Junction 12, Bedfordshire) (Temporary Restriction and Prohibition of Traffic) Order 2006 No. 2006/2711. - Enabling power: Road Traffic Regulation Act 1984, s. 14 (1) (a). - Made: 02.10.2006. Coming into force: 09.10.2006. Effect: None. Territorial extent & classification: E. Local *Unpublished*

The M1 Motorway (Junction 13) Northbound Entry Slip Road (Temporary Prohibition of Traffic) Order 2006 No. 2006/902. - Enabling power: Road Traffic Regulation Act 1984, s. 14 (1) (a). - Made: 20.03.2006. Coming into force: 27.03.2006. Effect: None. Territorial extent & classification: E. Local *Unpublished*

The M1 Motorway (Junction 13) Northbound Exit Slip Road (Temporary Restriction and Prohibition of Traffic) Order 2006 No. 2006/3133. - Enabling power: Road Traffic Regulation Act 1984, s. 14 (1) (a). - Made: 09.10.2006. Coming into force: 16.10.2006. Effect: None. Territorial extent & classification: E. Local *Unpublished*

The M1 Motorway (Junction 15a and 17, Northamptonshire) (Temporary Restriction and Prohibition of Traffic) Order 2006 No. 2006/2291. - Enabling power: Road Traffic Regulation Act 1984, ss. 14 (1) (a) (7). - Made: 15.08.2006. Coming into force: 22.08.2006. Effect: None. Territorial extent & classification: E. Local *Unpublished*

The M1 Motorway (Junction 16 - Junction 17, Daventry) (Temporary 50 Miles Per Hour Speed Restriction) Order 2006 No. 2006/3378. - Enabling power: Road Traffic Regulation Act 1984, s. 14 (1) (a). - Made: 11.12.2006. Coming into force: 18.12.2006. Effect: None. Territorial extent & classification: E. Local *Unpublished*

The M1 Motorway (Junction 16) Northbound Entry Slip Road (Temporary Prohibition of Traffic) Order 2006 No. 2006/1857. - Enabling power: Road Traffic Regulation Act 1984, s. 14 (1) (a). - Made: 05.06.2006. Coming into force: 12.06.2006. Effect: None. Territorial extent & classification: E. Local *Unpublished*

The M1 Motorway (Junction 16 to 15A, Northamptonshire) (Temporary 50 Miles Per Hour speed Restriction) Order 2006 No. 2006/2092. - Enabling power: Road Traffic Regulation Act 1984, ss. 14 (1) (a). - Made: 21.07.2006. Coming into force: 28.07.2006. Effect: None. Territorial extent & classification: E. Local *Unpublished*

The M1 Motorway (Junction 19, Leicestershire) Southbound Entry Slip Road (Temporary Restriction and Prohibition of Traffic) Order 2006 No. 2006/2058. - Enabling power: Road Traffic Regulation Act 1984, ss. 14 (1) (a) (7). - Made: 17.07.2006. Coming into force: 24.07.2006. Effect: None. Territorial extent & classification: E. Local *Unpublished*

The M1 Motorway (Junction 19) (Northbound Entry Slip Road) (Temporary Prohibition of Traffic) Order 2006 No. 2006/2873. - Enabling power: Road Traffic Regulation Act 1984, s. 14 (1) (a). - Made: 16.10.2006. Coming into force: 23.10.2006. Effect: None. Territorial extent & classification: E. Local *Unpublished*

The M1 Motorway (Junction 24A) and the A50 Trunk Road (Lockington) (Temporary Restriction and Prohibition of Traffic) Order 2006 No. 2006/2033. - Enabling power: Road Traffic Regulation Act 1984, ss. 14 (1) (a). - Made: 07.07.2006. Coming into force: 14.07.2006. Effect: None. Territorial extent & classification: E. Local *Unpublished*

The M1 Motorway (Junction 24A) (Northbound Entry Slip Road) (Temporary Prohibition of Traffic) Order 2006 No. 2006/2546. - Enabling power: Road Traffic Regulation Act 1984, s. 14 (1) (a). - Made: 15.09.2006. Coming into force: 22.09.2006. Effect: None. Territorial extent & classification: E. Local *Unpublished*

The M1 Motorway (Junction 24A) (Southbound Exit Slip Road) (Temporary Prohibition of Traffic) Order 2006 No. 2006/993. - Enabling power: Road Traffic Regulation Act 1984, s. 14 (1) (a). - Made: 20.03.2006. Coming into force: 27.03.2006. Effect: None. Territorial extent & classification: E. Local *Unpublished*

The M1 Motorway (Junction 24), the A6, the A50 and the A453 Trunk Roads (Temporary Prohibition and Restriction of Traffic) Order 2006 No. 2006/3515. - Enabling power: Road Traffic Regulation Act 1984, s. 14 (1) (a). - Made: 29.12.2006. Coming into force: 05.01.2007. Effect: None. Territorial extent & classification: E. Local *Unpublished*

The M1 Motorway (Junction 24), the A6, the A50 and the A453 Trunk Roads (Temporary Prohibition and Restriction of Traffic) Order 2006 No. 2006/2115. - Enabling power: Road Traffic Regulation Act 1984, s. 14 (1) (a). - Made: 21.07.2006. Coming into force: 28.07.2006. Effect: None. Territorial extent & classification: E. Local *Unpublished*

The M1 Motorway (Junction 25) (Southbound Entry Slip Road) (Temporary Prohibition of Traffic) Order 2006 No. 2006/3177. - Enabling power: Road Traffic Regulation Act 1984, s. 14 (1) (a). - Made: 24.11.2006. Coming into force: 01.12.2006. Effect: None. Territorial extent & classification: E. Local *Unpublished*

The M1 Motorway (Junction 28) and A38 Trunk Road (Temporary Restriction of Traffic) Order 2006 No. 2006/2882. - Enabling power: Road Traffic Regulation Act 1984, s. 14 (1) (a). - Made: 23.10.2006. Coming into force: 30.10.2006. Effect: None. Territorial extent & classification: E. Local *Unpublished*

The M1 Motorway (Junction 28) (Temporary Prohibition of Traffic) Order 2006 No. 2006/1411. - Enabling power: Road Traffic Regulation Act 1984, s. 14 (1) (a). - Made: 17.05.2006. Coming into force: 24.05.2006. Effect: None. Territorial extent & classification: E. Local *Unpublished*

The M1 Motorway (Junction 29, Derbyshire) (Temporary Restriction and Prohibition of Traffic) Order 2006 No. 2006/293. - Enabling power: Road Traffic Regulation Act 1984, s. 14 (1) (a). - Made: 03.02.2006. Coming into force: 10.02.2006. Effect: None. Territorial extent & classification: E. Local *Unpublished*

The M1 Motorway (Junction 30) (Southbound Entry Slip Road) (Temporary Prohibition of Traffic) Order 2006 No. 2006/3014. - Enabling power: Road Traffic Regulation Act 1984, s. 14 (1) (a). - Made: 06.11.2006. Coming into force: 13.11.2006. Effect: None. Territorial extent & classification: E. Local *Unpublished*

The M1 Motorway (Junction 31 to Junction 32) and the M18 Motorway (Temporary Restriction and Prohibition of Traffic) Order 2006 No. 2006/3448. - Enabling power: Road Traffic Regulation Act 1984, s. 14 (1) (a) (7). - Made: 18.12.2006. Coming into force: 02.01.2007. Effect: None. Territorial extent & classification: E. Local *Unpublished*

The M1 Motorway (Junction 32 to Junction 33) and the M18 Motorway (Temporary Prohibition of Traffic) Order 2006 No. 2006/2025. - Enabling power: Road Traffic Regulation Act 1984, s. 14 (1) (a). - Made: 19.07.2006. Coming into force: 30.07.2006. Effect: None. Territorial extent & classification: E. Local *Unpublished*

The M1 Motorway (Junction 32 to Junction 33) and the M18 Motorway (Temporary Restriction and Prohibition of Traffic) Order 2006 No. 2006/1584. - Enabling power: Road Traffic Regulation Act 1984, s. 14 (1) (a) (7). - Made: 16.05.2006. Coming into force: 30.05.2006. Effect: None. Territorial extent & classification: E. Local *Unpublished*

The M1 Motorway (Junction 33 and Junction 35) (Temporary Prohibition of Traffic) Order 2006 No. 2006/1817. - Enabling power: Road Traffic Regulation Act 1984, s. 14 (1) (a). - Made: 16.06.2006. Coming into force: 29.07.2006. Effect: None. Territorial extent & classification: E. Local *Unpublished*

The M1 Motorway (Junction 33, Brinsworth) (Temporary Prohibition of Traffic) Order 2006 No. 2006/1485. - Enabling power: Road Traffic Regulation Act 1984, s. 14 (1) (a). - Made: 25.04.2006. Coming into force: 07.05.2006. Effect: None. Territorial extent & classification: E. Local *Unpublished*

The M1 Motorway (Junction 33, Southbound Exit Slip Road) (Temporary Prohibition of Traffic) Order 2006 No. 2006/1225. - Enabling power: Road Traffic Regulation Act 1984, s. 14 (1) (a). - Made: 24.03.2006. Coming into force: 07.05.2006. Effect: None. Territorial extent & classification: E. Local *Unpublished*

The M1 Motorway (Junction 34 to Junction 35) (Temporary 50 Miles Per Hour Speed Restriction) Order 2006 No. 2006/2043. - Enabling power: Road Traffic Regulation Act 1984, ss. 14 (1) (b). - Made: 21.07.2006. Coming into force: 02.08.2006. Effect: None. Territorial extent & classification: E. Local *Unpublished*

The M1 Motorway (Junction 35A, Southbound Entry Slip Road) (Temporary Prohibition of Traffic) (No. 2) Order 2006 No. 2006/2768. - Enabling power: Road Traffic Regulation Act 1984, s. 14 (1) (a). - Made: 06.10.2006. Coming into force: 19.10.2006. Effect: None. Territorial extent & classification: E. Local *Unpublished*

The M1 Motorway (Junction 35A, Southbound Entry Slip Road) (Temporary Prohibition of Traffic) Order 2006 No. 2006/1287. - Enabling power: Road Traffic Regulation Act 1984, s. 14 (1) (a). - Made: 05.05.2006. Coming into force: 17.05.2006. Effect: None. Territorial extent & classification: E. Local *Unpublished*

The M1 Motorway (Junction 35A) (Temporary Prohibition of Traffic) Order 2006 No. 2006/1137. - Enabling power: Road Traffic Regulation Act 1984, s. 14 (1) (a). - Made: 18.04.2006. Coming into force: 27.04.2006. Effect: None. Territorial extent & classification: E. Local *Unpublished*

The M1 Motorway (Junction 35A to Junction 39) (Temporary Restriction and Prohibition of Traffic) Order 2006 No. 2006/3029. - Enabling power: Road Traffic Regulation Act 1984, s. 14 (1) (a) (7). - Made: 20.10.2006. Coming into force: 31.10.2006. Effect: None. Territorial extent & classification: E. Local *Unpublished*

The M1 Motorway (Junction 36) (Temporary Prohibition of Traffic) Order 2006 No. 2006/2355. - Enabling power: Road Traffic Regulation Act 1984, s. 14 (1) (a). - Made: 22.08.2006. Coming into force: 03.09.2006. Effect: None. Territorial extent & classification: E. Local *Unpublished*

Road traffic: Traffic regulation

The M1 Motorway (Junction 36 to Junction 37) (Temporary Restriction and Prohibition of Traffic) Order 2006 No. 2006/2853. - Enabling power: Road Traffic Regulation Act 1984, s. 14 (1) (a) (7). - Made: 18.10.2006. Coming into force: 29.10.2006. Effect: None. Territorial extent & classification: E. Local *Unpublished*

The M1 Motorway (Junction 38, Northbound Entry Slip Road) (Temporary Prohibition of Traffic) Order 2006 No. 2006/1409. - Enabling power: Road Traffic Regulation Act 1984, s. 14 (1) (a). - Made: 09.05.2006. Coming into force: 21.05.2006. Effect: None. Territorial extent & classification: E. Local *Unpublished*

The M1 Motorway (Junction 39, Junction 40 and Junction 41) (Temporary Prohibition of Traffic) Order 2006 No. 2006/1822. - Enabling power: Road Traffic Regulation Act 1984, s. 14 (1) (a). - Made: 16.06.2006. Coming into force: 29.06.2006. Effect: None. Territorial extent & classification: E. Local *Unpublished*

The M1 Motorway (Junction 40, Southbound Exit Slip Road) (Temporary Prohibition of Traffic) Order 2006 No. 2006/2026. - Enabling power: Road Traffic Regulation Act 1984, ss. 14 (1) (a). - Made: 11.07.2006. Coming into force: 23.07.2006. Effect: None. Territorial extent & classification: E. Local *Unpublished*

The M1 Motorway (Junction 41, Northbound Exit Slip Road) (Temporary Prohibition of Traffic) Order 2006 No. 2006/1889. - Enabling power: Road Traffic Regulation Act 1984, s. 14 (1) (a). - Made: 04.07.2006. Coming into force: 16.07.2006. Effect: None. Territorial extent & classification: E. Local *Unpublished*

The M1 Motorway (Junction 42, Lofthouse Interchange) (Temporary Restriction and Prohibition of Traffic) Order 2006 No. 2006/696. - Enabling power: Road Traffic Regulation Act 1984, s. 14 (1) (a). - Made: 24.02.2006. Coming into force: 09.03.2006. Effect: None. Territorial extent & classification: E. Local *Unpublished*

The M1 Motorway (Junction 44, Rothwell, Haigh) (Temporary Prohibition of Traffic) (No. 2) Order 2006 No. 2006/2580. - Enabling power: Road Traffic Regulation Act 1984, s. 14 (1) (a). - Made: 18.09.2006. Coming into force: 29.09.2006. Effect: None. Territorial extent & classification: E. Local *Unpublished*

The M1 Motorway (Junction 44, Rothwell Haigh) (Temporary Prohibition of Traffic) Order 2006 No. 2006/1288. - Enabling power: Road Traffic Regulation Act 1984, s. 14 (1) (a). - Made: 09.05.2006. Coming into force: 22.05.2006. Effect: None. Territorial extent & classification: E. Local *Unpublished*

The M1 Motorway (Junction 46, Austhorpe) (Temporary Prohibition of Traffic) (No. 2) Order 2006 No. 2006/2589. - Enabling power: Road Traffic Regulation Act 1984, s. 14 (1) (a). - Made: 11.09.2006. Coming into force: 22.09.2006. Effect: None. Territorial extent & classification: E. Local *Unpublished*

The M1 Motorway (Junction 46, Austhorpe) (Temporary Prohibition of Traffic) Order 2006 No. 2006/1599. - Enabling power: Road Traffic Regulation Act 1984, s. 14 (1) (a). - Made: 05.06.2006. Coming into force: 17.06.2006. Effect: None. Territorial extent & classification: E. Local *Unpublished*

The M1 Motorway (Junction 46, Austhorpe) (Temporary Restriction and Prohibition of Traffic) Order 2006 No. 2006/2421. - Enabling power: Road Traffic Regulation Act 1984, s. 14 (1) (a). - Made: 29.08.2006. Coming into force: 10.09.2006. Effect: None. Territorial extent & classification: E. Local *Unpublished*

The M1 Motorway (Junction 47, Parlington) (Temporary Prohibition of Traffic) (No. 2) Order 2006 No. 2006/1570. - Enabling power: Road Traffic Regulation Act 1984, s. 14 (1) (a). - Made: 30.05.2006. Coming into force: 13.06.2006. Effect: None. Territorial extent & classification: E. Local *Unpublished*

The M1 Motorway (Junction 47, Parlington) (Temporary Prohibition of Traffic) (No. 3) Order 2006 No. 2006/2458. - Enabling power: Road Traffic Regulation Act 1984, s. 14 (1) (a). - Made: 01.09.2006. Coming into force: 15.09.2006. Effect: None. Territorial extent & classification: E. Local *Unpublished*

The M1 Motorway (Junction 47, Parlington) (Temporary Prohibition of Traffic) Order 2006 No. 2006/1377. - Enabling power: Road Traffic Regulation Act 1984, s. 14 (1) (a). - Made: 12.05.2006. Coming into force: 24.05.2006. Effect: None. Territorial extent & classification: E. Local *Unpublished*

The M1 Motorway (Junctions 1 to 3, Slip Roads) (Temporary Prohibition of Traffic) Order 2006 No. 2006/889. - Enabling power: Road Traffic Regulation Act 1984, s. 14 (1) (a). - Made: 20.03.2006. Coming into force: 01.04.2006. Effect: None. Territorial extent & classification: E. Local *Unpublished*

The M1 Motorway (Junctions 11 and 12) Slip Roads (Bedfordshire) (Temporary Prohibition of Traffic) Order 2006 No. 2006/2017. - Enabling power: Road Traffic Regulation Act 1984, s. 14 (1) (a). - Made: 10.07.2006. Coming into force: 17.07.2006. Effect: None. Territorial extent & classification: E. Local *Unpublished*

The M1 Motorway (Junctions 12 - 11) (Temporary Restriction of Traffic) Order 2006 No. 2006/2653. - Enabling power: Road Traffic Regulation Act 1984, s. 14 (1) (a) (7). - Made: 25.09.2006. Coming into force: 02.10.2006. Effect: None. Territorial extent & classification: E. Local *Unpublished*

The M1 Motorway (Junctions 15A and 16) (Temporary Restriction and Prohibition of Traffic) Order 2006 No. 2006/1828. - Enabling power: Road Traffic Regulation Act 1984, s. 14 (1) (a). - Made: 27.06.2006. Coming into force: 04.07.2006. Effect: None. Territorial extent & classification: E. Local *Unpublished*

The M1 Motorway (Junctions 18 - 19) (Temporary Prohibition and Restriction of Traffic) Order 2006 No. 2006/2063. - Enabling power: Road Traffic Regulation Act 1984, ss. 14 (1) (a) (7). - Made: 20.07.2006. Coming into force: 22.07.2006. Effect: None. Territorial extent & classification: E. Local *Unpublished*

The M1 Motorway (Junctions 20 - 21, Leicestershire) (Temporary 40 Miles Per Hour Speed Restriction) Order 2006 No. 2006/2022. - Enabling power: Road Traffic Regulation Act 1984, s. 14 (1) (a). - Made: 17.07.2006. Coming into force: 24.07.2006. Effect: None. Territorial extent & classification: E. Local *Unpublished*

The M1 Motorway (Leicester Forest East Service Area) (Slip Road) (Temporary Prohibition of Traffic) Order 2006 No. 2006/3490. - Enabling power: Road Traffic Regulation Act 1984, s. 14 (1) (a). - Made: 27.12.2006. Coming into force: 03.01.2007. Effect: None. Territorial extent & classification: E. Local *Unpublished*

The M1 Motorway (Little Linford - Gayhurst Road Bridge, Milton Keynes, Buckinghamshire) (Temporary Restriction of Traffic) Order 2006 No. 2006/1202. - Enabling power: Road Traffic Regulation Act 1984, s. 14 (1) (a) (7). - Made: 24.04.2006. Coming into force: 01.05.2006. Effect: None. Territorial extent & classification: E. Local *Unpublished*

The M1 Motorway (South of Junction 25, Long Eaton, Derbyshire) (Temporary Restriction and Prohibition of Traffic) Order 2006 No. 2006/2047. - Enabling power: Road Traffic Regulation Act 1984, ss. 14 (1) (a) (7). - Made: 03.07.2006. Coming into force: 10.07.2006. Effect: None. Territorial extent & classification: E. Local *Unpublished*

The M1 Motorway (Trowell, Nottinghamshire) (Temporary Restriction and Prohibition of Traffic) Order 2006 No. 2006/3013. - Enabling power: Road Traffic Regulation Act 1984, s. 14 (1) (a) (7). - Made: 06.11.2006. Coming into force: 13.11.2006. Effect: None. Territorial extent & classification: E. Local *Unpublished*

The M1 Motorway (Willen Road Bridge, Milton Keynes, Buckinghamshire) (Temporary Restriction of Traffic) Order 2006 No. 2006/1369. - Enabling power: Road Traffic Regulation Act 1984, s. 14 (1) (a) (7). - Made: 16.05.2006. Coming into force: 23.05.2006. Effect: None. Territorial extent & classification: E. Local *Unpublished*

The M2 Motorway and the A2 Trunk Road (Junction 7, Brenley Corner) (Temporary Restriction and Prohibition of Traffic) Order 2006 No. 2006/27. - Enabling power: Road Traffic Regulation Act 1984, s. 14 (1) (a). - Made: 03.01.2006. Coming into force: 07.01.2006. Effect: None. Territorial extent & classification: E. Local *Unpublished*

The M2 Motorway (Junction 3, Londonbound Carriageway) (Temporary Prohibition of Traffic) Order 2006 No. 2006/2769. - Enabling power: Road Traffic Regulation Act 1984, s. 14 (1) (a). - Made: 09.10.2006. Coming into force: 14.10.2006. Effect: None. Territorial extent & classification: E. Local *Unpublished*

The M2 Motorway (Junction 5, Londonbound Slip Roads) (Temporary Prohibition of Traffic) Order 2006 No. 2006/2721. - Enabling power: Road Traffic Regulation Act 1984, s. 14 (1) (a). - Made: 02.10.2006. Coming into force: 07.10.2006. Effect: None. Territorial extent & classification: E. Local *Unpublished*

The M2 Motorway (Junctions 3 - 5) (Temporary Restriction and Prohibition of Traffic) Order 2006 No. 2006/1212. - Enabling power: Road Traffic Regulation Act 1984, s. 14 (1) (a) (7). - Made: 24.04.2006. Coming into force: 29.04.2006. Effect: None. Territorial extent & classification: E. Local *Unpublished*

The M2 Motorway (Junctions 4 - 3, Londonbound Carriageway) (Temporary Restriction of Traffic) Order 2006 No. 2006/3253. - Enabling power: Road Traffic Regulation Act 1984, s. 14 (1) (a) (7). - Made: 04.12.2006. Coming into force: 06.01.2007. Effect: None. Territorial extent & classification: E. Local *Unpublished*

The M2 Motorway (Junctions 6 - 7) (Temporary Prohibition of Traffic) Order 2006 No. 2006/2770. - Enabling power: Road Traffic Regulation Act 1984, s. 14 (1) (a). - Made: 09.10.2006. Coming into force: 14.10.2006. Effect: None. Territorial extent & classification: E. Local *Unpublished*

The M2 Motorway (West of Junction 6) (Temporary Restriction of Traffic) Order 2006 No. 2006/81. - Enabling power: Road Traffic Regulation Act 1984, s. 14 (1) (a) (7). - Made: 16.01.2006. Coming into force: 21.01.2006. Effect: None. Territorial extent & classification: E. Local *Unpublished*

The M3 Motorway (Junction 2 - Thorpe Interchange) (Temporary Prohibition of Traffic) Order 2006 No. 2006/895. - Enabling power: Road Traffic Regulation Act 1984, s. 14 (1) (a). - Made: 20.03.2006. Coming into force: 25.03.2006. Effect: None. Territorial extent & classification: E. Local *Unpublished*

The M3 Motorway (Junction 2, Westbound) (Temporary Prohibition of Traffic) Order 2006 No. 2006/1886. - Enabling power: Road Traffic Regulation Act 1984, s. 14 (1) (a). - Made: 10.07.2006. Coming into force: 15.07.2006. Effect: None. Territorial extent & classification: E. Local *Unpublished*

The M3 Motorway (Junction 3, Eastbound Entry Slip Road) (Temporary Prohibition of Traffic) Order 2006 No. 2006/3032. - Enabling power: Road Traffic Regulation Act 1984, s. 14 (1) (a). - Made: 13.11.2006. Coming into force: 18.11.2006. Effect: None. Territorial extent & classification: E. Local *Unpublished*

The M3 Motorway (Junction 3, Exit Slip Roads) (Temporary Prohibition of Traffic) Order 2006 No. 2006/2551. - Enabling power: Road Traffic Regulation Act 1984, s. 14 (1) (a). - Made: 18.09.2006. Coming into force: 23.09.2006. Effect: None. Territorial extent & classification: E. Local *Unpublished*

Road traffic: Traffic regulation

The M3 Motorway (Junction 3 - Lightwater, Slip Road) (Temporary Prohibition of Traffic) Order 2006 No. 2006/975. - Enabling power: Road Traffic Regulation Act 1984, s. 14 (1) (a). - Made: 27.03.2006. Coming into force: 01.04.2006. Effect: None. Territorial extent & classification: E. Local *Unpublished*

The M3 Motorway (Junction 4A - A325 Roundabout) (Temporary Restriction of Traffic) Order 2006 No. 2006/2151. - Enabling power: Road Traffic Regulation Act 1984, s. 14 (1) (a). - Made: 31.07.2006. Coming into force: 05.08.2006. Effect: None. Territorial extent & classification: E. Local *Unpublished*

The M3 Motorway (Junction 4A, Westbound Entry Slip Road) (Temporary Prohibition of Traffic) Order 2006 No. 2006/2586. - Enabling power: Road Traffic Regulation Act 1984, s. 14 (1) (a). - Made: 11.09.2006. Coming into force: 16.09.2006. Effect: None. Territorial extent & classification: E. Local *Unpublished*

The M3 Motorway (Junction 4, Eastbound Entry Slip Road) (Temporary Prohibition of Traffic) Order 2006 No. 2006/3185. - Enabling power: Road Traffic Regulation Act 1984, s. 14 (1) (a). - Made: 27.11.2006. Coming into force: 02.12.2006. Effect: None. Territorial extent & classification: E. Local *Unpublished*

The M3 Motorway (Junction 4, Eastbound Exit Slip Road) (Temporary Prohibition of Traffic) Order 2006 No. 2006/2772. - Enabling power: Road Traffic Regulation Act 1984, s. 14 (1) (a). - Made: 09.10.2006. Coming into force: 14.10.2006. Effect: None. Territorial extent & classification: E. Local *Unpublished*

The M3 Motorway (Junction 6, Eastbound) (Temporary Prohibition of Traffic) Order 2006 No. 2006/2461. - Enabling power: Road Traffic Regulation Act 1984, s. 14 (1) (a) (7). - Made: 04.09.2006. Coming into force: 09.09.2006. Effect: None. Territorial extent & classification: E. Local *Unpublished*

The M3 Motorway (Junction 6) (Temporary Restriction and Prohibition of Traffic) (No. 2) Order 2006 No. 2006/2639. - Enabling power: Road Traffic Regulation Act 1984, s. 14 (1) (a), sch. 9, para. 27 (1). - Made: 25.09.2006. Coming into force: 30.09.2006. Effect: S.I. 2005/3086; 2006/971 revoked. Territorial extent & classification: E. Local *Unpublished*

The M3 Motorway (Junction 6) (Temporary Restriction and Prohibition of Traffic) Order 2006 No. 2006/971. - Enabling power: Road Traffic Regulation Act 1984, s. 14 (1) (a), sch. 9, para. 27 (1). - Made: 27.03.2006. Coming into force: 01.04.2006. Effect: S.I. 2005/3086 revoked. Territorial extent & classification: E. Local. - Revoked by S.I. 2006/2639 (Unpublished) *Unpublished*

The M3 Motorway (Junction 6, Westbound Exit Slip Road) (Temporary Prohibition of Traffic) Order 2006 No. 2006/2726. - Enabling power: Road Traffic Regulation Act 1984, s. 14 (1) (a). - Made: 02.10.2006. Coming into force: 07.10.2006. Effect: None. Territorial extent & classification: E. Local *Unpublished*

The M3 Motorway (Junction 10, Southbound Entry Slip Road) (Temporary Prohibition of Traffic) Order 2006 No. 2006/3186. - Enabling power: Road Traffic Regulation Act 1984, s. 14 (1) (a). - Made: 27.11.2006. Coming into force: 02.12.2006. Effect: None. Territorial extent & classification: E. Local *Unpublished*

The M3 Motorway (Junction 12, Northbound Entry Slip Road) (Temporary Prohibition of Traffic) Order 2006 No. 2006/3437. - Enabling power: Road Traffic Regulation Act 1984, s. 14 (1) (a). - Made: 18.12.2006. Coming into force: 30.12.2006. Effect: None. Territorial extent & classification: E. Local *Unpublished*

The M3 Motorway (Junctions 2 - 3) (Temporary Prohibition of Traffic) Order 2006 No. 2006/2874. - Enabling power: Road Traffic Regulation Act 1984, s. 14 (1) (a). - Made: 23.10.2006. Coming into force: 28.10.2006. Effect: None. Territorial extent & classification: E. Local *Unpublished*

The M3 Motorway (Junctions 3 and 4, Slip Roads) (Temporary Prohibition of Traffic) Order 2006 No. 2006/3444. - Enabling power: Road Traffic Regulation Act 1984, s. 14 (1) (a). - Made: 18.12.2006. Coming into force: 23.12.2006. Effect: None. Territorial extent & classification: E. Local *Unpublished*

The M3 Motorway (Junctions 4 to 5) (Temporary Restriction and Prohibition of Traffic) Order 2006 No. 2006/28. - Enabling power: Road Traffic Regulation Act 1984, s. 14 (1) (a). - Made: 03.01.2006. Coming into force: 07.01.2006. Effect: None. Territorial extent & classification: E. Local *Unpublished*

The M4 Motorway (Junction 3, Eastbound Exit Slip Road (Temporary Prohibition of Traffic) Order 2006 No. 2006/906. - Enabling power: Road Traffic Regulation Act 1984, s. 14 (1) (a). - Made: 20.03.2006. Coming into force: 01.04.2006. Effect: None. Territorial extent & classification: E. Local. - Revoked by S.I. 2006/2069 (Unpublished) *Unpublished*

The M4 Motorway (Junction 4, Link Roads) (Temporary Prohibition of Traffic) Order 2006 No. 2006/2460. - Enabling power: Road Traffic Regulation Act 1984, s. 14 (1) (a). - Made: 04.09.2006. Coming into force: 09.09.2006. Effect: None. Territorial extent & classification: E. Local *Unpublished*

The M4 Motorway (Junction 4) (Temporary Restriction of Traffic) Order 2006 No. 2006/1315. - Enabling power: Road Traffic Regulation Act 1984, s. 14 (1) (a) (7). - Made: 02.05.2006. Coming into force: 06.05.2006. Effect: None. Territorial extent & classification: E. Local *Unpublished*

The M4 Motorway (Junction 5, Westbound Carriageway) (Temporary Prohibition of Traffic) Order 2006 No. 2006/1973. - Enabling power: Road Traffic Regulation Act 1984, s. 14 (1) (a). - Made: 17.07.2006. Coming into force: 22.07.2006. Effect: None. Territorial extent & classification: E. Local *Unpublished*

Road traffic: Traffic regulation

The M4 Motorway (Junction 8/9, Exit Slip Roads) (Temporary Prohibition of Traffic) Order 2006 No. 2006/2560. - Enabling power: Road Traffic Regulation Act 1984, s. 14 (1) (a). - Made: 18.09.2006. Coming into force: 23.09.2006. Effect: None. Territorial extent & classification: E. Local *Unpublished*

The M4 Motorway (Junction 10, Link Roads) (Temporary Prohibition of Traffic) Order 2006 No. 2006/3037. - Enabling power: Road Traffic Regulation Act 1984, s. 14 (1) (a). - Made: 06.11.2006. Coming into force: 11.11.2006. Effect: None. Territorial extent & classification: E. Local *Unpublished*

The M4 Motorway (Junction 11, Westbound Entry Slip Road) (Temporary Prohibition of Traffic) Order 2006 No. 2006/2771. - Enabling power: Road Traffic Regulation Act 1984, s. 14 (1) (a). - Made: 09.10.2006. Coming into force: 14.10.2006. Effect: None. Territorial extent & classification: E. Local *Unpublished*

The M4 Motorway (Junction 11, Westbound Exit Slip Road) (Temporary Prohibition of Traffic) Order 2006 No. 2006/3187. - Enabling power: Road Traffic Regulation Act 1984, s. 14 (1) (a). - Made: 27.11.2006. Coming into force: 02.12.2006. Effect: None. Territorial extent & classification: E. Local *Unpublished*

The M4 Motorway (Junction 13, Chieveley Interchange) (Temporary 40 Miles Per Hour Speed Restriction) Order 2006 No. 2006/2201. - Enabling power: Road Traffic Regulation Act 1984, s. 14 (1) (a). - Made: 07.08.2006. Coming into force: 12.08.2006. Effect: None. Territorial extent & classification: E. Local *Unpublished*

The M4 Motorway (Junction 14 - 15) (Temporary Restriction and Prohibition of Traffic) Order 2006 No. 2006/2775. - Enabling power: Road Traffic Regulation Act 1984, s. 14 (1) (a) (7). - Made: 09.10.2006. Coming into force: 14.10.2006. Effect: None. Territorial extent & classification: E. Local *Unpublished*

The M4 Motorway (Junction 15, Almondsbury Interchange) (Temporary Prohibition of Traffic) Order 2006 No. 2006/2205. - Enabling power: Road Traffic Regulation Act 1984, s. 14 (1) (a). - Made: 08.08.2006. Coming into force: 11.08.2006. Effect: None. Territorial extent & classification: E. Local *Unpublished*

The M4 Motorway (Junction 16) (Temporary Prohibition and Restriction of Traffic) Order 2006 No. 2006/2095. - Enabling power: Road Traffic Regulation Act 1984, ss. 14 (1) (a) (7). - Made: 25.07.2006. Coming into force: 28.07.2006. Effect: None. Territorial extent & classification: E. Local *Unpublished*

The M4 Motorway (Junction 20, M4 Westbound to M5 Northbound, Almondsbury Interchange) (Temporary Prohibition of Traffic) (Number 2) Order 2006 No. 2006/2340. - Enabling power: Road Traffic Regulation Act 1984, s. 14 (1) (a). - Made: 22.08.2006. Coming into force: 25.08.2006. Effect: None. Territorial extent & classification: E. Local *Unpublished*

The M4 Motorway (Junction 20 - M4 Westbound to M5 Northbound, Almondsbury Interchange) (Temporary Prohibition of Traffic) Order 2006 No. 2006/1993. - Enabling power: Road Traffic Regulation Act 1984, s. 14 (1) (a). - Made: 18.07.2006. Coming into force: 21.07.2006. Effect: None. Territorial extent & classification: E. Local *Unpublished*

The M4 Motorway (Junction 22) (Temporary Prohibition of Traffic) Order 2006 No. 2006/1147. - Enabling power: Road Traffic Regulation Act 1984, s. 14 (1) (a). - Made: 18.04.2006. Coming into force: 21.04.2006. Effect: None. Territorial extent & classification: E. Local *Unpublished*

The M4 Motorway (Junctions 1 - 3) (Temporary Prohibition of Traffic) Order 2006 No. 2006/192. - Enabling power: Road Traffic Regulation Act 1984, s. 14 (1) (a). - Made: 23.01.2006. Coming into force: 30.01.2006. Effect: None. Territorial extent & classification: E. Local *Unpublished*

The M4 Motorway (Junctions 1 to 3) (Temporary Prohibition of Traffic) Order 2006 No. 2006/890. - Enabling power: Road Traffic Regulation Act 1984, s. 14 (1) (a). - Made: 20.03.2006. Coming into force: 01.04.2006. Effect: None. Territorial extent & classification: E. Local *Unpublished*

The M4 Motorway (Junctions 3 - 5, Link and Slip Roads) (Temporary Prohibition of Traffic) Order 2006 No. 2006/2069. - Enabling power: Road Traffic Regulation Act 1984, ss. 14 (1) (a). - Made: 24.07.2006. Coming into force: 02.08.2006. Effect: S.I. 2006/906 revoked. Territorial extent & classification: E. Local *Unpublished*

The M4 Motorway (Junctions 4 - 4A) (Temporary Prohibition of Traffic) Order 2006 No. 2006/2204. - Enabling power: Road Traffic Regulation Act 1984, s. 14 (1) (a). - Made: 07.08.2006. Coming into force: 12.08.2006. Effect: None. Territorial extent & classification: E. Local *Unpublished*

The M4 Motorway (Junctions 5 - 4B) (Temporary Restriction and Prohibition of Traffic) Order 2006 No. 2006/3181. - Enabling power: Road Traffic Regulation Act 1984, s. 14 (1) (a) (7). - Made: 27.11.2006. Coming into force: 02.12.2006. Effect: None. Territorial extent & classification: E. Local *Unpublished*

The M4 Motorway (Junctions 5 - 6) (Temporary Prohibition of Traffic) Order 2006 No. 2006/2109. - Enabling power: Road Traffic Regulation Act 1984, s. 14 (1) (a), sch. 9, para. 27 (1). - Made: 24.07.2006. Coming into force: 29.07.2006. Effect: S.I. 2005/3533 revoked. Territorial extent & classification: E. Local *Unpublished*

The M4 Motorway (Junctions 8/9 - 10) (Temporary Restriction and Prohibition of Traffic) Order 2006 No. 2006/2154. - Enabling power: Road Traffic Regulation Act 1984, s. 14 (1) (a) (7). - Made: 31.07.2006. Coming into force: 05.08.2006. Effect: None. Territorial extent & classification: E. Local *Unpublished*

The M4 Motorway (Junctions 14 - 18) (Temporary Prohibition and Restriction of Traffic) Order 2006 No. 2006/3484. - Enabling power: Road Traffic Regulation Act 1984, s. 14 (1) (a) (7). - Made: 27.12.2006. Coming into force: 29.12.2006. Effect: None. Territorial extent & classification: E. Local *Unpublished*

The M4 Motorway (Junctions 15 - 17 Slip Roads) (Temporary Prohibition of Traffic) Order 2006 No. 2006/2099. - Enabling power: Road Traffic Regulation Act 1984, ss. 14 (1) (a). - Made: 25.07.2006. Coming into force: 28.07.2006. Effect: None. Territorial extent & classification: E. Local *Unpublished*

The M4 Motorway (Junctions 16 - 15) (Temporary Prohibition and Restriction of Traffic) Order 2006 No. 2006/2342. - Enabling power: Road Traffic Regulation Act 1984, s. 14 (1) (a). - Made: 22.08.2006. Coming into force: 25.08.2006. Effect: None. Territorial extent & classification: E. Local *Unpublished*

The M4 Motorway (Junctions 16 - 17) (Temporary Prohibition and Restriction of Traffic) Order 2006 No. 2006/1372. - Enabling power: Road Traffic Regulation Act 1984, s. 14 (1) (a) (7). - Made: 12.05.2006. Coming into force: 27.05.2006. Effect: None. Territorial extent & classification: E. Local *Unpublished*

The M4 Motorway (Junctions 18 - 17) (Temporary Prohibition and Restriction of Traffic) Order 2006 No. 2006/19. - Enabling power: Road Traffic Regulation Act 1984, s. 14 (1) (a) (7). - Made: 04.01.2006. Coming into force: 06.01.2006. Effect: None. Territorial extent & classification: E. Local *Unpublished*

The M4 Motorway (Junctions 18 - 19) (Temporary Prohibition and Restriction of Traffic) Order 2006 No. 2006/2094. - Enabling power: Road Traffic Regulation Act 1984, ss. 14 (1) (a) (7). - Made: 25.07.2006. Coming into force: 28.07.2006. Effect: None. Territorial extent & classification: E. Local *Unpublished*

The M4 Motorway (Junctions19 - 21) and the M32 Motorway (Junction 2 to M4) (Temporary Prohibition and Restriction of Traffic) Order 2006 No. 2006/2716. - Enabling power: Road Traffic Regulation Act 1984, s. 14 (1) (a) (7). - Made: 03.10.2006. Coming into force: 05.10.2006. Effect: None. Territorial extent & classification: E. Local *Unpublished*

The M4 Motorway (Junctions 20 - 21) (Temporary Restriction of Traffic) Order 2006 No. 2006/2101. - Enabling power: Road Traffic Regulation Act 1984, s. 14 (1) (a) (7). - Made: 25.07.2006. Coming into force: 28.07.2006. Effect: None. Territorial extent & classification: E. Local *Unpublished*

The M4 Motorway (Leigh Delamere Service Area) (Temporary Prohibition of Traffic) Order 2006 No. 2006/414. - Enabling power: Road Traffic Regulation Act 1984, s. 14 (1) (a). - Made: 20.02.2006. Coming into force: 25.02.2006. Effect: None. Territorial extent & classification: E. Local *Unpublished*

The M4 Motorway (Rogiet Toll Plaza) (Temporary 50 MPH Speed Restriction) Order 2006 No. 2006/2999. - Enabling power: Road Traffic Regulation Act 1984, s. 14 (1) (b). - Made: 31.10.2006. Coming into force: 03.11.2006. Effect: None. Territorial extent & classification: E. Local *Unpublished*

The M5 and M6 Motorways (South of Walsall) (Temporary Restriction and Prohibition of Traffic) Order 2006 No. 2006/375. - Enabling power: Road Traffic Regulation Act 1984, s. 14 (1) (a) (7). - Made: 03.02.2006. Coming into force: 10.02.2006. Effect: None. Territorial extent & classification: E. Local *Unpublished*

The M5 and M50 Motorways (M5 Junction 8) (Temporary Restriction and Prohibition of Traffic) Order 2006 No. 2006/3482. - Enabling power: Road Traffic Regulation Act 1984, s. 14 (1) (a). - Made: 22.12.2006. Coming into force: 29.12.2006. Effect: None. Territorial extent & classification: E. Local *Unpublished*

The M5 Motorway (Junction 1) (Northbound Entry Slip Road) (Temporary Prohibition of Traffic) Order 2006 No. 2006/1725. - Enabling power: Road Traffic Regulation Act 1984, s. 14 (1) (a). - Made: 26.06.2006. Coming into force: 03.07.2006. Effect: None. Territorial extent & classification: E. Local *Unpublished*

The M5 Motorway (Junction 1) (Slip Roads) (Temporary Restriction and Prohibition of Traffic) Order 2006 No. 2006/2219. - Enabling power: Road Traffic Regulation Act 1984, s. 14 (1) (a). - Made: 28.07.2006. Coming into force: 04.08.2006. Effect: None. Territorial extent & classification: E. Local *Unpublished*

The M5 Motorway (Junction 1) (Temporary Restriction of Traffic) Order 2006 No. 2006/323. - Enabling power: Road Traffic Regulation Act 1984, s. 14 (1) (a) (7). - Made: 06.02.2006. Coming into force: 13.02.2006. Effect: None. Territorial extent & classification: E. Local *Unpublished*

The M5 Motorway (Junction 2) and the A4123 Trunk Road (Oldbury) (Temporary Prohibition of Traffic) Order 2006 No. 2006/1113. - Enabling power: Road Traffic Regulation Act 1984, s. 14 (1) (a). - Made: 27.03.2006. Coming into force: 03.04.2006. Effect: None. Territorial extent & classification: E. Local *Unpublished*

The M5 Motorway (Junction 2, Oldbury) (Temporary Restriction and Prohibition of Traffic) Order 2006 No. 2006/283. - Enabling power: Road Traffic Regulation Act 1984, s. 14 (1) (a). - Made: 30.01.2006. Coming into force: 06.02.2006. Effect: None. Territorial extent & classification: E. Local *Unpublished*

The M5 Motorway (Junction 3) (Northbound Exit Slip Road) (Temporary Prohibition of Traffic) Order 2006 No. 2006/1655. - Enabling power: Road Traffic Regulation Act 1984, s. 14 (1) (a). - Made: 12.06.2006. Coming into force: 19.06.2006. Effect: None. Territorial extent & classification: E. Local *Unpublished*

The M5 Motorway (Junction 3) (Southbound Entry Slip Road) (Temporary Prohibition of Traffic) Order 2005 No. 2006/9. - Enabling power: Road Traffic Regulation Act 1984, s. 14 (1) (a). - Made: 03.01.2006. Coming into force: 10.01.2006. Effect: None. Territorial extent & classification: E. Local *Unpublished*

The M5 Motorway (Junction 3) (Temporary Prohibition of Traffic) Order 2006 No. 2006/2042. - Enabling power: Road Traffic Regulation Act 1984, ss. 14 (1) (a). - Made: 10.07.2006. Coming into force: 17.07.2006. Effect: None. Territorial extent & classification: E. Local *Unpublished*

The M5 Motorway (Junction 4 - Junction 4A) M42 Motorway (Junction 1 - M5 Junction 4A) (Temporary Restriction and Prohibition of Traffic) Order 2006 No. 2006/1868. - Enabling power: Road Traffic Regulation Act 1984, s. 14 (1) (a) (7). - Made: 30.06.2006. Coming into force: 07.07.2006. Effect: None. Territorial extent & classification: E. Local *Unpublished*

The M5 Motorway (Junction 5) (Northbound Exit Slip Road) (Temporary Prohibition of Traffic) Order 2006 No. 2006/458. - Enabling power: Road Traffic Regulation Act 1984, s. 14 (1) (a). - Made: 13.02.2006. Coming into force: 20.02.2006. Effect: None. Territorial extent & classification: E. Local *Unpublished*

The M5 Motorway (Junction 5) (Slip Roads) (Temporary Prohibition of Traffic) Order 2006 No. 2006/707. - Enabling power: Road Traffic Regulation Act 1984, s. 14 (1) (a). - Made: 24.02.2006. Coming into force: 03.03.2006. Effect: None. Territorial extent & classification: E. Local *Unpublished*

The M5 Motorway (Junction 6, Worcestershire) (Temporary Restriction of Traffic) Order 2006 No. 2006/3050. - Enabling power: Road Traffic Regulation Act 1984, s. 14 (1) (a). - Made: 23.10.2006. Coming into force: 30.10.2006. Effect: None. Territorial extent & classification: E. Local *Unpublished*

The M5 Motorway (Junction 7) (Southbound Exit Slip Road) (Temporary Prohibition and Restriction of Traffic) Order 2006 No. 2006/3509. - Enabling power: Road Traffic Regulation Act 1984, s. 14 (1) (a). - Made: 29.12.2006. Coming into force: 05.01.2007. Effect: None. Territorial extent & classification: E. Local *Unpublished*

The M5 Motorway (Junction 9) (Slip Roads) and the A46 Trunk Road (Temporary Prohibition and Restriction of Traffic) Order 2006 No. 2006/2147. - Enabling power: Road Traffic Regulation Act 1984, s. 14 (1) (a). - Made: 21.07.2006. Coming into force: 28.07.2006. Effect: None. Territorial extent & classification: E. Local *Unpublished*

The M5 Motorway (Junction 12 Northbound and Southbound Exit Slip Roads) (Temporary Prohibition of Traffic) Order 2006 No. 2006/2638. - Enabling power: Road Traffic Regulation Act 1984, s. 14 (1) (a). - Made: 25.09.2006. Coming into force: 29.09.2006. Effect: None. Territorial extent & classification: E. Local *Unpublished*

The M5 Motorway (Junction 12) (Temporary Prohibition of Traffic) Order 2006 No. 2006/1479. - Enabling power: Road Traffic Regulation Act 1984, s. 14 (1) (a). - Made: 30.05.2006. Coming into force: 02.06.2006. Effect: None. Territorial extent & classification: E. Local *Unpublished*

The M5 Motorway (Junction 12) (Temporary Prohibition of Traffic) Order 2006 No. 2006/21. - Enabling power: Road Traffic Regulation Act 1984, s. 14 (1) (a). - Made: 04.01.2006. Coming into force: 07.01.2006. Effect: None. Territorial extent & classification: E. Local *Unpublished*

The M5 Motorway (Junction 17 Northbound Entry Slip Road) (Temporary Prohibition of Traffic) Order 2006 No. 2006/2343. - Enabling power: Road Traffic Regulation Act 1984, s. 14 (1) (a). - Made: 22.08.2006. Coming into force: 25.08.2006. Effect: None. Territorial extent & classification: E. Local *Unpublished*

The M5 Motorway (Junction 18 - Avonmouth) (Temporary Prohibition of Traffic) Order 2006 No. 2006/1309. - Enabling power: Road Traffic Regulation Act 1984, s. 14 (1) (a) (c). - Made: 02.05.2006. Coming into force: 05.05.2006. Effect: None. Territorial extent & classification: E. Local *Unpublished*

The M5 Motorway (Junction 21 Slip Roads) (Temporary Prohibition of Traffic) Order 2006 No. 2006/1991. - Enabling power: Road Traffic Regulation Act 1984, s. 14 (1) (a). - Made: 18.07.2006. Coming into force: 21.07.2006. Effect: None. Territorial extent & classification: E. Local *Unpublished*

The M5 Motorway (Junction 22 Slip Roads) (Temporary Prohibition of Traffic) Order 2006 No. 2006/2341. - Enabling power: Road Traffic Regulation Act 1984, s. 14 (1) (a). - Made: 22.08.2006. Coming into force: 25.08.2006. Effect: None. Territorial extent & classification: E. Local *Unpublished*

The M5 Motorway (Junction 22) (Temporary Prohibition of Traffic) Order 2006 No. 2006/1207. - Enabling power: Road Traffic Regulation Act 1984, s. 14 (1) (a). - Made: 21.04.2006. Coming into force: 26.04.2006. Effect: None. Territorial extent & classification: E. Local *Unpublished*

The M5 Motorway (Junction 23) (Temporary Restriction of Traffic) Order 2006 No. 2006/381. - Enabling power: Road Traffic Regulation Act 1984, s. 14 (1) (a) (7). - Made: 13.02.2006. Coming into force: 17.02.2006. Effect: None. Territorial extent & classification: E. Local *Unpublished*

The M5 Motorway (Junction 26) (Temporary Prohibition of Traffic) Order 2006 No. 2006/3475. - Enabling power: Road Traffic Regulation Act 1984, s. 14 (1) (a). - Made: 22.12.2006. Coming into force: 29.12.2006. Effect: None. Territorial extent & classification: E. Local *Unpublished*

The M5 Motorway (Junction 27) (Temporary Prohibition of Traffic) Order 2006 No. 2006/3130. - Enabling power: Road Traffic Regulation Act 1984, s. 14 (1) (a). - Made: 22.11.2006. Coming into force: 29.11.2006. Effect: None. Territorial extent & classification: E. Local *Unpublished*

The M5 Motorway (Junction 28) (Temporary Prohibition of Traffic) Order 2006 No. 2006/20. - Enabling power: Road Traffic Regulation Act 1984, s. 14 (1) (a). - Made: 04.01.2006. Coming into force: 07.01.2006. Effect: None. Territorial extent & classification: E. Local *Unpublished*

The M5 Motorway (Junction 28) (Temporary Prohibition of Traffic) Order 2006 No. 2006/1048. - Enabling power: Road Traffic Regulation Act 1984, s. 14 (1) (a). - Made: 03.04.2006. Coming into force: 08.04.2006. Effect: None. Territorial extent & classification: E. Local *Unpublished*

The M5 Motorway (Junctions 1 to 2) (Temporary Prohibition and Restriction of Traffic) Order 2006 No. 2006/3354. - Enabling power: Road Traffic Regulation Act 1984, s. 14 (1) (a) (7). - Made: 08.12.2006. Coming into force: 15.12.2006. Effect: None. Territorial extent & classification: E. Local *Unpublished*

The M5 Motorway (Junctions 5 - 6) (Temporary Restriction and Prohibition of Traffic) Order 2006 No. 2006/1588. - Enabling power: Road Traffic Regulation Act 1984, s. 14 (1) (a) (7). - Made: 05.06.2006. Coming into force: 12.06.2006. Effect: None. Territorial extent & classification: E. Local *Unpublished*

The M5 Motorway (Junctions 9- 11A) (Temporary Restriction of Traffic) Order 2006 No. 2006/382. - Enabling power: Road Traffic Regulation Act 1984, s. 14 (1) (a) (7). - Made: 13.02.2006. Coming into force: 17.02.2006. Effect: None. Territorial extent & classification: E. Local *Unpublished*

The M5 Motorway (Junctions 11, 11A & 13A Slip Roads) (Temporary Prohibition of Traffic) Order 2006 No. 2006/2100. - Enabling power: Road Traffic Regulation Act 1984, s. 14 (1) (a). - Made: 25.07.2006. Coming into force: 28.07.2006. Effect: None. Territorial extent & classification: E. Local *Unpublished*

The M5 Motorway (Junctions 11A - 11) (Temporary Restriction of Traffic) Order 2006 No. 2006/1478. - Enabling power: Road Traffic Regulation Act 1984, s. 14 (1) (a) (7). - Made: 30.05.2006. Coming into force: 02.06.2006. Effect: None. Territorial extent & classification: E. Local *Unpublished*

The M5 Motorway (Junctions 12 - 14) (Temporary Restriction of Traffic) Order 2006 No. 2006/2096. - Enabling power: Road Traffic Regulation Act 1984, ss. 14 (1) (a) (7). - Made: 25.07.2006. Coming into force: 28.07.2006. Effect: None. Territorial extent & classification: E. Local *Unpublished*

The M5 Motorway (Junctions 13 - 15) (Temporary Restriction and Prohibition of Traffic) Order 2006 No. 2006/2206. - Enabling power: Road Traffic Regulation Act 1984, s. 14 (1) (a) (7). - Made: 08.08.2006. Coming into force: 11.08.2006. Effect: None. Territorial extent & classification: E. Local *Unpublished*

The M5 Motorway (Junctions 14 & 16 Slip Roads) (Temporary Prohibition of Traffic) Order 2006 No. 2006/2097. - Enabling power: Road Traffic Regulation Act 1984, ss. 14 (1) (a). - Made: 25.07.2006. Coming into force: 28.07.2006. Effect: None. Territorial extent & classification: E. Local *Unpublished*

The M5 Motorway (Junctions 23-25 Slip Roads) (Temporary Prohibition of Traffic) Order 2006 No. 2006/1992. - Enabling power: Road Traffic Regulation Act 1984, s. 14 (1) (a). - Made: 18.07.2006. Coming into force: 21.07.2006. Effect: None. Territorial extent & classification: E. Local *Unpublished*

The M5 Motorway (Junctions 25 - 26) (Temporary Prohibition and Restriction of Traffic) Order 2006 No. 2006/1145. - Enabling power: Road Traffic Regulation Act 1984, s. 14 (1) (a) (7). - Made: 18.04.2006. Coming into force: 22.04.2006. Effect: None. Territorial extent & classification: E. Local *Unpublished*

The M5 Motorway (Junctions 28 - 31) (Temporary Prohibition and Restriction of Traffic) Order 2006 No. 2006/2747. - Enabling power: Road Traffic Regulation Act 1984, s. 14 (1) (a) (7). - Made: 11.10.2006. Coming into force: 14.10.2006. Effect: None. Territorial extent & classification: E. Local *Unpublished*

The M5 Motorway (Junctions 28 and 30 Slip Roads) (Temporary Prohibition of Traffic) Order 2006 No. 2006/1994. - Enabling power: Road Traffic Regulation Act 1984, s. 14 (1) (a). - Made: 18.07.2006. Coming into force: 21.07.2006. Effect: None. Territorial extent & classification: E. Local *Unpublished*

The M5 Motorway (North of Junction 4) (Temporary Prohibition of Traffic) Order 2006 No. 2006/1612. - Enabling power: Road Traffic Regulation Act 1984, s. 14 (1) (a) (7). - Made: 07.06.2006. Coming into force: 14.06.2006. Effect: None. Territorial extent & classification: E. Local *Unpublished*

The M5 Motorway (Ray Hall Interchange/M6 Junction 8) (Temporary Restriction and Prohibition of Traffic) Order 2006 No. 2006/284. - Enabling power: Road Traffic Regulation Act 1984, s. 14 (1) (a) (7). - Made: 31.01.2006. Coming into force: 07.02.2006. Effect: None. Territorial extent & classification: E. Local *Unpublished*

The M5 Motorway (Sedgemoor Services Slip Roads) (Temporary Prohibition of Traffic) Order 2006 No. 2006/1990. - Enabling power: Road Traffic Regulation Act 1984, s. 14 (1) (a). - Made: 18.07.2006. Coming into force: 21.07.2006. Effect: None. Territorial extent & classification: E. Local *Unpublished*

The M5 Motorway (Taunton Deane Service Area) (Temporary Prohibition of Traffic) Order 2006 No. 2006/450. - Enabling power: Road Traffic Regulation Act 1984, s. 14 (1) (a). - Made: 21.02.2006. Coming into force: 25.02.2006. Effect: None. Territorial extent & classification: E. Local *Unpublished*

The M6 and M5 Motorways (Ray Hall Interchange) (Temporary Prohibition and Restriction of Traffic) Order 2006 No. 2006/2668. - Enabling power: Road Traffic Regulation Act 1984, s. 14 (1) (a) (7). - Made: 22.09.2006. Coming into force: 29.09.2006. Effect: None. Territorial extent & classification: E. Local *Unpublished*

The M6 and M69 Motorways (M6 Junction 2) and the A46 Trunk Road (Temporary Restriction and Prohibition of Traffic) Order 2006 No. 2006/2548. - Enabling power: Road Traffic Regulation Act 1984, s. 14 (1) (a). - Made: 15.09.2006. Coming into force: 22.09.2006. Effect: None. Territorial extent & classification: E. Local *Unpublished*

The M6 Motorway and A74 Trunk Road (Junction 44, Greymoorhill Interchange Southbound Carriageway) (Temporary Prohibition and Restriction of Traffic) Order 2006 No. 2006/529. - Enabling power: Road Traffic Regulation Act 1984, s. 14 (1) (a). - Made: 21.02.2006. Coming into force: 19.03.2006. Effect: None. Territorial extent & classification: E. Local *Unpublished*

The M6 Motorway (Birmingham to Walsall) (Temporary Restriction and Prohibition of Traffic) Order 2006 No. 2006/1569. - Enabling power: Road Traffic Regulation Act 1984, s. 14 (1) (a) (7). - Made: 19.05.2006. Coming into force: 26.05.2006. Effect: None. Territorial extent & classification: E. Local *Unpublished*

The M6 Motorway (Borrowbeck Viaduct) (Temporary Prohibition and Restriction of Traffic) Order 2006 No. 2006/3154. - Enabling power: Road Traffic Regulation Act 1984, s. 14 (1) (a) (7). - Made: 22.11.2006. Coming into force: 25.11.2006. Effect: None. Territorial extent & classification: E. Local *Unpublished*

The M6 Motorway (Bromford, Birmingham) (Temporary Restriction and Prohibition of Traffic) Order 2006 No. 2006/3052. - Enabling power: Road Traffic Regulation Act 1984, s. 14 (1) (a) (7). - Made: 20.10.2006. Coming into force: 27.10.2006. Effect: None. Territorial extent & classification: E. Local *Unpublished*

The M6 Motorway (Deerslack Bridge) (No. 2) (Temporary Restriction and Prohibition of Traffic) Order 2006 No. 2006/2754. - Enabling power: Road Traffic Regulation Act 1984, s. 14 (1) (a) (7). - Made: 10.10.2006. Coming into force: 03.11.2006. Effect: None. Territorial extent & classification: E. Local *Unpublished*

The M6 Motorway (Doxey, Staffordshire) (Temporary Prohibition of Traffic) Order 2006 No. 2006/1559. - Enabling power: Road Traffic Regulation Act 1984, s. 14 (1) (b). - Made: 26.05.2006. Coming into force: 02.06.2006. Effect: None. Territorial extent & classification: E. Local *Unpublished*

The M6 Motorway (Eamont Bridge) (Temporary Prohibition and Restriction of Traffic) Order 2006 No. 2006/187. - Enabling power: Road Traffic Regulation Act 1984, s. 14 (1) (a) (7). - Made: 23.01.2006. Coming into force: 17.02.2006. Effect: None. Territorial extent & classification: E. Local *Unpublished*

The M6 Motorway (Gravelly Hill Interchange, Birmingham) (Slip Roads) (Temporary Prohibition of Traffic) Order 2006 No. 2006/1572. - Enabling power: Road Traffic Regulation Act 1984, s. 14 (1) (a). - Made: 19.05.2006. Coming into force: 26.05.2006. Effect: None. Territorial extent & classification: E. Local *Unpublished*

The M6 Motorway (Gravelly Hill Interchange, Birmingham) (Temporary Restriction and Prohibition of Traffic) Order 2006 No. 2006/1306. - Enabling power: Road Traffic Regulation Act 1984, s. 14 (1) (a) (7). - Made: 28.04.2006. Coming into force: 05.05.2006. Effect: None. Territorial extent & classification: E. Local *Unpublished*

The M6 Motorway (Hutton Bridge Parapet Replacement Between Junctions 36 and 37) (Temporary Restriction of Traffic) Order 2006 No. 2006/2478. - Enabling power: Road Traffic Regulation Act 1984, s. 14 (1) (a) (7). - Made: 05.09.2006. Coming into force: 30.09.2006. Effect: None. Territorial extent & classification: E. Local *Unpublished*

The M6 Motorway (Junction 1, Warwickshire) (Slip Roads) (Temporary Prohibition of Traffic) Order 2006 No. 2006/3000. - Enabling power: Road Traffic Regulation Act 1984, s. 14 (1) (a). - Made: 31.10.2006. Coming into force: 07.11.2006. Effect: None. Territorial extent & classification: E. Local *Unpublished*

The M6 Motorway (Junction 2) (Northbound Exit Slip Road) (Temporary Prohibition of Traffic) Order 2006 No. 2006/2673. - Enabling power: Road Traffic Regulation Act 1984, s. 14 (1) (a). - Made: 15.09.2006. Coming into force: 22.09.2006. Effect: None. Territorial extent & classification: E. Local *Unpublished*

The M6 Motorway (Junction 2 to 3) (Temporary Prohibition of Traffic) Order 2006 No. 2006/2519. - Enabling power: Road Traffic Regulation Act 1984, s. 14 (1) (a). - Made: 29.08.2006. Coming into force: 05.09.2006. Effect: None. Territorial extent & classification: E. Local *Unpublished*

The M6 Motorway (Junction 3) (Southbound Exit Slip Road) (Temporary Prohibition of Traffic) Order 2006 No. 2006/2572. - Enabling power: Road Traffic Regulation Act 1984, s. 14 (1) (a). - Made: 11.09.2006. Coming into force: 18.09.2006. Effect: None. Territorial extent & classification: E. Local *Unpublished*

The M6 Motorway (Junction 3 to 1, Warwickshire) (Temporary Prohibition and Restriction of Traffic) Order 2006 No. 2006/2756. - Enabling power: Road Traffic Regulation Act 1984, s. 14 (1) (a) (7). - Made: 11.09.2006. Coming into force: 18.09.2006. Effect: None. Territorial extent & classification: E. Local *Unpublished*

The M6 Motorway (Junction 4) (Slip Roads) and the A446 Trunk Road (Temporary Prohibition and Restriction of Traffic) Order 2006 No. 2006/1774. - Enabling power: Road Traffic Regulation Act 1984, s. 14 (1) (a). - Made: 23.06.2006. Coming into force: 30.06.2006. Effect: None. Territorial extent & classification: E. Local *Unpublished*

The M6 Motorway (Junction 4, Warwickshire) (Temporary Prohibition of Traffic) Order 2006 No. 2006/3204. - Enabling power: Road Traffic Regulation Act 1984, s. 14 (1) (a) (7). - Made: 17.11.2006. Coming into force: 24.11.2006. Effect: None. Territorial extent & classification: E. Local *Unpublished*

The M6 Motorway (Junction 5) (Southbound Entry Slip Road) (Temporary Restriction and Prohibition of Traffic) Order 2006 No. 2006/3507. - Enabling power: Road Traffic Regulation Act 1984, s. 14 (1) (a). - Made: 29.12.2006. Coming into force: 05.01.2007. Effect: None. Territorial extent & classification: E. Local *Unpublished*

The M6 Motorway (Junction 6, Birmingham) (Slip Road) (Temporary Prohibition of Traffic) Order 2006 No. 2006/286. - Enabling power: Road Traffic Regulation Act 1984, s. 14 (1) (a). - Made: 30.01.2006. Coming into force: 06.02.2006. Effect: None. Territorial extent & classification: E. Local *Unpublished*

The M6 Motorway (Junction 7) (Southbound Entry Slip Road) (Temporary Prohibition and Restriction of Traffic) Order 2006 No. 2006/3141. - Enabling power: Road Traffic Regulation Act 1984, s. 14 (1) (a). - Made: 20.11.2006. Coming into force: 27.11.2006. Effect: None. Territorial extent & classification: E. Local *Unpublished*

The M6 Motorway (Junction 8) (Ray Hall Interchange) (Temporary Prohibition of Traffic) Order 2006 No. 2006/288. - Enabling power: Road Traffic Regulation Act 1984, s. 14 (1) (a). - Made: 03.02.2006. Coming into force: 10.02.2006. Effect: None. Territorial extent & classification: E. Local *Unpublished*

The M6 Motorway (Junction 9 - Junction 10) (Temporary Restriction and Prohibition of Traffic) Order 2006 No. 2006/3024. - Enabling power: Road Traffic Regulation Act 1984, s. 14 (1) (a) (7). - Made: 10.11.2006. Coming into force: 17.11.2006. Effect: None. Territorial extent & classification: E. Local *Unpublished*

The M6 Motorway (Junction 9) (Southbound Entry Slip Road) (Temporary Prohibition of Traffic) Order 2006 No. 2006/2044. - Enabling power: Road Traffic Regulation Act 1984, ss. 14 (1) (a). - Made: 10.07.2006. Coming into force: 17.07.2006. Effect: None. Territorial extent & classification: E. Local *Unpublished*

The M6 Motorway (Junction 10A - Junction 13) and the M54 Motorway (Junction 1 - Junction 2) (Slip Roads) (Temporary Prohibition of Traffic) Order 2006 No. 2006/1988. - Enabling power: Road Traffic Regulation Act 1984, s. 14 (1) (a). - Made: 14.07.2006. Coming into force: 21.07.2006. Effect: None. Territorial extent & classification: E. Local *Unpublished*

The M6 Motorway (Junction 10) (Entry Slip Roads) (Temporary Prohibition and Restriction of Traffic) Order 2006 No. 2006/3140. - Enabling power: Road Traffic Regulation Act 1984, s. 14 (1) (a) (7). - Made: 20.11.2006. Coming into force: 27.11.2006. Effect: None. Territorial extent & classification: E. Local *Unpublished*

The M6 Motorway (Junction 10) (Northbound Entry Slip Road) (Temporary Prohibition of Traffic) Order 2006 No. 2006/449. - Enabling power: Road Traffic Regulation Act 1984, s. 14 (1) (a). - Made: 13.02.2006. Coming into force: 20.02.2006. Effect: None. Territorial extent & classification: E. Local *Unpublished*

The M6 Motorway (Junction 10) (Southbound Entry Slip Road) (Temporary Prohibition of Traffic) Order 2006 No. 2006/3059. - Enabling power: Road Traffic Regulation Act 1984, s. 14 (1) (a). - Made: 16.10.2006. Coming into force: 23.10.2006. Effect: None. Territorial extent & classification: E. Local *Unpublished*

The M6 Motorway (Junction 11) (Southbound Entry Slip Road) (Temporary Restriction and Prohibition of Traffic) Order 2006 No. 2006/3453. - Enabling power: Road Traffic Regulation Act 1984, s. 14 (1) (a). - Made: 20.12.2006. Coming into force: 27.12.2006. Effect: None. Territorial extent & classification: E. Local *Unpublished*

The M6 Motorway (Junction 12) and the A5 Trunk Road (Gailey to Brownhills) (Temporary Restriction and Prohibition of Traffic) Order 2006 No. 2006/3058. - Enabling power: Road Traffic Regulation Act 1984, s. 14 (1) (a). - Made: 16.10.2006. Coming into force: 23.10.2006. Effect: None. Territorial extent & classification: E. Local *Unpublished*

The M6 Motorway (Junction 12 - North of Junction 13) (Temporary Restriction and Prohibition of Traffic) Order 2006 No. 2006/3513. - Enabling power: Road Traffic Regulation Act 1984, s. 14 (1) (a) (7). - Made: 22.12.2006. Coming into force: 29.12.2006. Effect: None. Territorial extent & classification: E. Local *Unpublished*

The M6 Motorway (Junction 13) (Slip Roads) (Temporary Prohibition of Traffic) Order 2006 No. 2006/289. - Enabling power: Road Traffic Regulation Act 1984, s. 14 (1) (a). - Made: 03.02.2006. Coming into force: 10.02.2006. Effect: None. Territorial extent & classification: E. Local *Unpublished*

The M6 Motorway (Junction 14) (Northbound Exit Slip Road) (Temporary Prohibition of Traffic) (No. 2) Order 2006 No. 2006/3514. - Enabling power: Road Traffic Regulation Act 1984, s. 14 (1) (a). - Made: 29.12.2006. Coming into force: 05.01.2007. Effect: None. Territorial extent & classification: E. Local *Unpublished*

The M6 Motorway (Junction 14) (Northbound Exit Slip Road) (Temporary Prohibition of Traffic) Order 2006 No. 2006/2549. - Enabling power: Road Traffic Regulation Act 1984, s. 14 (1) (a). - Made: 12.09.2006. Coming into force: 19.09.2006. Effect: None. Territorial extent & classification: E. Local *Unpublished*

The M6 Motorway (Junction 14, Stafford) (Temporary Restriction and Prohibition of Traffic) Order 2006 No. 2006/1564. - Enabling power: Road Traffic Regulation Act 1984, s. 14 (1) (a). - Made: 22.05.2006. Coming into force: 29.05.2006. Effect: None. Territorial extent & classification: E. Local *Unpublished*

The M6 Motorway (Junction 16, Staffordshire) (Temporary Restriction and Prohibition of Traffic) Order 2006 No. 2006/2561. - Enabling power: Road Traffic Regulation Act 1984, s. 14 (1) (a). - Made: 18.09.2006. Coming into force: 25.09.2006. Effect: None. Territorial extent & classification: E. Local *Unpublished*

The M6 Motorway (Junction 17, Northbound Entry Slip Road) (Temporary Prohibition of Traffic) Order 2006 No. 2006/1876. - Enabling power: Road Traffic Regulation Act 1984, s. 14 (1) (a). - Made: 03.07.2006. Coming into force: 28.07.2006. Effect: None. Territorial extent & classification: E. Local *Unpublished*

The M6 Motorway (Junction 17 Southbound Entry Slip Road and Junctions 16 to 17 Northbound and Southbound Carriageways) (Temporary Prohibition and Restriction of Traffic) Order 2006 No. 2006/2611. - Enabling power: Road Traffic Regulation Act 1984, s. 14 (1) (a) (7). - Made: 08.09.2006. Coming into force: 01.10.2006. Effect: None. Territorial extent & classification: E. Local *Unpublished*

The M6 Motorway (Junction 19, Northbound Exit Slip Road) (Temporary Prohibition of Traffic) Order 2006 No. 2006/628. - Enabling power: Road Traffic Regulation Act 1984, s. 14 (1) (a). - Made: 27.02.2006. Coming into force: 19.03.2006. Effect: None. Territorial extent & classification: E. Local *Unpublished*

The M6 Motorway (Junction 20, Northbound Entry Slip Road) (Temporary Prohibition of Traffic) Order 2006 No. 2006/3069. - Enabling power: Road Traffic Regulation Act 1984, s. 14 (1) (a). - Made: 20.10.2006. Coming into force: 19.11.2006. Effect: None. Territorial extent & classification: E. Local *Unpublished*

The M6 Motorway (Junction 20, Northbound Exit Slip Road) (Temporary Prohibition of Traffic) Order 2006 No. 2006/2856. - Enabling power: Road Traffic Regulation Act 1984, s. 14 (1) (a). - Made: 16.10.2006. Coming into force: 14.11.2006. Effect: None. Territorial extent & classification: E. Local *Unpublished*

The M6 Motorway (Junction 20, Southbound Link Roads to M56 Westbound and Eastbound) (Temporary Prohibition of Traffic) Order 2006 No. 2006/1148. - Enabling power: Road Traffic Regulation Act 1984, s. 14 (1) (a). - Made: 17.04.2006. Coming into force: 07.05.2006. Effect: None. Territorial extent & classification: E. Local *Unpublished*

The M6 Motorway Junction 21A (Northbound Link Road to the M62 Eastbound) (Temporary Prohibition of Traffic) Order 2006 No. 2006/1156. - Enabling power: Road Traffic Regulation Act 1984, s. 14 (1) (a). - Made: 17.04.2006. Coming into force: 07.05.2006. Effect: None. Territorial extent & classification: E. Local *Unpublished*

The M6 Motorway Junction 21A (Northbound Link Road to the M62 Eastbound) (Temporary Prohibition of Traffic) Order 2006 (No. 2) No. 2006/2359. - Enabling power: Road Traffic Regulation Act 1984, s. 14 (1) (a). - Made: 14.08.2006. Coming into force: 07.09.2006. Effect: None. Territorial extent & classification: E. Local *Unpublished*

The M6 Motorway Junction 21A (Northbound Link Road to the M62, Westbound) (Temporary Prohibition of Traffic) Order 2006 No. 2006/2593. - Enabling power: Road Traffic Regulation Act 1984, s. 14 (1) (a). - Made: 08.09.2006. Coming into force: 05.10.2006. Effect: None. Territorial extent & classification: E. Local *Unpublished*

The M6 Motorway (Junction 21, Northbound and Southbound Entry Slip Roads) (Temporary Prohibition of Traffic) Order 2006 No. 2006/1149. - Enabling power: Road Traffic Regulation Act 1984, s. 14 (1) (a). - Made: 17.04.2006. Coming into force: 09.05.2006. Effect: None. Territorial extent & classification: E. Local *Unpublished*

The M6 Motorway (Junction 22, Northbound and Southbound Entry and Exit Slip Roads) (Temporary Prohibition of Traffic) Order 2006 No. 2006/1875. - Enabling power: Road Traffic Regulation Act 1984, s. 14 (1) (a). - Made: 03.07.2006. Coming into force: 27.07.2006. Effect: None. Territorial extent & classification: E. Local *Unpublished*

The M6 Motorway (Junction 22, Southbound Entry Slip Road) (Temporary Prohibition of Traffic) Order 2006 No. 2006/1353. - Enabling power: Road Traffic Regulation Act 1984, s. 14 (1) (a). - Made: 08.05.2006. Coming into force: 01.06.2006. Effect: None. Territorial extent & classification: E. Local *Unpublished*

The M6 Motorway (Junction 26, Eastern Roundabout, Southbound Exit Slip Road and Link Roads to the A577) (Temporary Prohibition of Traffic) Order 2006 No. 2006/2544. - Enabling power: Road Traffic Regulation Act 1984, s. 14 (1) (a). - Made: 11.09.2006. Coming into force: 05.10.2006. Effect: None. Territorial extent & classification: E. Local *Unpublished*

The M6 Motorway (Junction 27, Northbound and Southbound Carriageway and Slip Roads) (Temporary Prohibition and Restriction of Traffic) Order 2006 No. 2006/3054. - Enabling power: Road Traffic Regulation Act 1984, s. 14 (1) (a). - Made: 16.10.2006. Coming into force: 09.11.2006. Effect: None. Territorial extent & classification: E. Local *Unpublished*

The M6 Motorway (Junction 27, Northbound Exit Slip Road) (Temporary Prohibition of Traffic) Order 2006 No. 2006/3153. - Enabling power: Road Traffic Regulation Act 1984, s. 14 (1) (a). - Made: 21.11.2006. Coming into force: 15.12.2006. Effect: None. Territorial extent & classification: E. Local *Unpublished*

The M6 Motorway (Junction 27, Southbound Entry Slip Road) (Temporary Prohibition of Traffic) Order 2006 No. 2006/2244. - Enabling power: Road Traffic Regulation Act 1984, s. 14 (1) (a). - Made: 07.08.2006. Coming into force: 31.08.2006. Effect: None. Territorial extent & classification: E. Local *Unpublished*

The M6 Motorway (Junction 28. Northbound Main Carraigeway) (Temporary Prohibition of Traffic) Order 2006 No. 2006/1798. - Enabling power: Road Traffic Regulation Act 1984, s. 14 (1) (b). - Made: 19.06.2006. Coming into force: 01.07.2006. Effect: None. Territorial extent & classification: E. Local *Unpublished*

The M6 Motorway (Junction 29, Northbound Entry and Southbound Exit Slip Roads) (Temporary Prohibition of Traffic) Order 2006 No. 2006/2175. - Enabling power: Road Traffic Regulation Act 1984, s. 14 (1) (a). - Made: 31.07.2006. Coming into force: 28.08.2006. Effect: None. Territorial extent & classification: E. Local *Unpublished*

The M6 Motorway (Junction 29, Northbound Link Road to the M6 Junction 29A) (Temporary Prohibition of Traffic) Order 2006 No. 2006/2543. - Enabling power: Road Traffic Regulation Act 1984, s. 14 (1) (a). - Made: 18.09.2006. Coming into force: 15.10.2006. Effect: None. Territorial extent & classification: E. Local *Unpublished*

The M6 Motorway (Junction 29, Southbound Entry Slip Road) (Temporary Prohibition of Traffic) Order 2006 No. 2006/2442. - Enabling power: Road Traffic Regulation Act 1984, s. 14 (1) (a). - Made: 21.08.2006. Coming into force: 14.09.2006. Effect: None. Territorial extent & classification: E. Local *Unpublished*

The M6 Motorway (Junction 31-30, Southbound Main Carriageway) (Temporary Restriction of Traffic) Order 2006 No. 2006/384. - Enabling power: Road Traffic Regulation Act 1984, s. 14 (1) (a) (7). - Made: 10.02.2006. Coming into force: 05.03.2006. Effect: None. Territorial extent & classification: E. Local *Unpublished*

The M6 Motorway (Junction 31A Southbound Main Carriageway and Entry Slip Road) (Temporary Prohibition and Restriction of Traffic) Order 2006 No. 2006/720. - Enabling power: Road Traffic Regulation Act 1984, s. 14 (1) (a) (7). - Made: 07.03.2006. Coming into force: 28.03.2006. Effect: None. Territorial extent & classification: E. Local *Unpublished*

The M6 Motorway (Junction 33 Northbound and Southbound Main Carriageways, Northbound Entry and Exit Slip Roads) (Temporary Restriction of Traffic) Order 2006 No. 2006/233. - Enabling power: Road Traffic Regulation Act 1984, s. 14 (1) (a). - Made: 30.01.2006. Coming into force: 28.02.2006. Effect: None. Territorial extent & classification: E. Local *Unpublished*

The M6 Motorway (Junction 33 Southbound Exit Slip Road) (Temporary Prohibition of Traffic) Order 2006 No. 2006/1724. - Enabling power: Road Traffic Regulation Act 1984, s. 14 (1) (a). - Made: 23.06.2006. Coming into force: 17.07.2006. Effect: None. Territorial extent & classification: E. Local *Unpublished*

The M6 Motorway (Junction 34, Northbound Entry and Exit Slip Roads) (Temporary Prohibition of Traffic) Order 2006 No. 2006/2734. - Enabling power: Road Traffic Regulation Act 1984, s. 14 (1) (a). - Made: 26.09.2006. Coming into force: 22.10.2006. Effect: None. Territorial extent & classification: E. Local *Unpublished*

The M6 Motorway (Junction 34, Northbound Main Carriageway and Entry Slip Road) (Temporary Prohibition and Restriction of Traffic) Order 2006 No. 2006/477. - Enabling power: Road Traffic Regulation Act 1984, s. 14 (1) (a). - Made: 21.02.2006. Coming into force: 17.03.2006. Effect: None. Territorial extent & classification: E. Local *Unpublished*

The M6 Motorway (Junction 34, Southbound Exit and Entry Slip Roads) (No. 2) (Temporary Prohibition of Traffic) Order 2006 No. 2006/2779. - Enabling power: Road Traffic Regulation Act 1984, s. 14 (1) (a). - Made: 10.10.2006. Coming into force: 05.11.2006. Effect: None. Territorial extent & classification: E. Local *Unpublished*

The M6 Motorway (Junction 34, Southbound Exit and Entry Slip Roads) (Temporary Prohibition of Traffic) Order 2006 No. 2006/2247. - Enabling power: Road Traffic Regulation Act 1984, s. 14 (1) (a). - Made: 08.08.2006. Coming into force: 03.09.2006. Effect: None. Territorial extent & classification: E. Local *Unpublished*

The M6 Motorway (Junction 36, Town Head Bridge Parapet Upgrade) (Temporary Restriction of Traffic) Order 2006 No. 2006/7. - Enabling power: Road Traffic Regulation Act 1984, s. 14 (1) (a) (7). - Made: 03.01.2006. Coming into force: 26.01.2006. Effect: None. Territorial extent & classification: E. Local *Unpublished*

The M6 Motorway (Junction 40, Castletown Bridge, Northbound and Southbound Carriageways) (Temporary Restriction of Traffic) Order 2006 No. 2006/475. - Enabling power: Road Traffic Regulation Act 1984, s. 14 (1) (a) (7). - Made: 21.02.2006. Coming into force: 19.03.2006. Effect: None. Territorial extent & classification: E. Local *Unpublished*

The M6 Motorway (Junction 42 to 41, Southwaite Services) (Temporary Restriction of Traffic) Order 2006 No. 2006/3093. - Enabling power: Road Traffic Regulation Act 1984, s. 14 (1) (a). - Made: 14.11.2006. Coming into force: 08.12.2006. Effect: None. Territorial extent & classification: E. Local *Unpublished*

The M6 Motorway (Junction 44, Greaymoorhill) and A74 Trunk Road and A7 Circulatory Carriageway (Temporary Restriction of Traffic) Order 2006 No. 2006/1320. - Enabling power: Road Traffic Regulation Act 1984, s. 14 (1) (a). - Made: 02.05.2006. Coming into force: 31.05.2006. Effect: None. Territorial extent & classification: E. Local *Unpublished*

The M6 Motorway (Junctions 3 - 4, Warwickshire) (Temporary Restriction of Traffic) Order 2006 No. 2006/3228. - Enabling power: Road Traffic Regulation Act 1984, s. 14 (1) (a) (7). - Made: 27.11.2006. Coming into force: 04.12.2006. Effect: None. Territorial extent & classification: E. Local *Unpublished*

The M6 Motorway (Junctions 4 - 4A) (Temporary Restriction and Prohibition of Traffic) Order 2006 No. 2006/321. - Enabling power: Road Traffic Regulation Act 1984, s. 14 (1) (a) (7). - Made: 06.02.2006. Coming into force: 13.02.2006. Effect: None. Territorial extent & classification: E. Local *Unpublished*

The M6 Motorway (Junctions 10 - 10A) (Temporary Prohibition of Traffic) Order 2006 No. 2006/1652. - Enabling power: Road Traffic Regulation Act 1984, s. 14 (1) (a) (7). - Made: 14.06.2006. Coming into force: 21.06.2006. Effect: None. Territorial extent & classification: E. Local *Unpublished*

The M6 Motorway (Junctions 11 - 13, Staffordshire) (Temporary Restriction and Prohibition of Traffic) Order 2006 No. 2006/667. - Enabling power: Road Traffic Regulation Act 1984, s. 14 (1) (a) (7). - Made: 20.02.2006. Coming into force: 27.02.2006. Effect: None. Territorial extent & classification: E. Local *Unpublished*

The M6 Motorway (Junctions 11A - 13) (Temporary Restriction and Prohibition of Traffic) Order 2006 No. 2006/2399. - Enabling power: Road Traffic Regulation Act 1984, s. 14 (1) (a) (7). - Made: 18.08.2006. Coming into force: 25.08.2006. Effect: None. Territorial extent & classification: E. Local *Unpublished*

The M6 Motorway (Junctions 14 - 15, Staffordshire) (Temporary Restriction and Prohibition of Traffic) Order 2006 No. 2006/75. - Enabling power: Road Traffic Regulation Act 1984, s. 14 (1) (a). - Made: 06.01.2006. Coming into force: 13.01.2006. Effect: None. Territorial extent & classification: E. Local *Unpublished*

The M6 Motorway (Junctions 14 - 15) (Temporary Prohibition of Traffic) Order 2006 No. 2006/1650. - Enabling power: Road Traffic Regulation Act 1984, s. 14 (1) (a) (7). - Made: 16.06.2006. Coming into force: 23.06.2006. Effect: None. Territorial extent & classification: E. Local *Unpublished*

The M6 Motorway (Junctions 15 - 16) (Temporary 40 Miles Per Hour Speed Restriction) Order 2006 No. 2006/285. - Enabling power: Road Traffic Regulation Act 1984, s. 14 (1) (a). - Made: 30.01.2006. Coming into force: 06.02.2006. Effect: None. Territorial extent & classification: E. Local *Unpublished*

The M6 Motorway (Junctions 16 - 15, Staffordshire) (Temporary Prohibition of Traffic) Order 2006 No. 2006/2667. - Enabling power: Road Traffic Regulation Act 1984, s. 14 (1) (a) (7). - Made: 15.09.2006. Coming into force: 22.09.2006. Effect: None. Territorial extent & classification: E. Local *Unpublished*

The M6 Motorway (Junctions 17 to 19, Northbound Carriageway) (Temporary Prohibition and Restriction of Traffic) Order 2006 No. 2006/2124. - Enabling power: Road Traffic Regulation Act 1984, s. 14 (1) (a) (7). - Made: 21.07.2006. Coming into force: 18.08.2006. Effect: None. Territorial extent & classification: E. Local *Unpublished*

The M6 Motorway (Junctions 24 - 25 Norhbound and Southbound Carriageways and Junction 25 Southbound Entry Slip Road) (Temporary Prohibition and Restriction of Traffic) Order 2006 No. 2006/3196. - Enabling power: Road Traffic Regulation Act 1984, s. 14 (1) (a) (7). - Made: 27.11.2006. Coming into force: 02.12.2006. Effect: None. Territorial extent & classification: E. Local *Unpublished*

The M6 Motorway (Junctions 27-28 Charnock Richard Services, Northbound and Southbound Carriageways) (Temporary Restriction of Traffic) Order 2006 No. 2006/2240. - Enabling power: Road Traffic Regulation Act 1984, s. 14 (1) (a) (7). - Made: 07.08.2006. Coming into force: 03.09.2006. Effect: None. Territorial extent & classification: E. Local *Unpublished*

The M6 Motorway Junctions 30, 31 and 31A Northbound Main Carriageway and Exit Slip Roads (And M61 Motorway Northbound Carriageway) (Temporary Prohibition and Restriction of Traffic) Order 2006 No. 2006/2753. - Enabling power: Road Traffic Regulation Act 1984, s. 14 (1) (a) (7). - Made: 10.10.2006. Coming into force: 05.11.2006. Effect: None. Territorial extent & classification: E. Local *Unpublished*

The M6 Motorway (Junctions 30 - 31a, Southbound Carriageway) (Cuerdale Lane Bridge) (Temporary Restriction of Traffic) Order 2006 No. 2006/3047. - Enabling power: Road Traffic Regulation Act 1984, s. 14 (1) (a). - Made: 20.10.2006. Coming into force: 16.11.2006. Effect: None. Territorial extent & classification: E. Local *Unpublished*

The M6 Motorway (Junctions 30 to 44), M55 and A74(M) Motorways and A74 Trunk Road (Temporary Variable Speed LImit) Order 2006 No. 2006/732. - Enabling power: Road Traffic Regulation Act 1984, s. 14 (1) (a) (7). - Made: 06.03.2006. Coming into force: 31.03.2006. Effect: None. Territorial extent & classification: E. Local *Unpublished*

The M6 Motorway (Junctions 32-33, Keepers and Woodacre Great Wood Footbridges and Woodacre Lane Bridge) (Temporary Restriction of Traffic) Order 2006 No. 2006/3070. - Enabling power: Road Traffic Regulation Act 1984, s. 14 (1) (a) (7). - Made: 24.10.2006. Coming into force: 19.11.2006. Effect: None. Territorial extent & classification: E. Local *Unpublished*

The M6 Motorway (Junctions 32-33, Keepers and Woodacre Great Wood Footbridges) (Temporary Restriction of Traffic) Order 2006 No. 2006/3502. - Enabling power: Road Traffic Regulation Act 1984, s. 14 (1) (a) (7). - Made: 28.12.2006. Coming into force: 20.01.2007. Effect: None. Territorial extent & classification: E. Local *Unpublished*

The M6 Motorway (Junctions 32 - 33 Northbound Carriageway, Matshead Bridge) (Temporary Prohibition and Restriction of Traffic) Order 2006 No. 2006/3462. - Enabling power: Road Traffic Regulation Act 1984, s. 14 (1) (a) (7). - Made: 12.12.2006. Coming into force: 07.01.2007. Effect: None. Territorial extent & classification: E. Local *Unpublished*

The M6 Motorway (Low Hurst Bank Southbound) (Temporary Restriction of Traffic) Order 2006 No. 2006/2732. - Enabling power: Road Traffic Regulation Act 1984, s. 14 (1) (a) (7). - Made: 26.09.2006. Coming into force: 22.10.2006. Effect: None. Territorial extent & classification: E. Local *Unpublished*

The M6 Motorway (M1 Junction 19) (Slip Roads) (Temporary Prohibition of Traffic) Order 2006 No. 2006/3203. - Enabling power: Road Traffic Regulation Act 1984, s. 14 (1) (a). - Made: 24.11.2006. Coming into force: 01.12.2006. Effect: None. Territorial extent & classification: E. Local *Unpublished*

The M6 Motorway (North of Junction 4) (Temporary Restriction and Prohibition of Traffic) Order 2006 No. 2006/322. - Enabling power: Road Traffic Regulation Act 1984, s. 14 (1) (a) (7). - Made: 06.02.2006. Coming into force: 13.02.2006. Effect: None. Territorial extent & classification: E. Local *Unpublished*

The M6 Motorway (Shap Fell Northbound Resurfacing) (Temporary Restriction and Prohibition of Traffic) Order 2006 No. 2006/2760. - Enabling power: Road Traffic Regulation Act 1984, s. 14 (1) (a) (7). - Made: 10.10.2006. Coming into force: 05.11.2006. Effect: None. Territorial extent & classification: E. Local *Unpublished*

The M6 Motorway (South of Junction 6) (Temporary Restriction and Prohibition of Traffic) Order 2006 No. 2006/420. - Enabling power: Road Traffic Regulation Act 1984, s. 14 (1) (a) (7). - Made: 10.02.2006. Coming into force: 17.02.2006. Effect: None. Territorial extent & classification: E. Local *Unpublished*

The M6 Motorway (South of Junction 14) (Temporary Prohibition of Traffic) Order 2006 No. 2006/1989. - Enabling power: Road Traffic Regulation Act 1984, s. 14 (1) (a) (7). - Made: 14.07.2006. Coming into force: 21.07.2006. Effect: None. Territorial extent & classification: E. Local *Unpublished*

The M6 Motorway (South of Junction 16) (Temporary Prohibition of Traffic) Order 2006 No. 2006/3512. - Enabling power: Road Traffic Regulation Act 1984, s. 14 (1) (a) (7). - Made: 29.12.2006. Coming into force: 05.01.2007. Effect: None. Territorial extent & classification: E. Local *Unpublished*

The M6 Motorway (Weedford Park and Great Wyrley Toll Plazas) (Temporary 30 Miles Per Hour Speed Restriction) Order 2006 No. 2006/1042. - Enabling power: Road Traffic Regulation Act 1984, s. 14 (1) (b). - Made: 03.04.2006. Coming into force: 10.04.2006. Effect: None. Territorial extent & classification: E. Local *Unpublished*

The M6 Motorway (Yarnfield Lane, Near Stone, Staffordshire) (Temporary Prohibition of Traffic) Order 2006 No. 2006/1558. - Enabling power: Road Traffic Regulation Act 1984, s. 14 (1) (b). - Made: 26.05.2006. Coming into force: 02.06.2006. Effect: None. Territorial extent & classification: E. Local *Unpublished*

The M10 and the M1 Motorways (Junctions 7 - 8) (Temporary Restriction of Traffic) Order 2006 No. 2006/1481. - Enabling power: Road Traffic Regulation Act 1984, s. 14 (1) (a) (7). - Made: 30.05.2006. Coming into force: 03.06.2006. Effect: None. Territorial extent & classification: E. Local *Unpublished*

The M11 Motorway (Junction 4, Westbound Exit Link Road) (Temporary Prohibition of Traffic) Order 2006 No. 2006/3134. - Enabling power: Road Traffic Regulation Act 1984, s. 14 (1) (a). - Made: 20.11.2006. Coming into force: 27.11.2006. Effect: None. Territorial extent & classification: E. Local *Unpublished*

The M11 Motorway (Junction 5, Southbound Entry Slip Road) (Temporary Prohibition of Traffic) Order 2006 No. 2006/1292. - Enabling power: Road Traffic Regulation Act 1984, s. 14 (1) (a). - Made: 08.05.2006. Coming into force: 17.05.2006. Effect: None. Territorial extent & classification: E. Local *Unpublished*

The M11 Motorway (Junction 7 - Junction 8, Essex) (Temporary 50 Miles Per Hour Speed Restriction) Order 2006 No. 2006/1215. - Enabling power: Road Traffic Regulation Act 1984, s. 14 (1) (a). - Made: 21.04.2006. Coming into force: 28.04.2006. Effect: None. Territorial extent & classification: E. Local *Unpublished*

The M11 Motorway (Junction 8 - 10) (Temporary Restriction and Prohibition of Traffic) Order 2006 No. 2006/330. - Enabling power: Road Traffic Regulation Act 1984, s. 14 (1). - Made: 23.01.2006. Coming into force: 30.01.2006. Effect: None. Territorial extent & classification: E. Local *Unpublished*

The M11 Motorway (Junction 9A - Junction 9, Cambridgeshire) (Temporary Prohibition of Traffic) Order 2006 No. 2006/2110. - Enabling power: Road Traffic Regulation Act 1984, s. 14 (1) (a). - Made: 24.07.2006. Coming into force: 31.07.2006. Effect: None. Territorial extent & classification: E. Local *Unpublished*

The M11 Motorway (Junction 10, Cambridgeshire) (Temporary Restriction and Prohibition of Traffic) (No. 2) Order 2006 No. 2006/2160. - Enabling power: Road Traffic Regulation Act 1984, s. 14 (1) (a). - Made: 31.07.2006. Coming into force: 07.08.2006. Effect: None. Territorial extent & classification: E. Local *Unpublished*

The M11 Motorway (Junction 10, Cambridgeshire) (Temporary Restriction and Prohibition of Traffic) Order 2006 No. 2006/1730. - Enabling power: Road Traffic Regulation Act 1984, s. 14 (1) (a). - Made: 16.06.2006. Coming into force: 23.06.2006. Effect: None. Territorial extent & classification: E. Local *Unpublished*

The M11 Motorway (Junction 10 to Junction 11) (Temporary Restriction and Prohibition of Traffic) Order 2006 No. 2006/3033. - Enabling power: Road Traffic Regulation Act 1984, s. 14 (1) (a). - Made: 27.10.2006. Coming into force: 03.11.2006. Effect: None. Territorial extent & classification: E. Local *Unpublished*

The M11 Motorway (Junction 12 - 13, Cambridgeshire) (Temporary Prohibition of Traffic) Order 2006 No. 2006/710. - Enabling power: Road Traffic Regulation Act 1984, s. 14 (1) (a). - Made: 06.03.2006. Coming into force: 13.03.2006. Effect: None. Territorial extent & classification: E. Local *Unpublished*

The M11 Motorway (Junction 12, Cambridgeshire) (Temporary Prohibition of Traffic) Order 2006 No. 2006/160. - Enabling power: Road Traffic Regulation Act 1984, s. 14 (1). - Made: 23.01.2006. Coming into force: 30.01.2006. Effect: None. Territorial extent & classification: E. Local *Unpublished*

The M11 Motorway (Junction 12) Northbound Entry Slip Road (Temporary Prohibition of Traffic) Order 2006 No. 2006/2598. - Enabling power: Road Traffic Regulation Act 1984, s. 14 (1) (a). - Made: 11.09.2006. Coming into force: 18.09.2006. Effect: None. Territorial extent & classification: E. Local *Unpublished*

The M11 Motorway (Junction 13) Southbound Entry Slip Road (Temporary Prohibition of Traffic) Order 2006 No. 2006/2481. - Enabling power: Road Traffic Regulation Act 1984, s. 14 (1) (a). - Made: 04.09.2006. Coming into force: 11.09.2006. Effect: None. Territorial extent & classification: E. Local *Unpublished*

The M11 Motorway (Junctions 4 -5, Northbound) (Temporary Restriction and Prohibition of Traffic) Order 2006 No. 2006/412. - Enabling power: Road Traffic Regulation Act 1984, s. 14 (1) (a) (7). - Made: 20.02.2006. Coming into force: 25.02.2006. Effect: None. Territorial extent & classification: E. Local *Unpublished*

The M11 Motorway (Junctions 4 - 7) (Temporary Prohibition of Traffic) Order 2006 No. 2006/2199. - Enabling power: Road Traffic Regulation Act 1984, s. 14 (1) (a), sch. 9, para. 27 (1). - Made: 07.08.2006. Coming into force: 14.08.2006. Effect: S.I. 2006/1292, 3192, 3210 revoked. Territorial extent & classification: E. Local *Unpublished*

The M11 Motorway (Junctions 5 - 4, Southbound Carriageway) (Temporary Restriction of Traffic) Order 2006 No. 2006/278. - Enabling power: Road Traffic Regulation Act 1984, s. 14 (1) (a) (7). - Made: 30.01.2006. Coming into force: 04.02.2006. Effect: None. Territorial extent & classification: E. Local *Unpublished*

The M11 Motorway (Junctions 6 - 4, Southbound) (Temporary Restriction and Prohibition of Traffic) Order 2006 No. 2006/3183. - Enabling power: Road Traffic Regulation Act 1984, s. 14 (1) (a) (7). - Made: 27.11.2006. Coming into force: 02.12.2006. Effect: None. Territorial extent & classification: E. Local *Unpublished*

The M11 Motorway (Junctions 8 and 8A) and the A120 Trunk Road (Thremhall Avenue, Essex) (Temporary Restriction and Prohibition of Traffic) Order 2006 No. 2006/2437. - Enabling power: Road Traffic Regulation Act 1984, s. 14 (1) (a). - Made: 22.08.2006. Coming into force: 29.08.2006. Effect: None. Territorial extent & classification: E. Local *Unpublished*

The M11 Motorway (Southbound Entry Slip Road) (Junction 10) (Temporary Prohibition of Traffic) Order 2006 No. 2006/3308. - Enabling power: Road Traffic Regulation Act 1984, s. 14 (1) (a). - Made: 04.12.2006. Coming into force: 11.12.2006. Effect: None. Territorial extent & classification: E. Local *Unpublished*

The M11 Motorway (Strethall Bridleway Overbridge, Great Chesterford, Essex and Cambridgeshire) (Temporary Prohibition of Traffic) Order 2006 No. 2006/3377. - Enabling power: Road Traffic Regulation Act 1984, s. 14 (1) (a). - Made: 11.12.2006. Coming into force: 18.12.2006. Effect: None. Territorial extent & classification: E. Local *Unpublished*

The M18 Motorway and the A1(M) Motorway (Wadworth Interchange) (Temporary Prohibition of Traffic) Order 2006 No. 2006/2714. - Enabling power: Road Traffic Regulation Act 1984, s. 14 (1) (a). - Made: 03.10.2006. Coming into force: 15.10.2006. Effect: None. Territorial extent & classification: E. Local *Unpublished*

The M18 Motorway and the A1(M) Motorway (Wadworth Interchange) (Temporary Prohibition of Traffic) Order 2006 No. 2006/2258. - Enabling power: Road Traffic Regulation Act 1984, s. 14 (1) (a). - Made: 28.07.2006. Coming into force: 10.08.2006. Effect: None. Territorial extent & classification: E. Local *Unpublished*

The M18 Motorway and the M180 Motorway (North Ings Roundabout) (Temporary Prohibition of Traffic) Order 2006 No. 2006/385. - Enabling power: Road Traffic Regulation Act 1984, s. 14 (1) (a). - Made: 07.02.2006. Coming into force: 19.02.2006. Effect: None. Territorial extent & classification: E. Local *Unpublished*

The M18 Motorway (Junction 1, Bramley) (Temporary Prohibition of Traffic) Order 2006 No. 2006/1107. - Enabling power: Road Traffic Regulation Act 1984, s. 14 (1) (a). - Made: 11.04.2006. Coming into force: 23.04.2006. Effect: None. Territorial extent & classification: E. Local *Unpublished*

The M18 Motorway (Junction 3 to Junction 2) (Temporary Prohibition of Traffic) Order 2006 No. 2006/901. - Enabling power: Road Traffic Regulation Act 1984, s. 14 (1) (a). - Made: 22.03.2006. Coming into force: 26.03.2006. Effect: None. Territorial extent & classification: E. Local *Unpublished*

The M18 Motorway (Junction 4 to Junction 5) (Temporary Restriction and Prohibition of Traffic) Order 2006 No. 2006/2854. - Enabling power: Road Traffic Regulation Act 1984, s. 14 (1) (a) (7). - Made: 17.10.2006. Coming into force: 29.10.2006. Effect: None. Territorial extent & classification: E. Local *Unpublished*

The M18 Motorway (Junction 6) (Temporary Prohibition of Traffic) Order 2006 No. 2006/3174. - Enabling power: Road Traffic Regulation Act 1984, s. 14 (1) (a). - Made: 06.11.2006. Coming into force: 19.11.2006. Effect: None. Territorial extent & classification: E. Local *Unpublished*

The M20 and M26 Motorways (Junctions 4 - 2/2A) (Temporary Prohibition of Traffic) Order 2006 No. 2006/2583. - Enabling power: Road Traffic Regulation Act 1984, s. 14 (1) (a) (7). - Made: 11.09.2006. Coming into force: 16.09.2006. Effect: None. Territorial extent & classification: E. Local *Unpublished*

Road traffic: Traffic regulation

The M20 Motorway and the A20 Trunk Road (Cheriton Interchange - Western Heights Roundabout) (Temporary Restriction and Prohibition of Traffic) Order 2006 No. 2006/149. - Enabling power: Road Traffic Regulation Act 1984, s. 14 (1) (a). - Made: 23.01.2006. Coming into force: 28.01.2006. Effect: None. Territorial extent & classification: E. Local *Unpublished*

The M20 Motorway and the A20 Trunk Road (Junctions 1 - 2, Coastbound) (Temporary Restriction and Prohibition of Traffic) Order 2006 No. 2006/1885. - Enabling power: Road Traffic Regulation Act 1984, s. 14 (1) (a) (7). - Made: 10.07.2006. Coming into force: 15.07.2006. Effect: None. Territorial extent & classification: E. Local *Unpublished*

The M20 Motorway and the A20 Trunk Road (Junctions 1 - 2, Westbound Entry Slip Roads) (Temporary Prohibition of Traffic) Order 2006 No. 2006/2105. - Enabling power: Road Traffic Regulation Act 1984, s. 14 (1) (a), sch. 9, para. 27 (1). - Made: 24.07.2006. Coming into force: 02.08.2006. Effect: S.I. 2006/805 revoked. Territorial extent & classification: E. Local *Unpublished*

The M20 Motorway and the A20 Trunk Road (Roundhil Tunnels) (Temporary Restriction and Prohibition of Traffic) Order 2006 No. 2006/3182. - Enabling power: Road Traffic Regulation Act 1984, s. 14 (1) (a). - Made: 27.11.2006. Coming into force: 06.12.2006. Effect: None. Territorial extent & classification: E. Local *Unpublished*

The M20 Motorway and the A2070 and A292 Trunk Roads (Junctions 9 - 10) (Temporary Restriction and Prohibition of Traffic and Pedestrians) Order 2006 No. 2006/2330. - Enabling power: Road Traffic Regulation Act 1984, s. 14 (1) (a) (7). - Made: 21.08.2006. Coming into force: 26.08.2006. Effect: None. Territorial extent & classification: E. Local *Unpublished*

The M20 Motorway (Junction 1) (Temporary Restriction of Traffic) Order 2006 No. 2006/156. - Enabling power: Road Traffic Regulation Act 1984, s. 14 (1) (a) (7). - Made: 23.01.2006. Coming into force: 28.01.2006. Effect: None. Territorial extent & classification: E. Local *Unpublished*

The M20 Motorway (Junction 2, Westbound Entry Slip Road) (Temporary Prohibition of Traffic) Order 2006 No. 2006/805. - Enabling power: Road Traffic Regulation Act 1984, s. 14 (1) (a). - Made: 13.03.2006. Coming into force: 22.03.2006. Effect: None. Territorial extent & classification: E. Local. - Revoked by S.I. 2006/2105 (Unpublished) *Unpublished*

The M20 Motorway (Junction 4) (Temporary Restriction and Prohibition of Traffic) (No. 2) Order 2006 No. 2006/1132. - Enabling power: Road Traffic Regulation Act 1984, s. 14 (1) (a) (7). - Made: 18.04.2006. Coming into force: 24.04.2006. Effect: S.I. 2006/534 revoked. Territorial extent & classification: E. Local *Unpublished*

The M20 Motorway (Junction 4) (Temporary Restriction and Prohibition of Traffic) Order 2006 No. 2006/534. - Enabling power: Road Traffic Regulation Act 1984, s. 14 (1) (a). - Made: 27.02.2006. Coming into force: 04.03.2006. Effect: None. Territorial extent & classification: E. Local *Unpublished*

The M20 Motorway (Junction 8, Londonbound Carriageway) (Temporary 50 Miles Per Hour Speed Restriction) Order 2006 No. 2006/3439. - Enabling power: Road Traffic Regulation Act 1984, s. 14 (1) (a). - Made: 18.12.2006. Coming into force: 06.01.2007. Effect: None. Territorial extent & classification: E. Local *Unpublished*

The M20 Motorway (Junction 11, Coastbound Exit Slip Road) (Temporary Prohibition of Traffic) Order 2006 No. 2006/1314. - Enabling power: Road Traffic Regulation Act 1984, s. 14 (1) (a). - Made: 02.05.2006. Coming into force: 06.05.2006. Effect: None. Territorial extent & classification: E. Local *Unpublished*

The M20 Motorway (Junction 11, Slip Roads) (Temporary Prohibition of Traffic) Order 2006 No. 2006/1884. - Enabling power: Road Traffic Regulation Act 1984, s. 14 (1) (a). - Made: 10.07.2006. Coming into force: 15.07.2006. Effect: None. Territorial extent & classification: E. Local *Unpublished*

The M20 Motorway (Junctions 4 - 5, Coastbound Carriageway) (Temporary 50 Miles Per Hour Speed Restriction) Order 2006 No. 2006/388. - Enabling power: Road Traffic Regulation Act 1984, s. 14 (1) (a). - Made: 13.02.2006. Coming into force: 18.02.2006. Effect: None. Territorial extent & classification: E. Local *Unpublished*

The M20 Motorway (Junctions 4 - 7) (Temporary Restriction and Prohibition of Traffic) Order 2006 No. 2006/155. - Enabling power: Road Traffic Regulation Act 1984, s. 14 (1) (a). - Made: 23.01.2006. Coming into force: 28.01.2006. Effect: None. Territorial extent & classification: E. Local. - Revoked by S.I. 2007/7 (Unpublished) *Unpublished*

The M20 Motorway (Junctions 8 - 9) (Temporary Restriction of Traffic) Order 2006 No. 2006/2413. - Enabling power: Road Traffic Regulation Act 1984, s. 14 (1) (a) (7). - Made: 29.08.2006. Coming into force: 02.09.2006. Effect: None. Territorial extent & classification: E. Local *Unpublished*

The M20 Motorway (West of Junction 9) (Temporary 50 Miles Per Hour Speed Restriction) Order 2006 No. 2006/1313. - Enabling power: Road Traffic Regulation Act 1984, s. 14 (1) (a). - Made: 02.05.2006. Coming into force: 06.05.2006. Effect: None. Territorial extent & classification: E. Local *Unpublished*

The M23 and M25 Motorways (Merstham Interchange) (Temporary Prohibition of Traffic) Order 2006 No. 2006/1769. - Enabling power: Road Traffic Regulation Act 1984, s. 14 (1) (a). - Made: 26.06.2006. Coming into force: 05.07.2006. Effect: None. Territorial extent & classification: E. Local. - Revoked by S.I. 2006/2588 (Unpublished) *Unpublished*

Road traffic: Traffic regulation

The M23 Motorway and the A23 Trunk Road (Junction 11, Pease Pottage) (Temporary Restriction and Prohibition of Traffic) Order 2006 No. 2006/3359. - Enabling power: Road Traffic Regulation Act 1984, s. 14 (1) (a). - Made: 11.12.2006. Coming into force: 16.12.2006. Effect: None. Territorial extent & classification: E. Local *Unpublished*

The M23 Motorway (Junction 8, Southbound Link Road) (Temporary Prohibition of Traffic) Order 2006 No. 2006/2584. - Enabling power: Road Traffic Regulation Act 1984, s. 14 (1) (a). - Made: 11.09.2006. Coming into force: 16.09.2006. Effect: None. Territorial extent & classification: E. Local *Unpublished*

The M23 Motorway (Junction 9, Northbound Exit Slip Road) (Temporary Prohibition of Traffic) Order 2006 No. 2006/148. - Enabling power: Road Traffic Regulation Act 1984, s. 14 (1) (a). - Made: 23.01.2006. Coming into force: 28.01.2006. Effect: None. Territorial extent & classification: E. Local *Unpublished*

The M23 Motorway (Junctions 8 - 10) (Temporary Restriction and Prohibition of Traffic) Order 2006 No. 2006/527. - Enabling power: Road Traffic Regulation Act 1984, s. 14 (1) (a) (7). - Made: 20.02.2006. Coming into force: 25.02.2006. Effect: None. Territorial extent & classification: E. Local *Unpublished*

The M23 Motorway (Junctions 10 - 9, Northbound) (Temporary 50 Miles Per Hour Speed Restriction) Order 2006 No. 2006/2556. - Enabling power: Road Traffic Regulation Act 1984, s. 14 (1) (a). - Made: 18.09.2006. Coming into force: 23.09.2006. Effect: None. Territorial extent & classification: E. Local *Unpublished*

The M25 and M3 Motorways (Thorpe Interchange, Link Roads) (Temporary Prohibition of Traffic) Order 2006 No. 2006/25. - Enabling power: Road Traffic Regulation Act 1984, s. 14 (1) (a). - Made: 03.01.2006. Coming into force: 07.01.2006. Effect: None. Territorial extent & classification: E. Local *Unpublished*

The M25 and M4 Motorways (Thorney Interchange) (Temporary Prohibition of Traffic) Order 2006 No. 2006/254. - Enabling power: Road Traffic Regulation Act 1984, s. 14 (1) (a) (7). - Made: 30.01.2006. Coming into force: 07.02.2006. Effect: None. Territorial extent & classification: E. Local *Unpublished*

The M25 and M23 Motorways (Merstham Interchange, Link Roads) (Temporary Prohibition of Traffic) Order 2006 No. 2006/1375. - Enabling power: Road Traffic Regulation Act 1984, s. 14 (1) (a). - Made: 15.05.2006. Coming into force: 24.05.2006. Effect: None. Territorial extent & classification: E. Local. - Revoked by S.I. 2006/2588 (Unpublished) *Unpublished*

The M25 Motorway and the A3 Trunk Road (Wisley Interchange at Junction 10 and Ockham Junction) (Temporary Prohibition of Traffic) Order 2006 No. 2006/2552. - Enabling power: Road Traffic Regulation Act 1984, s. 14 (1) (a). - Made: 18.09.2006. Coming into force: 23.09.2006. Effect: None. Territorial extent & classification: E. Local *Unpublished*

The M25 Motorway and the A12 Trunk Road (Junction 28) (Temporary Restriction and Prohibition of Traffic) Order 2006 No. 2006/1352. - Enabling power: Road Traffic Regulation Act 1984, s. 14 (1) (a). - Made: 10.05.2006. Coming into force: 13.05.2006. Effect: None. Territorial extent & classification: E. Local *Unpublished*

The M25 Motorway and the A282 Trunk Road (Junctions 26 - 31) (Temporary Prohibition of Traffic) Order 2006 No. 2006/2878. - Enabling power: Road Traffic Regulation Act 1984, s. 14 (1) (a). - Made: 23.10.2006. Coming into force: 01.11.2006. Effect: S.I. 2005/3060, 3141, 3211; 2006/893, 977, 1101 revoked. Territorial extent & classification: E. Local *Unpublished*

The M25 Motorway and the A282 Trunk Road (Junctions 29, 30 and 31, Slip Roads) (Temporary Prohibition of Traffic) Order 2006 No. 2006/893. - Enabling power: Road Traffic Regulation Act 1984, s. 14 (1) (a). - Made: 20.03.2006. Coming into force: 01.04.2006. Effect: None. Territorial extent & classification: E. Local. - Revoked by S.I. 2006/2878 (Unpublished) *Unpublished*

The M25 Motorway and the A405 Trunk Road (Junction 21A - M1 Junction 6) (Temporary Restriction and Prohibition of Traffic) Order 2006 No. 2006/1376. - Enabling power: Road Traffic Regulation Act 1984, s. 14 (1) (a). - Made: 15.05.2006. Coming into force: 20.05.2006. Effect: None. Territorial extent & classification: E. Local *Unpublished*

The M25 Motorway and the A3113 Trunk Road (Junction 14) (Temporary 50 Miles Per Hour Speed Restriction) Order 2006 No. 2006/2846. - Enabling power: Road Traffic Regulation Act 1984, s. 14 (1) (a). - Made: 16.10.2006. Coming into force: 21.10.2006. Effect: None. Territorial extent & classification: E. Local *Unpublished*

The M25 Motorway and the M26 Motorway (Junction 5) (Temporary Restriction and Prohibition of Traffic) Order 2006 No. 2006/1897. - Enabling power: Road Traffic Regulation Act 1984, s. 14 (1) (a) (7). - Made: 17.07.2006. Coming into force: 22.07.2006. Effect: None. Territorial extent & classification: E. Local *Unpublished*

The M25 Motorway (Bell Common Tunnel) (Temporary Restriction and Prohibition of Traffic) Order 2006 No. 2006/1430. - Enabling power: Road Traffic Regulation Act 1984, s. 14 (1) (a) (7), sch. 9, para. 27 (1). - Made: 22.05.2006. Coming into force: 04.06.2006. Effect: S.I. 2005/2312 revoked. Territorial extent & classification: E. Local *Unpublished*

The M25 Motorway (Clacket Lane Services, Clockwise) (Temporary Restriction and Prohibition of Traffic) Order 2006 No. 2006/1045. - Enabling power: Road Traffic Regulation Act 1984, s. 14 (1) (a) (7). - Made: 03.04.2006. Coming into force: 08.04.2006. Effect: None. Territorial extent & classification: E. Local *Unpublished*

Road traffic: Traffic regulation

The M25 Motorway (Junction 1) (Temporary Restriction and Prohibition of Traffic) Order 2006 No. 2006/1553. - Enabling power: Road Traffic Regulation Act 1984, s. 14 (1) (a) (7). - Made: 30.05.2006. Coming into force: 06.06.2006. Effect: None. Territorial extent & classification: E. Local *Unpublished*

The M25 Motorway (Junction 2, Clockwise Carriageway) (Temporary Prohibition of Traffic) Order 2006 No. 2006/1606. - Enabling power: Road Traffic Regulation Act 1984, s. 14 (1) (a). - Made: 12.06.2006. Coming into force: 23.06.2006. Effect: None. Territorial extent & classification: E. Local *Unpublished*

The M25 Motorway (Junction 2, Clockwise Carriageway) (Temporary Prohibition of Traffic) Order 2006 No. 2006/80. - Enabling power: Road Traffic Regulation Act 1984, s. 14 (1) (a). - Made: 16.01.2006. Coming into force: 21.01.2006. Effect: None. Territorial extent & classification: E. Local *Unpublished*

The M25 Motorway (Junction 4, Slip Roads) (Temporary Prohibition of Traffic) Order 2006 No. 2006/2106. - Enabling power: Road Traffic Regulation Act 1984, s. 14 (1) (a). - Made: 24.07.2006. Coming into force: 29.07.2006. Effect: None. Territorial extent & classification: E. Local *Unpublished*

The M25 Motorway (Junction 4, Spur Road) (Temporary Restriction and Prohibition of Traffic) Order 2006 No. 2006/2876. - Enabling power: Road Traffic Regulation Act 1984, s. 14 (1) (a) (7). - Made: 23.10.2006. Coming into force: 28.10.2006. Effect: None. Territorial extent & classification: E. Local *Unpublished*

The M25 Motorway (Junction 5, Clockwise Carriageway) (Temporary Prohibition of Traffic) Order 2006 No. 2006/1102. - Enabling power: Road Traffic Regulation Act 1984, s. 14 (1) (a). - Made: 10.04.2006. Coming into force: 19.04.2006. Effect: None. Territorial extent & classification: E. Local *Unpublished*

The M25 Motorway (Junction 5, Slip Roads) (Temporary Prohibition of Traffic) Order 2006 No. 2006/807. - Enabling power: Road Traffic Regulation Act 1984, s. 14 (1) (a). - Made: 13.03.2006. Coming into force: 22.03.2006. Effect: None. Territorial extent & classification: E. Local *Unpublished*

The M25 Motorway (Junction 6) (Temporary Restriction and Prohibition of Traffic) Order 2006 No. 2006/1649. - Enabling power: Road Traffic Regulation Act 1984, s. 14 (1) (a) (7). - Made: 19.06.2006. Coming into force: 24.06.2006. Effect: None. Territorial extent & classification: E. Local *Unpublished*

The M25 Motorway (Junction 7, Merstham Interchange) (Temporary Restriction and Prohibition of Traffic) Order 2006 No. 2006/154. - Enabling power: Road Traffic Regulation Act 1984, s. 14 (1) (a) (7). - Made: 23.01.2006. Coming into force: 28.01.2006. Effect: None. Territorial extent & classification: E. Local *Unpublished*

The M25 Motorway (Junction 7, Southbound Link Roads) (Temporary Prohibition of Traffic) Order 2006 No. 2006/1605. - Enabling power: Road Traffic Regulation Act 1984, s. 14 (1) (a). - Made: 12.06.2006. Coming into force: 17.06.2006. Effect: None. Territorial extent & classification: E. Local *Unpublished*

The M25 Motorway (Junction 8, Clockwise Exit Slip Road) (Temporary Prohibition of Traffic) Order 2006 No. 2006/1216. - Enabling power: Road Traffic Regulation Act 1984, s. 14 (1) (a). - Made: 24.04.2006. Coming into force: 01.05.2006. Effect: None. Territorial extent & classification: E. Local. - Revoked by S.I. 2006/2588 (Unpublished) *Unpublished*

The M25 Motorway (Junction 8, Clockwise) (Temporary Restriction and Prohibition of Traffic) Order 2006 No. 2006/2155. - Enabling power: Road Traffic Regulation Act 1984, s. 14 (1) (a) (7). - Made: 31.06.2006. Coming into force: 05.08.2006. Effect: None. Territorial extent & classification: E. Local *Unpublished*

The M25 Motorway (Junction 8, Entry Slip Roads) (Temporary Prohibition of Traffic) Order 2006 No. 2006/806. - Enabling power: Road Traffic Regulation Act 1984, s. 14 (1) (a). - Made: 13.03.2006. Coming into force: 22.03.2006. Effect: None. Territorial extent & classification: E. Local. - Revoked by S.I. 2006/2588 (Unpublished) *Unpublished*

The M25 Motorway (Junction 9, Anti-clockwise Exit Slip Road) (Temporary Prohibition of Traffic) Order 2006 No. 2006/2773. - Enabling power: Road Traffic Regulation Act 1984, s. 14 (1) (a). - Made: 09.10.2006. Coming into force: 14.10.2006. Effect: None. Territorial extent & classification: E. Local *Unpublished*

The M25 Motorway (Junction 9, Carriageways) (Temporary 50 Miles Per Hour Speed Restriction) Order 2006 No. 2006/253. - Enabling power: Road Traffic Regulation Act 1984, s. 14 (1) (a). - Made: 30.01.2006. Coming into force: 02.02.2006. Effect: None. Territorial extent & classification: E. Local *Unpublished*

The M25 Motorway (Junction 9, Entry Slip Roads) (Temporary Prohibition of Traffic) Order 2006 No. 2006/251. - Enabling power: Road Traffic Regulation Act 1984, s. 14 (1) (a). - Made: 30.01.2006. Coming into force: 02.02.2006. Effect: None. Territorial extent & classification: E. Local *Unpublished*

The M25 Motorway (Junction 9, Entry Slip Roads) (Temporary Prohibition of Traffic) Order 2006 No. 2006/1373. - Enabling power: Road Traffic Regulation Act 1984, s. 14 (1) (a) (7). - Made: 15.05.2006. Coming into force: 24.05.2006. Effect: None. Territorial extent & classification: E. Local. - Revoked by S.I. 2006/2588 (Unpublished) *Unpublished*

The M25 Motorway (Junction 12, Anti-Clockwise Exit Link Road) (Temporary Prohibition of Traffic) Order 2006 No. 2006/3135. - Enabling power: Road Traffic Regulation Act 1984, s. 14 (1) (a). - Made: 20.11.2006. Coming into force: 25.11.2006. Effect: None. Territorial extent & classification: E. Local *Unpublished*

The M25 Motorway (Junction 13, Clockwise Carriageway) (Temporary Prohibition of Traffic) Order 2006 No. 2006/2328. - Enabling power: Road Traffic Regulation Act 1984, s. 14 (1) (a). - Made: 21.08.2006. Coming into force: 26.08.2006. Effect: None. Territorial extent & classification: E. Local *Unpublished*

The M25 Motorway (Junction 13, Slip Roads) (Temporary Prohibition of Traffic) Order 2006 No. 2006/1210. - Enabling power: Road Traffic Regulation Act 1984, s. 14 (1) (a). - Made: 24.04.2006. Coming into force: 01.05.2006. Effect: None. Territorial extent & classification: E. Local. - Revoked by S.I. 2006/2588 (Unpublished) *Unpublished*

The M25 Motorway (Junction 14 and Terminal 5 Spur Roads) (Temporary Prohibition of Traffic) Order 2006 No. 2006/1887. - Enabling power: Road Traffic Regulation Act 1984, s. 14 (1) (a). - Made: 10.07.2006. Coming into force: 17.07.2006. Effect: None. Territorial extent & classification: E. Local *Unpublished*

The M25 Motorway (Junction 14, Clockwise Slip Road) (Temporary Prohibition of Traffic) Order 2006 No. 2006/298. - Enabling power: Road Traffic Regulation Act 1984, s. 14 (1) (a). - Made: 06.02.2006. Coming into force: 11.02.2006. Effect: None. Territorial extent & classification: E. Local *Unpublished*

The M25 Motorway (Junction 16, Anti-clockwise) (Temporary Restriction and Prohibition of Traffic) Order 2006 No. 2006/2729. - Enabling power: Road Traffic Regulation Act 1984, s. 14 (1) (a) (7). - Made: 02.10.2006. Coming into force: 07.10.2006. Effect: None. Territorial extent & classification: E. Local *Unpublished*

The M25 Motorway (Junction 16, Link Roads) (Temporary Prohibition of Traffic) Order 2006 No. 2006/260. - Enabling power: Road Traffic Regulation Act 1984, s. 14 (1) (a) (7). - Made: 30.01.2006. Coming into force: 07.02.2006. Effect: None. Territorial extent & classification: E. Local *Unpublished*

The M25 Motorway (Junction 17, Slip Roads) (Temporary Prohibition of Traffic) Order 2006 No. 2006/1044. - Enabling power: Road Traffic Regulation Act 1984, s. 14 (1) (a). - Made: 03.04.2006. Coming into force: 13.04.2006. Effect: None. Territorial extent & classification: E. Local. - Revoked by S.I. 2006/2331 (Unpublished) *Unpublished*

The M25 Motorway (Junction 18, Northbound Slip Roads) (Temporary Prohibition of Traffic) Order 2006 No. 2006/896. - Enabling power: Road Traffic Regulation Act 1984, s. 14 (1) (a). - Made: 20.03.2006. Coming into force: 01.04.2006. Effect: None. Territorial extent & classification: E. Local. - Revoked by S.I. 2006/2331 (Unpublished) *Unpublished*

The M25 Motorway (Junction 19, Clockwise Exit Slip/Link Road) (Temporary Prohibition of Traffic) Order 2006 No. 2006/1311. - Enabling power: Road Traffic Regulation Act 1984, s. 14 (1) (a). - Made: 02.05.2006. Coming into force: 06.05.2006. Effect: None. Territorial extent & classification: E. Local *Unpublished*

The M25 Motorway (Junction 19, Spur Road) (Temporary 50 Miles Per Hour Speed Restriction) Order 2006 No. 2006/1647. - Enabling power: Road Traffic Regulation Act 1984, s. 14 (1) (a). - Made: 19.06.2006. Coming into force: 24.06.2006. Effect: None. Territorial extent & classification: E. Local *Unpublished*

The M25 Motorway (Junction 20, Clockwise) (Temporary Restriction and Prohibition of Traffic) Order 2006 No. 2006/3061. - Enabling power: Road Traffic Regulation Act 1984, s. 14 (1) (a) (7). - Made: 30.10.2006. Coming into force: 04.11.2006. Effect: None. Territorial extent & classification: E. Local *Unpublished*

The M25 Motorway (Junction 20, Slip Roads) (Temporary Prohibition of Traffic) Order 2006 No. 2006/2257. - Enabling power: Road Traffic Regulation Act 1984, s. 14 (1) (a). - Made: 14.08.2006. Coming into force: 19.08.2006. Effect: None. Territorial extent & classification: E. Local *Unpublished*

The M25 Motorway (Junction 21, Clockwise Entry Slip Road) (Temporary Prohibition of Traffic) Order 2006 No. 2006/1208. - Enabling power: Road Traffic Regulation Act 1984, s. 14 (1) (a). - Made: 24.04.2006. Coming into force: 04.05.2006. Effect: None. Territorial extent & classification: E. Local. - Revoked by S.I. 2006/2331 (Unpublished) *Unpublished*

The M25 Motorway (Junction 21, Clockwise Link Road) (Temporary Prohibition of Traffic) Order 2006 No. 2006/1218. - Enabling power: Road Traffic Regulation Act 1984, s. 14 (1) (a). - Made: 24.04.2006. Coming into force: 03.05.2006. Effect: None. Territorial extent & classification: E. Local. - Revoked by S.I. 2006/2331 (Unpublished) *Unpublished*

The M25 Motorway (Junction 22, Westbound Exit Slip Road) (Temporary Prohibition of Traffic) Order 2006 No. 2006/907. - Enabling power: Road Traffic Regulation Act 1984, s. 14 (1) (a). - Made: 20.03.2006. Coming into force: 01.04.2006. Effect: None. Territorial extent & classification: E. Local *Unpublished*

The M25 Motorway (Junction 24, Anti-clockwise Entry Slip Road) (Temporary Prohibition of Traffic) Order 2006 No. 2006/2845. - Enabling power: Road Traffic Regulation Act 1984, s. 14 (1) (a). - Made: 16.10.2006. Coming into force: 21.10.2006. Effect: None. Territorial extent & classification: E. Local *Unpublished*

The M25 Motorway (Junction 25, Entry Slip Roads) (Temporary Prohibition of Traffic) Order 2006 No. 2006/976. - Enabling power: Road Traffic Regulation Act 1984, s. 14 (1) (a), sch. 9, para. 27 (1). - Made: 27.03.2006. Coming into force: 01.04.2006. Effect: None. Territorial extent & classification: E. Local. - Revoked by S.I. 2006/2331 (Unpublished) *Unpublished*

The M25 Motorway (Junction 26, Slip Roads) (Temporary Prohibition of Traffic) Order 2006 No. 2006/977. - Enabling power: Road Traffic Regulation Act 1984, s. 14 (1) (a). - Made: 27.03.2006. Coming into force: 01.04.2006. Effect: None. Territorial extent & classification: E. Local. - Revoked by S.I. 2006/2878 (Unpublished) *Unpublished*

The M25 Motorway (Junction 28, Anti-Clockwise Exit Slip Road) (Temporary Prohibition of Traffic) Order 2006 No. 2006/702. - Enabling power: Road Traffic Regulation Act 1984, s. 14 (1) (a). - Made: 06.03.2006. Coming into force: 11.03.2006. Effect: None. Territorial extent & classification: E. Local *Unpublished*

The M25 Motorway (Junction 28, Clockwise Entry Slip Road) (Temporary Prohibition of Traffic) Order 2006 No. 2006/1101. - Enabling power: Road Traffic Regulation Act 1984, s. 14 (1) (a). - Made: 10.04.2006. Coming into force: 19.04.2006. Effect: None. Territorial extent & classification: E. Local. - Revoked by S.I. 2006/2878 (Unpublished) *Unpublished*

The M25 Motorway (Junctions 6 - 7, Clockwise Carriageway) (Temporary Restriction of Traffic) Order 2006 No. 2006/153. - Enabling power: Road Traffic Regulation Act 1984, s. 14 (1) (a) (7). - Made: 23.01.2006. Coming into force: 28.01.2006. Effect: None. Territorial extent & classification: E. Local *Unpublished*

The M25 Motorway (Junctions 6 - 7, Clockwise) (Temporary Restriction and Prohibition of Traffic) Order 2006 No. 2006/2877. - Enabling power: Road Traffic Regulation Act 1984, s. 14 (1) (a) (7). - Made: 23.10.2006. Coming into force: 28.10.2006. Effect: None. Territorial extent & classification: E. Local *Unpublished*

The M25 Motorway (Junctions 8 - 10, Clockwise) (Temporary Prohibition of Traffic) Order 2006 No. 2006/2463. - Enabling power: Road Traffic Regulation Act 1984, s. 14 (1) (a). - Made: 04.09.2006. Coming into force: 09.09.2006. Effect: None. Territorial extent & classification: E. Local *Unpublished*

The M25 Motorway (Junctions 8 - 10) (Temporary Restriction and Prohibition of Traffic) Order 2006 No. 2006/1573. - Enabling power: Road Traffic Regulation Act 1984, s. 14 (1) (a). - Made: 05.06.2006. Coming into force: 10.06.2006. Effect: None. Territorial extent & classification: E. Local *Unpublished*

The M25 Motorway (Junctions 10 - 11, Clockwise Carriageway) (Temporary 50 Miles Per Hour Speed Restriction) Order 2006 No. 2006/535. - Enabling power: Road Traffic Regulation Act 1984, s. 14 (1) (a) (7). - Made: 27.02.2006. Coming into force: 04.03.2006. Effect: None. Territorial extent & classification: E. Local *Unpublished*

The M25 Motorway (Junctions 10 - 14) (Temporary Prohibition of Traffic) Order 2006 No. 2006/152. - Enabling power: Road Traffic Regulation Act 1984, s. 14 (1) (a). - Made: 23.01.2006. Coming into force: 28.01.2006. Effect: None. Territorial extent & classification: E. Local *Unpublished*

The M25 Motorway (Junctions 14 - 15) (Temporary Restriction and Prohibition of Traffic) Order 2006 No. 2006/1732. - Enabling power: Road Traffic Regulation Act 1984, s. 14 (1) (a) (7). - Made: 26.06.2006. Coming into force: 01.07.2006. Effect: None. Territorial extent & classification: E. Local *Unpublished*

The M25 Motorway (Junctions 15 - 16, Clockwise) (Temporary Restriction of Traffic) Order 2006 No. 2006/3161. - Enabling power: Road Traffic Regulation Act 1984, s. 14 (1) (a) (7). - Made: 20.11.2006. Coming into force: 25.11.2006. Effect: None. Territorial extent & classification: E. Local *Unpublished*

The M25 Motorway (Junctions 16 - 15, Anti-Clockwise Carriageway) (Temporary 50 Miles Per Hour Speed Restriction) Order 2006 No. 2006/704. - Enabling power: Road Traffic Regulation Act 1984, s. 14 (1) (a). - Made: 06.03.2006. Coming into force: 11.03.2006. Effect: None. Territorial extent & classification: E. Local *Unpublished*

The M25 Motorway (Junctions 17 - 18) (Temporary Restriction and Prohibition of Traffic) Order 2006 No. 2006/1131. - Enabling power: Road Traffic Regulation Act 1984, s. 14 (1) (a) (7). - Made: 18.04.2006. Coming into force: 22.04.2006. Effect: None. Territorial extent & classification: E. Local *Unpublished*

The M25 Motorway (Junctions 17 - 25) (Temporary Prohibition of Traffic) Order 2006 No. 2006/2331. - Enabling power: Road Traffic Regulation Act 1984, s. 14 (1) (a), sch. 9, para. 27 (1). - Made: 21.08.2006. Coming into force: 01.09.2006. Effect: S.I. 2005/3010, 3018, 3019; 2006/896, 907, 976, 1044, 1208, 1218 revoked. Territorial extent & classification: E. Local *Unpublished*

The M25 Motorway (Junctions 25-26) (Temporary Restriction of Traffic) Order 2006 No. 2006/974. - Enabling power: Road Traffic Regulation Act 1984, s. 14 (1) (a) (7). - Made: 27.03.2006. Coming into force: 01.04.2006. Effect: None. Territorial extent & classification: E. Local *Unpublished*

The M25 Motorway (Junctions 28 - 27, Anti-Clockwise Carriageway) (Temporary Restriction of Traffic) (No. 2) Order 2006 No. 2006/2464. - Enabling power: Road Traffic Regulation Act 1984, s. 14 (1) (a) (7). - Made: 04.09.2006. Coming into force: 09.09.2006. Effect: None. Territorial extent & classification: E. Local *Unpublished*

The M25 Motorway (Junctions 28 - 27, Anti-Clockwise Carriageway) (Temporary Restriction of Traffic) Order 2006 No. 2006/2335. - Enabling power: Road Traffic Regulation Act 1984, s. 14 (1) (a) (7). - Made: 21.08.2006. Coming into force: 26.08.2006. Effect: None. Territorial extent & classification: E. Local *Unpublished*

The M25 Motorway (Junctions 29 - 30) (Temporary Restriction of Traffic) Order 2006 No. 2006/1213. - Enabling power: Road Traffic Regulation Act 1984, s. 14 (1) (a) (7). - Made: 24.04.2006. Coming into force: 29.04.2006. Effect: None. Territorial extent & classification: E. Local *Unpublished*

The M25 Motorway (Marker Posts 80.6 - 97.0) (Temporary Restriction and Prohibition of Traffic) Order 2003 and the M25 Motorway (Marker Posts 80.6 - 97.0) (Temporary Restriction and Prohibition of Traffic) Order 2003 Variation Order 2005 Revocation Order 2006 No. 2006/2336. - Enabling power: Road Traffic Regulation Act 1984, ss. 14 (1) (a) (7), 15 (2), sch. 9, para. 27 (1). - Made: 21.08.2006. Coming into force: 01.09.2006. Effect: S.I. 2003/3219; 2005/2138 revoked. Territorial extent & classification: E. Local *Unpublished*

The M25 Motorway (Marker Posts 143.7 - 151.8) (Temporary Restriction and Prohibition of Traffic) (No. 2) Order 2006 No. 2006/1312. - Enabling power: Road Traffic Regulation Act 1984, ss. 14 (1) (a) (7), 15 (2). - Made: 02.05.2006. Coming into force: 06.05.2006. Effect: S.I. 2006/82 revoked. Territorial extent & classification: E. Local *Unpublished*

The M25 Motorway (Marker posts 143.7 - 151.8) (Temporary Restriction and Prohibition of Traffic) Order 2006 No. 2006/82. - Enabling power: Road Traffic Regulation Act 1984, ss. 14 (1) (a) (7), 15 (2). - Made: 16.01.2006. Coming into force: 01.02.2006. Effect: None. Territorial extent & classification: E. Local. - Revoked by S.I. 2006/1312 *Unpublished*

The M25 Motorway (Merstham Interchange) (Temporary 50 Miles Per Hour Speed Restriction) Order 2006 No. 2006/3356. - Enabling power: Road Traffic Regulation Act 1984, s. 14 (1) (a). - Made: 11.12.2006. Coming into force: 23.12.2006. Effect: None. Territorial extent & classification: E. Local *Unpublished*

The M25 Motorway, the M23 Motorway and the M3 Motorway (M25 Junctions 7 - 13, Slip/Link Roads) (Temporary Restriction and Prohibition of Traffic) Order 2006 No. 2006/2588. - Enabling power: Road Traffic Regulation Act 1984, s. 14 (1) (a) (7), sch. 9, para. 27 (1). - Made: 11.09.2006. Coming into force: 22.09.2006. Effect: S.I. 2005/3015; 2006/806, 1210, 1216, 1373, 1375, 1769 revoked. Territorial extent & classification: E. Local *Unpublished*

The M25 Motorway (West of Junction 6 - Junction 7) (Temporary Restriction of Traffic) Order 2006 No. 2006/2333. - Enabling power: Road Traffic Regulation Act 1984, s. 14 (1) (a) (7). - Made: 21.08.2006. Coming into force: 26.08.2006. Effect: None. Territorial extent & classification: E. Local *Unpublished*

The M26 Motorway (M25 Junction 5 - Junction 2A) (Temporary Prohibition of Traffic) Order 2006 No. 2006/410. - Enabling power: Road Traffic Regulation Act 1984, s. 14 (1) (a). - Made: 20.02.2006. Coming into force: 25.02.2006. Effect: None. Territorial extent & classification: E. Local *Unpublished*

The M27 Motorway (Junction 3, Westbound Exit Slip Road) (Temporary Prohibition of Traffic) Order 2006 No. 2006/3066. - Enabling power: Road Traffic Regulation Act 1984, s. 14 (1) (a). - Made: 30.10.2006. Coming into force: 04.11.2006. Effect: None. Territorial extent & classification: E. Local *Unpublished*

The M27 Motorway (Junction 4, Bassett Wood Bridge) (Temporary 50 Miles Per Hour Speed Restriction) Order 2006 No. 2006/2728. - Enabling power: Road Traffic Regulation Act 1984, s. 14 (1) (a). - Made: 02.10.2006. Coming into force: 07.10.2006. Effect: None. Territorial extent & classification: E. Local *Unpublished*

The M27 Motorway (Junction 4, Westbound Carriageway) (Temporary Prohibition of Traffic) Order 2006 No. 2006/1574. - Enabling power: Road Traffic Regulation Act 1984, s. 14 (1) (a). - Made: 05.06.2006. Coming into force: 10.06.2006. Effect: None. Territorial extent & classification: E. Local *Unpublished*

The M27 Motorway (Junction 11, Westbound Entry Slip Road) (Temporary Prohibition of Traffic) Order 2006 No. 2006/1128. - Enabling power: Road Traffic Regulation Act 1984, s. 14 (1) (a). - Made: 18.04.2006. Coming into force: 22.04.2006. Effect: None. Territorial extent & classification: E. Local *Unpublished*

The M27 Motorway (Junction 12) (Temporary Prohibition of Traffic) Order 2006 No. 2006/413. - Enabling power: Road Traffic Regulation Act 1984, s. 14 (1) (a). - Made: 20.02.2006. Coming into force: 25.02.2006. Effect: None. Territorial extent & classification: E. Local *Unpublished*

The M27 Motorway (Junctions 3 and 5, Slip Roads) (Temporary Prohibition of Traffic) Order 2006 No. 2006/3441. - Enabling power: Road Traffic Regulation Act 1984, s. 14 (1) (a). - Made: 18.12.2006. Coming into force: 30.12.2006. Effect: None. Territorial extent & classification: E. Local *Unpublished*

The M32 Motorway (Junction 1 Northbound Entry Slip Road) (Temporary Prohibition of Traffic) Order 2006 No. 2006/2344. - Enabling power: Road Traffic Regulation Act 1984, s. 14 (1) (a). - Made: 22.08.2006. Coming into force: 25.08.2006. Effect: None. Territorial extent & classification: E. Local *Unpublished*

The M40 Motorway (Junction 1A, Link Roads) (Temporary Prohibition of Traffic) Order 2006 No. 2006/26. - Enabling power: Road Traffic Regulation Act 1984, s. 14 (1) (a). - Made: 03.01.2006. Coming into force: 07.01.2006. Effect: None. Territorial extent & classification: E. Local *Unpublished*

The M40 Motorway (Junction 1A, Westbound Link Road) (Temporary Prohibition of Traffic) Order 2006 No. 2006/1731. - Enabling power: Road Traffic Regulation Act 1984, s. 14 (1) (a). - Made: 26.06.2006. Coming into force: 01.07.2006. Effect: None. Territorial extent & classification: E. Local *Unpublished*

The M40 Motorway (Junction 4 Handy Cross, High Wycombe, Buckinghamshire) (Temporary Prohibition of Traffic) Order 2006 No. 2006/2050. - Enabling power: Road Traffic Regulation Act 1984, ss. 14 (1) (a). - Made: 10.07.2006. Coming into force: 17.07.2006. Effect: None. Territorial extent & classification: E. Local *Unpublished*

The M40 Motorway (Junction 9, Oxfordshire) (Temporary Prohibition of Traffic) Order 2006 No. 2006/1106. - Enabling power: Road Traffic Regulation Act 1984, s. 14 (1) (a). - Made: 07.04.2006. Coming into force: 14.04.2006. Effect: None. Territorial extent & classification: E. Local *Unpublished*

The M40 Motorway (Junction 10, Ardley Roundabout, Oxfordshire) (Temporary Prohibition of Traffic) Order 2006 No. 2006/3307. - Enabling power: Road Traffic Regulation Act 1984, s. 14 (1) (a). - Made: 04.12.2006. Coming into force: 11.12.2006. Effect: None. Territorial extent & classification: E. Local *Unpublished*

Road traffic: Traffic regulation

The M40 Motorway (Junction 10 - Junction 11) (Temporary Restriction and Prohibition of Traffic) Order 2006 No. 2006/3091. - Enabling power: Road Traffic Regulation Act 1984, s. 14 (1) (a) (7). - Made: 06.11.2006. Coming into force: 13.11.2006. Effect: None. Territorial extent & classification: E. Local *Unpublished*

The M40 Motorway (Junction 15) (Slip Roads) (Temporary Prohibition of Traffic) Order 2006 No. 2006/24. - Enabling power: Road Traffic Regulation Act 1984, s. 14 (1) (a). - Made: 04.01.2006. Coming into force: 11.01.2006. Effect: None. Territorial extent & classification: E. Local *Unpublished*

The M40 Motorway (Junction 15) (Temporary Prohibition of Traffic) Order 2006 No. 2006/1591. - Enabling power: Road Traffic Regulation Act 1984, s. 14 (1) (a) (7). - Made: 05.06.2006. Coming into force: 12.06.2006. Effect: None. Territorial extent & classification: E. Local *Unpublished*

The M40 Motorway (Junctions 1 - 15, Buckinghamshire, Oxfordshire and Warwickshire) (Temporary Restriction of Traffic) Order 2006 No. 2006/1615. - Enabling power: Road Traffic Regulation Act 1984, s. 14 (1) (a). - Made: 05.06.2006. Coming into force: 12.06.2006. Effect: None. Territorial extent & classification: E. Local *Unpublished*

The M40 Motorway (Junctions 1A - 13, Warwickshire, Northamptonshire, Oxfordshire and Buckinghamshire) (Temporary 50 Miles Per Hour Speed Restriction) Order 2006 No. 2006/3487. - Enabling power: Road Traffic Regulation Act 1984, s. 14 (1) (a). - Made: 20.12.2006. Coming into force: 03.01.2007. Effect: None. Territorial extent & classification: E. Local *Unpublished*

The M40 Motorway (Junctions 9 - 10) (Temporary Restriction and Prohibition of Traffic) Order 2006 No. 2006/165. - Enabling power: Road Traffic Regulation Act 1984, s. 14 (1). - Made: 23.01.2006. Coming into force: 30.01.2006. Effect: None. Territorial extent & classification: E. Local *Unpublished*

The M40 Motorway (North of Junction 15) (Temporary Restriction and Prohibition of Traffic) Order 2006 No. 2006/423. - Enabling power: Road Traffic Regulation Act 1984, s. 14 (1) (a) (7). - Made: 13.02.2006. Coming into force: 20.02.2006. Effect: None. Territorial extent & classification: E. Local *Unpublished*

The M40 Motorway (Southbound Carriageway, Junction 15 - Junction 14, Warwickshire) (Temporary Restriction of Traffic) Order 2006 No. 2006/1677. - Enabling power: Road Traffic Regulation Act 1984, s. 14 (1) (a) (7). - Made: 30.05.2006. Coming into force: 06.06.2006. Effect: None. Territorial extent & classification: E. Local *Unpublished*

The M40 Motorway (Treadway Hill Overbridge, Buckinghamshire) (Temporary Restriction and Prohibition of Traffic) Order 2006 No. 2006/3137. - Enabling power: Road Traffic Regulation Act 1984, s. 14 (1) (a) (7). - Made: 13.11.2006. Coming into force: 20.11.2006. Effect: None. Territorial extent & classification: E. Local *Unpublished*

The M42 Motorway and the A5 Trunk Road (M42 Junction 10 to Dordon, Warwickshire) (Temporary Prohibition and Restriction of Traffic) Order 2006 No. 2006/2870. - Enabling power: Road Traffic Regulation Act 1984, s. 14 (1) (a). - Made: 16.10.2006. Coming into force: 23.10.2006. Effect: None. Territorial extent & classification: E. Local *Unpublished*

The M42 Motorway (East of Junction 1 - M5 Junction 4A) (Temporary Restriction and Prohibition of Traffic) Order 2006 No. 2006/730. - Enabling power: Road Traffic Regulation Act 1984, s. 14 (1) (a) (7). - Made: 03.03.2006. Coming into force: 10.03.2006. Effect: None. Territorial extent & classification: E. Local *Unpublished*

The M42 Motorway (Junction 1 - M5 Junction 4A) (Temporary Prohibition of Traffic) Order 2006 No. 2006/1563. - Enabling power: Road Traffic Regulation Act 1984, s. 14 (1) (a) (7). - Made: 23.05.2006. Coming into force: 30.05.2006. Effect: None. Territorial extent & classification: E. Local *Unpublished*

The M42 Motorway (Junction 1 - M5 Junction 4A) (Temporary Prohibition of Traffic) Order 2006 No. 2006/3456. - Enabling power: Road Traffic Regulation Act 1984, s. 14 (1) (a). - Made: 20.12.2006. Coming into force: 27.12.2006. Effect: None. Territorial extent & classification: E. Local *Unpublished*

The M42 Motorway (Junction 2) (Southbound Entry Slip Road) (Temporary Prohibition of Traffic) Order 2006 No. 2006/2574. - Enabling power: Road Traffic Regulation Act 1984, s. 14 (1) (a). - Made: 19.09.2006. Coming into force: 26.09.2006. Effect: None. Territorial extent & classification: E. Local *Unpublished*

The M42 Motorway (Junction 2) (Temporary Prohibition of Traffic) Order 2006 No. 2006/1720. - Enabling power: Road Traffic Regulation Act 1984, s. 14 (1) (a) (7). - Made: 06.06.2006. Coming into force: 13.06.2006. Effect: None. Territorial extent & classification: E. Local *Unpublished*

The M42 Motorway (Junction 3) (Slip Road) (Temporary Prohibition and Restriction of Traffic) Order 2006 No. 2006/3142. - Enabling power: Road Traffic Regulation Act 1984, s. 14 (1) (a). - Made: 17.11.2006. Coming into force: 24.11.2006. Effect: None. Territorial extent & classification: E. Local *Unpublished*

The M42 Motorway (Junction 3) (Slip Road) (Temporary Prohibition of Traffic) Order 2006 No. 2006/442. - Enabling power: Road Traffic Regulation Act 1984, s. 14 (1) (a). - Made: 10.02.2006. Coming into force: 17.02.2006. Effect: None. Territorial extent & classification: E. Local *Unpublished*

The M42 Motorway (Junction 3) (Temporary Restriction and Prohibition of Traffic) Order 2006 No. 2006/2218. - Enabling power: Road Traffic Regulation Act 1984, s. 14 (1) (a) (7). - Made: 28.07.2006. Coming into force: 04.08.2006. Effect: None. Territorial extent & classification: E. Local *Unpublished*

Road traffic: Traffic regulation

The M42 Motorway (Junction 6) and the A45 Trunk Road (Slip Roads) (Warwickshire) (Temporary Prohibition and Restriction of Traffic) Order 2006 No. 2006/2150. - Enabling power: Road Traffic Regulation Act 1984, s. 14 (1) (a). - Made: 21.07.2006. Coming into force: 28.07.2006. Effect: None. Territorial extent & classification: E. Local *Unpublished*

The M42 Motorway (Junction 6 - Junction 7A) (Temporary Prohibition of Traffic) Order 2006 No. 2006/2148. - Enabling power: Road Traffic Regulation Act 1984, s. 14 (1) (a). - Made: 24.07.2006. Coming into force: 31.07.2006. Effect: None. Territorial extent & classification: E. Local *Unpublished*

The M42 Motorway (Junction 7) (Link Road) (Temporary Prohibition of Traffic) Order 2006 No. 2006/1191. - Enabling power: Road Traffic Regulation Act 1984, s. 14 (1) (a). - Made: 18.04.2006. Coming into force: 25.04.2006. Effect: None. Territorial extent & classification: E. Local *Unpublished*

The M42 Motorway (Junction 8) (Link Road) (Temporary Prohibition of Traffic) Order 2006 No. 2006/3353. - Enabling power: Road Traffic Regulation Act 1984, s. 14 (1) (a). - Made: 08.12.2006. Coming into force: 15.12.2006. Effect: None. Territorial extent & classification: E. Local *Unpublished*

The M42 Motorway (Junction 9) (Northbound Entry Slip Road) (Temporary Prohibition of Traffic) Order 2006 No. 2006/1194. - Enabling power: Road Traffic Regulation Act 1984, s. 14 (1) (a). - Made: 18.04.2006. Coming into force: 25.04.2006. Effect: None. Territorial extent & classification: E. Local *Unpublished*

The M42 Motorway (Junction 9) (Temporary Prohibition of Traffic) Order 2006 No. 2006/1865. - Enabling power: Road Traffic Regulation Act 1984, s. 14 (1) (a). - Made: 03.07.2006. Coming into force: 10.07.2006. Effect: None. Territorial extent & classification: E. Local *Unpublished*

The M42 Motorway (Junction 10) and the A5 Trunk Road (Temporary Restriction and Prohibition of Traffic) Order 2006 No. 2006/3025. - Enabling power: Road Traffic Regulation Act 1984, s. 14 (1) (a). - Made: 10.11.2006. Coming into force: 17.11.2006. Effect: None. Territorial extent & classification: E. Local *Unpublished*

The M42 Motorway (Junction 11) (Temporary Prohibition of Traffic) Order 2006 No. 2006/995. - Enabling power: Road Traffic Regulation Act 1984, s. 14 (1) (a). - Made: 20.03.2006. Coming into force: 27.03.2006. Effect: None. Territorial extent & classification: E. Local *Unpublished*

The M42 Motorway (Junctions 3 - 3A) (Temporary Prohibition of Traffic) Order 2006 No. 2006/1590. - Enabling power: Road Traffic Regulation Act 1984, s. 14 (1) (a) (7). - Made: 02.06.2006. Coming into force: 09.06.2006. Effect: None. Territorial extent & classification: E. Local *Unpublished*

The M42 Motorway (Junctions 3A - 3) (Temporary Prohibition of Traffic) Order 2006 No. 2006/1562. - Enabling power: Road Traffic Regulation Act 1984, s. 14 (1) (a) (7). - Made: 24.05.2006. Coming into force: 31.05.2006. Effect: None. Territorial extent & classification: E. Local *Unpublished*

The M42 Motorway (Junctions 7 - 7A) (Temporary Restriction and Prohibition of Traffic) Order 2006 No. 2006/1780. - Enabling power: Road Traffic Regulation Act 1984, s. 14 (1) (a) (7). - Made: 16.06.2006. Coming into force: 23.06.2006. Effect: None. Territorial extent & classification: E. Local *Unpublished*

The M42 Motorway (Junctions 8 and 9) (Temporary Prohibition of Traffic) Order 2006 No. 2006/727. - Enabling power: Road Traffic Regulation Act 1984, s. 14 (1) (a). - Made: 03.03.2006. Coming into force: 10.03.2006. Effect: None. Territorial extent & classification: E. Local *Unpublished*

The M42 Motorway (Junctions 9 - 6), the M6 Motorway (Junction 4A) and the M6 Toll Motorway (Temporary Prohibition of Traffic) Order 2006 No. 2006/2024. - Enabling power: Road Traffic Regulation Act 1984, s. 14 (1) (a). - Made: 17.07.2006. Coming into force: 24.07.2006. Effect: None. Territorial extent & classification: E. Local *Unpublished*

The M42 Motorway (Junctions 10 - 9, Warwickshire) (Temporary Restriction of Traffic) Order 2006 No. 2006/1783. - Enabling power: Road Traffic Regulation Act 1984, s. 14 (1) (a). - Made: 19.06.2006. Coming into force: 26.06.2006. Effect: None. Territorial extent & classification: E. Local *Unpublished*

The M42 Motorway (Junctions 10 - 11, Warwickshire) (Restriction on Use of Right Hand or Off Side Lane) (Experimental) Order 2006 No. 2006/1037. - Enabling power: Road Traffic Regulation Act 1984, ss. 9(1) to (3), 10 (1) (2). - Made: 27.03.2006. Coming into force: 09.04.2006. Effect: None. Territorial extent & classification: E. Local *Unpublished*

The M42 Motorway (Linthurst, East of Junction 1) (Temporary Restriction and Prohibition of Traffic) Order 2006 No. 2006/3023. - Enabling power: Road Traffic Regulation Act 1984, s. 14 (1) (a) (7). - Made: 10.11.2006. Coming into force: 17.11.2006. Effect: None. Territorial extent & classification: E. Local *Unpublished*

The M42 Motorway (South of Junction 11) and A42 Trunk Road (Leicestershire) (Temporary Restriction and Prohibition of Traffic) Order 2006 No. 2006/282. - Enabling power: Road Traffic Regulation Act 1984, s. 14 (1) (a) (7). - Made: 27.01.2006. Coming into force: 03.02.2006. Effect: None. Territorial extent & classification: E. Local *Unpublished*

The M45 Motorway (Dunchurch Roundabout, Warwickshire and Northamptonshire) (Temporary 50 Miles Per Hour Speed Restriction) Order 2006 No. 2006/3035. - Enabling power: Road Traffic Regulation Act 1984, s. 14 (1) (a). - Made: 30.10.2006. Coming into force: 06.11.2006. Effect: None. Territorial extent & classification: E. Local *Unpublished*

The M45 Motorway (Dunchurch, Warwickshire and Northamptonshire) (Temporary 50 Miles Per Hour Speed Limit) Order 2006 No. 2006/2609. - Enabling power: Road Traffic Regulation Act 1984, s. 14 (1) (a). - Made: 18.09.2006. Coming into force: 25.09.2006. Effect: None. Territorial extent & classification: E. Local *Unpublished*

The M48 Motorway (Junction 1, Aust) (Temporary Prohibition of Traffic) Order 2006 No. 2006/546. - Enabling power: Road Traffic Regulation Act 1984, s. 14 (1) (a). - Made: 28.02.2006. Coming into force: 04.03.2006. Effect: None. Territorial extent & classification: E. Local *Unpublished*

The M48 Motorway (Junctions 1 - 2, Servern Bridge) (Temporary Restriction of Traffic) Order 2006 No. 2006/2998. - Enabling power: Road Traffic Regulation Act 1984, s. 14 (1) (b). - Made: 31.10.2006. Coming into force: 03.11.2006. Effect: None. Territorial extent & classification: E. Local *Unpublished*

The M48 Motorway (Junctions 1 - 2) (Severn Bridge) (Temporary Prohibition and Restriction of Traffic) Order 2006 No. 2006/77. - Enabling power: Road Traffic Regulation Act 1984, s. 14 (1) (b), sch. 9, para. 27 (1). - Made: 10.01.2006. Coming into force: 14.01.2006. Effect: S.I. 2005/1503 revoked. Territorial extent & classification: E. Local *Unpublished*

The M48 Motorway (Junctions 1 - 2, Severn Bridge) (Temporary Prohibition and Restriction of Traffic) Order 2006 No. 2006/2031. - Enabling power: Road Traffic Regulation Act 1984, ss. 14 (1) (a). - Made: 11.07.2006. Coming into force: 14.07.2006. Effect: None. Territorial extent & classification: E. Local *Unpublished*

The M48 Motorway (Junctions 1 - 2, Severn Bridge) (Temporary Prohibition of Traffic) Order 2006 No. 2006/2592. - Enabling power: Road Traffic Regulation Act 1984, s. 14 (1) (a). - Made: 12.09.2006. Coming into force: 15.09.2006. Effect: None. Territorial extent & classification: E. Local *Unpublished*

The M48 Motorway (Junctions 2 - 1, Severn Bridge) (Temporary Prohibition of Traffic) Order 2006 No. 2006/1473. - Enabling power: Road Traffic Regulation Act 1984, s. 14 (1) (a). - Made: 25.05.2006. Coming into force: 31.05.2006. Effect: None. Territorial extent & classification: E. Local *Unpublished*

The M48 Motorway (M4 Junction 21 to M48 Junction 2) (Temporary Prohibition of Traffic) Order 2006 No. 2006/1779. - Enabling power: Road Traffic Regulation Act 1984, s. 14 (1) (a). - Made: 20.06.2006. Coming into force: 22.06.2006. Effect: None. Territorial extent & classification: E. Local *Unpublished*

The M48 Motorway (Near Aust, Gloucestershire) (Temporary Prohibition of Traffic) Order 2006 No. 2006/2420. - Enabling power: Road Traffic Regulation Act 1984, s. 14 (1) (a). - Made: 29.08.2006. Coming into force: 01.09.2006. Effect: None. Territorial extent & classification: E. Local *Unpublished*

The M49 Motorway and M5 Motorway (Junction 18A) and M4 Motorway (Junction 22) (Temporary Prohibition of Traffic) Order 2006 No. 2006/2346. - Enabling power: Road Traffic Regulation Act 1984, s. 14 (1) (a). - Made: 22.08.2006. Coming into force: 25.08.2006. Effect: None. Territorial extent & classification: E. Local *Unpublished*

The M49 Motorway and M5 Motorway (Junction 18A) (Temporary Prohibition of Traffic) Order 2006 No. 2006/1146. - Enabling power: Road Traffic Regulation Act 1984, s. 14 (1) (a). - Made: 18.04.2006. Coming into force: 21.04.2006. Effect: None. Territorial extent & classification: E. Local *Unpublished*

The M50 and M5 Motorways (M50 Junction 2 to M5 Junction 8) (Temporary Restriction and Prohibition of Traffic) Order 2006 No. 2006/1729. - Enabling power: Road Traffic Regulation Act 1984, s. 14 (1) (a). - Made: 26.06.2006. Coming into force: 03.07.2006. Effect: None. Territorial extent & classification: E. Local *Unpublished*

The M50 Motorway and A449 Trunk Road (Ross-on-Wye, Herefordshire) (Temporary Restriction and Prohibition of Traffic) Order 2006 No. 2006/1112. - Enabling power: Road Traffic Regulation Act 1984, s. 14 (1) (a). - Made: 30.03.2006. Coming into force: 06.04.2006. Effect: None. Territorial extent & classification: E. Local *Unpublished*

The M50 Motorway (Junction 1, Worcestsershire) (Temporary Prohibition of Traffic) Order 2006 No. 2006/2019. - Enabling power: Road Traffic Regulation Act 1984, s. 14 (1) (a) (7). - Made: 17.07.2006. Coming into force: 24.07.2006. Effect: None. Territorial extent & classification: E. Local *Unpublished*

The M50 Motorway (Junctions 2 to 1) (Temporary Prohibition of Traffic) Order 2006 No. 2006/3051. - Enabling power: Road Traffic Regulation Act 1984, s. 14 (1) (a). - Made: 23.10.2006. Coming into force: 30.10.2006. Effect: None. Territorial extent & classification: E. Local *Unpublished*

The M50 Motorway (Junctions 2 to 4) (Temporary Prohibition of Traffic) Order 2006 No. 2006/2045. - Enabling power: Road Traffic Regulation Act 1984, ss. 14 (1) (a). - Made: 10.07.2006. Coming into force: 17.07.2006. Effect: None. Territorial extent & classification: E. Local *Unpublished*

The M50 Motorway (Junctions 3 - 4, Herefordshire) (Temporary 40 Miles Per Hour Speed Restriction) Order 2006 No. 2006/12. - Enabling power: Road Traffic Regulation Act 1984, s. 14 (1) (a). - Made: 03.01.2006. Coming into force: 10.01.2006. Effect: None. Territorial extent & classification: E. Local *Unpublished*

The M53 Motorway (Junction 2, Northbound Entry Slip Road) (Temporary Prohibition of Traffic) Order 2006 No. 2006/2648. - Enabling power: Road Traffic Regulation Act 1984, s. 14 (1) (a). - Made: 22.09.2006. Coming into force: 22.10.2006. Effect: None. Territorial extent & classification: E. Local *Unpublished*

Road traffic: Traffic regulation

The M53 Motorway (Junction 2, Southbound Entry Slip Road) (Temporary Prohibition of Traffic) Order 2006 No. 2006/1595. - Enabling power: Road Traffic Regulation Act 1984, s. 14 (1) (a). - Made: 26.05.2006. Coming into force: 21.06.2006. Effect: None. Territorial extent & classification: E. Local *Unpublished*

The M53 Motorway (Junction 2, Southbound Exit Slip Road) (Temporary Prohibition of Traffic) Order 2006 No. 2006/2445. - Enabling power: Road Traffic Regulation Act 1984, s. 14 (1) (a). - Made: 25.08.2006. Coming into force: 24.09.2006. Effect: None. Territorial extent & classification: E. Local *Unpublished*

The M53 Motorway (Junction 3, Southbound Carriageway and Entry Slip Road) (Temporary Prohibition and Restriction of Traffic) Order 2006 No. 2006/3461. - Enabling power: Road Traffic Regulation Act 1984, s. 14 (1) (a) (7). - Made: 08.12.2006. Coming into force: 07.01.2007. Effect: None. Territorial extent & classification: E. Local *Unpublished*

The M53 Motorway (Junction 3, Southbound Entry Slip Road) (Temporary Prohibition of Traffic) Order 2006 No. 2006/1596. - Enabling power: Road Traffic Regulation Act 1984, s. 14 (1) (a). - Made: 26.05.2006. Coming into force: 20.06.2006. Effect: None. Territorial extent & classification: E. Local *Unpublished*

The M53 Motorway (Junction 6, Closure of Northbound Exit and Entry Slip Roads) (Temporary Prohibition of Traffic) Order 2006 No. 2006/1104. - Enabling power: Road Traffic Regulation Act 1984, s. 14 (1) (a). - Made: 07.04.2006. Coming into force: 04.05.2006. Effect: None. Territorial extent & classification: E. Local *Unpublished*

The M53 Motorway (Junction 8, Northbound Exit Slip Road) (Temporary Prohibition of Traffic) Order 2006 No. 2006/2438. - Enabling power: Road Traffic Regulation Act 1984, s. 14 (1) (a). - Made: 21.08.2006. Coming into force: 17.09.2006. Effect: None. Territorial extent & classification: E. Local *Unpublished*

The M53 Motorway (Junction 11, Northbound Link Road to the M56 Eastbound) (Temporary Prohibition of Traffic) Order 2006 No. 2006/1356. - Enabling power: Road Traffic Regulation Act 1984, s. 14 (1) (a). - Made: 08.05.2006. Coming into force: 01.06.2006. Effect: None. Territorial extent & classification: E. Local *Unpublished*

The M53 Motorway (Junction 11, Southbound Link Road to the M56 Eastbound) (Temporary Prohibition of Traffic) Order 2006 No. 2006/3460. - Enabling power: Road Traffic Regulation Act 1984, s. 14 (1) (a). - Made: 08.12.2006. Coming into force: 07.01.2007. Effect: None. Territorial extent & classification: E. Local *Unpublished*

The M53 Motorway (Junctions 5 to 9, Northbound and Southbound Main Carriageway Closures) (Temporary Prohibition of Traffic) Order 2006 No. 2006/470. - Enabling power: Road Traffic Regulation Act 1984, s. 14 (1) (a). - Made: 20.02.2006. Coming into force: 19.03.2006. Effect: None. Territorial extent & classification: E. Local *Unpublished*

The M54 Motorway and the A5 Trunk Road (Telford to Shrewsbury, Shropshire) (Temporary Prohibition of Traffic) Order 2006 No. 2006/2248. - Enabling power: Road Traffic Regulation Act 1984, s. 14 (1) (a). - Made: 07.08.2006. Coming into force: 14.08.2006. Effect: None. Territorial extent & classification: E. Local *Unpublished*

The M54 Motorway (Junction 1) (Eastbound Exit Slip Road) (Temporary Prohibition of Traffic) Order 2006 No. 2006/705. - Enabling power: Road Traffic Regulation Act 1984, s. 14 (1) (a). - Made: 24.02.2006. Coming into force: 03.03.2006. Effect: None. Territorial extent & classification: E. Local *Unpublished*

The M54 Motorway (Junction 2) (Slip Roads) (Temporary Prohibition of Traffic) Order 2006 No. 2006/198. - Enabling power: Road Traffic Regulation Act 1984, s. 14 (1) (a). - Made: 23.01.2006. Coming into force: 30.01.2006. Effect: None. Territorial extent & classification: E. Local *Unpublished*

The M54 Motorway (Junctions 2 - 7) (Temporary Prohibition of Traffic) Order 2006 No. 2006/1365. - Enabling power: Road Traffic Regulation Act 1984, s. 14 (1) (a). - Made: 08.05.2006. Coming into force: 15.05.2006. Effect: None. Territorial extent & classification: E. Local *Unpublished*

The M55 Motorway and M6 Motorway (Junctions 32 - 33, Northbound and Southbound Carriageway and Slip Roads) (Temporary Prohibition and Restriction of Traffic) Order 2006 No. 2006/2858. - Enabling power: Road Traffic Regulation Act 1984, s. 14 (1) (a) (7). - Made: 17.10.2006. Coming into force: 12.11.2006. Effect: None. Territorial extent & classification: E. Local *Unpublished*

The M55 Motorway (Eastbound Link Road to the Northbound M6 Motorway - Junction 32) (Temporary Prohibition of Traffic) Order 2006 No. 2006/1801. - Enabling power: Road Traffic Regulation Act 1984, s. 14 (1) (a). - Made: 27.06.2006. Coming into force: 25.07.2006. Effect: None. Territorial extent & classification: E. Local *Unpublished*

The M55 Motorway (Eastbound Link Road to the Southbound M6 Motorway - Junction 32) (Temporary Prohibition of Traffic) Order 2006 No. 2006/1802. - Enabling power: Road Traffic Regulation Act 1984, s. 14 (1) (a). - Made: 27.06.2006. Coming into force: 26.07.2006. Effect: None. Territorial extent & classification: E. Local *Unpublished*

The M55 Motorway (Junction 1, Broughton Circle Interchange) (Temporary Restriction of Traffic) Order 2006 No. 2006/1. - Enabling power: Road Traffic Regulation Act 1984, s. 14 (1) (a). - Made: 03.01.2006. Coming into force: 29.01.2006. Effect: None. Territorial extent & classification: E. Local *Unpublished*

The M55 Motorway (Junction 1, Eastbound and Westbound Main Carriageways and Westbound Entry Slip Road) (Sign Gantry and Safety Barrier Upgrade) (Temporary Restriction of Traffic) Order 2006 No. 2006/297. - Enabling power: Road Traffic Regulation Act 1984, s. 14 (1) (a) (7). - Made: 06.02.2006. Coming into force: 05.03.2006. Effect: None. Territorial extent & classification: E. Local *Unpublished*

The M55 Motorway (Junction 1, Eastbound Link Road to the Southbound M6 Motorway) and M6 Motorway (Junction 32, Southbound Main Carriageway) (Temporary Restriction and Prohibition of Traffic) Order 2006 No. 2006/189. - Enabling power: Road Traffic Regulation Act 1984, s. 14 (1) (a). - Made: 24.01.2006. Coming into force: 19.02.2006. Effect: None. Territorial extent & classification: E. Local *Unpublished*

The M55 Motorway (Junction 1, Eastbound Main Carriageway) (Temporary Prohibition and Restriction of Traffic) Order 2006 No. 2006/3403. - Enabling power: Road Traffic Regulation Act 1984, s. 14 (1) (a) (7). - Made: 08.12.2006. Coming into force: 02.01.2007. Effect: None. Territorial extent & classification: E. Local *Unpublished*

The M55 Motorway (Junction 1 Eastbound & Westbound Exit Slip Roads) (Temporary Prohibition of Traffic) Order 2006 No. 2006/229. - Enabling power: Road Traffic Regulation Act 1984, s. 14 (1) (a). - Made: 23.01.2006. Coming into force: 30.01.2006. Effect: None. Territorial extent & classification: E. Local *Unpublished*

The M55 Motorway (Junction 3. Pier Upgrade) (Temporary Restriction of Traffic) Order 2006 No. 2006/3075. - Enabling power: Road Traffic Regulation Act 1984, s. 14 (1) (a) (7). - Made: 31.10.2006. Coming into force: 12.11.2006. Effect: None. Territorial extent & classification: E. Local *Unpublished*

The M55 Motorway (Junctions 1 to 3 Westbound Carriageway) (Temporary Restriction of Traffic) Order 2006 No. 2006/2048. - Enabling power: Road Traffic Regulation Act 1984, ss. 14 (1) (a). - Made: 11.07.2006. Coming into force: 05.08.2006. Effect: None. Territorial extent & classification: E. Local *Unpublished*

The M55 Motorway (Junctions 3 to 1, Eastbound and Westbound Main Carriageways) (Temporary Restriction of Traffic) Order 2006 No. 2006/1633. - Enabling power: Road Traffic Regulation Act 1984, s. 14 (1) (a) (7). - Made: 09.06.2006. Coming into force: 02.07.2006. Effect: None. Territorial extent & classification: E. Local *Unpublished*

The M55 Motorway (Junctions 3 to 1) (Safety Barrier Upgrade) (Temporary Restriction and Prohibition of Traffic) Order 2006 No. 2006/860. - Enabling power: Road Traffic Regulation Act 1984, s. 14 (1) (a). - Made: 16.03.2006. Coming into force: 18.03.2006. Effect: None. Territorial extent & classification: E. Local *Unpublished*

The M56 Motorway (Junction 1 Eastbound Exit Slip Road to the A34 Northbound) (Temporary Prohibition of Traffic) Order 2006 No. 2006/1222. - Enabling power: Road Traffic Regulation Act 1984, s. 14 (1) (a). - Made: 24.03.2006. Coming into force: 16.05.2006. Effect: None. Territorial extent & classification: E. Local *Unpublished*

The M56 Motorway (Junction 1 Westbound Entry Slip Road From the A34 Southbound) (Temporary Prohibition of Traffic) Order 2006 No. 2006/1153. - Enabling power: Road Traffic Regulation Act 1984, s. 14 (1) (a). - Made: 14.04.2006. Coming into force: 11.05.2006. Effect: None. Territorial extent & classification: E. Local *Unpublished*

The M56 Motorway (Junction 2 Eastbound Entry Slip Road) (Temporary Prohibition of Traffic) Order 2006 No. 2006/3207. - Enabling power: Road Traffic Regulation Act 1984, s. 14 (1) (a). - Made: 10.11.2006. Coming into force: 11.12.2006. Effect: None. Territorial extent & classification: E. Local *Unpublished*

The M56 Motorway (Junction 5 Northbound Exit Slip Road) (Temporary Prohibition of Traffic) Order 2006 No. 2006/1219. - Enabling power: Road Traffic Regulation Act 1984, s. 14 (1) (a). - Made: 20.04.2006. Coming into force: 18.05.2006. Effect: None. Territorial extent & classification: E. Local *Unpublished*

The M56 Motorway (Junction 7 Westbound Exit slip Road, Bowden Interchange) (Temporary Prohibition of Traffic) Order 2006 No. 2006/1124. - Enabling power: Road Traffic Regulation Act 1984, s. 14 (1) (a). - Made: 10.04.2006. Coming into force: 04.05.2006. Effect: None. Territorial extent & classification: E. Local *Unpublished*

The M56 Motorway (Junction 11 - 14, Eastbound and Westbound Carriageways and Slip Roads) (Temporary Prohibition and Restriction of Traffic) Order 2006 No. 2006/1186. - Enabling power: Road Traffic Regulation Act 1984, s. 14 (1) (a). - Made: 18.04.2006. Coming into force: 21.04.2006. Effect: None. Territorial extent & classification: E. Local *Unpublished*

The M56 Motorway (Junction 11, Eastbound Entry Slip Road) (Temporary Prohibition of Traffic) Order 2006 No. 2006/1325. - Enabling power: Road Traffic Regulation Act 1984, s. 14 (1) (a). - Made: 04.05.2006. Coming into force: 04.06.2006. Effect: None. Territorial extent & classification: E. Local *Unpublished*

The M56 Motorway (Junction 11, Eastbound Main Carriageway) (Temporary Prohibition of Traffic) Order 2006 No. 2006/3006. - Enabling power: Road Traffic Regulation Act 1984, s. 14 (1) (a). - Made: 27.10.2006. Coming into force: 26.11.2006. Effect: None. Territorial extent & classification: E. Local *Unpublished*

The M56 Motorway (Junction 12, Eastbound Entry Slip Road) (Temporary Prohibition of Traffic) Order 2006 No. 2006/3155. - Enabling power: Road Traffic Regulation Act 1984, s. 14 (1) (a). - Made: 17.11.2006. Coming into force: 27.11.2006. Effect: None. Territorial extent & classification: E. Local *Unpublished*

Road traffic: Traffic regulation

The M56 Motorway (Junction 12, Eastbound Exit Slip Road and Main Carriageway) (Temporary Prohibition and Restriction of Traffic) Order 2006 No. 2006/3019. - Enabling power: Road Traffic Regulation Act 1984, s. 14 (1) (a) (7). - Made: 27.10.2006. Coming into force: 25.11.2006. Effect: None. Territorial extent & classification: E. Local *Unpublished*

The M56 Motorway Junction 15 (Westbound to M53 Junction 11 Northbound Link) and M53 Motorway (Junction 10 Northbound Exit Slip Road) (Temporary Prohibition of Traffic) Order 2006 No. 2006/1578. - Enabling power: Road Traffic Regulation Act 1984, s. 14 (1) (a). - Made: 19.05.2006. Coming into force: 15.06.2006. Effect: None. Territorial extent & classification: E. Local *Unpublished*

The M57 Motorway (A5036 Dunnings Bridge Road) Switch Island (Temporary Restriction of Traffic) Order 2006 No. 2006/1245. - Enabling power: Road Traffic Regulation Act 1984, s. 14 (1) (b). - Made: 25.04.2006. Coming into force: 09.05.2006. Effect: None. Territorial extent & classification: E. Local *Unpublished*

The M57 Motorway (Junction 4 Southbound Entry Slip Road) (Temporary Prohibition of Traffic) Order 2006 No. 2006/2483. - Enabling power: Road Traffic Regulation Act 1984, s. 14 (1) (a). - Made: 29.08.2006. Coming into force: 24.09.2006. Effect: None. Territorial extent & classification: E. Local *Unpublished*

The M57 Motorway (Junction 6, Southbound Main Carriageway and Entry Slip Road) (Temporary Prohibition and Restriction of Traffic) Order 2006 No. 2006/429. - Enabling power: Road Traffic Regulation Act 1984, s. 14 (1) (a) (7). - Made: 06.02.2006. Coming into force: 03.03.2006. Effect: None. Territorial extent & classification: E. Local *Unpublished*

The M60 Motorway (Junction 1 Anticlockwise Entry Slip Road) (Temporary Prohibition of Traffic) Order 2006 No. 2006/1154. - Enabling power: Road Traffic Regulation Act 1984, s. 14 (1) (a). - Made: 14.04.2006. Coming into force: 09.05.2006. Effect: None. Territorial extent & classification: E. Local *Unpublished*

The M60 Motorway (Junction 3, Anticlockwise Entry Slip Road from A34) (No. 2) (Temporary Prohibition of Traffic) Order 2006 No. 2006/2733. - Enabling power: Road Traffic Regulation Act 1984, s. 14 (1) (a). - Made: 18.09.2006. Coming into force: 22.09.2006. Effect: None. Territorial extent & classification: E. Local *Unpublished*

The M60 Motorway (Junction 3, Anticlockwise Entry Slip road from A34) (Temporary Prohibition of Traffic) Order 2006 No. 2006/852. - Enabling power: Road Traffic Regulation Act 1984, s. 14 (1) (a). - Made: 17.03.2006. Coming into force: 02.04.2006. Effect: None. Territorial extent & classification: E. Local *Unpublished*

The M60 Motorway (Junction 4, Clockwise Entry Slip Road From A34) (Temporary Prohibition of Traffic) Order 2006 No. 2006/1826. - Enabling power: Road Traffic Regulation Act 1984, s. 14 (1) (a). - Made: 23.06.2006. Coming into force: 23.07.2006. Effect: None. Territorial extent & classification: E. Local *Unpublished*

The M60 Motorway (Junction 11, Anticlockwise Exit Slip) (Temporary Prohibition of Traffic) Order 2006 No. 2006/1221. - Enabling power: Road Traffic Regulation Act 1984, s. 14 (1) (a). - Made: 18.04.2006. Coming into force: 17.05.2006. Effect: None. Territorial extent & classification: E. Local *Unpublished*

The M60 Motorway (Junction 12 Anticlockwise, Link Roads From M602 Westbound and M62 Eastbound) (Temporary Prohibition of Traffic) Order 2006 No. 2006/1139. - Enabling power: Road Traffic Regulation Act 1984, s. 14 (1) (a) (7). - Made: 18.04.2006. Coming into force: 22.04.2006. Effect: None. Territorial extent & classification: E. Local *Unpublished*

The M60 Motorway (Junction 13, Clockwise and Anticlockwise Entry Slip Roads) (Temporary Prohibition of Traffic) Order 2006 No. 2006/1126. - Enabling power: Road Traffic Regulation Act 1984, s. 14 (1) (a). - Made: 10.04.2006. Coming into force: 08.05.2006. Effect: None. Territorial extent & classification: E. Local *Unpublished*

The M60 Motorway (Junction 16 Clockwise Entry Slip Road) (Temporary Prohibition of Traffic) Order 2006 No. 2006/3208. - Enabling power: Road Traffic Regulation Act 1984, s. 14 (1) (a). - Made: 13.11.2006. Coming into force: 11.12.2006. Effect: None. Territorial extent & classification: E. Local *Unpublished*

The M60 Motorway (Junction 19, Anticlockwise Entry Slip Road and Clockwise Exit Slip Road) (Temporary Prohibition of Traffic) Order 2006 No. 2006/466. - Enabling power: Road Traffic Regulation Act 1984, s. 14 (1) (a). - Made: 17.02.2006. Coming into force: 19.03.2006. Effect: None. Territorial extent & classification: E. Local *Unpublished*

The M60 Motorway (Junction 20 Anticlockwise Entry Slip Roads) (Temporary Prohibition of Traffic) Order 2006 No. 2006/1125. - Enabling power: Road Traffic Regulation Act 1984, s. 14 (1) (a). - Made: 10.04.2006. Coming into force: 09.05.2006. Effect: None. Territorial extent & classification: E. Local *Unpublished*

The M60 Motorway (Junction 21, Anticlockwise Entry Slip Road and Main Carriageway) (Temporary Prohibition and Restriction of Traffic) Order 2006 No. 2006/693. - Enabling power: Road Traffic Regulation Act 1984, s. 14 (1) (a) (7). - Made: 03.03.2006. Coming into force: 26.03.2006. Effect: None. Territorial extent & classification: E. Local *Unpublished*

The M60 Motorway (Junction 21, Anticlockwise Entry Slip Road from the A663) (Temporary Prohibition of Traffic) Order 2006 No. 2006/1155. - Enabling power: Road Traffic Regulation Act 1984, s. 14 (1) (a). - Made: 13.04.2006. Coming into force: 10.05.2006. Effect: None. Territorial extent & classification: E. Local *Unpublished*

The M60 Motorway (Junction 23, Clockwise and Anticlockwise Main Carriageways and Slip Roads) (Temporary Prohibition and Restriction of Traffic) Order 2006 No. 2006/1803. - Enabling power: Road Traffic Regulation Act 1984, s. 14 (1) (a) (7). - Made: 15.06.2006. Coming into force: 02.07.2006. Effect: None. Territorial extent & classification: E. Local *Unpublished*

Road traffic: Traffic regulation

The M60 Motorway (Junction 24 - 25, Clockwise Main Carriageway) (Temporary Restriction of Traffic) Order 2006 No. 2006/2857. - Enabling power: Road Traffic Regulation Act 1984, s. 14 (1) (b). - Made: 16.10.2006. Coming into force: 22.10.2006. Effect: None. Territorial extent & classification: E. Local *Unpublished*

The M60 Motorway (Junction 25, Anticlockwise Entry and Exit Slip Roads) (Temporary Prohibition of Traffic) Order 2006 No. 2006/383. - Enabling power: Road Traffic Regulation Act 1984, s. 14 (1) (a). - Made: 10.02.2006. Coming into force: 09.03.2006. Effect: None. Territorial extent & classification: E. Local *Unpublished*

The M60 Motorway (Junction 27 Clockwise Entry Slip Road) (Temporary Prohibition of Traffic) Order 2006 No. 2006/2412. - Enabling power: Road Traffic Regulation Act 1984, s. 14 (1) (a). - Made: 18.08.2006. Coming into force: 31.08.2006. Effect: None. Territorial extent & classification: E. Local *Unpublished*

The M60 Motorway (Junctions 3 - 27, Clockwise and Anticlockwise Main Carriageways and Slip Roads) (Temporary Prohibition and Restriction of Traffic) Amendment Order 2006 No. 2006/3021. - Enabling power: Road Traffic Regulation Act 1984, s. 14 (1) (a). - Made: 10.11.2006. Coming into force: 11.12.2006. Effect: S.I. 2006/2558 amended. Territorial extent & classification: E. Local *Unpublished*

The M60 Motorway (Junctions 3 - 27, Clockwise and Anticlockwise Main Carriageways and Slip Roads) (Temporary Prohibition and Restriction of Traffic) Order 2006 No. 2006/2558. - Enabling power: Road Traffic Regulation Act 1984, s. 14 (1) (a) (7). - Made: 18.09.2006. Coming into force: 14.09.2006. Effect: None. Territorial extent & classification: E. Local *Unpublished*

The M60 Motorway (Junctions 19 to 20, Clockwise and Anticlockwise Carriageway Hardshoulder Running) (Temporary Prohibition and Restriction of Traffic) Order 2006 No. 2006/627. - Enabling power: Road Traffic Regulation Act 1984, s. 14 (1) (a) (7). - Made: 17.02.2006. Coming into force: 15.03.2006. Effect: None. Territorial extent & classification: E. Local *Unpublished*

The M60 Motorway (Junctions 22 to 24, Anticlockwise Main Carriageway) (Temporary Restriction of Traffic) Order 2006 No. 2006/2279. - Enabling power: Road Traffic Regulation Act 1984, s. 14 (1) (b). - Made: 11.08.2006. Coming into force: 22.08.2006. Effect: None. Territorial extent & classification: E. Local *Unpublished*

The M60 Motorway (Junctions 22 to 24, Clockwise and Anticlockwise Main Carriageways and Slip Roads) (Temporary Prohibition and Restriction of Traffic) Order 2006 No. 2006/847. - Enabling power: Road Traffic Regulation Act 1984, s. 14 (1) (a) (7). - Made: 13.03.2006. Coming into force: 02.04.2006. Effect: None. Territorial extent & classification: E. Local *Unpublished*

The M61 J9/M65 J2 Motorways (Link Road To And From Walton Summit Industrial Park) (Temporary Prohibition of Traffic) Order 2006 No. 2006/2440. - Enabling power: Road Traffic Regulation Act 1984, s. 14 (1) (a). - Made: 28.08.2006. Coming into force: 21.09.2006. Effect: None. Territorial extent & classification: E. Local *Unpublished*

The M61 Motorway (Junction 1, Southbound Link Road to the Anticlockwise M60 Motorway - Junction 15) (Temporary Prohibition of Traffic) Order 2006 No. 2006/275. - Enabling power: Road Traffic Regulation Act 1984, s. 14 (1) (a). - Made: 20.01.2006. Coming into force: 05.02.2006. Effect: None. Territorial extent & classification: E. Local *Unpublished*

The M61 Motorway (Junction 2 Southbound Link Road to A580 Eastbound) (Temporary Prohibition of Traffic) Order 2006 No. 2006/1310. - Enabling power: Road Traffic Regulation Act 1984, s. 14 (1) (a). - Made: 01.05.2006. Coming into force: 24.05.2006. Effect: None. Territorial extent & classification: E. Local *Unpublished*

The M61 Motorway (Junction 3, Southbound Exit Slip Road) (Temporary Prohibition of Traffic) Order 2006 No. 2006/1323. - Enabling power: Road Traffic Regulation Act 1984, s. 14 (1) (a). - Made: 24.04.2006. Coming into force: 18.05.2006. Effect: None. Territorial extent & classification: E. Local *Unpublished*

The M61 Motorway (Junction 6, Bolton West Services, Southbound Carriageway) (Temporary Prohibition and Restriction of Traffic) Order 2006 No. 2006/3485. - Enabling power: Road Traffic Regulation Act 1984, s. 14 (1) (a). - Made: 19.12.2006. Coming into force: 14.01.2007. Effect: None. Territorial extent & classification: E. Local *Unpublished*

The M61 Motorway (Junction 6 Northbound Carriageway) (Temporary Prohibition of Traffic) Order 2006 No. 2006/1634. - Enabling power: Road Traffic Regulation Act 1984, ss. 14 (1) (a). - Made: 13.06.2006. Coming into force: 09.07.2006. Effect: None. Territorial extent & classification: E. Local *Unpublished*

The M61 Motorway (Junction 6 Northbound Entry Slip Road) (Temporary Prohibition of Traffic) Order 2006 No. 2006/691. - Enabling power: Road Traffic Regulation Act 1984, s. 14 (1) (a). - Made: 03.03.2006. Coming into force: 30.03.2006. Effect: None. Territorial extent & classification: E. Local *Unpublished*

The M61 Motorway (Junction 6 Northbound Exit Slip Road) (Temporary Prohibition of Traffic) Order 2006 No. 2006/848. - Enabling power: Road Traffic Regulation Act 1984, ss. 14 (1) (a). - Made: 13.03.2006. Coming into force: 06.04.2006. Effect: None. Territorial extent & classification: E. Local *Unpublished*

The M61 Motorway (Junction 9, Northbound Exit Slip Road to M65 Eastbound) (Temporary Prohibition of Traffic) Order 2006 No. 2006/2553. - Enabling power: Road Traffic Regulation Act 1984, s. 14 (1) (a). - Made: 11.09.2006. Coming into force: 05.10.2006. Effect: None. Territorial extent & classification: E. Local *Unpublished*

Road traffic: Traffic regulation

The M61 Motorway (Junction 9 Southbound Entry Slip Road) (Temporary Prohibition of Traffic) Order 2006 No. 2006/2410. - Enabling power: Road Traffic Regulation Act 1984, s. 14 (1) (a). - Made: 21.08.2006. Coming into force: 14.09.2006. Effect: None. Territorial extent & classification: E. Local *Unpublished*

The M61 Motorway (Junction 9 Southbound Exit Slip Road) (Temporary Prohibition of Traffic) Order 2006 No. 2006/2441. - Enabling power: Road Traffic Regulation Act 1984, s. 14 (1) (a). - Made: 21.08.2006. Coming into force: 14.09.2006. Effect: None. Territorial extent & classification: E. Local *Unpublished*

The M61 Motorway (Junctions 5-6 Northbound Carriageway) (Temporary Prohibition and Restriction of Traffic) Order 2006 No. 2006/2159. - Enabling power: Road Traffic Regulation Act 1984, ss. 14 (1) (a) (7). - Made: 18.07.2006. Coming into force: 13.08.2006. Effect: None. Territorial extent & classification: E. Local *Unpublished*

The M61 Motorway (Kearsley Spur) (Temporary Prohibition of Traffic) (No. 2) Order 2006 No. 2006/1426. - Enabling power: Road Traffic Regulation Act 1984, s. 14 (1) (a). - Made: 16.05.2006. Coming into force: 09.06.2006. Effect: None. Territorial extent & classification: E. Local *Unpublished*

The M61 Motorway (Kearsley Spur) (Temporary Prohibition of Traffic) Order 2006 No. 2006/186. - Enabling power: Road Traffic Regulation Act 1984, s. 14 (1) (a). - Made: 23.01.2006. Coming into force: 10.02.2006. Effect: None. Territorial extent & classification: E. Local *Unpublished*

The M61 Motorway (Northbound Entry Slip Road From the Westbound A580) (Temporary Prohibition of Traffic) Order 2006 No. 2006/3483. - Enabling power: Road Traffic Regulation Act 1984, s. 14 (1) (a). - Made: 22.12.2006. Coming into force: 17.01.2007. Effect: None. Territorial extent & classification: E. Local *Unpublished*

The M61 Motorway (Northbound Link Road from the A580 at Junction 14 of the M60) (Temporary Restriction of Traffic) Order 2006 No. 2006/1635. - Enabling power: Road Traffic Regulation Act 1984, s. 14 (1) (b). - Made: 07.06.2006. Coming into force: 12.06.2006. Effect: None. Territorial extent & classification: E. Local *Unpublished*

The M62 Motorway and the M1 Motorway (Lofthouse Interchange) (Temporary Restriction and Prohibition of Traffic) Order 2006 No. 2006/1818. - Enabling power: Road Traffic Regulation Act 1984, s. 14 (1) (a). - Made: 20.06.2006. Coming into force: 02.07.2006. Effect: None. Territorial extent & classification: E. Local *Unpublished*

The M62 Motorway (Junction 7 Eastbound and Westbound Exit and Entry Slip Roads) (Temporary Restriction of Traffic) Order 2006 No. 2006/1246. - Enabling power: Road Traffic Regulation Act 1984, s. 14 (1) (a). - Made: 20.04.2006. Coming into force: 17.05.2006. Effect: None. Territorial extent & classification: E. Local *Unpublished*

The M62 Motorway (Junction 7 Eastbound Exit Slip Road) (Temporary Prohibition of Traffic) Order 2006 No. 2006/2644. - Enabling power: Road Traffic Regulation Act 1984, s. 14 (1) (a). - Made: 25.09.2006. Coming into force: 03.10.2006. Effect: None. Territorial extent & classification: E. Local *Unpublished*

The M62 Motorway (Junction 8, Westbound Entry Slip Road) (Temporary Prohibition of Traffic) Order 2006 No. 2006/1321. - Enabling power: Road Traffic Regulation Act 1984, s. 14 (1) (a). - Made: 28.04.2006. Coming into force: 30.05.2006. Effect: None. Territorial extent & classification: E. Local *Unpublished*

The M62 Motorway (Junction 9. Eastbound Entry Slip Road) (Temporary Prohibition of Traffic) Order 2006 No. 2006/1355. - Enabling power: Road Traffic Regulation Act 1984, s. 14 (1) (a). - Made: 05.05.2006. Coming into force: 31.05.2006. Effect: None. Territorial extent & classification: E. Local *Unpublished*

The M62 Motorway (Junction 9. Westbound Entry Slip Road) (Temporary Prohibition of Traffic) Order 2006 No. 2006/1354. - Enabling power: Road Traffic Regulation Act 1984, s. 14 (1) (a). - Made: 05.05.2006. Coming into force: 01.06.2006. Effect: None. Territorial extent & classification: E. Local *Unpublished*

The M62 Motorway (Junction 11, Eastbound Access and Westbound Exit Slip Roads) (Temporary Prohibition and Restriction of Traffic) Order 2006 No. 2006/1604. - Enabling power: Road Traffic Regulation Act 1984, s. 14 (1) (a) (7). - Made: 30.05.2006. Coming into force: 22.06.2006. Effect: None. Territorial extent & classification: E. Local *Unpublished*

The M62 Motorway (Junction 11, Eastbound Entry Slip Road) (Temporary Prohibition of Traffic) Order 2006 No. 2006/1322. - Enabling power: Road Traffic Regulation Act 1984, s. 14 (1) (a). - Made: 28.04.2006. Coming into force: 29.05.2006. Effect: None. Territorial extent & classification: E. Local *Unpublished*

The M62 Motorway (Junction 20, Circulatory Carriageway and Slip Roads) and the A627 Motorway (Southbound and Northbound Main Carriageways) (Temporary Prohibition and Restriction of Traffic) Order 2006 No. 2006/476. - Enabling power: Road Traffic Regulation Act 1984, s. 14 (1) (a) (7). - Made: 20.02.2006. Coming into force: 16.03.2006. Effect: None. Territorial extent & classification: E. Local *Unpublished*

The M62 Motorway (Junction 21, Eastbound and Westbound Entry and Exit Slip Roads) (Temporary Prohibition and Restriction of Traffic) Order 2006 No. 2006/424. - Enabling power: Road Traffic Regulation Act 1984, s. 14 (1) (a) (7). - Made: 13.02.2006. Coming into force: 06.03.2006. Effect: None. Territorial extent & classification: E. Local *Unpublished*

The M62 Motorway (Junction 24, Ainley Top) (Temporary Prohibition of Traffic) Order 2006 No. 2006/1824. - Enabling power: Road Traffic Regulation Act 1984, s. 14 (1) (a). - Made: 20.06.2006. Coming into force: 02.07.2006. Effect: None. Territorial extent & classification: E. Local *Unpublished*

The M62 Motorway (Junction 24) (Temporary Prohibition of Traffic) Order 2006 No. 2006/256. - Enabling power: Road Traffic Regulation Act 1984, s. 14 (1) (a). - Made: 27.01.2006. Coming into force: 08.02.2006. Effect: None. Territorial extent & classification: E. Local *Unpublished*

The M62 Motorway (Junction 25 and Junction 26) (Temporary Prohibition of Traffic) Order 2006 No. 2006/1816. - Enabling power: Road Traffic Regulation Act 1984, s. 14 (1) (a). - Made: 16.06.2006. Coming into force: 29.07.2006. Effect: None. Territorial extent & classification: E. Local *Unpublished*

The M62 Motorway (Junction 25 to Junction 26) (Temporary Restriction and Prohibition of Traffic) Order 2006 No. 2006/1891. - Enabling power: Road Traffic Regulation Act 1984, s. 14 (1) (a). - Made: 04.07.2006. Coming into force: 16.07.2006. Effect: None. Territorial extent & classification: E. Local *Unpublished*

The M62 Motorway (Junction 28, Tingley) (Temporary Prohibition of Traffic) Order 2006 No. 2006/1019. - Enabling power: Road Traffic Regulation Act 1984, s. 14 (1) (a). - Made: 24.03.2006. Coming into force: 05.04.2006. Effect: None. Territorial extent & classification: E. Local *Unpublished*

The M62 Motorway (Junction 29, Lofthouse Interchange) (Temporary Prohibition of Traffic) Order 2006 No. 2006/1024. - Enabling power: Road Traffic Regulation Act 1984, s. 14 (1) (a). - Made: 24.03.2006. Coming into force: 04.04.2006. Effect: None. Territorial extent & classification: E. Local *Unpublished*

The M62 Motorway (Junction 29, Lofthouse Interchange) (Temporary Restriction and Prohibition of Traffic) Order 2006 No. 2006/36. - Enabling power: Road Traffic Regulation Act 1984, s. 14 (1) (a) (7). - Made: 06.01.2006. Coming into force: 19.01.2006. Effect: None. Territorial extent & classification: E. Local *Unpublished*

The M62 Motorway (Junction 30 to Junction 31) (Temporary Restriction of Traffic) Order 2006 No. 2006/2351. - Enabling power: Road Traffic Regulation Act 1984, s. 14 (1) (a) (7). - Made: 22.08.2006. Coming into force: 03.09.2006. Effect: None. Territorial extent & classification: E. Local *Unpublished*

The M62 Motorway (Junction 31 to Junction 32) (Temporary Prohibition of Traffic) Order 2006 No. 2006/2339. - Enabling power: Road Traffic Regulation Act 1984, s. 14 (1) (a). - Made: 21.08.2006. Coming into force: 01.09.2006. Effect: None. Territorial extent & classification: E. Local *Unpublished*

The M62 Motorway (Junction 32) (Temporary Prohibition of Traffic) Order 2006 No. 2006/2263. - Enabling power: Road Traffic Regulation Act 1984, s. 14 (1) (a). - Made: 08.08.2006. Coming into force: 20.08.2006. Effect: None. Territorial extent & classification: E. Local *Unpublished*

The M62 Motorway (Junction 33, Ferrybridge) (Temporary Restriction and Prohibition of Traffic) Order 2003 (Revocation) Order 2006 No. 2006/1830. - Enabling power: Road Traffic Regulation Act 1984, ss. 14 (1) (a) (7), 15 (2), 122A. - Made: 29.06.2006. Coming into force: 01.07.2006. Effect: S.I. 2003/1009 revoked. Territorial extent & classification: E. Local *Unpublished*

The M62 Motorway (Junction 33, Westbound Exit Slip Road) (Temporary Prohibition of Traffic) Order 2006 No. 2006/1815. - Enabling power: Road Traffic Regulation Act 1984, s. 14 (1) (a). - Made: 27.06.2006. Coming into force: 09.07.2006. Effect: None. Territorial extent & classification: E. Local *Unpublished*

The M62 Motorway (Junction 34 and Junction 35) (Temporary Restriction of Traffic) Order 2006 No. 2006/2634. - Enabling power: Road Traffic Regulation Act 1984, s. 14 (1) (a) (7). - Made: 25.09.2006. Coming into force: 01.10.2006. Effect: None. Territorial extent & classification: E. Local *Unpublished*

The M62 Motorway (Junction 34) (Temporary Prohibition of Traffic) Order 2006 No. 2006/453. - Enabling power: Road Traffic Regulation Act 1984, s. 14 (1) (a). - Made: 14.02.2006. Coming into force: 24.02.2006. Effect: None. Territorial extent & classification: E. Local *Unpublished*

The M62 Motorway (Junction 36, Airmyn) (Temporary Prohibition of Traffic) Order 2006 No. 2006/2259. - Enabling power: Road Traffic Regulation Act 1984, s. 14 (1) (a). - Made: 28.07.2006. Coming into force: 10.08.2006. Effect: None. Territorial extent & classification: E. Local *Unpublished*

The M62 Motorway (Junction 37, Howden) (Temporary Prohibition of Traffic) Order 2006 No. 2006/262. - Enabling power: Road Traffic Regulation Act 1984, s. 14 (1) (a) (b). - Made: 31.01.2006. Coming into force: 13.02.2006. Effect: None. Territorial extent & classification: E. Local *Unpublished*

The M62 Motorway (Junctions 20 to 21 Eastbound and Westbound Carriageways and Entry and Exit Slip Roads) (Temporary Prohibition of Traffic) Order 2006 No. 2006/2054. - Enabling power: Road Traffic Regulation Act 1984, ss. 14 (1) (a). - Made: 04.07.2006. Coming into force: 28.07.2006. Effect: None. Territorial extent & classification: E. Local *Unpublished*

The M62 Motorway (Junctions 20 to 21 Eastbound and Westbound Carriageways) (Temporary Prohibition and Restriction of Traffic) Order 2006 No. 2006/694. - Enabling power: Road Traffic Regulation Act 1984, s. 14 (1) (a). - Made: 03.03.2006. Coming into force: 23.03.2006. Effect: None. Territorial extent & classification: E. Local *Unpublished*

The M65 Motorway (Junction 1 Eastbound Entry Slip Road) (Temporary Prohibition of Traffic) Order 2006 No. 2006/2242. - Enabling power: Road Traffic Regulation Act 1984, s. 14 (1) (a). - Made: 07.08.2006. Coming into force: 31.08.2006. Effect: None. Territorial extent & classification: E. Local *Unpublished*

Road traffic: Traffic regulation

The M65 Motorway (Junction 1 Westbound Entry Slip Road) (Temporary Prohibition of Traffic) Order 2006 No. 2006/2360. - Enabling power: Road Traffic Regulation Act 1984, s. 14 (1) (a). - Made: 14.08.2006. Coming into force: 07.09.2006. Effect: None. Territorial extent & classification: E. Local *Unpublished*

The M65 Motorway (Junction 2 Eastbound Entry Slip Road) (Temporary Prohibition of Traffic) Order 2006 No. 2006/2439. - Enabling power: Road Traffic Regulation Act 1984, s. 14 (1) (a). - Made: 21.08.2006. Coming into force: 14.09.2006. Effect: None. Territorial extent & classification: E. Local *Unpublished*

The M65 Motorway (Junction 2, Eastbound Exit Slip Road and Circulatory Carriageway) (Temporary Prohibition and Restriction of Traffic) (No. 2) Order 2006 No. 2006/2484. - Enabling power: Road Traffic Regulation Act 1984, s. 14 (1) (a) (7). - Made: 01.09.2006. Coming into force: 01.10.2006. Effect: None. Territorial extent & classification: E. Local *Unpublished*

The M65 Motorway (Junction 2 Eastbound Exit Slip Road and Circulatory Carriageway) (Temporary Prohibition and Restriction of Traffic) Order 2006 No. 2006/1514. - Enabling power: Road Traffic Regulation Act 1984, s. 14 (1) (a). - Made: 29.05.2006. Coming into force: 25.06.2006. Effect: None. Territorial extent & classification: E. Local *Unpublished*

The M65 Motorway (Junction 2 Eastbound Link Road From the A6) (Temporary Prohibition of Traffic) Order 2006 No. 2006/3074. - Enabling power: Road Traffic Regulation Act 1984, s. 14 (1) (a). - Made: 09.10.2006. Coming into force: 05.11.2006. Effect: None. Territorial extent & classification: E. Local *Unpublished*

The M65 Motorway (Junction 2 Westbound Entry Slip Road) (Temporary Prohibition of Traffic) Order 2006 No. 2006/2443. - Enabling power: Road Traffic Regulation Act 1984, s. 14 (1) (a). - Made: 28.08.2006. Coming into force: 21.09.2006. Effect: None. Territorial extent & classification: E. Local *Unpublished*

The M65 Motorway (Junction 3 Eastbound Entry Slip Road) (Temporary Prohibition of Traffic) Order 2006 No. 2006/2245. - Enabling power: Road Traffic Regulation Act 1984, s. 14 (1) (a). - Made: 07.08.2006. Coming into force: 31.08.2006. Effect: None. Territorial extent & classification: E. Local *Unpublished*

The M65 Motorway (Junction 3 Westbound Entry Slip Road) (Temporary Prohibition of Traffic) Order 2006 No. 2006/2467. - Enabling power: Road Traffic Regulation Act 1984, s. 14 (1) (a). - Made: 14.08.2006. Coming into force: 07.09.2006. Effect: None. Territorial extent & classification: E. Local *Unpublished*

The M65 Motorway (Junction 4 Eastbound Entry Slip Road) (Temporary Prohibition of Traffic) Order 2006 No. 2006/2468. - Enabling power: Road Traffic Regulation Act 1984, s. 14 (1) (a). - Made: 14.08.2006. Coming into force: 07.09.2006. Effect: None. Territorial extent & classification: E. Local *Unpublished*

The M65 Motorway (Junction 4 Westbound Entry Slip Road) (Temporary Prohibition of Traffic) Order 2006 No. 2006/2241. - Enabling power: Road Traffic Regulation Act 1984, s. 14 (1) (a). - Made: 14.08.2006. Coming into force: 07.09.2006. Effect: None. Territorial extent & classification: E. Local *Unpublished*

The M65 Motorway (Junction 5 Eastbound Entry Slip Road) (Temporary Prohibition of Traffic) Order 2006 No. 2006/2246. - Enabling power: Road Traffic Regulation Act 1984, s. 14 (1) (a). - Made: 07.08.2006. Coming into force: 31.08.2006. Effect: None. Territorial extent & classification: E. Local *Unpublished*

The M65 Motorway (Junction 5 Westbound Entry Slip Road) (Temporary Prohibition of Traffic) Order 2006 No. 2006/2361. - Enabling power: Road Traffic Regulation Act 1984, s. 14 (1) (a). - Made: 14.08.2006. Coming into force: 07.09.2006. Effect: None. Territorial extent & classification: E. Local *Unpublished*

The M65 Motorway (Junction 5 Westbound Exit Slip Road) (Temporary Prohibition of Traffic) Order 2006 No. 2006/2444. - Enabling power: Road Traffic Regulation Act 1984, s. 14 (1) (a). - Made: 28.08.2006. Coming into force: 21.09.2006. Effect: None. Territorial extent & classification: E. Local *Unpublished*

The M65 Motorway (Junction 6 Eastbound Exit Slip Road) (Temporary Prohibition of Traffic) Order 2006 No. 2006/2515. - Enabling power: Road Traffic Regulation Act 1984, s. 14 (1) (a). - Made: 04.09.2006. Coming into force: 28.09.2006. Effect: None. Territorial extent & classification: E. Local *Unpublished*

The M66 Motorway and A56 Trunk Road (Northbound Carriageway and Slip Roads) (Temporary Prohibition of Traffic) Order 2006 No. 2006/1247. - Enabling power: Road Traffic Regulation Act 1984, s. 14 (1) (a). - Made: 17.04.2006. Coming into force: 04.05.2006. Effect: None. Territorial extent & classification: E. Local *Unpublished*

The M66 Motorway and M62 Motorway (Junction 18, Eastbound Entry Slip Roads) (Temporary Prohibition of Traffic) Order 2006 No. 2006/2859. - Enabling power: Road Traffic Regulation Act 1984, s. 14 (1) (a). - Made: 18.10.2006. Coming into force: 22.10.2006. Effect: None. Territorial extent & classification: E. Local *Unpublished*

The M66 Motorway (Junction 2, Southbound Entry Slip Road) (Temporary Prohibition of Traffic) Order 2006 No. 2006/1151. - Enabling power: Road Traffic Regulation Act 1984, s. 14 (1) (a). - Made: 14.04.2006. Coming into force: 07.05.2006. Effect: None. Territorial extent & classification: E. Local *Unpublished*

The M66 Motorway (Junction 4 Northbound Entry Slip Road) (Temporary Prohibition of Traffic) Order 2006 No. 2006/2844. - Enabling power: Road Traffic Regulation Act 1984, s. 14 (1) (a). - Made: 09.10.2006. Coming into force: 16.10.2006. Effect: None. Territorial extent & classification: E. Local *Unpublished*

Road traffic: Traffic regulation

The M66 Motorway (Junction 4 Southbound Exit Slip Road to M60/M62) (Simester Roundabout) (Temporary Prohibition of Traffic) Order 2006 No. 2006/2781. - Enabling power: Road Traffic Regulation Act 1984, s. 14 (1) (a). - Made: 09.10.2006. Coming into force: 15.10.2006. Effect: None. Territorial extent & classification: E. Local *Unpublished*

The M66 Motorway (Junctions 0 to 2, Southbound Carriageway and Junction 1, Southbound Entry Slip Road) (Temporary Prohibition of Traffic) Order 2006 No. 2006/2411. - Enabling power: Road Traffic Regulation Act 1984, s. 14 (1) (a). - Made: 22.08.2006. Coming into force: 14.09.2006. Effect: None. Territorial extent & classification: E. Local *Unpublished*

The M67 Motorway (Junction 2, Eastbound Entry Slip Road) (Temporary Prohibition of Traffic) Order 2006 No. 2006/2485. - Enabling power: Road Traffic Regulation Act 1984, s. 14 (1) (a). - Made: 01.09.2006. Coming into force: 01.10.2006. Effect: None. Territorial extent & classification: E. Local *Unpublished*

The M69 Motorway (Junction 1) and the A5 Trunk Road (Near Hinckley) (Temporary Restriction and Prohibition of Traffic) Order 2006 No. 2006/3494. - Enabling power: Road Traffic Regulation Act 1984, s. 14 (1) (a). - Made: 20.10.2006. Coming into force: 27.10.2006. Effect: None. Territorial extent & classification: E. Local *Unpublished*

The M69 Motorway (Junction 1) (Slip Road) (Temporary Prohibition of Traffic) Order 2006 No. 2006/996. - Enabling power: Road Traffic Regulation Act 1984, s. 14 (1) (a). - Made: 20.03.2006. Coming into force: 27.03.2006. Effect: None. Territorial extent & classification: E. Local *Unpublished*

The M69 Motorway (Junction with the A46, Coventry) (Temporary Prohibition of Traffic) Order 2006 No. 2006/1782. - Enabling power: Road Traffic Regulation Act 1984, s. 14 (1) (b). - Made: 16.06.2006. Coming into force: 23.06.2006. Effect: None. Territorial extent & classification: E. Local *Unpublished*

The M161 Motorway (Junction 6 Southbound Carriageway) (Temporary Prohibition of Traffic) Order 2006 No. 2006/2594. - Enabling power: Road Traffic Regulation Act 1984, s. 14 (1) (a). - Made: 29.08.2006. Coming into force: 24.09.2006. Effect: None. Territorial extent & classification: E. Local *Unpublished*

The M180 Motorway (Junction 2, Woodhouse) (Temporary Prohibition of Traffic) Order 2006 No. 2006/1821. - Enabling power: Road Traffic Regulation Act 1984, s. 14 (1) (a). - Made: 27.06.2006. Coming into force: 09.07.2006. Effect: None. Territorial extent & classification: E. Local *Unpublished*

The M181 Motorway (Midmoor Interchange to Frodingham Roundabout) (Temporary Prohibition of Traffic) Order 2006 No. 2006/2260. - Enabling power: Road Traffic Regulation Act 1984, s. 14 (1) (a). - Made: 01.08.2006. Coming into force: 13.08.2006. Effect: None. Territorial extent & classification: E. Local *Unpublished*

The M271 Motorway (M27 Junction 3 - Redbridge Roundabout) (Temporary Prohibition of Traffic) Order 2006 No. 2006/2156. - Enabling power: Road Traffic Regulation Act 1984, s. 14 (1) (a) (7). - Made: 31.07.2006. Coming into force: 05.08.2006. Effect: None. Territorial extent & classification: E. Local *Unpublished*

The M602 Motorway (Junction 1 Westbound Exit Slip Road) and M62 Motorway (Temporary Prohibition and Restriction of Traffic) Order 2006 No. 2006/3060. - Enabling power: Road Traffic Regulation Act 1984, s. 14 (1) (a) (7). - Made: 16.10.2006. Coming into force: 09.11.2006. Effect: None. Territorial extent & classification: E. Local *Unpublished*

The M602 Motorway (Westbound Link Road to the M60 Motorway Clockwise at Junction 12) (Temporary Prohibition of Traffic) Order 2006 No. 2006/1223. - Enabling power: Road Traffic Regulation Act 1984, s. 14 (1) (a). - Made: 24.03.2006. Coming into force: 22.05.2006. Effect: None. Territorial extent & classification: E. Local *Unpublished*

The M621 Motorway (Gildersome Interchange) (Temporary Restriction and Prohibition of Traffic) Order 2006 No. 2006/1819. - Enabling power: Road Traffic Regulation Act 1984, s. 14 (1) (a) (7). - Made: 20.06.2006. Coming into force: 02.07.2006. Effect: None. Territorial extent & classification: E. Local *Unpublished*

The M621 Motorway (Junction 1, Islington) (Temporary Prohibition of Traffic) Order 2006 No. 2006/2061. - Enabling power: Road Traffic Regulation Act 1984, ss. 14 (1) (a). - Made: 18.07.2006. Coming into force: 30.07.2006. Effect: None. Territorial extent & classification: E. Local *Unpublished*

The M621 Motorway (Junction 3 to Junction 7) (Temporary Prohibition of Traffic) Order 2006 No. 2006/1098. - Enabling power: Road Traffic Regulation Act 1984, s. 14 (1) (a). - Made: 07.04.2006. Coming into force: 20.04.2006. Effect: None. Territorial extent & classification: E. Local *Unpublished*

The M621 Motorway (Junction 4, Hunslet) (Temporary Prohibition of Traffic) Order 2006 No. 2006/1136. - Enabling power: Road Traffic Regulation Act 1984, s. 14 (1) (a), 15 (2). - Made: 18.04.2006. Coming into force: 27.04.2006. Effect: None. Territorial extent & classification: E. Local *Unpublished*

The M621 Motorway (Junction 4, Hunslet) (Temporary Prohibition of Traffic) Order 2006 No. 2006/263. - Enabling power: Road Traffic Regulation Act 1984, s. 14 (1) (a). - Made: 31.01.2006. Coming into force: 11.02.2006. Effect: None. Territorial extent & classification: E. Local *Unpublished*

The M621 Motorway (Junction 6 to Junction 7) (Temporary Restriction and Prohibition of Traffic) Order 2006 No. 2006/626. - Enabling power: Road Traffic Regulation Act 1984, s. 14 (1) (a). - Made: 24.02.2006. Coming into force: 07.03.2006. Effect: None. Territorial extent & classification: E. Local *Unpublished*

The M621 Motorway (M62 Motorway to Junction 1) (Temporary Restriction of Traffic) Order 2006 No. 2006/2104. - Enabling power: Road Traffic Regulation Act 1984, s. 14 (1) (a) (7). - Made: 24.07.2006. Coming into force: 06.08.2006. Effect: None. Territorial extent & classification: E. Local *Unpublished*

Road traffic, England

The A404 Trunk Road (Maidenhead Thicket to Handy Cross) (Closure of Layby) Order 2006 No. 2006/579. - Enabling power: Road Traffic Regulation Act 1984, ss. 1 (1), 2 (1) (2). - Issued: 15.03.2006. Made: 24.02.2006. Coming into force: 13.03.2006. Effect: None. Territorial extent & classification: E. Local. - 2p.: 30 cm. - 978-0-11-074205-2 *£3.00*

The Bus Lane Contraventions (Approved Local Authorities) (England) (Amendment) (No. 2) Order 2006 No. 2006/1447. - Enabling power: Transport Act 2000, s. 144 (3) (b) (14). - Issued: 07.06.2006. Made: 31.05.2006. Laid: 06.06.2006. Coming into force: 04.07.2006. Effect: S.I. 2005/2755 amended. Territorial extent & classification: E. General. - With correction slip dated August 2006. - 4p.: 30 cm. - 978-0-11-074643-2 *£3.00*

The Bus Lane Contraventions (Approved Local Authorities) (England) (Amendment) (No. 3) Order 2006 No. 2006/1516. - Enabling power: Transport Act 2000, s. 144 (3) (b) (14). - Issued: 23.06.2006. Made: 13.06.2006. Laid: 16.06.2006. Coming into force: 11.07.2006. Effect: S.I. 2005/2755 amended. Territorial extent & classification: E. General. - With correction slip dated August 2006. - 4p.: 30 cm. - 978-0-11-074705-7 *£3.00*

The Bus Lane Contraventions (Approved Local Authorities) (England) (Amendment) (No. 4) Order 2006 No. 2006/2632. - Enabling power: Transport Act 2000, s. 144 (3) (b) (14). - Issued: 12.10.2006. Made: 04.10.2006. Laid: 06.10.2006. Coming into force: 02.11.2006. Effect: S.I. 2005/2755 amended. Territorial extent & classification: E. General. - 4p.: 30 cm. - 978-0-11-075158-0 *£3.00*

The Bus Lane Contraventions (Approved Local Authorities) (England) (Amendment) (No. 5) Order 2006 No. 2006/2820. - Enabling power: Transport Act 2000, s. 144 (3) (b) (14). - Issued: 03.11.2006. Made: 24.10.2006. Laid: 27.10.2006. Coming into force: 28.11.2006. Effect: S.I. 2005/2755 amended. Territorial extent & classification: E. General. - 4p.: 30 cm. - 978-0-11-075221-1 *£3.00*

The Bus Lane Contraventions (Approved Local Authorities) (England) (Amendment) (No. 6) Order 2006 No. 2006/3212. - Enabling power: Transport Act 2000, s. 144 (3) (b) (14). - Issued: 11.12.2006. Made: 01.12.2006. Laid: 06.12.2006. Coming into force: 03.01.2007. Effect: S.I. 2005/2755 amended. Territorial extent & classification: E. General. - 2p.: 30 cm. - 978-0-11-075414-7 *£3.00*

The Bus Lane Contraventions (Approved Local Authorities) (England) (Amendment) (No. 7) Order 2006 No. 2006/3425. - Enabling power: Transport Act 2000, ss. 144 (3) (b) (14). - Issued: 29.12.2006. Made: 20.12.2006. Laid: 21.12.2006. Coming into force: 02.02.2007. Effect: S.I. 2005/2755 amended. Territorial extent & classification: E. General. - 2p.: 30 cm. - 978-0-11-075582-3 *£3.00*

The Bus Lane Contraventions (Approved Local Authorities) (England) (Amendment) (No. 8) Order 2006 No. 2006/3419. - Enabling power: Transport Act 2000, ss. 144 (3) (b) (14). - Issued: 29.12.2006. Made: 19.12.2006. Laid: 21.12.2006. Coming into force: 06.02.2007. Effect: S.I. 2005/2755 amended. Territorial extent & classification: E. General. - 2p.: 30 cm. - 978-0-11-075580-9 *£3.00*

The Bus Lane Contraventions (Approved Local Authorities) (England) (Amendment) Order 2006 No. 2006/593. - Enabling power: Transport Act 2000, ss. 144 (3) (b) (14). - Issued: 14.03.2006. Made: 07.03.2006. Laid: 10.03.2006. Coming into force: 04.04.2006. Effect: S.I. 2005/2755 amended. Territorial extent & classification: E. General. - With correction slip dated August 2006. - 4p.: 30 cm. - 978-0-11-074191-8 *£3.00*

The M6 Toll (Speed Limit) Regulations 2006 No. 2006/1185. - Enabling power: Road Traffic Regulation Act 1984, s. 17 (2) (3). - Issued: 19.05.2006. Made: 13.04.2006. Laid: 03.05.2006. Coming into force: 25.05.2006. Effect: S.I. 2003/2188 revoked. Territorial extent & classification: E. Local. - 4p.: 30 cm. - 978-0-11-074580-0 *£3.00*

The M53 Motorway (Bidston Moss Viaduct) (50 Miles per Hour Speed Limit) Regulations 2006 No. 2006/2912. - Enabling power: Road Traffic Regulation Act 1984, s. 17 (2) (3). - Issued: 13.11.2006. Made: 06.11.2006. Laid: 08.11.2006. Coming into force: 12.12.2006. Effect: None. Territorial extent & classification: E. General. - 2p.: 30 cm. - 978-0-11-075264-8 *£3.00*

The Quiet Lanes and Home Zones (England) Regulations 2006 No. 2006/2082. - Enabling power: Transport Act 2000, s. 268. - Issued: 07.08.2006. Made: 26.07.2006. Laid: 31.07.2006. Coming into force: 21.08.2006. Effect: None. Territorial extent & classification: E. General. - 12p.: 30 cm. - 978-0-11-074966-2 *£3.00*

The Road Traffic (Permitted Parking Area and Special Parking Area) (Borough of Bracknell Forest) Order 2006 No. 2006/592. - Enabling power: Road Traffic Act 1991, sch. 3, paras 1 (1), 2 (1). - Issued: 15.03.2006. Made: 07.03.2006. Laid: 10.03.2006. Coming into force: 03.04.2006. Effect: 1984 c. 27; 1991 c. 40 modified in relation to parking areas as specified in schs. 1 & 2. Territorial extent & classification: E. General. - 12p.: 30 cm. - 978-0-11-074199-4 *£3.00*

The Road Traffic (Permitted Parking Area and Special Parking Area) (Borough of Warrington) Order 2006 No. 2006/3421. - Enabling power: Road Traffic Act 1991, sch. 3, paras 1 (1), 2 (1) 3 (3). - Issued: 29.12.2006. Made: 19.12.2006. Laid: 21.12.2006. Coming into force: 05.02.2007. Effect: 1984 c. 27; 1991 c. 40 modified in relation to parking areas as specified in schs. 1 & 2. Territorial extent & classification: E. General- 8p.: 30 cm. - 978-0-11-075570-0 £3.00

The Road Traffic (Permitted Parking Area and Special Parking Area) (City of Derby) Order 2006 No. 2006/1445. - Enabling power: Road Traffic Act 1991, sch. 3, paras 1 (1), 2 (1). - Issued: 07.06.2006. Made: 31.05.2006. Laid: 06.06.2006. Coming into force: 03.07.2006. Effect: 1984 c. 27; 1991 c. 40 modified in relation to parking areas as specified in sch. 1 & 2. Territorial extent & classification: E. General. - 8p.: 30 cm. - 978-0-11-074639-5 £3.00

The Road Traffic (Permitted Parking Area and Special Parking Area) (City of Kingston upon Hull) Order 2006 No. 2006/1515. - Enabling power: Road Traffic Act 1991, sch. 3, paras 1 (1), 2 (1). - Issued: 30.06.2006. Made: 13.06.2006. Laid: 16.06.2006. Coming into force: 10.07.2006. Effect: 1984 c. 27; 1991 c. 40 modified in relation to parking areas as specified in sch. 1 & 2. Territorial extent & classification: E. General. - 8p.: 30 cm. - 978-0-11-074747-7 £3.00

The Road Traffic (Permitted Parking Area and Special Parking Area) (City of Leicester) Order 2006 No. 2006/3211. - Enabling power: Road Traffic Act 1991, sch. 3, paras 1 (1), 2 (1), 3 (3). - Issued: 11.12.2006. Made: 01.12.2006. Laid: 06.12.2006. Coming into force: 02.01.2007. Effect: 1984 c. 27; 1991 c. 40 modified in relation to parking areas as specified in schs. 1 & 2. Territorial extent & classification: E. General. - 8p.: 30 cm. - 978-0-11-075411-6 £3.00

The Road Traffic (Permitted Parking Area and Special Parking Area) (City of Wolverhampton) Order 2006 No. 2006/3420. - Enabling power: Road Traffic Act 1991, sch. 3, paras 1 (1), 2 (1) 3 (3). - Issued: 29.12.2006. Made: 19.12.2006. Laid: 21.12.2006. Coming into force: 05.02.2007. Effect: 1984 c. 27; 1991 c. 40 modified in relation to parking areas as specified in schs. 1 & 2. Territorial extent & classification: E. General- 8p.: 30 cm. - 978-0-11-075569-4 £3.00

The Road Traffic (Permitted Parking Area and Special Parking Area) (County of Shropshire) Order 2006 No. 2006/2819. - Enabling power: Road Traffic Act 1991, sch. 3, paras 1 (1), 2 (1), 3 (3). - Issued: 03.11.2006. Made: 24.10.2006. Laid: 27.10.2006. Coming into force: 27.11.2006. Effect: 1984 c. 27; 1991 c. 40 modified in relation to parking areas as specified in sch. 1 & 2. Territorial extent & classification: E. General. - 8p.: 30 cm. - 978-0-11-075220-4 £3.00

The Road Traffic (Permitted Parking Area and Special Parking Area) (County of Surrey) (Borough of Surrey Heath) Order 2006 No. 2006/851. - Enabling power: Road Traffic Act 1991, sch. 3, paras 1 (1), 2 (1). - Issued: 27.03.2006. Made: 16.03.2006. Laid: 24.03.2006. Coming into force: 20.04.2006. Effect: 1984 c. 27; 1991 c. 40 modified in relation to parking areas as specified in sch. 2 & 3. Territorial extent & classification: E. General. - 12p., col. maps: 30 cm. - 978-0-11-074379-0 £6.50

The Road Traffic (Permitted Parking Area and Special Parking Area) (County of Surrey) (District of Tandridge) Order 2006 No. 2006/2319. - Enabling power: Road Traffic Act 1991, sch. 3, paras 1 (1), 2 (1), 3 (3). - Issued: 06.09.2006. Made: 29.08.2006. Laid: 31.08.2006. Coming into force: 28.09.2006. Effect: 1984 c. 27; 1991 c. 40 modified in relation to parking areas as specified in sch. 1 & 2. Territorial extent & classification: E. General. - 8p.: 30 cm. - 978-0-11-075054-5 £3.00

The Road Traffic (Permitted Parking Area and Special Parking Area) (County of Warwickshire) (Borough of Rugby) Order 2006 No. 2006/2356. - Enabling power: Road Traffic Act 1991, sch. 3, paras 1 (1), 2 (1), 3 (3). - Issued: 07.09.2006. Made: 31.08.2006. Laid: 04.09.2006. Coming into force: 02.10.2006. Effect: 1984 c. 27; 1991 c. 40 modified in relation to parking areas as specified in sch. 1 & 2. Territorial extent & classification: E. General. - 8p.: 30 cm. - 978-0-11-075062-0 £3.00

The Road Traffic (Permitted Parking Area and Special Parking Area) (County of Wiltshire) (Districts of Kennet and North Wiltshire) Order 2006 No. 2006/2134. - Enabling power: Road Traffic Act 1991, sch. 3, paras 1 (1), 2 (1). - Issued: 08.08.2006. Made: 01.08.2006. Laid: 03.08.2006. Coming into force: 04.09.2006. Effect: 1984 c. 27; 1991 c. 40 modified in relation to parking areas as specified in sch. 1 & 2. Territorial extent & classification: E. General. - 8p.: 30 cm. - 978-0-11-074969-3 £3.00

The Road Traffic (Permitted Parking Area and Special Parking Area) (Metropolitan Borough of Calderdale) Order 2006 No. 2006/2631. - Enabling power: Road Traffic Act 1991, sch. 3, paras 1 (1), 2 (1), 3 (3). - Issued: 12.10.2006. Made: 04.10.2006. Laid: 06.10.2006. Coming into force: 01.11.2006. Effect: 1984 c. 27; 1991 c. 40 modified in relation to parking areas as specified in sch. 1 & 2. Territorial extent & classification: E. General. - 8p.: 30 cm. - 978-0-11-075157-3 £3.00

The Road Traffic (Permitted Parking Area and Special Parking Area) (Metropolitan Borough of Kirklees) Order 2006 No. 2006/1446. - Enabling power: Road Traffic Act 1991, sch. 3, paras 1 (1), 2 (1). - Issued: 07.06.2006. Made: 31.05.2006. Laid: 06.06.2006. Coming into force: 03.07.2006. Effect: 1984 c. 27; 1991 c. 40 modified in relation to parking areas as specified in sch. 1 & 2. Territorial extent & classification: E. General. - 8p.: 30 cm. - 978-0-11-074642-5 £3.00

The Road Traffic (Permitted Parking Area and Special Parking Area) (Metropolitan Borough of South Tyneside) Order 2006 No. 2006/3424. - Enabling power: Road Traffic Act 1991, sch. 3, paras 1 (1), 2 (1) 3 (3). - Issued: 29.12.2006. Made: 20.12.2006. Laid: 21.12.2006. Coming into force: 01.02.2007. Effect: 1984 c. 27; 1991 c. 40 modified in relation to parking areas as specified in schs. 1 & 2. Territorial extent & classification: E. General- 8p.: 30 cm. - 978-0-11-075581-6 £3.00

Road traffic, England and Wales

The A249 Trunk Road (Iwade Bypass to Queensborough Improvement) (24 Hours Clearway) Order 2006 No. 2006/1956. - Enabling power: Road Traffic Regulation Act 1984, ss. 1 (1), 2 (1) (2), 4 (1). - Issued: 28.07.2006. Made: 14.07.2006. Coming into force: 31.07.2006. Effect: None. Territorial extent & classification: E/W. Local. - 4p.: 30 cm. - 978-0-11-074924-2 £3.00

The A249 Trunk Road (Iwade Bypass to Queensborough Improvement) (50 Miles Per Hour Speed Limit) Order 2006 No. 2006/1346. - Enabling power: Road Traffic Regulations Act 1984, ss. 84 (1) (a), 2, 122A. - Issued: 23.05.2006. Made: 10.05.2006. Coming into force: 30.05.2006. Effect: None. Territorial extent & classification: E/W. Local. - 2p.: 30 cm. - 978-0-11-074593-0 £3.00

The A249 Trunk Road (Iwade Bypass to Queensborough Improvement) (Derestriction) Order 2006 No. 2006/1955. - Enabling power: Road Traffic Regulations Act 1984, ss. 82 (2), 83 (1). - Issued: 27.05.2006. Made: 14.07.2006. Coming into force: 31.07.2006. Effect: None. Territorial extent & classification: E/W. Local. - 2p.: 30 cm. - 978-0-11-074925-9 £3.00

The A249 Trunk Road (Iwade Bypass to Queensborough Improvement) (Prohibition of Certain Classes of Traffic and Pedestrians) Order 2006 No. 2006/1347. - Enabling power: Road Traffic Regulations Act 1984, ss. 1 (1), 2 (1) (2), 122A. - Issued: 23.05.2006. Made: 10.05.2006. Coming into force: 30.05.2006. Effect: None. Territorial extent & classification: E/W. Local. - 2p.: 30 cm. - 978-0-11-074594-7 £3.00

The A249 Trunk Road (Iwade Bypass to Queensborough Improvement) (Prohibition of Left and Right Hand Turns) Order 2006 No. 2006/1345. - Enabling power: Road Traffic Regulations Act 1984, ss. 1 (1), 2 (10, 2 (2), 122A. - Issued: 23.05.2006. Made: 10.05.2006. Coming into force: 30.05.2006. Effect: None. Territorial extent & classification: E/W. Local. - 2p.: 30 cm. - 978-0-11-074592-3 £3.00

The Personal Injuries (NHS Charges) (General) and Road Traffic (NHS Charges) (Amendment) Regulations 2006 No. 2006/3388. - Enabling power: Road Traffic (NHS Charges) Act 1999, s. 16 (2) & Health and Social Care (Community Health and Standards) Act 2003, ss. 151 (8) (9), 153 (10) (11), 160 (1) to (3), 162 (3), 163, 164 (4), 195 (1) (2), sch. 10, para. 8. - Issued: 21.12.2006. Made: 12.12.2006. Laid: 19.12.2006. Coming into force: 29.01.2007. Effect: S.I. 2005/475 amended. Territorial extent & classification: E/W. General. - 8p.: 30 cm. - 978-0-11-075548-9 £3.00

The Personal Injuries (NHS Charges) (Reviews and Appeals) and Road Traffic (NHS Charges) (Reviews and Appeals) (Amendment) Regulations 2006 No. 2006/3398. - Enabling power: Road Traffic (NHS Charges) Act 1999, ss. 7 (4), 16 (2) and Health and Social Care (Community Health and Standards) Act 2003, ss. 153 (2) (5) (7) (8), 163 (1), 195 (1) (2). - Issued: 21.12.2006. Made: 12.12.2006. Laid: 19.12.2006. Coming into force: 29.01.2007. Effect: S.I. 1999/786 amended. Territorial extent & classification: E/W. General. - 12p.: 30 cm. - 978-0-11-075549-6 £3.00

The Road Traffic (NHS Charges) Amendment Regulations 2006 No. 2006/401. - Enabling power: Road Traffic (NHS Charges) Act 1999, ss. 3 (2) (4), 16 (2), 17. - Issued: 28.02.2006. Made: 19.02.2006. Laid: 28.02.2006. Coming into force: 01.04.2006. Effect: S.I. 1999/785 amended. Territorial extent & classification: E/W. General. - 2p.: 30 cm. - 978-0-11-074089-8 £3.00

The School Crossing Patrol Sign (England and Wales) Regulations 2006 No. 2006/2215. - Enabling power: Road Traffic Regulation Act 1984, s. 28 (4). - Issued: 18.08.2006. Made: 10.08.2006. Laid: 14.08.2006. Coming into force: 04.09.2006. Effect: S.I. 2002/3020 revoked. Territorial extent & classification: E/W. General. - 4p., col. ill.: 30 cm. - 978-0-11-075015-6 £3.00

Road traffic, Wales

The Road Traffic (Permitted Parking Area and Special Parking Area) (County Borough of Conwy) Order 2006 No. 2006/1791 (W.187). - Enabling power: Road Traffic Act 1991, sch. 3, paras. 1 (1), 2 (1), 3 (3). - Issued: 12.07.2006. Made: 04.07.2006. Coming into force: 01.09.2006. Effect: 1984 c. 38; 1991 c. 40 modified in relation to the parking area specified. Territorial extent & classification: W. General. - In English and Welsh. Welsh title: Gorchymyn Traffig Ffyrdd (Ardal Barcio a Ganiateir ac Ardal Barcio Arbennig) (Bwrdeistref Sirol Conwy) (Cymru) 2006. - 12p.: 30 cm. - 978-0-11-091382-7 £3.00

Road traffic, Wales: Speed limits

The A40 Trunk Road (Withybush, Haverfordwest, Pembrokeshire) (40 mph and 50 mph Speed Limits) Order 2006 No. 2006/1740 (W.180). - Enabling power: Road Traffic Regulation Act 1984, s. 84 (1) (2). - Made: 01.07.2006. Coming into force: 10.07.2006. Effect: None. Territorial extent & classification: W. Local. - In English and Welsh *Unpublished*

The A470 Trunk Road (Abercynon Roundabout, Rhondda Cynon Taf) (50 mph Speed Limit) Order 2006 No. 2006/1159 (W.114). - Enabling power: Road Traffic Regulation Act 1984, ss. 84 (1) (2). - Made: 19.04.2006. Coming into force: 28.04.2006. Effect: S.I. 1985/1760 partially revoked. Territorial extent & classification: W. Local. - In English and Welsh *Unpublished*

The A470 Trunk Road (Coryton, Cardiff to Taff's Well, Rhondda Cynon Taf) (50 MPH Speed Limit) Order 2006 No. 2006/833 (W.76). - Enabling power: Road Traffic Regulation Act 1984, s. 84 (1) (2). - Made: 18.01.2006. Coming into force: 23.01.2006. Effect: None. Territorial extent & classification: W. Local. - In English and Welsh *Unpublished*

The A483 Trunk Road (Crossgates, near Llandrindod Wells, Powys) (50 mph Speed Limit) Order 2006 No. 2006/1444 (W.143). - Enabling power: Road Traffic Regulation Act 1984, s. 84 (1) (2). - Made: 10.05.2006. Coming into force: 22.05.2006. Effect: S.I.1994/1979 revoked. Territorial extent & classification: W. Local. - In English and Welsh *Unpublished*

The A483 Trunk Road (Garth Road, Builth Wells, Powys) (30 and 40 MPH Speed Limits) Order 2006 No. 2006/1180 (W.115). - Enabling power: Road Traffic Regulation Act 1984, ss. 84 (1) (2), s. 124, sch. 9, para. 27. - Made: 25.04.2006. Coming into force: 02.05.2006. Effect: S.I. 1979/376 revoked. Territorial extent & classification: W. Local. - In English and Welsh *Unpublished*

The A487 Trunk Road (Caernarfon, Gwynedd) (Restricted Roads and 40 MPH Speed Limit) Order 1994 (Variation) Order 2006 No. 2006/2833 (W.254). - Enabling power: Road Traffic Regulation Act 1984, ss. 82 (2), 83 (1), 84 (1) (2), 124, sch. 9, para. 27. - Made: 19.10.2006. Coming into force: 01.11.2006. Effect: S.I. 1994/3330 varied & 2000/1253 (W.68) revoked. Territorial extent & classification: W. Local. - In English and Welsh *Unpublished*

The A487 Trunk Road (Tremadog, Gwynedd) (40 mph Speed Limit) Order 2006 No. 2006/1079 (W.111). - Enabling power: Road Traffic Regulation Act 1984, ss. 84 (1) (2), 124, sch. 9, para. 27. - Made: 01.04.2006. Coming into force: 10.04.2006. Effect: S.I. 1988/1266; 1999/1530 revoked. Territorial extent & classification: W. Local. - In English and Welsh *Unpublished*

The A4076 Trunk Road (Johnston, Haverfordwest, Pembrokeshire) (50 MPH Speed Limit) Order 2006 No. 2006/319 (W.40). - Enabling power: Road Traffic Regulation Act 1984, s. 84 (1) (2). - Made: 08.02.2006. Coming into force: 20.02.2006. Effect: None. Territorial extent & classification: W. Local. - In English and Welsh *Unpublished*

The Cardiff to Glan Conwy Trunk Road (A470) (Llan Ffestiniog, Blaenau Ffestiniog, Gwynedd) (30 mph Speed Limit) Order 2006 No. 2006/1083 (W.112). - Enabling power: Road Traffic Regulation Act 1984, s. 84 (1) (2). - Made: 10.04.2006. Coming into force: 18.04.2006. Effect: None. Territorial extent & classification: W. Local. - In English and Welsh *Unpublished*

The London - Holyhead Trunk Road (A5) (Bethesda, Bangor, Gwynedd) (40 MPH Speed Limit) Order 2006 No. 2006/1502 (W.146). - Enabling power: Road Traffic Regulation Act 1984, ss. 84 (1) (2), 124, sch. 9, para. 27. - Made: 07.06.2006. Coming into force: 13.06.2006. Effect: S.I. 1980/785 revoked. Territorial extent & classification: W. Local. - In English and Welsh *Unpublished*

Road traffic, Wales: Traffic regulation

The A5 & A494 Trunk Roads (Druids Junction, West of Corwen, Denbighshire) (Temporary 40 mph Speed Limits) Order 2006 No. 2006/3149 (W.290). - Enabling power: Road Traffic Regulation Act 1984, ss. 14 (1) (4). - Made: 27.11.2006. Coming into force: 04.12.2006. Effect: None. Territorial extent & classification: W. Local. - In English and Welsh *Unpublished*

The A5 Trunk Road (Carrog, Llidiart Y Parc, Corwen, Denbighshire) (Temporary 40 mph Speed Limit) Order 2006 No. 2006/2305 (W.207). - Enabling power: Road Traffic Regulation Act 1984, ss. 14 (1) (4). - Made: 24.08.2006. Coming into force: 04.09.2006. Effect: None. Territorial extent & classification: W. Local. - In English and Welsh *Unpublished*

The A5 Trunk Road (Halfway Bridge, Bethesda, Gwynedd) (Temporary 40 MPH Speed Limits) Order 2006 No. 2006/2621 (W.223). - Enabling power: Road Traffic Regulation Act 1984, ss. 14 (1) (4). - Made: 27.09.2006. Coming into force: 02.10.2006. Effect: None. Territorial extent & classification: W. Local. - In English and Welsh *Unpublished*

The A5 Trunk Road (Llyn Ogwen, North of Capel Curig, Conwy County Borough) (Temporary Traffic Restrictions) Order 2006 No. 2006/469 (W.54). - Enabling power: Road Traffic Regulation Act 1984, s. 14 (1) (4). - Made: 23.02.2006. Coming into force: 06.03.2006. Effect: None. Territorial extent & classification: W. Local. - In English and Welsh *Unpublished*

The A5 Trunk Road (Llyn Ogwen to Pont Rhyd Goch, Nr Capel Curig, Gwynedd) (Temporary Traffic Restrictions) Order 2006 No. 2006/2296 (W.205). - Enabling power: Road Traffic Regulation Act 1984, ss. 14 (1) (4). - Made: 23.08.2006. Coming into force: 04.09.2006. Effect: None. Territorial extent & classification: W. Local. - In English and Welsh *Unpublished*

The A5 Trunk Road (Pentrefoelas, Conwy) (Temporary Traffic Restrictions) Order 2006 No. 2006/603 (W.67). - Enabling power: Road Traffic Regulation Act 1984, ss. 14 (1) (4). - Made: 06.03.2006. Coming into force: 06.03.2006. Effect: None. Territorial extent & classification: W. Local. - In English and Welsh *Unpublished*

The A5 Trunk Road (Ty Nant to Dinmael (Glyn Bends), East of Cerrigydrudion, Conwy) (Temporary Traffic Restrictions) Order 2006 No. 2006/2666 (W.228). - Enabling power: Road Traffic Regulation Act 1984, s. 14 (1) (4) (5). - Made: 05.10.2006. Coming into force: 09.10.2006. Effect: None. Territorial extent & classification: W. Local. - In English and Welsh *Unpublished*

The A5 Trunk Road (Ty Nant to Dinmael (Glyn Bends), East of Cerrigydrudion, Conwy) (Temporary Traffic Restrictions) Order 2006 No. 2006/1759 (W.182). - Enabling power: Road Traffic Regulation Act 1984, s. 14 (1) (4) (5). - Made: 03.07.2006. Coming into force: 07.07.2006. Effect: None. Territorial extent & classification: W. Local. - In English and Welsh *Unpublished*

The A40/A48 Trunk Roads (West of Meifrim Junction to South of Llangunnor Roundabout and East of Pensarn Roundabout, Carmarthenshire) (Temporary 40 mph Speed Limit) Order 2006 No. 2006/2489 (W.215). - Enabling power: Road Traffic Regulation Act 1984, s. 14 (1) (4). - Made: 11.09.2006. Coming into force: 18.09.2006. Effect: None. Territorial extent & classification: W. Local. - In English and Welsh *Unpublished*

The A40 Trunk Road (Gibraltar Tunnels to County Boundary, Monmouthshire) (Temporary 40 mph Speed Limit) Order 2006 No. 2006/2306 (W.208). - Enabling power: Road Traffic Regulation Act 1984, s. 14 (1) (4). - Made: 16.08.2006. Coming into force: 03.09.2006. Effect: None. Territorial extent & classification: W. Local. - In English and Welsh *Unpublished*

The A40 Trunk Road (High Street, Fishguard, Monmouthshire) (Temporary Prohibition of Vehicles) (No. 2) Order 2006 No. 2006/2970 (W.269). - Enabling power: Road Traffic Regulation Act 1984, s. 14 (1) (4). - Made: 13.11.2006. Coming into force: 27.11.2006. Effect: None. Territorial extent & classification: W. Local. - In English and Welsh *Unpublished*

The A40 Trunk Road (High Street, Fishguard, Monmouthshire) (Temporary Prohibition of Vehicles) Order 2006 No. 2006/2276 (W.202). - Enabling power: Road Traffic Regulation Act 1984, s. 14 (1) (4). - Made: 21.08.2006. Coming into force: 04.09.2006. Effect: None. Territorial extent & classification: W. Local. - In English and Welsh *Unpublished*

The A40 Trunk Road (Llansantffraed, Talybont-on-Usk, Powys) (Temporary 30 MPH Speed Limit) Order 2006 No. 2006/2863 (W.257). - Enabling power: Road Traffic Regulation Act 1984, s. 14 (1) (4). - Made: 26.10.2006. Coming into force: 01.11.2006. Effect: None. Territorial extent & classification: W. Local. - In English and Welsh *Unpublished*

The A40 Trunk Road (Mitchel Troy Picnic Site, Southwest of Monmouth, Monmouthshire) (Prohibition and Restriction of Waiting) Order 2006 No. 2006/2614 (W.221). - Enabling power: Road Traffic Regulation Act 1984, s. 1 (1), 2 (1) (2), 4 (2). - Made: 26.09.2006. Coming into force: 02.10.2006. Effect: None. Territorial extent & classification: W. Local. - In English and Welsh *Unpublished*

The A40 Trunk Road (Mitchel Troy Picnic Site, Southwest of Monmouth, Monmouthshire) (Temporary Prohibition of Vehicles) Order 2006 No. 2006/3 (W.2). - Enabling power: Road Traffic Regulation Act 1984, s. 14 (1) (4). - Made: 04.01.2006. Coming into force: 16.01.2006. Effect: None. Territorial extent & classification: W. Local. - In English and Welsh *Unpublished*

The A40 Trunk Road (Raglan Interchange to Monmouth, Monmouthshire) (Temporary Prohibition of Cyclists) Order 2006 No. 2006/1280 (W.125). - Enabling power: Road Traffic Regulation Act 1984, s. 14 (1) (4). - Made: 09.05.2006. Coming into force: 10.05.2006. Effect: None. Territorial extent & classification: W. Local. - In English and Welsh *Unpublished*

The A40 Trunk Road (Tangiers Lay-by, Haverfordwest, Pembrokeshire) (Prohibition of Waiting and Prohibition of Right Hand Turns) Order 2006 No. 2006/2067 (W.197). - Enabling power: Road Traffic Regulation Act 1984, s. 1 (1), 2 (1) (2). - Made: 20.07.2006. Coming into force: 26.07.2006. Effect: None. Territorial extent & classification: W. Local. - In English and Welsh *Unpublished*

The A44 Trunk Road (Primrose Hill Junction, Llanbadarn Fawr, Aberystwyth, Ceredigion) (Temporary Prohibition of Vehicles) Order 2006 No. 2006/2812 (W.244). - Enabling power: Road Traffic Regulation Act 1984, s. 14 (1) (4). - Made: 13.10.2006. Coming into force: 20.10.2006. Effect: None. Territorial extent & classification: W. Local. - In English and Welsh *Unpublished*

The A48 and A483 Trunk Roads and M4 Motorway (North of Cross Hands to South of Pont Abraham, Camarthenshire) (Temporary 40 MPH Speed Limit) Order 2006 No. 2006/2295 (W.204). - Enabling power: Road Traffic Regulation Act 1984, s. 14 (1) (4) (7). - Made: 30.01.2006. Coming into force: 10.02.2006. Effect: None. Territorial extent & classification: W. Local. - In English and Welsh *Unpublished*

The A48 Trunk Road (Pontardulais Road Junction, Cross Hands, Camarthenshire) (Prohibition of U-Turns) Order 2006 No. 2006/238 (W.35). - Enabling power: Road Traffic Regulation Act 1984, ss. 1 (1), 2 (1) (2). - Made: 30.01.2006. Coming into force: 10.02.2006. Effect: None. Territorial extent & classification: W. Local. - In English and Welsh *Unpublished*

The A55 Trunk Road (Abergele, Conwy to St Asaph, Denbighshire) (Temporary Traffic Restrictions) Order 2006 No. 2006/2694 (W.229). - Enabling power: Road Traffic Regulation Act 1984, ss. 14 (1) (4). - Made: 10.10.2006. Coming into force: 16.10.2006. Effect: None. Territorial extent & classification: W. Local. - In English and Welsh *Unpublished*

The A55 Trunk Road (Bangor, Gwynedd) (Temporary Prohibition of Vehicles) Order 2006 No. 2006/1600 (W.154). - Enabling power: Road Traffic Regulation Act 1984, s. 14 (1) (4). - Made: 16.06.2006. Coming into force: 22.06.2006. Effect: None. Territorial extent & classification: W. Local. - In English and Welsh *Unpublished*

The A55 Trunk Road (Britannia Bridge, Gwynedd and Anglesey) (Temporary Prohibition of Vehicles) Order 2006 No. 2006/1271 (W.120). - Enabling power: Road Traffic Regulation Act 1984, ss. 14 (1) (4). - Made: 02.05.2006. Coming into force: 14.05.2006. Effect: None. Territorial extent & classification: W. Local. - In English and Welsh *Unpublished*

The A55 Trunk Road (Conwy Tunnel, Conwy) (Temporary Traffic Restrictions) Order 2006 No. 2006/53 (W.10). - Enabling power: Road Traffic Regulation Act 1984, ss. 14 (1) (4) (7). - Made: 10.01.2006. Coming into force: 22.02.2006. Effect: None. Territorial extent & classification: W. Local. - In English and Welsh *Unpublished*

The A55 Trunk Road (Holywell Bypass, Flintshire) (Temporary Traffic Restrictions) Order 2006 No. 2006/2274 (W.201). - Enabling power: Road Traffic Regulation Act 1984, ss. 14 (1) (4). - Made: 22.08.2006. Coming into force: 04.09.2006. Effect: None. Territorial extent & classification: W. Local. - In English and Welsh *Unpublished*

The A55 Trunk Road (Junction 1, Kingsland Roundabout, Holyhead - Junction 6, Nant Turnpike Interchange, Llangefni, Isle of Anglesey) (Temporary Prohibition of Vehicles and 40 mph Speed Limit) Order 2006 No. 2006/2532 (W.216). - Enabling power: Road Traffic Regulation Act 1984, ss. 14 (1) (4). - Made: 18.09.2006. Coming into force: 01.10.2006. Effect: None. Territorial extent & classification: W. Local. - In English and Welsh *Unpublished*

The A55 Trunk Road (Junction 33, Northop Interchange, Flintshire) (Temporary Prohibition of Vehicles) Order 2006 No. 2006/2534 (W.217). - Enabling power: Road Traffic Regulation Act 1984, s. 14 (1) (4). - Made: 15.09.2006. Coming into force: 29.09.2006. Effect: None. Territorial extent & classification: E. Local. - In English and Welsh *Unpublished*

The A55 Trunk Road (Pen-y-clip Tunnel, Conwy) (Temporary Traffic Restrictions) (No. 2) Order 2006 No. 2006/2605 (W.218). - Enabling power: Road Traffic Regulation Act 1984, ss. 14 (1) (4) (7). - Made: 22.09.2006. Coming into force: 01.10.2006. Effect: None. Territorial extent & classification: W. Local. - In English and Welsh *Unpublished*

The A55 Trunk Road (Pen-y-clip Tunnel, Conwy) (Temporary Traffic Restrictions) Order 2006 No. 2006/121 (W.15). - Enabling power: Road Traffic Regulation Act 1984, ss. 14 (1) (4) (7). - Made: 24.01.2006. Coming into force: 30.01.2006. Effect: None. Territorial extent & classification: W. Local. - In English and Welsh *Unpublished*

The A55 Trunk Road (Tal-y-bont, Bangor, Gwynedd) (Temporary 40 MPH Speed Limit) Order 2006 No. 2006/1494 (W.144). - Enabling power: Road Traffic Regulation Act 1984, ss. 14 (1) (4). - Made: 02.06.2006. Coming into force: 05.06.2006. Effect: None. Territorial extent & classification: W. Local. - In English and Welsh *Unpublished*

The A55 Trunk Road (Westbound Carriageway, Junction 24 to Junction 27, Asaph, Denbighshire) (Temporary Prohibition of Vehicles) Order 2006 No. 2006/205 (W.34). - Enabling power: Road Traffic Regulation Act 1984, ss. 14 (1) (4). - Made: 31.01.2006. Coming into force: 06.02.2006. Effect: None. Territorial extent & classification: W. Local. - In English and Welsh *Unpublished*

The A465 Trunk Road (Cefn Coed to Dowlais) (Temporary Prohibition of Cyclists and 30 mph Speed Limit) Order 2006 No. 2006/2308 (W.209). - Enabling power: Road Traffic Regulation Act 1984, s. 14 (1) (4). - Made: 16.08.2006. Coming into force: 04.09.2006. Effect: None. Territorial extent & classification: W. Local. - In English and Welsh *Unpublished*

The A465 Trunk Road (Galon Uchaf, Merthyr Tydfil) (Temporary Prohibition of Vehicles) Order 2006 No. 2006/240 (W.36). - Enabling power: Road Traffic Regulation Act 1984, s. 14 (1) (4). - Made: 02.02.2006. Coming into force: 10.02.2006. Effect: None. Territorial extent & classification: W. Local. - In English and Welsh *Unpublished*

The A465 Trunk Road (Galon Uchaf, Merthyr Tydfil) (Temporary Prohibition of Vehicles) Order 2006 No. 2006/2371 (W.211). - Enabling power: Road Traffic Regulation Act 1984, s. 14 (1) (4). - Made: 04.09.2006. Coming into force: 18.09.2006. Effect: None. Territorial extent & classification: W. Local. - In English and Welsh *Unpublished*

The A465 Trunk Road (Garnlydan, Brynmawr, Blaenau Gwent) (Prohibition of Right Hand Turns and U-Turns) Order 2006 No. 2006/318 (W.39). - Enabling power: Road Traffic Regulation Act 1984, ss. 1 (1), 2 (1) (2). - Made: 09.02.2006. Coming into force: 14.02.2006. Effect: None. Territorial extent & classification: W. Local. - In English and Welsh *Unpublished*

Road traffic, Wales: Traffic regulation

The A465 Trunk Road (Gilwern to Abergavenny, Monmouthshire) (Temporary Prohibition of Pedestrians) Order 2006 No. 2006/146 (W.21). - Enabling power: Road Traffic Regulation Act 1984, s. 14 (1) (4). - Made: 25.01.2006. Coming into force: 27.01.2006. Effect: None. Territorial extent & classification: W. Local. - In English and Welsh *Unpublished*

The A465 Trunk Road (Govilon, Monmouthshire) (Temporary Prohibition of Vehicles) (No. 2) Order 2006 No. 2006/3219 (W.292). - Enabling power: Road Traffic Regulation Act 1984, s. 14 (1) (4). - Made: 05.12.2006. Coming into force: 14.12.2006. Effect: None. Territorial extent & classification: W. Local. - In English and Welsh *Unpublished*

The A465 Trunk Road (Govilon, Monmouthshire) (Temporary Prohibition of Vehicles) Order 2006 No. 2006/1443 (W.142). - Enabling power: Road Traffic Regulation Act 1984, s. 14 (1) (4). - Made: 31.05.2006. Coming into force: 08.06.2006. Effect: None. Territorial extent & classification: W. Local. - In English and Welsh *Unpublished*

The A465 Trunk Road (Nant Ffrwd Viaduct, Near Merthyr Tydfil) (Temporary 40 MPH Speed Limit) Order 2006 No. 2006/2795 (W.234). - Enabling power: Road Traffic Regulation Act 1984, s. 14 (1) (4). - Made: 17.10.2006. Coming into force: 31.10.2006. Effect: None. Territorial extent & classification: W. Local. - In English and Welsh *Unpublished*

The A465 Trunk Road (Nantybwch, Tredegar, Blaenau Gwent) (Temporary Traffic Restrictions) Order 2006 No. 2006/910 (W.86). - Enabling power: Road Traffic Regulation Act 1984, s. 14 (1) (4). - Made: 21.03.2006. Coming into force: 27.03.2006. Effect: None. Territorial extent & classification: W. Local. - In English and Welsh *Unpublished*

The A465 Trunk Road (Neath Interchange, Saltings Viaduct, Neath Port Talbot) (Temporary Prohibition of Vehicles) Order 2006 No. 2006/2365 (W.210). - Enabling power: Road Traffic Regulation Act 1984, s. 14 (1) (4). - Made: 29.08.2006. Coming into force: 10.09.2006. Effect: None. Territorial extent & classification: W. Local. - In English and Welsh *Unpublished*

The A465 Trunk Road (Pont Neath Vaughan Viaduct, Rhondda Cynon Taff) (Temporary 40 MPH Speed Limit) Order 2006 No. 2006/145 (W.20). - Enabling power: Road Traffic Regulation Act 1984, s. 14 (1) (4). - Made: 25.01.2006. Coming into force: 06.02.2006. Effect: None. Territorial extent & classification: W. Local. - In English and Welsh *Unpublished*

The A470 Trunk Road (Coryton, Cardiff) (Prohibition of Waiting) Order 2006 No. 2006/1158 (W.113). - Enabling power: Road Traffic Regulation Act 1984, ss. 1 (1), 2 (1) (2), 4 (2). - Made: 21.04.2006. Coming into force: 24.04.2006. Effect: None. Territorial extent & classification: W. Local. - In English and Welsh *Unpublished*

The A470 Trunk Road (Coryton, Cardiff to Nantgarw Junction, Rhondda Cynon Taf) (Prohibition of Cyclists) Order 2006 No. 2006/1181 (W.116). - Enabling power: Road Traffic Regulation Act 1984, ss. 1 (1), 2 (1) (2). - Made: 25.04.2006. Coming into force: 02.05.2006. Effect: None. Territorial extent & classification: W. Local. - In English and Welsh *Unpublished*

The A470 Trunk Road (Glan y Mor to Pentrefelin, Conwy) (Temporary Traffic Restrictions) Order 2006 No. 2006/581 (W.65). - Enabling power: Road Traffic Regulation Act 1984, s. 14 (1) (4). - Made: 03.03.2006. Coming into force: 06.03.2006. Effect: None. Territorial extent & classification: W. Local. - In English and Welsh *Unpublished*

The A470 Trunk Road (Nantgarw Interchange, Rhondda Cynon Taf) (Temporary Prohibition of Vehicles) Order 2006 No. 2006/403 (W.52). - Enabling power: Road Traffic Regulation Act 1984, s. 14 (1) (4). - Made: 14.02.2006. Coming into force: 25.02.2006. Effect: None. Territorial extent & classification: W. Local. - In English and Welsh *Unpublished*

The A470 Trunk Road (Nantgarw Interchange, Rhondda Cynon Taf) (Temporary Traffic Restrictions) Order 2006 No. 2006/2487 (W.213). - Enabling power: Road Traffic Regulation Act 1984, s. 14 (1) (4). - Made: 11.09.2006. Coming into force: 16.09.2006. Effect: None. Territorial extent & classification: W. Local. - In English and Welsh *Unpublished*

The A470 Trunk Road (Nantgarw Interchange to Bridge Street Interchange, Rhondda Cynon Taff) (Temporary 50 MPH Speed Limit and Prohibition of Cyclists) Order 2006 No. 2006/2903 (W.259). - Enabling power: Road Traffic Regulation Act 1984, s. 14 (1) (4). - Made: 31.10.2006. Coming into force: 13.11.2006. Effect: None. Territorial extent & classification: W. Local. - In English and Welsh *Unpublished*

The A477 Trunk Road (Backe Road Junction, West of St. Clears, Carmarthenshire) (Temporary 10 MPH Speed Limit) Order 2006 No. 2006/2419 (W.212). - Enabling power: Road Traffic Regulation Act 1984, s. 14 (1) (4). - Made: 07.09.2006. Coming into force: 18.01.2006. Effect: None. Territorial extent & classification: W. Local. - In English and Welsh *Unpublished*

The A483 Trunk Road (Gresford, Wrexham) (Temporary Traffic Restrictions) Order 2006 No. 2006/374 (W.50). - Enabling power: Road Traffic Regulation Act 1984, s. 14 (1) (4). - Made: 14.02.2006. Coming into force: 20.02.2006. Effect: None. Territorial extent & classification: W. Local. - In English and Welsh *Unpublished*

The A483 Trunk Road (Rhosmaen/Bridge Street, Llandeilo, Carmarthenshire) (Temporary Traffic Restrictions) Order 2006 No. 2006/926 (W.88). - Enabling power: Road Traffic Regulation Act 1984, s. 14 (1) (4). - Made: 24.03.2006. Coming into force: 27.03.2006. Effect: None. Territorial extent & classification: W. Local. - In English and Welsh *Unpublished*

The A483 Trunk Road (Rhosmaen Street, Llandeilo, Carmarthenshire) (Temporary Prohibition of Vehicles) Order 2006 No. 2006/2277 (W.203). - Enabling power: Road Traffic Regulation Act 1984, s. 14 (1) (4). - Made: 21.08.2006. Coming into force: 04.09.2006. Effect: None. Territorial extent & classification: W. Local. - In English and Welsh *Unpublished*

The A487 Trunk Road (Mill Street, Aberystwyth, Ceredigion) (Temporary Prohibition of Vehicles) Order 2006 No. 2006/2 (W.1). - Enabling power: Road Traffic Regulation Act 1984, s. 14 (1) (4). - Made: 03.01.2006. Coming into force: 09.01.2006. Effect: None. Territorial extent & classification: W. Local. - In English and Welsh *Unpublished*

The A487 Trunk Road (Vergam Terrace, Fishguard, Pembrokeshire) (Temporary Prohibition of Vehicles) Order 2006 No. 2006/2624 (W.224). - Enabling power: Road Traffic Regulation Act 1984, s. 14 (1) (4). - Made: 02.10.2006. Coming into force: 16.10.2006. Effect: None. Territorial extent & classification: W. Local. - In English and Welsh *Unpublished*

The A487 Trunk Road (West Street, Fishguard, Pembrokeshire) (Temporary Prohibition of Vehicles) Order 2006 No. 2006/2488 (W.214). - Enabling power: Road Traffic Regulation Act 1984, s. 14 (1) (4). - Made: 11.09.2006. Coming into force: 25.09.2006. Effect: None. Territorial extent & classification: W. Local. - In English and Welsh *Unpublished*

The A494/A550 Trunk Road (Deeside, Flintshire) (Temporary 40 MPH Speed Limit) Order 2006 No. 2006/2834 (W.255). - Enabling power: Road Traffic Regulation Act 1984, ss. 14 (1) (4). - Made: 24.10.2006. Coming into force: 31.10.2006. Effect: None. Territorial extent & classification: W. Local. - In English and Welsh *Unpublished*

The A494/A550 Trunk Road (Deeside Park Interchange, Queensferry) (Temporary 40 and 50 mph Variable Speed Limit) Order 2006 No. 2006/951 (W.100). - Enabling power: Road Traffic Regulation Act 1984, s. 14 (1) (4). - Made: 28.03.2006. Coming into force: 01.04.2006. Effect: None. Territorial extent & classification: W. Local. - In English and Welsh *Unpublished*

The A494 Trunk Road (Ruthin, Denbighshire) (Temporary 30 mph Speed Limit) Order 2006 No. 2006/1286 (W.126). - Enabling power: Road Traffic Regulation Act 1984, s. 14 (1) (4). - Made: 10.05.2006. Coming into force: 22.05.2006. Effect: None. Territorial extent & classification: W. Local. - In English and Welsh *Unpublished*

The A494 Trunk Road (Ruthin, Denbighshire) (Temporary Traffic Restrictions) Order 2006 No. 2006/2884 (W.258). - Enabling power: Road Traffic Regulation Act 1984, ss. 14 (1) (4). - Made: 30.10.2006. Coming into force: 06.11.2006. Effect: None. Territorial extent & classification: W. Local. - In English and Welsh *Unpublished*

The A4042 Trunk Road (Little Mill Junction, Monmouthshire) (Temporary 40 MPH Speed Limit) Order 2006 No. 2006/2273 (W.200). - Enabling power: Road Traffic Regulation Act 1984, ss. 14 (1) (4). - Made: 21.08.2006. Coming into force: 03.09.2006. Effect: None. Territorial extent & classification: W. Local. - In English and Welsh *Unpublished*

The A4060 Trunk Road (Triangle Business Park Roundabout to Mountain Hare Roundabout, Merthyr Tydfil) (Temporary 40 MPH Speed Limit) Order 2006 No. 2006/348 (W.43). - Enabling power: Road Traffic Regulation Act 1984, s. 14 (1) (4). - Made: 01.02.2006. Coming into force: 10.02.2006. Effect: None. Territorial extent & classification: W. Local. - In English and Welsh *Unpublished*

The London to Fishguard Trunk Road (A40) (Llansantffraed, Talybont-on-Usk Junction Improvement Side Roads) Order 2006 No. 2006/1708 (W.170). - Enabling power: Highways Act 1980, ss. 14, 125, 268. - Made: 19.06.2006. Coming into force: 28.06.2006. Effect: None. Territorial extent & classification: W. Local. - In English and Welsh *Unpublished*

##########**The London to Holyhead Trunk Road (A5) (Pont Melin Rug Improvement) Order 2006 No. 2006/3115 (W.288).** - Enabling power: Highways Act 1980, s. 10. - Made: 23.11.2006. Coming into force: 07.12.2006. Effect: S.I. 1939/400 amended. Territorial extent & classification: W. Local. - In English and Welsh *Unpublished*

The M4 Motorway (Brombil Lane Underpass (Junction 39), Neath Port Talbot) (Temporary Traffic Restrictions) Order 2006 No. 2006/299 (W.38). - Enabling power: Road Traffic Regulation Act 1984, s. 14 (1) (4) (7). - Made: 08.02.2006. Coming into force: 17.02.2006. Effect: None. Territorial extent & classification: W. Local. - In English and Welsh *Unpublished*

The M4 Motorway (Brynglas Tunnels, Newport) (Temporary Prohibition of Vehicles and 40MPH Speed Limit) Order 2006 No. 2006/32 (W.6). - Enabling power: Road Traffic Regulation Act 1984, s. 14 (1) (4) (7). - Made: 09.01.2006. Coming into force: 13.01.2006. Effect: None. Territorial extent & classification: W. Local. - In English and Welsh *Unpublished*

The M4 Motorway (Eastbound and Westbound Exit Slip Roads at Junction 26, Malpas, Newport) (Temporary Prohibition of Vehicles) Order 2006 No. 2006/402 (W.51). - Enabling power: Road Traffic Regulation Act 1984, s. 14 (1) (4). - Made: 20.02.2006. Coming into force: 22.02.2006. Effect: None. Territorial extent & classification: W. Local. - In English and Welsh *Unpublished*

Road traffic, Wales: Traffic regulation

The M4 Motorway (Eastbound and Westbound Slip Roads at Junction 38, Margam, Neath Port Talbot) (Temporary Prohibition of Vehicles) Order 2006 No. 2006/411 (W.53). - Enabling power: Road Traffic Regulation Act 1984, s. 14 (1) (4). - Made: 21.02.2006. Coming into force: 03.03.2006. Effect: None. Territorial extent & classification: W. Local. - In English and Welsh *Unpublished*

The M4 Motorway (Eastbound Off-Slip Road at Junction 34, Miskin, Rhondda Cynon Taf and Vale of Glamorgan) (Temporary Prohibition of Vehicles) Order 2006 No. 2006/2606 (W.219). - Enabling power: Road Traffic Regulation Act 1984, s. 14 (1) (4). - Made: 22.09.2006. Coming into force: 30.09.2006. Effect: None. Territorial extent & classification: W. Local. - In English and Welsh *Unpublished*

The M4 Motorway (Eastbound On-Slip Road at Junction 36, Sarn, Bridgend) (Temporary Prohibition of Vehicles) Order 2006 No. 2006/2615 (W.222). - Enabling power: Road Traffic Regulation Act 1984, s. 14 (1) (4). - Made: 26.09.2006. Coming into force: 06.10.2006. Effect: None. Territorial extent & classification: W. Local. - In English and Welsh *Unpublished*

The M4 Motorway (Junction 24, Coldra, Newport) (Temporary Prohibition of Vehicles) (No. 2) Order 2006 No. 2006/4 (W.3). - Enabling power: Road Traffic Regulation Act 1984, s. 14 (1) (4). - Made: 04.01.2006. Coming into force: 16.01.2006. Effect: None. Territorial extent & classification: W. Local. - In English and Welsh *Unpublished*

The M4 Motorway (Junction 24, Coldra, Newport) (Temporary Prohibition of Vehicles) Order 2006 No. 2006/52 (W.9). - Enabling power: Road Traffic Regulation Act 1984, s. 14 (1) (4). - Made: 06.01.2006. Coming into force: 16.01.2006. Effect: None. Territorial extent & classification: W. Local. - In English and Welsh *Unpublished*

The M4 Motorway (Junction 24, Coldra, to East of Junction 23A, Magor, Newport) (Temporary Prohibition of Vehicles and 50 MPH Speed Limit) Order 2006 No. 2006/2297 (W.206). - Enabling power: Road Traffic Regulation Act 1984, s. 14 (1) (4). - Made: 23.08.2006. Coming into force: 03.09.2006. Effect: None. Territorial extent & classification: W. Local. - In English and Welsh *Unpublished*

The M4 Motorway (Junction 32 Coryton, Cardiff - Junction 33 Capel Llanilltern, Cardiff) (Temporary Prohibition of Vehicles and 50 MPH Speed Limit) Order 2006 No. 2006/1637 (W.155). - Enabling power: Road Traffic Regulation Act 1984, s. 14 (1) (4). - Made: 20.06.2006. Coming into force: 01.07.2006. Effect: None. Territorial extent & classification: W. Local. - In English and Welsh *Unpublished*

The M4 Motorway (Junction 43, Llandarcy, Neath Port Talbot) (Temporary Prohibition of Vehicles) Order 2006 No. 2006/513 (W.62). - Enabling power: Road Traffic Regulation Act 1984, s. 14 (1) (4). - Made: 27.02.2006. Coming into force: 03.03.2006. Effect: None. Territorial extent & classification: W. Local *Unpublished*

The M4 Motorway (Junction 43, Llandarcy, Neath Port Talbot) (Temporary Prohibition of Vehicles) Order 2006 No. 2006/3436 (W.312). - Enabling power: Road Traffic Regulation Act 1984, s. 14 (1) (4). - Made: 21.12.2006. Coming into force: 12.01.2007. Effect: None. Territorial extent & classification: W. Local. - In English and Welsh *Unpublished*

The M4 Motorway (Junction 45, Ynysforgan to Junction 46, Llangyfelach, Swansea) (Temporary Traffic Restrictions) Order 2006 No. 2006/911 (W.87). - Enabling power: Road Traffic Regulation Act 1984, s. 14 (1) (4) (7). - Made: 22.032006. Coming into force: 24.03.2006. Effect: None. Territorial extent & classification: W. Local. - In English and Welsh *Unpublished*

The M4 Motorway (Westbound Exit and Eastbound Entry Slip Roads at Junction 25A, Grove Park, Newport) (Temporary Prohibition of Vehicles) Order 2006 No. 2006/118 (W.33). - Enabling power: Road Traffic Regulation Act 1984, s. 14 (1) (4). - Made: 31.01.2006. Coming into force: 08.02.2006. Effect: None. Territorial extent & classification: W. Local. - In English and Welsh *Unpublished*

The M4 Motorway (Westbound Off Slip Road at Junction 42, Earlswood, Neath Port Talbot) (Temporary Prohibition of Vehicles) Order 2006 No. 2006/509 (W.61). - Enabling power: Road Traffic Regulation Act 1984, s. 14 (1) (4). - Made: 28.02.2006. Coming into force: 13.03.2006. Effect: None. Territorial extent & classification: W. Local *Unpublished*

The M4 Motorway (Westbound On-Slip Road at Junction 39, Groes, Neath Port Talbot) (Temporary Prohibition of Vehicles) Order 2006 No. 2006/350 (W.44). - Enabling power: Road Traffic Regulation Act 1984, s. 14 (1) (4). - Made: 14.02.2006. Coming into force: 17.02.2006. Effect: None. Territorial extent & classification: W. Local. - In English and Welsh *Unpublished*

Rural affairs, England and Wales

The Natural Environment and Rural Communities Act 2006 (Commencement No. 3 and Transitional Provisions) Order 2006 No. 2006/2541 (C.86). - Enabling power: Natural Environment and Rural Communities Act 2006, s. 107 (2) (6) (b) (7) (b) (8) (b) (c). Bringing into operation various provisions of the 2006 Act on 01.10.2006, in accord. with art. 2. - Issued: 28.09.2006. Made: 20.09.2006. Effect: None. Territorial extent & classification: UK [but parts E/W only]. General. - 8p.: 30 cm. - 978-0-11-075132-0 £3.00

Savings banks

The National Savings Bank (Amendment) Regulations 2006 No. 2006/1066. - Enabling power: National Savings Bank Act 1971, s. 2. - Issued: 19.05.2006. Made: 16.05.2006. Laid: 16.05.2006. Coming into force: 06.06.2006 except for regs 4, 5, 6, 7, 8, 12, 13; 01.10.2006 for regs 4, 5, 6, 7, 8, 12, 13. Effect: S.I. 1972/764 amended. Territorial extent & classification: E/W/S/NI. General. - 4p.: 30 cm. - 978-0-11-074582-4 £3.00

Sea fisheries, England

The Sea Fishing (Enforcement of Annual Community and Third Country Fishing Measures) (England) Order 2006 No. 2006/1970. - Enabling power: Fisheries Act 1981, s. 30 (2). - Issued: 27.07.2006. Made: 18.07.2006. Laid: 24.07.2006. Coming into force: 15.08.2006. Effect: S.I. 2005/617 amended & S.I. 2004/1237 revoked. Territorial extent & classification: E. General. - EC note: This Order makes provision for the enforcement of certain restrictions and obligations relating to sea fishing by Community vessels and third country vessels which are contained in Council Regulation (EC) no. 51/2006. - 16p.: 30 cm. - 978-0-11-074909-9 £3.00

The Sea Fishing (Marking and Identification of Passive Fishing Gear and Beam Trawls) (England) Order 2006 No. 2006/1549. - Enabling power: Fisheries Act 1981, s. 30 (2). - Issued: 22.06.2006. Made: 13.06.2006. Laid: 16.06.2006. Coming into force: 10.07.2006. Effect: None. Territorial extent & classification: E. General. - EC note: This Order makes provision for the enforcement of Community restrictions and other obligations relating to the marking and identification of passive gear and beam trawls deployed by fishing vessels as set out in Commission Regulation (EC) No. 356/2005 as amended. In the context of this Order passive gear means longlines, gillnets, entangling nets, trammel nets, drifting gillnets and any associated anchoring, floating or navigational gear. - 8p.: 30 cm. - 978-0-11-074713-2 £3.00

The Sea Fishing (Restriction on Days at Sea) (Monitoring, Inspection and Surveillance) Order 2006 No. 2006/1327. - Enabling power: Fisheries Act 1981, s. 30 (2). - Issued: 25.05.2006. Made: 11.05.2006. Laid: 12.05.2006. Coming into force: 01.06.2006. Effect: S. I. 2005/393 amended. Territorial extent & classification: E. General. - EC note: This Order provides for the administration and enforcement of the provisions of Annex IIA and IIC ("the Annexes") to Council Regulation (EC) no. 51/2006 fixing for 2006 the fishing opportunities and associated conditions for certain fish stocks and groups of fish stocks, applicable in Community waters and for Community vessels, in waters where catch limitations are required. - 16p.: 30 cm. - 978-0-11-074577-0 £3.00

Sea fisheries, Wales

The Fishing Boats (Satellite-Tracking Devices) (Wales) Scheme 2006 No. 2006/2799 (W.238). - Enabling power: Fisheries Act 1981, s. 15. - Issued: 30.10.2006. Made: 18.10.2006. Coming into force: 20.10.2006. Effect: None. Territorial extent & classification: W. General. - EC note: These Regs make provision for funding satellite-tracking devices on fishing boats (over 15 metres) which are administered in Wales as a result of Commission regulation 2244/2003. - In English and Welsh. Welsh title: Cynllun Cychod Pysgota (Dyfeisiau Olrhain Drwy Loeren) (Cymru) 2006. - 12p.: 30 cm. - 978-0-11-091414-5 £3.00

The Registration of Fish Buyers and Sellers and Designation of Fish Auction Sites (Wales) Regulations 2006 No. 2006/1495 (W.145). - Enabling power: European Communities Act 1972, s. 2 (2). - Issued: 19.06.2006. Made: 06.06.2006. Coming into force: 09.06.2006. Effect: None. Territorial extent & classification: W. General. - EC note: These Regs make provision for the administration and enforcement of art. 22 of Council Regulation 2371/2002 (the CFP Regulation) and art. 9 of Council Regulation 2847/93 which impose requirements relating to the first marketing and purchasing of fish (first sale fish). - In English & Welsh. Welsh title: Rheoliadau Cofrestru Prynwyr a Gwerthwyr Pysgod a Dynodi Safleoedd Arwerthu Pysgod (Cymru) 2006. - 20p.: 30 cm. - 978-0-11-091349-0 £3.50

The Sea Fisheries (Northern Hake Stock) Wales 2006 No. 2006/1796 (W.191). - Enabling power: Fisheries Act 1981, s. 30 (2). - Issued: 13.07.2006. Made: 05.07.2006. Coming into force: 07.07.2006. Effect: None. Territorial extent & classification: W. General. - In English & Welsh. Welsh title: Gorchymyn Pysgota Môr (Stoc o Gedduon Gogleddol) (Cymru) 2006. - 16p.: 30 cm. - 978-0-11-091381-0 £3.00

The Sea Fishing (Enforcement of Community Satellite Monitoring Measures) (Wales) Order 2006 No. 2006/2798 (W.237). - Enabling power: Fisheries Act 1981, s. 30 (2). - Issued: 26.10.2006. Made: 18.10.2006. Coming into force: 20.10.2006. Effect: S.I. 2000/1078 (W.71); 2002/677 (W.74) revoked. Territorial extent & classification: W. General. - With correction slip dated February 2007 which corrects the made date to 18.10.2006. EC note: Provides for the enforcement in Wales of Commission Regulation (EC) 2244/2003 laying down detaiiled provisions regarding satellite-based Vessel Monitoring Systems. - In English and Welsh. Welsh title: Gorchymyn Pysgota Môr (Gorfodi Mesurau Cymunedol ar gyfer Monitro drwy Loeren) (Cymru) 2006. - 16p.: 30 cm. - 978-0-11-091412-1 £3.00

Secure training centres, England and Wales

The Criminal Justice and Public Order Act 1994 (Suspension of Custody Officer Certificate) (Amendment) Regulations 2006 No. 2006/1050. - Enabling power: Criminal Justice and Public Order Act 1994, sch. 2, para. 3. - Issued: 10.04.2006. Made: 03.04.2006. Laid: 07.04.2006. Coming into force: 02.05.2006. Effect: S.I. 1998/474 amended. Territorial extent & classification: E/W. General. - This Statutory Instrument has been made in consequence of a defect in S.I. 1998/474 (ISBN 0110656067) and is being issued free of charge to all known recipients of that Statutory Instrument. - 2p.: 30 cm. - 978-0-11-074467-4 £3.00

Security industry

The Private Security Industry Act 2001 (Duration of Licence) (No. 2) Order 2006 No. 2006/3411. - Enabling power: Private Security Industry Act 2001, s. 8 (8) (b). - Issued: 05.01.2007. Made: 18.12.2006. Laid: 21.12.2006. Coming into force: 01.02.2007. Effect: S.I. 2006/427 revoked with savings. Territorial extent & classification: E/W/S. General. - 4p.: 30 cm. - 978-0-11-075563-2 £3.00

The Private Security Industry (Licences) (Amendment) Regulations 2006 No. 2006/3410. - Enabling power: Private Security Industry Act 2001, ss. 8, 9, 24 (1) (5). - Issued: 09.01.2007. Made: 18.12.2006. Laid: 21.12.2006. Coming into force: 01.02.2007. Effect: S.I. 2004/255 amended. Territorial extent & classification: E/W/S. General. - 4p.: 30 cm. - 978-0-11-075592-2 £3.00

Security industry, England and Wales

The Private Security Industry Act 2001 (Amendments to Schedule 2) Order 2006 No. 2006/1831. - Enabling power: Private Security Industry Act 2001, sch. 2, paras 1 (2), 7 (2). - Issued: 14.07.2006. Made: 10.07.2006. Coming into force: 11.07.2006. Effect: 2001 c. 12 amended. Territorial extent & classification: E/W. General. - Supersedes draft SI (ISBN 011074697X) issued 19.06.2006. - 8p.: 30 cm. - 978-0-11-074823-8 £3.00

The Private Security Industry Act 2001 (Approved Contractor Scheme) Regulations 2006 No. 2006/425. - Enabling power: Private Security Industry Act 2001, s. 15 (3) (a) (8). - Issued: 28.02.2006. Made: 15.02.2006. Laid: 27.02.2006. Coming into force: 20.03.2006. Effect: None. Territorial extent & classification: E/W. General. - 4p.: 30 cm. - 978-0-11-074091-1 £3.00

The Private Security Industry Act 2001 (Commencement No. 10) Order 2006 No. 2006/392 (C.10). - Enabling power: Private Security Industry Act 2001, s. 26 (2). Bringing into operation various provisions of the 2001 Act on 20.03.2006. - Issued: 24.02.2006. Made: 15.02.2006. Effect: None. Territorial extent & classification: E/W. General. - 4p.: 30 cm. - 978-0-11-074084-3 £3.00

The Private Security Industry Act 2001 (Designated Activities) (Amendment No. 2) Order 2006 No. 2006/1804. - Enabling power: Private Security Industry Act 2001, ss. 3 (3). - Issued: 11.07.2006. Made: 06.07.2006. Laid: 07.07.2006. Coming into force: 11.07.2006. Effect: S.I. 2006/426 amended & S.I. 2006/824 revoked. Territorial extent & classification: E/W. General. - This Statutory Instrument is being issued free of charge to all known recipients of S.I. 2006/824 (ISBN 0110743601). - 2p.: 30 cm. - 978-0-11-074815-3 £3.00

The Private Security Industry Act 2001 (Designated Activities) (Amendment) Order 2006 No. 2006/824. - Enabling power: Private Security Industry Act 2001, ss. 3 (3), 24 (5). - Issued: 23.03.2006. Made: 17.03.2006. Laid: 17.03.2006. Coming into force: 20.03.2006. Effect: S.I. 2006/426 amended. Territorial extent & classification: E/W. General. - This Statutory Instrument has been made in consequence of a defect in SI 2006/426 and is being issued free of charge to all known recipients of that Statutory Instrument. Revoked by S.I. 2006/1804 (ISBN 0110748158). - 4p.: 30 cm. - 978-0-11-074360-8 £3.00

The Private Security Industry Act 2001 (Designated Activities) Order 2006 No. 2006/426. - Enabling power: Private Security Industry Act 2001, s. 3 (3). - Issued: 28.02.2006. Made: 15.02.2006. Laid: 27.02.2006. Coming into force: 20.03.2006. Effect: S.I. 2005/2251 revoked. Territorial extent & classification: E/W. General. - 2p.: 30 cm. - 978-0-11-074093-5 £3.00

The Private Security Industry Act 2001 (Duration of Licence) Order 2006 No. 2006/427. - Enabling power: Private Security Industry Act 2001, s. 8 (8) (b). - Issued: 28.02.2006. Made: 15.02.2006. Laid: 27.02.2006. Coming into force: 20.03.2006. Effect: S.I. 2005/235 revoked. Territorial extent & classification: E/W. General. - 4p.: 30 cm. - 978-0-11-074092-8 £3.00

The Private Security Industry Act 2001 (Exemption) (Aviation Security) Regulations 2006 No. 2006/428. - Enabling power: Private Security Industry Act 2001, s. 4. - Issued: 28.02.2006. Made: 18.02.2006. Laid: 27.02.2006. Coming into force: 20.03.2006. Effect: None. Territorial extent & classification: E/W. General. - 4p.: 30 cm. - 978-0-11-074094-2 £3.00

Seeds

The Forest Reproductive Material (Great Britain) (Amendment) Regulations 2006 No. 2006/2530. - Enabling power: European Communities Act 1972, s. 2 (2). - Issued: 20.09.2006. Made: 15.09.2006. Laid: 18.09.2006. Coming into force: 09.10.2006. Effect: S.I. 2002/3026 amended. Territorial extent & classification: E/W/S. General. - EC note: Implements Commission Decision 2005/942/EC authorising Member States to take decisions under Directive 1999/105/EC on assurances afforded in respect of forest reproductive material produced in third countries and Commission Regulation 69/2004/EC authorising derogations from certain provisions of Council Directive 1999/105/EC in respect of the marketing of forest reproductive material derived from certain basic material. - 8p.: 30 cm. - 978-0-11-075122-1 £3.00

Seeds, England

The Cereal Seed (England) and Fodder Plant Seed (England) (Amendment) Regulations 2006 No. 2006/1678. - Enabling power: Plant Varieties and Seeds Act 1964, ss. 16 (1) (1A) (3) (4). - Issued: 30.06.2006. Made: 25.06.2006. Laid: 28.06.2006. Coming into force: 19.07.2006. Effect: S.I. 2002/3172, 3173 amended. Territorial extent & classification: E. General. - EC note: These regulations implement Commission Directive 2006/55/EC, amending Annex III to Council Directive as regards the maximum weight of seed lots. - 2p.: 30 cm. - 978-0-11-074754-5 £3.00

The Seed (England) (Amendments for Tests and Trials etc.) Regulations 2006 No. 2006/2314. - Enabling power: Plant Varieties and Seeds Act 1964, ss. 16 (1) (1A) (2) (3) (5), 36. - Issued: 04.09.2006. Made: 24.08.2006. Laid: 30.08.2006. Coming into force: 23.09.2006. Effect: S.I. 2002/3171, 3172, 3173, 3174, 3175 amended. Territorial extent & classification: E. General. - With correction slip dated September 2006. EC note: These regulations give effect to Commission Decision 2004/842/EC. - 20p.: 30 cm. - 978-0-11-075051-4 £3.50

The Seed Potatoes (England) Regulations 2006 No. 2006/1161. - Enabling power: Plant Varieties and Seeds Act 1964, ss. 16 (1) (1A) (2) (3) (4) (5), 36. - Issued: 02.05.2006. Made: 21.04.2006. Laid: 25.04.2006. Coming into force: 16.05.2006. Effect: 1964 c. 14 modified & S.I. 1991/2206; 1992/1031; 1993/1878; 1994/2592; 1997/1474; 2000/1788 revoked. Territorial extent & classification: Extends to E/W but applies only to E. General. - EC note: Give effect to Council Directive 2002/56/EC on the marketing of seed potatoes, and Commission Decision 2004/842/EC which sets out the conditions on which seed potatoes which have not yet been added to a national list may be marketed for test and trial purposes. - 36p.: 30 cm. - 978-0-11-074521-3 £6.50

The Seed Potatoes (Fees) (England) Regulations 2006 No. 2006/1160. - Enabling power: Plant Varieties and Seeds Act 1964, s. 16 (1) (1A) (e). - Issued: 28.04.2006. Made: 21.04.2006. Laid: 25.04.2006. Coming into force: 17.05.2006. Effect: S.I. 2004/1316 revoked. Territorial extent & classification: Extends to E/W but applies only to E. General. - 4p.: 30 cm. - 978-0-11-074520-6 £3.00

Seeds, Wales

The Cereal Seed (Wales) and Fodder Plant Seed (Wales) (Amendment) Regulations 2006 No. 2006/3250 (W.294). - Enabling power: Plant Varieties and Seeds Act 1964, s. 16 (1) (1A) (3) (4). - Issued: 13.12.2006. Made: 05.12.2006. Coming into force: 20.12.2006. Effect: S.I. 2005/1207 (W. 79), 3036 (W. 224) amended. Territorial extent & classification: W. General. - EC note: Implements Commission Directive 2006/55/EC amending Annex III to Council Directive 66/402/EEC as regards the maximum weight of seed lots. - In English and Welsh. Welsh title: Rheoliadau Hadau Yd (Cymru) a Hadau Planhigion Porthiant (Cymru) (Diwygio) 2006. - 4p.: 30 cm. - 978-0-11-091465-7 £3.00

The Seed Potatoes (Fees) (Wales) (No. 2) Regulations 2006 No. 2006/2961 (W.267). - Enabling power: Plant Varieties and Seeds Act 1964, s. 16 (1) (1A) (e). - Issued: 20.11.2006. Made: 07.11.2006. Coming into force: 16.11.2006. Effect: S.I. 2006/519 (W.63) revoked. Territorial extent & classification: W. General. - In English and Welsh. Welsh title: Rheoliadau Tatws Hadyd (Ffioedd) (Cymru) (Rhif 2) 2006. - 8p.: 30 cm. - 978-0-11-091436-7 £3.00

The Seed Potatoes (Fees) (Wales) Regulations 2006 No. 2006/519 (W.63). - Enabling power: Plant Varieties and Seeds Act 1964, s. 16 (1) (1A) (e). - Issued: 09.03.2006. Made: 28.02.2006. Coming into force: 03.03.2006. Effect: S.I. 1998/1228 revoked in relation to Wales. Territorial extent & classification: W. General. - Revoked by S.I. 2006/2961 (W.267) (ISBN 0110914368). - In English and Welsh. Welsh title: Rheoliadau Tatws Hadyd (Ffioedd) (Cymru) 2006. - 8p.: 30 cm. - 978-0-11-091291-2 £3.00

The Seed Potatoes (Wales) Regulations 2006 No. 2006/2929 (W.264). - Enabling power: Plant Varieties and Seeds Act 1964, ss. 16 (1) (1A) (2) (3) (4) (5), 36. - Issued: 20.11.2006. Made: 07.11.2006. Coming into force: 15.11.2006. Effect: S.I. 1991/2206; 1992/1031; 1993/1878; 1994/2592; 1997/1474; 2001/3666 revoked in relation to Wales. Territorial extent & classification: W. General. - EC note: These Regulations give effect, in Wales, to Council Directive 2002/56/EC on the marketing of seed potatoes, and to Commission Decision 2004/842/EC- In English and Welsh. Welsh title: Rheoliadau Tatws Hadyd (Cymru) 2006. - 64p.: 30 cm. - 978-0-11-091432-9 £10.50

Serious Organised Crime Agency

The Serious Organised Crime and Police Act 2005 (Application and Modification of Certain Enactments to Designated Staff of SOCA) Order 2006 No. 2006/987.
- Enabling power: Serious Organised Crime and Police Act 2005, ss. 52 (1), 172 (2). - Issued: 05.04.2006. Made: 29.03.2006. Coming into force: 01.04.2006. Effect: 1971 c.77; 1984 c.60; 1999 c.33; 2003 c.38 amended. Territorial extent & classification: E/W/S/NI. General. - Supersedes draft S.I. (ISBN 0110741099) issued 06.03.2006. - 8p.: 30 cm. - 978-0-11-074434-6 £3.00

The Serious Organised Crime and Police Act 2005 (Commencement No. 5 and Transitional and Transitory Provisions and Savings) Order 2006 No. 2006/378 (C.9). - Enabling power: Serious Organised Crime and Police Act 2005, s. 178 (8) (9) (10). Bringing into operation various provisions of the 2005 Act in accord. with arts. 2, 3, 4, 5, 6, 7. - Issued: 22.02.2006. Made: 15.02.2006. Effect: None. Territorial extent & classification: E/W/S/NI [parts to E/W or NI only]. General. - 12p.: 30 cm. - 978-0-11-074072-0 £3.00

The Serious Organised Crime and Police Act 2005 (Consequential and Supplementary Amendments to Secondary Legislation) Order 2006 No. 2006/594. - Enabling power: Serious Organised Crime and Police Act 2005, s. 173 (1). - Issued: 10.03.2006. Made: 06.03.2006. Laid: 09.03.2006. Coming into force: 01.04.2006. Effect: 44 instruments amended & S.I. 2002/1298 revoked. Territorial extent & classification: E/W/S/NI. General. - 16p.: 30 cm. - 978-0-11-074188-8 £3.00

The Serious Organised Crime and Police Act 2005 (Delegation under section 43) Order 2006 No. 2006/100.
- Enabling power: Serious Organised Crime and Police Act 2005, s. 44 (2). - Issued: 27.01.2006. Made: 23.01.2006. Laid: 25.01.2006. Coming into force: 01.03.2006. Effect: None. Territorial extent & classification: E/W/S/NI. General. - 2p.: 30 cm. - 978-0-11-073932-8 £3.00

Sex discrimination, England

The Sex Discrimination Act 1975 (Public Authorities) (Statutory Duties) Order 2006 No. 2006/2930. - Enabling power: Sex Discrimination Act 1975, ss. 76B (1), 76C (2). - Issued: 13.11.2006. Made: 07.11.2006. Laid: 10.11.2006. Coming into force: 06.04.2007. Effect: None. Territorial extent & classification: E. General. - 8p.: 30 cm. - 978-0-11-075282-2 £3.00

Social care

The Appointments Commission Regulations 2006 No. 2006/2380. - Enabling power: Health Act 2006, ss. 65, 79 (3), sch. 4, paras 2 (b) (d), 3 (3) (b), 7 (1) (2), 10 (3) (c) (5) (6), 18 (2) (b). - Issued: 11.09.2006. Made: 04.09.2006. Laid: 05.09.2006. Coming into force: 01.10.2006. Effect: S.I. 2001/794 revoked. Territorial extent & classification: E/W/S/NI. General. - 12p.: 30 cm. - 978-0-11-075076-7 £3.00

Social care, England

The Care Standards Act 2000 (Establishments and Agencies) (Miscellaneous Amendments) Regulations 2006 No. 2006/1493. - Enabling power: Care Standards Act 2000, ss. 22 (1) (2) (d) (f) (5) (a) (7) (a) (l), 25, 118 (5) to (7). - Issued: 09.06.2006. Made: 06.06.2006. Laid: 09.06.2006. Coming into force: 01.07.2006 for all purposes except regulation 2 (2) to (5) (9); 01.09.2006 for the purposes of regulation 2 (2) to (5) (9). Effect: S.I. 2001/3965; 2002/3212, 3214; 2004/2071 amended. Territorial extent & classification: E. General. - 8p.: 30 cm. - 978-0-11-074660-9 £3.00

The Commission for Social Care Inspection (Fees and Frequency of Inspections) (Amendment) Regulations 2006 No. 2006/517. - Enabling power: Care Standards Act 2000, ss. 12 (2), 15 (3), 16 (3), 31 (7), 45 (4), 118 (5) (6) & Children Act 1989, s. 87D (2). - Issued: 03.03.2006. Made: 28.02.2006. Laid: 03.03.2006. Coming into force: 01.04.2006. Effect: S.I. 2004/662 amended & S.I. 2005/575 revoked. Territorial extent & classification: E. General. - 4p.: 30 cm. - 978-0-11-074133-8 £3.00

The Health and Social Care (Community Health and Standards) Act 2003 Commencement (No. 9) Order 2006 No. 2006/1680 (C.57). - Enabling power: Health and Social Care (Community Health and Standards) Act 2003, ss. 195 (1), 199 (1). Bringing into operation various provisions of the 2003 Act on 27.06.2006; 01.09.2006. - Issued: 30.06.2006. Made: 26.06.2006. Effect: None. Territorial extent & classification: E/W. Applies in relation the England only apart from article 2 (2) which applies in relation to England and Wales. General. - 8p.: 30 cm. - 978-0-11-074762-0 £3.00

The Local Authority Social Services Complaints (England) Regulations 2006 No. 2006/1681. - Enabling power: Health and Social Care (Community Health and Standards Act) 2003, ss. 113 (1), 114 (1) (2), 115 (1) (2) (4) (5) (6), 195 (1) (b). - Issued: 29.06.2006. Made: 27.06.2006. Laid: 29.06.2006. Coming into force: 01.09.2006. Effect: None. Territorial extent & classification: E. General. - 12p.: 30 cm. - 978-0-11-074764-4 £3.00

The National Care Standards Commission (Commission for Social Care Inspection) (Fees) (Adoption Agencies, Adoption Support Agencies and Local Authority Fostering Functions) (Amendment) Regulations 2006 No. 2006/578. - Enabling power: Care Standards Act 2000, ss. 12 (2), 15 (3), 16 (3), 118 (5) (6) & Health and Social Care (Community Health and Standards Act) 2003, s. 86 (1). - Issued: 10.03.2006. Made: 06.03.2006. Laid: 10.03.2006. Coming into force: 01.04.2006. Effect: S.I. 2003/368 amended. Territorial extent & classification: E. General. - 4p.: 30 cm. - 978-0-11-074172-7 £3.00

Social care, England and Wales

The Health Act 2006 (Commencement No. 1 and Transitional Provisions) Order 2006 No. 2006/2603 (C.88). - Enabling power: Health Act 2006, ss. 79 (3), 83 (3) (7) (8). Bringing into operation various provisions of the 2006 Act on 28.09.2006 and 01.10.2006. - Issued: 29.09.2006. Made: 22.09.2006. Effect: None. Territorial extent & classification: E/W. General. - 8p.: 30 cm. - 978-0-11-075136-8 £3.00

The Protection of Children and Vulnerable Adults and Care Standards Tribunal (Amendment) Regulations 2006 No. 2006/1930. - Enabling power: Protection of Children Act 1999, s. 9 (2) (3) (b) (d) (3B). - Issued: 24.07.2006. Made: 13.07.2006. Laid: 24.07.2006. Coming into force: 01.10.2006. Effect: S.I. 2002/816 amended. Territorial extent & classification: E/W. General. - 4p.: 30 cm. - 978-0-11-074863-4 £3.00

Social care, Wales

The Care Standards Act 2000 and the Children Act 1989 (Abolition of Fees) (Wales) Regulations 2006 No. 2006/878 (W.83). - Enabling power: Care Standards Act 2000, ss. 12 (2), 15 (3), 16 (3), 22 (7), 118 (5) to (7) & Children Act 1989, ss. 79F, 87D, 104 (4), sch. 9A, para. 7 & Health and Social Care (Community Health and Standards) Act 2003, s. 94 (6). - Issued: 29.03.2006. Made: 21.03.2006. Coming into force: 01.04.2006. Effect: S.I. 2002/919 (W.107), 2935 (W.277), 3161 (W.296); 2003/237 (W.35), 781 (W.92), 2527 (W. 242); 2004/219 (W.23), 1756 (W.188) amended & S.I. 2002/921 (W.109) revoked. Territorial extent & classification: W. General. - In English and Welsh. Welsh title: Rheoliadau Deddf Safonau Gofal 2000 a Deddf Plant 1989 (Dileu Ffioedd) (Cymru) 2006. - 4p.: 30 cm. - 978-0-11-091304-9 £3.00

The Care Standards Act 2000 and the Children Act 1989 (Regulatory Reform and Complaints) (Wales) Regulations 2006 No. 2006/3251 (W.295). - Enabling power: Children Act 1989, ss. 23 (2) (a) (9), 59 (2), 79C, 104 (4), sch. 2, para. 12; Care Standards Act 2000, ss. 14 (1) (d), 16, 22, 25, 33, 42 (1), 48 (1), 50, 118 (1) (5) to (7) and Adoption and Children Act 2002, ss. 2 (6) (b), 9(1) (3), 10, 140 (1). - Issued: 14.12.2006. Made: 05.12.2006. Coming into force: 01.01.2007. Effect: S.I. 2002/324 (W.37), 327 (W.40), 812 (W.92), 919 (W.107); 2003/237 (W.35), 781 (W.92), 2527 (W.242); 2004/219 (W.23), 1756 (W.188); 2005/1514 (W.118) amended. Territorial extent & classification: W. General. - In English and Welsh. Welsh title: Rheoliadau Deddf Safonau Gofal 2000 a Deddf Plant 1989 (Diwygio Rheoleiddiol a Chwynion) (Cymru) 2006. - 48p.: 30 cm. - 978-0-11-091467-1 £7.50

The Children (Private Arrangements for Fostering) (Wales) Regulations 2006 No. 2006/940 (W.89). - Enabling power: Children Act 1989 ss. 67 (2) (2A) (6), 104 (4), sch. 8, para. 7. - Issued: 05.04.2006. Made: 28.03.2006. Coming into force: 01.04.2006. Effect: S.I. 1991/2050 revoked with savings in relation to Wales. Territorial extent & classification: W. General. - In English and Welsh. Welsh title: Rheoliadau Plant (Trefniadau Preifat ar gyfer Maethu) (Cymru) 2006. - 16p.: 30 cm. - 978-0-11-091308-7 £3.00

The Children (Secure Accommodation) (Amendment) (Wales) Regulations 2006 No. 2006/2986 (W.276). - Enabling power: Children Act 1989, ss. 25 (7), 104 (1) (4), sch. 4, para. 4 (1) (a), sch. 5, para. 7 (1) (a) (4), sch. 6, para. (10) (1) (a). - Issued: 28.11.2006. Made: 14.11.2006. Coming into force: 16.11.2006. Effect: S.I. 1991/1505 amended in relation to Wales. Territorial extent & classification: W. General. - With correction slip dated February 2007. - In English and Welsh. Welsh title: Rheoliadau Plant (Llety Diogel) (Diwygio) (Cymru) 2006. - 4p.: 30 cm. - 978-0-11-091448-0 £3.00

The Independent Review of Determinations (Adoption) (Wales) Regulations 2006 No. 2006/3100 (W.284). - Enabling power: Adoption and Children Act 2002, ss. 9, 12. - Issued: 05.12.2006. Made: 21.11.2006. Coming into force: 31.12.2006. Effect: S.I. 2005/2689 (W. 189) amended & S.I. 2005/1819 (W.147) revoked. Territorial extent & classification: W. General. - In English and Welsh. Welsh title: Rheoliadau Adolygu Penderfyniadau'n Annibynnol (Mabwysiadu) (Cymru) 2006. - 16p.: 30 cm. - 978-0-11-091450-3 £3.00

Social security

The Child Benefit and Guardian's Allowance (Miscellaneous Amendments) Regulations 2006 No. 2006/203. - Enabling power: Social Security Administration Act 1992, ss. 1 (1) (b), 5 (1) (a) (b) (h) (i) (p), 71 (6); Social Security Administration (Northern Ireland) Act 1992, ss. 1 (1) (b), 5 (1) (a) (b) (h) (i) (p), 69 (6) & Tax Credits Act 2002, ss. 58, 65 (1) (2) (7) (9). - Issued: 08.02.2006. Made: 01.02.2006. Laid: 02.02.2006. Coming into force: 10.04.2006. Effect: S.I. 2003/492, 494 amended. Territorial extent & classification: E/W/S/NI. General. - 4p.: 30 cm. - 978-0-11-074003-4 £3.00

The Child Benefit (General) Regulations 2006 No. 2006/223. - Enabling power: Social Security Contributions and Benefits Act 1992, ss. 142 (2), 143 (3) (c) (4) (5), 144 (1), 145A (1), 146(3), 147 (1) (2) (4) to (6), 175 (3) to (5), sch. 9, paras 1, 2 (2), 3, sch. 10, para. 5, 6 (1); Social Security Contributions and Benefits (Northern Ireland) Act 1992, ss. 138 (2), 139 (4) (5), 140 (1), 141 (1), 141A (1), 142 (3), 143 (1) (2) (4) (5) (6), 171 (3) (4) (5), sch. 9, paras 1, 2 (2), 3, sch. 10, paras 5, 6 (1); Social Security Administration Act 1992, s. 13 (1C); Social Security Administration (Northern Ireland) Act 1992, s. 11 (1C) & Finance Act 1999, s. 133 (1). - Issued: 08.02.2006. Made: 02.02.2006. Laid: 03.02.2006. Coming into force: 10.04.2006. Effect: S.I. 2005/2078 (S.9), 2919 amended and S.I. 2003/493; 2004/1244 revoked. Territorial extent & classification: E/W/S/NI. General. - With correction slip dated February 2006. - 24p.: 30 cm. - 978-0-11-074006-5 £4.00

The Child Benefit (Rates) Regulations 2006 No. 2006/965. - Enabling power: Social Security Contributions and Benefits Act 1992, ss. 145, 147 (1), 175 (4) & Social Security Contributions and Benefits (Northern Ireland) Act 1992, ss. 141, 171 (1) (4), 173 (1). - Issued: 04.04.2006. Made: 29.03.2006. Coming into force: 10.04.2006 in accord. with reg. 1. Effect: S.I. 1993/965; 1996/1803; 2000/1483; 2005/2919 & S.R. 1993/169; 1996/288; 2001/108 amended & S.I. 1976/1267 (with saving); 1991/502; 1998/1581; S.R. 1976/223 (with saving); 1991/82; 1998/239 revoked. Territorial extent & classification: E/W/S/NI. General. - Supersedes draft SI (ISBN 0110740319) issued 17.02.2006. - 8p.: 30 cm. - 978-0-11-074430-8 £3.00

The Council Tax Benefit (Persons who have attained the qualifying age for state pension credit) Regulations 2006 No. 2006/216. - Enabling power: Social Security Contributions and Benefits Act 1992, ss. 123 (1) (e), 131 (3) (b) (5) (c) (ii) (7) (b) (10), 132, 133 (3) (4), 134, 135 (1) (2) (6), 136, 136A (3) (4) (a), 137 (1) (2) (a) to (d) (l) (m), 175 (1) (3) to (6) & Social Security Administration Act 1992, ss. 1 (1) (1C), 6 (1) (a) to (d) (g) to (r) (u), 7 (2), 7A, 76 (1) to (3) (6) (8), 77 (1), 122E (3) (4), 128A, 138 (1) (9), 139 (6) (b), 189 (1) (3) to (6), 191 & Social Security Act 1998, ss. 34, 79 (1) (4), 84. - Issued: 10.02.2006. Made: 02.02.2006. Laid: 10.02.2006. Coming into force: 06.03.2006. Effect: These regulations are made for the purpose only of consolidating other regulations revoked in the Housing Benefit and Council Tax Benefit (Consequential Provisions) Regulations (S.I. 2006/217). Territorial extent & classification: E/W/S. General. - 94p.: 30 cm. - 978-0-11-074020-1 £13.50

The Council Tax Benefit Regulations 2006 No. 2006/215. - Enabling power: Social Security Contributions and Benefits Act 1992, ss. 123 (1) (e), 131 (3) (b) (5) (c) (ii) (7) (b) (10), 132, 133 (3) (4), 134 (1), 135 (1) (2) (6), 136, 137 (1) (2) (a) to (d) (l) (m), 175 (1) (3) to (6) & Social Security Administration Act 1992, ss. 1 (1) (1C), 6 (1) (a) to (d) (g) to (r) (u), 7 (2), 7A, 76 (1) to (3) (6) (8), 77 (1), 122E (3) (4), 128A, 138 (1) (9), 139 (6) (b), 189 (1) (3) to (6), 191 & Social Security Act 1998, ss. 34, 79 (1) (4), 84. - Issued: 10.02.2006. Made: 02.02.2006. Laid: 10.02.2006. Coming into force: 06.03.2006. Effect: These regulations are made for the purpose only of consolidating other regulations revoked in the Housing Benefit and Council Tax Benefit (Consequential Provisions) Regulations (S.I. 2006/217). Territorial extent & classification: E/W/S. General. - 110p.: 30 cm. - 978-0-11-074018-8 £15.50

The Employment Zones (Allocation to Contractors) Pilot Regulations 2006 No. 2006/962. - Enabling power: Welfare Reform and Pensions Act 1999, ss. 60 (1) to (3) (9), 83 (4) (6) (9) & Jobseekers Act 1995, ss. 19 (10) (c), 29 (1) (3) (5), 36 (2) (4). - Issued: 05.04.2006. Made: 30.03.2006. Coming into force: 24.04.2006. Effect: S.I. 1996/207 amended. Territorial extent & classification: E/W/S. General. - These Regs. shall cease to have effect on 23rd April 2007 unless revoked with effect from an earlier date. Supersedes the draft S.I. (ISBN 0110740238) issued 15.02.2006. - 12p.: 30 cm. - 978-0-11-074446-9 £3.00

The Employment Zones (Amendment) Regulations 2006 No. 2006/1000. - Enabling power: Welfare Reform and Pensions Act 1999, ss. 60 (1) (2) (9), 83 (4) (6). - Issued: 05.04.2006. Made: 30.03.2006. Laid: 03.04.2006. Coming into force: 24.04.2006. Effect: S.I. 2003/2438 amended. Territorial extent & classification: E/W/S. General. - 4p.: 30 cm. - 978-0-11-074445-2 £3.00

The Guardian's Allowance (General) (Amendment) Regulations 2006 No. 2006/204. - Enabling power: Social Security Contributions and Benefits Act 1992, s. 77 (3) (8) (9) & Social Security Contributions and Benefits (Northern Ireland) Act 1992, s. 77 (3) (8) (9). - Issued: 08.02.2006. Made: 02.02.2006. Laid: 03.02.2006. Coming into force: 10.04.2006. Effect: S.I. 2003/495 amended. Territorial extent & classification: E/W/S/NI. General. - 4p.: 30 cm. - 978-0-11-074004-1 £3.00

The Guardian's Allowance Up-rating Order 2006 No. 2006/957. - Enabling power: Social Security Administration Act 1992, s. 150 (2). - Issued: 03.04.2006. Made: 29.03.2006. Coming into force: 10.04.2006. Effect: 1992 c.4 amended. Territorial extent & classification: E/W/S. General. - 2p.: 30 cm. - 978-0-11-074423-0 £3.00

The Guardian's Allowance Up-rating Regulations 2006 No. 2006/1034. - Enabling power: Social Security Contributions and Benefits Act 1992, ss. 113 (1), 122 (1), 175 (3) (4) & Social Security Administration Act 1992, ss. 155 (3), 189 (4) (5), 191 & Social Security Contributions and Benefits (Northern Ireland) Act 1992, ss. 113 (1), 121 (1), 171 (3) (4) & Social Security Administration (Northern Ireland) Act 1992, ss. 135 (3), 165 (4) (5), 167 (1). - Issued: 07.04.2006. Made: 04.04.2006. Laid: 04.04.2006. Coming into force: 10.04.2006. Effect: None. Territorial extent & classification: E/W/S/NI. General. - 4p.: 30 cm. - 978-0-11-074464-3 *£3.00*

The Housing Benefit (Amendment) Regulations 2006 No. 2006/644. - Enabling power: Social Security Administration Act 1992, ss. 134 (1A), 189 (4) to (7) & Child Support, Pensions and Social Security Act 2000, s. 68, sch. 7, paras 3 (1), 20. - Issued: 15.03.2006. Made: 08.03.2006. Laid: 13.03.2006. Coming into force: 03.04.2006. Effect: S.I. 2001/1002; 2006/213, 214 amended. Territorial extent & classification: E/W/S. General. - 4p.: 30 cm. - 978-0-11-074251-9 *£3.00*

The Housing Benefit and Council Tax Benefit (Amendment) (No. 2) Regulations 2006 No. 2006/2967. - Enabling power: Social Security Administration Act 1992, ss. 5 (1) (a) (j), 6 (1) (a) (j), 189 (1) (4), 191. - Issued: 20.11.2006. Made: 14.11.2006. Laid: 20.11.2006. Coming into force: 20.12.2006. Effect: S.I. 2006/213, 214, 215, 216 amended. Territorial extent & classification: E/W/S. General. - 8p.: 30 cm. - 978-0-11-075309-6 *£3.00*

The Housing Benefit and Council Tax Benefit (Amendment) Regulations 2006 No. 2006/2813. - Enabling power: Social Security Administration Act 1992, ss. 134 (8) (b), 139 (6) (b). - Issued: 27.10.2006. Made: 19.10.2006. Laid: 27.10.2006. Coming into force: 20.11.2006. Effect: S.I. 2006/213, 214, 215, 216 amended. Territorial extent & classification: E/W/S. General. - 4p.: 30 cm. - 978-0-11-075213-6 *£3.00*

The Housing Benefit and Council Tax Benefit (Consequential Provisions) Regulations 2006 No. 2006/217. - Enabling power: Social Security Contributions and Benefits Act 1992, ss. 123 (1) (d) (e), 130 (2) to (4), 131 (3) (b) (5) (c) (ii) (7) (b) (10), 132, 133 (3) (4), 134, 135 (1) (2) (6), 136, 136A (3) (4) (a), 137 (1) (2) (c) to (f) (l) (m), 175 (1) (3) to (6); Social Security Administration Act 1992, ss. 1 (1) (1C), 5 (1) (a) to (d) (g) to (r) (6), 6 (1) (a) to (d) (g) to (r) (u), 7 (2), 7A, 75, 76 (1) to (3) (6) (8), 77 (1), 113, 122E (3) (4), 126A, 128A, 134 (1A) (8) (b), 138 (1) (9), 139 (6) (b), 189 (1) (3) to (6), 191; Housing Act 1996, s. 122 (3) (5) & Social Security Act 1998, ss. 34, 79 (1) (4), 84. - Issued: 10.02.2006. Made: 02.02.2006. Laid: 10.02.2006. Coming into force: 06.03.2006. Effect: 42 statutory instruments amended (see schedule 2) & 133 partially revoked and 84 fully revoked (schedule 1, subject to any relevant savings in schedule 3) & transitory modifications are given in schedule 4. Territorial extent & classification: E/W/S. General. - 89p.: 30 cm. - 978-0-11-074021-8 *£13.50*

The Housing Benefit (Persons who have attained the qualifying age for state pension credit) Regulations 2006 No. 2006/214. - Enabling power: Social Security Contributions and Benefits Act 1992, ss. 123 (1) (d), 130 (2) to (4), 134, 135 (1) (2) (6), 136, 136A (3) (4) (a), 137, 175 (1) (3) to (6); Social Security Administration Act 1992, ss. 1 (1) (1C), 5 (1) (a) to (d) (g) to (r) (6), 7 (2), 7A, 75, 113, 122E (3) (4), 126A, 128A, 134 (1A) (8) (b), 189 (1) (3) to (6), 191; Housing Act 1996, s. 122 (3) (5) & Social Security Act 1998, ss. 34, 79 (1) (4), 84. - Issued: 10.02.2006. Made: 02.02.2006. Laid: 10.02.2006. Coming into force: 06.03.2006. Effect: These regulations are made for the purpose only of consolidating other regulations revoked in the Housing Benefit and Council Tax Benefit (Consequential Provisions) Regulations (S.I. 2006/217). Territorial extent & classification: E/W/S. General. - 132p.: 30 cm. - 978-0-11-074017-1 *£17.50*

The Housing Benefit Regulations 2006 No. 2006/213. - Enabling power: Social Security Contributions and Benefits Act 1992, ss. 123 (1) (d), 130 (2) to (4), 134, 135 (1) (2) (6), 136, 137, 175 (1) (3) to (6) & Social Security Administration Act 1992, ss. 1 (1) (1C), 5 (1) (a) to (d) (g) to (r) (6), 7 (2), 7A, 75, 113, 122E (3) (4), 126A, 128A, 134 (1A) (8) (b), 189 (1) (3) to (6), 191 & Housing Act 1996, s. 122 (3) (5) & Social Security Act 1998, ss. 34, 79 (1) (4), 84. - Issued: 10.02.2006. Made: 02.02.2006. Laid: 10.02.2006. Coming into force: 06.03.2006. Effect: These regulations are made for the purpose only of consolidating other regulations revoked in the Housing Benefit and Council Tax Benefit (Consequential Provisions) Regulations (S.I. 2006/217). Territorial extent & classification: E/W/S. General. - 153p.: 30 cm. - 978-0-11-074016-4 *£22.00*

The Income-related Benefits (Subsidy to Authorities) Amendment (No. 2) Order 2006 No. 2006/559. - Enabling power: Social Security Administration Act 1992, ss. 140B, 140F (2), 189 (1) (4) (5) (7). - Issued: 09.03.2006. Made: 02.03.2006. Laid: 09.03.2006. Coming into force: 01.04.2006. Effect: S.I. 1998/562 amended. in relation to England and Wales. Territorial extent & classification: E/W/S. General. - 8p.: 30 cm. - 978-0-11-074162-8 *£3.00*

The Income-related Benefits (Subsidy to Authorities) Amendment Order 2006 No. 2006/54. - Enabling power: Social Security Administration Act 1992, ss. 140B, 140C (1) (3) (4), 140F (2), 189 (1) (4) (5) (7). - Issued: 19.01.2006. Made: 11.01.2006. Laid: 19.01.2006. Coming into force: 09.02.2006. Effect: S.I. 1998/562 amended. Territorial extent & classification: E/W/S. General. - 16p.: 30 cm. - 978-0-11-073905-2 *£3.00*

The Northern Ireland Act 1998 (Modification) Order 2006 No. 2006/2659. - Enabling power: Northern Ireland Act 1998, s. 87 (7). - Issued: 24.10.2006. Made: 10.10.2006. Laid: 24.10.2006. Coming into force: 15.11.2006. Effect: 1998 c.47 modified. Territorial extent & classification: E/W/S/NI. General. - 4p.: 30 cm. - 978-0-11-075172-6 *£3.00*

Social security

The Pensions Act 2004 (PPF Payments and FAS Payments) (Consequential Provisions) Order 2006 No. 2006/343. - Enabling power: Pensions Act 2004, ss. 315 (5), 319 (2) (a). - Issued: 20.02.2006. Made: 13.02.2006. Coming into force: 14.02.2006 in accord. with art. 1 (1). Effect: 1992 c.4; 1995 c.18; 2002 c.16 amended. Territorial extent & classification: E/W/S/NI. General. - Supersedes draft SI (ISBN 0110738829) issued on 09.01.2006. - 8p.: 30 cm. - 978-0-11-074038-6 £3.00

The Pneumoconiosis, Byssinosis and Miscellaneous Diseases Benefit (Amendment) Scheme 2006 No. 2006/638. - Enabling power: Social Security Contributions and Benefits Act 1992, sch. 8, para. 4. - Issued: 14.03.2006. Made: 07.03.2006. Laid: 14.03.2006. Coming into force: 06.04.2006. Effect: S.I. 1983/136 amended. Territorial extent & classification: E/W/S. General. - 4p.: 30 cm. - 978-0-11-074212-0 £3.00

The Pneumoconiosis etc. (Workers' Compensation) (Payment of Claims) (Amendment) Regulations 2006 No. 2006/829. - Enabling power: Pneumoconiosis etc. (Workers' Compensation) Act 1979, ss. 1 (1) (2) (4), 7. - Issued: 23.03.2006. Made: 15.03.2006. Coming into force: 01.04.2006. Effect: S.I. 1988/668 amended. Territorial extent & classification: E/W/S. General. - 8p.: 30 cm. - 978-0-11-074366-0 £3.00

The Social Fund (Application for Review) (Amendment) Regulations 2006 No. 2006/961. - Enabling power: Social Security Act 1998, s. 38 (1) (3). - Issued: 03.04.2006. Made: 29.03.2006. Laid: 03.04.2006. Coming into force: 24.04.2006. Effect: S.I. 1988/34 amended. Territorial extent & classification: E/W/S. General. - 2p.: 30 cm. - 978-0-11-074422-3 £3.00

The Social Fund Cold Weather Payments (General) Amendment Regulations 2006 No. 2006/2655. - Enabling power: Social Security Contributions and Benefits Act 1992, ss. 138 (2) (4), 175 (1) (3) (4). - Issued: 10.10.2006. Made: 29.09.2006. Laid: 10.10.2006. Coming into force: 01.11.2006. Effect: S.I. 1988/1724 amended. Territorial extent & classification: E/W/S. General. - 12p.: 30 cm. - 978-0-11-075150-4 £3.00

The Social Security Act 1998 (Commencement No. 14) Order 2006 No. 2006/2376 (C.82). - Enabling power: Social Security Act 1998, ss. 79 (3) (4), 87 (2). Bringing into operation various provisions of the 1998 Act on 01.10.2006. - Issued: 08.09.2006. Made: 04.09.2006. Effect: None. Territorial extent & classification: E/W/S. General. - 8p.: 30 cm. - 978-0-11-075073-6 £3.00

The Social Security Act 1998 (Commencement Nos. 9 and 11) (Amendment) Order 2006 No. 2006/2540. - Enabling power: Social Security Act 1998, s. 87 (2) (3). - Issued: 02.10.2006. Made: 20.09.2006. Coming into force: 16.10.2006. Effect: S.I. 1999/2422 (C.61), 2860 (C.75) amended. Territorial extent & classification: E/W/S. General. - 4p.: 30 cm. - 978-0-11-075130-6 £3.00

The Social Security Act 1998 (Prescribed Benefits) Regulations 2006 No. 2006/2529. - Enabling power: Social Security Act 1998, ss. 8 (3) (h), 79 (1), 84. - Issued: 21.09.2006. Made: 14.09.2006. Laid: 21.09.2006. Coming into force: 16.10.2006. Effect: None. Territorial extent & classification: E/W/S. General. - 2p.: 30 cm. - 978-0-11-075121-4 £3.00

The Social Security (Adult Learning Option) Amendment Regulations 2006 No. 2006/2144. - Enabling power: Social Security Contributions and Benefits Act 1992, ss. 30C (3), 123 (1) (a), 124 (1) (e), 137 (1), 175 (1) (3) to (5). - Issued: 08.08.2006. Made: 02.08.2006. Laid: 08.08.2006. Coming into force: 01.09.2006. Effect: S.I. 1987/1967; 1994/2946 amended. Territorial extent & classification: E/W/S (though only those who live in the areas where ALO is offered, currently only England, will be affected by these regulations). General. - 4p.: 30 cm. - 978-0-11-074984-6 £3.00

The Social Security Benefits Up-rating Order 2006 No. 2006/645. - Enabling power: Social Security Administration Act 1992, ss. 150, 151, 189 (1) (4) (5). - Issued: 16.03.2006. Made: 09.03.2006. Coming into force: In accord. with art. 1. Effect: 1965 c.51; 1992 c.4; 1993 c.48 & S.I. 1978/393; 1986/1960; 1987/1967, 1969, 1971; 1991/2890; 1992/1814; 1994/2946; 1995/310; 1996/207; 2002/1792, 2818 amended & S.I. 2005/522 revoked. Territorial extent & classification: E/W/S. General. - Supersedes the draft S.I. (ISBN 0110739272) issued on 25.01.2006. - 48p.: 30 cm. - 978-0-11-074258-8 £7.50

The Social Security Benefits Up-rating Regulations 2006 No. 2006/712. - Enabling power: Social Security Contributions and Benefits Act 1992, ss. 90, 113 (1), 122 (1) 175 (1) (3) & Social Security Administration Act 1992, ss. 155 (3), 189 (1) (4), 191. - Issued: 16.03.2006. Made: 09.03.2006. Laid: 16.03.2005. Coming into force: 10.04.2006. Effect: S.I. 1977/343 amended & S.I. 2005/632 revoked. Territorial extent & classification: E/W/S. General. - 4p.: 30 cm. - 978-0-11-074270-0 £3.00

The Social Security (Bulgaria and Romania) Amendment Regulations 2006 No. 2006/3341. - Enabling power: Social Security Contributions and Benefits Act 1992, ss. 123 (1) (a) (d) (e), 131 (3) (b), 135 (1) (2), 137 (1) (2), 175 (1) (3); Jobseekers Act 1995, ss. 4 (5) (12), 35 (1), 36 (2), sch. 1, para. 11 & State Pension Credit Act 2002, ss. 1 (5) (a), 17 (1). - Issued: 21.12.2006. Made: 14.12.2006. Laid: 15.12.2006. Coming into force: 01.01.2007. Effect: S.I. 1987/1967; 1996/207; 2002/1792; 2006/213, 214, 215, 216 amended. Territorial extent & classification: E/W/S. General. - 8p.: 30 cm. - 978-0-11-075504-5 £3.00

The Social Security (Categorisation of Earners) (Amendment) Regulations 2006 No. 2006/1530. - Enabling power: Social Security Contributions and Benefits Act 1992, s. 2 (2) (a) (2A). - Issued: 16.06.2006. Made: 13.06.2006. Laid: 14.06.2006. Coming into force: 05.07.2006. Effect: S.I. 1978/1689 amended. Territorial extent & classification: E/W/S. General. - With correction slip dated September 2006. - 2p.: 30 cm. - 978-0-11-074693-7 £3.00

The Social Security (Claims and Payments) Amendment (No. 2) Regulations 2006 No. 2006/3188. - Enabling power: Social Security Administration Act 1992, ss. 5 (1) (p), 189 (1) (4) (6), 191. - Issued: 06.12.2006. Made: 28.11.2006. Laid: 06.12.2006. Coming into force: 27.12.2006. Effect: S.I. 1987/1968 amended. Territorial extent & classification: E/W/S. General. - 4p.: 30 cm. - 978-0-11-075396-6 *£3.00*

The Social Security (Claims and Payments) Amendment Regulations 2006 No. 2006/551. - Enabling power: Social Security Administration Act 1992, ss. 15A (2) (b), 189 (1) (4), 191. - Issued: 08.03.2006. Made: 02.03.2006. Laid: 08.03.2006. Coming into force: 01.04.2006. Effect: S.I. 1987/1968 amended. Territorial extent & classification: E/W/S. General. - 2p.: 30 cm. - 978-0-11-074150-5 *£3.00*

The Social Security (Contributions) (Amendment No. 2) Regulations 2006 No. 2006/576. - Enabling power: Social Security Contributions and Benefits Act 1992, ss. 3 (2) (3), 10 (9), sch. 1, para. 7B & Social Security Contributions and Benefits (Northern Ireland) Act 1992, ss. 3 (2) (3), 10 (9), sch. 1, para. 7B. - Issued: 16.03.2006. Made: 09.03.2006. Laid: 10.03.06. Coming into force: 06.04.06. Effect: S.I. 2001/1004 amended. Territorial extent & classification: E/W/S/NI. General. - 8p.: 30 cm. - 978-0-11-074253-3 *£3.00*

The Social Security (Contributions) (Amendment No. 3) Regulations 2006 No. 2006/883. - Enabling power: Social Security Contributions and Benefits Act 1992, s. 3 (2) (3) & Social Security Contributions and Benefits (Northern Ireland) Act 1992, ss. 3 (2) (3). - Issued: 28.03.2006. Made: 22.03.2006. Laid: 22.03.2006. Coming into force: 06.04.2006. Effect: S.I. 2001/1004 amended. Territorial extent & classification: E/W/S/NI. General. - 2p.: 30 cm. - 978-0-11-074393-6 *£3.00*

The Social Security (Contributions) (Amendment No. 4) Regulations 2006 No. 2006/2003. - Enabling power: Social Security Contributions and Benefits Act 1992, s. 3 (2) (3) & Social Security Contributions and Benefits (Northern Ireland) Act 1992, s. 3 (2) (3). - Issued: 28.07.2006. Made: 24.07.2006. Laid: 24.07.2006. Coming into force: 14.08.2006. Effect: S.I. 2001/1004 amended. Territorial extent & classification: E/W/S/NI. General. - 4p.: 30 cm. - 978-0-11-074928-0 *£3.00*

The Social Security (Contributions) (Amendment No. 5) Regulations 2006 No. 2006/2829. - Enabling power: Social Security Contributions and Benefits Act 1992, s. 3 (2) (3) & Social Security Contributions and Benefits (Northern Ireland) Act 1992, s. 3 (2) (3). - Issued: 30.10.2006. Made: 25.10.2006. Laid: 26.10.2006. Coming into force: 16.11.2006. Effect: S.I. 2001/1004 amended. Territorial extent & classification: E/W/S/NI. General. - 4p.: 30 cm. - 978-0-11-075226-6 *£3.00*

The Social Security (Contributions) (Amendment No. 6) Regulations 2006 No. 2006/2924. - Enabling power: Social Security Contributions and Benefits Act 1992, s. 3 (2) (3), 175 (1A) (5) & Social Security Contributions and Benefits (Northern Ireland) Act 1992, s. 3 (2) (3), 171 (5). - Issued: 14.11.2006. Made: 08.11.2006. Laid: 09.11.2006. Coming into force: 14.11.2006. Effect: S.I. 2001/1004 amended. Territorial extent & classification: E/W/S/NI. General. - 4p.: 30 cm. - 978-0-11-075281-5 *£3.00*

The Social Security (Contributions) (Amendment) Regulations 2006 No. 2006/127. - Enabling power: Social Security Contributions and Benefits Act 1992, ss. 5, 122 (1), 175 (3) (4) & Social Security Contributions and Benefits (Northern Ireland) Act 1992, ss. 5, 121 (1), 171 (3) (4) (10). - Issued: 30.01.2006. Made: 24.01.2006. Laid: 25.01.2006. Coming into force: 06.04.2006. Effect: S.I. 2001/1004 amended. Territorial extent & classification: E/W/S/NI. General. - 4p.: 30 cm. - 978-0-11-073939-7 *£3.00*

The Social Security (Contributions) (Re-rating and National Insurance Funds Payments) Order 2006 No. 2006/624. - Enabling power: Social Security Administration Act 1992, ss. 141 (4) (5), 142 (2) (3), 143 (1) (3), 144 (2) & Social Security Administration (Northern Ireland) Act 1992, ss. 129, 165 (11A) & Social Security Act 1993, s. 2 (2) & S.I. 1993/592 (N.I. 2), art. 4 (3). - Issued: 13.03.2006. Made: 07.03.2006. Coming into force: 06.04.2006. Effect: 1992 c. 4, 8 amended. Territorial extent & classification: E/W/S/NI. General. - 4p.: 30 cm. - 978-0-11-074198-7 *£3.00*

The Social Security (Deferral of Retirement Pensions etc.) Regulations 2006 No. 2006/516. - Enabling power: Social Security Contributions and Benefits Act 1992, ss. 62 (1) (a) (c), 122 (1), 175 (3), sch. 5, paras, A1 (3) (a), 2 (2), 3C (4) (a), sch. 5A, para. 1 (3) (a) & Social Security Administration Act 1992, ss. 71 (6) (b), 189 (1) (4), 191 & Pensions Act 2004, s. 315 (2), sch. 11, para. 27. - Issued: 06.03.2006. Made: 27.02.2006. Laid: 06.03.2006. Coming into force: 06.04.2006. Effect: S.I. 1979/642; 1988/664; 2005/454, 469, 2677 amended. Territorial extent & classification: E/W/S. General. - 4p.: 30 cm. - 978-0-11-074132-1 *£3.00*

The Social Security (Graduated Retirement Benefit) (Consequential Provisions) Order 2006 No. 2006/2839. - Enabling power: Pensions Act 2004, s. 319 (2) (a). - Issued: 01.11.2006. Made: 25.10.2006. Coming into force: 26.10.2006 in accord. with art. 1. Effect: 1992 c.5 amended. Territorial extent & classification: E/W/S. General. - Supersedes draft SI (ISBN 0110748123) issued 11.07.2006. - 4p.: 30 cm. - 978-0-11-075230-3 *£3.00*

The Social Security (Incapacity Benefit Work-focused Interviews) Amendment (No. 2) Regulations 2006 No. 2006/3088. - Enabling power: Social Security Administration Act 1992, ss. 2A, 189 (1) (4) to (6) (7A), 191. - Issued: 24.11.2006. Made: 16.11.2006. Laid: 24.11.2006. Coming into force: 29.12.2006. Effect: S.I. 2003/2439 amended. Territorial extent & classification: E/W/S. General. - 4p.: 30 cm. - 978-0-11-075349-2 *£3.00*

Social security

The Social Security (Incapacity Benefit Work-focused Interviews) Amendment Regulations 2006 No. 2006/536. - Enabling power: Social Security Administration Act 1992, ss. 2A, 189 (1) (4) to (6) (7A), 191. - Issued: 06.03.2006. Made: 01.03.2006. Laid: 06.03.2006. Coming into force: 03.04.2006. Effect: S.I. 2003/2439 amended. Territorial extent & classification: E/W/S. General. - 4p.: 30 cm. - 978-0-11-074140-6 £3.00

The Social Security (Incapacity for Work) Amendment Regulations 2006 No. 2006/757. - Enabling power: Social Security Contributions and Benefits Act 1992, ss. 171D, 175 (1) (3) (4). - Issued: 20.03.2006. Made: 14.03.2006. Laid: 20.03.2006. Coming into force: 10.04.2006. Effect: S.I. 1995/311 amended. Territorial extent & classification: E/W/S. General. - 8p.: 30 cm. - 978-0-11-074316-5 £3.00

The Social Security (Income Support and Jobseeker's Allowance) Amendment Regulations 2006 No. 2006/1402. - Enabling power: Social Security Contributions and Benefits Act 1992, ss. 123 (1) (a), 124 (1) (e), 137 (1), 175 (1) (3) (4) & Jobseekers Act 1995, ss. 6 (2) (4), 7 (4), 8, 35 (1), 36 (2) (4), sch. 1, paras 8, 8A (1). - Issued: 30.05.2006. Made: 25.05.2006. Coming into force: 30.05.2006. Effect: S.I. 1987/1967; 1996/207 amended. Territorial extent & classification: E/W/S. General. - Supersedes draft SI (ISBN 0110745116) issued 24.04.2006. - 4p.: 30 cm. - 978-0-11-074614-2 £3.00

The Social Security (Industrial Injuries) (Dependency) (Permitted Earnings Limits) Order 2006 No. 2006/663. - Enabling power: Social Security Contributions and Benefits Act 1992, sch. 7, para. 4 (5). - Issued: 15.03.2006. Made: 09.03.2006. Laid: 15.03.2006. Coming into force: 12.04.2006. Effect: 1992 c. 4 amended. Territorial extent & classification: E/W/S. General. - 2p.: 30 cm. - 978-0-11-074240-3 £3.00

The Social Security (Industrial Injuries) (Prescribed Diseases) Amendment (No. 2) Regulations 2006 No. 2006/769. - Enabling power: Social Security Contributions and Benefits Act 1992, ss. 108 (2), 122 (1), 175 (1) to (4). - Issued: 22.03.2006. Made: 15.03.2006. Laid: 15.03.2006. Coming into force: 05.04.2006. Effect: S.I. 2006/586 amended. Territorial extent & classification: E/W/S. General. - This Statutory Instrument has been made in consequence of a defect in S.I. 2006/586 and is being issued free of charge to all known recipients of that Statutory Instrument. - 2p.: 30 cm. - 978-0-11-074350-9 £3.00

The Social Security (Industrial Injuries) (Prescribed Diseases) Amendment Regulations 2006 No. 2006/586. - Enabling power: Social Security Contributions and Benefits Act 1992, ss. 108(2), 109 (2), 122 (1), 175 (1) to (4), sch. 6, para. 1. - Issued: 10.03.2006. Made: 05.03.2006. Laid: 10.03.2006. Coming into force: 06.04.2006. Effect: S.I. 1985/967 amended. Territorial extent & classification: E/W/S. General. - 4p.: 30 cm. - 978-0-11-074178-9 £3.00

The Social Security (Lebanon) Amendment Regulations 2006 No. 2006/1981. - Enabling power: Social Security Contributions and Benefits Act 1992, ss. 123 (1) (a) (d) (e), 131 (3) (b), 135 (1) (2), 137 (1) (2), 175 (1) (3) (4) & Jobseekers Act 1995, ss. 4 (5) (12), 35 (1), 36 (2) (4), sch. 1, para. 11 & State Pension Credit Act 2002, ss. 1 (5) (a), 17 (1). - Issued: 28.07.2006. Made: 24.07.2006. Laid: 24.07.2006. Coming into force: 25.07.2006. Effect: S.I. 1987/1967; 1996/207; 2002/1792; 2006/213, 214, 215, 216 amended. Territorial extent & classification: E/W/S. General. - 4p.: 30 cm. - 978-0-11-074936-5 £3.00

The Social Security (Miscellaneous Amendments) (No. 2) Regulations 2006 No. 2006/832. - Enabling power: Social Security Administration Act 1992, ss. 5 (1) (a) to (c) (i) (j) (m) (p), 7A (1) (6) (d), 111A (1A) (1B) (1D) (1E), 112 (1A) to (1D), 189 (1) (4) to (6), 191 & Social Security Act 1998, ss. 9 (4), 10 (3) (6), 79 (1) (4), 84. - Issued: 27.03.2006. Made: 20.03.2006. Laid: 20.03.2006. Coming into force: In accord. with reg. 1. Effect: S.I. 1987/1968; 1996/207, 672; 1999/991; 2001/3252 amended & S.I. 1994/3196 revoked (10.04.2006). Territorial extent & classification: E/W/S. General. - 8p.: 30 cm. - 978-0-11-074375-2 £3.00

The Social Security (Miscellaneous Amendments) (No. 3) Regulations 2006 No. 2006/2377. - Enabling power: Social Security Administration Act 1992, ss. 5 (1) (a) to (c) (p), 189 (1) (4), 191 & Social Security Act 1998, ss. 10 (3) (6), 79 (1) (4), 84. - Issued: 08.09.2006. Made: 04.09.2006. Laid: 08.09.2006. Coming into force: 02.10.2006. Effect: S.I. 1987/1968; 1999/991 amended. Territorial extent & classification: E/W/S. General. - 4p.: 30 cm. - 978-0-11-075072-9 £3.00

The Social Security (Miscellaneous Amendments) (No. 4) Regulations 2006 No. 2006/2378. - Enabling power: Social Security Contributions and Benefits Act 1992, ss. 30A (2A), 30C (4), 30E (1), 47 (6), 64 (1), 68 (4), 71 (6), 86A (1), 122 (1), 123 (1) (a) (d) (e), 124 (1) (e), 135 (1), 136 (3) (5) (b) (c), 136A (3), 137 (1) (2) (h) (l), 171D, 171G (2), 175 (1) (3) to (5), sch. 7, para. 2 (3) & Social Security Administration Act 1992, ss. 5 (1) (l) (p), 189 (1) (4) (5) & Social Security (Incapacity for Work) Act 1994, s. 4 & Jobseekers Act 1995, ss. 4 (5), 7 (2) (a), 12 (2) (4) (b) (c), 35 (1), 36 (1) (2) (4), sch. 1, paras 1 (2) (b), 12, 16 (1) (a) (b) & Child Support, Pensions and Social Security Act 2000, sch. 7, paras. 4 (6), 20 (1) (3) & State Pension Credit Act 2002, ss. 1 (5) (a), 2 (3) (b), 7 (4), 15 (6) (a) (b), 17 (1) (2) (a), 19 (1). - Issued: 08.09.2006. Made: 04.09.2006. Laid: 08.09.2006. Coming into force: In accord. with reg. 1. Effect: S.I. 1979/642; 1982/1408; 1984/1303; 1987/1967, 1968; 1991/2740, 2890; 1994/2945, 2946; 1995/310, 311; 1996/207; 2002/1792; 2006/213, 214, 215, 216 amended. Territorial extent & classification: E/W/S. General. - 20p.: 30 cm. - 978-0-11-075074-3 £3.50

The Social Security (Miscellaneous Amendments) (No. 5) Regulations 2006 No. 2006/3274. - Enabling power: Social Security Contributions and Benefits Act 1992, ss. 123 (1) (a) (d), 135 (1), 137 (1) (2) (h), 175 (1) (3) to (5) & Jobseekers Act 1995, ss. 4 (5), 35 (1), 36 (1) (2) (4) & State Pension Credit Act 2002, ss. 2 (3) (b), 17 (1). - Issued: 14.12.2006. Made: 07.12.2006. Laid: 14.12.2006. Coming into force: 08.01.2007. Effect: S.I. 1987/1967; 1996/207; 2002/1792; 2006/213, 214 amended. Territorial extent & classification: E/W/S. General. - 4p.: 30 cm. - 978-0-11-075458-1 £3.00

The Social Security (Miscellaneous Amendments) Regulations 2006 No. 2006/588. - Enabling power: Social Security Contributions and Benefits Act 1992, ss. 123 (1) (a) (d) (e), 124 (1) (e), 131 (10) (b), 135 (1), 136 (5) (a) (b), 136A (3), 137 (1), 138 (1) (a) (4), 175 (1) (3) (4) & Social Security Administration Act 1992, ss. 5 (1) (k), 73 (1) (b), 189 (1) (4) (5) & Jobseekers Act 1995, ss. 12 (4) (a) (b), 35 (1), 36 (2) (4) & State Pension Credit Act 2002, ss. 2 (3) (b) (9), 13 (1) (a), 15 (1) (j), 17 (1). - Issued: 10.03.2006. Made: 07.03.2006. Laid: 10.03.2006. Coming into force: In accord. with reg. 1. Effect: S.I. 1987/1967; 1996/207; 2002/1792; 2005/2502, 3061, 3360; 2006/213, 214, 215, 216, 217 amended. Territorial extent & classification: E/W/S. General. - 12p.: 30 cm. - 978-0-11-074180-2 £3.00

The Social Security (National Insurance Numbers) Amendment Regulations 2006 No. 2006/2897. - Enabling power: Social Security Administration Act 1992, ss. 182C, 189 (1) (4) to (6). - Issued: 07.11.2006. Made: 01.11.2006. Laid: 07.11.2006. Coming into force: 11.12.2006, for the purpose of reg. 2(a); 01.03.2007, for the purpose of reg. 2(b). Effect: S.I. 2001/769 amended. Territorial extent & classification: E/W/S. General. - 4p.: 30 cm. - 978-0-11-075255-6 £3.00

The Social Security Pensions (Low Earnings Threshold) Order 2006 No. 2006/500. - Enabling power: Social Security Administration Act 1992, s. 148A. - Issued: 03.03.2006. Made: 27.02.2006. Laid: 03.03.2006. Coming into force: 06.04.2006. Effect: None. Territorial extent & classification: E/W/S. General. - 2p.: 30 cm. - 978-0-11-074120-8 £3.00

The Social Security (Persons from Abroad) Amendment (No. 2) Regulations 2006 No. 2006/2528. - Enabling power: Social Security Contributions and Benefits Act 1992, ss. 123 (1) (a) (d) (e), 131 (3) (b), 135 (1) (2), 137 (1) (2), 175 (1) (3) & Jobseekers Act 1995, ss. 4 (5) (12), 35 (1), 36 (2), sch. 1, para. 11 & State Pension Credit Act 2002, ss. 1 (5) (a), 17 (1). - Issued: 21.09.2006. Made: 14.09.2006. Laid: 18.09.2006. Coming into force: 09.10.2006. Effect: S.I. 1987/1967; 1996/207; 2002/1792; 2006/213, 214, 215, 216 amended. Territorial extent & classification: E/W/S. General. - 4p.: 30 cm. - 978-0-11-075120-7 £3.00

The Social Security (Persons from Abroad) Amendment Regulations 2006 No. 2006/1026. - Enabling power: Social Security Contributions and Benefits Act 1992, ss. 123(1) (a) (d) (e), 131 (3) (b), 135 (1) (2), 137 (1) (2), 138 (1) (a) (4), 175 (1) (3) (4) & Jobseekers Act 1995, ss. 4 (5) (12), 35 (1), 36 (2) (4), sch. 1, para. 11 & State Pension Credit Act 2002, ss. 1 (5) (a), 17 (1). - Issued: 07.04.2006. Made: 03.04.2006. Laid: 07.04.2006. Coming into force: 30.04.2006. Effect: S.I. 1987/1967; 1996/207; 2002/1792; 2005/3061; 2006/213, 214, 215, 216 amended & S.I. 1994/1807; 1996/2006; 2000/979; 2004/1232 revoked. Territorial extent & classification: E/W/S. General. - EC note: These regulations are made in consequence of Council Directive 2004/38/EC, the provisions of which are to be transposed by the Immigration (European Economic Area) Regulations 2006 (S.I. 2006/1003). - 16p.: 30 cm. - 978-0-11-074463-6 £3.00

The Social Security (PPF Payments and FAS Payments) (Consequential Amendments) Regulations 2006 No. 2006/1069. - Enabling power: Social Security Contributions and Benefits Act 1992, ss. 30DD (1) (c), 89 (1) (1A) (2), 122 (1), 175 (1) (3) (4) & Jobseekers Act 1995, ss. 4 (1) (b), 35 (1), 36 (1) to (4). - Issued: 10.04.2006. Made: 05.04.2006. Laid: 10.04.2006. Coming into force: 05.04.2006. Effect: S.I. 1977/343; 1994/2945, 2946; 1996/207 amended. Territorial extent & classification: E/W/S. General. - 4p.: 30 cm. - 978-0-11-074475-9 £3.00

The Social Security (Provisions relating to Qualifying Young Persons) (Amendment) Regulations 2006 No. 2006/692. - Enabling power: Social Security Contributions and Benefits Act 1992, ss. sections 82 (4), 85 (4), 86A, 90 (b), 114 (1), 122 (1) (5), 175 (1) (3), sch. 7, para. 6 (1) (b) (5) & Social Security Administration Act 1992, ss. 1 (1C), 189 (1) (4), 191. - Issued: 16.03.2006. Made: 09.03.2006. Laid: 16.03.2005. Coming into force: 10.04.2006. Effect: S.I. 1977/343; 1979/642; 1994/2945 amended. Territorial extent & classification: E/W/S. General. - 4p.: 30 cm. - 978-0-11-074269-4 £3.00

The Social Security Revaluation of Earnings Factors Order 2006 No. 2006/496. - Enabling power: Social Security Administration Act 1992, ss. 148 (3) (4), 189 (1) (4) (5). - Issued: 03.03.2006. Made: 27.02.2006. Laid: 03.03.2006. Coming into force: 06.04.2006. Effect: None. Territorial extent & classification: E/W/S. General. - 4p.: 30 cm. - 978-0-11-074119-2 £3.00

The Social Security (Students and Income-related Benefits) Amendment Regulations 2006 No. 2006/1752. - Enabling power: Social Security Contributions and Benefits Act 1992, ss. 123 (1) (a) (d) (e), 136 (3) (5) (b), 137 (1), 175 (1) (3) (4) & Jobseekers Act 1995, ss. 12 (1) (4) (b), 35 (1), 36 (2) (4). - Issued: 07.07.2006. Made: 03.07.2006. Laid: 07.07.2006. Coming into force: 01.08.2006 & 01.09.2006, in accord. with reg. 1 (2). Effect: S.I. 1987/1967; 1996/207; 2005/1807; 2006/213, 215 amended. Territorial extent & classification: E/W/S. General. - 4p.: 30 cm. - 978-0-11-074803-0 £3.00

Social security

The Social Security (Working Neighbourhoods) Miscellaneous Amendments Regulations 2006 No. 2006/909. - Enabling power: Social Security Administration Act 1992, ss. 2A, 2AA, 2B, 189 (1) (4) to (6) (7A), 191; Welfare Reform and Pensions Act 1999, ss. 60 (1) to (4) (9), 83 (4) (6) & Jobseekers Act 1995, s. 19 (10). - Issued: 29.03.2006. Made: 23.03.2006. Laid: 29.03.2006. Coming into force: 24.04.2006. Effect: S.I. 1996/206; 2000/1926; 2002/1703; 2003/1886; 2004/959 amended. Territorial extent & classification: E/W/S. General. - 4p.: 30 cm. - 978-0-11-074394-3 £3.00

The Social Security (Young Persons) Amendment Regulations 2006 No. 2006/718. - Enabling power: Social Security Contributions and Benefits Act 1992, ss. 123 (1) (a) (d) (e), 124 (1) (d) (e), 135 (1), 137 (1) (2) (e) (f) (i), 175 (1) (3) to (5) & Jobseekers Act 1995, ss. 3 (1) (f) (iii), 3A (1) (e) (ii), 4 (5), 35 (1), 36 (2) to (4), sch. 1, paras 8, 8A (1), 9C, 14 & State Pension Credit Act 2002, ss. 1 (5) (b), 2 (3) (b), 15 (3) (6), 17 (1) (2), 19 (1). - Issued: 20.03.2006. Made: 13.03.2006. Laid: 20.03.2006. Coming into force: 10.04.2006 in accord. with art. 1 (2). Effect: S.I. 1987/1967; 1996/207; 2002/1792; 2006/213, 214, 215, 216 amended. Territorial extent & classification: E/W/S. General. - With correction slip, dated April 2006. - 8p.: 30 cm. - 978-0-11-074277-9 £3.00

The Statutory Maternity Pay, Social Security (Maternity Allowance) and Social Security (Overlapping Benefits) (Amendment) Regulations 2006 No. 2006/2379. - Enabling power: Social Security Contributions and Benefits Act 1992, ss. 35 (3) (a) (i) (c), 165 (1) (3) (4) (7), 175 (1) (3) & Social Security Administration Act 1992, ss. 5 (1) (l), 73 (1) (a), 189 (1) (3) (4). - Issued: 08.09.2006. Made: 04.09.2006. Laid: 08.09.2006. Coming into force: 01.10.2006 in accord. with reg. 1 (2). Effect: S.I. 1979/597; 1986/1960; 1987/416 amended. Territorial extent & classification: E/W/S. General. - 8p.: 30 cm. - 978-0-11-075075-0 £3.00

The Statutory Sick Pay (General) Amendment Regulations 2006 No. 2006/799. - Enabling power: Social Security Contributions and Benefits Act 1992, s. 151 (4). - Issued: 22.03.2006. Made: 15.03.2006. Laid: 20.03.2006. Coming into force: 10.04.2006. Effect: S.I. 1982/894 amended. Territorial extent & classification: E/W/S. General. - 4p.: 30 cm. - 978-0-11-074348-6 £3.00

The Work and Families Act 2006 (Commencement No. 1) Order 2006 No. 2006/1682 (C.58). - Enabling power: Work and Families Act 2006, s. 19 (2) (3). Bringing into operation various provisions of the 2006 Act on 27.06.2006, 01.10.2006, 06.04.2007 in accord. with arts, 2, 3, 4. - Issued: 04.07.2006. Made: 25.06.2006. Effect: None. Territorial extent & classification: E/W/S/NI. General. - 2p.: 30 cm. - 978-0-11-074760-6 £3.00

The Workmen's Compensation (Supplementation) (Amendment) Scheme 2006 No. 2006/738. - Enabling power: Social Security Contributions and Benefits Act 1992, sch. 8, para. 2 & Social Security Administration Act 1992, sch. 9, para. 1. - Issued: 20.03.2006. Made: 13.03.2006. Laid: 20.03.2006. Coming into force: 12.04.2006. Effect: S.I. 1982/1489 amended. Territorial extent & classification: E/W/S. General. - 4p.: 30 cm. - 978-0-11-074313-4 £3.00

Social security, Northern Ireland

The Guardian's Allowance Up-rating (Northern Ireland) Order 2006 No. 2006/956. - Enabling power: Social Security Administration (Northern Ireland) Act 1992, s. 132 (2). - Issued: 03.04.2006. Made: 29.03.2006. Coming into force: 10.04.2006. Effect: 1992 c.7 amended. Territorial extent & classification: NI. General. - 2p.: 30 cm. - 978-0-11-074419-3 £3.00

The Social Security (Categorisation of Earners) (Amendment) (Northern Ireland) Regulations 2006 No. 2006/1531. - Enabling power: Social Security Contributions and Benefits (Northern Ireland) Act 1992, s. 2 (2) (a) (2A). - Issued: 16.06.2006. Made: 13.06.2006. Laid: 14.06.2006. Coming into force: 05.07.2006. Effect: S.R. 1978/401 amended. Territorial extent & classification: NI. General. - With correction slip dated September 2006. - 2p.: 30 cm. - 978-0-11-074694-4 £3.00

Social services, Wales

The Community Care, Services for Carers and Children's Services (Direct Payments) (Wales) Amendment Regulations 2006 No. 2006/2840 (W.256). - Enabling power: Health and Social Care Act 2001, ss. 57 (1) (3) (6) (7), 64 (6). - Issued: 01.11.2006. Made: 25.10.2006. Coming into force: 01.11.2006. Effect: S.I. 2004/1748 (W.185) amended. Territorial extent & classification: W. General. - In English and Welsh. Welsh title: Rheoliadau Diwygio Gofal Cymunedol, Gwasanaethau ar gyfer Gofalwyr a Gwasanaethau Plant (Taliadau Uniongyrchol) (Cymru) 2006. - With correction slip dated February 2007. - 4p.: 30 cm. - 978-0-11-091421-3 £3.00

Sports grounds and sporting events

The London Olympic Games and Paralympic Games Act 2006 (Commencement No. 1) Order 2006 No. 2006/1118 (C.38). - Enabling power: London Olympic Games and Paralympic Games Act 2006, s. 40 (2) to (4) (9). Bringing into operation certain provisions of the 2006 Act on 30.05.2006. - Issued: 25.04.2006. Made: 19.04.2006. Effect: None. Territorial extent & classification: E/W/S/NI. General. - 4p.: 30 cm. - 978-0-11-074507-7 £3.00

Sports grounds and sporting events, England

The Safety of Sports Grounds (Designation) Order 2006 No. 2006/218. - Enabling power: Safety of Sports Grounds Act 1975, s. 1 (1), 18 (2). - Issued: 07.02.2006. Made: 31.01.2006. Laid: 02.02.2006. Coming into force: 01.03.2006. Effect: S.I. 1986/1296 amended. Territorial extent & classification: E. General. - 2p.: 30 cm. - 978-0-11-074001-0 *£3.00*

Sports grounds and sporting events, England and Wales

The Football Spectators (2006 World Cup Control Period) Order 2006 No. 2006/988. - Enabling power: Football Spectators Act 1989, ss. 14 (6), 22A (2). - Issued: 05.04.2006. Made: 29.03.2006. Laid: 03.04.2006. Coming into force: 24.04.2006. Effect: None. Territorial extent & classification: E/W. General. - 2p.: 30 cm. - 978-0-11-074435-3 *£3.00*

The Football Spectators (Prescription) (Amendment) Order 2006 No. 2006/761. - Enabling power: Football Spectators Act 1989, ss. 14 (2), 22A. - Issued: 20.03.2006. Made: 14.03.2006. Laid: 20.03.2006. Coming into force: 10.04.2006. Effect: S.I. 2004/2409 amended. Territorial extent & classification: E/W. General. - 4p.: 30 cm. - 978-0-11-074339-4 *£3.00*

The Football Spectators (Seating) Order 2006 No. 2006/1661. - Enabling power: Football Spectators Act 1989, s. 11 (1) to (3). - Issued: 28.06.2006. Made: 22.06.2006. Laid: 23.06.2006. Coming into force: 17.07.2006. Effect: None. Territorial extent & classification: E/W. General. - 2p.: 30 cm. - 978-0-11-074745-3 *£3.00*

The Safety of Sports Grounds (Designation) (No. 2) Order 2006 No. 2006/1662. - Enabling power: Safety of Sports Grounds Act 1975, s. 1 (1), 18 (2). - Issued: 28.06.2006. Made: 22.06.2006. Laid: 23.06.2006. Coming into force: 17.07.2006. Effect: S.I. 1986/1296 amended. Territorial extent & classification: E/W. General. - 2p.: 30 cm. - 978-0-11-074746-0 *£3.00*

The Safety of Sports Grounds (Designation) (No. 3) Order 2006 No. 2006/1971. - Enabling power: Safety of Sports Grounds Act 1975, s. 1 (1). - Issued: 27.07.2006. Made: 19.07.2006. Laid: 21.07.2006. Coming into force: 11.08.2006. Effect: None. Territorial extent & classification: E/W. General. - 2p.: 30 cm. - 978-0-11-074910-5 *£3.00*

The Safety of Sports Grounds (Designation) (No. 4) Order 2006 No. 2006/3168. - Enabling power: Safety of Sports Grounds Act 1975, s. 1 (1). - Issued: 05.12.2006. Made: 27.11.2006. Laid: 29.11.2006. Coming into force: 20.12.2006. Effect: None. Territorial extent & classification: E/W. General. - 2p.: 30 cm. - 978-0-11-075393-5 *£3.00*

Stamp duty

The Stamp Duty and Stamp Duty Reserve Tax (Definition of Unit Trust Scheme and Open-ended Investment Company) (Amendment) Regulations 2006 No. 2006/746. - Enabling power: Finance Act 1999, sch. 19, para. 6A (4). - Issued: 21.03.2006. Made: 15.03.2006. Laid: 15.03.2006. Coming into force: 06.04.2006. Effect: S.I. 2001/964 amended. Territorial extent & classification: E/W/S/NI. General. - 8p.: 30 cm. - 978-0-11-074323-3 *£3.00*

The Stamp Duty and Stamp Duty Reserve Tax (Extension of Exceptions relating to Recognised Exchanges) Regulations 2006 No. 2006/139. - Enabling power: Finance (No.2) Act 2005, s. 50 (1) (4). - Issued: 01.02.2006. Made: 25.01.2006. Laid: 26.01.2006. Coming into force: 16.02.2006. Effect: None. Territorial extent & classification: E/W/S/NI. General. - 2p.: 30 cm. - 978-0-11-073953-3 *£3.00*

Stamp duty land tax

The Pension Protection Fund (Tax) Regulations 2006 No. 2006/575. - Enabling power: Finance Act 2005, s. 102. - Issued: 14.03.2006. Made: 09.03.2006. Laid: 10.03.2006. Coming into force: 06.04.2006. Effect: None. Territorial extent & classification: E/W/S/NI. General. - 14p.: 30 cm. - 978-0-11-074218-2 *£3.00*

The Stamp Duty Land Tax (Administration) (Amendment) Regulations 2006 No. 2006/776. - Enabling power: Finance Act 2003, s. 113 (2), sch. 11, para. 2. - Issued: 21.03.2006. Made: 15.03.2006. Laid: 16.03.2006. Coming into force: 17.04.2006. Effect: S.I. 2003/2837 amended. Territorial extent & classification: E/W/S/NI. General. - 4p.: 30 cm. - 978-0-11-074326-4 *£3.00*

The Stamp Duty Land Tax (Amendment to the Finance Act 2003) Regulations 2006 No. 2006/875. - Enabling power: Finance Act 2003, s. 50 (2) (3). - Issued: 28.03.2006. Made: 22.03.2006. Laid: 22.03.2006. Coming into force: 12.04.2006. Effect: 2003 c. 14 amended. Territorial extent & classification: E/W/S/NI. General. - 4p.: 30 cm. - 978-0-11-074383-7 *£3.00*

The Stamp Duty Land Tax (Electronic Communications) (Amendment) Regulations 2006 No. 2006/3427. - Enabling power: Finance Act 1999, ss. 132, 133 (2) & Finance Act 2003, s. 79 (1) (5) (6) (b) & Finance (No. 2) Act 2005, s. 47 (5) (6) (b). - Issued: 02.01.2007. Made: 20.12.2006. Laid: 21.12.2006. Coming into force: 31.01.2007. Effect: S.I. 2005/844 amended. Territorial extent & classification: E/W/S/NI. General. - 8p.: 30 cm. - 978-0-11-075576-2 *£3.00*

The Stamp Duty Land Tax (Variation of the Finance Act 2003) Regulations 2006 No. 2006/3237. - Enabling power: Finance Act 2003, s. 109. - Issued: 22.01.2007. Made: 06.12.2006 at 11.00 am. Laid: 06.12.2006 at 2.00 pm. Coming into force: 06.12.2006 at 2.00 pm. Effect: 2003 c. 14 varied. Territorial extent & classification: E/W/S/NI. General. - Approved by the House of Commons. Supersedes the S.I. of the same title and number (ISBN 9780110754321) issued 12.12.2006. - 8p.: 30 cm. - 978-0-11-075654-7 £3.00

The Stamp Duty Land Tax (Variation of the Finance Act 2003) Regulations 2006 No. 2006/3237. - Enabling power: Finance Act 2003, s. 109. - Issued: 12.12.2006. Made: 06.12.2006, 11.00 am. Laid: 06.12.2006, 2.00 pm. Coming into force: 06.12.2006, 2.00 pm. Effect: 2003 c. 14 amended. Territorial extent & classification: E/W/S/NI. General. - For approval by that House within twenty-eight days beginning with the day on which the Regulations were made, subject to extension for periods of dissolution, prorogation or adjournment for more than four days. Superseded by the S.I. of the same title and number (ISBN 9780110756547) issued on 22.01.2007. - 8p.: 30 cm. - 978-0-11-075432-1 £3.00

Stamp duty reserve tax

The Stamp Duty and Stamp Duty Reserve Tax (Definition of Unit Trust Scheme and Open-ended Investment Company) (Amendment) Regulations 2006 No. 2006/746. - Enabling power: Finance Act 1999, sch. 19, para. 6A (4). - Issued: 21.03.2006. Made: 15.03.2006. Laid: 15.03.2006. Coming into force: 06.04.2006. Effect: S.I. 2001/964 amended. Territorial extent & classification: E/W/S/NI. General. - 8p.: 30 cm. - 978-0-11-074323-3 £3.00

The Stamp Duty and Stamp Duty Reserve Tax (Extension of Exceptions relating to Recognised Exchanges) Regulations 2006 No. 2006/139. - Enabling power: Finance (No.2) Act 2005, s. 50 (1) (4). - Issued: 01.02.2006. Made: 25.01.2006. Laid: 26.01.2006. Coming into force: 16.02.2006. Effect: None. Territorial extent & classification: E/W/S/NI. General. - 2p.: 30 cm. - 978-0-11-073953-3 £3.00

Statistics of trade

The Statistics of Trade (Customs and Excise) (Amendment) Regulations 2006 No. 2006/3216. - Enabling power: European Communities Act 1972, s. 2 (2). - Issued: 08.12.2006. Made: 04.12.2006. Laid: 05.12.2006. Coming into force: 01.01.2007. Effect: S.I. 1992/2790 amended, S.I. 2005/3371 revoked. Territorial extent & classification: UK. General. - 4p.: 30 cm. - 978-0-11-075415-4 £3.00

Supreme Court of England and Wales

The Civil Procedure Act 1997 (Amendment) Order 2006 No. 2006/1847 (L.7). - Enabling power: Civil Procedure Act 1997, s. 2A (1). - Issued: 17.07.2006. Made: 10.07.2006. Laid: 12.07.2006. Coming into force: 01.09.2006. Effect: 1997 c. 12 amended. Territorial extent & classification: E/W. General. - 2p.: 30 cm. - 978-0-11-074836-8 £3.00

The Civil Procedure (Amendment No.2) Rules 2006 No. 2006/3132 (L.13). - Enabling power: Civil Procedure Act 1997, s. 2. - Issued: 29.11.2006. Made: 23.11.2006. Laid: 27.11.2006. Coming into force: 18.12.2006. Effect: S.I. 1998/3132 amended. Territorial extent & classification: E/W. General. - 4p.: 30 cm. - 978-0-11-075374-4 £3.00

The Civil Procedure (Amendment No.3) Rules 2006 No. 2006/3435 (L.15). - Enabling power: Civil Procedure Act 1997, s. 2. - Issued: 03.01.2007. Made: 19.12.2006. Laid: 21.12.2006. Coming into force: 06.04.2007. Effect: S.I. 1998/3132 amended. Territorial extent & classification: E/W. General. - 16p.: 30 cm. - 978-0-11-075578-6 £3.00

The Civil Procedure (Amendment) Rules 2006 No. 2006/1689 (L.6). - Enabling power: Civil Procedure Act 1997, s. 2. - Issued: 03.07.2006. Made: 26.06.2006. Laid: 27.06.2006. Coming into force: 02.10.2006. Effect: S.I. 1998/3132 amended. Territorial extent & classification: E/W. General. - 8p.: 30 cm. - 978-0-11-074765-1 £3.00

The Civil Proceedings Fees (Amendment) Order 2006 No. 2006/719 (L.4). - Enabling power: Courts Act 2003, s. 92 & Insolvency Act 1986, ss. 414, 415. - Issued: 20.03.2006. Made: 09.03.2006. Laid: 16.03.2006. Coming into force: 06.04.2006. Effect: S.I. 2004/3121 amended. Territorial extent & classification: E/W. General. - 4p.: 30 cm. - 978-0-11-074278-6 £3.00

The Constitutional Reform Act 2005 (Commencement No. 4) Order 2006 No. 2006/228 (C.5). - Enabling power: Constitutional Reform Act 2005, s. 148. Bringing into operation various provisions of the 2005 Act on 27.02.2006. - Issued: 08.02.2006. Made: 29.01.2006. Effect: None. Territorial extent & classification: Extends to UK but applies to E/W. General. - 2p.: 30 cm. - 978-0-11-074008-9 £3.00

The Constitutional Reform Act 2005 (Temporary Modifications) Order 2006 No. 2006/227. - Enabling power: Constitutional Reform Act 2005, s. 143 (1) (2) (a). - Issued: 08.02.2006. Made: 29.01.2006. Laid: 03.02.2006. Coming into force: 27.02.2006. Effect: 2005 c.4 temporarily modified in accord. with art. 2. Territorial extent & classification: Extends to UK but applies to E/W. General. - 2p.: 30 cm. - 978-0-11-074007-2 £3.00

The Courts Act 2003 (Consequential Amendment) Order 2006 No. 2006/1001. - Enabling power: Courts Act 2003, ss. 109 (4) (a) (5) (b). - Issued: 04.04.2006. Made: 29.03.2006. Coming into force: 06.04.2006. Effect: 1991 c.48 amended. Territorial extent & classification: E/W. General. - Supersedes draft. - 2p.: 30 cm. - 978-0-11-074447-6 £3.00

The Criminal Procedure (Amendment No. 2) Rules 2006 No. 2006/2636 (L.9). - Enabling power: Courts Act 2003, s. 69. - Issued: 11.10.2006. Made: 03.10.2006. Laid: 04.10.2006. Coming into force: 06.11.2006. Effect: S.I. 2005/384 (L.4) amended. Territorial extent and classification: E/W. General. - 12p.: 30 cm. - 978-0-11-075153-5 £3.00

The Criminal Procedure (Amendment) Rules 2006 No. 2006/353 (L.2). - Enabling power: Courts Act 2003, s. 69 & Juries Act 1974, ss. 9 (3), 9A (3). - Issued: 21.02.2006. Made: 09.02.2006. Laid: 15.02.2006. Coming into force: 03.04.2006. Effect: S.I. 2005/384 (L. 4) amended. Territorial extent and classification: E/W. General. - 16p.: 30 cm. - 978-0-11-074065-2 £3.00

The Family Proceedings (Amendment) (No. 2) Rules 2006 No. 2006/2080 (L.8). - Enabling power: Matrimonial and Family Proceedings Act 1984, s. 40 (1). - Issued: 01.08.2006. Made: 25.07.2006. Laid: 27.07.2006. Coming into force: 21.08.2006. Effect: S.I. 1991/1247 amended. Territorial extent & classification: E/W. General. - 4p.: 30 cm. - 978-0-11-074957-0 £3.00

The Family Proceedings (Amendment) Rules 2006 No. 2006/352 (L.1). - Enabling power: Matrimonial and Family Proceedings Act 1984, s. 40 (1). - Issued: 21.02.2006. Made: 10.02.2006. Laid: 15.02.2006. Coming into force: 03.04.2006. Effect: S.1.1991/1247 amended. Territorial extent & classification: E/W. General. - 12p.: 30 cm. - 978-0-11-074057-7 £3.00

The Family Proceedings Fees (Amendment) Order 2006 No. 2006/739 (L.5). - Enabling power: Courts Act 2003, s. 92. - Issued: 20.03.2006. Made: 07.03.2006. Laid: 16.03.2006. Coming into force: 06.04.2006. Effect: S.I. 2004/3114 amended. Territorial extent & classification: E/W. General. - 2p.: 30 cm. - 978-0-11-074306-6 £3.00

Sustainable development, Northern Ireland

The Northern Ireland (Miscellaneous Provisions) Act 2006 (Commencement No.2) Order 2006 No. 2006/2966 (C.104). - Enabling power: Northern Ireland (Miscellaneous Provisions) Act 2006, s. 31 (3). Bringing into operation various provisions of the 2005 Act on 01.12.2006 & 31.03.2007. - Issued: 20.11.2006. Made: 13.11.2006. Effect: None. Territorial extent & classification: NI. General. - 2p.: 30 cm. - 978-0-11-075306-5 £3.00

Tax credits

The Child Tax Credit (Amendment No. 2) Regulations 2006 No. 2006/1163. - Enabling power: Tax Credits Act 2002, ss. 8 (2), 65 (1) (7) (9). - Issued: 28.04.2006. Made: 25.04.2006. Laid: 25.04.2006. Coming into force: 24.05.2006. Effect: S.I. 2002/2007 amended. Territorial extent & classification: E/W/S/NI. General. - 2p.: 30 cm. - 978-0-11-074525-1 £3.00

The Child Tax Credits (Amendment) Regulations 2006 No. 2006/222. - Enabling power: Tax Credits Act 2002, ss. 8, 65 (1), 67. - Issued: 08.02.2006. Made: 02.02.2006. Laid: 03.02.2006. Coming into force: 06.04.2006. Effect: S.I. 2002/2007 amended. Territorial extent & classification: E/W/S/NI. General. - 4p.: 30 cm. - 978-0-11-074005-8 £3.00

The Tax Credits Act 2002 (Commencement and Transitional Provisions) Order 2006 No. 2006/3369 (C.124). - Enabling power: Tax Credits Act 2002, ss. 61, 62 (2). - Issued: 21.12.2006. Made: 14.12.2006. Coming into force: 14.12.2006. Effect: S.I. 2003/962; 2005/773 amended and S.I. 2005/1106, 776 revoked. Territorial extent & classification: E/W/S/NI. General. - 4p.: 30 cm. - 978-0-11-075527-4 £3.00

The Tax Credits (Claims and Notifications) (Amendment) Regulations 2006 No. 2006/2689. - Enabling power: Tax Credits Act 2002, ss. 6, 65 (2) (7), 67. - Issued: 13.10.2006. Made: 10.10.2006. Laid: 11.10.2006. Coming into force: 01.11.2006 & 06.04.2007 in accord. with reg. 1. Effect: S.I. 2002/2014 amended. Territorial extent & classification: E/W/S/NI. General. - 4p.: 30 cm. - 978-0-11-075170-2 £3.00

The Tax Credits (Miscellaneous Amendments) Regulations 2006 No. 2006/766. - Enabling power: Tax Credits Act 2002, ss. 3 (7), 7 (8) (9), 8 (2) (4), 10, 12, 65 (1) (3) (7) (9), 66. - Issued: 21.03.2006. Made: 14.03.2006. Laid: 15.03.2006. Coming into force: 06.04.2006. Effect: S.I. 2002/2005, 2006, 2007, 2014; 2003/654; 2004/1243 amended. Territorial extent & classification: E/W/S/NI. General. - 12p.: 30 cm. - 978-0-11-074322-6 £3.00

The Tax Credits Up-rating Regulations 2006 No. 2006/963. - Enabling power: Tax Credits Act 2002, ss. 7 (1) (a), 9, 11, 13, 65 (1). - Issued: 04.04.2006. Made: 29.03.2006. Coming into force: 06.04.2006. Effect: S.I.2002/2005, 2007, 2008 amended. Territorial extent & classification: E/W/S/NI. General. - 4p.: 30 cm. - 978-0-11-074428-5 £3.00

Taxes

The Mutual Assistance Provisions Order 2006 No. 2006/3283. - Enabling power: Finance Act 2003, s. 197 (5). - Issued: 14.12.2006. Made: 11.12.2006. Laid: 11.12.2006. Coming into force: 01.01.2007. Effect: 2003 c.14 amended. Territorial extent & classification: E/W/S/NI. General. - With correction slip dated January 2007. - 2p.: 30 cm. - 978-0-11-075465-9 £3.00

The Stamp Duty Land Tax (Amendment to the Finance Act 2003) Regulations 2006 No. 2006/875. - Enabling power: Finance Act 2003, s. 50 (2) (3). - Issued: 28.03.2006. Made: 22.03.2006. Laid: 22.03.2006. Coming into force: 12.04.2006. Effect: 2003 c. 14 amended. Territorial extent & classification: E/W/S/NI. General. - 4p.: 30 cm. - 978-0-11-074383-7 £3.00

The Taxation of Pension Schemes (Consequential Amendments of Occupational and Personal Pension Schemes Legislation) Order 2006 No. 2006/744. - Enabling power: Finance Act 2004, s. 281 (2). - Issued: 23.03.2006. Made: 14.03.2006. Laid: 15.03.2006. Coming into force: 06.04.2006. Effect: 40 instruments amended. Territorial extent & classification: E/W/S/NI. General. - 40p.: 30 cm. - 978-0-11-074341-7 £6.50

Taxes: Tonnage tax

The Tonnage Tax (Training Requirement) (Amendment) Regulations 2006 No. 2006/2229. - Enabling power: Finance Act 2000, sch. 22, paras 29, 31, 36. - Issued: 22.08.2006. Made: 14.08.2006. Laid: 17.08.2006. Coming into force: 01.10.2006. Effect: S.I. 2000/2129 amended. Territorial extent & classification: E/W/S/NI. General. - 2p.: 30 cm. - 978-0-11-075021-7 £3.00

Terms and conditions of employment

The Adoption and Children Act 2002 (Consequential Amendment to Statutory Adoption Pay) Order 2006 No. 2006/2012. - Enabling power: Adoption and Children Act 2002, ss. 140 (7), 142 (1). - Issued: 01.08.2006. Made: 23.07.2006. Coming into force: 01.09.2006. Effect: 1992 c.4 amended. Territorial extent & classification: E/W/S. General. - Supersedes draft SI (ISBN 0110747739) issued 04.07.2006. - 4p.: 30 cm. - 978-0-11-074935-8 £3.00

The Collective Redundancies (Amendment) Regulations 2006 No. 2006/2387. - Enabling power: European Communities Act 1972, s. 2 (2). - Issued: 14.09.2006. Made: 31.08.2006. Laid: 08.09.2006. Coming into force: 01.10.2006. Effect: 1992 c.52 amended. Territorial extent & classification: E/W/S. General. - EC note: These Regs are made in consequence of the judgement of the European Court Justice in Case C-188/03, Junk v Kühnel, which concerned the interpretation of Council Directive 98/59/EC on the approximation of the laws of the Member States relating to collective redundancies. - 2p.: 30 cm. - 978-0-11-075085-9 £3.00

The Employment Rights (Increase of Limits) Order 2006 No. 2006/3045. - Enabling power: Employment Relations Act 1999, s. 34. - Issued: 24.11.2006. Made: 14.11.2006. Laid: 20.11.2006. Coming into force: 01.02.2007. Effect: S.I. 2005/3352 revoked with saving. Territorial extent & classification: E/W/S. General. - 8p.: 30 cm. - 978-0-11-075337-9 £3.00

The European Cooperative Society (Involvement of Employees) Regulations 2006 No. 2006/2059. - Enabling power: European Communities Act 1972, s. 2 (2). - Issued: 04.08.2006. Made: 25.07.2006. Laid: 27.07.2006. Coming into force: 18.08.2006. Effect: 1996 c.17, c.18; 2002 c.22; S.I. 1996/1919 (N.I.16), 1921; 1999/3323; 2003/2902 amended. Territorial extent & classification: E/W/S/NI. General. - EC note: These Regulations implement Council Directive 2003/72/EC supplementing the Statute for a European Cooperative Society with regard to the involvement of employees. The Directive supplements Regulation 1435/2003/EC. - 48p.: 30 cm. - 978-0-11-074944-0 £7.50

The Flexible Working (Eligibility, Complaints and Remedies) (Amendment) Regulations 2006 No. 2006/3314. - Enabling power: Employment Rights Act 1996, ss. 80F (1) (b), 80F (8) (a) (10). - Issued: 20.12.2006. Made: 07.12.2006. Laid: 14.12.2006. Coming into force: 06.04.2007. Effect: S.I. 2002/3236 amended. Territorial extent & classification: E/W/S. General. - 4p.: 30 cm. - 978-0-11-075491-8 £3.00

The Information and Consultation of Employees (Amendment) Regulations 2006 No. 2006/514. - Enabling power: Employment Relations Act 2004, s. 42 (1) (3) (a) (4) (f) (9). - Issued: 07.03.2006. Made: 27.02.2006. Coming into force: 06.04.2006. Effect: S.I. 2004/3426 amended. Territorial extent & classification: GB. General. - Supersedes draft SI (ISBN 0110739019) issued 20.01.2006. - 4p.: 30 cm. - 978-0-11-074130-7 £3.00

The Maternity and Parental Leave etc. and the Paternity and Adoption Leave (Amendment) Regulations 2006 No. 2006/2014. - Enabling power: Employment Rights Act 1996, ss. 47C (2), 71 (3), 73 (2) (3), 74 (2) (3) (4), 75 (1) (2), 75A (2) (2A), 75B (2) (3), 75C, 75D (1), 99 (1). - Issued: 01.08.2006. Made: 23.07.2006. Coming into force: 01.10.2006. Effect: S.I. 1999/3312; 2002/2788 amended. Territorial extent & classification: E/W/S. General. - With correction slip, dated January 2007. Supersedes draft SI (ISBN 0110747720) issued 04.07.2006. - 8p.: 30 cm. - 978-0-11-074940-2 £3.00

The National Minimum Wage Regulations 1999 (Amendment) Regulations 2006 No. 2006/2001. - Enabling power: National Minimum Wage Act 1998, ss. 1 (3), 2, 3, 51. - Issued: 28.07.2006. Made: 20.07.2006. Coming into force: 01.10.2006. Effect: S.I. 1999/584; 2005/2019 amended. Territorial extent & classification: E/W/S/NI. General. - Supersedes draft S.I. (ISBN 011074652X) issued 14.06.2006. - 4p.: 30 cm. - 978-0-11-074918-1 £3.00

The Occupational and Personal Pension Schemes (Consultation by Employers and Miscellaneous Amendment) Regulations 2006 No. 2006/349. - Enabling power: Pensions Act 2004, ss. 10 (5) (a), 259 (1) (2), 260 (1), 261 (2) (4), 286 (1) (3) (g), 315 (2) (3) (5), 318 (1) (4) (a) (5). - Issued: 22.02.2006. Made: 15.02.2006. Coming into force: 06.04.2006 except for reg. 22; 16.02.2006 for reg. 22. Effect: 1996 c.18; S.I. 2005/1994 amended. Territorial extent & classification: E/W/S (with the exception of the amendment to the 2005 Regulations, which extends to Northern Ireland). General. - 20p.: 30 cm. - 978-0-11-074081-2 £3.50

The Occupational and Personal Pension Schemes (Miscellaneous Amendments) Regulations 2006 No. 2006/778. - Enabling power: Pension Schemes Act 1993, ss. 55 (2B), 101C (2), 113 (1) (d), 181 (1), 182 (2) (3) & Pension Schemes (Northern Ireland) Act 1993, ss. 51 (2B) (2ZA) & Pensions Act 1995, ss. 35 (3) (4), 40 (2), 41 (1), 47 (5) (6), 49 (1) (2) (4) (9) (b), 87 (1), 88 (1), 91 (5), 124 (1), 174 (2) (3) & Pensions Act 2004, ss. 259 (1), 260 (1), 315 (2), 318 (1). - Issued: 21.03.2006. Made: 14.03.2006. Laid: 16.03.2006. Coming into force: In accord. with reg. 1 (1). Effect: S.R. 1996/493; S.I. 1996/1172, 1715, 1975; 1997/785; 2000/1054, 2692; 2005/3378; 2006/349 amended. Territorial extent & classification: E/W/S/NI General. - 8p.: 30 cm. - 978-0-11-074337-0 £3.00

The Social Security Benefits Up-rating Order 2006 No. 2006/645. - Enabling power: Social Security Administration Act 1992, ss. 150, 151, 189 (1) (4) (5). - Issued: 16.03.2006. Made: 09.03.2006. Coming into force: In accord. with art. 1. Effect: 1965 c.51; 1992 c.4; 1993 c.48 & S.I. 1978/393; 1986/1960; 1987/1967, 1969, 1971; 1991/2890; 1992/1814; 1994/2946; 1995/310; 1996/207; 2002/1792, 2818 amended & S.I. 2005/522 revoked. Territorial extent & classification: E/W/S. General. - Supersedes the draft S.I. (ISBN 0110739272) issued on 25.01.2006. - 48p.: 30 cm. - 978-0-11-074258-8 £7.50

The Statutory Maternity Pay, Social Security (Maternity Allowance) and Social Security (Overlapping Benefits) (Amendment) Regulations 2006 No. 2006/2379. - Enabling power: Social Security Contributions and Benefits Act 1992, ss. 35 (3) (a) (i) (c), 165 (1) (3) (4) (7), 175 (1) (3) & Social Security Administration Act 1992, ss. 5 (1) (l), 73 (1) (a), 189 (1) (3) (4). - Issued: 08.09.2006. Made: 04.09.2006. Laid: 08.09.2006. Coming into force: 01.10.2006 in accord. with reg. 1 (2). Effect: S.I. 1979/597; 1986/1960; 1987/416 amended. Territorial extent & classification: E/W/S. General. - 8p.: 30 cm. - 978-0-11-075075-0 £3.00

The Statutory Paternity Pay and Statutory Adoption Pay (General) and the Statutory Paternity Pay and Statutory Adoption Pay (Weekly Rates) (Amendment) Regulations 2006 No. 2006/2236. - Enabling power: Social Security Contributions and Benefits Act 1992, ss. 171ZE (10A), 171ZN (2) (3) (6A) & Social Security Administration Act 1992, s. 5 (1) (l). - Issued: 24.08.2006. Made: 14.08.2006. Laid: 17.08.2006. Coming into force: 01.10.2006. Effect: S.I. 2002/2818, 2822 amended. Territorial extent & classification: E/W/S. General. - 4p.: 30 cm. - 978-0-11-075028-6 £3.00

The Statutory Sick Pay (General) Amendment Regulations 2006 No. 2006/799. - Enabling power: Social Security Contributions and Benefits Act 1992, s. 151 (4). - Issued: 22.03.2006. Made: 15.03.2006. Laid: 20.03.2006. Coming into force: 10.04.2006. Effect: S.I. 1982/894 amended. Territorial extent & classification: E/W/S. General. - 4p.: 30 cm. - 978-0-11-074348-6 £3.00

The Transfer of Undertakings (Protection of Employment) (Consequential Amendments) Regulations 2006 No. 2006/2405. - Enabling power: European Communities Act 1972, s. 2 (2) & Employment Relations Act 1999, s. 38. - Issued: 14.09.2006. Made: 06.09.2006. Laid: 08.09.2006. Coming into force: 01.10.2006. Effect: S.I. 2004/753, 1861, 3426 amended. Territorial extent & classification: E/W/S. General. - EC note: These regs implement, in Great Britain, Council Directive 2001/23/EC on the approximation of the law relating to business transfers, they are made under section 2(2) of the European Communities Act 1972. - 4p.: 30 cm. - 978-0-11-075093-4 £3.00

The Transfer of Undertakings (Protection of Employment) Regulations 2006 No. 2006/246. - Enabling power: European Communities Act 1972, s. 2 (2) & Employment Relations Act 1999, s. 38. - Issued: 15.02.2006. Made: 06.02.2006. Laid: 07.02.2006. Coming into force: 06.04.2006. Effect: 1993 c. 19; 1996 c. 18 & 21 other Acts amended; S.I. 1993/3160 (N.I. 15); 1994/2809 (N.I. 16); 1996/1919 (N.I. 16), 1921 (N.I. 18) amended & S.I. 1981/1794 revoked with savings, in accord. with arts 19-20 and schedule 2. Territorial extent & classification: E/W/S/NI. General. - EC note: These Regs implement Council Directive 2001/23/EC on the approximation of the law relating to business transfers. - 24p.: 30 cm. - 978-0-11-073992-2 £4.00

The Work and Families Act 2006 (Commencement No. 1) Order 2006 No. 2006/1682 (C.58). - Enabling power: Work and Families Act 2006, s. 19 (2) (3). Bringing into operation various provisions of the 2006 Act on 27.06.2006, 01.10.2006, 06.04.2007 in accord. with arts, 2, 3, 4. - Issued: 04.07.2006. Made: 25.06.2006. Effect: None. Territorial extent & classification: E/W/S/NI. General. - 2p.: 30 cm. - 978-0-11-074760-6 £3.00

The Work and Families Act 2006 (Commencement No. 2) Order 2006 No. 2006/2232 (C.76). - Enabling power: Work and Families Act 2006, s. 19 (2) (3). Bringing into operation various provisions of the 2006 Act on 01.10.2006 in accord with art. 2. - Issued: 22.08.2006. Made: 14.08.2006. Effect: None. Territorial extent & classification: E/W/S. General. - 2p.: 30 cm. - 978-0-11-075023-1 £3.00

The Working Time (Amendment) (No.2) Regulations 2006 No. 2006/2389. - Enabling power: European Communities Act 1972, s. 2 (2). - Issued: 14.09.2006. Made: 04.09.2006. Laid: 08.09.2006. Coming into force: 01.10.2006. Effect: S.I. 1998/1833 amended. Territorial extent & classification: E/W/S. General. - EC note: These Regulations amend the Working Time Regulations 1998 which implement Council Directive 2003/88/EC- 2p.: 30 cm. - 978-0-11-075087-3 £3.00

The Working Time (Amendment) Regulations 2006 No. 2006/99. - Enabling power: European Communities Act 1972, s. 2 (2). - Issued: 02.02.2006. Made: 23.01.2006. Laid: 24.01.2006. Coming into force: 06.04.2006. Effect: S.I. 1998/1833 amended. Territorial extent & classification: E/W/S. General. - 2p.: 30 cm. - 978-0-11-073930-4 *£3.00*

Town and country planning

The Planning and Compulsory Purchase Act 2004 (Commencement No. 9 and Consequential Provisions) Order 2006 No. 2006/1281 (C.43). - Enabling power: Planning and Compulsory Purchase Act 2004, ss. 121, 122. Bringing into operation various provisions of the 2004 Act on 07.06.2006 in accord. with arts. 2 to 4. - Issued: 17.05.2006. Made: 10.05.2006. Laid: 17.05.2006. Effect: 1990 c.8, c.9 amended & S.I. 1992/2832; 1995/419; 1999/1736, 1892 amended. Territorial extent & classification: E/W/S. General. - 8p.: 30 cm. - 978-0-11-074573-2 *£3.00*

The Town and Country Planning (Environmental Impact Assessment) (Amendment) Regulations 2006 No. 2006/3295. - Enabling power: European Communities Act 1972, s. 2 (2). - Issued: 18.12.2006. Made: 11.12.2006. Laid: 18.12.2006. Coming into force: 15.01.2007. Effect: S.I. 1999/293 amended in relation to England. Territorial extent & classification: E only, though reg 22 inserts provisions that also apply to Scotland, Wales and Northern Ireland. General. - EC note: These Regulations give effect to art. 3 of Directive 2003/35/EC ("the Directive") in so far as it affects public participation in the decision making process for applications and appeals relating to development for which environmental impact assessment is required. The Directive amends with regard to public participation and access to justice Council Directives 85/337/EEC as amended by Directive 97/11/EC and 96/61/EC. These Regulations also apply the requirements of Council Directive 85/337/EEC. - 12p.: 30 cm. - 978-0-11-075471-0 *£3.00*

Town and country planning, England

The Caravan Sites Act 1968 and Social Landlords (Permissible Additional Purposes) (England) Order 2006 (Definition of Caravan) (Amendment) (England) Order 2006 No. 2006/2374. - Enabling power: Caravan Sites Act 1968, s. 13 (3) & Housing Act 1996, s. 2 (7). - Issued: 08.09.2006. Made: 04.09.2006. Laid: 08.09.2006. Coming into force: 01.10.2006. Effect: 1960 c. 62; S.I. 2006/1968 amended. Territorial extent & classification: E. General. - 4p.: 30 cm. - 978-0-11-075070-5 *£3.00*

The Periodic Review of Mineral Planning Permissions (Conygar Quarry) Order 2006 No. 2006/226. - Enabling power: Environment Act 1995, sch. 14, para. 3A (1). - Issued: 09.02.2006. Made: 02.02.2006. Laid: 09.02.2006. Coming into force: 03.03.2006. Effect: None. Territorial extent & classification: E. General. - 2p.: 30 cm. - 978-0-11-074010-2 *£3.00*

The Planning and Compulsory Purchase Act 2004 (Commencement No. 8 and Saving) Order 2006 No. 2006/1061 (C.35). - Enabling power: Planning and Compulsory Purchase Act 2004, s. 121. Bringing into operation various provisions of the 2004 Act on 10.05.2006 & 10.08.2006. - Issued: 12.04.2006. Made: 05.04.2006. Effect: None. Territorial extent & classification: E. General. - 8p.: 30 cm. - 978-0-11-074481-0 *£3.00*

The Planning (Applications for Planning Permission, Listed Buildings and Conservation Areas) (Amendment) (England) Regulations 2006 No. 2006/1063. - Enabling power: Town and Country Planning Act 1990, s. 62 & Planning (Listed Buildings and Conservation Areas) Act 1990, s. 10 (3) to (5). - Issued: 12.04.2006. Made: 05.04.2006. Laid: 12.04.2006. Coming into force: 10.08.2006. Effect: S.I. 1988/1812; 1990/1519 amended. Territorial extent & classification: E. General. - 4p.: 30 cm. - 978-0-11-074483-4 *£3.00*

The Planning (Application to the Houses of Parliament) Order 2006 No. 2006/1469. - Enabling power: Town and Country Planning Act 1990, s. 293 (1) & Planning (Listed Buildings and Conservation Areas) Act 1990, s. 82C (3) (c) & Planning (Hazardous Substances) Act 1990, s. 31 (3). - Issued: 13.06.2006. Made: 06.06.2006. Coming into force: 07.06.2006 in accord. with art. 1 (1). Effect: None. Territorial extent & classification: E. General. - 4p.: 30 cm. - 978-0-11-074655-5 *£3.00*

The Planning (Listed Buildings, Conservation Areas and Hazardous Substances) (Amendment) (England) Regulations 2006 No. 2006/1283. - Enabling power: Planning (Listed Buildings and Conservation Areas) Act 1990, s. 82B (8) & Planning (Hazardous Substances) Act 1990, s. 30B (2) (3) (8) (b). - Issued: 17.05.2006. Made: 10.05.2006. Laid: 17.05.2006. Coming into force: 07.06.2006. Effect: S.I. 1990/1519; 1992/656 amended in relation to England. Territorial extent & classification: E. General. - 4p.: 30 cm. - 978-0-11-074575-6 *£3.00*

The Planning (National Security Directions and Appointed Representatives) (England) Rules 2006 No. 2006/1284. - Enabling power: Town and Country Planning Act 1990, s. 321 (7) & Planning (Listed Buildings and Conservation Areas) Act 1990, sch. 3, para. 6A (3) & Planning (Hazardous Substances) Act 1990, sch., para. 6A (3). - Issued: 17.05.2006. Made: 12.05.2006. Laid: 17.05.2006. Coming into force: 07.06.2006. Effect: None. Territorial extent & classification: E. General. - 8p.: 30 cm. - 978-0-11-074578-7 *£3.00*

The Town and Country Planning (Costs of Independent Examinations) (Standard Daily Amount) (England) Regulations 2006 No. 2006/3227. - Enabling power: Town and Country Planning Act 1990, s. 303A (5). - Issued: 11.12.2006. Made: 05.12.2006. Laid: 11.12.2006. Coming into force: 03.01.2007. Effect: None. Territorial extent & classification: E. General. - 4p.: 30 cm. - 978-0-11-075422-2 *£3.00*

The Town and Country Planning (Determination of Appeals by Appointed Persons) (Prescribed Classes) (Amendment) (England) Regulations 2006 No. 2006/2227. - Enabling power: Planning (Listed Buildings and Conservation Areas) Act 1990, s.93, sch. 3, para. 1. - Issued: 22.08.2006. Made: 14.08.2006. Laid: 22.08.2006. Coming into force: 01.10.2006. Effect: S.I. 1997/420 amended. Territorial extent & classification: E. General. - 4p.: 30 cm. - 978-0-11-075019-4 *£3.00*

The Town and Country Planning (Fees for Applications and Deemed Applications) (Amendment) (England) Regulations 2006 No. 2006/994. - Enabling power: Town and Country Planning Act 1990, s. 303. - Issued: 04.04.2006. Made: 30.03.2006. Coming into force: 06.04.2006. Effect: S.I. 1989/193 amended. Territorial extent & classification: E. General. - Supersedes draft S.I. (ISBN 0110739884) issued on 10.02.2006. - 4p.: 30 cm. - 978-0-11-074444-5 *£3.00*

The Town and Country Planning (General Development Procedure) (Amendment) (England) Order 2006 No. 2006/1062. - Enabling power: Town and Country Planning Act 1990, ss. 55 (2A) (2B), 59, 61 (1), 61A, 69, 78, sch. 4A, para. 1 (1) (2). - Issued: 12.04.2006. Made: 05.04.2006. Laid: 12.04.2006. Coming into force: In accord.with art. 1 (2) (3). Effect: S.I. 1995/419 amended. Territorial extent & classification: E. General. - 12p.: 30 cm. - 978-0-11-074482-7 *£3.00*

The Town and Country Planning (General Development Procedure) (Amendment) (No. 2) (England) Order 2006 No. 2006/2375. - Enabling power: Town and Country Planning Act 1990, ss. 59, 61 (1), 74 (1) (c), 333 (7). - Issued: 08.09.2006. Made: 04.09.2006. Laid: 08.09.2006. Coming into force: 01.10.2006. Effect: S.I. 1995/419 amended. Territorial extent & classification: E. General. - 4p.: 30 cm. - 978-0-11-075071-2 *£3.00*

The Town and Country Planning (General Permitted Development) (Amendment) (England) Order 2006 No. 2006/221. - Enabling power: Town and Country Planning Act 1990, ss. 59, 60, 333 (7). - Issued: 07.02.2006. Made: 23.01.2006. Laid: 07.02.2006. Coming into force: 06.04.2006. Effect: SI 1995/418 amended. Territorial extent & classification: E. General. - 2p.: 30 cm. - 978-0-11-074011-9 *£3.00*

The Town and Country Planning (Regional Spatial Strategies) (Examinations in Public) (Remuneration and Allowances) (England) (Revocation) Regulations 2006 No. 2006/3320. - Enabling power: Planning and Compulsory Purchase Act 2004, ss. 11 (2) (h), 122 (3). - Issued: 20.12.2006. Made: 12.12.2006. Laid: 20.12.2006. Coming into force: 21.01.2007. Effect: S.I. 2004/2209 revoked. Territorial extent & classification: E. General. - 2p.: 30 cm. - 978-0-11-075492-5 *£3.00*

The Town and Country Planning (Use Classes) (Amendment) (England) Order 2006 No. 2006/220. - Enabling power: Town and Country Planning Act 1990, ss. 55 (2) (f), 333 (7). - Issued: 07.02.2006. Made: 23.01.2006. Coming into force: 06.04.2006. Effect: S.I. 1987/764 amended. Territorial extent & classification: E. General. - 2p.: 30 cm. - 978-0-11-074013-3 *£3.00*

Town and country planning, England and Wales

The Town and Country Planning (Application of Subordinate Legislation to the Crown) Order 2006 No. 2006/1282. - Enabling power: Town and Country Planning Act 1990, ss. 55 (2) (f), 59, 60, 61 (1), 293A & Planning and Compulsory Purchase Act 2004, ss. 88, 122 (3). - Issued: 17.05.2006. Made: 10.05.2006. Laid: 17.05.2006. Coming into force: 07.06.2006. Effect: 19 S.I.s modified in accord. with arts. 5 to 46. Territorial extent & classification: E/W. General. - 56p.: 30 cm. - 978-0-11-074574-9 *£9.00*

Town and country planning, Wales

The Planning and Compulsory Purchase Act 2004 (Commencement No. 4 and Consequential, Transitional and Savings Provisions) (Wales) (Amendment No. 2) Order 2006 No. 2006/1700 (W.162) (C.59). - Enabling power: Planning and Compulsory Purchase Act 2004, ss. 121 (5), 122 (3). - Issued: 06.09.2006. Made: 29.06.2006. Coming into force: 30.06.2006. Effect: S.I. 2005/2722 (W.193) (C.110) amended. Territorial extent & classification: W. General. - In English and Welsh. Welsh title: Gorchmyn Deddf Cynllunio a Phrynu Gorfodol 2004 (Cychwyn Rhif 4 a Darpariaethau Canlyniadol a Throsiannol a Darpariaethau Arbed) (Cymru) (Diwygio Rhif 2) 2006. - 4p.: 30 cm. - 978-0-11-091398-8 *£3.00*

The Planning and Compulsory Purchase Act 2004 (Commencement No.4 and Consequential, Transitional and Savings Provisions) (Wales) (Amendment No.3) Order 2006 No. 2006/3119 (W.289). - Enabling power: Planning and Compulsory Purchase Act 2004, ss. 121 (5), 122 (3). - Issued: 04.12.2006. Made: 21.11.2006. Coming into force: 22.11.2006. Effect: S.I. 2005/2722 (W.193) (C.110) amended. Territorial extent & classification: W. General. - In English and Welsh. Welsh title: Gorchymyn Deddf Cynllunio a Phrynu Gorfodol 2004 (Cychwyn Rhif 4 a Darpariaethau Canlyniadol a Throsiannol a Darpariaethau Arbed) (Cymru) (Diwygio Rhif 3) 2006. - 4p.: 30 cm. - 978-0-11-091458-9 *£3.00*

Planning and Compulsory Purchase Act 2004 (Commencement No. 4 and Consequential, Transitional and Savings Provisions) (Wales) (Amendment) Order 2006 No. 2006/842 (W.77). - Enabling power: Planning and Compulsory Purchase Act 2004, ss. 121 (5), 122 (3) (b). - Issued: 25.04.2006. Made: 21.03.2006. Coming into force: 22.03.2006. Effect: S.I. 2005/2722 (W.193) (C.110) amended. Territorial extent & classification: W. General. - In English and Welsh. Welsh title: Gorchmyn Deddf Cynllunio a Phrynu Gorfodol 2004 (Cychwyn Rhif 4 a Darpariaethau Canlyniadol a Throsiannol a Darpariaethau Arbed) (Cymru) (Diwygio) 2006. - 4p.: 30 cm. - 978-0-11-091328-5 *£3.00*

The Planning and Compulsory Purchase Act 2004 (Commencement No. 7) Order 2006 No. 2006/931 (C.26). - Enabling power: Planning and Compulsory Purchase Act 2004, ss. 121 (1) (2), 122 (3). Bringing into operation various provisions of the 2004 Act on 01.04.2006 in relation to Wales, in accord. with art. 2. - Issued: 31.03.2006. Made: 27.03.2006. Effect: None. Territorial extent & classification: W. General. - 4p.: 30 cm. - 978-0-11-074408-7 £3.00

The Planning (Listed Buildings and Conservation Areas) (Amendment) (Wales) Regulations 2006 No. 2006/3316 (W.301). - Enabling power: Planning (Listed Buildings and Conservation Areas) Act 1990, ss. 10 (3) (4) (b) (5), 93 (1) (b). - Issued: 20.12.2006. Made: 12.12.2006. Coming into force: 30.06.2007. Effect: S.I. 1990/1519 amended. Territorial extent & classification: W. General. - In English and Welsh. Welsh title: Rheoliadau Cynllunio (Adeiladau Rhestredig ac Ardaloedd Cadwraeth) (Diwygio) (Cymru) 2006. - 4p.: 30 cm. - 978-0-11-091474-9 £3.00

The Planning (Listed Buildings, Conservation Areas and Hazardous Substances) (Amendments relating to Crown Land) (Wales) Regulations 2006 No. 2006/1388 (W.138). - Enabling power: Planning (Listed Buildings and Conservation Areas) Act 1990, ss. 82B (8), 93 & Planning (Hazardous Substances) Act 1990, s. 30B (2) (3) (8) (b). - Issued: 20.06.2006. Made: 23.05.2006. Coming into force: 07.06.2006. Effect: S.I. 1990/1519; 1992/656 amended in relation to Wales. Territorial extent & classification: W. General. - In English & Welsh. Welsh title: Rheoliadau Cynllunio (Adeiladau Rhestredig, Ardaloedd Cadwraeth a Sylweddau Peryglus (Diwygiadau sy'n ymwneud â Thir y Goron) (Cymru) 2006. - 8p.: 30 cm. - 978-0-11-091351-3 £3.00

The Planning (National Security Directions and Appointed Representatives) (Wales) Regulations 2006 No. 2006/1387 (W.137). - Enabling power: Town and Country Planning Act 1990, s. 321 (7) & Planning (Listed Buildings and Conservation Areas) Act 1990, sch. 3, para. 6A (3) & Planning (Hazardous Substances) Act 1990, sch., para. 6A (3). - Issued: 20.06.2006. Made: 23.05.2006. Coming into force: 07.06.2006. Effect: None. Territorial extent & classification: W. General. - In English and Welsh. Welsh title: Rheolidau Cynllunio (Cyfarwyddiadau Diogelwch Gwladol a Chynrychiolwyr Penodedig) (Cymru) 2006. - 16p.: 30 cm. - 978-0-11-091353-7 £3.00

The Town and Country Planning (Environmental Impact Assessment) (Amendment) (Wales) Regulations 2006 No. 2006/3009 (W.283). - Enabling power: European Communities Act 1972, s. 2 (2) & Town and Country Planning Act 1990, s. 71A. - Issued: 28.11.2006. Made: 21.11.2006. Coming into force: 30.11.2006. Effect: S.I. 1995/419; 1999/293 amended in relation to Wales. Territorial extent & classification: W. General. - EC note: Implement in Wales article 3 of Directive 2003/35/EC. This SI was printed as 2006/3009 in error and is superseded by S.I. 2006/3099 (W.283) (ISBN 0110914716). - In English and Welsh. Welsh title: Rheoliadau Cynllunio Gwlad a Thref (Asesu Effaith Amgylcheddol) (Diwygio) (Cymru) 2006. - 12p.: 30 cm. - 978-0-11-091449-7 £3.00

The Town and Country Planning (Environmental Impact Assessment) (Amendment) (Wales) Regulations 2006 No. 2006/3099 (W.283). - Enabling power: European Communities Act 1972, s. 2 (2) & Town and Country Planning Act 1990, s. 71A. - Issued: 18.12.2006. Made: 21.11.2006. Coming into force: 30.11.2006. Effect: S.I. 1995/419; 1999/293 amended in relation to Wales. Territorial extent & classification: W. General. - This Statutory Instrument has been printed in substitution of the SI of the same title (ISBN 011091449X), which was incorrectly published as SI 2006/3009 (W.283) on 28.11.2006 and is being issued free of charge to all known recipients of that Statutory Instrument EC note: Implements in Wales article 3 of Directive 2003/35/EC. - In English and Welsh. Welsh title: Rheoliadau Cynllunio Gwlad a Thref (Asesu Effaith Amgylcheddol) (Diwygio) (Cymru) 2006. - 12p.: 30 cm. - 978-0-11-091471-8 £3.00

The Town and Country Planning (Fees for Applications and Deemed Applications) (Amendment No. 2) (Wales) Regulations 2006 No. 2006/1052 (W.108). - Enabling power: Town and Country Planning Act 1990, s. 303. - Issued: 18.04.2006. Made: 04.04.2006. Coming into force: 06.04.2006. Effect: S.I. 1989/193 amended in relation to Wales. Territorial extent & classification: W. General. - In English and Welsh. Welsh title: Rheoliadau Cynllunio Gwlad a Thref (Ffioedd am Geisiadau a Cheisiadau Tybiedig) (Diwygio Rhif 2) (Cymru) 2006. - 8p.: 30 cm. - 978-0-11-091322-3 £3.00

The Town and Country Planning (Fees for Applications and Deemed Applications) (Amendment) (Wales) Regulations 2006 No. 2006/948 (W.97). - Enabling power: Town and Country Planning Act 1990, s. 303. - Issued: 11.04.2006. Made: 28.03.2006. Coming into force: 01.04.2006. Effect: S.I. 1989/193 amended in relation to Wales & S.I. 2004/2736 (W.243) revoked. Territorial extent & classification: W. General. - In English and Welsh. Welsh title: Rheoliadau Cynllunio Gwlad a Thref (Ffioedd ar Gyfer Ceisiadau a Cheisiadau Tybiedig) (Diwygio) (Cymru) 2006. - 12p.: 30 cm. - 978-0-11-091319-3 £3.00

The Town and Country Planning (General Development Procedure) (Amendment) (Wales) Order 2006 No. 2006/3390 (W.310). - Enabling power: Town and Country Planning Act 1990, ss. 59, 61 (1), 62, 69. - Issued: 22.12.2006. Made: 12.12.2006. Coming into force: 30.06.2007. Effect: S.I. 1995/419 amended in relation to Wales. Territorial extent & classification: W. General. - In English and Welsh. Welsh title: Gorchymyn Cynllunio Gwlad a Thref (Gweithdrefn Datblygu Cyffredinol) (Diwygio) (Cymru) 2006. - 4p.: 30 cm. - 978-0-11-091479-4 *£3.00*

The Town and Country Planning (General Permitted Development) (Amendment) (Wales) Order 2006 No. 2006/124 (W.17). - Enabling power: Town and Country Planning Act 1990, ss. 59, 60, 333 (7). - Issued: 31.01.2006. Made: 24.01.2006. Coming into force: 31.01.2006. Effect: S.I. 1995/418 amended. Territorial extent & classification: W. General. - In English and Welsh. Welsh title: Gorchymyn Cynllunio Gwlad a Thref (Datblygu Cyffredinol a Ganiateir) (Diwygio) (Cymru) 2006. - 8p.: 30 cm. - 978-0-11-091260-8 *£3.00*

The Town and Country Planning (Miscellaneous Amendments and Modifications relating to Crown Land) (Wales) Order 2006 No. 2006/1386 (W.136). - Enabling power: Town and Country Planning Act 1990, ss. 55 (2) (f), 59, 60, 61 (1), 293A (8) (9) (b), 333 (7). - Issued: 20.06.2006. Made: 23.05.2006. Coming into force: 07.06.2006. Effect: S.I. 1987/764; 1995/418, 419 amended in relation to Wales. Territorial extent & classification: W. General. - In English and Welsh. Welsh title: Gorchymyn Cynllunio Gwlad a Thref (Diwygiadau Amrywiol ac Addasiadau sy'n ymwneud â Thir y Goron) (Cymru) 2006. - 20p.: 30 cm. - 978-0-11-091352-0 *£3.50*

Trade descriptions

The Textile Products (Determination of Composition) Regulations 2006 No. 2006/3298. - Enabling power: European Communities Act 1972, s. 2 (2). - Issued: 20.12.2006. Made: 13.12.2006. Laid: 13.12.2006. Coming into force: 06.01.2007. Effect: S.I. 1976/202; 1988/1349 revoked. Territorial extent & classification: E/W/S/NI. General. - EC note: These Regulations implement Directive 96/73/EC on certain methods for the quantitative analysis of binary textile fibres as amended by 2006/2/EC and 73/44/EEC. - 4p.: 30 cm. - 978-0-11-075484-0 *£3.00*

The Textile Products (Indications of Fibre Content) (Amendment and Consolidation of Schedules of Textile Names and Allowances) Regulations 2006 No. 2006/3297. - Enabling power: European Communities Act 1972, s. 2 (2). - Issued: 20.12.2006. Made: 13.12.2006. Laid: 13.12.2006. Coming into force: 06.01.2007. Effect: S.I. 1986/26; 1988/1350 amended & S.I. 1998/1169; 2005/1401 revoked. Territorial extent & classification: E/W/S/NI. General. - EC note: These Regulations implement Directive 2006/3/EC amending, for the purposes of adapting to technical progress, Annexes I and II to Directive 96/74/EC on textile names. - 12p.: 30 cm. - 978-0-11-075482-6 *£3.00*

Trade marks

The Community Trade Mark Regulations 2006 No. 2006/1027. - Enabling power: Trade Marks Act 1994, s. 52. - Issued: 13.04.2006. Made: 05.04.2006. Laid: 06.04.2006. Coming into force: 29.04.2006. Effect: S.I. 2004/2332 amended & S.I. 1996/1908; 2004/949; 2005/440 revoked. Territorial extent & classification: E/W/S/NI. General. - EC note: These regulations make provision for the operation of Council Regulation (EC) no. 40/94 on the Community trade mark. - 8p.: 30 cm. - 978-0-11-074472-8 *£3.00*

The Olympics and Paralympics Association Rights (Appointment of Proprietors) Order 2006 No. 2006/1119. - Enabling power: Olympic Symbol etc. (Protection) Act 1995, ss. 1 (2) (2A) (3), 5A (2). - Issued: 25.04.2006. Made: 19.04.2006. Laid: 19.04.2006. Coming into force: 12.05.2006. Effect: S.I. 1995/2473 revoked. Territorial extent & classification: E/W/S/NI. General. - 8p.: 30 cm. - 978-0-11-074509-1 *£3.00*

The Paralympics Association Right (Paralympic Symbol) Order 2006 No. 2006/1120. - Enabling power: Olympic Symbol etc. (Protection) Act 1995, s. 18 (1). - Issued: 25.04.2006. Made: 19.04.2006. Laid: 19.04.2006. Coming into force: 12.05.2006. Effect: None. Territorial extent & classification: E/W/S/NI. General. - 4p., ill.: 30 cm. - 978-0-11-074510-7 *£3.00*

The Trade Marks (Amendment) Rules 2006 No. 2006/3039. - Enabling power: Trade Marks Act 1994, ss. 65, 78. - Issued: 24.11.2006. Made: 16.11.2006. Laid: 20.11.2006. Coming into force: 01.01.2007. Effect: S.I. 2000/136; 2001/3832 amended. Territorial extent & classification: E/W/S/NI/IoM. General. - 4p.: 30 cm. - 978-0-11-075336-2 *£3.00*

The Trade Marks (International Registration) (Amendment No.2) Order 2006 No. 2006/1080. - Enabling power: Trade Marks Act 1994, s. 54. - Issued: 19.04.2006. Made: 07.04.2006. Laid: 11.04.2006. Coming into force: 12.04.2006. Effect: S.I. 1996/714 amended. Territorial extent & classification: E/W/S/NI. General. - This Statutory Instrument has been printed to correct errors in S.I. 1996/714 caused by amendments made to that Statutory Instrument by S.I. 2006/763 (ISBN 0110743202). This Statutory Instrument is being issued free of charge to all known recipients of S.I. 2006/763. - 2p.: 30 cm. - 978-0-11-074487-2 *£3.00*

The Trade Marks (International Registration) (Amendment) Order 2006 No. 2006/763. - Enabling power: Trade Marks Act 1994, s. 54. - Issued: 20.03.2006. Made: 14.03.2006. Laid: 15.03.2006. Coming into force: 06.04.2006. Effect: SI 1996/714 amended. Territorial extent & classification: E/W/S/NI/IoM. General. - 2p.: 30 cm. - 978-0-11-074320-2 *£3.00*

Transfer of functions

The Constitutional Reform Act 2005 (Commencement No. 5) Order 2006 No. 2006/1014 (C.33). - Enabling power: Constitutional Reform Act 2005, s. 148. Bringing into operation various provisions of the 2005 Act on 03.04.2006, 02.10.2006 & 02.04.2007. - Issued: 06.04.2006. Made: 02.04.2006. Effect: None. Territorial extent & classification: E/W/S/NI. General. - 8p.: 30 cm. - 978-0-11-074457-5 £3.00

The Lord Chancellor (Transfer of Functions and Supplementary Provisions) (No.2) Order 2006 No. 2006/1016. - Enabling power: Constitutional Reform Act 2005, ss. 19, 143. - Issued: 06.04.2006. Made: 02.04.2006. Coming into force: 03.04.2006. Effect: 1876 c. 59; 1887 c. 70; 1984 c. 42; 1988 c. 48; 2002 c. 41; 2004 c. 7, c. 18, c. 33, c. 35; 2005 c. 2, c. 9, c. 18, c. 19; S.I. 1953/1849; 1962/2834; 2003/284; 2004/1193 amended. Territorial extent & classification: E/W/S/NI. General. - 12p.: 30 cm. - 978-0-11-074456-8 £3.00

The Lord Chancellor (Transfer of Functions and Supplementary Provisions) (No. 3) Order 2006 No. 2006/1640. - Enabling power: Constitutional Reform Act 2005, ss. 19, 140 (4) (b), 143. - Issued: 26.06.2006. Made: 21.06.2006. Coming into force: In accord. with art. 1. Effect: 1972 c. 48; 1975 c. 27; 1987 c. 45; 1991 c. 5; 2004 c. 36 & Church Commissioners Measure 1947 No. 2 & S.I. 1948/1 amended. Territorial extent & classification: E/W/S/NI. General. - Supersedes draft SI (ISBN 0110745906) issued 22.05.2006. - 8p.: 30 cm. - 978-0-11-074735-4 £3.00

The Lord Chancellor (Transfer of Functions and Supplementary Provisions) Order 2006 No. 2006/680. - Enabling power: Constitutional Reform Act 2005, ss. 19, 143. - Issued: 17.03.2006. Made: 10.03.2006. Laid: 13.03.06. Coming into force: 03.04.2006. Effect: 58 instruments amended. Territorial extent & classification: E/W/S/NI. General. - 20p.: 30 cm. - 978-0-11-074265-6 £3.00

Transport

The Docklands Light Railway (Silvertown and London City Airport Extension) (Exemptions etc.) Order 2006 No. 2006/2536. - Enabling power: Railways Act 1993, ss. 24 (1) (2) (11), 49 (2) to (5), 143 (4), 151 (5). - Issued: 04.10.2006. Made: 20.09.2006. Laid: 25.09.2006. Coming into force: 23.10.2006. Effect: S.I. 1994/607 amended. Territorial extent & classification: E/W/S. General. - 4p.: 30 cm. - 978-0-11-075126-9 £3.00

The Rail Vehicle Accessibility (Gatwick Express Class 458 Vehicles) Exemption Order 2006 No. 2006/933. - Enabling power: Disability Discrimination Act 1995, s. 47 (1) (b) (1A) (a) (4). - Issued: 06.04.2006. Made: 28.03.2006. Coming into force: 06.04.2006. Effect: None. Territorial extent & classification: E/W/S. General. - 4p.: 30 cm. - 978-0-11-074410-0 £3.00

The Railways (Access to Training Services) Regulations 2006 No. 2006/598. - Enabling power: European Communities Act 1972, s. 2 (2). - Issued: 20.03.2006. Made: 09.03.2006. Laid: 17.03.2006. Coming into force: 10.04.2006. Effect: None. Territorial extent & classification: E/W/S. General. - EC note: These Regulations implement, in part, art. 13 of Council Directive 2004/49/EC on safety on the Community's railways. - 4p.: 30 cm. - 978-0-11-074303-5 £3.00

The Railways Act 2005 (Amendment) Regulations 2006 No. 2006/556. - Enabling power: Railways Act 2005, sch. 3, para. 1 (4). - Issued: 10.03.2006. Made: 01.03.2006. Laid: 09.03.2006. Coming into force: 01.04.2006. Effect: 2005 c. 14 amended. Territorial extent & classification: E/W/S. General. - 4p.: 30 cm. - 978-0-11-074163-5 £3.00

The Railways (Substitute Road Services) (Exemptions) Order 2006 No. 2006/1935. - Enabling power: Transport Act 2000, s. 248 (4). - Issued: 25.07.2006. Made: 17.07.2006. Laid: 20.07.2006. Coming into force: 01.10.2006. Effect: None. Territorial extent & classification: E/W/S/NI. General. - 4p.: 30 cm. - 978-0-11-074867-2 £3.00

The Transport for London (Sloane Square House) Order 2006 No. 2006/2188. - Enabling power: Greater London Authority Act 1999, s. 163. - Issued: 16.08.2006. Made: 08.08.2006. Laid: 15.08.2006. Coming into force: 06.09.2006. Effect: None. Territorial extent & classification: E/W/S/NI. General. - 4p., map: 30 cm. - 978-0-11-075009-5 £3.00

The Transport Security (Electronic Communications) Order 2006 No. 2006/2190. - Enabling power: Electronic Communications Act 2000, ss. 8, 9. - Issued: 17.08.2006. Made: 08.08.2006. Laid: 14.08.2006. Coming into force: 30.09.2006. Effect: 1982 c.36; 1990 c.31; 1993 c.43; S.I. 1994/570; 2004/1495 amended. Territorial extent & classification: E/W/S/NI. General. - 12p.: 30 cm. - 978-0-11-075004-0 £3.00

Transport: Railways

The Closures Guidance (Railway Services in England and Wales) Order 2006 No. 2006/2836. - Enabling power: Railways Act 2005, ss. 43 (3) (a), 56 (5). - Issued: 03.11.2006. Made: 26.10.2006. Laid: 27.10.2006. Coming into force: 01.12.2006. Effect: None. Territorial extent & classification: E/W/S. General. - 2p.: 30 cm. - 978-0-11-075232-7 £3.00

The Closures Guidance (Railway Services in Scotland and England) Order 2006 No. 2006/2837. - Enabling power: Railways Act 2005, ss. 43 (3) (c), 56 (5). - Issued: 03.11.2006. Made: 26.10.2006. Laid: 27.10.2006. Laid before the Scottish Parliament: 27.10.2006. Coming into force: 01.12.2006. Effect: None. Territorial extent & classification: E/W/S. General. - 2p.: 30 cm. - 978-0-11-075233-4 £3.00

The Railways (Abolition of the Strategic Rail Authority) Order 2006 No. 2006/2925. - Enabling power: Railways Act 2005, s. 1 (10). - Issued: 15.11.2006. Made: 08.11.2006. Coming into force: 01.12.2006. Effect: None. Territorial extent & classification: E/W/S. General. - 2p.: 30 cm. - 978-0-11-075280-8 £3.00

The Railways Act 2005 (Commencement No. 5) Order 2006 No. 2006/266 (C.7). - Enabling power: Railways Act 2005, s. 60 (2). Bringing into operation various provisions of the 2005 Act on 07.02.2006 & 01.04.2006 in accord. with art. 2. - Issued: 15.02.2006. Made: 06.02.2006. Effect: None. Territorial extent & classification: E/W/S. General. - 8p.: 30 cm. - 978-0-11-073981-6 £3.00

The Railways Act 2005 (Commencement No. 6) Order 2006 No. 2006/1951 (C. 65). - Enabling power: Railways Act 2005, s. 60 (2). Bringing into operation various provisions of the 2005 Act on 01.08.2006. - Issued: 26.07.2006. Made: 12.07.2006. Effect: None. Territorial extent & classification: E/W/S/NI. General. - 8p.: 30 cm. - 978-0-11-074881-8 £3.00

The Railways Act 2005 (Commencement No. 7, Transitional and Saving Provisions) Order 2006 No. 2006/2911 (C.102). - Enabling power: Railways Act 2005, s. 60 (2) (3). Bringing into operation various provisions of the 2005 Act on 01.12.2006. - Issued: 13.11.2006. Made: 06.11.2006. Laid: 08.11.2006. Effect: None. Territorial extent & classification: E/W/S. General. - 12p.: 30 cm. - 978-0-11-075263-1 £3.00

The Railways (Interoperability) Regulations 2006 No. 2006/397. - Enabling power: European Communities Act 1972, s. 2 (2) & Transport Act 2000, s. 247. - Issued: 27.02.2006. Made: 16.02.2006. Laid: 23.02.2006. Coming into force: In accord.with reg. 1. Effect: S.I. 2002/1166 revoked (02.04.2006 with saving). Territorial extent & classification: E/W/S/NI. General. - EC note: These Regs give effect to 3 Directives concerning railway interoperability which have the purpose of establishing conditions for the inter-working of the trans-European rail system. They apply in relation to the UK parts of the trans-European rail system. S.I. 2002/1166 implemented Council Directive 96/48/EC (High speed Directive). These Regs revoke and replace the High Speed Regs with regulations that in addition implement Directive 2001/16/EC (the Conventional Directive) and Directive 2004/50/EC which made amendments to both the High-speed Directive and the Conventional Directive. - 40p.: 30 cm. - 978-0-11-074087-4 £6.50

Transport and works, England

The Borough of Poole (Poole Harbour Opening Bridges) Order 2006 No. 2006/2310. - Enabling power: Transport and Works Act 1992, ss. 3, 5, sch. 1, paras. 1 to 4, 7, 8, 10, 11, 13, 15, 16, 17 & S.I. 1992/3230, art. 2. - Issued: 04.09.2006. Made: 24.08.2006. Coming into force: 14.09.2006. Effect: 4 William 4 c.xlvi (1834); 9 & 10 Geo.5. c.xliv; 1965 c.xxx amended & 1973 c.26 modified & The Poole Bridge (Variation of Times of Opening) Order 1992 (Unnumbered) revoked. Territorial extent & classification: E. Local. - 36p.: 30 cm. - 978-0-11-075050-7 £6.50

The Docklands Light Railway (Stratford International Extension) Order 2006 No. 2006/2905. - Enabling power: Transport and Works Act 1992, ss. 1, 5, sch. 1, paras. 1 to 4, 7, 8, 10, 11, 15 to 17. - Issued: 13.11.2006. Made: 01.11.2006. Coming into force: 22.11.2006. Effect: None. Territorial extent & classification: E. Local. - 56p.: 30 cm. - 978-0-11-075269-3 £9.00

The Greater Manchester (Light Rapid Transit System) Order 2006 No. 2006/405. - Enabling power: Transport and Works Act 1992, ss. 1, 5, sch. 1, paras. 1 to 4, 6 to 13, 15 to 17. - Issued: 28.02.2006. Made: 20.02.2006. Coming into force: 13.03.2006. Effect: 1988 c. i amended & S.I. 1996/2714; 1997/1266; 1998/1936 amended. Territorial extent & classification: E. Local. - 4p.: 30 cm. - 978-0-11-074097-3 £3.00

The Luton Dunstable Translink Order 2006 No. 2006/3118. - Enabling power: Transport and Works Act 1992, ss. 1, 5, sch. 1, paras. 1 to 5, 7 to 13, 15 to 17. - Issued: 01.12.2006. Made: 22.11.2006. Coming into force: 13.12.2006. Effect: None. Territorial extent & classification: E. Local. - 53p.: 30 cm. - 978-0-11-075376-8 £9.00

The Network Rail (Thameslink 2000) Order 2006 No. 2006/3117. - Enabling power: Transport and Works Act 1992, ss. 1, 3, 5, sch. 1, paras. 1 to 5, 7, 8, 10, 11, 16, 17. - Issued: 01.12.2006. Made: 22.11.2006. Coming into force: 13.12.2006. Effect: None. Territorial extent & classification: E. Local. - 66p.: 30 cm. - 978-0-11-075377-5 £10.50

The Network Rail (West Coast Main Line) (Stowe Hill) Order 2006 No. 2006/3471. - Enabling power: Transport and Works Act 1992, ss. 1, 5, 13 (3), sch. 1, paras 3, 4, 7, 8, 11, 16. - Issued: 08.01.2007. Made: 22.12.2006. Coming into force: 12.01.2007. Effect: None. Territorial extent & classification: E. Local. - 8p.: 30 cm. - 978-0-11-075584-7 £3.00

The Port of Blyth (Battleship Wharf Railway) Order 2006 No. 2006/1518. - Enabling power: Transport and Works Act 1992, ss. 1, 5, sch. 1, paras 1, 2, 7, 8, 16. - Issued: 20.06.2006. Made: 12.06.2006. Coming into force: 03.07.2006. Effect: None. Territorial extent & classification: E. Local. - 12p.: 30 cm. - 978-0-11-074692-0 £3.00

Transport and works, England and Wales

The Transport and Works (Applications and Objections Procedure) (England and Wales) Rules 2006 No. 2006/1466. - Enabling power: Transport and Works Act 1992, ss. 6, 6A, 7 (3) (b) (c) (4), 10. - Issued: 14.06.2006. Made: 03.06.2006. Laid: 08.06.2006. Coming into force: 11.09.2006. Effect: S.I. 2000/2190 revoked with savings. Territorial extent & classification: E/W. General. - With correction slip dated July 2006. - 48p.: 30 cm. - 978-0-11-074665-4 £7.50

The Transport and Works (Assessment of Environmental Effects) Regulations 2006 No. 2006/958. - Enabling power: European Communities Act 1972, s. 2 (2). - Issued: 03.04.2006. Made: 28.03.2006. Laid: 30.03.2006. Coming into force: 20.04.2006. Effect: 1992 c. 42 amended. Territorial extent & classification: E/W. General. - EC note: These Regulations implement in part, the provisions of Directive 2003/35/EC. Art. 3 amends the public participation and access to justice provisions of Council Directive 85/337/EEC (as amended by Council Directive 97/11/EC), relating to the assessment of the effects of certain public and private projects on the environment. - 4p.: 30 cm. - 978-0-11-074425-4 £3.00

The Transport and Works (Model Clauses for Railways and Tramways) Order 2006 No. 2006/1954. - Enabling power: Transport and Works Act 1992, s. 8. - Issued: 28.07.2006. Made: 18.07.2006. Coming into force: 08.08.2006. Effect: S.I. 1992/3270 revoked. Territorial extent & classification: E/W. General. - 56p.: 30 cm. - 978-0-11-074923-5 £9.00

Transport and works, Wales

The Pontypool and Blaenavon Railway (Phase I) Order 2006 No. 2006/1691 (W.161). - Enabling power: Transport and Works Act 1992, ss. 1, 5, sch. 1, paras 1, 8, 15, 17. - Made: 20.06.2006. Coming into force: 21.06.2006. Effect: None. Territorial extent & classification: W. Local. - In English and Welsh *Unpublished*

Transport, England

The Borough of Poole (Poole Harbour Opening Bridges) Order 2006 No. 2006/2310. - Enabling power: Transport and Works Act 1992, ss. 3, 5, sch. 1, paras. 1 to 4, 7, 8, 10, 11, 13, 15, 16, 17 & S.I. 1992/3230, art. 2. - Issued: 04.09.2006. Made: 24.08.2006. Coming into force: 14.09.2006. Effect: 4 William 4 c.xlvi (1834); 9 & 10 Geo.5. c.xliv; 1965 c.xxx amended & 1973 c.26 modified & The Poole Bridge (Variation of Times of Opening) Order 1992 (Unnumbered) revoked. Territorial extent & classification: E. Local. - 36p.: 30 cm. - 978-0-11-075050-7 £6.50

The Docklands Light Railway (Stratford International Extension) Order 2006 No. 2006/2905. - Enabling power: Transport and Works Act 1992, ss. 1, 5, sch. 1, paras. 1 to 4, 7, 8, 10, 11, 15 to 17. - Issued: 13.11.2006. Made: 01.11.2006. Coming into force: 22.11.2006. Effect: None. Territorial extent & classification: E. Local. - 56p.: 30 cm. - 978-0-11-075269-3 £9.00

The Greater Manchester (Light Rapid Transit System) Order 2006 No. 2006/405. - Enabling power: Transport and Works Act 1992, ss. 1, 5, sch. 1, paras. 1 to 4, 6 to 13, 15 to 17. - Issued: 28.02.2006. Made: 20.02.2006. Coming into force: 13.03.2006. Effect: 1988 c. i amended & S.I. 1996/2714; 1997/1266; 1998/1936 amended. Territorial extent & classification: E. Local. - 4p.: 30 cm. - 978-0-11-074097-3 £3.00

The Luton Dunstable Translink Order 2006 No. 2006/3118. - Enabling power: Transport and Works Act 1992, ss. 1, 5, sch. 1, paras. 1 to 5, 7 to 13, 15 to 17. - Issued: 01.12.2006. Made: 22.11.2006. Coming into force: 13.12.2006. Effect: None. Territorial extent & classification: E. Local. - 53p.: 30 cm. - 978-0-11-075376-8 £9.00

The Network Rail (Thameslink 2000) Order 2006 No. 2006/3117. - Enabling power: Transport and Works Act 1992, ss. 1, 3, 5, sch. 1, paras. 1 to 5, 7, 8, 10, 11, 16, 17. - Issued: 01.12.2006. Made: 22.11.2006. Coming into force: 13.12.2006. Effect: None. Territorial extent & classification: E. Local. - 66p.: 30 cm. - 978-0-11-075377-5 £10.50

The Network Rail (West Coast Main Line) (Stowe Hill) Order 2006 No. 2006/3471. - Enabling power: Transport and Works Act 1992, ss. 1, 5, 13 (3), sch. 1, paras 3, 4, 7, 8, 11, 16. - Issued: 08.01.2007. Made: 22.12.2006. Coming into force: 12.01.2007. Effect: None. Territorial extent & classification: E. Local. - 8p.: 30 cm. - 978-0-11-075584-7 £3.00

The Port of Blyth (Battleship Wharf Railway) Order 2006 No. 2006/1518. - Enabling power: Transport and Works Act 1992, ss. 1, 5, sch. 1, paras 1, 2, 7, 8, 16. - Issued: 20.06.2006. Made: 12.06.2006. Coming into force: 03.07.2006. Effect: None. Territorial extent & classification: E. Local. - 12p.: 30 cm. - 978-0-11-074692-0 £3.00

Transport, England and Wales

The Disability Discrimination Act 1995 (Private Hire Vehicles) (Carriage of Guide Dogs, etc.) (England and Wales) (Amendment) Regulations 2006 No. 2006/1617. - Enabling power: Disability Discrimination Act 1995, ss. 37A (8) (b) (9), 67 (2). - Issued: 26.06.2006. Made: 16.06.2006. Laid: 22.06.2006. Coming into force: 17.07.2006. Effect: S.I. 2003/3122 amended. Territorial extent & classification: E/W. General. - This Statutory Instrument has been printed to correct errors in SI 2003/3122 (ISBN 0110482565) and is being issued free of charge to all known recipients of that Statutory Instrument. - 4p.: 30 cm. - 978-0-11-074718-7 £3.00

The Disability Discrimination Act 1995 (Taxis) (Carrying of Guide Dogs etc.) (England and Wales) (Amendment) Regulations 2006 No. 2006/1616. - Enabling power: Disability Discrimination Act 1995, ss. 37 (8) (b) (9), 67 (2). - Issued: 26.06.2006. Made: 16.06.2006. Laid: 22.06.2006. Coming into force: 17.07.2006. Effect: S.I. 2000/2990 amended. Territorial extent & classification: E/W. General. - This Statutory Instrument has been printed to correct errors in SI 2000/2990 (ISBN 0110187660) and is being issued free of charge to all known recipients of that Statutory Instrument. - 4p.: 30 cm. - 978-0-11-074717-0 £3.00

The Transport and Works (Applications and Objections Procedure) (England and Wales) Rules 2006 No. 2006/1466. - Enabling power: Transport and Works Act 1992, ss. 6, 6A, 7 (3) (b) (c) (4), 10. - Issued: 14.06.2006. Made: 03.06.2006. Laid: 08.06.2006. Coming into force: 11.09.2006. Effect: S.I. 2000/2190 revoked with savings. Territorial extent & classification: E/W. General. - With correction slip dated July 2006. - 48p.: 30 cm. - 978-0-11-074665-4 £7.50

The Transport and Works (Model Clauses for Railways and Tramways) Order 2006 No. 2006/1954. - Enabling power: Transport and Works Act 1992, s. 8. - Issued: 28.07.2006. Made: 18.07.2006. Coming into force: 08.08.2006. Effect: S.I. 1992/3270 revoked. Territorial extent & classification: E/W. General. - 56p.: 30 cm. - 978-0-11-074923-5 £9.00

The Tyne and Wear Passenger Transport Authority (Increase in Number of Members) Order 2006 No. 2006/582. - Enabling power: Local Government Act 1985, ss. 29 (2), 103 (1). - Issued: 13.03.2006. Made: 01.03.2006. Laid: 10.03.2006. Coming into force: 01.04.2006. Effect: 1985 c.51 amended. Territorial extent & classification: E/W. General. - 2p.: 30 cm. - 978-0-11-074181-9 £3.00

Transport, Wales

The Pontypool and Blaenavon Railway (Phase I) Order 2006 No. 2006/1691 (W.161). - Enabling power: Transport and Works Act 1992, ss. 1, 5, sch. 1, paras 1, 8, 15, 17. - Made: 20.06.2006. Coming into force: 21.06.2006. Effect: None. Territorial extent & classification: W. Local. - In English and Welsh *Unpublished*

The Regional Transport Planning (Wales) Order 2006 No. 2006/2993 (W.280). - Enabling power: Transport Act 2000, ss. 108, 109C, 113A. - Issued: 23.11.2006. Made: 15.11.2006. Coming into force: 23.11.2006. Effect: None. Territorial extent & classification: W. General. - In English and Welsh. Welsh title: Gorchymyn Cynllunio Trafnidiaeth Rhanbarthol (Cymru) 2006. - 8p.: 30 cm. - 978-0-11-091441-1 £3.00

The Traffic Management Act 2004 (Commencement No. 1) (Wales) Order 2006 No. 2006/2826 (W.249) (C.97). - Enabling power: Traffic Management Act 2004, s. 99 (1). Bringing into operation various provisions of the 2004 Act on 26.10.2006. - Issued: 03.11.2006. Made: 25.10.2006. Effect: None. Territorial extent & classification: W. General. - In English and Welsh. Welsh title: Gorchymyn Deddf Rheoli Traffig 2004 (Cychwyn Rhif 1) (Cymru) 2006. - 4p.: 30 cm. - 978-0-11-091426-8 £3.00

The Transport (Wales) Act 2006 (Commencement) Order 2006 No. 2006/1403 (W.140) (C.48). - Enabling power: Transport (Wales) Act 2006, ss. 12, 13. Bringing into force various provisions of the 2006 Act on 26.05.2006 in accord. with art. 2. - Issued: 01.06.2006. Made: 24.05.2006. Effect: None. Territorial extent & classification: W. General. - In English and Welsh. Welsh title: Gorchymyn Deddf Trafnidiaeth (Cymru) 2006 (Cychwyn) 2006. - 4p.: 30 cm. - 978-0-11-091344-5 £3.00

Tribunals and inquiries, England

The Town and Country Planning (Costs of Independent Examinations) (Standard Daily Amount) (England) Regulations 2006 No. 2006/3227. - Enabling power: Town and Country Planning Act 1990, s. 303A (5). - Issued: 11.12.2006. Made: 05.12.2006. Laid: 11.12.2006. Coming into force: 03.01.2007. Effect: None. Territorial extent & classification: E. General. - 4p.: 30 cm. - 978-0-11-075422-2 £3.00

United Nations

The Al-Qaida and Taliban (United Nations Measures) Order 2006 No. 2006/2952. - Enabling power: United Nations Act 1946, s. 1. - Issued: 20.11.2006. Made: 14.11.2006. Laid: 15.11.2006. Coming into force: 16.11.2006. Effect: S.I. 2002/111 amended & S.I. 2002/251 revoked. Territorial extent & classification: E/W/S/NI. General. - 16p.: 30 cm. - 978-0-11-075314-0 £3.00

The Lebanon and Syria (United Nations Measures) (Channel Islands) Order 2006 No. 2006/1250. - Enabling power: United Nations Act 1946, s. 1. - Issued: 16.05.2006. Made: 09.05.2006. Laid: 10.05.2006. Coming into force: 31.05.2006. Effect: None. Territorial extent & classification: CI/IoM. General. - 12p.: 30 cm. - 978-0-11-074564-0 £3.00

The Lebanon and Syria (United Nations Measures) (Isle of Man) Order 2006 No. 2006/1249. - Enabling power: United Nations Act 1946, s. 1. - Issued: 16.05.2006. Made: 09.05.2006. Laid: 10.05.2006. Coming into force: 31.05.2006. Effect: None. Territorial extent & classification: CI/IoM. General. - 12p.: 30 cm. - 978-0-11-074563-3 £3.00

The Lebanon and Syria (United Nations Measures) (Overseas Territories) Order 2006 No. 2006/311. - Enabling power: United Nations Act 1946, s. 1. - Issued: 20.02.2006. Made: 14.02.2006. Laid: 15.02.2006. Coming into force: 16.02.2006. Effect: None. Territorial extent & classification: Anguilla, Bermuda, British Antarctic Territory, British Indian Ocean Territory, Cayman Is., Falkland Is., Montserrat, Pitcairn, Henderson, Ducie & Oeno Is., St Helena & Dependencies, South Georgia & the South Sandwich Is., the Sovereign Base Areas of Akrotiri & Dhekelia (Cyprus), Turks & Caicos Is. & the Virgin Is. General. - 12p.: 30 cm. - 978-0-11-074050-8 *£3.00*

The North Korea (United Nations Measures) Order 2006 No. 2006/2958. - Enabling power: United Nations Act 1946, s. 1. - Issued: 20.11.2006. Made: 14.11.2006. Laid: 15.11.2006. Coming into force: 16.11.2006. Effect: None. Territorial extent & classification: E/W/S/NI. General. - 12p.: 30 cm. - 978-0-11-075313-3 *£3.00*

The North Korea (United Nations Measures) (Overseas Territories) Order 2006 No. 2006/3327. - Enabling power: United Nations Act 1946, s. 1. - Issued: 21.12.2006. Made: 14.12.2006. Laid: 15.12.2006. Coming into force: 16.12.2006. Effect: None. Territorial extent & classification: Anguilla, Bermuda, British Antarctic Territory, British Indian Ocean Territory, Cayman Islands, Falkland Islands, Montserrat, Pitcairn, Henderson, Ducie and Oeno Islands, St. Helena & Dependencies, South Georgia & South Sandwich Islands, The Sovereign Base Areas of Akrotiri & Dhekelia in the Island of Cyprus, Turks & Caicos Islands, Virgin Islands. General. - 20p.: 30 cm. - 978-0-11-075515-1 *£3.50*

The Sudan (United Nations Measures) Order 2006 No. 2006/1454. - Enabling power: United Nations Act 1946, s. 1. - Issued: 13.06.2006. Made: 07.06.2006. Laid: 08.06.2006. Coming into force: 09.06.2006. Effect: S.I. 2005/1259 revoked. Territorial extent & classification: E/W/S/NI. General. - 12p.: 30 cm. - 978-0-11-074667-8 *£3.00*

The Terrorism (United Nations Measures) Order 2006 No. 2006/2657. - Enabling power: United Nations Act 1946, s. 1. - Issued: 17.10.2006. Made: 10.10.2006. Laid: 11.10.2006. Coming into force: 12.10.2006. Effect: S.I. 2001/3801; 2002/111; 2005/3389 amended & S.I. 2001/3365; 2003/1297; 2005/1525 revoked. Territorial extent & classification: E/W/S/NI. General. - EC note: These Regs provide for enforcement of Reg. (EC) 2580/2001 on specific measures directed at certain persons and entities with a view to combating terrorism. Art. 3 provides that 'designated persons' are persons named in Council Decision 2006/379/EC. UN note: This Order gives effect in the UK to Resolution 1373 (2001) adopted by the Security Council of the UN (28.09.2001) relating to terrorism and resolution 1453 (2002) adopted on 20.12.2002 relating to humanitarian exemptions. - 16p.: 30 cm. - 978-0-11-075171-9 *£3.00*

The United Nations (International Tribunals) (Former Yugoslavia and Rwanda) (Amendment) (No. 2) Order 2006 No. 2006/3326. - Enabling power: United Nations Act 1946, s. 1. - Issued: 21.12.2006. Made: 14.12.2006. Laid: 21.12.2006. Coming into force: 22.01.2007. Effect: S.I. 2006/1923 amended. Territorial extent & classification: E/W/S/NI. General. - 2p.: 30 cm. - 978-0-11-075514-4 *£3.00*

The United Nations (International Tribunals) (Former Yugoslavia and Rwanda) (Amendment) Order 2006 No. 2006/1923. - Enabling power: United Nations Act 1946, s. 1. - Issued: 03.08.2006. Made: 19.07.2006. Laid: 31.07.2006. Coming into force: 22.08.2006. Effect: S.I. 1996/716, 1296 amended. Territorial extent & classification: E/W/S/NI. General. - 12p.: 30 cm. - 978-0-11-074892-4 *£3.00*

Urban development, England

The London Thames Gateway Development Corporation (Planning Functions) (Amendment) Order 2006 No. 2006/2186. - Enabling power: Local Government, Planning and Land Act 1980, s. 149 (1) (3) (11) (13). - Issued: 16.08.2006. Made: 09.08.2006. Laid: 16.08.2006. Coming into force: 07.09.2006. Effect: S.I. 2005/2721 amended. Territorial extent & classification: E. General. - 4p., map: 30 cm. - 978-0-11-075006-4 *£3.00*

The Olympic Delivery Authority (Planning Functions) Order 2006 No. 2006/2185. - Enabling power: Local Government, Planning and Land Act 1980, s. 149 (1) (3) (11) (13). - Issued: 16.08.2006. Made: 09.08.2006. Laid: 16.08.2006. Coming into force: 07.09.2006. Effect: None. Territorial extent & classification: E. General. - 4p., map: 30 cm. - 978-0-11-075007-1 *£3.00*

The West Northamptonshire Development Corporation (Planning Functions) Order 2006 No. 2006/616. - Enabling power: Local Government, Planning and Land Act 1980, s. 149 (1) (3) (11) (13). - Issued: 15.03.2006. Made: 03.03.2006. Laid: 15.03.2006. Coming into force: 06.04.2006. Effect: 1990 c.8 modified. Territorial extent & classification: E. General. - 8p., map: 30 cm. - 978-0-11-074200-7 *£3.00*

Value added tax

The Customs and Excise Duties (Travellers' Allowances and Personal Reliefs) (New Member States) (Amendment) Order 2006 No. 2006/3157. - Enabling power: Customs and Excise Duties (General Reliefs) Act 1979, s. 13 (1) (3). - Issued: 01.12.2006. Made: 28.11.2006. Laid: 29.11.2006. Coming into force: 01.01.2007. Effect: S.I. 2004/1002 amended. Territorial extent & classification: E/W/S/NI. General. - Order made by the Commissioners for Her Majesty's Revenue and Customs, laid before the House of Commons for approval by that House within twenty-eight days. Superseded by S.I. of same no. (ISBN 0110755014). - 4p.: 30 cm. - 978-0-11-075386-7 *£3.00*

The Customs and Excise Duties (Travellers' Allowances and Personal Reliefs) (New Member States) (Amendment) Order 2006 No. 2006/3157. - Enabling power: Customs and Excise Duties (General Reliefs) Act 1979, s. 13 (1) (3). - Issued: 19.12.2006. Made: 28.11.2006. Laid: 29.11.2006. Coming into force: 01.01.2007. Effect: S.I. 2004/1002 amended. Territorial extent & classification: E/W/S/NI. General. - Supersedes SI of same no. (ISBN 0110753860) issued 01.12.2006. - 4p.: 30 cm. - 978-0-11-075501-4 £3.00

The Finance Act 2006, section 18, (Appointed Day) Order 2006 No. 2006/2149 (C.72). - Enabling power: Finance Act 2006, s. 18 (4). Bringing into operation various provisions of the 2006 Act on 01.09.2006. - Issued: 14.08.2006. Made: 09.08.2006. Effect: None. Territorial extent & classification: E/W/S/NI. General. - 2p.: 30 cm. - 978-0-11-074999-0 £3.00

The Relief for Legacies Imported from Third Countries (Application) Order 2006 No. 2006/3158. - Enabling power: Customs and Excise Duties (General Reliefs) Act 1979, s. 7. - Issued: 01.12.2006. Made: 28.11.2006. Laid: 29.11.2006. Coming into force: 01.01.2007. Effect: S.I. 1992/3193 updated in respect of a reference to Directive 73/388/EC. Territorial extent & classification: E/W/S/NI. General. - 2p.: 30 cm. - 978-0-11-075385-0 £3.00

The Value Added Tax (Amendment) (No.2) Regulations 2006 No. 2006/2902. - Enabling power: Value Added Tax Act 1994, sch. 1, para. 17. - Issued: 08.11.2006. Made: 03.11.2006. Laid: 03.11.2006. Coming into force: 01.12.2006. Effect: S.I. 1995/2518 amended. Territorial extent & classification: E/W/S/NI. General. - 8p.: 30 cm. - 978-0-11-075257-0 £3.00

The Value Added Tax (Amendment) (No. 3) Regulations 2006 No. 2006/3292. - Enabling power: Value Added Tax Act 1994, ss. 14 (3), 16 (1), 25 (6), 93 (1) (2), sch. 11, paras 2 (3), 2A (2). - Issued: 15.12.2006. Made: 11.12.2006. Laid: 11.12.2006. Coming into force: 01.01.2007. Effect: S.I. 1995/2518 amended. Territorial extent & classification: E/W/S/NI. General. - With correction slip dated February 2007. - 8p.: 30 cm. - 978-0-11-075477-2 £3.00

The Value Added Tax (Amendment) Regulations 2006 No. 2006/587. - Enabling power: Value Added Tax Act 1994, ss. 16 (1), 25 (1), 37 (3), sch. 11, para. 2 (1) (11). - Issued: 10.03.2006. Made: 07.03.2006. Laid: 07.03.2006. Coming into force: 01.04.2006 for regs. 2, 3; 06.04.2006 for regs. 4, 5. Effect: S.I. 1995/2518 amended. Territorial extent & classification: E/W/S/NI. General. - 8p.: 30 cm. - 978-0-11-074177-2 £3.00

The Value Added Tax (Betting, Gaming and Lotteries) Order 2006 No. 2006/2685. - Enabling power: Value Added Tax Act 1994, ss. 31 (2), 96 (9). - Issued: 13.10.2006. Made: 09.10.2006. Laid: 10.10.2006. Coming into force: 01.11.2006. Effect: 1994 c.23 amended & S.I. 2005/3328 revoked. Territorial extent & classification: E/W/S/NI. General. - For approval of the House of Commons within 28 days. Superseded by the S.I. of the same number (ISBN 0110752546) issued on 07.11.2006. - 4p.: 30 cm. - 978-0-11-075167-2 £3.00

The Value Added Tax (Betting, Gaming and Lotteries) Order 2006 No. 2006/2685. - Enabling power: Value Added Tax Act 1994, ss. 31 (2), 96 (9). - Issued: 07.11.2006. Made: 09.10.2006. Laid: 10.10.2006. Coming into force: 01.11.2006. Effect: 1994 c.23 amended & S.I. 2005/3328 revoked. Territorial extent & classification: E/W/S/NI. General. - Approved by the House of Commons. - 4p.: 30 cm. - 978-0-11-075254-9 £3.00

The Value Added Tax (Cars) (Amendment) Order 2006 No. 2006/874. - Enabling power: Value Added Tax Act 1994, s. 5 (3). - Issued: 28.03.2006. Made: 22.03.2006. Laid: 22.03.2006. Coming into force: 13.04.2006. Effect: S.I. 1992/3122 amended. Territorial extent & classification: E/W/S/NI. General. - 2p.: 30 cm. - 978-0-11-074385-1 £3.00

The Value Added Tax (Consideration for Fuel Provided for Private Use) Order 2006 No. 2006/868. - Enabling power: Value Added Tax Act 1994, s. 57 (4). - Issued: 28.03.2005. Made: 22.03.2006. Laid: 22.03.2006. Coming into force: 01.05.2006. Effect: 1994 c. 23 amended. Territorial extent & classification: E/W/S/NI. General. - 2p.: 30 cm. - 978-0-11-074388-2 £3.00

The Value Added Tax (Gaming Machines) Order 2006 No. 2006/2686. - Enabling power: Value Added Tax Act 1994, s. 23 (7). - Issued: 16.10.2006. Made: 09.10.2006. Laid: 10.10.2006. Coming into force: 01.11.2006. Effect: 1994 c.23 amended. Territorial extent & classification: E/W/S/NI. General. - 4p.: 30 cm. - 978-0-11-075166-5 £3.00

The Value Added Tax (Increase of Registration Limits) Order 2006 No. 2006/876. - Enabling power: Value Added Tax Act 1994, sch. 1, para. 15, sch. 3, para. 9. - Issued: 28.03.2006. Made: 22.03.2006. Laid: 22.03.2006. Coming into force: 01.04.2006. Effect: 1994 c. 23 amended. Territorial extent & classification: E/W/S/NI. General. - 2p.: 30 cm. - 978-0-11-074390-5 £3.00

The Value Added Tax (Lifeboats) Order 2006 No. 2006/1750. - Enabling power: Value Added Tax Act 1994, s. 30 (4). - Issued: 10.07.2006. Made: 03.07.2006. Laid: 04.07.2006. Coming into force: 01.08.2006. Effect: 1994 c. 23 amended. Territorial extent & classification: E/W/S/NI. General. - 2p.: 30 cm. - 978-0-11-074797-2 £3.00

The Value Added Tax (Place of Supply of Services) (Amendment) Order 2006 No. 2006/1683. - Enabling power: Value Added Tax Act 1994, s. 7 (11). - Issued: 30.6.2006. Made: 26.06.2006 Laid: 27.06.2006. Coming into force: 01.08.2006. Effect: S.I. 1992/3121 amended. Territorial extent & classification: E/W/S/NI. General. - 2p.: 30 cm. - 978-0-11-074761-3 £3.00

The Value Added Tax (Reduced Rate) Order 2006 No. 2006/1472. - Enabling power: Value Added Tax Act 1994, ss. 29A, 96 (9). - Issued: 12.06.2006. Made: 06.06.2006. Laid: 07.06.2006. Coming into force: 01.07.2006. Effect: 1994 c. 23 amended. Territorial extent & classification: E/W/S/NI. General. - 4p.: 30 cm. - 978-0-11-074658-6 £3.00

The Value Added Tax (Refund of Tax) Order 2006 No. 2006/1793. - Enabling power: Value Added Tax Act 1994, s. 33 (3) (k). - Issued: 11.07.2006. Made: 05.07.2006. Laid: 06.07.2006. Coming into force: 01.08.2006. Effect: None. Territorial extent & classification: E/W/S/NI. General. - 2p.: 30 cm. - 978-0-11-074814-6 *£3.00*

The Value Added Tax (Special Provisions) (Amendment) (No.2) Order 2006 No. 2006/869. - Enabling power: Value Added Tax Act 1994, s. 5 (3). - Issued: 28.03.2006. Made: 22.03.2006. Laid: 22.03.2006. Coming into force: 13.04.2006. Effect: S.I. 1995/1268 amended. Territorial extent & classification: E/W/S/NI. General. - With correction slip dated June 2006. - 2p.: 30 cm. - 978-0-11-074389-9 *£3.00*

The Value Added Tax (Treatment of Transactions and Special Provisions) (Amendment) Order 2006 No. 2006/2187. - Enabling power: Value Added Tax Act 1994, ss. 5 (3), 50A, 97 (5). - Issued: 14.08.2006. Made: 09.08.2006. Laid: 10.08.2006. Coming into force: 01.09.2006. Effect: S.I. 1995/958, 1268 amended. Territorial extent & classification: E/W/S/NI. General. - 4p.: 30 cm. - 978-0-11-075000-2 *£3.00*

Veterinary surgeons

The Veterinary Surgeons and Veterinary Practitioners (Registration) (Amendment) Regulations Order of Council 2006 No. 2006/3255. - Enabling power: Veterinary Surgeons Act 1966, s. 11. - Issued: 13.12.2006. Made: 05.12.2006. Coming into force: 01.04.2007. Effect: S.I. 2005/3517 amended. Territorial extent & classification: E/W/S/NI. General. - 4p.: 30 cm. - 978-0-11-075440-6 *£3.00*

Water, England and Wales

The Protection of Water Against Agricultural Nitrate Pollution (England and Wales) (Amendment) Regulations 2006 No. 2006/1289. - Enabling power: European Communities Act 1972, s. 2 (2). - Issued: 16.05.2006. Made: 10.05.2006. Laid: 10.05.2006. Coming into force: 01.06.2006. Effect: S.I. 1996/888; 2002/2614 amended. Territorial extent & classification: E/W. General. - EC note: These Regulations make provision for implementing, in part, Art. 2 of Directive 2003/35/EC on public participation in respect of drawing up certain plans and programmes relating to the environment. The programmes to which that Article applies include action programmes in relation to nitrate vulnerable zones designated under Council Directive 91/676/EEC concerning the protection of waters against pollution caused by nitrates from agricultural sources. - 4p.: 30 cm. - 978-0-11-074568-8 *£3.00*

The Unfair Terms in Consumer Contracts (Amendment) and Water Act 2003 (Transitional Provision) Regulations 2006 No. 2006/523. - Enabling power: European Communities Act 1972, s. 2 (2) & Water Act 2003, s. 103 (1) (b) (2) (b). - Issued: 07.03.2006. Made: 01.03.2006. Laid: 03.03.2006. Coming into force: 01.04.2006. Effect: S.I. 1999/2083 amended. Territorial extent & classification: UK, except for reg. 3 which extends only to E/W. General. - 4p.: 30 cm. - 978-0-11-074137-6 *£3.00*

The Water Act 2003 (Commencement No. 6, Transitional Provisions and Savings) Order 2006 No. 2006/984 (C.30). - Enabling power: Water Act 2003, ss. 104 (6) (a), 105 (3) to (6). Bringing into operation various provisions of the 2003 Act on 01.04.2006. - Issued: 05.04.2006. Made: 30.03.2006. Effect: None. Territorial extent & classification: E/W. General. - 12p.: 30 cm. - 978-0-11-074437-7 *£3.00*

Water resources, England

The Mid Kent Water (Non-Essential Use) Drought Order 2006 No. 2006/1424. - Enabling power: Water Resources Act 1991, ss. 73 (1), 74 (2) (b) (5) (a), sch. 8, para. 2 (5). - Issued: 06.06.2006. Made: 25.05.2006. Coming into force: 26.05.2006. Effect: None. Territorial extent & classification: E. Local. - The authorisation given by this Order shall cease to have effect on 25th November 2006. - 4p.: 30 cm. - 978-0-11-074629-6 *£3.00*

The Southern Water Services (Kent Medway, Kent Thanet and Sussex Hastings) (Non-Essential Use) Drought Order 2006 No. 2006/1423. - Enabling power: Water Resources Act 1991, ss. 73 (1), 74 (2) (b) (5) (a), sch. 8, para. 2 (5). - Issued: 06.06.2006. Made: 25.05.2006. Coming into force: 26.05.2006. Effect: None. Territorial extent & classification: E. Local. - The authorisation given by this Order shall cease to have effect on 25th November 2006. - 4p.: 30 cm. - 978-0-11-074628-9 *£3.00*

The Southern Water Services (Sussex North and Sussex Coast) (Non-Essential Use) Drought Order 2006 No. 2006/1422. - Enabling power: Water Resources Act 1991, ss. 73 (1), 74 (2) (b) (5) (a), sch. 8, para. 2 (5). - Issued: 06.06.2006. Made: 25.05.2006. Coming into force: 26.05.2006. Effect: None. Territorial extent & classification: E. Local. - The authorisation given by this Order shall cease to have effect on 25th November 2006. - 4p.: 30 cm. - 978-0-11-074627-2 *£3.00*

The Sutton and East Surrey Water plc (Non-Essential Use) Drought Order 2006 No. 2006/1333. - Enabling power: Water Resources Act 1991, ss. 73 (1), 74 (2) (b), sch. 8, para. 2 (5). - Issued: 22.05.2006. Made: 15.05.2006. Coming into force: 16.05.2006. Effect: None. Territorial extent & classification: E. General. - 4p.: 30 cm. - 978-0-11-074583-1 *£3.00*

Water resources, England and Wales

The Water Resources (Abstraction and Impounding) Regulations 2006 No. 2006/641. - Enabling power: Water Resources Act 1991, ss. 25A (7) (a), 34, 36A (5), 37 (4) (6), 37A, 43 (2) (a) (3), 45, 51 (1C) (b) (1D), 52 (4), 55 (4), 59 (1), 64, 161B (5) (6) (7), 161C (3) (4), 189, 199 (1), 199A (2) (6), 219 (2) (d) (e) (f), 221 (1) & Water Act 2003, s. 3 (5). - Issued: 15.03.2006. Made: 07.03.2006. Laid: 10.03.2006. Coming into force: In accord. with art. 1 (2). Effect: S.I. 1965/534, 1092; 1989/336 revoked with saving. Territorial extent & classification: E/W. General. - 28p.: 30 cm. - 978-0-11-074208-3 £4.50

The Water Resources (Environmental Impact Assessment) (England and Wales) (Amendment) Regulations 2006 No. 2006/3124. - Enabling power: European Communities Act 1972, s. 2 (2). - Issued: 30.11.2006. Made: 21.11.2006. Laid: 28.11.2006. Coming into force: 31.12.2006. Effect: S.I. 2003/164 amended. Territorial extent & classification: E/W. General. - EC note: These Regulations implement the amendments to Directive 85/337/EEC made by article 3 of Directive 2003/35/EC. With correction slip dated February 2007. - 8p.: 30 cm. - 978-0-11-075370-6 £3.00

Water, Scotland

The Water Environment and Water Services (Scotland) Act 2003 (Consequential Provisions and Modifications) Order 2006 No. 2006/1054 (S.10). - Enabling power: Scotland Act 1998, ss. 104, 112 (1), 113. - Issued: 12.04.2006. Made: 31.03.2006. Coming into force: 01.04.2006. Effect: 1989 c. 29; 1996 c. 8 & S.I. 1996/1527 amended. Territorial extent & classification: S. General. - Supersedes draft SI (ISBN 0110699726) issued 03.03.2006. - 8p.: 30 cm. - 978-0-11-070249-0 £3.00

The Water Environment (Controlled Activities) (Scotland) Regulations 2005 (Notices in the Interests of National Security) Order 2006 No. 2006/661 (S.5). - Enabling power: Scotland Act 1998, ss. 104, 112 (1), 113. - Issued: 16.03.2006. Made: 09.03.2006. Laid: 15.03.2006. Coming into force: 05.04.2006. Effect: None. Territorial extent & classification: S. General. - 4p.: 30 cm. - 978-0-11-074257-1 £3.00

Weights and measures

The Measuring Instruments (Active Electrical Energy Meters) Regulations 2006 No. 2006/1679. - Enabling power: European Communities Act 1972, s. 2 (2). - Issued: 04.07.2006. Made: 21.06.2006. Laid: 27.06.2006. Coming into force: 31.07.2006 for regs 1, 2, 7, 9, 10, sch. 2, part 1; 30.10.2006 for remainder. Effect: 1989 c. 29; S.I. 1992/231 (NI. 1); 1998/1565, 1566; S.R. 1998/443, 444 amended. Territorial extent & classification: E/W/S/NI. General. - EC note: These Regulations implement Directive 2004/22/EC of the European Parliament and of the Council on measuring instruments in relation to active electrical energy meters. - 32p.: 30 cm. - 978-0-11-074759-0 £5.50

The Measuring Instruments (Amendment) Regulations 2006 No. 2006/2625. - Enabling power: European Communities Act 1972, s. 2 (2) & Weights and Measures Act 1985, ss. 15 (1), 86 (1) [in relation to Reg. 3 of the Regs]. - Issued: 12.10.2006. Made: 01.10.2006. Laid: 05.10.2006. Coming into force: 30.10.2006. Effect: S.I. 2006/1256, 1257, 1268, 1270 amended. Territorial extent & classification: E/W/S/NI [except for reg. 3 which does not apply to NI]. General. - This Statutory Instrument has been made in part because of defects in SI 2006/1256, SI 2006/1257, SI 2006/1268 and SI 2006/1270, and is being issued free of charge to all known recipients of those Statutory Instruments - EC note: These regs partially implement Directive 2004/22/EC. - 4p.: 30 cm. - 978-0-11-075147-4 £3.00

The Measuring Instruments (Automatic Catchweighers) Regulations 2006 No. 2006/1257. - Enabling power: European Communities Act 1972, s. 2 (2) & Weights and Measures Act 1985, ss. 15 (1), 86 (1). - Issued: 12.05.2006. Made: 28.04.2006. Laid: 05.05.2006. Coming into force: 30.05.2006 for regs 1, 2, 7, 9, 10 and sch. 2, part 1; 30.10.2006 for remainder. Effect: None. Territorial extent & classification: E/W/S/NI (except for part III which does not apply to NI). General. - EC note: These Regulations implement Directive 2004/22/EC on measuring instruments in relation to the class of automatic catchweighers within the category of automatic weighing instruments covered by the Directive. - 32p.: 30 cm. - 978-0-11-074550-3 £5.50

The Measuring Instruments (Automatic Discontinuous Totalisers) Regulations 2006 No. 2006/1255. - Enabling power: European Communities Act 1972, s. 2 (2) & Weights and Measures Act 1985, ss. 15 (1), 86 (1). - Issued: 12.05.2006. Made: 28.04.2006. Laid: 05.05.2006. Coming into force: 30.05.2006 for regs 1, 2, 7, 9, 10 and sch. 2, part 1; 30.10.2006 for remainder. Effect: None. Territorial extent & classification: E/W/S/NI (except for part III which does not apply to NI). General. - EC note: These Regulations implement Directive 2004/22/EC on measuring instruments in relation to the class of automatic discontinuous totalisers within the category of automatic weighing instruments covered by the Directive. - 32p.: 30 cm. - 978-0-11-074547-3 £5.50

The Measuring Instruments (Automatic Gravimetric Filling Instruments) Regulations 2006 No. 2006/1258. - Enabling power: European Communities Act 1972, s. 2 (2) & Weights and Measures Act 1985, s.15 (1), 86 (1). - Issued: 12.05.2006. Made: 28.04.2006. Laid: 05.05.2006. Coming into force: 30.05.2006 for regs 1, 2, 7, 9, 10 and sch. 2, part 1; 30.10.2006 for remainder. Effect: S.I. 2005/281 amended. Territorial extent & classification: E/W/S/NI (except for part III which does not apply to NI). General. - EC note: These Regulations implement Directive 2004/22/EC on measuring instruments in relation to the class of automatic gravimetric filling instruments within the category of automatic weighing instruments covered by the Directive. - 36p.: 30 cm. - 978-0-11-074548-0 £6.50

The Measuring Instruments (Automatic Rail-weighbridges) Regulations 2006 No. 2006/1256. - Enabling power: European Communities Act 1972, s. 2 (2) & Weights and Measures Act 1985, s.15 (1), 86 (1). - Issued: 12.05.2006. Made: 28.04.2006. Laid: 05.05.2006. Coming into force: 30.05.2006 for regs 1, 2, 7, 9, 10 and sch. 2, pt 1; 30.10.2006 for remainder. Effect: None. Territorial extent & classification: E/W/S/NI (except for part III which does not apply to NI). General. - EC note: These Regulations implement Directive 2004/22/EC on measuring instruments in relation to automatic rail-weighbridges. - 36p.: 30 cm. - 978-0-11-074549-7 £6.50

The Measuring Instruments (Beltweighers) Regulations 2006 No. 2006/1259. - Enabling power: European Communities Act 1972, s. 2 (2) & Weights and Measures Act 1985, ss. 15 (1), 86 (1). - Issued: 12.05.2006. Made: 28.04.2006. Laid: 05.05.2006. Coming into force: 30.05.2006 for regs 1, 2, 7, 9, 10 and sch. 2, part 1; 30.10.2006 for remainder. Effect: None. Territorial extent & classification: E/W/S/NI (except for part III which does not apply to NI). General. - EC note: These Regulations implement Directive 2004/22/EC on measuring instruments in relation to the class of beltweighers (also known as continuous totalisers) within the category of automatic weighing instruments covered by the Directive. - 32p.: 30 cm. - 978-0-11-074546-6 £5.50

The Measuring Instruments (Capacity Serving Measures) Regulations 2006 No. 2006/1264. - Enabling power: European Communities Act 1972, s. 2 (2) & Weights and Measures Act 1985, s. 15 (1), 86 (1). - Issued: 15.05.2006. Made: 28.04.2006. Laid: 08.05.2006. Coming into force: 30.05.2006 & 30.10.2006 in accord. with reg. 1 (2) (3). Effect: None. Territorial extent & classification: E/W/S/NI [except for part III which does not apply to NI]. General. - EC note: These Regs implement Directive 2004/22/EC on measuring instruments in relation to capacity serving measures covered by the Directive in so far as they are prescribed. - 32p.: 30 cm. - 978-0-11-074555-8 £5.50

The Measuring Instruments (Cold-water Meters) Regulations 2006 No. 2006/1268. - Enabling power: European Communities Act 1972, s. 2 (2) & Weights and Measures Act 1985, s. 15 (1), 86 (1). - Issued: 15.05.2006. Made: 28.04.2006. Laid: 08.05.2006. Coming into force: 30.05.2006 & 30.10.2006 in accord. with reg. 1 (2) (3). Effect: None. Territorial extent & classification: E/W/S/NI [except for part III which does not apply to NI]. General. - EC note: These Regulations implement Directive 2004/22/EC on measuring instruments in relation to cold-water meters. - 32p.: 30 cm. - 978-0-11-074556-5 £5.50

The Measuring Instruments (Exhaust Gas Analysers) Regulations 2006 No. 2006/2164. - Enabling power: European Communities Act 1972, s. 2 (2). - Issued: 14.08.2006. Made: 04.08.2006. Laid: 09.08.2006. Coming into force: 07.09.2006 for regs 1, 2, 7, 9, 10, sch. 2, Pt 1 and 30.10.2006 for remainder. Effect: None. Territorial extent & classification: E/W/S/NI. General. - EC note: These Regulations implement Directive 2004/22/EC on measuring instruments in relation to exhaust gas analysers, which are measuring instruments covered by the Directive. - 32p.: 30 cm. - 978-0-11-074985-3 £5.50

The Measuring Instruments (Gas Meters) Regulations 2006 No. 2006/2647. - Enabling power: European Communities Act 1972, s. 2 (2). - Issued: 12.10.2006. Made: 01.10.2006. Laid: 05.10.2006. Coming into force: 30.10.2006. Effect: 1986 c.44; S.I. 1983/684; 1996/275 (NI.2) modified. Territorial extent & classification: E/W/S/NI. General. - EC note: These Regulations implement Directive 2004/22/EC on measuring instruments in relation to gas meters. - 32p.: 30 cm. - 978-0-11-075149-8 £5.50

The Measuring Instruments (Liquid Fuel and Lubricants) (Amendment) Regulations 2006 No. 2006/2234. - Enabling power: Weights and Measures Act 1985, s. 15 (1), 86 (1). - Issued: 24.08.2006. Made: 15.08.2006. Laid: 17.08.2006. Coming into force: 30.10.2006. Effect: S.I. 1995/1014 amended. Territorial extent & classification: E/W/S. General. - 2p.: 30 cm. - 978-0-11-075025-5 £3,00

The Measuring Instruments (Liquid Fuel and Lubricants) Regulations 2006 No. 2006/1266. - Enabling power: European Communities Act 1972, s. 2 (2) & Weights and Measures Act 1985, s. 15 (1), 86 (1). - Issued: 15.05.2006. Made: 28.04.2006. Laid: 08.05.2006. Coming into force: 30.05.2006 & 30.10.2006 in accord. with reg. 1 (2) (3). Effect: None. Territorial extent & classification: E/W/S/NI [except for part III which does not apply to NI]. General. - EC note: These Regulations implement Directive 2004/22/EC on measuring instruments in relation to measuring systems. - 36p.: 30 cm. - 978-0-11-074553-4 £5.50

The Measuring Instruments (Liquid Fuel delivered from Road Tankers) Regulations 2006 No. 2006/1269. - Enabling power: European Communities Act 1972, s. 2 (2) & Weights and Measures Act 1985, s. 15 (1), 86 (1). - Issued: 15.05.2006. Made: 28.04.2006. Laid: 08.05.2006. Coming into force: 30.05.2006 & 30.10.2006 in accord. with reg. 1 (2) (3). Effect: None. Territorial extent & classification: E/W/S/NI [except for part III which does not apply to NI]. General. - EC note: These Regulations implement Directive 2004/22/EC on measuring instruments in relation to meter measuring systems. - 36p.: 30 cm. - 978-0-11-074557-2 £6.50

The Measuring Instruments (Material Measures of Length) Regulations 2006 No. 2006/1267. - Enabling power: European Communities Act 1972, s. 2 (2) & Weights and Measures Act 1985, s. 15 (1), 86 (1). - Issued: 15.05.2006. Made: 28.04.2006. Laid: 08.05.2006. Coming into force: 30.05.2006 & 30.10.2006 in accord. with reg. 1 (2) (3). Effect: None. Territorial extent & classification: E/W/S/NI [except for part III which does not apply to NI]. General. - EC note: These Regulations implement Directive 2004/22/EC on measuring instruments in relation to the class of material measures of length within the category of material measures covered by the Directive. - With correction slip dated July 2006. - 28p.: 30 cm. - 978-0-11-074554-1 £4.50

The Measuring Instruments (Non-Prescribed Instruments) Regulations 2006 No. 2006/1270. - Enabling power: European Communities Act 1972, s. 2 (2). - Issued: 15.05.2006. Made: 28.04.2006. Laid: 08.05.2006. Coming into force: 30.05.2006 & 30.10.2006 in accord. with reg. 1 (2) (3). Effect: None. Territorial extent & classification: E/W/S/NI [except for part III which does not apply to NI]. General. - EC note: Implements Directive 2004/22/EC on measuring instruments in relation to the legal metrological control of measuring instruments not regulated in the UK other than for use for trade for certain instruments as set out in regulation 3. These Regulations authorise the appointment of notified bodies to conduct conformity assessment of such instruments intended to be placed on the market or put into service in other member states. - 48p.: 30 cm. - 978-0-11-074558-9 £7.50

The Measuring Instruments (Taximeters) Regulations 2006 No. 2006/2304. - Enabling power: European Communities Act 1972, s. 2 (2). - Issued: 11.09.2006. Made: 24.08.2006. Laid: 29.08.2006. Coming into force: 29.09.2006 for regs 1, 2, 7, 9, 10, sch. 2, part 1; 30.10.2006 for remainder. Effect: None. Territorial extent & classification: E/W/S/NI. General. - EC note: These Regulations implement Directive 2004/22/EC on measuring instruments in relation to taximeters. - 32p.: 30 cm. - 978-0-11-075044-6 £5.50

The Weights and Measures (Packaged Goods) Regulations 2006 No. 2006/659. - Enabling power: Weights and Measures Act 1985, ss. 15 (1), 86 & European Communities Act 1972, s. 2 (2). - Issued: 22.03.2006. Made: 13.03.2006. Laid: 14.03.2006. Coming into force: 06.04.2006. Effect: 1985 c. 72; 2001 c. 16 & S.I. 1987/1538; 1988/120, 2040; 1994/1852; 1995/735; 2000/388, 932 amended & S.I. 1986/2049; 1992/1580; 1994/1258 revoked. Territorial extent & classification: E/W/S. General. - EC note: These Regulations re-implement the following Directives in whole or part: Council Directive 75/106/EEC (as amended); Council Directive 76/211/EEC as amended by Commission Directive 78/891/EEC and Council Directive 80/181/EEC (as amended). - 24p., ill.: 30 cm. - 978-0-11-074330-1 £4.00

Welsh Public Services Ombudsman

The Public Services Ombudsman (Wales) Act 2005 (Consequential Amendments to the Local Government Pension Scheme Regulations 1977 and Transitional Provisions) Order 2006 No. 2006/1011 (W.104). - Enabling power: Public Services Ombudsman (Wales) Act 2005, ss. 43 (1). - Issued: 09.05.2006. Made: 31.03.2006. Coming into force: 31.03.2006, at 16.03 hrs. Effect: S.I. 1997/1612 amended in relation to Wales. Territorial extent & classification: W. General. - 4p.: 30 cm. - 978-0-11-091331-5 £3.00

The Public Services Ombudsman (Wales) Act 2005 (Transitional Provisions and Consequential Amendments) Order 2006 No. 2006/362 (W.48). - Enabling power: Public Services Ombudsman (Wales) Act 2005, ss. 43 (1) (2), 44 (1). - Issued: 24.02.2006. Made: 14.02.2006. Coming into force: 01.04.2006. Effect: 1990/200; 1992/1812; 1993/3228; 1995/201; 1996/709; 2001/2281 (W.171), 2283 (W.172), 2284 (W.173), 2288 (W.176), 2289 (W.177), 2291 (W.179); 2003/437; 2005/1313 (W.95) amended & S.I. 2001/2275 (W.165) revoked & S.I. 1999/1791; 2004/2359 revoked in relation to Wales. Territorial extent & classification: W. General. - In English and Welsh. Welsh title: Gorchymyn Deddf Ombwdsmon Gwasanaethau Cyhoeddus (Cymru) 2005 (Darpariaethau Trosiannol a Diwygiadau Canlyniadol) 2006. - 12p.: 30 cm. - 978-0-11-091276-9 £3.00

The Public Services Ombudsman (Wales) (Jurisdiction and Transitional Provisions and Savings) Order 2006 No. 2006/363 (W.49). - Enabling power: Public Services Ombudsman (Wales) Act 2005, ss. 10 (2), 28 (2) (a), 41 (1) (3), 43 (1) (b), 44 (2) (b). - Issued: 22.02.2006. Made: 14.02.2006. Coming into force: 01.04.2006. Effect: 2005 c.10 amended. Territorial extent & classification: W. General. - In English and Welsh. Welsh title: Gorchymyn Ombwdsmon Gwasanaethau Cyhoeddus (Cymru) (Awdurdodaeth a Darpariaethau Trosiannol ac Arbedion) 2006. - 8p.: 30 cm. - 978-0-11-091275-2 £3.00

Wireless telegraphy

The Wireless Telegraphy (Guernsey) Order 2006 No. 2006/3325. - Enabling power: Wireless Telegraphy Act 1967, s. 15 (6); Broadcasting Act 1990, s. 204 (6); Intelligence Services Act 1994, s. 12 (4), Broadcasting Act 1996, s. 150 (4); Communications Act 2003, s. 411 (6) and Wireless Telegraphy Act 2006, ss. 118 (3) (6), 119 (3), sch. 8, para. 24. - Issued: 21.12.2006. Made: 14.12.2006. Coming into force: 08.02.2007. Effect: 2006 c.36 modified; S.I. 1994/1064; 2003/3195 modified and S.I. 1952/1900; 1967/1279; 1997/284 revoked as they relate to Guernsey; S.I. 1967/1274; 1998/1511 revoked. Territorial extent & classification: Guernsey. General. - 12p.: 30 cm. - 978-0-11-075520-5 £3.00

The Wireless Telegraphy (Jersey) Order 2006 No. 2006/3324. - Enabling power: Wireless Telegraphy Act 1967, s. 15 (6); Broadcasting Act 1990, s. 204 (6); Intelligence Services Act 1994, s. 12 (4), Broadcasting Act 1996, s. 150 (4); Communications Act 2003, s. 411 (6) and Wireless Telegraphy Act 2006, ss. 118 (3) (6), 119 (3), sch. 8, para. 24. - Issued: 21.12.2006. Made: 14.12.2006. Coming into force: 08.02.2007. Effect: 2006 c.36 modified; S.I. 2003/3197; 2004/308 amended and S.I. 1952/1900; 1967/1279; 1997/284 revoked as they relate to Jersey; S.I. 1967/1275; 1998/1512; 2003/3196 revoked. Territorial extent & classification: Jersey. General. - 16p.: 30 cm. - 978-0-11-075516-8 *£3.00*

Statutory Instruments

Arranged by Number

1	Road traffic
2 (W.1)	Road traffic, Wales
3 (W.2)	Road traffic, Wales
4 (W.3)	Road traffic, Wales
5	Public procurement, England and Wales
	Public procurement, Northern Ireland
6	Public procurement, England and Wales
	Public procurement, Northern Ireland
7	Road traffic
8	Road traffic
9	Road traffic
10	Road traffic
11	Road traffic
12	Road traffic
13	Road traffic
14	Food, England
15	Agriculture, England
	Food, England
16	Pensions
17	Road traffic
18	Copyright
	Rights in performances
19	Road traffic
20	Road traffic
21	Road traffic
22	Road traffic
23	Road traffic
24	Road traffic
25	Road traffic
26	Road traffic
27	Road traffic
28	Road traffic
29	Environmental protection
30 (W.4)	Education, Wales
31 (W.5)	Food, Wales
32 (W.6)	Road traffic, Wales
33	Pensions
34	Pensions
35	Copyright
36	Road traffic
37	Road traffic
38	Road traffic
39	Road traffic
40	Road traffic
41 (W.7)	Agriculture, Wales
42 (W.8)	Highways, Wales
43	Road traffic
44	Road traffic
45	Road traffic
46	Road traffic
47	Road traffic
48	Road traffic
49	Road traffic
50	Financial services
51 (C.1)	Education, England and Wales
52 (W.9)	Road traffic, Wales
53 (W.10)	Road traffic, Wales
54	Social security
55	Pensions
56	Road traffic
57	Proceeds of crime, England and Wales
	Proceeds of crime, Northern Ireland
58	Financial services and markets
59	Climate change levy
60	Climate change levy
61	Local government, England
62 (W.11)	Agriculture, Wales
63 (W.12)	Public bodies, Wales
64 (W.13)	Public bodies, Wales
65	Road traffic
66	Road traffic
67	Road traffic
68	Animals, England
69	Local government, England
70	Road traffic
71	Road traffic
72	Road traffic
73	Road traffic
74	Road traffic
75	Road traffic
76	Road traffic
77	Road traffic
78	Road traffic
79	Road traffic
80	Road traffic
81	Road traffic
82	Road traffic
83	Road traffic
84	Road traffic
85	Road traffic
86	Road traffic
87	Local government, England and Wales
88	Local government, England and Wales

89	Merchant shipping	137	Income tax
90	Children and young persons, England	138	Income tax
91	London government Contracting out, England	139	Stamp duty Stamp duty reserve tax
92	Cremation, England and Wales	140	Animals, England
93	Road traffic	141	Education
94	Road traffic	142	Road traffic
95	Road traffic	143	Road traffic
96	Road traffic	144	Excise
97	Road traffic	145 (W.20)	Road traffic, Wales
98	Road traffic	146 (W.21)	Road traffic, Wales
99	Terms and conditions of employment	147	Pensions
100	Serious Organised Crime Agency	148	Road traffic
101	Civil aviation	149	Road traffic
102	Civil aviation	150	Road traffic
103	Civil aviation	151	Road traffic
104	Civil aviation	152	Road traffic
105	Civil aviation	153	Road traffic
106	Civil aviation	154	Road traffic
107	Civil aviation	155	Road traffic
108	Civil aviation	156	Road traffic
109	Civil aviation	157	Road traffic
110	Civil aviation	158	Road traffic
111	Income tax Corporation tax	159	Road traffic
		160	Road traffic
112	Income tax Corporation tax	161	Road traffic
113	Agriculture, England	162	Road traffic
114	Road traffic	163	Road traffic
115	Road traffic	164	Road traffic
116 (W.14)	Agriculture, Wales	165	Road traffic
117	Civil aviation	166	Road traffic
118 (W.33)	Road traffic, Wales	167	Road traffic
119	Education, England and Wales Education, Northern Ireland	168	Animals, England
		169	Agriculture, England
120	Food	170	Energy conservation
121 (W.15)	Road traffic, Wales	171 (W.22)	Plant health, Wales
122	Police, England and Wales	172 (W.23) (C.2)	Education, Wales
123 (W.16)	Environmental protection, Wales	173 (W.24)	Education, Wales
124 (W.17)	Town and country planning, Wales	174 (W.25)	Education, Wales
125 (W.18)	Education, Wales	175 (W.26)	Education, Wales
126 (W.19)	Education, Wales	176 (W.27)	Education, Wales
127	Social security	177 (W.28)	Education, Wales
128	Education, England	178 (W.29)	Housing, Wales
129	Income tax	179 (W.30)	Animals, Wales
130	Income tax	180 (W.31)	Animals, Wales
131	Income tax	181 (W.32)	National Health Service, Wales
132	Income tax	182	Animals, England
133	Income tax	183	Animals, England
134	Income tax	184	Capital gains tax Corporation tax
135	Income tax		
136	Income tax	185	National Health Service, England

186	Road traffic
187	Road traffic
188	Road traffic
189	Road traffic
190	Road traffic
191	Road traffic
192	Road traffic
193	Road traffic
194	Road traffic
195	Road traffic
196	Road traffic
197	Road traffic
198	Road traffic
199	Child trust funds
200	National Health Service, England
201 (C.3)	Excise
202	Excise
203	Social security
204	Social security
205 (W.34)	Road traffic, Wales
206	Income tax
207	Income tax
208	Income tax
209	Income tax
210	Income tax
211	Income tax
212	Income tax
213	Social security
214	Social security
215	Social security
216	Social security
217	Social security
218	Sports grounds and sporting events, England
219	Disabled persons
220	Town and country planning, England
221	Town and country planning, England
222	Tax credits
223	Social security
224 (C.4)	Building and buildings, England and Wales
225	Agriculture, England
226	Town and country planning, England
227	Supreme Court of England and Wales
228 (C.5)	Supreme Court of England and Wales
229	Road traffic
230	Road traffic
231	Road traffic
232	Road traffic
233	Road traffic
234	Road traffic
235 (C.6)	Defence
236	Road traffic
237	Rating and valuation, England Council tax, England
238 (W.35)	Road traffic, Wales
239	Agriculture, England
240 (W.36)	Road traffic, Wales
241 (S.1)	Constitutional law Devolution, Scotland Broadcasting
242 (S.2)	Constitutional law Devolution, Scotland Charities
243	Income tax
244	Road traffic
245	Local government, England
246	Terms and conditions of employment
247	Local government, England
248	Local government, England
249 (W.37)	Local government, Wales
250	Government resources and accounts
251	Road traffic
252	Road traffic
253	Road traffic
254	Road traffic
255	Road traffic
256	Road traffic
257	Road traffic
258	Road traffic
259	Road traffic
260	Road traffic
261	Road traffic
262	Road traffic
263	Road traffic
264	Industrial and provident societies
265	Industrial and provident societies
266 (C.7)	Transport
267	Road traffic
268	Road traffic
269	Road traffic
270	Road traffic
271	Road traffic
272	Road traffic
273	Road traffic
274	Road traffic
275	Road traffic
276	Road traffic
277	Road traffic
278	Road traffic
279	Road traffic

280	Road traffic	327	Road traffic
281	Road traffic	328	Road traffic
282	Road traffic	329	Road traffic
283	Road traffic	330	Road traffic
284	Road traffic	331	Road traffic
285	Road traffic	332	Road traffic
286	Road traffic	333	Corporation tax
287	Road traffic	334	Employment and training
288	Road traffic	335	Employment and training
289	Road traffic	336	Health and safety
290	Road traffic	337	Pensions
291	Road traffic	338	Electronic communications
292	Road traffic	339	Electronic communications
293	Road traffic	340	Electronic communications
294	Road traffic	341	Electronic communications
295	Road traffic	342	Bee diseases, England
296	Road traffic	343	Pensions Social security
297	Road traffic	344 (W.41)	Council tax, Wales
298	Road traffic	345 (W.42) (C.8)	National Health Service, Wales
299 (W.38)	Road traffic, Wales	346	Intellectual property
300	Customs	347	Pensions
301	Agriculture, England	348 (W.43)	Road traffic, Wales
302	Highways, England	349	Pensions Terms and conditions of employment
303	Pensions	350 (W.44)	Road traffic, Wales
304 (S.3)	Constitutional law Devolution, Scotland	351	London government
305	National Health Service, England and Wales	352 (L.1)	Family proceedings, England and Wales Supreme Court of England and Wales County courts, England and Wales
306	Education, England		
307	European Communities	353 (L.2)	Supreme Court of England and Wales Magistrates' courts, England and Wales
308	Proceeds of crime Financial services		
309	International immunities and privileges	354	Competition
310	Overseas territories	355	Competition
311	United Nations	356	Offshore installations
312 (N.I.1)	Northern Ireland	357 (W.45)	Agriculture, Wales
313 (N.I.2)	Northern Ireland	358 (W.46)	National Health Service, Wales
314 (N.I.3)	Northern Ireland	359	National Health Service, England
315	Patents	360 (W.47)	National Health Service, Wales
316	Copyright Rights in performances	361	National Health Service, England and Wales
317	Designs	362 (W.48)	Welsh Public Services Ombudsman
318 (W.39)	Road traffic, Wales	363 (W.49)	Welsh Public Services Ombudsman
319 (W.40)	Road traffic, Wales	364	Income tax
320	Road traffic	365	Income tax
321	Road traffic	366	National Health Service, England
322	Road traffic	367	Housing, England
323	Road traffic	368	Housing, England
324	Road traffic	369	Housing, England
325	Road traffic	370	Housing, England
326	Road traffic	371	Housing, England
		372	Housing, England

373	Housing, England	417	Road traffic
374 (W.50)	Road traffic, Wales	418	Road traffic
375	Road traffic	419	Road traffic
376	Civil aviation	420	Road traffic
377	Civil aviation	421	Road traffic
378 (C.9)	Serious Organised Crime Agency Criminal law, England and Wales Criminal law, Northern Ireland Police, England and Wales	422	Road traffic
		423	Road traffic
		424	Road traffic
379	Road traffic	425	Security industry, England and Wales
380	Road traffic		
381	Road traffic	426	Security industry, England and Wales
382	Road traffic	427	Security industry, England and Wales
383	Road traffic		
384	Road traffic	428	Security industry, England and Wales
385	Road traffic		
386	Road traffic	429	Road traffic
387	Road traffic	430	Road traffic
388	Road traffic	431	Road traffic
389	Legal Services Commission, England and Wales	432	Road traffic
		433	Road traffic
390	Representation of the people, England and Wales	434	Road traffic
		435	Road traffic
391	Pensions	436	Road traffic
392 (C.10)	Security industry, England and Wales	437	Education, England
393 (C.11)	Environmental protection, England	438	Health and safety
		439	Road traffic
394	Animals, England	440	Road traffic
395	Medicines	441	Road traffic
396	National lottery	442	Road traffic
397	Transport	443	Road traffic
398	Highways, England	444	Road traffic
399	Highways, England	445	Road traffic
400	Immigration	446	Road traffic
401	National Health Service, England and Wales Road traffic, England and Wales	447	Road traffic
		448	Road traffic
402 (W.51)	Road traffic, Wales	449	Road traffic
403 (W.52)	Road traffic, Wales	450	Road traffic
404 (C.12)	Human tissue, England and Wales Human tissue, Northern Ireland	451	Road traffic
		452	Road traffic
405	Transport and works, England Transport, England	453	Road traffic
		454	Road traffic
406	Road traffic	455	Road traffic
407	Road traffic	456	Road traffic
408	Education, England	457	Road traffic
409	Education, England	458	Road traffic
410	Road traffic	459	Road traffic
411 (W.53)	Road traffic, Wales	460	Road traffic
412	Road traffic	461	Road traffic
413	Road traffic	462	Road traffic
414	Road traffic	463	Road traffic
415	Road traffic		
416	Road traffic		

464	Road traffic	512	Prevention and suppression of terrorism
465	Road traffic	513 (W.62)	Road traffic, Wales
466	Road traffic	514	Terms and conditions of employment
467	Pensions	515	Health care and associated professions
468	Education, England		
469 (W.54)	Road traffic, Wales	516	Social security
470	Road traffic	517	Social care, England Children and young persons, England
471	Road traffic		
472	Road traffic	518	Agriculture, England
473	Road traffic	519 (W.63)	Seeds, Wales
474	Road traffic	520 (W.64)	Education, Wales
475	Road traffic	521	Local government, England
476	Road traffic	522	Competition Consumer protection
477	Road traffic	523	Water, England and Wales Consumer protection
478	Road traffic		
479	National Health Service, England	524	Road traffic
480	Northern Ireland	525	Road traffic
481 (C.12)	National Health Service, England	526	Local government, England
482	Education, England	527	Road traffic
483	Education, England and Wales	528	Road traffic
484	Regulatory reform, England and Wales	529	Road traffic
		530	Road traffic
485 (W.55)	Food, Wales	531	Road traffic
486	National Health Service, England	532	Road traffic
487 (W.56)	National Health Service, Wales	533	Road traffic
488 (W.57)	National Health Service, Wales	534	Road traffic
489 (W.58)	National Health Service, Wales	535	Road traffic
490 (W.59)	National Health Service, Wales	536	Social security
491 (W.60)	National Health Service, Wales	537	Environmental protection, England
492	Rating and valuation, England	538	Human tissue, England and Wales Human tissue, Northern Ireland
493	Immigration		
494	Medicines Fees and charges	539	Public health, England
		540	Police, England and Wales
495	Rating and valuation, England	541	Betting, gaming and lotteries
496	Social security	542	Betting, gaming and lotteries
497	Income tax	543	Betting, gaming and lotteries, England and Wales
498	Income tax		
499	Income tax	544	Coroners, England
500	Social security	545	Road traffic
501	Magistrates' courts, England and Wales	546	Road traffic
		547	Road traffic
502	Magistrates' courts, England and Wales	548	Road traffic
		549	Road traffic
503	Local government, England	550	Road traffic
504	Local government, England	551	Social security
505	Local government, England	552	National Health Service, England
506	Food, England	553	Local government, England
507	Education, England	554	Harbours, docks, piers and ferries
508	Local government, England	555	Education, England
509 (W.61)	Road traffic, Wales	556	Transport
510	Local government, England	557	Health and safety
511	Education, England		

558	Pensions	601	Civil aviation
559	Social security	602	Representation of the people
560 (C.13)	Pensions	603 (W.67)	Road traffic, Wales
561	Insolvency, England and Wales	604	Fees and charges
562	National Health Service, England and Wales	605	Competition
563	National Health Service, England	606	Pensions
564	Local government, England	607	Ministers of the Crown
565	National lottery, England	608	European Communities
566	Pensions	609	Constitutional law Devolution, Scotland
567	Income tax	610	Overseas territories
568	Income tax	611 (N.I.4)	Northern Ireland
569	Income tax	612 (N.I. 5)	Northern Ireland
570	Income tax	613 (N.I.6)	Northern Ireland
571	Income tax	614	Income tax
572	Income tax	615 (W.68)	Local government, Wales
573	Income tax	616	Urban development, England
574	Income tax	617 (W.69)	Agriculture, Wales
575	Corporation tax Income tax Capital gains tax Inheritance tax Stamp duty land tax	618	Land drainage, England and Wales
		619	Electronic communications Broadcasting
		620	Police, England and Wales
576	Social security	621 (W.70)	Education, Wales
577	Excise	622	Insolvency, England and Wales
578	Children and young persons, England Social care, England	623	Government trading funds
		624	Social security
579	Road traffic, England	625	Road traffic
580	Pensions	626	Road traffic
581 (W.65)	Road traffic, Wales	627	Road traffic
582	Transport, England and Wales	628	Road traffic
583	Housing, England	629	Criminal law
584	Metropolitan and city districts	630	Race relations
585	Highways, England	631 (C. 14)	Betting, gaming and lotteries
586	Social security	632	National Health Service, England and Wales
587	Value added tax	633	National Health Service, England and Wales
588	Social security		
589	Food	634	National Health Service, England and Wales
590 (W.66)	Agriculture, Wales Food, Wales	635	National Health Service, England and Wales
591	Licences and licensing, England Rating and valuation, England	636	Betting, gaming and lotteries, England and Wales
592	Road traffic, England	637	Betting, gaming and lotteries
593	Local government, England Road traffic, England	638	Social security
594	Police Serious Organised Crime Agency	639 (C.15)	Civil partnership, England and Wales
595	Pensions	640	National Health Service, England and Wales
596	National Health Service, England	641	Water resources, England and Wales
597	Pensions	642	Cinemas and film
598	Transport	643	Cinemas and film
599	Health and safety	644	Social security
600	National Health Service, England and Wales	645	Social security

Number	Subject
	Terms and conditions of employment
646	Housing, England
647	Housing, England
648	Plant breeders' rights
649	Merchant shipping
650 (W.71)	Housing, Wales
651	Environmental protection, England
652	Building and buildings, England and Wales
653	Mental health, England and Wales
654	National lottery
655	Betting, gaming and lotteries
656 (C.16)	Environmental protection, England and Wales
657	European Communities
658	Employment
659	Weights and measures
660	Employment
661 (S.5)	Constitutional law Devolution, Scotland Environmental protection, Scotland Water, Scotland
662	Employment
663	Social security
664	Road traffic
665	Road traffic
666	Road traffic
667	Road traffic
668	Road traffic
669	Road traffic
670	Road traffic
671	Road traffic
672	Pensions
673	Pensions
674	National assistance services, England
675	National Health Service, England
676	Lord Chief Justice Judicial appointments and discipline
677	Lord Chief Justice Lord Chancellor Coroners, England and Wales
678	Judicial appointments and discipline
679	Judicial appointments and discipline
680	Lord Chancellor Lord Chief Justice Transfer of functions
681	Road traffic
682	Road traffic
683	Road traffic
684	Road traffic
685	Pensions
686	Pensions
687	Road traffic
688	Road traffic
689	Road traffic
690	Road traffic
691	Road traffic
692	Social security
693	Road traffic
694	Road traffic
695	Road traffic
696	Road traffic
697	Road traffic
698	Road traffic
699	Road traffic
700	Road traffic
701	Road traffic
702	Road traffic
703	Road traffic
704	Road traffic
705	Road traffic
706	Road traffic
707	Road traffic
708	Road traffic
709	Road traffic
710	Road traffic
711	Road traffic
712	Social security
713	Legal Services Commission, England and Wales
714	Pensions
715 (L.3)	Magistrates' courts, England and Wales
716	Local government, England
717	Pensions
718	Social security
719 (L.4)	Supreme Court of England and Wales County courts, England and Wales
720	Road traffic
721	Road traffic
722	Road traffic
723	Road traffic
724	Road traffic
725	Road traffic
726	Road traffic
727	Road traffic
728	Road traffic
729	Road traffic
730	Road traffic
731	Road traffic
732	Road traffic
733	Immigration
734 (S.6)	Insolvency, Scotland
735 (S.7)	Insolvency, Scotland
736	Education, England and Wales
737	Environmental protection

738	Social security
739 (L.5)	Family proceedings, England and Wales Supreme Court of England and Wales County courts, England and Wales
740	Police, England and Wales Pensions, England and Wales
741	Pensions
742	Pensions
743	Environmental protection, England
744	Taxes
745	Income tax
746	Stamp duty Stamp duty reserve tax
747	Pensions
748	Police, England and Wales
749	Pensions
750	Police, England and Wales
751 (C.17)	Police, England and Wales
752	Representation of the people, England and Wales Local government, England and Wales
753	Road traffic
754	Road traffic
755	Food
756	Food
757	Social security
758	Gender recognition
759	Pensions
760	Intellectual property
761	Sports grounds and sporting events, England and Wales
762 (W.72)	Food, Wales
763	Trade marks
764 (W.73)	Local government, Wales
765	Pensions
766	Tax credits
767 (W.74)	Agriculture, Wales
768 (W.75)(C.18)	Environmental protection, Wales
769	Social security
770	Environmental protection, England
771	Environmental protection, England
772 (S. 8)	Insolvency, Scotland
773	Land drainage, England
774	Land drainage, England
775	National Health Service, England
776	Stamp duty land tax
777	Income tax
778	Pensions Terms and conditions of employment
779	Dogs, England
780	Regulatory reform Forestry
781	Environmental protection, England
782	National Health Service, England
783	Environmental protection, England
784	Petroleum
785	National Health Service, England
786	National Health Service, England
787	National Health Service, England
788	National Health Service, England
789	Civil aviation
790	Civil aviation
791	Civil aviation
792	Civil aviation
793	Civil aviation
794	Civil aviation
795 (C. 19)	Environmental protection, England
796	Civil aviation
797	Civil aviation
798	Dogs, England
799	Social security Terms and conditions of employment
800	Civil aviation
801	Pensions
802	Pensions
803	Land drainage, England
804	Land drainage, England
805	Road traffic
806	Road traffic
807	Road traffic
808	Road traffic
809	Road traffic
810	Road traffic
811	Road traffic
812	Road traffic
813	Road traffic
814	Road traffic
815	Road traffic
816	Road traffic
817	Road traffic
818	Road traffic
819	Road traffic
820	Road traffic
821	Road traffic
822	Road traffic
823	Road traffic
824	Security industry, England and Wales
825	National Health Service, England
826	Land drainage, England
827	National Health Service, England
828	National Health Service, England
829	Social security

830	Housing, England	878 (W.83)	Social care, Wales
831	Housing, England		Children and young persons, Wales
832	Social security		Public health, Wales
833 (W.76)	Road traffic, Wales	879 (W.84)(C.21)	Education, Wales
834 (S. 9)	Representation of the people, Scotland	880	Lands tribunal, England and Wales
		881	*Cancelled*
835	Criminal law, England and Wales	882	Income tax
836 (C.22)	National Health Service, England and Wales	883	Social security
		884	Constitutional law
837	Children and young persons, England and Wales		Devolution, Wales
			Representation of the people, Wales
838	Education, England	885 (W.85)(C.23)	Children and young persons, Wales
839	Education, England	886	Local government, England
840	Education, England	887	Disabled persons
841	Education, England	888	Road traffic
842 (W.77)	Town and country planning, Wales	889	Road traffic
843	Corporation tax	890	Road traffic
844	Agriculture, England	891	Road traffic
845	Road traffic	892	Road traffic
846	Road traffic	893	Road traffic
847	Road traffic	894	Road traffic
848	Road traffic	895	Road traffic
849	Road traffic	896	Road traffic
850	Road traffic	897	Road traffic
851	Road traffic, England	898	Road traffic
852	Road traffic	899	Road traffic
853	Civil aviation	900	Road traffic
854	Civil aviation	901	Road traffic
855	Civil aviation	902	Road traffic
856	Civil aviation	903	Road traffic
857	Civil aviation	904	Road traffic
858	Civil aviation	905	Road traffic
859	Civil aviation	906	Road traffic
860	Road traffic	907	Road traffic
861	Road traffic	908	Road traffic
862	Road traffic	909	Social security
863	Road traffic	910 (W.86)	Road traffic, Wales
864	Animals, England	911 (W.87)	Road traffic, Wales
865	Landfill tax	912	Income tax
866 (W.78)	Animals, Wales	913	National Health Service, England
867 (W.79)	Animals, Wales	914	Medicines
868	Value added tax	915	Medicines
869	Value added tax	916	Civil aviation
870 (W.80)(C.20)	Children and young persons, Wales	917	Civil aviation
871	Capital gains tax	918	Civil aviation
872	Income tax	919	Pensions
873 (W.81)	Education, Wales	920	Pensions
874	Value added tax	921	Charities, England and Wales
875	Taxes	922	Highways, England
	Stamp duty land tax	923	Highways, England
876	Value added tax	924	Road traffic
877 (W.82)	Education, Wales	925	Pensions

926 (W.88)	Road traffic, Wales	971	Road traffic
927 (C.24)	Children and young persons, England	972	Road traffic
928 (C. 25)	Civil partnership, Northern Ireland	973	Road traffic
		974	Road traffic
929	Education, England and Wales	975	Road traffic
930	Education, England and Wales	976	Road traffic
931 (C.26)	Town and country planning, Wales	977	Road traffic
932	Police, England and Wales	978 (W.101)	Health care and associated professions, Wales
933	Disabled persons Transport	979 (W.102)	Local government, Wales
934 (C.27)	Environmental protection, England and Wales	980 (W.103)	Land drainage, Wales
935	Pensions	981	Income tax Corporation tax
936	Corporation tax	982 (C.29)	Income tax Corporation tax
937	Environmental protection, England and Wales	983	Children and young persons, England
938	Road traffic	984 (C.30)	Water, England and Wales
939	Highways, England	985	Agriculture, England and Wales Pesticides, England and Wales
940 (W.89)	Social care, Wales Children and young persons, Wales		
941 (W.90)	National Health Service, Wales	986	Dangerous drugs
942 (W.91)	National Health Service, Wales	987	Serious Organised Crime Agency
943 (W.92)	National Health Service, Wales	988	Sports grounds and sporting events, England and Wales
944 (W.93)	Local government, Wales	989	Agriculture, England
945 (W.94)	National Health Service, Wales	990	Countryside, England
946 (W.95)	National Health Service, Wales	991	Agriculture, England Countryside, England
947 (W.96)	National Health Service, Wales		
948 (W.97)	Town and country planning, Wales	992	Road traffic
949 (W.98)	Local government, Wales	993	Road traffic
950 (W.99)	Housing, Wales	994	Town and country planning, England
951 (W.100)	Road traffic, Wales	995	Road traffic
952	Offshore installations	996	Road traffic
953	Education, England	997	Road traffic
954	Climate change levy	998	Road traffic
955	Education, England and Wales	999	Road traffic
956	Social security, Northern Ireland	1000	Social security
957	Social security	1001	County courts, England and Wales Magistrates' courts, England and Wales Supreme Court of England and Wales
958	Transport and works, England and Wales		
959	Income tax Corporation tax	1002 (C.31)	Environmental protection, England and Wales
960	Government resources and accounts	1003	Immigration
961	Social security	1004	Electricity, England and Wales
962	Social security	1005	Disabled persons
963	Tax credits	1006	Criminal law, England and Wales
964	Income tax Corporation tax Capital gains tax	1007	Disabled persons
		1008	Ecclesiastical law, England and Wales
965	Social security	1009	Pensions
966	Pensions, England and Wales	1010	Health and safety
967	Road traffic	1011 (W.104)	Welsh Public Services Ombudsman
968	Road traffic	1012	Northern Ireland Constitutional law
969	Road traffic		
970	Road traffic		

1013 (C.32)	Prevention and suppression of terrorism	1055	Constitutional law Devolution, Scotland Criminal law
1014 (C.33)	Lord Chancellor Lord Chief Justice Judicial appointments and discipline Judicial appointments and removals, Northern Ireland Transfer of functions	1056	Constitutional law Devolution, Scotland National Health Service, Scotland
		1057	Health and safety
1015	Health care and associated professions Nurses and midwives	1058	Excise
		1059	Dogs, England
1016	Lord Chancellor Lord Chief Justice Transfer of functions	1060 (C.34)	Housing, England
		1061 (C.35)	Town and country planning, England
1017	Road traffic	1062	Town and country planning, England
1018	Road traffic	1063	Town and country planning, England
1019	Road traffic	1064 (W.110)	Local government, Wales
1020	Road traffic	1065	National Health Service, England
1021	Road traffic	1066	Savings banks
1022	Road traffic	1067	Education, England
1023	Road traffic	1068	Education, England
1024	Road traffic	1069	Social security
1025	Road traffic	1070	Proceeds of crime
1026	Social security	1071	International development
1027	Trade marks	1072	Education, England
1028	Intellectual property	1073	Education, Wales
1029	Intellectual property	1074	Road traffic
1030	Insolvency	1075	International immunities and privileges
1031	Employment and training	1076	Road traffic
1032	Electronic communications	1077	Housing, England
1033	Education, England	1078	Education, England
1034	Social security	1079 (W.111)	Road traffic, Wales
1035 (W.105)	Rating and valuation, Wales	1080	Trade marks
1036 (W.106)	Animals, Wales	1081	Police, Northern Ireland Northern Ireland
1037	Road traffic	1082 (C.36)	Equal opportunities and human rights
1038	Betting, gaming and lotteries	1083 (W.112)	Road traffic, Wales
1039	Copyright, Gibraltar	1084	Fire and rescue services, England
1040	Constitutional law Devolution, Scotland	1085 (C.37)	Police, England and Wales Proceeds of crime
1041	Representation of the people, Wales	1086	Civil aviation
1042	Road traffic	1087	Civil aviation
1043	Road traffic	1088	Civil aviation
1044	Road traffic	1089	Civil aviation
1045	Road traffic	1090	Civil aviation
1046	Road traffic	1091	Civil aviation
1047	Road traffic	1092	Civil aviation
1048	Road traffic	1093	Housing, England
1049	Road traffic	1094	Disabled persons
1050	Secure training centres, England and Wales	1095	Highways, England
		1096	Highways, England
1051 (W.107)	National assistance services, Wales	1097	Road traffic
1052 (W.108)	Town and country planning, Wales	1098	Road traffic
1053 (W.109)	Animals, Wales	1099	Road traffic
1054 (S.10)	Constitutional law Devolution, Scotland Water, Scotland	1100	Road traffic

1101	Road traffic	**1147**	Road traffic
1102	Road traffic	**1148**	Road traffic
1103	Road traffic	**1149**	Road traffic
1104	Road traffic	**1150**	Road traffic
1105	Road traffic	**1151**	Road traffic
1106	Road traffic	**1152**	Clean air, England
1107	Road traffic	**1153**	Road traffic
1108	Road traffic	**1154**	Road traffic
1109	Road traffic	**1155**	Road traffic
1110	Road traffic	**1156**	Road traffic
1111	Road traffic	**1157 (S.11)**	Civil aviation, Scotland
1112	Road traffic	**1158 (W.113)**	Road traffic, Wales
1113	Road traffic	**1159 (W.114)**	Road traffic, Wales
1114	Road traffic	**1160**	Seeds, England
1115	Constitutional law Devolution, Scotland Health	**1161**	Seeds, England
		1162	Income tax
1116	Criminal law, England and Wales Criminal law, Northern Ireland	**1163**	Tax credits
		1164	Education, England
1117	Road traffic	**1165**	Civil aviation
1118 (C.38)	Olympic Games and Paralympic Games Sports grounds and sporting events	**1166**	Civil aviation
		1167	Civil aviation
1119	Trade marks Commercial property	**1168**	Civil aviation
		1169	Civil aviation
1120	Trade marks Commercial property	**1170**	Civil aviation
1121	Civil partnership	**1171**	Civil aviation
1122	Civil aviation	**1172 (C.39)**	Rights of way, England
1123	Civil aviation	**1173**	Civil aviation
1124	Road traffic	**1174**	Civil aviation
1125	Road traffic	**1175**	Civil aviation
1126	Road traffic	**1176 (C.40)**	Natural environment, England and Wales Natural environment, Northern Ireland Rights of way, England
1127	Road traffic		
1128	Road traffic		
1129	Road traffic	**1177**	Highways, England and Wales
1130	Road traffic	**1178**	Protection of wrecks, England
1131	Road traffic	**1179**	Food
1132	Road traffic	**1180 (W.115)**	Road traffic, Wales
1133	Road traffic	**1181 (W.116)**	Road traffic, Wales
1134	Road traffic	**1182**	Corporation tax
1135	Harbours, docks, piers and ferries	**1183**	Companies
1136	Road traffic	**1184**	Education, England
1137	Road traffic	**1185**	Road traffic, England
1138	Road traffic	**1186**	Road traffic
1139	Road traffic	**1187**	Road traffic
1140	Road traffic	**1188**	Road traffic
1141	Road traffic	**1189**	Road traffic
1142	Road traffic	**1190**	Road traffic
1143	Road traffic	**1191**	Road traffic
1144	Road traffic	**1192**	Road traffic
1145	Road traffic	**1193**	Road traffic
1146	Road traffic		

1194	Road traffic		1243	Road traffic
1195	Road traffic		1244	Merchant shipping
1196	Road traffic		1245	Road traffic
1197	Animals, England		1246	Road traffic
1198	Consumer protection		1247	Road traffic
1199	Health care and associated professions Nurses and midwives		1248	Marine pollution
			1249	United Nations
1200	Animals, England		1250	United Nations
1201	Road traffic		1251	Constitutional law Devolution, Scotland Fire and rescue services
1202	Road traffic			
1203	Road traffic		1252 (N.I. 7)	Northern Ireland
1204	Road traffic		1253 (N.I.8)	Northern Ireland
1205	Road traffic		1254 (N.I.9)	Northern Ireland
1206	Road traffic		1255	Weights and measures
1207	Road traffic		1256	Weights and measures
1208	Road traffic		1257	Weights and measures
1209	Road traffic		1258	Weights and measures
1210	Road traffic		1259	Weights and measures
1211	Road traffic		1260	Human tissue, England and Wales Human tissue, Northern Ireland
1212	Road traffic			
1213	Road traffic		1261 (W.118)	Plant breeders' rights, Wales
1214	Road traffic		1262 (W.119)	Education, Wales
1215	Road traffic		1263	Housing, England
1216	Road traffic		1264	Weights and measures
1217	Road traffic		1265	Merchant shipping
1218	Road traffic		1266	Weights and measures
1219	Road traffic		1267	Weights and measures
1220	Road traffic		1268	Weights and measures
1221	Road traffic		1269	Weights and measures
1222	Road traffic		1270	Weights and measures
1223	Road traffic		1271 (W.120)	Road traffic, Wales
1224	Road traffic		1272	Insolvency, England and Wales
1225	Road traffic		1273	Consumer credit
1226 (W.117)	Animals, Wales		1274	Education, England and Wales
1227	Road traffic		1275 (W.121)	Local government, Wales
1228	Animals, England		1276	Industrial and provident societies
1229	Intellectual property		1277 (W.122)	Education, Wales
1230	Civil aviation		1278 (W.123)(C.41)	Education, Wales
1231	Civil aviation		1279 (W.124)(C.42)	Rights of way, Wales
1232	Civil aviation		1280 (W.125)	Road traffic, Wales
1233	Civil aviation		1281 (C.43)	Town and country planning
1234	Civil aviation		1282	Town and country planning, England and Wales
1235	Civil aviation			
1236	Civil aviation		1283	Town and country planning, England
1237	Road traffic		1284	Town and country planning, England
1238	Highways, England		1285	Highways, England
1239	Road traffic		1286 (W.126)	Road traffic, Wales
1240	Road traffic		1287	Road traffic
1241	Road traffic		1288	Road traffic
1242	Road traffic		1289	Water, England and Wales
			1290	Road traffic

1291	Road traffic	1339 (W.131)	Food, Wales
1292	Road traffic	1340	Protection of wrecks, England
1293 (W.127)	Animals, Wales	1341 (W.132)	Education, Wales
1294	Housing, England	1342	Protection of wrecks, England
1295	Pesticides, England and Wales	1343 (W.133)	Education, Wales
1296	Civil aviation	1344 (W.134)	Plant health, Wales
1297	Civil aviation	1345	Road traffic, England and Wales
1298	Civil aviation	1346	Road traffic, England and Wales
1299	Civil aviation	1347	Road traffic, England and Wales
1300	Civil aviation	1348	Excise
1301	Civil aviation	1349 (W.135)	Agriculture, Wales
1302	Civil aviation	1350	Civil aviation
1303	Civil aviation	1351	Road traffic
1304	Civil aviation	1352	Road traffic
1305	Civil aviation	1353	Road traffic
1306	Road traffic	1354	Road traffic
1307	Road traffic	1355	Road traffic
1308	Road traffic	1356	Road traffic
1309	Road traffic	1357	Agriculture
1310	Road traffic	1358	Corporation tax
1311	Road traffic	1359	*Cancelled*
1312	Road traffic	1360	*Cancelled*
1313	Road traffic	1361 (C.46)	Environmental protection, England
1314	Road traffic	1362	Road traffic
1315	Road traffic	1363	Road traffic
1316	Road traffic	1364	Road traffic
1317	Road traffic	1365	Road traffic
1318	Road traffic	1366	Road traffic
1319	Road traffic	1367	Road traffic
1320	Road traffic	1368	Road traffic
1321	Road traffic	1369	Road traffic
1322	Road traffic	1370	Road traffic
1323	Road traffic	1371	Road traffic
1324	Road traffic	1372	Road traffic
1325	Road traffic	1373	Road traffic
1326	Road traffic	1374	Road traffic
1327	Sea fisheries, England	1375	Road traffic
1328	Civil aviation	1376	Road traffic
1329	Civil aviation	1377	Road traffic
1330	Prevention and suppression of terrorism Northern Ireland	1378	Road traffic
		1379	Environmental protection, England
1331	Customs	1380	Environmental protection, England
1332	Land registration, England and Wales	1381	Environmental protection, England
		1382 (C.47)	Nature conservation, England and Wales
1333	Water resources, England		Natural environment, England and Wales
1334	Environmental protection, England		
1335 (W.128)	Education, Wales	1383	Pensions
1336 (W.129)(C.44)	Education, Wales	1384	Civil aviation
1337	Pensions	1385	National Health Service, England
1338 (W.130)(C.45)	Education, Wales	1386 (W.136)	Town and country planning, Wales

1387 (W.137)	Town and country planning, Wales	1437	Road traffic
1388 (W.138)	Town and country planning, Wales	1438	Pensions
1389 (W.139)	National Health Service, Wales	1439 (C.49)	Identity cards
1390	British nationality	1440	Healthcare and associated professions
1391	Electronic communications	1441	Healthcare and associated professions
1392	Protection of wrecks, England	1442	Police, England and Wales
1393	National Health Service, England	1443 (W.142)	Road traffic, Wales
1394	Animals, England	1444 (W.143)	Road traffic, Wales
1395	Civil aviation	1445	Road traffic, England
1396	Civil aviation	1446	Road traffic, England
1397	Civil aviation	1447	Local government, England Road traffic, England
1398	Civil aviation	1448	National Health Service, England
1399	Civil aviation	1449	Electromagnetic compatibility
1400	Civil aviation	1450	Dangerous drugs
1401	Food, England	1451	Highways, England
1402	Social security	1452	Charities
1403 (W.140)(C.48)	Transport, Wales	1453	Income tax
1404	Local government, England	1454	United Nations
1405	Local government, England	1455	Pensions
1406	Police, England and Wales	1456	Children and young persons
1407	National Health Service, England and Wales	1457	Parliament
1408	National Health Service, England	1458	Constitutional law Devolution, Wales
1409	Road traffic	1459 (N.I.10)	Northern Ireland
1410	Road traffic	1460	Education, England
1411	Road traffic	1461	European Communities
1412	Road traffic	1462	Local government, England
1413	Road traffic	1463	Environmental protection
1414	Road traffic	1464	Food, England
1415	Road traffic	1465	Income tax
1416	Road traffic	1466	Transport and works, England and Wales Transport, England and Wales Canals and inland waterways, England and Wales
1417	Highways, England		
1418	Highways, England	1467	Police, England and Wales
1419	Highways, England	1468	Protection of wrecks, England
1420 (W.141)	Education, Wales	1469	Town and country planning, England
1421	Immigration	1470	Protection of wrecks, England
1422	Water resources, England	1471	Animals, England
1423	Water resources, England	1472	Value added tax
1424	Water resources, England	1473	Road traffic
1425	Road traffic	1474	Road traffic
1426	Road traffic	1475	Road traffic
1427	Road traffic	1476	Road traffic
1428	Road traffic	1477	Road traffic
1429	Road traffic	1478	Road traffic
1430	Road traffic	1479	Road traffic
1431	Road traffic	1480	Road traffic
1432	Road traffic	1481	Road traffic
1433	Road traffic	1482	Road traffic
1434	Road traffic	1483	Road traffic
1435	Road traffic		
1436	Road traffic		

1484	Road traffic	1531	Social Security, Northern Ireland
1485	Road traffic	1532 (W.150)	Highways, Wales
1486	Road traffic	1533	Education, England
1487	Road traffic	1534 (W.151)	Food, Wales
1488	Road traffic	1535 (W.152)(C.54)	Housing, Wales
1489	Road traffic	1536 (W.153)	Animals, Wales
1490	Road traffic	1537 (C.55)	Judicial appointments and removals, Northern Ireland
1491	Road traffic	1538	Animals
1492	Environmental protection	1539	Animals
1493	Social care, England	1540	Food, England and Wales
1494 (W.144)	Road traffic, Wales	1541	Family proceedings, England and Wales
1495 (W.145)	Sea fisheries, Wales	1542	County courts, England and Wales
1496	British nationality	1543	Income tax Corporation tax Capital gains tax
1497 (C.50)	Immigration		
1498 (C.51)	Immigration	1544	Income tax Corporation tax Capital gains tax
1499	Agriculture, England Agriculture, Northern Ireland		
1500	Atomic energy and radioactive substances, England and Wales	1545	Highways, England
1501	National Health Service, England	1546	Highways, England
1502 (W.146)	Road traffic, Wales	1547	Museums and galleries
1503	Housing, England and Wales	1548	Immigration
1504	Education, England	1549	Sea fisheries, England
1505	Education, England	1550	National Health Service, England
1506	Animals, England	1551	Judicial appointments and discipline
1507	Education, England	1552	Road traffic
1508 (C. 52)	Consumer credit	1553	Road traffic
1509	Local government, England	1554	Road traffic
1510	Environmental protection	1555	Road traffic
1511 (W.147)	Animals, Wales	1556	Road traffic
1512 (W.148)	Animals, Wales	1557	Road traffic
1513 (W.149)	Animals, Wales	1558	Road traffic
1514	Road traffic	1559	Road traffic
1515	Road traffic, England	1560	Road traffic
1516	Local government, England Road traffic, England	1561	Road traffic
		1562	Road traffic
1517 (C.53)	Immigration	1563	Road traffic
1518	Transport and works, England Transport, England	1564	Road traffic
		1565	Road traffic
1519	Electricity Gas	1566	Road traffic
		1567	Road traffic
1520	Family law	1568	Road traffic
1521	Electricity	1569	Road traffic
1522	Civil aviation	1570	Road traffic
1523	Civil aviation	1571	Road traffic
1524	Civil aviation	1572	Road traffic
1525	Civil aviation	1573	Road traffic
1526	Civil aviation	1574	Road traffic
1527	Civil aviation	1575	Road traffic
1528	Civil aviation	1576	Road traffic
1529	Civil aviation		
1530	Social Security		

1577	Road traffic
1578	Road traffic
1579	Road traffic
1580	Road traffic
1581	Road traffic
1582	Road traffic
1583	Road traffic
1584	Road traffic
1585	Road traffic
1586	Road traffic
1587	Road traffic
1588	Road traffic
1589	Road traffic
1590	Road traffic
1591	Road traffic
1592	Road traffic
1593	Road traffic
1594	Road traffic
1595	Road traffic
1596	Road traffic
1597	Road traffic
1598	Road traffic
1599	Road traffic
1600 (W.154)	Road traffic, Wales
1601	Road traffic
1602	Road traffic
1603	Road traffic
1604	Road traffic
1605	Road traffic
1606	Road traffic
1607	Road traffic
1608	Road traffic
1609	Road traffic
1610	Road traffic
1611	Road traffic
1612	Road traffic
1613	Road traffic
1614	Road traffic
1615	Road traffic
1616	Disabled persons, England and Wales Transport, England and Wales
1617	Disabled persons, England and Wales Transport, England and Wales
1618	National Health Service, England
1619	National Health Service, England
1620	National Health Service, England
1621	National Health Service, England
1622	National Health Service, England
1623	National Health Service, England
1624	National Health Service, England
1625	National Health Service, England
1626	National Health Service, England
1627	National Health Service, England
1628	National Health Service, England
1629	Criminal law, England and Wales
1630	Chiropractors
1631	Road traffic
1632	Road traffic
1633	Road traffic
1634	Road traffic
1635	Road traffic
1636	Road traffic
1637 (W.155)	Road traffic, Wales
1638	Road traffic
1639	Income tax
1640	Lord Chancellor Transfer of functions
1641 (W.156)	Housing, Wales
1642 (W.157)	Housing, Wales
1643 (W.158)	Plant health, Wales
1644	Companies
1645	Road traffic
1646	Road traffic
1647	Road traffic
1648	Road traffic
1649	Road traffic
1650	Road traffic
1651	Road traffic
1652	Road traffic
1653	Road traffic
1654	Road traffic
1655	Road traffic
1656	Road traffic
1657	Road traffic
1658	Acquisition of land, England
1659	Human tissue
1660 (W.159)(C.56)	Education, Wales
1661	Sports grounds and sporting events, England and Wales
1662	Sports grounds and sporting events, England and Wales
1663	Healthcare and associated professions
1664	Healthcare and associated professions
1665	Healthcare and associated professions
1666	Healthcare and associated professions
1667	Healthcare and associated professions
1668	Healthcare and associated professions
1669	Healthcare and associated professions
1670	Healthcare and associated professions
1671	Healthcare and associated professions
1672 (W.160)	Fire and rescue services, Wales Pensions, Wales
1673	Education, England

1674	Education, England	1719	Customs
1675	Road traffic	1720	Road traffic
1676	Road traffic	1721	Disabled persons
1677	Road traffic	1722	Insolvency
1678	Seeds, England	1723	Highways, England
1679	Weights and measures	1724	Road traffic
1680 (C.57)	National Health Service, England and Wales Social care, England	1725	Road traffic
		1726	Road traffic
1681	Social care, England	1727	Road traffic
1682 (C.58)	Social security Terms and conditions of employment	1728	Road traffic
		1729	Road traffic
1683	Value added tax	1730	Road traffic
1684	Civil aviation	1731	Road traffic
1685	Civil aviation	1732	Road traffic
1686	Civil aviation	1733	Pensions
1687	Civil aviation	1734	Public health, England
1688	Civil aviation	1735	Environmental protection, England and Wales Environmental protection, Northern Ireland
1689 (L.6)	Supreme Court of England and Wales County courts, England and Wales		
1690	Pensions	1736 (C.60)	Highways, England
1691 (W.161)	Transport and works, Wales Transport, Wales	1737	Magistrates' courts, England and Wales
1692	Contracting out	1738	Children and young persons, England
1693	Land charges, England	1739	Education, England
1694	Representation of the people, England and Wales	1740 (W.180)	Road traffic, Wales
1695	Road traffic	1741	National Health Service, England
1696	Customs	1742	Agriculture, England and Wales Pesticides, England and Wales
1697	Highways, England	1743	Immigration
1698	Highways, England	1744	Education, England
1699	Proceeds of crime	1745	Education, England
1700 (W.162)(C.59)	Town and country planning, Wales	1746	Education, England
1701 (W.163)	Plant health, Wales	1747	Coroners, England
1702 (W.164)	Housing, Wales	1748	Revenue and customs, England and Wales
1703 (W.165)	Public health, Wales		
1704 (W.166)	Food, Wales	1749 (W.181)	National Health Service, Wales
1705 (W.167)	Children and young persons, Wales	1750	Value added tax
1706 (W.168)	Housing, Wales	1751	Education, England
1707 (W.169)	Housing, Wales	1752	Social security
1708 (W.170)	Road traffic, Wales	1753	Local government, England
1709 (W.171)	Housing, Wales	1754	Education, England
1710 (W.172)	Bee diseases, Wales	1755	Mobile homes, England
1711 (W.173)	Highways, Wales Acquisition of land, Wales	1756	Road traffic
		1757	Animals, England
1712 (W.174)	Housing, Wales	1758	Betting, gaming and lotteries
1713 (W.175)	Housing, Wales	1759 (W.182)	Road traffic, Wales
1714 (W.176)	Education, Wales	1760	Education, England
1715 (W.177)	Housing, Wales	1761 (W.183)	Animals, Wales
1716 (W.178)	Agriculture, Wales	1762 (W.184)	Animals, Wales
1717 (W.179)	Agriculture, Wales	1763	Road traffic
1718	Health care and associated professions	1764	Road traffic

1765	Road traffic	1814	Road traffic
1766	Road traffic	1815	Road traffic
1767	Road traffic	1816	Road traffic
1768	Road traffic	1817	Road traffic
1769	Road traffic	1818	Road traffic
1770	Road traffic	1819	Road traffic
1771	Road traffic	1820	Road traffic
1772	Road traffic	1821	Road traffic
1773	Road traffic	1822	Road traffic
1774	Road traffic	1823	Road traffic
1775	Road traffic	1824	Road traffic
1776	Road traffic	1825	Road traffic
1777	Road traffic	1826	Road traffic
1778	Road traffic	1827	Road traffic
1779	Road traffic	1828	Road traffic
1780	Road traffic	1829	Road traffic
1781	Road traffic	1830	Road traffic
1782	Road traffic	1831	Security industry, England and Wales
1783	Road traffic	1832	Mental capacity, England
1784	Road traffic	1833	Designs
1785	Education, England	1834	Customs
1786	Defence	1835 (C.61)	Criminal law, England and Wales Criminal law, Northern Ireland
1787	Excise	1836 (S.12)	Representation of the people, Scotland
1788	Defence		
1789 (W.185)	Acquisition of land, Wales	1837	National Health Service, England
1790 (W.186)	National Health Service, Wales	1838	Inquiries
1791 (W.187)	Road traffic, Wales	1839	Justices of the Peace, England and Wales
1792 (W.188)	National Health Service, Wales		
1793	Value added tax	1840	Civil aviation
1794 (W.189)	Education, Wales	1841	Civil aviation
1795 (W.190)	Education, Wales	1842	Civil aviation
1796 (W.191)	Sea fisheries, Wales	1843	Civil aviation
1797	Road traffic	1844	Civil aviation
1798	Road traffic	1845	Civil aviation
1799	Road traffic	1846	Customs
1800	Road traffic	1847 (L.7)	Supreme Court of England and Wales County courts, England and Wales
1801	Road traffic	1848	Climate change levy
1802	Road traffic	1849 (W.192)	Local government, Wales
1803	Road traffic	1850 (W.193)	Food, Wales
1804	Security industry, England and Wales	1851 (W.194)	Food, Wales
1805	Financial services and markets	1852 (W.195)	Fire and rescue services, Wales
1806	Electronic communications	1853	Road traffic
1807	Electronic communications	1854	Road traffic
1808	Electronic communications	1855	Road traffic
1809	Electronic communications	1856	Road traffic
1810	Fire and rescue services, England Pensions, England	1857	Road traffic
1811	Fire and rescue services, England Pensions, England	1858	Road traffic
		1859	Road traffic
1812	Education, England	1860	Road traffic
1813	Education, England	1861	Road traffic

1862	Road traffic	1911	Civil aviation
1863 (W.196)	Education, Wales	1912	Diplomatic Service
1864	Road traffic	1913	Caribbean and North Atlantic territories
1865	Road traffic		
1866	Road traffic	1914	Health care and associated professions
1867	Road traffic		
1868	Road traffic	1915 (NI.11)	Northern Ireland
1869	Clean air, England	1916 (N.I.12)	Northern Ireland
1870	Road traffic	1917	Children and young persons
1871 (C.62)	Criminal law, England and Wales	1918	Post Office
1872	Road traffic	1919	Prevention and suppression of terrorism
1873	Road traffic	1920	Education, England
1874	Investigatory powers	1921	Cinema and films
1875	Road traffic	1922	International immunities and privileges
1876	Road traffic		
1877	Road traffic	1923	United Nations
1878	Investigatory powers	1924	Income tax Corporation tax Capital gains tax
1879	Plant health, England		
1880	Road traffic	1925	Income tax Corporation tax Capital gains tax
1881	Road traffic		
1882	Road traffic	1926	Ministers of the Crown
1883	Road traffic	1927	Ministers of the Crown
1884	Road traffic	1928	Medicines
1885	Road traffic	1929	Children and young persons, England and Wales
1886	Road traffic		
1887	Road traffic	1930	Social care, England and Wales Children and young persons, England and Wales
1888	Road traffic		
1889	Road traffic	1931	Climate change levy
1890	Road traffic	1932	Family law, England and Wales Pensions, England and Wales
1891	Road traffic		
1892	Road traffic	1933 (C.63)	Public passenger transport
1893	Education, England	1934	Family law, England and Wales Pensions, England and Wales Civil partnership, England and Wales
1894	Education, England		
1895	Education, England		
1896	Education, England	1935	Transport
1897	Road traffic	1936 (C.64)	Prevention and suppression of terrorism
1898	Education, England		
1899	Education, England	1937	Road traffic
1900	Education, England	1938	Police, England and Wales
1901	Education, England	1939	Ecclesiastical law, England
1902	Education, England	1940	Ecclesiastical law, England
1903	Education, England	1941	Ecclesiastical law, England
1904	Education, England	1942	Ecclesiastical law, England
1905	Education, England	1943	Ecclesiastical law, England
1906	Education, England	1944 (N.I.13)	Northern Ireland
1907	International immunities and privileges	1945 (N.I.14)	Northern Ireland
		1946 (N.I.15)	Northern Ireland
1908	International immunities and privileges	1947 (N.I.16)	Northern Ireland
		1948	Housing, England
1909	Overseas territories	1949	Offshore installations
1910	Defence	1950	Derelict land, England
		1951 (C. 65)	Transport

1952	Medicines	1996	Health care and associated professions
1953	Energy conservation, England	1997 (C.68)	Human tissue, England Wales
1954	Transport and works, England and Wales		Human tissue, Northern Ireland
	Transport, England and Wales	1998	Road traffic
1955	Road traffic, England and Wales	1999	Excise
1956	Road traffic, England and Wales	2000	Gas
1957	Income tax	2001	Terms and conditions of employment
1958	Income tax	2002	Electricity
1959	Income tax	2003	Social security
1960	Income tax	2004	Income tax
1961	Income tax	2005	Education, England
1962	Income tax	2006 (C.69)	Environmental protection, England
1963	Income tax	2007	Housing, England
1964 (C.66)	Electricity	2008	Pensions, England and Wales
	Gas	2009	Education, England and Wales
1965	Pensions	2010	Electricity
1966	Disabled persons	2011	Gas
1967	Disabled persons	2012	Terms and conditions of employment
1968	Housing, England	2013	Health and safety
1969	Financial services and markets	2014	Terms and conditions of employment
1970	Sea fisheries, England	2015	Defence
1971	Sports grounds and sporting events, England and Wales	2016	Prevention and suppression of terrorism
1972 (C.67)	Representation of the people	2017	Road traffic
	Electoral Commission	2018	Road traffic
	Registration of political parties	2019	Road traffic
	Political parties	2020	Road traffic
	National election expenditure	2021	Road traffic
	Referendums	2022	Road traffic
1973	Road traffic	2023	Road traffic
1974	Regulatory reform	2024	Road traffic
	Designs	2025	Road traffic
1975	Designs	2026	Road traffic
1976	*Cancelled*	2027	Road traffic
1977	Merchant shipping	2028	Road traffic
1978	Road traffic	2029	Road traffic
1979	Excise	2030	Road traffic
1980	Excise	2031	Road traffic
1981	Social security	2032	Road traffic
1982	Road traffic	2033	Road traffic
1983	Road traffic	2034	Road traffic
1984	Road traffic	2035	Road traffic
1985	Road traffic	2036	Road traffic
1986	Road traffic	2037	Road traffic
1987	Road traffic	2038	Road traffic
1988	Road traffic	2039	Road traffic
1989	Road traffic	2040	Highways, England
1990	Road traffic	2041	Road traffic
1991	Road traffic	2042	Road traffic
1992	Road traffic	2043	Road traffic
1993	Road traffic		
1994	Road traffic		
1995	Road traffic		

2044	Road traffic
2045	Road traffic
2046	Road traffic
2047	Road traffic
2048	Road traffic
2049	Road traffic
2050	Road traffic
2051	Road traffic
2052	Road traffic
2053	Hovercraft
2054	Road traffic
2055	Merchant shipping
2056	Road traffic
2057	Road traffic
2058	Road traffic
2059	Terms and conditions of employment
2060	Road traffic
2061	Road traffic
2062	Road traffic
2063	Road traffic
2064	Electricity, England and Wales
2065	Customs
2066	Public health
2067 (W.197)	Road traffic, Wales
2068	Data protection
2069	Road traffic
2070	Road traffic
2071	Road traffic
2072	National Health Service, England
2073	National Health Service, England
2074	National Health Service, England
2075	Agriculture Countryside, England
2076	National Health Service, England
2077	National Health Service, England
2078	Cooperative societies
2079	Education, England
2080 (L.8)	Family proceedings, England and Wales Supreme Court of England and Wales County courts, England and Wales
2081	Children and young persons, England
2082	Road traffic, England
2083	Road traffic
2084	National Health Service, England
2085	Civil aviation
2086	Civil aviation
2087	Civil aviation
2088	Civil aviation
2089	Civil aviation
2090	Civil aviation
2091	Civil aviation
2092	Road traffic
2093	Road traffic
2094	Road traffic
2095	Road traffic
2096	Road traffic
2097	Road traffic
2098	Road traffic
2099	Road traffic
2100	Road traffic
2101	Road traffic
2102	Road traffic
2103	Road traffic
2104	Road traffic
2105	Road traffic
2106	Road traffic
2107	Road traffic
2108	Road traffic
2109	Road traffic
2110	Road traffic
2111	Road traffic
2112	Road traffic
2113	Road traffic
2114	Road traffic
2115	Road traffic
2116	Road traffic
2117	Road traffic
2118	Road traffic
2119	Road traffic
2120	Road traffic
2121	Road traffic
2122	Road traffic
2123	Road traffic
2124	Road traffic
2125	Medicines Fees and charges
2126	Animals, England
2127	Road traffic
2128 (W.198)	Animals, Wales
2129 (C.70)	Education, England and Wales
2130	Broadcasting
2131	Broadcasting Electronic communications
2132	Northern Ireland Constitutional law
2133	Education, England and Wales
2134	Road traffic, England
2135	Criminal law, England and Wales Criminal law, Northern Ireland
2136 (C.71)	Dangerous drugs, England and Wales

2137	Criminal law, England and Wales	2186	Urban development, England
2138	Criminal law, England and Wales	2187	Value added tax
2139	Education, England	2188	Local government Transport
2140	Land drainage, England	2189	Education, England
2141	Inheritance tax	2190	Transport
2142	Education, England	2191	Road traffic
2143	Rehabilitation of offenders, England and Wales	2192	Agriculture, England
2144	Social security	2193	Road traffic
2145	Commons, England	2194	Road traffic
2146	Road traffic	2195	Road traffic
2147	Road traffic	2196	Road traffic
2148	Road traffic	2197	Road traffic
2149 (C.72)	Value added tax	2198	Education, England
2150	Road traffic	2199	Road traffic
2151	Road traffic	2200	Highways, England
2152	Road traffic	2201	Road traffic
2153	Road traffic	2202	Road traffic
2154	Road traffic	2203	Road traffic
2155	Road traffic	2204	Road traffic
2156	Road traffic	2205	Road traffic
2157	Road traffic	2206	Road traffic
2158	Road traffic	2207	Road traffic
2159	Road traffic	2208	Road traffic
2160	Road traffic	2209	Road traffic
2161	Road traffic	2210	Road traffic
2162	Road traffic	2211	Animals, England
2163	Road traffic	2212	Education, England
2164	Weights and measures	2213	Road traffic
2165	Police, England and Wales	2214	Education, England and Wales
2166	Animals, England	2215	Road traffic, England and Wales
2167	Harbours, docks, piers and ferries	2216	Education, England and Wales
2168	Immigration	2217	Road traffic
2169	Human tissue, England and Wales Human tissue, Northern Ireland	2218	Road traffic
2170	Immigration	2219	Road traffic
2171	National Health Service, England	2220	Road traffic
2172	Highways, England	2221	Road traffic
2173	Highways, England	2222	Road traffic
2174	Road traffic	2223	Road traffic
2175	Road traffic	2224	Road traffic
2176	Road traffic	2225	Road traffic
2177 (C.73)	National lottery	2226 (C.75)	Immigration
2178	Dangerous drugs	2227	Town and country planning, England
2179	Highways, England	2228	Professional qualifications
2180	Highways, England	2229	Taxes
2181	Police, England and Wales	2230	Highways, England
2182 (C.74)	Police, England and Wales	2231	Consumer protection
2183	Merchant shipping	2232 (C.76)	Terms and conditions of employment
2184	Merchant shipping	2233	Income tax Corporation tax
2185	Urban development, England	2234	Weights and measures

2235	Income tax Corporation tax	2281	Road traffic
2236	Terms and conditions of employment	2282	Road traffic
2237 (W.199)	Animals, Wales	2283	Road traffic
2238	Environmental protection, England	2284	Road traffic
2239	Race relations	2285	Food
2240	Road traffic	2286	Road traffic
2241	Road traffic	2287	Road traffic
2242	Road traffic	2288	Road traffic
2243	Road traffic	2289	Food, England
2244	Road traffic	2290	Human rights
2245	Road traffic	2291	Road traffic
2246	Road traffic	2292	Road traffic
2247	Road traffic	2293	Road traffic
2248	Road traffic	2294	Road traffic
2249	Road traffic	2295 (W.204)	Road traffic, Wales
2250	Road traffic	2296 (W.205)	Road traffic, Wales
2251	Road traffic	2297 (W.206)	Road traffic, Wales
2252	Road traffic	2298	Agriculture, England
2253	Road traffic	2299	Prevention and suppression of terrorism
2254	Road traffic	2300	Civil aviation
2255	Road traffic	2301	Civil aviation
2256	Road traffic	2302	Civil aviation
2257	Road traffic	2303	Civil aviation
2258	Road traffic	2304	Weights and measures
2259	Road traffic	2305 (W.207)	Road traffic, Wales
2260	Road traffic	2306 (W.208)	Road traffic, Wales
2261	Highways, England	2307	Plant health, England
2262	Highways, England	2308 (W.209)	Road traffic, Wales
2263	Road traffic	2309 (C.79)	Defence
2264	Road traffic	2310	Transport and works, England Transport, England
2265	Road traffic	2311	Environmental protection, England
2266	Road traffic	2312	Rating and valuation, England
2267	Road traffic	2313	Rating and valuation, England
2268 (C.77)	Representation of the people Electoral Commission Registration of political parties Political parties National election expenditure Referendums	2314	Seeds, England
		2315	Justices of the Peace, England and Wales
		2316	Civil aviation
2269	Highways, England	2317	Education, England
2270	Highways, England	2318	Council tax, England
2271	Customs	2319	Road traffic, England
2272 (C.78)	Pensions	2320	Road traffic
2273 (W.200)	Road traffic, Wales	2321	International development
2274 (W.201)	Road traffic, Wales	2322	Civil aviation
2275	Mobile homes, England	2323	International development
2276 (W.202)	Road traffic, Wales	2324	International development
2277 (W.203)	Road traffic, Wales	2325	International development
2278	Police, England and Wales	2326	Defence
2279	Road traffic	2327	International development
2280	Housing, England	2328	Road traffic

2329	Road traffic	2375	Town and country planning, England
2330	Road traffic	2376 (C.82)	Social security
2331	Road traffic	2377	Social security
2332	Road traffic	2378	Social security
2333	Road traffic	2379	Terms and conditions of employment Social security
2334	Road traffic		
2335	Road traffic	2380	Public health National Health Service, England Social care
2336	Road traffic		
2337	Road traffic	2381	Education, England
2338	Road traffic	2382	Education, England
2339	Road traffic	2383	Financial services and markets
2340	Road traffic	2384	Prevention and suppression of terrorism
2341	Road traffic	2385	Proceeds of crime
2342	Road traffic	2386	Medicines
2343	Road traffic	2387	Terms and conditions of employment
2344	Road traffic	2388	Electricity, England and Wales
2345	Road traffic	2389	Terms and conditions of employment
2346	Road traffic	2390	National Health Service, England
2347	Road traffic	2391	Road traffic
2348	Road traffic	2392	Road traffic
2349	Road traffic	2393	Environmental protection
2350	Road traffic	2394	Road traffic
2351	Road traffic	2395	Road traffic
2352	Road traffic	2396	Road traffic
2353	Road traffic	2397	Road traffic
2354	Road traffic	2398	Road traffic
2355	Road traffic	2399	Road traffic
2356	Road traffic, England	2400	Road traffic
2357	Road traffic	2401	Road traffic
2358	Road traffic	2402	Road traffic
2359	Road traffic	2403	Road traffic
2360	Road traffic	2404	Road traffic
2361	Road traffic	2405	Terms and conditions of employment
2362	Agriculture, England	2406 (C.85)	Employment
2363	Legal Services Commission, England and Wales	2407	Medicines
2364	Legal Services Commission, England and Wales	2408	Employment and training
		2409	Road traffic
2365 (W.210)	Road traffic, Wales	2410	Road traffic
2366	Legal Services Commission, England and Wales	2411	Road traffic
		2412	Road traffic
2367 (C.80)	Excise	2413	Road traffic
2368	Excise	2414	Road traffic
2369	Consumer protection Electronic communications	2415	Road traffic
2370	Education, England	2416	Road traffic
2371 (W.211)	Road traffic, Wales	2417	Road traffic
2372 (C.81)	Consumer protection, England and Wales Consumer protection, Northern Ireland	2418	Road traffic
		2419 (W.212)	Road traffic, Wales
		2420	Road traffic
2373	Employment	2421	Road traffic
2374	Town and country planning, England	2422	Road traffic

2423	Road traffic	2473	Road traffic
2424	Designs	2474	Road traffic
2425	Road traffic	2475	Road traffic
2426	Road traffic	2476	Road traffic
2427	Road traffic	2477	Road traffic
2428	Road traffic	2478	Road traffic
2429	Road traffic	2479	Road traffic
2430	Road traffic	2480	Road traffic
2431	Road traffic	2481	Road traffic
2432	Road traffic	2482	Road traffic
2433	Road traffic	2483	Road traffic
2434	Road traffic	2484	Road traffic
2435	Road traffic	2485	Road traffic
2436	Road traffic	2486	Agriculture, England and Wales
2437	Road traffic	2487 (W.213)	Road traffic, Wales
2438	Road traffic	2488 (W.214)	Road traffic, Wales
2439	Road traffic	2489 (W.215)	Road traffic, Wales
2440	Road traffic	2490	Legal Services Commission, England and Wales
2441	Road traffic	2491 (C.83)	Legal Services Commission, England and Wales
2442	Road traffic	2492	Legal Services Commission, England and Wales
2443	Road traffic	2493	Legal Services Commission, England and Wales
2444	Road traffic	2494	Legal Services Commission, England and Wales
2445	Road traffic	2495	Education, England
2446	Road traffic	2496	Highways, England
2447	Road traffic	2497	Road traffic
2448	Road traffic	2498	Road traffic
2449	Road traffic	2499	Local government, England
2450	Road traffic	2500	Civil aviation
2451	Road traffic	2501	Civil aviation
2452	Road traffic	2502	Civil aviation
2453	Road traffic	2503	Highways, England
2454	Road traffic	2504 (C.84)	Commons, England
2455	Road traffic	2505	Road traffic
2456	Road traffic	2506	Road traffic
2457	Road traffic	2507	Road traffic
2458	Road traffic	2508	Road traffic
2459	Road traffic	2509	Road traffic
2460	Road traffic	2510	Road traffic
2461	Road traffic	2511	Road traffic
2462	Road traffic	2512	Road traffic
2463	Road traffic	2513	Road traffic
2464	Road traffic	2514	Road traffic
2465	Road traffic	2515	Road traffic
2466	Road traffic	2516	Road traffic
2467	Road traffic	2517	Road traffic
2468	Road traffic	2518	Road traffic
2469	Road traffic	2519	Road traffic
2470	Race relations		
2471	Race relations		
2472	Road traffic		

2520	Road traffic	2567	Road traffic
2521	Immigration Housing	2568	Road traffic
		2569	Road traffic
2522	Agriculture, England	2570	Road traffic
2523	Health and safety	2571	Road traffic
2524	National Health Service, England	2572	Road traffic
2525	Immigration	2573	Road traffic
2526	National Health Service, England	2574	Road traffic
2527	Housing, England	2575	Road traffic
2528	Social security	2576	Road traffic
2529	Social security	2577	Road traffic
2530	Seeds	2578	Road traffic
2531	Highways, England	2579	Road traffic
2532 (W.216)	Road traffic, Wales	2580	Road traffic
2533	Road traffic	2581	Road traffic
2534 (W.217)	Road traffic, Wales	2582	Road traffic
2535	Protection of wrecks, England	2583	Road traffic
2536	Transport	2584	Road traffic
2537	National Health Service, England	2585	Road traffic
2538	National Health Service, England	2586	Road traffic
2539	National Health Service, England	2587	Road traffic
2540	Social security	2588	Road traffic
2541 (C.86)	Agriculture Nature conservation Natural environment, England and Wales Rural affairs, England and Wales	2589	Road traffic
		2590	Road traffic
		2591	Road traffic
2542	Education, England	2592	Road traffic
2543	Road traffic	2593	Road traffic
2544	Road traffic	2594	Road traffic
2545	Road traffic	2595	Road traffic
2546	Road traffic	2596	Road traffic
2547	Road traffic	2597	Road traffic
2548	Road traffic	2598	Road traffic
2549	Road traffic	2599	Road traffic
2550	Road traffic	2600	Road traffic
2551	Road traffic	2601	Education, England
2552	Road traffic	2602 (C.87)	Identity cards
2553	Road traffic	2603 (C.88)	Public health, England and Wales Health care and associated professions, England and Wales National Health Service, England and Wales Social care, England and Wales
2554	Road traffic		
2555	Road traffic		
2556	Road traffic		
2557	Road traffic	2604	Harbours, docks, piers and ferries
2558	Road traffic	2605 (W.218)	Road traffic, Wales
2559	Road traffic	2606 (W.219)	Road traffic, Wales
2560	Road traffic	2607 (W.220)	Animals, Wales
2561	Road traffic	2608	Road traffic
2562	Road traffic	2609	Road traffic
2563	Housing, England	2610	Road traffic
2564	Road traffic	2611	Road traffic
2565	Road traffic	2612	Road traffic
2566	Road traffic	2613	Road traffic

2614 (W.221)	Road traffic, Wales
2615 (W.222)	Road traffic, Wales
2616	Defence
2617	Designs
2618	Local government, England
2619	Local government, England
2620	Local government, England
2621 (W.223)	Road traffic, Wales
2622	Civil aviation
2623	Road traffic
2624 (W.224)	Road traffic, Wales
2625	Weights and measures
2626	Channel Tunnel
2627	Channel Tunnel
2628	Landlord and tenant, England
2629 (W.225)	Environmental protection, Wales
2630 (C.89)	National lottery
2631	Road traffic, England
2632	Local government, England Road traffic, England
2633	Road traffic
2634	Road traffic
2635	Road traffic
2636 (L.9)	Supreme Court of England and Wales Magistrates' courts, England and Wales
2637	Road traffic
2638	Road traffic
2639	Road traffic
2640	Road traffic
2641	Road traffic
2642	Road traffic
2643	Road traffic
2644	Road traffic
2645 (W.226)	Housing, Wales
2646 (W.227)	Housing, Wales
2647	Weights and measures
2648	Road traffic
2649	Road traffic
2650	Road traffic
2651	Road traffic
2652	Road traffic
2653	Road traffic
2654	Road traffic
2655	Social security
2656	Cinemas and films
2657	United Nations
2658	Education, England
2659	Northern Ireland Social security
2660	Education, Wales
2661	Education, England
2662 (C.90)	Criminal law, England and Wales
2663	Betting, gaming and lotteries
2664	Probation, England and Wales
2665	Civil aviation
2666 (W.228)	Road traffic, Wales
2667	Road traffic
2668	Road traffic
2669	Road traffic
2670	Road traffic
2671	Road traffic
2672	Road traffic
2673	Road traffic
2674	Road traffic
2675	Road traffic
2676	Road traffic
2677	Road traffic
2678	Road traffic
2679	Fees and charges
2680	Road traffic
2681	Customs
2682	Customs
2683	Customs
2684	Child trust funds
2685	Value added tax
2686	Value added tax
2687	Food, England
2688 (C.91)	Northern Ireland Representation of the people, Northern Ireland
2689	Tax credits
2690	National Health Service, England
2691	National Health Service, England
2692	Pensions
2693	Excise
2694 (W.229)	Road traffic, Wales
2695	Plant health
2696	Plant health
2697	Plant health
2698 (W.230)	Agriculture, Wales
2699 (W.231)(C.92)	Commissioner for Older People, Wales
2700	Insurance premium tax
2701	Animals, England
2702	Animals, England
2703	Animals, England
2704	Clean air, England
2705	Food, England
2706	Road traffic
2707	Road traffic
2708	Road traffic

2709	Road traffic	2759	Road traffic
2710	Road traffic	2760	Road traffic
2711	Road traffic	2761	Road traffic
2712	Road traffic	2762	Road traffic
2713	Road traffic	2763	Civil aviation
2714	Road traffic	2764	Civil aviation
2715	Road traffic	2765	Civil aviation
2716	Road traffic	2766	Civil aviation
2717	Road traffic	2767	Civil aviation
2718	Road traffic	2768	Road traffic
2719	Road traffic	2769	Road traffic
2720	Road traffic	2770	Road traffic
2721	Road traffic	2771	Road traffic
2722	Road traffic	2772	Road traffic
2723	Road traffic	2773	Road traffic
2724	Road traffic	2774	Road traffic
2725	Road traffic	2775	Road traffic
2726	Road traffic	2776	Road traffic
2727	Road traffic	2777	Road traffic
2728	Road traffic	2778	Road traffic
2729	Road traffic	2779	Road traffic
2730	Road traffic	2780	Road traffic
2731	Road traffic	2781	Road traffic
2732	Road traffic	2782	Companies
2733	Road traffic	2783	Highways, England
2734	Road traffic	2784	Highways, England
2735	Road traffic	2785	Electronic communications
2736	Road traffic	2786	Electronic communications
2737	Road traffic	2787	Food, England
2738	Road traffic	2788 (L.10)	Immigration
2739	Health and safety	2789 (L.11)	Immigration
2740	Animals, England	2790	Fire and rescue services, England
2741	Road traffic	2791 (W.232)	National Health Service, Wales
2742	Road traffic	2792 (W.233)	Food, Wales
2743	Road traffic	2793	Broadcasting Electronic communications
2744	Road traffic	2794	Offshore installations
2745	Road traffic	2795 (W.234)	Road traffic, Wales
2746	Road traffic	2796 (W.235)	Landlord and tenant, Wales
2747	Road traffic	2797 (W.236)(C.93)	Environmental protection, Wales
2748	Road traffic	2798 (W.237)	Sea fisheries, Wales
2749	Road traffic	2799 (W.238)	Sea fisheries, Wales
2750	Road traffic	2800 (W.239)	Housing, Wales
2751	Road traffic	2801 (W.240)	Housing, Wales
2752	Road traffic	2802 (W.241)	Environmental protection, Wales
2753	Road traffic	2803 (W.242)	Animals, Wales
2754	Road traffic	2804 (W.243)	Education, Wales
2755	Road traffic	2805	Landlord and tenant, England and Wales
2756	Road traffic		Regulatory reform, England and Wales
2757	Road traffic		
2758	Road traffic	2806	Medicines

2807	Medicines	2853	Road traffic
2808	Agriculture, England	2854	Road traffic
2809	Registration of births, deaths and marriages, etc., England and Wales	2855	Road traffic
		2856	Road traffic
2810	Mental capacity, England	2857	Road traffic
2811 (C.94)	Criminal law	2858	Road traffic
2812 (W.244)	Road traffic, Wales	2859	Road traffic
2813	Social security	2860	Road traffic
2814 (C.95)	Mental capacity, England	2861	Highways, England
2815	Atomic energy and radioactive substances	2862	Highways, England
		2863 (W.257)	Road traffic, Wales
2816	Road traffic	2864	Corporation tax
2817 (C.96)	Food, England and Wales National Health Service, England and Wales	2865	Corporation tax
		2866	Corporation tax
		2867	Corporation tax
2818	Food	2868	Road traffic
2819	Road traffic, England	2869	Road traffic
2820	Local government, England Road traffic, England	2870	Road traffic
		2871	Road traffic
2821	Animals, England	2872	Road traffic
2822 (W.245)	Housing, Wales	2873	Road traffic
2823 (W.246)	Housing, Wales	2874	Road traffic
2824 (W.247)	Housing, Wales	2875	Road traffic
2825 (W.248)	Housing, Wales	2876	Road traffic
2826 (W.249) (C.97)	Transport, Wales	2877	Road traffic
2827	Registration of births, deaths and marriages, etc., England and Wales	2878	Road traffic
		2879	Road traffic
2828 (W.250)	Education, Wales	2880	Road traffic
2829	Social security	2881	Road traffic
2830 (W.251)	Food, Wales	2882	Road traffic
2831 (W.252)	Agriculture, Wales	2883	Mental capacity, England
2832 (W.253)	Plant health, Wales	2884 (W.258)	Road traffic, Wales
2833 (W.254)	Road traffic, Wales	2885 (C.99)	Defence
2834 (W.255)	Road traffic, Wales	2886	Defence
2835	Government trading funds	2887	Defence
2836	Transport	2888	Defence
2837	Transport	2889	Defence
2838 (C.98)	Immigration	2890	Defence
2839	Social security	2891	Defence
2840 (W.256)	Social services, Wales	2892	Pensions
2841	Agriculture, England	2893	Pensions
2842	Road traffic	2894	Electronic communications
2843	Road traffic	2895 (C.100)	Education, England
2844	Road traffic	2896	Education, England
2845	Road traffic	2897	Social security
2846	Road traffic	2898 (L.12)	Immigration
2847	Road traffic	2899	Immigration
2848	Road traffic	2900	*Cancelled*
2849	Road traffic	2901	Health care and associated professions Opticians
2850	Road traffic		
2851	Road traffic		
2852	Road traffic		

2902	Value added tax	2946	Education, England
2903	Road traffic, Wales	2947	Education, England
2904	Food, England	2948	Education, England
2905	Transport and works, England Transport, England	2949	Education, England
		2950	Marine pollution
2906 (C.101)	Employment	2951	Ministers of the Crown
2907	Consumer protection	2952	United Nations
2908	Immigration	2953 (N.I. 17)	Northern Ireland
2909	Competition Consumer protection Disclosure of information	2954 (N.I. 18)	Northern Ireland
		2955 (N.I. 19)	Northern Ireland
2910	Representation of the people, England and Wales	2956	Education, England
		2957 (N.I. 20)	Northern Ireland
2911 (C.102)	Transport	2958	United Nations
2912	Road Traffic	2959	Outer space
2913	Constitutional law Devolution, Scotland River, Scotland River, England and Wales	2960	Education, England
		2961 (W.267)	Seeds, Wales
2914	Pensions, England and Wales	2962	Civil aviation
2915	National lottery	2963	Civil aviation
2916	Consumer protection	2964 (C.103)	Betting, gaming and lotteries
2917	Defence	2965	Representation of the people
2918	Defence	2966 (C.104)	Criminal law, Northern Ireland Sustainable development, Northern Ireland
2919	National Health Service, England and Wales		
		2967	Social security
2920	County courts, England and Wales	2968	Electronic communications
2921	Agriculture, England Food, England	2969 (W.268)	Food, Wales
		2970 (W.269)	Road traffic, Wales
2922	Agriculture, England and Wales Pesticides, England and Wales	2971	Education, England
		2972	Representation of the people, England and Wales
2923 (W.260)	Food, Wales		
2924	Social security	2973	Representation of the people, England and Wales
2925	Transport		
2926 (W.261)	Animals, Wales	2974	Political parties, England and Wales
2927 (W.262)	Animals, Wales	2975	Financial services and markets
2928 (W.263)	Agriculture, Wales	2976	Education, England
2929 (W.264)	Seeds, Wales	2977	Education, England
2930	Sex discrimination, England	2978	Electricity, England and Wales
2931	Employment and training	2979 (W.270)	Clean air, Wales
2932 (W.265)	Highways, Wales	2980 (W.271)	Clean air, Wales
2933	Pesticides, England and Wales	2981 (W.272)	Animals, Wales
2934 (W.266)	Highways, Wales	2982 (W.273)	Food, Wales
2935	Road traffic	2983 (W.274)	Housing, Wales
2936	Highways, England	2984	Medicines
2937	Pensions	2985 (W.275)	National Health Service, Wales
2938	Education, England	2986 (W.276)	Social care, Wales
2939	Education, England	2987	Animals, England
2940	Education, England	2988 (W.277)	Environmental protection, Wales
2941	Education, England	2989 (W.278)	Environmental protection, Wales
2942	Education, England	2990 (C.105)	Children and young persons, England Education, England
2943	Education, England		
2944	Education, England	2991	Children and young persons, England Education, England
2945	Education, England		

2992 (W.279) (C.106)	Rights of way, Wales	3040	Road traffic
2993 (W.280)	Transport, Wales	3041	Road traffic
2994	Electronic communications	3042	Road traffic
2995	Road traffic	3043	Road traffic
2996	Road traffic	3044	Road traffic
2997	Road traffic	3045	Terms and conditions of employment
2998	Road traffic	3046	Road traffic
2999	Road traffic	3047	Road traffic
3000	Road traffic	3048	Road traffic
3001	Road traffic	3049	Road traffic
3002	Road traffic	3050	Road traffic
3003	Road traffic	3051	Road traffic
3004	Road traffic	3052	Road traffic
3005 (C.107)	Consumer protection, England and Wales	3053	Road traffic
3006	Road traffic	3054	Road traffic
3007	Road traffic	3055	Road traffic
3008	Road traffic	3056	Road traffic
3009	Road traffic	3057	Road traffic
3010	Road traffic	3058	Road traffic
3011	Road traffic	3059	Road traffic
3012	Road traffic	3060	Road traffic
3013	Road traffic	3061	Road traffic
3014	Road traffic	3062	Road traffic
3015	Road traffic	3063	Road traffic
3016	Road traffic	3064	Road traffic
3017	Road traffic	3065	Road traffic
3018	Road traffic	3066	Road traffic
3019	Road traffic	3067	Road traffic
3020	Road traffic	3068	Road traffic
3021	Road traffic	3069	Road traffic
3022	Road traffic	3070	Road traffic
3023	Road traffic	3071	Road traffic
3024	Road traffic	3072	Road traffic
3025	Road traffic	3073	Road traffic
3026	Road traffic	3074	Road traffic
3027	Road traffic	3075	Road traffic
3028	Road traffic	3076	Highways, England
3029	Road traffic	3077	Highways, England
3030	Road traffic	3078	Highways, England
3031	Road traffic	3079	Pensions
3032	Road traffic	3080	Road traffic
3033	Road traffic	3081	Road traffic
3034	Road traffic	3082	Road traffic
3035	Road traffic	3083	Road traffic
3036	Road traffic	3084	Road traffic
3037	Road traffic	3085	Road traffic
3038	Road traffic	3086	Pensions
3039	Trade marks	3087	National Health Service, England
		3088	Social security
		3089	Corporation tax

	Petroleum revenue tax	3135	Road traffic
3090	Road traffic	3136	Road traffic
3091	Road traffic	3137	Road traffic
3092	Road traffic	3138	Road traffic
3093	Road traffic	3139	Road traffic
3094	Consumer credit	3140	Road traffic
3095	Competition	3141	Road traffic
3096	Local government, England	3142	Road traffic
3097 (W.281)	Education, Wales	3143	Road traffic
3098 (W.282)	Education, Wales	3144 (C. 109)	Immigration
3099 (W.283)	Town and country planning, Wales	3145	Immigration
3100 (W.284)	Social care, Wales Children and young persons, Wales	3146	National lottery, England
		3147	Education, England
3101 (W.285)	Agriculture, Wales	3148	Dangerous drugs, England Dangerous drugs, Scotland
3102	Local government, England		
3103 (W.286)	Education, Wales	3149 (W.290)	Road traffic, Wales
3104	Civil aviation	3150	Education, England
3105	Pensions	3151	Education, England
3106	Forestry, England and Wales	3152	Pensions
3107	Insolvency	3153	Road traffic
3108 (W.287)	National Health Service, Wales	3154	Road traffic
3109	Local government, England	3155	Road traffic
3110	Local government, England	3156	Education, England
3111	Local government, England	3157	Customs Excise Value added tax
3112	Local government, England		
3113	Local government, England	3158	Customs Excise Value added tax
3114	Local government, England		
3115 (W.288)	Road traffic, Wales	3159	Excise
3116	Food, England	3160	Education, England
3117	Transport and works, England Transport, England	3161	Road traffic
		3162	Road traffic
3118	Transport and works, England Transport, England	3163	Highways, England
		3164	Highways, England
3119 (W.289)	Town and country planning, Wales	3165	Countryside, England
3120	Agriculture, England	3166 (W.291)	Animals, Wales
3121	Education, England	3167	Rating and valuation, England
3122	Education, England and Wales	3168	Sports grounds and sporting events, England and Wales
3123	National Health Service, England		
3124	Water resources, England and Wales	3169	Atomic energy and radioactive substances, England and Wales
3125 (C.108)	Dangerous drugs, England Dangerous drugs, Scotland National Health Service, England and Wales		
		3170	Capital gains tax Corporation tax
3126	Highways, England	3171	Education, England and Wales
3127	Road traffic	3172	Road traffic
3128	Road traffic	3173	Road traffic
3129	Road traffic	3174	Road traffic
3130	Road traffic	3175	Road traffic
3131	Road traffic	3176	Road traffic
3132 (L.13)	Supreme Court of England and Wales County courts, England and Wales	3177	Road traffic
		3178	Road traffic
3133	Road traffic	3179	Road traffic
3134	Road traffic	3180	Road traffic

3181	Road traffic	3230	Road traffic
3182	Road traffic	3231	Road traffic
3183	Road traffic	3232	Road traffic
3184	Road traffic	3233	Road traffic
3185	Road traffic	3234	Excise
3186	Road traffic	3235	Excise
3187	Road traffic	3236	Corporation tax
3188	Social security	3237	Stamp duty land tax
3189 (C.110)	Disabled persons	3238	Corporation tax
3190	Housing, England	3239	Corporation tax
3191 (C. 111)	Housing, England	3240 (C.116)	Income tax
3192	Road traffic	3241	Income tax
3193	Road traffic	3242	Housing, England
3194	Income tax	3243	Defence
3195	Child trust funds	3244	Defence
3196	Road traffic	3245 (W.293)	Food, Wales
3197	Education, England	3246	Highways, England
3198	*Cancelled*	3247	Animals, England
3199	Education, England	3248	Constitutional law Devolution, Scotland Food
3200 (C.112)	Criminal law		
3201 (C.113)	National lottery	3249	Animals, England
3202	National lottery	3250 (W.294)	Seeds, Wales
3203	Road traffic	3251 (W.295)	Social care, Wales Children and young persons, Wales
3204	Road traffic		
3205	Road traffic	3252	Registration of political parties
3206	Road traffic	3253	Road traffic
3207	Road traffic	3254	Agriculture, England
3208	Road traffic	3255	Veterinary surgeons
3209	Road traffic	3256 (W.296)	Agriculture, Wales
3210	Road traffic	3257 (W.297) (C.117)	Countryside, Wales Rights of way, Wales
3211	Road traffic, England	3258	Constitutional law Devolution, Scotland
3212	Local government, England Road traffic, England		
3213	Highways, England	3259	Compensation
3214	Professional qualifications	3260	Animals, England
3215	Immigration	3261	Income tax
3216	Statistics of trade	3262	Corporation tax
3217 (C.114)	Criminal law, England and Wales	3263 (C. 118)	Northern Ireland
3218	Corporation tax	3264	Medicines
3219 (W.292)	Road traffic, Wales	3265	Corporation tax Income tax
3220 (C.115)	Betting, gaming and lotteries	3266	Betting, gaming and lotteries
3221	Financial services and markets	3267	Betting, gaming and lotteries
3222	Corporation tax	3268 (W.298)	Representation of the people, Wales
3223	Merchant shipping	3269	Corporation tax
3224	Merchant shipping	3270	Corporation tax
3225	Merchant shipping	3271	Corporation tax
3226	Education, England	3272 (C.119)	Betting, gaming and lotteries
3227	Town and country planning, England Tribunals and inquiries, England	3273	Corporation tax
		3274	Social security
3228	Road traffic	3275	Immigration
3229	Road traffic		

3276	Road traffic	3319	Consumer protection, England and Wales
3277	Immigration	3320	Town and country planning, England
3278	Representation of the people, England and Wales	3321	Consumer protection, England and Wales
3279	Local government, England	3322	Consumer protection, England and Wales
3280	Local government, England		
3281	Cinemas and film	3323	Income tax Corporation tax Capital gains tax
3282	European Communities, Wales		
3283	Taxes Excise Recovery of taxes Insurance premium tax	3324	Broadcasting Electronic communications Wireless telegraphy
3284	Betting, gaming and lotteries	3325	Broadcasting Electronic communications Wireless telegraphy
3285	Betting, gaming and lotteries		
3286	Capital gains tax Corporation tax Income tax	3326	United Nations
		3327	United Nations
3287	Betting, gaming and lotteries	3328	Parliamentary Commissioner
3288	Income tax	3329	European Communities
3289	Environmental protection	3330	Local government, England
3290	Rehabilitation of offenders, England and Wales	3331	Dangerous drugs
		3332	National Health Service, England
3291	Capital gains tax	3333	Legal services, England and Wales
3292	Value added tax	3334	Constitutional law Devolution, Wales
3293	Betting, gaming and lotteries		
3294	Libraries	3335	Constitutional law
3295	Town and country planning	3336 (N.I.21)	Northern Ireland
3296	Corporation tax	3337 (N.I. 22)	Northern Ireland
3297	Trade descriptions	3338	Constitutional law Devolution, Scotland National Health Service
3298	Trade descriptions		
3299	Road traffic	3339 (W.302)(C.120)	Local government, Wales
3300	Highways, England	3340	Housing, England
3301	Highways, England	3341	Social security
3302	Highways, England	3342 (W.303)	Agriculture, Wales
3303	Civil aviation	3343 (W.304)	Agriculture, Wales
3304	Representation of the people, England and Wales	3344 (W.305)	Food, Wales
		3345 (W.306)	Rating and valuation, Wales
3305	Representation of the people, England and Wales	3346	Education, England
		3347 (W.307)	Rating and valuation, Wales
3306	National Health Service, England	3348	Civil aviation
3307	Road traffic	3349	Civil aviation
3308	Road traffic	3350	Civil aviation
3309 (W.299)	Animals, Wales	3351	Civil aviation
3310 (W.300)	Animals, Wales	3352	Civil aviation
3311	Environmental protection	3353	Road traffic
3312	Petroleum revenue tax	3354	Road traffic
3313	Petroleum revenue tax Corporation tax	3355	Road traffic
3314	Terms and conditions of employment	3356	Road traffic
3315	Environmental protection, England and Wales	3357	Road traffic
		3358	Road traffic
3316 (W.301)	Town and country planning, Wales	3359	Road traffic
3317	Immigration	3360 (C.121)	Children and young persons, England
3318	Building and buildings, England and Wales	3361 (C.122)	Betting, gaming and lotteries

3362	Legal services, England and Wales	3406	Representation of the people
3363	Consumer protection	3407	Constitutional law Devolution, Scotland Animals, England and Wales
3364 (C.123)	Police, England and Wales Extradition Criminal law, England and Wales	3408	Education, England
3365	Police, England and Wales	3409	Education, England
3366 (W.308)	National Health Service, Wales	3410	Security industry
3367	Food	3411	Security industry
3368	Public health, England	3412 (C.128)	Representation of the people
3369 (C.124)	Tax credits	3413	Financial services and markets
3370	Pensions	3414	Financial services and markets
3371	Consumer protection	3415	Police, England and Wales Pensions, England and Wales
3372	Consumer protection	3416 (C.129)	National election expenditure Political parties Representation of the people
3373	National Health Service, England		
3374	Pensions	3417	Local government, England
3375	Highways, England	3418	Electromagnetic compatibility
3376	Road traffic	3419	Local government, England Road traffic, England
3377	Road traffic		
3378	Road traffic	3420	Road traffic, England
3379	Road traffic	3421	Road traffic, England
3380	Road traffic	3422 (C. 130)	Criminal law, Northern Ireland
3381	Road traffic	3423 (C.131)	Criminal law, England and Wales Criminal law, Northern Ireland
3382	Road traffic		
3383 (W.309)	Highways, Wales	3424	Road traffic, England
3384	Financial services and markets	3425	Local government, England Road traffic, England
3385	Financial services and markets		
3386	Financial services and markets	3426	Excise
3387	Corporation tax	3427	Stamp duty land tax
3388	National Health Service, England and Wales Road traffic, England and Wales	3428 (C.132)	Companies
		3429	Companies
		3430	Cinema and film
3389	Corporation tax	3431	Road traffic
3390 (W.310)	Town and country planning, Wales	3432	Fire and rescue services, England Pensions, England
3391	Betting, gaming and lotteries		
3392 (W.311)	Rating and valuation, Wales	3433	Fire and rescue services, England Pensions, England
3393	Immigration		
3394	Rating and valuation, England	3434	Fire and rescue services, England Pensions, England
3395	Council tax, England Rating and valuation, England	3435 (L.15)	Supreme Court of England and Wales County courts, England and Wales
3396	Council tax, England		
3397 (C.125)	National Health Service, England and Wales	3436 (W.312)	Road traffic, Wales
		3437	Road traffic
3398	National Health Service, England and Wales Road traffic, England and Wales	3438	Road traffic
		3439	Road traffic
3399 (C.126)	Corporation tax Income tax	3440	Road traffic
		3441	Road traffic
3400 (C. 127)	Education, England	3442	Road traffic
3401	Road traffic	3443	Road traffic
3402	Road traffic	3444	Road traffic
3403	Road traffic	3445	Road traffic
3404	Road traffic	3446	Road traffic
3405 (L.14)	Magistrates' courts, England and Wales	3447	Road traffic

3448	Road traffic
3449	Police, England and Wales
3450	Local government, England
3451	Extradition
3452 (W.313)	Animals, Wales
3453	Road traffic
3454	Road traffic
3455	Road traffic
3456	Road traffic
3457	Road traffic
3458	Road traffic
3459	Road traffic
3460	Road traffic
3461	Road traffic
3462	Road traffic
3463	Road traffic
3464	Road traffic
3465	Highways, England
3466	Highways, England
3467	Local government, England
3468	Local government, England
3469	Local government, England
3470	Local government, England
3471	Transport and works, England Transport, England
3472	Agriculture, England Food, England
3473 (C.133)	Mental capacity, England
3474	Mental capacity, England
3475	Road traffic
3476	Road traffic
3477	Road traffic
3478	Road traffic
3479	Road traffic
3480	Road traffic
3481	Road traffic
3482	Road traffic
3483	Road traffic
3484	Road traffic
3485	Road traffic
3486	Road traffic
3487	Road traffic
3488	Road traffic
3489	Road traffic
3490	Road traffic
3491	Road traffic
3492	Road traffic
3493	Road traffic
3494	Road traffic
3495	Civil aviation
3496	Civil aviation
3497	Civil aviation
3498	Civil aviation
3499	Civil aviation
3500	Road traffic
3501	Road traffic
3502	Road traffic
3503	Road traffic
3504	Road traffic
3505	Road traffic
3506	Road traffic
3507	Road traffic
3508	Road traffic
3509	Road traffic
3510	Road traffic
3511	Health care and associated professions
3512	Road traffic
3513	Road traffic
3514	Road traffic
3515	Road traffic

Subsidiary Numbers

Commencement orders (bring an act or part of an act into operation)

51 (C.1)
172 (W.23) (C.2)
201 (C.3)
224 (C.4)
228 (C.5)
235 (C.6)
266 (C.7)
345 (W.42) (C.8)
378 (C.9)
392 (C.10)
393 (C.11)
404 (C.12)
481 (C.12)
560 (C.13)
631 (C. 14)
639 (C.15)
656 (C.16)
751 (C.17)
768 (W.75)(C.18)
795 (C. 19)
836 (C.22)

870 (W.80)(C.20)
879 (W.84)(C.21)
885 (W.85)(C.23)
927 (C.24)
928 (C. 25)
931 (C.26)
934 (C.27)
982 (C.29)
984 (C.30)
1002 (C.31)
1013 (C.32)
1014 (C.33)
1060 (C.34)
1061 (C.35)
1082 (C.36)
1085 (C.37)
1118 (C.38)
1172 (C.39)
1176 (C.40)
1278 (W.123) (C.41)
1279 (W.124) (C.42)
1281 (C.43)
1336 (W.129) (C.44)
1338 (W.130) (C.45)
1361 (C.46)
1382 (C.47)
1403 (W.140) (C.48)
1439 (C.49)
1497 (C.50)
1498 (C.51)
1508 (C. 52)
1517 (C.53)
1535 (W.152) (C.54)
1537 (C.55)
1660 (W.159) (C.56)
1680 (C.57)
1682 (C.58)
1700 (W.162) (C.59)
1736 (C.60)
1835 (C.61)
1871 (C.62)
1933 (C.63)
1936 (C.64)
1951 (C. 65)
1964 (C.66)
1972 (C.67)
1997 (C.68)
2006 (C.69)

2129 (C.70)
2136 (C.71)
2149 (C.72)
2177 (C.73)
2182 (C.74)
2226 (C.75)
2232 (C.76)
2268 (C.77)
2272 (C.78)
2309 (C.79)
2367 (C.80)
2372 (C.81)
2376 (C.82)
2406 (C.85)
2491 (C.83)
2504 (C.84)
2541 (C.86)
2602 (C.87)
2603 (C.88)
2630 (C.89)
2662 (C.90)
2688 (C.91)
2699 (W.231) (C.92)
2797 (W.236)(C.93)
2811 (C.94)
2814 (C.95)
2817 (C.96)
2826 (W.249) (C.97)
2838 (C.98)
2885 (C.99)
2895 (C.100)
2906 (C.101)
2911 (C.102)
2964 (C.103)
2966 (C.104)
2990 (C.105)
2992 (W.279) (C.106)
3005 (C.107)
3125 (C.108)
3144 (C. 109)
3189 (C.110)
3191 (C. 111)
3200 (C.112)
3201 (C.113)
3217 (C.114)
3220 (C.115)
3240 (C.116)
3257 (W.297) (C.117)

3263 (C. 118)
3272 (C.119)
3339 (W.302) (C.120)
3360 (C.121)
3361 (C.122)
3364 (C.123)
3369 (C.124)
3397 (C.125)
3399 (C.126)
3400 (C. 127)
3412 (C.128)
3416 (C.129)
3422 (C. 130)
3423 (C.131)
3428 (C.132)
3473 (C.133)

Instruments relating to fees or procedure in courts in England and Wales

352 (L.1)
353 (L.2)
715 (L.3)
719 (L.4)
739 (L.5)
1689 (L.6)
1847 (L.7)
2080 (L.8)
2636 (L.9)
2788 (L.10)
2789 (L.11)
2898 (L.12)
3132 (L.13)
3405 (L.14)
3435 (L.15)

Certain orders in Council relating to Northern Ireland

312 (N.I.1)
313 (N.I.2)
314 (N.I.3)
611 (N.I.4)
612 (N.I. 5)
613 (N.I.6)
1252 (N.I.7)
1253 (N.I.8)
1254 (N.I.9)
1254 (N.I.9)
1459 (N.I.10)

1915 (NI.11)
1916 (N.I.12)
1944 (N.I.13)
1945 (N.I.14)
1946 (N.I.15)
1947 (N.I.16)
2953 (N.I.17)
2954 (N.I.18)
2955 (N.I.19)
2957 (N.I.20)
3336 (N.I.21)
3337 (N.I.22)

Instruments that extend only to Scotland

241 (S.1)
242 (S.2)
304 (S.3)
661 (S.5)
734 (S.6)
735 (S.7)
772 (S.8)
834 (S.9)
1054 (S.10)
1157 (S.11)
1836 (S.12)

Instruments that extend only to Wales

2 (W.1)
3 (W.2)
4 (W.3)
30 (W.4)
31 (W.5)
32 (W.6)
41 (W.7)
42 (W.8)
52 (W.9)
53 (W.10)
62 (W.11)
63 (W.12)
64 (W.13)
116 (W.14)
118 (W.33)
121 (W.15)
123 (W.16)
124 (W.17)
125 (W.18)
126 (W.19)
145 (W.20)

146 (W.21)
171 (W.22)
172 (W.23) (C.2)
173 (W.24)
174 (W.25)
175 (W.26)
176 (W.27)
177 (W.28)
178 (W.29)
179 (W.30)
180 (W.31)
181 (W.32)
205 (W.34)
238 (W.35)
240 (W.36)
249 (W.37)
299 (W.38)
318 (W.39)
319 (W.40)
344 (W.41)
345 (W.42) (C.8)
348 (W.43)
350 (W.44)
357 (W.45)
358 (W.46)
360 (W.47)
362 (W.48)
363 (W.49)
374 (W.50)
402 (W.51)
403 (W.52)
411 (W.53)
469 (W.54)
485 (W.55)
487 (W.56)
488 (W.57)
489 (W.58)
490 (W.59)
491 (W.60)
509 (W.61)
513 (W.62)
519 (W.63)
520 (W.64)
581 (W.65)
590 (W.66)
603 (W.67)
615 (W.68)
617 (W.69)

621 (W.70)
650 (W.71)
762 (W.72)
764 (W.73)
767 (W.74)
768 (W.75)(C.18)
833 (W.76)
842 (W.77)
866 (W.78)
867 (W.79)
870 (W.80)(C.20)
873 (W.81)
877 (W.82)
878 (W.83)
879 (W.84)(C.21)
885 (W.85)(C.23)
910 (W.86)
911 (W.87)
926 (W.88)
940 (W.89)
941 (W.90)
942 (W.91)
943 (W.92)
944 (W.93)
945 (W.94)
946 (W.95)
947 (W.96)
948 (W.97)
949 (W.98)
950 (W.99)
951 (W.100)
978 (W.101)
979 (W.102)
980 (W.103)
1011 (W.104)
1035 (W.105)
1036 (W.106)
1051 (W.107)
1052 (W.108)
1053 (W.109)
1064 (W.110)
1079 (W.111)
1083 (W.112)
1158 (W.113)
1159 (W.114)
1180 (W.115)
1181 (W.116)
1226 (W.117)

1261 (W.118)	1704 (W.166)
1262 (W.119)	1705 (W.167)
1271 (W.120)	1706 (W.168)
1275 (W.121)	1707 (W.169)
1277 (W.122)	1708 (W.170)
1278 (W.123) (C.41)	1709 (W.171)
1279 (W.124) (C.42)	1710 (W.172)
1280 (W.125)	1711 (W.173)
1286 (W.126)	1712 (W.174)
1293 (W.127)	1713 (W.175)
1335 (W.128)	1714 (W.176)
1336 (W.129) (C.44)	1715 (W.177)
1338 (W.130) (C.45)	1716 (W.178)
1339 (W.131)	1717 (W.179)
1341 (W.132)	1740 (W.180)
1343 (W.133)	1749 (W.181)
1344 (W.134)	1759 (W.182)
1349 (W.135)	1761 (W.183)
1386 (W.136)	1762 (W.184)
1387 (W.137)	1789 (W.185)
1388 (W.138)	1790 (W.186)
1389 (W.139)	1791 (W.187)
1403 (W.140) (C.48)	1792 (W.188)
1420 (W.141)	1794 (W.189)
1443 (W.142)	1795 (W.190)
1444 (W.143)	1796 (W.191)
1494 (W.144)	1849 (W.192)
1495 (W.145)	1850 (W.193)
1502 (W.146)	1851 (W.194)
1511 (W.147)	1852 (W.195)
1512 (W.148)	1863 (W.196)
1513 (W.149)	2067 (W.197)
1532 (W.150)	2128 (W.198)
1534 (W.151)	2237 (W.199)
1535 (W.152) (C.54)	2273 (W.200)
1536 (W.153)	2274 (W.201)
1600 (W.154)	2276 (W.202)
1637 (W.155)	2277 (W.203)
1641 (W.156)	2295 (W.204)
1642 (W.157)	2296 (W.205)
1643 (W.158)	2297 (W.206)
1660 (W.159) (C.56)	2305 (W.207)
1672 (W.160)	2306 (W.208)
1691 (W.161)	2308 (W.209)
1700 (W.162) (C.59)	2365 (W.210)
1701 (W.163)	2371 (W.211)
1702 (W.164)	2419 (W.212)
1703 (W.165)	2487 (W.213)

2488 (W.214)
2489 (W.215)
2532 (W.216)
2534 (W.217)
2605 (W.218)
2606 (W.219)
2607 (W.220)
2614 (W.221)
2615 (W.222)
2621 (W.223)
2624 (W.224)
2629 (W.225)
2645 (W.226)
2646 (W.227)
2666 (W.228)
2694 (W.229)
2698 (W.230)
2699 (W.231) (C.92)
2791 (W.232)
2792 (W.233)
2795 (W.234)
2796 (W.235)
2797 (W.236)(C.93)
2798 (W.237)
2799 (W.238)
2800 (W.239)
2801 (W.240)
2802 (W.241)
2803 (W.242)
2804 (W.243)
2812 (W.244)
2822 (W.245)
2823 (W.246)
2823 (W.254)
2824 (W.247)
2825 (W.248)
2826 (W.249) (C.97)
2828 (W.250)
2830 (W.251)
2831 (W.252)
2832 (W.253)
2834 (W.255)
2840 (W.256)
2863 (W.257)
2884 (W.258)
2923 (W.260)
2926 (W.261)
2927 (W.262)

2928 (W.263)
2929 (W.264)
2932 (W.265)
2932 (W.265)
2934 (W.266)
2961 (W.267)
2969 (W.268)
2970 (W.269)
2979 (W.270)
2980 (W.271)
2981 (W.272)
2982 (W.273)
2983 (W.274)
2985 (W.275)
2986 (W.276)
2988 (W.277)
2989 (W.278)
2992 (W.279) (C.106)
2993 (W.280)
3009 (W.283)
3097 (W.281)
3098 (W.282)
3099 (W.283)
3100 (W.284)
3101 (W.285)
3103 (W.286)
3108 (W.287)
3115 (W.288)
3119 (W.289)
3149 (W.290)
3166 (W.291)
3219 (W.292)
3245 (W.293)
3250 (W.294)
3251 (W.295)
3256 (W.296)
3257 (W.297) (C.117)
3268 (W.298)
3309 (W.299)
3310 (W.300)
3316 (W.301)
3339 (W.302) (C.120)
3342 (W.303)
3343 (W.304)
3344 (W.305)
3345 (W.306)
3347 (W.307)
3366 (W.308)

3383 (W.309)
3390 (W.310)
3392 (W.311)

3436 (W.312)
3452 (W.313)

Instruments that extend only to Wales

Scottish Legislation

Other statutory publications

Office of the Queen's Printer for Scotland.

The acts of the Scottish Parliament 2005: with lists of the acts, tables and index. - ix, 660p.: hdbk: 31 cm. - 978-0-11-840432-7 £79.00

Scottish statutory instruments 2005. - 4v. (xvii, 3802p.): hdbk: 31 cm. - Contents: Vol 1 Nos 1 to 257, 1st January to 12th May; Vol 2 Nos 260 to 459, 17th May to 22nd September; Vol 3 Nos 460 to 599, 22nd September to 28th November; Vol. 4 Nos 604 to 663, 29th November to 31st December. - 978-0-11-840433-4 £350.00 for four volumes not sold separately

Acts of the Scottish Parliament

Acts of the Scottish Parliament 2006

Animal Health and Welfare (Scotland) Act 2006: 2006 asp 11. - iii, 63p.: 30 cm. - Royal assent, 11th July 2006. An Act of the Scottish Parliament to amend the Animal Health Act 1981, including by making provision for preventing the spread of disease; to make provision for the welfare of animals, including the prevention of harm. Explanatory notes have been produced to assist in the understanding of this Act and are available separately (ISBN 0105911038). - 978-0-10-590101-3 £10.50

Budget (Scotland) Act 2006: 2006 asp 5. - ii, 20, [1]p.: 30 cm. - Royal assent, 21st March 2006. An Act of the Scottish Parliament to make provision, for financial year 2006/07, for use of resources by the Scottish Administration and certain bodies whose expenditure is payable out of the Scottish Consolidated Fund, for authorising the payment of sums out of the Fund and for the maximum amounts of borrowing by certain statutory bodies; to make provision, for financial year 2007/08, for authorising the payment of sums out of the Fund on a temporary basis. Explanatory notes have been produced to assist in the understanding of this Act and will be available separately. - 978-0-10-590095-5 £4.50

Edinburgh Tram (Line One) Act 2006: 2006 asp 7. - iv, 64p.: 30 cm. - Royal assent, 8th May 2006. An Act of the Scottish Parliament to authorise the construction and operation of a tram line in Edinburgh forming a loop from St Andrew Square, along Leith Walk to Leith, west to Granton, south to Haymarket and back to St Andrew Square via Princes Street. Explanatory notes have been produced to assist in the understanding of this Act and will be available separately. - 978-0-10-590097-9 £10.50

Edinburgh Tram (Line Two) Act 2006: 2006 asp 6. - iv, 60, [1]p.: 30 cm. - Royal assent, 27th April 2006. An Act of the Scottish Parliament to authorize the construction and operation of a tram line in Edinburgh following a western course from St Andrew Square, via Princes Street, Haymarket, Murrayfield and South Gyle to Edinburgh Airport and Newbridge. Explanatory notes have been produced to assist in the understanding of this Act and will be available separately. - 978-0-10-590096-2 £10.50

Family Law (Scotland) Act 2006: 2006 asp 2. - iii, 34p.: 30 cm. - An Act of the Scottish Parliament to amend the law in relation to marriage, divorce and the jurisdiction of the courts in certain consistorial actions; to amend the Matrimonial Homes (Family Protection) (Scotland) Act 1981; to amend the law relating to the domicile of persons who are under 16 years of age; to make further provision as respects responsibilities and rights in relation to children; to make provision conferring rights in relation to property, succession and claims in damages for person living or having lived together as if husband and wife or civil partners; to amend part 3 of the Civil Partnership Act 2004; to make further provision in relation to persons entitled to damages under the Damages (Scotland) Act 1976; to make provision in relation to certain rules of private international law relating to family law; to make incompetent actions for declarator of freedom and putting to silence. Royal assent on 20th January 2006. Explanatory Notes have been produced to assist in the understanding of this Act and are available separately (ISBN 0105910848). - 978-0-10-590092-4 £7.00

Housing (Scotland) Act 2006: 2006 asp 1. - viii, 128p.: 30 cm. - Royal assent, 5th January 2006. An Act of the Scottish Parliament to make provision about housing standards; to confer a right to adapt rented houses to meet the needs of disabled occupants; to provide for the giving of assistance by local authorities in connection with work carried out in relation to houses; to require certain information to be made available on the sale of houses; to regulate the multiple occupation of houses and certain other types of living accommodation; to make provision about mobile homes; to make provision about matters to be considered by local authorities when assessing suitability of persons to act as a landlord. Explanatory notes have been produced to assist in the understanding of this Act and are available separately (ISBN 0105910805). - 978-0-10-590091-7 £19.50

Human Tissue (Scotland) Act 2006:2006 asp 4. - iii, 52p.: 30 cm. - Royal assent, 16th March 2006. An Act of the Scottish Parliament to make provision in relation to activities involving human tissue. Explanatory notes have been produced to assist in the understanding of this Act and are available separately (ISBN 010591083X). - 978-0-10-590094-8 *£9.00*

Interests of Members of the Scottish Parliament Act 2006:2006 asp 12. - ii, 13p.: 30 cm. - Royal assent, 13th July 2006. An Act of the Scottish Parliament to make provision (including provision for the purposes of section 39 of the Scotland Act 1998) about the registration and declaration of interests of members of the Scottish Parliament and the prohibition of advocacy by such members in return for payment or benefit in kind. Explanatory notes have been produced to assist in the understanding of this Act and are available separately (ISBN 0105910899). - 978-0-10-590102-0 *£3.50*

Joint Inspection of Children's Services and Inspection of Social Work Services (Scotland) Act 2006:2006 asp 3. - [12]p.: 30 cm. - An Act of the Scottish Parliament to make provision for the carrying out of joint inspections of the provision of services to children; and to make provision as to the appointment of persons to act as social work inspectors and their functions. Royal assent, 22nd February 2006. Explanatory notes have been produced to assist in the understanding of this Act and are available separately (ISBN 0105910910). - 978-0-10-590093-1 *£3.00*

Local Electoral Administration and Registration Services (Scotland) Act 2006:2006 asp 14. - iii, 52p.: 30 cm. - Royal assent, 1st August 2006. An Act of the Scottish Parliament to make provision in relation to the administration and conduct of local government elections; to reorganise local registration services; to amend the law in relation to the registration of births and deaths and the procedure in relation to marriages and civil partnerships; to provide for the recording of certain events occurring outwith Scotland in relation to persons who have a Scottish connection; to make available certain information and records held by the Registrar General. Explanatory notes have been produced to assist in the understanding of this Act and will be available separately. - 978-0-10-590104-4 *£9.00*

Planning etc. (Scotland) Act 2006:2006 asp 17. - iii, 95p., print on demand: 30 cm. - Royal assent, 20th December 2006. An Act of the Scottish Parliament to make further provision relating to town and country planning; to make provision for business improvement districts. Explanatory notes have been produced to assist in the understanding of this Act and are available separately (ISBN 9780105910930). Copies are supplied by TSO's On-demand publishing service. - 978-0-10-590107-5 *£15.00*

Police, Public Order and Criminal Justice (Scotland) Act 2006:2006 asp 10. - v, 110p.: 30 cm. - Royal assent, 4 July 2006. An Act of the Scottish Parliament to make further provision about the police, to make further provision about public order and safety; to make further provision about criminal justice. Explanatory notes to the Act have been produced to assist in the understanding of the Act and are available separately (ISBN 0105910902). - 978-0-10-590100-6 *£17.50*

Scottish Commission for Human Rights Act 2006:2006 asp 16. - ii, 18p.: 30 cm. - Royal assent, 8th December 2006. An Act of the Scottish Parliament to provide for the establishment and functions of the Scottish Commission for Human Rights. Explanatory notes have been produced to assist in the understanding of this Act and are available separately (ISBN 9780105910985). - 978-0-10-590106-8 *£4.00*

Scottish Schools (Parental Involvement) Act 2006:2006 asp 8. - ii, 15p.: 30 cm. - Royal assent, 14th June 2006. An Act of the Scottish Parliament to make further provision for the involvement of parents in their children's education and in school education generally; to provide for the establishment of councils to represent the parents of pupils attending public schools; to abolish School Boards; to make further provision as regards the appointment of headteachers and deputy headteachers; to make further provision as regards the content of the development plan for a school. Explanatory Notes have been produced to assist in the understanding of this Act and are available separately (ISBN 0105910872). - 978-0-10-590098-6 *£3.50*

Senior Judiciary (Vacancies and Incapacity) (Scotland) Act 2006:2006 asp 9. - [8]p.: 30 cm. - An Act of the Scottish Parliament to make provision for the exercise of functions during vacancies in the offices of Lord President of the Court of Session and Lord Justice Clerk and the incapacity of the holders of those offices. Royal assent on 27th June 2006. Explanatory Notes have been produced to assist in the understanding of this Act and are available separately (ISBN 0105910880). - 978-0-10-590099-3 *£3.00*

Tourist Boards (Scotland) Act 2006:2006 asp 15. - [12]p.: 30 cm. - Royal assent, 30th November 2006. An Act of the Scottish Parliament to rename the Scottish Tourist Board, to increase the maximum number of members on that body and to abolish area tourist boards. Explanatory notes have been produced to assist in the understanding of this Act and are available separately (ISBN 0105910929). - 978-0-10-590105-1 *£3.00*

Waverley Railway (Scotland) Act 2006:2006 asp 13. - iii, 86p.: 30 cm. - Royal assent, 24th July 2006. An Act of the Scottish Parliament to authorise the reconstruction of a railway from a point in Midlothian immediately south of Newcraighall in the City of Edinburgh to Tweedbank in Scottish Borders, including stations at Shawfair, Eskbank, Newtongrange, Gorebridge, Stow, Galashiels and Tweedbank; to make provision concerning planning agreements and developer contributions relating to the railway. Explanatory notes have been produced to assist in the understanding of this Act and will be available separately. - 978-0-10-590103-7 £13.50

Acts of the Scottish Parliament - Explanatory notes 2006

Animal Health and Welfare (Scotland) Act 2006 (asp 11):explanatory notes. - 32p.: 30 cm. - These notes relate to the Animal Health and Welfare (Scotland) Act 2006 (asp 11) (ISBN 9780105901013) which received Royal assent on 11 July 2006. - 978-0-10-591103-6 £5.50

Family Law (Scotland) Act 2006 (asp 2):explanatory notes. - 13p., pod: 30 cm. - This document relates to the Family Law (Scotland) Act 2006 (asp 2) (ISBN 0105900923) which received Royal assent on 20 January 2006. - Copies are supplied from TSO's On-Demand Publishing Service. - 978-0-10-591084-8 £3.00

Housing (Scotland) Act 2006 (asp 1):explanatory notes. - 36p.: 30 cm. - These notes relate to the Housing (Scotland) Act 2006 (asp 1) (ISBN 0105900915) which received Royal assent on 5 January 2006. - 978-0-10-591080-0 £6.50

Human Tissue (Scotland) Act 2006 (asp 4):explanatory notes. - 31, [3]p.: 30 cm. - This document relates to the Human Tissue (Scotland) Act 2006 (asp 4) (ISBN 010590094X) which received Royal assent on 16 March 2006. - 978-0-10-591083-1 £6.50

Interests of Members of the Scottish Parliament Act 2006 (asp 12):explanatory notes. - 24p.: 30 cm. - This document relates to the Interests of Members of the Scottish Parliament Act 2006 (asp 12) (ISBN 0105901024) which received Royal assent on 13 July 2006. - 978-0-10-591089-3 £4.00

Joint Inspection of Children's Services and Inspection of Social Work Services (Scotland) Act 2006 (asp 3): explanatory notes. - 8p.: 30 cm. - This document relates to the Joint Inspection of Children's Services and Inspection of Social Work Services (Scotland) Act 2006 (asp 3) (ISBN 0105900931) which received Royal assent on 22 February 2006. - 978-0-10-591091-6 £3.00

Planning etc. (Scotland) Act 2006 (asp 17):explanatory notes. - 35p.: 30 cm. - This document relates to the Planning etc. (Scotland) Act 2006 (asp 17) (ISBN 9780105901075) which received Royal assent on 20 December 2006. - 978-0-10-591093-0 £6.50

Police, Public Order and Criminal Justice (Scotland) Act 2006 (asp 10):explanatory notes. - 61p.: 30 cm. - These notes relate to the Police, Public Order and Criminal Justice (Scotland) Act 2006 (asp 10) (ISBN 0105901008) which received Royal assent on 4 July 2006. - 978-0-10-591090-9 £10.50

Scottish Commission for Human Rights Act 2006 (asp 16):explanatory notes. - 12p.: 30 cm. - These notes relate to the Scottish Commission for Human Rights Act 2006 (asp 16) (ISBN 0105901067) which received Royal assent on 2 November 2006. - 978-0-10-591098-5 £3.00

Scottish Schools (Parental Involvement) Act 2006 (asp 8):explanatory notes. - 12p.: 30 cm. - This document relates to the Scottish Schools (Parental Involvement) Act 2006 (asp 8) (ISBN 0105900982) which received Royal assent on 14 June 2006. - 978-0-10-591087-9 £3.00

Senior Judiciary (Vacancies and Incapacity) (Scotland) Act 2006 (asp 9):explanatory notes. - 4p.: 30 cm. - This document relates to the Senior Judiciary (Vacancies and Incapacity) (Scotland) Act 2006 (asp 9) (ISBN 0105900990) which received Royal assent on 27th June 2006. - 978-0-10-591088-6 £3.00

Tourist Boards (Scotland) Act 2006 (asp 15):explanatory notes. - [8]p.: 30 cm. - These notes relate to the Tourist Boards (Scotland) Act 2006 (asp 15) (ISBN 0105901059) which received Royal assent on 30 November 2006. - 978-0-10-591092-3 £3.00

Scottish Statutory Instruments
By Subject Heading

Agriculture

The Beef Carcase (Classification) (Scotland) Amendment Regulations 2006 No. 2006/118. - Enabling power: European Communities Act 1972, s. 2 (2). - Issued: 15.03.2006. Made: 07.03.2006. Laid before the Scottish Parliament: 09.03.2006. Coming into force: 31.03.2006. Effect: S.S.I. 2004/280 amended. Territorial extent & classification: S. General. - EC note: These regs relate to the administration and enforcement of the Community system of classification of beef carcases as required by Commission Regulation 344/91 laying down detailed rules for applying Council Regulation 1186/90 to extend the scope of the Community scale for the classification of carcases of adult bovine animals. They provide for the execution and enforcement of certain Community instruments, in particular, Regulation 854/2004 laying down specific rules for the organisation of official controls on products of animal origin intended for human consumption. - 4p.: 30 cm. - 978-0-11-070037-3 £3.00

The Common Agricultural Policy (Wine) (Scotland) Amendment Regulations 2006 No. 2006/311. - Enabling power: European Communities Act 1972, s. 2 (2). - Issued: 20.06.2006. Made: 07.06.2006. Laid before the Scottish Parliament: 08.06.2006. Coming into force: 01.07.2006. Effect: S.S.I. 2002/325 amended. Territorial extent & classification: S. General. - 16p.: 30 cm. - 978-0-11-070659-7 *£3.00*

The EC Fertilisers (Scotland) Regulations 2006 No. 2006/543. - Enabling power: European Communities Act 1972, s. 2 (2). - Issued: 16.11.2006. Made: 09.11.2006. Laid before the Scottish Parliament: 10.11.2006. Coming into force: 04.12.2006. Effect: None. Territorial extent & classification: S. General. - EC Note: Implement in Scotland Regulation (EC) No. 2003/2003 relating to fertilisers. - 12p.: 30 cm. - 978-0-11-071169-0 *£3.00*

The Environmental Impact Assessment (Agriculture) (Scotland) Regulations 2006 No. 2006/582. - Enabling power: European Communities Act 1972, s. 2 (2). - Issued: 07.12.2006. Made: 29.11.2006. Laid before the Scottish Parliament: 30.11.2006. Coming into force: 01.01.2007. Effect: S.S.I. 2002/6 revoked. Territorial extent & classification: S. General. - EC note: These Regulations implement, in relation to projects on uncultivated land and semi-natural areas and projects restructuring rural land holdings in Scotland, Council Directive 85/337/EEC (as amended by Council Directives 97/11/EC and 2003/35/EC) on the assessment of the effects of certain public and private projects on the environment and Council Directive 92/43/EEC (as last amended by the Act concerning conditions of accession of the Czech Republic and other states and the adjustments to the Treaties on which the European Union is founded) on the conservation of natural habitats and of wild fauna and flora insofar as it applies to such projects. - 28p.: 30 cm. - 978-0-11-071337-3 *£4.50*

The Environmental Impact Assessment (Scotland) Amendment Regulations 2006 No. 2006/614. - Enabling power: European Communities Act 1972, s. 2 (2) and Town and Country Planning (Scotland) Act 1997, s. 40. - Issued: 05.01.2007. Made: 21.12.2006. Laid before the Scottish Parliament: 22.12.2006. Coming into force: 01.02.2007. Effect: 1984 c.54; S.I. 1999/367 amended in relation to Scotland; S.S.I. 1999/1, 43; 2006/582 amended. Territorial extent & classification: S. General. - Copies are supplied by TSO's On-demand publishing service. With correction slip dated February 2007. EC note: These Regulations implement in Scotland the amendments made by Article 3 of Council Directive 2003/35/EC with regard to public participation and access to justice to Council Directive 85/337/EEC. - 24p.: 30 cm. - 978-0-11-071472-1 *£4.00*

The Feeding Stuffs (Scotland) Amendment and the Feeding Stuffs (Sampling and Analysis) Amendment (Scotland) Regulations 2006 No. 2006/16. - Enabling power: Agriculture Act 1970, ss. 66 (1), 74A, 84 & European Communities Act 1972, s. 2 (2). - Issued: 24.01.2006. Made: 17.01.2006. Laid before the Scottish Parliament: 19.01.2006. Coming into force: 16.02.2006. Effect: S.I. 1999/1663 (in relation to Scotland) & S.S.I. 2005/605 amended. Territorial extent & classification: S. General. - EC note: These Regs. implement Commission Directives 2005/6/EC (amending 71/250/EEC); 2005/7/EC (amending 2002/70/EC); 2005/8/EC (amending Annex 1 to Directive 2002/32/EC). - 4p.: 30 cm. - 978-0-11-069908-0 *£3.00*

The Feeding Stuffs (Scotland) Amendment Regulations 2006 No. 2006/516. - Enabling power: Agriculture Act 1970, ss. 66 (1), 68 (1), 69 (1), 74 (1), 74A. - Issued: 31.10.2006. Made: 24.10.2006. Laid before the Scottish Parliament: 25.10.2006. Coming into force: 17.11.2006. Effect: S.S.I. 2005/605 amended and S.S.I. 2000/453; 2003/312 revoked. Territorial extent & classification: S. General. - EC note: The provisions of the 2000 Regulations were intended to implement in Scotland article 1.4 and article 1.1(b) respectively of Directive 2002/2/EC of the European Parliament and of the Council Directive 79/373/EEC on the circulation of compound feedingstuffs. The European Court of Justice has now ruled that article 1.4 of Directive 2002/2/EC is legally valid, whereas article 1.1(b) is not. - 4p.: 30 cm. - 978-0-11-071110-2 *£3.00*

The Feeding Stuffs (Scotland) and the Feed (Hygiene and Enforcement) (Scotland) Amendment Regulations 2006 No. 2006/578. - Enabling power: Agriculture Act 1970, ss. 66 (1), 74 (1), 74A, 84 & European Communities Act 1972, s. 2 (2). - Issued: 11.12.2006. Made: 29.11.2006. Laid before the Scottish Parliament: 30.11.2006. Coming into force: 26.12.2006. Effect: S.S.I. 2005/605, 608 amended. Territorial extent & classification: S. General. - EC note: These Regulations provide for the implementation of the following EC Directives: Commission Directive 2005/86/EC amending Annex I to Directive 2002/32/EC on undesirable substances in animal feed as regards camphechlor; Commission Directive 2005/87/EC amending Annex I to Directive 2002/32/EC on undesirable substances in animal feed as regards lead, fluorine and cadmium and Commission Directive 2006/13/EC amending Annexes I and II to Directive 2002/32/EC on undesirable substances in animal feed as regards dioxins and dioxin-like PCBs. The Regulations also implement a provision contained in Council Directive 79/373/EEC on the circulation of compound feedingstuffs as last amended by Council Regulation 807/2003. This provision relates to the limits of variation for the declaration of the moisture content of compound pet foods. - 12p.: 30 cm. - 978-0-11-071339-7 *£3.00*

The Land Management Contracts (Menu Scheme) (Scotland) Amendment Regulations 2006 No. 2006/213. - Enabling power: European Communities Act 1972, s. 2 (2). - Issued: 27.04.2006. Made: 20.04.2006. Laid before the Scottish Parliament: 21.04.2006. Coming into force: 15.05.2006. Effect: S.S.I. 2005/225 amended. Territorial extent & classification: S. General. - 4p.: 30 cm. - 978-0-11-070352-7 £3.00

The Less Favoured Area Support Scheme (Scotland) Amendment Regulations 2006 No. 2006/601. - Enabling power: European Communities Act 1972, s. 2 (2). - Issued: 20.12.2006. Made: 14.12.2006. Laid before the Scottish Parliament: 15.12.2006. Coming into force: 22.12.2006. Effect: S.S.I. 2005/569 amended. Territorial extent & classification: S. General. - 4p.: 30 cm. - 978-0-11-071408-0 £3.00

The Older Cattle (Disposal) (Scotland) Amendment Regulations 2006 No. 2006/82. - Enabling power: European Communities Act 1972, s. 2 (2). - Issued: 07.03.2006. Made: 27.02.2006. Laid: 28.02.2006. Coming into force: 22.03.2006. Effect: S.S.I. 2006/4 amended. Territorial extent & classification: S. General. - This Scottish Statutory Instrument has been made in consequence of a defect in S.S.I. 2006/4 and is being issued free of charge to all known recipients of that instrument. - 4p.: 30 cm. - 978-0-11-069978-3 £3.00

The Older Cattle (Disposal) (Scotland) Regulations 2006 No. 2006/4. - Enabling power: European Communities Act 1972, s. 2 (2). - Issued: 16.01.2006. Made: 09.01.2006. Laid before the Scottish Parliament: 10.01.2006. Coming into force: 23.01.2006. Effect: S.I. 1996/1193 revoked in relation to Scotland. Territorial extent & classification: S. General. - EC note: These regs make provision for the enforcement of Commission Regulation No. 716/96, adopting exceptional support measures for the beef market in the UK following the entry into force of Commission Regulation No. 2109/2005. The Commission Regulation provides for a Community co-financed scheme authorising the UK competent authority to purchase any bovine animal born or reared within the UK before 1st August 1996 which does not exhibit any clinical sign of BSE and which was, during a period of at least six months prior to its sale, present on a holding located in the UK. The Commission Regulation also contains provisions relating to the slaughter and disposal of such animals. - 8p.: 30 cm. - 978-0-11-069897-7 £3.00

The Pesticides (Maximum Residue Levels in Crops, Food and Feeding Stuffs) (Scotland) Amendment (No.2) Regulations 2006 No. 2006/312. - Enabling power: European Communities Act 1972, s. 2 (2). - Issued: 20.06.2006. Made: 07.06.2006. Laid before the Scottish Parliament: 08.06.2006. Coming into force: 27.07.2006 except for reg. 4; 15.09.2006 for reg. 4, in accord. with reg. 1. Effect: S.S.I. 2005/599 amended. Territorial extent & classification: S. General. - EC note: These Regulations implement Commission Directives 2006/4/EC; 2006/9/EC and 2006/30/EC. - 20p.: 30 cm. - 978-0-11-070660-3 £3.50

The Pesticides (Maximum Residue Levels in Crops, Food and Feeding Stuffs) (Scotland) Amendment (No. 3) Regulations 2006 No. 2006/548. - Enabling power: European Communities Act 1972, s. 2 (2). - Issued: 24.11.2006. Made: 16.11.2006. Laid before the Scottish Parliament: 17.11.2006. Coming into force: In accord. with reg. 1 (3) to (7). Effect: S.S.I. 2005/599; 2006/151 amended. Territorial extent & classification: S. General. - EC note: These Regulations implement Commission Directives 2006/53/EC, 2006/59/EC, 2006/60/EC and 2006/61/EC. - 48p.: 30 cm. - 978-0-11-071184-3 £7.50

The Pesticides (Maximum Residue Levels in Crops, Food and Feeding Stuffs) (Scotland) Amendment Regulations 2006 No. 2006/151. - Enabling power: European Communities Act 1972, s. 2 (2). - Issued: 25.04.2006. Made: 14.03.2006. Laid before the Scottish Parliament: 15.03.2006. Coming into force: In accord. with reg. 1(2) to (4). Effect: S.S.I. 2005/599 amended. Territorial extent & classification: S. General. - This S.S.I. has been printed in substitution of the S.S.I. of the same number (issued on 07.04.2006) and is being issued free of charge to all known recipients of that instrument. EC note: These Regulations implement Commission Directives 2005/70/EC, 2005/74/EC and 2005/76/EC. - 28p., tables: 30 cm. - 978-0-11-070210-0 £4.00

The Pig Carcase (Grading) Amendment (Scotland) Regulations 2006 No. 2006/451. - Enabling power: European Communities Act 1972, s. 2 (2). - Issued: 11.09.2006. Made: 01.09.2006. Laid before the Scottish Parliament: 04.09.2006. Coming into force: 26.09.2006. Effect: S.I. 1994/2155 amended in relation to Scotland. Territorial extent and classification: S. General. - EC note: These Regulations, which apply in relation to Scotland only, amend the 1994 Regulations to incorporate amendments made by Commission Decision no. 2006/374. - 4p.: 30 cm. - 978-0-11-070994-9 £3.00

The Products of Animal Origin (Third Country Imports) (Scotland) Amendment Regulations 2006 No. 2006/156. - Enabling power: European Communities Act 1972, s. 2 (2). - Issued: 23.03.2006. Made: 16.03.2006. Laid before the Scottish Parliament: 16.03.2006. Coming into force: 17.03.2006. Effect: S.S.I. 2002/445 amended. Territorial extent & classification: S. General. - EC note: These Regulations implement Council Directive 97/78/EC, which lays down the principles governing the organisation of veterinary checks on products entering the Community from third countries. They also give effect to the restriction on the importation of feathers from certain third countries contained in Commission Decision 2006/7/EC as amended by Commission Decision 2006/183/EC. - 4p.: 30 cm. - 978-0-11-070137-0 £3.00

Anatomy

The Anatomy (Scotland) Regulations 2006 No. 2006/334. - Enabling power: Anatomy Act 1984, ss. 3 (5), 5 (6), 6A (12), 8 (1), 11 (4) (7). - Issued: 23.06.2006. Made: 07.06.2006. Laid before the Scottish Parliament: 09.06.2006. Coming into force: 01.09.2006. Effect: S.I. 1988/44, 198 revoked with savings. Territorial extent & classification: S. General. - 12p.: 30 cm. - 978-0-11-070690-0 £3.00

The Anatomy (Specified Persons and Museums for Public Display) (Scotland) Order 2006 No. 2006/328. - Enabling power: Anatomy Act 1984, s. 6A (2). - Issued: 21.06.2006. Made: 07.06.2006. Laid before the Scottish Parliament: 09.06.2006. Coming into force: 01.09.2006. Effect: None. Territorial extent & classification: S. General. - 4p.: 30 cm. - 978-0-11-070703-7 £3.00

The Human Tissue (Scotland) Act 2006 (Anatomy Act 1984 Transitional Provisions) Order 2006 No. 2006/340. - Enabling power: Human Tissue (Scotland) Act 2006, s. 58. - Issued: 26.06.2006. Made: 07.06.2006. Laid before the Scottish Parliament: 09.06.2006. Coming into force: 01.09.2006. Effect: None. Territorial extent & classification: S. General. - 8p.: 30 cm. - 978-0-11-070737-2 £3.00

Animals

The Animal Health and Welfare (Scotland) Act 2006 (Commencement No. 1, Savings and Transitional Provisions) Order 2006 No. 2006/482 (C.41). - Enabling power: Animal Health and Welfare (Scotland) Act 2006, s. 55 (1). Bringing into operation various provisions of the 2006 Act on 06.10.2006. - Issued: 09.10.2006. Made: 28.09.2006. Effect: None. Territorial extent & classification: S. General. - 4p.: 30 cm. - 978-0-11-071060-0 £3.00

The Avian Influenza (H5N1 in Wild Birds) (Scotland) Amendment Order 2006 No. 2006/237. - Enabling power: Animal Health Act 1981, ss. 1, 7 (1), 8 (1). - Issued: 10.05.2006. Made: 27.04.2006. Coming into force: 28.04.2006. Effect: S.S.I. 2006/196 amended. Territorial extent & classification: S. General. - 16p.: 30 cm. - 978-0-11-070411-1 £3.00

The Avian Influenza (H5N1 in Wild Birds) (Scotland) Order 2006 No. 2006/196. - Enabling power: Animal Health Act 1981, ss. 1, 7 (1), 8 (1), 87 (5) (a). - Issued: 19.04.2006. Made: 05.04.2006. Coming into force: 05.04.2006. Effect: None. Territorial extent & classification: S. General. - EC note: These regs implement Commission Decision 2006/115/EC concerning certain protection measures in relation to highly pathogenic avian influenza in wild birds in the Community and repealing Decisions 2006/86/EC, 2006/90/EC, 2006/91/EC, 2006/94/EC, 2006/104/EC and 2006/105/EC. - 20p.: 30 cm. - 978-0-11-070264-3 £3.50

Animals: Animal health

The Animal Health and Welfare (Scotland) Act 2006 (Consequential Provisions) Order 2006 No. 2006/536. - Enabling power: Animal Health and Welfare (Scotland) Act 2006, s. 53 (1). - Issued: 13.11.2006. Made: 02.11.2006. Coming into force: 03.11.2006. Effect: 16 UK Acts amended; 2002 asp 6; S.I. 1995/731 amended. Territorial extent & classification: S. General. - 8p.: 30 cm. - 978-0-11-071128-7 £3.00

The Animals and Animal Products (Import and Export) (Scotland) Amendment (No. 2) Regulations 2006 No. 2006/450. - Enabling power: European Communities Act 1972, s. 2 (2). - Issued: 08.09.2006. Made: 30.08.2006. Laid before the Scottish Parliament: 01.09.2006. Coming into force: 02.09.2006. Effect: S.S.I. 2000/216 amended. Territorial extent & classification: S. General. - EC note: These Regs implement Commission Decision 2006/542/EC on animal health conditions and veterinary certification for the re-entry of registered horses for racing, competition and cultural events after temporary export. - 2p.: 30 cm. - 978-0-11-070987-1 £3.00

The Animals and Animal Products (Import and Export) (Scotland) Amendment Regulations 2006 No. 2006/335. - Enabling power: European Communities Act 1972, s. 2 (2) & Finance Act 1973, s. 56 (1) (2). - Issued: 23.06.2006. Made: 07.06.2006. Laid before the Scottish Parliament: 08.06.2006. Coming into force: 17.06.2006. Effect: S.S.I. 2000/216 amended. Territorial extent & classification: S. General. - With correction slip dated September 2006. EC note: Implements Commission Decision 2000/666/EC laying down the animal health requirements and the veterinary certification for the import of birds, other than poultry and the conditions for quarantine and Council Directive 2004/68/EC laying down animal health rules for the importation into and transit through the Community of certain live ungulate animals. Amendments have also been made to the 2000 Regulations to include reference to the Common Veterinary Entry Document pursuant to Commission Regulation (EC) No. 282/2004 introducing a document for the declaration of, and veterinary checks on, animals from third countries entering the Community. - 12p.: 30 cm. - 978-0-11-070689-4 £3.00

The Avian Influenza and Influenza of Avian Origin in Mammals (Scotland) Order 2006 No. 2006/336. - Enabling power: Animal Health Act 1981, ss. 1, 7, 8 (1), 11, 15 (5), 17 (1), 23, 25, 28, 32 (2), 35 (1) (3), 38 (1), 83 (2), 87 (2) (5) (a), 88 (2). - Issued: 23.06.2006. Made: 07.06.2006. Coming into force: 01.07.2006. Effect: S.I. 1978/32 amended in relation to Scotland and S.S.I. 2003/354 amended. Territorial extent & classification: S. General. - This Order transposes Council Directive 2005/94/EC on Community measures for the control of avian influenza and repealing Directive 92/40/EC, other than Chapter IX and certain slaughter provisions. - 52p.: 30 cm. - 978-0-11-070708-2 £9.00

The Avian Influenza (Preventive Measures) (Scotland) Amendment Regulations 2006 No. 2006/399. - Enabling power: European Communities Act 1972, s. 2 (2). - Issued: 20.07.2006. Made: 20.06.2006. Laid before the Scottish Parliament: 14.07.2006. Coming into force: 22.06.2006. Effect: S.S.I. 2005/530 amended. Territorial extent & classification: S. General. - EC note: The principal Regulations give effect to Commission Decision 2005/734/EC which has been subsequently amended by Commission Decision 2006/405/EC to extend the period of application of its measures to 31st December 2006. These Regulations, by replacing the definition of the Commission Decision in the principal Regulations, give effect to this amendment. - 2p.: 30 cm. - 978-0-11-070873-7 £3.00

The Avian Influenza (Slaughter and Vaccination) (Scotland) Regulations 2006 No. 2006/337. - Enabling power: European Communities Act 1972, s. 2 (2). - Issued: 23.06.2006. Made: 07.06.2006. Laid before the Scottish Parliament: 08.06.2006. Coming into force: 01.07.2006. Effect: None. Territorial extent & classification: S. General. - EC note: These Regulations transpose for Scotland Council Directive 2005/94/EC on Community measures for the control of avian influenza repealing Directive 92/40/EEC insofar as it deals with vaccination against avian influenza, preventive eradication and imposing a duty to slaughter birds on infected premises. - 20p.: 30 cm. - 978-0-11-070714-3 £3.50

The Diseases of Animals (Approved Disinfectants) Amendment (Scotland) Order 2006 No. 2006/352. - Enabling power: Animal Health Act 1981, ss. 1, 7, 23 (f) (g). - Issued: 20.06.2006. Made: 11.06.2006. Coming into force: 16.06.2006. Effect: S.I. 1978/32 amended in relation to Scotland & S.S.I. 2005/587 revoked. Territorial extent & classification: S. General. - 12p.: 30 cm. - 978-0-11-070649-8 £3.00

The Foot-and-Mouth Disease (Scotland) Order 2006 No. 2006/44. - Enabling power: Animal Health Act 1981, ss. 1, 7 (1), 8 (1), 13, 15 (3) (4), 17 (1), 23, 25, 26, 28, 34 (7), 83 (2), 87 (2) (5). - Issued: 13.02.2006. Made: 06.02.2006. Coming into force: 23.02.2006. Effect: S.I. 1978/32 amended in relation to Scotland & S.S.I. 2001/297, 390; 2002/34 amended & S.I. 1983/1950; 1993/3119 revoked in relation to Scotland & S.S.I. 2001/52, 55, 101 revoked. Territorial extent & classification: S. General. - EC note: This Order, read with the Animal Health Act 1981 (c.22) partially transposes for Scotland Council Directive 2003/85/EC on Community measures for the control of foot-and-mouth disease repealing Directive 85/511/EEC and Decisions 89/531/EEC and 91/665/EEC and amending Directive 92/46/EEC. - 68p.: 30 cm. - 978-0-11-069933-2 £10.50

The Foot-and-Mouth Disease (Slaughter and Vaccination) (Scotland) Regulations 2006 No. 2006/45. - Enabling power: European Communities Act 1972, s. 2 (2). - Issued: 13.02.2006. Made: 06.02.2006. Laid before the Scottish Parliament: 07.02.2006. Coming into force: 23.02.2006. Effect: S.S.I. 2005/653 amended & S.I. 1972/1509 revoked in relation to Scotland & S.S.I. 2001/261 revoked. Territorial extent & classification: S. General. - EC note: These Regs transpose for Scotland, Council Directive 2003/85/EC on Community measures for the control of foot-and-mouth disease insofar as it deals with vaccination against foot-and-mouth disease and the provision of additional slaughter powers. - 36p.: 30 cm. - 978-0-11-069934-9 £6.50

The Products of Animal Origin (Third Country Imports) (Scotland) Amendment (No. 2) Regulations 2006 No. 2006/419. - Enabling power: European Communities Act 1972, s. 2 (2). - Issued: 16.08.2006. Made: 09.08.2006. Laid before the Scottish Parliament: 10.08.2006. Coming into force: 11.08.2006. Effect: S.S.I. 2002/445 amended. Territorial extent & classification: S. General. - EC note: These Regs amend the 2002 Regs (which implemented Council Directive 97/78/EC, which lays down the principles governing the organisation of veterinary checks on products entering the Community from third countries) to refer to Commission Decision 2006/522/EC which further amends Decision 2005/760/EC and Decision 2006/521/EC which further amends Decision 2006/7/EC. These Regulations also update the reference to Regulation 1774/2002 laying down health rules concerning animal by products not intended for human consumption. - 4p.: 30 cm. - 978-0-11-070906-2 £3.00

The Sheep and Goats (Identification and Traceability) (Scotland) Amendment (No. 2) Regulations 2006 No. 2006/594. - Enabling power: European Communities Act 1972, s. 2 (2). - Issued: 18.12.2006. Made: 11.12.2006. Laid before the Scottish Parliament: 11.12.2006. Coming into force: 21.12.2006 for regs 1 & 9; 22.12.2006 for regs 2 to 8. Effect: S.S.I. 2006/73 amended & S.S.I. 2006/577 revoked (21.12.2006). Territorial extent & classification: S. General. - EC note: These Regulations relate to the provision for the administration and enforcement of Council Regulation 21/2004 (establishing a system for the identification and registration of ovine and caprine animals and amending Regulation 1782/2003 and Directives 92/102/EEC and 64/432/EEC). - 4p.: 30 cm. - 978-0-11-071371-7 £3.00

The Sheep and Goats (Identification and Traceability) (Scotland) Regulations 2006 No. 2006/73. - Enabling power: European Communities Act 1972, s. 2 (2). - Issued: 02.03.2006. Made: 23.02.2006. Laid before the Scottish Parliament: 24.02.2006. Coming into force: 20.03.2006. Effect: S.S.I. 2002/221 amended & S.S.I. 2000/418; 2002/38, 39, 531; 2003/228 revoked. Territorial extent & classification: S. General. - EC note: These Regulations make provision for the administration and enforcement of Council Regulation (EC) No. 21/2004 (establishing a system for the identification and registration of ovine and caprine animals and amending Regulation (EC) No. 1782/2003 and Directives 92/102/EEC and 64/432/EEC). - 24p.: 30 cm. - 978-0-11-069971-4 £4.00

Animals: Animal health

The Transmissible Spongiform Encephalopathies (Scotland) Regulations 2006 No. 2006/530. - Enabling power: European Communities Act 1972, s. 2 (2). - Issued: 20.11.2006. Made: 01.11.2006. Laid before the Scottish Parliament: 02.11.2006. Coming into force: 24.11.2006. Effect: S.I. 1995/614; 1997/2964; S.S.I. 2001/189; 2003/411; 2004/6; 2005/605, 616; 2006/3 amended and S.I. 1997/2965, 3062; 1998/2405, 2431; 1999/539 revoked in relation to Scotland & S.S.I. 2000/344, 345; 2001/3, 4, 73, 86, 276, 287, 288, 383; 2002/255; 2003/198; 2004/277; 2005/173, 469; 2006/46, 231, 430 revoked. Territorial extent & classification: S. General. - EC note: These Regulations make provision for the administration and enforcement of Regulation (EC) 9999/2001 laying down rules for the prevention, control and eradication of certain transmissible spongiform encephalopathies, as amended by the EU instruments listed in Schedule 1. - 56p.: 30 cm. - 978-0-11-071159-1 £9.00

The TSE (Scotland) Amendment (No. 2) Regulations 2006 No. 2006/231. - Enabling power: European Communities Act 1972, s. 2 (2). - Issued: 26.05.2006. Made: 02.05.2006. Laid before the Scottish Parliament: 02.05.2006. Coming into force: 03.05.2006. Effect: S.S.I. 2000/62, 216; 2002/255; 2006/3 amended & S.I. 1999/1103, 1554 revoked in relation to Scotland & S.S.I. 2000/184; 2002/449; 2005/218 revoked. Territorial extent & classification: S. General. - Revoked by S.S.I. 2006/530 (ISBN 0110711599). EC note: Amends S.S.I. 2002/255 which gave effect in Scotland to the enforcement and administration of Reg no. 999/2001 laying down rules for the prevention, control and eradication of certain transmissible spongiform encephalopathies. - 20p.: 30 cm. - 978-0-11-070551-4 £3.50

The TSE (Scotland) Amendment (No. 3) Regulations 2006 No. 2006/430. - Enabling power: European Communities Act 1972, s. 2 (2). - Issued: 23.08.2006. Made: 16.08.2006. Laid before the Scottish Parliament: 17.08.2006. Coming into force: 18.08.2006. Effect: S.S.I. 2002/255 amended. Territorial extent & classification: S. General. - Revoked by S.S.I. 2006/530 (ISBN 0110711599). EC note: Amends the 2002 Regs in order to apply a derogation available to member states in point 13 of Annex XI of Regulation (EC) no. 999/2001 (the Community TSE Regulation). - 4p.: 30 cm. - 978-0-11-070917-8 £3.00

The TSE (Scotland) Amendment Regulations 2006 No. 2006/46. - Enabling power: European Communities Act 1972, s. 2 (2). - Issued: 14.02.2006. Made: 07.02.2006. Laid before the Scottish Parliament: 07.02.2006. Coming into force: 10.03.2006. Effect: S.S.I. 2002/255 amended. Territorial extent & classification: S. General. - Revoked by S.S.I. 2006/530 (ISBN 0110711599). EC note: These Regulations amend the TSE (Scotland) Regulations 2002 (S.I. 2002/255) which give effect in Scotland to the enforcement and administration of Regulation (EC) No. 999/2001 laying down rules for the prevention, control and eradication of certain transmissible spongiform encephalopathies. Annex VII was replaced by regulation 1492/2004. - 8p.: 30 cm. - 978-0-11-069937-0 £3.00

The Welfare of Animals (Transport) (Scotland) Regulations 2006 No. 2006/606. - Enabling power: European Communities Act 1972, s. 2 (2). - Issued: 28.12.2006. Made: 15.12.2006. Laid before the Scottish Parliament: 18.12.2006. Coming into force: 25.01.2007. Effect: S.I. 1975/1024; 1981/1051; 1997/1480; 1998/2537; 1999/1622 revoked in so far as they relate to Scotland. Territorial extent & classification: S. General. - With correction slip, dated March 2007. EC note: These Regulations, which apply in Scotland only, revoke the Welfare of Animals (Transport) Order 1997, which implemented Council Directive 91/628/EEC on the protection of animals during transport, and make provision for the administration and enforcement of Council Regulation (EC) No. 1/2005 on the protection of animals during transport and related operations and amending Directives 64/432/EEC and 93/119/EC and Regulation (EC) No. 1255/97. They also makes provision in Scotland for the administration and enforcement of Council Regulation 1255/97 concerning Community criteria for staging points and amending the route plan referred to in the Annex to Directive 91/628/EEC. With correction slip dated March 2007. - 12p.: 30 cm. - 978-0-11-071428-8 £3.00

Betting, gaming and lotteries

The Gambling Act 2005 (Licensing Authority Policy Statement) (Scotland) Regulations 2006 No. 2006/154. - Enabling power: Gambling Act 2005, s. 349 (4) (5). - Issued: 22.03.2006. Made: 15.03.2006. Laid before the Scottish Parliament: 15.03.2006. Coming into force: 23.04.2006. Effect: None. Territorial extent & classification: S. General. - 4p.: 30 cm. - 978-0-11-070124-0 £3.00

The Gaming Act (Variation of Fees) (Scotland) Order 2006 No. 2006/249. - Enabling power: Gambling Act 1968, s. 48 (5). - Issued: 16.05.2006. Made: 09.05.2006. Laid before the Scottish Parliament: 09.05.2006. Coming into force: 01.06.2006. Effect: 1968 c.65 amended. Territorial extent & classification: S. General. - 4p.: 30 cm. - 978-0-11-070442-5 £3.00

Building and buildings

The Building (Forms) (Scotland) Amendment Regulations 2006 No. 2006/163. - Enabling power: Building (Scotland) Act 2003, s. 36. - Issued: 29.03.2006. Made: 21.03.2006. Laid before the Scottish Parliament: 22.03.2006. Coming into force: 01.05.2006. Effect: S.S.I. 2005/172 amended. Territorial extent & classification: S. General. - 36p.: 30 cm. - 978-0-11-070188-2 £6.50

The Building (Scotland) Amendment Regulations 2006 No. 2006/534. - Enabling power: Building (Scotland) Act 2003, ss. 1, 2, 8 (8), 54, 56, sch. 1. - Issued: 10.11.2006. Made: 02.11.2006. Laid before the Scottish Parliament: 03.11.2006. Coming into force: 01.05.2007. Effect: S.S.I. 2004/406 amended. Territorial extent & classification: S. General. - Copies are supplied by TSO's on-demand publishing service. This SSI has been amended by SSI 2007/166 (ISBN 9780110720265) which is being supplied free of charge to all known recipients of 2006/534. - 28p.: 30 cm. - 978-0-11-071127-0 £4.50

Charities

The Charities Accounts (Scotland) Regulations 2006 No. 2006/218. - Enabling power: Charities and Trustee Investment (Scotland) Act 2005, s. 44 (4) (5). - Issued: 02.05.2006. Made: 24.04.2006. Laid before the Scottish Parliament: 25.04.2006. Coming into force: 17.05.2006. Effect: None. Territorial extent & classification: S. General. - 16p.: 30 cm. - 978-0-11-070356-5 £3.00

The Charities and Trustee Investment (Scotland) Act 2005 (Commencement No. 2) Order 2006 No. 2006/74 (C.9). - Enabling power: Charities and Trustee Investment (Scotland) Act 2005, ss. 103 (2), 107 (2). Bringing into operation various provisions of the 2005 Act on 24.02.2006. - Issued: 03.03.2006. Made: 23.02.2006. Effect: None. Territorial extent & classification: S. General. - 4p.: 30 cm. - 978-0-11-069968-4 £3.00

The Charities and Trustee Investment (Scotland) Act 2005 (Commencement No. 3, Transitional and Savings Provision) Order 2006 No. 2006/189 (C.18). - Enabling power: Charities and Trustee Investment (Scotland) Act 2005, ss. 103 (2), 107 (2). Bringing into operation various provisions of the 2005 Act on 01.04.2006, 24. 04. 2006. - Issued: 10.04.2006. Made: 31.03.2006. Effect: None. Territorial extent & classification: S. General. - 8p.: 30 cm. - 978-0-11-070243-8 £3.00

The Charity Test (Specified Bodies) (Scotland) Order 2006 No. 2006/219. - Enabling power: Charities and Trustee Investment (Scotland) Act 2005, s. 7 (5). - Issued: 02.05.2006. Made: 21.04.2006. Coming into force: 24.04.2006. Effect: 2005 asp 10 disapplied in relation to the bodies specified in the schedule. Territorial extent & classification: S. General. - Supersedes draft SSI (ISBN 0110699599) issued 23.02.2006. - 4p.: 30 cm. - 978-0-11-070375-6 £3.00

The Further and Higher Education (Scotland) Act 1992 Modification Order 2006 No. 2006/216. - Enabling power: Charities and Trustee Investment (Scotland) Act 2005, s. 102 (a). - Issued: 28.04.2006. Made: 20.04.2006. Coming into force: 24.04.2006. Effect: 1992 c. 37 modified. Territorial extent & classification: S. General. - 2p.: 30 cm. - 978-0-11-070353-4 £3.00

The Protection of Charities Assets (Exemption) (Scotland) Order 2006 No. 2006/220. - Enabling power: Charities and Trustee Investment (Scotland) Act 2005, s. 19 (8) (9). - Issued: 02.05.2006. Made: 21.04.2006. Coming into force: 24.04.2006. Effect: 2005 asp 10 disapplied in relation to the property owned by the bodies specified in the Order. Territorial extent & classification: S. General. - Supersedes draft SSI (ISBN 0110699602) issued 23.02.2006. - 8p.: 30 cm. - 978-0-11-070374-9 £3.00

The Scottish Charity Appeals Panel Rules 2006 No. 2006/571. - Enabling power: Charities and Trustee Investment (Scotland) Act 2005, sch. 2, para. 4 (1). - Issued: 05.12.2006. Made: 29.11.2006. Laid before the Scottish Parliament: 30.11.2006. Coming into force: 31.12.2006. Effect: None. Territorial extent & classification: S. General. - 12p.: 30 cm. - 978-0-11-071274-1 £3.00

The Scottish Charity Register (Transitional) Order 2006 No. 2006/188. - Enabling power: Charities and Trustee Investment (Scotland) Act 2005, s. 99 (3). - Issued: 10.04.2006. Made: 31.03.2006. Laid before the Scottish Parliament: 31.03.2006. Coming into force: 01.04.2006. Effect: 2003 asp 10, section 3 (3) disapplied until 23.08.2007. Territorial extent & classification: S. General. - 2p.: 30 cm. - 978-0-11-070245-2 £3.00

Children and young persons

The Children (Protection at Work) (Scotland) Regulations 2006 No. 2006/140. - Enabling power: European Communities Act 1972, s. 2 (2). - Issued: 27.03.2006. Made: 08.03.2006. Laid before the Scottish Parliament: 10.03.2006. Coming into force: 18.04.2006. Effect: 1937 c.37 amended. Territorial extent & classification: S. General. - EC note: These Regulations give further effect in Scotland, to Council Directive 94/33/EC on the protection of young people at work. - 4p.: 30 cm. - 978-0-11-070164-6 £3.00

The Intensive Support and Monitoring (Scotland) Regulations 2006 No. 2006/15. - Enabling power: Children (Scotland) Act 1995, ss. 17, 31, 70 (12) (13) (14) (17), 103. - Issued: 24.01.2006. Made: 17.01.2006. Laid before the Scottish Parliament: 18.01.2006. Coming into force: 20.02.2006 except for reg 1 (3); 16.04.2006 for reg. 1 (3). Effect: S.S.I. 2005/129, 201 revoked on 16.04.2006. Territorial extent & classification: S. General. - 8p.: 30 cm. - 978-0-11-069909-7 £3.00

The Joint Inspections (Scotland) Amendment Regulations 2006 No. 2006/365. - Enabling power: Joint Inspection of Children's Services and Inspection of Social Work Services (Scotland) Act 2006, s. 3 (1) (f). - Issued: 29.06.2006. Made: 22.05.2006. Coming into force: 23.05.2006. Effect: S.S.I. 2006/263 amended. Territorial extent & classification: S. General. - This Scottish Statutory Instrument has been made in consequence of a defect in S.S.I. 2006/263 (ISBN 0110704924) and is being issued free of charge to all known recipients of that instrument. - 2p.: 30 cm. - 978-0-11-070765-5 £3.00

The Joint Inspections (Scotland) Regulations 2006 No. 2006/263. - Enabling power: Joint Inspection of Children's Services and Inspection of Social Work Services (Scotland) Act 2006, ss. 3 (1), 6 (2). - Issued: 23.05.2006. Made: 15.05.2006. Coming into force: 16.05.2006. Effect: None. Territorial extent & classification: S. General. - This instrument has been amended by SSI 2006/365 (ISBN 0110707656) which is being issued free of charge to all known recipients of SSI 2006/263. - 8p.: 30 cm. - 978-0-11-070492-0 *£3.00*

The Parental Responsibilities and Parental Rights Agreement (Scotland) Amendment Regulations 2006 No. 2006/255. - Enabling power: Children (Scotland) Act 1995, ss. 4 (2), 103 (2). - Issued: 18.05.2006. Made: 11.05.2006. Laid before the Scottish Parliament: 12.05.2006. Coming into force: 03.06.2006. Effect: S.I. 1996/2549 amended. Territorial extent & classification: S. General. - 8p.: 30 cm. - 978-0-11-070488-3 *£3.00*

Civil partnership

The Civil Partnership Act 2004 (Consequential Amendments) (Scotland) Order 2006 No. 2006/379. - Enabling power: Civil Partnership Act 2004, s. 259 (1) to (3). - Issued: 05.07.2006. Made: 27.06.2006. Coming into force: 30.06.2006. Effect: 1991 c.55; 2003 asp 9 amended. Territorial extent & classification: S. General. - Supersedes draft S.S.I. (ISBN 0110705335) issued 30.05.2006. - 4p.: 30 cm. - 978-0-11-070811-9 *£3.00*

The Civil Partnership (Attestation) (Scotland) Regulations 2006 No. 2006/574. - Enabling power: Civil Partnership Act 2004, ss. 88 (5), 92 (2). - Issued: 06.12.2006. Made: 29.11.2006. Laid before the Scottish Parliament: 30.11.2006. Coming into force: 01.01.2007. Effect: None. Territorial extent & classification: S. General. - 2p.: 30 cm. - 978-0-11-071305-2 *£3.00*

The Civil Partnership Family Homes (Form of Consent) (Scotland) Regulations 2006 No. 2006/115. - Enabling power: Civil Partnership Act 2004, ss. 106 (3) (a) (i), 258 (2). - Issued: 14.03.2006. Made: 07.03.2006. Laid before the Scottish Parliament: 08.03.2006. Coming into force: 30.03.2006. Effect: None. Territorial extent & classification: S. General. - 4p.: 30 cm. - 978-0-11-069998-1 *£3.00*

The Registration Services (Fees, etc.) (Scotland) Regulations 2006 No. 2006/575. - Enabling power: Registration of Births, Deaths and Marriages (Scotland) Act 1965, ss.28A (4), 37 (1), 38 (2) (3), 39C, 39D (1), 39E (3), 43 (8), 47, 54 (1); Marriage (Scotland) Act 1977, ss. 3 (1), 19 (2); Civil Partnership Act 2004, ss. 88 (1), 95 (4), 122 (4), 134 (2) & Local Electoral Administration and Registration Services (Scotland) Act 2006, ss. 58 (5) (8), 61 (2) (a). - Issued: 06.12.2006. Made: 29.11.2006. Laid before the Scottish Parliament: 30.11.2006. Coming into force: 01.01.2007. Effect: S.I. 1998/643, 3191 & S.S.I. 2000/447; 2002/390; 2003/89; 2005/100, 556 revoked. Territorial extent & classification: S. General. - 16p.: 30 cm. - 978-0-11-071313-7 *£3.00*

Construction

The Construction Contracts (Scotland) Exclusion Amendment Order 2006 No. 2006/513. - Enabling power: Housing Grants, Construction and Regeneration Act 1996, s. 106 (1) (b). - Issued: 26.10.2006. Made: 18.10.2006. Coming into force: 19.10.2006. Effect: S.I. 1998/686 amended. Territorial extent & classification: S. General. - 2p.: 30 cm. - 978-0-11-071106-5 *£3.00*

Consumer protection

The Tobacco Advertising and Promotion Act 2002 (Commencement No. 10) (Scotland) Order 2006 No. 2006/473 (C.40). - Enabling power: Tobacco Advertising and Promotion Act 2002, s. 22 (1) (2). Bringing into operation various provisions of the 2002 Act on 28.09.2006, in accord. with art. 2. - Issued: 27.09.2006. Made: 14.09.2006. Effect: None. Territorial extent & classification: S. General. - 4p.: 30 cm. - 978-0-11-071041-9 *£3.00*

Council tax

The Council Tax (Electronic Communications) (Scotland) Order 2006 No. 2006/67. - Enabling power: Electronic Communications Act 2000, ss. 8, 9. - Issued: 27.02.2006. Made: 20.02.2006. Laid before the Scottish Parliament: 21.02.2006. Coming into force: 01.04.2006. Effect: S.I. 1992/1332 amended. Territorial extent & classification: S. General. - 4p.: 30 cm. - 978-0-11-069965-3 *£3.00*

The Council Tax (Exempt Dwellings) (Scotland) Amendment Order 2006 No. 2006/402. - Enabling power: Local Government Finance Act 1992, ss. 72 (5) to (7), 113 (2). - Issued: 21.07.2006. Made: 29.06.2006. Laid before the Scottish Parliament: 17.07.2006. Coming into force: 01.10.2006. Effect: S.I. 1992/1332; 1997/728 amended. Territorial extent & classification: S. General. - 4p.: 30 cm. - 978-0-11-070884-3 *£3.00*

Court of Session

Act of Sederunt (Rules of the Court of Session Amendment) (Miscellaneous) 2006 No. 2006/83. - Enabling power: Court of Session Act 1988, s. 5. - Issued: 07.03.2006. Made: 24.02.2006. Coming into force: 17.03.2006. Effect: S.I. 1994/1443 amended. Territorial extent & classification: S. General. - 12p.: 30 cm. - 978-0-11-069979-0 *£3.00*

Act of Sederunt (Rules of the Court of Session Amendment No.2) (Fees of Shorthand Writers) 2006 No. 2006/87. - Enabling power: Court of Session Act 1988, s. 5. - Issued: 06.03.2006. Made: 24.02.2006. Coming into force: 01.05.2006. Effect: S.I. 1994/1443 amended. Territorial extent & classification: S. General. - 4p.: 30 cm. - 978-0-11-069983-7 *£3.00*

Act of Sederunt (Rules of the Court of Session Amendment No. 2) (UNCITRAL Model Law on Cross-Border Insolvency) 2006 No. 2006/199. - Enabling power: Court of Session Act 1988, s. 5. - Issued: 13.04.2006. Made: 03.04.2006. Coming into force: 06.04.2006. Effect: S.I. 1994/1443 amended. Territorial extent & classification: S. General. - 8p.: 30 cm. - 978-0-11-070261-2 £3.00

Act of Sederunt (Rules of the Court of Session Amendment No. 3) (Family Law (Scotland) Act 2006) 2006 No. 2006/206. - Enabling power: Court of Session Act 1988, s. 5. - Issued: 25.04.2006. Made: 12.04.2006. Coming into force: 04.05.2006. Effect: S.I. 1994/1443 amended. Territorial extent & classification: S. General. - 8p.: 30 cm. - 978-0-11-070267-4 £3.00

Act of Sederunt (Rules of the Court of Session Amendment No. 4) (Fees of Solicitors) 2006 No. 2006/294. - Enabling power: Court of Session Act 1988, s. 5. - Issued: 07.06.2006. Made: 26.05.2006. Coming into force: 01.07.2006. Effect: S.I. 1994/1443 amended Territorial extent & classification: S. General. - 8p.: 30 cm. - 978-0-11-070563-7 £3.00

Criminal law

The Antisocial Behaviour etc. (Scotland) Act 2004 (Commencement and Savings) Amendment Order 2006 No. 2006/104 (C.13). - Enabling power: Antisocial Behaviour etc. (Scotland) Act 2004, ss. 141 (2), 145 (2). Bringing into operation various provisions of the 2004 Act on 31.03.2006. - Issued: 13.03.2006. Made: 06.03.2006. Effect: S.S.I. 2004/420 amended. Territorial extent & classification: S. General. - 2p.: 30 cm. - 978-0-11-069995-0 £3.00

The Bail Conditions (Methods of Monitoring Compliance and Specification of Devices) (Scotland) Regulations 2006 No. 2006/7. - Enabling power: Criminal Procedure (Scotland) Act 1995, ss. 24B (1) (b), 24D (4). - Issued: 19.01.2006. Made: 11.01.2006. Laid before the Scottish Parliament: 13.01.2006. Coming into force: 20.02.2006 except for para. 1 (3); 16.04.2006 for para. 1 (3). Effect: S.S.I. 2005/142 revoked (16.04.2006). Territorial extent & classification: S. General. - 4p.: 30 cm. - 978-0-11-069901-1 £3.00

The Community Justice Authorities (Establishment, Constitution and Proceedings) (Scotland) Order 2006 No. 2006/182. - Enabling power: Management of Offenders etc. (Scotland) Act 2005, s. 3 (1). - Issued: 06.04.2006. Made: 30.03.2006. Coming into force: 03.04.2006. Effect: None. Territorial extent & classification: S. General. - 8p.: 30 cm. - 978-0-11-070226-1 £3.00

The Crime (International Co-operation) Act 2003 (Commencement No. 2) (Scotland) Order 2006 No. 2006/281 (C.27). - Enabling power: Crime (International Co-operation) Act 2003, s. 94 (3) (a). Bringing into operation various provisions of the 2003 Act on 11.06.2006 in accord. with art. 2. - Issued: 31.05.2006. Made: 24.05.2006. Effect: None. Territorial extent & classification: S. General. - 2p.: 30 cm. - 978-0-11-070552-1 £3.00

The Criminal Justice (Scotland) Act 2003 (Commencement No. 7) Order 2006 No. 2006/85 (C.10). - Enabling power: Criminal Justice (Scotland) Act 2003, s. 89 (2) (3). Bringing into operation various provisions of the 2003 Act on 02.04.2006. - Issued: 06.03.2006. Made: 21.02.2006. Effect: None. Territorial extent & classification: S. General. - 2p.: 30 cm. - 978-0-11-069981-3 £3.00

The Criminal Justice (Scotland) Act 2003 (Commencement No. 8) Order 2006 No. 2006/168 (C.17). - Enabling power: Criminal Justice (Scotland) Act 2003, s. 89 (2) (3). Bringing into operation various provisions of the 2003 Act on 01.04.2006. - Issued: 29.03.2006. Made: 22.03.2006. Effect: None. Territorial extent & classification: S. General. - Copies are supplied from TSO's On-Demand Publishing Service. - 4p.: 30 cm. - 978-0-11-070198-1 £3.00

The Criminal Justice (Scotland) Act 2003 (Commencement No. 9) Order 2006 No. 2006/332 (C.30). - Enabling power: Criminal Justice (Scotland) Act 2003, s. 89 (2) (3). Bringing into operation various provisions of the 2003 Act on 19.06.2006 & 20.06.2006 in accord. with art. 2. - Issued: 21.06.2006. Made: 07.06.2006. Effect: None. Territorial extent & classification: S. General. - 4p.: 30 cm. - 978-0-11-070697-9 £3.00

The Home Detention Curfew Licence (Prescribed Standard Conditions) (Scotland) Order 2006 No. 2006/315. - Enabling power: Prisoners and Criminal Proceedings (Scotland) Act 1993, s. 12AA (3) (5). - Issued: 19.06.2006. Made: 08.06.2006. Laid before the Scottish Parliament: 08.06.2006. Coming into force: 03.07.2006. Effect: None. Territorial extent & classification: S. General. - 4p.: 30 cm. - 978-0-11-070629-0 £3.00

The Management of Offenders etc. (Scotland) Act 2005 (Commencement No. 1) Order No. 2006/48 (C.6). - Enabling power: Management of Offenders etc. (Scotland) Act 2005, s. 24 (2) (3). Bringing into operation various provisions of the 2005 Act on 08.02.2006 & 03.04.2006. - Issued: 14.02.2006. Made: 07.02.2006. Effect: None. Territorial extent & classification: S. General. - 4p.: 30 cm. - 978-0-11-069938-7 £3.00

The Management of Offenders etc. (Scotland) Act 2005 (Commencement No. 2) Order 2006 No. 2006/331 (C.29). - Enabling power: Management of Offenders etc. (Scotland) Act 2005, s. 24 (2) (3). Bringing into operation various provisions of the 2005 Act on 20.06.2006; 03.07.2006 in accord. with art. 3. - Issued: 22.06.2006. Made: 07.06.2006. Effect: None. Territorial extent & classification: S. General. - 4p.: 30 cm. - 978-0-11-070707-5 £3.00

The Management of Offenders etc. (Scotland) Act 2005 (Commencement No. 3) Order 2006 No. 2006/545 (C.42). - Enabling power: Management of Offenders etc. (Scotland) Act 2005, s. 24 (2) (3). Bringing into operation various provisions of the 2005 Act on 01.12.2006; 02.04.2007 in accord. with art. 2. - Issued: 22.11.2006. Made: 14.11.2006. Effect: None. Territorial extent & classification: S. General. - 2p.: 30 cm. - 978-0-11-071172-0 £3.00

The Management of Offenders etc. (Scotland) Act 2005 (Designation of Partner Bodies) Order 2006 No. 2006/63. - Enabling power: Management of Offenders etc. (Scotland) Act 2005, s. 3 (23). - Issued: 22.02.2006. Made: 14.02.2006. Laid before the Scottish Parliament: 16.02.2006. Coming into force: 03.04.2006. Effect: None. Territorial extent & classification: S. General. - 4p.: 30 cm. - 978-0-11-069951-6 £3.00

The Management of Offenders etc. (Scotland) Act 2005 (Supplementary Provisions) Order 2006 No. 2006/389. - Enabling power: Management of Offenders etc. (Scotland) Act 2005, s. 22 (1) (2). - Issued: 10.07.2006. Made: 29.06.2006. Coming into force: 30.06.2006 in accord. with art. 1 (1). Effect: 1980 c. 55; S.I. 2005/1515 amended. Territorial extent & classification: S. General. - Supersedes draft S.S.I. (ISBN 0110704894) issued 18.05.2006. - 4p.: 30 cm. - 978-0-11-070836-2 £3.00

The Police, Public Order and Criminal Justice (Scotland) Act 2006 (Commencement No. 1) Order 2006 No. 2006/432 (C.34). - Enabling power: Police, Public Order and Criminal Justice (Scotland) Act 2006, s. 104 (1). Bringing into operation various provisions of the 2006 Act on 01.09.2006. - Issued: 24.08.2006. Made: 16.08.2006. Effect: None. Territorial extent & classification: S. General. - 4p.: 30 cm. - 978-0-11-070922-2 £3.00

The Police, Public Order and Criminal Justice (Scotland) Act 2006 (Commencement No. 2) Order 2006 No. 2006/607 (C.46). - Enabling power: Police, Public Order and Criminal Justice (Scotland) Act 2006, s. 104 (1). Bringing into operation various provisions of the 2006 Act on 01.01.2007. - Issued: 29.12.2006. Made: 13.12.2006. Effect: None. Territorial extent & classification: S. General. - 8p.: 30 cm. - 978-0-11-071429-5 £3.00

The Private Landlord Registration (Information and Fees) (Scotland) Amendment Regulations 2006 No. 2006/28. - Enabling power: Antisocial Behaviour etc. (Scotland) Act 2004, s. 83 (3). - Issued: 02.02.2006. Made: 25.01.2006. Laid before the Scottish Parliament: 26.01.2005. Coming into force: 31.01.2006. Effect: S.S.I. 2005/558 amended. Territorial extent & classification: S. General. - 4p.: 30 cm. - 978-0-11-069917-2 £3.00

The Restriction of Liberty Order (Scotland) Regulations 2006 No. 2006/8. - Enabling power: Criminal Procedure (Scotland) Act 1995, ss. 245A (8), 245C (3). - Issued: 19.01.2006. Made: 11.01.2006. Laid before the Scottish Parliament: 13.01.2006. Coming into force: 20.02.2006 except for reg 1 (3); 16.04.2006 for reg 1 (3). Effect: S.I. 1998/1802 revoked (16.04.2006). Territorial extent & classification: S. General. - 8p.: 30 cm. - 978-0-11-069902-8 £3.00

The Risk Assessment and Minimisation (Accreditation Scheme) (Scotland) Order 2006 No. 2006/190. - Enabling power: Criminal Justice (Scotland) Act 2003, s. 11 (1) (1A). - Issued: 07.04.2006. Made: 29.03.2006. Coming into force: 30.03.2006. Effect: None. Territorial extent & classification: S. General. - 12p.: 30 cm. - 978-0-11-070234-6 £3.00

The Serious Organised Crime and Police Act 2005 (Commencement No. 2) (Scotland) Order 2006 No. 2006/166 (C.15). - Enabling power: Serious Organised Crime and Police Act 2005, s. 178 (3) (4) (5) (9). Bringing into operation various provisions of the 2005 Act on 01.04.2006; 01.05.2006. - Issued: 29.03.2006. Made: 22.03.2006. Effect: None. Territorial extent & classification: S. General. - Copies are supplied from TSO's On-Demand Publishing Service. - 8p.: 30 cm. - 978-0-11-070195-0 £3.00

The Serious Organised Crime and Police Act 2005 (Specified Persons for Financial Reporting Orders) (Scotland) Order 2006 No. 2006/170. - Enabling power: Serious Organised Crime and Police Act 2005, s. 79 (9). - Issued: 29.03.2006. Made: 22.03.2006. Laid before the Scottish Parliament: 23.03.2006. Coming into force: 01.05.2006. Effect: None. Territorial extent & classification: S. General. - 4p.: 30 cm. - 978-0-11-070201-8 £3.00

Crofters, cottars and small landholders

The Croft House Grant (Scotland) Regulations 2006 No. 2006/214. - Enabling power: Crofters (Scotland) Act 1993, ss. 42, 44, 45. - Issued: 12.07.2006. Made: 20.04.2006. Laid before the Scottish Parliament: 21.04.2006. Coming into force: 15.05.2006. Effect: S.I. 1990/944 revoked. Territorial extent & classification: S. General. - 12p.: 30 cm. - 978-0-11-070857-7 £3.00

The Crofting Counties Agricultural Grants (Scotland) Scheme 2006 No. 2006/24. - Enabling power: Crofters (Scotland) Act 1993, ss. 42 (1) (2) (3), 46 (4). - Issued: 30.01.2006. Made: 18.01.2006. Laid before the Scottish Parliament: 24.01.2006. Coming into force: 25.01.2006. Effect: S.I. 1988/559; 1992/3291; 1994/1013 revoked. Territorial extent & classification: S. General. - 8p.: 30 cm. - 978-0-11-069912-7 £3.00

District Courts

Act of Adjournal (Criminal Procedure Rules Amendment No. 4) (Miscellaneous) 2006 No. 2006/436. - Enabling power: Criminal Procedure (Scotland) Act 1995, s. 305. - Issued: 30.08.2006. Made: 22.08.2006. Coming into force: 01.09.2006. Effect: S.I. 1996/513 amended. Territorial extent & classification: S. General. - 8p.: 30 cm. - 978-0-11-070926-0 £3.00

Education

The Academic Awards and Distinctions (The Robert Gordon University) (Scotland) Order of Council 2006 No. 2006/452. - Enabling power: Further and Higher Education (Scotland) Act 1992, ss. 48, 60 (3). - Issued: 07.09.2006. Made: 04.09.2006. Laid before the Scottish Parliament: 11.09.2006. Coming into force: 04.10.2006. Effect: S.I. 1992/1189 amended. Territorial extent & classification: S. General. - 4p.: 30 cm. - 978-0-11-070995-6 £3.00

The Additional Support Needs Tribunals for Scotland (Practice and Procedure) Rules 2006 No. 2006/88. - Enabling power: Education (Additional Support for Learning) (Scotland) Act 2004, ss. 17 (4), 34 (2), sch. 1, para. 11. - Issued: 07.03.2006. Made: 28.02.2006. Laid before the Scottish Parliament: 01.03.2006. Coming into force: 27.03.2006. Effect: S.S.I. 2005/514 revoked. Territorial extent & classification: S. General. - These Rules supersede S.S.I. 2005/514 and are being issued free of charge to all known recipients of that instrument. - 24p.: 30 cm. - 978-0-11-069984-4 £4.00

The Designation of Institutions of Higher Education (Scotland) Amendment Order 2006 No. 2006/398. - Enabling power: Further and Higher Education (Scotland) Act 1992, ss. 44, 60. - Issued: 20.07.2006. Made: 13.07.2006. Laid before the Scottish Parliament: 14.07.2006. Coming into force: 17.07.2006. Effect: S.I. 1992/1025 amended. Territorial extent & classification: S. General. - This Scottish Statutory Instrument has been made in consequence of a defect in S.S.I. 2006/279 (ISBN 0110705270) and is being issued free of charge to all known recipients of that instrument. - 4p.: 30 cm. - 978-0-11-070879-9 £3.00

The Designation of Institutions of Higher Education (Scotland) Order 2006 No. 2006/279. - Enabling power: Further and Higher Education (Scotland) Act 1992, s. 44. - Issued: 30.05.2006. Made: 23.05.2006. Laid before the Scottish Parliament: 23.05.2006. Coming into force: 13.06.2006. Effect: S.I. 1992/1025 amended. Territorial extent & classification: S. General. - 2p.: 30 cm. - 978-0-11-070527-9 £3.00

The Education (Appeal Committee Procedures) (Scotland) Amendment Regulations 2006 No. 2006/322. - Enabling power: Education (Scotland) Act 1980, ss. 28D (3), 28H (5) & Education (Additional Support for Learning) (Scotland) Act 2004, s. 34, sch. 2, para. 6 (6). - Issued: 21.06.2006. Made: 08.06.2006. Laid before the Scottish Parliament: 08.06.2006. Coming into force: 30.06.2006. Effect: S.I. 1982/1736 amended. Territorial extent & classification: S. General. - 4p.: 30 cm. - 978-0-11-070676-4 £3.00

The Education (Assisted Places) (Scotland) Amendment Regulations 2006 No. 2006/317. - Enabling power: Education (Scotland) Act 1980, ss. 75A (9) (10), 75B. - Issued: 19.06.2006. Made: 08.06.2006. Laid before the Scottish Parliament: 09.06.2006. Coming into force: 01.08.2006. Effect: S.S.I. 2001/222 amended. Territorial extent & classification: S. General. - 4p.: 30 cm. - 978-0-11-070636-8 £3.00

The Education (Graduate Endowment, Student Fees and Support) (Scotland) Amendment Regulations 2006 No. 2006/323. - Enabling power: Education (Scotland) Act 1980, ss. 49 (3), 73 (f), 73B, 74 (1) & Education (Fees and Awards) Act 1983, ss. 1, 2 & Education (Graduate Endowment and Student Support) (Scotland) Act 2001, s. 1. - Issued: 21.06.2006. Made: 06.06.2006. Laid before the Scottish Parliament: 08.06.2006. Coming into force: 30.06.2006. Effect: S.I. 1992/580; 1995/1739; 1997/93; 1999/1131; S.S.I. 2000/200; 2001/280; 2004/273 amended. Territorial extent & classification: S. General. - 60p.: 30 cm. - 978-0-11-070677-1 £9.00

The Education (Student Loans) Amendment (Scotland) Regulations 2006 No. 2006/316. - Enabling power: Education (Student Loans) Act 1990, s. 1 (7), sch. 2, para. 1 (1) (a). - Issued: 19.06.2006. Made: 06.06.2006. Laid before the Scottish Parliament: 07.06.2006. Coming into force: 01.08.2006. Effect: S.I. 1998/211 amended in relation to Scotland. Territorial extent & classification: S. General. - 4p.: 30 cm. - 978-0-11-070630-6 £3.00

The Education (Student Loans for Tuition Fees) (Repayment and Allowances) (Scotland) Amendment Regulations 2006 No. 2006/326. - Enabling power: Education (Scotland) Act 1990, ss. 73 (f), 73B, 74 (1). - Issued: 21.06.2006. Made: 08.06.2006. Laid before the Scottish Parliament: 09.06.2006. Coming into force: 01.07.2006. Effect: S.S.I. 1999/1131; 2000/110 amended. Territorial extent & classification: S. General. - 4p.: 30 cm. - 978-0-11-070711-2 £3.00

The Education (Student Loans for Tuition Fees) (Scotland) Regulations 2006 No. 2006/333. - Enabling power: Education (Scotland) Act 1980, ss. 73 (f), 73B, 74 (1). - Issued: 23.06.2006. Made: 07.06.2006. Laid before the Scottish Parliament: 08.06.2006. Coming into force: 01.07.2006. Effect: None. Territorial extent & classification: S. General. - 20p.: 30 cm. - 978-0-11-070696-2 £3.50

The Fundable Bodies (Scotland) Order 2006 No. 2006/480. - Enabling power: Further and Higher Education (Scotland) Act 2005, ss. 7 (1), 34 (2) (a). - Issued: 09.10.2006. Made: 28.09.2006. Coming into force: 30.09.2006. Effect: 2005 asp 6 modified. Territorial extent & classification: S. General. - 4p.: 30 cm. - 978-0-11-071061-7 *£3.00*

The Registration of Independent Schools (Scotland) Regulations 2006 No. 2006/324. - Enabling power: Education (Scotland) Act 1980, ss. 98 (3), 98A (2). - Issued: 21.06.2006. Made: 08.06.2006. Laid before the Scottish Parliament: 08.06.2006. Coming into force: 01.07.2006. Effect: S.S.I. 2005/571 revoked. Territorial extent & classification: S. General. - 8p.: 30 cm. - 978-0-11-070688-7 *£3.00*

The Robert Gordon University (Establishment) (Scotland) Order 2006 No. 2006/276. - Enabling power: Further and Higher Education (Scotland) Act 1992, ss. 46, 60. - Issued: 30.05.2006. Made: 23.05.2006. Laid before the Scottish Parliament: 23.05.2006. Coming into force: 13.06.2006. Effect: None. Territorial extent & classification: S. General. - 2p.: 30 cm. - 978-0-11-070526-2 *£3.00*

The Robert Gordon University (Scotland) Amendment Order of Council 2006 No. 2006/404. - Enabling power: Further and Higher Education (Scotland) Act 1992, ss. 45, 60. - Issued: 27.07.2006. Made: 17.07.2006. Laid before the Scottish Parliament: 20.07.2006. Coming into force: 21.07.2006. Effect: S.S.I. 2006/298 amended. Territorial extent & classification: S. General. - This Scottish statutory instrument has been made in consequence of a defect in S.S.I. 2006/298 (ISBN 0110706056) and is being issued free of charge to all known recipients of that instrument. This amending order revokes the revocation of S.I. 1993/1157 (ISBN 0110341570) by S.S.I. 2006/298. - 4p.: 30 cm. - 978-0-11-070885-0 *£3.00*

The Robert Gordon University (Scotland) Order of Council 2006 No. 2006/298. - Enabling power: Further and Higher Education (Scotland) Act 1992, ss. 45, 60. - Issued: 09.06.2006. Made: 30.05.2006. Laid before the Scottish Parliament: 06.06.2006. Coming into force: 28.06.2006. Effect: S.I. 1993/1157 revoked. Territorial extent & classification: S. General- With correction slip dated September 2006. - 8p.: 30 cm. - 978-0-11-070605-4 *£3.00*

The Robert Gordon University (Transfer and Closure) (Scotland) Order 2006 No. 2006/461. - Enabling power: Further and Higher Education (Scotland) Act 1992, ss. 47 (1) 1(A) (2) (4) (6). - Issued: 18.09.2006. Made: 11.09.2006. Laid before the Scottish Parliament: 12.09.2006. Coming into force: 04.10.2006. Effect: S.I. 1981/1221 revoked. Territorial extent & classification: S. General. - 4p.: 30 cm. - 978-0-11-071009-9 *£3.00*

The Scottish Schools (Parental Involvement) Act 2006 (Commencement No. 1) Order 2006 No. 2006/454 (C.36). - Enabling power: Scottish Schools (Parental Involvement) Act 2006, s. 24 (2). Bringing into operation various provisions of the 2006 Act on 12.09.2006 in acc.with art. 2. - Issued: 12.09.2006. Made: 05.09.2006. Effect: None. Territorial extent & classification: S. General. - 2p.: 30 cm. - 978-0-11-070999-4 *£3.00*

The Standards in Scotland's Schools etc. Act 2000 (Commencement No. 8 and Savings) Order 2006 No. 2006/232 (C.20). - Enabling power: Standards in Scotland's Schools etc. Act 2000, s. 61 (2) (3) (4). Bringing into operation various provisions of the 2000 Act on 01.07.2006. in acc.with art. 2. - Issued: 08.05.2006. Made: 28.04.2006. Effect: None. Territorial extent & classification: S. General. - 4p.: 30 cm. - 978-0-11-070376-3 *£3.00*

The St Mary's Music School (Aided Places) (Scotland) Amendment Regulations 2006 No. 2006/318. - Enabling power: Education (Scotland) Act 1980, ss. 73 (f), 74 (1). - Issued: 19.06.2006. Made: 08.06.2006. Laid before the Scottish Parliament: 09.06.2006. Coming into force: 01.08.2006. Effect: S.S.I. 2001/223 amended. Territorial extent & classification: S. General. - 4p.: 30 cm. - 978-0-11-070639-9 *£3.00*

The Student Fees (Specification) (Scotland) Order 2006 No. 2006/401. - Enabling power: Further and Higher Education (Scotland) Act 2005, ss. 9 (6) (7), 34 (2). - Issued: 21.07.2006. Made: 28.06.2006. Coming into force: 03.07.2006. Effect: None. Territorial extent & classification: S. General. - 4p.: 30 cm. - 978-0-11-070880-5 *£3.00*

The Teaching Council (Scotland) (Legal Assessor) Rules 2006 No. 2006/455. - Enabling power: Teaching Council (Scotland) Act 1965, ss. 10 (6), 12 (7), sch. 2, para. 3. - Issued: 12.09.2006. Made: 02.09.2006. Coming into force: 22.09.2006. Effect: S.I. 1981/721 revoked. Territorial extent & classification: S. General. - 4p.: 30 cm. - 978-0-11-071000-6 *£3.00*

Electricity

The Electricity (Applications for Consent) Amendment (Scotland) Regulations 2006 No. 2006/18. - Enabling power: Electricity Act 1989, ss. 36 (8), 60 (3), sch. 8, para. 1 (3). - Issued: 26.01.2006. Made: 16.01.2006. Laid before the Scottish Parliament: 20.01.2006. Coming into force: 13.03.2006. Effect: S.I. 1990/455 amended in relation to Scotland. Territorial extent & classification: S. General. - 4p.: 30 cm. - 978-0-11-069911-0 *£3.00*

The Renewables Obligation (Scotland) Order 2006 No. 2006/173. - Enabling power: Electricity Act 1989, ss. 32 to 32C. - Issued: 30.03.2006. Made: 20.03.2006. Coming into force: 01.04.2006. Effect: S.S.I. 2005/185 revoked with savings. Territorial extent & classification: S. General. - 40p.: 30 cm. - 978-0-11-070209-4 *£6.50*

Electronic communications

The Electronic Communications (Scotland) Order 2006 No. 2006/367. - Enabling power: Electronic Communications Act 2000, ss. 8, 9. - Issued: 03.07.2006. Made: 22.06.2006. Coming into force: 23.06.2006 in accord. with art. 1 (1). Effect: 1981 c.37; 1980 c.44; 1985 c.63; 1996 c.58; 2005 asp 5, 7 amended & S.S.I. 2000/200 amended. Territorial extent & classification: S. General. - Supersedes draft S.S.I. (ISBN 0110704681) issued 17.05.2006. - 8p.: 30 cm. - 978-0-11-070766-2 £3.00

Energy conservation

The Home Energy Efficiency Scheme (Scotland) Regulations 2006 No. 2006/570. - Enabling power: Social Security Act 1990, s. 15. - Issued: 06.12.2006. Made: 29.11.2006. Laid before the Scottish Parliament: 30.11.2006. Coming into force: 01.01.2007. Effect: S.I. 1997/790 (in relation to Scotland); 1999/1018 & S.S.I. 2001/267; 2003/284, 529; 2004/188; 2005/144 revoked with savings. Territorial extent & classification: S. General. - 12p.: 30 cm. - 978-0-11-071270-3 £3.00

Enforcement

The Diligence against Earnings (Variation) (Scotland) Regulations 2006 No. 2006/116. - Enabling power: Debtors (Scotland) Act 1987, ss. 49 (7) (a), 53 (3), 63 (6), 71. - Issued: 14.03.2006. Made: 07.03.2006. Laid before the Scottish Parliament: 08.03.2006. Coming into force: 05.04.2006. Effect: 1987 c.18 amended. Territorial extent & classification: S. General. - 8p.: 30 cm. - 978-0-11-070028-1 £3.00

Environmental protection

The Antisocial Behaviour etc. (Scotland) Act 2004 (Commencement and Savings) Amendment Order 2006 No. 2006/104 (C.13). - Enabling power: Antisocial Behaviour etc. (Scotland) Act 2004, ss. 141 (2), 145 (2). Bringing into operation various provisions of the 2004 Act on 31.03.2006. - Issued: 13.03.2006. Made: 06.03.2006. Effect: S.S.I. 2004/420 amended. Territorial extent & classification: S. General. - 2p.: 30 cm. - 978-0-11-069995-0 £3.00

The Environmental Assessment (Scotland) Act 2005 (Commencement and Savings) Order 2006 No. 2006/19 (C.2). - Enabling power: Environmental Assessment (Scotland) Act 2005, ss. 22 (2), 26. Bringing into operation various provisions of the 2005 Act on 20.02.2006. - Issued: 03.02.2006. Made: 19.01.2006. Effect: None. Territorial extent & classification: S. General. - 2p.: 30 cm. - 978-0-11-069922-6 £3.00

The Environmental Noise (Scotland) Regulations 2006 No. 2006/465. - Enabling power: European Communities Act 1972, s. 2 (2). - Issued: 20.09.2006. Made: 12.09.2006. Laid before the Scottish Parliament: 13.09.2006. Coming into force: 05.10.2006. Effect: None. Territorial extent & classification: S. General. - EC note: Implements Directive 2002/49/EC relating to the assessment and management of environmental noise. - 24p.: 30 cm. - 978-0-11-071012-9 £4.00

The Waste Management Licensing Amendment (Scotland) Regulations 2006 No. 2006/541. - Enabling power: European Communities Act 1972, s. 2 (2). - Issued: 16.11.2006. Made: 08.11.2006. Laid before the Scottish Parliament: 09.11.2006. Coming into force: 01.12.2006. Effect: 1995 c. 25; S.I. 1994/1056 amended in relation to Scotland. Territorial extent & classification: S. General. - These Regulations transpose the requirements of Articles 4 and 11 of the Waste Framework Directive (formerly Directive 75/442/EEC and now consolidated as Directive 2006/12/EC, and Article 3 of the Hazardous Waste Directive (91/689/EC as amended by Council Directive 94/31/EC and Regulation (EC) No. 166/2006 of the European Parliament and of the Council). The Regulations also implement Commission Decision 2000/532/EC (as amended by Commission Decisions 2001/118/EC, 2001/119/EC and 2001/573/EC) establishing a list of wastes pursuant to Article 1(a) of the Waste Framework Directive and Article 1(4) of the Hazardous Waste Directive. The list of wastes contained within that Decision is known as the European Waste Catalogue. - 56p.: 30 cm. - 978-0-11-071157-7 £9.00

The Waste Management Licensing (Water Environment) (Scotland) Regulations 2006 No. 2006/128. - Enabling power: Water Environment and Water Services (Scotland) Act 2003, ss. 20, 36 (2) (3), sch. 2. - Issued: 16.03.2006. Made: 08.03.2006. Laid before the Scottish Parliament: 09.03.2006. Coming into force: 01.04.2006. Effect: S.I. 1994/1056 amended in relatin to Scotland. Territorial extent & classification: S. General. - 4p.: 30 cm. - 978-0-11-070078-6 £3.00

The Water Environment and Water Services (Scotland) Act 2003 (Designation of Responsible Authorities and Functions) Order 2006 No. 2006/126. - Enabling power: Water Environment and Water Services (Scotland) Act 2003, s. 2 (8). - Issued: 16.03.2006. Made: 08.03.2006. Laid before the Scottish Parliament: 09.03.2006. Coming into force: 01.04.2006. Effect: None. Territorial extent & classification: S. General. - 4p.: 30 cm. - 978-0-11-070075-5 £3.00

The Water Environment (Consequential and Savings Provisions) (Scotland) Order 2006 No. 2006/181. - Enabling power: Water Environment and Water Services (Scotland) Act 2003, ss. 36 (3), 37. - Issued: 05.04.2006. Made: 29.03.2006. Coming into force: 01.04.2006. Effect: 1961 c. 41; 1964 c. 40; 1974 c. 40; 1980 c. 45; 1990 c. 43; 1991 c. iv, c. 28, c. 34; 1993 c. 12; 1994 c. iii; 1995 c. 25, c. 46; 2003 asp 15; 2004 asp 10 amended & S.I. 1993/1155; 1996/973; 1999/1750 amended & 1951 c. 66 repealed with savings; 1965 c. 13 repealed & S.I. 1973/1846; 1983/1182; 1984/864, 865; 1986/1623; 1993/1154, 1156; 1995/2382; S.S.I. 2000/432; 2003/168 revoked. Territorial extent & classification: S. General. - Superseded by the draft S.S.I. (ISBN 0110699564) issued 23.02.2006. - 12p.: 30 cm. - 978-0-11-070222-3 *£3.00*

The Water Environment (Consequential Provisions) (Scotland) Order 2006 No. 2006/127. - Enabling power: Water Environment and Water Services (Scotland) Act 2003, ss.36 (3), 37. - Issued: 16.03.2006. Made: 08.03.2006. Laid before the Scottish Parliament: 09.03.2006. Coming into force: 01.04.2006. Effect: S.I. 1993/1155; S.S.I. 2000/323; 2005/22, 225, 569 amended & S.I. 1987/1782; 1998/2746 revoked. Territorial extent & classification: S. General. - 4p.: 30 cm. - 978-0-11-070077-9 *£3.00*

The Water Environment (Controlled Activities) (Third Party Representations etc) (Scotland) Regulations 2006 No. 2006/553. - Enabling power: Water Environment and Water Services (Scotland) Act 2003, s. 20, sch. 2. - Issued: 27.11.2006. Made: 21.11.2006. Laid before the Scottish Parliament: 22.11.2006. Coming into force: 14.12.2006. Effect: S.S.I. 2005/348 amended. Territorial extent & classification: S. General. - 8p.: 30 cm. - 978-0-11-071196-6 *£3.00*

The Water Environment (Oil Storage) (Scotland) Regulations 2006 No. 2006/133. - Enabling power: Water Environment and Water Services (Scotland) Act 2003, ss. 20, 36 (2) (3), sch. 2. - Issued: 24.03.2006. Made: 08.03.2006. Laid before the Scottish Parliament: 10.03.2006. Coming into force: 01.04.2006. Effect: S.S.I. 2003/531 amended. Territorial extent & classification: S. General. - 8p.: 30 cm. - 978-0-11-070175-2 *£3.00*

The Water Environment (Relevant Enactments) Order 2006 No. 2006/554. - Enabling power: Water Environment and Water Services (Scotland) Act 2003, s. 2 (8). - Issued: 28.11.2006. Made: 21.11.2006. Laid before the Scottish Parliament: 22.11.2006. Coming into force: 14.12.2006. Effect: None. Territorial extent & classification: S. General. - 4p.: 30 cm. - 978-0-11-071197-3 *£3.00*

Ethical standards

The Ethical Standards in Public Life etc. (Scotland) Act 2000 (Codes of Conduct for Members of certain Scottish Public Authorities) Order 2006 No. 2006/26. - Enabling power: Ethical Standards in Public Life etc. (Scotland) Act 2000, s. 32 (1). - Issued: 30.01.2006. Made: 24.01.2006. Laid before the Scottish Parliament: 25.01.2006. Coming into force: 01.04.2006. Effect: None. Territorial extent & classification: S. General. - 4p.: 30 cm. - 978-0-11-069913-4 *£3.00*

Family law

The Divorce and Dissolution etc. (Pension Protection Fund) (Scotland) Regulations 2006 No. 2006/254. - Enabling power: Family Law (Scotland) Act 1985, s. 10 (8B). - Issued: 18.05.2006. Made: 11.05.2006. Laid before the Scottish Parliament: 12.05.2006. Coming into force: 03.06.2006. Effect: None. Territorial extent & classification: S. General. - 4p.: 30 cm. - 978-0-11-070484-5 *£3.00*

The Divorce (Religious Bodies) (Scotland) Regulations 2006 No. 2006/253. - Enabling power: Divorce (Scotland) Act 1976, s. 3A (7). - Issued: 18.05.2006. Made: 11.05.2006. Laid before the Scottish Parliament: 12.05.2006. Coming into force: 03.06.2006. Effect: None. Territorial extent & classification: S. General. - 2p.: 30 cm. - 978-0-11-070487-6 *£3.00*

The Family Law (Scotland) Act 2006 (Commencement, Transitional Provisions and Savings) Order 2006 No. 2006/212 (C.19). - Enabling power: Family Law (Scotland) Act 2006, s. 46(2) (3). Bringing into operation various provisions on 04.05.2006. - Issued: 27.04.2006. Made: 19.04.2006. Effect: None. Territorial extent & classification: S. General. - 4p.: 30 cm. - 978-0-11-070319-0 *£3.00*

The Family Law (Scotland) Act 2006 (Consequential Modifications) Order 2006 No. 2006/384. - Enabling power: Family Law (Scotland) Act 2006, s. 44 (1) (2). - Issued: 06.07.2006. Made: 29.06.2006. Coming into force: 30.06.2006. Effect: 1964 c.41; 1968 c.70; 1977 c.15; 1981 c. 59; 1984 c.56; 1985 c.37; 2004 c.33 amended. Territorial extent & classification: S. General. - Supersedes draft S.S.I. (ISBN 0110708075) issued 25.05.2006. - 4p.: 30 cm. - 978-0-11-070807-2 *£3.00*

Farriers Registration Council

The Farriers (Registration) Act 1975 (Commencement No. 4) (Scotland) Order 2006 No. 2006/581 (C.44). - Enabling power: Farriers (Registration) Act 1975, s. 19 (3). Bringing into operation various provisions of the 1975 Act on 30.03.2007, in accord. with art. 2. - Issued: 12.12.2006. Made: 04.12.2006. Effect: None. Territorial extent & classification: S. General. - 2p.: 30 cm. - 978-0-11-071352-6 *£3.00*

Feudal tenure

The Abolition of Feudal Tenure etc. (Scotland) Act 2000 (Specified Day) Order 2006 No. 2006/109. - Enabling power: Abolition of Feudal Tenure etc. (Scotland) Act 2000, s. 20 (6) (b). - Issued: 14.03.2006. Made: 07.03.2006. Laid before the Scottish Parliament: 08.03.2006. Coming into force: 31.03.2006. Effect: None. Territorial extent & classification: S. General. - 2p.: 30 cm. - 978-0-11-070020-5 *£3.00*

Fire safety

The Fire Safety (Scotland) Regulations 2006 No. 2006/456. - Enabling power: Fire (Scotland) Act 2005, ss. 57, 58, 59 (2), 61 (8), 75 (b), 76 (6), 88 (2). - Issued: 13.09.2006. Made: 05.09.2006. Laid before the Scottish Parliament: 07.09.2006. Coming into force: 01.10.2006. Effect: None. Territorial extent & classification: S. General. - EC note: These Regs impose a number of specific duties in relation to fire safety measures so as to give effect in Scotland to Council Directives 89/391/EEC; 91/383/EEC; 89/654/EEC, 94/33/EC, 98/24/EC and 99/92/EC. - 20p.: 30 cm. - 978-0-11-071001-3 *£3.50*

The Fire (Scotland) Act 2005 (Commencement No. 3 and Savings) Order 2006 No. 2006/458 (C.37). - Enabling power: Fire (Scotland) Act 2005, ss. 88 (2) (b), 90. Bringing into operation various provisions of the 2005 Act on 01.10.2006. - Issued: 13.09.2006. Made: 05.09.2006. Effect: None. Territorial extent & classification: S. General. - 4p.: 30 cm. - 978-0-11-071003-7 *£3.00*

The Fire (Scotland) Act 2005 (Consequential Modifications and Savings) (No. 2) Order 2006 No. 2006/457. - Enabling power: Fire (Scotland) Act 2005, ss. 87 (1), 88 (2) (a). - Issued: 13.09.2006. Made: 05.09.2006. Laid before the Scottish Parliament: 07.09.2006. Coming into force: 01.10.2006. Effect: S.I. 1977/500; 1987/37; 1996/1513, 1592 modified in relation to Scotland & S.I. 1996/3256; S.S.I. 2002/114 modified & S.I. 1996/341; 1999/3242 amended in relation to Scotland & S.I. 1976/2003; 1997/1840 (with savings); 1999/1877 revoked in relation to Scotland & S.I. 1990/683 revoked. Territorial extent & classification: S. General. - 8p.: 30 cm. - 978-0-11-071002-0 *£3.00*

The Fire (Scotland) Act 2005 (Consequential Modifications and Savings) Order 2006 No. 2006/475. - Enabling power: Fire (Scotland) Act 2005, ss. 87, 88 (2). - Issued: 06.10.2006. Made: 28.09.2006. Coming into force: 01.10.2006 in accord. with art. 1. Effect: 23 acts amended and 1973 c. 11 repealed. Territorial extent & classification: S. General. - 16p.: 30 cm. - 978-0-11-071045-7 *£3.00*

Fire services

The Firefighters' Compensation Scheme (Scotland) Order 2006 No. 2006/338. - Enabling power: Fire and Rescue Services Act 2004, ss. 34 (1) to (5) (8), 60 (2). - Issued: 26.06.2006. Made: 08.06.2006. Laid before the Scottish Parliament: 09.06.2006. Coming into force: 01.07.2006. Effect: None. Territorial extent & classification: S. General. - 40p.: 30 cm. - 978-0-11-070756-3 *£6.50*

The Firefighters' Pension Scheme Amendment (Scotland) Order 2006 No. 2006/342. - Enabling power: Fire Services Act 1947, s. 26(1) to (5) & Superannuation Act 1972, ss. 12, 16. - Issued: 26.06.2006. Made: 08.06.2006. Laid before the Scottish Parliament: 09.06.2006. Coming into force: 01.07.2006. Effect: S.I. 1992/129 amended in relation to Scotland. Territorial extent & classification: S. General. - 20p.: 30 cm. - 978-0-11-070729-7 *£3.50*

Fish farming

The Environmental Impact Assessment (Scotland) Amendment Regulations 2006 No. 2006/614. - Enabling power: European Communities Act 1972, s. 2 (2) and Town and Country Planning (Scotland) Act 1997, s. 40. - Issued: 05.01.2007. Made: 21.12.2006. Laid before the Scottish Parliament: 22.12.2006. Coming into force: 01.02.2007. Effect: 1984 c.54; S.I. 1999/367 amended in relation to Scotland; S.S.I. 1999/1, 43; 2006/582 amended. Territorial extent & classification: S. General. - Copies are supplied by TSO's On-demand publishing service. With correction slip dated February 2007. EC note: These Regulations implement in Scotland the amendments made by Article 3 of Council Directive 2003/35/EC with regard to public participation and access to justice to Council Directive 85/337/EEC. - 24p.: 30 cm. - 978-0-11-071472-1 *£4.00*

Food

The Ceramic Articles in Contact with Food (Scotland) Regulations 2006 No. 2006/230. - Enabling power: Food Safety Act 1990, ss. 6 (4), 16 (2), 17 (1), 26 (1) (a), 2 (a) (3), 31, 48 (1) & Consumer Protection Act 1987, s. 11. - Issued: 10.05.2006. Made: 28.04.2006. Laid before the Scottish Parliament: 28.04.2006. Coming into force: In accord. with reg. 1 (2) on 20.05.2006 & 20.05.2007. Effect: S.S.I. 2005/616 amended & S.I. 1988/1647 revoked in relation to Scotland (20.05.2006). Territorial extent & classification: S. General. - EC note: Implements Council Directive 84/500/EEC as amended by Commission Directive 2005/31/EC regarding a declaration of compliance and performance criteria of the analytical method for ceramic articles intended to come into contact with foodstuffs. - 12p.: 30 cm. - 978-0-11-070393-0 *£3.00*

The Contaminants in Food (Scotland) Regulations 2006 No. 2006/306. - Enabling power: Food Safety Act 1990, ss. 6 (4), 16 (1) (a) (e) (f), 17 (2), 26 (1) (a) (2) (e) (3), 31 (1) (2) (b) (c) (f), 48 (1). - Issued: 20.06.2006. Made: 07.06.2006. Laid before the Scottish Parliament: 07.06.2006. Coming into force: 01.07.2006. Effect: 1990 c. 16 modified & S.I. 1990/2463 amended in relation to Scotland & S.S.I. 2005/606 revoked. Territorial extent & classification: S. General. - EC note: These Regulations make provision for the execution and enforcement of Commission Regulation (EC) 466/2001 (as corrected and amended) setting maximum levels of contaminants in foodstuffs. - 8p.: 30 cm. - 978-0-11-070651-1 *£3.00*

The Curd Cheese (Restriction on Placing on the Market) (Scotland) Regulations 2006 No. 2006/512. - Enabling power: European Communities Act 1972, s. 2 (2). - Issued: 26.10.2006. Made: 19.10.2006. Laid before the Scottish Parliament: 19.10.2006. Coming into force: 20.10.2006. Effect: None. Territorial extent & classification: S. General. - EC note: These Regulations, implement in relation to Scotland, Commission Decision 2006/694/EC prohibiting the placing on the market of curd cheese manufactured in a dairy establishment in the United Kingdom. - 4p.: 30 cm. - 978-0-11-071099-0 *£3.00*

The Dairy Produce Quotas (Scotland) Amendment Regulations 2006 No. 2006/119. - Enabling power: European Communities Act 1972, s. 2 (2). - Issued: 14.03.2006. Made: 07.03.2006. Laid before the Scottish Parliament: 09.03.2006. Coming into force: 31.03.2006. Effect: S.S.I. 2005/91 amended. Territorial extent & classification: S. General. - This Scottish Statutory Instrument has been made in consequence of defects in S.S.I. 2005/91 and is being issued free of charge to all known recipients of that instrument. - 4p.: 30 cm. - 978-0-11-070029-8 *£3.00*

The Fishery Products (Official Controls Charges) (Scotland) Regulations 2006 No. 2006/579. - Enabling power: European Communities Act 1972, s. 2 (2). - Issued: 11.12.2006. Made: 29.11.2006. Laid before the Scottish Parliament: 30.11.2006. Coming into force: 01.01.2007. Effect: S.S.I. 2005/597 revoked. Territorial extent & classification: S. General. - EC note: These Regulations provide for the execution and enforcement in relation to Scotland of Articles 26 and 27 of Regulation 882/2004 on official controls performed to ensure the verification of compliance with feed and food law, animal health and animal welfare rules, so far as those provisions require fees to be collected to cover the costs occasioned by official controls performed on fishery products under Annex III to Regulation 854/2004 laying down specific rules for the organisation of official controls on products of animal origin intended for human consumption. - 12p.: 30 cm. - 978-0-11-071340-3 *£3.00*

The Fish Labelling (Scotland) Amendment Regulations 2006 No. 2006/105. - Enabling power: Food Safety Act 1990, ss. 16 (1) (e) (f), 17 (2), 26 (1) (a). - Issued: 14.03.2006. Made: 06.03.2006. Laid before the Scottish Parliament: 07.03.2006. Coming into force: 06.04.2006. Effect: S.S.I. 2003/145 amended. Territorial extent & classification: S. General. - 12p.: 30 cm. - 978-0-11-069996-7 *£3.00*

The Food (Emergency Control) (Scotland) Revocation Regulations 2006 No. 2006/459. - Enabling power: European Communities Act 1972, s. 2(2). - Issued: 14.09.2006. Made: 07.09.2006. Laid before the Scottish Parliament: 08.09.2006. Coming into force: 01.10.2006. Effect: S.S.I. 2002/424, 425; 2003/396, 413, 414, 418, 419, 558; 2004/210; 2005/70 revoked. Territorial extent & classification: S. General. - 4p.: 30 cm. - 978-0-11-071007-5 *£3.00*

The Food for Particular Nutritional Uses (Addition of Substances for Specific Nutritional Purposes) (Scotland) Amendment Regulations 2006 No. 2006/556. - Enabling power: Food Safety Act 1990, ss. 16 (1) (f), 17 (1), 48 (1). - Issued: 30.11.2006. Made: 22.11.2006. Laid before the Scottish Parliament: 23.11.2006. Coming into force: 31.12.2006. Effect: S.S.I. 2002/397 amended. Territorial extent & classification: S. General. - EC note: Implements, in relation to Scotland, Commission Directive 2006/34/EC amending the Annex to Directive 2001/15/EC as regards the inclusion of certain substances. - 4p.: 30 cm. - 978-0-11-071209-3 *£3.00*

The Food Hygiene (Scotland) Regulations 2006 No. 2006/3. - Enabling power: European Communities Act 1972, s. 2 (2). - Issued: 16.01.2006. Made: 09.01.2006. Laid before the Scottish Parliament: 10.01.2006. Coming into force: 11.01.2006. Effect: S.I. 1995/614, 3124; 1996/1499, 3124; 1997/2964; 1998/871, 2424; 1999/1103 & S.S.I. 1999/186; 2000/62; 2002/255; 2003/311, 411; 2005/332, 616 amended & S.S.I. 2005/505 revoked. Territorial extent & classification: S. General. - EC note: These regs provide for the execution and enforcement of Regulations No. 852/2004; 853/2004; 854/2004 and implement these Commission Regulations 2073/2005; 2074/2005; 2075/2005; 2076/2005. - 44p.: 30 cm. - 978-0-11-069898-4 *£7.50*

The Meat (Official Controls Charges) (Scotland) Regulations 2006 No. 2006/580. - Enabling power: European Communities Act 1972, s. 2 (2). - Issued: 12.12.2006. Made: 29.11.2006. Laid before the Scottish Parliament: 30.11.2006. Coming into force: 01.01.2007. Effect: S.S.I. 2005/607 revoked. Territorial extent & classification: S. General. - EC note: These Regulations provide for the execution and enforcement in Scotland of Articles 26 and 27 of Regulation (EC) No. 882/2004 on official controls performed to ensure the verification of compliance with feed and food law, animal health and animal welfare rules in so far as those provisions require fees to be collected to cover the costs occasioned by official controls performed, first, on meat of domestic ungulates, meat from poultry and lagomorphs, meat of farmed game and meat of wild game under Regulation (EC) No. 854/2004 laying down specific rules for the organisation of official controls on products of animal origin intended for human consumption and, second, to verify compliance with the animal welfare rules set out in Council Directive 93/119/EC in so far as they apply in relation to animals slaughtered for human consumption at slaughterhouses. - 12p.: 30 cm. - 978-0-11-071350-2 *£3.00*

The Plastic Materials and Articles in Contact with Food (Scotland) (No. 2) Regulations 2006 No. 2006/517. - Enabling power: Food Safety Act 1990, ss. 6 (4), 16 (2), 17 (1) (2), 26 (1) (a) (3), 31, 48 (1). - Issued: 06.11.2006. Made: 25.10.2006. Laid before the Scottish Parliament: 26.10.2006. Coming into force: 19.11.2006. Effect: S.I. 1990/2463; S.S.I. 2005/243 amended & S.S.I. 2006/314 revoked. Territorial extent & classification: S. General. - EC note: The principal Directives implemented by these Regulations are: Council Directive 82/711/EEC, as amended by Commission Directives 93/8/EEC and 97/48/EC; Council Directive 85/572/EEC; Commission Directive 2002/72/EC, as amended by Commission Directives 2004/1/EC, 2004/19/EC and 2005/79/EC. - 36p.: 30 cm. - 978-0-11-071115-7 *£6.50*

The Plastic Materials and Articles in Contact with Food (Scotland) Regulations 2006 No. 2006/314. - Enabling power: Food Safety Act 1990, ss. 6 (4), 16 (2), 17 (1) (2), 26 (1) (a) (3), 31 (2), 48 (1). - Issued: 19.06.2006. Made: 07.06.2006. Laid before the Scottish Parliament: 07.06.2006. Coming into force: 30.06.2006. Effect: S.I. 1990/2463 & S.S.I. 2005/243 amended & S.I. 1998/1376 revoked in so far as it relates to Scotland & S.S.I. 2000/431; 2002/498; 2003/9; 2004/524; 2005/92 revoked. Territorial extent & classification: S. General. - Revoked by S.S.I. 2006/517 (ISBN 0110711157). EC note: These Regulations provide for the execution and enforcement of Commission Regulation 1895/2005 and also provide for the continued implementation of the following Directives, Council Directive 82/711/EEC (as amended by 93/8/EEC & 97/48/EC); 85/572/EEC; 2002/72/EC (as amended by 2004/1/EC & 2004/19/EC). - 80p.: 30 cm. - 978-0-11-070613-9 *£12.00*

The Rice Products (Restriction on First Placing on the Market) (Scotland) Regulations 2006 No. 2006/542. - Enabling power: European Communities Act 1972, s. 2 (2). - Issued: 16.11.2006. Made: 08.11.2006. Laid before the Scottish Parliament: 09.11.2006. Coming into force: 10.11.2006. Effect: None. Territorial extent & classification: S. General. - EC note: These Regulations implement in relation to Scotland Commission Decision 2006/601/EC on emergency measures regarding the non-authorised genetically modified organism "LL RICE 601" in rice products as amended by Commission Decision 2006/754/EC- 4p.: 30 cm. - 978-0-11-071168-3 *£3.00*

Forestry

The Environmental Impact Assessment (Scotland) Amendment Regulations 2006 No. 2006/614. - Enabling power: European Communities Act 1972, s. 2 (2) and Town and Country Planning (Scotland) Act 1997, s. 40. - Issued: 05.01.2007. Made: 21.12.2006. Laid before the Scottish Parliament: 22.12.2006. Coming into force: 01.02.2007. Effect: 1984 c.54; S.I. 1999/367 amended in relation to Scotland; S.S.I. 1999/1, 43; 2006/582 amended. Territorial extent & classification: S. General. - Copies are supplied by TSO's On-demand publishing service. With correction slip dated February 2007. EC note: These Regulations implement in Scotland the amendments made by Article 3 of Council Directive 2003/35/EC with regard to public participation and access to justice to Council Directive 85/337/EEC. - 24p.: 30 cm. - 978-0-11-071472-1 *£4.00*

Gaelic language

The Gaelic Language (Scotland) Act 2005 Commencement Order 2006 No. 2006/31 (C.3). - Enabling power: Gaelic Language (Scotland) Act 2005, s. 13 (2). Bringing into operation various provisions of the 2005 Act on 13.02.2006. - Issued: 02.02.2006. Made: 25.01.2006. Effect: None. Territorial extent & classification: S. General. - 2p.: 30 cm. - 978-0-11-069918-9 *£3.00*

Harbours, docks, piers and ferries

The Highland Council (Raasay) Harbour Revision Order 2006 No. 2006/17. - Enabling power: Harbours Act 1964, s. 14. - Issued: 31.01.2006. Made: 17.01.2006. Coming into force: 18.01.2006. Effect: None. Territorial extent & classification: S. Local. - 20p., col. map: 30 cm. - 978-0-11-069910-3 *£3.50*

High Court of Justiciary

Act of Adjournal (Criminal Procedure Rules Amendment No. 2) (Financial Reporting Orders) 2006 No. 2006/205. - Enabling power: Criminal Procedure (Scotland) Act 1995, s. 305. - Issued: 25.04.2006. Made: 12.04.2006. Coming into force: 01.05.2006. Effect: S.I. 1996/513 amended. Territorial extent & classification: S. General. - 8p.: 30 cm. - 978-0-11-070275-9 *£3.00*

Act of Adjournal (Criminal Procedure Rules Amendment No. 3) (Risk Assessment Orders and Orders for Lifelong Restriction) 2006 No. 2006/302. - Enabling power: Criminal Procedure (Scotland) Act 1995, s. 305. - Issued: 08.06.2006. Made: 31.05.2006. Coming into force: 20.06.2006. Effect: S.I. 1996/513 amended. Territorial extent & classification: S. General. - 12p.: 30 cm. - 978-0-11-070606-1 *£3.00*

Act of Adjournal (Criminal Procedure Rules Amendment No. 4) (Miscellaneous) 2006 No. 2006/436. - Enabling power: Criminal Procedure (Scotland) Act 1995, s. 305. - Issued: 30.08.2006. Made: 22.08.2006. Coming into force: 01.09.2006. Effect: S.I. 1996/513 amended. Territorial extent & classification: S. General. - 8p.: 30 cm. - 978-0-11-070926-0 *£3.00*

Act of Adjournal (Criminal Procedure Rules Amendment) (Vulnerable Witnesses (Scotland) Act 2004) 2006 No. 2006/76. - Enabling power: Criminal Procedure (Scotland) Act 1995, s. 305. - Issued: 06.03.2006. Made: 24.02.2006. Coming into force: 01.04.2006. Effect: S.I. 1996/513 amended. Territorial extent & classification: S. General. - 8p.: 30 cm. - 978-0-11-069975-2 *£3.00*

The Vulnerable Witnesses (Scotland) Act 2004 (Commencement No. 3, Savings and Transitional Provisions) Order 2006 No. 2006/59 (C.8). - Enabling power: Vulnerable Witnesses (Scotland) Act 2004, s. 25. Bringing into operation various provisions of the 2004 Act on 01.04.2006. - Issued: 20.02.2006. Made: 09.02.2006. Effect: None. Territorial extent & classification: S. General. - Copies are supplied from TSO's On-Demand Publishing Service. - 8p.: 30 cm. - 978-0-11-069948-6 *£3.00*

Housing

The Housing Revenue Account General Fund Contribution Limits (Scotland) Order 2006 No. 2006/64. - Enabling power: Housing (Scotland) Act 1987, s. 204. - Issued: 14.01.2005. Made: 14.02.2005. Laid before the Scottish Parliament: 07.02.2005. Coming into force: 17.03.2005. Effect: None. Territorial extent & classification: S. General. - 2p.: 30 cm. - 978-0-11-069954-7 *£3.00*

The Housing (Scotland) Act 2006 (Commencement No. 1) Order 2006 No. 2006/14 (C.1). - Enabling power: Housing (Scotland) Act 2006, s. 195 (3). Bringing into operation various provisions of the 2006 act on 29.01.2006. - Issued: 23.01.2006. Made: 16.01.2006. Effect: None. Territorial extent & classification: S. General. - 2p.: 30 cm. - 978-0-11-069906-6 *£3.00*

The Housing (Scotland) Act 2006 (Commencement No. 2) Order 2006 No. 2006/252 (C.24). - Enabling power: Housing (Scotland) Act 2006, ss. 191 (2), 195 (3). Bringing into operation various provisions of the 2006 Act on 17.05.2006. - Issued: 18.05.2006. Made: 11.05.2006. Effect: None. Territorial extent & classification: S. General. - 2p.: 30 cm. - 978-0-11-070483-8 *£3.00*

The Housing (Scotland) Act 2006 (Commencement No. 3) Order 2006 No. 2006/395 (C.33). - Enabling power: Housing (Scotland) Act 2006, ss. 191 (2), 195 (3). Bringing into operation various provisions of the 2006 Act on 05.07.2006 & 04.12.2006. - Issued: 10.07.2006. Made: 29.06.2006. Effect: None. Territorial extent & classification: S. General. - 2p.: 30 cm. - 978-0-11-070854-6 *£3.00*

The Housing (Scotland) Act 2006 (Commencement No. 4) Order 2006 No. 2006/569 (C.43). - Enabling power: Housing (Scotland) Act 2006, ss. 191 (2), 195 (3). Bringing into operation various provisions of the 2006 Act on 04.12.2006. - Issued: 06.12.2006. Made: 27.11.2006. Effect: None. Territorial extent & classification: S. General. - 2p.: 30 cm. - 978-0-11-071269-7 *£3.00*

The Private Landlord Registration (Information and Fees) (Scotland) Amendment Regulations 2006 No. 2006/28. - Enabling power: Antisocial Behaviour etc. (Scotland) Act 2004, s. 83 (3). - Issued: 02.02.2006. Made: 25.01.2006. Laid before the Scottish Parliament: 26.01.2005. Coming into force: 31.01.2006. Effect: S.S.I. 2005/558 amended. Territorial extent & classification: S. General. - 4p.: 30 cm. - 978-0-11-069917-2 *£3.00*

The Registered Social Landlords (Purposes or Objects) (Scotland) Order 2006 No. 2006/211. - Enabling power: Housing (Scotland) Act 2001, ss. 58 (5), 109 (2) (a). - Issued: 26.04.2006. Made: 19.04.2006. Laid before the Scottish Parliament: 21.04.2006. Coming into force: 15.05.2006. Effect: 2001 asp 10 amended. Territorial extent & classification: S. General. - 4p.: 30 cm. - 978-0-11-070318-3 *£3.00*

Human tissue

The Adults with Incapacity (Removal of Regenerative Tissue for Transplantation) (Form of Certificate) (Scotland) (No. 2) Regulations 2006 No. 2006/368. - Enabling power: Human Tissue (Scotland) Act 2006, s. 18 (2). - Issued: 04.07.2006. Made: 27.06.2006. Laid before the Scottish Parliament: 28.06.2006. Coming into force: 01.09.2006. Effect: S.S.I. 2006/343 revoked. Territorial extent & classification: S. General. - This Scottish Statutory Instrument has been made in consequence of a defect in S.S.I. 2006/343 and is being issued free of charge to all known recipients of that instrument. - 4p.: 30 cm. - 978-0-11-070767-9 £3.00

The Adults with Incapacity (Removal of Regenerative Tissue for Transplantation) (Form of Certificate) (Scotland) Regulations 2006 No. 2006/343. - Enabling power: Human Tissue (Scotland) Act 2006, s. 18 (2). - Issued: 26.06.2006. Made: 08.06.2006. Laid before the Scottish Parliament: 09.06.2006. Coming into force: 01.09.2006. Effect: None. Territorial extent & classification: S. General. - Revoked by S.S.I. 2006/368 (ISBN 0110707672). - 4p.: 30 cm. - 978-0-11-070726-6 £3.00

The Approval of Research on Organs No Longer Required for Procurator Fiscal Purposes (Specified Persons) (Scotland) Order 2006 No. 2006/310. - Enabling power: Human Tissue (Scotland) Act 2006, ss. 40 (2) (c), 48 (2). - Issued: 20.06.2006. Made: 06.06.2006. Laid before the Scottish Parliament: 07.06.2006. Coming into force: 01.09.2006. Effect: None. Territorial extent & classification: S. General. - 4p.: 30 cm. - 978-0-11-070650-4 £3.00

The Human Organ and Tissue Live Transplants (Scotland) Regulations 2006 No. 2006/390. - Enabling power: Human Tissue (Scotland) Act 2006, ss. 17 (3) (4) (5) (7), 18 (2), 59 (1) (b). - Issued: 10.07.2006. Made: 29.06.2006. Coming into force: 01.09.2006. Effect: None. Territorial extent & classification: S. General. - 16p.: 30 cm. - 978-0-11-070832-4 £3.00

The Human Tissue (Removal of Body Parts by an Authorised Person) (Scotland) Regulations 2006 No. 2006/327. - Enabling power: Human Tissue (Scotland) Act 2006, s. 11 (1) (b) (2). - Issued: 21.06.2006. Made: 07.06.2006. Laid before the Scottish Parliament: 08.06.2006. Coming into force: 01.09.2006. Effect: None. Territorial extent & classification: S. General. - 2p.: 30 cm. - 978-0-11-070704-4 £3.00

The Human Tissue (Scotland) Act 2006 (Anatomy Act 1984 Transitional Provisions) Order 2006 No. 2006/340. - Enabling power: Human Tissue (Scotland) Act 2006, s. 58. - Issued: 26.06.2006. Made: 07.06.2006. Laid before the Scottish Parliament: 09.06.2006. Coming into force: 01.09.2006. Effect: None. Territorial extent & classification: S. General. - 8p.: 30 cm. - 978-0-11-070737-2 £3.00

The Human Tissue (Scotland) Act 2006 (Commencement) Order 2006 No. 2006/251 (C.23). - Enabling power: Human Tissue (Scotland) Act 2006, s. 62 (2) (3). Bringing into operation various provisions of the 2006 Act on 12.05.2006 & 01.09.2006 in accord with arts. 2 & 3. - Issued: 17.05.2006. Made: 10.05.2006. Effect: None. Territorial extent & classification: S. General. - 8p.: 30 cm. - 978-0-11-070478-4 £3.00

The Human Tissue (Scotland) Act 2006 (Maintenance of Records and Supply of Information Regarding the Removal and Use of Body Parts) Regulations 2006 No. 2006/344. - Enabling power: Human Tissue (Scotland) Act 2006, s. 19 (1). - Issued: 26.06.2006. Made: 08.06.2006. Laid before the Scottish Parliament: 09.06.2006. Coming into force: 01.09.2006. Effect: None. Territorial extent & classification: S. General. - 8p.: 30 cm. - 978-0-11-070728-0 £3.00

The Human Tissue (Scotland) Act (Human Organ Transplants Act 1989 Transitional and Savings Provisions) Order 2006 No. 2006/420. - Enabling power: Human Tissue (Scotland) Act 2006, s. 58. - Issued: 17.08.2006. Made: 08.08.2006. Laid before the Scottish Parliament: 11.08.2006. Coming into force: 01.09.2006. Effect: None. Territorial extent & classification: S. General. - 4p.: 30 cm. - 978-0-11-070907-9 £3.00

The Human Tissue (Specification of Posts) (Scotland) Order 2006 No. 2006/309. - Enabling power: Human Tissue (Scotland) Act 2006, ss. 41 (2) (b), 59 (1) (b). - Issued: 20.06.2006. Made: 06.06.2006. Laid before the Scottish Parliament: 07.06.2006. Coming into force: 01.09.2006. Effect: None. Territorial extent & classification: S. General. - 2p.: 30 cm. - 978-0-11-070658-0 £3.00

Investigatory powers

The Regulation of Investigatory Powers (Prescription of Offices, Ranks and Positions) (Scotland) Amendment Order 2006 No. 2006/466. - Enabling power: Regulation of Investigatory Powers (Scotland) Act 2000, ss. 8 (1), 9 (3). - Issued: 19.09.2006. Made: 12.09.2006. Laid before the Scottish Parliament: 13.09.2006. Coming into force: 05.10.2006. Effect: S.S.I. 2000/343 amended. Territorial extent & classification: S. General. - 2p.: 30 cm. - 978-0-11-071014-3 £3.00

Land drainage

The Environmental Impact Assessment (Scotland) Amendment Regulations 2006 No. 2006/614. - Enabling power: European Communities Act 1972, s. 2 (2) and Town and Country Planning (Scotland) Act 1997, s. 40. - Issued: 05.01.2007. Made: 21.12.2006. Laid before the Scottish Parliament: 22.12.2006. Coming into force: 01.02.2007. Effect: 1984 c.54; S.I. 1999/367 amended in relation to Scotland; S.S.I. 1999/1, 43; 2006/582 amended. Territorial extent & classification: S. General. - Copies are supplied by TSO's On-demand publishing service. With correction slip dated February 2007. EC note: These Regulations implement in Scotland the amendments made by Article 3 of Council Directive 2003/35/EC with regard to public participation and access to justice to Council Directive 85/337/EEC. - 24p.: 30 cm. - 978-0-11-071472-1 £4.00

Land reform

The Community Right to Buy (Definition of Excluded Land) (Scotland) Order 2006 No. 2006/486. - Enabling power: Land Reform (Scotland) Act 2003, s. 33 (2). - Issued: 11.10.2006. Made: 03.10.2006. Coming into force: 04.10.2006, in accord. with art. 1 (1). Effect: S.S.I. 2004/296 revoked. Territorial extent & classification: S. - Supersedes draft SSI (ISBN 0110708121) issued 07.07.2006. - 4p.: 30 cm. - 978-0-11-071070-9 £3.00

Land registration

The Automated Registration of Title to Land (Electronic Communications) (Scotland) Order 2006 No. 2006/491. - Enabling power: Electronic Communications Act 2000, ss. 8, 9 (5) (6). - Issued: 11.10.2006. Made: 04.10.2006. Coming into force: 05.10.2006 in accord. with art. 1 (1). Effect: 1979 c.33; 1995 c. 7 amended. Territorial extent & classification: S. General. - Supersedes draft SSI (ISBN 0110707559) issued on 22.06.2006. - 8p.: 30 cm. - 978-0-11-071071-6 £3.00

The Land Registration (Scotland) Rules 2006 No. 2006/485. - Enabling power: Land Registration (Scotland) Act 1979, s. 27 (1). - Issued: 26.10.2006. Made: 04.10.2006. Laid: 05.10.2006. Coming into force: 14.11.2006 & 22.01.2007 in accord. with rule 1. Effect: S.I. 1980/1413; 1982/974; 1995/248; 1998/3100; S.S.I. 2004/476 revoked (14.11.2006). Territorial extent & classification: S. General. - 64p.: 30 cm. - 978-0-11-071088-4 £25.00

Legal aid and advice

The Advice and Assistance (Assistance by Way of Representation) (Scotland) Amendment (No. 2) Regulations 2006 No. 2006/615. - Enabling power: Legal Aid (Scotland) Act 1986, ss. 9 (1) (2) (a) (c) (d), 37 (1). - Issued: 08.01.2007. Made: 21.12.2006. Coming into force: 22.12.2006 in accord. with reg. 1. Effect: S.S.I. 2003/179 amended. Territorial extent & classification: S. General. - 4p.: 30 cm. - 978-0-11-071477-6 £3.00

The Advice and Assistance (Assistance by Way of Representation) (Scotland) Amendment Regulations 2006 No. 2006/345. - Enabling power: Legal Aid (Scotland) Act 1986, s. 9 (1) (2) (a) (b) (c) (dd) (de). - Issued: 26.06.2006. Made: 08.06.2006. Coming into force: 12.06.2006. Effect: S.S.I. 2003/179 amended. Territorial extent & classification: S. General. - 4p.: 30 cm. - 978-0-11-070738-9 £3.00

The Advice and Assistance (Financial Conditions) (Scotland) Regulations 2006 No. 2006/179. - Enabling power: Legal Aid (Scotland) Act 1986, ss. 11 (2), 36 (1) (2) (b). - Issued: 04.04.2006. Made: 28.03.2006. Coming into force: 10.04.2006. Effect: 1986 c.47 amended & S.S.I. 2005/163 revoked with saving. Territorial extent & classification: S. General. - Supersedes draft S.S.I. (ISBN 0110699521) issued on 22.02.2006. - 4p.: 30 cm. - 978-0-11-070211-7 £3.00

The Advice and Assistance (Scotland) Amendment (No. 2) Regulations 2006 No. 2006/233. - Enabling power: Legal Aid (Scotland) Act 1986, s. 33 (2) (b) (3) (a) (b) (f). - Issued: 09.05.2006. Made: 02.02.2006. Laid before the Scottish Parliament: 03.05.2006. Coming into force: 12.06.2006. Effect: S.I. 1996/2447 amended. Territorial extent & classification: S. General. - 2p.: 30 cm. - 978-0-11-070391-6 £3.00

The Advice and Assistance (Scotland) Amendment Regulations 2006 No. 2006/60. - Enabling power: Legal Aid (Scotland) Act 1986, s. 12 (3). - Issued: 21.02.2006. Made: 14.02.2006. Laid before the Scottish Parliament: 16.02.2006. Coming into force: 10.04.2006. Effect: S.I. 1996/2447 amended. Territorial extent & classification: S. General. - 2p.: 30 cm. - 978-0-11-069949-3 £3.00

The Civil Legal Aid (Financial Conditions) (Scotland) Regulations 2006 No. 2006/178. - Enabling power: Legal Aid (Scotland) Act 1986, s. 36 (1) (2) (b). - Issued: 04.04.2006. Made: 28.03.2006. Coming into force: 10.04.2006. Effect: 1986 c.47 amended & S.S.I. 2005/162 revoked with saving. Territorial extent & classification: S. General. - Supersedes ISBN 011069953X. - 4p.: 30 cm. - 978-0-11-070220-9 £3.00

The Civil Legal Aid (Scotland) Amendment (No. 2) Regulations 2006 No. 2006/325. - Enabling power: Legal Aid (Scotland) Act 1986, s. 36 (1) (2) (d) (e) (h). - Issued: 21.06.2006. Made: 08.06.2006. Laid before the Scottish Parliament: 09.06.2006. Coming into force: 01.08.2006. Effect: S.S.I. 2002/494 amended. Territorial extent & classification: S. General. - 4p.: 30 cm. - 978-0-11-070679-5 £3.00

The Civil Legal Aid (Scotland) Amendment Regulations 2006 No. 2006/61. - Enabling power: Legal Aid (Scotland) Act 1986, ss. 17 (2B), 36 (1). - Issued: 21.02.2006. Made: 14.02.2006. Laid before the Scottish Parliament: 16.02.2006. Coming into force: 10.04.2006. Effect: S.S.I. 2002/494 amended. Territorial extent & classification: S. General. - 2p.: 30 cm. - 978-0-11-069950-9 £3.00

The Criminal Legal Aid (Scotland) (Fees) Amendment Regulations 2006 No. 2006/515. - Enabling power: Legal Aid (Scotland) Act 1986, ss. 33 (2) (a) (3) (a) (b) (f). - Issued: 31.10.2006. Made: 24.10.2006. Laid before the Scottish Parliament: 25.10.2006. Coming into force: 16.11.2006. Effect: S.I. 1989/1491 amended. Territorial extent & classification: S. General. - 4p.: 30 cm. - 978-0-11-071108-9 £3.00

The Criminal Legal Aid (Scotland) (Prescribed Proceedings) Amendment Regulations 2006 No. 2006/616. - Enabling power: Legal Aid (Scotland) Act 1986, s. 21 (2). - Issued: 08.01.2007. Made: 21.12.2006. Coming into force: 22.12.2006 in accord. with reg. 1. Effect: S.I. 1997/3069 amended. Territorial extent and classification: S. General. - Supersedes draft S.S.I. (ISBN 0110711823) issued 21.11.2006. - 2p.: 30 cm. - 978-0-11-071476-9 £3.00

The Criminal Legal Aid (Summary Justice Pilot Courts and Bail Conditions) (Scotland) Regulations 2006 No. 2006/234. - Enabling power: Legal Aid (Scotland) Act 1986, ss. 33 (2) (a) (3) (a) (b) (f) (3A) (a), 41A. - Issued: 09.05.2006. Made: 02.05.2006. Laid before the Scottish Parliament: 03.05.2006. Coming into force: 12.06.2006. Effect: S.I. 1989/1491; 1999/491 amended. Territorial extent & classification: S. General. - 4p.: 30 cm. - 978-0-11-070392-3 £3.00

Licenses and licensing

The Civic Government (Scotland) Act 1982 (Licensing of Skin Piercing and Tattooing) Amendment Order 2006 No. 2006/604. - Enabling power: Civic Government (Scotland) Act 1982, s. 44 (1) (b) (2). - Issued: 22.12.2006. Made: 11.12.2006. Coming into force: 12.12.2006. Effect: S.S.I. 2006/43 amended. Territorial extent & classification: S. General. - 8p.: 30 cm. - 978-0-11-071423-3 £3.00

The Civic Government (Scotland) Act 1982 (Licensing of Skin Piercing and Tattooing) Order 2006 No. 2006/43. - Enabling power: Civic Government (Scotland) Act 1982, s. 44 (1) (b) (2). - Issued: 09.02.2006. Made: 01.02.2006. Coming into force: 02.02.2006 in acc. with art. 1. Effect: 1982 c.45 modified. Territorial extent & classification: S. General. - Approved by a resolution of the Scottish Parliament. Supersedes draft S.S.I. (ISBN 011069872X) issued on 19.12.2005. - 8p.: 30 cm. - 978-0-11-069927-1 £3.00

Licensing (Liquor)

The Licensing (Scotland) Act 2005 (Commencement No. 1 and Transitional Provisions) Order 2006 No. 2006/239 (C.21). - Enabling power: Licensing (Scotland) Act 2005, ss. 146 (2), 150 (2). Bringing into operation various provisions of the 2005 Act on 01.06.2006. - Issued: 11.05.2006. Made: 04.05.2006. Effect: None. Territorial extent & classification: S. General. - Revoked by S.S.I. 2006/286 (C.28) (ISBN 0110705610) which is being issued free of charge to all known recipients of 2006/239 (C.21). - 4p.: 30 cm. - 978-0-11-070418-0 £3.00

Licensing (liquor)

The Licensing (Scotland) Act 2005 (Commencement No. 2 and Transitional Provisions) Order 2006 No. 2006/286 (C.28). - Enabling power: Licensing (Scotland) Act 2005, ss. 146 (2), 150 (2). Bringing into operation various provisions of the 2005 Act on 01.06.2006 in accord. with art. 2. - Issued: 02.06.2006. Made: 25.05.2006. Effect: S.S.I. 2006/239 (C.21) revoked. Territorial extent & classification: S. General. - This Scottish Statutory Instrument has been made in consequence of a defect in S.S.I. 2006/239 (ISBN 0110704185) and is being issued free of charge to all known recipients of that instrument. - 4p.: 30 cm. - 978-0-11-070561-3 £3.00

Local government

The Aberdeen City (Electoral Arrangements) Order 2006 No. 2006/511. - Enabling power: Local Government (Scotland) Act 1973, s. 17 (2). - Issued: 26.10.2006. Made: 18.10.2006. Coming into force: 10.11.2006. Effect: None. Territorial extent & classification: S. General. - 4p.: 30 cm. - 978-0-11-071100-3 £3.00

The Aberdeenshire (Electoral Arrangements) Order 2006 No. 2006/416. - Enabling power: Local Government (Scotland) Act 1973, s. 17 (2). - Issued: 08.08.2006. Made: 31.07.2006. Coming into force: 11.08.2006. Effect: None. Territorial extent & classification: S. General. - 4p.: 30 cm. - 978-0-11-070905-5 £3.00

The Angus (Electoral Arrangements) Order 2006 No. 2006/393. - Enabling power: Local Government (Scotland) Act 1973, s. 17 (2). - Issued: 10.07.2006. Made: 29.06.2006. Coming into force: 21.07.2006. Effect: None. Territorial extent & classification: S. General. - 4p.: 30 cm. - 978-0-11-070850-8 £3.00

The Antisocial Behaviour etc. (Scotland) Act 2004 (Commencement and Savings) Amendment Order 2006 No. 2006/104 (C.13). - Enabling power: Antisocial Behaviour etc. (Scotland) Act 2004, ss. 141 (2), 145 (2). Bringing into operation various provisions of the 2004 Act on 31.03.2006. - Issued: 13.03.2006. Made: 06.03.2006. Effect: S.S.I. 2004/420 amended. Territorial extent & classification: S. General. - 2p.: 30 cm. - 978-0-11-069995-0 £3.00

The Argyll and Bute (Electoral Arrangements) Order 2006 No. 2006/378. - Enabling power: Local Government (Scotland) Act 1973, s. 17 (2). - Issued: 05.07.2006. Made: 22.06.2006. Coming into force: 14.07.2006. Effect: None. Territorial extent & classification: S. General. - 4p.: 30 cm. - 978-0-11-070803-4 £3.00

The City of Edinburgh (Electoral Arrangements) Order 2006 No. 2006/537. - Enabling power: Local Government (Scotland) Act 1973, s. 17 (2). - Issued: 13.11.2006. Made: 02.11.2006. Coming into force: 17.11.2006. Effect: None. Territorial extent & classification: S. General. - 4p.: 30 cm. - 978-0-11-071129-4 £3.00

The Clackmannanshire (Electoral Arrangements) Order 2006 No. 2006/472. - Enabling power: Local Government (Scotland) Act 1973, s. 17 (2). - Issued: 22.09.2006. Made: 13.09.2006. Coming into force: 07.10.2006. Effect: None. Territorial extent & classification: S. General. - 4p.: 30 cm. - 978-0-11-071032-7 £3.00

The Council Tax (Electronic Communications) (Scotland) Order 2006 No. 2006/67. - Enabling power: Electronic Communications Act 2000, ss. 8, 9. - Issued: 27.02.2006. Made: 20.02.2006. Laid before the Scottish Parliament: 21.02.2006. Coming into force: 01.04.2006. Effect: S.I. 1992/1332 amended. Territorial extent & classification: S. General. - 4p.: 30 cm. - 978-0-11-069965-3 £3.00

The Dumfries and Galloway (Electoral Arrangements) Order 2006 No. 2006/434. - Enabling power: Local Government (Scotland) Act 1973, s. 17 (2). - Issued: 29.08.2006. Made: 16.08.2006. Coming into force: 04.09.2006. Effect: None. Territorial extent & classification: S. General. - 4p.: 30 cm. - 978-0-11-070925-3 £3.00

The Dundee City (Electoral Arrangements) Order 2006 No. 2006/375. - Enabling power: Local Government (Scotland) Act 1973, s. 17 (2). - Issued: 05.07.2006. Made: 22.06.2006. Coming into force: 14.07.2006. Effect: None. Territorial extent & classification: S. General. - 4p.: 30 cm. - 978-0-11-070785-3 £3.00

The East Ayrshire (Electoral Arrangements) Order 2006 No. 2006/428. - Enabling power: Local Government (Scotland) Act 1973, s. 17 (2). - Issued: 22.08.2006. Made: 10.08.2006. Coming into force: 04.09.2006. Effect: None. Territorial extent & classification: S. General. - 4p.: 30 cm. - 978-0-11-070914-7 £3.00

The East Dunbartonshire (Electoral Arrangements) Order 2006 No. 2006/374. - Enabling power: Local Government (Scotland) Act 1973, s. 17 (2). - Issued: 05.07.2006. Made: 22.06.2006. Coming into force: 14.07.2006. Effect: None. Territorial extent & classification: S. General. - 4p.: 30 cm. - 978-0-11-070784-6 £3.00

The East Lothian (Electoral Arrangements) Order 2006 No. 2006/359. - Enabling power: Local Government (Scotland) Act 1973, s. 17 (2). - Issued: 26.06.2006. Made: 14.06.2006. Coming into force: 03.07.2006. Effect: None. Territorial extent & classification: S. General. - 4p.: 30 cm. - 978-0-11-070736-5 £3.00

The East Renfrewshire (Electoral Arrangements) Order 2006 No. 2006/391. - Enabling power: Local Government (Scotland) Act 1973, s. 17 (2). - Issued: 10.07.2006. Made: 29.06.2006. Coming into force: 21.07.2006. Effect: None. Territorial extent & classification: S. General. - 4p.: 30 cm. - 978-0-11-070837-9 £3.00

The Ethical Standards in Public Life etc. (Scotland) Act 2000 (Codes of Conduct for Members of certain Scottish Public Authorities) Order 2006 No. 2006/26. - Enabling power: Ethical Standards in Public Life etc. (Scotland) Act 2000, s. 32 (1). - Issued: 30.01.2006. Made: 24.01.2006. Laid before the Scottish Parliament: 25.01.2006. Coming into force: 01.04.2006. Effect: None. Territorial extent & classification: S. General. - 4p.: 30 cm. - 978-0-11-069913-4 £3.00

The Falkirk (Electoral Arrangements) Order 2006 No. 2006/392. - Enabling power: Local Government (Scotland) Act 1973, s. 17 (2). - Issued: 10.07.2006. Made: 29.06.2006. Coming into force: 21.07.2006. Effect: None. Territorial extent & classification: S. General. - 4p.: 30 cm. - 978-0-11-070845-4 £3.00

The Fife (Electoral Arrangements) Order 2006 No. 2006/510. - Enabling power: Local Government (Scotland) Act 1973, s. 17 (2). - Issued: 25.10.2006. Made: 18.10.2006. Coming into force: 03.11.2006. Effect: None. Territorial extent & classification: S. General. - 4p.: 30 cm. - 978-0-11-071105-8 £3.00

The Glasgow City (Electoral Arrangements) Order 2006 No. 2006/546. - Enabling power: Local Government (Scotland) Act 1973, s. 17 (2). - Issued: 22.11.2006. Made: 14.11.2006. Coming into force: 28.11.2006. Effect: None. Territorial extent & classification: S. General. - 4p.: 30 cm. - 978-0-11-071177-5 £3.00

The Highland (Electoral Arrangements) Order 2006 No. 2006/481. - Enabling power: Local Government (Scotland) Act 1973, s. 17 (2). - Issued: 06.10.2006. Made: 27.09.2006. Coming into force: 16.10.2006. Effect: None. Territorial extent & classification: S. General. - 4p.: 30 cm. - 978-0-11-071059-4 £3.00

The Inverclyde (Electoral Arrangements) Order 2006 No. 2006/373. - Enabling power: Local Government (Scotland) Act 1973, s. 17 (2). - Issued: 05.07.2006. Made: 22.06.2006. Coming into force: 14.07.2006. Effect: None. Territorial extent & classification: S. General. - 4p.: 30 cm. - 978-0-11-070782-2 £3.00

The Local Governance (Scotland) Act 2004 (Commencement No. 3) Order 2006 No. 2006/470 (C.39). - Enabling power: Local Governance (Scotland) Act 2004, ss. 16 (2), 17 (2). Bringing into force certain provisions of the 2004 Act on 14.09.2006 in accord. with art. 2. - Issued: 20.09.2006. Made: 13.09.2006. Effect: None. Territorial extent and classification: S. General. - 2p.: 30 cm. - 978-0-11-071025-9 £3.00

The Local Governance (Scotland) Act 2004 (Severance Payments) Regulations 2006 No. 2006/471. - Enabling power: Local Governance (Scotland) Act 2004, ss. 12, 16 (2). - Issued: 22.09.2006. Made: 14.09.2006. Laid before the Scottish Parliament: 15.09.2006. Coming into force: 07.10.2006. Effect: None. Territorial extent & classification: S. General. - 8p.: 30 cm. - 978-0-11-071031-0 £3.00

The Local Government (Discretionary Payments and Injury Benefits) (Scotland) Amendment Regulations 2006 No. 2006/609. - Enabling power: Superannuation Act 1972, ss. 7, 12, 24. - Issued: 29.12.2006. Made: 19.12.2006. Laid before the Scottish Parliament: 21.12.2006. Coming into force: 29.01.2007. Effect: S.I. 1998/192 amended. Territorial extent & classification: S. General. - 4p.: 30 cm. - 978-0-11-071464-6 £3.00

The Local Government Finance (Scotland) Order 2006 No. 2006/29. - Enabling power: Local Government Finance Act 1992, sch. 12, paras 1, 9 (4). - Issued: 21.02.2006. Made: 25.01.2006. Laid before the Scottish Parliament: 26.01.2005. Coming into force: In accord. with art. 1. Effect: S.S.I. 2005/19 amended. Territorial extent & classification: S. General. - Approved by the Scottish Parliament. The original for approval SI was issued 02.02.2006. - 8p.: 30 cm. - 978-0-11-069916-5 £3.00

The Local Government in Scotland Act 2003 (Commencement No. 3) Order 2006 No. 2006/89 (C.11). - Enabling power: Local Government in Scotland Act 2003, s. 62 (2). Bringing into force certain provisions of the 2003 Act on 20.03.2006, 03.07.2006. - Issued: 08.03.2006. Made: 28.02.2006. Effect: None. Territorial extent and classification: S. General. - 2p.: 30 cm. - 978-0-11-069985-1 £3.00

The Midlothian (Electoral Arrangements) Order 2006 No. 2006/460. - Enabling power: Local Government (Scotland) Act 1973, s. 17 (2). - Issued: 26.06.2006. Made: 05.09.2006. Coming into force: 30.09.2006. Effect: None. Territorial extent & classification: S. General. - 4p.: 30 cm. - 978-0-11-071008-2 £3.00

The Moray (Electoral Arrangements) Order 2006 No. 2006/372. - Enabling power: Local Government (Scotland) Act 1973, s. 17 (2). - Issued: 05.07.2006. Made: 22.06.2006. Coming into force: 14.07.2006. Effect: None. Territorial extent & classification: S. General. - 4p.: 30 cm. - 978-0-11-070772-3 £3.00

The Na h-Eileanan an Iar (Electoral Arrangements) Order 2006 No. 2006/558. - Enabling power: Local Government (Scotland) Act 1973, s. 17 (2). - Issued: 30.11.2006. Made: 20.11.2006. Coming into force: 28.11.2006. Effect: None. Territorial extent & classification: S. General. - 4p.: 30 cm. - 978-0-11-071198-0 £3.00

The Non-Domestic Rating (Electronic Communications) (Scotland) Order 2006 No. 2006/201. - Enabling power: Electronic Communications Act 2000, ss. 8, 9. - Issued: 13.04.2006. Made: 31.03.2006. Coming into force: 01.04.2006. Effect: 1973 c.65 amended. Territorial extent & classification: S. General. - 4p.: 30 cm. - 978-0-11-070263-6 £3.00

The North Ayrshire (Electoral Arrangements) Order 2006 No. 2006/427. - Enabling power: Local Government (Scotland) Act 1973, s. 17 (2). - Issued: 22.08.2006. Made: 10.08.2006. Coming into force: 04.09.2006. Effect: None. Territorial extent & classification: S. General. - 4p.: 30 cm. - 978-0-11-070908-6 £3.00

The North Lanarkshire (Electoral Arrangements) Order 2006 No. 2006/532. - Enabling power: Local Government (Scotland) Act 1973, s. 17 (2). - Issued: 16.11.2006. Made: 01.11.2006. Coming into force: 17.11.2006. Effect: None. Territorial extent & classification: S. General. - 4p.: 30 cm. - 978-0-11-071161-4 £3.00

The Orkney Islands (Electoral Arrangements) Order 2006 No. 2006/394. - Enabling power: Local Government (Scotland) Act 1973, s. 17 (2). - Issued: 10.07.2006. Made: 27.06.2006. Coming into force: 14.07.2006. Effect: None. Territorial extent & classification: S. General. - 4p.: 30 cm. - 978-0-11-070852-2 £3.00

The Perth and Kinross (Electoral Arrangements) Order 2006 No. 2006/370. - Enabling power: Local Government (Scotland) Act 1973, s. 17 (2). - Issued: 05.07.2006. Made: 22.06.2006. Coming into force: 14.07.2006. Effect: None. Territorial extent & classification: S. General. - 4p.: 30 cm. - 978-0-11-070768-6 £3.00

The Private Landlord Registration (Information and Fees) (Scotland) Amendment Regulations 2006 No. 2006/28. - Enabling power: Antisocial Behaviour etc. (Scotland) Act 2004, s. 83 (3). - Issued: 02.02.2006. Made: 25.01.2006. Laid before the Scottish Parliament: 26.01.2005. Coming into force: 31.01.2006. Effect: S.S.I. 2005/558 amended. Territorial extent & classification: S. General. - 4p.: 30 cm. - 978-0-11-069917-2 £3.00

The Renfrewshire (Electoral Arrangements) Order 2006 No. 2006/551. - Enabling power: Local Government (Scotland) Act 1973, s. 17 (2). - Issued: 27.11.2006. Made: 17.11.2006. Coming into force: 28.11.2006. Effect: None. Territorial extent & classification: S. General. - 4p.: 30 cm. - 978-0-11-071194-2 £3.00

Local government

The Scottish Borders (Electoral Arrangements) Order 2006 No. 2006/533. - Enabling power: Local Government (Scotland) Act 1973, s. 17 (2). - Issued: 17.11.2006. Made: 31.10.2006. Coming into force: 10.11.2006. Effect: None. Territorial extent & classification: S. General. - 4p.: 30 cm. - 978-0-11-071167-6 £3.00

The Shetland Islands (Electoral Arrangements) Order 2006 No. 2006/562. - Enabling power: Local Government (Scotland) Act 1973, s. 17 (2). - Issued: 01.12.2006. Made: 22.11.2006. Coming into force: 28.11.2006. Effect: None. Territorial extent & classification: S. General. - 4p.: 30 cm. - 978-0-11-071262-8 £3.00

The South Ayrshire (Electoral Arrangements) Order 2006 No. 2006/429. - Enabling power: Local Government (Scotland) Act 1973, s. 17 (2). - Issued: 22.08.2006. Made: 10.08.2006. Coming into force: 04.09.2006. Effect: None. Territorial extent & classification: S. General. - 4p.: 30 cm. - 978-0-11-070916-1 £3.00

The South Lanarkshire (Electoral Arrangements) Order 2006 No. 2006/377. - Enabling power: Local Government (Scotland) Act 1973, s. 17 (2). - Issued: 05.07.2006. Made: 22.06.2006. Coming into force: 14.07.2006. Effect: None. Territorial extent & classification: S. General. - 4p.: 30 cm. - 978-0-11-070801-0 £3.00

The Stirling (Electoral Arrangements) Order 2006 No. 2006/376. - Enabling power: Local Government (Scotland) Act 1973, s. 17 (2). - Issued: 05.07.2006. Made: 22.06.2006. Coming into force: 14.07.2006. Effect: None. Territorial extent & classification: S. General. - 4p.: 30 cm. - 978-0-11-070795-2 £3.00

The West Dunbartonshire (Electoral Arrangements) Order 2006 No. 2006/547. - Enabling power: Local Government (Scotland) Act 1973, s. 17 (2). - Issued: 22.11.2006. Made: 14.11.2006. Coming into force: 28.11.2006. Effect: None. Territorial extent & classification: S. General. - 4p.: 30 cm. - 978-0-11-071178-2 £3.00

The West Lothian (Electoral Arrangements) Order 2006 No. 2006/535. - Enabling power: Local Government (Scotland) Act 1973, s. 17 (2). - Issued: 09.11.2006. Made: 31.10.2006. Coming into force: 10.11.2006. Effect: None. Territorial extent & classification: S. General. - 4p.: 30 cm. - 978-0-11-071126-3 £3.00

Marriage

The Marriage (Approval of Places) (Scotland) Amendment Regulations 2006 No. 2006/573. - Enabling power: Marriage (Scotland) Act 1977, s. 18A (1) (2). - Issued: 06.12.2006. Made: 29.11.2006. Laid before the Scottish Parliament: 30.11.2006. Coming into force: 01.01.2007. Effect: S.S.I. 2002/260 amended. Territorial extent & classification: S. General. - 4p.: 30 cm. - 978-0-11-071283-3 £3.00

The Registration Services (Fees, etc.) (Scotland) Regulations 2006 No. 2006/575. - Enabling power: Registration of Births, Deaths and Marriages (Scotland) Act 1965, ss.28A (4), 37 (1), 38 (2) (3), 39C, 39D (1), 39E (3), 43 (8), 47, 54 (1); Marriage (Scotland) Act 1977, ss. 3 (1), 19 (2); Civil Partnership Act 2004, ss. 88 (1), 95 (4), 122 (4), 134 (2) & Local Electoral Administration and Registration Services (Scotland) Act 2006, ss. 58 (5) (8), 61 (2) (a). - Issued: 06.12.2006. Made: 29.11.2006. Laid before the Scottish Parliament: 30.11.2006. Coming into force: 01.01.2007. Effect: S.I. 1998/643, 3191 & S.S.I. 2000/447; 2002/390; 2003/89; 2005/100, 556 revoked. Territorial extent & classification: S. General. - 16p.: 30 cm. - 978-0-11-071313-7 £3.00

Mental health

The Mental Health (Care and Treatment) (Scotland) Act 2003 (Transitional and Savings Provisions) Amendment Order 2006 No. 2006/221. - Enabling power: Mental Health (Care and Treatment) (Scotland) Act 2003, s. 332. - Issued: 03.05.2006. Made: 24.04.2006. Laid before the Scottish Parliament: 26.04.2006. Coming into force: 22.05.2006. Effect: S.S.I. 2005/452 amended. Territorial extent & classification: S. General. - 2p.: 30 cm. - 978-0-11-070373-2 £3.00

The Mental Health (Form of Documents) (Scotland) Regulations 2006 No. 2006/12. - Enabling power: Mental Health (Care and Treatment) (Scotland) Act 2003, s. 325. - Issued: 20.01.2006. Made: 12.01.2006. Laid before the Scottish Parliament: 13.01.2006. Coming into force: 06.02.2006. Effect: S.S.I. 2005/444 revoked. Territorial extent & classification: S. General. - 24p.: 30 cm. - 978-0-11-069903-5 £4.00

The Mental Health (Recall or Variation of Removal Order) (Scotland) Regulations 2006 No. 2006/11. - Enabling power: Mental Health (Care and Treatment) (Scotland) Act 2003, s. 295 (5) (b). - Issued: 20.01.2006. Made: 12.01.2006. Laid before the Scottish Parliament: 13.01.2006. Coming into force: 06.02.2006. Effect: None. Territorial extent & classification: S. General. - 2p.: 30 cm. - 978-0-11-069904-2 £3.00

The Mental Health (Relevant Health Board for Patients Detained in Conditions of Excessive Security) (Scotland) Regulations 2006 No. 2006/172. - Enabling power: Mental Health (Care and Treatment) (Scotland) Act 2003, s. 273. - Issued: 30.03.2006. Made: 22.03.2006. Laid before the Scottish Parliament: 23.03.2006. Coming into force: 01.05.2006. Effect: None. Territorial extent & classification: S. General. - 4p.: 30 cm. - 978-0-11-070203-2 £3.00

The Mental Health Tribunal for Scotland (Practice and Procedure) (No. 2) Amendment Rules 2006 No. 2006/171. - Enabling power: Mental Health (Care and Treatment) (Scotland) Act 2003, ss. 21 (4), 326 (2), sch. 2, para. 10. - Issued: 30.03.2006. Made: 22.03.2006. Laid before the Scottish Parliament: 23.03.2006. Coming into force: 01.05.2006. Effect: S.S.I. 2005/519 amended. Territorial extent & classification: S. General. - 8p.: 30 cm. - 978-0-11-070202-5 £3.00

National assistance services

The National Assistance (Assessment of Resources) Amendment (Scotland) Regulations 2006 No. 2006/113. - Enabling power: National Assistance Act 1948, s. 22 (5). - Issued: 15.03.2006. Made: 06.03.2006. Laid before the Scottish Parliament: 08.03.2006. Coming into force: 10.04.2006. Effect: S.I. 1992/2977 amended in relation to Scotland & S.S.I. 2005/82 revoked. Territorial extent & classification: S. General. - 4p.: 30 cm. - 978-0-11-070000-7 £3.00

The National Assistance (Sums for Personal Requirements) (Scotland) Regulations 2006 No. 2006/114. - Enabling power: National Assistance Act 1948, s. 22 (4). - Issued: 15.03.2006. Made: 06.03.2006. Laid before the Scottish Parliament: 08.03.2006. Coming into force: 10.04.2006. Effect: S.S.I. 2005/84 revoked. Territorial extent & classification: S. General. - 4p.: 30 cm. - 978-0-11-069999-8 £3.00

National Health Service

The Functions of Health Boards (Scotland) Amendment Order 2006 No. 2006/132. - Enabling power: National Health Service (Scotland) Act 1978, ss. 2 (1) (a), 105 (7). - Issued: 17.03.2006. Made: 09.03.2006. Laid before the Scottish Parliament: 10.03.2006. Coming into force: 01.04.2006. Effect: S.I. 1991/570 amended. Territorial extent & classification: S. General. - 4p.: 30 cm. - 978-0-11-070097-7 £3.00

The National Health Service (Charges for Drugs and Appliances) (Scotland) Amendment (No. 2) Regulations 2006 No. 2006/246. - Enabling power: National Health Service (Scotland) Act 1978, ss. 27 (2), 69 (1), 105 (7), 108 (1). - Issued: 16.05.2006. Made: 09.05.2006. Laid before the Scottish Parliament: 09.05.2006. Coming into force: 31.05.2006. Effect: S.S.I. 2001/430 amended. Territorial extent & classification: S. General. - 4p.: 30 cm. - 978-0-11-070452-4 £3.00

The National Health Service (Charges for Drugs and Appliances) (Scotland) Amendment Regulations 2006 No. 2006/149. - Enabling power: National Health Service (Scotland) Act 1978, ss. 27 (2), 69 (1) (2), 105 (7), 108 (1). - Issued: 23.03.2006. Made: 14.03.2006. Laid before the Scottish Parliament: 16.03.2006. Coming into force: 01.04.2006. Effect: S.S.I. 2001/430 amended. Territorial extent & classification: S. General. - 8p.: 30 cm. - 978-0-11-070138-7 £3.00

The National Health Service (Charges to Overseas Visitors) (Scotland) Amendment Regulations 2006 No. 2006/141. - Enabling power: National Health Service (Scotland) Act 1978, ss. 98, 105 (7), 108 (1). - Issued: 20.03.2006. Made: 09.03.2006. Laid before the Scottish Parliament: 10.03.2006. Coming into force: 01.04.2006. Effect: S.I. 1989/364 amended. Territorial extent & classification: S. General. - 4p.: 30 cm. - 978-0-11-070100-4 £3.00

The National Health Service (Constitution of Health Boards) (Scotland) Amendment Order 2006 No. 2006/32. - Enabling power: National Health Service (Scotland) Act 1978, ss. 2 (1) (a), 105 (6) (7). - Issued: 03.02.2006. Made: 26.01.2006. Coming into force: 01.04.2006. Effect: S.I. 1974/267 amended. Territorial extent & classification: S. General. - 2p.: 30 cm. - 978-0-11-069920-2 £3.00

The National Health Service (Dental Charges) (Scotland) Amendment Regulations 2006 No. 2006/131. - Enabling power: National Health Service (Scotland) Act 1978, 70A (1), 71 (1), 71A, 105 (7), 108 (1) & National Health Service (Primary Care) Act 1997, ss. 20 (1), 39 (2), 40 (2). - Issued: 16.03.2006. Made: 08.03.2006. Laid before the Scottish Parliament: 10.03.2006. Coming into force: 01.04.2006. Effect: S.S.I. 2003/158 amended. Territorial extent & classification: S. General. - 4p.: 30 cm. - 978-0-11-070083-0 £3.00

The National Health Service (Discipline Committees) (Scotland) Regulations 2006 No. 2006/330. - Enabling power: National Health Service (Scotland) Act 1978, ss. 17P, 25 (2), 26 (2), 27 (2), 29 (1), 105 (7), 106 (a), 108 (1) & Health and Medicines Act 1988, s. 17. - Issued: 21.06.2006. Made: 07.06.2006. Laid before the Scottish Parliament: 08.06.2006. Coming into force: 01.07.2006. Effect: S.I. 2002/3135 amended & S.I. 1992/434; 1994/3038; 1996/938; 1998/1424; S.S.I. 1999/53; 2005/118, 434; 2006/139 revoked. Territorial extent & classification: S. General. - 32p.: 30 cm. - 978-0-11-070698-6 £4.50

The National Health Service (Functions of the Common Services Agency) (Scotland) Amendment (No. 2) Order 2006 No. 2006/603. - Enabling power: National Health Service (Scotland) Act 1978, s. 10 (3) (5), 105 (7). - Issued: 22.12.2006. Made: 14.12.2006. Coming into force: 18.12.2006. Effect: S.I. 1974/467 amended & S.S.I. 2006/560 revoked. Territorial extent & classification: S. General. - This Scottish Statutory Instrument has been printed to correct errors in S.S.I. 2006/560 (ISBN 0110712188) and is being issued free of charge to all known recipients of that instrument. - 4p.: 30 cm. - 978-0-11-071419-6 £3.00

The National Health Service (Functions of the Common Services Agency) (Scotland) Amendment Order 2006 No. 2006/560. - Enabling power: National Health Service (Scotland) Act 1978, s. 10 (4). - Issued: 01.12.2006. Made: 23.11.2006. Coming into force: 18.12.2006. Effect: S.I. 1974/467 amended. Territorial extent & classification: S. General. - 2p.: 30 cm. - 978-0-11-071218-5 £3.00

The National Health Service (General Dental Services) (Scotland) Amendment (No. 2) Regulations 2006 No. 2006/321. - Enabling power: National Health Service (Scotland) Act 1978, ss. 25 (1) (2), 105 (7), 108 (1). - Issued: 21.06.2006. Made: 07.06.2006. Laid before the Scottish Parliament: 08.06.2006. Coming into force: 01.07.2006. Effect: S.I. 1996/177 amended. Territorial extent & classification: S. General. - 4p.: 30 cm. - With correction slip dated September 2006. - 978-0-11-070671-9 £3.00

The National Health Service (General Dental Services) (Scotland) Amendment Regulations 2006 No. 2006/137. - Enabling power: National Health Service (Scotland) Act 1978, ss. 25 (1) (2), 28A, 105 (7), 108 (1). - Issued: 27.03.2006. Made: 09.03.2006. Laid before the Scottish Parliament: 10.03.2006. Coming into force: 01.04.2006. Effect: S.I. 1996/177 amended. Territorial extent & classification: S. General. - 8p.: 30 cm. - 978-0-11-070168-4 £3.00

The National Health Service (General Medical Services Contracts) (Scotland) Amendment Regulations 2006 No. 2006/247. - Enabling power: National Health Service (Scotland) Act 1978, ss. 17K, 17N, 28 (1), 105 (7), 108 (1). - Issued: 16.05.2006. Made: 09.05.2006. Laid before the Scottish Parliament: 09.05.2006. Coming into force: 31.05.2006. Effect: S.S.I. 2004/115 amended. Territorial extent & classification: S. General. - 4p.: 30 cm. - 978-0-11-070465-4 £3.00

The National Health Service (General Ophthalmic Services) (Scotland) Amendment Regulations 2006 No. 2006/42. - Enabling power: National Health Service (Scotland) Act 1978, ss. 26, 28A, 28B, 105 (7), 108 (1). - Issued: 08.02.2006. Made: 01.02.2006. Laid before the Scottish Parliament: 02.02.2006. Coming into force: 06.03.2006. Effect: S.I. 1986/965 amended. Territorial extent & classification: S. General. - Revoked by S.S.I. 2006/135 (ISBN 0110700988) with savings. - 4p.: 30 cm. - 978-0-11-069928-8 £3.00

The National Health Service (General Ophthalmic Services) (Scotland) Amendment Regulations 2006 No. 2006/329. - Enabling power: National Health Service (Scotland) Act 1978, ss. 26, 105 (7), 108 (1). - Issued: 21.06.2006. Made: 07.06.2006. Laid before the Scottish Parliament: 08.06.2006. Coming into force: 01.07.2006. Effect: S.S.I. 2006/135 amended. Territorial extent & classification: S. General. - 4p.: 30 cm. - 978-0-11-070702-0 £3.00

The National Health Service (General Ophthalmic Services) (Scotland) Regulations 2006 No. 2006/135. - Enabling power: National Health Service (Scotland) Act 1978, ss. 26, 28A, 32A (7), 32D, 34, 105 (7), 106 (a), 108 (1). - Issued: 20.03.2006. Made: 10.03.2006. Laid before the Scottish Parliament: 10.03.2006. Coming into force: 01.04.2006. Effect: S.I. 1991/534; 1992/531 amended & S.S.I. 2002/86; 2004/212 amended & S.I. 1986/965; 1988/543; 1989/387, 1177; 1990/1048; 1995/704; 1996/843, 2353; 1999/55, 725 & S.S.I. 2001/62; 2003/201, 432; 2004/36, 98, 169; 2005/128; 2006/42 revoked with savings. Territorial extent & classification: S. General. - 52p.: 30 cm. - 978-0-11-070098-4 £9.00

The National Health Service (Optical Charges and Payments) (Scotland) Amendment Regulations 2006 No. 2006/138. - Enabling power: National Health Service (Scotland) Act 1978, ss. 26, 70 (1), 73 (a), 74 (a), 105 (7), 108 (1), sch. 11, paras 2, 2A. - Issued: 27.03.2006. Made: 09.03.2006. Laid before the Scottish Parliament: 10.03.2006. Coming into force: 01.04.2006. Effect: S.I. 1998/642 amended. Territorial extent & classification: S. General. - 8p.: 30 cm. - 978-0-11-070186-8 £3.00

The National Health Service (Pharmaceutical Services) (Scotland) Amendment (No. 2) Regulations 2006 No. 2006/245. - Enabling power: National Health Service (Scotland) Act 1978, ss. 27 (1) (2), 105 (7), 108 (1). - Issued: 16.05.2006. Made: 09.05.2006. Laid before the Scottish Parliament: 09.05.2006. Coming into force: 31.05.2006. Effect: S.I. 1995/414 amended. Territorial extent & classification: S. General. - 4p.: 30 cm. - 978-0-11-070444-9 £3.00

The National Health Service (Pharmaceutical Services) (Scotland) Amendment (No. 3) Regulations 2006 No. 2006/320. - Enabling power: National Health Service (Scotland) Act 1978, ss. 27 (1) (2), 28A, 105 (7), 108 (1). - Issued: 21.06.2006. Made: 07.06.2006. Laid before the Scottish Parliament: 07.06.2006. Coming into force: 01.07.2006. Effect: S.I. 1995/414 amended. Territorial extent & classification: S. General. - 4p.: 30 cm. - 978-0-11-070667-2 £3.00

The National Health Service (Pharmaceutical Services) (Scotland) Amendment Regulations 2006 No. 2006/143. - Enabling power: National Health Service (Scotland) Act 1978, ss. 27 (1) (2), 105 (7), 108 (1) & Smoking Health and Social Care (Scotland) Act 2005, s. 39. - Issued: 22.03.2006. Made: 10.03.2006. Laid before the Scottish Parliament: 10.03.2006. Coming into force: 01.04.2006. Effect: S.I. 1995/414 amended. Territorial extent & classification: S. General. - 4p.: 30 cm. - 978-0-11-070125-7 £3.00

The National Health Service (Primary Medical Services Performers Lists) (Scotland) Amendment Regulations 2006 No. 2006/136. - Enabling power: National Health Service (Scotland) Act 1978, ss. 17P, 105 (7), 108 (1). - Issued: 20.03.2006. Made: 09.03.2006. Laid before the Scottish Parliament: 10.03.2006. Coming into force: 01.04.2006. Effect: S.S.I. 2004/114 amended. Territorial extent & classification: S. General. - 4p.: 30 cm. - 978-0-11-070103-5 £3.00

The National Health Service (Primary Medical Services Section 17C Agreements) (Scotland) Amendment Regulations 2006 No. 2006/248. - Enabling power: National Health Service (Scotland) Act 1978, ss. 17E, 28 (1), 105 (7), 108 (1). - Issued: 16.05.2006. Made: 09.05.2006. Laid before the Scottish Parliament: 09.05.2006. Coming into force: 31.05.2006. Effect: S.S.I. 2004/116 amended. Territorial extent & classification: S. General. - 4p.: 30 cm. - 978-0-11-070466-1 £3.00

The National Health Service (Service Committees and Tribunal) (Scotland) Amendment Regulations 2006 No. 2006/139. - Enabling power: National Health Service (Scotland) Act 1978, ss. 26 (2), 105 (7), 108 (1). - Issued: 20.03.2006. Made: 13.03.2006. Laid before the Scottish Parliament: 13.03.2006. Coming into force: 01.04.2006. Effect: S.I. 1992/434 amended. Territorial extent & classification: S. General. - Revoked by S.S.I. 2006/330 (ISBN 0110706986). - 4p.: 30 cm. - 978-0-11-070102-8 £3.00

The National Health Service (Superannuation Scheme and Additional Voluntary Contributions) (Scotland) Amendment Regulations 2006 No. 2006/307. - Enabling power: Superannuation Act 1972, s. 10, 12, sch. 3. - Issued: 12.06.2006. Made: 05.06.2006. Laid before the Scottish Parliament: 07.06.2006. Coming into force: 30.06.2006. Effect: S.I. 1995/365; 1998/1451 amended. Territorial extent & classification: S. General. - 16p.: 30 cm. - 978-0-11-070611-5 £3.00

The National Health Service (Superannuation Scheme and Compensation for Premature Retirement) (Scotland) Amendment Regulations 2006 No. 2006/561. - Enabling power: Superannuation Act 1972, ss. 10, 12, 24, sch. 3. - Issued: 30.11.2006. Made: 20.11.2006. Laid before the Scottish Parliament: 27.11.2006. Coming into force: 22.12.2006. Effect: S.I. 1995/365; S.S.I. 2003/344 amended. Territorial extent & classification: S. General. - EC note: These Regulations take account of the age discrimination aspect of EC Directive 2000/78 on equal treatment and employment and vocational training. - 8p.: 30 cm. - 978-0-11-071219-2 £3.00

The National Health Service (Travelling Expenses and Remission of Charges) (Scotland) Amendment (No. 2) Regulations 2006 No. 2006/183. - Enabling power: National Health Service (Scotland) Act 1978, ss. 75A, 105 (7), 108 (1). - Issued: 07.04.2006. Made: 30.03.2006. Laid before the Scottish Parliament: 31.03.2006. Coming into force: 01.04.2006, 01.05.2006 in accord. with reg. 1 (2) (3). Effect: S.S.I. 2003/460 amended & S.I. 2006/142 revoked (01.04.2006). Territorial extent & classification: S. General. - This Scottish Statutory Instrument has been made in consequence of a defect in S.S.I. 2006/142 (ISBN 0110701593) and is being issued free of charge to all known recipients of that instrument. - 4p.: 30 cm. - 978-0-11-070235-3 £3.00

The National Health Service (Travelling Expenses and Remission of Charges) (Scotland) Amendment (No. 3) Regulations 2006 No. 2006/440. - Enabling power: National Health Service (Scotland) Act 1978, ss. 75A, 105 (7), 108 (1). - Issued: 08.09.2006. Made: 30.08.2006. Laid before the Scottish Parliament: 30.08.2006. Coming into force: 01.09.2006. Effect: S.S.I. 2003/460 amended. Territorial extent & classification: S. General. - 4p.: 30 cm. - 978-0-11-070986-4 £3.00

The National Health Service (Travelling Expenses and Remission of Charges) (Scotland) Amendment Regulations 2006 No. 2006/142. - Enabling power: National Health Service (Scotland) Act 1978, ss. 75A, 105 (7), 108 (1). - Issued: 24.03.2006. Made: 10.03.2006. Laid before the Scottish Parliament: 10.03.2006. Coming into force: 01.04.2006. Effect: S.S.I. 2003/460 amended. Territorial extent & classification: S. General. - 4p.: 30 cm. - 978-0-11-070159-2 £3.00

The National Health Service (Tribunal) (Scotland) Amendment Regulations 2006 No. 2006/122. - Enabling power: National Health Service (Scotland) Act 1978, ss. 29 (4), 29A (5), 32, 32C (2), 105 (7), 106 (a), 108 (1). - Issued: 15.03.2006. Made: 07.03.2006. Laid before the Scottish Parliament: 09.03.2006. Coming into force: 01.04.2006. Effect: S.S.I. 2004/38 amended. Territorial extent & classification: S. General. - 16p.: 30 cm. - 978-0-11-070058-8 £3.00

The National Health Service (Variation of the Areas of Greater Glasgow and Highland Health Boards) (Scotland) Order 2006 No. 2006/33. - Enabling power: National Health Service (Scotland) Act 1978, ss. 2 (3) (4), 105 (7). - Issued: 03.02.2006. Made: 26.01.2006. Laid before the Scottish Parliament: 27.01.2006. Coming into force: 01.03.2006 except for arts. 3, 10, 11, 12 & 01.04.2006 for arts 3, 10, 11, 12. Effect: None. Territorial extent & classification: S. General. - 8p.: 30 cm. - 978-0-11-069921-9 £3.00

The National Waiting Times Centre Board (Scotland) Amendment Order 2006 No. 2006/144. - Enabling power: National Health Service (Scotland) Act 1978, ss. 2 (1) (b) (1C), 105 (7). - Issued: 21.03.2006. Made: 10.03.2006. Laid before the Scottish Parliament: 10.03.2006. Coming into force: 01.04.2006. Effect: S.S.I. 2002/305 amended. Territorial extent & classification: S. General. - 4p.: 30 cm. - 978-0-11-070123-3 £3.00

The NHS Education for Scotland Amendment Order 2006 No. 2006/79. - Enabling power: National Health Service (Scotland) Act 1978, ss. 2 (1) (b) (1C), 105 (6). - Issued: 06.03.2006. Made: 27.02.2006. Laid before the Scottish Parliament: 28.02.2006. Coming into force: 23.03.2006. Effect: S.S.I. 2002/103 amended. Territorial extent & classification: S. General. - 2p.: 30 cm. - 978-0-11-069974-5 £3.00

The Personal Injuries (NHS Charges) (Amounts) (Scotland) Regulations 2006 No. 2006/588. - Enabling power: Health and Social Care (Community Health and Standards) Act 2003, ss. 153 (2) (5) (7) (8), 163 (1), 168, 195 (1) (2). - Issued: 08.12.2006. Made: 29.11.2006. Coming into force: 29.01.2007. Effect: None. Territorial extent & classification: S. General. - 8p.: 30 cm. - 978-0-11-071338-0 £3.00

The Personal Injuries (NHS Charges) (General) (Scotland) Regulations 2006 No. 2006/592. - Enabling power: Health and Social Care (Community Health and Standards) Act 2003, ss. 151 (8) (9), 153 (10) (11), 160 (1) to (3), 162 (3), 163, 164 (4), 168, 195 (1) (2), sch. 10, para. 8. - Issued: 29.12.2006. Made: 13.12.2006. Laid before the Scottish Parliament: 15.12.2006-. Coming into force: 29.01.2007. Effect: None. Territorial extent & classification: S. General. - 8p.: 30 cm. - 978-0-11-071446-2 £3.00

The Personal Injuries (NHS Charges) (Reviews and Appeals) (Scotland) Regulations 2006 No. 2006/593. - Enabling power: Health and Social Care (Community Health and Standards) Act 2003, ss. 156 (1) (2) (4), 157, 158 (7), 168, 195 (1) (2). - Issued: 29.12.2006. Made: 13.12.2006. Laid before the Scottish Parliament: 15.12.2006. Coming into force: 29.01.2007. Effect: None. Territorial extent & classification: S. General. - 8p.: 30 cm. - 978-0-11-071445-5 £3.00

The Primary Medical Services (Scotland) Act 2004 (Modification of the National Health Service (Scotland) Act 1978) Order 2006 No. 2006/30. - Enabling power: Primary Medical Services (Scotland) Act 2004, s. 7 (1) (2). - Issued: 02.02.2006. Made: 24.01.2006. Coming into force: 01.02.2006. Effect: 1978 (c.29) modified. Territorial extent & classification: S. General. - 4p.: 30 cm. - 978-0-11-069915-8 £3.00

The Road Traffic (NHS Charges) Amendment (Scotland) Regulations 2006 No. 2006/84. - Enabling power: Road Traffic (NHS Charges) Act 1999, ss. 3 (2) (4),16 (2) (a) (b). - Issued: 07.03.2006. Made: 27.02.2006. Laid before the Scottish Parliament: 28.02.2006. Coming into force: 01.04.2006. Effect: S.I. 1999/785 amended. Territorial extent & classification: S. General. - 4p.: 30 cm. - 978-0-11-069980-6 £3.00

The Smoking, Health and Social Care (Scotland) Act 2005 (Commencement No. 4) Order 2006 No. 2006/121 (C.14). - Enabling power: Smoking, Health and Social Care (Scotland) Act 2005, ss. 40 (1), 43 (3) (4). Bringing into operation various provisions of the 2005 Act on 07.03.2006, 01.04.2006, in accord. with art. 3. - Issued: 15.03.2006. Made: 06.02.2006. Effect: None. Territorial extent & classification: S. General. - 8p.: 30 cm. - 978-0-11-070059-5 £3.00

Olympic games and paralympic games

The London Olympic Games and Paralympic Games Act 2006 (Commencement) (Scotland) Order 2006 No. 2006/611 (C.47). - Enabling power: London Olympic Games and Paralympic Games Act 2006, s. 40 (3). Bringing into operation various provisions of the 2006 Act on 31.12.2006. - Issued: 29.12.2006. Made: 10.12.2006. Effect: None. Territorial extent & classification: S. General. - 2p.: 30 cm. - 978-0-11-071469-1 £3.00

Opticians

The Sight Testing (Examination and Prescription) Amendment (Scotland) Regulations 2006 No. 2006/134. - Enabling power: Opticians Act 1989, s. 26 (1) (3). - Issued: 20.03.2006. Made: 09.03.2006. Laid before the Scottish Parliament: 10.03.2006. Coming into force: 01.04.2006. Effect: S.I. 1989/1230 amended. Territorial extent & classification: S. General. - 2p.: 30 cm. - 978-0-11-070110-3 £3.00

Pensions

The Firefighters' Compensation Scheme (Scotland) Order 2006 No. 2006/338. - Enabling power: Fire and Rescue Services Act 2004, ss. 34 (1) to (5) (8), 60 (2). - Issued: 26.06.2006. Made: 08.06.2006. Laid before the Scottish Parliament: 09.06.2006. Coming into force: 01.07.2006. Effect: None. Territorial extent & classification: S. General. - 40p.: 30 cm. - 978-0-11-070756-3 £6.50

The Firefighters' Pension Scheme Amendment (Scotland) Order 2006 No. 2006/342. - Enabling power: Fire Services Act 1947, s. 26(1) to (5) & Superannuation Act 1972, ss. 12, 16. - Issued: 26.06.2006. Made: 08.06.2006. Laid before the Scottish Parliament: 09.06.2006. Coming into force: 01.07.2006. Effect: S.I. 1992/129 amended in relation to Scotland. Territorial extent & classification: S. General. - 20p.: 30 cm. - 978-0-11-070729-7 £3.50

The Local Government Pension Scheme (Scotland) Amendment (No. 2) Regulations 2006 No. 2006/468. - Enabling power: Superannuation Act 1972, ss. 7, 12. - Issued: 20.09.2006. Made: 12.09.2006. Laid before the Scottish Parliament: 14.09.2006. Coming into force: In accord. with reg. 1 (3). Effect: S.I. 1998/366 amended. Territorial extent & classification: S. General. - 12p.: 30 cm. - 978-0-11-071023-5 £3.00

The Local Government Pension Scheme (Scotland) Amendment (No. 3) Regulations 2006 No. 2006/514. - Enabling power: Superannuation Act 1972, ss. 7, 12. - Issued: 30.10.2006. Made: 24.10.2006. Laid before the Scottish Parliament: 26.10.2006. Coming into force: 01.10.2006 & 01.12.2006 in accord. with reg. 1 (3). Effect: S.I. 1998/366 amended. Territorial extent & classification: S. General. - 8p.: 30 cm. - 978-0-11-071107-2 £3.00

The Local Government Pension Scheme (Scotland) Amendment Regulations 2006 No. 2006/123. - Enabling power: Superannuation Act 1972, s. 7. - Issued: 16.03.2006. Made: 08.03.2006. Laid before the Scottish Parliament: 09.03.2006. Coming into force: 01.04.2006. Effect: S.I. 1998/366 amended. Territorial extent & classification: S. General. - 4p.: 30 cm. - 978-0-11-070064-9 £3.00

The Police Pensions Amendment (Scotland) Regulations 2006 No. 2006/285. - Enabling power: Police Pensions Act 1976, s. 1. - Issued: 02.06.2006. Made: 24.05.2006. Laid before the Scottish Parliament: 31.05.2006. Coming into force: 22.06.2006. Effect: S.I. 1987/257; 1991/1304 amended. Territorial extent & classification: S. General. - 12p.: 30 cm. - 978-0-11-070560-6 £3.00

The Teachers' Superannuation (Scotland) Amendment (No. 2) Regulations 2006 No. 2006/605. - Enabling power: Superannuation Act 1972, s. 9, 12, 24. - Issued: 29.12.2006. Made: 12.12.2006. Laid before the Scottish Parliament: 18.12.2006. Coming into force: 29.01.2007. Effect: S.I. 1995/2814 (S. 207); 1996/2317; S.S.I. 2005/393 amended. Territorial extent & classification: S. General. - 4p.: 30 cm. - 978-0-11-071425-7 £3.00

The Teachers' Superannuation (Scotland) Amendment Regulations 2006 No. 2006/308. - Enabling power: Superannuation Act 1972, s. 9, 12. - Issued: 12.06.2006. Made: 05.06.2006. Laid before the Scottish Parliament: 07.06.2006. Coming into force: 30.06.2006. Effect: S.I. 1995/2814 (S. 207); S.S.I. 2005/393 amended Territorial extent & classification: S. General. - 12p.: 30 cm. - 978-0-11-070609-2 £3.00

Pesticides

The Pesticides (Maximum Residue Levels in Crops, Food and Feeding Stuffs) (Scotland) Amendment (No.2) Regulations 2006 No. 2006/312. - Enabling power: European Communities Act 1972, s. 2 (2). - Issued: 20.06.2006. Made: 07.06.2006. Laid before the Scottish Parliament: 08.06.2006. Coming into force: 27.07.2006 except for reg. 4; 15.09.2006 for reg. 4, in accord. with reg. 1. Effect: S.S.I. 2005/599 amended. Territorial extent & classification: S. General. - EC note: These Regulations implement Commission Directives 2006/4/EC; 2006/9/EC and 2006/30/EC. - 20p.: 30 cm. - 978-0-11-070660-3 £3.50

The Pesticides (Maximum Residue Levels in Crops, Food and Feeding Stuffs) (Scotland) Amendment (No. 3) Regulations 2006 No. 2006/548. - Enabling power: European Communities Act 1972, s. 2 (2). - Issued: 24.11.2006. Made: 16.11.2006. Laid before the Scottish Parliament: 17.11.2006. Coming into force: In accord. with reg. 1 (3) to (7). Effect: S.S.I. 2005/599; 2006/151 amended. Territorial extent & classification: S. General. - EC note: These Regulations implement Commission Directives 2006/53/EC, 2006/59/EC, 2006/60/EC and 2006/61/EC. - 48p.: 30 cm. - 978-0-11-071184-3 £7.50

The Pesticides (Maximum Residue Levels in Crops, Food and Feeding Stuffs) (Scotland) Amendment Regulations 2006 No. 2006/151. - Enabling power: European Communities Act 1972, s. 2 (2). - Issued: 25.04.2006. Made: 14.03.2006. Laid before the Scottish Parliament: 15.03.2006. Coming into force: In accord. with reg. 1(2) to (4). Effect: S.S.I. 2005/599 amended. Territorial extent & classification: S. General. - This S.S.I. has been printed in substitution of the S.S.I. of the same number (issued on 07.04.2006) and is being issued free of charge to all known recipients of that instrument. EC note: These Regulations implement Commission Directives 2005/70/EC, 2005/74/EC and 2005/76/EC. - 28p., tables: 30 cm. - 978-0-11-070210-0 £4.00

The Plant Protection Products (Scotland) Amendment (No. 2) Regulations 2006 No. 2006/449. - Enabling power: European Communities Act 1972, s. 2 (2). - Issued: 07.09.2006. Made: 30.08.2006. Laid before the Scottish Parliament: 04.09.2006. Coming into force: 26.09.2006. Effect: S.S.I. 2005/331 amended & S.S.I. 2006/241 revoked. Territorial extent & classification: S. General. - EC note: These Regulations amend the definition of the Directive in the principal Regulations so as to implement Commission Directives 2006/39/EC, 2006/41/EC, 2006/45/EC and 2006/64/EC which amend Annex 1 to the Directive (regulation 3). - 8p.: 30 cm. - 978-0-11-070968-0 £3.00

The Plant Protection Products (Scotland) Amendment (No. 3) Regulations 2006 No. 2006/576. - Enabling power: European Communities Act 1972, s. 2 (2). - Issued: 15.01.2007. Made: 29.11.2006. Laid before the Scottish Parliament: 30.11.2006. Coming into force: 22.12.2006. Effect: S.S.I. 2005/331 amended & S.S.I. 2006/449 revoked. Territorial extent & classification: S. General. - EC note: These Regs amend the definition of "the Directive (Council Directive 91/414/EEC)" in the principal regulations (S.S.I. 2005/331) so as to implement Commission Directives 2006/74/EC, 2006/75/EC, 2006/76/EC, 2006/85/EC which amend Annex 1 to the Directive (reg. 3). - 8p.: 30 cm. - 978-0-11-071478-3 £3.00

The Plant Protection Products (Scotland) Amendment Regulations 2006 No. 2006/241. - Enabling power: European Communities Act 1972, s. 2 (2). - Issued: 15.05.2006. Made: 04.05.2006. Laid before the Scottish Parliament: 09.05.2006. Coming into force: 01.06.2006. Effect: S.S.I. 2005/331 amended. Territorial extent & classification: S. General. - Revoked by S.S.I. 2006/449 (ISBN 0110709683). EC note: Implements Commission Directives 2005/53/EC, 2005/54/EC, 2005/57/EC, 2005/58/EC, 2005/72/EC, 2006/5/EC, 2006/6/EC, 2006/10/EC, 2006/16/EC and 2006/19/EC. - 8p.: 30 cm. - 978-0-11-070426-5 £3.00

Pilotage

The Perth (Pilotage Powers) Order 2006 No. 2006/49. - Enabling power: Pilotage Act 1987, s. 1 (4). - Issued: 15.02.2006. Made: 07.02.2006. Laid before the Scottish Parliament: 08.02.2006. Coming into force: 01.04.2006. Effect: None. Territorial extent & classification: S. General. - 4p.: 30 cm. - 978-0-11-069936-3 £3.00

Plant health

The Plant Health (Potatoes) (Scotland) Order 2006 No. 2006/319. - Enabling power: Plant Health Act 1967, ss. 3, 4 (1). - Issued: 19.06.2006. Made: 07.06.2006. Laid before the Scottish Parliament: 08.06.2006. Coming into force: In accord. with art. 1 (1) (2). Effect: None. Territorial extent & classification: S. General. - 8p.: 30 cm. - 978-0-11-070648-1 £3.00

The Plant Health (Scotland) Amendment Order 2006 No. 2006/474. - Enabling power: Plant Health Act 1967, ss. 2, 3, 4 (1). - Issued: 28.09.2006. Made: 21.09.2006. Laid before the Scottish Parliament: 22.09.2006. Coming into force: 31.10.2006. Effect: S.S.I. 2005/613 amended. Territorial extent & classification: S. General. - EC note: Implements Directives 2005/77/EC; 2006/35/EC; Decisions 2005/870/EC; 2006/464/EC; 2006/473/EC. - 8p.: 30 cm. - 978-0-11-071042-6 £3.00

The Potatoes Originating in Egypt (Scotland) Amendment Regulations 2006 No. 2006/27. - Enabling power: European Communities Act 1972, s. 2 (2). - Issued: 31.01.2006. Made: 24.01.2006. Laid before the Scottish Parliament: 26.01.2006. Coming into force: 28.02.2006. Effect: S.S.I. 2004/111 amended. Territorial extent & classification: S. General. - EC note: These Regulations implement in Scotland Commission Decision 2005/840/EC amending Commission Decision 2004/4/EC authorising Member States temporarily to take emergency measures against the dissemination of Pseudomonas solanacearum (Smith) Smith (now referred to as Ralstonia solanacearum (Smith) Yabuuchi et al.) as regards Egypt. - 2p.: 30 cm. - 978-0-11-069914-1 *£3.00*

Police

The Antisocial Behaviour etc. (Scotland) Act 2004 (Commencement and Savings) Amendment Order 2006 No. 2006/104 (C.13). - Enabling power: Antisocial Behaviour etc. (Scotland) Act 2004, ss. 141 (2), 145 (2). Bringing into operation various provisions of the 2004 Act on 31.03.2006. - Issued: 13.03.2006. Made: 06.03.2006. Effect: S.S.I. 2004/420 amended. Territorial extent & classification: S. General. - 2p.: 30 cm. - 978-0-11-069995-0 *£3.00*

The Police Act 1997 Amendment (Scotland) Order 2006 No. 2006/50. - Enabling power: Serious Organised Crime and Police Act 2005, s. 173 (1) (a) (5) (b) (ii) (iii). - Issued: 15.02.2006. Made: 06.02.2006. Coming into force: 07.02.2006. Effect: 1997 c. 50 amended in relation to Scotland. Territorial extent & classification: S. General. - 4p.: 30 cm. - 978-0-11-069940-0 *£3.00*

The Police Act 1997 (Criminal Records) (Registration) (Scotland) Regulations 2006 No. 2006/97. - Enabling power: Police Act 1997, ss. 120 (3), 120A (7), 124A (4), 125 (5). - Issued: 10.03.2006. Made: 02.03.2006. Laid before the Scottish Parliament: 06.03.2006. Coming into force: 01.04.2006. Effect: S.S.I. 2002/23 revoked. Territorial extent & classification: S. General. - 8p.: 30 cm. - 978-0-11-069990-5 *£3.00*

The Police Act 1997 (Criminal Records) (Scotland) Amendment Regulations 2006 No. 2006/521. - Enabling power: Police Act 1997, ss. 112 (1) (a), 113A (1) (a), 113B (1) (a), 114 (1) (a), 116 (1) (a). - Issued: 07.11.2006. Made: 26.10.2006. Laid before the Scottish Parliament: 01.11.2006. Coming into force: 15.12.2006. Effect: S.S.I. 2006/96 amended. Territorial extent & classification: S. General. - 8p., col. forms: 30 cm. - 978-0-11-071120-1 *£9.40*

The Police Act 1997 (Criminal Records) (Scotland) Regulations 2006 No. 2006/96. - Enabling power: Police Act 1997, ss. 112 (1) (2) (a) (3), 113A (1) (3) (a) (6), 113B (1) (2) (b) (3) (a) (9), 113C (1) (b) (d), 113D (1) (b), 114 (1), 116 (1) (2) (b), 118 (2) (a) (3), 119 (7), 125 (5). - Issued: 10.03.2006. Made: 02.03.2006. Laid before the Scottish Parliament: 06.03.2006. Coming into force: 01.04.2006. Effect: S.S.I. 2002/143, 217; 2004/526 revoked. Territorial extent & classification: S. General. - 16p.: 30 cm. - 978-0-11-069991-2 *£3.00*

The Police Grant (Scotland) Order 2006 No. 2006/91. - Enabling power: Police (Scotland) Act 1967, s. 32 (3) (5). - Issued: 08.03.2006. Made: 27.02.2006. Laid before the Scottish Parliament: 02.03.2006. Coming into force: 01.04.2006. Effect: None. Territorial extent & classification: S. General. - 2p.: 30 cm. - 978-0-11-069986-8 *£3.00*

The Police Grant (Variation) (Scotland) Order 2006 No. 2006/39. - Enabling power: Police (Scotland) Act 1967, s. 32 (3) (5). - Issued: 07.02.2005. Made: 26.01.2006. Laid before the Scottish Parliament: 01.02.2006. Coming into force: 09.03.2006. Effect: S.I. 1998/611, 891; 1999/953; S.S.I. 2000/73; 2001/74; 2002/116; 2003/172; 2004/120; 2005/107 amended. Territorial extent & classification: S. General. - 8p.: 30 cm. - 978-0-11-069926-4 *£3.00*

The Police (Injury Benefit) (Scotland) Regulations 2006 No. 2006/610. - Enabling power: Police Pensions Act 1976, ss. 1, 6, 7, 8. - Issued: 29.12.2006. Made: 19.12.2006. Laid before the Scottish Parliament: 21.12.2006. Coming into force: 01.02.2007. Effect: S.I. 1987/256, 257; S.S.I. 2005/495 amended; S.I. 1987/156 revoked. Territorial extent & classification: S. General. - 44p.: 30 cm. - 978-0-11-071465-3 *£7.50*

The Police (Minimum Age for Appointment) (Scotland) Regulations 2006 No. 2006/552. - Enabling power: Police (Scotland) Act 1967, ss. 26, 27. - Issued: 27.11.2006. Made: 20.11.2006. Laid before the Scottish Parliament: 21.11.2006. Coming into force: 23.11.2006. Effect: S.I. 1968/208; S.S.I. 2004/257 amended. Territorial extent & classification: S. General. - 4p.: 30 cm. - 978-0-11-071195-9 *£3.00*

The Police Pensions Amendment (Scotland) Regulations 2006 No. 2006/285. - Enabling power: Police Pensions Act 1976, s. 1. - Issued: 02.06.2006. Made: 24.05.2006. Laid before the Scottish Parliament: 31.05.2006. Coming into force: 22.06.2006. Effect: S.I. 1987/257; 1991/1304 amended. Territorial extent & classification: S. General. - 12p.: 30 cm. - 978-0-11-070560-6 *£3.00*

The Police, Public Order and Criminal Justice (Scotland) Act 2006 (Commencement No. 1) Order 2006 No. 2006/432 (C.34). - Enabling power: Police, Public Order and Criminal Justice (Scotland) Act 2006, s. 104 (1). Bringing into operation various provisions of the 2006 Act on 01.09.2006. - Issued: 24.08.2006. Made: 16.08.2006. Effect: None. Territorial extent & classification: S. General. - 4p.: 30 cm. - 978-0-11-070922-2 *£3.00*

The Police, Public Order and Criminal Justice (Scotland) Act 2006 (Commencement No. 2) Order 2006 No. 2006/607 (C.46). - Enabling power: Police, Public Order and Criminal Justice (Scotland) Act 2006, s. 104 (1). Bringing into operation various provisions of the 2006 Act on 01.01.2007. - Issued: 29.12.2006. Made: 13.12.2006. Effect: None. Territorial extent & classification: S. General. - 8p.: 30 cm. - 978-0-11-071429-5 *£3.00*

The Serious Organised Crime and Police Act 2005 (Commencement No. 2) (Scotland) Order 2006 No. 2006/166 (C.15). - Enabling power: Serious Organised Crime and Police Act 2005, s. 178 (3) (4) (5) (9). Bringing into operation various provisions of the 2005 Act on 01.04.2006; 01.05.2006. - Issued: 29.03.2006. Made: 22.03.2006. Effect: None. Territorial extent & classification: S. General. - Copies are supplied from TSO's On-Demand Publishing Service. - 8p.: 30 cm. - 978-0-11-070195-0 £3.00

The Serious Organised Crime and Police Act 2005 (Consequential and Supplementary Amendments) (Scotland) Order 2006 No. 2006/129. - Enabling power: Serious Organised Crime and Police Act 2005, ss. 173 (1) to (3) (5) (a). - Issued: 16.03.2006. Made: 08.03.2006. Laid before the Scottish Parliament: 09.03.2006. Coming into force: 01.04.2006. Effect: S.I. 1986/1078; 1989/1796; 1993/176; 1995/2507; 1997/2400; 1999/1319; 2002/3113 (all amended in relation to Scotland); S.S.I. 2002/62; 2005/494, 565 amended. Territorial extent & classification: S. General. - Copies are supplied from TSO's On-Demand Publishing Service. - 8p.: 30 cm. - 978-0-11-070065-6 £3.00

Prisons

The Prisons and Young Offenders Institutions (Scotland) Amendment Rules 2006 No. 2006/5. - Enabling power: Prisons (Scotland) Act 1989, s. 39. - Issued: 17.01.2006. Made: 10.01.2006. Laid: 11.01.2006. Coming into force: 02.02.2006. Effect: SI 1994/1931 amended. - Revoked by S.S.I. 2006/94 (ISBN 0110699882). - 2p.: 30 cm. - 978-0-11-069900-4 £3.00

The Prisons and Young Offenders Institutions (Scotland) Rules 2006 No. 2006/94. - Enabling power: Prisons (Scotland) Act 1989, s. 39. - Issued: 13.03.2006. Made: 02.03.2006. Laid before the Scottish Parliament: 03.03.2006. Coming into force: 26.03.2006. Effect: S.I. 1994/1931 (with savings); 1996/32; 1997/2007; 1998/1589, 2504; 1999/374 & S.S.I. 2000/187; 2002/107; 2003/242; 2006/5 revoked. Territorial extent & classification: S. General. - Copies are supplied from TSO's On-Demand Publishing Service. - 88p.: 30 cm. - 978-0-11-069988-2 £13.50

Public bodies

The Public Appointments and Public Bodies etc. (Scotland) Act 2003 (Treatment of Office or Body as Specified Authority) Order 2006 No. 2006/303. - Enabling power: Public Appointments and Public Bodies etc. (Scotland) Act 2003, s. 3 (3). - Issued: 09.06.2006. Made: 31.05.2006. Coming into force: 01.06.2006. Effect: None. Territorial extent & classification: S. General. - Supersedes draft S.I. (ISBN 0110703375) issued on 27.04.2006. - 2p.: 30 cm. - 978-0-11-070608-5 £3.00

The Public Appointments and Public Bodies etc. (Scotland) Act 2003 (Treatment of Office or Body as Specified Authority) (Scottish Legal Complaints Commission) Order 2006 No. 2006/612. - Enabling power: Public Appointments and Public Bodies etc. (Scotland) Act 2003, s. 3 (3). - Issued: 03.01.2007. Made: 20.12.2006. Coming into force: 21.12.2006. Effect: None. Territorial extent & classification: S. General. - Supersedes draft SSI (ISBN 0110711386) issued 13.11.2006. - 2p.: 30 cm. - 978-0-11-071470-7 £3.00

The Public Appointments and Public Bodies etc. (Scotland) Act 2003 (Treatment of Public Transport Users' Committee for Scotland as Specified Authority and Amendment of Specified Authorities) Order 2006 No. 2006/363. - Enabling power: Public Appointments and Public Bodies etc. (Scotland) Act 2003, s. 3 (2) (3). - Issued: 27.06.2006. Made: 20.06.2006. Coming into force: In accord. with art. 1 (2) (3). Effect: 2003 asp 4 modified. Territorial extent & classification: S. General. - Supersedes draft SSI (ISBN 0110704754) issued 17.05.2006. - 4p.: 30 cm. - 978-0-11-070757-0 £3.00

Public finance and accountability

The Budget (Scotland) Act 2005 Amendment (No. 2) Order 2006 No. 2006/162. - Enabling power: Budget (Scotland) Act 2005, s. 7 (1). - Issued: 28.03.2006. Made: 16.03.2006. Coming into force: 17.03.2006. Effect: 2005 asp 4 amended. Territorial extent & classification: S. General. - 4p.: 30 cm. - 978-0-11-070187-5 £3.00

The Budget (Scotland) Act 2005 Amendment Order 2006 No. 2006/56. - Enabling power: Budget (Scotland) Act 2005, s. 7 (1). - Issued: 17.02.2006. Made: 08.02.2006. Coming into force: 09.02.2006. Effect: 2005 asp 4 amended. Territorial extent & classification: S. General. - 4p.: 30 cm. - 978-0-11-069942-4 £3.00

The Budget (Scotland) Act 2006 Amendment Order 2006 No. 2006/589. - Enabling power: Budget (Scotland) Act 2006, s. 7 (1). - Issued: 12.12.2006. Made: 04.12.2006. Coming into force: 05.12.2006. Effect: 2006 asp 5 amended. Territorial extent & classification: S. General. - Supersedes draft SI (ISBN 0110711149) issued 01.11.2006. - 4p.: 30 cm. - 978-0-11-071351-9 £3.00

Public health

The Civic Government (Scotland) Act 1982 (Licensing of Skin Piercing and Tattooing) Amendment Order 2006 No. 2006/604. - Enabling power: Civic Government (Scotland) Act 1982, s. 44 (1) (b) (2). - Issued: 22.12.2006. Made: 11.12.2006. Coming into force: 12.12.2006. Effect: S.S.I. 2006/43 amended. Territorial extent & classification: S. General. - 8p.: 30 cm. - 978-0-11-071423-3 £3.00

The Civic Government (Scotland) Act 1982 (Licensing of Skin Piercing and Tattooing) Order 2006 No. 2006/43. - Enabling power: Civic Government (Scotland) Act 1982, s. 44 (1) (b) (2). - Issued: 09.02.2006. Made: 01.02.2006. Coming into force: 02.02.2006 in acc. with art. 1. Effect: 1982 c.45 modified. Territorial extent & classification: S. General. - Approved by a resolution of the Scottish Parliament. Supersedes draft S.S.I. (ISBN 011069872X) issued on 19.12.2005. - 8p.: 30 cm. - 978-0-11-069927-1 £3.00

The Health Protection Agency (Scottish Health Functions) Order 2006 No. 2006/559. - Enabling power: Health Protection Agency Act 2004, s. 2 (7). - Issued: 01.12.2006. Made: 23.11.2006. Laid before the Scottish Parliament: 24.11.2006. Coming into force: 18.12.2006. Effect: None. Territorial extent & classification: S. General. - 4p.: 30 cm. - 978-0-11-071217-8 £3.00

The Prohibition of Smoking in Certain Premises (Scotland) Regulations 2006 No. 2006/90. - Enabling power: Smoking, Health and Social Care (Scotland) Act 2005, ss. 3 (3), 4 (2) (3) (6) (7), 40 (1) (b), sch. 1, paras 2, 4 (1), 5 (2), 12. - Issued: 08.03.2006. Made: 28.02.2006. Coming into force: 26.03.2006 at 0600 hours. Effect: None. Territorial extent & classification: S. General. - 12p.: 30 cm. - 978-0-11-069987-5 £3.00

The Smoking, Health and Social Care (Scotland) Act 2005 (Commencement No. 3) Order 2006 No. 2006/47 (C.5). - Enabling power: Smoking, Health and Social Care (Scotland) Act 2005, s. 43 (3) (4). Bringing into operation various provisions of the 2005 Act on 07.02.2006, in accord. with art. 2. - Issued: 13.02.2006. Made: 06.02.2006. Effect: None. Territorial extent & classification: S. General. - 2p.: 30 cm. - 978-0-11-069935-6 £3.00

The Smoking, Health and Social Care (Scotland) Act 2005 (Consequential Amendments) Order 2006 No. 2006/95. - Enabling power: Smoking, Health and Social Care (Scotland) Act 2005, s. 39. - Issued: 20.03.2006. Made: 03.03.2006. Laid before the Scottish Parliament: 03.03.2006. Coming into force: 26.03.2006 at 0600 hours. Effect: S.I. 1984/467 amended. Territorial extent & classification: S. General. - 2p.: 30 cm. - 978-0-11-070117-2 £3.00

Public health: Contamination of food

The Food Protection (Emergency Prohibitions) (Amnesic Shellfish Poisoning) (East Coast) (Scotland) Order 2005 Revocation Order 2006 No. 2006/102. - Enabling power: Food and Environment Protection Act 1985, s. 1 (1) (2). - Issued: 13.03.2006. Made: 06.03.2006. Laid before the Scottish Parliament: 07.03.2006. Coming into force: 06.03.2006 at 1630 hours in accord with art. 1. Effect: S.S.I. 2005/498 revoked. Territorial extent & classification: S. General. - 2p.: 30 cm. - 978-0-11-069993-6 £3.00

The Food Protection (Emergency Prohibitions) (Amnesic Shellfish Poisoning) (West Coast) (No. 6) (Scotland) Order 2005 Revocation Order 2006 No. 2006/69. - Enabling power: Food and Environment Protection Act 1985, s. 1 (1) (2). - Issued: 28.02.2006. Made: 22.02.2006. Laid before the Scottish Parliament: 23.02.2006. Coming into force: 22.02.2006 at 1630 hours in accord with art. 1. Effect: S.S.I. 2005/384 revoked. Territorial extent & classification: S. General. - 2p.: 30 cm. - 978-0-11-069967-7 £3.00

The Food Protection (Emergency Prohibitions) (Amnesic Shellfish Poisoning) (West Coast) (No. 7) (Scotland) Order 2005 Revocation Order 2006 No. 2006/235. - Enabling power: Food and Environment Protection Act 1985, s. 1 (1) (2). - Issued: 09.05.2006. Made: 28.04.2006. Laid before the Scottish Parliament: 03.05.2006. Coming into force: 28.04.2006 at 1630 hours in accord with art. 1. Effect: S.S.I. 2005/391 revoked. Territorial extent & classification: S. General. - 2p.: 30 cm. - 978-0-11-070405-0 £3.00

The Food Protection (Emergency Prohibitions) (Amnesic Shellfish Poisoning) (West Coast) (No. 8) (Scotland) Order 2005 Revocation Order 2006 No. 2006/191. - Enabling power: Food and Environment Protection Act 1985, s. 1 (1) (2). - Issued: 10.04.2006. Made: 31.03.2006. Laid before the Scottish Parliament: 03.04.2006. Coming into force: 31.03.2006 at 1630 hours in accord with art. 1. Effect: S.S.I. 2005/410 revoked. Territorial extent & classification: S. General. - 2p.: 30 cm. - 978-0-11-070236-0 £3.00

The Food Protection (Emergency Prohibitions) (Amnesic Shellfish Poisoning) (West Coast) (No. 11) (Scotland) Order 2005 Partial Revocation Order 2006 No. 2006/202. - Enabling power: Food and Environment Protection Act 1985, s. 1 (1) (2), 24 (3). - Issued: 19.04.2006. Made: 10.04.2006. Laid before the Scottish Parliament: 11.04.2006. Coming into force: 10.04.2006 at 1600 hours in accord with art. 1. Effect: S.S.I. 2005/455 partially revoked. Territorial extent & classification: S. General. - Revoked by S.S.I. 2006/260 (ISBN 0110704916) on 15.05.2006 at 16.30 hours. - 2p.: 30 cm. - 978-0-11-070265-0 £3.00

The Food Protection (Emergency Prohibitions) (Amnesic Shellfish Poisoning) (West Coast) (No. 11) (Scotland) Order 2005 Revocation Order 2006 No. 2006/260. - Enabling power: Food and Environment Protection Act 1985, s. 1 (1) (2). - Issued: 22.05.2006. Made: 15.05.2006. Laid before the Scottish Parliament: 16.05.2006. Coming into force: 15.05.2006 at 1630 hours in accord with art. 1. Effect: S.S.I. 2005/455; 2006/202 revoked. Territorial extent & classification: S. General. - 2p.: 30 cm. - 978-0-11-070491-3 £3.00

The Food Protection (Emergency Prohibitions) (Amnesic Shellfish Poisoning) (West Coast) (No. 12) (Scotland) Order 2005 Revocation Order 2006 No. 2006/6. - Enabling power: Food and Environment Protection Act 1985, s. 1 (1) (2). - Issued: 17.01.2006. Made: 11.01.2006. Laid before the Scottish Parliament: 12.01.2006. Coming into force: 11.01.2006 at 1630 hours in accord with art. 1. Effect: S.S.I. 2005/497 revoked. Territorial extent & classification: S. General. - 2p.: 30 cm. - 978-0-11-069899-1 *£3.00*

The Food Protection (Emergency Prohibitions) (Amnesic Shellfish Poisoning) (West Coast) (No. 13) (Scotland) Order 2005 Partial Revocation Order 2006 No. 2006/236. - Enabling power: Food and Environment Protection Act 1985, ss. 1 (1) (2), 24 (3). - Issued: 09.05.2006. Made: 28.04.2006. Laid before the Scottish Parliament: 03.05.2006. Coming into force: 28.04.2006 at 1630 hours in accord with art. 1. Effect: S.S.I. 2005/520 partially revoked. Territorial extent & classification: S. General. - Revoked at 1630 hours by S.S.I. 2006/242 (ISBN 0110704193) on 05.05.2006. - 2p.: 30 cm. - 978-0-11-070401-2 *£3.00*

The Food Protection (Emergency Prohibitions) (Amnesic Shellfish Poisoning) (West Coast) (No. 13) (Scotland) Order 2005 Revocation Order 2006 No. 2006/242. - Enabling power: Food and Environment Protection Act 1985, s. 1 (1) (2). - Issued: 15.05.2006. Made: 05.05.2006. Laid before the Scottish Parliament: 08.05.2006. Coming into force: 05.05.2006 at 1630 hours in accord with art. 1. Effect: S.S.I. 2005/520; 2006/236 revoked. Territorial extent & classification: S. General. - 2p.: 30 cm. - 978-0-11-070419-7 *£3.00*

The Food Protection (Emergency Prohibitions) (Amnesic Shellfish Poisoning) (West Coast) (No. 14) (Scotland) Order 2005 Partial Revocation Order 2006 No. 2006/103. - Enabling power: Food and Environment Protection Act 1985, s. 1 (1) (2), 24 (3). - Issued: 13.03.2006. Made: 06.03.2006. Laid before the Scottish Parliament: 07.03.2006. Coming into force: 06.03.2006 at 1630 hours in accord with art. 1. Effect: S.S.I. 2005/529 partially revoked. Territorial extent & classification: S. General. - Revoked by S.S.I. 2006/203 (ISBN 0110702662) at 1600 hours on 10.04.2006. - 2p.: 30 cm. - 978-0-11-069992-9 *£3.00*

The Food Protection (Emergency Prohibitions) (Amnesic Shellfish Poisoning) (West Coast) (No. 14) (Scotland) Order 2005 Revocation Order 2006 No. 2006/203. - Enabling power: Food and Environment Protection Act 1985, s. 1 (1) (2). - Issued: 19.04.2006. Made: 10.04.2006. Laid before the Scottish Parliament: 11.04.2006. Coming into force: 10.04.2006 at 1600 hours in accord with art. 1. Effect: S.S.I. 2005/529; 2006/103 revoked. Territorial extent & classification: S. General. - 2p.: 30 cm. - 978-0-11-070266-7 *£3.00*

The Food Protection (Emergency Prohibitions) (Amnesic Shellfish Poisoning) (West Coast) (No. 15) (Scotland) Order 2005 Revocation Order 2006 No. 2006/41. - Enabling power: Food and Environment Protection Act 1985, s. 1 (1) (2). - Issued: 07.02.2006. Made: 01.02.2006. Laid before the Scottish Parliament: 02.02.2006. Coming into force: 01.02.2006 at 1630 hours in accord with art. 1. Effect: S.S.I. 2005/575 revoked. Territorial extent & classification: S. General. - 2p.: 30 cm. - 978-0-11-069924-0 *£3.00*

The Food Protection (Emergency Prohibitions) (Amnesic Shellfish Poisoning) (West Coast) (No. 16) (Scotland) Order 2005 Partial Revocation Order 2006 No. 2006/145. - Enabling power: Food and Environment Protection Act 1985, s. 1 (1) (2), 24 (3). - Issued: 20.03.2006. Made: 10.03.2006. Laid before the Scottish Parliament: 13.03.2006. Coming into force: 10.03.2006 at 1630 hours in accord. with art. 1. Effect: S.S.I. 2005/579 partially revoked. Territorial extent & classification: S. General. - Revoked by S.S.I. 2006/192 (ISBN 0110702425) on 31.03.2006 at 16.30. - 2p.: 30 cm. - 978-0-11-070101-1 *£3.00*

The Food Protection (Emergency Prohibitions) (Amnesic Shellfish Poisoning) (West Coast) (No. 16) (Scotland) Order 2005 Revocation Order 2006 No. 2006/192. - Enabling power: Food and Environment Protection Act 1985, s. 1 (1) (2). - Issued: 10.04.2006. Made: 31.03.2006. Laid before the Scottish Parliament: 03.04.2006. Coming into force: 31.03.2006 at 1630 hours in accord with art. 1. Effect: S.S.I. 2005/579; 2006/145 revoked. Territorial extent & classification: S. General. - 2p.: 30 cm. - 978-0-11-070242-1 *£3.00*

The Food Protection (Emergency Prohibitions) (Amnesic Shellfish Poisoning) (West Coast) (No. 17) (Scotland) Order 2005 Revocation Order 2006 No. 2006/66. - Enabling power: Food and Environment Protection Act 1985, s. 1 (1) (2). - Issued: 23.02.2006. Made: 16.02.2006. Laid before the Scottish Parliament: 17.02.2006. Coming into force: 16.02.2006 at 1530 hours in accord with art. 1. Effect: S.S.I. 2005/585 revoked. Territorial extent & classification: S. General. - 2p.: 30 cm. - 978-0-11-069961-5 *£3.00*

The Food Protection (Emergency Prohibitions) (Amnesic Shellfish Poisoning) (West Coast) (No. 18) (Scotland) Order 2005 Revocation Order 2006 No. 2006/169. - Enabling power: Food and Environment Protection Act 1985, s. 1 (1) (2). - Issued: 30.03.2006. Made: 22.03.2006. Laid before the Scottish Parliament: 23.03.2006. Coming into force: 22.03.2006 at 1600 hours in accord with art. 1. Effect: S.S.I. 2005/626 revoked. Territorial extent & classification: S. General. - 4p.: 30 cm. - 978-0-11-070199-8 *£3.00*

The Food Protection (Emergency Prohibitions) (Paralytic Shellfish Poisoning) (Orkney) (No. 2) (Scotland) Order 2005 Revocation Order 2006 No. 2006/38. - Enabling power: Food and Environment Protection Act 1985, s. 1 (1) (2). - Issued: 07.02.2006. Made: 30.01.2006. Laid before the Scottish Parliament: 31.01.2006. Coming into force: 30.01.2006 at 1630 hours in accord with art. 1. Effect: S.S.I. 2005/548 revoked. Territorial extent & classification: S. General. - 2p.: 30 cm. - 978-0-11-069923-3 £3.00

The Food Protection (Emergency Prohibitions) (Radioactivity in Sheep) Partial Revocation (Scotland) Order 2006 No. 2006/52. - Enabling power: Food and Environment Protection Act 1985, ss. 1 (1) (2), 24 (3). - Issued: 16.02.2006. Made: 09.02.2006. Laid before the Scottish Parliament: 09.02.2006. Coming into force: 10.02.2006. Effect: S.I. 1991/20 amended in relation in Scotland. Territorial extent & classification: S. General. - 4p.: 30 cm. - 978-0-11-069944-8 £3.00

Public passenger transport

The Public Service Vehicles (Conduct of Drivers, Inspectors, Conductors and Passengers) Amendment (Scotland) Regulations 2006 No. 2006/613. - Enabling power: Public Passenger Vehicles Act 1981, ss. 24 (1), 25 (1). - Issued: 29.12.2006. Made: 20.12.2006. Laid before the Scottish Parliament: 22.12.2006. Coming into force: 01.02.2007. Effect: S.I. 1990/1020 amended in relation to Scotland. Territorial extent & classification: S. General. - 4p.: 30 cm. - 978-0-11-071471-4 £3.00

Public procurement

The Public Contracts (Scotland) Regulations 2006 No. 2006/1. - Enabling power: European Communities Act 1972, s. 2 (2). - Issued: 13.01.2006. Made: 04.01.2006. Laid before the Scottish Parliament: 05.01.2006. Coming into force: 31.01.2006. Effect: 1993 c. 51; 1996/974; 1997/1744; 1999/506, 1042, 1820; 2001/1149; 2002/881; S.S.I. 2003/242 amended in relation to Scotland & S.I. 1991/2680; 1993/3228; 1995/201; 2000/2009; 2003/46 revoked (with saving) in relation to Scotland. Territorial extent & classification: S. General. - EC note: These regs implement, for Scotland, Directive 2004/18/EC on the co-ordination of procedures for the award of public works contracts, public supply contracts and public services contracts. They also provide remedies for breaches of these Regulations, in order to implement Council Directive 89/665/EEC. - 88p.: 30 cm. - 978-0-11-069896-0 £13.50

The Utilities Contracts (Scotland) Regulations 2006 No. 2006/2. - Enabling power: European Communities Act 1972, s. 2 (2). - Issued: 13.01.2006. Made: 04.01.2006. Laid before the Scottish Parliament: 05.01.2006. Coming into force: 31.01.2006. Effect: S.I. 1996/2911; 2001/2418 revoked (with saving). Territorial extent & classification: S. General. - EC note: These regs implement, for Scotland, Directive 2004/17/EC co-ordinating the procurement procedures of entities operating in the water, energy, transport and postal services sectors. They also provide remedies for breaches of these Regulations, in order to implement Council Directive 92/13/EEC. - 68p.: 30 cm. - 978-0-11-069895-3 £10.50

Race relations

The Race Relations Act 1976 (Statutory Duties) (Scotland) Amendment Order 2006 No. 2006/467. - Enabling power: Race Relations Act 1976, ss. 71 (2) (3), 74 (4). - Issued: 20.09.2006. Made: 13.09.2006. Laid before the Scottish Parliament: 14.09.2006. Coming into force: 07.10.2006. Effect: S.S.I. 2002/62 amended. Territorial extent & classification: S. General. - 4p.: 30 cm. - 978-0-11-071019-8 £3.00

Rating and valuation

The Council Tax (Electronic Communications) (Scotland) Order 2006 No. 2006/67. - Enabling power: Electronic Communications Act 2000, ss. 8, 9. - Issued: 27.02.2006. Made: 20.02.2006. Laid before the Scottish Parliament: 21.02.2006. Coming into force: 01.04.2006. Effect: S.I. 1992/1332 amended. Territorial extent & classification: S. General. - 4p.: 30 cm. - 978-0-11-069965-3 £3.00

The Non-Domestic Rate (Scotland) Order 2006 No. 2006/92. - Enabling power: Local Government (Scotland) Act 1975, ss. 7B (1), 37 (1). - Issued: 08.03.2006. Made: 01.03.2006. Laid before the Scottish Parliament: 02.03.2006. Coming into force: 01.04.2006. Effect: None. Territorial extent & classification: S. General. - 2p.: 30 cm. - 978-0-11-069989-9 £3.00

The Non-Domestic Rates (Levying) (Scotland) (No. 2) Regulations 2006 No. 2006/158. - Enabling power: Local Government etc. (Scotland) Act 1994, s. 153. - Issued: 24.03.2006. Made: 16.03.2006. Laid before the Scottish Parliament: 17.03.2006. Coming into force: 01.04.2006. Effect: S.S.I. 2005/126 (with savings); 2006/124 revoked. Territorial extent & classification: S. General. - 16p.: 30 cm. - 978-0-11-070160-8 £3.00

The Non-Domestic Rating (Electronic Communications) (Scotland) Order 2006 No. 2006/201. - Enabling power: Electronic Communications Act 2000, ss. 8, 9. - Issued: 13.04.2006. Made: 31.03.2006. Coming into force: 01.04.2006. Effect: 1973 c.65 amended. Territorial extent & classification: S. General. - 4p.: 30 cm. - 978-0-11-070263-6 £3.00

The Non Domestic Rating (Rural Areas and Rateable Value Limits) (Scotland) Amendment Order 2006 No. 2006/125. - Enabling power: Local Government and Rating Act 1997, sch. 2, para. 1 (3) (c). - Issued: 16.03.2006. Made: 08.03.2006. Laid before the Scottish Parliament: 09.03.2006. Coming into force: 01.04.2006. Effect: S.S.I. 2005/103 amended. Territorial extent & classification: S. General. - 8p.: 30 cm. - 978-0-11-070069-4 £3.00

The Non-Domestic Rating (Telecommunications and Canals) (Scotland) Amendment Order 2006 No. 2006/557. - Enabling power: Valuation and Rating (Scotland) Act 1956, s. 6A. - Issued: 29.11.2006. Made: 22.11.2006. Laid before the Scottish Parliament: 23.11.2006. Coming into force: 01.01.2007. Effect: S.I. 1995/239 amended. Territorial extent & classification: S. General. - 4p.: 30 cm. - 978-0-11-071199-7 £3.00

The Valuation and Rating (Exempted Classes) (Scotland) Order 2006 No. 2006/180. - Enabling power: Valuation and Rating (Exempted Classes) (Scotland) Act 1976, s. 1. - Issued: 05.04.2006. Made: 28.03.2006. Coming into force: 01.04.2006. Effect: None. Territorial extent & classification: S. General. - 4p.: 30 cm. - 978-0-11-070221-6 £3.00

Registers and records

The Fees in the Registers of Scotland Amendment Order 2006 No. 2006/600. - Enabling power: Land Registers (Scotland) Act 1868, s. 25. - Issued: 21.12.2006. Made: 13.12.2006. Coming into force: 22.01.2007. Effect: S.I. 1995/1945 amended. Territorial extent & classification: S. General. - 12p.: 30 cm. - 978-0-11-071384-7 £3.00

The Register of Sasines (Application Procedure) Amendment Rules 2006 No. 2006/568. - Enabling power: Abolition of Feudal Tenure etc. (Scotland) Act 2000, s. 5 (2). - Issued: 05.12.2006. Made: 28.11.2006. Laid before the Scottish Parliament: 29.11.2006. Coming into force: 22.01.2007. Effect: S.S.I. 2004/318 amended. Territorial extent & classification: S. General. - 8p., col. forms: 30 cm. - 978-0-11-071263-5 £9.50

The Register of Sasines (Methods of Operation) (Scotland) Regulations 2006 No. 2006/164. - Enabling power: Register of Sasines (Scotland) Act 1987, s. 1. - Issued: 29.03.2006. Made: 21.03.2006. Laid before the Scottish Parliament: 22.03.2006. Coming into force: 30.04.2006. Effect: S.I. 1989/909 revoked. Territorial extent & classification: S. General. - 8p.: 30 cm. - 978-0-11-070189-9 £3.00

Registration of births, deaths, marriages, etc.

The Local Electoral Administration and Registration Services (Scotland) Act 2006 (Commencement No.1 and Transitional Provision) Order 2006 No. 2006/469 (C.38). - Enabling power: Local Electoral Administration and Registration Services (Scotland) Act 2006, ss. 61 (2), 63 (2). Bringing into operation various provisions of the 2006 Act on 01.10.2006 & 01.01.2007, in accord. with arts. 2, 3. - Issued: 21.09.2006. Made: 13.09.2006. Effect: None. Territorial extent & classification: S. General. - 12p.: 30 cm. - 978-0-11-071024-2 £3.00

The National Health Service Central Register (Scotland) Regulations 2006 No. 2006/484. - Enabling power: Local Electoral Administration and Registration Services (Scotland) Act 2006, ss. 57 (2) (f) (3) (i) (4) (6) (7), 61 (2). - Issued: 10.10.2006. Made: 03.10.20006. Laid before the Scottish Parliament: 04.10.2006. Coming into force: 11.11.2006. Effect: None. Territorial extent & classification: S. General. - 8p.: 30 cm. - 978-0-11-071062-4 £3.00

The Registration of Births, Still-births, Deaths and Marriages (Prescription of Forms and Errors) (Scotland) Regulations 2006 No. 2006/598. - Enabling power: Registration of Births, Deaths and Marriages (Scotland) Act 1965, ss. 19 (2), 39E (4), 40 (1), 42 (3), 43 (3) to (5), 54 (1) (b). - Issued: 19.12.2006. Made: 12.12.2006. Coming into force: 01.01.2007. Effect: S.I. 1997/1782, 2348 amended. Territorial extent & classification: S. General. - 12p.: 30 cm. - 978-0-11-071376-2 £3.00

The Registration Services (Attestation and Authentication) (Scotland) Regulations 2006 No. 2006/597. - Enabling power: Registration of Births, Deaths and Marriages (Scotland) Act 1965, ss. 15 (1) (2), 16 (1) (c), 18 (1) (a), 21 (2) (a), 24, 25 (1) (c), 41, 54 (1)(b), 54A and Marriage (Scotland) Act 1977, ss. 3 (3A), 5 (1), 24A (2). - Issued: 19.12.2006. Made: 12.12.2006. Coming into force: 01.01.2007. Effect: None. Territorial extent & classification: S. General. - 4p.: 30 cm. - 978-0-11-071373-1 £3.00

The Registration Services (Consequential Provisions) (Scotland) Order 2006 No. 2006/596. - Enabling power: Local Electoral Administration and Registration Services (Scotland) Act 2006, s. 62 (1) (a) (2). - Issued: 20.12.2006. Made: 12.12.2006. Coming into force: 01.01.2007. Effect: 1972 c.11; 1984 c.14; 1986 c.9; 1991 c.50; 2004 c.7; S.R. & O. 1935/247 amended. Territorial extent & classification: S. General. - Supersedes draft SI (ISBN 011071153X) issued 15.11.2006. - 4p.: 30 cm. - 978-0-11-071372-4 £3.00

The Registration Services (Fees, etc.) (Scotland) Regulations 2006 No. 2006/575. - Enabling power: Registration of Births, Deaths and Marriages (Scotland) Act 1965, ss.28A (4), 37 (1), 38 (2) (3), 39C, 39D (1), 39E (3), 43 (8), 47, 54 (1); Marriage (Scotland) Act 1977, ss. 3 (1), 19 (2); Civil Partnership Act 2004, ss. 88 (1), 95 (4), 122 (4), 134 (2) & Local Electoral Administration and Registration Services (Scotland) Act 2006, ss. 58 (5) (8), 61 (2) (a). - Issued: 06.12.2006. Made: 29.11.2006. Laid before the Scottish Parliament: 30.11.2006. Coming into force: 01.01.2007. Effect: S.I. 1998/643, 3191 & S.S.I. 2000/447; 2002/390; 2003/89; 2005/100, 556 revoked. Territorial extent & classification: S. General. - 16p.: 30 cm. - 978-0-11-071313-7 £3.00

Rehabilitation of offenders

The Rehabilitation of Offenders Act 1974 (Exclusions and Exceptions) (Amendment) (Scotland) Order 2006 No. 2006/194. - Enabling power: Rehabilitation of Offenders Act 1974, ss. 4 (4), 7 (4), 10 (1). - Issued: 10.04.2006. Made: 30.03.2006. Coming into force: In accord. with art 1 (2). Effect: S.S.I. 2003/231 amended. Territorial extent & classification: S. General. - With correction slip dated August 2006. - 4p.: 30 cm. - 978-0-11-070246-9 £3.00

River: Salmon and freshwater fisheries

The Assynt - Coigach Area Protection Variation Order 2006 No. 2006/488. - Enabling power: Salmon and Freshwater Fisheries (Consolidation) (Scotland) Act 2003, s. 48 (1). - Issued: 11.10.2006. Made: 05.10.2006. Coming into force: 06.10.2006. Effect: S.S.I. 2004/260 amended. Territorial extent & classification: S. General. - 2p.: 30 cm. - 978-0-11-071076-1 £3.00

The Conservation of Salmon (Collection of Statistics) (Scotland) Regulations 2006 No. 2006/572. - Salmon and Freshwater Fisheries (Consolidation) (Scotland) Act 2003, s. 38 (1) (5) (a), sch. 1, para 7 (b). - Issued: 20.12.2006. Made: 27.11.2006. Laid before the Scottish Parliament: 30.11.2006. Coming into force: 01.01.2007. Effect: None. Territorial extent & classification: S. General. - 4p.: 30 cm. - 978-0-11-071383-0 £3.00

The Northern Salmon Fishery District Designation Order 2006 No. 2006/447. - Enabling power: Salmon and Freshwater Fisheries (Consolidation) (Scotland) Act 2003, ss. 34 (2), 35, sch. 1. - Issued: 07.09.2006. Made: 31.08.2006. Coming into force: 01.09.2006. Effect: None. Territorial extent & classification: S. General. - 4p.: 30 cm. - 978-0-11-070964-2 £3.00

Road and bridges, Scotland

The A83 Trunk Road (Tarbert) (Special Event) (Temporary Prohibition of Waiting) Order 2006 No. 2006/259. - Enabling power: Roads (Scotland) Act 1984, s. 62 (1). - Made: 12.05.2006. Coming into force: 26.05.2006. Effect: None. Territorial extent & classification: S. Local *Unpublished*

Roads and bridges

The A7 Trunk Road (Auchenrivock Improvement) Order 2006 No. 2006/565. - Enabling power: Roads (Scotland) Act 1984, s. 5 (2). - Made: 23.11.2006. Coming into force: 01.12.2006. Effect: None. Territorial extent & classification: S. Local *Unpublished*

The A7 Trunk Road (Auchenrivock Improvement) (Side Roads) Order 2006 No. 2006/566. - Enabling power: Roads (Scotland) Act 1984, s. 12 (1). - Made: 23.11.2006. Coming into force: 01.12.2006. Effect: None. Territorial extent & classification: S. Local *Unpublished*

The A8 Trunk Road (East Hamilton Street, Greenock) (Stopping Up) Order 2006 No. 2006/25. - Enabling power: Roads (Scotland) Act 1984, ss. 1 (1), 12 (1). - Made: 23.01.2006. Coming into force: 07.02.2006. Effect: None. Territorial extent & classification: S. Local *Unpublished*

The A9 Trunk Road (Ballinluig Junction Improvement) (Side Roads) Order 2006 No. 2006/348. - Enabling power: Roads (Scotland) Act 1984, s. 12 (1). - Made: 08.06.2006. Coming into force: 16.06.2006. Effect: None. Territorial extent & classification: S. Local *Unpublished*

The A9 Trunk Road (Ballinluig Junction Improvement) (Slip Roads) Order 2006 No. 2006/349. - Enabling power: Roads (Scotland) Act 1984, ss. 5 (2), 143 (1). - Made: 08.06.2006. Coming into force: 16.06.2006. Effect: None. Territorial extent & classification: S. Local *Unpublished*

The A9 Trunk Road (Helmsdale to Ord of Caithness Improvements - Phase 2) (Side Roads) (Variation) Order 2006 No. 2006/529. - Enabling power: Roads (Scotland) Act 1984, s. 12 (1). - Made: 30.10.2006. Coming into force: 10.11.2006. Effect: S.S.I. 2004/354 varied. Territorial extent & classification: S. Local *Unpublished*

The A76 Trunk Road (Glenairlie Improvement) Order 2006 No. 2006/462. - Enabling power: Roads (Scotland) Act 1984, s. 5 (2). - Made: 08.09.2006. Coming into force: 15.09.2006. Effect: None. Territorial extent & classification: S. Local *Unpublished*

The A76 Trunk Road (Glenairlie Improvement) (Side Roads) Order 2006 No. 2006/463. - Enabling power: Roads (Scotland) Act 1984, s. 12 (1). - Made: 08.09.2006. Coming into force: 15.09.2006. Effect: None. Territorial extent & classification: S. Local *Unpublished*

The A77 Trunk Road (Haggstone Climbing Lane) (Side Roads) Order 2006 No. 2006/369. - Enabling power: Roads (Scotland) Act 1984, s. 12 (1). - Made: 26.06.2006. Coming into force: 07.07.2006. Effect: None. Territorial extent & classification: S. Local *Unpublished*

The A80/M73 Special Roads (Moodiesburn Bypass) Scheme 2006 No. 2006/500. - Enabling power: Roads (Scotland) Act 1984, s. 7. - Made: 06.10.2006. Coming into force: 13.10.2006. Effect: None. Territorial extent & classification: S. Local *Unpublished*

The A80/M73 Special Roads (Moodiesburn Bypass) (Side Roads) Order 2006 No. 2006/501. - Enabling power: Roads (Scotland) Act 1984, s. 9. - Made: 06.10.2006. Coming into force: 13.10.2006. Effect: None. Territorial extent & classification: S. Local *Unpublished*

The A80 Special Road (Auchenkilns to Haggs) Appropriation Order 2006 No. 2006/499. - Enabling power: Roads (Scotland) Act 1984, s. 9 (1). - Made: 06.10.2006. Coming into force: 13.10.2006. Effect: None. Territorial extent & classification: S. Local *Unpublished*

The A80 Special Road (Auchenkilns to Haggs) Scheme 2006 No. 2006/497. - Enabling power: Roads (Scotland) Act 1984, s. 7. - Made: 06.10.2006. Coming into force: 13.10.2006. Effect: None. Territorial extent & classification: S. Local *Unpublished*

The A80 Special Road (Mollinsburn to Auchenkilns) Appropriation Order 2006 No. 2006/496. - Enabling power: Roads (Scotland) Act 1984, s. 9 (1). - Made: 06.10.2006. Coming into force: 13.10.2006. Effect: None. Territorial extent & classification: S. Local *Unpublished*

The A80 Trunk Road (Auchenkilns to Haggs) (Side Roads) Order 2006 No. 2006/498. - Enabling power: Roads (Scotland) Act 1984, s. 9. - Made: 06.10.2006. Coming into force: 13.10.2006. Effect: None. Territorial extent & classification: S. Local *Unpublished*

The A80 Trunk Road (Mollinsburn to Auchenkilns) (Side Roads) Order 2006 No. 2006/494. - Enabling power: Roads (Scotland) Act 1984, s. 12 (1). - Made: 06.10.2006. Coming into force: 13.10.2006. Effect: None. Territorial extent & classification: S. Local *Unpublished*

The A82 Trunk Road (Aonachan Lay-by, Spean Bridge) (Stopping Up) Order 2006 No. 2006/53. - Enabling power: Roads (Scotland) Act 1984, s. 68 (1). - Made: 07.02.2006. Coming into force: 23.02.2006. Effect: None. Territorial extent & classification: S. Local *Unpublished*

The A82 Trunk Road (Balloch to Tarbet Cycle Routes) (Redetermination of Means of Exercise of Public Right of Passage) Order 2006 No. 2006/305. - Enabling power: Roads (Scotland) Act 1984, ss. 2 (1), 152 (2). - Made: 05.06.2006. Coming into force: 15.06.2006. Effect: None. Territorial extent & classification: S. Local *Unpublished*

The A737 Trunk Road (Roadhead Roundabout Improvement) Order 2006 No. 2006/422. - Enabling power: Roads (Scotland) Act 1984, s. 5 (2). - Made: 11.08.2006. Coming into force: 25.08.2006. Effect: None. Territorial extent & classification: S. Local *Unpublished*

The A737 Trunk Road (Roadhead Roundabout Improvement) (Side Roads) Order 2006 No. 2006/423. - Enabling power: Roads (Scotland) Act 1984, s. 12 (1). - Made: 11.08.2006. Coming into force: 25.08.2006. Effect: None. Territorial extent & classification: S. Local *Unpublished*

The A830 Trunk Road (Arisaig - Loch nan Uamh) (Side Roads) (Variation) Order 2006 No. 2006/489. - Enabling power: Roads (Scotland) Act 1984, s. 12 (1). - Made: 03.10.2006. Coming into force: 13.10.2006. Effect: S.S.I. 2005/538 varied. Territorial extent & classification: S. Local *Unpublished*

The A830 Trunk Road (Arisaig - Loch nan Uamh) (Variation) Order 2006 No. 2006/490. - Enabling power: Roads (Scotland) Act 1984, s. 5 (2). - Made: 03.10.2006. Coming into force: 13.10.2006. Effect: S.S.I. 2005/537 varied. Territorial extent & classification: S. Local *Unpublished*

The Environmental Impact Assessment (Scotland) Amendment Regulations 2006 No. 2006/614. - Enabling power: European Communities Act 1972, s. 2 (2) and Town and Country Planning (Scotland) Act 1997, s. 40. - Issued: 05.01.2007. Made: 21.12.2006. Laid before the Scottish Parliament: 22.12.2006. Coming into force: 01.02.2007. Effect: 1984 c.54; S.I. 1999/367 amended in relation to Scotland; S.S.I. 1999/1, 43; 2006/582 amended. Territorial extent & classification: S. General. - Copies are supplied by TSO's On-demand publishing service. With correction slip dated February 2007. EC note: These Regulations implement in Scotland the amendments made by Article 3 of Council Directive 2003/35/EC with regard to public participation and access to justice to Council Directive 85/337/EEC. - 24p.: 30 cm. - 978-0-11-071472-1 £4.00

The Erskine Bridge (Temporary Suspension of Tolls) Order 2006 No. 2006/157. - Enabling power: Erskine Bridge Tolls Act 1968, s. 6. - Issued: 24.03.2006. Made: 16.03.2006. Laid before the Scottish Parliament: 16.03.2006. Coming into force: 01.04.2006. Effect: None. Territorial extent & classification: S. General. - Copies are supplied from TSO's On-Demand Publishing Service. - 4p.: 30 cm. - 978-0-11-070170-7 £3.00

The M8/A8 Trunk Road (Greenock Road/Port Glasgow Road Junction, Greenock) (Temporary Prohibition of Specified Turns) Order 2006 No. 2006/100. - Enabling power: Road Traffic Regulation Act 1984, s. 14 (1) (a). - Made: 06.03.2006. Coming into force: 20.03.2006. Effect: None. Territorial extent & classification: S. Local *Unpublished*

The M8/A8 Trunk Road (Rue End Street/Dellington Street Junction, Greenock) (Temporary Prohibition of Specified Turns) Order 2006 No. 2006/150. - Enabling power: Road Traffic Regulation Act 1984, s. 14 (1) (a). - Made: 08.03.2006. Coming into force: 20.03.2006. Effect: None. Territorial extent & classification: S. Local *Unpublished*

Roads and bridges

The M77 Special Road (Fenwick to Malletsheugh and Glasgow Southern Orbital) Trunking Order 2006 No. 2006/567. - Enabling power: Roads (Scotland) Act 1984, ss. 5 (2), 143 (1). - Made: 24.11.2006. Coming into force: 08.11.2006. Effect: None. Territorial extent & classification: S. Local *Unpublished*

The M80/A80 Trunk Roads (Stepps to Moodiesburn) Detrunking Order 2006 No. 2006/502. - Enabling power: Roads (Scotland) Act 1984, s. 5 (2). - Made: 06.10.2006. Coming into force: In accord.with art. 1. Effect: None. Territorial extent & classification: S. Local *Unpublished*

The M80/M73 Special Roads (Mollinsburn to Auchenkilns) Scheme 2006 No. 2006/493. - Enabling power: Roads (Scotland) Act 1984, s. 7. - Made: 06.10.2006. Coming into force: 13.10.2006. Effect: None. Territorial extent & classification: S. Local *Unpublished*

The Stepps Bypass (M80) (City of Glasgow District Boundary to Crow Wood) (Connecting Roads) Special Road (Revocation) Scheme 2006 No. 2006/503. - Enabling power: Roads (Scotland) Act 1984, ss. 7, 145. - Made: 06.10.2006. Coming into force: In accord.with art. 1. Effect: The Stepps Bypass (M80) (City of Glasgow District Boundary to Crow Wood) (Connecting Roads) Special Road Scheme 1987 is revoked. Territorial extent & classification: S. Local *Unpublished*

The Stepps Bypass (M80) (City of Glasgow District Boundary to Crow Wood) Special Road (Variation) Scheme 2006 No. 2006/504. - Enabling power: Roads (Scotland) Act 1984, ss. 7, 145. - Made: 06.10.2006. Coming into force: In accord.with art. 1. Effect: The Stepps Bypass (M80) (City of Glasgow District Boundary to Crow Wood) (Connecting Roads) Special Road Scheme 1987 is varied. Territorial extent & classification: S. Local *Unpublished*

Road traffic

The A80 Trunk Roads (Mollinsburn to Auchenkilns) (Prohibition of Specified Turns) Order 2006 No. 2006/495. - Enabling power: Road Traffic Regulation Act 1984, s. 1 (1). - Made: 06.10.2006. Coming into force: 13.10.2006. Effect: None. Territorial extent & classification: S. Local *Unpublished*

The Road Traffic (NHS Charges) Amendment (Scotland) Regulations 2006 No. 2006/84. - Enabling power: Road Traffic (NHS Charges) Act 1999, ss. 3 (2) (4),16 (2) (a) (b). - Issued: 07.03.2006. Made: 27.02.2006. Laid before the Scottish Parliament: 28.02.2006. Coming into force: 01.04.2006. Effect: S.I. 1999/785 amended. Territorial extent & classification: S. General. - 4p.: 30 cm. - 978-0-11-069980-6 *£3.00*

The Road Traffic (Permitted Parking Area and Special Parking Area) (City of Glasgow, Perth and Kinross Council, Aberdeen City Council, Dundee City Council and South Lanarkshire Council) Designation Amendment Order 2006 No. 2006/446. - Enabling power: Road Traffic Act 1991, sch. 3, paras. 1 (1), 2 (1), 3 (3). - Issued: 06.09.2006. Made: 30.08.2006. Laid before the Scottish Parliament: 01.09.2006. Coming into force: 01.10.2006. Effect: S.S.I. 1999/59; 2002/398; 2003/70; 2004/87; 2005/11 amended. Territorial extent & classification: S. General. - 4p.: 30 cm. - 978-0-11-070955-0 *£3.00*

Road traffic: Speed limits

The A7 Trunk Road (Hawick) (30mph Speed Limit) Variation and Hawick High School and Wilton Primary School (Part-time 20mph Speed Limit) Order 2006 No. 2006/356. - Enabling power: Road Traffic Regulation Act 1984, s. 84 (1) (a) (c). - Made: 13.06.2006. Coming into force: 21.06.2006. Effect: S.I. 1975/436 varied. Territorial extent & classification: S. Local *Unpublished*

The A7 Trunk Road (Selkirk) (30 mph Speed Limit) Variation and Selkirk High School and St Joseph's Primary School (Part-time 20 mph Speed Limit) Order 2006 No. 2006/564. - Enabling power: Road Traffic Regulation Act 1984, s. 84 (1) (a) (c). - Made: 17.11.2006. Coming into force: 01.12.2006. Effect: S.S.I. 2003/549 varied & S.I. 1996/2170 revoked. Territorial extent & classification: S. Local *Unpublished*

The A9 Trunk Road (Golspie) (30mph Speed Limit) Variation and Golspie High School (Part-time 20mph Speed Limit) Order 2006 No. 2006/228. - Enabling power: Road Traffic Regulation Act 1984, s. 84 (1) (a) (c). - Made: 27.04.2006. Coming into force: 08.05.2006. Effect: S.S.I. 2002/394 varied. Territorial extent & classification: S. Local *Unpublished*

The A9 Trunk Road (Portree) (30 mph and 40 mph Speed Limits) Variation and Portree High School (Part-time 20 mph Speed Limit) Order 2006 No. 2006/261. - Enabling power: Road Traffic Regulation Act 1984, ss. 82 (2) (a), 83 (1), 84 (1) (a) (c). - Made: 15.05.2006. Coming into force: 01.06.2006. Effect: The Highland Regional Council (Portree, Skye) (Restricted Roads and 40 mph Speed Limit) Order 1990 varied. Territorial extent & classification: S. Local *Unpublished*

The A68 Trunk Road (Dalkeith) (30 mph Speed Limit) Variation and St David's Primary School (Part-time 20 mph Speed Limit) Order 2006 No. 2006/563. - Enabling power: Road Traffic Regulation Act 1984, s. 84 (1) (a) (c). - Made: 17.11.2006. Coming into force: 01.12.2006. Effect: S.I. 2004/540 varied. Territorial extent & classification: S. Local *Unpublished*

The A68 Trunk Road (Pathhead) (30mph Speed Limit) Variation and Pathhead Primary School (Part-time 20mph Speed Limit) Order 2006 No. 2006/258. - Enabling power: Road Traffic Regulation Act 1984, s. 84 (1) (a) (c). - Made: 12.05.2006. Coming into force: 23.05.2006. Effect: S.I. 1992/2747 varied. Territorial extent & classification: S. Local *Unpublished*

The A76 Trunk Road (Cumnock) (30mph Speed Limit) Variation and Castle Primary School (Part-time 20mph Speed Limit) Order 2006 No. 2006/438. - Enabling power: Road Traffic Regulation Act 1984, s. 84 (1) (a) (c). - Made: 25.08.2006. Coming into force: 04.092006. Effect: S.I. 1975/766 varied. Territorial extent & classification: S. Local *Unpublished*

The A77 Trunk Road (British Seniors Open Golf Championship, Turnberry) (Temporary 30mph Speed Limit) Order 2006 No. 2006/408. - Enabling power: Road Traffic Regulation Act 1984, s. 88 (1) (a) (2). - Made: 21.07.2006. Coming into force: 22.07.2006. Effect: None. Territorial extent & classification: S. Local *Unpublished*

The A77 Trunk Road (Girvan) (30mph Speed Limit) Variation and Sacred Heart and Invergarven Primary Schools (Part-time 20mph Speed Limit) Order 2006 No. 2006/433. - Enabling power: Road Traffic Regulation Act 1984, s. 84 (1) (a) (c). - Made: 18.08.2006. Coming into force: 28.08.2006. Effect: S.I. 1975/766 varied. Territorial extent & classification: S. Local *Unpublished*

The A77 Trunk Road (Whitletts Roundabout) (50mph Speed Limit) Order 2006 No. 2006/426. - Enabling power: Road Traffic Regulation Act 1984, s. 84 (1) (a). - Made: 14.08.2006. Coming into force: 21.08.2006. Effect: None. Territorial extent & classification: S. Local *Unpublished*

The A78 Trunk Road Greenock Schools (Part-time 20mph Speed Limit) Order 2006 No. 2006/439. - Enabling power: Road Traffic Regulation Act 1984, s. 84 (1) (a) (c). - Made: 29.08.2006. Coming into force: 11.09.2006. Effect: None. Territorial extent & classification: S. Local *Unpublished*

The A80 Trunk Road (Auchenkilns Junction) (Speed Limit) Order 2006 No. 2006/417. - Enabling power: Road Traffic Regulation Act 1984, s. 84 (1) (a). - Made: 04.08.2006. Coming into force: 11.08.2006. Effect: None. Territorial extent & classification: S. Local *Unpublished*

The A82 Trunk Road (Drumnadrochit & Lewiston) (30mph and 40mph Speed Limit) Order 2006 No. 2006/624. - Enabling power: Road Traffic Regulation Act 1984, s. 84 (1) (a). - Made: 19.12.2006. Coming into force: 05.01.2007. Effect: S.S.I. 2000/27, 377 revoked. Territorial extent & classification: S. Local *Unpublished*

The A82 Trunk Road (Fort William) (30mph Speed Limit) Variation and Fort William Primary School (Part-time 20mph Speed Limit) Order 2006 No. 2006/20. - Enabling power: Road Traffic Regulation Act 1984, s. 84 (1) (a). - Made: 19.01.2006. Coming into force: 02.02.2006. Effect: S.I. 1975/764 varied. Territorial extent & classification: S. Local *Unpublished*

The A82 Trunk Road (Scottish Open Golf Tournament, Loch Lomond) (Temporary 30mph Speed Limit) Order 2006 No. 2006/371. - Enabling power: Road Traffic Regulation Act 1984, s. 88 (1) (a) (2). - Made: 27.06.2006. Coming into force: 12.07.2006. Effect: None. Territorial extent & classification: S. Local *Unpublished*

The A85 Trunk Road (Connel) (30mph Speed Limit) Variation and Achaleven Primary School (Part-time 20mph Speed Limit) Order 2006 No. 2006/262. - Enabling power: Road Traffic Regulation Act 1984, s. 84 (1) (a) (c). - Made: 15.05.2006. Coming into force: 01.06.2006. Effect: S.I 1995/1345 varied. Territorial extent & classification: S. Local *Unpublished*

The A85 Trunk Road (Lochawe) (30mph Speed Limit) Order 2006 No. 2006/483. - Enabling power: Road Traffic Regulation Act 1984, s. 84 (1). - Made: 28.09.2006. Coming into force: 05.10.2006. Effect: S.I. 1981/1454 revoked. Terr. extent & class.: S. Local *Unpublished*

The A86 Trunk Road (Newtownmore) (30mph Speed Limit) Variation and Newtownmore Primary School (Part-time 20mph Speed Limit) Order 2006 No. 2006/10. - Enabling power: Road Traffic Regulation Act 1984, s. 84 (1) (a) (c). - Made: 12.01.2006. Coming into force: 26.01.2006. Effect: S.S.I. 2002/53 varied. Territorial extent & classification: S. Local *Unpublished*

The A86 Trunk Road (Roybridge) (30mph Speed Limit) and Roybridge Primary School (Part-time 20mph Speed Limit) Order 2006 No. 2006/204. - Enabling power: Road Traffic Regulation Act 1984, ss. 82 (2) (a), 83 (1), 84 (1) (a) (c). - Made: 11.04.2006. Coming into force: 28.04.2006. Effect: S.S.I. 2003/3113 revoked. Territorial extent & classification: S. Local *Unpublished*

The A86 Trunk Road (Spean Bridge) (30mph Speed Limit) Variation and Spean Bridge Primary School (Part-time 20mph Speed Limit) Order 2006 No. 2006/9. - Enabling power: Road Traffic Regulation Act 1984, s. 84 (1) (a) (c). - Made: 11.01.2006. Coming into force: 25.01.2006. Effect: S.S.I. 2002/377 varied. Territorial extent & classification: S. Local *Unpublished*

The A87 Trunk Road (Invergarry) (40mph Speed Limit) Variation and Invergarry Primary School (Part-time 20mph Speed Limit) Order 2006 No. 2006/175. - Enabling power: Road Traffic Regulation Act 1984, s. 84 (1) (a) (c). - Made: 24.03.2006. Coming into force: 07.04.2006. Effect: S.I. 1982/1473 varied. Territorial extent & classification: S. Local *Unpublished*

The A87 Trunk Road (Inverinate) (40mph Speed Limit) Variation and Loch Duich Primary School (Part-time 20mph Speed Limit) Order 2006 No. 2006/362. - Enab. power: Road Traffic Reg. Act 1984, s. 84(1)(a)(c). - Made: 19.06.2006. CiF: 03.07.2006. Effect: S.I. 1994/1694 varied. Terr. ex. & class.: S. Local *Unpub'd*

The A87 Trunk Road (Uig, Isle of Skye) (30mph and 40mph Speed Limit) Variation and Uig Primary School (Part-time 20mph Speed Limit) Order 2006 No. 2006/165. - Enabling power: Road Traffic Regulation Act 1984, s. 84 (1) (a) (c). - Made: 21.03.2006. Coming into force: 06.04.2006. Effect: S.S.I. 2003/555 varied. Territorial extent & classification: S. Local *Unpublished*

The A90 Trunk Road (Ellon Road, Aberdeen) (40 mph Speed Limit) Order 2006 No. 2006/407. - Enabling power: Road Traffic Regulation Act 1984, s. 84 (1) (a). - Made: 17.07.2006. Coming into force: 31.07.2006. Effect: None. Territorial extent & classification: S. Local *Unpublished*

The A90 Trunk Road (Kingsway, Dundee) (Temporary 40mph Speed Restriction) Order 2006 No. 2006/229. - Enabling power: Road Traffic Regulation Act 1984, s. 88 (1) (a) (2). - Made: 28.04.2006. Coming into force: 13.05.2006. Effect: None. Territorial extent & classification: S. Local *Unpublished*

The A90 Trunk Road (Schoolhill Development) (Temporary 40mph Speed Limit) Order 2006 No. 2006/625. - Enabling power: Road Traffic Regulation Act 1984, s. 84 (1) (a). - Made: 21.12.2006. Coming into force: 04.01.2007. Effect: None. Territorial extent & classification: S. Local *Unpublished*

The A90 Trunk Road (The Parkway, Bridge of Don, Aberdeen) (50 mph Speed Limit) Order 2006 No. 2006/405. - Enabling power: Road Traffic Regulation Act 1984, s. 84 (1) (a). - Made: 17.07.2006. Coming into force: 31.07.2006. Effect: None. Territorial extent & classification: S. Local *Unpublished*

The A92 Trunk Road (Freuchie) (40 mph Speed Limit) Order 2006 No. 2006/520. - Enabling power: Road Traffic Regulation Act 1984, s. 84 (1) (a). - Made: 23.10.2006. Coming into force: 06.11.2006. Effect: The Fife Regional Council (Speed Limits) (Consolidation) (Revocation) Order 1992 varied & S.I. 1999/17 revoked. Territorial extent & classification: S. Local *Unpublished*

The A95 Trunk Road (Cromdale Village) (30mph Speed Limit) Order 2006 No. 2006/161. - Enabling power: Road Traffic Regulation Act 1984, s. 84 (1) (a). - Made: 17.03.2006. Coming into force: 30.03.2006. Effect: The Highland Regional Council (A95 Cromdale) (40mph Speed Limit) Order 1992 revoked. Territorial extent & classification: S. Local *Unpublished*

The A96 Trunk Road (Fochabers) (30mph Speed Limit) Variation and Milnes Primary School (Part-time 20 mph Speed Limit) Order 2006 No. 2006/526. - Enabling power: Road Traffic Regulation Act 1984, s. 84 (1) (a) (c). - Made: 30.10.2006. Coming into force: 13.11.2006. Effect: S.I. 1994/2344 varied. Territorial extent & classification: S. Local *Unpublished*

The A96 Trunk Road (Nairn) (30mph Speed Limit) Variation and Rosebank Primary School (Part-time 20mph Speed Limit) Order 2006 No. 2006/357. - Enabling power: Road Traffic Regulation Act 1984, s. 84 (1) (a) (c). - Made: 09.06.2006. Coming into force: 23.06.2006. Effect: S.I. 1975/820 varied. Territorial extent & classification: S. Local *Unpublished*

The A702 Trunk Road (Biggar Road, Edinburgh) (40 mph Speed Limit) Order 2006 No. 2006/400. - Enabling power: Road Traffic Regulation Act 1984, s. 84 (1) (a). - Made: 13.07.2006. Coming into force: 27.07.2006. Effect: None. Territorial extent & classification: S. Local *Unpublished*

The A702 Trunk Road (Hillend) (40mph Speed Limit) Order 2006 No. 2006/623. - Enabling power: Road Traffic Regulation Act 1984, s. 84 (1) (a). - Made: 15.12.2006. Coming into force: 29.12.2006. Effect: None. Territorial extent & classification: S. Local *Unpublished*

The A702 Trunk Road (West Linton) (30mph Speed Limit) Variation and West Linton Primary School (Part-time 20mpoh Speed Limit) Order 2006 No. 2006/256. - Enabling power: Road Traffic Regulation Act 1984, s. 84 (1) (a) (c). - Made: 11.05.2006. Coming into force: 31.05.2006. Effect: S.I. 1978/498 varied. Territorial extent & classification: S. Local *Unpublished*

The A725 Trunk Road (Shawhead to Whirlies Roundabout) (40mph, 50mph and 60mph Speed Limit) Order 2006 No. 2006/62. - Enabling power: Road Traffic Regulation Act 1984, s. 84 (1) (a). - Made: 15.02.2006. Coming into force: 01.03.2006. Effect: None. Territorial extent & classification: S. Local *Unpublished*

The A737 Trunk Road (Kilwinning) (30mph Speed Limit) Variation and Kilwinning Academy and Abbey Primary School (Part-time 20mpoh Speed Limit) Order 2006 No. 2006/267. - Enabling power: Road Traffic Regulation Act 1984, s. 84 (1) (a) (c). - Made: 17.05.2006. Coming into force: 06.06.2006. Effect: Strathclyde Regional Council (Restricted Roads) (Transitional) Order 1985 varied. Territorial extent & classification: S. Local *Unpublished*

The A830 Trunk Road (30mph Corpach and Banavie Primary School Part-time 20mph Speed Limit) Order 2006 No. 2006/21. - Enabling power: Road Traffic Regulation Act 1984, s. 82 (2) (a), 83 (1), 84 (1) (a) (c). - Made: 19.01.2006. Coming into force: 02.02.2006. Effect: S.I. 1993/2435 amended. Territorial extent & classification: S. Local *Unpublished*

The A830 Trunk Road (30mph Lochybridge and Lochaber High School Part-time 20mph Speed Limit) Order 2006 No. 2006/22. - Enabling power: Road Traffic Regulation Act 1984, ss. 82 (2) (a), 83 (1), 84 (1) (a) (c). - Made: 19.01.2006. Coming into force: 02.02.2006. Effect: S.I. 1974/947 amended & S.I. 1980/659; 1992/1263 revoked. Territorial extent & classification: S. Local *Unpublished*

The A977 Trunk Road (Kincardine Toll Road) (Temporary 30mph Speed Limit) Order 2006 No. 2006/159. - Enabling power: Road Traffic Regulation Act 1984, s. 88 (1) (a). - Made: 17.03.2006. Coming into force: 01.04.2006. Effect: None. Territorial extent & classification: S. Local *Unpublished*

The M8/A8 Trunk Road (Chapleton Street to Anderson Street, Port Glasgow) (Temporary 40 mph Speed Limit) Order 2006 No. 2006/492. - Enabling power: Road Traffic Regulation Act 1984, s. 14 (1) (4). - Made: 05.10.2006. Coming into force: 16.10.2006. Effect: None. Territorial extent & classification: S. Local *Unpublished*

The M90/A90 Trunk Road (Persley Bridge, Aberdeen) (30 mph Speed Limit) 2006 No. 2006/406. - Enabling power: Road Traffic Regulation Act 1984, s. 84 (1) (a). - Made: 17.07.2006. Coming into force: 31.07.2006. Effect: None. Territorial extent & classification: S. Local *Unpublished*

The M90 Motorway (Gairneybridge to Milnathort) (Temporary 50mph Speed Restriction) 2006 No. 2006/351. - Enabling power: Road Traffic Regulation Act 1984, s. 88 (1) (a) (2). - Made: 23.06.2006. Coming into force: 07.07.2006. Effect: None. Territorial extent & classification: S. Local *Unpublished*

Road traffic: Traffic regulation

The A8 Trunk Road (Ratho Street, Greenock) (Temporary Prohibition of Specified Turns) Order 2006 No. 2006/23. - Enabling power: Road Traffic Regulation Act 1984, s. 14 (1) (a). - Made: 20.01.2006. Coming into force: 31.01.2006. Effect: None. Territorial extent & classification: S. Local *Unpublished*

The A9 Trunk Road (Auchterarder, Perthshire) (Temporary Prohibition of Specified Turns) (No. 2) Order 2006 No. 2006/271. - Enabling power: Road Traffic Regulation Act 1984, s. 14 (1) (a). - Made: 22.05.2006. Coming into force: 01.06.2006. Effect: None. Territorial extent & classification: S. Local *Unpublished*

The A9 Trunk Road (Auchterarder, Perthshire) (Temporary Prohibition of Specified Turns) Order 2006 No. 2006/54. - Enabling power: Road Traffic Regulation Act 1984, s. 14 (1) (a). - Made: 10.02.2006. Coming into force: 24.02.2006. Effect: None. Territorial extent & classification: S. Local *Unpublished*

The A9 Trunk Road (Ballinluig Junction Improvement) (Prohibition of Specified Turns) Order 2006 No. 2006/350. - Enabling power: Road Traffic Regulation Act 1984, s. 1 (1). - Made: 08.06.2006. Coming into force: 16.06.2006. Effect: None. Territorial extent & classification: S. Local *Unpublished*

The A9 Trunk Road (Greenloaning, Perthshire) (Temporary Prohibition of Specified Turns) Order 2006 No. 2006/590. - Enabling power: Road Traffic Regulation Act 1984, s. 14 (1) (a). - Made: 29.11.2006. Coming into force: 13.11.2006. Effect: None. Territorial extent & classification: S. Local *Unpublished*

The A9 Trunk Road (Schoolhill Development) (Temporary Prohibition of Specified Turns) Order 2006 No. 2006/277. - Enabling power: Road Traffic Regulation Act 1984, s. 14 (1) (a). - Made: 22.05.2006. Coming into force: 01.06.2006. Effect: None. Territorial extent & classification: S. Local *Unpublished*

The A9 Trunk Road (Tore) (Temporary Prohibition of Specified Turns) Order 2006 No. 2006/217. - Enabling power: Road Traffic Regulation Act 1984, s. 14 (1) (a). - Made: 21.04.2006. Coming into force: 01.05.2006. Effect: None. Territorial extent & classification: S. Local *Unpublished*

The A68 Trunk Road (Bongate, Jedburgh) (Prohibition of Waiting) Order 2006 No. 2006/544. - Enabling power: Road Traffic Regulation Act 1984, s. 1 (1). - Made: 02.11.2006. Coming into force: 16.11.2006. Effect: None. Territorial extent & classification: S. Local *Unpublished*

The A74(M) Motorway (Junction 20, Northbound on Slip at Eaglesfield) (Temporary Prohibition of Traffic) Order 2006 No. 2006/519. - Enabling power: Road Traffic Regulation Act 1984, s. 14 (1) (a). - Made: 26.10.2006. Coming into force: 10.11.2006. Effect: None. Territorial extent & classification: S. Local *Unpublished*

The A77 Trunk Road (Central Reserve) (Prohibition of Specified Turns) Order 2006 No. 2006/147. - Enabling power: Road Traffic Regulation Act 1984, s. 1 (1). - Made: 08.03.2006. Coming into force: 17.03.2006. Effect: None. Territorial extent & classification: S. Local *Unpublished*

The A77 Trunk Road (Dalrymple Street, Girvan) (Special Event) (Temporary Prohibition of Traffic) Order 2006 No. 2006/555. - Enabling power: Road Traffic Regulation Act 1984, s. 16A. - Made: 17.11.2006. Coming into force: 01.12.2006. Effect: None. Territorial extent & classification: S. Local *Unpublished*

The A77 Trunk Road (Lendalfoot Picnic Area) (Special Event) (Temporary Prohibition of Traffic) Order 2006 No. 2006/409. - Enabling power: Road Traffic Regulation Act 1984, s. 16A. - Made: 21.07.2006. Coming into force: 22.07.2006. Effect: None. Territorial extent & classification: S. Local *Unpublished*

The A77 Trunk Road (Maybole) (Prohibition of Waiting and Loading/Unloading) Order 2006 No. 2006/160. - Enabling power: Road Traffic Regulation Act 1984, ss. 1 (1), 124 (1) (d). - Made: 17.03.2006. Coming into force: 07.04.2006. Effect: S.I. 1974/1174 revoked. Territorial extent & classification: S. Local *Unpublished*

The A77 Trunk Road (Whitletts Roundabout) (Prohibition of Specified Turns) Order 2006 No. 2006/425. - Enabling power: Road Traffic Regulation Act 1984, s. 1 (1). - Made: 14.08.2006. Coming into force: 21.08.2006. Effect: None. Territorial extent & classification: S. Local *Unpublished*

The A78 Trunk Road (Eglinton Interchange to Pennyburn Roundabout) (Temporary Prohibition of Traffic) Order 2006 No. 2006/99. - Enabling power: Road Traffic Regulation Act 1984, s. 14 (1) (a). - Made: 03.03.2006. Coming into force: 13.03.2006. Effect: None. Territorial extent & classification: S. Local *Unpublished*

The A78 Trunk Road (Inverkip Street, Greenock) (Temporary Prohibition of Traffic) Order 2006 No. 2006/93. - Enabling power: Road Traffic Regulation Act 1984, s. 14 (1) (a). - Made: 02.03.2006. Coming into force: 10.03.2006. Effect: None. Territorial extent & classification: S. Local *Unpublished*

The A78 Trunk Road (Inverkip Street, Greenock) (Temporary Prohibition of Traffic, Temporary Prohibition of Waiting or Loading, Temporary One Way Operation and Temporary Prohibition of Specified Turns) Order 2006 No. 2006/421. - Enabling power: Road Traffic Regulation Act 1984, s. 14 (1) (a). - Made: 11.08.2006. Coming into force: 25.08.2006. Effect: None. Territorial extent & classification: S. Local *Unpublished*

The A78 Trunk Road (Inverkip Street, Greenock) (Temporary Prohibition of Traffic, Temporary Prohibition of Waiting or Loading, Temporary Prohibition of Entry, Temporary One Way Operation and Temporary Prohibition of Pedestrians) Order 2006 No. 2006/396. - Enabling power: Road Traffic Regulation Act 1984, s. 14 (1) (a). - Made: 07.07.2006. Coming into force: 13.07.2006. Effect: None. Territorial extent & classification: S. Local *Unpublished*

The A78 Trunk Road (Longhill, Skelmorlie) (Temporary Prohibition of Specified Turns) Order 2006 No. 2006/507. - Enabling power: Road Traffic Regulation Act 1984, s. 14 (1) (a). - Made: 13.10.2006. Coming into force: 23.10.2006. Effect: None. Territorial extent & classification: S. Local *Unpublished*

The A78 Trunk Road (Pennyburn Roundabout to Longford Avenue, Kilwinning) (Temporary Prohibition of Traffic) Order 2006 No. 2006/98. - Enabling power: Road Traffic Regulation Act 1984, s. 14 (1) (a). - Made: 03.03.2006. Coming into force: 13.03.2006. Effect: None. Territorial extent & classification: S. Local *Unpublished*

The A82 Trunk Road (Lairig Eilde Bridge, Glencoe) (Temporary Prohibition of Traffic and Temporary Speed Restriction) Order 2005 No. 2006/177. - Enabling power: Road Traffic Regulation Act 1984, s. 14 (1) (4). - Made: 28.03.2006. Coming into force: 02.04.2006. Effect: None. Territorial extent & classification: S. Local *Unpublished*

The A82 Trunk Road (Stoneymollan Roundabout, Balloch) (Temporary Prohibition of Specified Turns) Order 2006 No. 2006/13. - Enabling power: Road Traffic Regulation Act 1984, s. 14 (1) (a). - Made: 13.01.2006. Coming into force: 23.01.2006. Effect: None. Territorial extent & classification: S. Local *Unpublished*

The A86 Trunk Road (Dalwhinnie Junction to Creag Meagaidh) (Temporary Prohibition of Traffic) Order 2006 No. 2006/208. - Enabling power: Road Traffic Regulation Act 1984, s. 14 (1) (a). - Made: 19.042006. Coming into force: 01.04.2006. Effect: None. Territorial extent & classification: S. Local *Unpublished*

The A90 Trunk Road (Hilton Drive and Manor Avenue Junctions, Aberdeen) (Prohibition of Specified Turns) Order 2006 No. 2006/238. - Enabling power: Road Traffic Regulation Act 1984, s. 1 (1). - Made: 03.05.2006. Coming into force: 11.05.2006. Effect: None. Territorial extent & classification: S. Local *Unpublished*

The A90 Trunk Road (Mill of Marcus, Angus) (Temporary Prohibition of Specified Turns) Order 2006 No. 2006/550. - Enabling power: Road Traffic Regulation Act 1984, s. 14 (1) (a). - Made: 10.11.2006. Coming into force: 01.12.2006. Effect: None. Territorial extent & classification: S. Local *Unpublished*

The A90 Trunk Road (Nether Careston, Angus) (Temporary Prohibition of Specified Turns) Order 2006 No. 2006/366. - Enabling power: Road Traffic Regulation Act 1984, s. 14 (1) (a). - Made: 23.06.2006. Coming into force: 16.07.2006. Effect: None. Territorial extent & classification: S. Local *Unpublished*

The A90 Trunk Road (Perth to Dundee) (Temporary Prohibition of Traffic, Temporary Prohibition of Overtaking and Temporary Speed Restriction) Order 2006 No. 2006/280. - Enabling power: Road Traffic Regulation Act 1984, s. 14 (1) (4). - Made: 15.05.2006. Coming into force: 22.05.2006. Effect: None. Territorial extent & classification: S. Local *Unpublished*

The A90 Trunk Road (Petterden, Angus) (Temporary Prohibition of Specified Turns) Order 2006 No. 2006/304. - Enabling power: Road Traffic Regulation Act 1984, s. 14 (1). - Made: 02.06.2006. Coming into force: 11.06.2006. Effect: None. Territorial extent & classification: S. Local *Unpublished*

The A90 Trunk Road (Schoolhill Development) (Temporary 50mph Speed Limit) Order 2006 No. 2006/278. - Enabling power: Road Traffic Regulation Act 1984, s. 14 (1) (4). - Made: 22.05.2006. Coming into force: 01.06.2006. Effect: None. Territorial extent & classification: S. Local *Unpublished*

The A92/A972 Trunk Road (Kingsway, Dundee) (Temporary Prohibition of Specified Turns) Order 2006 No. 2006/364. - Enabling power: Road Traffic Regulation Act 1984, s. 14 (1) (a). - Made: 22.06.2006. Coming into force: 01.07.2006. Effect: None. Territorial extent & classification: S. Local *Unpublished*

The A92 Trunk Road (Forgan Roundabout, Fife) (Temporary Prohibition of Specified Turns) Order 2006 No. 2006/346. - Enabling power: Road Traffic Regulation Act 1984, s. 14 (1) (a). - Made: 07.06.2006. Coming into force: 19.06.2006. Effect: None. Territorial extent & classification: S. Local *Unpublished*

The A96 Trunk Road (Ladyhill Road Car Park, Elgin) (Prohibition of Specified Turns) Order 2006 No. 2006/591. - Enabling power: Road Traffic Regulation Act 1984, s. 1 (1). - Made: 04.12.2006. Coming into force: 18.12.2006. Effect: None. Territorial extent & classification: S. Local *Unpublished*

The A702 Trunk Road (Biggar High Street) (Special Event) (Temporary Prohibition of Traffic) Order 2006 No. 2006/595. - Enabling power: Road Traffic Regulation Act 1984, s. 16A. - Made: 08.12.2006. Coming into force: 30.12.2006. Effect: None. Territorial extent & classification: S. Local *Unpublished*

Road traffic: Traffic regulation

The A702 Trunk Road (Hillend) (Prohibition of Waiting) Order 2006 No. 2006/622. - Enabling power: Road Traffic Regulation Act 1984, s. 1 (1). - Made: 15.12.2006. Coming into force: 29.12.2006. Effect: None. Territorial extent & classification: S. Local *Unpublished*

The A720 Trunk Road (Calder Junction to Baberton Junction) (Temporary Prohbition of Overtaking and Temporary Speed Restriction) Order 2006 No. 2006/174. - Enabling power: Road Traffic Regulation Act 1984, s. 14 (1) (4). - Made: 20.03.2006. Coming into force: 27.03.2006. Effect: None. Territorial extent & classification: S. Local *Unpublished*

The A725/A726 Trunk Road (Carmunnock Bypass, Kingsway) (Temporary Prohibition of Pedestrians) Order 2006 No. 2006/435. - Enabling power: Road Traffic Regulation Act 1984, s. 14 (1) (a). - Made: 23.08.2006. Coming into force: 01.09.2006. Effect: None. Territorial extent & classification: S. Local *Unpublished*

The A725/A726 Trunk Road (Queensway) (Temporary Prohibition of Pedestrians) Order 2006 No. 2006/358. - Enabling power: Road Traffic Regulation Act 1984, s. 14 (1) (a). - Made: 16.06.2006. Coming into force: 26.06.2006. Effect: None. Territorial extent & classification: S. Local *Unpublished*

The A725/A726 Trunk Road (Righead Roundabout) (Temporary Prohibition of Specified Turns and Temporary Prohibition of Pedestrians) Order 2006 No. 2006/617. - Enabling power: Road Traffic Regulation Act 1984, s. 14 (1) (a). - Made: 21.12.2006. Coming into force: 15.01.2007. Effect: None. Territorial extent & classification: S. Local *Unpublished*

The A726 Trunk Road (Paisley to East Kilbride) (Central Reserve) (Prohibition of Specified Turns) Order 2006 No. 2006/148. - Enabling power: Road Traffic Regulation Act 1984, s. 1 (1). - Made: 08.03.2006. Coming into force: 17.03.2006. Effect: None. Territorial extent & classification: S. Local *Unpublished*

The A726 Trunk Road (Paisley to East Kilbride) Detrunking Order 2006 No. 2006/146. - Enabling power: Roads (Scotland) Act 1984, ss. 5 (2), 143 (1). - Made: 08.03.2006. Coming into force: 17.03.2006. Effect: None. Territorial extent & classification: S. Local *Unpublished*

The A876 Trunk Road (Upper Forth Crossing at Kincardine) (Temporary Prohibition of Traffic, Temporary Prohibition of Overtaking and Temporary Speed Restriction) Order 2006 No. 2006/300. - Enabling power: Road Traffic Regulation Act 1984, s. 14 (1) (4). - Made: 24.05.2006. Coming into force: 05.06.2006. Effect: None. Territorial extent & classification: S. Local *Unpublished*

The A977 Trunk Road (Upper Forth Crossing at Kincardine) (Temporary Prohibition of Traffic, Temporary Prohibition of Overtaking and Temporary Speed Restriction) Order 2006 No. 2006/301. - Enabling power: Road Traffic Regulation Act 1984, s. 14 (1) (a). - Made: 24.05.2006. Coming into force: 05.06.2006. Effect: None. Territorial extent & classification: S. Local *Unpublished*

The M8/A8 Trunk Road (Bogston Lane to Mackenzie Street, Greenock) (Temporary Prohibition of Specified Turns) Order 2006 No. 2006/403. - Enabling power: Road Traffic Regulation Act 1984, s. 14 (1) (a). - Made: 14.07.2006. Coming into force: 24.07.2006. Effect: None. Territorial extent & classification: S. Local *Unpublished*

The M8/A8 Trunk Road (Port Glasgow) (Temporary Speed Limit, Temporary Prohibition of Specified Turns and Temporary Prohibition of Pedestrians) Order 2006 No. 2006/380. - Enabling power: Road Traffic Regulation Act 1984, s. 14 (1) (2) (4). - Made: 29.06.2006. Coming into force: 07.07.2006. Effect: None. Territorial extent & classification: S. Local *Unpublished*

The M8/A8 Trunk Road (William Street, Port Glasgow Road, Belhaven Street and Anderson Street, Port Glasgow) (Temporary Prohibition of Specified Turns) Order 2006 No. 2006/176. - Enabling power: Road Traffic Regulation Act 1984, s. 14 (1) (a). - Made: 27.03.2006. Coming into force: 06.04.2006. Effect: None. Territorial extent & classification: S. Local *Unpublished*

The M9/A9 Trunk Road (Artafallie Junction) (Temporary Prohbition of Specified Turns) Order 2006 No. 2006/240. - Enabling power: Road Traffic Regulation Act 1984, s. 14 (1) (a). - Made: 04.05.2006. Coming into force: 15.05.2006. Effect: None. Territorial extent & classification: S. Local *Unpublished*

The M9/A9 Trunk Road (Between Junction 5 and Junction 6) (Temporary Prohbition of Traffic, Temporary Prohbition of Overtaking and Temporary Speed Restriction) Order 2006 No. 2006/215. - Enabling power: Road Traffic Regulation Act 1984, s. 14 (1) (4). - Made: 20.04.2006. Coming into force: 25.04.2006. Effect: None. Territorial extent & classification: S. Local *Unpublished*

The M9 Trunk Road (Junction 1A (Kirkliston) (Northbound Off Slip Road to Humbie Railway Bridge) (Temporary Prohibition of Traffic, Temporary Prohibition of Overtaking and Temporary Speed Restriction) 2006 No. 2006/518. - Enabling power: Road Traffic Regulation Act 1984, s. 14 (1) (a). - Made: 20.10.2006. Coming into force: 30.10.2006. Effect: None. Territorial extent & classification: S. Local *Unpublished*

The M74 Motorway (Junction 12, Millbank) (Temporary Prohibition of Traffic) (No. 2) Order 2006 No. 2006/283. - Enabling power: Road Traffic Regulation Act 1984, s. 14 (1) (a). - Made: 24.05.2006. Coming into force: 06.06.2006. Effect: None. Territorial extent & classification: S. Local *Unpublished*

The M74 Motorway (Junction 12, Millbank) (Temporary Prohibition of Traffic) Order 2006 No. 2006/222. - Enabling power: Road Traffic Regulation Act 1984, s. 14 (1) (a). - Made: 26.04.2006. Coming into force: 05.05.2006. Effect: None. Territorial extent & classification: S. Local *Unpublished*

Road traffic: Traffic regulation

The M74 Motorway (Junction 12 Northbound) (Temporary 40mph Speed Limit) (No. 2) Order 2006 No. 2006/282. - Enabling power: Road Traffic Regulation Act 1984, s. 14 (1) (4). - Made: 24.05.2006. Coming into force: 06.06.2006. Effect: None. Territorial extent & classification: S. Local *Unpublished*

The M74 Motorway (Junction 12 Northbound) (Temporary 40mph Speed Limit) Order 2006 No. 2006/223. - Enabling power: Road Traffic Regulation Act 1984, s. 14 (1) (4). - Made: 26.04.2006. Coming into force: 05.05.2006. Effect: None. Territorial extent & classification: S. Local *Unpublished*

The M74 Motorway (Junction 13, Northbound Off Slip at Abington) (Temporary Prohibition of Traffic) Order 2006 No. 2006/353. - Enabling power: Road Traffic Regulation Act 1984, s. 14 (1) (a). - Made: 13.06.2006. Coming into force: 23.06.2006. Effect: None. Territorial extent & classification: S. Local *Unpublished*

The M74 Motorway (Junction 14, Elvanfoot) (Temporary Prohibition of Traffic) Order 2006 No. 2006/347. - Enabling power: Road Traffic Regulation Act 1984, s. 14 (1) (a). - Made: 09.06.2006. Coming into force: 23.06.2006. Effect: None. Territorial extent & classification: S. Local *Unpublished*

The M74 Motorway (Junction 19, Northbound On Slip at Ecclefechan) (Temporary Prohibition of Traffic) Order 2006 No. 2006/354. - Enabling power: Road Traffic Regulation Act 1984, s. 14 (1) (a). - Made: 13.06.2006. Coming into force: 23.06.2006. Effect: None. Territorial extent & classification: S. Local *Unpublished*

The M74 Motorway (Junction 22, Southbound Off Slip at Gretna Green) (Temporary Prohibition of Traffic) Order 2006 No. 2006/355. - Enabling power: Road Traffic Regulation Act 1984, s. 14 (1) (a). - Made: 13.06.2006. Coming into force: 23.06.2006. Effect: None. Territorial extent & classification: S. Local *Unpublished*

The M77/A77 Trunk Road (Bogend Toll) (Temporary Prohibition of Specified Turns) Order 2006 No. 2006/424. - Enabling power: Road Traffic Regulation Act 1984, s. 14 (1) (a). - Made: 15.08.2006. Coming into force: 28.08.2006. Effect: None. Territorial extent & classification: S. Local *Unpublished*

The M77/A77 Trunk Road (Junction 5 (Maidenhill) to Junction 2 (Barrhead Road)) (Temporary Prohibition of Traffic) Order 2006 No. 2006/193. - Enabling power: Road Traffic Regulation Act 1984, s. 14 (1) (a). - Made: 03.04.2006. Coming into force: 14.04.2006. Effect: None. Territorial extent & classification: S. Local *Unpublished*

The M77/A77 Trunk Road (Whitletts Roundabout to Dutchhouse Roundabout, Ayr Bypass) (Prohibition of Specified Turns) Order 2006 No. 2006/508. - Enabling power: Road Traffic Regulation Act 1984, s. 1 (1). - Made: 13.10.2006. Coming into force: 23.10.2006. Effect: None. Territorial extent & classification: S. Local *Unpublished*

The M80/A80 Trunk Road (Junction 5 to Junction 9) (Temporary Width Restriction of Traffic) Order 2006 No. 2006/418. - Enabling power: Road Traffic Regulation Act 1984, s. 14 (1) (a). - Made: 04.08.2006. Coming into force: 20.08.2006. Effect: None. Territorial extent & classification: S. Local *Unpublished*

The M90/A90 Trunk Road (Glendoick, near Perth) (Temporary Prohibition of Specified Turns) Order 2006 No. 2006/68. - Enabling power: Road Traffic Regulation Act 1984, s. 14 (1) (a). - Made: 21.02.2006. Coming into force: 01.03.2006. Effect: None. Territorial extent & classification: S. Local *Unpublished*

The M90/A90 Trunk Road (Hilton Drive and Manor Avenue Junctions, Aberdeen) (Temporary Prohibition of Specified Turns) Order 2006 No. 2006/65. - Enabling power: Road Traffic Regulation Act 1984, s. 14 (1) (a). - Made: 15.02.2006. Coming into force: 01.03.2006. Effect: None. Territorial extent & classification: S. Local *Unpublished*

The M876 Special Road (Upper Forth Crossing at Kincardine) (Temporary Prohibition of Traffic, Temporary Prohibition of Overtaking and Temporary Speed Restriction) Order 2006 No. 2006/299. - Enabling power: Road Traffic Regulation Act 1984, s. 14 (1) (4). - Made: 24.05.2006. Coming into force: 05.06.2006. Effect: None. Territorial extent & classification: S. Local *Unpublished*

The North East Unit Trunk Roads Area (Temporary Prohibitions of Traffic, Temporary Prohibitions of Overtaking and Temporary Speed Restrictions) (No. 1) Order 2006 No. 2006/36. - Enabling power: Road Traffic Regulation Act 1984, s. 14 (1) (4). - Made: 30.01.2006. Coming into force: 01.02.2006. Effect: None. Territorial extent & classification: S. Local *Unpublished*

The North East Unit Trunk Roads Area (Temporary Prohibitions of Traffic, Temporary Prohibitions of Overtaking and Temporary Speed Restrictions) (No. 2) Order 2006 No. 2006/80. - Enabling power: Road Traffic Regulation Act 1984, s. 14 (1) (4). - Made: 27.01.2006. Coming into force: 01.03.2006. Effect: None. Territorial extent & classification: S. Local *Unpublished*

The North East Unit Trunk Roads Area (Temporary Prohibitions of Traffic, Temporary Prohibitions of Overtaking and Temporary Speed Restrictions) (No. 3A) Order 2006 No. 2006/195. - Enabling power: Road Traffic Regulation Act 1984, s. 14 (1) (4). - Made: 04.04.2006. Coming into force: 06.04.2006. Effect: S.S.I. 2006/187 revoked. Territorial extent & classification: S. Local *Unpublished*

The North East Unit Trunk Roads Area (Temporary Prohibitions of Traffic, Temporary Prohibitions of Overtaking and Temporary Speed Restrictions) (No. 3) Order 2006 No. 2006/187. - Enabling power: Road Traffic Regulation Act 1984, s. 14 (1) (4). - Made: 30.03.2006. Coming into force: 01.04.2006. Effect: None. Territorial extent & classification: S. Local. - Revoked by S.S.I. 2006/195 (Unpublished) *Unpublished*

The North East Unit Trunk Roads Area (Temporary Prohibitions of Traffic, Temporary Prohibitions of Overtaking and Temporary Speed Restrictions) (No. 4) Order 2006 No. 2006/224. - Enabling power: Road Traffic Regulation Act 1984, s. 14 (1) (4). - Made: 27.04.2006. Coming into force: 01.05.2006. Effect: None. Territorial extent & classification: S. Local *Unpublished*

The North East Unit Trunk Roads Area (Temporary Prohibitions of Traffic, Temporary Prohibitions of Overtaking and Temporary Speed Restrictions) (No. 5) Order 2006 No. 2006/290. - Enabling power: Road Traffic Regulation Act 1984, s. 14 (1) (4). - Made: 30.05.2006. Coming into force: 01.06.2006. Effect: None. Territorial extent & classification: S. Local *Unpublished*

The North East Unit Trunk Roads Area (Temporary Prohibitions of Traffic, Temporary Prohibitions of Overtaking and Temporary Speed Restrictions) (No. 6) Order 2006 No. 2006/387. - Enabling power: Road Traffic Regulation Act 1984, s. 14 (1) (4). - Made: 29.06.2006. Coming into force: 01.07.2006. Effect: None. Territorial extent & classification: S. Local *Unpublished*

The North East Unit Trunk Roads Area (Temporary Prohibitions of Traffic, Temporary Prohibitions of Overtaking and Temporary Speed Restrictions) (No. 7) Order 2006 No. 2006/412. - Enabling power: Road Traffic Regulation Act 1984, s. 14 (1) (4). - Made: 28.07.2006. Coming into force: 01.08.2006. Effect: None. Territorial extent & classification: S. Local *Unpublished*

The North East Unit Trunk Roads Area (Temporary Prohibitions of Traffic, Temporary Prohibitions of Overtaking and Temporary Speed Restrictions) (No. 8) Order 2006 No. 2006/444. - Enabling power: Road Traffic Regulation Act 1984, s. 14 (1) (4). - Made: 30.08.2006. Coming into force: 01.09.2006. Effect: None. Territorial extent & classification: S. Local *Unpublished*

The North East Unit Trunk Roads Area (Temporary Prohibitions of Traffic, Temporary Prohibitions of Overtaking and Temporary Speed Restrictions) (No. 9) Order 2006 No. 2006/479. - Enabling power: Road Traffic Regulation Act 1984, s. 14 (1) (4). - Made: 28.09.2006. Coming into force: 01.10.2006. Effect: None. Territorial extent & classification: S. Local *Unpublished*

The North East Unit Trunk Roads Area (Temporary Prohibitions of Traffic, Temporary Prohibitions of Overtaking and Temporary Speed Restrictions) (No. 10) Order 2006 No. 2006/525. - Enabling power: Road Traffic Regulation Act 1984, s. 14 (1) (4). - Made: 30.10.2006. Coming into force: 01.11.2006. Effect: None. Territorial extent & classification: S. Local *Unpublished*

The North East Unit Trunk Roads Area (Temporary Prohibitions of Traffic, Temporary Prohibitions of Overtaking and Temporary Speed Restrictions) (No. 11) Order 2006 No. 2006/583. - Enabling power: Road Traffic Regulation Act 1984, s. 14 (1) (4). - Made: 29.11.2006. Coming into force: 01.12.2006. Effect: None. Territorial extent & classification: S. Local *Unpublished*

The North East Unit Trunk Roads Area (Temporary Prohibitions of Traffic, Temporary Prohibitions of Overtaking and Temporary Speed Restrictions) (No. 12) Order 2006 No. 2006/618. - Enabling power: Road Traffic Regulation Act 1984, s. 14 (1) (4). - Made: 28.12.2006. Coming into force: 01.01.2007. Effect: None. Territorial extent & classification: S. Local *Unpublished*

The North West Unit Trunk Roads Area (Temporary Prohibitions of Traffic, Temporary Prohibitions of Overtaking and Temporary Speed Restrictions) (No. 1) Order 2006 No. 2006/34. - Enabling power: Road Traffic Regulation Act 1984, s. 14 (1) (4). - Made: 30.01.2006. Coming into force: 01.02.2006. Effect: None. Territorial extent & classification: S. Local *Unpublished*

The North West Unit Trunk Roads Area (Temporary Prohibitions of Traffic, Temporary Prohibitions of Overtaking and Temporary Speed Restrictions) (No. 2) Order 2006 No. 2006/77. - Enabling power: Road Traffic Regulation Act 1984, s. 14 (1) (4). - Made: 27.01.2006. Coming into force: 01.03.2006. Effect: None. Territorial extent & classification: S. Local *Unpublished*

The North West Unit Trunk Roads Area (Temporary Prohibitions of Traffic, Temporary Prohibitions of Overtaking and Temporary Speed Restrictions) (No. 3) Order 2006 No. 2006/186. - Enabling power: Road Traffic Regulation Act 1984, s. 14 (1) (4). - Made: 30.03.2006. Coming into force: 01.04.2006. Effect: None. Territorial extent & classification: S. Local *Unpublished*

The North West Unit Trunk Roads Area (Temporary Prohibitions of Traffic, Temporary Prohibitions of Overtaking and Temporary Speed Restrictions) (No. 4) Order 2006 No. 2006/225. - Enabling power: Road Traffic Regulation Act 1984, s. 14 (1) (4). - Made: 27.04.2006. Coming into force: 01.05.2006. Effect: None. Territorial extent & classification: S. Local *Unpublished*

The North West Unit Trunk Roads Area (Temporary Prohibitions of Traffic, Temporary Prohibitions of Overtaking and Temporary Speed Restrictions) (No. 5) Order 2006 No. 2006/289. - Enabling power: Road Traffic Regulation Act 1984, s. 14 (1) (4). - Made: 30.05.2006. Coming into force: 01.06.2006. Effect: None. Territorial extent & classification: S. Local *Unpublished*

The North West Unit Trunk Roads Area (Temporary Prohibitions of Traffic, Temporary Prohibitions of Overtaking and Temporary Speed Restrictions) (No. 6) Order 2006 No. 2006/385. - Enabling power: Road Traffic Regulation Act 1984, s. 14 (1) (4). - Made: 29.06.2006. Coming into force: 01.07.2006. Effect: None. Territorial extent & classification: S. Local *Unpublished*

The North West Unit Trunk Roads Area (Temporary Prohibitions of Traffic, Temporary Prohibitions of Overtaking and Temporary Speed Restrictions) (No. 7) Order 2006 No. 2006/413. - Enabling power: Road Traffic Regulation Act 1984, s. 14 (1) (4). - Made: 28.07.2006. Coming into force: 01.08.2006. Effect: None. Territorial extent & classification: S. Local *Unpublished*

Road traffic: Traffic regulation

The North West Unit Trunk Roads Area (Temporary Prohibitions of Traffic, Temporary Prohibitions of Overtaking and Temporary Speed Restrictions) (No. 8) Order 2006 No. 2006/443. - Enabling power: Road Traffic Regulation Act 1984, s. 14 (1) (4). - Made: 30.08.2006. Coming into force: 01.09.2006. Effect: None. Territorial extent & classification: S. Local *Unpublished*

The North West Unit Trunk Roads Area (Temporary Prohibitions of Traffic, Temporary Prohibitions of Overtaking and Temporary Speed Restrictions) (No. 9) Order 2006 No. 2006/478. - Enabling power: Road Traffic Regulation Act 1984, s. 14 (1) (4). - Made: 28.09.2006. Coming into force: 01.10.2006. Effect: None. Territorial extent & classification: S. Local *Unpublished*

The North West Unit Trunk Roads Area (Temporary Prohibitions of Traffic, Temporary Prohibitions of Overtaking and Temporary Speed Restrictions) (No. 10) Order 2006 No. 2006/524. - Enabling power: Road Traffic Regulation Act 1984, s. 14 (1) (4). - Made: 30.10.2006. Coming into force: 01.11.2006. Effect: None. Territorial extent & classification: S. Local *Unpublished*

The North West Unit Trunk Roads Area (Temporary Prohibitions of Traffic, Temporary Prohibitions of Overtaking and Temporary Speed Restrictions) (No. 11) Order 2006 No. 2006/584. - Enabling power: Road Traffic Regulation Act 1984, s. 14 (1) (4). - Made: 29.11.2006. Coming into force: 01.12.2006. Effect: None. Territorial extent & classification: S. Local *Unpublished*

The North West Unit Trunk Roads Area (Temporary Prohibitions of Traffic, Temporary Prohibitions of Overtaking and Temporary Speed Restrictions) (No. 12) Order 2006 No. 2006/619. - Enabling power: Road Traffic Regulation Act 1984, s. 14 (1) (4). - Made: 28.12.2006. Coming into force: 01.01.2007. Effect: None. Territorial extent & classification: S. Local *Unpublished*

The South East Unit Trunk Roads Area (Temporary Prohibitions of Traffic, Temporary Prohibitions of Overtaking and Temporary Speed Restrictions) (No. 1) Order 2006 No. 2006/35. - Enabling power: Road Traffic Regulation Act 1984, s. 14 (1) (4). - Made: 30.01.2006. Coming into force: 01.02.2006. Effect: None. Territorial extent & classification: S. Local *Unpublished*

The South East Unit Trunk Roads Area (Temporary Prohibitions of Traffic, Temporary Prohibitions of Overtaking and Temporary Speed Restrictions) (No. 2) Order 2006 No. 2006/81. - Enabling power: Road Traffic Regulation Act 1984, s. 14 (1) (4). - Made: 27.02.2006. Coming into force: 01.03.2006. Effect: None. Territorial extent & classification: S. Local *Unpublished*

The South East Unit Trunk Roads Area (Temporary Prohibitions of Traffic, Temporary Prohibitions of Overtaking and Temporary Speed Restrictions) (No. 3) Order 2006 No. 2006/185. - Enabling power: Road Traffic Regulation Act 1984, s. 14 (1) (4). - Made: 30.03.2006. Coming into force: 01.04.2006. Effect: None. Territorial extent & classification: S. Local *Unpublished*

The South East Unit Trunk Roads Area (Temporary Prohibitions of Traffic, Temporary Prohibitions of Overtaking and Temporary Speed Restrictions) (No. 4) Order 2006 No. 2006/227. - Enabling power: Road Traffic Regulation Act 1984, s. 14 (1) (4). - Made: 27.04.2006. Coming into force: 01.05.2006. Effect: None. Territorial extent & classification: S. Local *Unpublished*

The South East Unit Trunk Roads Area (Temporary Prohibitions of Traffic, Temporary Prohibitions of Overtaking and Temporary Speed Restrictions) (No. 5) Order 2006 No. 2006/288. - Enabling power: Road Traffic Regulation Act 1984, s. 14 (1) (4). - Made: 30.05.2006. Coming into force: 01.06.2006. Effect: None. Territorial extent & classification: S. Local *Unpublished*

The South East Unit Trunk Roads Area (Temporary Prohibitions of Traffic, Temporary Prohibitions of Overtaking and Temporary Speed Restrictions) (No. 6) Order 2006 No. 2006/388. - Enabling power: Road Traffic Regulation Act 1984, s. 14 (1) (4). - Made: 29.06.2006. Coming into force: 01.07.2006. Effect: None. Territorial extent & classification: S. Local *Unpublished*

The South East Unit Trunk Roads Area (Temporary Prohibitions of Traffic, Temporary Prohibitions of Overtaking and Temporary Speed Restrictions) (No. 7) Order 2006 No. 2006/414. - Enabling power: Road Traffic Regulation Act 1984, s. 14 (1) (4). - Made: 28.07.2006. Coming into force: 01.08.2006. Effect: None. Territorial extent & classification: S. Local *Unpublished*

The South East Unit Trunk Roads Area (Temporary Prohibitions of Traffic, Temporary Prohibitions of Overtaking and Temporary Speed Restrictions) (No. 8) Order 2006 No. 2006/442. - Enabling power: Road Traffic Regulation Act 1984, s. 14 (1) (4). - Made: 30.08.2006. Coming into force: 01.09.2006. Effect: None. Territorial extent & classification: S. Local *Unpublished*

The South East Unit Trunk Roads Area (Temporary Prohibitions of Traffic, Temporary Prohibitions of Overtaking and Temporary Speed Restrictions) (No. 9) Order 2006 No. 2006/477. - Enabling power: Road Traffic Regulation Act 1984, s. 14 (1) (4). - Made: 28.09.2006. Coming into force: 01.10.2006. Effect: None. Territorial extent & classification: S. Local *Unpublished*

The South East Unit Trunk Roads Area (Temporary Prohibitions of Traffic, Temporary Prohibitions of Overtaking and Temporary Speed Restrictions) (No. 10) Order 2006 No. 2006/523. - Enabling power: Road Traffic Regulation Act 1984, s. 14 (1) (4). - Made: 30.10.2006. Coming into force: 01.11.2006. Effect: None. Territorial extent & classification: S. Local *Unpublished*

The South East Unit Trunk Roads Area (Temporary Prohibitions of Traffic, Temporary Prohibitions of Overtaking and Temporary Speed Restrictions) (No. 11) Order 2006 No. 2006/585. - Enabling power: Road Traffic Regulation Act 1984, s. 14 (1) (4). - Made: 29.11.2006. Coming into force: 01.12.2006. Effect: None. Territorial extent & classification: S. Local *Unpublished*

Road traffic: Traffic regulation

The South East Unit Trunk Roads Area (Temporary Prohibitions of Traffic, Temporary Prohibitions of Overtaking and Temporary Speed Restrictions) (No. 12) Order 2006 No. 2006/621. - Enabling power: Road Traffic Regulation Act 1984, s. 14 (1) (4). - Made: 28.12.2006. Coming into force: 01.01.2007. Effect: None. Territorial extent & classification: S. Local *Unpublished*

The South West Unit Trunk Roads Area (Temporary Prohibitions of Traffic, Temporary Prohibitions of Overtaking and Temporary Speed Restrictions) (No. 1) Order 2006 No. 2006/37. - Enabling power: Road Traffic Regulation Act 1984, s. 14 (1) (4). - Made: 30.01.2006. Coming into force: 01.02.2006. Effect: None. Territorial extent & classification: S. Local *Unpublished*

The South West Unit Trunk Roads Area (Temporary Prohibitions of Traffic, Temporary Prohibitions of Overtaking and Temporary Speed Restrictions) (No. 2) Order 2006 No. 2006/78. - Enabling power: Road Traffic Regulation Act 1984, s. 14 (1) (4). - Made: 27.02.2006. Coming into force: 01.03.2006. Effect: None. Territorial extent & classification: S. Local *Unpublished*

The South West Unit Trunk Roads Area (Temporary Prohibitions of Traffic, Temporary Prohibitions of Overtaking and Temporary Speed Restrictions) (No. 3) Order 2006 No. 2006/184. - Enabling power: Road Traffic Regulation Act 1984, s. 14 (1) (4). - Made: 30.03.2006. Coming into force: 01.04.2006. Effect: None. Territorial extent & classification: S. Local *Unpublished*

The South West Unit Trunk Roads Area (Temporary Prohibitions of Traffic, Temporary Prohibitions of Overtaking and Temporary Speed Restrictions) (No. 4) Order 2006 No. 2006/226. - Enabling power: Road Traffic Regulation Act 1984, s. 14 (1) (4). - Made: 27.04.2006. Coming into force: 01.05.2006. Effect: None. Territorial extent & classification: S. Local *Unpublished*

The South West Unit Trunk Roads Area (Temporary Prohibitions of Traffic, Temporary Prohibitions of Overtaking and Temporary Speed Restrictions) (No. 5) Order 2006 No. 2006/287. - Enabling power: Road Traffic Regulation Act 1984, s. 14 (1) (4). - Made: 30.05.2006. Coming into force: 01.06.2006. Effect: None. Territorial extent & classification: S. Local *Unpublished*

The South West Unit Trunk Roads Area (Temporary Prohibitions of Traffic, Temporary Prohibitions of Overtaking and Temporary Speed Restrictions) (No. 6) Order 2006 No. 2006/386. - Enabling power: Road Traffic Regulation Act 1984, s. 14 (1) (4). - Made: 29.06.2006. Coming into force: 01.07.2006. Effect: None. Territorial extent & classification: S. Local *Unpublished*

The South West Unit Trunk Roads Area (Temporary Prohibitions of Traffic, Temporary Prohibitions of Overtaking and Temporary Speed Restrictions) (No. 7) Order 2006 No. 2006/415. - Enabling power: Road Traffic Regulation Act 1984, s. 14 (1) (4). - Made: 28.07.2006. Coming into force: 01.08.2006. Effect: None. Territorial extent & classification: S. Local *Unpublished*

The South West Unit Trunk Roads Area (Temporary Prohibitions of Traffic, Temporary Prohibitions of Overtaking and Temporary Speed Restrictions) (No. 8) Order 2006 No. 2006/441. - Enabling power: Road Traffic Regulation Act 1984, s. 14 (1) (4). - Made: 30.08.2006. Coming into force: 01.09.2006. Effect: None. Territorial extent & classification: S. Local *Unpublished*

The South West Unit Trunk Roads Area (Temporary Prohibitions of Traffic, Temporary Prohibitions of Overtaking and Temporary Speed Restrictions) (No. 9) Order 2006 No. 2006/476. - Enabling power: Road Traffic Regulation Act 1984, s. 14 (1) (4). - Made: 28.09.2006. Coming into force: 01.10.2006. Effect: None. Territorial extent & classification: S. Local *Unpublished*

The South West Unit Trunk Roads Area (Temporary Prohibitions of Traffic, Temporary Prohibitions of Overtaking and Temporary Speed Restrictions) (No. 10) Order 2006 No. 2006/522. - Enabling power: Road Traffic Regulation Act 1984, s. 14 (1) (4). - Made: 30.10.2006. Coming into force: 01.11.2006. Effect: None. Territorial extent & classification: S. Local *Unpublished*

The South West Unit Trunk Roads Area (Temporary Prohibitions of Traffic, Temporary Prohibitions of Overtaking and Temporary Speed Restrictions) (No. 11) Order 2006 No. 2006/586. - Enabling power: Road Traffic Regulation Act 1984, s. 14 (1) (4). - Made: 29.11.2006. Coming into force: 01.12.2006. Effect: None. Territorial extent & classification: S. Local *Unpublished*

The South West Unit Trunk Roads Area (Temporary Prohibitions of Traffic, Temporary Prohibitions of Overtaking and Temporary Speed Restrictions) (No. 12) Order 2006 No. 2006/620. - Enabling power: Road Traffic Regulation Act 1984, s. 14 (1) (4). - Made: 28.12.2006. Coming into force: 01.01.2007. Effect: None. Territorial extent & classification: S. Local *Unpublished*

Sea fisheries

The Inshore Fishing (Prohibition of Fishing for Cockles) (Scotland) (No. 2) Order 2006 No. 2006/383. - Enabling power: Inshore Fishing (Scotland) Act 1984, s. 1. - Issued: 11.07.2006. Made: 30.06.2006. Laid before the Scottish Parliament: 30.06.2006. Coming into force: 01.07.2006. Effect: S.S.I. 2006/58 revoked. Territorial extent & classification: S. General. - Revoked by S.S.I. 2006/487 (ISBN 0110710894). - 4p.: 30 cm. - 978-0-11-070855-3 *£3.00*

The Inshore Fishing (Prohibition of Fishing for Cockles) (Scotland) (No. 3) Order 2006 No. 2006/487. - Enabling power: Inshore Fishing (Scotland) Act 1984, s. 1. - Issued: 12.10.2006. Made: 05.10.2006. Laid before the Scottish Parliament: 05.10.2006. Coming into force: 12.11.2006. Effect: S.S.I. 2006/383 revoked. Territorial extent & classification: S. General. - 8p., 1 map: 30 cm. - 978-0-11-071089-1 £3.00

The Inshore Fishing (Prohibition of Fishing for Cockles) (Scotland) Order 2006 No. 2006/58. - Enabling power: Inshore Fishing (Scotland) Act 1984, s. 1. - Issued: 20.02.2006. Made: 10.02.2006. Laid before the Scottish Parliament: 10.02.2006. Coming into force: 13.03.2006. Effect: S.I. 1995/1373 & S.S.I. 2001/449; 2005/140 revoked. Territorial extent & classification: S. General. - Revoked by S.S.I. 2006/383 (ISBN 0110708555)- 8p., map: 30 cm. - 978-0-11-069946-2 £3.00

The Lobsters (Goat Island) (Scotland) Order 2006 No. 2006/506. - Enabling power: Sea Fisheries (Shellfish) Act 1976, s. 12 (1) (3) (3A). - Made: 12.10.2006. Coming into force: 13.10.2006. Effect: None. Territorial extent & classification: S. Local. - Revoked by S.S.I. 2006/587 (Unpublished) *Unpublished*

The Lobsters (Goat Island) (Scotland) Revocation Order 2006 No. 2006/587. - Enabling power: Sea Fisheries (Shellfish) Act 1976, s. 12 (1) (3) (3A) (8). - Made: 29.11.2006. Coming into force: 30.11.2006. Effect: S.S.I 2006/506 revoked. Territorial extent & classification: S. Local *Unpublished*

The Regulation of Scallop Dredges (Scotland) Revocation Order 2006 No. 2006/549. - Enabling power: Sea Fish(Conservation) Act 1967, ss. 3, 15 (3). - Issued: 23.11.2006. Made: 16.11.2006. Laid before the Scottish Parliament: 17.11.2006. Coming into force: 09.12.2006. Effect: S.S.I. 2005/371 revoked. Territorial extent & classification: S. General. - 2p.: 30 cm. - 978-0-11-071183-6 £3.00

The Sea Fishing (Enforcement of Community Quota and Third Country Fishing Measures) (Scotland) Order 2006 No. 2006/244. - Enabling power: Fisheries Act 1981, s. 30 (2). - Issued: 15.05.2006. Made: 09.05.2006. Laid before the Scottish Parliament: 09.05.2006. Coming into force: 31.05.2006. Effect: S.S.I. 2005/311 revoked with savings. Territorial extent & classification: S. General. - EC note: This Order makes provision for the enforcement of certain enforceable Community restrictions and other obligations relating to sea fishing by Community vessels and third country vessels set out in Council Regulation (EC) 51/2006. - 20p.: 30 cm. - 978-0-11-070443-2 £3.50

The Sea Fishing (Marking and Identification of Passive Fishing Gear and Beam Trawls) (Scotland) Order 2006 No. 2006/284. - Enabling power: Fisheries Act 1981, s. 30 (2). - Issued: 02.06.2006. Made: 24.05.2006. Laid before the Scottish Parliament: 30.05.2006. Coming into force: 21.06.2006. Effect: None. Territorial extent & classification: S. General. - EC note: Provides for the enforcement, in Scotland and the Scottish zone, of Commission Regulation no. 356/2005, as amended by Regulation no. 1805/2005, laying down detailed provisions regarding the marking and identification of passive fishing gear and beam trawls. - 12p.: 30 cm. - 978-0-11-070557-6 £3.00

The Sea Fishing (Northern Hake Stock) (Scotland) Order 2006 No. 2006/505. - Enabling power: Fisheries Act 1981, s. 30 (2). - Issued: 19.10.2006. Made: 11.10.2006. Laid before the Scottish Parliament: 12.10.2006. Coming into force: 14.11.2006. Effect: S.S.I. 2006/341 amended. Territorial extent & classification: S. General. - EC note: This Order provides for the enforcement in Scotland of the monitoring, inspection and surveillance provisions in Council Regulation 811/2004 which establishes a recovery plan for the northern hake stock which inhabits the hake recovery zone as defined in Article 1 of the Council Regulation. - 12p.: 30 cm. - 978-0-11-071090-7 £3.00

The Sea Fishing (Restriction on Days at Sea) (Scotland) Order 2006 No. 2006/341. - Enabling power: Fisheries Act 1981, s. 30 (2). - Issued: 26.06.2006. Made: 08.06.2006. Laid before the Scottish Parliament: 08.06.2006. Coming into force: 30.06.2006. Effect: S.S.I. 2000/7 amended & S.S.I. 2005/90 revoked. Territorial extent & classification: S. General. - EC note: This Order provides for the enforcement in Scotland of the provisions of Annex IIa and IIc to Council Regulation 51/2006 fixing for certain fish stocks and groups of fish stocks the fishing opportunities in Community waters for 2006 and the monitoring, inspection and surveillance provisions in Council Regulation 423/2004. - 20p.: 30 cm. - 978-0-11-070727-3 £3.50

Sea fisheries: Conservation of sea fish

The Prohibition of Fishing with Multiple Trawls (No. 2) (Scotland) Amendment Order 2006 No. 2006/602. - Enabling power: Sea Fish (Conservation) Act 1967, s. 5. - Issued: 21.12.2006. Made: 14.12.2006. Laid before the Scottish Parliament: 15.12.2006. Coming into force: 22.01.2007. Effect: S.S.I. 2000/405 amended and S.S.I. 2003/166 revoked. Territorial extent & classification: S. General. - 4p.: 30 cm. - 978-0-11-071416-5 £3.00

The Sea Fish (Prohibited Methods of Fishing) (Firth of Clyde) Order 2006 No. 2006/51. - Enabling power: Sea Fish (Conservation) Act 1967, ss. 5 (1) (c), 15 (3), 22 (2). - Issued: 15.02.2006. Made: 08.02.2006. Laid before the Scottish Parliament: 09.02.2006. Coming into force: 14.02.2006. Effect: S.S.I. 2005/67 revoked. Territorial extent & classification: S. General. - 8p.: 30 cm. - 978-0-11-069941-7 £3.00

Sea fisheries: Shellfish

The Solway Firth Regulated Fishery (Scotland) Order 2006 No. 2006/57. - Enabling power: Sea Fisheries (Shellfish) Act 1967, s. 1. - Issued: 20.02.2006. Made: 10.02.2006. Laid before the Scottish Parliament: 10.02.2006. Coming into force: 13.03.2006. Effect: None. Territorial extent & classification: S. General. - 12p., map: 30 cm. - 978-0-11-069945-5 £3.00

Security industry

The Private Security Industry Act 2001 (Commencement No. 1) (Scotland) Order 2006 No. 2006/382 (C.32). - Enabling power: Private Security Industry Act 2001, s. 26 (2). Bringing into operation various provisions of the 2001 Act on 06.07.2006. - Issued: 13.07.2006. Made: 04.07.2006. Effect: None. Territorial extent & classification: S. General. - 2p.: 30 cm. - 978-0-11-070856-0 £3.00

The Serious Organised Crime and Police Act 2005 (Commencement No. 7) Order 2006 No. 2006/381 (C.31). - Enabling power: Serious Organised Crime and Police Act 2005, s. 178 (6) (b) (9). Bringing into operation various provisions of the 2005 Act on 30.06.2006; 06.07.2006 in accord. with art. 2. - Issued: 06.07.2006. Made: 28.06.2006. Effect: None. Territorial extent & classification: S. General. - 8p.: 30 cm. - 978-0-11-070806-5 £3.00

Seeds

The Cereal Seed (Scotland) and Fodder Plant Seed (Scotland) Amendment Regulations 2006 No. 2006/448. - Enabling power: Plant Varieties and Seeds Act 1964, ss. 16 (1) (1A) (3), 36. - Issued: 06.09.2006. Made: 30.08.2006. Laid before the Scottish Parliament: 04.09.2006. Coming into force: 26.09.2006. Effect: S.S.I. 2005/328; 329 amended. Territorial extent & classification: S. General. - EC note: These Regs implement Commission Directive 2006/55/EC, amending Annex III to Council Directive 66/402/EEC as regards the maximum weight of seed lots. - 4p.: 30 cm. - 978-0-11-070967-3 £3.00

The Seed Potatoes (Fees) (Scotland) Amendment Regulations 2006 No. 2006/264. - Enabling power: Plant Varieties and Seeds Act 1964, s. 16 (1) (1A) (e). - Issued: 25.05.2006. Made: 17.05.2006. Laid before the Scottish Parliament: 19.05.2006. Coming into force: 12.06.2006. Effect: S.S.I. 2005/279 amended. Territorial extent & classification: S. General. - 4p.: 30 cm. - 978-0-11-070493-7 £3.00

The Seed (Registration, Licensing and Enforcement) (Scotland) Regulations 2006 No. 2006/313. - Enabling power: Plant Varieties and Seeds Act 1964, ss. 16 (1) to (5A), 24 (5), 26(2) (3), 36. - Issued: 20.06.2006. Made: 07.06.2006. Laid before the Scottish Parliament: 08.06.2006. Coming into force: 01.07.2006. Effect: S.S.I. 2002/526; 2004/317; 2005/328, 329 amended & S.I. 1985/980; 1987/1098; 1990/611; 1993/2530 revoked in relation to Scotland, with savings. Territorial extent & classification: S. General. - EC note: The Regulations revoke and replace earlier regulations. There are new requirements relating to supervision of licensed personnel as a result of the introduction of corresponding requirements into the Seed Marketing Directives (as defined in regulation 2) by Council Directive 2004/117/EC (regulation 32). These Regulations are in line with Council Directive 2004/117/EC which makes permanent a longstanding experiment on the use of licensed personnel in the regulation of seed marketing. - 40p.: 30 cm. - 978-0-11-070661-0 £6.50

The Seeds (Fees) (Scotland) Amendment Regulations 2006 No. 2006/70. - Enabling power: Plant Varieties and Seeds Act 1964, ss. 16 (1) (1A) (e), 36. - Issued: 28.02.2006. Made: 22.02.2006. Laid before the Scottish Parliament: 23.02.2006. Coming into force: 17.03.2006. Effect: S.S.I. 2002/526; 2004/317; 2005/328 amended. Territorial extent and classification: S. General. - 4p.: 30 cm. - 978-0-11-069966-0 £3.00

Serious Organised Crime Agency

The Serious Organised Crime and Police Act 2005 (Consequential and Supplementary Amendments) (Scotland) Order 2006 No. 2006/129. - Enabling power: Serious Organised Crime and Police Act 2005, ss. 173 (1) to (3) (5) (a). - Issued: 16.03.2006. Made: 08.03.2006. Laid before the Scottish Parliament: 09.03.2006. Coming into force: 01.04.2006. Effect: S.I. 1986/1078; 1989/1796; 1993/176; 1995/2507; 1997/2400; 1999/1319; 2002/3113 (all amended in relation to Scotland); S.S.I. 2002/62; 2005/494, 565 amended. Territorial extent & classification: S. General. - Copies are supplied from TSO's On-Demand Publishing Service. - 8p.: 30 cm. - 978-0-11-070065-6 £3.00

Sheriff Court

Act of Adjournal (Criminal Procedure Rules Amendment No. 2) (Financial Reporting Orders) 2006 No. 2006/205. - Enabling power: Criminal Procedure (Scotland) Act 1995, s. 305. - Issued: 25.04.2006. Made: 12.04.2006. Coming into force: 01.05.2006. Effect: S.I. 1996/513 amended. Territorial extent & classification: S. General. - 8p.: 30 cm. - 978-0-11-070275-9 £3.00

Act of Adjournal (Criminal Procedure Rules Amendment No. 4) (Miscellaneous) 2006 No. 2006/436. - Enabling power: Criminal Procedure (Scotland) Act 1995, s. 305. - Issued: 30.08.2006. Made: 22.08.2006. Coming into force: 01.09.2006. Effect: S.I. 1996/513 amended. Territorial extent & classification: S. General. - 8p.: 30 cm. - 978-0-11-070926-0 £3.00

Act of Adjournal (Criminal Procedure Rules Amendment) (Vulnerable Witnesses (Scotland) Act 2004) 2006 No. 2006/76. - Enabling power: Criminal Procedure (Scotland) Act 1995, s. 305. - Issued: 06.03.2006. Made: 24.02.2006. Coming into force: 01.04.2006. Effect: S.I. 1996/513 amended. Territorial extent & classification: S. General. - 8p.: 30 cm. - 978-0-11-069975-2 £3.00

Act of Sederunt (Chancery Procedure Rules) 2006 No. 2006/292. - Enabling power: Titles to Land Consolidation (Scotland) Act 1868, s. 51 & Sheriff Courts (Scotland) Act 1971, s. 32. - Issued: 06.06.2006. Made: 26.05.2006. Coming into force: 02.06.2006. Effect: S.I. 1996/2184 revoked. Territorial extent & classification: S. General. - 16p.: 30 cm. - 978-0-11-070573-6 £3.00

Act of Sederunt (Child Care and Maintenance Rules 1997) (Amendment) (Adoption and Children Act 2002) 2006 No. 2006/411. - Enabling power: Sheriff Courts (Scotland) Act 1971, s. 32. - Issued: 01.08.2006. Made: 21.07.2006. Coming into force: 18.08.2006. Effect: S.I. 1997/291 (S.19) amended. Territorial extent & classification: S. General. - 8p.: 30 cm. - 978-0-11-070904-8 £3.00

Act of Sederunt (Child Care and Maintenance Rules) Amendment (Vulnerable Witnesses (Scotland) Act 2004) 2006 No. 2006/75. - Enabling power: Sheriff Courts (Scotland) Act 1971, s. 32. - Issued: 06.03.2006. Made: 24.02.2006. Coming into force: 01.04.2006. Effect: S.I. 1997/291 (S.19) amended. Territorial extent & classification: S. General. - 8p.: 30 cm. - 978-0-11-069976-9 £3.00

Act of Sederunt (Fees of Messengers-at-Arms) 2006 No. 2006/540. - Enabling power: Execution of Diligence (Scotland) Act 1926, s. 6 & Court of Session Act 1988, s. 5. - Issued: 15.11.2006. Made: 07.11.2006. Coming into force: 01.01.2007. Effect: S.S.I. 2002/566 amended Territorial extent & classification: S. General. - 8p.: 30 cm. - 978-0-11-071156-0 £3.00

Act of Sederunt (Fees of Sheriff Officers) 2006 No. 2006/539. - Enabling power: Sheriff Courts (Scotland) Act 1907, s. 40 and Execution of Diligence (Scotland) Act 1926, s. 6. - Issued: 14.11.2006. Made: 07.11.2006. Laid before the Scottish Parliament: 09.11.2006. Coming into force: 01.01.2007. Effect: S.S.I. 2002/567 amended Territorial extent & classification: S. General. - 8p.: 30 cm. - 978-0-11-071155-3 £3.00

Act of Sederunt (Fees of Shorthand Writers in the Sheriff Court) (Amendment) 2006 No. 2006/86. - Enabling power: Sheriff Courts (Scotland) Act 1907, s. 40. - Issued: 06.03.2006. Made: 24.02.2006. Laid before the Scottish Parliament: 28.02.2006. Coming into force: 01.05.2006. Effect: S.I. 1992/1878 amended. Territorial extent & classification: S. General. - 4p.: 30 cm. - 978-0-11-069982-0 £3.00

Act of Sederunt (Fees of Solicitors in the Sheriff Court) (Amendment) 2006 No. 2006/295. - Enabling power: Sheriff Courts (Scotland) Act 1907, s. 40. - Issued: 07.06.2006. Made: 26.05.2006. Laid before the Scottish Parliament: 31.05.2006. Coming into force: 01.07.2006. Effect: S.I. 1993/3080 amended Territorial extent & classification: S. General. - 12p.: 30 cm. - 978-0-11-070571-2 £3.00

Act of Sederunt (Jurisdiction, Recognition and Enforcement of Judgments in Matrimonial Matters and Matters of Parental Responsibility Rules) 2006 No. 2006/397. - Enabling power: Sheriff Courts (Scotland) Act 1971, s. 32. - Issued: 18.07.2006. Made: 07.07.2006. Coming into force: 01.08.2006. Effect: None. Territorial extent & classification: S. General. - 12p.: 30 cm. - 978-0-11-070872-0 £3.00

Act of Sederunt (Ordinary Cause and Summary Application Rules) Amendment (Miscellaneous) 2006 No. 2006/410. - Enabling power: Sheriff Courts (Scotland) Act 1971, s. 32. - Issued: 01.08.2006. Made: 21.07.2006. Coming into force: 18.08.2006. Effect: 1907 c.51 amended. Territorial extent & classification: S. General. - 8p.: 30 cm. - 978-0-11-070903-1 £3.00

Act of Sederunt (Ordinary Cause Rules) Amendment (Causes Relating to Articles 81 and 82 of the Treaty Establishing the European Community) 2006 No. 2006/293. - Enabling power: Sheriff Courts (Scotland) Act 1971, s. 32. - Issued: 06.06.2006. Made: 26.05.2006. Coming into force: 16.06.2006. Effect: 1907 c.51 amended. Territorial extent & classification: S. General. - 4p.: 30 cm. - 978-0-11-070574-3 £3.00

Act of Sederunt (Ordinary Cause Rules) Amendment (Family Law (Scotland) Act 2006 etc.) 2006 No. 2006/207. - Enabling power: Sheriff Courts (Scotland) Act 1971, s. 32. - Issued: 26.04.2006. Made: 12.04.2006. Coming into force: 04.05.2006. Effect: 1907 c.51 amended. Territorial extent & classification: S. General. - 24p.: 30 cm. - 978-0-11-070272-8 £4.00

Act of Sederunt (Ordinary Cause, Summary Application, Summary Cause and Small Claim Rules) Amendment (Equality Act 2006 etc.) 2006 No. 2006/509. - Enabling power: Sheriff Courts (Scotland) Act 1971, s. 32; Sex Discrimination Act 1975, s. 66B; Race Relations Act 1976, s. 67A; Disability Discrimination Act 1995, s. 59A & Equality Act 2006, s. 71. - Issued: 24.10.2006. Made: 13.10.2006. Coming into force: 03.11.2006. Effect: 1907 c. 51 & S.I. 1999/929; S.S.I. 2002/132, 133 amended. Territorial extent & classification: S. General. - 12p.: 30 cm. - 978-0-11-071098-3 £3.00

Act of Sederunt (Sheriff Court Bankruptcy Rules 1996) Amendment (UNCITRAL Model Law on Cross-Border Insolvency) 2006 No. 2006/197. - Enabling power: Sheriff Courts (Scotland) Act 1971, s. 32. - Issued: 12.04.2006. Made: 03.04.2006. Coming into force: 06.04.2006. Effect: S.I. 1996/2507 amended. Territorial extent & classification: S. General. - 8p.: 30 cm. - 978-0-11-070259-9 £3.00

Act of Sederunt (Sheriff Court Caveat Rules) 2006 No. 2006/198. - Enabling power: Sheriff Courts (Scotland) Act 1971, s. 32. - Issued: 12.04.2006. Made: 03.04.2006. Coming into force: 28.04.2006. Effect: 1907 c.51 & S.I. 1986/2297; 1999/929 amended. Territorial extent & classification: S. General. - 4p.: 30 cm. - 978-0-11-070260-5 £3.00

Act of Sederunt (Sheriff Court Company Insolvency Rules 1986) Amendment (UNCITRAL Model Law on Cross-Border Insolvency) 2006 No. 2006/200. - Enabling power: Sheriff Courts (Scotland) Act 1971, s. 32. - Issued: 13.04.2006. Made: 03.04.2006. Coming into force: 06.04.2006. Effect: S.I. 1986/2297 amended. Territorial extent & classification: S. General. - 4p.: 30 cm. - 978-0-11-070262-9 £3.00

Act of Sederunt (Summary Applications, Statutory Applications and Appeals etc. Rules) Amendment (Miscellaneous) 2006 No. 2006/437. - Enabling power: Sheriff Courts (Scotland) Act 1971, s. 32. - Issued: 31.08.2006. Made: 22.08.2006. Coming into force: 01.09.2006. Effect: S.I. 1999/929 amended. Territorial extent & classification: S. General. - 4p.: 30 cm. - 978-0-11-070929-1 £3.00

The Maximum Number of Part-Time Sheriffs (Scotland) Order 2006 No. 2006/257. - Enabling power: Sheriff Courts (Scotland) Act 1971, s. 11A (5). - Issued: 22.05.2006. Made: 09.05.2006. Coming into force: 10.05.2006 in accord. with art. 1. Effect: 1971 c. 58 amended. Territorial extent & classification: S. General. - 2p.: 30 cm. - 978-0-11-070490-6 £3.00

The Vulnerable Witnesses (Scotland) Act 2004 (Commencement No. 3, Savings and Transitional Provisions) Order 2006 No. 2006/59 (C.8). - Enabling power: Vulnerable Witnesses (Scotland) Act 2004, s. 25. Bringing into operation various provisions of the 2004 Act on 01.04.2006. - Issued: 20.02.2006. Made: 09.02.2006. Effect: None. Territorial extent & classification: S. General. - Copies are supplied from TSO's On-Demand Publishing Service. - 8p.: 30 cm. - 978-0-11-069948-6 £3.00

Social care

The Regulation of Care (Applications and Provision of Advice) (Scotland) Amendment Order 2006 No. 2006/272. - Enabling power: Regulation of Care (Scotland) Act 2001, ss. 7 (2) (a), 14 (3). - Issued: 30.05.2006. Made: 19.05.2006. Laid before the Scottish Parliament: 22.05.2006. Coming into force: 20.06.2006. Effect: S.S.I. 2002/113 amended. Territorial extent & classification: S. General. - 2p.: 30 cm. - 978-0-11-070520-0 £3.00

The Regulation of Care (Fees) (Scotland) Amendment Order 2006 No. 2006/273. - Enabling power: Regulation of Care (Scotland) Act 2001, s. 24 (1). - Issued: 30.05.2006. Made: 19.05.2006. Laid before the Scottish Parliament: 22.05.2006. Coming into force: 20.06.2006. Effect: S.S.I. 2005/97 amended. Territorial extent & classification: S. General. - 4p.: 30 cm. - 978-0-11-070521-7 £3.00

The Regulation of Care (Requirements as to Care Services) (Scotland) Amendment Regulations 2006 No. 2006/274. - Enabling power: Regulation of Care (Scotland) Act 2001, s. 29 (1) (2) (c) (e) (7) (c) (o). - Issued: 30.05.2006. Made: 19.05.2006. Laid before the Scottish Parliament: 22.05.2006. Coming into force: 20.06.2006. Effect: S.S.I. 2002/114 amended. Territorial extent & classification: S. General. - 4p.: 30 cm. - 978-0-11-070522-4 £3.00

The Regulation of Care (Scotland) Act 2001 (Commencement No. 7 and Transitional Provisions) Order 2006 No. 2006/275 (C.26). - Enabling power: Regulation of Care (Scotland) Act 2001, s. 81 (2) to (4). Bringing into operation various provisions of the 2001 Act on 20.06.2006. - Issued: 30.05.2006. Made: 19.05.2006. Effect: None. Territorial extent & classification: S. General. - 8p.: 30 cm. - 978-0-11-070516-3 £3.00

The Regulation of Care (Social Service Workers) (Scotland) Amendment Order 2006 No. 2006/453. - Enabling power: Regulation of Care (Scotland) Act 2001, s. 44 (1) (b). - Issued: 12.09.2006. Made: 05.09.2006. Laid before the Scottish Parliament: 06.09.2006. Coming into force: 02.10.2006. Effect: S.S.I. 2005/318 amended. Territorial extent & classification: S. General. - 4p.: 30 cm. - 978-0-11-070998-7 £3.00

The Social Work Inspections (Scotland) Regulations 2006 No. 2006/531. - Enabling power: Joint Inspection of Children's Services and Inspection of Social Work Services (Scotland) Act 2006, ss. 5 (3), 6 (1) (2). - Issued: 17.11.2006. Made: 02.11.2006. Coming into force: 03.11.2006. Effect: None. Territorial extent & classification: S. General. - 8p.: 30 cm. - 978-0-11-071160-7 £3.00

Special roads

The A80/M73 Special Roads (Moodiesburn Bypass) Scheme 2006 No. 2006/500. - Enabling power: Roads (Scotland) Act 1984, s. 7. - Made: 06.10.2006. Coming into force: 13.10.2006. Effect: None. Territorial extent & classification: S. Local *Unpublished*

The A80/M73 Special Roads (Moodiesburn Bypass) (Side Roads) Order 2006 No. 2006/501. - Enabling power: Roads (Scotland) Act 1984, s. 9. - Made: 06.10.2006. Coming into force: 13.10.2006. Effect: None. Territorial extent & classification: S. Local *Unpublished*

The A80 Special Road (Auchenkilns to Haggs) Scheme 2006 No. 2006/497. - Enabling power: Roads (Scotland) Act 1984, s. 7. - Made: 06.10.2006. Coming into force: 13.10.2006. Effect: None. Territorial extent & classification: S. Local *Unpublished*

The M77 Special Road (Fenwick to Malletsheugh and Glasgow Southern Orbital) Trunking Order 2006 No. 2006/567. - Enabling power: Roads (Scotland) Act 1984, ss. 5 (2), 143 (1). - Made: 24.11.2006. Coming into force: 08.11.2006. Effect: None. Territorial extent & classification: S. Local *Unpublished*

Sports grounds and sporting events

The London Olympic Games and Paralympic Games Act 2006 (Commencement) (Scotland) Order 2006 No. 2006/611 (C.47). - Enabling power: London Olympic Games and Paralympic Games Act 2006, s. 40 (3). Bringing into operation various provisions of the 2006 Act on 31.12.2006. - Issued: 29.12.2006. Made: 10.12.2006. Effect: None. Territorial extent & classification: S. General. - 2p.: 30 cm. - 978-0-11-071469-1 £3.00

Title conditions

The Title Conditions (Scotland) Act 2003 (Conservation Bodies) Amendment (No. 2) Order 2006 No. 2006/130. - Enabling power: Title Conditions (Scotland) Act 2003, s. 38 (7). - Issued: 17.03.2006. Made: 09.03.2006. Laid before the Scottish Parliament: 09.03.2006. Coming into force: 31.03.2006. Effect: S.S.I. 2003/453 amended. Territorial extent & classification: S. General. - 2p.: 30 cm. - 978-0-11-070095-3 £3.00

The Title Conditions (Scotland) Act 2003 (Conservation Bodies) Amendment Order 2006 No. 2006/110. - Enabling power: Title Conditions (Scotland) Act 2003, s. 38 (4). - Issued: 14.03.2006. Made: 07.03.2006. Laid before the Scottish Parliament: 08.03.2006. Coming into force: 31.03.2006. Effect: S.S.I. 2003/453 amended. Territorial extent & classification: S. General. - 2p.: 30 cm. - 978-0-11-070006-9 £3.00

The Title Conditions (Scotland) Act 2003 (Rural Housing Bodies) Amendment Order 2006 No. 2006/108. - Enabling power: Title Conditions (Scotland) Act 2003, s. 43 (5). - Issued: 14.03.2006. Made: 07.03.2006. Laid before the Scottish Parliament: 08.03.2006. Coming into force: 31.03.2006. Effect: S.S.I. 2004/477 amended. Territorial extent & classification: S. General. - 4p.: 30 cm. - 978-0-11-070026-7 £3.00

Town and country planning

The Environmental Impact Assessment (Scotland) Amendment Regulations 2006 No. 2006/614. - Enabling power: European Communities Act 1972, s. 2 (2) and Town and Country Planning (Scotland) Act 1997, s. 40. - Issued: 05.01.2007. Made: 21.12.2006. Laid before the Scottish Parliament: 22.12.2006. Coming into force: 01.02.2007. Effect: 1984 c.54; S.I. 1999/367 amended in relation to Scotland; S.S.I. 1999/1, 43; 2006/582 amended. Territorial extent & classification: S. General. - Copies are supplied by TSO's On-demand publishing service. With correction slip dated February 2007. EC note: These Regulations implement in Scotland the amendments made by Article 3 of Council Directive 2003/35/EC with regard to public participation and access to justice to Council Directive 85/337/EEC. - 24p.: 30 cm. - 978-0-11-071472-1 £4.00

The Planning and Compulsory Purchase Act 2004 (Commencement No. 1) (Scotland) Order 2006 No. 2006/101 (C.12). - Enabling power: Planning and Compulsory Purchase Act 2004, ss. 121 (4), 122 (3). Bringing into operation various provisions of the 2004 Act on 20.03.2006. - Issued: 13.03.2006. Made: 03.03.2006. Effect: None. Territorial extent & classification: S. General. - 8p.: 30 cm. - 978-0-11-069994-3 £3.00

The Planning and Compulsory Purchase Act 2004 (Commencement No. 2 and Consequential Provisions) (Scotland) Order 2006 No. 2006/243 (C.22). - Enabling power: Planning and Compulsory Purchase Act 2004, ss. 121 (4), 122 (3). Bringing into operation various provisions of the 2004 Act on 11.05.2006. - Issued: 15.05.2006. Made: 06.05.2006. Effect: 1997 c.8, c.9 amended. Territorial extent & classification: S. General. - 8p.: 30 cm. - 978-0-11-070441-8 £3.00

The Planning and Compulsory Purchase Act 2004 (Commencement No. 3) (Scotland) Order 2006 No. 2006/268 (C.25). - Enabling power: Planning and Compulsory Purchase Act 2004, s. 121 (4). Bringing into operation various provisions of the 2004 Act on 12.06.2006, in accord. with art. 3. - Issued: 25.05.2006. Made: 17.05.2006. Effect: None. Territorial extent & classification: S. General. - Copies are supplied from TSO's On-Demand Publishing Service. - 8p.: 30 cm. - 978-0-11-070512-5 £3.00

The Planning and Compulsory Purchase Act 2004 (Transitional Provisions) (Scotland) Order 2006 No. 2006/269. - Enabling power: Planning and Compulsory Purchase Act 2004, ss. 119 (2), 122 (3). - Issued: 30.05.2006. Made: 19.05.2006. Laid before the Scottish Parliament: 22.05.2006. Coming into force: 12.06.2006. Effect: 1997 c.10 amended. Territorial extent & classification: S. General. - 8p.: 30 cm. - 978-0-11-070525-5 £3.00

The Planning (National Security Directions and Appointed Representatives) (Scotland) Rules 2006 No. 2006/265. - Enabling power: Town and Country Planning (Scotland) Act 1997, s. 265A (6) (b). - Issued: 25.05.2006. Made: 17.05.2006. Laid before the Scottish Parliament: 19.05.2006. Coming into force: 12.06.2006. Effect: None. Territorial extent & classification: S. General. - 12p.: 30 cm. - 978-0-11-070495-1 £3.00

The Town and Country Planning (Application of Subordinate Legislation to the Crown) (Inquiries Procedure) (Scotland) Order 2006 No. 2006/339. - Enabling power: Planning and Compulsory Purchase Act 2004, ss. 98, 122 (3). - Issued: 26.06.2006. Made: 07.06.2006. Laid before the Scottish Parliament: 09.06.2006. Coming into force: 01.07.2006. Effect: S.I. 1997/750, 796 amended. Territorial extent & classification: S. General. - 16p.: 30 cm. - 978-0-11-070715-0 £3.00

The Town and Country Planning (Application of Subordinate Legislation to the Crown) (Scotland) Order 2006 No. 2006/270. - Enabling power: Town and Country Planning (Scotland) Act 1997, ss. 26 (2) (f), 30, 31 (1) & Planning and Compulsory Purchase Act 2004, ss. 98, 122 (3). - Issued: 25.05.2006. Made: 17.05.2006. Laid before the Scottish Parliament: 19.05.2006. Coming into force: 12.05.2006. Effect: S.I. 1975/1204; 1984/467; 1987/1529; 1992/223, 224; 1993/323; 1994/2716; 1997/3061; 1999/1736; S.S.I. 1999/1 amended. Territorial extent & classification: S. General. - 24p.: 30 cm. - 978-0-11-070513-2 £4.00

The Town and Country Planning (Listed Buildings and Buildings in Conservation Areas) (Amendment) (Scotland) Regulations 2006 No. 2006/266. - Enabling power: Planning (Listed Buildings and Conservation Areas) (Scotland) Act 1997, s. 73B (8). - Issued: 25.05.2006. Made: 17.05.2006. Laid before the Scottish Parliament: 19.05.2006. Coming into force: 12.06.2006. Effect: S.I. 1987/1529 amended. Territorial extent & classification: S. General. - 4p.: 30 cm. - 978-0-11-070503-3 £3.00

Transport

The Bus User Complaints Tribunal Regulations Revocation Regulations 2006 No. 2006/608. - Enabling power: Transport (Scotland) Act 2001, ss. 41 (1), 81 (2). - Issued: 29.12.2006. Made: 19.12.2006. Coming into force: In accord. with art 1. Effect: S.S.I. 2002/199 revoked with savings. Territorial extent & classification: S. General. - Supersedes draft SSI (ISBN 0110711548) issued on 14.11.2006. - 4p.: 30 cm. - 978-0-11-071463-9 £3.00

The National Bus Travel Concession Scheme for Older and Disabled Persons (Eligible Persons and Eligible Services) (Scotland) Order 2006 No. 2006/117. - Enabling power: Transport (Scotland) Act 2005, ss. 40 (7), 52 (4). - Issued: 14.03.2006. Made: 07.03.2006. Laid before the Scottish Parliament: 08.03.2006. Coming into force: 01.04.2006. Effect: None. Territorial extent & classification: S. General. - 8p.: 30 cm. - 978-0-11-070038-0 £3.00

The National Bus Travel Concession Scheme for Older and Disabled Persons (Scotland) Order 2006 No. 2006/107. - Enabling power: Transport (Scotland) Act 2005, ss. 40 (1) (3) (4), 52 (4). - Issued: 14.03.2006. Made: 07.03.2006. Coming into force: 01.04.2006. Effect: None. Territorial extent & classification: S. General. - Copies are supplied from TSO's On-Demand Publishing Service. - 8p.: 30 cm. - 978-0-11-070030-4 £3.00

The Public Transport Users' Committee for Scotland Order 2006 No. 2006/250. - Enabling power: Transport (Scotland) Act 2005, ss. 41 (1) (2), 42 (3), 52 (4). - Issued: 16.05.2006. Made: 10.05.2006. Laid before the Scottish Parliament: 11.05.2006. Coming into force: In accord. with art. 1. Effect: None. Territorial extent & classification: S. General. - 8p.: 30 cm. - 978-0-11-070467-8 £3.00

The Regional Transport Strategies (Health Boards) (Scotland) Order 2006 No. 2006/528. - Enabling power: Transport (Scotland) Act 2005, s. 8 (3). - Issued: 08.11.2006. Made: 31.10.2006. Laid before the Scottish Parliament: 02.11.2006. Coming into force: 01.01.2007. Effect: None. Territorial extent & classification: S. General. - 4p.: 30 cm. - 978-0-11-071125-6 £3.00

The Road User Charging Schemes (Keeping of Accounts and Relevant Expenses) (Scotland) Regulations 2005 Revocation Regulations 2006 No. 2006/431. - Enabling power: Transport (Scotland) Act 2001, sch. 1, paras 1, 4. - Issued: 24.08.2006. Made: 17.08.2006. Laid before the Scottish Parliament: 18.08.2006. Coming into force: 30.09.2006. Effect: S.S.I. 2005/654 revoked. Territorial extent & classification: S. General. - This Scottish Statutory Instrument has been made in consequence of a defect in S.S.I. 2005/654 (ISBN 0110698835) and is being issued free of charge to all known recipients of that instrument. - 2p.: 30 cm. - 978-0-11-070923-9 £3.00

The Strathclyde Passenger Transport Area (Variation) Order 2006 No. 2006/112. - Enabling power: Local Government etc. (Scotland) Act 1994, s. 40 (8). - Issued: 13.03.2006. Made: 07.03.2006. Laid before the Scottish Parliament: 08.03.2006. Coming into force: In accord. with art 1. Effect: S.I. 1995/1971 amended. Territorial extent & classification: S. General. - 4p.: 30 cm. - 978-0-11-070003-8 £3.00

The Transfer of Functions from the Strathclyde Passenger Transport Authority and the Strathclyde Passenger Transport Executive to the West of Scotland Transport Partnership Order 2006 No. 2006/106. - Enabling power: Transport (Scotland) Act 2005, ss. 10 (1), 52 (4). - Issued: 13.03.2006. Made: 07.03.2006. Coming into force: 01.04.2006. Effect: None. Territorial extent & classification: S. General. - 4p.: 30 cm. - 978-0-11-069997-4 £3.00

The Transfer of Functions to the Shetland Transport Partnership Order 2006 No. 2006/527. - Enabling power: Transport (Scotland) Act 2005, ss. 10 (1), 52 (4). - Issued: 08.11.2006. Made: 31.10.2006. Coming into force: 01.11.2006. Effect: None. Territorial extent & classification: S. General. - 8p.: 30 cm. - 978-0-11-071123-2 £3.00

The Transfer of Functions to the South-West of Scotland Transport Partnership Order 2006 No. 2006/538. - Enabling power: Transport (Scotland) Act 2005, ss. 10 (1), 52 (4). - Issued: 14.11.2006. Made: 06.11.2006. Coming into force: 07.11.2006. Effect: None. Territorial extent & classification: S. General. - 8p.: 30 cm. - 978-0-11-071145-4 £3.00

The Transfer of Property, Rights and Liabilities from the Strathclyde Passenger Transport Authority and the Strathclyde Passenger Transport Executive to the West of Scotland Transport Partnership Order 2006 No. 2006/111. - Enabling power: Transport (Scotland) Act 2005, ss. 15 (5), 52 (4). - Issued: 13.03.2006. Made: 07.03.2006. Laid before the Scottish Parliament: 08.03.2006. Coming into force: 01.04.2006. Effect: None. Territorial extent & classification: S. General. - 4p.: 30 cm. - 978-0-11-070005-2 £3.00

Water

The Water Environment and Water Services (Scotland) Act 2003 (Commencement No. 4) Order 2006 No. 2006/55 (C.7). - Enabling power: Water Environment and Water Services (Scotland) Act 2003, s. 38 (1). Bringing into operation various provisions of the 2003 Act on 06.03.2006. - Issued: 16.02.2006. Made: 08.02.2006. Effect: None. Territorial extent & classification: S. General. - 2p.: 30 cm. - 978-0-11-069943-1 £3.00

The Water Environment and Water Services (Scotland) Act 2003 (Designation of Responsible Authorities and Functions) Order 2006 No. 2006/126. - Enabling power: Water Environment and Water Services (Scotland) Act 2003, s. 2 (8). - Issued: 16.03.2006. Made: 08.03.2006. Laid before the Scottish Parliament: 09.03.2006. Coming into force: 01.04.2006. Effect: None. Territorial extent & classification: S. General. - 4p.: 30 cm. - 978-0-11-070075-5 £3.00

The Water Environment (Consequential and Savings Provisions) (Scotland) Order 2006 No. 2006/181. - Enabling power: Water Environment and Water Services (Scotland) Act 2003, ss. 36 (3), 37. - Issued: 05.04.2006. Made: 29.03.2006. Coming into force: 01.04.2006. Effect: 1961 c. 41; 1964 c. 40; 1974 c. 40; 1980 c. 45; 1990 c. 43; 1991 c. iv, c. 28, c. 34; 1993 c. 12; 1994 c. iii; 1995 c. 25, c. 46; 2003 asp 15; 2004 asp 10 amended & S.I. 1993/1155; 1996/973; 1999/1750 amended & 1951 c. 66 repealed with savings; 1965 c. 13 repealed & S.I. 1973/1846; 1983/1182; 1984/864, 865; 1986/1623; 1993/1154, 1156; 1995/2382; S.S.I. 2000/432; 2003/168 revoked. Territorial extent & classification: S. General. - Superseded by the draft S.S.I. (ISBN 0110699564) issued 23.02.2006. - 12p.: 30 cm. - 978-0-11-070222-3 £3.00

The Water Environment (Consequential Provisions) (Scotland) Order 2006 No. 2006/127. - Enabling power: Water Environment and Water Services (Scotland) Act 2003, ss.36 (3), 37. - Issued: 16.03.2006. Made: 08.03.2006. Laid before the Scottish Parliament: 09.03.2006. Coming into force: 01.04.2006. Effect: S.I. 1993/1155; S.S.I. 2000/323; 2005/22, 225, 569 amended & S.I. 1987/1782; 1998/2746 revoked. Territorial extent & classification: S. General. - 4p.: 30 cm. - 978-0-11-070077-9 £3.00

The Water Environment (Controlled Activities) (Third Party Representations etc) (Scotland) Regulations 2006 No. 2006/553. - Enabling power: Water Environment and Water Services (Scotland) Act 2003, s. 20, sch. 2. - Issued: 27.11.2006. Made: 21.11.2006. Laid before the Scottish Parliament: 22.11.2006. Coming into force: 14.12.2006. Effect: S.S.I. 2005/348 amended. Territorial extent & classification: S. General. - 8p.: 30 cm. - 978-0-11-071196-6 £3.00

The Water Environment (Oil Storage) (Scotland) Regulations 2006 No. 2006/133. - Enabling power: Water Environment and Water Services (Scotland) Act 2003, ss. 20, 36 (2) (3), sch. 2. - Issued: 24.03.2006. Made: 08.03.2006. Laid before the Scottish Parliament: 10.03.2006. Coming into force: 01.04.2006. Effect: S.S.I. 2003/531 amended. Territorial extent & classification: S. General. - 8p.: 30 cm. - 978-0-11-070175-2 £3.00

The Water Environment (Relevant Enactments) Order 2006 No. 2006/554. - Enabling power: Water Environment and Water Services (Scotland) Act 2003, s. 2 (8). - Issued: 28.11.2006. Made: 21.11.2006. Laid before the Scottish Parliament: 22.11.2006. Coming into force: 14.12.2006. Effect: None. Territorial extent & classification: S. General. - 4p.: 30 cm. - 978-0-11-071197-3 £3.00

Water industry

The Sewerage Nuisance (Code of Practice) (Scotland) Order 2006 No. 2006/155. - Enabling power: Water Services etc. (Scotland) Act 2005, ss. 25 (1) (3), 34 (2). - Issued: 23.03.2006. Made: 15.03.2006. Laid before the Scottish Parliament: 16.03.2006. Coming into force: 22.04.2006. Effect: None. Territorial extent & classification: S. General. - 8p.: 30 cm. - 978-0-11-070135-6 £3.00

The Water Services and Sewerage Services Licences (Scotland) Order 2006 No. 2006/464. - Enabling power: Water Services etc. (Scotland) Act 2005, ss. 13 (6), 18 (3), 20 (8), 34 (2), sch. 2, paras. 1 (1) (4), 12 (1). - Issued: 20.09.2006. Made: 12.09.2006. Laid before the Scottish Parliament: 13.09.2006. Coming into force: 05.10.2006. Effect: 2005 asp 3 modified. Territorial extent & classification: S. General. - 8p.: 30 cm. - 978-0-11-071011-2 £3.00

The Water Services etc. (Scotland) Act 2005 (Commencement No. 2) Order 2006 No. 2006/40 (C.4). - Enabling power: Water Services etc. (Scotland) Act 2005, s. 37 (2) (3). Bringing into operation various provisions of the 2005 Act on 10.02.2006. - Issued: 08.02.2006. Made: 01.02.2006. Effect: None. Territorial extent & classification: S. General. - 2p.: 30 cm. - 978-0-11-069925-7 £3.00

The Water Services etc. (Scotland) Act 2005 (Commencement No. 3 and Savings) Order 2006 No. 2006/167 (C.16). - Enabling power: Water Services etc. (Scotland) Act 2005, ss. 34(2), 37(2) (3). Bringing into operation various provisions of the 2005 Act on 01.04.2006 & 22.04.2006. - Issued: 30.03.2006. Made: 22.03.2006. Effect: None. Territorial extent & classification: S. General. - 8p.: 30 cm. - 978-0-11-070196-7 £3.00

The Water Services etc. (Scotland) Act 2005 (Commencement No. 4) Order 2006 No. 2006/445 (C.35). - Enabling power: Water Services etc. (Scotland) Act 2005, ss. 34 (2), 37 (2). Bringing into operation various provisions of the 2005 Act on 07.09.2006 in accord. with art. 2. - Issued: 06.09.2006. Made: 30.08.2006. Effect: None. Territorial extent & classification: S. General. - 4p.: 30 cm. - 978-0-11-070930-7 £3.00

The Water Services etc. (Scotland) Act 2005 (Commencement No. 5) Order 2006 No. 2006/599 (C. 45). - Enabling power: Water Services etc. (Scotland) Act 2005, ss. 34(2), 37(2). Bringing into operation various provisions of the 2005 Act on 08.01.2007. - Issued: 20.12.2006. Made: 13.12.2006. Effect: None. Territorial extent & classification: S. General. - 4p.: 30 cm. - 978-0-11-071382-3 £3.00

Water supply

The Private Water Supplies (Grants) (Scotland) Regulations 2006 No. 2006/210. - Enabling power: Local Government in Scotland Act 2003, s. 47. - Issued: 26.04.2006. Made: 19.04.2006. Laid before the Scottish Parliament: 20.04.2006. Coming into force: 03.07.2006. Effect: None. Territorial extent & classification: S. General. - 8p.: 30 cm. - 978-0-11-070283-4 £3.00

The Private Water Supplies (Notices) (Scotland) Regulations 2006 No. 2006/297. - Enabling power: European Communities Act 1972, s. 2 (2). - Issued: 07.06.2006. Made: 30.05.2006. Coming into force: 03.07.2006. Effect: 1980 c. 45 amended. Territorial extent & classification: S. General. - EC note: These Regulations modify section 76G of the 1980 Act to place a duty on local authorities to serve notices in the case of Type A supplies (as defined in the 2006 Regulations). Type A supplies are those which must satisfy the water quality standards set out in Council Directive 98/83/EC on the quality of waterintended for human consumption. In the case of Type B supplies,to which the Directive does not apply, local authorities retain their powers to serve notices. - 4p.: 30 cm. - 978-0-11-070575-0 £3.00

The Private Water Supplies (Scotland) Regulations 2006 No. 2006/209. - Enabling power: Water (Scotland) Act 1980, ss. 76F (5) to (8), 76J, 101 (1) (1A), 109 (1). - Issued: 27.04.2006. Made: 19.04.2006. Laid before the Scottish Parliament: 20.4.2005. Coming into force: 03.07.2006. Effect: S.S.I. 2001/207 amended & S.I. 1992/575 (with savings); 1998/1856 (S.99) revoked. Territorial extent & classification: S. General. - EC note: These Regs implement Council Directive 98/83/EC insofar as it concerns private water supplies. With correction slip dated June 2006. - 60p.: 30 cm. - 978-0-11-070284-1 £9.00

The Provision of Water and Sewerage Services (Reasonable Cost) (Scotland) Regulations 2006 No. 2006/120. - Enabling power: Sewerage (Scotland) Act 1968, s. 1 (3C) & Water (Scotland) Act 1980, s. 6 (2D). - Issued: 15.03.2006. Made: 08.03.2006. Laid before the Scottish Parliament: 09.03.2006. Coming into force: 01.04.2006. Effect: None. Territorial extent & classification: S. General. - 8p.: 30 cm. - 978-0-11-070063-2 £3.00

The Scottish Water (Abhainn Dhubh) Water Order 2006 No. 2006/360. - Enabling power: Water (Scotland) Act 1980, ss. 17 (1), 29 (1), 107 (1) (b). - Issued: 27.06.2006. Made: 16.06.2006. Coming into force: 21.06.2006. Effect: S.I. 1963/1589 revoked with effect 31.12.2007. Territorial extent & classification: S. General. - 4p.: 30 cm. - 978-0-11-070735-8 £3.00

The Scottish Water (Allt an Lagain) Water Order 2006 No. 2006/152. - Enabling power: Water (Scotland) Act 1980, ss. 17 (1), 29 (1), 107 (1) (b). - Issued: 21.03.2006. Made: 13.03.2006. Coming into force: 14.03.2006. Effect: 1980 c. 45 modified & S.I. 1954/1343 revoked with effect 31.12.2007. Territorial extent & classification: S. General. - 4p.: 30 cm. - 978-0-11-070127-1 £3.00

The Scottish Water (Loch Braigh Horrisdale) Water Order 2006 No. 2006/296. - Enabling power: Water (Scotland) Act 1980, ss. 17 (1), 29 (1), 107 (1) (b). - Issued: 07.06.2006. Made: 30.05.2006. Coming into force: 02.06.2006. Effect: County of Ross and Cromarty (Loch Braigh Horrisdale, Badachro) Water Order 1961 revoked (31.12.2007). Territorial extent & classification: S. General. - 4p.: 30 cm. - 978-0-11-070572-9 £3.00

The Scottish Water (Tomich Boreholes) Water Order 2006 No. 2006/361. - Enabling power: Water (Scotland) Act 1980, ss. 17 (1), 29 (1), 107 (1) (b). - Issued: 27.06.2006. Made: 16.06.2006. Coming into force: 21.06.2006. Effect: S.I. 1966/477; 1971/2174 revoked with effect 31.12.2007. Territorial extent & classification: S. General. - 4p.: 30 cm. - 978-0-11-070734-1 £3.00

The Scottish Water (Unapool Burn) Water Order 2006 No. 2006/153. - Enabling power: Water (Scotland) Act 1980, ss. 17 (1), 29 (1), 107 (1) (b). - Issued: 21.03.2006. Made: 13.03.2006. Coming into force: 14.03.2006. Effect: 1980 c. 45 modified & S.I. 1967/730 revoked with effect 31.12.2007. Territorial extent & classification: S. General. - 4p.: 30 cm. - 978-0-11-070126-4 £3.00

The Water and Sewerage Charges (Exemption and Reduction) (Scotland) Regulations 2006 No. 2006/72. - Enabling power: Water Industry (Scotland) Act 2002, s. 40. - Issued: 02.03.2006. Made: 22.02.2006. Laid before the Scottish Parliament: 23.02.2006. Coming into force: 01.04.2006. Effect: S.S.I. 2002/167 amended. Territorial extent & classification: S. General. - 4p.: 30 cm. - 978-0-11-069969-1 £3.00

The Water Services Charges (Billing and Collection) (Scotland) Order 2006 No. 2006/71. - Enabling power: Water Industry (Scotland) Act 2002, s. 37. - Issued: 02.03.2006. Made: 22.02.2006. Laid before the Scottish Parliament: 23.02.2006. Coming into force: 01.04.2006. Effect: None. Territorial extent & classification: S. General. - 8p.: 30 cm. - 978-0-11-069970-7 £3.00

Young offender institutions

The Prisons and Young Offenders Institutions (Scotland) Rules 2006 No. 2006/94. - Enabling power: Prisons (Scotland) Act 1989, s. 39. - Issued: 13.03.2006. Made: 02.03.2006. Laid before the Scottish Parliament: 03.03.2006. Coming into force: 26.03.2006. Effect: S.I. 1994/1931 (with savings); 1996/32; 1997/2007; 1998/1589, 2504; 1999/374 & S.S.I. 2000/187; 2002/107; 2003/242; 2006/5 revoked. Territorial extent & classification: S. General. - Copies are supplied from TSO's On-Demand Publishing Service. - 88p.: 30 cm. - 978-0-11-069988-2 £13.50

Young offenders institutions

The Prisons and Young Offenders Institutions (Scotland) Amendment Rules 2006 No. 2006/5. - Enabling power: Prisons (Scotland) Act 1989, s. 39. - Issued: 17.01.2006. Made: 10.01.2006. Laid: 11.01.2006. Coming into force: 02.02.2006. Effect: SI 1994/1931 amended. - Revoked by S.S.I. 2006/94 (ISBN 0110699882). - 2p.: 30 cm. - 978-0-11-069900-4 £3.00

Scottish Statutory Instruments

Arranged by Number

1	Public procurement
2	Public procurement
3	Food
4	Agriculture
5	Prisons Young offenders institutions
6	Public health
7	Criminal law
8	Criminal law
9	Road traffic
10	Road traffic
11	Mental health
12	Mental health
13	Road traffic
14 (C.1)	Housing
15	Children and young persons
16	Agriculture
17	Harbours, docks, piers and ferries
18	Electricity
19 (C.2)	Environmental protection
20	Road traffic
21	Road traffic
22	Road traffic
23	Road traffic
24	Crofters, cottars and small landholders
25	Roads and bridges
26	Local government Ethical standards
27	Plant health
28	Housing Criminal law Local government
29	Local government
30	National Health Service
31 (C.3)	Gaelic language
32	National Health Service
33	National Health Service
34	Road traffic
35	Road traffic
36	Road traffic
37	Road traffic
38	Public health
39	Police
40 (C.4)	Water industry
41	Public health
42	National Health Service
43	Licenses and licensing
44	Public health Animals
45	Animals
46	Animals
47 (C.5)	Public health
48 (C.6)	Criminal law
49	Pilotage
50	Police
51	Sea fisheries
52	Public health
53	Roads and bridges
54	Road traffic
55 (C.7)	Water
56	Public finance and accountability
57	Sea fisheries
58	Sea fisheries
59 (C.8)	High Court of Justiciary Sheriff Court
60	Legal aid and advice
61	Legal aid and advice
62	Road traffic
63	Criminal law
64	Housing
65	Road traffic
66	Public health
67	Local government Council tax Rating and valuation
68	Road traffic
69	Public health
70	Seeds
71	Water supply
72	Water supply
73	Animals
74 (C.9)	Charities
75	Sheriff Court
76	High Court of Justiciary Sheriff Court
77	Road traffic
78	Road traffic
79	National Health Service
80	Road traffic
81	Road traffic
82	Agriculture
83	Court of Session
84	National Health Service Road traffic
85 (C.10)	Criminal law
86	Sheriff Court
87	Court of Session
88	Education
89 (C.11)	Local government

90	Public health	135	National Health Service
91	Police	136	National Health Service
92	Rating and valuation	137	National Health Service
93	Road traffic	138	National Health Service
94	Prisons Young offender institutions	139	National Health Service
		140	Children and young persons
95	Public health	141	National Health Service
96	Police	142	National Health Service
97	Police	143	National Health Service
98	Road traffic	144	National Health Service
99	Road traffic	145	Public health
100	Roads and bridges	146	Road traffic
101 (C.12)	Town and country planning	147	Road traffic
102	Public health	148	Road traffic
103	Public health	149	National Health Service
104 (C.13)	Criminal law Police Local government Environmental protection	150	Roads and bridges
		151	Agriculture Pesticides
105	Food	152	Water supply
106	Transport	153	Water supply
107	Transport	154	Betting, gaming and lotteries
108	Title conditions	155	Water industry
109	Feudal tenure	156	Agriculture
110	Title conditions	157	Roads and bridges
111	Transport	158	Rating and valuation
112	Transport	159	Road traffic
113	National assistance services	160	Road traffic
114	National assistance services	161	Road traffic
115	Civil partnership	162	Public finance and accountability
116	Enforcement	163	Building and buildings
117	Transport	164	Registers and records
118	Agriculture	165	Road traffic
119	Food	166 (C.15)	Criminal law Police
120	Water supply		
121 (C.14)	National Health Service	167 (C.16)	Water industry
122	National Health Service	168 (C.17)	Criminal law
123	Pensions	169	Public health
124	*Revoked before issuing by SSI 2006/158*	170	Criminal law
		171	Mental health
125	Rating and valuation	172	Mental health
126	Environmental protection Water	173	Electricity
		174	Road traffic
127	Environmental protection Water	175	Road traffic
128	Environmental protection	176	Road traffic
129	Police Serious Organised Crime Agency	177	Road traffic
		178	Legal aid and advice
130	Title conditions	179	Legal aid and advice
131	National Health Service	180	Rating and valuation
132	National Health Service	181	Environmental protection Water
133	Environmental protection Water		
		182	Criminal law
134	Opticians		

183	National Health Service	231	Animals
184	Road traffic	232 (C.20)	Education
185	Road traffic	233	Legal aid and advice
186	Road traffic	234	Legal aid and advice
187	Road traffic	235	Public health
188	Charities	236	Public health
189 (C.18)	Charities	237	Animals
190	Criminal law	238	Road traffic
191	Public health	239 (C.21)	Licensing (Liquor)
192	Public health	240	Road traffic
193	Road traffic	241	Pesticides
194	Rehabilitation of offenders	242	Public health
195	Road traffic	243 (C.22)	Town and country planning
196	Animals	244	Sea fisheries
197	Sheriff Court	245	National Health Service
198	Sheriff Court	246	National Health Service
199	Court of Session	247	National Health Service
200	Sheriff Court	248	National Health Service
201	Local government Rating and valuation	249	Betting, gaming and lotteries
		250	Transport
202	Public health	251 (C.23)	Human tissue
203	Public health	252 (C.24)	Housing
204	Road traffic	253	Family law
205	High Court of Justiciary Sheriff Court	254	Family law
		255	Children and young persons
206	Court of Session	256	Road traffic
207	Sheriff Court	257	Sheriff Court
208	Road traffic	258	Road traffic
209	Water supply	259	Road and bridges, Scotland
210	Water supply	260	Public health
211	Housing	261	Road traffic
212 (C.19)	Family law	262	Road traffic
213	Agriculture	263	Children and young persons
214	Crofters, cottars and small landholders	264	Seeds
215	Road traffic	265	Town and country planning
216	Charities	266	Town and country planning
217	Road traffic	267	Road traffic
218	Charities	268 (C.25)	Town and country planning
219	Charities	269	Town and country planning
220	Charities	270	Town and country planning
221	Mental health	271	Road traffic
222	Road traffic	272	Social care
223	Road traffic	273	Social care
224	Road traffic	274	Social care
225	Road traffic	275 (C.26)	Social care
226	Road traffic	276	Education
227	Road traffic	277	Road traffic
228	Road traffic	278	Road traffic
229	Road traffic	279	Education
230	Food	280	Road traffic

281 (C.27)	Criminal law		330	National Health Service
282	Road traffic		331 (C.29)	Criminal law
283	Road traffic		332 (C.30)	Criminal law
284	Sea fisheries		333	Education
285	Police Pensions		334	Anatomy
			335	Animals
286 (C.28)	Licensing (liquor)		336	Animals
287	Road traffic		337	Animals
288	Road traffic		338	Fire services Pensions
289	Road traffic			
290	Road traffic		339	Town and country planning
291	*Revoked before issuing*		340	Human tissue Anatomy
292	Sheriff Court			
293	Sheriff Court		341	Sea fisheries
294	Court of Session		342	Fire services Pensions
295	Sheriff Court		343	Human tissue
296	Water supply		344	Human tissue
297	Water supply		345	Legal aid and advice
298	Education		346	Road traffic
299	Road traffic		347	Road traffic
300	Road traffic		348	Roads and bridges
301	Road traffic		349	Roads and bridges
302	High Court of Justiciary		350	Road traffic
303	Public bodies		351	Road traffic
304	Road traffic		352	Animals
305	Roads and bridges		353	Road traffic
306	Food		354	Road traffic
307	National Health Service		355	Road traffic
308	Pensions		356	Road traffic
309	Human tissue		357	Road traffic
310	Human tissue		358	Road traffic
311	Agriculture		359	Local government
312	Agriculture Pesticides		360	Water supply
			361	Water supply
313	Seeds		362	Road traffic
314	Food		363	Public bodies
315	Criminal law		364	Road traffic
316	Education		365	Children and young persons
317	Education		366	Road traffic
318	Education		367	Electronic communications
319	Plant health		368	Human tissue
320	National Health Service		369	Roads and bridges
321	National Health Service		370	Local government
322	Education		371	Road traffic
323	Education		372	Local government
324	Education		373	Local government
325	Legal aid and advice		374	Local government
326	Education		375	Local government
327	Human tissue		376	Local government
328	Anatomy		377	Local government
329	National Health Service			

378	Local government	428	Local government
379	Civil partnership	429	Local government
380	Road traffic	430	Animals
381 (C.31)	Security industry	431	Transport
382 (C.32)	Security industry	432 (C.34)	Police Criminal law
383	Sea fisheries	433	Road traffic
384	Family law	434	Local government
385	Road traffic	435	Road traffic
386	Road traffic	436	High Court of Justiciary Sheriff Court District Courts
387	Road traffic	437	Sheriff Court
388	Road traffic	438	Road traffic
389	Criminal law	439	Road traffic
390	Human tissue	440	National Health Service
391	Local government	441	Road traffic
392	Local government	442	Road traffic
393	Local government	443	Road traffic
394	Local government	444	Road traffic
395 (C.33)	Housing	445 (C.35)	Water industry
396	Road traffic	446	Road traffic
397	Sheriff Court	447	River
398	Education	448	Seeds
399	Animals	449	Pesticides
400	Road traffic	450	Animals
401	Education	451	Agriculture
402	Council tax	452	Education
403	Road traffic	453	Social care
404	Education	454 (C.36)	Education
405	Road traffic	455	Education
406	Road traffic	456	Fire safety
407	Road traffic	457	Fire safety
408	Road traffic	458 (C.37)	Fire safety
409	Road traffic	459	Food
410	Sheriff Court	460	Local government
411	Sheriff Court	461	Education
412	Road traffic	462	Roads and bridges
413	Road traffic	463	Roads and bridges
414	Road traffic	464	Water industry
415	Road traffic	465	Environmental protection
416	Local government	466	Investigatory powers
417	Road traffic	467	Race relations
418	Road traffic	468	Pensions
419	Animals	469 (C.38)	Registration of births, deaths, marriages, etc.
420	Human tissue	470 (C.39)	Local government
421	Road traffic	471	Local government
422	Roads and bridges	472	Local government
423	Roads and bridges	473 (C.40)	Consumer protection
424	Road traffic	474	Plant health
425	Road traffic		
426	Road traffic		
427	Local government		

475	Fire safety		523	Road traffic
476	Road traffic		524	Road traffic
477	Road traffic		525	Road traffic
478	Road traffic		526	Road traffic
479	Road traffic		527	Transport
480	Education		528	Transport
481	Local government		529	Roads and bridges
482 (C.41)	Animals		530	Animals
483	Road traffic, Scotland		531	Social care
484	Registration of births, deaths, marriages, etc.		532	Local government
			533	Local government
485	Land registration		534	Building and buildings
486	Land reform		535	Local government
487	Sea fisheries		536	Animals
488	River		537	Local government
489	Roads and bridges		538	Transport
490	Roads and bridges		539	Sheriff Court
491	Land registration		540	Sheriff Court
492	Road traffic		541	Environmental protection
493	Roads and bridges		542	Food
494	Roads and bridges		543	Agriculture
495	Road traffic		544	Road traffic
496	Roads and bridges		545 (C.42)	Criminal law
497	Roads and bridges Special roads		546	Local government
			547	Local government
498	Roads and bridges		548	Agriculture Pesticides
499	Roads and bridges			
500	Roads and bridges Special roads		549	Sea fisheries
			550	Road traffic
501	Roads and bridges Special roads		551	Local government
			552	Police
502	Roads and bridges		553	Environmental protection Water
503	Roads and bridges			
504	Roads and bridges		554	Environmental protection Water
505	Sea fisheries			
506	Sea fisheries		555	Road traffic
507	Road traffic		556	Food
508	Road traffic		557	Rating and valuation
509	Sheriff Court		558	Local government
510	Local government		559	Public health
511	Local government		560	National Health Service
512	Food		561	National Health Service
513	Construction		562	Local government
514	Pensions		563	Road traffic
515	Legal aid and advice		564	Road traffic
516	Agriculture		565	Roads and bridges
517	Food		566	Roads and bridges
518	Road traffic		567	Roads and bridges Special roads
519	Road traffic			
520	Road traffic		568	Registers and records
521	Police		569 (C.43)	Housing
522	Road traffic		570	Energy conservation

571	Charities
572	River
573	Marriage
574	Civil partnership
575	Registration of births, deaths, marriages, etc. Marriage Civil partnership
576	Pesticides
577	*Revoked before issuing by SSI 2006/594*
578	Agriculture
579	Food
580	Food
581 (C.44)	Farriers Registration Council
582	Agriculture
583	Road traffic
584	Road traffic
585	Road traffic
586	Road traffic
587	Sea fisheries
588	National Health Service
589	Public finance and accountability
590	Road traffic
591	Road traffic
592	National Health Service
593	National Health Service
594	Animals
595	Road traffic
596	Registration of births, deaths, marriages, etc.
597	Registration of births, deaths, marriages, etc.
598	Registration of births, deaths, marriages, etc.
599 (C. 45)	Water industry
600	Registers and records
601	Agriculture
602	Sea fisheries
603	National Health Service
604	Licenses and licensing Public health
605	Pensions
606	Animals
607 (C.46)	Police Criminal law
608	Transport
609	Local government
610	Police
611 (C.47)	Olympic games and paralympic games Sports grounds and sporting events
612	Public bodies
613	Public passenger transport
614	Town and country planning Land drainage Roads and bridges Fish farming Forestry Agriculture
615	Legal aid and advice
616	Legal aid and advice
617	Road traffic
618	Road traffic
619	Road traffic
620	Road traffic
621	Road traffic
622	Road traffic
623	Road traffic
624	Road traffic
625	Road traffic

List of Scottish Commencement Orders

14 (C.1)
19 (C.2)
31 (C.3)
40 (C.4)
47 (C.5)
48 (C.6)
55 (C.7)
59 (C.8)
74 (C.9)
85 (C.10)
89 (C.11)
101 (C.12)
104 (C.13)
121 (C.14)
166 (C.15)
167 (C.16)
168 (C.17)
189 (C.18)
212 (C.19)
232 (C.20)
239 (C.21)
243 (C.22)
251 (C.23)
252 (C.24)
268 (C.25)
275 (C.26)
281 (C.27)
286 (C.28)
331 (C.29)
332 (C.30)
381 (C.31)

382 (C.32)
395 (C.33)
432 (C.34)
445 (C.35)
454 (C.36)
458 (C.37)
469 (C.38)
470 (C.39)

473 (C.40)
482 (C.41)
545 (C.42)
569 (C.43)
581 (C.44)
599 (C.45)
607 (C.46)
611 (C.47)

Northern Ireland Legislation

Other statutory publications

Statutory Publications Office.

Chronological table of statutory rules Northern Ireland: covering the legislation to 31 December 2004. - [approx. 860 pages]: looseleaf with binder holes: 30 cm. - 978-0-337-08774-5 £75.00

Chronological table of statutory rules Northern Ireland: covering the legislation to 31 December 2005. - 2nd ed. - [approx. 800 pages]: looseleaf with binder holes: 30 cm. - 978-0-337-08833-9 £70.00

Northern Ireland statutes 2005: [binder]. - 1 binder: 31 cm. - 978-0-337-08846-9 £25.00

The statutes revised: Northern Ireland. - Final cumulative supplement to 31 December 2005. - 2nd ed. - xi, 660p.: looseleaf with binder holes: 25 cm. - This is the final cumulative supplement to Statutes revised Northern Ireland 2nd edition. The material held in this volume has been integrated into the UK Statute Law Database. Northern Ireland legislation from 1 January 2006 is available online at www.statutelaw.gov.uk. Effects will be applied directly to the text of primary legislation there. - 978-0-337-08873-5 £65.00

The statutory rules of Northern Ireland 2005

Part 2: Nos. 151-300. - xiii, p. 947-1783: hdbk: 31 cm. - 978-0-337-09491-0 £675.00

Part 3: Nos. 301-450. - xiii, p. 1785-2672: hdbk: 31 cm. - 978-0-337-09492-7 £595.00

Part 4: Nos. 451-590. - xxxiv, p. 2673-3799: hdbk: 31 cm. - 978-0-337-09493-4 £675.00

The statutory rules of Northern Ireland 2006

Part 1: Nos. 1-150. - 2 v. (xiv, p. 1-1306): hdbk: 31 cm. - 978-0-337-09600-6 £750.00

Part 2: Nos. 151-300. - 2 v. (xiii, p. 1307-2740): hdbk: 31 cm. - 978-0-337-09601-3 £835.00

Part 3: Nos. 301-450. - 2 v. (xiii, p. 2741-3935): hdbk: 31 cm. - 978-0-337-09602-0 £700.00

Title page, index and tables to Northern Ireland statutes volume 2005. - lxvii p.: looseleaf with binder holes: 30 cm. - 978-0-337-08845-2 £20.00

Statutory Rules of Northern Ireland

By Subject Heading

Access to justice

The Access to Justice (Northern Ireland) Order 2003 (Commencement No. 5) Order (Northern Ireland) 2006 No. 2006/27 (C.2). - Enabling power: S.I. 2003/435 (N.I. 10), art. 1 (2). Bringing into operation various provisions of the 2003 Order on 20.03.2006. - Issued: 07.03.2006. Made: 31.01.2006. Coming into operation: 20.03.2006. Effect: None. - 4p: 30 cm. - 978-0-337-96374-2 £3.00

Age discrimination

The Employment Equality (Age) (Amendment No. 2) Regulations (Northern Ireland) 2006 No. 2006/453. - Enabling power: European Communities Act 1972, s. 2 (2). - Issued: 20.11.2006. Made: 13.11.2006. Coming into operation: 01.12.2006. Effect: S.R. 2006/261 amended. - EC note: These Regs amend the Employment Equality (Age) Regulations (Northern Ireland) 2006 (S.R. 2006/261) which implement the Council Directive 2000/78/EC establishing a general framework for equal treatment in employment and occupation. These Regulations deal with provisions relating to pensions. - 16p.: 30 cm. - 978-0-337-96709-2 £3.00

The Employment Equality (Age) (Amendment) Regulations (Northern Ireland) 2006 No. 2006/395. - Enabling power: European Communities Act 1972, s. 2 (2). - Issued: 04.10.2006. Made: 28.09.2006. Coming into operation: 30.09.2006. Effect: S.R. 2006/261 amended. - EC note: These Regs amend the 2006 Regs which implement Council Directive 2000/78/EC establishing a general framework for equal treatment in employment and occupation. - 4p.: 30 cm. - 978-0-337-96657-6 £3.00

The Employment Equality (Age) Regulations (Northern Ireland) 2006 No. 2006/261. - Enabling power: European Communities Act 1972, s. 2 (2). - Issued: 20.06.2006. Made: 13.06.2006. Coming into operation: In accord. with reg. 1. Effect: 1972 c. 9 (N.I.); 1992 c. 7 & S.I. 1981/231 (N.I.10); 1994/766 (N.I. 5); 1996/1919 (N.I. 16), 1921 (N.I. 18); 1998/1506 (N.I.10), 3162 (N.I. 21); 2003/2902 (N.I. 15) & S.R. 1980/121; 1982/263; 1987/30; 1996/604; 2000/405; 2002/378; 2003/497; 2004/521; 2005/150 amended & S.R.& O. (N.I.) 1965/246 revoked. - EC note: These Regulations implement, in Northern Ireland, Council Directive 2000/78/EC establishing a general framework for equal treatment in employment so far as it relates to discrimination on the grounds of age. - 68p.: 30 cm. - 978-0-337-96550-0 £9.00

The Industrial Tribunals (Interest on Awards in Age Discrimination Cases) Regulations (Northern Ireland) 2006 No. 2006/262. - Enabling power: European Communities Act 1972, s. 2 (2). - Issued: 19.06.2006. Made: 13.06.2006. Coming into operation: 01.10.2006. Effect: None. - EC note: These Regs. ensure that the remedies available under the Age Regs comply with art. 17 of Council Directive 2000/78/EC establishing a general framework for equal treatment in employment so far as it relates to discrimination on grounds of age. - 4p.: 30 cm. - 978-0-337-96551-7 £3.00

Agriculture

The Agricultural Wages (Abolition of Permits to Infirm and Incapacitated Persons) Regulations (Northern Ireland) 2006 No. 2006/429. - Enabling power: European Communities Act 1972, s. 2 (2). - Issued: 03.11.2006. Made: 30.10.2006. Coming into operation: 01.12.2006. Effect: 1998 c. 39; S.I. 1977/2151 (N.I.22) amended. - EC note: These Regulations implement provisions of Council Directive 2000/78/EC establishing a general framework for equal treatment in employment and occupation in so far as it relates to disability discrimination in the payment of agricultural wages. They are also a consequence of the revocation of regulation 6 of the Disability Discrimination (Employment) Regulations (Northern Ireland) 1996 (SR 1996 No 419) by regulation 3 of the Disability Discrimination (Employment Field) (Leasehold Premises) Regulations (Northern Ireland) 2004 (SR 2004 No 374). - 4p.: 30 cm. - 978-0-337-96693-4 £3.00

The Agriculture (2004 Order) (Commencement and Appointed Day) Order (Northern Ireland) 2006 No. 2006/172 (C.11). - Enabling power: S.I. 2004/3327 (N.I.23), art. 1 (3). Bringing into operation various provisions of the 2004 Order on 01.04.2006. - Issued: 07.04.2006. Made: 31.03.2006. Coming into operation: -. Effect: None. - 2p: 30 cm. - 978-0-337-96473-2 £3.00

The Agriculture (Weather Aid 2002) (Amendment) Scheme (Northern Ireland) 2006 No. 2006/232. - Enabling power: Agriculture (Temporary Assistance) Act (Northern Ireland) 1954, ss. 1 (1), 2 (1). - Issued: 30.05.2006. Made: 23.05.2006. Coming into operation: 15.06.2006. Effect: S.R. 2005/468 amended. - 4p: 30 cm. - 978-0-337-96520-3 £3.00

The Common Agricultural Policy Single Payment and Support Schemes (Amendment) Regulations (Northern Ireland) 2006 No. 2006/211. - Enabling power: European Communities Act 1972, s. 2 (2). - Issued: 26.05.2006. Made: 10.05.2006. Coming into operation: 10.05.2006. Effect: S.R. 2005/256 amended. - EC note: Amends S.R. 2005/256 which made provision in Northern Ireland for the administration of Council Reg. no. 1782/2003 and Commission Reg nos. 795/2004, 796/2004 and 1973/2004. - 4p.: 30 cm. - 978-0-337-96515-9 £3.00

The Common Agricultural Policy Single Payment and Support Schemes (Cross Compliance) (Amendment) Regulations (Northern Ireland) 2006 No. 2006/459. - Enabling power: European Communities Act 1972, s. 2 (2). - Issued: 23.11.2006. Made: 17.11.2006. Coming into operation: 15.12.2006. Effect: S.R. 2005/6 amended. - EC note: These Regs designate the Department of Agriculture, the Department of the Environment and the Health and Safety Executive for Northern Ireland as the authorities responsible for carrying out controls on certain specified requirements or standards set out in Council Regulation (EC) No. 1782/2003 and Commission Regulation (EC) No. 796/2004 in relation to cross compliance under the new system of direct support schemes (including the Single Payment Scheme) under the Common Agricultural Policy, which came into force on 1st January 2005. - 4p.: 30 cm. - 978-0-337-96716-0 £3.00

The Common Agricultural Policy Single Payment and Support Schemes (Set-aside) (Amendment) Regulations (Northern Ireland) 2006 No. 2006/200. - Enabling power: European Communities Act 1972, s. 2 (2). - Issued: 04.05.2006. Made: 26.04.2006. Coming into operation: 15.05.2006. Effect: S.R. 2005/310 amended. - EC note: These regs relate to the provision in Northern Ireland for the administration of Council Regulation (EC) No. 1782/2003, Commission Regulation (EC) No. 795/2004 and Commission Regulation (EC) No. 1973/2004 in relation to the obligation to set aside land under the new Single Farm Payment Scheme for farmers. - 8p.: 30 cm. - 978-0-337-96490-9 £3.00

Countryside Management (Amendment) Regulations (Northern Ireland) 2006 No. 2006/208. - Enabling power: S.I. 1995/3212 (N.I. 21), art. 3 & European Communities Act 1972, s. 2 (2). - Issued: 15.05.2006. Made: 09.05.2006. Coming into operation: 03.07.2006. Effect: S.R. 2005/268 amended. - 4p: 30 cm. - 978-0-337-96495-4 £3.00

The Curd Cheese (Restriction on Placing on the Market) (Amendment) Regulations (Northern Ireland) 2006 No. 2006/493. - Enabling power: European Communities Act 1972, s. 2 (2). - Issued: 07.12.2006. Made: 01.12.2006. Coming into operation: 08.01.2007. Effect: S.R. 2006/415 amended. - 4p.: 30 cm. - 978-0-337-96743-6 £3.00

EC Fertilisers Regulations (Northern Ireland) 2006 No. 2006/503. - Enabling power: European Communities Act 1972, s. 2 (2). - Issued: 11.12.2006. Made: 06.12.2006. Coming into force: 01.02.2007. Effect: None. - EC note: These Regulations implement in Northern Ireland, Regulation 2003/2003 relating to fertilisers. - 12p.: 30 cm. - 978-0-337-96752-8 £3.00

The Eggs (Marketing Standards) (Amendment) Regulations (Northern Ireland) 2006 No. 2006/287. - Enabling power: European Communities Act 1972, s. 2 (2). - Issued: 05.07.2006. Made: 29.06.2006. Coming into operation: 30.06.2006. Effect: S.R. 1995/382 amended. - 4p.: 30 cm. - 978-0-337-96571-5 £3.00

Environmental Impact Assessment (Uncultivated Land and Semi-Natural Areas) Regulations (Northern Ireland) 2006 No. 2006/90. - Enabling power: European Communities Act 1972, s. 2 (2). - Issued: 30.03.2006. Made: 02.03.2006. Coming into operation: 17.04.2006. Effect: S.R. 2001/435 revoked with saving. - EC note: Implements Directive 2003/35/EC providing for public participation in certain environmental decision-making, which amends Directive 85/337/EC as amended by Directive 97/11/EC. - 28p: 30 cm. - 978-0-337-96397-1 *£4.50*

Environmentally Sensitive Areas Designation (Amendment) Order (Northern Ireland) 2006 No. 2006/209. - Enabling power: S.I. 1987/458 (N.I. 3), art. 3 (1) (3). - Issued: 15.05.2005. Made: 09.05.2006. Coming into operation: 03.07.2006. Effect: S.R. 2005/276 amended. - 4p: 30 cm. - 978-0-337-96496-1 *£3.00*

Farm Nutrient Management Scheme (Northern Ireland) 2006 No. 2006/537. - Enabling power: S.I. 1987/166 (N.I. 1), art. 16 (1) (2). - Issued: 08.01.2007. Made: 21.12.2006. Coming into operation: 21.12.2006. Effect: S.R. 2005/5 amended. - 8p: 30 cm. - 978-0-337-96785-6 *£3.00*

Farm Subsidies (Review of Decisions) (Amendment) Regulations (Northern Ireland) 2006 No. 2006/303. - Enabling power: European Communities Act 1972, s. 2 (2). - Issued: 19.07.2006. Made: 04.07.2006. Coming into operation: 04.07.2006. Effect: S.R. 2001/391 amended. - 4p.: 30 cm. - 978-0-337-96587-6 *£3.00*

The Feeding Stuffs (Amendment) Regulations (Northern Ireland) 2006 No. 2006/427. - Enabling power: Agriculture Act 1970, ss. 66 (1), 68 (1), 69 (1), 74 (1), 74A. - Issued: 31.10.2006. Made: 24.10.2006. Coming into operation: 17.11.2006. Effect: S.R. 2001/47; 2003/306; 2005/545 amended. - EC note: These regs relate to the implementation, in relation to Northern Ireland, Article 1.4 and Article 1.1(b) respectively of Directive 2002/2/EC amending Council Directive 79/373/EEC on the circulation of compound feedingstuffs. - 4p: 30 cm. - 978-0-337-96691-0 *£3.00*

The Feeding Stuffs and the Feeding Stuffs (Sampling and Analysis) (Amendment) Regulations (Northern Ireland) 2006 No. 2006/18. - Enabling power: Agriculture Act 1970, ss. 66 (1), 74A, 77 (4), 78 (6), 84. - Issued: 10.02.2006. Made: 25.01.2006. Coming into operation: 16.02.2006. Effect: S.R. 1999/296; 2005/545 amended. - EC note: These Regs implement Commission Directive 2005/6/EC (amending Directive 71/250/EEC); 2002/7/EC (amending Directive 2002/70/EC), 2002/8/EC (amending Annex 1 to Directive 2002/32/EC). - 4p: 30 cm. - 978-0-337-96325-4 *£3.00*

The Feed (Specified Undesirable Substances) Regulations (Northern Ireland) 2006 No. 2006/471. - Enabling power: Agriculture Act 1970, ss. 66 (1), 74A, 84 & European Communities Act 1972, s. 2 (2). - Issued: 29.11.2006. Made: 23.11.2006. Coming into operation: 26.12.2006 Effect: S.R. 2005/545, 546 amended. - EC note: These Regs provide for the implementation of Directives 2005/86/EC and 2005/87/EC (which amend Annex I to Directive 2002/32/EC) and 2006/13/EC (which amends Annexes I and II to Directive 2002/32/EC), on undesirable substances in animal feed; and also implement a provision contained in Directive 79/373/EC on the circulation of compound feedingstuffs, as last amended by Regulation (EC) no. 807/2003. - 12p: 30 cm. - 978-0-337-96727-6 *£3.00*

Less Favoured Area Compensatory Allowances Regulations (Northern Ireland) 2006 No. 2006/52. - Enabling power: European Communities Act 1972, s. 2 (2). - Issued: 10.03.2006. Made: 16.02.2006. Coming into operation: 16.02.2006. Effect: S.R. 2001/391 amended. - EC note: These Regulations implement Commission Regulation 817/2004 laying down detailed rules for the application of Council Regulation 1257/1999 as last amended by Council Regulation (EC) No. 2223/2004 on support for rural development from the European Agricultural Guidance and Guarantee Fund (EAGGF). They also implement Measure 2 of the Northern Ireland Rural Development Programme as amended. - 12p.: 30 cm. - 978-0-337-96383-4 *£3.00*

The Official Feed and Food Controls Regulations (Northern Ireland) 2006 No. 2006/2. - Enabling power: European Communities Act 1972, s. 2 (2). - Issued: 18.01.2006. Made: 10.01.2006. Coming into operation: 11.01.2006 Effect: S.R. 2005/574 revoked. - EC note: These Regs provide for the execution and enforcement of Reg. No. 882/2004, and they also impose prohibitions on the introduction of certain feed and food into Northern Ireland in the light of Article 11 of Reg. No. 178/2002, as last amended by Reg. No. 1642/2003 and as read with Article 10 of Reg. No. 852/2004. - 28p: 30 cm. - 978-0-337-96311-7 *£4.50*

Organic Farming (Conversion of Animal Housing) (Amendment) Scheme (Northern Ireland) 2006 No. 2006/81. - Enabling power: S.I. 1987/166 (N.I. 1), art. 16 (1) (2). - Issued: 14.03.2006. Made: 22.02.2006. Coming into operation: 31.03.2006. Effect: S.R. 2003/472 amended. - 2p.: 30 cm. - 978-0-337-96392-6 *£3.00*

Pesticides (Maximum Residue Levels in Crops, Food and Feeding Stuffs) Regulations (Northern Ireland) 2006 No. 2006/220. - Enabling power: European Communities Act 1972, s. 2 (2) & Food and Environment Protection Act 1985, s. 16 (2). - Issued: 26.05.2006. Made: 12.05.2006. Coming into operation: 30.06.2006. Effect: S.R. 2002/20, 27, 250; 2003/123, 379, 435; 2004/200, 367; 2005/51, 401 revoked. - EC note: These Regs specify new maximum residue levels in implementation of Commission Directives 2005/37/EC, 2005/46/EC, 2005/48/EC, 2005/70/EC, 2005/74/EC, 2005/76/EC, 2006/4/EC, 2006/9/EC and 2006/30/EC; and in accordance with Council Directive 90/642/EEC. - 256p.: 30 cm. - 978-0-337-96511-1 *£26.00*

Agriculture

The Pig Carcase (Grading) (Amendment) Regulations (Northern Ireland) 2006 No. 2006/253. - Enabling power: European Communities Act 1972, s. 2 (2). - Issued: 12.06.2006. Made: 06.06.2006. Coming into operation: 14.07.2006. Effect: S.R. 1994/384 amended. - EC note: These Regulations amend the 1994 Regulations so as to take account of Commission Decision 2004/370/EC. - 2p.: 30 cm. - 978-0-337-96539-5 £3.00

The Products of Animal Origin (Third Country Imports) Regulations (Northern Ireland) 2006 No. 2006/291. - Enabling power: European Communities Act 1972, s. 2 (2). - Issued: 07.07.2006. Made: 30.06.2006. Coming into operation: 24.07.2006. Effect: S.R. 2004/464; 2005/554 revoked. - EC note: These Regs continue to implement for Northern Ireland Council Directive 97/78/EC. Commission Decision 2002/349/EC specifies the products of animal origian to which the Directive applies - meat, fish (including shellfish), milk and products made from these, together with egg products and a large number of animal by-products, including casings, skins, bones and blood - from third countries. - 52p.: 30 cm. - 978-0-337-96574-6 £7.50

The Rice Products (Restriction on First Placing on the Market) Regulations (Northern Ireland) 2006 No. 2006/443. - Enabling power: European Communities Act 1972, s. 2 (2). - Issued: 15.11.2006. Made: 09.11.2006. Coming into operation: 09.11.2006. Effect: None. - EC note: These Regulations implement Commission Decision 2006/601/EC on emergency measures regarding the non-authorised genetically modified organism "LL RICE 601" in rice products as amended by Commission Decision 2006/754/EC. - 4p.: 30 cm. - 978-0-337-96702-3 £3.00

The Sea Fishing (Restriction on Days at Sea) (Monitoring, Inspection and Surveillance) Order (Northern Ireland) 2006 No. 2006/300. - Enabling power: Fisheries Act 1981, s. 30 (2). - Issued: 10.07.2006. Made: 04.07.2006. Coming into operation: 01.08.2006. Effect: S. I. 2005/393 amended. - EC note: This Order provides in Northern Ireland and in relation to Northern Ireland fishing boats for the administration and enforcement of the provisions of Annex IIA and IIC to Council Regulation (EC) No 51/2006 fixing for 2006 the fishing opportunities and associated conditions for certain fish stocks and groups of fish stocks, applicable in Community waters and, for Community vessels, in waters where catch limitations are required. - 16p.: 30 cm. - 978-0-337-96577-7 £3.00

The Seed Potatoes (Tuber Inspection Fees) (Amendment) Regulations (Northern Ireland) 2006 No. 2006/330. - Enabling power: Seeds Act (Northern Ireland) 1965, s. 1. - Issued: 10.08.2006. Made: 04.08.2006. Coming into operation: 28.08.2006. Effect: S.R. 2006/187 amended. - 2p.: 30 cm. - 978-0-337-96604-0 £3.00

The Seed Potatoes (Tuber Inspection Fees) Regulations (Northern Ireland) 2006 No. 2006/187. - Enabling power: Seeds Act (Northern Ireland) 1965, s. 1. - Issued: 25.04.2006. Made: 19.04.2006. Coming into operation: 28.08.2006. Effect: S.R. 1982/236; 2005/370 revoked. - 4p.: 30 cm. - 978-0-337-96484-8 £3.00

The Sheep and Goats (Records, Identification and Movement) (Amendment) Order (Northern Ireland) 2006 No. 2006/508. - Enabling power: S.I. 1981/1115 (N.I. 22), arts 5 (1)(b), 19 (e) (g), 44, 60 (1). - Issued: 19.12.2006. Made: 06.12.2006. Coming into operation: 31.12.2006. Effect: S.R. 2005/535 amended. - 8p: 30 cm. - 978-0-337-96760-3 £3.00

Agriculture: Pesticides

Pesticides (Maximum Residue Levels in Crops, Food and Feeding Stuffs) (Amendment) Regulations (Northern Ireland) 2006 No. 2006/501. - Enabling power: European Communities Act 1972, s. 2 (2). - Issued: 13.12.2006. Made: 05.12.2006. Coming into operation: 18.01.2007. Effect: S.R. 2006/220 amended. - EC note: The Regulations implement, for Northern Ireland, Commission Directives 2006/53/EC, 2006/59/EC, 2006/60/EC and 2006/61/EC. - 32p.: 30 cm. - 978-0-337-96751-1 £5.50

Animal health

The Transmissible Spongiform Encephalopathies Regulations (Northern Ireland) 2006 No. 2006/202. - Enabling power: European Communities Act 1972, s. 2 (2). - Issued: 08.05.2006. Made: 02.05.2006. Coming into operation: 03.05.2006. Effect: S.R. 2000/78; 2003/495; 2005/78 amended & 21 instruments revoked. - EC note: These Regulations revoke and remake with amendments the TSE Regulations (Northern Ireland) 2002 (S.R. 2002/225) and enforce Regulation 999/2001, laying down rules for the prevention, control and eradication of certain transmissible spongiform encephalopathies as amended by and as read with the provisions in Schedule 1. - 48p.: 30 cm. - 978-0-337-96491-6 £7.50

Animals

The Animals and Animal Products (Import and Export) (Amendment No. 2) Regulations (Northern Ireland) 2006 No. 2006/346. - Enabling power: European Communities Act 1972, s. 2 (2) & Finance Act 1973, s. 56 (1) (2) (5). - Issued: 29.08.2006. Made: 23.08.2006. Coming into operation: 01.09.2006. Effect: S.R. 2005/78 amended. - Revoked by S.R. 2006/401 (ISBN 0337966680). EC note: The Regulations update Schedule 4 of S.R. 2005/78, in order to bring the implementation of Community instruments as up-to-date as possible. The changes made to Schedule 4 are in relation to the countries from which imports are permitted of captive birds going to approved bodies, institutes or centres and lists instruments covering trade in captive birds going to approved bodies, institutes or centres. - 4p: 30 cm. - 978-0-337-96617-0 £3.00

The Animals and Animal Products (Import and Export) (Amendment) Regulations (Northern Ireland) 2006 No. 2006/105. - Enabling power: European Communities Act 1972, s. 2 (2) & Finance Act 1973, s. 56 (1) (2) (5). - Issued: 22.03.2006. Made: 10.03.2006. Coming into operation: 01.04.2006. Effect: S.R. 2005/78 amended. - Revoked by S.R. 2006/401 (ISBN 0337966680). EC note: The Regulations provide a statutory basis for the Northern Ireland Poultry Health Assurance Scheme, which is implemented by the Department in order to ensure compliance with the rules set out in Annex II to Council Directive 90/539/EEC (on animal health conditions governing intra-Community trade in, and imports from third countries of, poultry and hatching eggs). - 8p: 30 cm. - 978-0-337-96411-4 *£3.00*

The Animals and Animal Products (Import and Export) Regulations (Northern Ireland) 2006 No. 2006/401. - Enabling power: European Communities Act 1972, s. 2 (2) and Finance Act 1973, s. 56 (1) (2) (5). - Issued: 12.10.2006. Made: 05.10.2006. Coming into operation: 01.11.2006. Effect: 10 S.R.s disapplied; S.R. 2005/78 partially revoked and S.R. 2005/446; 2006/105, 346 revoked. - 56p.: 30 cm. - 978-0-337-96668-2 *£9.00*

The Diseases of Animals (Amendment) Regulations (Northern Ireland) 2006 No. 2006/41. - Enabling power: European Communities Act 1972, s. 2 (2). - Issued: 24.02.2006. Made: 17.02.2006. Coming into operation: 23.02.2006. Effect: S.I. 1981/1115 (N.I. 22) amended. - 4p: 30 cm. - 978-0-337-96355-1 *£3.00*

The Sales, Markets and Lairs (Amendment) Order (Northern Ireland) 2006 No. 2006/241. - Enabling power: S.I. 1981/1115 (N.I. 22), arts. 19, 21, 60 (1). - Issued: 08.06.2006. Made: 02.06.2006. Coming into operation: 28.06.2006. Effect: S.R. 1975/294 amended. - 4p: 30 cm. - 978-0-337-96528-9 *£3.00*

The Salmonella in Turkey Flocks and Herds of Slaughter Pigs (Survey Powers) Regulations (Northern Ireland) 2006 No. 2006/492. - Enabling power: European Communities Act 1972, s. 2 (2). - Issued: 07.12.2006. Made: 01.12.2006. Coming into operation: 22.12.2006. Effect: S.R. 2005/132, 584 revoked. - EC note: These Regulations provide a power of entry to inspectors to undertake the sampling required by Commission Decision 2006/662/EC concerning a financial contribution by the Community towards a baseline survey on the prevalence of Salmonella spp. in turkeys to be carried out in the Member States and in herds of slaughter pigs as required by Commission Decision 2006/668/EC. - 4p: 30 cm. - 978-0-337-96742-9 *£3.00*

Animals: Animal health

The Foot-and-Mouth Disease (Control of Vaccination) Regulations (Northern Ireland) 2006 No. 2006/43. - Enabling power: European Communities Act 1972, s. 2 (2). - Issued: 24.02.2006. Made: 17.02.2006. Coming into operation: 23.02.2006. Effect: None. - EC note: These Regulations transpose for Northern Ireland Council Directive 2003/85/EC on Community measures for the control of foot-and-mouth disease insofar as it deals with vaccination against foot-and-mouth disease. - 32p: 30 cm. - 978-0-337-96356-8 *£5.50*

The Foot-and-Mouth Disease Regulations (Northern Ireland) 2006 No. 2006/42. - Enabling power: European Communities Act 1972, s. 2 (2). - Issued: 07.03.2006. Made: 17.02.2006. Coming into operation: 23.02.2006. Effect: S.R. 1972/16 amended & S.R. & O. (N.I.) 1962/209; 1968/14, 29, 34 & S.R. 2001/82, 83, 239; 2002/44 revoked. - EC note: These Regulations transpose for Northern Ireland Council Directive 2003/85/EC on Community measures for the control of foot-and-mouth disease repealing Directive 85/511/EEC and Decisions 89/531/EEC and 91/665/EEC and amending Directive 92/46/EEC. The Regulations transpose the Directive except insofar as it deals with vaccination against foot-and-mouth disease. - 64p: 30 cm. - 978-0-337-96357-5 *£9.00*

The Welfare of Animals (Transport) Regulations (Northern Ireland) 2006 No. 2006/538. - Enabling power: European Communities Act 1972, s. 2 (2). - Issued: 05.01.2007. Made: 21.12.2006. Coming into operation: 05.01.2007. Effect: S.R. 1997/346; 1999/326, 380 revoked. - EC note: These Regs make provision for the administration and enforcement of Council Regulation (EC) No. 1/2005 on the protection of animals during transport and related operations and amending Directives 64/432/EEC and 93/119/EC and Regulation (EC) No 1255/97. It also makes provision for the administration and enforcement of Council Regulation 1255/97 concerning Community criteria for staging points and amending the route plan referred to in the Annex to Directive 91/628/EEC. - 12p: 30 cm. - 978-0-337-96787-0 *£3.00*

Building regulations

The Building (Amendment No. 2) Regulations (Northern Ireland) 2006 No. 2006/440. - Enabling power: S.I. 1979/1709 (N.I. 16), arts 3, 5 (1) (2) (3), sch. 1, paras 2, 6, 9, 13, 16, 17, 18, 21, 22. - Issued: 14.11.2006. Made: 09.11.2006. Coming into operation: 30.11.2006. Effect: S.R. 2000/389; 2006/355 amended. - 8p.: 30 cm. - 978-0-337-96700-9 *£3.00*

The Building (Amendment) Regulations (Northern Ireland) 2006 No. 2006/355. - Enabling power: S.I. 1979/1709 (N.I. 16), arts 3, 5 (1) (2) (3), sch. 1, paras 2, 6, 9, 13, 15, 16, 17, 18, 19, 20, 21, 22. - Issued: 05.09.2006. Made: 31.08.2006. Coming into operation: 30.11.2006. Effect: S.R. 2000/389 amended. - 20p.: 30 cm. - 978-0-337-96626-2 *£3.50*

Children

The Children (Prescribed Orders - Isle of Man and Guernsey) Regulations (Northern Ireland) 2006 No. 2006/480. - Enabling power: S.I. 1995/755 (N.I. 2), art. 180. - Issued: 04.12.2006. Made: 27.11.2006. Coming into operation: 21.12.2006. Effect: S.R. 1996/528 revoked. - 4p: 30 cm. - 978-0-337-96730-6 £3.00

The Employment of Children (Amendment) Regulations (Northern Ireland) 2006 No. 2006/212. - Enabling power: S.I. 1995/755 (N.I. 2), art. 136 (1). - Issued: 16.05.2006. Made: 03.05.2006. Coming into operation: 08.06.2006. Effect: S.R. 1996/477 amended. - 4p: 30 cm. - 978-0-337-96500-5 £3.00

Child support

The Child Support (Miscellaneous Amendments) Regulations (Northern Ireland) 2006 No. 2006/273. - Enabling power: S.I. 1991/2628 (N.I. 23), arts. 16 (1), 18 (4), 29 (2) (3), 32, 34, 37A (3), 48 (4), sch. 1, para. 11. - Issued: 26.06.2006. Made: 21.06.2006. Coming into operation: In accord. with reg. 1. Effect: S.R. 1992/339, 390; 1999/162; 2001/15, 17 amended. - 8p.: 30 cm. - 978-0-337-96558-6 £3.00

Civil partnership

The Dissolution etc. (Pension Protection Fund) Regulations (Northern Ireland) 2006 No. 2006/311. - Enabling power: Civil Partnership Act 2004, sch. 15, paras. 27, 30, 31. - Issued: 25.07.2006. Made: 19.07.2006. Coming into operation: 14.08.2006. Effect: 2004 c.33; S.R. 2005/484 modified. - 8p.: 30 cm. - 978-0-337-96590-6 £3.00

Companies

The Companies (1986 Order) (Investment Companies and Accounting and Audit Amendments) Regulations (Northern Ireland) 2006 No. 2006/137. - Enabling power: European Communities Act 1972, s. 2 (2) & S.I. 1986/1032 (N.I.6), art. 265. - Issued: 28.03.2005. Made: 16.03.2006. Coming into operation: 01.04.2006. Effect: S.I. 1986/1032 (N.I.6); S.R. 2004/307 amended. - 8p: 30 cm. - 978-0-337-96442-8 £3.00

The Companies (1986 Order) (Operating and Financial Review) (Repeal) Regulations (Northern Ireland) 2006 No. 2006/94. - Enabling power: S.I. 1986/1032 (N.I. 6), art. 265. - Issued: 22.03.2006. Made: 08.03.2006. Coming into operation: 31.03.2006. Effect: S.I. 1986/1032 (N.I. 6) amended. - 8p: 30 cm. - 978-0-337-96401-5 £3.00

The Companies (1986 Order) (Small Companies' Accounts and Audit) Regulations (Northern Ireland) 2006 No. 2006/438. - Enabling power: S.I. 1986/1032 (N.I. 6), art. 265. - Issued: 13.11.2006. Made: 07.11.2006. Coming into operation: 01.12.2006. Effect: S.I. 1986/1032 (N.I. 6) & S.R. 2004/307 amended. - 8p: 30 cm. - 978-0-337-96698-9 £3.00

The Companies (Audit, Investigations and Community Enterprise) (2005 Order) (Commencement No. 1 and Transitional Provision) Order (Northern Ireland) 2006 No. 2006/93 (C.6). - Enabling power: S.I. 2005/1967 (N.I. 17), art. 1. Bringing into operation various provisions of the 2005 Order on 06.04.2006. - Issued: 23.03.2006. Made: 08.03.2006. Coming into operation: -. Effect: None. - 4p: 30 cm. - 978-0-337-96400-8 £3.00

The Companies (Revision of Defective Accounts and Report) (Amendment) Regulations (Northern Ireland) 2006 No. 2006/139. - Enabling power: S.I. 1986/1032 (N.I. 6), art. 253 (3) (4). - Issued: 28.03.2006. Made: 16.03.2006. Coming into operation: 01.04.2006. Effect: S.R. 1991/268 amended. - 8p: 30 cm. - 978-0-337-96440-4 £3.00

The Companies (Summary Financial Statement) (Amendment) Regulations (Northern Ireland) 2006 No. 2006/138. - Enabling power: S.I. 1986/1032 (N.I.6), art. 259 (1) (2) (3). - Issued: 28.03.2006. Made: 16.03.2006. Coming into operation: 01.04.2006. Effect: S.R. 1996/179 amended. - 12p: 30 cm. - 978-0-337-96439-8 £3.00

Companies: Partnerships

The Partnerships and Unlimited Companies (Accounts) (Amendment) Regulations (Northern Ireland) 2006 No. 2006/354. - Enabling power: European Communities Act 1972, s. 2 (2). - Issued: 06.09.2006. Made: 31.08.2006. Coming into operation: 01.10.2006. Effect: S.R. 1994/133 amended. - 4p: 30 cm. - 978-0-337-96625-5 £3.00

Consumer protection

The Consumer Protection (Code of Practice for Traders on Price Indications) Approval Order (Northern Ireland) 2006 No. 2006/371. - Enabling power: S.I. 1987/2049 (N.I. 20), art. 18. - Issued: 27.09.2006. Made: 15.09.2006. Coming into operation: 30.10.2006. Effect: S.R. 1989/56 revoked. - 16p.: 30 cm. - 978-0-337-96650-7 £3.00

Contracting out

The Contracting Out (Functions Relating to Child Support) Order (Northern Ireland) 2006 No. 2006/286. - Enabling power: S.I. 1996/1632 (N.I. 11), art. 17 (1). - Issued: 05.07.2006. Made: 28.06.2006. Coming into operation: 03.07.2006. Effect: None. - 4p.: 30 cm. - 978-0-337-96570-8 £3.00

Contracting out: Child support

The Contracting Out (Functions Relating to Child Support) (Amendment) Order (Northern Ireland) 2006 No. 2006/433. - Enabling power: S.I. 1996/1632 (N.I. 11), art, 17 (1) (3). - Issued: 07.11.2006. Made: 02.11.2006. Coming into operation: 03.11.2006. Effect: S.R. 2006/286 amended. - This Statutory Rule has been made to amend provisions in S.R. 2006 No. 286 (ISBN 0337965706) and is being issued free of charge to all known recipients of that Statutory Rule. - 2p: 30 cm. - 978-0-337-96694-1 *£3.00*

County courts

The County Court (Amendment) Rules (Northern Ireland) 2006 No. 2006/521. - Enabling power: S.I. 1980/397 (N.I.3), art. 47. - Issued: 05.01.2007. Made: 14.12.2006. Coming into operation: 08.01.2007. Effect: S.R. 1981/225 amended. - EC note: These Regs implement the European Directive on the Enforcement of Intellectual Property Rights (Directive 2004/48/EC) by making provision for the court to make an interim order making the continuation of an alleged infringement of an intellectual property right subject to guarantees, by providing that where the court grants a remedy before the issue of proceedings, the remedy shall only be granted on terms providing for the issue of a civil bill and by amending the procedure relating to applications under the Copyright Design and Patents Act 1988 and the Trade Marks Act 1994. - 28p: 30 cm. - 978-0-337-96774-0 *£4.50*

The Family Proceedings (Amendment) Rules (Northern Ireland) 2006 No. 2006/304. - Enabling power: S.I. 1993/1576 (N.I. 6), art. 12. - Issued: 14.07.2006. Made: 04.07.2006. Coming into operation: 01.08.2006. Effect: S.R. 1996/322 amended. - 4p.: 30 cm. - 978-0-337-96585-2 *£3.00*

Credit unions

The Credit Unions (Deposits and Loans) Order (Northern Ireland) 2006 No. 2006/78. - Enabling power: S.I. 1985/1205 (N.I. 12), arts. 26 (4), 28 (2) (4). - Issued: 09.03.2006. Made: 02.03.2006. Coming into operation: 01.04.2006. Effect: S.I. 1985/1205 (N.I. 12) amended & S.R. 1993/429 revoked. - 4p.: 30 cm. - 978-0-337-96382-7 *£3.00*

The Credit Unions (Limit on Membership) Order (Northern Ireland) 2006 No. 2006/76. - Enabling power: S.I. 1985/1205 (N.I. 12), art. 13 (3). - Issued: 09.03.2006. Made: 02.03.2006. Coming into operation: 01.04.2006. Effect: S.I. 1985/1205 (N.I. 12) amended. - 2p.: 30 cm. - 978-0-337-96381-0 *£3.00*

The Credit Unions (Limit on Shares) Order (Northern Ireland) 2006 No. 2006/77. - Enabling power: S.I. 1985/1205 (N.I. 12), art. 14 (4). - Issued: 09.03.2006. Made: 02.03.2006. Coming into operation: 01.04.2006. Effect: S.I. 1985/1205 (N.I. 12) amended & S.R. 1993/428 revoked. - 2p.: 30 cm. - 978-0-337-96380-3 *£3.00*

Criminal evidence

The Criminal Justice (Evidence) (Northern Ireland) Order 2004 (Categories of Offences) Order 2006 No. 2006/62. - Enabling power: S.I. 2004/1501 (N.I. 10), art. 8 (4) (b). - Issued: 02.03.2006. Made: 01.03.2006. Laid: 06.03.2006. Coming into operation: 03.04.2006. Effect: None. - 8p.: 30 cm. - 978-0-337-96365-0 *£3.00*

The Criminal Justice (Evidence) (Northern Ireland) Order 2004 (Commencement No. 3) Order 2006 No. 2006/63 (C.5). - Enabling power: S.I. 2004/1501 (N.I. 10), art. 1 (3). Bringing into operation various provisions of the 2004 Order on 03.04.2006. - Issued: 02.03.2006. Made: 17.02.2006. Coming into operation: -. Effect: None. - 2p.: 30 cm. - 978-0-337-96367-4 *£3.00*

Criminal procedure

The Criminal Justice (2003 Order) (Commencement No. 3) Order (Northern Ireland) 2006 No. 2006/451 (C.27). - Enabling power: S.I. 2003/1247 (N.I. 13), art. 1 (3). Bringing into operation certain provisions of the 2003 Order on 13.11.2006. - Issued: 16.11.2006. Made: 09.11.2006. Coming into operation: -. Effect: None. - 2p.: 30 cm. - 978-0-337-96707-8 *£3.00*

The Criminal Justice (2005 Order) (Commencement No. 2) Order (Northern Ireland) 2006 No. 2006/368 (C.21). - Enabling power: S.I. 2005/1965 (N.I. 15), art. 1 (2). Bringing into operation various provisions of the 2005 Order on 18.09.2006. - Issued: 18.09.2006. Made: 13.09.2006. Coming into operation: -. Effect: None. - 2p: 30 cm. - 978-0-337-96637-8 *£3.00*

Dangerous drugs

The Misuse of Drugs (Amendment) (No. 2) Regulations (Northern Ireland) 2006 No. 2006/214. - Enabling power: Misuse of Drugs Act 1971, ss. 7, 10, 22, 31. - Issued: 22.05.2006. Made: 11.05.2006. Coming into operation: 01.06.2006. Effect: S.R. 2002/1 amended. - 4p: 30 cm. - 978-0-337-96508-1 *£3.00*

The Misuse of Drugs (Amendment) (No. 3) Regulations (Northern Ireland) 2006 No. 2006/264. - Enabling power: Misuse of Drugs Act 1971, ss. 7, 10, 22, 31. - Issued: 04.07.2006. Made: 14.06.2006. Coming into operation: 07.07.2006 except for regs 8 (1), 11; 01.01.2007 for regs 8 (1), 11, in accord. with reg. 2. Effect: S.R. 2002/1 amended. - 8p: 30 cm. - 978-0-337-96555-5 *£3.00*

The Misuse of Drugs (Amendment) (No. 4) Regulations (Northern Ireland) 2006 No. 2006/334. - Enabling power: Misuse of Drugs Act 1971, ss. 7, 10, 31. - Issued: 01.09.2006. Made: 11.08.2006. Coming into operation: 01.09.2006. Effect: S.R. 2002/1; 2006/264 amended. - This Statutory Rule has been made in consequence of defects in Statutory Rule 2006/264 (ISBN 0337965552) and is being issued free of charge to all known recipients of that Statutory Rule. - 4p: 30 cm. - 978-0-337-96610-1 *£3.00*

The Misuse of Drugs (Amendment) Regulations (Northern Ireland) 2006 No. 2006/44. - Enabling power: Misuse of Drugs Act 1971, ss. 7, 10, 22, 31. - Issued: 01.02.2006. Made: 15.02.2006. Coming into operation: 08.03.2006. Effect: S.R. 2002/1 amended. - 2p: 30 cm. - 978-0-337-96346-9 £3.00

Dangerous wild animals

The Dangerous Wild Animals (2004 Order) (Commencement No. 1) Order (Northern Ireland) 2006 No. 2006/416 (C.23). - Enabling power: S.I. 2004/1993 (N.I.16), art. 1 (3). Bringing various provisions of the 2004 Order into operation on 04.12.2006. - Issued: 14.11.2006. Made: 08.11.2006. Coming into operation: -. Effect: None. - This Statutory Rule is being issued free of charge to all known recipients of SR 2006 No 416 (C.23) (same ISBN) which originally published on 24th October 2006. - 2p.: 30 cm. - 978-0-337-96678-1 £3.00

The Dangerous Wild Animals (2004 Order) (Commencement No. 2) Order (Northern Ireland) 2006 No. 2006/496 (C.31). - Enabling power: S.I. 2004/1993 (N.I.16), art. 1 (3). Bringing various provisions of the 2004 Order into operation on 28.12.2006. - Issued: 08.12.2006. Made: 01.12.2006. Coming into operation: -. Effect: S.R. 2006/416 (C.23) revoked. - This Statutory Rule is being issued free of charge to all known recipients of S.R. 2006/416 (C.23). - 2p.: 30 cm. - 978-0-337-96744-3 £3.00

The Dangerous Wild Animals (Fees) (No.2) Order (Northern Ireland) 2006 No. 2006/497. - Enabling power: S.I. 2004/1993 (N.I.16), art. 3 (2). - Issued: 08.12.2006. Made: 01.12.2006. Coming into operation: 28.12.2006. Effect: S.R. 2006/417 revoked. - This Statutory Rule is being issued free of charge to all known recipients of S.R. 2006/417. - 2p.: 30 cm. - 978-0-337-96745-0 £3.00

The Dangerous Wild Animals (Fees) Order (Northern Ireland) 2006 No. 2006/417. - Enabling power: S.I. 2004/1993 (N.I.16), art. 3 (2). - Issued: 14.11.2006. Made: 08.11.2006. Coming into operation: 04.12.2006. Effect: None. - This Statutory Rule is being issued free of charge to all known recipients of SR 2006 No 417 (same ISBN) which was originally published on 24th October 2006. - 2p.: 30 cm. - 978-0-337-96679-8 £3.00

Disabled persons

The Disability Discrimination (2006 Order) (Commencement No. 1) Order (Northern Ireland) 2006 No. 2006/289 (C.16). - Enabling power: S.I. 2006/312 (N.I.1), art. 1 (2). Bringing into operation various provisions of the 2006 Order on 03.07.2006. - Issued: 06.07.2005. Made: 30.06.2006. Coming into operation: -. Effect: None. - 4p.: 30 cm. - 978-0-337-96572-2 £3.00

The Disability Discrimination (2006 Order) (Commencement No. 2) Order (Northern Ireland) 2006 No. 2006/470 (C.29). - Enabling power: S.I. 2006/312 (N.I.1), art. 1 (2). Bringing into operation various provisions of the 2006 Order on 01.01.2007. - Issued: 29.11.2006. Made: 23.11.2006. Coming into operation: -. Effect: None. - 4p.: 30 cm. - 978-0-337-96726-9 £3.00

The Disability Discrimination (Services and Premises) (Amendment) Regulations (Northern Ireland) 2006 No. 2006/46. - Enabling power: Disability Discrimination Act 1995, ss. 19 (5) (c), 67 (1), 68 (1). - Issued: 23.02.2006. Made: 15.02.2006. Coming into operation: 20.03.2006. Effect: S.R. 1996/557 amended. - 2p: 30 cm. - 978-0-337-96345-2 £3.00

The Special Educational Needs and Disability (Northern Ireland) Order 2005 (Amendment) (Further and Higher Education) Regulations (Northern Ireland) 2006 No. 2006/332. - Enabling power: European Communities Act 1972, s. 2 (2). - Issued: 14.08.2006. Made: 09.08.2006. Coming into operation: In accord. with reg. 1 (2) (3). Effect: S.I. 2005/1117 (N.I.6) amended. - EC note: These Regulations implement (in Northern Ireland) the provisions of Council Directive 2000/78/EC, establishing a general framework for equal treatment in employment and occupation, so far as it relates to disability discrimination but only insofar as the Directive's obligations impact upon Chapter II of Part III of the Special Educational Needs and Disability (Northern Ireland) Order 2005 (S.I. 2005/1117 (N.I. 6)). - 12p.: 30 cm. - 978-0-337-96606-4 £3.00

Drainage

Drainage (Environmental Impact Assessment) Regulations (Northern Ireland) 2006 No. 2006/34. - Enabling power: European Communities Act 1972, s. 2 (2). - Issued: 20.02.2006. Made: 09.02.2006. Coming into operation: 20.03.2006. Effect: S.I. 1973/69 (N.I. 1); 1999/662 (N.I. 6) amended & S.R. 2001/394 revoked (with saving). - EC note: These Regulations (which revoke and re-enact with amendments the 2001 Regulations) implement the further changes to Council Directive 85/337/EEC made by Council Directive 2003/35/EC. - 28p.: 30 cm. - 978-0-337-96338-4 £4.50

The Drainage Trusts (Dissolution) Order (Northern Ireland) 2006 No. 2006/281. - Enabling power: S.I. 1973/69 (N.I. 1), art. 29A. - Issued: 30.06.2006. Made: 26.06.2006. Coming into operation: 31.07.2006. Effect: None. - 4p.: 30 cm. - 978-0-337-96564-7 £3.00

Education

The Disability Discrimination (Code of Practice) (Further and Higher Education) (Appointed Day) Order (Northern Ireland) 2006 No. 2006/17. - Enabling power: Disability Discrimination Act 1995, ss. 54A (6) (a), 67 (2) (3) (a). - Issued: 02.02.2006. Made: 25.01.2006. Coming into operation: 30.01.2006. Effect: None. - 2p: 30 cm. - 978-0-337-96324-7 £3.00

The Disability Discrimination (Code of Practice) (Schools) (Appointed Day) Order (Northern Ireland) 2006 No. 2006/16. - Enabling power: Disability Discrimination Act 1995, ss. 54A (6) (a), 67 (2) (3) (a). - Issued: 02.02.2005. Made: 25.01.2006. Coming into operation: 30.01.2006. Effect: None. - 2p: 30 cm. - 978-0-337-96323-0 £3.00

Education (Prohibition from Teaching or Working with Children) Regulations (Northern Ireland) 2006 No. 2006/51. - Enabling power: S.I. 1986/594 (N.I.3), arts 70 (1) (2), 88A (1) (2), 134. - Issued: 23.02.2005. Made: 16.02.2006. Coming into operation: 03.04.2006. Effect: None. - 4p: 30 cm. - 978-0-337-96350-6 £3.00

The Education (Student Loans) (Amendment) (No. 2) Regulations (Northern Ireland) 2006 No. 2006/329. - Enabling power: S.I. 1990/1506(N.I. 11), art. 3 (5), sch. 2, para. 1 (1). - Issued: 10.08.2006. Made: 04.08.2006. Coming into operation: 05.08.2006. Effect: S.R. 1998/58 amended. - 4p.: 30 cm. - 978-0-337-96603-3 £3.00

The Education (Student Loans) (Amendment) Regulations (Northern Ireland) 2006 No. 2006/307. - Enabling power: S.I. 1990/1506 (N.I. 11), art. 3 (5), sch. 2, para. 1 (1). - Issued: 21.07.2006. Made: 17.07.2006. Coming into operation: 01.08.2006. Effect: S.R. 1998/58; 2005/351, 435 amended. - 12p.: 30 cm. - 978-0-337-96588-3 £3.00

The Education (Student Loans) (Repayment) (Amendment) (No. 2) Regulations (Northern Ireland) 2006 No. 2006/331. - Enabling power: S.I. 1998/1760 (N.I. 14), arts 3 (2), 8 (4). - Issued: 14.08.2006. Made: 08.08.2006. Coming into operation: 01.09.2006. Effect: S.R. 2000/121 amended. - 8p: 30 cm. - 978-0-337-96605-7 £3.00

The Education (Student Loans) (Repayment) (Amendment) Regulations (Northern Ireland) 2006 No. 2006/28. - Enabling power: S.I. 1998/1760 (N.I. 14), arts 3 (2), 8 (4). - Issued: 10.02.2006. Made: 02.02.2006. Coming into operation: 06.04.2006. Effect: S.R. 2000/121 amended. - 4p: 30 cm. - 978-0-337-96333-9 £3.00

The Education (Student Support) (2005 Regulations) (Amendment) Regulations (Northern Ireland) 2006 No. 2006/252. - Enabling power: S.I. 1998/1760 (N.I. 14), arts, 3, 8 (4). - Issued: 20.06.2006. Made: 06.06.2006. Coming into operation: 29.06.2006. Effect: S.R. 2005/340, 445 amended. - Revoked by S.R. 2006/312 (ISBN 0337965919). - 16p.: 30 cm. - 978-0-337-96538-8 £3.00

The Education (Student Support) (Amendment) Regulations (Northern Ireland) 2006 No. 2006/383. - Enabling power: S.I. 1998/1760 (N.I. 14), arts 3, 8 (4). - Issued: 26.09.2006. Made: 19.09.2006. Coming into operation: 20.09.2006. Effect: S.R. 2006/312 amended. - 4p.: 30 cm. - 978-0-337-96648-4 £3.00

The Education (Student Support) Regulations (Northern Ireland) 2006 No. 2006/312. - Enabling power: S.I. 1998/1760 (N.I. 14), arts, 3, 8 (4). - Issued: 28.07.2006. Made: 18.07.2006. Coming into operation: 01.09.2006. Effect: S.R. 2005/340 [with savings], 445; 2006/252 revoked. - 104p.: 30 cm. - 978-0-337-96591-3 £13.50

The Education (Supply of Student Support Information to Governing Bodies) Regulations (Northern Ireland) 2006 No. 2006/403. - Enabling power: S.I. 2005/1116 (N.I. 5), arts 13 (1) to (5), 14 (4). - Issued: 13.10.2006. Made: 09.10.2006. Coming into operation: 10.10.2006. Effect: None. - 4p.: 30 cm. - 978-0-337-96670-5 £3.00

The Further Education (Student Support) (Cross-Border Eligibility) Regulations (Northern Ireland) 2006 No. 2006/422. - Enabling power: S.I. 1998/1760 (N.I. 14), arts 3 (2), 8 (4). - Issued: 26.10.2006. Made: 19.10.2006. Coming into operation: 12.11.2006. Effect: None. - 4p.: 30 cm. - 978-0-337-96689-7 £3.00

Grammar Schools (Charges) (Amendment) Regulations (Northern Ireland) 2006 No. 2006/511. - Enabling power: S.I. 1989/2406 (N.I. 20), art. 132 (2) (3). - Issued: 14.12.2006. Made: 11.12.2006. Coming into operation: 01.09.2007. Effect: S.R. 1992/171 amended & S.R. 2005/361 revoked. - 2p.: 30 cm. - 978-0-337-96762-7 £3.00

The Higher Education (2005 Order) (Commencement) Order (Northern Ireland) 2006 No. 2006/30 (C.3). - Enabling power: S.I. 2005/1116 (N.I.5), art. 1 (3). Bringing into operation various provisions of the 2005 Order on 13.02.2006. - Issued: 15.02.2006. Made: 06.02.2006. Coming into operation: -. Effect: None. - 2p.: 30 cm. - 978-0-337-96335-3 £3.00

The Student Fees (Amounts) (Amendment) Regulations (Northern Ireland) 2006 No. 2006/455. - Enabling power: S.I. 2005/1116 (N.I. 5), arts. 4 (8), 14 (4). - Issued: 21.11.2006. Made: 15.11.2006. Coming into operation: 01.09.2007. Effect: None. - 2p.: 30 cm. - 978-0-337-96713-9 £3.00

The Student Fees (Qualifying Courses and Persons) Regulations (Northern Ireland) 2006 No. 2006/384. - Enabling power: S.I. 2005/1116 (N.I. 5), arts. 4 (8), 14 (4). - Issued: 25.09.2006. Made: 19.09.2006. Coming into operation: 20.09.2006. Effect: None. - 4p.: 30 cm. - 978-0-337-96649-1 £3.00

Students Awards (Amendment) Regulations (Northern Ireland) 2006 No. 2006/378. - Enabling power: S.I. 1986/594 (N.I. 3), arts. 50 (1) (2), 134 (1). - Issued: 21.09.2006. Made: 15.09.2006. Coming into operation: 30.04. 2006; 01.09.2006, in accord. with reg. 2. Effect: S.R. 2005/466 amended. - 12p.: 30 cm. - 978-0-337-96644-6 £3.00

Teachers' (Eligibility) (Amendment) Regulations (Northern Ireland) 2006 No. 2006/441. - Enabling power: S.I. 1986/594 (N.I. 3), arts. 70 (1) (2), 134 (1). - Issued: 23.11.2006. Made: 09.11.2006. Coming into operation: 10.11.2006. Effect: S.R. 1997/312 amended. - 2p.: 30 cm. - 978-0-337-96714-6 £3.00

The Teachers' Superannuation (Miscellaneous Amendments) (No. 2) Regulations (Northern Ireland) 2006 No. 2006/366. - Enabling power: S.I. 1972/1073 (N.I. 10), art. 11 (1) (2) (3) (3A), sch. 3, paras 1, 3, 4, 5, 6, 8, 11, 13. - Issued: 02.10.2006. Made: 13.09.2006. Coming into operation: In accord. with reg. 1. Effect: S.R. 1996/260; 1998/333 amended. - 4p: 30 cm. - 978-0-337-96655-2 £3.00

The Teachers' Superannuation (Miscellaneous Amendments) Regulations (Northern Ireland) 2006 No. 2006/163. - Enabling power: S.I. 1972/1073 (N.I. 10), art. 11 (1) (2) (3) (3A), sch. 3, paras 1, 3, 4, 5, 6, 8, 11, 13. - Issued: 25.04.2006. Made: 29.03.2006. Coming into operation: 06.04.2006. Effect: S.R. 1996/260; 1998/333 amended. - 8p: 30 cm. - 978-0-337-96482-4 £3.00

Electricity

Energy (Amendment) Order (Northern Ireland) 2006 No. 2006/424. - Enabling power: S.I. 2003/419 (N.I.6), art. 56 (1). - Issued: 26.10.2006. Made: 20.10.2006. Coming into operation: 01.12.2006. Effect: S.I. 2003/419 (N.I.6) amended. - 4p.: 30 cm. - 978-0-337-96687-3 £3.00

Renewables Obligation Order (Northern Ireland) 2006 No. 2006/56. - Enabling power: S.I. 2003/419 (N.I. 6), arts. 52 to 55, 66 (3). - Issued: 01.03.2006. Made: 16.02.2006. Coming into operation: 01.04.2006. Effect: S.R 2005/38 revoked with savings. - EC note: This Order re-enacts the provisions of the 2005 Order which gave effect to Article 3.1 of the European Directive on the promotion of electricity produced from renewable energy sources in the internal market (Directive 2001/77/EC). - 32p: 30 cm. - 978-0-337-96354-4 £5.50

Employer's liability

The Employer's Liability (Compulsory Insurance) (Amendment) Regulations (Northern Ireland) 2006 No. 2006/298. - Enabling power: S.I. 1972/963 (N.I. 6), arts. 7 (c), 10 (1). - Issued: 07.07.2006. Made: 03.07.2006. Coming into operation: 28.08.2006. Effect: S.R. 1999/448 amended & S.R. 2005/392 revoked. - 8p.: 30 cm. - 978-0-337-96576-0 £3.00

Employment

Collective Redundancies (Amendment) Regulations (Northern Ireland) 2006 No. 2006/369. - Enabling power: European Communities Act 1972, s. 2 (2). - Issued: 19.09.2006. Made: 13.09.2006. Coming into operation: 08.10.2006. Effect: S.I. 1996/1919 (N.I. 16) amended. - 2p.: 30 cm. - 978-0-337-96638-5 £3.00

The Employment Protection (Continuity of Employment) (Amendment) Regulations (Northern Ireland) 2006 No. 2006/357. - Enabling power: S.I. 1996/1919 (N.I. 16), art. 15 (1). - Issued: 11.09.2006. Made: 05.09.2006. Coming into operation: 01.10.2006. Effect: S.R. 1996/604 amended. - 2p.: 30 cm. - 978-0-337-96628-6 £3.00

Employment Rights (Increase of Limits) Order (Northern Ireland) 2006 No. 2006/75. - Enabling power: S.I. 1999/2790 (N.I. 9), arts. 33 (1) to (4), 39 (3). - Issued: 14.03.2006. Made: 01.03.2006. Coming into operation: 26.03.2006. Effect: S.R. 2005/12 revoked with saving. - 8p.: 30 cm. - 978-0-337-96390-2 £3.00

The Gangmasters (Appeals) (Amendment) Regulations (Northern Ireland) 2006 No. 2006/235. - Enabling power: Gangmasters (Licensing) Act 2004, ss. 10, 25 (2). - Issued: 02.06.2006. Made: 25.05.2006. Coming into operation: 19.06.2006. Effect: S.R. 2006/189 amended. - 2p: 30 cm. - 978-0-337-96523-4 £3.00

The Gangmasters (Appeals) Regulations (Northern Ireland) 2006 No. 2006/189. - Enabling power: Gangmasters (Licensing) Act 2004, ss. 10, 25 (2). - Issued: 26.04.2006. Made: 20.04.2006. Coming into operation: 15.05.2006. Effect: None. - 12p.: 30 cm. - 978-0-337-96485-5 £3.00

The Gangmasters Licensing (Exclusions) Regulations (Northern Ireland) 2006 No. 2006/340. - Enabling power: Gangmasters (Licensing) Act 2004, s. 6 (2). - Issued: 23.08.2006. Made: 17.08.2006. Coming into operation: 11.09.2006. Effect: None. - 8p: 30 cm. - 978-0-337-96614-9 £3.00

The Information and Consultation of Employees (Amendment) Regulations (Northern Ireland) 2006 No. 2006/86. - Enabling power: Employment Relations Act 2004, s. 43 (1) (3) (a) (4) (e) (f) (9). - Issued: 13.03.2006. Made: 06.03.2006. Coming into operation: 06.04.2006. Effect: S.R. 2005/47 amended. - 4p: 30 cm. - 978-0-337-96387-2 £3.00

The Labour Relations Agency (Flexible Working) Arbitration Scheme Order (Northern Ireland) 2006 No. 2006/206. - Enabling power: S.I. 1992/807 (N.I. 5), art. 84A (2) (6). - Issued: 18.05.2006. Made: 02.05.2006. Coming into operation: 21.05.2006. Effect: None. - 28p: 30 cm. - 978-0-337-96499-2 £4.50

Public Interest Disclosure (Prescribed Persons) (Amendment) Order (Northern Ireland) 2006 No. 2006/458. - Enabling power: S.I. 1996/1919 (N.I. 16), art. 67F. - Issued: 23.11.2006. Made: 17.11.2006. Coming into operation: 10.12.2006. Effect: S.R. 1999/401 amended & S.R. 2004/261 revoked. - 8p.: 30 cm. - 978-0-337-96715-3 £3.00

The Service Provision Change (Protection of Employment) Regulations (Northern Ireland) 2006 No. 2006/177. - Enabling power: European Communities Act 1972, s. 2 (2) & S.I. 1999/2790 (N.I. 9), arts. 37 (2), 39 (3). - Issued: 10.04.2006. Made: 03.04.2006. Coming into operation: 06.04.2006. Effect: S.I. 1996/1919 (N.I. 16), 1921 (N.I. 18); 2006/246 amended. - 20p: 30 cm. - 978-0-337-96474-9 £3.50

The Social Security Benefits Up-rating Order (Northern Ireland) 2006 No. 2006/109. - Enabling power: Social Security Administration (Northern Ireland) Act 1992, ss. 132, 165 (1) (4) (5). - Issued: 28.03.2006. Made: 10.03.2006. Coming into operation: In accord. with art. 1. Effect: 1992 c. 7; 1993 c. 49; S.R. 1978/105; 1987/30, 459, 460, 461; 1992/32; 1994/461; 1995/35; 1996/198; 2002/380; 2003/28, 197 amended & S.R. 2005/82 revoked (13.04.2006). - 40p: 30 cm. - 978-0-337-96413-8 £6.50

The Working Time (Amendment No.2) Regulations (Northern Ireland) 2006 No. 2006/389. - Enabling power: European Communities Act 1972, s. 2 (2). - Issued: 29.09.2006. Made: 22.09.2006. Coming into operation: 01.10.2006. Effect: S.R. 1998/386 amended. - 2p.: 30 cm. - 978-0-337-96654-5 *£3.00*

The Working Time (Amendment) Regulations (Northern Ireland) 2006 No. 2006/135. - Enabling power: European Communities Act 1972, s. 2 (2). - Issued: 27.03.2006. Made: 15.03.2006. Coming into operation: 06.04.2006. Effect: S.R. 1998/386 amended. - 2p.: 30 cm. - 978-0-337-96437-4 *£3.00*

Employment: Work and families

The Maternity and Parental Leave etc. (Amendment) Regulations (Northern Ireland) 2006 No. 2006/372. - Enabling power: S.I. 1996/1919 (N.I. 16), arts 70C (2), 103 (3), 105 (2) (3), 106 (2) (3) (4), 107, 131 (1), 251 (6). - Issued: 20.09.2006. Made: 15.09.2006. Coming into operation: 01.10.2006. Effect: S.R. 1999/471 amended. - 8p.: 25 cm. - 978-0-337-96640-8 *£3.00*

The Paternity and Adoption Leave (Amendment) Regulations (Northern Ireland) 2006 No. 2006/373. - Enabling power: S.I. 1996/1919 (N.I.16), arts 70C (2), 107A (2) (2A), 107B (2) (3), 107C, 107D, 131 (1), 251 (6). - Issued: 20.09.2006. Made: 15.09.2006. Coming into operation: 01.10.2006. Effect: S.R. 2002/377 amended. - 8p.: 30 cm. - 978-0-337-96641-5 *£3.00*

The Statutory Paternity Pay and Statutory Adoption Pay (Amendment) Regulations (Northern Ireland) 2006 No. 2006/374. - Enabling power: Social Security Contributions and Benefits (Northern Ireland) Act 1992, ss. 167ZE (10A), 167ZJ (8), 167ZN (2) (3) (6A), 167ZS (8), 171 (4) & Social Security Administration (Northern Ireland) Act 1992, s. 5 (1) (m). - Issued: 20.09.2006. Made: 15.09.2006. Coming into operation: 01.10.2006. Effect: S.R. 2002/378, 380 amended. - 4p.: 30 cm. - 978-0-337-96642-2 *£3.00*

The Work and Families (Northern Ireland) Order 2006 (Commencement No. 1) Order (Northern Ireland) 2006 No. 2006/344 (C.17). - Enabling power: S.I. 2006/1947 (N.I.16), art. 1 (3) (4). Bringing into operation various provisions of the 2006 Order on 01.09.2006, 01.10.2006, 06.04.2007. - Issued: 25.08.2006. Made: 21.08.2006. Coming into operation: -. Effect: None. - 4p.: 30 cm. - 978-0-337-96615-6 *£3.00*

Energy conservation

The Domestic Energy Efficiency Grants (Amendment No. 5) Regulations (Northern Ireland) 2006 No. 2006/183. - Enabling power: S.I. 1990/1511 (N.I. 15), art. 17 (1) (2) (3) (4). - Issued: 13.04.2006. Made: 04.04.2006. Coming into operation: 08.05.2006. Effect: S.R. 2002/56 amended. - 2p.: 30 cm. - 978-0-337-96477-0 *£3.00*

Environmental protection

The Environmental Noise Regulations (Northern Ireland) 2006 No. 2006/387. - Enabling power: European Communities Act 1972, s. 2 (2). - Issued: 28.09.2006. Made: 21.09.2006. Coming into operation: 20.10.2006. Effect: None. - EC note: These Regs implement, in relation to Northern Ireland, Directive 2002/49/EC relating to the assessment and management of environmental noise. - 32p.: 30 cm. - 978-0-337-96651-4 *£5.50*

The Nitrates Action Programme Regulations (Northern Ireland) 2006 No. 2006/489. - Enabling power: European Communities Act 1972, s. 2 (2) & S.I. 1997/2778 (N.I. 19), arts 32, 44, 72. - Issued: 07.12.2006. Made: 01.12.2006. Coming into operation: 01.01.2007. Effect: S.R. 2003/319, 493 amended and S.R. 1999/156; 2003/259; 2005/306 revoked. - EC note: These Regulations give further effect to Council Directive 91/676/EEC concerning the protection of waters against pollution caused by nitrates from agricultural sources and Council Directive 2003/35/EC on public participation in respect of the drawing up of certain plans and programmes relating to the environment. - 24p.: 30 cm. - 978-0-337-96740-5 *£4.00*

The Ozone Depleting Substances (Qualifications) Regulations (Northern Ireland) 2006 No. 2006/321. - Enabling power: European Communities Act 1972, s. 2 (2). - Issued: 03.08.2006. Made: 28.07.2006. Coming into operation: 31.08.2006. Effect: None. - EC note: These Regulations give effect to the provisions in Arts 16.5, 17.1 and 17.2 of Regulation 2037/2000 on substances that deplete the ozone layer (as amended by Regulations 2038/2000, 2039/2000, 1804/2003 and 2077/2004 and Decisions 2003/160/EC, 2004/232/EC and 2005/625/EC). They relate to minimum qualifications for those working on the recovery, recycling, reclamation or destruction of controlled substances and the prevention and minimising of leakages of controlled substances. - 8p.: 30 cm. - 978-0-337-96600-2 *£3.00*

Phosphorus (Use in Agriculture) Regulations (Northern Ireland) 2006 No. 2006/488. - Enabling power: S.I. 1997/2778 (N.I. 19), arts 32, 44, 74. - Issued: 07.12.2006. Made: 01.12.2006. Coming into operation: 01.01.2007. Effect: None. - 8p: 30 cm. - 978-0-337-96741-2 *£3.00*

The Pollution Prevention and Control (Miscellaneous Amendments) Regulations (Northern Ireland) 2006 No. 2006/98. - Enabling power: S.I. 2002 No. 3153 (N.I. 7), art. 4. - Issued: 30.03.2006. Made: 09.03.2006. Coming into operation: 23.04.2006. Effect: S.R. 2003/46 amended. - EC note: Implements, in Northern Ireland, amendments to the public participation provisions in Directive 96/61/EC made by art. 4 of Directive 2003/35/EC and amending Directives 85/337/EEC and 96/61/EC. - 12p: 30 cm. - 978-0-337-96456-5 *£3.00*

The Radioactive Contaminated Land Regulations (Northern Ireland) 2006 No. 2006/345. - Enabling power: European Communities Act 1972, s. 2 (2). - Issued: 29.08.2006. Made: 22.08.2006. Coming into operation: 22.09.2006. Effect: None. - EC note: These Regs implement arts 48, 53 of Council Directive 96/29/Euratom laying down basic safety standards for the protection of the health of workers and the general public against the dangers arising from ionising radiation. - 8p.: 30 cm. - 978-0-337-96616-3 £3.00

The Waste Electrical and Electronic Equipment (Charges) Regulations (Northern Ireland) 2006 No. 2006/509. - Enabling power: European Communities Act 1972, s. 2 (2) & Finance Act 1973, s. 56 (1) (2). - Issued: 15.12.2006. Made: 11.12.2006. Coming into operation: 02.01.2007. Effect: None. - 4p.: 30 cm. - 978-0-337-96763-4 £3.00

Waste Electrical and Electronic Equipment (Waste Management Licensing) Regulations (Northern Ireland) 2006 No. 2006/519. - Enabling power: European Communities Act 1972, s. 2 (2) & S.I. 1997/2778 (N.I. 19), arts 2 (8), 4 (3), 6 (6). - Issued: 20.12.2006. Made: 14.12.2006. Coming into operation: 05.01.2007. Effect: S.R. 2003/493 amended. - 12p.: 30 cm. - 978-0-337-96770-2 £3.00

The Waste Management Regulations (Northern Ireland) 2006 No. 2006/280. - Enabling power: European Communities Act 1972, s. 2 (2) & S.I. 1997/2778 (N.I. 19), arts 2 (3), 4 (3), 38 (3) (a), 77. - Issued: 30.06.2006. Made: 26.06.2006. Coming into operation: 31.07.2006. Effect: S.I. 1997/2778 (N.I. 19); S.R. 1998/401; 1999/362; 2002/248; 2003/46, 493, 496; 2005/300 amended. - 16p.: 30 cm. - 978-0-337-96563-0 £3.00

Water Abstraction and Impoundment (Licensing) Regulations (Northern Ireland) 2006 No. 2006/482. - Enabling power: S.I. 1999/662 (N.I. 6), arts 20 (1) (3) (4), 30 (1), 61 (2). - Issued: 06.12.2006. Made: 27.11.2006. Coming into operation: 01.02.2007. Effect: None. - 20p: 30 cm. - 978-0-337-96733-7 £3.50

European Communities

The Animals and Animal Products (Import and Export) (Amendment No. 2) Regulations (Northern Ireland) 2006 No. 2006/346. - Enabling power: European Communities Act 1972, s. 2 (2) & Finance Act 1973, s. 56 (1) (2) (5). - Issued: 29.08.2006. Made: 23.08.2006. Coming into operation: 01.09.2006. Effect: S.R. 2005/78 amended. - Revoked by S.R. 2006/401 (ISBN 0337966680). EC note: The Regulations update Schedule 4 of S.R. 2005/78, in order to bring the implementation of Community instruments as up-to-date as possible. The changes made to Schedule 4 are in relation to the countries from which imports are permitted of captive birds going to approved bodies, institutes or centres and lists instruments covering trade in captive birds going to approved bodies, institutes or centres. - 4p: 30 cm. - 978-0-337-96617-0 £3.00

The Animals and Animal Products (Import and Export) (Amendment) Regulations (Northern Ireland) 2006 No. 2006/105. - Enabling power: European Communities Act 1972, s. 2 (2) & Finance Act 1973, s. 56 (1) (2) (5). - Issued: 22.03.2006. Made: 10.03.2006. Coming into operation: 01.04.2006. Effect: S.R. 2005/78 amended. - Revoked by S.R. 2006/401 (ISBN 0337966680). EC note: The Regulations provide a statutory basis for the Northern Ireland Poultry Health Assurance Scheme, which is implemented by the Department in order to ensure compliance with the rules set out in Annex II to Council Directive 90/539/EEC (on animal health conditions governing intra-Community trade in, and imports from third countries of, poultry and hatching eggs). - 8p: 30 cm. - 978-0-337-96411-4 £3.00

The Animals and Animal Products (Import and Export) Regulations (Northern Ireland) 2006 No. 2006/401. - Enabling power: European Communities Act 1972, s. 2 (2) and Finance Act 1973, s. 56 (1) (2) (5). - Issued: 12.10.2006. Made: 05.10.2006. Coming into operation: 01.11.2006. Effect: 10 S.R.s disapplied; S.R. 2005/78 partially revoked and S.R. 2005/446; 2006/105, 346 revoked. - 56p.: 30 cm. - 978-0-337-96668-2 £9.00

The Diseases of Animals (Amendment) Regulations (Northern Ireland) 2006 No. 2006/41. - Enabling power: European Communities Act 1972, s. 2 (2). - Issued: 24.02.2006. Made: 17.02.2006. Coming into operation: 23.02.2006. Effect: S.I. 1981/1115 (N.I. 22) amended. - 4p: 30 cm. - 978-0-337-96355-1 £3.00

The Passenger and Goods Vehicles (Recording Equipment) (Amendment) Regulations (Northern Ireland) 2006 No. 2006/274. - Enabling power: European Communities Act 1972, s. 2 (2). - Issued: 28.06.2006. Made: 21.06.2006. Coming into operation: 31.07.2006. Effect: S.R. 1996/145 amended. - EC note: These Regulations modify the provisions of the 1996 Regs to take account of the new digital tachograph provided for by Council Regulation (EC) No. 2135/98, which amended Regulation (EEC) No. 3821/85 on recording equipment in road transport. They also amend the definition of the 'Community Recording Equipment Regulation' to include reference to Regulation (EC) 561/2006. - 12p.: 30 cm. - 978-0-337-96559-3 £3.00

European communities

The Salmonella in Turkey Flocks and Herds of Slaughter Pigs (Survey Powers) Regulations (Northern Ireland) 2006 No. 2006/492. - Enabling power: European Communities Act 1972, s. 2 (2). - Issued: 07.12.2006. Made: 01.12.2006. Coming into operation: 22.12.2006. Effect: S.R. 2005/132, 584 revoked. - EC note: These Regulations provide a power of entry to inspectors to undertake the sampling required by Commission Decision 2006/662/EC concerning a financial contribution by the Community towards a baseline survey on the prevalence of Salmonella spp. in turkeys to be carried out in the Member States and in herds of slaughter pigs as required by Commission Decision 2006/668/EC. - 4p: 30 cm. - 978-0-337-96742-9 £3.00

European Communities

The Transmissible Spongiform Encephalopathies Regulations (Northern Ireland) 2006 No. 2006/202. - Enabling power: European Communities Act 1972, s. 2 (2). - Issued: 08.05.2006. Made: 02.05.2006. Coming into operation: 03.05.2006. Effect: S.R. 2000/78; 2003/495; 2005/78 amended & 21 instruments revoked. - EC note: These Regulations revoke and remake with amendments the TSE Regulations (Northern Ireland) 2002 (S.R. 2002/225) and enforce Regulation 999/2001, laying down rules for the prevention, control and eradication of certain transmissible spongiform encephalopathies as amended by and as read with the provisions in Schedule 1. - 48p.: 30 cm. - 978-0-337-96491-6 £7.50

The Water Resources (Environmental Impact Assessment) (Amendment) Regulations (Northern Ireland) 2006 No. 2006/483. - Enabling power: European Communities Act 1972, s. 2 (2). - Issued: 04.12.2006. Made: 27.11.2006. Coming into operation: 01.02.2007. Effect: S.R. 2005/32 amended. - EC note: Implements, in part, Article 2 of Directive 2003/35/EC on public participation in respect of drawing up certain plans or programmes relating to the environment. That Article amends Council Directive 85/337/EEC on the assessment of the effects of certain public and private projects on the environment. - 8p: 30 cm. - 978-0-337-96734-4 £3.00

Fair employment

Fair Employment (Specification of Public Authorities) (Amendment) Order (Northern Ireland) 2006 No. 2006/504. - Enabling power: S.I. 1998/3162 (N.I. 21), arts 50, 51. - Issued: 11.12.2006. Made: 06.12.2006. Coming into operation: 01.01.2007. Effect: S.R. 2004/494 amended. - 8p: 30 cm. - 978-0-337-96753-5 £3.00

Family law

The Child Support (Miscellaneous Amendments) Regulations (Northern Ireland) 2006 No. 2006/273. - Enabling power: S.I. 1991/2628 (N.I. 23), arts. 16 (1), 18 (4), 29 (2) (3), 32, 34, 37A (3), 48 (4), sch. 1, para. 11. - Issued: 26.06.2006. Made: 21.06.2006. Coming into operation: In accord. with reg. 1. Effect: S.R. 1992/339, 390; 1999/162; 2001/15, 17 amended. - 8p.: 30 cm. - 978-0-337-96558-6 £3.00

The Dissolution etc. (Pension Protection Fund) Regulations (Northern Ireland) 2006 No. 2006/311. - Enabling power: Civil Partnership Act 2004, sch. 15, paras. 27, 30, 31. - Issued: 25.07.2006. Made: 19.07.2006. Coming into operation: 14.08.2006. Effect: 2004 c.33; S.R. 2005/484 modified. - 8p.: 30 cm. - 978-0-337-96590-6 £3.00

The Divorce etc. (Pension Protection Fund) Regulations (Northern Ireland) 2006 No. 2006/310. - Enabling power: S.I. 1978/1045 (N.I.15), art. 27E (5) (8) (9). - Issued: 25.07.2006. Made: 19.07.2006. Coming into operation: 14.08.2006. Effect: S.I. 1978/1045 (N.I.15); 2000/210 modified. - 8p.: 30 cm. - 978-0-337-96589-0 £3.00

Family proceedings

The Family Proceedings (Amendment) Rules (Northern Ireland) 2006 No. 2006/304. - Enabling power: S.I. 1993/1576 (N.I. 6), art. 12. - Issued: 14.07.2006. Made: 04.07.2006. Coming into operation: 01.08.2006. Effect: S.R. 1996/322 amended. - 4p.: 30 cm. - 978-0-337-96585-2 £3.00

Fees and charges

Measuring Instruments (EEC Requirements) (Verification Fees) Regulations (Northern Ireland) 2006 No. 2006/35. - Enabling power: Finance Act 1973, s. 56 (1). - Issued: 02.03.2006. Made: 10.02.2006. Coming into operation: 01.04.2006. Effect: S.R. 2005/117 revoked with savings. - 4p: 30 cm. - 978-0-337-96339-1 £3.00

Fire and rescue services

The Fire and Rescue Services (2006 Order) (Commencement No. 1) Order (Northern Ireland) 2006 No. 2006/257 (C.15). - Enabling power: S.I. 2006/1254 (N.I. 9), art. 1 (3). - Issued: 15.06.2006. Made: 09.06.2006. Coming into operation: 01.07.2006. Effect: None. - 2p.: 30 cm. - 978-0-337-96546-3 £3.00

Fire services: Discipline

Fire Services (Discipline) (Revocation) Regulations (Northern Ireland) 2006 No. 2006/250. - Enabling power: S.I. 1984/1821 (N.I. 11), arts. 9 (5), 52 (1). - Issued: 12.06.2006. Made: 17.05.2006. Coming into operation: 01.06.2006. Effect: S.R. 1985/288 revoked with saving. - 2p.: 30 cm. - 978-0-337-96536-4 £3.00

Fire services: Superannuation

The Firemen's Pension Scheme Order (Northern Ireland) 2006 No. 2006/210. - Enabling power: S.I. 1984/1821 (N.I. 11), art. 10 (1) (3) (4) (5). - Issued: 23.05.2006. Made: 08.05.2006. Coming into force: 01.04.2006. Effect: S.R. & O. (N.I.) 1971/33; 1972/157, 379; 1973/1 revoked (in so far as still having effect) & S.R. & O. 1973/393; S.R. 1975/358; 1976/216; 1978/24, 100; 1979/87, 88, 310; 1980/62, 91, 208; 1981/143, 320; 1982/18; 1983/116; 1984/99; 1987/424; 1988/144, 185; 1989/383; 1991/312, 447 revoked. - 112p: 30 cm. - 978-0-337-96497-8 £15.50

Fisheries

Eel Fishing (Licence Duties) Regulations (Northern Ireland) 2006 No. 2006/513. - Enabling power: Fisheries Act (Northern Ireland) 1966, ss. 15 (1), 19 (1). - Issued: 18.12.2006. Made: 12.12.2006. Coming into operation: 01.01.2007. Effect: S.R. 2005/456 revoked. - 4p: 30 cm. - 978-0-337-96765-8 *£3.00*

Fisheries (Amendment) Byelaws (Northern Ireland) 2006 No. 2006/517. - Enabling power: Fisheries Act (Northern Ireland) 1966, ss. 26 (1), 37, 51 (2), 52 (2), 70 (1) (2), 71 (2) (g), 72 (1), 89, 95, 97, 114 (1) (b), 115 (1) (b). - Issued: 05.01.2007. Made: 13.12.2006. Coming into operation: 01.01.2007. Effect: S.R. 2003/525 amended. - 8p: 30 cm. - 978-0-337-96768-9 *£3.00*

Infected Waters (Infectious Pancreatic Necrosis) (Revocation) Order (Northern Ireland) 2006 No. 2006/57. - Enabling power: Diseases of Fish Act (Northern Ireland) 1967, s. 1 (1). - Issued: 28.02.2006. Made: 17.02.2006. Coming into operation: 07.04.2006. Effect: S.R. 2003/243 revoked. - 2p.: 30 cm. - 978-0-337-96362-9 *£3.00*

Public Angling Estate (Amendment) Byelaws (Northern Ireland) 2006 No. 2006/224. - Enabling power: Fisheries Act (Northern Ireland) 1966, s. 26 (1). - Issued: 24.05.2006. Made: 18.05.2006. Coming into operation: 03.06.2006. Effect: S.R. 2005/267 amended. - 4p: 30 cm. - 978-0-337-96516-6 *£3.00*

Food

Animals and Animal Products (Examination for Residues and Maximum Residue Limits) (Amendment) Regulations (Northern Ireland) 2006 No. 2006/263. - Enabling power: European Communities Act 1972, s. 2 (2) & S.I. 1991/762 (N.I. 7), arts 15 (1) (a), (b) (f) (3), 16 (1) (2), 25 (1) (2) (a) (3), 26 (3), 30 (9), 31 (3), 32 (1), 47 (2), sch. 1, para. 7. - Issued: 19.06.2006. Made: 12.06.2006. Coming into operation: 14.07.2006. Effect: S.R. 1998/237 amended. - EC note: Transposes directives and updates the 1998 Regs - S.R. 1998/237. - 8p.: 30 cm. - 978-0-337-96552-4 *£3.00*

The Ceramic Articles in Contact with Food Regulations (Northern Ireland) 2006 No. 2006/217. - Enabling power: S.I. 1991/762 (N.I. 7), arts. 15 (2), 16 (1), 25 (1) (a) (2) (a) (3), 26 (3), 47 (1). - Issued: 19.05.2006. Made: 05.05.2006. Coming into operation: 20.05.2006 except for reg. 3 (3) (a) (b) (4); 20.05.2007 for reg. 3 (3) (a) (b) (4). Effect: S.R. 2006/2 amended. - EC note: These Regulations implement Council Directive 84/500/EEC on ceramic articles intended to come into contact with foodstuffs as amended by Commission Directive 2005/31/EC regarding a declaration of compliance and performance criteria of the analytical method for ceramic articles intended to come into contact with foodstuffs. - 8p.: 30 cm. - 978-0-337-96505-0 *£3.00*

The Contaminants in Food Regulations (Northern Ireland) 2006 No. 2006/256. - Enabling power: S.I. 1991/762 (N.I.7), arts. 15 (1) (a) (e) (f), 16 (1) (2), 25 (1) (a) (2) (e) (3), 26 (3), 32 (1) (2) (b) (c) (f), 47 (2). - Issued: 15.06.2006. Made: 08.06.2006. Coming into operation: 01.07.2006. Effect: S.R. 2005/538 revoked. - EC note: These Regs make provision for the execution and enforcement of Commission Regulation 466/2001 setting maximum levels for contaminants in foodstuffs. - 8p: 30 cm. - 978-0-337-96545-6 *£3.00*

The Curd Cheese (Restriction on Placing on the Market) (Amendment) Regulations (Northern Ireland) 2006 No. 2006/493. - Enabling power: European Communities Act 1972, s. 2 (2). - Issued: 07.12.2006. Made: 01.12.2006. Coming into operation: 08.01.2007. Effect: S.R. 2006/415 amended. - 4p.: 30 cm. - 978-0-337-96743-6 *£3.00*

The Curd Cheese (Restriction on Placing on the Market) Regulations (Northern Ireland) 2006 No. 2006/415. - Enabling power: European Communities Act 1972, s. 2 (2). - Issued: 25.10.2006. Made: 18.10.2006. Coming into operation: 18.10.2006. Effect: None. - EC note: These Regulations implement Commission Decision 2006/694/EC prohibiting the placing on the market of curd cheese manufactured in a dairy establishment in the United Kingdom. - 8p.: 30 cm. - 978-0-337-96681-1 *£3.00*

Dairy Produce Quotas (Amendment) Regulations (Northern Ireland) 2006 No. 2006/60. - Enabling power: European Communities Act 1972, s. 2 (2). - Issued: 02.03.2006. Made: 22.02.2006. Coming into operation: 31.03.2006. Effect: S.R. 2005/70 amended. - 4p.: 30 cm. - 978-0-337-96366-7 *£3.00*

The Fishery Products (Official Controls Charges) Regulations (Northern Ireland) 2006 No. 2006/485. - Enabling power: European Communities Act 1972, s. 2 (2). - Issued: 05.12.2006. Made: 29.11.2006. Coming into operation: 01.01.2007. Effect: SR 2005/524 revoked. - EC note: These Regs provide for the execution and enforcement in relation to Northern Ireland of arts. 26, 27 of REG (EC) no. 882/2004 on official controls performed to ensure the verification of compliance with feed and food law, animal health and animal welfare rules. - 12p: 30 cm. - 978-0-337-96736-8 *£3.00*

The Fish Labelling (Amendment) Regulations (Northern Ireland) 2006 No. 2006/116. - Enabling power: S.I. 1991/762 (N.I.7) arts. 15 (1) (e) (f), 16 (2), 25 (1) (3), 26 (3), 47 (2). - Issued: 23.03.2006. Made: 06.03.2006. Coming into operation: 06.04.2006. Effect: S.R. 2003/160 amended. - 12p.: 30 cm. - 978-0-337-96421-3 *£3.00*

The Food Benefit Schemes (2003 Order) (Commencement) (Amendment) Order (Northern Ireland) 2006 No. 2006/437 (C.26). - Enabling power: S.I. 2003/3202 (N.I. 19), art. 1 (3). Bringing into operation various provisions of the 2003 Order on 27.11.2006. - Issued: 15.11.2006. Made: 03.11.2006. Coming into operation: -. Effect: S.R. 2006/418 (C. 24) amended. - 4p.: 30 cm. - 978-0-337-96703-0 *£3.00*

The Food Benefit Schemes (2003 Order) (Commencement) Order (Northern Ireland) 2006 No. 2006/418 (C.24). - Enabling power: S.I. 2003/3202 (N.I. 19), art. 1 (3). Bringing into operation various provisions of the 2003 Order on 06.11.2006. - Issued: 25.10.2005. Made: 17.10.2006. Coming into operation: -. Effect: None. - 2p.: 30 cm. - 978-0-337-96680-4 £3.00

The Food (Emergency Control) (Revocation) Regulations (Northern Ireland) 2006 No. 2006/351. - Enabling power: European Communities Act 1972, s. 2 (2). - Issued: 06.09.2006. Made: 30.08.2006. Coming into operation: 01.10.2006. Effect: S.R. 2002/293, 307; 2003/353, 360, 377 revoked. - 4p.: 30 cm. - 978-0-337-96622-4 £3.00

The Food for Particular Nutritional Uses (Addition of Substances for Specific Nutritional Purposes) (Amendment) Regulations (Northern Ireland) 2006 No. 2006/481. - Enabling power: S.I. 1991/762 (N.I.7), arts 15 (1) (f), 16 (1), 25 (3), 26 (3), 47 (2). - Issued: 01.12.2006. Made: 24.11.2006. Coming into operation: 31.12.2006. Effect: S.R. 2002/264 amended. - 4p: 30 cm. - 978-0-337-96731-3 £3.00

The Food Hygiene Regulations (Northern Ireland) 2006 No. 2006/3. - Enabling power: European Communities Act 1972, s. 2 (2). - Issued: 07.02.2006. Made: 10.01.2006. Coming into operation: 11.01.2006. Effect: S.R. 1996/49, 383; 1997/540; 1999/418; 2003/300 amended & S.R. 1995/396; 2005/356 revoked. - EC note: These regs provide for the execution and enforcement in relation to Northern Ireland of certain Community instruments, Community Regulations 852/2004, 853/2004, 854/2004, 2073/2005 and 2075/2005. - 40p: 30 cm. - 978-0-337-96312-4 £6.50

The Healthy Start Scheme and Day Care Food Scheme Regulations (Northern Ireland) 2006 No. 2006/478. - Enabling power: S.I. 1988/594 (N.I. 2), art. 13 (1) to (4) (6) (8) & Social Security Contributions and Benefits (Northern Ireland) Act 1992, s. 171 (2) to (5). - Issued: 11.01.2007. Made: 23.11.2006. Coming into operation: 27.11.2006. Effect: S.R. 1988/137 revoked with savings. - 20p.: 30 cm. - 978-0-337-96788-7 £3.50

The Meat (Official Controls Charges) Regulations (Northern Ireland) 2006 No. 2006/454. - Enabling power: European Communities Act 1972, s. 2 (2). - Issued: 20.11.2006. Made: 13.11.2006. Coming into force: 01.01.2007. Effect: S.R. 2005/549 revoked. - EC note: These Regulations provide for the execution and enforcement in relation to Northern Ireland of Articles 26 and 27 of Regulation (EC) No. 882/2004 on official controls performed to ensure the verification of compliance with feed and food law, animal health and animal welfare rules- 12p.: 30 cm. - 978-0-337-96711-5 £3.00

The Official Feed and Food Controls Regulations (Northern Ireland) 2006 No. 2006/2. - Enabling power: European Communities Act 1972, s. 2 (2). - Issued: 18.01.2006. Made: 10.01.2006. Coming into operation: 11.01.2006 Effect: S.R. 2005/574 revoked. - EC note: These Regs provide for the execution and enforcement of Reg. No. 882/2004, and they also impose prohibitions on the introduction of certain feed and food into Northern Ireland in the light of Article 11 of Reg. No. 178/2002, as last amended by Reg. No. 1642/2003 and as read with Article 10 of Reg. No. 852/2004. - 28p: 30 cm. - 978-0-337-96311-7 £4.50

The Plastic Materials and Articles in Contact with Food (No 2) Regulations (Northern Ireland) 2006 No. 2006/420. - Enabling power: S.I. 1991/762 (N.I.7), arts 15 (2), 16 (1) (2), 25 (1) (a) (3), 32 (2), 47 (2). - Issued: 30.10.2006. Made: 19.10.2006. Coming into operation: 19.11.2006. Effect: S.R. 1991/198; 2005/210 amended & S.R. 2006/251 revoked. - EC note: The principal Directives implemented by these Regulations are: Council Directive 82/711/EEC as amended by Commission Directives 93/8/EEC and 97/48/EC; Council Directive 85/572/EEC; Commission Directive 2002/72/EC as amended by Commission Directives 2004/1/EC, 2004/19/EC and 2005/79/EC. - 36p.: 30 cm. - 978-0-337-96685-9 £6.50

The Plastic Materials and Articles in Contact with Food Regulations (Northern Ireland) 2006 No. 2006/251. - Enabling power: S.I. 1991/762 (N.I. 7), arts 15 (2), 16 (1) (2), 25 (1) (a) (3), 32, 47 (2). - Issued: 20.06.2006. Made: 05.06.2006. Coming into operation: 30.06.2006. Effect: S.R. 1991/198; 2005/210 amended & S.R. 1998/264; 2000/402; 2002/316; 2003/2; 2004/493; 2005/49 revoked. - Revoked by S.R. 2006/420 (ISBN 0337966850). EC note: These Regs continue to implement Council Directives 82/711/EEC, 85/572/EEC and Commission Directive 2002/72/EC. They also provide for the execution and enforcement of Commission Regulation 1895/2005. - 76p.: 30 cm. - 978-0-337-96537-1 £10.50

The Rice Products (Restriction on First Placing on the Market) Regulations (Northern Ireland) 2006 No. 2006/443. - Enabling power: European Communities Act 1972, s. 2 (2). - Issued: 15.11.2006. Made: 09.11.2006. Coming into operation: 09.11.2006. Effect: None. - EC note: These Regulations implement Commission Decision 2006/601/EC on emergency measures regarding the non-authorised genetically modified organism "LL RICE 601" in rice products as amended by Commission Decision 2006/754/EC. - 4p.: 30 cm. - 978-0-337-96702-3 £3.00

Forestry

Environmental Impact Assessment (Forestry) Regulations (Northern Ireland) 2006 No. 2006/518. - Enabling power: European Communities Act 1972, s. 2 (2). - Issued: 21.12.2006. Made: 07.12.2006. Coming into operation: 04.01.2007. Effect: S.R. 2000/84 revoked with savings. - EC note: These Regs implement amendments made to Council Directive 85/337/EEC (as amended by Directive 97/11/EC) by Council Directive 2003/35/EC (that provides for public participation in certain environmental decision making). - 32p.: 30 cm. - 978-0-337-96769-6 £5.50

Game

Game Preservation (Special Protection for Irish Hares) Order (Northern Ireland) 2006 No. 2006/114. - Enabling power: Game Preservation Act (Northern Ireland) 1928, ss. 7C (1), 7F (1). - Issued: 23.03.2006. Made: 09.03.2006. Coming into operation: 17.04.2006. Effect: None. - 2p: 30 cm. - 978-0-337-96418-3 £3.00

Gas

The Gas (Designation of Pipelines) Order (Northern Ireland) 2006 No. 2006/404. - Enabling power: S.I. 2003/419 (N.I.6), art. 59 (1) to (3) (5) (6). - Issued: 16.10.2006. Made: 10.10.2006. Coming into operation: 01.11.2006. Effect: None. - 4p.: 30 cm. - 978-0-337-96671-2 £3.00

Gas Order 1996 (Amendment) Regulations (Northern Ireland) 2006 No. 2006/358. - Enabling power: European Communities Act 1972, s. 2 (2). - Issued: 11.09.2006. Made: 05.09.2006. Coming into operation: 01.10.2006. Effect: S.I. 1996/275 (N.I. 2); S.I. 2003/419 (N.I. 6) amended & S.R. 2002/291 revoked. - EC note: These Regulations amend the Gas (Northern Ireland) Order 1996 to ensure that it conforms with the requirements of Directive 2003/55/EC of the European Parliament and of the Council concerning common rules for the internal market in natural gas. This Directive is to be read with Commission Decision PH(2005) 0791which grants derogations from Articles 18, 23(1)(b) and 24 in relation to supplies of gas to customers in certain geographical areas in Northern Ireland. - 12p.: 30 cm. - 978-0-337-96629-3 £3.00

Government resources and accounts

The Whole of Government Accounts (Designation of Bodies) (Northern Ireland) Order 2006 No. 2006/226. - Enabling power: Government Resources and Accounts Act (Northern Ireland) 2001, s. 15 (1). - Issued: 08.06.2006. Made: 22.05.2006. Coming into operation: 14.06.2006. Effect: None. - 8p.: 30 cm. - 978-0-337-96529-6 £3.00

Health and personal social services

The Belfast Health and Social Services Trust (Establishment) Order (Northern Ireland) 2006 No. 2006/292. - Enabling power: S.I. 1991/194 (N.I. 1), art. 10 (1), sch. 3, paras 3, 3A, 4, 5. - Issued: 10.07.2006. Made: 22.06.2006. Coming into operation: 01.08.2006. Effect: None. - 8p.: 30 cm. - 978-0-337-96578-4 £3.00

The Care Tribunal (Amendment) Regulations (Northern Ireland) 2006 No. 2006/342. - Enabling power: S.I. 2003/431 (N.I. 9), arts. 44 (2) (3), 48 (2), sch. 2, para. 2 (4). - Issued: 30.08.2006. Made: 17.08.2006. Coming into operation: 29.09.2006. Effect: S.R. 2005/178 amended. - 4p.: 30 cm. - 978-0-337-96619-4 £3.00

The Charges for Drugs and Appliances (Amendment) Regulations (Northern Ireland) 2006 No. 2006/145. - Enabling power: S.I. 1972/1265 (N.I. 14), arts. 98, 106, sch. 15. - Issued: 27.03.2006. Made: 20.03.2006. Coming into operation: 01.04.2006. Effect: S.R. 1997/382 amended. - 4p.: 30 cm. - 978-0-337-96447-3 £3.00

The Health and Personal Social Services (Assessment of Resources) (Amendment) Regulations (Northern Ireland) 2006 No. 2006/103. - Enabling power: S.I. 1972/1265 (N.I. 14), arts. 36 (6), 99 (5). - Issued: 21.03.2006. Made: 10.03.2006. Coming into operation: 10.04.2006. Effect: S.R. 1993/127 amended. - 4p.: 30 cm. - 978-0-337-96405-3 £3.00

The Health and Personal Social Services (Primary Medical Services) (Miscellaneous Amendments) Regulations (Northern Ireland) 2006 No. 2006/319. - Enabling power: S.I. 1972/1265 (N.I. 14), arts 15C (1) (b) (iii), 57B, 57E, 57F, 57G, 106, 107 (6) & S.I. 1991/194 (N.I. 1), art 8 (6). - Issued: 10.08.2006. Made: 25.07.2006. Coming into operation: 15.08.2006. Effect: S.R. 2004/140, 149 amended. - 4p.: 30 cm. - 978-0-337-96598-2 £3.00

The Health and Personal Social Services (Superannuation Scheme and Injury Benefits) (Amendment) Regulations (Northern Ireland) 2006 No. 2006/159. - Enabling power: S.I. 1972/1073 (N.I. 10), arts 12 (1) (2) (3), 14 (1) (2), sch. 3. - Issued: 04.04.2006. Made: 24.03.2006. Coming into operation: 24.04.2006. Effect: S.R. 1995/95; 2001/367 amended. - 4p: 30 cm. - 978-0-337-96462-6 £3.00

The Health and Personal Social Services (Superannuation Scheme, Injury Benefits and Additional Voluntary Contributions) (Amendment) Regulations (Northern Ireland) 2006 No. 2006/410. - Enabling power: S.I. 1972/1073 (N.I. 10), arts 12, 14, sch. 3. - Issued: 20.10.2006. Made: 12.10.2006. Coming into operation: 31.10.2006. Effect: S.R. 1995/95; 1999/294; 2001/367 amended. - 16p: 30 cm. - 978-0-337-96677-4 £3.00

The Northern Health and Social Services Trust (Establishment) Order (Northern Ireland) 2006 No. 2006/295. - Enabling power: S.I. 1991/194 (N.I. 1), art. 10 (1), sch. 3, paras 3, 3A, 4, 5. - Issued: 10.07.2006. Made: 22.06.2006. Coming into operation: 01.08.2006. Effect: None. - 8p.: 30 cm. - 978-0-337-96581-4 £3.00

The Northern Ireland Social Care Council (Description of Social Care Workers) Order (Northern Ireland) 2006 No. 2006/396. - Enabling power: Health and Personal Social Services Act (Northern Ireland) 2001, ss. 3 (1) (b), 57 (3). - Issued: 04.10.2006. Made: 28.09.2006. Coming into operation: 24.10.2006. Effect: None. - 4p.: 30 cm. - 978-0-337-96658-3 £3.00

The Northern Ireland Social Care Council (Social Care Workers) Regulations (Northern Ireland) 2006 No. 2006/394. - Enabling power: Health and Personal Social Services Act (Northern Ireland) 2001, ss. 2 (2) (3), 57 (3). - Issued: 04.10.2006. Made: 28.09.2006. Coming into operation: 23.10.2006. Effect: None. - 4p.: 30 cm. - 978-0-337-96656-9 £3.00

The Optical Charges and Payments (Amendment) Regulations (Northern Ireland) 2006 No. 2006/106. - Enabling power: S.I. 1972/1265 (N.I. 14), arts. 62, 98, 106, 107 (6), sch. 15. - Issued: 23.03.2006. Made: 10.03.2006. Coming into operation: 01.04.2006. Effect: S.R. 1997/191 amended. - 8p: 30 cm. - 978-0-337-96419-0 £3.00

The Regulation and Improvement Authority (Fees and Frequency of Inspections) (Amendment) Regulations (Northern Ireland) 2006 No. 2006/341. - Enabling power: S.I. 2003/431 (N.I. 9), arts. 17 (3), 48 (2). - Issued: 30.08.2006. Made: 17.08.2006. Coming into operation: 29.09.2006. Effect: S.R. 2005/182 amended. - 4p.: 30 cm. - 978-0-337-96620-0 £3.00

The South Eastern Health and Social Services Trust (Establishment) Order (Northern Ireland) 2006 No. 2006/293. - Enabling power: S.I. 1991/194 (N.I. 1), art. 10 (1), sch. 3, paras 3, 3A, 4, 5. - Issued: 10.07.2006. Made: 22.06.2006. Coming into operation: 01.08.2006. Effect: None. - 8p.: 30 cm. - 978-0-337-96579-1 £3.00

The Southern Health and Social Services Trust (Establishment) Order (Northern Ireland) 2006 No. 2006/294. - Enabling power: S.I. 1991/194 (N.I. 1), art. 10 (1), sch.3, paras 3, 3A, 4, 5. - Issued: 10.07.2006. Made: 22.06.2006. Coming into operation: 01.08.2006. Effect: None. - 8p.: 30 cm. - 978-0-337-96580-7 £3.00

The Travelling Expenses and Remission of Charges (Amendment No. 2) Regulations (Northern Ireland) 2006 No. 2006/190. - Enabling power: S.I. 1972/1265 (N.I. 14), arts. 45, 98, 106, 107 (6), sch. 15, paras 1 (b), 1B. - Issued: 27.04.2006. Made: 21.04.2006. Coming into operation: 01.05.2006. Effect: S.R. 2004/91 amended. - 4p.: 30 cm. - 978-0-337-96486-2 £3.00

The Travelling Expenses and Remission of Charges (Amendment No. 3) Regulations (Northern Ireland) 2006 No. 2006/333. - Enabling power: S.I. 1972/1265 (N.I. 14), arts. 45, 98, 106, 107 (6), sch. 15, paras 1 (b), 1B. - Issued: 17.08.2006. Made: 14.08.2006. Coming into operation: 01.09.2006. Effect: S.R. 2004/91 amended. - 4p.: 30 cm. - 978-0-337-96607-1 £3.00

The Travelling Expenses and Remission of Charges (Amendment) Regulations (Northern Ireland) 2006 No. 2006/136. - Enabling power: S.I. 1972/1265 (N.I. 14), arts. 45, 98, 106, 107 (6), sch. 15, paras 1 (b), 1B. - Issued: 27.03.2006. Made: 16.03.2006. Coming into operation: 01.04.2006. Effect: S.R. 2004/91 amended. - 4p.: 30 cm. - 978-0-337-96438-1 £3.00

The Western Health and Social Services Trust (Establishment) Order (Northern Ireland) 2006 No. 2006/296. - Enabling power: S.I. 1991/194 (N.I. 1), art. 10 (1), sch. 3, paras 3, 3A, 4, 5. - Issued: 10.07.2006. Made: 22.06.2006. Coming into operation: 01.08.2006. Effect: None. - 8p.: 30 cm. - 978-0-337-96582-1 £3.00

Health and safety

The Agriculture (Safety of Children and Young Persons) Regulations (Northern Ireland) 2006 No. 2006/335. - Enabling power: S.I. 1978/1039 (N.I. 9), arts. 17 (1) (2) (3) (6), 55 (2), sch. 3, para. 13. - Issued: 18.08.2006. Made: 15.08.2006. Coming into operation: 31.10.2006. Effect: S.R. 1993/477 amended & S.R. 1981/6; 1983/355 revoked. - 8p.: 30 cm. - 978-0-337-96608-8 £3.00

The Carriage of Dangerous Goods and Use of Transportable Pressure Equipment (Amendment) Regulations (Northern Ireland) 2006 No. 2006/525. - Enabling power: S.I. 1978/1039 (N.I. 9), arts. 17 (1) to (6), 40 (2) to (4), 54 (1), 55 (2), sch. 3, paras 1 (1) to (4), 2, 3 (1), 5, 14 (1), 15, 19. - Issued: 21.12.2006. Made: 18.12.2006. Coming into operation: 01.02.2007. Effect: S.R. 2005/523; 2006/173 amended. - EC note: Implements Commission Directive 2004/89/EC adapting for the fifth time to technical progress Council Directive; Commission Directive 2004/110/EC adapting for the sixth time to technical progress Council Directive 96/49/EC96/49/EC;; Commission Directive 2004/111/EC adapting for the fifth time to technical progress Council Directive 94/55/EC. - 20p: 30 cm. - 978-0-337-96776-4 £3.50

The Carriage of Dangerous Goods and Use of Transportable Pressure Equipment Regulations (Northern Ireland) 2006 No. 2006/173. - Enabling power: S.I. 1978/1039 (N.I. 9), arts. 17 (1) to (6), 40 (2) to (4), 55 (2), sch. 3, paras 1 (1) to (4), 2, 3 (1), 5, 13, 14 (1), 15, 19. - Issued: 12.04.2006. Made: 31.03.2006. Coming into operation: 01.08.2006. Effect: 1929 c. 13 (NI) & S.R. 1991/509; 1992/71; 1994/6; 1996/119; 1997/248, 455; 1998/131; 2001/436; 2002/301; 2003/33, 34, 35, 152; 2004/222; 2005/523 amended & S.R. 1992/15, 79; 1997/247, 249; 1998/448; 2000/119; 2002/34; 2003/386, 533 revoked. - EC note: These Regulations implement, for Northern Ireland and regarding the carriage of dangerous goods other than explosives, three Directives. First, Council Directive 94/55/EC on the transport of dangerous goods by road (as amended by Directives 2000/61/EC, 2003/28/EC). Secondly Council Directive 96/49/EC on the transport of dangerous goods by rail (as amended by Directives 2000/62/EC, 2003/29/EC). Thirdly these Regulations implement Council Directive 1999/36/EC concerning transportable pressure equipment ("the Transportable Pressure Equipment Directive"). - 100p: 30 cm. - 978-0-337-96476-3 £13.50

The Carriage of Explosives (Amendment) Regulations (Northern Ireland) 2006 No. 2006/520. - Enabling power: S.I. 1978/1039 (N.I. 9), arts. 17 (1) to (6), 40 (2) to (4), 55 (2), sch. 3, paras. 1 (1) to (4), 2, 3 (1), 5, 13, 14 (1), 15, 19. - Issued: 11.01.2007. Made: 13.12.2006. Coming into operation: 01.02.2007. Effect: S.R. 2006/182 amended & S.I. 1919/809 amended. - EC note: These Regulations amend (S.R. 2006 No. 182) (the Carriage Regulations) to implement the following Directives: Commission Directive 2004/89/EC; Commission Directive 2004/110/EC; Council Directive 96/49/EC; Commission Directive 2004/111/EC; Council Directive 94/55/EC. - 8p.: 30 cm. - 978-0-337-96771-9 £3.00

The Carriage of Explosives Regulations (Northern Ireland) 2006 No. 2006/182. - Enabling power: S.I. 1978/1039 (N.I. 9), arts. 17 (1) to (6), 40 (2) to (4), 55 (2), sch. 3, paras. 1 (1) to (4), 2, 3 (1), 5, 13, 14 (1), 15, 19. - Issued: 20.04.2006. Made: 31.03.2006. Coming into operation: 01.08.2006. Effect: S.R. 1979/290; 1991/516; 1995/87 amended & S.R. 1993/268; 1997/474, 475; 2000/171; 2001/387, 390 revoked. - EC note: Implements Council Directive 94/55/EC on transport of dangerous goods by road (as amended by Directive 2000/61/EC and Commission Directive 2003/28/EC) and implements Council Directive 96/49/EC on the transport of dangerous goods by rail (as amended by Directive 2000/62/EC and Commission Directive 2003/29/EC). - 48p., col. ill.: 30 cm. - 978-0-337-96479-4 £7.50

The Control of Noise at Work Regulations (Northern Ireland) 2006 No. 2006/1. - Enabling power: S.I. 1978/1039 (N.I. 9), arts. 17 (1) (2) (5), 55 (2), sch. 3, paras 1 (1), 7 (1), 8, 10, 12 (2) (3), 13, 14 (1), 15, 19. - Issued: 26.01.2006. Made: 10.01.2006. Coming into operation: 06.04.2006. Effect: S.R. 1993/20; 1996/119, 228; 1998/47; 1999/150, 305 amended & S.R. 1990/147 revoked. - EC note: These Regs implement, as regards Northern Ireland, Directive 2003/10/EC on the minimum health and safety requirements regarding the exposure of workers to the risks arising from physical agents (noise) (seventeenth individual Directive within the meaning of article 16(1) of Directive 89/391/EEC). - 20p.: 30 cm. - 978-0-337-96309-4 £3.50

The Genetically Modified Organisms (Contained Use) (Amendment) Regulations (Northern Ireland) 2006 No. 2006/524. - Enabling power: S.I. 1978/1039 (N.I. 9), arts 17 (1) (2), 40 (2) (4), 55 (2), sch. 3, paras 1 (1) (2), 10, 14 (1), 15. - Issued: 21.12.2006. Made: 18.12.2006. Coming into operation: 01.05.2007 for reg. 3 (12) to (16); 01.02.2007 for all other purposes. Effect: S.R. 2001/295; 2005/523 amended. - 8p.: 30 cm. - 978-0-337-96777-1 £3.00

The Management of Health and Safety at Work (Amendment) Regulations (Northern Ireland) 2006 No. 2006/255. - Enabling power: European Communities Act 1972, s. 2 (2) & S.I. 1978/1039 (N.I. 9), arts 2 (5), 17 (1) (2) (3) (5), 43 (2), 54 (1), 55 (2), sch. 3, paras 5 (1), 6, 7 (1), 8, 9, 11, 13, 14, 15, 17 (a). - Issued: 14.06.2006. Made: 08.06.2006. Coming into operation: 17.07.2006. Effect: S.R. 2000/388 amended. - 4p.: 30 cm. - 978-0-337-96544-9 £3.00

The Manufacture and Storage of Explosives Regulations (Northern Ireland) 2006 No. 2006/425. - Enabling power: S.I. 1978/1039 (N.I. 9), arts. 17 (1) (2) (4) (5), 40 (2) (4), 53 (1), 54 (1), 55 (2), sch. 3, paras 1 (1) (2) (3), 6, 10, 13, 14 (1), 15, 17, 19. - Issued: 27.10.2006. Made: 19.10.2006. Coming into operation: 01.12.2006. Effect: 11 Acts & 26 Statutory Instruments amended, 1924 c. 5 repealed, 34 Statutory Instruments revoked & S.R. & O. (N.I.) 1925/81 partially revoked, in accord. with sch. 6 & 7. - 60p., tables: 30 cm. - 978-0-337-96688-0 £9.00

Quarries (Explosives) Regulations (Northern Ireland) 2006 No. 2006/204. - Enabling power: S.I. 1978/1039 (N.I. 9), arts. 17 (1) (2) (3) (a) (5) (b), 55 (2), sch. 3, paras 1 (1), 2, 5, 13, 15, 19, 20 (b). - Issued: 09.06.2006. Made: 02.05.2006. Coming into operation: 01.08.2006. Effect: S.R. 2006/182 amended & S.R. 1991/233 revoked. - EC note: The Regulations give effect in relation to quarries to Council Directive 92/104/EEC concerning minimum requirements for improving the health and safety protection of workers in surface and underground mineral extracting industries. - 8p.: 30 cm. - 978-0-337-96493-0 £3.00

Quarries Regulations (Northern Ireland) 2006 No. 2006/205. - Enabling power: S.I. 1978/1039 (N.I. 9), arts. 17 (1) (2) (3) (5), 55 (2), sch. 3, paras 1 (1) (2), 2 (1) (2), 5, 7, 8, 11, 13, 14 (1), 15, 17, 19, 20 (b). - Issued: 10.05.2006. Made: 02.05.2006. Coming into operation: 01.08.2006, 01.08.2007 & 01.08.2008 in accord. with reg. 1. Effect: S.I. 1983/150 (NI.4) amended & S.R. 1979/437; 1991/13; 1993/37; 1995/296; 1997/455; 1999/90; 2000/375; 2004/63, 222; 2006/173 amended & S.R. 1962/180; 1963/41; 1992/216; 1995/378 revoked (01.08.2006). - EC note: The Regulations give effect to Council Directive 92/104/EEC concerning minimum requirements for improving the health and safety protection of workers in surface and underground mineral extracting industries. - 28p.: 30 cm. - 978-0-337-96494-7 *£4.50*

Health and safety: Transport

The Railways (Safety Management) Regulations (Northern Ireland) 2006 No. 2006/237. - Enabling power: S.I. 1978/1039 (N.I. 9), arts. 17 (1) (2) (4) (5) (6) (b), 55 (2), sch. 3, paras. 1 (1) (a) (c) (2), 5, 6, 7 (1), 13, 14 (1), 15. - Issued: 05.06.2006. Made: 25.05.2006. Coming into operation: 30.06.2006. Effect: None. - EC note: Part 2 and Reg 18 of the Regulations implement, insofar as they apply to any railway in relation to Northern Ireland, Directive 2004/49/EC on safety on the Community's railways and amending Council Directive 95/18/EC on the licensing of transport undertakings and Directive 2001/14/EC on the allocation of infrastructure capacity and the levying of charges for use of infrastructure and safety certification except in relation to access to training facilities, placing in service of in-use rolling stock and accident and incident investigation. - 28p.: 30 cm. - 978-0-337-96524-1 *£4.50*

Health services charges

The Recovery of Health Services Charges (Amounts) Regulations (Northern Ireland) 2006 No. 2006/507. - Enabling power: S.I. 2006/1944 (N.I. 13), arts 2, 5 (2) (5) (7) (8), 19 (3). - Issued: 22.12.2006. Made: 06.12.2006. Coming into operation: 29.01.2007. Effect: None. - 8p: 30 cm. - 978-0-337-96755-9 *£3.00*

The Recovery of Health Services Charges (General) Regulations (Northern Ireland) 2006 No. 2006/536. - Enabling power: S.I. 2006/1944 (N.I. 13), arts 2, 4 (9), 5 (10) (11), 12 (1) to (3), 14 (3), 15, 16 (4), 19 (3), sch. 1, para 8. - Issued: 08.01.2007. Made: 21.12.2006. Coming into operation: 29.01.2007. Effect: None. - 8p: 30 cm. - 978-0-337-96783-2 *£3.00*

Housing

The Allocation of Housing and Homelessness (Eligibility) Regulations (Northern Ireland) 2006 No. 2006/397. - Enabling power: S.I. 1981/156 (N.I. 3), art. 22A (3) & S.I. 1988/1990 (N.I. 23), art. 7A (2). - Issued: 04.10.2006. Made: 28.09.2006. Coming into operation: 01.11.2006. Effect: S.R. 2004/198, 199 revoked with savings. - EC note: These Regs take account of the implementation of Directive 2004/38/EC (which makes changes to the rights of free movement of citizens of the EU and their family members) by the Immigration (European Economic Area) Regulations 2006 (S.I. 2006/1003, ISBN 0110744659). - 8p.: 30 cm. - 978-0-337-96659-0 *£3.00*

The Housing Benefit (Amendment) Regulations (Northern Ireland) 2006 No. 2006/462. - Enabling power: Social Security Administration (Northern Ireland) Act 1992, ss. 5 (1) (a) (k), 165 (1) (4). - Issued: 24.11.2006. Made: 21.11.2006. Coming into operation: 20.12.2006. Effect: S.R. 2006/405, 406 amended. - 4p.: 30 cm. - 978-0-337-96719-1 *£3.00*

The Housing Benefit (Consequential Provisions) (Amendment) Regulations (Northern Ireland) 2006 No. 2006/449. - Enabling power: Social Security Contributions and Benefits (Northern Ireland) Act 1992, ss. 122 (1) (d), 132A (3), 171 (1) (3) (4). - Issued: 16.11.2006. Made: 10.11.2006. Coming into operation: 19.11.2006. Effect: S.R. 2006/407 amended. - This Statutory Rule is made in consequence of a defect in S.R. 2006 No. 407 (ISBN 0337966761) and is being issued free of charge to all known recipients of that Statutory Rule. - 2p.: 30 cm. - 978-0-337-96705-4 *£3.00*

The Housing Benefit (Consequential Provisions) Regulations (Northern Ireland) 2006 No. 2006/407. - Enabling power: Social Security Contributions and Benefits (Northern Ireland) Act 1992, ss. 122 (1) (d), 129 (2) (3) (4), 130, 131 (1) (2) (6), 132, 132A (3) (4) (a), 133 (2), 171 (1) (3) to (5) & Social Security Administration (Northern Ireland) Act 1992, ss. 1 (1) (1C), 5 (1) (a) to (d), (g) to (t) (5), 73, 107, 119A, 126 (4) (5), 165 (1) (4) to (6) & S.I. 1998/1506 (N.I. 10), arts 34, 74 (1) (3). - Issued: 25.10.2006. Made: 12.10.2006. Coming into operation: 20.11.2006. Effect: 153 amended & 96 revoked. - 56p.: 30 cm. - 978-0-337-96676-7 *£7.50*

The Housing Benefit (Electronic Communications) Order (Northern Ireland) 2006 No. 2006/463. - Enabling power: Electronic Communications Act (Northern Ireland) 2001, ss. 1, 2. - Issued: 27.11.2006. Made: 21.11.2006. Coming into operation: 20.12.2006. Effect: S.R. 2006/405, 406 amended. - 8p.: 30 cm. - 978-0-337-96720-7 *£3.00*

The Housing Benefit (Persons who have attained the qualifying age for state pension credit) Regulations (Northern Ireland) 2006 No. 2006/406. - Enabling power: Social Security Contributions and Benefits (Northern Ireland) Act 1992, ss. 122 (1) (d), 129 (2) (3) (4), 130, 131 (1) (2) (6), 132, 132A (3) (4) (a), 133, 171 (1) (3) to (5) & Social Security Administration (Northern Ireland) Act 1992, ss. 1 (1) (1C), 5 (1) (a) to (d) (g) to (t) (5), 73, 107, 119A, 126 (4) (5), 165 (1) & (4) to (6) & S.I. 1998/1506 (N.I.10), arts 34, 74 (1) (3). - Issued: 25.10.2005. Made: 12.10.2006. Coming into operation: 20.11.2006. Effect: None. - 124p.: 30 cm. - 978-0-337-96675-0 £17.50

The Housing Benefit Regulations (Northern Ireland) 2006 No. 2006/405. - Enabling power: Social Security Contributions and Benefits (Northern Ireland) Act 1992, ss. 122 (1) (d), 129 (2) (3) (4), 130, 131 (1) (2) (6), 132, 133, 171 (1) (3) to (5) & Social Security Administration (Northern Ireland) Act 1992, ss. 1 (1) (1C), 5 (1) (a) to (d) (g) to (t) (5), 73, 107, 119A, 126(4) (5) 165 (1) (4) to (6) & S.I. 1998/1506 (N.I.10), arts 34, 74 (1) (3). - Issued: 25.10.2005. Made: 12.10.2006. Coming into operation: 20.11.2006. Effect: None. - 152p.: 30 cm. - 978-0-337-96674-3 £22.00

The Housing Renewal Grants (Reduction of Grant) (Amendment) Regulations (Northern Ireland) 2006 No. 2006/452. - Enabling power: S.I. 1992/1725 (N.I.15), art. 47. - Issued: 16.11.2006. Made: 10.11.2006. Coming into operation: 18.12.2006. Effect: S.R. 2004/8 amended. - 16p.: 30 cm. - 978-0-337-96708-5 £3.00

The Social Security Benefits Up-rating Order (Northern Ireland) 2006 No. 2006/109. - Enabling power: Social Security Administration (Northern Ireland) Act 1992, ss. 132, 165 (1) (4) (5). - Issued: 28.03.2006. Made: 10.03.2006. Coming into operation: In accord. with art. 1. Effect: 1992 c. 7; 1993 c. 49; S.R. 1978/105; 1987/30, 459, 460, 461; 1992/32; 1994/461; 1995/35; 1996/198; 2002/380; 2003/28, 197 amended & S.R. 2005/82 revoked (13.04.2006). - 40p: 30 cm. - 978-0-337-96413-8 £6.50

The Social Security (Bulgaria and Romania) (Amendment) Regulations (Northern Ireland) 2006 No. 2006/523. - Enabling power: Social Security Contributions and Benefits (Northern Ireland) Act 1992, ss. 122 (1) (a) (d), 131 (1) (2), 133 (2), 171 (1) (3); S.I. 1995/2705 (N.I. 15), art. 6 (5) (12), sch. 1, para. 11 and State Pension Credit Act (Northern Ireland) 2002, ss. 1 (5) (a), 19 (1) (3). - Issued: 21.12.2006. Made: 14.12.2006. Coming into operation: 01.01.2007. Effect: S.R. 1987/459; 1996/198; 2003/28; 2006/405, 406 amended. - 4p.: 30 cm. - 978-0-337-96773-3 £3.00

The Social Security (Deferral of Retirement Pensions, Shared Additional Pension and Graduated Retirement Benefit) (Miscellaneous Provisions) Regulations (Northern Ireland) 2006 No. 2006/104. - Enabling power: Social Security Contributions and Benefits (Northern Ireland) Act 1992, ss. 62 (1) (a) (c), 132 (4) (a) (b), 171 (1) (3) to (5), sch. 5, paras A1 (1) (3), 3C (2) (4), sch. 5A, para. 1 (1) (3) & Social Security Administration (Northern Ireland) Act 1992, ss. 5 (1) (j), 165 (1) (4) (6) & S.I. 1998/1506 (N.I. 10), arts. 10, 11 (3) (6), 12 (1), 18 (1), 74 (1) & Child Support, Pensions and Social Security Act (Northern Ireland) 2000, sch. 7, para. 3 (1), 4 (3) (5), 20 (1) (3) & State Pension Credit Act (Northern Ireland) 2002, ss. 15 (6) (a) (b), 19 (1) to (3) & S.I. 2005/255 (N.I. 1), sch. 9, para. 22. - Issued: 22.03.2006. Made: 09.03.2006. Coming into operation: 06.04.2006. Effect: S.R. 1987/461, 465; 1999/162; 2001/213; 2003/28; 2005/121, 123 amended. - 16p: 30 cm. - 978-0-337-96410-7 £3.00

The Social Security (Lebanon) (Amendment) Regulations (Northern Ireland) 2006 No. 2006/320. - Enabling power: Social Security Contributions and Benefits (Northern Ireland) Act 1992, ss. 122 (1) (a) (d), 131 (1) (2), 133 (2), 171 (1) (3) (4) & S.I. 1995/2705 (N.I. 15), arts. 6 (5) (12), 36 (2), sch. 1, para. 11 & State Pension Credit Act (Northern Ireland) 2002, ss. 1 (5) (a), 19 (1) (2) (a) (3). - Issued: 02.08.2006. Made: 27.07.2006. Coming into operation: 28.07.2006. Effect: S.R. 1987/459, 461; 1996/198; 2003/28 amended. - These Regulations shall cease to have effect on 30th January 2007. - 4p.: 30 cm. - 978-0-337-96599-9 £3.00

The Social Security (Miscellaneous Amendments No. 4) Regulations (Northern Ireland) 2006 No. 2006/359. - Enabling power: Social Security Contributions and Benefits (Northern Ireland) Act 1992, ss. 30A (2A), 30C (4), 30E (1), 47 (6), 64 (1), 68 (4), 71 (6), 86A (1), 122 (1) (a) (d), 123 (1) (e), 129 (4), 131 (1), 132 (3) (4) (b) (c), 132A (3), 133 (2) (h), 167D, 171(1) (3) to (5), sch. 7, para. 2 (3) & Social Security Administration (Northern Ireland) Act 1992, ss. 5 (1) (m), 165 (1) (4) (5) & S.I. 1994/1898 (N.I. 12), art. 6 & S.I. 1995/2705 (N.I. 15), arts. 6 (5), 8 (4), 9 (2) (a) (4), 14 (2) (4) (b) (c), 36 (2), sch. 1, paras 1 (2) (b), 8, 8A (1), 12, 16 (1) & Child Support, Pensions and Social Security Act (Northern Ireland) 2000, sch. 7, paras 4 (5), 20 (1) (3) & State Pension Credit Act (Northern Ireland) 2002, ss. 1 (5) (a), 2 (3) (b), 7 (4), 15 (6) (a) (b), 17 (2) (a), 19 (1) to (3). - Issued: 19.09.2006. Made: 07.09.2006. Coming into operation: In accord. with reg. 1. Effect: S.R. 1979/243; 1984/92, 317; 1987/459, 461; 1990/131, 136; 1992/20, 32; 1993/165, 373; 1994/327, 335, 461, 485; 1995/35, 41; 1996/198, 199; 1997/165, 412; 2000/4; 2002/132, 299; 2003/28; 2005/458; 2006/150, 234 amended and S.R. 2005/415 revoked (09.10.2006). - 20p: 30 cm. - 978-0-337-96633-0 £3.50

The Social Security (Miscellaneous Amendments No. 5) Regulations (Northern Ireland) 2006 No. 2006/510. - Enabling power: Social Security Contributions and Benefits (Northern Ireland) Act 1992, ss. 122 (1) (a) (d), 131 (1), 133 (2) (h), 171 (1) (3) to (5); S.I. 1995/2705 (N.I. 15), arts 6 (5), 36 (2) and State Pension Credit Act (Northern Ireland) 2002, s. 2 (3) (b), 19 (1) (3). - Issued: 14.12.2006. Made: 08.12.2006. Coming into operation: 08.01.2007. Effect: S.R. 1987/459; 1996/198; 2003/28; 2006/405, 406 amended. - 4p.: 30 cm. - 978-0-337-96761-0 £3.00

The Social Security (Miscellaneous Amendments) Regulations (Northern Ireland) 2006 No. 2006/97. - Enabling power: Social Security Contributions and Benefits (Northern Ireland) Act 1992, ss.122 (1) (a) (d), 123 (1) (e), 131 (1), 132 (4) (a) (b), 132A (3), 134 (1) (a), 171 (1) (3) (4) & Social Security Administration (Northern Ireland) Act 1992, ss. 5 (1) (l), 165(1) (4) (5) & S.I. 1995/2705 (N.I. 15), arts. 14(4)(a) (b), 36(2) & State Pension Credit Act (Northern Ireland) 2002, ss. 2 (3) (b) (9), 13 (1) (a), 15 (1) (j), 19 (1) (2) (a) (3). - Issued: 21.03.2006. Made: 09.03.2006. Coming into operation: In accord. with reg. 1. Effect: S.R. 1987/459, 461; 1996/198; 2003/28; 2005/506 amended. - 8p: 30 cm. - 978-0-337-96403-9 £3.00

The Social Security (Persons from Abroad) (Amendment No. 2) Regulations (Northern Ireland) 2006 No. 2006/379. - Enabling power: Social Security Contributions and Benefits (Northern Ireland) Act 1992, ss. 122 (1) (a) (d), 131 (1) (2), 133 (2), 171 (1) (3) & S.I. 1995/2705 (N.I. 15), arts 6 (5) (12), sch. 1, para. 11 & State Pension Credit Act (Northern Ireland) 2002, ss. 1 (5) (a), 19 (1) (3). - Issued: 21.09.2006. Made: 15.09.2006. Coming into operation: 09.10.2006. Effect: S.R. 1987/459, 461; 1996/198; 2003/28; amended. - 4p: 30 cm. - 978-0-337-96645-3 £3.00

The Social Security (Persons from Abroad) (Amendment) Regulations (Northern Ireland) 2006 No. 2006/178. - Enabling power: Social Security Contributions and Benefits (Northern Ireland) Act 1992, ss. 122 (1) (a) (d), 131 (1) (2), 133 (2), 134 (1) (a), 171 (1) (3) (4) & S.I. 1995/2705 (N.I. 15), arts 6 (5) (12), 36 (2), sch. 1, para. 11 & State Pension Credit Act (Northern Ireland) 2002, ss. 1 (5) (a), 19 (1) (2) (a) (3). - Issued: 10.04.2006. Made: 03.04.2006. Coming into operation: 30.04.2006. Effect: S.R. 1987/459, 461; 1996/198; 2003/28; 2005/506 amended & S.R. 1994/266; 1996/375; 2000/125; 2004/197 revoked. - EC note: These Regulations amend the income-related benefits regulations and the Social Fund regulations in consequence of the Council Directive 2004/38/EC the provisions of which are to be transposed by the Immigration (European Economic Area) Regulations 2006. - 12p: 30 cm. - 978-0-337-96475-6 £3.00

The Social Security (Students and Income-related Benefits) (Amendment) Regulations (Northern Ireland) 2006 No. 2006/301. - Enabling power: Social Security Contributions and Benefits (Northern Ireland) Act 1992, ss. 122 (1) (a) (d), 132 (3) (4) (b), 171 (1) (3) (4) & S.I. 1995/2705 (N.I. 15), arts 14 (1) (4) (b), 36 (2). - Issued: 10.07.2006. Made: 04.07.2006. Coming into operation: In accord. with reg. 1. Effect: S.R. 1987/459, 461; 1996/198 amended & S.R. 2005/332 revoked. - 8p.: 30 cm. - 978-0-337-96583-8 £3.00

The Social Security (Young Persons) (Amendment) Regulations (Northern Ireland) 2006 No. 2006/128. - Enabling power: Social Security Contributions and Benefits (Northern Ireland) Act 1992, ss. 122 (1) (a) (d), 123 (1) (d) (e), 131 (1), 133 (2) (e) (f) (i), 171 (1) (3) to (5); S.I. 1995/2705 (N.I. 15), arts 5 (1) (f) (iii), 5A (1) (e) (ii), 6 (5), 36 (1) (2), Sch. 1, paras 8, 8A (1), 9C, 14; State Pension Credit Act (Northern Ireland) 2002, ss. 1 (5) (b), 2 (3) (b), 15 (3) (6), 17 (2), 19 (1) (2) (a) (3). - Issued: 24.03.2006. Made: 13.03.2006. Coming into operation: In accord. with reg. 1. Effect: S.R. 1987/459, 461; 1996/198; 2003/28 amended. - 8p.: 30 cm. - 978-0-337-96430-5 £3.00

Industrial and provident societies

The Community Benefit Societies (Restriction on Use of Assets) Regulations (Northern Ireland) 2006 No. 2006/258. - Enabling power: S.I. 2006/314 (N.I. 3), art. 9. - Issued: 15.06.2006. Made: 12.06.2006. Coming into operation: 31.07.2006. Effect: 1969 c. 24 modified. - 12p.: 30 cm. - 978-0-337-96547-0 £3.00

The Industrial and Provident Societies (2006 Order) (Commencement) Order (Northern Ireland) 2006 No. 2006/242 (C.13). - Enabling power: S.I. 2006/314 (NI. 3), art. 1 (3). Bringing into operation various provisions of the 2006 Order on 01.07.2006. - Issued: 08.06.2006. Made: 05.06.2006. Coming into operation: -. Effect: None. - 2p: 30 cm. - 978-0-337-96530-2 £3.00

Industrial relations

The Employment Code of Practice (Access and Unfair Practices during Recognition and Derecognition Ballots) (Appointed Day) Order (Northern Ireland) 2006 No. 2006/100. - Enabling power: S.I. 1992/807 (N.I. 5), art. 95 (1) to (6) (14). - Issued: 21.03.2006. Made: 09.03.2006. Coming into operation: 19.03.2006. Effect: None. - 2p: 30 cm. - 978-0-337-96408-4 £3.00

The Employment Code of Practice (Industrial Action Ballots and Notice to Employers) (Appointed Day) Order (Northern Ireland) 2006 No. 2006/101. - Enabling power: S.I. 1992/807 (N.I. 5), art. 95 (1) to (6) (14). - Issued: 22.03.2006. Made: 09.03.2006. Coming into operation: 19.03.2006. Effect: None. - 2p: 30 cm. - 978-0-337-96409-1 £3.00

The Employment Protection (Code of Practice) (Disclosure of Information) (Appointed Day) Order (Northern Ireland) 2006 No. 2006/423. - Enabling power: S.I. 1992/807 (N.I. 5), art. 90 (13). - Issued: 27.10.2006. Made: 20.10.2006. Coming into operation: 12.11.2006, in accord. with art. 2. Effect: S.R. 1978/233 revoked. - 2p: 30 cm. - 978-0-337-96690-3 £3.00

Industrial training

The Industrial Training Levy (Construction Industry) Order (Northern Ireland) 2006 No. 2006/277. - Enabling power: S.I. 1984/1159 (N.I. 9), arts, 23 (2) (3), 24 (3) (4). - Issued: 29.06.2006. Made: 23.06.2006. Coming into operation: 31.08.2006. Effect: None. - 8p.: 30 cm. - 978-0-337-96561-6 £3.00

Industrial tribunals

The Industrial Tribunals (Interest on Awards in Age Discrimination Cases) Regulations (Northern Ireland) 2006 No. 2006/262. - Enabling power: European Communities Act 1972, s. 2 (2). - Issued: 19.06.2006. Made: 13.06.2006. Coming into operation: 01.10.2006. Effect: None. - EC note: These Regs. ensure that the remedies available under the Age Regs comply with art. 17 of Council Directive 2000/78/EC establishing a general framework for equal treatment in employment so far as it relates to discrimination on grounds of age. - 4p.: 30 cm. - 978-0-337-96551-7 £3.00

Insolvency

The Insolvency (2005 Order) (Commencement No. 1) Order (Northern Ireland) 2006 No. 2006/21 (C.1). - Enabling power: S.I. 2005/1455 (N.I. 10), art. 1 (3). Bringing into operation various provisions of the 2005 Order on 27.03.2006. - Issued: 10.02.2006. Made: 02.02.2006. Coming into operation: -. Effect: None. - 2p: 30 cm. - 978-0-337-96332-2 £3.00

The Insolvency (2005 Order) (Transitional Provisions and Savings) Order (Northern Ireland) 2006 No. 2006/22. - Enabling power: S.I. 2005/1455 (N.I. 10), art. 29 (1) (2). - Issued: 10.02.2006. Made: 02.02.2006. Coming into operation: 27.03.2006. Effect: None. - 8p: 30 cm. - 978-0-337-96331-5 £3.00

The Insolvency (Amendment) Regulations (Northern Ireland) 2006 No. 2006/23. - Enabling power: S.R. 1991/364, rule 12.01 & S.I. 1989/2405 (N.I. 19), art 359, sch. 5, para. 27, sch. 6, para. 28. - Issued: 10.02.2006. Made: 02.02.2006. Coming into operation: 27.03.2006. Effect: S.R. 1996/574 amended. - 8p: 30 cm. - 978-0-337-96330-8 £3.00

The Insolvency (Amendment) Rules (Northern Ireland) 2006 No. 2006/47. - Enabling power: Registration of Deeds Act 1970, s. 19 (3) & S.I. 1989/2405 (N.I. 19), art 359. - Issued: 10.03.2006. Made: 09.02.2006. Coming into operation: 27.03.2006. Effect: S.R. 1991/364 amended. - 260p: 30 cm. - 978-0-337-96358-2 £28.00

Insolvency (Deposits) Order (Northern Ireland) 2006 No. 2006/55. - Enabling power: S.I. 1989/2405 (N.I. 19), art. 361 (2) (3). - Issued: 24.02.2006. Made: 16.02.2006. Coming into operation: 27.03.2006. Effect: S.R. 1991/384; 1996/577 revoked. - 4p: 30 cm. - 978-0-337-96353-7 £3.00

The Insolvency (Fees) Order (Northern Ireland) 2006 No. 2006/54. - Enabling power: S.I. 1989/2405 (N.I. 19), art. 361 (1) (3) (4). - Issued: 24.02.2006. Made: 16.02.2006. Coming into operation: 27.03.2006. Effect: S.R. 1991/385 (except in relation to any case where a winding-up or bankruptcy order is made under the 1989 Order before the commencement date); 1992/398; 1996/576 revoked. - 8p: 30 cm. - 978-0-337-96352-0 £3.00

The Insolvency (Monetary Limits) (Amendment) Order (Northern Ireland) 2006 No. 2006/26. - Enabling power: S.I. 1989/2405 (N.I. 19), art. 362 (1) (b). - Issued: 10.02.2006. Made: 02.02.2006. Coming into operation: 27.03.2006. Effect: S.R. 1991/386 amended. - 4p: 30 cm. - 978-0-337-96327-8 £3.00

The Insolvency (Northern Ireland) Order 1989 (Amendment) Regulations (Northern Ireland) 2006 No. 2006/370. - Enabling power: European Communities Act 1972, s. 2 (2). - Issued: 20.09.2006. Made: 14.09.2006. Coming into operation: 18.10.2006. Effect: S.I. 1989/2405 (N.I. 19) amended. - With correction slip dated September 2006 which amends the coming into operation date to 18 October 2006. - 4p.: 30 cm. - 978-0-337-96639-2 £3.00

The Insolvency (Northern Ireland) Order 1989, Article 59A (Appointed Date) Order (Northern Ireland) 2006 No. 2006/24. - Enabling power: S.I. 1989/2405 (N.I. 19), art. 59A (3) (a) (4). - Issued: 10.02.2006. Made: 02.02.2006. Coming into operation: 27.03.2006. Effect: None. - 2p: 30 cm. - 978-0-337-96329-2 £3.00

The Insolvency (Northern Ireland) Order 1989 (Prescribed Part) Order (Northern Ireland) 2006 No. 2006/25. - Enabling power: S.I. 1989/2405 (N.I. 19), art. 150A (2) (3) (7). - Issued: 10.02.2006. Made: 02.02.2006. Coming into operation: 27.03.2006. Effect: None. - 4p.: 30 cm. - 978-0-337-96328-5 £3.00

The Insolvency (Northern Ireland) Order 2005 (Minor and Consequential Amendments) Order (Northern Ireland) 2006 No. 2006/61. - Enabling power: S.I. 2005/1455 (N.I. 10), arts. 3 (4), 30. - Issued: 08.03.2006. Made: 22.02.2006. Coming into operation: 27.03.2006. Effect: S.I. 1989/2405 (N.I. 19); 2001/1757 amended & S.R. 1982/263; 1987/30; 1991/443; 1994/424; 1996/252; 1999/115, 454; 2002/378; 2003/357; 2005/126 amended. - 12p: 30 cm. - 978-0-337-96364-3 £3.00

The Insolvency Practitioners and Insolvency Account (Fees) Order (Northern Ireland) 2006 No. 2006/53. - Enabling power: S.I. 1989/2405 (N.I.19), art. 361A (1) (2) (3). - Issued: 01.03.2006. Made: 16.02.2006. Coming into operation: 27.03.2006. Effect: None. - 8p: 30 cm. - 978-0-337-96351-3 £3.00

The Insolvency Practitioners Regulations (Northern Ireland) 2006 No. 2006/33. - Enabling power: S.I. 1989/2405 (N.I.19), arts. 349 (3), 351 (3), 352 (2) (3), 363. - Issued: 08.03.2006. Made: 09.02.2006. Coming into operation: 27.03.2006. Effect: S.R. 1991/302; 1993/317, 454; 2003/547 revoked. - 20p: 30 cm. - 978-0-337-96336-0 £3.50

Insolvency Regulations (Northern Ireland) 1996 (Electronic Communications) Order (Northern Ireland) 2006 No. 2006/461. - Enabling power: Electronic Communications Act (Northern Ireland) 2001, ss. 1, 2. - Issued: 24.11.2006. Made: 20.11.2006. Coming into operation: 29.12.2006. Effect: S.R. 1996/574 amended. - 4p.: 30 cm. - 978-0-337-96718-4 £3.00

The Insolvent Partnerships (Amendment) Order (Northern Ireland) 2006 No. 2006/515. - Enabling power: S.I. 1989/2405 (N.I. 19), art. 364 & S.I. 2002/3150 (N.I. 4), art. 24 (1). - Issued: 08.01.2007. Made: 13.12.2006. Coming into operation: 08.01.2007. Effect: S.R. 1995/225 amended. - 44p: 30 cm. - 978-0-337-96767-2 £7.50

Insurance

The Insurance Accounts Directive (Miscellaneous Insurance Undertakings) (Amendment) Regulations (Northern Ireland) 2006 No. 2006/353. - Enabling power: European Communities Act 1972, s. 2 (2). - Issued: 06.09.2006. Made: 31.08.2006. Coming into operation: 01.10.2006. Effect: S.R. 1994/429 amended. - EC note: Amends the 1994 Regulations in order to ensure the full application to insurance undertakings of Regulation 1606/2002 (the IAS Regulation) and Directive 2003/51/EC (amending Directives 78/660/EEC, 83/349/EEC, 86/635/EEC and 91/674/EEC) (the Accounts Modernisation Directive). - 4p.: 30 cm. - 978-0-337-96624-8 £3.00

Intercountry adoption

The Adoption of Children from Overseas and Intercountry Adoption (Hague Convention) (Amendment) Regulations (Northern Ireland) 2006 No. 2006/336. - Enabling power: Adoption (Intercountry Aspects) Act (Northern Ireland) 2001, ss. 1 (1) (3) (5) & S.I. 1987/2203 (N.I. 22), arts. 10 (1), 16A, 58ZA. - Issued: 21.08.2006. Made: 15.08.2006. Coming into operation: 21.08.2006. Effect: S.R. 2002/144; 2003/16 amended. - 4p.: 30 cm. - 978-0-337-96609-5 £3.00

Justice

The Justice (Northern Ireland) Act 2002 (Addition of Listed Judicial Offices etc.) Order 2006 No. 2006/469. - Enabling power: Justice (Northern Ireland) Act 2002, ss. 2 (2) (a), 19 (4) (a). - Issued: 08.01.2007. Made: 23.11.2006. Coming into operation: 18.12.2006 except for rule 3; 01.04.2007 for rule 3. Effect: 2002 c.26 amended. - 4p: 30 cm. - 978-0-337-96725-2 £3.00

The Justice (Northern Ireland) Act 2002 (Commencement No.11) Order 2006 No. 2006/124 (C.8). - Enabling power: Justice (Northern Ireland) Act 2002, s. 87. Bringing into operation various provisions of the 2002 Act on 03.04.2006. - Issued: 24.03.2006. Made: 08.03.2006. Coming into operation: -. Effect: None. - 8p.: 30 cm. - 978-0-337-96429-9 £3.00

Laganside

The Laganside Corporation Dissolution Order (Northern Ireland) 2006 No. 2006/527. - Enabling power: S.I. 1989/490 (N.I.2), art. 9. - Issued: 18.01.2007. Made: 18.12.2006. Coming into operation: 01.04.2007; 01.07.2007 in accord. with art. 1 (2) to (4). Effect: S.I. 1989/490 (N.I. 2) amended. - 8p: 30 cm. - 978-0-337-96779-5 £3.00

The River Lagan Tidal Navigation and General Bye-laws (Northern Ireland) 2006 No. 2006/526. - Enabling power: S.I. 1989/490 (N.I. 2), art. 19. - Issued: 05.01.2007. Made: 18.12.2006. Coming into operation: 01.04.2007. Effect: None. - 12p: 30 cm. - 978-0-337-96778-8 £3.00

Landlord and tenant

The Private Tenancies (2006 Order) (Commencement) Order (Northern Ireland) 2006 No. 2006/428 (C.25). - Enabling power: S.I. 2006/1459 (N.I. 10), art. 1 (3). Bringing into operation certain provisions of the 2006 Order on 06.11.2006 & 01.04.2007. - Issued: 03.11.2006. Made: 24.10.2006. Coming into operation: -. Effect: None. - 2p.: 30 cm. - 978-0-337-96692-7 £3.00

Registered Rents (Increase) Order (Northern Ireland) 2006 No. 2006/58. - Enabling power: S.I. 1978/1050 (N.I. 20), art. 33 (2A) (2B). - Issued: 27.02.2006. Made: 17.02.2006. Coming into operation: 06.03.2006. Effect: None. - 2p.: 30 cm. - 978-0-337-96361-2 £3.00

Lands Tribunal

Lands Tribunal (Salaries) Order (Northern Ireland) 2006 No. 2006/265. - Enabling power: Lands Tribunal and Compensation Act (Northern Ireland) 1964, s. 2 (5) & Administrative and Financial Provisions Act (Northern Ireland) 1962, s. 18. - Issued: 21.06.2006. Made: 15.06.2006. Coming into operation: 24.07.2006. Effect: S.R. 2005/269 revoked. - 4p.: 30 cm. - 978-0-337-96554-8 £3.00

Lands Tribunal (Superannuation) (Amendment) Order (Northern Ireland) 2006 No. 2006/260. - Enabling power: Lands Tribunal and Compensation Act (Northern Ireland) 1964, s. 2 (5). - Issued: 20.06.2006. Made: 12.06.2006. Coming into operation: 04.07.2006. Effect: S.R. 1976/46 amended. - 4p.: 30 cm. - 978-0-337-96553-1 £3.00

Legal aid and advice

Legal Advice and Assistance (Amendment No. 2) Regulations (Northern Ireland) 2006 No. 2006/193. - Enabling power: S.I. 1981/228 (N.I. 8), arts 7(2), 22, 27. - Issued: 28.04.2006. Made: 20.04.2006. Coming into operation: 22.05.2006. Effect: S.R. 1981/366 amended & S.R. 2006/118 revoked. - This Statutory Rule has been made to correct an error in S.R. 2006 No. 118 (ISBN 033796422X) and is being issued free of charge to all known recipients of that Statutory Rule. - 4p.: 30 cm. - 978-0-337-96489-3 £3.00

Legal Advice and Assistance (Amendment) Regulations (Northern Ireland) 2006 No. 2006/118. - Enabling power: S.I. 1981/228 (N.I. 8), arts 7(2), 22, 27. - Issued: 23.03.2006. Made: 01.03.2006. Coming into operation: 10.04.2006. Effect: S.R. 1981/366 amended & S.R. 2005/67 revoked. - Revoked by SR 2006/193 (ISBN 0337964890) which is being sent free of charge to all known recipients. - 4p.: 30 cm. - 978-0-337-96422-0 £3.00

Legal Advice and Assistance (Financial Conditions) Regulations (Northern Ireland) 2006 No. 2006/117. - Enabling power: S.I. 1981/228 (N.I. 8), arts. 3 (2), 7 (3), 22, 27. - Issued: 24.03.2006. Made: 01.03.2006. Coming into operation: 10.04.2006. Effect: S.I. 1981/228 (N.I. 8) amended & S.R. 2005/65 revoked. - 4p: 30 cm. - 978-0-337-96424-4 £3.00

Legal Aid (Assessment of Resources) (Amendment) Regulations (Northern Ireland) 2006 No. 2006/80. - Enabling power: S.I. 1981/228 (N.I. 8), arts 14, 22, 27. - Issued: 14.03.2006. Made: 18.02.2006. Coming into operation: 27.03.2006. Effect: S.R. 1981/189 amended. - 2p: 30 cm. - 978-0-337-96395-7 £3.00

Legal Aid (Financial Conditions) Regulations (Northern Ireland) 2006 No. 2006/119. - Enabling power: S.I. 1981/228 (N.I. 8), arts. 9 (2), 12 (2), 22, 27. - Issued: 24.03.2006. Made: 01.03.2006. Coming into operation: 10.04.2006. Effect: S.I. 1981/228 (N.I. 8) amended & S.R. 2005/66 revoked with savings. - 4p: 30 cm. - 978-0-337-96423-7 £3.00

Legal Aid (General) (Amendment) Regulations (Northern Ireland) 2006 No. 2006/79. - Enabling power: S.I. 1981/228 (N.I. 8), arts 22, 27. - Issued: 14.03.2006. Made: 18.02.2006. Coming into operation: 27.03.2006. Effect: S.R. 1965/217 amended. - 2p.: 30 cm. - 978-0-337-96394-0 £3.00

The Legal Aid in Criminal Proceedings (Costs) (Amendment) Rules (Northern Ireland) 2006 No. 2006/245. - Enabling power: S.I. 1981/228 (N.I. 8), art. 36 (3). - Issued: 15.06.2006. Made: 26.05.2006. Coming into operation: 01.07.2006. Effect: S.R. 1992/314 amended. - 2p.: 30 cm. - 978-0-337-96535-7 £3.00

Local government

The Local Government (2005 Order) (Commencement No. 2 and Savings) Order (Northern Ireland) 2006 No. 2006/151 (C.10). - Enabling power: S.I. 2005/1968 (NI 18), art. 1 (2). Bringing into operation various provisions of the 2005 Order on 01.04.2006, in accord. with art. 2. - Issued: 28.03.2006. Made: 22.03.2006. Coming into operation: -. Effect: None. - 4p: 30 cm. - 978-0-337-96454-1 £3.00

Local Government (Accounts and Audit) (Amendment) Regulations (Northern Ireland) 2006 No. 2006/522. - Enabling power: S.I. 2005/1968 (N.I. 18), art. 24. - Issued: 20.12.2006. Made: 14.12.2006. Coming into operation: 01.04.2007. Effect: S.R. 2006/89 amended. - 4p: 30 cm. - 978-0-337-96772-6 £3.00

Local Government (Accounts and Audit) Regulations (Northern Ireland) 2006 No. 2006/89. - Enabling power: S.I. 2005/1968 (N.I. 18), art. 24. - Issued: 13.03.2006. Made: 07.03.2006. Coming into operation: 01.04.2006. Effect: None. - 8p: 30 cm. - 978-0-337-96389-6 £3.00

Local Government Companies (Best Value) Order (Northern Ireland) 2006 No. 2006/500. - Enabling power: Local Government (Best Value) Act (Northern Ireland) 2002, s. 3 (2). - Issued: 21.12.2006. Made: 05.12.2006. Coming into operation: 22.01.2007. Effect: None. - 4p: 30 cm. - 978-0-337-96750-4 £3.00

The Local Government (General Grant) (Amendment) Regulations (Northern Ireland) 2006 No. 2006/39. - Enabling power: S.I. 2002/3149 (N.I. 3), art. 4. - Issued: 01.03.2006. Made: 10.02.2006. Coming into operation: 01.04.2006. Effect: S.R. 2003/58 amended. - This Statutory Rule is being issued free of charge to all known recipients of SR 2006 no. 39 (previously issued 21.02.2006), which contained an error. - 2p: 30 cm. - 978-0-337-96341-4 £3.00

Local Government Pension Scheme (Amendment No. 2) Regulations (Northern Ireland) 2006 No. 2006/112. - Enabling power: S.I. 1972/1073 (N.I. 10), arts. 9, 14, sch. 3. - Issued: 23.03.20065. Made: 10.03.2006. Coming into operation: 01.04.2006. Effect: S.R. 2002/352 amended. - 4p: 30 cm. - 978-0-337-96420-6 £3.00

Local Government Pension Scheme (Civil Partnership) (Amendment) Regulations (Northern Ireland) 2006 No. 2006/6. - Enabling power: S.I. 1972/1073 (N.I. 10), arts 9, 14, sch. 3. - Issued: 25.01.2006. Made: 13.01.2006. Coming into operation: 10.02.2006. Effect: S.R. 2001/279; 2002/352, 353; 2003/61 amended. - 8p: 30 cm. - 978-0-337-96317-9 £3.00

Local Government Pension Scheme (Management and Investment of Funds) (Amendment) Regulations (Northern Ireland) 2006 No. 2006/400. - Enabling power: S.I. 1972/1073 (N.I. 10), art. 9, sch. 3. - Issued: 10.10.2006. Made: 04.10.2006. Coming into operation: 06.11.2006. Effect: S.R. 2000/178 amended. - 4p: 30 cm. - 978-0-337-96667-5 £3.00

Lord Chancellor

The Lord Chancellor (Consequential Provisions) Order (Northern Ireland) 2006 No. 2006/115. - Enabling power: Constitutional Reform Act 2005, s. 143. - Issued: 28.03.2006. Made: 13.03.2006. Coming into operation: 03.04.2006. Effect: S.R. 1981/225; 1992/314; 1996/300 amended. - 4p: 30 cm. - 978-0-337-96428-2 *£3.00*

Lord Chief Justice

The Lord Chancellor (Consequential Provisions) Order (Northern Ireland) 2006 No. 2006/115. - Enabling power: Constitutional Reform Act 2005, s. 143. - Issued: 28.03.2006. Made: 13.03.2006. Coming into operation: 03.04.2006. Effect: S.R. 1981/225; 1992/314; 1996/300 amended. - 4p: 30 cm. - 978-0-337-96428-2 *£3.00*

Magistrates' courts

The Magistrates' Courts (Amendment) Rules (Northern Ireland) 2006 No. 2006/413. - Enabling power: S.I. 1981/1675 (N.I. 26), art. 13 & S.I. 1989/1341 (N.I. 12), art. 80A (7). - Issued: 26.10.2006. Made: 17.10.2006. Coming into operation: In accord. with rule 1. Effect: S.R. 1984/225 amended. - 8p.: 30 cm. - 978-0-337-96682-8 *£3.00*

The Magistrates' Courts (Anti-social Behaviour Orders) (Amendment) Rules (Northern Ireland) 2006 No. 2006/414. - Enabling power: S.I. 1981/1675 (N.I. 26), art. 13. - Issued: 26.10.2006. Made: 17.10.2006. Coming into operation: 15.11.2006. Effect: S.R. 2004/324 amended. - 8p.: 30 cm. - 978-0-337-96683-5 *£3.00*

Northern Ireland Departments

The Departments (Transfer of Functions) Order (Northern Ireland) 2006 No. 2006/192. - Enabling power: S.I.1999/283 (NI 1), art. 8. - Issued: 28.04.2006. Made: 03.04.2006. Coming into operation: 28.05.2006. Effect: None. - 4p: 30 cm. - 978-0-337-96488-6 *£3.00*

Partnerships: Limited Liability Partnerships

Limited Liability Partnerships (Amendment) Regulations (Northern Ireland) 2006 No. 2006/377. - Enabling power: Limited Liability Partnerships Act (Northern Ireland) 2002, ss. 10, 11, 13. - Issued: 21.09.2006. Made: 15.09.2006. Coming into operation: 01.10.2006. Effect: S.R. 2004/307 amended. - 12p.: 30 cm. - 978-0-337-96643-9 *£3.00*

Pensions

The Dissolution etc. (Pension Protection Fund) Regulations (Northern Ireland) 2006 No. 2006/311. - Enabling power: Civil Partnership Act 2004, sch. 15, paras. 27, 30, 31. - Issued: 25.07.2006. Made: 19.07.2006. Coming into operation: 14.08.2006. Effect: 2004 c.33; S.R. 2005/484 modified. - 8p.: 30 cm. - 978-0-337-96590-6 *£3.00*

The Divorce etc. (Pension Protection Fund) Regulations (Northern Ireland) 2006 No. 2006/310. - Enabling power: S.I. 1978/1045 (N.I.15), art. 27E (5) (8) (9). - Issued: 25.07.2006. Made: 19.07.2006. Coming into operation: 14.08.2006. Effect: S.I. 1978/1045 (N.I.15); 2000/210 modified. - 8p.: 30 cm. - 978-0-337-96589-0 *£3.00*

The Employment Equality (Age) (Amendment No. 2) Regulations (Northern Ireland) 2006 No. 2006/453. - Enabling power: European Communities Act 1972, s. 2 (2). - Issued: 20.11.2006. Made: 13.11.2006. Coming into operation: 01.12.2006. Effect: S.R. 2006/261 amended. - EC note: These Regs amend the Employment Equality (Age) Regulations (Northern Ireland) 2006 (S.R. 2006/261) which implement the Council Directive 2000/78/EC establishing a general framework for equal treatment in employment and occupation. These Regulations deal with provisions relating to pensions. - 16p.: 30 cm. - 978-0-337-96709-2 *£3.00*

The Guaranteed Minimum Pensions Increase Order (Northern Ireland) 2006 No. 2006/108. - Enabling power: Pension Schemes (Northern Ireland) Act 1993, s. 105. - Issued: 21.03.2006. Made: 10.03.2006. Coming into operation: 06.04.2006. Effect: None. - 2p: 30 cm. - 978-0-337-96404-6 *£3.00*

The Judicial Pensions (Additional Voluntary Contributions) (Amendment) Regulations (Northern Ireland) 2006 No. 2006/126. - Enabling power: County Courts Act (Northern Ireland) 1959, s. 127A; Resident Magistrates' Pensions Act (Northern Ireland) 1960, s. 9A & Judicial Pensions Act (Northern Ireland) 1951, s. 11A. - Issued: 29.03.2006. Made: 06.03.2006. Coming into operation: 06.04.2006. Effect: S.R. 1995/189 amended. - 4p: 30 cm. - 978-0-337-96432-9 *£3.00*

The Judicial Pensions (Northern Ireland) (Widows' and Children's Benefits) (Amendment) Regulations 2006 No. 2006/125. - Enabling power: Administration of Justice Act 1973, ss. 10 (8), sch. 3. - Issued: 28.03.2006. Made: 01.03.2006. Coming into operation: 06.04.2006. Effect: S.R. 1987/101 amended. - 4p: 30 cm. - 978-0-337-96431-2 *£3.00*

The Judicial Pensions (Spouses' and Children's Benefits) (Amendment) Regulations (Northern Ireland) 2006 No. 2006/170. - Enabling power: Administration of Justice Act 1973, s. 10 (8), sch. 3. - Issued: 07.04.2006. Made: 22.03.2006. Coming into operation: 06.04.2006. Effect: S.R. 1993/40 amended. - 4p: 30 cm. - 978-0-337-96471-8 *£3.00*

The Occupational and Personal Pension Schemes (Consultation by Employers) Regulations (Northern Ireland) 2006 No. 2006/48. - Enabling power: S.I. 2005/255 (N.I. 1), arts. 2 (5) (a) (6), 7 (5) (a), 236 (1) (2), 237 (1), 238 (2) (4), 287 (1) (3). - Issued: 23.02.2006. Made: 16.02.2006. Coming into operation: 06.04.2006. Effect: S.I. 1996/1919 (N.I. 16), 1921 (N.I. 18) amended. - 20p: 30 cm. - 978-0-337-96347-6 £3.50

The Occupational and Personal Pension Schemes (Miscellaneous Amendments) Regulations (Northern Ireland) 2006 No. 2006/141. - Enabling power: Pension Schemes (Northern Ireland) Act 1993, s. 97C (2), 109 (1) (d), 177 (2) to (4); S.I.1995/3213 (N.I. 22), arts 35 (3) (4), 40 (2), 47 (5) (6), 49 (1) (2) (4) (9) (b), 85 (1), 86 (1), 89 (5), 166 (1) to (3) & S.I. 2005/255 (N.I. 1), arts 236 (1), 237 (1). - Issued: 27.03.2006. Made: 16.03.2006. Coming into operation: In accord. with reg 1. Effect: S.R. 1997/40, 94, 153; 2000/146, 349; 2005/569; 2006/48 amended. - 8p: 30 cm. - 978-0-337-96446-6 £3.00

The Occupational Pension Schemes (Consultation by Employers) (Modification for Multi-employer Schemes) Regulations (Northern Ireland) 2006 No. 2006/4. - Enabling power: S.I. 2005/255 (N.I. 1), arts. 280 (1) (b), 287 (1) (3). - Issued: 18.01.2006. Made: 11.01.2006. Coming into operation: 02.02.2006 Effect: S.I. 2005/255 (N.I. 1) modified. - 2p: 30 cm. - 978-0-337-96313-1 £3.00

The Occupational Pension Schemes (Contracting-out) (Amendment) Regulations (Northern Ireland) 2006 No. 2006/223. - Enabling power: Pension Schemes (Northern Ireland) Act 1993, ss. 17 (1), 177 (2) to (4). - Issued: 23.05.2006. Made: 17.05.2006. Coming into operation: 14.06.2006. Effect: S.R. 1996/493 amended. - 2p: 30 cm. - 978-0-337-96513-5 £3.00

The Occupational Pension Schemes (Cross-border Activities) (Amendment) Regulations (Northern Ireland) 2006 No. 2006/160. - Enabling power: S.I. 2005/255 (N.I. 1), arts. 264 (12), 265 (1). - Issued: 04.04.2006. Made: 27.03.2006. Coming into operation: 28.03.2006. Effect: S.R. 2005/581 amended & S.R. 2006/65 revoked. - 4p.: 30 cm. - 978-0-337-96464-0 £3.00

The Occupational Pension Schemes (Early Leavers: Cash Transfer Sums and Contribution Refunds) Regulations (Northern Ireland) 2006 No. 2006/49. - Enabling power: Pension Schemes (Northern Ireland) Act 1993, ss. 97AC (2) (a), 97AE (2), 97AF, 109A, 177 (2) (3), 178. - Issued: 23.02.2006. Made: 16.02.2006. Coming into operation: 06.04.2006. Effect: None. - 8p: 30 cm. - 978-0-337-96348-3 £3.00

The Occupational Pension Schemes (Fraud Compensation Levy) Regulations (Northern Ireland) 2006 No. 2006/85. - Enabling power: S.I. 1995/3213 (N.I. 22), arts. 10 (3), 75 (10), 87 (2) & S.I. 2005/255 (N.I. 1), arts. 171 (1) (4) (6) (11), 287 (2) (3). - Issued: 13.03.2006. Made: 06.03.2006. Coming into operation: 01.04.2006. Effect: S.R. 2005/168 amended. - 8p: 30 cm. - 978-0-337-96386-5 £3.00

The Occupational Pension Schemes (Levies) (Amendment) Regulations (Northern Ireland) 2006 No. 2006/162. - Enabling power: S.I. 2005/255 (N.I. 1), arts. 103 (1) (3), 110 (1) (b), 164 (8) (a), 191 (3) (4). - Issued: 04.04.2006. Made: 28.03.2006. Coming into operation: 01.04.2006. Effect: S.R. 2005/147 amended. - 4p: 30 cm. - 978-0-337-96466-4 £3.00

The Occupational Pension Schemes (Levy Ceiling) Order (Northern Ireland) 2006 No. 2006/132. - Enabling power: S.I. 2005/255 (N.I. 1), art. 161. - Issued: 22.03.2006. Made: 15.03.2006. Coming into operation: 16.04.2006. Effect: None. - 2p: 30 cm. - 978-0-337-96435-0 £3.00

The Occupational Pension Schemes (Member-nominated Trustees and Directors) Regulations (Northern Ireland) 2006 No. 2006/148. - Enabling power: S.I. 2005/255 (N.I. 1), arts. 218 (8) (c), 219 (10), 220 (2), 287 (2) (3). - Issued: 28.03.2006. Made: 21.03.2006. Coming into operation: 06.04.2006, in accord. with art. 1 (1). Effect: S.R. 1997/160; 1999/486; 2000/262; 2003/256 & S.R. 1996/431; 2002/279 revoked. - 8p: 30 cm. - 978-0-337-96451-0 £3.00

The Occupational Pension Schemes (Modification of Schemes) Regulations (Northern Ireland) 2006 No. 2006/149. - Enabling power: S.I. 1995/3213 (N.I. 22), arts 67 (1) (b) (3) (b), 67C (7) (a) (ii), 67D (4) (5), 68 (2) (e) (5), 166 (1) to (3). - Issued: 28.03.2006. Made: 21.03.2006. Coming into operation: In accord. with art. 1 (1) Effect: 2004 c. 12 modified & S.R. 1997/160; 1999/486; 2002/109; 2005/433, 536 amended & S.R. 1997/97 revoked (06.04.2006). - 8p: 30 cm. - 978-0-337-96450-3 £3.00

The Occupational Pension Schemes (Payments to Employer) Regulations (Northern Ireland) 2006 No. 2006/161. - Enabling power: S.I. 1995/3213 (N.I. 22), arts. 37 (3) (a) (b) (g) (4) (5) (8), 76 (2) (3) (d) (8), 122 (3), 166 (1) to (3) & S.I. 2005/255 (N.I. 1), art. 228 (6) (a). - Issued: 04.04.2006. Made: 27.03.2006. Coming into operation: 06.04.2006. Effect: S.R. 1997/160; 2005/171 amended & S.R. 1997/96, 473 revoked & S.I. 1995/3213 (N.I. 22) modified. - 16p.: 30 cm. - 978-0-337-96463-3 £3.00

The Occupational Pension Schemes (Pension Protection Levies) (Transitional Period and Modification for Multi-employer Schemes) Regulations (Northern Ireland) 2006 No. 2006/84. - Enabling power: S.I. 2005/255 (N.I. 1), arts. 163 (1) (a) (3), 287 (2) (3). - Issued: 13.03.2006. Made: 06.03.2006. Coming into operation: 30.03.2006. Effect: S.I. 2005/255 (N.I. 1) amended. - 8p: 30 cm. - 978-0-337-96385-8 £3.00

The Occupational Pension Schemes (Republic of Ireland Schemes Exemption (Revocation) and Tax Exempt Schemes (Miscellaneous Amendments)) Regulations (Northern Ireland) 2006 No. 2006/65. - Enabling power: Pension Schemes (Northern Ireland) 1993, ss. 109, 164 (1) (4), 170, 176 (4), 177 (2) (3) & S.I. 1995/3213 (N.I. 22), arts. 10 (3), 27, 37 (10), 38 (3) (b), 40 (1) (2), 41 (1) (6), 47 (5), 49 (2) (3), 50 (7), 68 (2) (e) (5), 69 (6), 73 (2) (b), 75 (1) (b) (5) (6D) (b) (i) (10), 75A (1) to (4), 76 (8), 85 (1), 87 (2), 115, 116, 122 (3), 166 (1) to (3) & S.I. 2005/255 (N.I. 1), arts. 34 (1) (b), 48 (1) (b) (7) (a), 55 (5), 264, 265 (1), 287 (2) (3). - Issued: 06.03.2006. Made: 27.02.2006. Coming into operation: In accord. with reg. 1. Effect: S.R. 1996/621; 1997/40, 94, 98; 2005/92, 93, 168, 171, 173, 568, 581 amended & S.R. 2000/382 revoked. - Revoked by S.R. 2006/160 (ISBN 0337964645). - 8p.: 30 cm. - 978-0-337-96369-8 £3.00

The Occupational Pension Schemes (Trustees' Knowledge and Understanding) Regulations (Northern Ireland) 2006 No. 2006/120. - Enabling power: S.I. 2005/255 (N.I. 1), art. 226 (2) (a). - Issued: 24.03.2006. Made: 13.03.2006. Coming into operation: 06.04.2006. Effect: None. - 4p: 30 cm. - 978-0-337-96425-1 £3.00

The Occupational Pension Schemes (Winding up Procedure Requirement) Regulations (Northern Ireland) 2006 No. 2006/297. - Enabling power: European Communities Act 1972, s. 2 (2) & Pension Schemes (Northern Ireland) Act 1993, ss. 109 (1), 177 (2) to (4) & S.I. 2005/255 (N.I. 1), arts 55 (2) (h), 64 (2) (a), 287 (3). - Issued: 06.07.2005. Made: 03.07.2006. Coming into operation: 24.07.2006. Effect: S.I. 2005/255 (N.I. 1); S.R. 1997/98; 2005/93, 568 amended. - EC note: These Regs implement para. (c) of art. 16.2 of the European Union Directive 2003/41/EC on the activities and supervision of institutions for occupational retirement provision. - 4p.: 30 cm. - 978-0-337-96575-3 £3.00

The Occupational Pensions (Revaluation) Order (Northern Ireland) 2006 No. 2006/467. - Enabling power: Pension Schemes (Northern Ireland) Act 1993, sch. 2, para. 2 (1). - Issued: 28.11.2006. Made: 22.11.2006. Coming into operation: 01.01.2007. Effect: None. - 2p: 30 cm. - 978-0-337-96724-5 £3.00

The Pension Protection Fund (General and Miscellaneous Amendments) Regulations (Northern Ireland) 2006 No. 2006/155. - Enabling power: S.I. 2005/255 (N.I. 1), arts. 110 (1) (b), 135 (9) (b), 145 (6) (7), 147 (3) (4) (a) (ii) (b) (ii) (6) (a), 150 (5), 152 (1) (2) (a) to (c) (e) (f), 154 (2) (3), 155 (4), 162 (3), 164 (5) (8) (a), 287 (2) (3), sch. 6. para. 24 (1) (2). - Issued: 31.03.2006. Made: 24.03.2006. Coming into operation: 01.04.2006, 06.04.2006 in accord. with reg. 1 (1). Effect: S.R. 2005/126, 131, 149 amended. - 16p.: 30 cm. - 978-0-337-96457-2 £3.00

The Pension Protection Fund (Insolvent Partnerships) (Amendment of Insolvency Events) Order (Northern Ireland) 2006 No. 2006/529. - Enabling power: S.I. 2005/255 (N.I. 1), art. 105 (7). - Issued: 08.01.2007. Made: 19.12.2006. Coming into operation: 09.01.2007. Effect: S.I. 2005/255 (NI. 1) amended. - 2p: 30 cm. - 978-0-337-96782-5 £3.00

The Pension Protection Fund (Levy Ceiling) Regulations (Northern Ireland) 2006 No. 2006/409. - Enabling power: S.I. 2005/255 (N.I. 1), art. 160 (4). - Issued: 19.10.2006. Made: 12.10.2006. Coming into operation: 20.11.2006. Effect: None. - 2p.: 30 cm. - 978-0-337-96673-6 £3.00

The Pension Protection Fund (Pension Compensation Cap) Order (Northern Ireland) 2006 No. 2006/50. - Enabling power: S.I. 2005/255 (N.I. 1), sch. 6, paras. 26 (7), 27. - Issued: 23.02.2006. Made: 16.02.2006. Coming into operation: 01.04.2006. Effect: S.R. 2005/136 revoked. - 2p: 30 cm. - 978-0-337-96349-0 £3.00

The Pension Protection Fund (Pension Sharing) Regulations (Northern Ireland) 2006 No. 2006/282. - Enabling power: S.I. 2005/255 (N.I. 1), arts. 199, 287 (2) (3). - Issued: 03.07.2006. Made: 27.06.2006. Coming into operation: 01.08.2006. Effect: S.I. 1999/3147 (NI.11); 2005/255 (NI. 1) modified. - 4p: 30 cm. - 978-0-337-96565-4 £3.00

The Pension Protection Fund (Provision of Information) (Amendment) Regulations (Northern Ireland) 2006 No. 2006/140. - Enabling power: S.I. 2005/255 (N.I. 1), arts. 172, 185 (1), 287 (2) (3). - Issued: 27.03.2006. Made: 16.03.2006. Coming into operation: 06.04.2006. Effect: S.R. 2005/129 amended. - 4p.: 30 cm. - 978-0-337-96444-2 £3.00

The Pension Protection Fund (Reviewable Matters and Review and Reconsideration of Reviewable Matters) (Amendment) Regulations (Northern Ireland) 2006 No. 2006/156. - Enabling power: S.I. 2005/255 (N.I. 1), arts. 188 (2) (a) (4) (a), 189 (2) (5) (a). - Issued: 31.03.2006. Made: 24.03.2006. Coming into operation: 06.04.2006. Effect: S.I. 2005/255 (N.I. 1); S.R. 2005/127, 138 amended. - 4p.: 30 cm. - 978-0-337-96458-9 £3.00

The Pension Protection Fund (Risk-based Pension Protection Levy) Regulations (Northern Ireland) 2006 No. 2006/92. - Enabling power: S.I. 2005/255 (N.I. 1), arts. 158 (3) (b), 287 (2). - Issued: 15.03.2006. Made: 08.03.2006. Coming into operation: 09.03.2006. Effect: None. - 2p: 30 cm. - 978-0-337-96399-5 £3.00

The Pensions (2004 Act and 2005 Order) (PPF Payments and FAS Payments) (Consequential Provisions) Order (Northern Ireland) 2006 No. 2006/37. - Enabling power: S.I. 2005/255 (N.I. 1), arts 287 (3), 290 (2). - Issued: 22.02.2006. Made: 13.02.2006. Coming into operation: 14.02.2006. Effect: 1992 c. 7; 2002 c. 14 (N.I.); S.I. 1995/2705 (N.I. 15) amended. - 8p: 30 cm. - 978-0-337-96340-7 £3.00

The Pensions (2005 Order) (Codes of Practice) (Early Leavers, Late Payment of Contributions and Trustee Knowledge and Understanding) (Appointed Day) Order (Northern Ireland) 2006 No. 2006/231. - Enabling power: S.I. 2005/255 (N.I. 1), art. 86 (7). Appoints 30.05.2006 as the date for the coming into effect of the Pensions Regulator Code of Practice Nos 4, 5, 6, and 7. - Issued: 30.05.2006. Made: 23.05.2006. Coming into operation: -. Effect: None. - 2p.: 30 cm. - 978-0-337-96519-7 £3.00

The Pensions (2005 Order) (Codes of Practice) (Member-nominated Trustees and Directors and Internal Controls) (Appointed Day) Order (Northern Ireland) 2006 No. 2006/460. - Enabling power: S.I. 2005/255 (N.I. 1), art. 86 (7). Bringing into operation various provisions of the 2005 Order on 22.11.2006. - Issued: 24.11.2006. Made: 20.11.2006. Coming into operation: -. Effect: None. - 2p.: 30 cm. - 978-0-337-96717-7 £3.00

The Pensions (2005 Order) (Commencement No. 8 and Appointed Day) Order (Northern Ireland) 2006 No. 2006/45 (C.4). - Enabling power: S.I. 2005/255 (N.I. 1), arts. 1 (2), 86 (7). Bringing into operation various provisions of the 2005 Order on 15.02.2006. - Issued: 23.02.2006. Made: 14.02.2006. Coming into operation: -. Effect: None. - 12p: 30 cm. - 978-0-337-96344-5 £3.00

The Pensions (2005 Order) (Commencement No. 9) Order (Northern Ireland) 2006 No. 2006/95 (C.7). - Enabling power: S.I. 2005/255 (N.I. 1), art. 1 (2). Bringing into operation various provisions of the 2005 Order on 09.03.2006, 01.04.2006, 06.04.2006. - Issued: 15.03.2006. Made: 08.03.2006. Coming into operation: -. Effect: None. - 12p: 30 cm. - 978-0-337-96402-2 £3.00

The Pensions (2005 Order) (Commencement No. 10 and Savings) Order (Northern Ireland) 2006 No. 2006/352 (C.19). - Enabling power: S.I. 2005/255 (N.I. 1), arts. 1 (2) (6) (b), 287 (3). Bringing into operation various provisions of the 2005 Order in accord. with art 2. - Issued: 06.09.2006. Made: 30.08.2006. Coming into operation: -. Effect: None. - 12p: 30 cm. - 978-0-337-96623-1 £3.00

The Pensions (2005 Order) (Disclosure of Restricted Information) (Amendment of Specified Persons) Order (Northern Ireland) 2006 No. 2006/444. - Enabling power: S.I. 2005/255 (N.I. 1), arts 81 (2) (a), 182 (2) (a). - Issued: 15.11.2006. Made: 09.11.2006. Coming into operation: 07.12.2006. Effect: S.I. 2005/255 (N.I. 1) amended. - 4p.: 30 cm. - 978-0-337-96704-7 £3.00

Pensions Increase (Review) Order (Northern Ireland) 2006 No. 2006/127. - Enabling power: S.I. 1975/1503 (N.I. 15), art. 69 (1) (2) (5) (5ZA). - Issued: 04.04.2006. Made: 14.03.2006. Coming into operation: 10.04.2006. Effect: None. - 8p: 30 cm. - 978-0-337-96465-7 £3.00

The Personal Pension Schemes (Appropriate Schemes) (Amendment) Regulations (Northern Ireland) 2006 No. 2006/20. - Enabling power: Pension Schemes (Northern Ireland) Act 1993, ss. 5 (5) (a), 177 (4). - Issued: 10.02.2006. Made: 31.01.2006. Coming into operation: 06.04.2006. Effect: S.R. 1997/139 amended. - 4p: 30 cm. - 978-0-337-96326-1 £3.00

Superannuation (Agri-food and Biosciences Institute) Order (Northern Ireland) 2006 No. 2006/188. - Enabling power: S.I. 1972/1073 (N.I. 10), art. 3 (4) (7). - Issued: 22.05.2006. Made: 20.04.2006. Coming into operation: 15.05.2006. Effect: S.I. 1972/1073 (N.I. 10) amended (with effect from 01.04.2006). - 2p.: 30 cm. - 978-0-337-96509-8 £3.00

Superannuation (Chief Electoral Officer for Northern Ireland) (Amendment) Order (Northern Ireland) 2006 No. 2006/393. - Enabling power: S.I. 1972/1073 (N.I. 10), art. 3 (4) (7). - Issued: 11.10.2006. Made: 27.09.2006. Coming into operation: 25.10.2006. Effect: S.I. 2006/181 amended. - 2p.: 30 cm. - 978-0-337-96666-8 £3.00

Superannuation (Chief Electoral Officer for Northern Ireland) Order (Northern Ireland) 2006 No. 2006/181. - Enabling power: S.I. 1972/1073 (N.I. 10), art. 3 (4) (7). - Issued: 28.04.2006. Made: 05.04.2006. Coming into operation: 28.04.2006. Effect: S.I. 1972/1073 (N.I. 10) amended. - 2p.: 30 cm. - 978-0-337-96487-9 £3.00

Pesticides

Pesticides (Maximum Residue Levels in Crops, Food and Feeding Stuffs) Regulations (Northern Ireland) 2006 No. 2006/220. - Enabling power: European Communities Act 1972, s. 2 (2) & Food and Environment Protection Act 1985, s. 16 (2). - Issued: 26.05.2006. Made: 12.05.2006. Coming into operation: 30.06.2006. Effect: S.R. 2002/20, 27, 250; 2003/123, 379, 435; 2004/200, 367; 2005/51, 401 revoked. - EC note: These Regs specify new maximum residue levels in implementation of Commission Directives 2005/37/EC, 2005/46/EC, 2005/48/EC, 2005/70/EC, 2005/74/EC, 2005/76/EC, 2006/4/EC, 2006/9/EC and 2006/30/EC; and in accordance with Council Directive 90/642/EEC. - 256p.: 30 cm. - 978-0-337-96511-1 £26.00

Plant Protection Products (Amendment) Regulations (Northern Ireland) 2006 No. 2006/278. - Enabling power: European Communities Act 1972, s. 2 (2). - Issued: 29.06.2006. Made: 23.06.2006. Coming into operation: 31.07.2006. Effect: S.R. 2005/526 amended. - 8p.: 30 cm. - 978-0-337-96562-3 £3.00

Pharmacy

Pharmaceutical Society of Northern Ireland (General) (Amendment No. 2) Regulations (Northern Ireland) 2006 No. 2006/240. - Enabling power: S.I. 1976/1213 (N.I. 22), art. 5 (1) (f). - Issued: 09.06.2006. Made: 30.05.2006. Coming into operation: 01.07.2006. Effect: S.R. 1994/202 amended. - 4p: 30 cm. - 978-0-337-96532-6 £3.00

The Pharmaceutical Society of Northern Ireland (General) (Amendment) Regulations (Northern Ireland) 2006 No. 2006/207. - Enabling power: S.I. 1976/1213 (N.I. 22), art. 5. - Issued: 18.05.2006. Made: 08.05.2006. Coming into operation: 01.06.2006. Effect: S.R. 1994/202 amended. - 4p: 30 cm. - 978-0-337-96498-5 £3.00

Planning

Planning (Application of Subordinate Legislation to the Crown) Order (Northern Ireland) 2006 No. 2006/218. - Enabling power: S.I. 2006/1252 (N.I.7), art. 24. - Issued: 19.05.2006. Made: 15.05.2006. Coming into operation: 10.06.2006. Effect: S.R. 1988/5; 1992/263, 448; 1993/275, 278; 2003/444; 2004/458 amended. - 36p.: 30 cm. - 978-0-337-96506-7 *£5.50*

Planning (Claims for Compensation) Regulations (Northern Ireland) 2006 No. 2006/238. - Enabling power: S.I. 1991/1220 (N.I. 11), art. 129 (1) & S.I. 1972/1634 (N.I. 17), art. 67A. - Issued: 06.06.2006. Made: 31.05.2006. Coming into operation: 03.07.2006. Effect: None. - 2p: 30 cm. - 978-0-337-96526-5 *£3.00*

Planning (Conservation Areas) (Consultation) Regulations (Northern Ireland) 2006 No. 2006/290. - Enabling power: S.I. 1991/1220 (N.I. 11), arts 50 (3) (c), 129 (1). - Issued: 11.07.2006. Made: 30.06.2006. Coming into operation: 31.07.2006. Effect: None. - 2p: 30 cm. - 978-0-337-96573-9 *£3.00*

Planning (Development Plans) (Amendment) Regulations (Northern Ireland) 2006 No. 2006/382. - Enabling power: S.I. 1991/1220 (N.I. 11), arts. 5 (6), 6 (5), 10, 129 (1). - Issued: 22.09.2006. Made: 18.09.2006. Coming into operation: 17.10.2006. Effect: S.R. 1991/119 amended. - 2p.: 30 cm. - 978-0-337-96647-7 *£3.00*

The Planning (Electronic Communications) Order (Northern Ireland) 2006 No. 2006/276. - Enabling power: Electronic Communications Act (Northern Ireland) 2001, ss. 1, 2 (6). - Issued: 28.06.2006. Made: 22.06.2006. Coming into operation: 01.08.2006. Effect: S.I. 1991/1220 (N.I. 11) amended & S.R. 1988/5; 1991/119; 1992/263, 448; 1993/275, 278; 1999/73; 2003/444 amended. - 20p: 30 cm. - 978-0-337-96560-9 *£3.50*

The Planning (General Development) (Amendment No. 2) Order (Northern Ireland) 2006 No. 2006/348. - Enabling power: S.I. 1991/1220 (N.I. 11), art. 13. - Issued: 30.08.2006. Made: 24.08.2006. Coming into operation: 21.09.2006. Effect: S.R. 1993/278 amended. - 8p: 30 cm. - 978-0-337-96621-7 *£3.00*

Planning (General Development) (Amendment) Order (Northern Ireland) 2006 No. 2006/219. - Enabling power: S.I. 1991/1220 (N.I. 11), art. 13 & S.I. 1972/1634 (N.I. 17), art. 67B (5). - Issued: 19.05.2006. Made: 15.05.2006. Coming into operation: 10.06.2006. Effect: S.R. 1993/278 amended. - 2p: 30 cm. - 978-0-337-96507-4 *£3.00*

The Planning (Inquiry Procedure) (Amendment) Rules (Northern Ireland) 2006 No. 2006/259. - Enabling power: S.I. 1991/1220 (N.I. 11), art. 123 (2). - Issued: 16.06.2006. Made: 12.06.2006. Coming into operation: 19.06.2006. Effect: S.R. 2006/213 amended. - 2p.: 30 cm. - 978-0-337-96548-7 *£3.00*

The Planning (Inquiry Procedure) Rules (Northern Ireland) 2006 No. 2006/213. - Enabling power: S.I. 1991/1220 (N.I. 11), art. 123 (2). - Issued: 17.05.2006. Made: 11.05.2006. Coming into operation: 10.06.2006. Effect: None. - 16p.: 30 cm. - 978-0-337-96504-3 *£3.00*

The Planning (Issue of Certificate) Rules (Northern Ireland) 2006 No. 2006/266. - Enabling power: S.I. 1991/1220 (N.I. 11), art. 123B (3). - Issued: 22.06.2006. Made: 16.06.2006. Laid: 21.06.2006. Coming into operation: 17.07.2006. Effect: None. - 4p.: 30 cm. - 978-0-337-96556-2 *£3.00*

The Planning (National Security Directions and Appointed Representatives) (Amendment) Rules (Northern Ireland) 2006 No. 2006/285. - Enabling power: S.I. 1991/1220 (N.I. 11), art. 123A (6). - Issued: 04.07.2006. Made: 28.06.2006. Coming into operation: 24.07.2006. Effect: S.R. 2006/215 amended. - 2p: 30 cm. - 978-0-337-96567-8 *£3.00*

The Planning (National Security Directions and Appointed Representatives) Rules (Northern Ireland) 2006 No. 2006/215. - Enabling power: S.I. 1991/1220 (N.I. 11), art. 123A (6). - Issued: 23.05.2006. Made: 16.05.2006. Coming into operation: 10.06.2006. Effect: None. - 8p: 30 cm. - 978-0-337-96514-2 *£3.00*

The Planning Reform (2006 Order) (Commencement No.1) Order (Northern Ireland) 2006 No. 2006/222 (C.12). - Enabling power: S.I. 2006/1252 (N.I.7), art. 1 (3). Bringing into operation various provisions of the 2006 Order on 18.05.2006. - Issued: 22.05.2006. Made: 17.05.2006. Coming into operation: -. Effect: None. - 2p: 30 cm. - 978-0-337-96512-8 *£3.00*

The Planning Reform (2006 Order) (Commencement No.2) Order (Northern Ireland) 2006 No. 2006/381 (C.22). - Enabling power: S.I. 2006/1252 (N.I.7), art. 1 (3). Bringing into operation various provisions of the 2006 Order on 17.10.2006. - Issued: 22.09.2006. Made: 18.09.2006. Coming into operation: -. Effect: None. - 2p: 30 cm. - 978-0-337-96646-0 *£3.00*

Planning Appeals Commission procedures

Planning Appeals Commission (Decisions on Appeals and Making of Reports) (No. 2) Rules (Northern Ireland) 2006 No. 2006/233. - Enabling power: S.I. 1991/1220 (N.I.11), art. 111 (5) (5A) (5B). - Issued: 30.05.2006. Made: 24.05.2006. Coming into operation: 14.06.2006. Effect: S.R. 2003/254; 2006/225 revoked. - 4p: 30 cm. - 978-0-337-96521-0 *£3.00*

Planning Appeals Commission (Decisions on Appeals and Making of Reports) Rules (Northern Ireland) 2006 No. 2006/225. - Enabling power: S.I.1991/1220 (N.I.11), art. 111 (5) (5A) (5B). - Issued: 25.05.2006. Made: 19.05.2006. Coming into operation: 09.06.2006. Effect: S.R. 2003/254 revoked. - Revoked by S.I. 2006/233 (ISBN 0337965218). - 4p: 30 cm. - 978-0-337-96517-3 *£3.00*

Plant health

The Plant Health (Amendment No. 2) Order (Northern Ireland) 2006 No. 2006/435. - Enabling power: Plant Health Act (Northern Ireland) 1967, ss. 2, 3, 4 (1). - Issued: 08.11.2006. Made: 02.11.2006. Coming into operation: 01.12.2006. Effect: S.R. 2006/82 amended. - EC note: Implements Commission Directive 2006/35/EC amending Annexes I to IV to Council Directive 2000/29/EC; Commission Decision 2006/473/EC recognising certain third countries and areas as being free from Xanthomonas campestris (all strains pathogenic to Citrus), Cercospora angolensis Carv. et Mendes and Guignardia citricarpa Kiely (all strains pathogenic to Citrus); and Commission Decision 2006/464/EC on provisional emergency measures to prevent the introduction into and the spread within the Community of Dryocosmus kuriphilus Yasumatsu. - 8p: 30 cm. - 978-0-337-96696-5 £3.00

Plant Health (Amendment) Order (Northern Ireland) 2006 No. 2006/165. - Enabling power: Plant Health Act (Northern Ireland) 1967, ss. 2, 3 (1), 4 (1). - Issued: 04.04.2006. Made: 29.03.2006. Coming into operation: 01.05.2006. Effect: S.R. 2006/82 amended. - 4p.: 30 cm. - 978-0-337-96467-1 £3.00

The Plant Health Order (Northern Ireland) 2006 No. 2006/82. - Enabling power: Plant Health Act (Northern Ireland) 1967, ss. 2, 3, 4 (1). - Issued: 10.04.2006. Made: 06.03.2006. Coming into operation: 31.03.2006. Effect: S.R. 2001/188 amended & S.R. 1993/256; 1994/28; 1995/164, 250, 494; 1996/204, 249; 1997/110, 397; 1998/16, 146, 315; 1999/24; 2000/126; 2001/437; 2002/273; 2003/235, 458; 2004/415; 2005/204 revoked. - EC note: This Order implements Council Directive 2002/89/EC (amending Directive 2000/29/EC); Commission Directives 2004/103/EC; 2004/105/EC; 2005/16/EC; 2005/17/EC and Commission Decisions 2005/260/EC and 2005/870/EC. - 132p.: 30 cm. - 978-0-337-96388-9 £17.50

The Plant Health (Wood and Bark) Order (Northern Ireland) 2006 No. 2006/66. - Enabling power: Plant Health Act (Northern Ireland) 1967, ss. 2, 3, 3A, 3B, 4(1). - Issued: 28.03.2006. Made: 27.02.2006. Coming into operation: 31.03.2006. Effect: S.R. 1993/460; 1996/18; 1997/11; 1999/389; 2001/401; 2002/285 revoked. - EC note: This Order implements Commission Directive 2002/36/EC, amending certain annexes to Council Directive 2000/29/EC; Council Directive 2002/89/EC, amending Directive 2000/29/EC; Commission Decision 2004/278/EC; Commission Directive 2004/102/EC; Commission Directive 2004/103; Commission Directive 2004/105/EC; Council Directive 2005/15/EC; Commission Directive 2005/17/EC; Commission Decision 2005/260/EC. - 60p: 30 cm. - 978-0-337-96379-7 £9.00

The Potatoes Originating in Egypt (Amendment No.2) Regulations (Northern Ireland) 2006 No. 2006/512. - Enabling power: European Communities Act 1972, s. 2 (2). - Issued: 15.12.2006. Made: 08.12.2006. Coming into operation: 01.01.2007. Effect: S.R. 2004/183 amended & S.R. 2006/107 revoked. - EC note: These regulations insert , into the definition of the Decision, Commission Decision 2006/749/EC. - 4p.: 30 cm. - 978-0-337-96764-1 £3.00

The Potatoes Originating in Egypt (Amendment) Regulations (Northern Ireland) 2006 No. 2006/107. - Enabling power: European Communities Act 1972, s. 2 (2). - Issued: 23.03.2006. Made: 10.03.2006. Coming into operation: 10.04.2006. Effect: S.R. 2004/183 amended & S.R. 2005/460 revoked. - EC note: These Regulations insert into the definition of the Decision, Commission Decision 2005/840/EC which amends and corrects the Decision (regulation 2). Decision 2005/840/EC renews the framework within which potatoes may be imported from Egypt into the territory of the European Community during the 2005/2006 season. - 4p: 30 cm. - 978-0-337-96417-6 £3.00

Police

Police (Recruitment) (Amendment) Regulations (Northern Ireland) 2006 No. 2006/69. - Enabling power: Police (Northern Ireland) Act 1998, ss. 25, 26 & Police (Northern Ireland) Act 2000, ss. 41, 43, 44. - Issued: 08.03.2006. Made: 23.02.2006. Coming into operation: 31.03.2006. Effect: S.R. 2001/140 amended. - 2p.: 30 cm. - 978-0-337-96372-8 £3.00

Police Service of Northern Ireland and Police Service of Northern Ireland Reserve (Full-Time) (Severance) Amendment Regulations 2006 No. 2006/19. - Enabling power: Police (Northern Ireland) 1998, ss. 25 (2) (k), 26. - Issued: 22.02.2005. Made: 23.01.2006. Laid: 02.02.2006. Coming into operation: 27.02.2006. Effect: S.R. 2003/60 amended. - 4p: 30 cm. - 978-0-337-96342-1 £3.00

Police Service of Northern Ireland and Police Service of Northern Ireland Reserve (Injury Benefit) Regulations 2006 No. 2006/268. - Enabling power: Police (Northern Ireland) Act 1998, ss, 25. 26. - Issued: 28.03.2007. Made: 20.06.2006. Coming into operation: 25.07.2006. Effect: S.R. 1988/374; 2006/123 amended & S.R. 1988/376 revoked. - This S.R. has been printed in substitution of the S.R. of the same number and ISBN (originally published 04.07.2006) and is being issued free of charge to all known recipients of that Statutory Rule. - 36p: 30 cm. - 978-0-337-96569-2 £5.50

The Police Service of Northern Ireland Pensions (Amendment No. 2) Regulations 2006 No. 2006/152. - Enabling power: Police (Northern Ireland) Act 1998, s. 25. - Issued: 30.03.2006. Made: 23.03.2006. Coming into operation: 05.04.2006. Effect: S.I. 1988/374; 1993/249 amended. - 12p: 30 cm. - 978-0-337-96455-8 £3.00

The Police Service of Northern Ireland Pensions (Amendment) Regulations 2006 No. 2006/123. - Enabling power: Police (Northern Ireland) Act 1998, s. 25. - Issued: 24.03.2006. Made: 06.03.2006. Coming into operation: 01.04.2006. Effect: S.R. 1988/374, 379 amended. - 16p: 30 cm. - 978-0-337-96426-8 £3.00

The Police Service of Northern Ireland Pensions (Pension Sharing) Regulations 2006 No. 2006/122. - Enabling power: Police (Northern Ireland) Act 1998, s. 25. - Issued: 23.03.2006. Made: 06.03.2006. Coming into operation: 31.03.2006. Effect: S.R. 1988/374, 379; 1993/249; 1994/197 amended. - 16p: 30 cm. - 978-0-337-96427-5 £3.00

The Police Service of Northern Ireland Reserve (Full-time) Severance Regulations 2006 No. 2006/313. - Enabling power: Police (Northern Ireland) Act 1998, s. 26 (1) (2) (g) (5). - Issued: 27.07.2006. Made: 18.07.2006. Laid: 24.07.2006. Coming into operation: 17.08.2006. Effect: S.R. 1988/375 modified. - 16p.: 30 cm. - 978-0-337-96592-0 £3.00

Public health

The Producer Responsibility Obligations (Packaging Waste) Regulations (Northern Ireland) 2006 No. 2006/356. - Enabling power: European Communities Act 1972, s. 2 (2) & S.I. 1998/1762 (N.I. 16), arts. 3-5, 7(2). - Issued: 11.09.2006. Made: 04.09.2006. Coming into operation: 09.10.2006. Effect: S.R. 1999/115, 496; 2002/239; 2004/106; 2005/329 revoked. - EC note: These Regulations impose on producers the obligation to recover and recycle packaging waste, and related obligations, in order for the United Kingdom to attain the recovery and recycling targets set out in article 6 (1) of Council Directive 94/62/EC on packaging and packaging waste as amended by Council Regulation (EC) no. 1882/2003, Council Directive 2004/12/EC and Council Directive 2005/20/EC. - 56p.: 30 cm. - 978-0-337-96627-9 £7.50

Radioactive substances

The Radioactive Contaminated Land Regulations (Northern Ireland) 2006 No. 2006/345. - Enabling power: European Communities Act 1972, s. 2 (2). - Issued: 29.08.2006. Made: 22.08.2006. Coming into operation: 22.09.2006. Effect: None. - EC note: These Regs implement arts 48, 53 of Council Directive 96/29/Euratom laying down basic safety standards for the protection of the health of workers and the general public against the dangers arising from ionising radiation. - 8p.: 30 cm. - 978-0-337-96616-3 £3.00

Rates

The Housing Benefit (Amendment) Regulations (Northern Ireland) 2006 No. 2006/462. - Enabling power: Social Security Administration (Northern Ireland) Act 1992, ss. 5 (1) (a) (k), 165 (1) (4). - Issued: 24.11.2006. Made: 21.11.2006. Coming into operation: 20.12.2006. Effect: S.R. 2006/405, 406 amended. - 4p.: 30 cm. - 978-0-337-96719-1 £3.00

The Housing Benefit (Consequential Provisions) (Amendment) Regulations (Northern Ireland) 2006 No. 2006/449. - Enabling power: Social Security Contributions and Benefits (Northern Ireland) Act 1992, ss. 122 (1) (d), 132A (3), 171 (1) (3) (4). - Issued: 16.11.2006. Made: 10.11.2006. Coming into operation: 19.11.2006. Effect: S.R. 2006/407 amended. - This Statutory Rule is made in consequence of a defect in S.R. 2006 No. 407 (ISBN 0337966761) and is being issued free of charge to all known recipients of that Statutory Rule. - 2p.: 30 cm. - 978-0-337-96705-4 £3.00

The Housing Benefit (Consequential Provisions) Regulations (Northern Ireland) 2006 No. 2006/407. - Enabling power: Social Security Contributions and Benefits (Northern Ireland) Act 1992, ss. 122 (1) (d), 129 (2) (3) (4), 130, 131 (1) (2) (6), 132, 132A (3) (4) (a), 133 (2), 171 (1) (3) to (5) & Social Security Administration (Northern Ireland) Act 1992, ss. 1 (1) (1C), 5 (1) (a) to (d), (g) to (t) (5), 73, 107, 119A, 126 (4) (5), 165 (1) (4) to (6) & S.I. 1998/1506 (N.I. 10), arts 34, 74 (1) (3). - Issued: 25.10.2006. Made: 12.10.2006. Coming into operation: 20.11.2006. Effect: 153 amended & 96 revoked. - 56p.: 30 cm. - 978-0-337-96676-7 £7.50

The Housing Benefit (Electronic Communications) Order (Northern Ireland) 2006 No. 2006/463. - Enabling power: Electronic Communications Act (Northern Ireland) 2001, ss. 1, 2. - Issued: 27.11.2006. Made: 21.11.2006. Coming into operation: 20.12.2006. Effect: S.R. 2006/405, 406 amended. - 8p.: 30 cm. - 978-0-337-96720-7 £3.00

The Housing Benefit (Persons who have attained the qualifying age for state pension credit) Regulations (Northern Ireland) 2006 No. 2006/406. - Enabling power: Social Security Contributions and Benefits (Northern Ireland) Act 1992, ss. 122 (1) (d), 129 (2) (3) (4), 130, 131 (1) (2) (6), 132, 132A (3) (4) (a), 133, 171 (1) (3) to (5) & Social Security Administration (Northern Ireland) Act 1992, ss. 1 (1) (1C), 5 (1) (a) to (d) (g) to (t) (5), 73, 107, 119A, 126 (4) (5), 165 (1) & (4) to (6) & S.I. 1998/1506 (N.I.10), arts 34, 74 (1) (3). - Issued: 25.10.2005. Made: 12.10.2006. Coming into operation: 20.11.2006. Effect: None. - 124p.: 30 cm. - 978-0-337-96675-0 £17.50

The Housing Benefit Regulations (Northern Ireland) 2006 No. 2006/405. - Enabling power: Social Security Contributions and Benefits (Northern Ireland) Act 1992, ss. 122 (1) (d), 129 (2) (3) (4), 130, 131 (1) (2) (6), 132, 133, 171 (1) (3) to (5) & Social Security Administration (Northern Ireland) Act 1992, ss. 1 (1) (1C), 5 (1) (a) to (d) (g) to (t) (5), 73, 107, 119A, 126(4) (5) 165 (1) (4) to (6) & S.I. 1998/1506 (N.I.10), arts 34, 74 (1) (3). - Issued: 25.10.2005. Made: 12.10.2006. Coming into operation: 20.11.2006. Effect: None. - 152p.: 30 cm. - 978-0-337-96674-3 £22.00

Rates (Amendment) (2006 Order) (Commencement No. 1) Order (Northern Ireland) 2006 No. 2006/464 (C.28). - Enabling power: S.I. 2006/2954 (N.I.18), art. 1 (3). Bringing into operation various provisions of the 2006 Order in accordance with art. 2. - Issued: 27.11.2006. Made: 22.11.2006. Coming into operation: -. Effect: None. - 8p.: 30 cm. - 978-0-337-96723-8 £3.00

The Rates (Automatic Telling Machines) (Designation of Rural Areas) Order (Northern Ireland) 2006 No. 2006/516. - Enabling power: S.I. 1977/2157 (N.I. 28), art. 42 (1G). - Issued: 19.12.2006. Made: 13.12.2006. Coming into operation: 01.04.2007. Effect: None. - 4p.: 30 cm. - 978-0-337-96766-5 £3.00

Rates (Capital Values, etc.) (2006 Order) (Commencement) Order (Northern Ireland) 2006 No. 2006/146 (C.9). - Enabling power: S.I. 2006/611 (N.I. 4), art. 1 (3). Bringing into operation various provisions of the 2006 Order on 01.04.2006. - Issued: 27.03.2006. Made: 21.03.2006. Coming into operation: -. Effect: None. - 2p: 30 cm. - 978-0-337-96449-7 £3.00

The Rates (Making and Levying of Different Rates) Regulations (Northern Ireland) 2006 No. 2006/498. - Enabling power: S.I. 1977/2157 (N.I. 28), art. 6 (6). - Issued: 08.12.2006. Made: 05.12.2006. Coming into operation: 28.12.2006. Effect: S.R. 1997/50; 2002/409 revoked with savings. - 4p.: 30 cm. - 978-0-337-96748-1 £3.00

Rates (Regional Rates) Order (Northern Ireland) 2006 No. 2006/7. - Enabling power: S.I. 1977/2157 (N.I. 28), arts 7 (1), 27 (4). - Issued: 20.01.2006. Made: 16.01.2006. Coming into operation: 01.04.2006 Effect: None. - 2p: 30 cm. - 978-0-337-96316-2 £3.00

Rates (Transitional Provisions) Order (Northern Ireland) 2006 No. 2006/468. - Enabling power: S.I. 2006/2954 (N.I. 18), art. 40 (1). - Issued: 29.11.2006. Made: 23.11.2006. Coming into operation: 01.12.2006 Effect: None. - 4p: 30 cm. - 978-0-337-96728-3 £3.00

The Social Security Benefits Up-rating Order (Northern Ireland) 2006 No. 2006/109. - Enabling power: Social Security Administration (Northern Ireland) Act 1992, ss. 132, 165 (1) (4) (5). - Issued: 28.03.2006. Made: 10.03.2006. Coming into operation: In accord. with art. 1. Effect: 1992 c. 7; 1993 c. 49; S.R. 1978/105; 1987/30, 459, 460, 461; 1992/32; 1994/461; 1995/35; 1996/198; 2002/380; 2003/28, 197 amended & S.R. 2005/82 revoked (13.04.2006). - 40p: 30 cm. - 978-0-337-96413-8 £6.50

The Social Security (Bulgaria and Romania) (Amendment) Regulations (Northern Ireland) 2006 No. 2006/523. - Enabling power: Social Security Contributions and Benefits (Northern Ireland) Act 1992, ss. 122 (1) (a) (d), 131 (1) (2), 133 (2), 171 (1) (3); S.I. 1995/2705 (N.I. 15), art. 6 (5) (12), sch. 1, para. 11 and State Pension Credit Act (Northern Ireland) 2002, ss. 1 (5) (a), 19 (1) (3). - Issued: 21.12.2006. Made: 14.12.2006. Coming into operation: 01.01.2007. Effect: S.R. 1987/459; 1996/198; 2003/28; 2006/405, 406 amended. - 4p.: 30 cm. - 978-0-337-96773-3 £3.00

The Social Security (Deferral of Retirement Pensions, Shared Additional Pension and Graduated Retirement Benefit) (Miscellaneous Provisions) Regulations (Northern Ireland) 2006 No. 2006/104. - Enabling power: Social Security Contributions and Benefits (Northern Ireland) Act 1992, ss. 62 (1) (a) (c), 132 (4) (a) (b), 171 (1) (3) to (5), sch. 5, paras A1 (1) (3), 3C (2) (4), sch. 5A, para. 1 (1) (3) & Social Security Administration (Northern Ireland) Act 1992, ss. 5 (1) (j), 165 (1) (4) (6) & S.I. 1998/1506 (N.I. 10), arts. 10, 11 (3) (6), 12 (1), 18 (1), 74 (1) & Child Support, Pensions and Social Security Act (Northern Ireland) 2000, sch. 7, para. 3 (1), 4 (3) (5), 20 (1) (3) & State Pension Credit Act (Northern Ireland) 2002, ss. 15 (6) (a) (b), 19 (1) to (3) & S.I. 2005/255 (N.I. 1), sch. 9, para. 22. - Issued: 22.03.2006. Made: 09.03.2006. Coming into operation: 06.04.2006. Effect: S.R. 1987/461, 465; 1999/162; 2001/213; 2003/28; 2005/121, 123 amended. - 16p: 30 cm. - 978-0-337-96410-7 £3.00

The Social Security (Lebanon) (Amendment) Regulations (Northern Ireland) 2006 No. 2006/320. - Enabling power: Social Security Contributions and Benefits (Northern Ireland) Act 1992, ss. 122 (1) (a) (d), 131 (1) (2), 133 (2), 171 (1) (3) (4) & S.I. 1995/2705 (N.I. 15), arts. 6 (5) (12), 36 (2), sch. 1, para. 11 & State Pension Credit Act (Northern Ireland) 2002, ss. 1 (5) (a), 19 (1) (2) (a) (3). - Issued: 02.08.2006. Made: 27.07.2006. Coming into operation: 28.07.2006. Effect: S.R. 1987/459, 461; 1996/198; 2003/28 amended. - These Regulations shall cease to have effect on 30th January 2007. - 4p.: 30 cm. - 978-0-337-96599-9 £3.00

The Social Security (Miscellaneous Amendments No. 4) Regulations (Northern Ireland) 2006 No. 2006/359. - Enabling power: Social Security Contributions and Benefits (Northern Ireland) Act 1992, ss. 30A (2A), 30C (4), 30E (1), 47 (6), 64 (1), 68 (4), 71 (6), 86A (1), 122 (1) (a) (d), 123 (1) (e), 129 (4), 131 (1), 132 (3) (4) (b) (c), 132A (3), 133 (2) (h), 167D, 171(1) (3) to (5), sch. 7, para. 2 (3) & Social Security Administration (Northern Ireland) Act 1992, ss. 5 (1) (m), 165 (1) (4) (5) & S.I. 1994/1898 (N.I. 12), art. 6 & S.I. 1995/2705 (N.I. 15), arts. 6 (5), 8 (4), 9 (2) (a) (4), 14 (2) (4) (b) (c), 36 (2), sch. 1, paras 1 (2) (b), 8, 8A (1), 12, 16 (1) & Child Support, Pensions and Social Security Act (Northern Ireland) 2000, sch. 7, paras 4 (5), 20 (1) (3) & State Pension Credit Act (Northern Ireland) 2002, ss. 1 (5) (a), 2 (3) (b), 7 (4), 15 (6) (a) (b), 17 (2) (a), 19 (1) to (3). - Issued: 19.09.2006. Made: 07.09.2006. Coming into operation: In accord. with reg. 1. Effect: S.R. 1979/243; 1984/92, 317; 1987/459, 461; 1990/131, 136; 1992/20, 32; 1993/165, 373; 1994/327, 335, 461, 485; 1995/35, 41; 1996/198, 199; 1997/165, 412; 2000/4; 2002/132, 299; 2003/28; 2005/458; 2006/150, 234 amended and S.R. 2005/415 revoked (09.10.2006). - 20p: 30 cm. - 978-0-337-96633-0 *£3.50*

The Social Security (Miscellaneous Amendments No. 5) Regulations (Northern Ireland) 2006 No. 2006/510. - Enabling power: Social Security Contributions and Benefits (Northern Ireland) Act 1992, ss. 122 (1) (a) (d), 131 (1), 133 (2) (h), 171 (1) (3) to (5); S.I. 1995/2705 (N.I. 15), arts 6 (5), 36 (2) and State Pension Credit Act (Northern Ireland) 2002, s. 2 (3) (b), 19 (1) (3). - Issued: 14.12.2006. Made: 08.12.2006. Coming into operation: 08.01.2007. Effect: S.R. 1987/459; 1996/198; 2003/28; 2006/405, 406 amended. - 4p.: 30 cm. - 978-0-337-96761-0 *£3.00*

The Social Security (Miscellaneous Amendments) Regulations (Northern Ireland) 2006 No. 2006/97. - Enabling power: Social Security Contributions and Benefits (Northern Ireland) Act 1992, ss.122 (1) (a) (d), 123 (1) (e), 131 (1), 132 (4) (a) (b), 132A (3), 134 (1) (a), 171 (1) (3) (4) & Social Security Administration (Northern Ireland) Act 1992, ss. 5 (1) (l), 165(1) (4) (5) & S.I. 1995/2705 (N.I. 15), arts. 14(4)(a) (b), 36(2) & State Pension Credit Act (Northern Ireland) 2002, ss. 2 (3) (b) (9), 13 (1) (a), 15 (1) (j), 19 (1) (2) (a) (3). - Issued: 21.03.2006. Made: 09.03.2006. Coming into operation: In accord. with reg. 1. Effect: S.R. 1987/459, 461; 1996/198; 2003/28; 2005/506 amended. - 8p: 30 cm. - 978-0-337-96403-9 *£3.00*

The Social Security (Persons from Abroad) (Amendment No. 2) Regulations (Northern Ireland) 2006 No. 2006/379. - Enabling power: Social Security Contributions and Benefits (Northern Ireland) Act 1992, ss. 122 (1) (a) (d), 131 (1) (2), 133 (2), 171 (1) (3) & S.I. 1995/2705 (N.I. 15), arts 6 (5) (12), sch. 1, para. 11 & State Pension Credit Act (Northern Ireland) 2002, ss. 1 (5) (a), 19 (1) (3). - Issued: 21.09.2006. Made: 15.09.2006. Coming into operation: 09.10.2006. Effect: S.R. 1987/459, 461; 1996/198; 2003/28; amended. - 4p: 30 cm. - 978-0-337-96645-3 *£3.00*

The Social Security (Persons from Abroad) (Amendment) Regulations (Northern Ireland) 2006 No. 2006/178. - Enabling power: Social Security Contributions and Benefits (Northern Ireland) Act 1992, ss. 122 (1) (a) (d), 131 (1) (2), 133 (2), 134 (1) (a), 171 (1) (3) (4) & S.I. 1995/2705 (N.I. 15), arts 6 (5) (12), 36 (2), sch. 1, para. 11 & State Pension Credit Act (Northern Ireland) 2002, ss. 1 (5) (a), 19 (1) (2) (a) (3). - Issued: 10.04.2006. Made: 03.04.2006. Coming into operation: 30.04.2006. Effect: S.R. 1987/459, 461; 1996/198; 2003/28; 2005/506 amended & S.R. 1994/266; 1996/375; 2000/125; 2004/197 revoked. - EC note: These Regulations amend the income-related benefits regulations and the Social Fund regulations in consequence of the Council Directive 2004/38/EC the provisions of which are to be transposed by the Immigration (European Economic Area) Regulations 2006. - 12p: 30 cm. - 978-0-337-96475-6 *£3.00*

The Social Security (Students and Income-related Benefits) (Amendment) Regulations (Northern Ireland) 2006 No. 2006/301. - Enabling power: Social Security Contributions and Benefits (Northern Ireland) Act 1992, ss. 122 (1) (a) (d), 132 (3) (4) (b), 171 (1) (3) (4) & S.I. 1995/2705 (N.I. 15), arts 14 (1) (4) (b), 36 (2). - Issued: 10.07.2006. Made: 04.07.2006. Coming into operation: In accord. with reg. 1. Effect: S.R. 1987/459, 461; 1996/198 amended & S.R. 2005/332 revoked. - 8p.: 30 cm. - 978-0-337-96583-8 *£3.00*

The Social Security (Young Persons) (Amendment) Regulations (Northern Ireland) 2006 No. 2006/128. - Enabling power: Social Security Contributions and Benefits (Northern Ireland) Act 1992, ss. 122 (1) (a) (d), 123 (1) (d) (e), 131 (1), 133 (2) (e) (f) (i), 171 (1) (3) to (5); S.I. 1995/2705 (N.I. 15), arts 5 (1) (f) (iii), 5A (1) (e) (ii), 6 (5), 36 (1) (2), Sch. 1, paras 8, 8A (1), 9C, 14; State Pension Credit Act (Northern Ireland) 2002, ss. 1 (5) (b), 2 (3) (b), 15 (3) (6), 17 (2), 19 (1) (2) (a) (3). - Issued: 24.03.2006. Made: 13.03.2006. Coming into operation: In accord. with reg. 1. Effect: S.R. 1987/459, 461; 1996/198; 2003/28 amended. - 8p.: 30 cm. - 978-0-337-96430-5 *£3.00*

Recovery of health service charges

The Recovery of Health Services Charges (2006 Order) (Commencement) Order (Northern Ireland) 2006 No. 2006/484 (C.30). - Enabling power: S.I. 2006/1944 (N.I. 13), art. 1 (2). Bringing into operation various provisions of the 2006 Order on 04.12.2006; 29.01.2007. - Issued: 04.12.2006. Made: 28.11.2006. Coming into operation: -. Effect: None. - 2p: 30 cm. - 978-0-337-96735-1 *£3.00*

Roads

The Motorways Traffic (Amendment) Regulations (Northern Ireland) 2006 No. 2006/83. - Enabling power: S.I. 1993/3160 (N.I.15), art. 20 (3). - Issued: 15.03.2006. Made: 02.03.2006. Coming into operation: 13.04.2006. Effect: S.R. 1984/160 amended. - 4p.: 30 cm. - 978-0-337-96398-8 *£3.00*

Roads: Street works

The Street Works (Reinstatement) (Amendment) Regulations (Northern Ireland) 2006 No. 2006/412. - Enabling power: S.I. 1995/3210 (N.I. 19), arts 31 (1) (2), 59 (2). - Issued: 25.10.2005. Made: 17.10.2006. Coming into operation: 27.11.2006. Effect: S.R. 1998/425 amended. - 4p.: 30 cm. - 978-0-337-96686-6 £3.00

Road traffic

The Road Traffic (Health Services Charges) (Amendment) Regulations (Northern Ireland) 2006 No. 2006/67. - Enabling power: Health and Personal Social Services Act (Northern Ireland) 2001, ss. 25 (2) (4), 37, 57 (1) (3). - Issued: 06.03.2006. Made: 27.02.2006. Coming into operation: 01.04.2006. Effect: S.R. 2001/125 amended. - 2p.: 30 cm. - 978-0-337-96371-1 £3.00

Road traffic and vehicles

The Goods Vehicles (Testing) (Amendment) Regulations (Northern Ireland) 2006 No. 2006/495. - Enabling power: S.I. 1995/2994 (N.I. 18), arts 67 (1) (m), 72 (3), 110 (2). - Issued: 12.12.2006. Made: 04.12.2006. Coming into operation: 16.01.2007. Effect: S.R. 2003/304 amended. - 2p.: 30 cm. - 978-0-337-96756-6 £3.00

The Immobilisation and Release of Vehicles Charge) Regulations (Northern Ireland) 2006 No. 2006/339. - Enabling power: S.I. 2005/1964 (N.I. 14), art. 20 (2) (c). - Issued: 22.08.2006. Made: 16.08.2006. Coming into operation: 30.10.2006. Effect: None. - 2p.: 30 cm. - 978-0-337-96611-8 £3.00

The Immobilisation and Removal of Vehicles (Prescribed Conditions) Regulations (Northern Ireland) 2006 No. 2006/479. - Enabling power: S.I. 2005/1964 (N.I. 14), arts. 18 (1) (b), 21 (1) (b). - Issued: 29.11.2006. Made: 24.11.2006. Coming into operation: 01.01.2007. Effect: None. - 2p.: 30 cm. - 978-0-337-96729-0 £3.00

The Motor Hackney Carriages (Belfast) (Amendment) By-Laws (Northern Ireland) 2006 No. 2006/284. - Enabling power: S.I. 1981/154 (N.I. 1), art. 65 (1) (2). - Issued: 04.07.2006. Made: 28.06.2006. Coming into operation: 27.07.2006. Effect: By-laws relating to motor hackney carriages standing or plying for hire made by the Council of the County Borough of Belfast on 4th June 1951 (the relevant amending byelaws are S.R. 1984/298; 2004/441), amended & S.R. 2004/441 revoked. - 4p.: 30 cm. - 978-0-337-96568-5 £3.00

The Motor Hackney Carriages (Belfast) (Amendment No. 2) By-Laws (Northern Ireland) 2006 No. 2006/450. - Enabling power: S.I. 1981/154 (N.I. 1), art. 65 (1) (2). - Issued: 16.11.2006. Made: 10.11.2006. Coming into operation: 18.11.2006. Effect: By-laws relating to Motor Hackney Carriages standing or plying for hire made by the Council of the County Borough of Belfast on 04.06.1951 amended. - 2p.: 30 cm. - 978-0-337-96706-1 £3.00

The Motor Vehicles (Approval) (Amendment) Regulations (Northern Ireland) 2006 No. 2006/343. - Enabling power: S.I. 1981/154 (N.I. 1), arts. 31A (1), 31D (1), 218 (1). - Issued: 31.08.2006. Made: 18.08.2006. Coming into operation: 04.10.2006. Effect: S.R. 2001/172 amended. - 60p.: 30 cm. - 978-0-337-96618-7 £9.00

The Motor Vehicles (Construction and Use) (Amendment No. 2) Regulations (Northern Ireland) 2006 No. 2006/246. - Enabling power: S.I. 1995/2994 (N.I. 18), arts 55 (1), 110 (2). - Issued: 14.06.2006. Made: 06.06.2006. Coming into operation: 19.07.2006. Effect: S.R. 1999/454 amended. - EC note: Modifies the 1999 regulations so that compliance with Directive 2001/85/EC, is offered as an alternative as it requires that the United Kingdom shall not refuse or prohibit sale or entry into service of a vehicle, or of bodywork intended to be part of the vehicle which may be type approved separately, if the requirements of the Directive and its Annexes are met, and if such refusal or prohibition of sale is on grounds relating to that Directive. - 4p.: 30 cm. - 978-0-337-96540-1 £3.00

The Motor Vehicles (Construction and Use) (Amendment No. 3) Regulations (Northern Ireland) 2006 No. 2006/328. - Enabling power: S.I. 1995/2994 (N.I. 18), arts 55 (1) (2) (6), 110 (2). - Issued: 08.08.2006. Made: 02.08.2006. Coming into operation: 01.10.2006. Effect: S.R. 1999/454 amended and S.R. 2005/402 revoked. - 4p.: 30 cm. - 978-0-337-96601-9 £3.00

The Motor Vehicles (Construction and Use) (Amendment) Regulations (Northern Ireland) 2006 No. 2006/32. - Enabling power: S.I. 1995/2994 (N.I. 18), arts. 55 (1) (2) (6), 110 (2). - Issued: 15.02.2006. Made: 08.02.2006. Coming into operation: 04.05.2006. Effect: S.R. 1999/454 amended. - 4p.: 30 cm. - 978-0-337-96334-6 £3.00

The Motor Vehicles (Taxi Drivers' Licences) (Fees) (Amendment) Regulations (Northern Ireland) 2006 No. 2006/408. - Enabling power: S.I. 1981/154 (N.I. 1), arts. 79A (2), 218 (1). - Issued: 19.10.2006. Made: 12.10.2006. Coming into operation: 24.11.2006. Effect: S.R. 1991/454 amended & S.R. 1996/304 revoked. - 4p.: 30 cm. - 978-0-337-96672-9 £3.00

The Motor Vehicle Testing (Amendment) Regulations (Northern Ireland) 2006 No. 2006/494. - Enabling power: S.I. 1995/2994 (N. I. 18), arts 63 (5), 72 (1) (2), 110 (2). - Issued: 12.12.2006. Made: 04.12.2006. Coming into operation: 16.01.2007. Effect: S.R. 2003/303 amended & S.R. 2003/518 revoked. - 4p.: 30 cm. - 978-0-337-96757-3 £3.00

The Motorways Traffic (Amendment) Regulations (Northern Ireland) 2006 No. 2006/83. - Enabling power: S.I. 1993/3160 (N.I.15), art. 20 (3). - Issued: 15.03.2006. Made: 02.03.2006. Coming into operation: 13.04.2006. Effect: S.R. 1984/160 amended. - 4p.: 30 cm. - 978-0-337-96398-8 £3.00

The Off-Street Parking (Amendment No. 2) Order (Northern Ireland) 2006 No. 2006/363. - Enabling power: S.I. 2005/1964 (N.I. 14), art. 43. - Issued: 15.09.2006. Made: 08.09.2006. Coming into operation: 30.10.2006. Effect: S.R. 2000/384 (which was not printed) amended. - 12p.: 30 cm. - 978-0-337-96635-4 £3.00

The On-Street Parking (Amendment) Order (Northern Ireland) 2006 No. 2006/362. - Enabling power: S.I. 2005/1964 (N.I. 14), art. 43. - Issued: 15.09.2006. Made: 08.09.2006. Coming into operation: 30.10.2006. Effect: S.R. 2000/383 (which was not printed) amended. - 2p.: 30 cm. - 978-0-337-96634-7 £3.00

The Passenger and Goods Vehicles (Recording Equipment) (Amendment) Regulations (Northern Ireland) 2006 No. 2006/274. - Enabling power: European Communities Act 1972, s. 2 (2). - Issued: 28.06.2006. Made: 21.06.2006. Coming into operation: 31.07.2006. Effect: S.R. 1996/145 amended. - EC note: These Regulations modify the provisions of the 1996 Regs to take account of the new digital tachograph provided for by Council Regulation (EC) No. 2135/98, which amended Regulation (EEC) No. 3821/85 on recording equipment in road transport. They also amend the definition of the 'Community Recording Equipment Regulation' to include reference to Regulation (EC) 561/2006. - 12p.: 30 cm. - 978-0-337-96559-3 £3.00

The Penalty Charges (Exemption from Criminal Proceedings) (Amendment) Regulations (Northern Ireland) 2006 No. 2006/432. - Enabling power: S.I. 2005/1964 (N.I. 14), art. 4 (7). - Issued: 07.11.2006. Made: 27.10.2006. Coming into operation: 30.10.2006. Effect: S.R. 2006/376 amended. - 2p: 30 cm. - 978-0-337-96695-8 £3.00

The Penalty Charges (Exemption from Criminal Proceedings) Regulations (Northern Ireland) 2006 No. 2006/376. - Enabling power: S.I. 2005/1964 (N.I. 14), art. 4 (7). - Issued: 06.10.2006. Made: 15.09.2006. Coming into operation: 30.10.2006. Effect: None. - 2p.: 30 cm. - 978-0-337-96662-0 £3.00

The Penalty Charges (Prescribed Amounts) Regulations (Northern Ireland) 2006 No. 2006/338. - Enabling power: S.I. 2005/1964 (N.I. 14), art. 4 (4). - Issued: 22.08.2006. Made: 16.08.2006. Coming into operation: 30.10.2006. Effect: None. - 2p.: 30 cm. - 978-0-337-96613-2 £3.00

The Public Service Vehicles Accessibility (Amendment) Regulations (Northern Ireland) 2006 No. 2006/249. - Enabling power: Disability Discrimination Act 1995, ss. 40, 41. - Issued: 14.06.2006. Made: 06.06.2006. Coming into operation: 19.07.2006. Effect: S.R. 2003/37 amended. - EC note: These regs modify the 2003 regs so that compliance with Directive 2001/85/EC, is offered as an alternative as it requires that the United Kingdom shall not refuse or prohibit the sale or entry into service of a vehicle, or of bodywork intended to be part of the vehicle (which may be type approved separately), if the requirements of the Directive and its Annexes are met, and if such refusal is on grounds relating to that Directive. - 4p.: 30 cm. - 978-0-337-96543-2 £3.00

The Public Service Vehicles (Amendment) Regulations (Northern Ireland) 2006 No. 2006/247. - Enabling power: S.I. 1981/154 (N.I. 1), arts 61 (1), 66 (1), 218 (1). - Issued: 14.06.2006. Made: 06.06.2006. Coming into operation: 19.07.2006. Effect: S.R. 1985/123 amended. - EC note: These Regulations amend regulation 6 of the Public Service Vehicles Regulations (Northern Ireland) 1985 to include Directive 2001/85/EC in the list of statutory requirements. This will allow buses to meet the requirements of the Directive as an alternative to the requirements of the Public Service Vehicles (Conditions of Fitness, Equipment and Use) Regulations (Northern Ireland) 1995. - 2p.: 30 cm. - 978-0-337-96542-5 £3.00

The Public Service Vehicles (Conditions of Fitness, Equipment and Use) (Amendment No. 2) Regulations (Northern Ireland) 2006 No. 2006/248. - Enabling power: S.I. 1995/2994 (N.I. 18), arts 55 (1), 110 (2). - Issued: 14.06.2006. Made: 06.06.2006. Coming into operation: 19.07.2006. Effect: S.R. 1995/447 amended. - EC note: These regs modify the 1995 regs so that compliance with Directive 2001/85/EC, is offered as an alternative as it requires that the United Kingdom shall not refuse or prohibit sale or entry into service of a bus or coach, or of bodywork intended to be part of the vehicle which may be type approved separately, if the requirements of the Directive and its Annexes are met, and if such refusal or prohibition of sale is on grounds relating to that Directive. - 2p.: 30 cm. - 978-0-337-96541-8 £3.00

The Public Service Vehicles (Conditions of Fitness, Equipment and Use) (Amendment) Regulations (Northern Ireland) 2006 No. 2006/74. - Enabling power: S.I. 1995/2994 (N.I. 18), arts. 55 (1) (2) (6), 110 (2). - Issued: 14.03.2006. Made: 01.03.2006. Coming into operation: 13.04.2006. Effect: S.R. 1995/447 amended. - 2p.: 30 cm. - 978-0-337-96384-1 £3.00

The Removal, Storage and Disposal of Vehicles (Prescribed Charges) Regulations (Northern Ireland) 2006 No. 2006/337. - Enabling power: S.I. 2005/1964 (N.I. 14), art. 23 (7) (c). - Issued: 22.08.2006. Made: 16.08.2006. Coming into operation: 30.10.2006. Effect: None. - 2p.: 30 cm. - 978-0-337-96612-5 £3.00

The Taxis (Enniskillen) Bye-Laws (Northern Ireland) 2006 No. 2006/73. - Enabling power: S.I. 1981/154 (N.I. 1), art. 65 (1) (2). - Issued: 08.03.2006. Made: 01.03.2006. Coming into operation: 13.04.2006. Effect: None. - 4p.: 30 cm. - 978-0-337-96378-0 £3.00

The Traffic Management (2005 Order) (Commencement) Order (Northern Ireland) 2006 No. 2006/347 (C.18). - Enabling power: S.I. 2005/1964 (N.I. 14), art. 1 (3). Bringing into operation various provisions of the 2005 Order on 30.10.2006. - Issued: 13.09.2006. Made: 23.08.2006. Coming into operation: -. Effect: None. - 4p.: 30 cm. - 978-0-337-96630-9 £3.00

The Traffic Management (Proceedings before Adjudicators) Regulations (Northern Ireland) 2006 No. 2006/421. - Enabling power: S.I. 2005/1964 (N.I. 14), art. 30 (1) (2). - Issued: 27.10.2006. Made: 19.10.2006. Coming into operation: 15.11.2006. Effect: None. - 20p.: 30 cm. - 978-0-337-96684-2 £3.50

The Traffic Signs (Amendment) Regulations (Northern Ireland) 2006 No. 2006/399. - Enabling power: S.I. 1997/276 (N.I. 2), art. 28 (2). - Issued: 10.10.2006. Made: 02.10.2006. Coming into operation: 13.11.2006. Effect: S.R. 1997/386 amended. - 8p.: 30 cm. - 978-0-337-96663-7 £3.00

The Zebra, Pelican and Puffin Pedestrian Crossings Regulations (Northern Ireland) 2006 No. 2006/164. - Enabling power: S.I. 1997/276 (N.I. 2), arts. 28 (2), 59 (3). - Issued: 07.04.2005. Made: 28.03.2006. Coming into operation: 09.05.2006. Effect: S.R. 1974/15; 1989/145; 1990/400; 1991/350; 1992/131 revoked. - 32p, figs: 30 cm. - 978-0-337-96468-8 £5.50

Salaries

The Salaries (Assembly Ombudsman and Commissioner for Complaints) Order (Northern Ireland) 2006 No. 2006/442. - Enabling power: S.I. 1996/1298 (N.I.8), art. 5 (1) (2) & S.I. 1996/1297 (N.I.7), art. 4 (1) (2). - Issued: 15.11.2006. Made: 02.11.2006. Coming into operation: 07.12.2006. Effect: S.R. 2005/234 revoked. - 2p.: 30 cm. - 978-0-337-96701-6 £3.00

Salaries (Comptroller and Auditor General) Order (Northern Ireland) 2006 No. 2006/302. - Enabling power: S.I. 1987/460 (N.I. 5), art. 4 (1). - Issued: 10.07.2006. Made: 26.06.2006. Coming into operation: 21.08.2006. Effect: S.R. 2005/489 revoked. - 2p.: 30 cm. - 978-0-337-96584-5 £3.00

Seeds

The Seed Potatoes (Crop Fees) Regulations (Northern Ireland) 2006 No. 2006/186. - Enabling power: Seeds Act (Northern Ireland) 1965, s. 1. - Issued: 25.04.2006. Made: 19.04.2006. Coming into operation: 10.05.2006. Effect: S.R. 2004/181; 2005/156 revoked. - 4p.: 30 cm. - 978-0-337-96483-1 £3.00

Sexual orientation discrimination

Equality Act (Sexual Orientation) (Amendment) (Northern Ireland) Regulations 2006 No. 2006/466. - Enabling power: Equality Act 2006, s. 82 (1) (3) (4) (5). - Issued: 19.12.2006. Made: 22.11.2006. Coming into operation: 01.01.2007. Effect: S.R. 2006/439 amended. - 2p: 30 cm. - 978-0-337-96737-5 £3.00

The Equality Act (Sexual Orientation) Regulations (Northern Ireland) 2006 No. 2006/439. - Enabling power: Equality Act 2006, ss. 82 (1) (3) (4) (5). - Issued: 14.11.2006. Made: 08.11.2006. Coming into operation: 01.01.2007. Effect: None. - 32p.: 30 cm. - 978-0-337-96699-6 £5.50

Social security

The Housing Benefit (Consequential Provisions) (Amendment) Regulations (Northern Ireland) 2006 No. 2006/449. - Enabling power: Social Security Contributions and Benefits (Northern Ireland) Act 1992, ss. 122 (1) (d), 132A (3), 171 (1) (3) (4). - Issued: 16.11.2006. Made: 10.11.2006. Coming into operation: 19.11.2006. Effect: S.R. 2006/407 amended. - This Statutory Rule is made in consequence of a defect in S.R. 2006 No. 407 (ISBN 0337966761) and is being issued free of charge to all known recipients of that Statutory Rule. - 2p.: 30 cm. - 978-0-337-96705-4 £3.00

The Housing Benefit (Consequential Provisions) Regulations (Northern Ireland) 2006 No. 2006/407. - Enabling power: Social Security Contributions and Benefits (Northern Ireland) Act 1992, ss. 122 (1) (d), 129 (2) (3) (4), 130, 131 (1) (2) (6), 132, 132A (3) (4) (a), 133 (2), 171 (1) (3) to (5) & Social Security Administration (Northern Ireland) Act 1992, ss. 1 (1) (1C), 5 (1) (a) to (d), (g) to (t) (5), 73, 107, 119A, 126 (4) (5), 165 (1) (4) to (6) & S.I. 1998/1506 (N.I. 10), arts 34, 74 (1) (3). - Issued: 25.10.2006. Made: 12.10.2006. Coming into operation: 20.11.2006. Effect: 153 amended & 96 revoked. - 56p.: 30 cm. - 978-0-337-96676-7 £7.50

The Pensions (2004 Act and 2005 Order) (PPF Payments and FAS Payments) (Consequential Provisions) Order (Northern Ireland) 2006 No. 2006/37. - Enabling power: S.I. 2005/255 (N.I. 1), arts 287 (3), 290 (2). - Issued: 22.02.2006. Made: 13.02.2006. Coming into operation: 14.02.2006. Effect: 1992 c. 7; 2002 c. 14 (N.I.); S.I. 1995/2705 (N.I. 15) amended. - 8p: 30 cm. - 978-0-337-96340-7 £3.00

Pneumoconiosis, etc., (Workers' Compensation) (Payment of Claims) (Amendment) Regulations (Northern Ireland) 2006 No. 2006/87. - Enabling power: S.I.1979/925 (N.I.9), arts. 2 (2), 3 (3), 4 (3), 11 (1) (4). - Issued: 21.03.2006. Made: 06.03.2006. Coming into operation: 16.04.2006. Effect: S.R. 1988/242 amended. - 8p: 30 cm. - 978-0-337-96391-9 £3.00

The Social Fund (Application for Review) (Amendment) Regulations (Northern Ireland) 2006 No. 2006/169. - Enabling power: S.I. 1998/1506 (N.I. 10), art. 38 (1) (3). - Issued: 07.04.2005. Made: 31.03.2006. Coming into operation: 24.04.2006. Effect: S.R. 1988/20; 1999/472 (C. 36) amended. - 4p: 30 cm. - 978-0-337-96472-5 £3.00

The Social Security (1998 Order) (Commencement No. 13) Order (Northern Ireland) 2006 No. 2006/360 (C.20). - Enabling power: S.I. 1998/1506 (NI.10), art. 1 (2). Bringing into operation various provisions of the 1998 Order on 01.10.2006 in accord. with art. 2. - Issued: 14.09.2006. Made: 08.09.2006. Coming into operation: -. Effect: None. - 2p.: 30 cm. - 978-0-337-96632-3 £3.00

The Social Security (1998 Order) (Commencement Nos. 8 and 10) (Amendment) Order (Northern Ireland) 2006 No. 2006/402. - Enabling power: S.I. 1998/1506 (N.I. 10), art. 1 (2) (4). - Issued: 13.10.2006. Made: 09.10.2006. Coming into operation: 16.10.2006 in accord. with art. 1 (2). Effect: S.R. 1992/38; 1995/35; 1999/371 (C.28), 428 (C.32) amended. - 4p.: 30 cm. - 978-0-337-96669-9 £3.00

The Social Security (1998 Order) (Prescribed Benefits) Regulations (Northern Ireland) 2006 No. 2006/388. - Enabling power: S.I. 1998/1506 (NI.10), arts 9 (3) (h), 74 (1). - Issued: 27.09.2006. Made: 22.09.2006. Coming into operation: 16.10.2006. Effect: None. - 4p.: 30 cm. - 978-0-337-96652-1 £3.00

The Social Security Benefits Up-rating Order (Northern Ireland) 2006 No. 2006/109. - Enabling power: Social Security Administration (Northern Ireland) Act 1992, ss. 132, 165 (1) (4) (5). - Issued: 28.03.2006. Made: 10.03.2006. Coming into operation: In accord. with art. 1. Effect: 1992 c. 7; 1993 c. 49; S.R. 1978/105; 1987/30, 459, 460, 461; 1992/32; 1994/461; 1995/35; 1996/198; 2002/380; 2003/28, 197 amended & S.R. 2005/82 revoked (13.04.2006). - 40p: 30 cm. - 978-0-337-96413-8 £6.50

The Social Security Benefits Up-rating Regulations (Northern Ireland) 2006 No. 2006/110. - Enabling power: Social Security Contributions and Benefits (Northern Ireland) Act 1992, ss. 90, 113 (1) (a), 171 (1) (3) & Social Security Administration (Northern Ireland) Act 1992, ss. 135 (3), 165 (1) (4). - Issued: 22.03.2006. Made: 10.03.2006. Coming into operation: 10.04.2006. Effect: S.R. 1977/74 amended & S.R. 2005/96 revoked. - 4p: 30 cm. - 978-0-337-96414-5 £3.00

The Social Security (Bulgaria and Romania) (Amendment) Regulations (Northern Ireland) 2006 No. 2006/523. - Enabling power: Social Security Contributions and Benefits (Northern Ireland) Act 1992, ss. 122 (1) (a) (d), 131 (1) (2), 133 (2), 171 (1) (3); S.I. 1995/2705 (N.I. 15), art. 6 (5) (12), sch. 1, para. 11 and State Pension Credit Act (Northern Ireland) 2002, ss. 1 (5) (a), 19 (1) (3). - Issued: 21.12.2006. Made: 14.12.2006. Coming into operation: 01.01.2007. Effect: S.R. 1987/459; 1996/198; 2003/28; 2006/405, 406 amended. - 4p.: 30 cm. - 978-0-337-96773-3 £3.00

The Social Security (Claims and Payments) (Amendment) Regulations (Northern Ireland) 2006 No. 2006/91. - Enabling power: Social Security Administration (Northern Ireland) Act 1992, ss. 13A (2) (b), 165 (1). - Issued: 14.03.2006. Made: 07.03.2006. Coming into operation: 01.04.2006. Effect: S.R. 1987/465 amended & S.R. 2005/362 revoked. - 4p.: 30 cm. - 978-0-337-96396-4 £3.00

The Social Security (Deferral of Retirement Pensions etc.) Regulations (Northern Ireland) 2006 No. 2006/113. - Enabling power: Social Security Contributions and Benefits (Northern Ireland) Act 1992, ss. 171 (3), sch. 5, para. 2 (2) & Social Security Administration (Northern Ireland) Act 1992, ss. 69 (6) (b), 165 (1) (4) & S.I. 2005/255 (N.I. 1), sch. 9, para. 22. - Issued: 22.03.2006. Made: 10.03.2006. Coming into operation: 06.04.2006. Effect: S.R. 1979/243; 1988/142; 2005/123 amended & S.R. 1992/318 revoked. - 4p: 30 cm. - 978-0-337-96415-2 £3.00

The Social Security (Deferral of Retirement Pensions, Shared Additional Pension and Graduated Retirement Benefit) (Miscellaneous Provisions) Regulations (Northern Ireland) 2006 No. 2006/104. - Enabling power: Social Security Contributions and Benefits (Northern Ireland) Act 1992, ss. 62 (1) (a) (c), 132 (4) (a) (b), 171 (1) (3) to (5), sch. 5, paras A1 (1) (3), 3C (2) (4), sch. 5A, para. 1 (1) (3) & Social Security Administration (Northern Ireland) Act 1992, ss. 5 (1) (j), 165 (1) (4) (6) & S.I. 1998/1506 (N.I. 10), arts. 10, 11 (3) (6), 12 (1), 18 (1), 74 (1) & Child Support, Pensions and Social Security Act (Northern Ireland) 2000, sch. 7, para. 3 (1), 4 (3) (5), 20 (1) (3) & State Pension Credit Act (Northern Ireland) 2002, ss. 15 (6) (a) (b), 19 (1) to (3) & S.I. 2005/255 (N.I. 1), sch. 9, para. 22. - Issued: 22.03.2006. Made: 09.03.2006. Coming into operation: 06.04.2006. Effect: S.R. 1987/461, 465; 1999/162; 2001/213; 2003/28; 2005/121, 123 amended. - 16p: 30 cm. - 978-0-337-96410-7 £3.00

The Social Security (Electronic Communications) (Miscellaneous Benefits) Order (Northern Ireland) 2006 No. 2006/203. - Enabling power: Electronic Communications Act (Northern Ireland) 2001, ss. 1, 2. - Issued: 09.05.2006. Made: 02.05.2006. Coming into operation: 26.05.2006. Effect: S.R. 1987/465 amended. - 4p.: 30 cm. - 978-0-337-96492-3 £3.00

The Social Security (Incapacity Benefit Work-focused Interviews) (Amendment No. 2) Regulations (Northern Ireland) 2006 No. 2006/398. - Enabling power: Social Security Administration (Northern Ireland) Act 1992, ss. 2A (1), 165 (4) to (6) (7A). - Issued: 04.10.2006. Made: 29.09.2006. Coming into operation: 30.10.2006. Effect: S.R. 2005/414 amended. - 12p.: 30 cm. - 978-0-337-96660-6 £3.00

The Social Security (Incapacity Benefit Work-focused Interviews) (Amendment) Regulations (Northern Ireland) 2006 No. 2006/167. - Enabling power: Social Security Administration (Northern Ireland) Act 1992, ss. 2A (1), 165 (4) to (6) (7A). - Issued: 07.04.2005. Made: 30.03.2006. Coming into operation: 24.04.2006. Effect: S.R. 2005/414 amended. - 8p: 30 cm. - 978-0-337-96470-1 £3.00

The Social Security (Incapacity for Work) (Amendment) Regulations (Northern Ireland) 2006 No. 2006/150. - Enabling power: Social Security Contributions and Benefits (Northern Ireland) Act 1992, ss. 167D, 171 (1) (3) (4). - Issued: 28.03.2006. Made: 22.03.2006. Coming into operation: 10.04.2006. Effect: S.R. 1995/41, 149; 1996/601; 1998/324; 1999/428 (C. 32); 2000/4, 86, 109; 2005/415 amended. - 8p.: 30 cm. - 978-0-337-96453-4 £3.00

The Social Security (Income Support and Jobseeker's Allowance) (Amendment) Regulations (Northern Ireland) 2006 No. 2006/234. - Enabling power: Social Security Contributions and Benefits (Northern Ireland) Act 1992, ss. 122 (1) (a), 123 (1) (e), 171 (1) (3) (4) & S.I. 1995/2705 (N.I. 15), arts. 8 (2) (4), 9 (4), 10, 36 (2), sch. 1, paras 8, 8A (1). - Issued: 31.05.2006. Made: 25.05.2006. Coming into operation: 30.05.2006. Effect: S.R. 1987/459; 1996/198 amended. - 4p.: 30 cm. - 978-0-337-96522-7 £3.00

The Social Security (Industrial Injuries) (Dependency) (Permitted Earnings Limits) Order (Northern Ireland) 2006 No. 2006/111. - Enabling power: Social Security Contributions and Benefits (Northern Ireland) Act 1992, ss. 171 (1) (3), sch. 7, para. 4 (5). - Issued: 23.03.2006. Made: 10.03.2006. Coming into operation: 12.04.2006. Effect: 1992 c.7 amended & S.R. 2005/95 revoked. - 2p: 30 cm. - 978-0-337-96416-9 £3.00

The Social Security (Industrial Injuries) (Prescribed Diseases) (Amendment No. 2) Regulations (Northern Ireland) 2006 No. 2006/133. - Enabling power: Social Security Contributions and Benefits (Northern Ireland) Act 1992, ss.108 (2), 171 (1) to (4). - Issued: 27.03.2006. Made: 15.03.2006. Coming into operation: 05.04.2006. Effect: S.R. 2006/96 amended. - This Statutory Rule has been made in consequence of a defect in S.R. 2006 No. 96 and is being issued free of charge to all known recipients of that Statutory Rule. - 2p.: 30 cm. - 978-0-337-96436-7 £3.00

The Social Security (Industrial Injuries) (Prescribed Diseases) (Amendment) Regulations (Northern Ireland) 2006 No. 2006/96. - Enabling power: Social Security Contributions and Benefits (Northern Ireland) Act 1992, ss. 108 (2), 109 (2), 171 (1) to (4), sch. 6, para. 1. - Issued: 21.03.2006. Made: 08.03.2006. Coming into operation: 06.04.2006. Effect: S.R. 1986/179; 1997/158; 2003/63 amended. - 4p: 30 cm. - 978-0-337-96406-0 £3.00

The Social Security (Lebanon) (Amendment) Regulations (Northern Ireland) 2006 No. 2006/320. - Enabling power: Social Security Contributions and Benefits (Northern Ireland) Act 1992, ss. 122 (1) (a) (d), 131 (1) (2), 133 (2), 171 (1) (3) (4) & S.I. 1995/2705 (N.I. 15), arts. 6 (5) (12), 36 (2), sch. 1, para. 11 & State Pension Credit Act (Northern Ireland) 2002, ss. 1 (5) (a), 19 (1) (2) (a) (3). - Issued: 02.08.2006. Made: 27.07.2006. Coming into operation: 28.07.2006. Effect: S.R. 1987/459, 461; 1996/198; 2003/28 amended. - These Regulations shall cease to have effect on 30th January 2007. - 4p.: 30 cm. - 978-0-337-96599-9 £3.00

The Social Security (Miscellaneous Amendments No. 2) Regulations (Northern Ireland) 2006 No. 2006/168. - Enabling power: Social Security Adminstration (Northern Ireland) Act 1992, ss. 5 (1) (a) to (c) (j) (k) (n) (q), 5A (1) (6) (c), 71 (1) (b), 105A (1A) (1B) (1D) (1E), 106 (1A) to (1D), 165 (1) (4) to (6) & S.I. 1998/1506 (N.I. 10), arts. 10 (4), 11 (3) (6), 74 (1) (3). - Issued: 07.04.2006. Made: 31.03.2006. Coming into operation: In accord. with reg. 1. Effect: S.R. 1987/465; 1989/40; 1996/85, 198; 1999/162, 472 (C.36), 473; 2000/215; 2001/420; 2002/67; 2005/46, 139, 580 amended & S.R. 1994/484 revoked (10.04.2006). - 12p.: 30 cm. - 978-0-337-96469-5 £3.00

The Social Security (Miscellaneous Amendments No. 3) Regulations (Northern Ireland) 2006 No. 2006/365. - Enabling power: Social Security Administration (Northern Ireland) Act 1992, ss. 5 (1) (a) to (c) (q), 165 (1) (4) (6) & S.I. 1998/1506 (N.I. 10), arts 11 (3) (6), 74 (1) (3). - Issued: 15.09.2006. Made: 11.09.2006. Coming into operation: 02.10.2006. Effect: S.R. 1987/465; 1990/398; 1991/488; 1999/162; 2002/67; 2003/191; 2005/46 amended. - 8p.: 30 cm. - 978-0-337-96636-1 £3.00

The Social Security (Miscellaneous Amendments No. 4) Regulations (Northern Ireland) 2006 No. 2006/359. - Enabling power: Social Security Contributions and Benefits (Northern Ireland) Act 1992, ss. 30A (2A), 30C (4), 30E (1), 47 (6), 64 (1), 68 (4), 71 (6), 86A (1), 122 (1) (a) (d), 123 (1) (e), 129 (4), 131 (1), 132 (3) (4) (b) (c), 132A (3), 133 (2) (h), 167D, 171(1) (3) to (5), sch. 7, para. 2 (3) & Social Security Administration (Northern Ireland) Act 1992, ss. 5 (1) (m), 165 (1) (4) (5) & S.I. 1994/1898 (N.I. 12), art. 6 & S.I. 1995/2705 (N.I. 15), arts. 6 (5), 8 (4), 9 (2) (a) (4), 14 (2) (4) (b) (c), 36 (2), sch. 1, paras 1 (2) (b), 8, 8A (1), 12, 16 (1) & Child Support, Pensions and Social Security Act (Northern Ireland) 2000, sch. 7, paras 4 (5), 20 (1) (3) & State Pension Credit Act (Northern Ireland) 2002, ss. 1 (5) (a), 2 (3) (b), 7 (4), 15 (6) (a) (b), 17 (2) (a), 19 (1) to (3). - Issued: 19.09.2006. Made: 07.09.2006. Coming into operation: In accord. with reg. 1. Effect: S.R. 1979/243; 1984/92, 317; 1987/459, 461; 1990/131, 136; 1992/20, 32; 1993/165, 373; 1994/327, 335, 461, 485; 1995/35, 41; 1996/198, 199; 1997/165, 412; 2000/4; 2002/132, 299; 2003/28; 2005/458; 2006/150, 234 amended and S.R. 2005/415 revoked (09.10.2006). - 20p: 30 cm. - 978-0-337-96633-0 £3.50

The Social Security (Miscellaneous Amendments No. 5) Regulations (Northern Ireland) 2006 No. 2006/510. - Enabling power: Social Security Contributions and Benefits (Northern Ireland) Act 1992, ss. 122 (1) (a) (d), 131 (1), 133 (2) (h), 171 (1) (3) to (5); S.I. 1995/2705 (N.I. 15), arts 6 (5), 36 (2) and State Pension Credit Act (Northern Ireland) 2002, s. 2 (3) (b), 19 (1) (3). - Issued: 14.12.2006. Made: 08.12.2006. Coming into operation: 08.01.2007. Effect: S.R. 1987/459; 1996/198; 2003/28; 2006/405, 406 amended. - 4p.: 30 cm. - 978-0-337-96761-0 £3.00

The Social Security (Miscellaneous Amendments) Regulations (Northern Ireland) 2006 No. 2006/97. - Enabling power: Social Security Contributions and Benefits (Northern Ireland) Act 1992, ss.122 (1) (a) (d), 123 (1) (e), 131 (1), 132 (4) (a) (b), 132A (3), 134 (1) (a), 171 (1) (3) (4) & Social Security Administration (Northern Ireland) Act 1992, ss. 5 (1) (l), 165(1) (4) (5) & S.I. 1995/2705 (N.I. 15), arts. 14(4)(a) (b), 36(2) & State Pension Credit Act (Northern Ireland) 2002, ss. 2 (3) (b) (9), 13 (1) (a), 15 (1) (j), 19 (1) (2) (a) (3). - Issued: 21.03.2006. Made: 09.03.2006. Coming into operation: In accord. with reg. 1. Effect: S.R. 1987/459, 461; 1996/198; 2003/28; 2005/506 amended. - 8p: 30 cm. - 978-0-337-96403-9 £3.00

The Social Security (National Insurance Numbers) (Amendment) Regulations (Northern Ireland) 2006 No. 2006/436. - Enabling power: Social Security Administration (Northern Ireland) Act 1992, ss. 158C, 165 (1) (4) to (6). - Issued: 09.11.2006. Made: 03.11.2006. Coming into force: 11.12.2006 except reg 2 (b) & 01.03.2007 for reg 2 (b). In accord. with art. 1 (1). Effect: S.R. 2001/102 amended. - 4p.: 30 cm. - 978-0-337-96697-2 £3.00

The Social Security Pensions (Low Earnings Threshold) Order (Northern Ireland) 2006 No. 2006/71. - Enabling power: Social Security Administration (Northern Ireland) Act 1992, s. 130A. - Issued: 08.03.2006. Made: 01.03.2006. Coming into operation: 06.04.2006. Effect: None. - 2p.: 30 cm. - 978-0-337-96375-9 £3.00

The Social Security (Persons from Abroad) (Amendment No. 2) Regulations (Northern Ireland) 2006 No. 2006/379. - Enabling power: Social Security Contributions and Benefits (Northern Ireland) Act 1992, ss. 122 (1) (a) (d), 131 (1) (2), 133 (2), 171 (1) (3) & S.I. 1995/2705 (N.I. 15), arts 6 (5) (12), sch. 1, para. 11 & State Pension Credit Act (Northern Ireland) 2002, ss. 1 (5) (a), 19 (1) (3). - Issued: 21.09.2006. Made: 15.09.2006. Coming into operation: 09.10.2006. Effect: S.R. 1987/459, 461; 1996/198; 2003/28; amended. - 4p: 30 cm. - 978-0-337-96645-3 £3.00

The Social Security (Persons from Abroad) (Amendment) Regulations (Northern Ireland) 2006 No. 2006/178. - Enabling power: Social Security Contributions and Benefits (Northern Ireland) Act 1992, ss. 122 (1) (a) (d), 131 (1) (2), 133 (2), 134 (1) (a), 171 (1) (3) (4) & S.I. 1995/2705 (N.I. 15), arts 6 (5) (12), 36 (2), sch. 1, para. 11 & State Pension Credit Act (Northern Ireland) 2002, ss. 1 (5) (a), 19 (1) (2) (a) (3). - Issued: 10.04.2006. Made: 03.04.2006. Coming into operation: 30.04.2006. Effect: S.R. 1987/459, 461; 1996/198; 2003/28; 2005/506 amended & S.R. 1994/266; 1996/375; 2000/125; 2004/197 revoked. - EC note: These Regulations amend the income-related benefits regulations and the Social Fund regulations in consequence of the Council Directive 2004/38/EC the provisions of which are to be transposed by the Immigration (European Economic Area) Regulations 2006. - 12p: 30 cm. - 978-0-337-96475-6 £3.00

The Social Security (PPF Payments and FAS Payments) (Consequential Amendments) Regulations (Northern Ireland) 2006 No. 2006/184. - Enabling power: Social Security Contributions and Benefits (Northern Ireland) Act 1992, ss. 30DD (1) (c), 89 (1) (1A) (2), 171 (1) (3) (4) & S.I. 1995/2705 (N.I. 15), arts 6 (1) (b), 36 (1) (2). - Issued: 13.04.2006. Made: 10.04.2006. Coming into operation: 05.05.2006. Effect: S.R. 1977/74; 1992/83; 1994/461, 485; 1996/198 amended. - 4p: 30 cm. - 978-0-337-96478-7 £3.00

The Social Security (Preparation for Employment Programme 50 to 59 Pilot) Regulations (Northern Ireland) 2006 No. 2006/70. - Enabling power: S.I. 1995/2705 (N.I. 15), arts. 21 (10) (c), 31 (1) (3), 36 (2). - Issued: 07.03.2006. Made: 28.02.2006. Coming into operation: 03.04.2006. Effect: None. - 4p.: 30 cm. - 978-0-337-96373-5 £3.00

The Social Security (Provisions relating to Qualifying Young Persons) (Amendment) Regulations (Northern Ireland) 2006 No. 2006/158. - Enabling power: Social Security Contributions and Benefits (Northern Ireland) Act 1992, ss. 82 (4), 85 (4), 86A, 90 (b), 114 (1), 121 (5), 171 (1) (3), sch. 7, para. 6 (1) (b) (5) & Social Security Administration (Northern Ireland) Act 1992, ss. 1 (1C), 165 (1) (4). - Issued: 31.03.2006. Made: 27.03.2006. Coming into operation: 10.04.2006. Effect: S.R. 1977/74; 1979/243; 1994/485 amended. - 4p.: 30 cm. - 978-0-337-96461-9 £3.00

The Social Security Revaluation of Earnings Factors Order (Northern Ireland) 2006 No. 2006/72. - Enabling power: Social Security Administration (Northern Ireland) Act 1992, ss. 130, 165 (1) (4) (5). - Issued: 08.03.2006. Made: 01.03.2006. Coming into operation: 06.04.2006. Effect: None. - 4p.: 30 cm. - 978-0-337-96376-6 £3.00

The Social Security (Students and Income-related Benefits) (Amendment) Regulations (Northern Ireland) 2006 No. 2006/301. - Enabling power: Social Security Contributions and Benefits (Northern Ireland) Act 1992, ss. 122 (1) (a) (d), 132 (3) (4) (b), 171 (1) (3) (4) & S.I. 1995/2705 (N.I. 15), arts 14 (1) (4) (b), 36 (2). - Issued: 10.07.2006. Made: 04.07.2006. Coming into operation: In accord. with reg. 1. Effect: S.R. 1987/459, 461; 1996/198 amended & S.R. 2005/332 revoked. - 8p.: 30 cm. - 978-0-337-96583-8 £3.00

The Social Security (Young Persons) (Amendment) Regulations (Northern Ireland) 2006 No. 2006/128. - Enabling power: Social Security Contributions and Benefits (Northern Ireland) Act 1992, ss. 122 (1) (a) (d), 123 (1) (d) (e), 131 (1), 133 (2) (e) (f) (i), 171 (1) (3) to (5); S.I. 1995/2705 (N.I. 15), arts 5 (1) (f) (iii), 5A (1) (e) (ii), 6 (5), 36 (1) (2), Sch. 1, paras 8, 8A (1), 9C, 14; State Pension Credit Act (Northern Ireland) 2002, ss. 1 (5) (b), 2 (3) (b), 15 (3) (6), 17 (2), 19 (1) (2) (a) (3). - Issued: 24.03.2006. Made: 13.03.2006. Coming into operation: In accord. with reg. 1. Effect: S.R. 1987/459, 461; 1996/198; 2003/28 amended. - 8p.: 30 cm. - 978-0-337-96430-5 £3.00

The Statutory Maternity Pay, Social Security (Maternity Allowance) and Social Security (Overlapping Benefits) (Amendment) Regulations (Northern Ireland) 2006 No. 2006/361. - Enabling power: Social Security Contributions and Benefits (Northern Ireland) Act 1992, ss. 35 (3) (a) (i) (c), 161 (1) (3) (4) (7), 171 (1) (3) and Social Security Administration (Northern Ireland) Act 1992, ss. 5 (1) (m), 71 (1) (a), 165 (1) (3) (4). - Issued: 14.09.2006. Made: 08.09.2006. Coming into operation: In accord. with reg. 1 (2), 01.10.2006. Effect: S.R. 1979/242; 1987/30, 170; 1994/191; 1995/150; 1996/289; 2002/354 amended. - 8p.: 30 cm. - 978-0-337-96631-6 £3.00

The Workmen's Compensation (Supplementation) (Amendment) Regulations (Northern Ireland) 2006 No. 2006/131. - Enabling power: Social Security Contributions and Benefits (Northern Ireland) Act 1992, s. 171 (4), sch. 8, para. 2 & Social Security Administration (Northern Ireland) Act 1992, sch. 6, para. 1. - Issued: 27.03.2006. Made: 14.03.2006. Coming into operation: 12.04.2006. Effect: S.R. 1983/101 amended & S.R. 2005/142 revoked. - 8p.: 30 cm. - 978-0-337-96434-3 £3.00

Statutory maternity pay

The Social Security Benefits Up-rating Order (Northern Ireland) 2006 No. 2006/109. - Enabling power: Social Security Administration (Northern Ireland) Act 1992, ss. 132, 165 (1) (4) (5). - Issued: 28.03.2006. Made: 10.03.2006. Coming into operation: In accord. with art. 1. Effect: 1992 c. 7; 1993 c. 49; S.R. 1978/105; 1987/30, 459, 460, 461; 1992/32; 1994/461; 1995/35; 1996/198; 2002/380; 2003/28, 197 amended & S.R. 2005/82 revoked (13.04.2006). - 40p: 30 cm. - 978-0-337-96413-8 £6.50

The Statutory Maternity Pay, Social Security (Maternity Allowance) and Social Security (Overlapping Benefits) (Amendment) Regulations (Northern Ireland) 2006 No. 2006/361. - Enabling power: Social Security Contributions and Benefits (Northern Ireland) Act 1992, ss. 35 (3) (a) (i) (c), 161 (1) (3) (4) (7), 171 (1) (3) and Social Security Administration (Northern Ireland) Act 1992, ss. 5 (1) (m), 71 (1) (a), 165 (1) (3) (4). - Issued: 14.09.2006. Made: 08.09.2006. Coming into operation: In accord. with reg. 1 (2), 01.10.2006. Effect: S.R. 1979/242; 1987/30, 170; 1994/191; 1995/150; 1996/289; 2002/354 amended. - 8p.: 30 cm. - 978-0-337-96631-6 £3.00

Statutory sick pay

The Social Security Benefits Up-rating Order (Northern Ireland) 2006 No. 2006/109. - Enabling power: Social Security Administration (Northern Ireland) Act 1992, ss. 132, 165 (1) (4) (5). - Issued: 28.03.2006. Made: 10.03.2006. Coming into operation: In accord. with art. 1. Effect: 1992 c. 7; 1993 c. 49; S.R. 1978/105; 1987/30, 459, 460, 461; 1992/32; 1994/461; 1995/35; 1996/198; 2002/380; 2003/28, 197 amended & S.R. 2005/82 revoked (13.04.2006). - 40p: 30 cm. - 978-0-337-96413-8 £6.50

The Statutory Sick Pay (General) (Amendment) Regulations (Northern Ireland) 2006 No. 2006/142. - Enabling power: Social Security Contributions and Benefits (Northern Ireland) Act 1992, s. 147 (4). - Issued: 27.03.2006. Made: 16.03.2006. Coming into operation: 10.04.2006. Effect: S.R. 1982/263 amended. - 4p.: 30 cm. - 978-0-337-96445-9 £3.00

Supreme Court

The Criminal Appeal (Retrial for Serious Offences) (Amendment) Rules (Northern Ireland) 2006 No. 2006/11. - Enabling power: Judicature (Northern Ireland) Act 1978, s. 55 & Criminal Justice Act 2003, s. 93. - Issued: 15.02.2006. Made: 19.01.2006. Coming into operation: 13.02.2006. Effect: S.R. 2005/158 amended. - 8p: 30 cm. - 978-0-337-96320-9 £3.00

The Family Proceedings (Amendment) Rules (Northern Ireland) 2006 No. 2006/304. - Enabling power: S.I. 1993/1576 (N.I. 6), art. 12. - Issued: 14.07.2006. Made: 04.07.2006. Coming into operation: 01.08.2006. Effect: S.R. 1996/322 amended. - 4p.: 30 cm. - 978-0-337-96585-2 £3.00

Supreme Court: Procedure

The Rules of the Supreme Court (Northern Ireland) (Amendment No.2) 2006 No. 2006/305. - Enabling power: Judicature (Northern Ireland) Act 1978, ss. 55, 55A, 57. - Issued: 14.07.2006. Made: 05.07.2006. Coming into operation: 31.07.2006. Effect: S.R. 1980/346 amended. - 4p.: 30 cm. - 978-0-337-96586-9 £3.00

Supreme Court, Northern Ireland

The Criminal Appeal (Prosecution Appeals) (Amendment) Rules (Northern Ireland) 2006 No. 2006/12. - Enabling power: Judicature (Northern Ireland) Act 1978, s. 55 & S.I. 2004/1500 (N.I. 9), art. 32. - Issued: 15.02.2006. Made: 19.01.2006. Coming into operation: 13.02.2006. Effect: S.R. 2005/159 amended. - 8p: 30 cm. - 978-0-337-96319-3 £3.00

The Criminal Appeal (Trial without jury where danger of jury tampering and Trial by jury of sample counts only) Rules (Northern Ireland) 2006 No. 2006/487. - Enabling power: Judicature (Northern Ireland) Act 1978, ss. 55, 55A & Criminal Justice Act 2003, s. 49 & Domestic Violence Crime and Victims Act 2004, s. 20. - Issued: 08.01.2007. Made: 30.11.2006. Coming into operation: 08.01.2007. Effect: None. - 20p.: 30 cm. - 978-0-337-96747-4 £3.50

Supreme Court, Northern Ireland: Procedure

The Crown Court (Amendment) Rules (Northern Ireland) 2006 No. 2006/499. - Enabling power: Judicature (Northern Ireland) Act 1978, ss. 52 (1), 53A & Criminal Justice Act 2003, s. 49 & Domestic Violence, Crime and Victims Act 2004, s. 20 & S.I. 1989/1341 (N.I. 12), art. 80A (7). - Issued: 08.01.2007. Made: 05.12.2006. Coming into operation: 08.01.2007. Effect: S.R. 1979/90 amended. - 24p.: 30 cm. - 978-0-337-96749-8 £4.00

The Rules of the Supreme Court (Northern Ireland) (Amendment) 2006 No. 2006/10. - Enabling power: Judicature (Northern Ireland) Act 1978, s. 55 & Proceeds of Crime Act 2002, s. 446. - Issued: 15.02.2005. Made: 19.01.2006. Coming into operation: 13.02.2006. Effect: S.R. 1980/346 amended. - 8p: 30 cm. - 978-0-337-96321-6 £3.00

The Rules of the Supreme Court (Northern Ireland) (Amendment No.3) 2006 No. 2006/486. - Enabling power: Judicature (Northern Ireland) Act 1978, ss. 55, 55A & Damages Act 1996, ss. 2 (8), 2A. - Issued: 08.12.2006. Made: 28.11.2006. Coming into operation: 08.01.2007. Effect: S.R. 1980/346 amended. - EC note: Amends the principal regs in consequence of Directive 2004/48/EC and Council Reg. (EC) no. 2201/2003. - 12p.: 30 cm. - 978-0-337-96746-7 £3.00

Tax credits

The Tax Credits (Approval of Home Child Care Providers) Scheme (Northern Ireland) 2006 No. 2006/64. - Enabling power: Tax Credits Act 2002, ss. 12 (5) (7) (8), 65 (9). - Issued: 02.03.2006. Made: 23.02.2006. Coming into operation: 06.04.2006. Effect: None. - 4p.: 30 cm. - 978-0-337-96368-1 £3.00

Terms and conditions of employment

The Agricultural Wages (Abolition of Permits to Infirm and Incapacitated Persons) Regulations (Northern Ireland) 2006 No. 2006/429. - Enabling power: European Communities Act 1972, s. 2 (2). - Issued: 03.11.2006. Made: 30.10.2006. Coming into operation: 01.12.2006. Effect: 1998 c. 39; S.I. 1977/2151 (N.I.22) amended. - EC note: These Regulations implement provisions of Council Directive 2000/78/EC establishing a general framework for equal treatment in employment and occupation in so far as it relates to disability discrimination in the payment of agricultural wages. They are also a consequence of the revocation of regulation 6 of the Disability Discrimination (Employment) Regulations (Northern Ireland) 1996 (SR 1996 No 419) by regulation 3 of the Disability Discrimination (Employment Field) (Leasehold Premises) Regulations (Northern Ireland) 2004 (SR 2004 No 374). - 4p.: 30 cm. - 978-0-337-96693-4 £3.00

The Occupational and Personal Pension Schemes (Consultation by Employers) Regulations (Northern Ireland) 2006 No. 2006/48. - Enabling power: S.I. 2005/255 (N.I. 1), arts. 2 (5) (a) (6), 7 (5) (a), 236 (1) (2), 237 (1), 238 (2) (4), 287 (1) (3). - Issued: 23.02.2006. Made: 16.02.2006. Coming into operation: 06.04.2006. Effect: S.I. 1996/1919 (N.I. 16), 1921 (N.I. 18) amended. - 20p: 30 cm. - 978-0-337-96347-6 £3.50

The Occupational and Personal Pension Schemes (Miscellaneous Amendments) Regulations (Northern Ireland) 2006 No. 2006/141. - Enabling power: Pension Schemes (Northern Ireland) Act 1993, s. 97C (2), 109 (1) (d), 177 (2) to (4); S.I.1995/3213 (N.I. 22), arts 35 (3) (4), 40 (2), 47 (5) (6), 49 (1) (2) (4) (9) (b), 85 (1), 86 (1), 89 (5), 166 (1) to (3) & S.I. 2005/255 (N.I. 1), arts 236 (1), 237 (1). - Issued: 27.03.2006. Made: 16.03.2006. Coming into operation: In accord. with reg 1. Effect: S.R. 1997/40, 94, 153; 2000/146, 349; 2005/569; 2006/48 amended. - 8p: 30 cm. - 978-0-337-96446-6 £3.00

Transfer of functions

The Lord Chancellor (Consequential Provisions) Order (Northern Ireland) 2006 No. 2006/115. - Enabling power: Constitutional Reform Act 2005, s. 143. - Issued: 28.03.2006. Made: 13.03.2006. Coming into operation: 03.04.2006. Effect: S.R. 1981/225; 1992/314; 1996/300 amended. - 4p: 30 cm. - 978-0-337-96428-2 £3.00

Unauthorised encampments

The Unauthorised Encampments (2005 Order) (Commencement) Order (Northern Ireland) 2006 No. 2006/244 (C.14). - Enabling power: S.I. 2005/1961 (N.I.11), art. 1 (3). Bringing into operation various provisions of the 2005 Order on 19.07.2006. - Issued: 12.06.2006. Made: 05.06.2006. Coming into operation: -. Effect: None. - 2p.: 30 cm. - 978-0-337-96534-0 £3.00

The Unauthorised Encampments (Retention and Disposal of Vehicles) Regulations (Northern Ireland) 2006 No. 2006/243. - Enabling power: S.I. 2005/1961 (NI.11), art. 9 (2). - Issued: 12.06.2006. Made: 05.06.2006. Coming into operation: 19.07.2006. Effect: None. - 8p.: 30 cm. - 978-0-337-96533-3 £3.00

Water and sewerage

The Water Resources (Environmental Impact Assessment) (Amendment) Regulations (Northern Ireland) 2006 No. 2006/483. - Enabling power: European Communities Act 1972, s. 2 (2). - Issued: 04.12.2006. Made: 27.11.2006. Coming into operation: 01.02.2007. Effect: S.R. 2005/32 amended. - EC note: Implements, in part, Article 2 of Directive 2003/35/EC on public participation in respect of drawing up certain plans or programmes relating to the environment. That Article amends Council Directive 85/337/EEC on the assessment of the effects of certain public and private projects on the environment. - 8p: 30 cm. - 978-0-337-96734-4 £3.00

Weights and measures

The Weighing Equipment (Automatic Catchweighing Instruments) Regulations (Northern Ireland) 2006 No. 2006/154. - Enabling power: S.I. 1981/231 (N.I. 10), art. 13 (1). - Issued: 31.03.2006. Made: 24.03.2006. Coming into operation: 08.05.2006. Effect: S.R. 2006/5 amended & SR & O 1967/237 amended. - These Regulations implement in Northern Ireland, International Recommendation OIML R51 of the Organisation Internationale de Metrologie Legale. - 16p: 30 cm. - 978-0-337-96460-2 £3.00

The Weighing Equipment (Beltweighters) Regulations (Northern Ireland) 2006 No. 2006/157. - Enabling power: S.I. 1981/231 (N.I. 10), arts. 9 (1) (3) (4), 10 (6), 13 (1). - Issued: 31.03.2006. Made: 24.03.2006. Coming into operation: 01.06.2006. Effect: S.R. 1985/319 revoked. - These Regulations replace with amendments the 1985 Regs in light of the International Recommendation 50-1, issued by the International Organisation of Legal Metrology. - 12p: 30 cm. - 978-0-337-96459-6 £3.00

The Weighing Equipment (Non-automatic Weighing Machines) Regulations (Northern Ireland) 2006 No. 2006/5. - Enabling power: S.I. 1981/231 (N.I. 10), arts 9 (1) (3), 10 (6), 13 (1). - Issued: 25.01.2006. Made: 13.01.2006. Coming into operation: 13.02.2006. Effect: S.R. 1991/266; 1995/228 amended & S.R. 1992//537; 1996/320 revoked. - 32p.: 30 cm. - 978-0-337-96314-8 £5.50

Weights and Measures (Passing as Fit for Use for Trade and Adjustment Fees) Regulations (Northern Ireland) 2006 No. 2006/36. - Enabling power: S.I. 1981/231 (N.I. 10), arts. 9 (3), 43. - Issued: 02.03.2006. Made: 10.02.2006. Coming into operation: 01.04.2006. Effect: S.R. 2005/118 revoked with savings. - 8p: 30 cm. - 978-0-337-96343-8 £3.00

Welfare foods

The Welfare Foods (Amendment No. 2) Regulations (Northern Ireland) 2006 No. 2006/477. - Enabling power: S.I. 1988/594 (N.I. 2), art. 13 (3) (4) & Social Security Contributions and Benefits (Northern Ireland) Act 1992, s. 171 (2) to (5). - Issued: 12.12.2006. Made: 23.11.2006. Coming into operation: 27.11.2006. Effect: S.R. 1988/137 amended. - 4p.: 30 cm. - 978-0-337-96758-0 £3.00

The Welfare Foods (Amendment) Regulations (Northern Ireland) 2006 No. 2006/180. - Enabling power: S.I. 1988/594 (N.I. 2), art. 13 (3) (4) & Social Security Contributions and Benefits (Northern Ireland) Act 1992, s. 171 (2) to (5). - Issued: 21.04.2006. Made: 04.04.2006. Coming into operation: 06.04.2006. Effect: S.R. 1988/137 amended. - 2p.: 30 cm. - 978-0-337-96481-7 £3.00

Statutory Rules of Northern Ireland

Arranged by Number

Statutory rules 2006
[Those marked * were of a local nature and publication was not required]

1	Health and safety
2	Agriculture
	Food
3	Food
4	Pensions
5	Weights and measures
6	Local government
7	Rates
8	*
9	*
10	Supreme Court, Northern Ireland
11	Supreme Court
12	Supreme Court, Northern Ireland
13	*
14	*
15	*
16	Education
17	Education
18	Agriculture
19	Police
20	Pensions
21 (C.1)	Insolvency
22	Insolvency
23	Insolvency
24	Insolvency
25	Insolvency
26	Insolvency
27 (C.2)	Access to justice
28	Education
29	*
30 (C.3)	Education
31	*
32	Road traffic and vehicles
33	Insolvency
34	Drainage
35	Fees and charges
36	Weights and measures
37	Social security
	Pensions
38	*
39	Local government
40	*
41	European Communities
42	Animals
43	Animals
	Animals
44	Dangerous drugs
45 (C.4)	Pensions
46	Disabled persons
47	Insolvency
48	Pensions
	Terms and conditions of employment
49	Pensions
50	Pensions
51	Education
52	Agriculture
53	Insolvency
54	Insolvency
55	Insolvency
56	Electricity
57	Fisheries
58	Landlord and tenant
59	*
60	Food
61	Insolvency
62	Criminal evidence
63 (C.5)	Criminal evidence
64	Tax credits
65	Pensions
66	Plant health
67	Road traffic
68	*
69	Police
70	Social security
71	Social security
72	Social security
73	Road traffic and vehicles
74	Road traffic and vehicles
75	Employment
76	Credit unions
77	Credit unions
78	Credit unions
79	Legal aid and advice
80	Legal aid and advice
81	Agriculture
82	Plant health
83	Roads
	Road traffic and vehicles
84	Pensions
85	Pensions
86	Employment
87	Social security
88	*
89	Local government

Welfare foods

90	Agriculture	132	Pensions
91	Social security	133	Social security
92	Pensions	134	*
93 (C.6)	Companies	135	Employment
94	Companies	136	Health and personal social services
95 (C.7)	Pensions	137	Companies
96	Social security	138	Companies
97	Housing Rates Social security	139	Companies
		140	Pensions
98	Environmental protection	141	Pensions Terms and conditions of employment
99	*	142	Statutory sick pay
100	Industrial relations	143	*
101	Industrial relations	144	*
102	*	145	Health and personal social services
103	Health and personal social services	146 (C.9)	Rates
104	Housing Rates Social security	147	*
		148	Pensions
105	European Communities Animals	149	Pensions
		150	Social security
106	Health and personal social services	151 (C.10)	Local government
107	Plant health	152	Police
108	Pensions	153	*
109	Social security Statutory maternity pay Statutory sick pay Employment Housing Rates	154	Weights and measures
		155	Pensions
		156	Pensions
110	Social security	157	Weights and measures
111	Social security	158	Social security
112	Local government	159	Health and personal social services
113	Social security	160	Pensions
114	Game	161	Pensions
115	Lord Chancellor Lord Chief Justice Transfer of functions	162	Pensions
		163	Education
		164	Road traffic and vehicles
116	Food	165	Plant health
117	Legal aid and advice	166	*
118	Legal aid and advice	167	Social security
119	Legal aid and advice	168	Social security
120	Pensions	169	Social security
121	*	170	Pensions
122	Police	171	*
123	Police	172 (C.11)	Agriculture
124 (C.8)	Justice	173	Health and safety
125	Pensions	174	*
126	Pensions	175	*
127	Pensions	176	*
128	Housing Rates Social security	177	Employment
		178	Housing Rates Social security
129	*		
130	*	179	*
131	Social security		

180	Welfare foods	228	*
181	Pensions	229	*
182	Health and safety	230	*
183	Energy conservation	231	Pensions
184	Social security	232	Agriculture
185	*	233	Planning Appeals Commission procedures
186	Seeds	234	Social security
187	Agriculture	235	Employment
188	Pensions	236	*
189	Employment	237	Health and safety
190	Health and personal social services	238	Planning
191	*	239	*
192	Northern Ireland Departments	240	Pharmacy
193	Legal aid and advice	241	Animals
194	*	242 (C.13)	Industrial and provident societies
195	*	243	Unauthorised encampments
196	*	244 (C.14)	Unauthorised encampments
197	*	245	Legal aid and advice
198	*	246	Road traffic and vehicles
199	*	247	Road traffic and vehicles
200	Agriculture	248	Road traffic and vehicles
201	*	249	Road traffic and vehicles
202	European Communities Animal health	250	Fire services
203	Social security	251	Food
204	Health and safety	252	Education
205	Health and safety	253	Agriculture
206	Employment	254	*
207	Pharmacy	255	Health and safety
208	Agriculture	256	Food
209	Agriculture	257 (C.15)	Fire and rescue services
210	Fire services	258	Industrial and provident societies
211	Agriculture	259	Planning
212	Children	260	Lands Tribunal
213	Planning	261	Age discrimination
214	Dangerous drugs	262	Industrial tribunals Age discrimination
215	Planning	263	Food
216	*	264	Dangerous drugs
217	Food	265	Lands Tribunal
218	Planning	266	Planning
219	Planning	267	*
220	Agriculture Pesticides	268	Police
221	*	269	*
222 (C.12)	Planning	270	*
223	Pensions	271	*
224	Fisheries	272	*
225	Planning Appeals Commission procedures	273	Family law Child support
226	Government resources and accounts	274	European Communities Road traffic and vehicles
227	*		

275	*		Social security
276	Planning	321	Environmental protection
277	Industrial training	22	*
278	Pesticides	323	*
279	*	324	*
280	Environmental protection	325	*
281	Drainage	326	*
282	Pensions	327	*
283	*	328	Road traffic and vehicles
284	Road traffic and vehicles	329	Education
285	Planning	330	Agriculture
286	Contracting out	331	Education
287	Agriculture	332	Disabled persons
288	*	333	Health and personal social services
289 (C.16)	Disabled persons	334	Dangerous drugs
290	Planning	335	Health and safety
291	Agriculture	336	Intercountry adoption
292	Health and personal social services	337	Road traffic and vehicles
293	Health and personal social services	338	Road traffic and vehicles
294	Health and personal social services	339	Road traffic and vehicles
295	Health and personal social services	340	Employment
296	Health and personal social services	341	Health and personal social services
297	Pensions	342	Health and personal social services
298	Employer's liability	343	Road traffic and vehicles
299	*	344 (C.17)	Employment
300	Agriculture	345	Radioactive substances Environmental protection
301	Housing Rates Social security	346	European Communities Animals
302	Salaries	347 (C.18)	Road traffic and vehicles
303	Agriculture	348	Planning
304	Family proceedings Supreme Court County courts	349	*
		350	*
305	Supreme Court	351	Food
306	*	352 (C.19)	Pensions
307	Education	353	Insurance
308	*	354	Companies
309	*	355	Building regulations
310	Family law Pensions	356	Public health
		357	Employment
311	Family law Pensions Civil partnership	358	Gas
		359	Housing Rates Social security
312	Education		
313	Police	360 (C.20)	Social security
314	*	361	Statutory maternity pay Social security
315	*		
316	*	362	Road traffic and vehicles
317	*	363	Road traffic and vehicles
318	*	364	*
319	Health and personal social services	365	Social security
320	Housing Rates	366	Education

367	*	413	Magistrates' courts
368 (C.21)	Criminal procedure	414	Magistrates' courts
369	Employment	415	Food
370	Insolvency	416 (C.23)	Dangerous wild animals
371	Consumer protection	417	Dangerous wild animals
372	Employment	418 (C.24)	Food
373	Employment	419	*
374	Employment	420	Food
375	*	421	Road traffic and vehicles
376	Road traffic and vehicles	422	Education
377	Partnerships	423	Industrial relations
378	Education	424	Electricity
379	Housing Rates Social security	425	Health and safety
		426	*
380	*	427	Agriculture
381 (C.22)	Planning	428 (C.25)	Landlord and tenant
382	Planning	429	Agriculture Terms and conditions of employment
383	Education	430	*
384	Education	431	*
385	*	432	Road traffic and vehicles
386	*	433	Contracting out
387	Environmental protection	434	*
388	Social security	435	Plant health
389	Employment	436	Social security
390	*	437 (C.26)	Food
391	*	438	Companies
392	*	439	Sexual orientation discrimination
393	Pensions	440	Building regulations
394	Health and personal social services	441	Education
395	Age discrimination	442	Salaries
396	Health and personal social services	443	Agriculture Food
397	Housing	444	Pensions
398	Social security	445	*
399	Road traffic and vehicles	446	*
400	Local government	447	*
401	European Communities Animals	448	*
402	Social security	449	Housing Rates Social security
403	Education	450	Road traffic and vehicles
404	Gas	451 (C.27)	Criminal procedure
405	Housing Rates	452	Housing
406	Housing Rates	453	Pensions Age discrimination
407	Housing Rates Social security	454	Food
		455	Education
408	Road traffic and vehicles	456	*
409	Pensions	457	*
410	Health and personal social services	458	Employment
411	*	459	Agriculture
412	Roads		

460	Pensions	507	Health services charges
461	Insolvency	508	Agriculture
462	Housing Rates	509	Environmental protection
463	Housing Rates	510	Social security Housing Rates
464 (C.28)	Rates	511	Education
465	*	512	Plant health
466	Sexual orientation discrimination	513	Fisheries
467	Pensions	514	*
468	Rates	515	Insolvency
469	Justice	516	Rates
470 (C.29)	Disabled persons	517	Fisheries
471	Agriculture	518	Forestry
472	*	519	Environmental protection
473	*	520	Health and safety
474	*	521	County courts
475	*	522	Local government
476	*	523	Social security Housing Rates
477	Welfare foods	524	Health and safety
478	Food	525	Health and safety
479	Road traffic and vehicles	526	Laganside
480	Children	527	Laganside
481	Food	528	*
482	Environmental protection	529	Pensions
483	European Communities Water and sewerage	530	*
484 (C.30)	Recovery of health service charges	531	*
485	Food	532	*
486	Supreme Court, Northern Ireland	533	*
487	Supreme Court, Northern Ireland	534	*
488	Environmental protection	535	*
489	Environmental protection	536	Health services charges
490	*	537	Agriculture
491	*	538	Animals
492	European communities Animals		
493	Agriculture Food		
494	Road traffic and vehicles		
495	Road traffic and vehicles		
496 (C.31)	Dangerous wild animals		
497	Dangerous wild animals		
498	Rates		
499	Supreme Court, Northern Ireland		
500	Local government		
501	Agriculture		
502	*		
503	Agriculture		
504	Fair employment		
505	*		
506	*		

List of Commencement Orders 2006

21 (C.1)
27 (C.2)
30 (C.3)
45 (C.4)
63 (C.5)
93 (C.6)
95 (C.7)
124 (C.8)
146 (C.9)
151 (C.10)
172 (C.11)
222 (C.12)
242 (C.13)

244 (C.14)
257 (C.15)
289 (C.16)
344 (C.17)
347 (C.18)
352 (C.19)
360 (C.20)
368 (C.21)
381 (C.22)

416 (C.23)
418 (C.24)
428 (C.25)
437 (C.26)
451 (C.27)
464 (C.28)
470 (C.29)
484 (C.30)
496 (C.31)

Alphabetical Index

A

Aberdeen City Council: Electoral arrangements: Scotland 360
Aberdeen City Council: Road traffic: Permitted & special parking area: Scotland 377
Aberdeenshire: Electoral arrangements: Scotland 360
Abhainn Dhubh: Scottish Water: Scotland 394
Abolition of Feudal Tenure etc. (Scotland) Act 2000: Specified day: Scotland. 354
Absent voting: Transitional provisions: England & Wales 164
Access to justice: 2003 Order: Commencement: Northern Ireland 404
Access: Countryside: Exclusions & restrictions: England 51
Accession: Immigration & worker authorisation 107
Acquisition of land: Compensation: Home loss payments: Prescribed amounts: England 12
Acquisition of land: Compensation: Home loss payments: Prescribed amounts: Wales 13
Acquisition of land: Wales. 13, 101
Act of Adjournal: Criminal procedure: Rules: Amendments: Scotland. 350, 357, 389
Act of Adjournal: Criminal procedure: Rules: Financial reporting orders: Scotland 357, 388
Act of Adjournal: Criminal procedure: Rules: Risk assessment Orders: Orders for lifelong restriction: Scotland 357
Act of Adjournal: Criminal procedure: Rules: Vulnerable Witnesses (Scotland) Act 2004: Scotland 357, 389
Act of Sederunt: Chancery procedure rules: Sheriff Court: Scotland 389
Act of Sederunt: Child care & maintenance rules: Vulnerable Witnesses (Scotland) Act 2004: Scotland 389
Act of Sederunt: Court of Session: Messengers-at-Arms: Fees: Scotland. 389
Act of Sederunt: Court of Session: Rules: Scotland 347
Act of Sederunt: Court of Session: Rules: Solicitor's fees: Scotland 348
Act of Sederunt: Court of Session: Shorthand writers: Fees: Scotland 347
Act of Sederunt: Family Law (Scotland) Act 2006: Scotland 348
Act of Sederunt: Ordinary cause rules: Causes relating to articles 81 & 82 of the Treaty Establishing the European Community: Sheriff Court: Scotland. 389
Act of Sederunt: Ordinary cause, summary application, summary cause & small claim rules: Amendments: Scotland 389
Act of Sederunt: Sheriff Court: Caveat Rules: Scotland. 390
Act of Sederunt: Sheriff Court: Child care & maintenance rules: Scotland 389
Act of Sederunt: Sheriff Court: Companies: Insolvency rules: Scotland 390
Act of Sederunt: Sheriff Court: Matrimonial & parental responsibility matters: Jurisdiction, recognition & enforcement of judgments: Scotland 389
Act of Sederunt: Sheriff Court: Ordinary cause & summary application rules: Scotland. 389
Act of Sederunt: Sheriff Court: Ordinary cause rules: Family Law (Scotland) Act 2006: Scotland 389
Act of Sederunt: Sheriff Court: Sheriff officers: Fees: Scotland 389
Act of Sederunt: Sheriff Court: Shorthand writers: Fees: Scotland 389
Act of Sederunt: Sheriff Court: Solicitor's fees: Scotland. 389
Act of Sederunt: Summary applications, statutory applications & appeals: Rules: Sheriff Court: Scotland 390
Act of Sederunt: UNCITRAL Model law: Cross-border insolvency: Scotland 348
Additional Support Needs Tribunals for Scotland: Practice & procedure: Scotland 350
Additional voluntary contributions: Superannuation scheme: National Health Service: Scotland 366
Adoption & Children Act 2002: Statutory adoption pay: Consequential amendment. 277
Adoption & paternity leave: Northern Ireland 414
Adoption agencies & adoption support agencies: Inspections: Fees 31, 265
Adoption pay: Statutory 278
Adoption, maternity & paternity leave: Employment: Acts 9
Adoption, maternity & paternity leave: Employment: Acts: Explanatory notes 11
Adoption: Independent Review of Determinations: Wales 32, 266
Adoption: Inter-country adoption: Acts 4
Adoption: Inter-country adoption: Acts: Explanatory notes 9
Adoption: Inter-country adoption: Children: Overseas territories: Hague Convention: Amendments: Northern Ireland. 426
Adoption: Statutory paternity & adoption pay: Northern Ireland 414
Adult learning option: Social security 269
Adults & children: Vulnerable groups: Safeguarding: Acts 8
Adults & children: Vulnerable groups: Safeguarding: Acts: Explanatory notes 11
Adults with incapacity: Removal of regenerative tissue for transplantation: Form of certificate: Scotland 358
Adults: Vulnerable adults: Care Standards Tribunal: Disqualification orders: Review: England & Wales 31
Adults: Vulnerable adults: Care Standards Tribunal: England & Wales 31, 266

Advice & assistance: Assistance by way of representation: Scotland 359
Advice & assistance: Financial conditions: Scotland 359
Advice & assistance: Representation: Assistance by way of: Amendments: Scotland 359
Advisory Board on the Registration of Homoeopathic Products 127
African Development Bank: African Development Fund: Tenth replenishment 117
African Development Fund: Multilateral debt relief initiative 117
Age discrimination: Cases: Industrial tribunals: Interest on awards: Northern Ireland 405, 425
Age discrimination: Employment 77
Age discrimination: Employment & training 77
Age discrimination: Employment: Northern Ireland 404, 428
Agricultural & forestry tractors: Emission of gaseous & particulate pollutants 78
Agricultural grants: Crofting counties: Scotland. 349
Agricultural holdings: Units of production: England 119
Agricultural holdings: Units of production: Wales 119
Agricultural nitrate pollution: Water: Protection 289
Agricultural tenancies: Regulatory reform: England & Wales. 119, 163
Agriculture: 2004 Order: Commencements: Northern Ireland 405
Agriculture: Agricultural wages: Permits: Infirm & incapacitated persons: Abolition: Northern Ireland 405, 444
Agriculture: Animal origin: Products: Third country imports: Wales 18
Agriculture: Animals & animal products: Import & export: Wales. 22, 23
Agriculture: Beef carcases: Classification: Scotland 340
Agriculture: Cattle: Older cattle: Disposal: Scotland 342
Agriculture: Common Agricultural Policy: Single payment & support schemes. 13
Agriculture: Common Agricultural Policy: Single payment & support schemes: Cross compliance: Northern Ireland 405
Agriculture: Common Agricultural Policy: Single payment & support schemes: Northern Ireland 405
Agriculture: Common Agricultural Policy: Single payment & support schemes: Reductions from payments: England 13
Agriculture: Common Agricultural Policy: Single payment & support schemes: Set-aside: Northern Ireland 405
Agriculture: Common Agricultural Policy: Single payment scheme: Set-aside: Wales 16
Agriculture: Common Agricultural Policy: Support schemes: Single payments: Cross compliance: Wales. 16
Agriculture: Common Agricultural Policy: Support schemes: Single payments: Wales 16
Agriculture: Common Agricultural Policy: Wine: England & Northern Ireland 14, 16
Agriculture: Common Agricultural Policy: Wine: Scotland. 341
Agriculture: Common Agricultural Policy: Wine: Wales. 17
Agriculture: Countryside: Management: Northern Ireland 405
Agriculture: EC fertilisers: England & Wales. 16
Agriculture: Eggs: Marketing standards: Northern Ireland 405
Agriculture: England Rural Development Programme: Project-based schemes: Closures 14
Agriculture: Environmental & countryside stewardships: England. 14, 51
Agriculture: Environmental impact assessment: England. 14
Agriculture: Environmental impact assessment: Scotland 341, 354, 356, 359, 376, 391
Agriculture: Environmental impact assessment: Uncultivated land & semi-natural areas: Northern Ireland. 406
Agriculture: Environmental stewardship & organic products. 13, 51
Agriculture: Environmentally sensitive areas: Designation: Northern Ireland 406
Agriculture: Farm Nutrient Management Scheme: Northern Ireland 406
Agriculture: Farm subsidies: Decisions: Review: Northern Ireland. 406
Agriculture: Feed & food: Official controls: England 15, 90
Agriculture: Feed & food: Official controls: Northern Ireland. 406, 418
Agriculture: Feed: Hygiene & enforcement: Scotland. 341
Agriculture: Feed: Specified undesirable substances: England. 14
Agriculture: Feed: Specified undesirable substances: Northern Ireland. 406
Agriculture: Feed: Specified undesirable substances: Wales 17
Agriculture: Feeding stuffs: Enforcement: Wales. 17
Agriculture: Feeding stuffs: England 14
Agriculture: Feeding stuffs: Northern Ireland 406
Agriculture: Feeding stuffs: Sampling & analysis: England 14
Agriculture: Feeding stuffs: Sampling & analysis: Scotland 341
Agriculture: Feeding stuffs: Sampling & analysis: Wales 17
Agriculture: Feeding stuffs: Scotland 341
Agriculture: Feeding stuffs: Wales 17
Agriculture: Feedings stuffs & feeding stuffs sampling & analysis: Northern Ireland 406
Agriculture: Fertilisers: European Communities: Northern Ireland. 405
Agriculture: Fertilisers: European Communities: Scotland 341
Agriculture: Health & safety: Children & young persons: Northern Ireland 420
Agriculture: Hill farm allowance: England 14, 15
Agriculture: Home-Grown Cereals Authority: Levy: Rate 13

Agriculture: Land management contracts: Menu scheme: Scotland. 342
Agriculture: Less favoured area support scheme: Scotland 342
Agriculture: Less favoured areas: Compensatory allowances: Northern Ireland 406
Agriculture: Natural Environment & Rural Communities Act 2006: Commencements. 13, 141, 261
Agriculture: Official controls: England 15, 90
Agriculture: Older cattle: Disposal: Wales 18
Agriculture: Organic farming: Animal housing: Conversion: Northern Ireland. 406
Agriculture: Paying Agency: National Assembly for Wales 18
Agriculture: Pesticides: Maximum residue levels: Crops, food & feeding stuffs: England & Wales 16, 152
Agriculture: Pesticides: Maximum residue levels: Crops, food & feeding stuffs: Northern Ireland 406, 407, 431
Agriculture: Pesticides: Maximum residue levels: Crops, food & feeding stuffs: Scotland 342, 368
Agriculture: Phosphorus: Use: Northern Ireland. 414
Agriculture: Pig carcases: Grading: England 15
Agriculture: Pig carcases: Grading: Northern Ireland 407
Agriculture: Pig carcases: Grading: Scotland 342
Agriculture: Products of animal origin: Third country imports: England. 15
Agriculture: Products of animal origin: Third country imports: Northern Ireland 407
Agriculture: Products of animal origin: Third country imports: Scotland. 342
Agriculture: Rice products: Marketing: Restrictions: England 15, 91
Agriculture: Rice products: Marketing: Restrictions: Northern Ireland 407, 418
Agriculture: Rural development programmes: Wales. 18
Agriculture: Seed potatoes: Tuber inspection fees: Northern Ireland 407
Agriculture: Sheep & goats: Records, identification & movement: Northern Ireland. 407
Agriculture: Single payment & support schemes: Cross-compliance: England 13
Agriculture: Subsidies & grants schemes: Appeals: Wales 16
Agriculture: Tir Cynnal: Wales 18
Agriculture: Tir Gofal: Wales 18
Agriculture: Weather aid 2002 scheme: Northern Ireland 405
Agri-food & Biosciences Institute: Superannuation: Northern Ireland 431
Air Force Act 1955: Continuation. 56
Air Force: Disablement & death: Service pensions 147
Air Force: Service pensions 147
Air navigation 33
Air navigation: Dangerous goods 33
Air navigation: Flying restrictions: Abergele 33
Air navigation: Flying restrictions: Arsingworth 33
Air navigation: Flying restrictions: Beating the Retreat Ceremony. 33
Air navigation: Flying restrictions: Biggin Hill. 33
Air navigation: Flying restrictions: Blackburn 33
Air navigation: Flying restrictions: Bournemouth 33
Air navigation: Flying restrictions: Burnham Overy Staithe 33
Air navigation: Flying restrictions: Christchurch 33
Air navigation: Flying restrictions: Dover & the English Channel 34
Air navigation: Flying restrictions: Dunsfold 34
Air navigation: Flying restrictions: Duxford 34
Air navigation: Flying restrictions: Eastbourne 34
Air navigation: Flying restrictions: Elvington. 34
Air navigation: Flying restrictions: Farnborough 34
Air navigation: Flying restrictions: Happisburth 34
Air navigation: Flying restrictions: Hawick. 34
Air navigation: Flying restrictions: Hendon. 34
Air navigation: Flying restrictions: Her Majesty, the Queen's 80th birthday flypast. 34
Air navigation: Flying restrictions: Her Majesty, the Queen's 80th Birthday flypast 34
Air navigation: Flying restrictions: High Wycombe 34, 35
Air navigation: Flying restrictions: HMP Channings Wood 35
Air navigation: Flying restrictions: Hullavington. 35
Air navigation: Flying restrictions: Inverkeithing. 35
Air navigation: Flying restrictions: Isle of Wight 35
Air navigation: Flying restrictions: Jet formation display teams 35
Air navigation: Flying restrictions: Keevil 35
Air navigation: Flying restrictions: Kemble. 35
Air navigation: Flying restrictions: Kesgrave. 35
Air navigation: Flying restrictions: Kew Palace 35
Air navigation: Flying restrictions: Llangeitho 36
Air navigation: Flying restrictions: Lowestoft 36
Air navigation: Flying restrictions: Manchester. 36

Air navigation: Flying restrictions: Margate 36
Air navigation: Flying restrictions: Mark Cross, East Sussex. 36
Air navigation: Flying restrictions: Morecombe Bay 36
Air navigation: Flying restrictions: Muston. 36
Air navigation: Flying restrictions: Nacton 36
Air navigation: Flying restrictions: North east London 36
Air navigation: Flying restrictions: Northern North Sea 36
Air navigation: Flying restrictions: Orford Ness 36
Air navigation: Flying restrictions: Peterborough. 37
Air navigation: Flying restrictions: Plymouth. 37
Air navigation: Flying restrictions: Popular Flying Association Rally 37
Air navigation: Flying restrictions: RAF Brize Norton 37
Air navigation: Flying restrictions: RAF Fairford 37
Air navigation: Flying restrictions: Remembrance Sunday 37
Air navigation: Flying restrictions: Rough Tower 37
Air navigation: Flying restrictions: Royal Air Force Leuchars 37
Air navigation: Flying restrictions: Royal Air Force Waddington 37
Air navigation: Flying restrictions: Royal Albert Hall 37
Air navigation: Flying restrictions: Sandhurst 37
Air navigation: Flying restrictions: Silverstone & Turweston 37
Air navigation: Flying restrictions: Smailholm 37
Air navigation: Flying restrictions: Southampton Water 37
Air navigation: Flying restrictions: Southend 38
Air navigation: Flying restrictions: Southern North Sea 38
Air navigation: Flying restrictions: Southport. 38
Air navigation: Flying restrictions: St Austell 38
Air navigation: Flying restrictions: St. Andrews 38
Air navigation: Flying restrictions: Stapleford 38
Air navigation: Flying restrictions: Staplehurst 38
Air navigation: Flying restrictions: State Opening of Parliament. 38
Air navigation: Flying restrictions: Stonehenge. 38
Air navigation: Flying restrictions: Stratford 38
Air navigation: Flying restrictions: Sunderland 38
Air navigation: Flying restrictions: Thursley 38
Air navigation: Flying restrictions: Tower of London 38
Air navigation: Flying restrictions: Trooping of the Colour Ceremony 39
Air navigation: Flying restrictions: Wales & southern England 39
Air navigation: Flying restrictions: Warwickshire 39
Air navigation: Flying restrictions: West Wales Airport 39
Air navigation: Flying restrictions: Weston Park 39
Air navigation: Flying restrictions: Weston-Super-Mare 39
Air navigation: Flying restrictions: Whittlesea 39
Air navigation: Flying restrictions: Wycombe Air Park 39
Air navigation: Overseas territories 33
Air passenger duty: Rate: Qualifying territories 83
Air pollution: Ships: Prevention 127
Air Travel Trust: Funding: Acts 4
Air Travel Trust: Funding: Acts: Explanatory notes 9
Aircraft: Third-country aircraft: Safety: Civil aviation 40
Airports: Slots: Allocation. 39
Alcoholic Liquor Duties Act 1979: Schedule 2A, para. 1(3): Amendment 83
Allt an Lagain: Scottish Water: Scotland 394
Al-Qaida & Taliban: United Nations: Measures. 286
Amesbury Church of England Voluntary Controlled Primary School: Religious character: Designation 62
Amnesic shellfish poisoning: Food protection: East Coast: Scotland 371
Amnesic shellfish poisoning: Food protection: West Coast: Scotland 371, 372
Anatomy Act 1984: Transitional provisions: Human Tissue (Scotland) Act 2006: Scotland 343, 358
Anatomy: Scotland 343
Anatomy: Specific persons & museums for public display: Scotland 343
Ancient Monuments Board for Wales: Abolition 158
Anglian region: General drainage charges 119
Angus: Electoral arrangements: Scotland 360
Animal by-products: Wales 22
Animal Health & Welfare (Scotland) Act 2006: Commencements: Scotland 343
Animal Health & Welfare (Scotland) Act 2006: Consequential Provisions: England and Wales 22, 42, 58

Animal Health & Welfare (Scotland) Act 2006: Consequential provisions: Scotland 343
Animal health: Animal by-products: Wales. 22
Animal health: Animals & animal products: Import & export: England 19
Animal health: Animals & animal products: Import & export: England: Scotland 343
Animal health: Animals & animal products: Import & export: Scotland 343
Animal health: Animals & animal products: Import & export: Wales 22, 23
Animal health: Avian influenza & influenza of avian origin: Mammals: England 19, 20
Animal health: Avian influenza & influenza of avian origin: Mammals: Scotland 343
Animal health: Avian influenza & influenza of avian origin: Mammals: Wales 23
Animal health: Avian influenza: Poultry: England 20
Animal health: Avian influenza: Poultry: Wales 23
Animal health: Avian influenza: Preventive measures: England 20
Animal health: Avian influenza: Preventive measures: Scotland 344
Animal health: Avian influenza: Preventive measures: Wales 23
Animal health: Avian influenza: Slaughter & vaccination: Scotland 344
Animal health: Avian influenza: Vaccination: England. 20
Animal health: Avian influenza: Vaccination: Wales. 23, 24
Animal health: Avian influenza: Wild birds: England 20
Animal health: Avian influenza: Wild birds: Scotland 343
Animal health: Avian influenza: Wild birds: Wales 23
Animal health: Bovine spongiform encephalopathy: Compensation: Wales 24
Animal health: Brucellosis: Wales 24
Animal health: Cattle: Compensation: England. 20
Animal health: Cattle: Database: Amendments 19
Animal health: Cattle: Identification: Amendments 19
Animal health: Diseases: Approved disinfectants: England 20
Animal health: Diseases: Approved disinfectants: Scotland. 344
Animal health: Enzootic bovine leukosis: Wales 24
Animal health: Equine infectious anaemia: Compensation: England. 20
Animal health: Foot & mouth disease: England 21
Animal health: Foot & mouth disease: Scotland. 344
Animal health: Foot & mouth disease: Slaughter & vaccination: Scotland 344
Animal health: Foot & mouth disease: Vaccination: Control: England. 21
Animal health: Foot & mouth disease: Vaccination: Control: Northern Ireland 408
Animal health: Foot & mouth disease: Vaccination: Control: Wales. 24
Animal health: Foot & mouth disease: Wales. 24
Animal health: Horses: Zootechnical standards: Wales. 22
Animal health: Products: Animal origin: Third country imports: Scotland 344
Animal health: Salmonella: Broiler flocks: Survey powers: Wales. 24
Animal health: Salmonella: Laying flocks: Survey powers: England 21
Animal health: Salmonella: Turkey flocks & slaughter pigs: Survey powers: England 21
Animal health: Sheep & goats: Identification & traceability: Scotland 344
Animal health: Sheep & goats: Records, identification & movement: England 21
Animal health: Sheep & goats: Records, identification & movement: Wales 24, 25
Animal health: Sheep & goats: Transmissible spongiform encephalopathies: Compensation: Wales 25
Animal health: Specified animal pathogens: England 21
Animal health: Specified diseases: Notification & slaughter: Wales 25
Animal health: Specified pathogens: Wales. 25
Animal health: Transmissible spongiform encephalopathies: England. 21
Animal health: Transmissible spongiform encephalopathies: Northern Ireland 407, 416
Animal health: Transmissible spongiform encephalopathies: Scotland 345
Animal health: Transmissible spongiform encephalopathies: Wales 22
Animal health: Tuberculosis: England 21
Animal health: Tuberculosis: Wales 25
Animal housing: Conversion: Organic farming: Northern Ireland 406
Animal welfare: Acts 4
Animal welfare: Acts: Explanatory notes 9
Animals & animal products: Import & export: England 19
Animals & animal products: Import & export: Northern Ireland 407, 408, 415
Animals & animal products: Import & export: Scotland 343
Animals & animal products: Import & export: Wales 22, 23
Animals & animal products: Residues & maximum residue limits: Examinations: Northern Ireland 417
Animals: Animal Health & Welfare (Scotland) Act 2006: Consequential provisions: Scotland 343
Animals: Dangerous wild animals: 2004 Order: Commencements: Northern Ireland 411
Animals: Dangerous wild animals: Fees: Northern Ireland 411
Animals: Diseases: Approved disinfectants. 24

Animals: Diseases: Northern Ireland 408, 415
Animals: Gatherings: England 19
Animals: Health & welfare: Acts: Explanatory notes: Scotland. 340
Animals: Health & welfare: Acts: Scotland 338
Animals: Health: Welfare: Transport 22
Animals: Horses: Zootechnical standards: England. 19
Animals: Official controls: England. 15, 90
Animals: Products of animal origin: Third country imports: England 15
Animals: Products of animal origin: Third country imports: Northern Ireland 407
Animals: Products of animal origin: Third country imports: Scotland 342
Animals: Products of animal origin: Third country imports: Wales 18
Animals: Sales, markets & lairs: Northern Ireland 408
Animals: Salmonella: Turkey flocks & slaughter pigs: Survey powers: Northern Ireland. 408, 415
Animals: Specified diseases: Notification & slaughter 21
Animals: Welfare: Slaughter or killing 22
Animals: Welfare: Transport: Northern Ireland 408
Animals: Welfare: Transport: Scotland 345
Anti-social Behaviour Act 2003: Commencement 79
Anti-social Behaviour Act 2003: Commencements: England & Wales 52
Anti-social Behaviour Act 2003: Commencements: Wales. 70
Antisocial Behaviour etc. (Scotland) Act 2004: Commencements: Scotland 348, 352, 360, 369
Anti-social behaviour orders: Magistrates' courts: Rules: Northern Ireland 428
Anti-social behaviour: Parenting orders: Wales. 72
Appointments Commission: National Health Service. 131, 159, 265
Appropriation: Acts. 4
Archaeology: Wrecks: Protection: Designation: England 158
Archbishop Courtenay Primary School: Religious character: Designation 62
Argyll & Bute: Electoral arrangements: Scotland 361
Armed Forces & Reserve Forces: Pensions Appeal Tribunals: Compensation scheme: Rights of appeal . . . 150
Armed Forces Act 2001: Commencement 56
Armed forces: Acts 4
Armed forces: Acts: Explanatory notes. 9
Armed Forces: Compensation schemes 146
Armed Forces: Compensation schemes: Excluded benefits: Tax purposes 109
Armed Forces: Entry, search & seizure 56
Armed Forces: Pension schemes: Amendment 146
Armed Forces: Pension schemes: Pensions increase 150
Armed Forces: Redundancy schemes 146
Armorial bearings: Local authorities. 123
Arms decommissioning: Amnesty period: Northern Ireland 143
Army Act 1955: Continuation. 56
Army: Disablement & death: Service pensions 147
Army: Service pensions 147
Artists: Resale rights 117
Asbestos: Control 94
Asian Development Bank: Asian Development Fund: Eighth replenishment. 117
Assembly Ombudsman: Salaries: Northern Ireland 439
Assistants to Justices' Clerks: Magistrates' courts. 126
Association of Law Costs Draftsmen: England & Wales 120
Assynt-Coigach area: Salmon & freshwater fisheries: Protection: Scotland 375
Asylum & Immigration (Treatment of Claimants, etc.) Act 2004: Commencement 107
Asylum & immigration: Acts. 6
Asylum & immigration: Acts: Explanatory notes. 10
Asylum & immigration: Refugees or persons in need of international protection: Qualification 109
Asylum & immigration: Safe countries: First list 108
Asylum & immigration: Tribunals: Fast track procedure 107
Asylum & immigration: Tribunals: Procedure: Amendments 107
Asylum: Designated states 107, 108
Asylum: Nationality, Immigration & Asylum Act 2002: Commencements. 109
Asylum: Nationality, Immigration & Asylum Act 2002: Juxtaposed controls 109
Asylum: Support 108
Atomic energy & radioactive substances: Emergency exemption: England & Wales 25
Atomic energy & radioactive substances: Nuclear industries: Security 25
Atomic energy & radioactive substances: Testing instruments: Exemptions: England & Wales. 25
Authorised investment funds: Taxes. 28, 47, 109

Automatic catchweighers: Weights & measures. 290
Automatic discontinuous totalisers: Weights & measures. 290
Automatic rail-weighbridges: Weights & measures 291
Automatic telling machines: Rural areas: Designation: Rates: Northern Ireland 435
Avian influenza & influenza of avian origin: Mammals: England 19, 20
Avian influenza & influenza of avian origin: Mammals: Wales 23
Avian influenza: Mammals: Scotland 343
Avian influenza: Poultry: England 20
Avian influenza: Poultry: Wales 23
Avian influenza: Preventive measures: England 20
Avian influenza: Preventive measures: Scotland 344
Avian influenza: Preventive measures: Wales 23
Avian influenza: Slaughter & vaccination: Scotland 344
Avian influenza: Vaccination: England 20
Avian influenza: Vaccination: Wales 23
Avian influenza: Wild birds: England. 20
Avian influenza: Wild birds: Scotland 343
Avian influenza: Wild birds: Wales 23
Aviation: Civil: Acts 4
Aviation: Civil: Acts: Explanatory notes 9
Aviation: Civil: Air navigation 33
Aviation: Civil: Air navigation: Overseas territories 33
Aviation: Civil: Air passenger duty: Rate: Qualifying territories. 83
Avon Ambulance Service: National Health Service Trust. 132
Awards for All (England) Joint Scheme: Authorisation: National lottery. 141
Awards: Students: Northern Ireland 412
Awdurdod Gwasanaethau Busnes y GIG: NHS Business Services Authority: Membership & procedure 137

B

Bail conditions: Devices: Compliance monitoring & specification: Methods: Scotland 348
Banking: Clearing houses: Regulatory provisions: Acts 7
Banking: Clearing houses: Regulatory provisions: Acts: Explanatory notes 10
Banks: Former authorised institutions: Insolvency 115
Bark: Plant health: Northern Ireland 433
Battleship Wharf railway: Port of Blyth 284, 285
Bee diseases & pests control: England 25
Bee diseases & pests control: Wales 26
Beef carcases: Classification: Scotland 340
Beer: Excise 83
Belarus: Restrictive measures: Funds, financial assets or economic resources: Overseas territories 145
Belfast: Health & Social Services Trust: Establishment: Northern Ireland 419
Belfast: Motor hackney carriages: By-laws: Northern Ireland 437
Belford St Mary's Church of England Voluntary Aided Middle School: Religious character: Designation 62
Beltweighers: Weights & measures 291
Bermuda: Outer Space Act 1986: Extension. 145
Best value authorities: Power to trade: Local government: Wales 125
Betting, gaming & lotteries: Gambling Act 1968: Fees: Variation: Scotland 345
Betting, gaming & lotteries: Gambling Act 2005: Commencements 26
Betting, gaming & lotteries: Gambling Act 2005: Commencements & transitional provisions 26
Betting, gaming & lotteries: Gambling Act 2005: Licensing authority policy statement. 27
Betting, gaming & lotteries: Gambling Act 2005: Licensing authority policy statement: Scotland. 345
Betting, gaming & lotteries: Gambling Act 2005: Licensing Authority: Policy statement 26
Betting, gaming & lotteries: Gambling Act 2005: Part 5: Modification: Personal licences 27
Betting, gaming & lotteries: Gambling Act 2005: Relevant offences 26
Betting, gaming & lotteries: Gambling Act 2005: Small-scale operator: Definition 26
Betting, gaming & lotteries: Gambling Act 2005: Transitional provisions 26
Betting, gaming & lotteries: Gambling Appeals Tribunal: Fees 26
Betting, gaming & lotteries: Gambling Appeals Tribunal: Rules. 26
Betting, gaming & lotteries: Gambling: Operating licences & single-machine permit fees 27
Betting, gaming & lotteries: Gambling: Personal licence fees 27
Betting, gaming & lotteries: Gaming Act 1968: Fees: Variation 27
Betting, gaming & lotteries: Gaming Act 1968: Fees: Variation: England & Wales. 27
Betting, gaming & lotteries: Gaming Act 1968: Monetary limits: Variation 27
Betting, gaming & lotteries: Lotteries: Gambling Commission: Fees 27
Betting, gaming & lotteries: Olympic lotteries: Payments out of fund 27

Betting, gaming & lotteries: Value added tax 288
Bidston Church of England Primary School: Religious character: Designation 62
Big lottery fund: Prescribed expenditure. 140
Biogas: Fuel-testing: Excise rebate 84
Birds: Avian influenza *see* Avian influenza
Birmingham Children's Hospital: National Health Service Trust. 131
Births, deaths, marriages, etc.: Registration *see* Registration .....
Blessed Trinity RC College: Religious character: Designation. 62
Blood: Safety & quality 94
Blyth: Port: Battleship Wharf railway 284, 285
Boatmasters: Qualifications & hours of work: Inland waterway & limited coastal operations 130
Body parts: Removal & use: Maintenance of records & supply of information: Human Tissue (Scotland) Act 2006: Scotland. 358
Boilers: Efficiency. 77
Bosnia & Herzegovina: Export control 54
Botswana: Double taxation: Relief. 29, 47, 110
Bournemouth-Swanage motor road & ferry: Revision of charges & traffic classifications 100
Bovine spongiform encephalopathy: Compensation: Wales 24
Bovine tuberculosis: Animal health: England. 21
Bovines: Brucellosis: Animal health: Wales 24
Bovines: Enzootic bovine leukosis: Animal health: Wales 24
Bovines: Tuberculosis: Animal health: Wales 25
Brackla & Coity Higher: Bridgend: Local government 124
Bracknell Forest (Borough): Permitted & special parking areas 253
Bradford Cathedral Community College: Religious character: Designation 62
Bradford: Parish electoral arrangements: Local government 121
Bradford: Parishes: Local government. 121
Bridgend: Brackla & Coity Higher: Local government 124
British citizenship: Designated service 27
British film: Definition 32
British nationality: British citizenship: Designated service 27
British nationality: Proof of paternity 27
British Olympic Association: Association rights: Appointment of proprietors 41, 282
British Paralympic Association: Association rights: Appointment of proprietors. 41, 282
British Paralympic Association: Association rights: Paralympic symbol 41, 282
Broadcasting: Digital terrestrial sound: Technical service 27, 75
Broadcasting: Gaelic Language (Scotland) Act 2005: Consequential modifications. 28, 43, 58
Broadcasting: Radio: Multiplex services: Digital capacity: Required percentage 28
Broadcasting: Television licensing 27, 75
Broadcasting: Television: Licensable content services 28, 75
Broadcasting: Wireless telegraphy: Guernsey 28, 75, 292
Broadcasting: Wireless telegraphy: Jersey. 28, 75, 293
Broadland, District: Whole Council elections 122
Broads Internal Drainage Board 119
Broiler flocks: Salmonella: Survey powers: England 21
Broiler flocks: Salmonella: Survey powers: Wales 24
Brucellosis: Animal health: Wales 24
BSE *see* Bovine spongiform encephalopathy 24
Buckinghamshire Mental Health: National Health Service Trust 131
Budget (Scotland) Act 2005: Amendments: Scotland 370
Budget (Scotland) Act 2006: Amendments: Scotland 370
Budget statements: Education: England. 63
Budget: Acts: Scotland. 338
Budget: Northern Ireland. 142
Building & buildings: Building & approved inspectors: England & Wales 28
Building & buildings: Forms: Scotland 345
Building & buildings: Scotland 346
Building & buildings: Sustainable & Secure Buildings Act 2004: Commencement 28
Building regulations: Northern Ireland 408
Building regulations: Scotland. 346
Buildings: Listed buildings & buildings in conservation areas: Town & country planning: Scotland 392
Bulgaria: Social security 269
Bulgaria: Social security: Northern Ireland 423, 435, 440
Bunkers Convention: Merchant shipping: Oil pollution 129
Burma: Sale, supply, export, technical assistance, financing & financial assistance: Customs: Penalties & licences 54
Bus lane contraventions: Approved local authorities 121, 122, 253

Bus User Complaints Tribunal: Scotland 392
Buses: Travel concession scheme: Older & disabled persons: Eligible persons & services: Scotland 392
Buses: Travel concession scheme: Older & disabled persons: Scotland 392
Business: Regulated sector: Proceeds of Crime Act 2002. 157
Business: Regulated sector: Terrorism Act 2000 156
Bute: Argyll & Bute: Electoral arrangements: Scotland. 361
Byssinosis: Miscellaneous disease benefit. 269
Byways: Restricted: Application & consequential amendment of provisions: England & Wales 101

C

Cadishead Primary School: School session times. 62
Calderdale (Metropolitan Borough): Permitted & special parking areas 254
Cambridgeshire County Council: Cambridge Riverside Foot/Cycle Bridge: Construction. 100
Canals & inland waterways: Transport & works: Applications & objections: Procedure: England & Wales. 28, 285, 286
Canals & telecommunications: Non-domestic rating: Scotland 374
Canterbury City Council: Armorial bearings 123
CAP *see* Common Agricultural Policy 13
Capacity serving measures: Weights & measures 291
Capital allowances: Energy-saving plant & machinery 47, 109
Capital allowances: Environmentally beneficial plant & machinery 47, 109
Capital finance & accounting: Wales 124
Capital gains tax see *also* Taxes
Capital gains tax: Annual exempt amount 29
Capital gains tax: Authorised investment funds 28, 47, 109
Capital gains tax: Avoidance schemes: Arrangements: Prescribed descriptions 29, 50, 114
Capital gains tax: Avoidance schemes: Information. 29, 50, 114
Capital gains tax: Chargeable gains: Gilt-edged securities 29, 50
Capital gains tax: Double taxation: Relief: Botswana 29, 47, 110
Capital gains tax: Double taxation: Relief: Japan 29, 47, 110
Capital gains tax: Double taxation: Relief: Poland 29, 47, 110
Capital gains tax: Gilt-edged securities 29, 50
Capital gains tax: Pension Protection Fund 29, 49, 111, 115, 274
Capital gains tax: Permanent interest bearing share: Definitions 29
Capital gains tax: Savings income: Information: Reporting. 29, 50, 114
Capital requirements: Financial services & markets 86
Caravans: Definitions: England 279
Care Standards Act 2000: Care services: Fees: Abolition: Wales 31, 159, 266
Care Standards Act 2000: Establishments & agencies. 265
Care Standards Act 2000: Regulatory reform & complaints: Wales 31, 266
Care Standards Tribunal: Children & vulnerable adults: England & Wales. 31, 266
Care Standards Tribunal: Disqualification orders: Review: Children & vulnerable adults: England & Wales 31
Care Tribunal: Regulations: Amendments: Northern Ireland 419
Care: Regulation of Care (Scotland) Act 2001: Commencements: Scotland 390
Care: Regulation: Applications & provision of advice: Scotland 390
Care: Regulation: Fees: Scotland 390
Care: Regulation: Requirements as to care services: Scotland 390
Careers & related services: Inspection: Wales 73
Carers: Services for: Community care: Children's services: Direct payments: Wales 273
Caribbean & North Atlantic territories: Turks & Caicos Islands: Constitution. 29
Caribbean Development Bank: Unified Special Development Fund: Sixth replenishment. 117
Carmarthenshire: Community Health Councils National Health Service: Wales 138
Carrington Spur, Trafford: Special roads scheme 100
Cars: Value added tax 288
Castle Point: Parishes: Local government 122
Catchweighers: Automatic: Weights & measures 290
Cathedrals: Care. 61
Cattle: Compensation: England 20
Cattle: Database: Amendments 19
Cattle: Identification: Amendments. 19
Cattle: Older cattle: Disposal: Scotland 342
Cattle: Older cattle: Disposal: Wales 18
Central Leeds Learning Federation: School session times: Changes 62
Ceramic articles: Food: Contact : Scotland 354
Ceramic articles: Food: Contact: England. 88
Ceramic articles: Food: Contact: Northern Ireland 417

Ceramic articles: Food: Contact: Wales... 91
Cereal: Seeds: England.. 264
Cereal: Seeds: Scotland 388
Cereal: Seeds: Wales.. 264
Cereals marketing: Home-Grown Cereals Authority: Levy: Rate 13
Chancery procedure rules: Sheriff Court: Act of Sederunt: Scotland 389
Channel Tunnel: International arrangements 29
Channel Tunnel: Miscellaneous provisions... 29
Charities & Trustee Investment (Scotland) Act 2005: Commencements: Scotland........................... 346
Charities & Trustee Investment (Scotland) Act 2005: Consequential modifications................. 30, 43, 58
Charities: Accounts: Scotland 346
Charities: Acts 4
Charities: Acts: Explanatory notes 9
Charities: Assets protection: Exemptions: Scotland.. 346
Charities: Charity test: Specified bodies: Scotland 346
Charities: Cheadle Royal Hospital, Manchester... 30
Charities: Exemption 30
Charities: Further & Higher Education (Scotland) Act 1992: Modification: Scotland 346
Charities: Scottish Charity Appeals Panel: Rules: Scotland.. 346
Cheadle Royal Hospital, Manchester 30
Cheese: Curd cheese: Marketing restrictions: England 89
Cheese: Curd cheese: Marketing restrictions: Northern Ireland 405, 417
Cheese: Curd cheese: Marketing restrictions: Scotland 355
Cheese: Curd cheese: Marketing restrictions: Wales 91
Chickens: Salmonella: Broiler flocks: Survey powers: England 21
Chickens: Salmonella: Broiler flocks: Survey powers: Wales 24
Chief Electoral Officer for Northern Ireland: Superannuation: Northern Ireland......................... 431
Child Abduction & Custody Act 1985: Jersey 30
Child benefit 266
Child benefit: General 267
Child benefit: Rates 267
Child care & maintenance rules: Sheriff Court: Act of Sederunt: Scotland.............................. 389
Child care & maintenance rules: Vulnerable Witnesses (Scotland) Act 2004: Act of Sederunt: Scotland 389
Child care: Providers: Approval: Tax credits: Schemes: Northern Ireland 444
Child minding: Registration fees: England 30
Child support: Amendments: Northern Ireland... 409, 416
Child support: Contracting out: Northern Ireland 409, 410
Child support: Family law.. 85
Child support: Functions: Contracting out 46
Child tax credits 276
Child trust funds... 32
Child trust funds: Amendments 32
Childcare Act 2006: Commencements: England 30
Childcare: Acts 4
Childcare: Acts: Explanatory notes.. 9
Childcare: Vouchers & employer contracted childcare: Income tax: Exempt amounts 110
Children & adults: Vulnerable groups: Safeguarding: Acts 8
Children & adults: Vulnerable groups: Safeguarding: Acts: Explanatory notes 11
Children & young persons: Adoption agencies, adoption support agencies & local authority fostering functions: Inspection: Fees 31, 265
Children & young persons: Adoption: Independent Review of Determinations: Wales 32, 266
Children & young persons: Care services: Fees: Abolition: Wales 31, 159, 266
Children & young persons: Care Standards Tribunal: Disqualification orders: Review: England & Wales..... 31
Children & young persons: Care Standards Tribunal: England & Wales............................ 31, 266
Children & young persons: Child Abduction & Custody Act 1985: Jersey 30
Children & young persons: Child minding & day care: Registration fees: England 30
Children & young persons: Childcare Act 2006: Commencements: England 30
Children & young persons: Children Act 1989: Representations procedure: England 30
Children & young persons: Children Act 2004: Commencements: England............................ 30
Children & young persons: Children Act 2004: Commencements: Wales 31
Children & young persons: Children boards: Local safeguarding: Wales 32
Children & young persons: Commission for Social Care Inspection: Fees & frequency of inspections ... 30, 265
Children & young persons: Education & Inspections Act 2006: Commencements 30, 63
Children & young persons: Family Law Act 1986: Dependent Territories............................. 30
Children & young persons: Fostering services: Private arrangements: Wales 32, 266
Children & young persons: Health & safety: Agriculture: Northern Ireland 420

Children & young persons: Information sharing index: England 30
Children & young persons: Intensive support & monitoring: Scotland 346
Children & young persons: Local safeguarding children boards: England 30
Children & young persons: Office for Standards in Education, Children's services & Skills: Transitional provisions 31, 67
Children & young persons: Parental Responsibilities & Parental Rights Agreement: Scotland 347
Children & young persons: Prescribed orders: Northern Ireland, Guernsey & Isle of Man 31
Children & young persons: Protection: At work: Scotland 346
Children & young persons: Secure accommodation: Wales 266
Children & young persons: Services: Joint inspections: Scotland 346, 347
Children & young persons: Social security: Amendments: Northern Ireland 424, 436, 442
Children Act 1989: Care services: Fees: Abolition: Wales 31, 159, 266
Children Act 1989: Regulatory reform & complaints: Wales 31, 266
Children Act 1989: Representations procedure: England 30
Children Act 2004: Commencements: England 30
Children Act 2004: Commencements: Wales 31
Children boards: Local safeguarding: Wales 32
Children: Adoption: Overseas territories: Hague Convention: Amendments: Northern Ireland 426
Children: Childcare: Acts 4
Children: Childcare: Acts: Explanatory notes 9
Children: Employment: Northern Ireland 409
Children: Looked after: Schools: Admission: England 63
Children: Needs: Parental separation: Contact disputes: Acts 4
Children: Needs: Parental separation: Contact disputes: Acts: Explanatory notes 9
Children: Prescribed orders: Isle of Man & Guernsey: Northern Ireland 409
Children: Proceedings: Allocation: England & Wales 85
Children's services: Community care: Services for carers: Direct payments: Wales 273
Children's services: Inspection: Acts: Explanatory notes: Scotland 340
Children's services: Inspection: Acts: Scotland 339
Chiropractors: General Chiropractic Council: Professional Conduct & Health Committees: Rules 32
Christ College, Cheltenham: Religious character: Designation 62
Chronological tables: Statutes 12
Church of England: General Synod: Measures 11
Church of England: General Synod: Measures: Bound volumes 12
Church of England: General Synod: Measures: Tables & index 12
Church of England: Legal aid 62
Churches Conservation Trust: Grants to 62
Churchfields, The Village School: Religious character: Designation 62
Cider: Excise 83
Cinema & film: British film: Definition 32
Cinema & films: Certification 32
Cinema & films: Films: Co-production agreements 32
Cinemas & film: Films: Certification 32
Cinemas & films: European Convention on Cinematographic Co-production 32
Cinemas: British film: Definition 32
City & Hackney: National Health Service primary care trust 132
City of Glasgow: Road traffic: Permitted & special parking area: Scotland 377
Civic Government (Scotland) Act 1982: Licensing: Skin piercing & tattooing: Scotland 360, 370, 371
Civil aviation: Acts 4
Civil aviation: Acts: Explanatory notes 9
Civil aviation: Air navigation 33
Civil aviation: Air navigation: Dangerous goods 33
Civil aviation: Air navigation: Overseas territories 33
Civil aviation: Air passenger duty: Rate: Qualifying territories 83
Civil aviation: Airports: Slots: Allocation 39
Civil aviation: Flying restrictions 33, 34, 35, 36, 37, 38, 39
Civil aviation: Provision of information to passengers 39
Civil aviation: Single European sky: National supervisory authority: Functions 40
Civil aviation: Third-country aircraft: Safety 40
Civil aviation: Transport Act 2000: Consequential amendments: Scotland 40
Civil courts: England & Wales 51
Civil legal aid: Financial conditions: Scotland 359
Civil legal aid: Scotland 359, 360
Civil Partnership Act 2004: Commencements 40
Civil Partnership Act 2004: Consequential amendments: Scotland 347
Civil Partnership Act 2004: Relationships arising 40
Civil partnership: Attestation: Scotland 347

Civil partnership: Dissolution.: Pensions 40, 85, 151
Civil partnership: Dissolution: Pension Protection Fund: Northern Ireland 409, 416, 428
Civil partnership: Family homes: Forms of consent: Scotland 347
Civil partnership: Local government: Pension schemes: Northern Ireland 427
Civil partnership: Registration services: Fees: Scotland 347, 363, 375
Civil Procedure Act 1997: Amendment: England & Wales. 51, 275
Civil procedure: Rules 51, 52, 275
Civil procedure: Rules: England & Wales. 52, 275
Civil proceedings: Fees: England & Wales 52, 275
Civil registration: Local electoral administration & registration services: Acts: Commencements: Scotland 374
Civil registration: Local electoral administration & registration services: Acts: Scotland 339
Clackmannanshire: Electoral arrangements: Scotland. 361
Claims management services: Regulated: Compensation. 46
Clean air: Smoke control areas: Authorised fuels: England. 40
Clean air: Smoke control areas: Authorised fuels: Wales. 40
Clean air: Smoke control areas: Exempted fireplaces: England 40
Clean air: Smoke control areas: Exempted fireplaces: Wales. 40
Clean Neighbourhoods & Environment Act 2005: Commencements 79, 80, 81
Clean Neighbourhoods & Environment Act 2005: Commencements: Wales 81
Clearing houses: Banking: Regulatory provisions: Acts 7
Clearing houses: Banking: Regulatory provisions: Acts: Explanatory notes 10
Clifton Suspension Bridge Tolls: Revision 100
Climate change agreements: Eligible facilities 41
Climate change agreements: Eligible facilities 41
Climate change levy: Agreements: Amendments 41
Climate change levy: Agreements: Energy-intensive Installations 41
Climate change levy: Climate change agreements: Eligible facilities 41
Climate change levy: General: Amendments 41
Climate change: Sustainable energy: Acts 4
Climate change: Sustainable energy: Acts: Explanatory notes. 9
Clinical negligence scheme: National Health Service: England. 133
Cockles: Inshore fishing: Prohibition: Scotland 386, 387
Cold weather payments: Social Fund 269
Cold-water meters: Weights & measures 291
Collective redundancies 277
Commercial property: British Paralympic Association: Association rights: Paralympic symbol. 41, 282
Commercial property: London Olympic & Paralympic Games 2012: Association rights: Appointment of proprietors 41, 282
Commission for Patient & Public Involvement in Health: Membership & procedure: England 132
Commission for Social Care Inspection: Fees. 31, 265
Commission for Social Care Inspection: Fees & frequency of inspections 30, 265
Commissioner for Complaints: Salaries: Northern Ireland 439
Commissioner for Older People (Wales) Act 2006: Commencements 41
Commissioner for older people: Wales: Acts. 4
Commissioner for older people: Wales: Acts: Explanatory notes 9
Commissioner for Victims & Survivors for Northern Ireland. 144
Common Agricultural Policy: Single payment & support schemes. 13
Common Agricultural Policy: Single payment & support schemes: Cross-compliance: England 13
Common Agricultural Policy: Single payment & support schemes: Cross-compliance: Northern Ireland 405
Common Agricultural Policy: Single payment & support schemes: Cross-compliance: Wales 16
Common Agricultural Policy: Single payment & support schemes: Northern Ireland 405
Common Agricultural Policy: Single payment & support schemes: Reductions from payments: England 13
Common Agricultural Policy: Single payment & support schemes: Set-aside: Northern Ireland. 405
Common Agricultural Policy: Single payment & support schemes: Wales 16
Common Agricultural Policy: Single payment scheme: Set-aside: Wales 16
Common Agricultural Policy: Wine: England & Northern Ireland 14, 16
Common Agricultural Policy: Wine: Scotland 341
Common Agricultural Policy: Wine: Wales 17
Common land: Registration, management & protection: Acts 5
Common land: Registration, management & protection: Acts: Explanatory notes 9
Commons Act 2006: Commencements 41
Commons Services Agency: National Health Service: Functions: Scotland 364
Commons: Severance of rights: England 41
Commonwealth countries & Ireland: Immunities & privileges 117
Communications Act 2003: Network or service: Persistent misuse: Maximum penalty 75
Communications: Television licensing 27, 75

Community & youth work: Education & training: Inspection: Wales 73
Community benefit societies: Assets: Restrictions on use. 114
Community benefit societies: Assets: Restrictions on use: Northern Ireland 424
Community care: Services for carers: Children's services: Direct payments: Wales 273
Community drivers' hours & working time: Road tankers 166
Community Health Councils: National Health Service: Carmarthenshire: Wales. 138
Community justice authorities: Establishment, constitution & proceedings: Scotland 348
Community Legal Service: Financial 120
Community Legal Service: Financial: Amendments 120
Community Legal Service: Funding: Amendments: England & Wales. 120
Community Legal Service: Funding: Family proceedings: Counsel: England & Wales 120
Community order: Review: Specified courts: Liverpool & Salford 52
Community right to buy: Definition of excluded Land: Scotland. 359
Companies Act 2006: Commencements 41
Companies: 1986 Order: Investment companies & accounting & audit amendments: Northern Ireland 409
Companies: 1986 Order: Operating & financial review: Repeals: Northern Ireland 409
Companies: 1986 Order: Small companies' accounts & audit: Northern Ireland 409
Companies: Accounts & reports: Defective: Revision: Northern Ireland 409
Companies: Acts: Explanatory notes 9
Companies: Audit, investigations & community enterprise: 2005 Order: Commencements: Northern Ireland 409
Companies: Disclosure of information: Designated authorities. 42
Companies: Insolvency 115
Companies: Insolvency rules: Sheriff Court: Act of Sederunt: Scotland 390
Companies: Insolvency: Banks: Former authorised institutions. 115
Companies: Insolvency: Cross-border. 115
Companies: Insolvency: Scotland 116
Companies: Law: Reform: Acts 5
Companies: Local government: Best value: Northern Ireland. 427
Companies: Partnerships & unlimited companies: Accounts: Northern Ireland 409
Companies: Registrar, languages & trading disclosures 42
Companies: Small & medium-sized: Accounts & audit 41
Companies: Summary financial statements: Northern Ireland. 409
Companies: Takeover bids: Directives: Implementation 42
Compensation Act 2006: Commencements. 46
Compensation: Claims management services. 46
Compensation: Claims management services: Regulated 46
Compensation: Mesothelioma claims: Contribution 42
Compensation: Negligence: Claims: Acts 5
Compensation: Negligence: Claims: Acts: Explanatory notes 9
Compensation: Specification of benefits: England & Wales 46
Competition Act 1998: Public policy exclusion. 42
Competition: Enterprise Act 2002: Enforcement undertakings. 42
Competition: Enterprise Act 2002: Enforcement undertakings & orders. 42
Competition: Enterprise Act 2002: Part 9: Restrictions on disclosure of information 42, 45, 61
Competition: Enterprise Act 2002: Water Services Regulation Authority 42, 45
Comptroller & Auditor General: Salaries: Northern Ireland. 439
Conservation areas: Listed buildings: Planning permission: Applications 279
Conservation areas: Planning: Consultation: Northern Ireland 432
Conservation areas: Planning: Crown land: Amendments: Wales. 281
Conservation areas: Wales. 281
Conservation Boards: Pension schemes: Pensions increase 150
Conservation bodies: Title Conditions (Scotland) Act 2003: Amendments: Scotland 391
Conservation: Ancient Monuments Board for Wales: Abolition 158
Conservation: Historic Buildings Council for Wales: Abolition 158
Consolidated Fund: Acts 5
Constitutional law: Animal Health & Welfare (Scotland) Act 2006: Consequential Provisions: England and Wales 22, 42, 58
Constitutional law: Charities & Trustee Investment (Scotland) Act 2005: Consequential modifications 30, 43, 58
Constitutional law: Gaelic Language (Scotland) Act 2005: Consequential modifications 28, 43, 58
Constitutional law: Management of Offenders etc. (Scotland) Act 2005: Consequential modifications. 43, 52, 58
Constitutional law: National Assembly for Wales: Disqualifications. 43
Constitutional law: National Assembly for Wales: Representation of the people. 43, 59, 165
Constitutional law: National Assembly for Wales: Transfer of functions 43, 59, 60
Constitutional law: Northern Ireland Act 2000: Modification. 43, 143
Constitutional law: Prohibition of Smoking in Certain Premises (Scotland) Regulations 2006: Consequential provisions 44, 59, 94
Constitutional law: River Tweed. 44, 59, 166
Constitutional law: Scotland Act 1998: Agency arrangements 43, 59, 87

Constitutional law: Scotland Act 1998: Agency arrangements: Specifications 43, 58, 89, 131
Constitutional law: Scotland Act 1998: Schedule 5: Modifications 43, 59
Constitutional law: Scotland Act 1998: Transfer of functions to the Scottish Ministers etc. 44, 59
Constitutional law: Smoking, Health & Social Care (Scotland) Act 2005: Consequential amendments 44, 59, 138
Constitutional law: Smoking, Health & Social Care (Scotland) Act 2005: Consequential provisions 44, 59, 94
Constitutional law: Water Environment & Water Services (Scotland) Act 2003: Consequential provisions & modifications . . 44, 59, 290
Constitutional law: Water Environment (Controlled Activities) (Scotland) Regulations 2005: Notices in the interests of national security
. . . . 44, 59, 81, 290
Constitutional Reform Act 2005: Commencements 118, 125, 126, 275, 283
Constitutional Reform Act 2005: Commencements: Northern Ireland 118
Constitutional Reform Act 2005: Supplementary provisions 118
Constitutional Reform Act 2005: Temporary modifications 275
Construction industry: Industrial training: Levy: Northern Ireland 425
Construction: Contracts: Exclusion: Scotland 347
Consular fees 60
Consumer contracts: Unfair terms: Consumer protection: Water Act 2003 . . . . 46, 289
Consumer Credit Act 2006: Commencements 44
Consumer credit: Acts 5
Consumer credit: Acts: Explanatory notes 9
Consumer credit: Enforcement, default & termination notices 44
Consumer credit: Exempt agreements 44
Consumer protection: Compensation Act 2006: Commencements 46
Consumer protection: Compensation: Claims management services 46
Consumer protection: Compensation: Claims management services: Regulated 46
Consumer protection: Compensation: Specification of benefits: England & Wales 46
Consumer protection: Consumer contracts: Unfair terms 46, 289
Consumer protection: Cosmetic products: Safety 44, 45
Consumer protection: Dangerous substances & preparations: Safety 45
Consumer protection: Enterprise Act 2002: Amendment 45
Consumer protection: Enterprise Act 2002: Part 8 Community infringements specified UK laws 45
Consumer protection: Enterprise Act 2002: Part 8 notice to OFT of intended prosecution specified enactments 45
Consumer protection: Enterprise Act 2002: Part 9: Restrictions on disclosure of information 42, 45, 61
Consumer protection: Enterprise Act 2002: Water Services Regulation Authority 42, 45
Consumer protection: Price indications: Traders: Code of practice: Approval: Northern Ireland 409
Consumer protection: Tobacco Advertising & Promotion Act 2002: Amendments 45, 75
Consumer protection: Tobacco Advertising & Promotion Act 2002: Commencements 46
Consumer protection: Tobacco Advertising & Promotion Act 2002: Commencements: Scotland 347
Consumer protection: Water Act 2003: Transitional provisions 46, 289
Contaminants: food: Northern Ireland 417
Contaminants: Food: Wales 91
Contaminated land: England 79
Contaminated land: Radioactive contaminated land: Enactments: Modification: England 80
Contaminated land: Wales 82
Contracting out: Child support functions 46
Contracting out: Child support functions: Northern Ireland 410
Contracting out: Transport for London: Investment & highway functions: Best value 46, 125
Contracting-out: Child support functions: Northern Ireland 409
Controlled drugs: Management & use: Supervision 56
Conwy: Permitted parking area: Wales 255
Conygar Quarry: Mineral planning permissions: Periodic review 279
Cooperative societies: European Cooperative Society 46
Copyright & performances: Application to other countries 46, 165
Copyright: Educational recording of broadcasts & cable programmes: Licensing scheme: Certification: Educational Recording Agency
Ltd. 47
Copyright: Gibraltar 47
Copyright: Performances: Moral rights 47, 165
Corby (Borough): Electoral changes 121
Coroners: Discipline: Designation 47, 125, 126
Coroners' districts: Gloucestershire 47
Coroners' districts: Suffolk 47
Corporation tax: Acts: Amendments 48
Corporation tax: Authorised investment funds 28, 47, 109
Corporation tax: Avoidance schemes: Arrangements: Prescribed descriptions 29, 50, 114
Corporation tax: Avoidance schemes: Information 29, 50, 114
Corporation tax: Capital allowances: Environmentally beneficial plant & machinery 47, 109

Corporation tax: Chargeable gains: Gilt-edged securities. 29, 50
Corporation tax: Disposals & appropriations: Nomination scheme 49, 152
Corporation tax: Double taxation: Relief: Botswana 29, 47, 110
Corporation tax: Double taxation: Relief: Japan. 29, 47, 110
Corporation tax: Double taxation: Relief: Poland 29, 47, 110
Corporation tax: Finance (No. 2) Act 2005: Section 17 (1): Appointed day 48, 110
Corporation tax: Finance Act 2002: Schedule 26, parts 2 & 9 48
Corporation tax: Finance Act 2006: Section 53 (2): Films & sound recordings: Appointed day 48, 110
Corporation tax: Finance Act 2006: Section 53 (2): Films & sound recordings: Power to alter dates 48, 110
Corporation tax: Gilt-edged securities 29, 50
Corporation tax: Income Tax (Trading & Other Income) Act 2005: Consequential amendments 48, 111
Corporation tax: Insurance companies: Amendments. 48
Corporation tax: Investment trusts & venture capital trusts: Definition of capital profits, gains or losses 48
Corporation tax: Lloyd's sourcebook: Finance Act 1993 & Finance Act 1994: Amendment 48
Corporation tax: Lloyd's Underwriters: Double taxation relief: Corporate members 49
Corporation tax: Lloyd's Underwriters: Limited liability underwriting: Conversion to. 48, 111
Corporation tax: Lloyd's Underwriters: Scottish Limited Partnerships 49, 111
Corporation tax: Loan relationships & derivative contracts: Accounting practice: Change 49
Corporation tax: Loan relationships & derivative contracts: Disregard & bringing into account of profits & losses 49
Corporation tax: Loan relationships & derivative contracts: Profits & losses: Disregard & bringing into account 49
Corporation tax: Non-resident insurance companies: Overseas losses: Group relief: Corporation Tax Acts: Modification 48
Corporation tax: Oil: Market value 49, 152
Corporation tax: Overseas life insurance companies 49
Corporation tax: Pension Protection Fund 29, 49, 111, 115, 274
Corporation tax: Real estate investment trusts: Breach of conditions. 50
Corporation tax: Real estate investment trusts: Group trusts: Financial statements 50
Corporation tax: Real estate investment trusts: Joint ventures 50
Corporation tax: Real estate investment trusts: Taxes: Assessment & recovery 49
Corporation tax: Savings income: Information: Reporting 29, 50, 114
Corporation tax: Securitisation companies: Taxation. 50
Corporation tax: Tonnage tax: Financial year 2006: Exception. 50
Corporation tax: Unit trust schemes & offshore funds: Non-qualifying investments test. 50, 114
Cosmetic products: Safety. 44, 45
Council benefit: Amendments 268
Council tax benefit 267, 268
Council tax benefit: Electronic communications 75
Council tax benefit: State pension credit: Qualifying age 267
Council tax: Amendments: England. 50, 161
Council tax: Demand notices: England 161
Council tax: Discount disregards: Amendments: England 50
Council tax: Electronic communications: England 51, 161
Council tax: Electronic communications: Scotland 347, 361, 373
Council tax: Exempt dwellings: England 50
Council tax: Exempt dwellings: Scotland 347
Council tax: Local authorities: Calculations: Alteration: Wales 51
Council tax: Valuation lists: Acts: England 5
Council tax: Valuation lists: Acts: Explanatory notes: England 10
Counter Fraud & Security Management Service: Abolition. 138
Countryside & Rights of Way Act 2000: Commencements 165
Countryside & Rights of Way Act 2000: Commencements: Wales 51, 166
Countryside stewardship: England 14, 51
Countryside: Access: Exclusions & restrictions: England 51
Countryside: Management: Northern Ireland 405
Countryside: National Park Authorities: England. 51
County courts: Civil courts: England & Wales 51
County courts: Civil Procedure Act 1997: Amendment: England & Wales. 51, 275
County courts: Civil procedure: Rules: England & Wales. 51, 52, 275
County courts: Civil proceedings: Fees: England & Wales 52, 275
County courts: Courts Act 2003: Consequential amendment 52, 126, 275
County courts: Family proceedings: England & Wales 52, 85, 276
County courts: Family proceedings: Fees: England & Wales 52, 85, 276
County courts: Family proceedings: Rules: England & Wales 52, 85, 276
County courts: Family proceedings: Rules: Northern Ireland. 410, 416, 443
County courts: Rules: Northern Ireland 410
County Durham & Darlington Priority Services: National Health Service Trust 136
Court of Protection: Rules 129

Court of Session: Act of Sederunt: Family Law (Scotland) Act 2006: Scotland 348
Court of Session: Act of Sederunt: UNCITRAL Model law: Cross-border insolvency: Scotland 348
Court of Session: Messengers-at-Arms: Fees: Act of Sederunt: Scotland. 389
Court of Session: Rules: Act of Sederunt: Scotland 347
Court of Session: Rules: Solicitor's fees: Act of Sederunt: Scotland 348
Court of Session: Shorthand writers: Fees: Act of Sederunt: Scotland 347
Courts Act 2003: Consequential amendment. 52, 126, 275
Courts: Magistrates' courts: Criminal procedure: Rules: England & Wales 126, 276
Courts-martial: Prosecution appeals. 56, 57
Courts-martial: Royal Navy, Army & Royal Air Force: Evidence: Rules 57
Coventry & Warwickshire Partnership: National Health Service Trust 132
Crawley Down Village CE School: Religious character: Designation 63
Credit unions: Deposits & loans: Northern Ireland 410
Credit unions: Loans: Maximum interest rate 114
Credit unions: Membership: Limits: Northern Ireland. 410
Credit unions: Shares: Limits: Northern Ireland 410
Cremation: England & Wales 52
Crime & Disorder Act 1998: Intervention orders 53
Crime & Disorder Act 1998: Relevant authorities & relevant persons 53
Crime (International Co-operation) Act 2003: Commencement 52
Crime (International Co-operation) Act 2003: Commencements: Scotland 348
Crime prevention: Designated areas 100
Crime: Violent crime: Reduction: Acts 9
Crime: Violent crime: Reduction: Acts: Explanatory notes 11
Criminal appeals: Prosecution appeals: Northern Ireland 443
Criminal appeals: Serious offences: Retrial: Northern Ireland 443
Criminal appeals: Supreme Court, Northern Ireland: Jury trials: Northern Ireland 443
Criminal Defence Service Act 2006: Commencements 120
Criminal Defence Service: Acts 5
Criminal Defence Service: Acts: Explanatory notes 10
Criminal Defence Service: England & Wales 120
Criminal Defence Service: Financial eligibility: England & Wales 120
Criminal Defence Service: Funding 120
Criminal Defence Service: Representation orders & consequential amendments 120
Criminal Defence Service: Representation orders, appeals. etc.. 120
Criminal evidence: Criminal Justice (Evidence) (Northern Ireland) Order 2004: Commencements: Northern Ireland 410
Criminal evidence: Criminal Justice (Evidence) (Northern Ireland) Order 2004: Offences: Categories: Northern Ireland 410
Criminal Justice & Public Order Act 1994: Armed Forces: Application to 57
Criminal Justice & Public Order Act 1994: Custody Officer Certificate: Suspension 263
Criminal Justice (Evidence) (Northern Ireland) Order 2004: Commencements: Northern Ireland 410
Criminal Justice (Evidence) (Northern Ireland) Order 2004: Offences: Categories: Northern Ireland 410
Criminal Justice (Scotland) Act 2003: Commencements: Scotland 348
Criminal Justice Act 1988: Application: Service courts: Evidence 57
Criminal Justice Act 1988: Sentencing: Reviews: England, Wales & Northern Ireland 53
Criminal Justice Act 2003: Commencements 53, 54, 154
Criminal Justice Act 2003: Commencements: Northern Ireland 54
Criminal justice: 2003 Order: Commencements: Northern Ireland 410
Criminal justice: 2005 Order: Commencements: Northern Ireland 410
Criminal justice: Acts. 8
Criminal justice: Acts: Explanatory notes. 10
Criminal justice: Acts: Explanatory notes: Scotland. 340
Criminal justice: Acts: Scotland 339
Criminal law: Anti-social Behaviour Act 2003: Commencements: England & Wales 52
Criminal law: Antisocial Behaviour etc. (Scotland) Act 2004: Commencements: Scotland 348, 352, 360, 369
Criminal law: Bail conditions: Devices: Compliance monitoring & specification: Methods: Scotland 348
Criminal law: Community justice authorities: Establishment, constitution & proceedings: Scotland 348
Criminal law: Community order: Review: Specified courts: Liverpool & Salford 52
Criminal law: Crime & Disorder Act 1998: Intervention orders 53
Criminal law: Crime & Disorder Act 1998: Relevant authorities & relevant persons 53
Criminal law: Crime (International Co-operation) Act 2003: Commencements: Scotland 348
Criminal law: Criminal Justice Act 1988: Sentencing: Reviews: England, Wales & Northern Ireland 53
Criminal law: Criminal justice: 2005 Order: Commencements: Northern Ireland 410
Criminal law: Domestic Violence, Crime & Victims Act 2004: Commencements 53, 54
Criminal law: Emergency workers: Protection: Acts 5
Criminal law: Fraud Act 2006: Commencements 52

Criminal law: Home detention curfew licence: Prescribed standard conditions: Scotland 348
Criminal law: Liberty: Restriction: Scotland 349
Criminal law: Management of Offenders etc. (Scotland) Act 2005: Commencements: Scotland 348, 349
Criminal law: Management of Offenders etc. (Scotland) Act 2005: Consequential modifications. 43, 52, 58
Criminal law: Management of Offenders etc. (Scotland) Act 2005: Partner bodies: Designation: Scotland 349
Criminal law: Management of Offenders etc. (Scotland) Act 2005: Supplementary provisions: Scotland 349
Criminal law: Northern Ireland (Miscellaneous Provisions) Act 2006: Commencements 54, 276
Criminal law: Offenders: Risk assessment & minimisation: Accreditation schemes: Scotland. 349
Criminal law: Police & Justice Act 2006: Commencements 53, 85, 155
Criminal law: Police, Public Order & Criminal Justice (Scotland) Act 2006: Commencements: Scotland 349, 369
Criminal law: Private landlords: Registration: Information & fees: Scotland 349, 357, 362
Criminal law: Serious Organised Crime & Police Act 2005: Appeals under s. 74 . . . . 53, 54
Criminal law: Serious Organised Crime & Police Act 2005: Application & modification of enactments: England & Wales 53
Criminal law: Serious Organised Crime & Police Act 2005: Commencements 53, 54, 155, 265
Criminal law: Serious Organised Crime & Police Act 2005: Commencements: Scotland. 349, 370
Criminal law: Serious Organised Crime & Police Act 2005: Financial reporting orders: Specified persons: Scotland 349
Criminal legal aid: Fees: Scotland 360
Criminal legal aid: Prescribed proceedings: Scotland 360
Criminal legal aid: Summary justice pilot courts & bail conditions: Scotland 360
Criminal procedure: Criminal justice: 2003 Order: Commencements: Northern Ireland 410
Criminal procedure: Rules: England & Wales 126, 276
Criminal procedure: Rules: Financial reporting orders: Act of Adjournal: Scotland 357, 388
Criminal procedure: Rules: Risk assessment Orders: Orders for lifelong restriction: Act of Adjournal: Scotland 357
Criminal procedure: Rules: Vulnerable Witnesses (Scotland) Act 2004: Act of Adjournal: Scotland 357, 389
Criminal proceedings: Traffic management: Penalty charges: Exemptions: Northern Ireland 438
Criminal records: Police Act 1997. 154
Criminal records: Police Act 1997: Scotland 369
Criminal records: Registration: Police Act 1997: Scotland 369
Crofters, cottars & small landholders: Croft house grant: Scotland 349
Crofters, cottars & small landholders: Crofting counties: Agricultural grants scheme: Scotland 349
Crofting counties: Agricultural grants scheme: Scotland 349
Crofts: Croft house grant: Scotland 349
Crops, food & feeding stuffs: Pesticides: Maximum residue levels: England & Wales 16, 152
Crops, food & feeding stuffs: Pesticides: Maximum residue levels: Northern Ireland 406, 407, 431
Crops, food & feeding stuffs: Pesticides: Maximum residue levels: Scotland. 342, 368
Crops: Seed potatoes: Crop fees: Northern Ireland 439
Crown Court: Rules: Northern Ireland. 444
Curd cheese: Marketing restrictions: England 89
Curd cheese: Marketing restrictions: Northern Ireland. 405, 417
Curd cheese: Marketing restrictions: Scotland. 355
Curd cheese: Marketing restrictions: Wales. 91
Curriculum: Science: Key stage 4: Disapplication: Wales 72
Customs & excise duties: Travellers' allowances & personal reliefs: New member states 54, 83, 287, 288
Customs & excise: Air passenger duty: Rate: Qualifying territories 83
Customs & excise: Trade: Statistics 275
Customs & revenue: Complaints & misconduct. 165
Customs: Export control. 54, 55
Customs: Export control: Bosnia & Herzegovina. 54
Customs: Export control: Lebanon 55
Customs: Export control: Liberia 55
Customs: Export control: Radioactive sources 55
Customs: Export control: Security & para-military goods 55
Customs: Free zones: Designations 55
Customs: Sale, supply, export, technical assistance, financing & financial assistance: Burma: Penalties & licences 54
Customs: Technical assistance, financing & financial assistance: Lebanon: Penalties & licences. 55
Customs: Technical assistance: Control. 55
Customs: Third countries: Legacies imported from: Relief: Application 55, 84, 288

D

Dairy produce: Quotas. 89
Dairy produce: Quotas: Northern Ireland 417
Dairy produce: Quotas: Scotland 355
Dairy produce: Quotas: Wales 92
Dangerous drugs: Controlled drugs: Management & use: Supervision. 56
Dangerous drugs: Drugs Act 2005: Commencements 56

Dangerous drugs: Health Act 2006: Commencements 56, 137
Dangerous drugs: Misuse of drugs 55, 56
Dangerous drugs: Misuse of Drugs Act 1971: Amendments 55
Dangerous drugs: Misuse of drugs: Northern Ireland 410, 411
Dangerous goods: Air navigation 33
Dangerous goods: Carriage: Northern Ireland 420, 421
Dangerous substances & preparations: Controls 78
Dangerous substances & preparations: Safety 45
Dangerous wild animals: 2004 Order: Commencements: Northern Ireland. 411
Dangerous wild animals: Fees: Northern Ireland 411
Dartford - Thurrock Crossing: Amendments 100
Data protection: Sensitive personal data: Processing 56
Day care food scheme: Healthy start scheme: Northern Ireland. 418
Day care: Registration fees: England 30
Debt: Multilateral debt relief initiative: African Development Fund 117
Defence: Armed Forces Act 2001: Commencement 56
Defence: Army, Air Force & Navy discipline acts: Continuation 56
Defence: Courts-martial: Prosecution appeals 56, 57
Defence: Courts-martial: Royal Navy, Army & Royal Air Force: Evidence: Rules 57
Defence: Criminal Justice & Public Order Act 1994: Armed Forces: Application to 57
Defence: Criminal Justice Act 1988: Application: Service courts: Evidence. 57
Defence: Police & Criminal Evidence Act 1984: Armed Forces: Application to. 57
Defence: Protection of Military Remains Act 1986: Vessels & controlled sites: Designations 57
Defence: Royal Marines: Terms of service 57
Defence: Royal Navy: Ratings: Terms of service. 57
Defence: Standing Civilian courts: Evidence: Rules 57
Defence: Youth Justice & Criminal Evidence Act 1999: Application: Courts-martial 57
Defence: Youth Justice & Criminal Evidence Act 1999: Application: Courts-Martial Appeal Court 57
Defence: Youth Justice & Criminal Evidence Act 1999: Application: Standing civilian courts 57
Defence: Youth Justice & Criminal Evidence Act 1999: Commencements 57
Dental charges: National Health Service: England 133
Dental charges: National Health Service: Scotland 364
Dental charges: National Health Service: Wales 139
Dental hygienists & therapists: General Dental Council: Professions complementary to dentistry 97
Dental Practice Board: Abolition: England & Wales 136
Dental public health: Local health boards: Functions: Wales 138
Dental public health: Primary care trusts: Functions: England 132
Dental services: General & personal: National Health Service: England & Wales 136
Dental services: General & personal: National Health Service: Wales 139
Dental services: General & personal: Transitional & consequential provisions: National Health Service: Wales 138
Dental services: General contracts & personal agreements: National Health Service: England 134
Dental services: General: Contracts: National Health Service: Wales. 139
Dental services: General: National Health Service: Scotland 364, 365
Dental services: Personal: Agreements: National Health Service: Wales 139, 140
Dental services: Primary care trusts, strategic health authorities & NHS Business Services Authority: Functions. 132
Dental services: Primary: Local health boards & NHS Business Services Authority: Wales 138
Dental Vocational Training Authority: Abolition 138
Dentists Act 1984 (Amendment) Order 2005: Transitional provisions 96, 97
Dentists: General Dental Council: Appointments Committee & appointment of members of committees 96, 97
Dentists: General Dental Council: Constitution. 96, 97
Dentists: General Dental Council: Fitness to practise: Rules 96, 97
Dentists: General Dental Council: Professions complementary to dentistry 97
Dentists: General Dental Council: Registration: Appeals: Rules 96, 97
Dentists: Professions complementary to dentistry: European qualifications 97
Departments: Transfer of functions: Northern Ireland. 428
Derby (City): Permitted & special parking areas 254
Derelict land: Clearance area: Briar's Lane, Hatfield 57
Design right: Semiconductor topographies 58
Designs: Convention countries 58
Designs: Registered Designs Act 1949: Amendment: Electronic communications 116
Designs: Registered: Fees 58
Designs: Registered: Regulatory reform 58, 162
Designs: Registered: Rules 58
Designs: Service & time limits. 116
Development corporations: West Northamptonshire Development Corporation: Planning functions 287

Development: International: Reporting & transparency: Acts 7
Devolution, Scotland: Animal Health & Welfare (Scotland) Act 2006: Consequential Provisions: England & Wales 22, 42, 58
Devolution, Scotland: Charities & Trustee Investment (Scotland) Act 2005: Consequential modifications. 30, 43, 58
Devolution, Scotland: Gaelic Language (Scotland) Act 2005: Consequential modifications 28, 43, 58
Devolution, Scotland: Management of Offenders etc. (Scotland) Act 2005: Consequential modifications 43, 52, 58
Devolution, Scotland: Prohibition of Smoking in Certain Premises (Scotland) Regulations 2006: Consequential provisions . . 44, 59, 94
Devolution, Scotland: River Tweed 44, 59, 166
Devolution, Scotland: Scotland Act 1998: Agency arrangements 43, 59, 87
Devolution, Scotland: Scotland Act 1998: Agency arrangements: Specifications 43, 58, 89, 131
Devolution, Scotland: Scotland Act 1998: Schedule 5: Modifications 43, 59
Devolution, Scotland: Scotland Act 1998: Transfer of functions to the Scottish Ministers etc. 44, 59
Devolution, Scotland: Smoking, Health & Social Care (Scotland) Act 2005: Consequential amendments 44, 59, 138
Devolution, Scotland: Smoking, Health & Social Care (Scotland) Act 2005: Consequential provisions 44, 59, 94
Devolution, Scotland: Water Environment & Water Services (Scotland) Act 2003: Consequential provisions & modifications 44, 59, 290
Devolution, Scotland: Water Environment (Controlled Activities) (Scotland) Regulations 2005: Notices in the interests of national
security 44, 59, 81, 290
Devolution, Wales: National Assembly for Wales: Representation of the people 43, 59, 165
Devolution, Wales: National Assembly for Wales: Transfer of functions 43, 59, 60
Devon & Somerset Fire & Rescue Authority: Combination scheme 87
Digital terrestrial sound: Broadcasting: Technical service 27, 75
Diligence against earnings: Variation: Scotland 352
Diocese of Bradford: Educational endowments. 63
Diocese of Lincoln: Educational endowments 63
Diocese of Manchester: Educational endowments 63
Diocese of York Whorlton Parochial School: Educational endowments 63
Diplomatic Service: Consular fees 60
Disability Discrimination Act 1995: Amendment: Further & higher education 60
Disability Discrimination Act 1995: Amendments: Northern Ireland. 142
Disability Discrimination Act 1995: Private hire vehicles: Carriage of guide dogs, etc.: England & Wales 61, 285
Disability Discrimination Act 1995: Taxis: Carriage of guide dogs, etc.: England & Wales 61, 286
Disability discrimination: 2006 Order: Commencements: Northern Ireland 411
Disability discrimination: Code of practice: Goods, facilities, services & premises: Revocation 60
Disability discrimination: Code of practice: Services, public functions, private clubs & premises: Appointed day 60
Disability discrimination: Code of practice: Supplement to Part 3: Transport Vehicles: Provision & use: Appointed day 60
Disability discrimination: Further & higher education: Codes of practice: Appointed days: Northern Ireland. 411
Disability discrimination: Public authorities: Duty to promote equality: Code of practice: Scotland: Appointed day. 60
Disability discrimination: Schools: Codes of practice: Appointed days: Northern Ireland 412
Disability Rights Commission Act 1999: Commencements 60
Disability: Discrimination: Acts 6
Disability: Discrimination: Acts: Explanatory notes 10
Disabled persons: Buses: Travel concession scheme: Eligible persons & services: Scotland. 392
Disabled persons: Disability Discrimination Act 1995: Amendment: Further & higher education 60
Disabled persons: Disability Discrimination Act 1995: Private hire vehicles: Carriage of guide dogs, etc.: England & Wales . . . 61, 285
Disabled persons: Disability Discrimination Act 1995: Taxis: Carriage of guide dogs, etc.: England & Wales 61, 286
Disabled persons: Disability discrimination: 2006 Order: Commencements: Northern Ireland 411
Disabled persons: Disability discrimination: Code of practice: Goods, facilities, services & premises: Revocation 60
Disabled persons: Disability discrimination: Code of practice: Services, public functions, private clubs & premises: Appointed day . . 60
Disabled persons: Disability discrimination: Code of practice: Supplement to Part 3: Transport Vehicles: Provision & use: Appointed day
. . . . 60
Disabled persons: Disability discrimination: Definition: Guidance. 60
Disabled persons: Disability discrimination: Definition: Guidance: Appointed day 60
Disabled persons: Disability discrimination: Premises 60
Disabled persons: Disability discrimination: Public authorities: Duty to promote equality: Code of practice: Scotland: Appointed day . 60
Disabled persons: Discrimination: Services & premises: Northern Ireland 411
Disabled persons: Rail vehicles: Gatwick Express class 458 vehicles: Accessibility: Exemptions 61, 283
Disabled persons: Special educational needs: Further & higher education: Northern Ireland 411
Disablement & death: Navy, army & air force: Service pensions 147
Disablement & death: Service pensions 147
Disclosure of information: Enterprise Act 2002: Part 9: Restrictions. 42, 45, 61
Discrimination: Age discrimination: Cases: Industrial tribunals: Interest on awards: Northern Ireland. 405, 425
Discrimination: Age discrimination: Employment 77
Discrimination: Disability Discrimination Act 1995: Amendment: Further & higher education. 60
Discrimination: Disability discrimination: 2006 Order: Commencements: Northern Ireland. 411
Discrimination: Disability discrimination: Code of practice: Goods, facilities, services & premises: Revocation. 60
Discrimination: Disability discrimination: Code of practice: Services, public functions, private clubs & premises: Appointed day . . . 60
Discrimination: Disability discrimination: Further & higher education: Codes of practice: Appointed days: Northern Ireland 411

Discrimination: Disability discrimination: Premises 60
Discrimination: Disability discrimination: Schools: Codes of practice: Appointed days: Northern Ireland 412
Discrimination: Disability discrimination: Services & premises: Northern Ireland. 411
Discrimination: Disability: Code of practice: Supplement to Part 3: Transport Vehicles: Provision & use: Appointed day 60
Discrimination: Disability: Definition: Guidance. 60
Discrimination: Disability: Definition: Guidance: Appointed day 60
Discrimination: Sex Discrimination Act 1975: Public authorities: Statutory duties. 265
Discrimination: Sexual orientation: Equality: Northern Ireland. 439
Diseases of Fish Act (Northern Ireland) 1967: Infected waters: Infectious pancreatic necrosis: Northern Ireland. 417
Disinfectants: Animal health: Diseases: Approved disinfectants: England. 20
District courts: Criminal procedure: Rules: Amendments: Act of Adjournal: Scotland 350, 357, 389
District of Broadland: Whole Council elections 122
Divorce & dissolution: Pension Protection Fund: Scotland 353
Divorce: Parental access to children: Contact disputes: Acts 4
Divorce: Parental access to children: Contact disputes: Acts: Explanatory notes 9
Divorce: Pension Protection Fund: Northern Ireland. 416, 428
Divorce: Pensions 85, 151
Divorce: Religious bodies: Scotland. 353
Docklands Light Railway: Silvertown & London City Airport Extension: Exemptions 283
Docklands Light Railway: Stratford International Extension 284, 285
Doctors: Medical Act 1983: Amendment 96
Doctors: Postgraduate Medical Education & Training Board: Fees: Rules. 96
Dogs: Control orders: Prescribed offences & penalties 61
Dogs: Controls: Designated land: Non-application: England 61
Dogs: Controls: Order procedures. 61
Domestic Violence, Crime & Victims Act 2004: Commencements 53, 54
Domestic Violence, Crime & Victims Act 2004: Victims' code of practice 52
Doncaster & South Humberside Healthcare: National Health Service Trust 132
Dover harbour: Revision 94
Drainage: Environmental impact assessment: Northern Ireland. 411
Drainage: Trusts: Dissolution: Northern Ireland. 411
Driving Standards Agency Trading Fund: Maximum borrowing 94
Drugs & appliances: Charges: National Health Service: Scotland 364
Drugs & appliances: Charges: National Health Service: Wales 139
Drugs & appliances: Charges: Northern Ireland. 419
Drugs Act 2005: Commencements 56
Drugs: Controlled drugs: Management & use: Supervision 56
Drugs: Misuse of drugs 55, 56
Drugs: Misuse of Drugs Act 1971: Amendments. 55
Drugs: Misuse of drugs: Northern Ireland 410, 411
Dumfries & Galloway: Electoral arrangements: Scotland. 361
Dunbartonshire: East Dunbartonshire: Electoral arrangements: Scotland. 361
Dunbartonshire: West Dunbartonshire: Electoral arrangements: Scotland 363
Dundee City Council: Road traffic: Permitted & special parking area: Scotland 377
Dundee City: Electoral arrangements: Scotland 361
Duty stamps 83
Duty stamps: Alcoholic Liquor Duties Act 1979: Schedule 2A, para. 1(3): Amendment 83
Dwellings: Exempt: Council tax: Scotland 347

E

Earnings factors: Revaluation: Social security. 272
Earnings factors: Revaluation: Social security: Northern Ireland 442
East Ayrshire: Electoral arrangements: Scotland 361
East Dunbartonshire: Electoral arrangements: Scotland. 361
East Kent: National Health Service Trust 133
East Lindsey: Parish electoral arrangements: Local government 122
East Lothian: Electoral arrangements: Scotland 361
East Midlands Ambulance Service: National Health Service Trust 132
East of England Ambulance Service: National Health Service Trust 132
East Renfrewshire: Electoral arrangements: Scotland 361
East Sussex County Healthcare: National Health Service Trust. 136
Eastbourne (Borough): Whole council elections. 121
EC fertilisers: England & Wales 16
Ecclesiastical law: Cathedrals: Care. 61

Ecclesiastical law: Church of England: Legal aid. 62
Ecclesiastical law: Churches Conservation Trust: Grants to 62
Ecclesiastical law: Judges, legal officers & others: Fees 61
Ecclesiastical law: Legal officers: Annual fees 61
Ecclesiastical law: Parochial fees 61
Edinburgh (City): Electoral arrangements: Scotland 361
Edinburgh: Trams: Public transport: Acts: Scotland. 338
Education & Inspections Act 2006: Commencements 30, 63
Education & training: Inspectors: Wales 72
Education & training: Youth & community work: Inspection: Wales 73
Education Act 2002: Commencements 71
Education Act 2002: Commencements: England 63
Education Act 2002: Transitional provisions: Consequential amendments. 71
Education Act 2005: Commencements 69, 71
Education: Additional Support Needs Tribunals for Scotland: Practice & procedure: Scotland 350
Education: Admission arrangements: Determination 71
Education: Admission arrangements: Objections 72
Education: Admission arrangements: Variation. 72
Education: Aided places: St Mary's Music School: Scotland 351
Education: Anti-social Behaviour Act 2003: Commencements: Wales 70
Education: Appeal Committee procedures: Scotland 350
Education: Aptitude for particular subjects: England 63
Education: Assisted places: England 63
Education: Assisted places: Incidental expenses: England 63
Education: Assisted places: Incidental expenses: Wales 71
Education: Assisted places: Scotland 350
Education: Assisted places: Wales 71
Education: Budget statements: England. 63
Education: Careers & related services: Inspection: Wales 73
Education: Central Leeds Learning Federation: School session times: Changes 62
Education: Chief Inspector of Schools: England 64
Education: Children: Looked after: Schools: Admission: England 63
Education: Designated institutions 64
Education: Diocese of Bradford: Educational endowments. 63
Education: Diocese of Lincoln: Educational endowments 63
Education: Diocese of Manchester: Educational endowments 63
Education: Diocese of York Whorlton Parochial School: Educational endowments 63
Education: Disqualification provisions: Bankruptcy & mental health 64
Education: Employment: Modification of enactments: Wales 72
Education: Fees & awards. 69
Education: Fees & awards: Wales. 72
Education: Financial reporting: Consistent 63
Education: Fundable bodies: Scotland. 351
Education: Further & higher education: Disability Discrimination Act 1995: Amendment 60
Education: Further & higher education: Disability discrimination: Codes of practice: Appointed days: Northern Ireland. 411
Education: Further education corporations: Revocation: Wales 73
Education: Further education: Designated institutions 64
Education: Further education: Designated institutions: Workers' Educational Association 69
Education: Further education: Providers: England 66
Education: Further education: Student support: Cross-border eligibility: Northern Ireland. 412
Education: General Teaching Council for Scotland: Legal assessor: Rules: Scotland 351
Education: General Teaching Council for Wales: Functions 73
Education: Graduate endowment, student fees & support: Scotland 350
Education: Grammar schools: Charges: Northern Ireland 412
Education: Hadley Learning Community: School governance 66
Education: Higher Education Act 2004: Commencements: Wales 73
Education: Higher education: 2005 Order: Commencement: Northern Ireland 412
Education: Higher education: Assembly learning grants & loans: Wales 71
Education: Higher education: Assembly learning grants: Wales 71
Education: Higher education: Institutions: Designation: Scotland 350
Education: Independent schools: Registration: Scotland 351
Education: Individual pupils: Information: England 64
Education: Individual pupils: Information: Prescribed persons: England. 64
Education: Individual pupils: Information: Wales 72
Education: Infant classes: Sizes: England. 64
Education: Inspections: Acts 5

Education: Inspections: Acts: Explanatory notes 10
Education: Institutions of Higher Education: Designation: Scotland 350
Education: Isle College: Dissolution 67
Education: Josiah Mason Sixth Form College, Erdington, Birmingham: Dissolution 67
Education: Local education authority performance targets: England. 65
Education: Maintained schools: Change of category: England 64
Education: Mandatory awards: England & Wales 69
Education: Merthyr Tydfil College: Dissolution: Wales 73
Education: Monkseaton Community High School: Governing body procedures. 67
Education: National curriculum: Key stage 4: Exceptions: England 65
Education: National curriculum: Science: Key stage 4: Disapplication: Wales 72
Education: New school: Admissions 73
Education: Newark & Sherwood College: Dissolution 67
Education: Newfield School: Change to school session times 67
Education: Nobel School: School session times: Changes 67
Education: Northern Ireland 142
Education: Office for Standards in Education, Children's Services & Skills: Transitional provisions. 31, 67
Education: Outturn statements: England 65
Education: Parenting orders: Anti-social behaviour: Wales 72
Education: People's College, Nottingham: Dissolution. 67
Education: Prohibition from teaching or working with children: Northern Ireland 412
Education: Provision: Information: England 64
Education: Pupil exclusions & appeals 65
Education: Pupil referral units: Application of enactments: England. 65
Education: Pupil registration: England 65
Education: Recognised awards: Richmond The American International University in London 65
Education: Robert Gordon University: Academic awards & distinctions: Scotland 350
Education: Robert Gordon University: Establishment: Scotland 351
Education: Robert Gordon University: Order of Council: Amendment: Scotland 351
Education: Robert Gordon University: Transfer & closure: Scotland. 351
Education: School day & school year: Wales. 72
Education: School inspection: Wales 72
Education: School lunches: Nutritional standards: England 65
Education: School performance & absence targets: Wales 72
Education: School teachers: Pay & conditions 69
Education: Schools: Staffing: England. 68
Education: Schools: Amesbury Church of England Voluntary Controlled Primary School: Religious character: Designation 62
Education: Schools: Archbishop Courtenay Primary School: Religious character: Designation. 62
Education: Schools: Belford St Mary's Church of England Voluntary Aided Middle School: Religious character: Designation. 62
Education: Schools: Bidston Church of England Primary School: Religious character: Designation 62
Education: Schools: Blessed Trinity RC College: Religious character: Designation. 62
Education: Schools: Bradford Cathedral Community College: Religious character: Designation 62
Education: Schools: Cadishead Primary School: School session times. 62
Education: Schools: Christ College, Cheltenham: Religious character: Designation. 62
Education: Schools: Churchfields, The Village School: Religious character: Designation. 62
Education: Schools: Crawley Down Village CE School: Religious character: Designation 63
Education: Schools: Disability discrimination: Codes of practice: Appointed days: Northern Ireland 412
Education: Schools: Farnsfield St Michael's Church of England Primary (Voluntary Aided) School: Religious character: Designation
. . . . 66
Education: Schools: Finance: England 67
Education: Schools: Five Lanes CofE VC Primary School: Religious character: Designation. 66
Education: Schools: Great & Little Preston Voluntary Controlled Church of England Primary School: Religious character: Designation
. . . . 66
Education: Schools: Holy Trinity Rosehill (VA) CE Primary School: Religious character: Designation 66
Education: Schools: Hope Hamilton CE Primary School: Religious character: Designation 66
Education: Schools: Hucknall National Church of England (VA) Primary School: Religious character: Designation 66
Education: Schools: Immanuel CofE Community College: Religious character: Designation. 66
Education: Schools: Inspectors: England 64
Education: Schools: Leatherhead Trinity Primary School: Religious character: Designation 67
Education: Schools: Lowick Church of England Voluntary Controlled First School: Religious character: Designation 67
Education: Schools: Orchard Primary School: Religious character: Designation 67
Education: Schools: Our Lady of Walsingham Catholic Primary School: Religious character: Designation 67
Education: Schools: Parental involvement: Acts: Explanatory notes: Scotland. 340
Education: Schools: Parental involvement: Acts: Scotland 339
Education: Schools: Performance information: England 65

Education: Schools: Performance targets: England 65
Education: Schools: Primary to secondary: Transition: Wales 73
Education: Schools: Religious character: Designation: Independent schools: England 63
Education: Schools: Sacred Heart RC Primary School: Religious character: Designation 67
Education: Schools: Saint Cecilia's, Wandsworth Church of England School: Religious character: Designation. 67
Education: Schools: Schools: Maintained schools: Staffing: Wales 73
Education: Schools: Shire Oak CofE Primary School: Religious character: Designation 68
Education: Schools: St Anne's RC Primary School: Religious character: Designation 68
Education: Schools: St Benedict's Catholic Primary School: Religious character: Designation 68
Education: Schools: St Georges VA Church Primary School: Religious character: Designation 68
Education: Schools: St John the Baptist Roman Catholic Primary School : Religious character: Designation 68
Education: Schools: St Peter's Church of England Junior & Infant School: Religious character: Designation 68
Education: Schools: St Teresa of Lisieux Catholic Infant School: Religious character: Designation 68
Education: Schools: Staffing: England 68
Education: Schools: Tauheedul Islam Girls High School: Religious character: Designation 68
Education: Schools: Teachers: Performance management: England 65
Education: Schools: Trinity CoE VC Primary School: Religious character: Designation 68
Education: Schools: Unity College: Religious character: Designation 69
Education: Schools: Westminster Church of England Primary School: Religious character: Designation. 69
Education: Scottish Schools (Parental Involvement) Act 2006: Commencements: Scotland 351
Education: Secondary schools: New: Proposals 65
Education: Single plan: Wales 73
Education: Special educational needs: England. 66
Education: Special needs: Further & higher education: Disabled persons: Northern Ireland 411
Education: Standards in Scotland's Schools etc. Act 2000: Commencements: Scotland 351
Education: Student fees: Amounts: England 68
Education: Student fees: Amounts: Northern Ireland 412
Education: Student fees: Inflation index 68
Education: Student fees: Qualifying courses & persons 68
Education: Student fees: Qualifying courses & persons: Northern Ireland 412
Education: Student fees: Specification: Scotland 351
Education: Student loans: England & Wales 70
Education: Student loans: Northern Ireland 412
Education: Student loans: Repayment. 70
Education: Student loans: Repayments: Northern Ireland. 412
Education: Student loans: Scotland 350
Education: Student loans: Tuition fees: Scotland 350
Education: Student support 66
Education: Student support: England & Wales 70
Education: Student support: England, Wales & Northern Ireland 70
Education: Student support: European institutions 66
Education: Student support: European Institutions 66
Education: Student support: Information: Governing bodies: Northern Ireland. 412
Education: Student support: Information: Supply to governing bodies. 62
Education: Student support: Information: Supply to governing bodies: Wales. 73
Education: Student support: Northern Ireland 412
Education: Students: Awards: Northern Ireland 412
Education: Teachers: Eligibility: Northern Ireland 412
Education: Teachers: Redundancy & premature retirement: Compensation 70
Education: Teachers: Superannuation: Northern Ireland 412, 413
Education: Teachers' pensions: Amendments 70
Education: Teachers' pensions: Reform amendments 70
Education: Tuition fees: Student loans: Repayment & allowances: Scotland 350
Education: Wales 73
Education: Widnes & Runcorn Sixth Form College: Dissolution 69
Education: Wimbledon School of Art Higher Education Corporation: Dissolution 69
Educational Recording Agency Ltd.: Copyright: Licensing scheme: Certification. 47
Eel fishing: Licence duties: Northern Ireland 417
Eggs: Marketing standards: England & Wales 91
Eggs: Marketing standards: Northern Ireland 405
Egypt: Potatoes: Originating in Egypt: Northern Ireland 433
Egypt: Potatoes: Originating in Egypt: Scotland 369
Elderly people: Commissioner: Wales: Acts 4
Elderly people: Commissioner: Wales: Acts: Explanatory notes 9
Elections: Absent voting: Transitional provisions: England & Wales. 164
Elections: Conduct: Acts 5

Elections: Conduct: Acts: Explanatory notes 10
Elections: Local electoral administration & registration services: Acts: Commencements: Scotland 374
Elections: Local electoral administration & registration services: Acts: Scotland 339
Elections: Local: Principal areas & parishes & communities: England & Wales 164
Elections: Policy development grants scheme 163
Electoral Administration Act 2006: Commencements 74, 131, 156, 162, 163
Electoral administration: Acts 5
Electoral administration: Acts: Explanatory notes 10
Electoral changes: Corby (Borough) 121
Electoral changes: Kettering (Borough) 121
Electoral changes: Lincoln (City) 122
Electoral changes: North Hertfordshire (District) 122
Electoral changes: North Kesteven (District) 122
Electoral changes: North Shropshire (District) 122
Electoral changes: South Northamptonshire (District) 122
Electoral changes: Tunbridge Wells (Borough) 121
Electoral changes: Waverley (Borough) 121
Electoral Commission: Electoral Administration Act 2006: Commencements 74, 131, 156, 162, 163
Electoral participation: Encouragement: Expenses: Reimbursement: England & Wales 164
Electoral registration: Acts 5
Electoral registration: Acts: Explanatory notes 10
Electrical & electronic equipment: Hazardous substances: Use restriction 78
Electrical & electronic equipment: Waste management licensing: Northern Ireland 415
Electrical & electronic equipment: Waste: Charges: Northern Ireland 415
Electricity Act 1989: Generation: Licence requirement: Exemption: England & Wales 74
Electricity Act 1989: Interconnector licence: Requirements: Exemptions 74
Electricity meters: Active 290
Electricity: Appeals: Time limits: Modification 74, 93
Electricity: Applications: Consent: Scotland 351
Electricity: Consents: Planning: Northern Ireland 142
Electricity: Energy Act 2004: Commencements 74, 93
Electricity: Non-fossil fuel sources: Arrangements: England & Wales 74
Electricity: Northern Ireland 413
Electricity: Offshore generating stations: Applications for consent 74
Electricity: Prepayment meter 74
Electricity: Renewables obligation: England & Wales 74
Electricity: Renewables obligation: Northern Ireland 413
Electricity: Renewables obligation: Scotland 351
Electricity: Safety, quality & continuity 74
Electromagnetic compatibility 75
Electromagnetic compatibility: European Communities 74
Electronic communications: Communications Act 2003: Network or service: Persistent misuse: Maximum penalty 75
Electronic communications: Digital terrestrial sound: Technical service 27, 75
Electronic communications: Housing benefit & council tax benefit 75
Electronic communications: Housing benefit: Northern Ireland 422, 434
Electronic communications: Intellectual property: Registered Designs Act 1949 & Patents Act 1977: Amendment 116
Electronic communications: Scotland 352
Electronic communications: Social security: Northern Ireland 440
Electronic communications: Stamp duty land tax 274
Electronic communications: Television licensing 27, 75
Electronic communications: Television: Licensable content services 28, 75
Electronic communications: Tobacco Advertising & Promotion Act 2002: Amendments 45, 75
Electronic communications: Transport 283
Electronic communications: Wireless telegraphy: Exemption 75
Electronic communications: Wireless telegraphy: Guernsey 28, 75, 292
Electronic communications: Wireless telegraphy: Jersey 28, 75, 293
Electronic communications: Wireless telegraphy: Licence award 75, 76
Electronic communications: Wireless telegraphy: Licence charges 76
Electronic communications: Wireless telegraphy: Licences: Number of: Limitation 76
Electronic communications: Wireless telegraphy: Licensing procedures 76
Electronic communications: Wireless telegraphy: Pre-consolidation amendments 76
Electronic communications: Wireless telegraphy: Register 76
Electronic communications: Wireless telegraphy: Spectrum access licences: Concurrent: Limitation 76
Electronic communications: Wireless telegraphy: Spectrum access licences: Limitation of number 76
Electronic communications: Wireless telegraphy: Spectrum trading 76

Emergency workers: Protection: Acts ... 5
Employees: Information & consultation: Northern Ireland ... 413
Employer's liability: Compulsory insurance: Northern Ireland ... 413
Employment & training: Age discrimination ... 77
Employment & training: Equality: Age discrimination ... 77
Employment & training: Industrial training levy: Construction Board ... 77
Employment & training: Industrial training levy: Engineering Construction Board ... 77
Employment programme: Preparation: Northern Ireland ... 442
Employment protection: Disclosure of information: Code of practice: Appointed day: Northern Ireland ... 425
Employment rights: Increase of limits : Northern Ireland ... 413
Employment rights: Limits: Increase ... 277
Employment zones ... 267
Employment zones: Allocation to contractors: Pilot ... 267
Employment: Access & unfair practices during recognition & derecognition ballots: Code of practice: Appointed day: Northern Ireland ... 424
Employment: Age discrimination: Industrial tribunals: Interest on awards: Northern Ireland ... 405, 425
Employment: Age discrimination: Northern Ireland ... 404, 428
Employment: Agricultural wages: Permits: Infirm & incapacitated persons: Abolition: Northern Ireland ... 405, 444
Employment: Children: Northern Ireland ... 409
Employment: Collective redundancies: Northern Ireland ... 413
Employment: Education: Modification of enactments: Wales ... 72
Employment: Employees: Information & consultation ... 277
Employment: Employees: Information & consultation: Northern Ireland ... 413
Employment: Flexible working: Eligibility, complaints & remedies ... 277
Employment: Gangmasters (Licensing) Act 2004: Commencements ... 76
Employment: Gangmasters: Appeals ... 76
Employment: Gangmasters: Appeals: Northern Ireland ... 413
Employment: Gangmasters: Licensing conditions ... 77
Employment: Gangmasters: Licensing exclusions ... 77
Employment: Gangmasters: Licensing: Exclusions: Northern Ireland ... 413
Employment: Industrial action ballots: Notice to employers: Code of practice: Appointed day: Northern Ireland ... 424
Employment: Labour Relations Agency: Flexible working: Arbitration scheme: Northern Ireland ... 413
Employment: Local government: Early termination: Discretionary compensation: England & Wales ... 151
Employment: Maternity & parental leave: Northern Ireland ... 414
Employment: Maternity, paternity & adoption leave: Acts ... 9
Employment: Maternity, paternity & adoption leave: Acts: Explanatory notes ... 11
Employment: Occupational & personal pension schemes: Amendments ... 147, 278
Employment: Occupational & personal pension schemes: Consultation by employers & amendments ... 147, 278
Employment: Paternity & adoption leave: Northern Ireland ... 414
Employment: Protection: Continuity of employment: Northern Ireland ... 413
Employment: Protection: Service provision change: Northern Ireland ... 413
Employment: Protection: Transfer of undertakings ... 278
Employment: Public interest disclosure: Prescribed persons: Northern Ireland ... 413
Employment: Race Relations: Code of Practice: Appointed day ... 160
Employment: Social security: Benefits up-rating: Northern Ireland ... 413, 423, 435, 440, 443
Employment: Statutory paternity pay & adoption pay: Northern Ireland ... 414
Employment: Statutory sick pay: General ... 273, 278
Employment: Terms & conditions: Occupational & personal pension schemes: Amendments: Northern Ireland ... 429, 444
Employment: Terms & conditions: Occupational & personal pension schemes: Consultation by employers: Northern Ireland ... 429, 444
Employment: Terms & conditions: Social security: Benefits up-rating ... 269, 278
Employment: Terms & conditions: Working time ... 279
Employment: Work & families: 2006 Order: Commencements: Northern Ireland ... 414
Employment: Work & families: Acts ... 9
Employment: Work & families: Acts: Explanatory notes ... 11
Employment: Working time: Northern Ireland ... 414
Energy Act 2004: Commencements ... 74, 93
Energy conservation: Boilers: Efficiency ... 77
Energy conservation: Domestic energy: Efficiency grants: Northern Ireland ... 414
Energy conservation: Home energy efficiency scheme: Scotland ... 352
Energy: Administration ... 116
Energy: Climate change: Sustainable energy: Acts ... 4
Energy: Climate change: Sustainable energy: Acts: Explanatory notes ... 9
Energy: Electricity: Northern Ireland ... 413
Energy: Electricity: Renewables obligation: England & Wales ... 74
Energy-saving items: Income tax ... 110
Enforcement: Diligence against earnings: Variation: Scotland ... 352

England Rural Development Programme: Project-based schemes: Closures 14
Enterprise Act 2002: Amendment. 45
Enterprise Act 2002: Disqualification from Office: General 115
Enterprise Act 2002: Enforcement undertakings 42
Enterprise Act 2002: Enforcement undertakings & orders 42
Enterprise Act 2002: Part 8 Community infringements specified UK laws 45
Enterprise Act 2002: Part 8 notice to OFT of intended prosecution specified enactments 45
Enterprise Act 2002: Part 9: Restrictions on disclosure of information. 42, 45, 61
Enterprise Act 2002: Water Services Regulation Authority 42, 45
Environment Act 1995: Commencements: England & Wales 81
Environment: Natural environment: Rural communities: Acts. 7
Environment: Natural environment: Rural communities: Acts: Explanatory notes. 10
Environment: Taxes: Landfill tax 119
Environmental Assessment (Scotland) Act 2005: Commencements: Scotland 352
Environmental impact assessment: Agriculture: England. 14
Environmental impact assessment: Agriculture: Scotland. 341
Environmental impact assessment: Drainage: Northern Ireland 411
Environmental impact assessment: Forestry: England & Wales 93
Environmental impact assessment: Forestry: Northern Ireland 419
Environmental impact assessment: Land drainage improvement works 119
Environmental impact assessment: Scotland 341, 354, 356, 359, 376, 391
Environmental impact assessment: Town & country planning: Wales 281
Environmental impact assessment: Uncultivated land & semi-natural areas: Northern Ireland. 406
Environmental impact assessment: Water resources: England & Wales 290
Environmental noise: Northern Ireland 414
Environmental noise: Scotland. 352
Environmental noise: Wales. 82
Environmental offences: Fixed penalty receipts: Use: England 79
Environmental Protection Act 1990: Isles of Scilly. 79
Environmental protection: Water Environment & Water Services (Scotland) Act 2003: Designation of responsible authorities &
functions: Scotland 352, 393
Environmental protection: Agricultural & forestry tractors: Emission of gaseous & particulate pollutants 78
Environmental protection: Anti-social Behaviour Act 2003: Commencement 79
Environmental protection: Antisocial Behaviour etc. (Scotland) Act 2004: Commencements: Scotland. 348, 352, 360, 369
Environmental protection: Clean Neighbourhoods & Environment Act 2005: Commencements 79, 80, 81
Environmental protection: Clean Neighbourhoods & Environment Act 2005: Commencements: Wales 81
Environmental protection: Contaminated land: England 79
Environmental protection: Contaminated land: Wales 82
Environmental protection: Dangerous substances & preparations: Controls 78
Environmental protection: Electrical & electronic equipment: Waste management licensing: Northern Ireland. 415
Environmental protection: Electrical & electronic equipment: Waste: Charges: Northern Ireland 415
Environmental protection: Environment Act 1995: Commencements: England & Wales 81
Environmental protection: Financial assistance. 81
Environmental protection: Greenhouse Gas Emissions Trading Scheme: Amendment 78
Environmental protection: Hazardous substances: Use restriction: Electrical & electronic equipment 78
Environmental protection: Highways: Gating orders: England. 80
Environmental protection: Joint waste disposal authorities: Recycling payments: Disapplication: England 80
Environmental protection: Mobile machinery: Non-road: Gaseous & particulate pollutants: Emissions 78
Environmental protection: Nitrates Action Programme: Northern Ireland 414
Environmental protection: Noise: England 79
Environmental protection: Noise: Northern Ireland 414
Environmental protection: Noise: Scotland 352
Environmental protection: Noise: Wales 82
Environmental protection: Offences: Fixed penalties 79
Environmental protection: Offences: Fixed penalty receipts: Use: England 79
Environmental protection: Oil: Storage: Scotland 353, 393
Environmental protection: Ozone depleting substances: Qualifications 78
Environmental protection: Ozone-depleting substances: Qualifications: Northern Ireland 414
Environmental protection: Packaging: Essential requirements 78
Environmental protection: Phosphorus: Agriculture: Use: Northern Ireland 414
Environmental protection: Pollution: Prevention & control 82
Environmental protection: Pollution: Prevention & control: England 80
Environmental protection: Pollution: Prevention & control: Northern Ireland 414
Environmental protection: Radioactive contaminated land: Enactments: Modification: England 80
Environmental protection: Radioactive contaminated land: Enactments: Modification: Wales 82

Environmental protection: Radioactive contaminated land: Northern Ireland 415, 434
Environmental protection: Statutory nuisances: Appeals 80
Environmental protection: Statutory nuisances: Artificial lighting: Relevant sports: Designations 80
Environmental protection: Statutory nuisances: Insects 80
Environmental protection: Waste electrical & electronic equipment 79
Environmental protection: Waste electrical & electronic equipment: Waste management licensing: England & Wales 81
Environmental protection: Waste management: England & Wales 81
Environmental protection: Waste management: Licensing: Scotland 352
Environmental protection: Waste management: Northern Ireland 415
Environmental protection: Waste recycling payments: England 80
Environmental protection: Waste: Household waste: Duty of care: Wales 82
Environmental protection: Water Environment (Controlled Activities) (Scotland) Regulations 2005: Notices in the interests of national
security 44, 59, 81, 290
Environmental protection: Water environment: Consequential provisions: Scotland 353, 393
Environmental protection: Water environment: Controlled activities: Third party representations, etc.: Scotland 353, 393
Environmental protection: Water environment: Relevant enactments: Scotland 353, 393
Environmental protection: Water environment: Waste management: Licensing: Scotland 352
Environmental protection: Water: Abstraction & impoundment: Licensing: Northern Ireland 415
Environmental protection: Water: Consequential & savings provisions: Scotland 353, 393
Environmental stewardship: England 13, 14, 51
Environmentally sensitive areas: Designation : Northern Ireland 406
Enzootic bovine leukosis: Animal health: Wales 24
Equal opportunities & human rights: Equality Act 2006: Commencements 82
Equal opportunities: Acts 6
Equal opportunities: Acts: Explanatory notes 10
Equality Act 2006: Commencements 82
Equality: Acts 6
Equality: Acts: Explanatory notes 10
Equality: Sexual orientation discrimination: Northern Ireland 439
Equine infectious anaemia: Compensation: England 20
Erskine Bridge: Tolls: Temporary suspension: Scotland 376
Ethical Standards in Public Life etc. (Scotland) Act 2000: Codes of conduct: Scottish public authorities members: Scotland . . . 353, 361
European Communities: Animals & animal products: Import & export: Northern Ireland 407, 408, 415
European Communities: Animals: Diseases: Northern Ireland 408, 415
European Communities: Community trade marks 282
European Communities: Designation 82
European Communities: Electromagnetic compatibility 74
European Communities: Nuclear reactors: Decommissioning: Environmental impact assessment 82
European Communities: Passenger & goods vehicles: Recording equipment: Northern Ireland 415, 438
European Communities: Professional qualifications: Recognition: Second general system 158
European Communities: Qualifications & experience: Recognition: Third general system 158
European Communities: Salmonella: Turkey flocks & slaughter pig herds: Survey powers: Northern Ireland 408, 415
European Communities: Structural Funds: National Assembly for Wales 83
European Communities: Transmissible spongiform encephalopathies: Northern Ireland 407, 416
European Communities: Treaties: Definition 82
European Communities: Water resources: Environmental impact assessment: Northern Ireland 416, 445
European Convention on Cinematographic Co-production 32
European Cooperative Society 46
European Cooperative Society: Employees: Involvement 277
European Economic Area: Homelessness: Allocation of housing & homelessness: Eligibility: Northern Ireland 422
European Economic Area: Immigration 108
European Organization for Nuclear Research: Immunities & privileges 117
European Parliament: Pensions: UK representatives 146
European qualifications: Health care & associated professions: Professions complementary to dentistry 97
European Union: Accessions: Acts 6
European Union: Accessions: Acts: Explanatory notes 10
Excise goods 84
Excise: Air passenger duty: Rate: Qualifying territories 83
Excise: Beer, cider & perry, spirits, wine & made-wine 83
Excise: Customs & excise duties: Travellers' allowances & personal reliefs: New member states 54, 83, 287, 288
Excise: Duties: Surcharges or rebates: Hydrocarbon oils 83, 84
Excise: Duty points: New member states 84
Excise: Duty stamps 83
Excise: Duty stamps: Alcoholic Liquor Duties Act 1979: Schedule 2A, para. 1(3): Amendment 83
Excise: Finance Act 2004: Duty stamps: Appointed day 84
Excise: Gaming duty 84

Excise: Hydrocarbon oil duties: Sulphur-free diesel: Biomass hydrogenation: Reliefs 84
Excise: Mutual assistance provisions 84, 116, 162, 276
Excise: Road fuel gas: Reliefs. 83
Excise: Third countries: Legacies imported from: Relief: Application 55, 84, 288
Excise: Tobacco products: Duty. 84
Excise: Tobacco products: Duty: Evasion: Finance Act 2006: Appointed day 84
Excise: Warehousekeepers & owners of warehoused goods 84
Exhaust gas analysers: Weights & measures 291
Explosives: Carriage: By road & rail: Health & safety: Northern Ireland. 421
Explosives: Manufacture & storage: Health & safety: Northern Ireland 421
Explosives: Quarries: Health & safety: Northern Ireland 421
Export control 55
Export control: Bosnia & Herzegovina 54
Export control: Lebanon. 55
Export control: Liberia 55
Export control: Radioactive sources. 55
Export control: Security & para-military goods. 55
Extradition Act 2003: Designations: Amendments 84
Extradition: Police & Justice Act 2006: Commencements 53, 85, 155

F

Fair employment: Public authorities: Specification: Northern Ireland 416
Falkirk: Electoral arrangements: Scotland. 361
Families: Employment: Leave: Acts 9
Families: Employment: Leave: Acts: Explanatory notes 11
Family homes: Forms of consent: Civil partnership: Scotland 347
Family Law (Scotland) Act 2006: Act of Sederunt: Scotland 348
Family Law (Scotland) Act 2006: Commencements: Scotland 353
Family Law (Scotland) Act 2006: Consequential modifications: Scotland 353
Family Law (Scotland) Act 2006: Sheriff Court: Ordinary cause rules: Act of Sederunt: Scotland 389
Family Law Act 1986: Dependent Territories 30
Family law: Acts: Explanatory notes: Scotland 340
Family law: Acts: Scotland 338
Family law: Child support. 85
Family law: Child support: Northern Ireland. 409, 416
Family law: Civil partnership: Dissolution: Pensions 40, 85, 151
Family law: Divorce & dissolution: Pension Protection Fund: Scotland 353
Family law: Divorce: Pensions. 85, 151
Family law: Divorce: Religious bodies: Scotland 353
Family law: Domestic Violence, Crime & Victims Act 2004: Victims' code of practice 52
Family proceedings: Children: Allocation: England & Wales 85
Family proceedings: England & Wales 52, 85, 276
Family proceedings: Fees 52, 85, 276
Family proceedings: Rules. 52, 85, 276
Family proceedings: Rules: Northern Ireland. 410, 416, 443
Farm Nutrient Management Scheme: Northern Ireland 406
Farm subsidies: Decisions: Review: Northern Ireland. 406
Farnsfield St Michael's Church of England Primary (Voluntary Aided) School: Religious character: Designation. 66
Farriers (Registration) Act 1975: Commencements: Scotland. 353
Farriers Registration Council: Farriers (Registration) Act 1975: Commencements: Scotland 353
Feed: Hygiene & enforcement: Scotland 341
Feed: Official controls: England 15, 90
Feed: Official controls: Northern Ireland. 406, 418
Feed: Official controls: Wales. 18, 92
Feed: Specified undesirable substances: England. 14
Feed: Specified undesirable substances: Northern Ireland. 406
Feed: Specified undesirable substances: Wales 17
Feeding stuffs, crops & food: Pesticides: Maximum residue levels: England & Wales. 16, 152
Feeding stuffs, crops & food: Pesticides: Maximum residue levels: Northern Ireland 406, 407, 431
Feeding stuffs, crops & food: Pesticides: Maximum residue levels: Scotland. 342, 368
Feeding stuffs: Enforcement: Wales 17
Feeding stuffs: England 14
Feeding stuffs: Northern Ireland 406
Feeding stuffs: Sampling & analysis: England 14

Feeding stuffs: Sampling & analysis: Northern Ireland 406
Feeding stuffs: Sampling & analysis: Scotland 341
Feeding stuffs: Sampling & analysis: Wales 17
Feeding stuffs: Scotland 341
Feeding stuffs: Wales 17
Fees & charges: Measuring instruments: EEC requirements 85
Fees & charges: Measuring instruments: EEC requirements: Verification: Northern Ireland. 416
Fees & charges: Medicines: Human use 85, 127
Fees & charges: Medicines: Human use: Medical devices 85, 127
Fees: Insolvency proceedings 115
Fertilisers: Agriculture: European Communities: Northern Ireland 405
Fertilisers: EC : England & Wales 16
Fertilisers: European Communities: Scotland 341
Feudal tenure: Abolition of Feudal Tenure etc. (Scotland) Act 2000: Specified day: Scotland. 354
Fife Council: Electoral arrangements: Scotland 361
Films & sound recordings: Appointed day: Income & corporation tax 48, 110
Films & sound recordings: Power to alter dates: Income & corporation tax 48, 110
Films: British film: Definition. 32
Films: Certification 32
Films: Co-production agreements 32
Finance (No. 2) Act 2005: Section 17 (1): Appointed day 48, 110
Finance Act 1993: Amendment: Lloyd's sourcebook. 48
Finance Act 1994: Amendment: Lloyd's sourcebook. 48
Finance Act 2002: Schedule 26, parts 2 & 9 48
Finance Act 2003: Amendment: Stamp duty land tax 274, 275, 276
Finance Act 2004: Duty stamps: Appointed day 84
Finance Act 2004: Section 77 (1) (7): Appointed day 110
Finance Act 2006. 6
Finance Act 2006: Section 18: Appointed day. 288
Finance Act 2006: Section 53 (1): Films & sound recordings: Appointed day 48, 110
Finance Act 2006: Section 53 (2): Films & sound recordings: Power to alter dates 48, 110
Finance Act 2006: Tobacco products duty: Evasion: Appointed day. 84
Finance: Acts 6
Financial assistance scheme: Amendments 146
Financial assistance scheme: Payments: Pensions Act 2004. . . . . 150, 269
Financial assistance scheme: Payments: Pensions Act 2004 & 2005 Orders: Northern Ireland. 430, 439
Financial assistance scheme: PPF payments & FAS payments: Northern Ireland 442
Financial assistance: Environmental purposes 81
Financial investigators: References: Proceeds of Crime Act 2002 157
Financial markets & insolvency: Settlement finality 86
Financial reporting orders: Criminal procedure: Rules: Act of Adjournal: Scotland 357, 388
Financial Services & Markets Act 2000 (Gibraltar) Order 2001: Amendment. 86
Financial Services & Markets Act 2000: Appointed representatives 86
Financial Services & Markets Act 2000: Confidential information: Disclosure 86
Financial Services & Markets Act 2000: Designated professional bodies 86
Financial Services & Markets Act 2000: EEA passport rights: Amendments 86
Financial Services & Markets Act 2000: Investment exchanges & clearing houses: Recognition requirements. . 86
Financial Services & Markets Act 2000: Markets in financial instruments: Modification of powers 86
Financial Services & Markets Act 2000: Regulated activities 87
Financial Services & Markets Act 2000: Regulated activities: Amendments 87
Financial services & markets: Capital requirements 86
Financial services: Clearing houses: Regulatory provisions: Acts 7
Financial services: Clearing houses: Regulatory provisions: Acts: Explanatory notes. 10
Financial services: Financial markets & insolvency: Settlement finality 86
Financial services: Investment exchanges: Regulatory provisions: Acts. 7
Financial services: Investment exchanges: Regulatory provisions: Acts: Explanatory notes. 10
Financial services: Proceeds of Crime Act 2002 & Money Laundering Regulations 2003: Amendment. . . . 86, 157
Fines: Collection: Final scheme: Magistrates' courts: England & Wales 126
Fire & rescue services: 2006 Order: Commencements: Northern Ireland 416
Fire & Rescue Services: Charging: Wales 88
Fire & rescue services: Devon & Somerset Fire & Rescue Authority: Combination scheme 87
Fire & rescue services: Discipline: Northern Ireland 416
Fire & rescue services: Firefighters' compensation schemes: England 88, 151
Fire & rescue services: Firefighters' pension schemes: England 88, 151
Fire & rescue services: Firefighters' pension schemes: Northern Ireland 416
Fire & rescue services: Firefighters' pension schemes: Scotland 354, 367

Fire & rescue services: Firefighters' pension schemes: Wales 88, 152
Fire & rescue services: National frameworks: England. 87
Fire & rescue services: Northern Ireland 142
Fire & rescue services: Scotland Act 1998: Agency arrangements. 43, 59, 87
Fire (Scotland) Act 2005: Commencements: Scotland 354
Fire (Scotland) Act 2005: Consequential modifications & savings: Scotland. 354
Fire safety: Fire (Scotland) Act 2005: Consequential modifications & savings: Scotland 354
Fire safety: Regulatory reform: England & Wales. 163
Fire safety: Scotland 354
Firefighters' compensation schemes: England. 88, 151
Firefighters' compensation schemes: Scotland. 354, 367
Firefighters' pension schemes: England 88, 151
Firefighters' pension schemes: Northern Ireland 416
Firefighters' pension schemes: Scotland 354, 367
Firefighters' pension schemes: Wales 88, 152
Fireplaces: Exempted: Smoke control areas: England 40
Fireplaces: Exempted: Smoke control areas: Wales 40
Firth of Clyde: Fishing: Prohibited methods: Scotland 387
Fish Auction Sites: Designation: Wales 262
Fish buyers & sellers: Registration: Wales 262
Fish farming: Environmental impact assessment: Scotland. 341, 354, 356, 359, 376, 391
Fish: Labelling: England 90
Fish: Labelling: Northern Ireland 417
Fish: Labelling: Scotland. 355
Fish: Labelling: Wales. 92
Fisheries: Byelaws: Amendments: Northern Ireland 417
Fisheries: Eel fishing: Licence duties: Northern Ireland. 417
Fisheries: Infected waters: Infectious pancreatic necrosis: Northern Ireland 417
Fisheries: Public Angling Estate: Byelaws: Northern Ireland 417
Fisheries: Salmon & freshwater fisheries: Assynt-Coigach area: Protection: Scotland 375
Fisheries: Salmon & freshwater: Northern salmon fishery district: Designation: Scotland. 375
Fishery products: Official controls: Charges: England 89
Fishery products: Official controls: Charges: Northern Ireland 417
Fishery products: Official controls: Charges: Scotland 355
Fishery products: Official controls: Charges: Wales 92
Fishing boats: Satellite-tracking devices: Wales. 262
Fishing vessels: Lifting operations & equipment 129
Fishing vessels: Work equipment: Provision & use 129
Fishing: Multiple trawls: Prohibition: Scotland 387
Fishing: Passive gear & beam trawls: Marking & identification: Scotland 387
Fishing: Prohibited methods: Firth of Clyde: Scotland 387
Five Lanes CofE VC Primary School: Religious character: Designation. 66
Flexible working: Eligibility, complaints & remedies. 277
Fodder plant seeds: Wales 264
Fodder plant: Seeds: England 264
Fodder plant: Seeds: Scotland 388
Food Benefit Schemes: 2003 Order: Commencements: Northern Ireland. 417
Food hygiene: Wales 92
Food protection: Emergency prohibitions: Amnesic shellfish poisoning: East Coast: Scotland 371
Food protection: Emergency prohibitions: Amnesic shellfish poisoning: West Coast: Scotland 371, 372
Food protection: Emergency prohibitions: Paralytic shellfish poisoning: Orkney: Scotland 373
Food protection: Emergency prohibitions: Sheep: Radioactivity: Scotland. 373
Food, feeding stuffs & crops: Pesticides: Maximum residue levels: England & Wales. 16, 152
Food, feeding stuffs & crops: Pesticides: Maximum residue levels: Northern Ireland 406, 407, 431
Food, feeding stuffs & crops: Pesticides: Maximum residue levels: Scotland. 342, 368
Food: Animals & animal products: Examination for residues & maximum residue limits. 88
Food: Animals & animal products: Residues & maximum residue limits: Examinations: Northern Ireland . . . 417
Food: Benefit schemes: 2003 Order: Commencements: Northern Ireland 418
Food: Ceramic articles: Contact: England. 88
Food: Ceramic articles: Contact: Northern Ireland 417
Food: Ceramic articles: Contact: Scotland. 354
Food: Ceramic articles: Contact: Wales. 91
Food: Contaminants: England. 89
Food: Contaminants: Northern Ireland. 417
Food: Contaminants: Scotland. 355

Food: Contaminants: Wales 91
Food: Curd cheese: Marketing restrictions: England 89
Food: Curd cheese: Marketing restrictions: Northern Ireland 405, 417
Food: Curd cheese: Marketing restrictions: Scotland 355
Food: Curd cheese: Marketing restrictions: Wales 91
Food: Dairy produce: Quotas 89
Food: Dairy produce: Quotas: Northern Ireland 417
Food: Dairy produce: Quotas: Scotland 355
Food: Dairy produce: Quotas: Wales 92
Food: Eggs: Marketing standards: Amendments: England & Wales 91
Food: Emergency controls: England 90
Food: Emergency controls: Wales 92
Food: Emergency controls: Northern Ireland 418
Food: Emergency controls: Scotland 355
Food: Fish: Labelling: England 90
Food: Fish: Labelling: Northern Ireland 417
Food: Fish: Labelling: Scotland 355
Food: Fish: Labelling: Wales 92
Food: Fishery products: Official controls: Charges: England 89
Food: Fishery products: Official controls: Charges: Northern Ireland 417
Food: Fishery products: Official controls: Charges: Scotland 355
Food: Fishery products: Official controls: Charges: Wales 92
Food: Health & Social Care (Community Health & Standards) Act 2003: Commencements 91, 137
Food: Healthy start scheme 89
Food: Healthy start scheme & welfare food 89
Food: Healthy start scheme: Day care food scheme: Northern Ireland 418
Food: Hygiene: England 90
Food: Hygiene: Northern Ireland 418
Food: Hygiene: Scotland 355
Food: Inspections & controls: Charges 89
Food: Kava-kava: Wales 92
Food: Meat: Official controls: Charges: England 90
Food: Meat: Official controls: Charges: Northern Ireland 418
Food: Meat: Official controls: Charges: Scotland 356
Food: Meat: Official controls: Charges: Wales 92
Food: Nutritional uses: England 90
Food: Nutritional uses: Northern Ireland 418
Food: Nutritional uses: Scotland 355
Food: Official controls: England 15, 90
Food: Official controls: Northern Ireland 406, 418
Food: Official controls: Wales 18, 92
Food: Olive oil: Marketing standards 89
Food: Pesticides: Maximum residue levels: Scotland 342, 368
Food: Plastic materials & articles: Contact: England 90, 91
Food: Plastic materials & articles: Contact: Northern Ireland 418
Food: Plastic materials & articles: Contact: Scotland 356
Food: Plastic materials & articles: Contact: Wales 93
Food: Residues surveillance: Charges 89
Food: Rice products: Marketing: Restrictions: England 15, 91, 93
Food: Rice products: Marketing: Restrictions: Northern Ireland 407, 418
Food: Rice products: Marketing: Restrictions: Scotland 356
Food: Rice products: Marketing: Restrictions: Wales 93
Food: Scotland Act 1998: Agency arrangements: Specifications 43, 58, 89
Food: Welfare food 89
Food: Welfare foods: Northern Ireland 445
Foot & mouth disease: Animal health: Scotland 344
Foot & mouth disease: England 21
Foot & mouth disease: Slaughter & vaccination: Animal health: Scotland 344
Foot & mouth disease: Vaccination: Control: England 21
Foot & mouth disease: Vaccination: Control: Northern Ireland 408
Foot & mouth disease: Vaccination: Control: Wales 24
Foot & mouth disease: Wales 24
Football spectators: Seating: Sports grounds & sporting events 274
Football: Spectators: 2006 World Cup: Control period 274
Football: Spectators: Prescription: England & Wales 274
Forestry: Environmental impact assessment: England & Wales 93

Forestry: Environmental impact assessment: Northern Ireland 419
Forestry: Environmental impact assessment: Scotland 341, 354, 356, 359, 376, 391
Forestry: Plant health. 153
Forestry: Plant health: Fees 153
Forestry: Regulatory reform 93, 162
Forestry: Wood: Packaging material marking 153
Forests: Reproductive material: Great Britain 264
Fostering services: Private arrangements: Wales 32, 266
Fostering: Local authority fostering functions: Inspections: Fees 31, 265
Fraud Act 2006: Commencements 52
Fraud: Acts 6
Fraud: Acts: Explanatory notes 10
Free zones: Designations 55
Friendly & Industrial & Provident Societies Act 1968: Audit exemptions 115
Fuel: Private use: Consideration: Value added tax 288
Fuels: Authorised: Smoke control areas: Wales. 40
Fuel-testing: Pilot projects: Biogas project: Excise rebate 84
Fundable bodies: Education: Scotland 351
Further & Higher Education (Scotland) Act 1992: Modification: Scotland 346
Further education corporations: Revocation: Wales 73
Further education: Providers: England 66
Further education: Student support: Cross-border eligibility: Northern Ireland 412

G

Gaelic Language (Scotland) Act 2005: Commencements: Scotland 356
Gaelic Language (Scotland) Act 2005: Consequential modifications 28, 43, 58
Galloway: Dumfries & Galloway: Electoral arrangements: Scotland 361
Gambling Act 1968: Fees: Variation: Scotland 345
Gambling Act 2005: Commencements 26
Gambling Act 2005: Commencements & transitional provisions. 26
Gambling Act 2005: Licensing Authority: Policy statement 26, 27
Gambling Act 2005: Licensing Authority: Policy statement: Scotland 345
Gambling Act 2005: Part 5: Modification: Personal licences 27
Gambling Act 2005: Relevant offences 26
Gambling Act 2005: Small-scale operator: Definition 26
Gambling Act 2005: Transitional provisions 26
Gambling Appeals Tribunal: Fees. 26
Gambling Appeals Tribunal: Rules 26
Gambling: Operating licences & single-machine permit fees. 27
Gambling: Personal licence fees 27
Game preservation: Irish hares: Special protection: Northern Ireland. 419
Gaming Act 1968: Fees: Variation 27
Gaming Act 1968: Fees: Variation: England & Wales 27
Gaming Act 1968: Monetary limits: Variation 27
Gaming duty 84
Gaming machines: Value added tax 288
Gangmasters (Licensing) Act 2004: Commencements 76
Gangmasters: Appeals 76
Gangmasters: Appeals: Northern Ireland 413
Gangmasters: Licensing conditions 77
Gangmasters: Licensing exclusions 77
Gangmasters: Licensing: Exclusions: Northern Ireland 413
Gas Act 1986: Interconnector licence: Requirements: Exemptions. 93
Gas meters: Measuring Instruments 291
Gas: Appeals: Time limits: Modification 74, 93
Gas: Energy Act 2004: Commencements 74, 93
Gas: Northern Ireland 419
Gas: Pipelines: Designation: Northern Ireland 419
Gas: Prepayment meters 93
Gateshead: Parishes: Local government 122
Gating orders: Highways: England 80
Gatwick Express class 458 vehicles: Accessibility: Exemptions 61, 283
Gender recognition: Application fees 93
General Chiropractic Council: Professional Conduct & Health Committees: Rules 32

General Dental Council: Appointments Committee & appointment of members of committees. 96, 97
General Dental Council: Committees: Constitution. 97
General Dental Council: Constitution. 96, 97
General Dental Council: Fitness to practise: Rules 96, 97
General Dental Council: Professions complementary to dentistry 97
General Dental Council: Professions complementary to dentistry: Business of dentistry 97
General Dental Council: Professions complementary to dentistry: Dental hygienists & therapists 97
General Dental Council: Professions complementary to dentistry: Qualifications & supervision of dental work 97
General Dental Council: Registration: Appeals: Rules 96, 97
General dental services: National Health Service: Contracts: Wales 139
General dental services: National Health Service: England 134
General dental services: National Health Service: England & Wales 136
General dental services: National Health Service: Transitional & consequential provisions: Wales. 138
General dental services: National Health Service: Wales 139
General lighthouse authorities: Beacons: Automatic identification system 129
General medical services: Contracts: National Health Service: Scotland 365
General ophthalmic services: National Health Service: Scotland 365
General ophthalmic services: Supplementary list: National Health Service: Wales. 140
General Optical Council: Continuing education & training 95, 145
General Osteopathic Council: Continuing professional development: Rules. 96
General Synod of the Church of England: Measures 11
General Synod of the Church of England: Measures: Bound volumes 12
General Synod of the Church of England: Measures: Tables & index 12
General Teaching Council for Scotland: Legal assessor: Rules: Scotland 351
General Teaching Council for Wales: Functions 73
Generation: Electricity: Licence requirement: Exemption: England & Wales 74
Genetically modified organisms: Contained use: Northern Ireland 421
Gibraltar: Copyright. 47
Gibraltar: Tax information exchange agreements 114
Gilt-edged securities: Capital gains tax 29, 50
Gilt-edged securities: Chargeable gains: Capital gains tax 29, 50
Glasgow (City): Road traffic: Permitted & special parking area: Scotland 377
Glasgow City Council: Electoral arrangements: Scotland. 361
Glasgow: Greater Glasgow Health Board: Area: Variation: Scotland. 366
Gloucestershire Ambulance Service: National Health Service Trust 132
Gloucestershire: Coroners' districts. 47
Goats & sheep: Records, identification & movement: Wales. 24, 25
Goats & sheep: Transmissible spongiform encephalopathies: Compensation: Wales 25
Goats: Identification & traceability: Scotland 344
Goats: Records, identification & movement: England 21
Goats: Records, identification & movement: Northern Ireland 407
Goods & passenger vehicles: Recording equipment: Northern Ireland 415, 438
Goods vehicles: Recording equipment. 168
Goods vehicles: Recording equipment: Fitting dates 168
Goods vehicles: Recording equipment: Tachograph cards 168
Goods vehicles: Testing: Northern Ireland 437
Goods vehicles: Type approval 168
Government accounts: Designation of bodies: Northern Ireland 419
Government resources & accounts: Designation of bodies: Northern Ireland. 419
Government resources & accounts: Special health authorities: Audit 93
Government resources & accounts: Special health authorities: Summarised accounts 93
Government trading funds: Driving Standards Agency Trading Fund: Maximum borrowing 94
Government trading funds: Ordnance Survey Trading Fund: Maximum borrowing. 94
Government: Wales: Acts 6
Government: Wales: Acts: Explanatory notes 10
Grammar schools: Charges: Northern Ireland 412
Gravimetric filling instruments: Automatic: Weights & measures 290
Great & Little Preston Voluntary Controlled Church of England Primary School: Religious character: Designation. 66
Great Western Ambulance Service: National Health Service Trust 132
Greater Glasgow Health Board: Area: Variation: Scotland 366
Greater London Authority: Grants for precept calculations: Allocation. 125
Greater Manchester: Light rapid transit systems 284, 285
Greenhouse Gas Emissions Trading Scheme: Amendment. 78
Guardian's allowance 266
Guardian's allowance: General 267
Guardian's allowance: Up-rating. 267, 268

Guardian's allowance: Up-rating: Northern Ireland 273
Guide dogs: Carriage of: Private hire vehicles: Disability Discrimination Act 1995: England & Wales 61, 285
Guide dogs: Carriage of: Taxis: Disability Discrimination Act 1995: England & Wales 61, 286
Gwaed a Thrawsblaniadau'r GIG: NHS Blood & Transplant: Membership & procedures 137
Gypsies & travellers: Caravans: Definitions: England 279

H

H5N1 *see* Avian influenza
Hadley Learning Community: School governance 66
Hake: Northern hake stock: Sea fisheries: Scotland 387
Hake: Northern hake stock: Sea fisheries: Wales 262
Harbours, docks, piers & ferries: Dover: Harbour revision 94
Harbours, docks, piers & ferries: Highland Council: Raasay: Harbour revision: Scotland 356
Harbours, docks, piers & ferries: Hull 94
Harbours, docks, piers & ferries: Humber Sea Terminal Phase III: Harbour revision 94
Harbours, docks, piers & ferries: Port of Ipswich: Harbour revision 94
Harbours: Poole harbour: Opening bridges 284, 285
Hares: Irish: Special protection: Game preservation: Northern Ireland 419
Hazardous substances: Planning: Crown land: Wales 281
Hazardous substances: Use restriction: Electrical & electronic equipment 78
HBOS Group: Reorganisation: Local acts 11
Health & personal social services: Belfast Health & Social Services Trust: Establishment: Northern Ireland 419
Health & personal social services: Care Tribunal: Regulations: Amendments: Northern Ireland 419
Health & personal social services: Drugs & appliances: Charges: Northern Ireland 419
Health & personal social services: Northern Health & Social Services Trust: Northern Ireland 419
Health & personal social services: Northern Ireland Social Care Council: Social care workers: Description: Northern Ireland 420
Health & personal social services: Northern Ireland Social Care Council: Social care workers: Northern Ireland 420
Health & personal social services: Optical charges & payments: Northern Ireland 420
Health & personal social services: Primary medical services: Amendments: Northern Ireland 419
Health & personal social services: Regulation & Improvement Authority: Inspections: Fees & frequency: Northern Ireland 420
Health & personal social services: Resources: Assessment: Northern Ireland 419
Health & personal social services: South Eastern Health & Social Services Trust: Establishment: Northern Ireland 420
Health & personal social services: Southern Health & Social Services Trust: Establishment: Northern Ireland 420
Health & personal social services: Superannuation: Northern Ireland 419
Health & personal social services: Travel expenses & remission of charges: Northern Ireland 420
Health & personal social services: Western Health & Social Services Trust: Establishment: Northern Ireland 420
Health & safety: Agriculture: Children & young persons: Northern Ireland 420
Health & safety: Asbestos: Control 94
Health & safety: At work: Management: Northern Ireland 421
Health & safety: Blood: Safety & quality 94
Health & safety: Dangerous goods: Carriage: Northern Ireland 420, 421
Health & safety: Enforcing authority for railways & other guided transport systems 94
Health & safety: Explosives: Carriage: By road & rail: Northern Ireland 421
Health & safety: Explosives: Manufacture & storage: Northern Ireland 421
Health & safety: Explosives: Quarries: Northern Ireland 421
Health & safety: Fees 95
Health & safety: Genetically modified organisms: Contained use: Northern Ireland 421
Health & safety: Ionising radiation: Medical exposure 95
Health & safety: Management: At work 95
Health & safety: Noise: Control: At work: Northern Ireland 421
Health & safety: Quarries: Northern Ireland 422
Health & safety: Railways & other guided transport 95
Health & safety: Railways: Safety levies 95
Health & safety: Railways: Safety management: Northern Ireland 422
Health & safety: Rating system: Housing: Wales 104
Health & safety: Transportable pressure equipment: Use: Northern Ireland 420, 421
Health & Social Care (Community Health & Standards) Act 2003: Commencements 91, 137, 265
Health & Social Care (Community Health & Standards) Act 2003: Commencements: Wales 139
Health & Social Care Act 2001: Commencements 132
Health Act 2006: Commencements 56, 97, 136, 137, 159, 266
Health authorities: Membership & procedure: England 132
Health authorities: Special health authorities: Audit 93
Health authorities: Special: Summarised accounts 93
Health authorities: Strategic: Dental services: Functions 132

Health Boards: Constitution: Scotland. 364
Health Boards: Functions: Scotland 364
Health Boards: Greater Glasgow & Highland Health Boards: Areas: Variation: Scotland 366
Health boards: Regional transport strategies: Scotland 392
Health care & associated professions: General Optical Council: Continuing education & training 95, 145
Health care & associated professions: Health Act 2006: Commencements 97, 136, 159, 266
Health care & associated professions: Health professions Wales: Abolition: Wales 98
Health care & associated professions: Medical Act 1983: Amendment 96
Health care & associated professions: Nurses & midwives: Parts of & entries in the register 95, 144
Health care & associated professions: Nursing & Midwifery Council: Practice committees: Constitution. 95, 144
Health care & associated professions: Osteopaths: General Osteopathic Council: Continuing professional development: Rules. 96
Health care & associated professions: Postgraduate Medical Education & Training Board: Fees: Rules 96
Health care & associated professions: Professions complementary to dentistry: European qualifications. 97
Health care: Private & voluntary: England 159
Health professions Wales: Abolition: Wales 98
Health professions: Register: Parts of & entries 96
Health Protection Agency: Scottish health functions: Scotland 371
Health Service Commissioner for England: Special health authorities 132, 137
Health Service: National Trusts 131, 132, 133, 134, 135, 136
Health services: Charges: Recovery: 2006 Order: Commencements: Northern Ireland. 436
Health services: Charges: Recovery: Amounts: Northern Ireland. 422
Health services: Charges: Recovery: Northern Ireland. 144, 422
Health services: Charges: Road traffic: Northern Ireland 437
Health services: National Health Service: Redress: Tort liability: Acts 7
Health services: National Health Service: Redress: Tort liability: Acts: Explanatory notes 10
Health start scheme: Healthy start food: Description: Wales 139
Health: Acts. 6
Health: Acts: Explanatory notes. 10
Health: Animals: Transmissible spongiform encephalopathies: Wales. 22
Health: Ionising radiation: Medical exposure. 95
Health: Local health boards: Establishment: Wales 139
Health: National Health Service: Acts 7
Health: Prohibition of Smoking in Certain Premises (Scotland) Regulations 2006: Consequential provisions 44, 59, 94
Health: Smoking, Health & Social Care (Scotland) Act 2005: Consequential provisions 44, 59, 94
Healthcare & associated professions: Dentists Act 1984 (Amendment) Order 2005: Transitional provisions. 96, 97
Healthcare & associated professions: General Dental Council: Appointments Committee & appointment of members of committees . 96, 97
Healthcare & associated professions: General Dental Council: Committees: Constitution 97
Healthcare & associated professions: General Dental Council: Constitution. 96, 97
Healthcare & associated professions: General Dental Council: Fitness to practise: Rules 96, 97
Healthcare & associated professions: General Dental Council: Professions complementary to dentistry 97
Healthcare & associated professions: General Dental Council: Professions complementary to dentistry: Business of dentistry 97
Healthcare & associated professions: General Dental Council: Professions complementary to dentistry: Dental hygienists & therapists 97
Healthcare & associated professions: General Dental Council: Professions complementary to dentistry: Qualifications & supervision of dental work 97
Healthcare & associated professions: General Dental Council: Registration: Appeals: Rules 96, 97
Healthcare & associated professions: Nursing & Midwifery Order 2001: Transitional provisions 96
Healthcare: Private & voluntary health care: Wales 159
Healthy start scheme 89
Healthy start scheme: Day care food scheme: Northern Ireland. 418
Hertfordshire: North Hertfordshire (District): Electoral changes 122
Herzegovina: Bosnia: Export control 54
High Court of Justiciary: Criminal procedure: Rules: Amendments: Act of Adjournal: Scotland 350, 357, 389
High Court of Justiciary: Criminal procedure: Rules: Financial reporting orders: Act of Adjournal: Scotland 357, 388
High Court of Justiciary: Criminal procedure: Rules: Risk assessment Orders: Orders for lifelong restriction: Act of Adjournal: Scotland 357
High Court of Justiciary: Criminal procedure: Rules: Vulnerable Witnesses (Scotland) Act 2004: Act of Adjournal: Scotland . . 357, 389
High Court of Justiciary: Vulnerable Witnesses (Scotland) Act 2004: Commencements: Scotland. 357, 390
Higher Education Act 2004: Commencements 70
Higher Education Act 2004: Commencements: Wales 73
Higher education: 2005 Order: Commencement: Northern Ireland 412
Higher education: Assembly learning grants & loans: Wales. 71
Higher education: Assembly learning grants: Wales 71
Higher education: Institutions: Designation: Scotland. 350
Highland Council: Electoral arrangements: Scotland 361
Highland Council: Raasay: Harbour revision: Scotland 356

Highland Health Board: Area: Variation: Scotland 366
Highways Stockton-on-Tees Borough Council: North Shore development: North Shore footbridge scheme 101
Highways, England. 100, 101
Highways: Cambridgeshire County Council: Cambridge Riverside Foot/Cycle Bridge: Construction. 100
Highways: Crime prevention: Designated areas. 100
Highways: Dartford - Thurrock Crossing: Amendments 100
Highways: England & Wales. 98, 99, 100, 101
Highways: Gating orders: England 80
Highways: Humber Bridge: Tolls & vehicle classification: Revision 100
Highways: Lincolnshire County Council: Car Dyke Crossing Bridge Scheme 2004: Confirmation instrument 100
Highways: Public rights of way: Registers: Wales 101
Highways: Restricted byways: Application & consequential amendment of provisions: England & Wales 101
Highways: Severn Bridges: Tolls 101
Highways: Special roads: England. 101
Highways: Street works: Inspection fees: Wales 101
Highways: Street works: Reinstatement: Wales 102
Highways: Traffic Management Act 2004: Commencements. 101
Highways: Trunk roads: A38: Dobwalls bypass 99
Highways: Trunk roads: A38: Dobwalls bypass: Detrunking. 99
Highways: Trunk roads: A65: Gargrave Bypass: 1990 & 1993 Orders. 99
Highways: Trunk roads: A65: Hellifield & Long Preston: Bypass & slip roads 99
Highways: Trunk roads: A550/A5117: M56 & A548 improvement: Connecting roads 100
Hill farm allowance: England 14, 15
Hinckley & Bosworth: Parishes: Local government. 122
Historic Buildings Council for Wales: Abolition 158
Holy Trinity Rosehill (VA) CE Primary School: Religious character: Designation 66
Home detention curfew licence: Prescribed standard conditions: Scotland 348
Home energy efficiency scheme: England 77
Home energy efficiency scheme: Scotland 352
Home information pack: Prescribed documents 104
Home loss payments: Prescribed amounts: England 12
Home loss payments: Prescribed amounts: Wales 13
Home-Grown Cereals Authority: Levy: Rate 13
Homelessness: Accommodation: Suitability: Wales. 104
Homelessness: Allocation of housing & homelessness: Eligibility: Northern Ireland 422
Homelessness: Allocation: England 102
Homelessness: Housing authority accommodation: Immigration control 102, 109
Homelessness: Housing: Allocation: Eligibility: England. 102
Homelessness: Housing: Allocation: England 102
Homelessness: Wales 104
Homoeopathic products: Advisory Board on the Registration of Homoeopathic Products 127
Homoeopathic products: National rules 127
Hope Hamilton CE Primary School: Religious character: Designation. 66
Horses: Zootechnical standards: England. 19
Horses: Zootechnical standards: Wales 22
Household waste: Duty of care: Wales 82
Housing (Scotland) Act 2006: Commencements: Scotland 357
Housing Act 2004: Commencements 102
Housing Act 2004: Commencements: England 102
Housing Act 2004: Commencements: Wales 104
Housing benefit 268
Housing benefit: Amendments. 268
Housing benefit: Consequential provisions: Northern Ireland 422, 434, 439
Housing benefit: Electronic communications 75
Housing benefit: Electronic communications: Northern Ireland 422, 434
Housing benefit: Northern Ireland 422, 423, 434, 435
Housing benefit: Pension credit: Qualifying age: Northern Ireland 423, 434
Housing benefits: State pension credit: Qualifying age 268
Housing Corporation: Delegation: Acts 6
Housing for Wales: Delegation: Acts. 6
Housing renewal grants: Forms: Wales 105
Housing renewal grants: Reduction of grant: Northern Ireland: Northern Ireland 423
Housing renewal grants: Wales 105
Housing Revenue Account General Fund: Contribution limits: Scotland 357
Housing: Accommodation needs: Assessment: Meaning of gypsies & travellers: England 103

Housing: Acts: Explanatory notes: Scotland. 340
Housing: Acts: Scotland 338
Housing: Allocation of housing & homelessness: Eligibility: Northern Ireland 422
Housing: Allocation: Eligibility: England. 102
Housing: Allocation: England 102
Housing: Allocation: Wales 104
Housing: Authority accommodation: Homelessness: Immigration control 102, 109
Housing: Bulgaria & Romania: Northern Ireland. 423, 435, 440
Housing: Children & young persons: Social security: Amendments: Northern Ireland 424, 436, 442
Housing: Empty dwelling management orders: Prescribed exceptions & requirements: England 103
Housing: Empty dwelling management orders: Prescribed exceptions & requirements: Wales 104
Housing: Empty dwelling management orders: Supplemental provisions: Wales 105
Housing: Health & safety: Rating system: Wales 104
Housing: Home information pack: Prescribed documents. 104
Housing: Homelessness: Accommodation: Suitability: Wales 104
Housing: Homelessness: Wales 104
Housing: Houses in multiple occupation: Licensing & management: Wales 105
Housing: Houses in multiple occupation: Licensing: Prescribed descriptions: England 103
Housing: Houses in multiple occupation: Licensing: Wales. 105
Housing: Houses in multiple occupation: Management 103
Housing: Houses in multiple occupation: Management: Wales 105
Housing: Houses in multiple occupation: Specified educational establishments 102
Housing: Houses in multiple occupation: Specified educational establishments: Wales 104
Housing: Houses: Licensing: Wales 105, 106
Housing: Housing benefit: Consequential provisions: Northern Ireland 422, 434, 439
Housing: Housing benefit: Northern Ireland 423, 435
Housing: Housing benefit: Pension credit: Qualifying age: Northern Ireland 423, 434
Housing: Interim management orders: Prescribed circumstances: England. 103
Housing: Interim management orders: Prescribed circumstances: Wales. 105
Housing: Introductory tenancies: Decisions to extend trial periods: Reviews: Wales. 105
Housing: Licensing & management 103
Housing: Management orders & empty dwelling management orders: Supplemental provisions: England 103
Housing: Northern Ireland 142
Housing: Private landlords: Registration: Information & fees: Scotland 349, 357, 362
Housing: Race Relations: Code of Practice: Appointed day. 160
Housing: Residential Property Tribunal: Fees: England. 103
Housing: Residential Property Tribunal: Fees: Wales 105
Housing: Residential Property Tribunal: Procedure: England. 103
Housing: Residential Property Tribunal: Procedure: Wales 105
Housing: Residential property: Management practice: Approval of codes 104
Housing: Retirement pensions: Deferral: Shared additional pension & graduated retirement benefit: Northern Ireland . . . 423, 435, 440
Housing: Right to buy: Designated rural areas & designated region: England 103
Housing: Right to buy: Priority of charges: England 103
Housing: Right to buy: Priority of charges: Wales 105
Housing: Rural housing bodies: Title Conditions (Scotland) Act 2003: Amendments: Scotland. 391
Housing: Selective licensing: Specified exemptions: England 103
Housing: Social housing: Grants to bodies other than registered social landlords: Additional purposes: England 104
Housing: Social landlords: Permissible additional purposes: England 104
Housing: Social landlords: Registered: Purposes or objects: Scotland 357
Housing: Social security: Amendments: Northern Ireland 423, 424, 436, 441, 442
Housing: Social security: Benefits up-rating: Northern Ireland 413, 423, 435, 440, 443
Housing: Social security: Lebanon: Northern Ireland. 423, 435, 441
Housing: Social security: Persons from abroad: Northern Ireland 424, 436, 442
Housing: Student accommodation: Approval 103
Housing: Student accommodation: Codes of management practice: Approval: Wales 104
Housing: Students & income-related benefits: Northern Ireland 424, 436, 442
Housing: Tenancies: Introductory: Review of decisions to extend a trial period: England 103
Hovercraft: Fees 106
Hucknall National Church of England (VA) Primary School: Religious character: Designation 66
Hull: Harbour revision. 94
Human organs & tissue: Acts: Explanatory notes: Scotland. 340
Human organs & tissue: Acts: Scotland 339
Human rights Act 1998: Proceedings: Proscribed Organisations Appeal Commission 106
Human rights: Equal opportunities: Equality Act 2006: Commencements 82
Human rights: Scottish Commission for Human Rights: Acts: Explanatory notes: Scotland 340
Human rights: Scottish Commission for Human Rights: Acts: Scotland 339

Human Tissue (Scotland) Act 2006: Anatomy Act 1984 transitional provisions: Scotland 343, 358
Human Tissue (Scotland) Act 2006: Body parts: Removal & use: Maintenance of records & supply of information: Scotland. 358
Human Tissue (Scotland) Act 2006: Commencements: Scotland 358
Human Tissue Act 2004: Commencements 106, 107
Human Tissue Act 2004: Entry & search powers: Information supply: England, Wales & Northern Ireland. 106, 107
Human Tissue Act 2004: Transplants: Ethical approval, exceptions from licensing & supply of information 106, 107
Human tissue: Adults with incapacity: Removal of regenerative tissue for transplantation: Form of certificate: Scotland 358
Human tissue: Body parts: Removal: Authorised persons: Scotland 358
Human tissue: Organ & tissue live transplants: Scotland 358
Human tissue: Organ transplants: Scotland 358
Human tissue: Organs: Research approval: Specified persons: Scotland 358
Human tissue: Persons who lack capacity to consent & transplants. 106
Human tissue: Specification of posts: Scotland 358
Humber Bridge: Tolls & vehicle classification: Revision 100
Humber Sea Terminal Phase III: Harbour revision 94
Humberside: Doncaster & South Humberside Healthcare: National Health Service Trust 132
Hydrocarbon oil duties: Sulphur-free diesel: Biomass hydrogenation: Reliefs. 84
Hydrocarbon oils: Excise: Duties: Surcharges or rebates 83, 84
Hygiene: Food hygiene: Wales 92

I

Identity Cards Act 2006: Commencements 107
Identity cards: Acts 6
Identity cards: Acts: Explanatory notes 10
Immanuel CofE Community College: Religious character: Designation 66
Immigration & asylum: Acts 6
Immigration & asylum: Acts: Explanatory notes 10
Immigration & asylum: Safe countries: First list 108
Immigration & asylum: Tribunals: Fast track procedure 107
Immigration control: Persons subject to: Housing authority accommodation: Homelessness 102, 109
Immigration Services Commissioner: Designated professional body: Fees 109
Immigration, Asylum & Nationality Act 2006: Commencements. 108
Immigration: Accession: Immigration & worker authorisation 107
Immigration: Asylum & Immigration (Treatment of Claimants, etc.) Act 2004: Commencement 107
Immigration: Asylum & Immigration Tribunals: Procedure: Amendments. 107
Immigration: Asylum: Designated states 107, 108
Immigration: Asylum: Support 108
Immigration: European Economic Area 108
Immigration: Leave to remain: Prescribed forms & procedures. 108
Immigration: Leave: Continuation: Notices 108
Immigration: Nationality, Immigration & Asylum Act 2002: Commencements 109
Immigration: Nationality, Immigration & Asylum Act 2002: Juxtaposed controls 109
Immigration: Notices. 109
Immigration: Passenger transit: Visas 109
Immigration: Physical data: Provision 109
Immigration: Refugees or persons in need of international protection: Qualification. 109
Immigration: Right of abode in the UK: Certificate of entitlement 108
Immigration: Travel bans: Designation 108
Immunities & privileges: European Organization for Nuclear Research 117
Immunities & privileges: International Criminal Court 117
Immunities & privileges: International: Commonwealth countries & Ireland. 117
Incapacity benefit: Work-focused interviews. 270, 271
Incapacity benefit: Work-focused interviews: Northern Ireland. 440
Incapacity for work: Social security 271
Incapacity for work: Social security: Northern Ireland 441
Income support 271
Income support: : Northern Ireland 441
Income tax *see also* Taxes
Income Tax (Trading & Other Income) Act 2005: Consequential amendments 48, 111
Income Tax (Trading & Other Income) Act 2005: Section 757 (2): Amendments: Interest & royalty payments: Exemptions 110
Income tax: Armed Forces & Reserve Forces: Compensation scheme: Excluded benefits 109
Income tax: Authorised investment funds 28, 47, 109
Income tax: Avoidance schemes: Arrangements: Prescribed descriptions 29, 50, 114
Income tax: Avoidance schemes: Information. 29, 50, 114

Income tax: Capital allowances: Energy-saving plant & machinery 47, 109
Income tax: Capital allowances: Environmentally beneficial plant & machinery 47, 109
Income tax: Double taxation: Relief: Botswana 29, 47, 110
Income tax: Double taxation: Relief: Japan 29, 47, 110
Income tax: Double taxation: Relief: Poland 29, 47, 110
Income tax: Energy-saving items 110
Income tax: Exempt amounts: Childcare vouchers & employer contracted childcare 110
Income tax: Exemptions: Interest & royalty payments: Income Tax (Trading & Other Income) Act 2005: Section 757 (2): Amendments
 110
Income tax: Finance (No. 2) Act 2005: Section 17 (1): Appointed day 48, 110
Income tax: Finance Act 2004: Section 77 (1) (7): Appointed day 110
Income tax: Finance Act 2006: Section 53 (2): Films & sound recordings: Appointed day 48, 110
Income tax: Finance Act 2006: Section 53 (2): Films & sound recordings: Power to alter dates 48, 110
Income tax: Indexation 110
Income tax: Individual savings accounts 111
Income tax: Judicial pensions 114
Income tax: Lloyd's Underwriters: Limited liability underwriting: Conversion to 48, 111
Income tax: Lloyd's Underwriters: Scottish Limited Partnerships 49, 111
Income tax: Partnerships: Contributions to a trade: Restrictions 111
Income tax: Pay As You Earn 110
Income tax: Pension benefits: Scheme administrator: Insurance company liability 111
Income tax: Pension funds pooling schemes 111
Income tax: Pension Protection Fund 29, 49, 111, 115, 274
Income tax: Pension schemes 114
Income tax: Pension schemes: Application of UK provisions to relevant non-UK schemes 112
Income tax: Pension schemes: Categories of country & requirements for overseas & recognised overseas schemes 111
Income tax: Pension schemes: Investment-regulated: Exception of tangible moveable property 111
Income tax: Pension schemes: Pension rates: Reduction 111
Income tax: Pension schemes: Qualifying & qualifying recognised overseas schemes & corresponding relief: Information requirements
 111
Income tax: Pension schemes: Registered: Authorised member payments 112
Income tax: Pension schemes: Registered: Authorised payments 112
Income tax: Pension schemes: Registered: Authorised payments: Transfer to Pension Protection Fund 112
Income tax: Pension schemes: Registered: Commencement lump sum: Meaning 113
Income tax: Pension schemes: Registered: Enhanced lifetime allowances 112, 113
Income tax: Pension schemes: Registered: Extension of Migrant Member Relief 113
Income tax: Pension schemes: Registered: Living accommodation: Co-ownership 112
Income tax: Pension schemes: Registered: Provision of information 113
Income tax: Pension schemes: Registered: Relevant annuities 113
Income tax: Pension schemes: Registered: Relevant excess: Surrender 113
Income tax: Pension schemes: Registered: Rules: Modification 113
Income tax: Pension schemes: Registered: Unauthorised payments 113
Income tax: Pension schemes: Registered: Up-rating percentages: Defined benefits arrangements & enhanced protection limits ... 113
Income tax: Pension schemes: Relevant migrant members 111
Income tax: Pension schemes: Relevant non-UK schemes: Application of UK provisions 112
Income tax: Pension schemes: Taxable property provisions 112
Income tax: Pension schemes: Transfers, reorganisations & winding up 111
Income tax: Pension schemes: Transitional provisions 114
Income tax: Registered & overseas pension schemes: Returns & information: Electronic communication 112
Income tax: Registered pension schemes: Annuities: Determining amount: Prescribed manner 113
Income tax: Registered pension schemes: Authorised arrears payments 112
Income tax: Registered pension schemes: Authorised member payments 112
Income tax: Registered pension schemes: Authorised reductions 112
Income tax: Registered pension schemes: Authorised surplus payments 112
Income tax: Registered pension schemes: Block transfers: Permitted membership period 112
Income tax: Registered pension schemes: Information: Provision 113
Income tax: Registered pension schemes: Splitting of schemes 113
Income tax: Registered pension schemes: Transfer of sums & assets 113
Income tax: Retirement benefits: Employer-financed: Excluded benefits: Tax purposes 110
Income tax: Savings income: Information: Reporting 29, 50, 114
Income tax: Tax information exchange agreements: Gibraltar 114
Income tax: Unit trust schemes & offshore funds: Non-qualifying investments test 50, 114
Income: Savings: Information: Reporting 29, 50, 114
Income-related benefits: Students 272
Income-related benefits: Students: Northern Ireland 424, 436, 442
Income-related benefits: Subsidy to authorities 268

Individual savings accounts: Income tax. 111
Industrial & provident societies: 2006 Order: Commencements: Northern Ireland. 424
Industrial & provident societies: Community benefit societies: Assets: Restrictions on use 114
Industrial & provident societies: Community benefit societies: Assets: Restrictions on use: Northern Ireland 424
Industrial & provident societies: Credit unions: Loans: Maximum interest rate 114
Industrial & provident societies: Friendly & Industrial & Provident Societies Act 1968: Audit exemptions. 115
Industrial & provident societies: Northern Ireland. 142
Industrial injuries: Dependency: Permitted earnings limits 271
Industrial injuries: Dependency: Permitted earnings limits: Northern Ireland 441
Industrial injuries: Prescribed diseases. 271
Industrial injuries: Prescribed diseases: Northern Ireland 441
Industrial relations: Employment protection: Disclosure of information: Code of practice: Appointed day: Northern Ireland 425
Industrial relations: Employment: Access & unfair practices during recognition & derecognition ballots: Code of practice: Appointed day: Northern Ireland 424
Industrial relations: Employment: Industrial action ballots: Notice to employers: Code of practice: Appointed day: Northern Ireland . 424
Industrial training levy: Construction Board 77
Industrial training levy: Construction industry: Northern Ireland 425
Industrial training levy: Engineering Construction Board 77
Industrial tribunals: Age discrimination: Cases: Interest on awards: Northern Ireland 405, 425
Infant classes: Sizes: England 64
Infected waters: Infectious pancreatic necrosis: Northern Ireland. 417
Influenza *see also* Avian influenza
Information sharing index: Children & young persons: England 30
Information: Access: Executive arrangements: Local authorities: England. 123
Information: Disclosure: Enterprise Act 2002: Part 9: Restrictions. 42, 45, 61
Inheritance tax: Accounts: Delivery: Excepted estates 115
Inheritance tax: Pension Protection Fund 29, 49, 111, 115, 274
Injury benefit: Police Service & Police Service Reserve: Northern Ireland 433
Inland waterway & limited coastal operations: Boatmasters: Qualifications & hours of work 130
Inquiries: Rules. 115
Insects: Statutory nuisances 80
Insolvency & financial markets: Settlement finality 86
Insolvency proceedings: Fees 115
Insolvency rules: Companies: Sheriff Court: Act of Sederunt: Scotland 390
Insolvency: 1989 Order, article 59A: Appointed Date: Northern Ireland 425
Insolvency: 1989 Order: Amendments: Northern Ireland 425
Insolvency: 1989 Order: Prescribed part: Northern Ireland 425
Insolvency: 2005 Order: Commencements: Northern Ireland 425
Insolvency: 2005 Order: Transitional provisions & savings: Northern Ireland 425
Insolvency: Banks: Former authorised institutions 115
Insolvency: Companies 115
Insolvency: Companies: Cross-border 115
Insolvency: Companies: Scotland 116
Insolvency: Cross-border 115
Insolvency: Deposits: Northern Ireland 425
Insolvency: Electronic communications: Northern Ireland 426
Insolvency: Energy: Administration 116
Insolvency: Enterprise Act 2002: Disqualification from Office: General 115
Insolvency: Fees: Northern Ireland 425
Insolvency: Individuals: Cross-border 115
Insolvency: Insolvent partnerships: England & Wales 115
Insolvency: Minor & consequential amendments: Northern Ireland 425
Insolvency: Monetary limits: Northern Ireland 425
Insolvency: Northern Ireland. 425
Insolvency: Partnerships: Amendments: Northern Ireland 426
Insolvency: Practitioners & accounts: Fees: Northern Ireland. 425
Insolvency: Practitioners: Northern Ireland 426
Insolvent partnerships: England & Wales 115
Insolvent partnerships: Insolvency events: Amendments: Pension Protection Fund: Northern Ireland. 430
Insurance companies: Corporation tax acts: Amendments 48
Insurance premium tax 116
Insurance premium tax: Mutual assistance provisions 84, 116, 162, 276
Insurance: Accounts Directive: Miscellaneous insurance undertakings: Northern Ireland 426
Insurance: Life: Overseas companies: Income tax 49
Insurance: Non-resident insurance companies: Overseas losses: Group relief: Corporation Tax Acts: Modification 48

Intellectual property: Artists: Resale rights 117
Intellectual property: Patents Act 1977: Amendment: Electronic communications. 116
Intellectual property: Patents: Trade marks & designs: Service & time limits 116
Intellectual property: Registered Designs Act 1949: Amendment: Electronic communications 116
Intellectual property: Rights: Enforcement 116
Intellectual property: Trade marks & designs: Address for service 116
Inter-country adoption: Children: Overseas territories: Hague Convention: Amendments: Northern Ireland 426
Interest: Exemptions: Income Tax (Trading & Other Income) Act 2005: Section 757 (2): Amendments 110
International Criminal Court: Immunities & privileges 117
International Development Association: 13th replenishment 117
International Development Association: Multilateral debt relief initiative 117
International development: African Development Bank: African Development Fund: Tenth replenishment 117
International development: African Development Fund: Multilateral debt relief initiative. 117
International development: Asian Development Bank: Asian Development Fund: Eighth replenishment 117
International development: Caribbean Development Bank: Unified Special Development Fund: Sixth replenishment 117
International development: Reporting & transparency: Acts. 7
International immunities & privileges: Commonwealth countries & Ireland 117
International immunities & privileges: European Organization for Nuclear Research 117
International immunities & privileges: International Criminal Court 117
International immunities & privileges: International Maritime Organisation: Immunities & privileges 117
International Maritime Organisation: Immunities & privileges 117
Inverclyde: Electoral arrangements: Scotland 361
Investigatory powers: Communications data: Regulation 118
Investigatory powers: Directed surveillance & covert human intelligence sources: Regulation 118
Investigatory powers: Regulation: Prescription of offices, ranks & positions: Scotland 358
Investment exchanges: Regulatory provisions: Acts 7
Investment exchanges: Regulatory provisions: Acts: Explanatory notes 10
Investment funds: Authorised: Taxes 47
Investment trusts & venture capital trusts: Definition of capital profits, gains or losses 48
Investment trusts: Real estate: Group trusts: Financial statements 50
Ionising radiation: Medical exposure 95
Ipswich, Port: Harbour revision. 94
Ireland: Commonwealth countries & Ireland: Immunities & privileges. 117
Irish hares: Special protection: Game preservation: Northern Ireland. 419
Isle College: Dissolution 67
Isle of Wight Healthcare: National Health Service trust. 132
Isle of Wight: National Health Service primary care trust. 132
Isle of Wight: Parish electoral arrangements: Local government 123
Isle of Wight: Parishes: Local government 123
Ivory Coast: Restrictive measures: Arms: Overseas territories 145

J

Japan: Double taxation: Relief. 29, 47, 110
Jersey: Child Abduction & Custody Act 1985 30
Jersey: Postal services 156
Jobseeker's allowance 271
Jobseekers' allowance: Employment zones 267
Jobseekers' allowance: Employment zones: Allocation to contractors: Pilot 267
Jobseeker's allowance: Northern Ireland 441
Joint inspections: Children & young persons: Services: Scotland 346, 347
Joint waste disposal authorities: Levies: England 124
Joint waste disposal authorities: Recycling payments: Disapplication: England 80
Josiah Mason Sixth Form College, Erdington, Birmingham: Dissolution 67
Judges, legal officers & others: Fees: Ecclesiastical law 61
Judicial appointments & discipline: Constitutional Reform Act 2005: Commencements. 118, 125, 126, 283
Judicial appointments & discipline: Offices: Modification 118
Judicial appointments & discipline: Permitted persons: Designation 118
Judicial appointments & discipline: Prescribed procedures 118, 126
Judicial appointments & removals: Constitutional Reform Act 2005: Commencements 118, 125, 126, 283
Judicial appointments & removals: Constitutional Reform Act 2005: Commencements: Northern Ireland 118
Judicial appointments: Senior: Vacancies & incapacity: Acts: Explanatory notes: Scotland 340
Judicial appointments: Senior: Vacancies & incapacity: Acts: Scotland 339
Judicial Pensions & Retirement Act 1993: Qualifying judicial offices: Addition. 147
Judicial pensions: Additional voluntary contributions 146
Judicial pensions: Additional voluntary contributions: Northern Ireland 428

Judicial pensions: Contributions 147
Judicial pensions: Spouses' & children's benefits: Northern Ireland 428
Judicial pensions: Widows' & children's benefits: Northern Ireland 428
Justice (Northern Ireland) Act 2002: Commencements: Northern Ireland 426
Justice (Northern Ireland) Act 2002: Listed judicial offices, etc.: Additions: Northern Ireland ... 426
Justice: Access: 2003 Order: Commencement: Northern Ireland 404
Justice: Criminal: Acts 8
Justice: Criminal: Acts: Explanatory notes 10
Justices of the Peace: Local justice areas 118
Justices' Clerks: Assistants: Magistrates' courts 126

K

Kava-kava: Food: Wales 92
Kennet (District): Wiltshire (County): Permitted & special parking areas 254
Kent & Medway: National Health Service & Social Care Partnership Trust 133
Kent Medway, Kent Thanet & Sussex Hastings: Water: Southern Water Services: Non-essential use: Drought order 289
Kent: East Kent: National Health Service & Social Care Partnership Trust 133
Kent: Mid Kent Water: Non-essential use: Drought order 289
Kent: West Kent: National Health Service & Social Care Partnership Trust 133
Kesteven: North Kesteven (District): Electoral changes 122
Kettering (Borough): Electoral changes 121
Kettering: Parishes: Local government 123
King's Lynn: Parishes: Local government 123
Kingston upon Hull (City): Permitted & special parking areas 254
Kinross: Perth & Kinross Council: Road traffic: Permitted & special parking area: Scotland 377
Kinross: Perth & Kinross: Electoral arrangements: Scotland 362
Kirklees (Metropolitan Borough): Permitted & special parking areas 254
Korea: North: United Nations: Measures 287
Korea: North: United Nations: Measures: Overseas territories 287

L

Labour Relations Agency: Flexible working: Arbitration scheme: Northern Ireland 413
Laganside Corporation: Dissolution: Northern Ireland 426
Laganside: River Lagan: Tidal navigation & general byelaws: Northern Ireland 426
Lanarkshire: North Lanarkshire: Electoral arrangements: Scotland 362
Lanarkshire: South Lanarkshire Council: Road traffic: Permitted & special parking area: Scotland ... 377
Lanarkshire: South Lanarkshire: Electoral arrangements: Scotland 363
Land charges: Constitutional Reform Act 2005: Supplementary provisions 118
Land drainage: Broads Internal Drainage Board 119
Land drainage: Environmental impact assessment: Scotland 341, 354, 356, 359, 376, 391
Land drainage: General drainage charges: Anglian region 119
Land drainage: Improvement works: Environmental assessment 119
Land drainage: North West Regional Flood Defence Committee 119
Land drainage: Severn-Trent Regional Flood Defence Committee 119
Land drainage: Waveney, Lower Yare, & Lothingland Internal Drainage Board 119
Land drainage: Welsh Regional Flood Defence Committee: Composition 119
Land drainage: Witham Third District Internal Drainage District 119
Land management contracts: Menu scheme: Scotland 342
Land reform: Community right to buy: Definition of excluded Land: Scotland 359
Land registration: Automated: Electronic communications: Scotland 359
Land registration: Fees: England & Wales 120
Land registration: Rules: Scotland 359
Land tax: Stamp duty: Electronic communications 274
Land: Contaminated land: England 79
Land: Contaminated land: Wales 82
Land: Environmental impact assessment: Agriculture: England 14
Land: Radioactive contaminated land: Enactments: Modification: England 80
Land: Radioactive contaminated land: Enactments: Modification: Wales 82
Land: Radioactive contaminated land: Northern Ireland 415, 434
Land: Uncultivated land & semi-natural areas: Environmental impact assessment: Northern Ireland .. 406
Landfill tax 119
Landlord & tenant: Agricultural holdings: Units of production: England 119
Landlord & tenant: Agricultural holdings: Units of production: Wales 119

Landlord & tenant: Agricultural tenancies: Regulatory reform: England & Wales 119, 163
Landlord & tenant: Private tenancies: 2006 Order: Commencements: Northern Ireland 426
Landlord & tenant: Registered rents: Increase: Northern Ireland 426
Landlords: Private landlords: Registration: Information & fees: Scotland 349, 357, 362
Landlords: Social landlords: Registered: Purposes or objects: Scotland 357
Lands Tribunal: Rules: England & Wales 120
Lands Tribunal: Salaries: Northern Ireland 426
Lands Tribunal: Superannuation: Northern Ireland 426
Law reform: Northern Ireland 143
Law: Companies: Reform: Acts 5
Law: Compensation: Negligence: Claims: Acts 5
Law: Compensation: Negligence: Claims: Acts: Explanatory notes 9
Law: Discrimination: Acts 6
Law: Discrimination: Acts: Explanatory notes 10
Law: Equality: Acts 6
Law: Equality: Acts: Explanatory notes 10
Law: Family law: Acts: Explanatory notes: Scotland 340
Law: Family law: Acts: Scotland 338
Leatherhead Trinity Primary School: Religious character: Designation 67
Lebanon: Export control 55
Lebanon: Social security 271
Lebanon: Social security: Northern Ireland 423, 435, 441
Lebanon: Technical assistance, financing & financial assistance: Customs: Penalties & licences 55
Lebanon: United Nations: Measures 287
Lebanon: United Nations: Measures: Channel Islands 286
Lebanon: United Nations: Measures: Isle of Man 286
Legal advice & assistance: Northern Ireland 427
Legal aid & advice: Advice & assistance: Assistance by way of representation: Scotland 359
Legal aid & advice: Advice & assistance: Financial conditions: Scotland 359
Legal aid & advice: Advice & assistance: Representation: Assistance by way of: Amendments: Scotland 359
Legal aid & advice: Advice & assistance: Scotland 359
Legal aid & advice: Civil legal aid: Financial conditions: Scotland 359
Legal aid & advice: Civil legal aid: Scotland 359, 360
Legal aid & advice: Criminal legal aid: Fees: Scotland 360
Legal aid & advice: Criminal legal aid: Summary justice pilot courts & bail conditions: Scotland 360
Legal aid & advice: Criminal proceedings: Costs: Northern Ireland 427
Legal aid & advice: Legal advice & assistance: Financial conditions: Northern Ireland 427
Legal aid & advice: Legal advice & assistance: Northern Ireland 427
Legal aid & advice: Legal aid: Financial conditions: Northern Ireland 427
Legal aid & advice: Resources: Assessment: Northern Ireland 427
Legal aid: Civil: Financial conditions: Scotland 359
Legal aid: Criminal Defence Service: Acts 5
Legal aid: Criminal Defence Service: Acts: Explanatory notes 10
Legal aid: Criminal: Prescribed proceedings: Scotland 360
Legal officers: Annual fees: Ecclesiastical law 61
Legal Services Commission: Community Legal Service: Financial 120
Legal Services Commission: Community Legal Service: Financial: Amendments 120
Legal Services Commission: Community Legal Service: Funding: Amendments: England & Wales 120
Legal Services Commission: Community Legal Service: Funding: Family proceedings: Counsel: England & Wales 120
Legal Services Commission: Criminal Defence Service Act 2006: Commencements 120
Legal Services Commission: Criminal Defence Service: England & Wales 120
Legal Services Commission: Criminal Defence Service: Financial eligibility: England & Wales 120
Legal Services Commission: Criminal Defence Service: Funding 120
Legal Services Commission: Criminal Defence Service: Representation orders & consequential amendments 120
Legal Services Commission: Criminal Defence Service: Representation orders, appeals. etc. 120
Legal Services Ombudsman: Jurisdiction 120
Legal services: Association of Law Costs Draftsmen: England & Wales 120
Legislative reform: Acts 7
Legislative reform: Acts: Explanatory notes 10
Leicester (City): Permitted & special parking areas 254
Leicester City Council: Local acts 11
Less favoured area support scheme: Agriculture: Scotland 342
Less favoured areas: Compensatory allowances: Agriculture: Northern Ireland 406
Liberia: Export control 55
Liberty: Restriction: Criminal law: Scotland 349
Libraries: Public Lending Right Scheme 1982: Variation: Commencement 121

Licences & licensing: Skin piercing & tattooing: Scotland 360, 370, 371
Licensing (Scotland) Act 2005: Commencements: Scotland 360
Licensing Act 2003: Public houses: Non-domestic rating: Consequential amendments: England 121, 161
Licensing Authority: Policy statement: Gambling Act 2005 . . . . 26, 27
Licensing Authority: Policy statement: Gambling Act 2005: Scotland 345
Life insurance: Overseas companies: Income tax 49
Lifeboats: Value added tax 288
Lifelong restriction Orders: Risk assessment Orders: Criminal procedure: Rules: Act of Adjournal: Scotland 357
Limited liability partnerships: Northern Ireland: Northern Ireland 428
Lincoln (City): Electoral changes 122
Lincolnshire County Council: Car Dyke Crossing Bridge Scheme 2004: Confirmation instrument 100
Liquid fuel & lubricants: Weights & measures 291
Liquid fuel delivered from road tankers: Weights & measures 291
Liquor: Licensing (Scotland) Act 2005: Commencements: Scotland 360
Listed buildings: Conservation areas: Planning permission: Applications 279
Listed buildings: Planning: Appointed persons: Determination of appeals: Prescribed classes: England 280
Listed buildings: Planning: Crown land: Amendments: Wales 281
Listed buildings: Wales 281
Liverpool City Council: Local acts 11
Llanelli/Dinefwr: Community Health Councils: National Health Service: Wales 138
Lloyd's sourcebook: Finance Act 1993 & Finance Act 1994: Amendment 48
Lloyd's Underwriters: Double taxation relief: Corporate members 49
Lloyd's Underwriters: Limited liability underwriting: Conversion to 48, 111
Lloyd's Underwriters: Scottish Limited Partnerships: Taxes 49, 111
Loan relationships & derivative contracts: Accounting practice: Change 49
Loan relationships & derivative contracts: Disregard & bringing into account of profits & losses 49
Loan relationships & derivative contracts: Profits & losses: Disregard & bringing into account 49
Loans: Maximum interest rate: Credit unions 114
Lobsters: Goat Is.: Sea fisheries: Scotland 387
Local authorities: Armorial bearings 123
Local authorities: Calculations: Alteration: Wales 51
Local authorities: Calculations: Requisite: Alteration: England 124
Local authorities: Capital finance & accounting: England 123
Local authorities: Capital finance & accounting: Wales 124
Local authorities: Categorisation 123
Local authorities: Executive arrangements: Information: Access: England 123
Local authorities: Fostering functions: Inspections: Fees 31, 265
Local authorities: Functions & responsibilities: England 123
Local authorities: Members & officers: Indemnities: Wales 124
Local authorities: Social services: Complaints: England 265
Local authorities: Standing orders: Wales 124
Local elections: Parishes & communities: England & Wales 164
Local elections: Principal areas & parishes & communities: England & Wales 164
Local elections: Principal areas: England & Wales 164
Local electoral administration & registration services: Acts: Commencements: Scotland 374
Local electoral administration & registration services: Acts: Scotland 339
Local Governance (Scotland) Act 2004: Severance payments: Scotland 362
Local Government Act 2003: Commencements: Wales 125
Local government *see also* Local authorities 123
Local government: 2005 Order: Commencement: Northern Ireland 427
Local government: Aberdeen City Council: Electoral arrangements: Scotland 360
Local government: Aberdeenshire: Electoral arrangements: Scotland 360
Local government: Accounts & audit: England 121
Local government: Accounts & audit: Northern Ireland 427
Local government: Angus: Electoral arrangements: Scotland 360
Local government: Antisocial Behaviour etc. (Scotland) Act 2004: Commencements: Scotland 348, 352, 360, 369
Local government: Argyll & Bute: Electoral arrangements: Scotland 361
Local government: Assistants for Political Groups: Remuneration: England 123
Local government: Best value authorities: Power to trade: England 123
Local government: Best value authorities: Power to trade: Wales 125
Local government: Best value: Performance indicators & standards: England 123
Local government: Boundaries: Northern Ireland 143
Local government: Bridgend: Brackla & Coity Higher 124
Local government: Bus lane contraventions: Approved local authorities 121, 122, 253
Local government: Clackmannanshire: Electoral arrangements: Scotland 361

Local government: Companies: Best value: Northern Ireland 427
Local government: Council tax: Electronic communications: Scotland 347, 361, 373
Local government: Discretionary payments & injury benefits: Scotland 362
Local government: District of Broadland: Whole Council elections 122
Local government: Dumfries & Galloway: Electoral arrangements: Scotland 361
Local government: Dundee City: Electoral arrangements: Scotland 361
Local government: East Ayrshire: Electoral arrangements: Scotland 361
Local government: East Dunbartonshire: Electoral arrangements: Scotland 361
Local government: East Lothian: Electoral arrangements: Scotland 361
Local government: East Renfrewshire: Electoral arrangements: Scotland 361
Local government: Eastbourne (Borough): Whole council elections 121
Local government: Edinburgh (City): Electoral arrangements: Scotland 361
Local government: Electoral changes: Corby (Borough) 121
Local government: Electoral changes: Kettering (Borough) 121
Local government: Electoral changes: Lincoln (City) 122
Local government: Electoral changes: North Hertfordshire (District) 122
Local government: Electoral changes: North Kesteven (District) 122
Local government: Electoral changes: North Shropshire (District) 122
Local government: Electoral changes: South Northamptonshire (District) 122
Local government: Electoral changes: Tunbridge Wells (Borough) 121
Local government: Electoral changes: Waverley (Borough) 121
Local government: Employment: Early termination: Discretionary compensation: England & Wales 151
Local government: Ethical Standards in Public Life etc. (Scotland) Act 2000: Codes of conduct: Scottish public authorities members: Scotland 353, 361
Local government: Falkirk: Electoral arrangements: Scotland 361
Local government: Fife Council: Electoral arrangements: Scotland 361
Local government: Finance: Council tax: Valuation lists: Acts: England 5
Local government: Finance: Council tax: Valuation lists: Acts: Explanatory notes: England 10
Local government: Finance: Scotland 362
Local government: General grant: Northern Ireland 427
Local government: Glasgow City Council: Electoral arrangements: Scotland 361
Local government: Highland Council: Electoral arrangements: Scotland 361
Local government: Improved plan: Wales 125
Local government: Information: Access: Variation 124
Local government: Inverclyde: Electoral arrangements: Scotland 361
Local government: Joint waste disposal authorities: Levies: England 124
Local government: Local authorities: Calculations: Requisite: Alteration: England 124
Local government: Local authorities: Capital finance & accounting: Wales 124
Local government: Local authorities: Executive arrangements: Information: Access: England 123
Local government: Local authorities: Functions & responsibilities: England 123
Local government: Local Governance (Scotland) Act 2003: Commencement: Scotland 362
Local government: Local Governance (Scotland) Act 2004: Commencement: Scotland 362
Local government: Midlothian: Electoral arrangements: Scotland 362
Local government: Moray: Electoral arrangements: Scotland 362
Local government: Na h-Eileanan an Iar: Electoral arrangements: Scotland 362
Local government: Non-domestic rating: Electronic communications: Scotland 362, 373
Local government: North Ayrshire: Electoral arrangements: Scotland 362
Local government: North Lanarkshire: Electoral arrangements: Scotland 362
Local government: Orkney Islands: Electoral arrangements: Scotland 362
Local government: Parish electoral arrangements: Bradford 121
Local government: Parish electoral arrangements: East Lindsey 122
Local government: Parish electoral arrangements: Isle of Wight 123
Local government: Parish electoral arrangements: Uttlesford 123
Local government: Parishes: Bradford 121
Local government: Parishes: Castle Point 122
Local government: Parishes: Gateshead 122
Local government: Parishes: Hinckley & Bosworth 122
Local government: Parishes: Isle of Wight 123
Local government: Parishes: Kettering 123
Local government: Parishes: King's Lynn & West Norfolk 123
Local government: Parishes: Rugby 123
Local government: Parishes: Stratford-on-Avon 123
Local government: Parishes: Tandridge 123
Local government: Parishes: Torbay 123
Local government: Parishes: Wealden 124
Local government: Parishes: Wear Valley 124

Local government: Pension schemes 151
Local government: Pension schemes: Amendments 151
Local government: Pension schemes: Civil partnership: Northern Ireland 427
Local government: Pension schemes: Funds: Management & investment: Northern Ireland 427
Local government: Pension schemes: Northern Ireland 427
Local government: Pension schemes: Public Services Ombudsman (Wales) Act 2005: Wales 292
Local government: Pension schemes: Scotland 367
Local government: Perth & Kinross: Electoral arrangements: Scotland 362
Local government: Private landlords: Registration: Information & fees: Scotland 349, 357, 362
Local government: Recreation grounds: Wormley Recreation Ground: Parish Council byelaws: Revocation: England .. 124
Local government: Relevant authorities: Standards Committee 124
Local government: Renfrewshire: Electoral arrangements: Scotland 362
Local government: Representation of the people: England & Wales 124, 164
Local government: Scottish Borders: Electoral arrangements: Scotland 363
Local government: Shetland Islands: Electoral arrangements: Scotland 363
Local government: South Ayrshire: Electoral arrangements: Scotland 363
Local government: South Lanarkshire: Electoral arrangements: Scotland 363
Local government: Standards Committees: Wales 125
Local government: Stirling: Electoral arrangements: Scotland 363
Local government: Transport for London: Sloane Square House 121, 283
Local government: West Dunbartonshire: Electoral arrangements: Scotland 363
Local government: West Lothian: Electoral arrangements: Scotland 363
Local health boards: Establishment: Wales 139
Local health boards: Functions: Dental public health: Wales 138
Local health boards: Functions: Primary dental services: Wales 138
Local justice areas 118
Local probations boards: Appointments & miscellaneous provisions 157
Local safeguarding children boards: England 30
Loch Braigh Horrisdale: Scottish Water: Scotland 394
London Ambulance Service: National Health Service Trust 133
London government: Greater London Authority: Grants for precept calculations: Allocation 125
London government: Transport for London: Investment & highway functions: Contracting out: Best value .. 46, 125
London Olympic Games & Paralympic Games Act 2006: Commencements 145, 273
London Olympic Games & Paralympic Games Act 2006: Commencements: Scotland 367, 391
London Olympic Games 2012: Association rights: Appointment of proprietors 41, 282
London Thames Gateway Development Corporation: Planning functions 287
London: Olympic & paralympic games: Acts 7
London: Olympic & paralympic games: Acts: Explanatory notes 10
London: Sloane Square House: Transport for London 121, 283
Lord Chancellor: Consequential provisions: Northern Ireland 428, 444
Lord Chancellor: Constitutional Reform Act 2005: Commencements 118, 125, 126, 283
Lord Chancellor: Coroners: Discipline: Designation 47, 125, 126
Lord Chancellor: Transfer of functions & supplementary provisions 125, 126, 283
Lord Chief Justice: Constitutional Reform Act 2005: Commencements 118, 125, 126, 283
Lord Chief Justice: Coroners: Discipline: Designation 47, 125, 126
Lord Chief Justice: Judicial appointments & discipline: Prescribed procedures 118, 126
Lord Chief Justice: Lord Chancellor: Consequential provisions: Northern Ireland 428, 444
Lord Chief Justice: Lord Chancellor: Transfer of functions & supplementary provisions 125, 126, 283
Lothian: East Lothian: Electoral arrangements: Scotland 361
Lothian: West Lothian: Electoral arrangements: Scotland 363
Lotteries: Gaming Board: Fees 27
Lotteries: National Lottery: Acts 7
Lotteries: National Lottery: Acts: Explanatory notes 10
Lowick Church of England Voluntary Controlled First School: Religious character: Designation 67
Luton Dunstable Translink: England 284, 285

M

Magistrates' courts: Assistants to Justices' Clerks 126
Magistrates' courts: Courts Act 2003: Consequential amendment 52, 126, 275
Magistrates' courts: Criminal procedure: Rules: England & Wales 126, 276
Magistrates' courts: Fees: England & Wales 127
Magistrates' courts: Fines: Collection 126
Magistrates' courts: Fines: Collection & discharge by unpaid work: Pilot schemes 126
Magistrates' courts: Fines: Collection: Final scheme: England & Wales 126

Magistrates' courts: Rules: Anti-social behaviour orders: Northern Ireland 428
Magistrates' courts: Rules: Northern Ireland 428
Maidstone Borough Council: Local acts 11
Maintained schools: Change of category: England 64
Mammals: Avian influenza & influenza of avian origin: England 19
Mammals: Avian influenza & influenza of avian origin: Wales 23
Mammals: Avian influenza: Scotland 343
Mammals: Avian influenza: Wales 23
Management of Offenders etc. (Scotland) Act 2005: Commencements: Scotland. 348, 349
Management of Offenders etc. (Scotland) Act 2005: Consequential modifications 43, 52, 58
Management of Offenders etc. (Scotland) Act 2005: Partner bodies: Designation: Scotland 349
Management of Offenders etc. (Scotland) Act 2005: Supplementary provisions: Scotland. 349
Manchester (Greater): Light rapid transit systems 284, 285
Manchester City Council: Mancunian Way: Special road scheme 101
Manchester County Council: Carrington Spur, Trafford: Special roads scheme 100
Mancunian Way: Special road scheme 101
Marine archaeology: Wrecks: Protection: Designation: England 158
Marine pollution: Prevention: Merchant shipping 127
Marketing: Eggs: Standards: Northern Ireland 405
Marriage: Places: Approval: Scotland 363
Marriages: Registration services: Fees: Scotland 347, 363, 375
Masters & seamen: Merchant shipping: Safety communications: Training, certification & minimum standards 130
Material measures of length: Weights & measures 292
Maternity & parental leave. 277
Maternity & parental leave: Northern Ireland 414
Maternity allowance 273, 278
Maternity pay: Statutory 273, 278
Maternity, paternity & adoption leave: Employment: Acts 9
Maternity, paternity & adoption leave: Employment: Acts: Explanatory notes 11
Matrimonial & parental responsibility matters: Jurisdiction, recognition & enforcement of judgments: Sheriff Court: Act of Sederunt: Scotland 389
Measuring instruments: Active electrical energy meters 290
Measuring instruments: Amendments 290
Measuring instruments: Automatic catchweighers 290
Measuring instruments: Automatic discontinuous totalisers. 290
Measuring instruments: Automatic gravimetric filling instruments 290
Measuring instruments: Automatic rail-weighbridges 291
Measuring instruments: Beltweighers 291
Measuring instruments: Capacity serving measures 291
Measuring instruments: Cold-water meters 291
Measuring instruments: EEC requirements: Fees 85
Measuring instruments: EEC requirements: Verification fees: Northern Ireland 416
Measuring instruments: Exhaust gas analysers 291
Measuring instruments: Gas meters 291
Measuring instruments: Liquid fuel & lubricants 291
Measuring instruments: Liquid fuel delivered from road tankers 291
Measuring instruments: Material measures of length 292
Measuring instruments: Non-prescribed instruments 292
Measuring instruments: Taximeters 292
Meat: Official controls: Charges: England 90
Meat: Official controls: Charges: Northern Ireland 418
Meat: Official controls: Charges: Scotland 356
Meat: Official controls: Charges: Wales 92
Medical Act 1983: Amendment 96
Medical devices: Medicines: Human use: Fees 85, 127
Medical research: Human organs & tissue: Acts: Explanatory notes: Scotland 340
Medical research: Human organs & tissue: Acts: Scotland 339
Medical services: General: Wales 139
Medical services: Primary: Amendments: Northern Ireland. 419
Medical services: Primary: National Health Service: Wales 140
Medicine: Human organs & tissue: Acts: Explanatory notes: Scotland 340
Medicine: Human organs & tissue: Acts: Scotland 339
Medicines: Advisory Board on the Registration of Homoeopathic Products 127
Medicines: Herbal medicinal products: Human use 128
Medicines: Human use: Administration & sale or supply 127
Medicines: Human use: Clinical trials 127

Medicines: Human use: Fees. 85, 127
Medicines: Human use: Homoeopathic products: National rules 127
Medicines: Human use: Medical devices: Fees 85, 127
Medicines: Human use: Prescribing: Amendments 128
Medicines: Pharmacies: Applications for registration & fees 128
Medicines: Radioactive substances: Administration. 127
Medicines: Sale or supply: Amendments 128
Medicines: Veterinary medicines 128
Medway: National Health Service primary care trust 133
Members & officers: Indemnities: Local authorities 124
Mental Capacity Act 2005: Appropriate bodies: England 128
Mental Capacity Act 2005: Appropriate body: England. 128
Mental Capacity Act 2005: Commencements 128
Mental Capacity Act 2005: Independent mental capacity advocates 129
Mental Capacity Act 2005: Independent mental capacity advocates: Role: Expansion. 128
Mental Health (Care & Treatment) (Scotland) Act 2003: Transitional & savings provisions: Scotland 363
Mental Health Tribunal for Scotland: Practice & procedure: Rules: Scotland 363
Mental health: Court of Protection: Rules 129
Mental health: Documents: Form: Scotland 363
Mental health: Patients detained in conditions of excessive security: Relevant health board: Scotland 363
Mental health: Recall or variation of removal: Scotland 363
Merchant shipping: Air pollution: Prevention 127
Merchant shipping: Fees 129
Merchant shipping: Fishing vessels: Lifting operations & equipment. 129
Merchant shipping: Fishing vessels: Work equipment: Provision & use 129
Merchant shipping: General lighthouse authorities: Beacons: Automatic identification system 129
Merchant shipping: Inland waterway & limited coastal operations: Boatmasters: Qualifications & hours of work 130
Merchant shipping: Light dues. 129
Merchant shipping: Local passenger vessels: Crew 129
Merchant shipping: Marine pollution: Prevention: Sewage & garbage 127
Merchant shipping: Oil pollution: Bunkers Convention 129
Merchant shipping: Pollution: Acts. 7
Merchant shipping: Pollution: Acts: Explanatory notes. 10
Merchant shipping: Pollution: Oil: Supplementary fund protocol. 129
Merchant shipping: Safety communications: Training, certification & minimum standards 130
Merthyr Tydfil College: Dissolution: Wales 73
Mesothelioma: Claims: Contribution: Compensation. 42
Messengers-at-Arms: Fees: Court of Session: Act of Sederunt: Scotland. 389
Metropolitan & city districts: Private hire vehicles: London 130
Mid Kent Water: Non-essential use: Drought order 289
Middlesbrough: National Health Service primary care trust. 133
Midlothian: Electoral arrangements: Scotland. 362
Midwifery: Nursing & Midwifery Council: Practice committees: Constitution. 95, 144
Midwifery: Nursing & Midwifery Order 2001: Transitional provisions 96
Military: Service pensions 147
Millennium Commission: Dissolution 141
Ministers of the Crown: Office of Her Majesty's Paymaster General: Transfer of functions 130
Ministers of the Crown: Secretary of State for Communities & Local Government 130
Ministers of the Crown: Statutory instruments: Transfer of functions 130
Ministers of the Crown: Transfer of functions: Third Sector, Communities & Equality 130
Misuse of Drugs Act 1971: Amendments 55
Mobile Homes Act 1983: Schedule 1: Amendment: England 130
Mobile homes: Written statement: England 130
Mobile machinery: Non-road: Gaseous & particulate pollutants: Emissions 78
Money Laundering Regulations 2003: Amendment 86, 157
Money laundering: Proceeds of Crime Act 2002 157
Monkseaton Community High School: Governing body procedures 67
Moral rights: Rights in performances 47, 165
Moray: Electoral arrangements: Scotland 362
Motor cycles: EC type approval 167
Motor hackney carriages: Belfast: Byelaws: Amendments: Northern Ireland. 437
Motor hackney carriages: By-laws: Belfast: Northern Ireland 437
Motor vehicles: Approval: Northern Ireland. 437
Motor vehicles: Cars: Driving instruction 166
Motor vehicles: Construction & use: Northern Ireland 437

Motor vehicles: Driving licences	167
Motor vehicles: EC type approval	167
Motor vehicles: Goods vehicles: Type approval	168
Motor vehicles: Immobilisation & release: Prescribed charges: Northern Ireland	437
Motor vehicles: Immobilisation & removal: Prescribed conditions: Northern Ireland	437
Motor vehicles: Removal, storage & disposal: Prescribed charges: Northern Ireland	438
Motor vehicles: Seat belts: Wearing of	167
Motor vehicles: Seat belts: Wearing of: Children	167
Motor vehicles: Taxi Drivers' licences: Fees: Amendments: Northern Ireland	437
Motor vehicles: Testing Vehicles: Motor: Testing: Northern Ireland	437
Motor vehicles: Tests	167
Motor vehicles: Type approval & approval marks: Fees	167
Motor vehicles: Value added tax	288
Motorways: A1(M)/A1: Redhouse interchange to Holmfield interchange & A162	173
Motorways: A1(M)/A14(M): Junction 14 to 17, slip roads, Cambridgeshire	171
Motorways: A1(M)/M18: Wadworth interchange	235
Motorways: A1(M): A5135 Junction - Junction 6	173
Motorways: A1(M): Biggleswade north roundabout, Bedfordshire	171
Motorways: A1(M): Blyth, Nottinghamshire	171
Motorways: A1(M): Bramham crossroads	171
Motorways: A1(M): Chesterton, Cambridgeshire	171
Motorways: A1(M): Clow Beck accommodation to the A1231 overbridge	171
Motorways: A1(M): Dishforth interchange to Baldersby interchange	173
Motorways: A1(M): Hatfield Tunnel	171
Motorways: A1(M): Junction 1, South Mimms	171
Motorways: A1(M): Junction 1-2	172
Motorways: A1(M): Junction 2, slip roads	171
Motorways: A1(M): Junction 3 - 6	172
Motorways: A1(M): Junction 3, 4, & 6	172
Motorways: A1(M): Junction 4 - 6, northbound	173
Motorways: A1(M): Junction 4, southbound entry slip road	171
Motorways: A1(M): Junction 6 - 4	173
Motorways: A1(M): Junction 6, Welwyn, Hertfordshire	171
Motorways: A1(M): Junction 7, Hertfordshire	171
Motorways: A1(M): Junction 8 - 9, Hertfordshire	173
Motorways: A1(M): Junction 8 - 9. Milksy Lane Underbridge, Hertfordshire	171
Motorways: A1(M): Junction 9	172
Motorways: A1(M): Junction 9, Hertfordshire	172
Motorways: A1(M): Junction 9, Hertfordshire, northbound exit slip road	172
Motorways: A1(M): Junction 9, Letchworth Gate, Hertfordshire	172
Motorways: A1(M): Junction 10 - 9, Hertfordshire	173
Motorways: A1(M): Junction 16, Stilton to junction 17, Haddon	172
Motorways: A1(M): Junction 38 to 37	172
Motorways: A1(M): Junction 50 to 60	172
Motorways: A1(M): Junction 57 to 56	172
Motorways: A1(M): Junction 57 to 56 & the A1	172
Motorways: A1(M): Junction 58 to 57	172
Motorways: A1(M): Junction 58 to junction 59	172
Motorways: A1(M): Junction 58, Burtree	172
Motorways: A1(M): Junction 61 to 60	172
Motorways: A1(M): Junction 61, Bowburn	172
Motorways: A1(M): Junction 63, Blind Lane interchange	172
Motorways: A1(M): Knebworth, Hertfordshire	173
Motorways: A1(M): Staindrop Road Bridge	173
Motorways: A1(M): Stamford to Peterborough	171
Motorways: A1(M): Wadworth interchange	171, 235
Motorways: A1: Bramham crossroads to Kirk Deighton junction & connecting roads	98
Motorways: A14(M)/A1(M): Junction 14 to 17, slip roads, Cambridgeshire	171
Motorways: A194(M): Blackfell Bridge	209
Motorways: A194(M): Havannah interchange	209
Motorways: A194(M): Springwell Bridge	209
Motorways: A3 (M): Havant/Portsmouth	178
Motorways: A3(M)/A3: Junction 2 - 1, northbound	178
Motorways: A3(M): Junction 2, southbound entry slip road	178
Motorways: A3(M): Junction 3 & 4, slip roads	178
Motorways: A3(M): Junction 3, southbound slip roads	178

Motorways: A404(M)/A404: Western Region Railway Bridge... 211
Motorways: A404(M): Junction 9A, exit slip roads.. 211
Motorways: A66(M): Blackwell Spur to Blackwell roundabout.. 206
Motorways: A74(M)... 233
Motorways: A74(M): Junction 20, northbound on slip at Eaglesfield..................................... 380
Motorways: M1/M10: Junction 7-8... 234
Motorways: M1/M10: Junctions 6 - 8 & M10 junction 1.. 219
Motorways: M1/M18: Junction 32-33... 221
Motorways: M1/M62: Lofthouse interchange.. 219
Motorways: M1/M69: M1 Junction 21, Leicestershire... 219
Motorways: M1: Courteenhall - Quinton Road Bridge, Northamptonshire.................................. 219
Motorways: M1: Junction 1, northbound entry slip road... 219
Motorways: M1: Junction 1 to 3: Slip roads.. 222
Motorways: M1: Junction 6 - 11..219, 220
Motorways: M1: Junction 6, slip roads... 220
Motorways: M1: Junction 8, southbound slip roads.. 220
Motorways: M1: Junction 10, southbound exit slip road... 220
Motorways: M1: Junction 11 & 12... 222
Motorways: M1: Junction 12, Bedfordshire.. 220
Motorways: M1: Junction 12-11... 222
Motorways: M1: Junction 13, northbound entry slip road.. 220
Motorways: M1: Junction 13, northbound exit slip road... 220
Motorways: M1: Junction 15A & 16.. 222
Motorways: M1: Junction 15a & 17, Northamptonshire.. 220
Motorways: M1: Junction 16 - 17, Daventry... 220
Motorways: M1: Junction 16 to 15A, Northamptonshire... 220
Motorways: M1: Junction 16, northbound entry slip road.. 220
Motorways: M1: Junction 18 - 19... 223
Motorways: M1: Junction 19, Leicestershire, southbound entry slip road.............................. 220
Motorways: M1: Junction 19, northbound entry slip road.. 220
Motorways: M1: Junction 20 - 21, Leicestershire... 223
Motorways: M1: Junction 21, Leicestershire.. 219
Motorways: M1: Junction 24 - A6/A50/A453.. 221
Motorways: M1: Junction 24: Roundabout junction of M1, A6, A50 & A453............................... 220
Motorways: M1: Junction 24A... 220
Motorways: M1: Junction 24A, northbound entry slip road... 220
Motorways: M1: Junction 24A: Southbound exit slip road.. 220
Motorways: M1: Junction 25, southbound entry slip road.. 221
Motorways: M1: Junction 28.. 221
Motorways: M1: Junction 29, Derbyshire.. 221
Motorways: M1: Junction 30, southboudn entry slip road.. 221
Motorways: M1: Junction 31 to 32.. 221
Motorways: M1: Junction 32 to 33.. 221
Motorways: M1: Junction 33 & 35... 221
Motorways: M1: Junction 33, Brinsworth.. 221
Motorways: M1: Junction 33, southbound exit slip road... 221
Motorways: M1: Junction 34 to 35.. 221
Motorways: M1: Junction 35A... 221
Motorways: M1: Junction 35A to 39... 221
Motorways: M1: Junction 35A, southbound entry slip road... 221
Motorways: M1: Junction 36.. 221
Motorways: M1: Junction 36 to 37.. 222
Motorways: M1: Junction 38, northbound entry slip road.. 222
Motorways: M1: Junction 39, 40 & 41... 222
Motorways: M1: Junction 4, northbound entry slip road... 219
Motorways: M1: Junction 40, southbound exit slip road... 222
Motorways: M1: Junction 41, northbound exit slip road... 222
Motorways: M1: Junction 42, Lofthouse interchange... 222
Motorways: M1: Junction 44, Rothwell Haigh.. 222
Motorways: M1: Junction 44, Rothwell, Haigh... 222
Motorways: M1: Junction 46, Austhorpe... 222
Motorways: M1: Junction 47, Parlington.. 222
Motorways: M1: Leicester Forest East Service Area, slip road.. 223
Motorways: M1: Little Linford - Gayhurst Road Bridge, Milton Keynes, Buckinghamshire................ 223
Motorways: M1: Lofthouse interchange..219, 249

Motorways: M1: M42 junction 11 to M1 junction 23A, Leicestershire........................ 219
Motorways: M1: South of junction 25, Long Eaton, Derbyshire........................ 223
Motorways: M1: Trowell, Nottinghamshire........................ 223
Motorways: M1: Willen Road Bridge, Milton Keynes, Buckinghamshire........................ 223
Motorways: M10/M1: Junction 7-8........................ 234
Motorways: M10/M1: Junctions 6 - 8 & M10 junction 1........................ 219
Motorways: M10: M1, junction 1........................ 219, 220
Motorways: M11:........................ 235
Motorways: M11: Hardwick-Girton, Cambridgeshire........................ 212
Motorways: M11: Junction 4 - 7........................ 235
Motorways: M11: Junction 4 -5, northbound........................ 235
Motorways: M11: Junction 4, westbound exit link road........................ 234
Motorways: M11: Junction 5 - 4, southbound carriageway........................ 235
Motorways: M11: Junction 5, southbound entry slip road........................ 234
Motorways: M11: Junction 6 - 4, southbound........................ 235
Motorways: M11: Junction 7 - 8, Essex........................ 234
Motorways: M11: Junction 8 - 10........................ 234
Motorways: M11: Junction 8 & 8A........................ 235
Motorways: M11: Junction 9A - 9, Cambridgeshire........................ 234
Motorways: M11: Junction 10 to 11........................ 234
Motorways: M11: Junction 10, Cambridgeshire........................ 234
Motorways: M11: Junction 10, southbound entry slip road........................ 235
Motorways: M11: Junction 12 -13, Cambridgeshire........................ 234
Motorways: M11: Junction 12, Cambridgeshire........................ 235
Motorways: M11: Junction 13, southbound entry slip road........................ 235
Motorways: M11: Spittals interchange to Girton interchange........................ 184
Motorways: M11: Strethall Bridleway Overbridge, Great Chesterford, Essex & Cambridgeshire........................ 235
Motorways: M120: Thremhall Avenue, Essex........................ 235
Motorways: M161: Junction 6, southbound carriageway........................ 252
Motorways: M18........................ 221
Motorways: M18/A1(M): Wadworth interchange........................ 235
Motorways: M18/M1: Junction 32-33........................ 221
Motorways: M18: Junction 1, Bramley........................ 235
Motorways: M18: Junction 3 to 2........................ 235
Motorways: M18: Junction 4 to 5........................ 235
Motorways: M18: Junction 6........................ 235
Motorways: M18: North Ings roundabout........................ 235
Motorways: M18: Wadworth interchange........................ 171, 235
Motorways: M180: Junction 2, Woodhouse........................ 252
Motorways: M180: North Ings roundabout........................ 235
Motorways: M181: Midmoor interchange to Frodingham roundabout........................ 252
Motorways: M2/A2: Junction 7, Brenley Corner........................ 223
Motorways: M2: Junction 3 - 5........................ 223
Motorways: M2: Junction 3, Londonbound carriageway........................ 223
Motorways: M2: Junction 4 - 3........................ 223
Motorways: M2: Junction 5, Londonbound slip roads........................ 223
Motorways: M2: Junction 6 - 7........................ 223
Motorways: M2: West of junction 6........................ 223
Motorways: M20: Cheriton interchange - Western Heights roundabout........................ 236
Motorways: M20: Junction 1........................ 236
Motorways: M20: Junction 1 - 2, coastbound........................ 236
Motorways: M20: Junction 11........................ 236
Motorways: M20: Junction 11, slip roads........................ 236
Motorways: M20: Junction 2, westbound entry slip road........................ 236
Motorways: M20: Junction 4........................ 236
Motorways: M20: Junction 4 - 5, coastbound carriageway........................ 236
Motorways: M20: Junction 4 - 7........................ 236
Motorways: M20: Junction 4-2/2A........................ 235
Motorways: M20: Junction 8 - 9........................ 236
Motorways: M20: Junction 8, Londonbound carriageway........................ 236
Motorways: M20: Junction 9 - east of junction 10, A20/A2070/A292........................ 236
Motorways: M20: Junctions 1 - 2, westbound entry slip roads........................ 236
Motorways: M20: Roundhill tunnels........................ 236
Motorways: M20: Swanley interchange........................ 188
Motorways: M20: West of junction 9........................ 236
Motorways: M23/A23: Junction 11, Pease Pottage........................ 237

Motorways: M23: Junction 8 - 10	237
Motorways: M23: Junction 8, southbound link road	237
Motorways: M23: Junction 9, northbound exit slip road	237
Motorways: M23: Junction 10 - 9, northbound	237
Motorways: M23: M25 junction 7 - 13, slip/link roads	241
Motorways: M23: Merstham interchange	236
Motorways: M23: Merstham interchange link roads	237
Motorways: M25	237
Motorways: M25/A2/A282: Dartford	177
Motorways: M25/M3: Thorpe interchange, link roads	237
Motorways: M25: A3113, junction 14	237
Motorways: M25: Bell Common Tunnel	237
Motorways: M25: Clacket Lane Services, clockwise	237
Motorways: M25: Junction 1	238
Motorways: M25: Junction 2, clockwise carriageway	238
Motorways: M25: Junction 4, slip roads	238
Motorways: M25: Junction 4, Spur Road	238
Motorways: M25: Junction 5, clockwise carriageway	238
Motorways: M25: Junction 5, slip roads	238
Motorways: M25: Junction 6	238
Motorways: M25: Junction 6 - 7, clockwise	240
Motorways: M25: Junction 6 - 7, clockwise carriageway	240
Motorways: M25: Junction 7 - 13, slip/link roads	241
Motorways: M25: Junction 7, Merstham interchange	238
Motorways: M25: Junction 7, southbound link roads	238
Motorways: M25: Junction 8 - 10	240
Motorways: M25: Junction 8- 10, clockwise	240
Motorways: M25: Junction 8, clockwise	238
Motorways: M25: Junction 8, clockwise exit slip road	238
Motorways: M25: Junction 8, entry slip roads	238
Motorways: M25: Junction 9, anti-clockwise exit slip road	238
Motorways: M25: Junction 9, carriageways	238
Motorways: M25: Junction 9, entry slip roads	238
Motorways: M25: Junction 10 - 11, clockwise carriageway	240
Motorways: M25: Junction 10 - 14	240
Motorways: M25: Junction 12, anti-clockwise exit link road	238
Motorways: M25: Junction 13, clockwise carriageway	239
Motorways: M25: Junction 13, slip roads	239
Motorways: M25: Junction 14	237
Motorways: M25: Junction 14 - 15	240
Motorways: M25: Junction 14 & terminal 5 spur roads	239
Motorways: M25: Junction 14, clockwise slip road	239
Motorways: M25: Junction 15 - 16, clockwise	240
Motorways: M25: Junction 16 - 15, anti-clockwise carriageway	240
Motorways: M25: Junction 16, anti-clockwise	239
Motorways: M25: Junction 16, link roads	239
Motorways: M25: Junction 17 - 25	240
Motorways: M25: Junction 17, slip roads	239
Motorways: M25: Junction 18: Northbound slip roads	239
Motorways: M25: Junction 19, clockwise exit slip/link road	239
Motorways: M25: Junction 19, spur road	239
Motorways: M25: Junction 20, clockwise	239
Motorways: M25: Junction 20, slip roads	239
Motorways: M25: Junction 21, clockwise entry slip road	239
Motorways: M25: Junction 21, clockwise link road	239
Motorways: M25: Junction 21A - M1 junction 6	237
Motorways: M25: Junction 22: Westbound exit slip road	239
Motorways: M25: Junction 24, anti-clockwise entry slip road	239
Motorways: M25: Junction 25 - 26	240
Motorways: M25: Junction 25: Entry slip roads	239
Motorways: M25: Junction 26 - 31	237
Motorways: M25: Junction 26: Slip roads	239
Motorways: M25: Junction 28	237
Motorways: M25: Junction 28 - 27, anti-clockwise carriageway	240
Motorways: M25: Junction 28, anti-clockwise exit slip road	240

Motorways: M25: Junction 28, clockwise entry slip road	240
Motorways: M25: Junction 29 - 30	240
Motorways: M25: Junction 29, 30 & 31: Slip roads	237
Motorways: M25: Marker post 143.7 - 151.8	241
Motorways: M25: Marker post 80.6 - 97.0	240
Motorways: M25: Merstham interchange	236, 241
Motorways: M25: Merstham interchange link roads	237
Motorways: M25: Swanley interchange	188
Motorways: M25: Thorney interchange	237
Motorways: M25: West of junction 6 - junction 7	241
Motorways: M25: Wisley Interchange at junction 10 & Ockham junction	237
Motorways: M26: Junction 17 - 18	240
Motorways: M26: Junction 5	237
Motorways: M26: M20, junction 4-2/2A	235
Motorways: M26: M25 junction 5 - junction 2A	241
Motorways: M27: Havant/Portsmouth	178
Motorways: M27: Junction 3 & 5, slip roads	241
Motorways: M27: Junction 3, westbound exit slip road	241
Motorways: M27: Junction 4, Bassett Wood Bridge	241
Motorways: M27: Junction 4, westbound carriageway	241
Motorways: M27: Junction 11, westbound entry slip road	241
Motorways: M27: Junction 12	241
Motorways: M271: M27 junction 3 - Redbridge roundabout	252
Motorways: M3/M25: Thorpe interchange, link roads	237
Motorways: M3: Junction 2 - 3	224
Motorways: M3: Junction 2, westbound	223
Motorways: M3: Junction 2: Thorpe interchange	223
Motorways: M3: Junction 3 - Lightwater, slip road	224
Motorways: M3: Junction 3 and 4, slip roads	224
Motorways: M3: Junction 3, eastbound entry slip road	223
Motorways: M3: Junction 3, exit slip roads	223
Motorways: M3: Junction 4 - 5	224
Motorways: M3: Junction 4, eastbound entry slip road	224
Motorways: M3: Junction 4, eastbound exit slip road	224
Motorways: M3: Junction 4A - A325 roundabout	224
Motorways: M3: Junction 4A, westbound entry slip road	224
Motorways: M3: Junction 6	224
Motorways: M3: Junction 6, eastbound	224
Motorways: M3: Junction 6, westbound exit slip road	224
Motorways: M3: Junction 10, southbound entry slip road	224
Motorways: M3: Junction 12, northbound entry slip road	224
Motorways: M3: M25 junction 7 - 13, slip/link roads	241
Motorways: M32: Junction 1, northbound entry slip road	241
Motorways: M32: Junction 2 to M4	226
Motorways: M4	244
Motorways: M4/A48/A483: North of Cross Hands to south of Pont Abraham, Camarthenshire	257
Motorways: M4: Brombil Lane underpass, junction 39, Neath Port Talbot	260
Motorways: M4: Brynglas Tunnels, Newport	260
Motorways: M4: Eastbound & westbound exit slip roads at junction 26, Malpas, Newport	260
Motorways: M4: Eastbound & westbound slip roads at junction 38, Margam, Neath Port Talbot	261
Motorways: M4: Eastbound off-slip road at junction 34, Miskin, Rhondda Cynon Taf & Vale of Glamorgan	261
Motorways: M4: Eastbound on-slip road at junction 36, Sarn, Bridgend	261
Motorways: M4: Junction 1 - 3	225
Motorways: M4: Junction 1 to 3	225
Motorways: M4: Junction 3 - 5, link and slip roads	225
Motorways: M4: Junction 3: Eastbound exit slip road	224
Motorways: M4: Junction 4	224
Motorways: M4: Junction 4 - 4A	225
Motorways: M4: Junction 4, link roads	224
Motorways: M4: Junction 5 - 4B	225
Motorways: M4: Junction 5 - 6	225
Motorways: M4: Junction 5, westbound carriageway	224
Motorways: M4: Junction 8/9 - 10	225
Motorways: M4: Junction 8/9, exit slip roads	225
Motorways: M4: Junction 11, westbound entry slip road	225
Motorways: M4: Junction 11, westbound exit slip road	225

Motorways: M4: Junction 13, Chieveley interchange	225
Motorways: M4: Junction 14 - 15	225
Motorways: M4: Junction 14 - 18	226
Motorways: M4: Junction 15 - 17, slip roads	226
Motorways: M4: Junction 15, Almondsbury interchange	225
Motorways: M4: Junction 16	225
Motorways: M4: Junction 16 - 15	226
Motorways: M4: Junction 16 - 17	226
Motorways: M4: Junction 18 - 17	226
Motorways: M4: Junction 18 - 19	226
Motorways: M4: Junction 19 - 21	226
Motorways: M4: Junction 20, Almondsbury interchange, westbound to M5 northbound	225
Motorways: M4: Junction 20, westbound to M5 northbound, Almondsbury interchange	225
Motorways: M4: Junction 20-21	226
Motorways: M4: Junction 21 to M48 junction 2	244
Motorways: M4: Junction 22	225, 244
Motorways: M4: Junction 24, Coldra, Newport	261
Motorways: M4: Junction 24, Coldra, to east of junction 23A, Magor, Newport	261
Motorways: M4: Junction 30 (Penwyn): Slip roads: Trunking scheme	101
Motorways: M4: Junction 32, Coryton, Cardiff - junction 33 Capl Llaniltern, Cardiff	261
Motorways: M4: Junction 42, westbound off slip road, Earlswood, Neath Port Talbot	261
Motorways: M4: Junction 43, Llandarcy, Neath Port Talbot	261
Motorways: M4: Junction 43,Llandarcy, Neath Port Talbot	261
Motorways: M4: Junction 45, Ynysforgan to junction 46, Llangyfelach, Swansea	261
Motorways: M4: Leigh Delamere Service Area	226
Motorways: M4: Link roads	225
Motorways: M4: Rogiet Toll Plaza	226
Motorways: M4: Theale to Winnersh section: Connecting roads scheme: Variation	100
Motorways: M4: Westbound exit & entry slip roads at junction 25A, Grove Park, Newport	261
Motorways: M4: Westbound on-slip road at junction 39, Groes, Neath Port Talbot	261
Motorways: M40/A404: Handy Cross	211
Motorways: M40: Junction 1 - 15, Buckinghamshire, Oxfordshire & Warwickshire	242
Motorways: M40: Junction 1A, link roads	241
Motorways: M40: Junction 1A, westbound link road	241
Motorways: M40: Junction 1A - 13, Warwickshire, Northamptonshire, Oxfordshire & Buckinghamshire	242
Motorways: M40: Junction 4, Handy Cross, High Wycombe, Buckinghamshire	241
Motorways: M40: Junction 9 - 10	242
Motorways: M40: Junction 9, Oxfordshire	241
Motorways: M40: Junction 10 - 11	242
Motorways: M40: Junction 10, Ardley roundabout, Oxfordshire	241
Motorways: M40: Junction 15	242
Motorways: M40: Junction 15, slip roads	242
Motorways: M40: North of junction 15	242
Motorways: M40: Southbound carriageway, junction 15 - 14, Warwickshire	242
Motorways: M40: Treadway Hill Overbridge, Buckinghamshire	242
Motorways: M42/A45: Junction 6	243
Motorways: M42: East of junction 1 - M5 junction 4A	242
Motorways: M42: Junction 1 - M5 junction 4A	227, 242
Motorways: M42: Junction 2	242
Motorways: M42: Junction 2, southbound entry slip road	242
Motorways: M42: Junction 3	242
Motorways: M42: Junction 3, slip road	242
Motorways: M42: Junction 3-3A	243
Motorways: M42: Junction 3A - 3	243
Motorways: M42: Junction 6-7A	243
Motorways: M42: Junction 7 - 7A	243
Motorways: M42: Junction 7, link road	243
Motorways: M42: Junction 8 & 9	243
Motorways: M42: Junction 8, link road	243
Motorways: M42: Junction 9	243
Motorways: M42: Junction 9 - 6	243
Motorways: M42: Junction 9: Northbound entry slip road	243
Motorways: M42: Junction 10	243
Motorways: M42: Junction 10 - 11, Warwickshire	243
Motorways: M42: Junction 10 - 9, Warwickshire	243

Motorways: M42: Junction 10 to Dordon, Warwickshire	242
Motorways: M42: Junction 11	243
Motorways: M42: Linthurst, east of junction 1	243
Motorways: M42: M42 junction 11 to M1 junction 23A, Leicestershire	219
Motorways: M42: South of junction 11	243
Motorways: M45: Dunchurch roundabout, Warwickshire & Northamptonshire	243
Motorways: M45: Dunchurch, Warwickshire & Northamptonshire	244
Motorways: M48: Junction 1 - 2, Severn Bridge	244
Motorways: M48: Junction 1, Aust	244
Motorways: M48: Junction 2 - 1, Severn Bridge	244
Motorways: M48: M4 junction 21 to M48 junction 2	244
Motorways: M48: Near Aust, Gloucestershire	244
Motorways: M49	244
Motorways: M5: Junction 1	226
Motorways: M5: Junction 1 to 2	228
Motorways: M5: Junction 1, slip roads	226
Motorways: M5: Junction 1: northbound entry slip road	226
Motorways: M5: Junction 2 & the A4123, Oldbury	226
Motorways: M5: Junction 2, Oldbury	226
Motorways: M5: Junction 3	227
Motorways: M5: Junction 3, northbound exit slip road	226
Motorways: M5: Junction 3, southbound entry slip road	227
Motorways: M5: Junction 4 - 4A	227
Motorways: M5: Junction 5 - 6	228
Motorways: M5: Junction 5, northbound exit slip road	227
Motorways: M5: Junction 5: Slip roads	227
Motorways: M5: Junction 6, Worcestershire	227
Motorways: M5: Junction 7, southbound exit slip road	227
Motorways: M5: Junction 8	226
Motorways: M5: Junction 9- 11A	228
Motorways: M5: Junction 9, slip roads	227
Motorways: M5: Junction 11, 11A & 13A slip roads	228
Motorways: M5: Junction 11A	212
Motorways: M5: Junction 11A-11	228
Motorways: M5: Junction 12	227
Motorways: M5: Junction 12 - 14	228
Motorways: M5: Junction 12, northbound & southbound exit slip roads	227
Motorways: M5: Junction 13 - 15	228
Motorways: M5: Junction 14 & 16, slip roads	228
Motorways: M5: Junction 17, northbound entry slip road	227
Motorways: M5: Junction 18 - Avonmouth	227
Motorways: M5: Junction 18A	244
Motorways: M5: Junction 21 slip roads	227
Motorways: M5: Junction 22	227
Motorways: M5: Junction 22, slip roads	227
Motorways: M5: Junction 23	227
Motorways: M5: Junction 23-25 slip roads	228
Motorways: M5: Junction 25 - 26	228
Motorways: M5: Junction 26	227
Motorways: M5: Junction 27	228
Motorways: M5: Junction 28	228
Motorways: M5: Junction 28 - 31	228
Motorways: M5: Junction 28 & 30	228
Motorways: M5: M50 junction 2 to M5 junction 8	244
Motorways: M5: North of junction 4	228
Motorways: M5: Ray Hall interchange	229
Motorways: M5: Ray Hall interchange/M6 junction 8	228
Motorways: M5: Sedgemoor services slip roads	228
Motorways: M5: South of Walsall	226
Motorways: M5: Taunton Deane Service Area	229
Motorways: M50: Junction 1, Worcestershire	244
Motorways: M50: Junction 2 to 1	244
Motorways: M50: Junction 2 to 4	244
Motorways: M50: Junction 2 to M5 junction 8	244
Motorways: M50: Junction 3 - 4, Herefordshire	244
Motorways: M50: M5 junction 8	226

Motorways: M50: Ross-on-Wye, Herefordshire 195, 244
Motorways: M53: Bidston Moss viaduct 253
Motorways: M53: Junction 2, northbound entry slip road. 244
Motorways: M53: Junction 2, southbound entry slip road. 245
Motorways: M53: Junction 2, southbound exit slip road 245
Motorways: M53: Junction 3, southbound carriageway & entry slip road 245
Motorways: M53: Junction 3, southbound entry slip road. 245
Motorways: M53: Junction 5 to 9: Northbound & southbound carriageway closures 245
Motorways: M53: Junction 6, closure of northbound exit & entry slip roads 245
Motorways: M53: Junction 8, northbound exit slip road 245
Motorways: M53: Junction 10, northbound exit slip road. 247
Motorways: M53: Junction 11, northbound link road to M56 eastbound 245
Motorways: M53: Junction 11, southbound link road to the M56 eastbound 245
Motorways: M54/A5: Telford to Shrewsbury, Shropshire 245
Motorways: M54: Junction 1 - 2, slip roads 230
Motorways: M54: Junction 1: Eastbound exit slip road 245
Motorways: M54: Junction 2 - 7. 245
Motorways: M54: Junction 2: Slip roads 245
Motorways: M55. 233
Motorways: M55: Eastbound link road to the northbound M6 junction 32 245
Motorways: M55: Eastbound link road to the southbound M6 junction 32 245
Motorways: M55: Junction 1 to 3, westbound carriageway 246
Motorways: M55: Junction 1, eastbound & westbound exit slip roads 246
Motorways: M55: Junction 1, eastbound & westbound main carriageways & westbound entry slip road 246
Motorways: M55: Junction 1, eastbound link road to the southbound M6 246
Motorways: M55: Junction 1, eastbound main carriageway. 246
Motorways: M55: Junction 3 - 1, eastbound & westbound main carriageways 246
Motorways: M55: Junction 3 to 1: Safety barrier upgrade 246
Motorways: M55: Junction 3, Pier Upgrade. 246
Motorways: M55: M 6 junction 32 - 33, northbound & southbound carriageway & slip roads. 245
Motorways: M56: Hapsford to Lea-by-Backford section: Connecting roads scheme: Partial revocation 101
Motorways: M56: Junction 1 eastbound exit slip road to the A34 northbound 246
Motorways: M56: Junction 1, westbound entry slip road from the A34 southbound 246
Motorways: M56: Junction 2, eastbound entry slip road 246
Motorways: M56: Junction 5 northbound exit slip road 246
Motorways: M56: Junction 7 westbound exit slip road, Bowden interchange 246
Motorways: M56: Junction 11 - 14, eastbound & westbound carriageways & slip roads. 246
Motorways: M56: Junction 11, eastbound entry slip road. 246
Motorways: M56: Junction 11, eastbound main carriageway 246
Motorways: M56: Junction 12, eastbound entry slip road. 246
Motorways: M56: Junction 12, eastbound exit slip road & main carriageway 247
Motorways: M56: Junction 15, westbound to M53 junction 11, northbound link. 247
Motorways: M57: A5036 Dunnings Bridge Rd., Switch Is.. 247
Motorways: M57: Junction 4, southbound entry slip road. 247
Motorways: M57: Junction 6, southbound main carriageway & entry slip road 247
Motorways: M6/A74: Harker Bridge 208
Motorways: M6: Birmingham to Walsall 229
Motorways: M6: Borrowbeck Viaduct. 229
Motorways: M6: Bromford, Birmingham 229
Motorways: M6: Carlisle to Guards Mill section: Connecting roads scheme 101
Motorways: M6: Deerslack Bridge 229
Motorways: M6: Doxey, Staffordshire 229
Motorways: M6: Eamont Bridge. 229
Motorways: M6: Extension project 208
Motorways: M6: Gravelly Hill Interchange, Birmingham. 229
Motorways: M6: Gravelly Hill interchange, Birmingham, slip roads 229
Motorways: M6: Hutton Bridge parapet: Replacement between junction 36 & 37. 229
Motorways: M6: Junction 1, Broughton Circle interchange. 245
Motorways: M6: Junction 1, Warwickshire, slip roads 229
Motorways: M6: Junction 2 229
Motorways: M6: Junction 2 - 3 229
Motorways: M6: Junction 2, northbound exit slip road 229
Motorways: M6: Junction 3 - 4, Warwickshire 232
Motorways: M6: Junction 3 to 1, Warwickshire. 229
Motorways: M6: Junction 3, southbound exit slip road 229

Motorways: M6: Junction 4 - 4A	232
Motorways: M6: Junction 4 slip roads & A446	230
Motorways: M6: Junction 4, Warwickshire	230
Motorways: M6: Junction 4A	243
Motorways: M6: Junction 5, southbound entry slip road	230
Motorways: M6: Junction 6, Birmingham	230
Motorways: M6: Junction 7, southbound entry slip road	230
Motorways: M6: Junction 8, Ray Hall interchange	230
Motorways: M6: Junction 9 - 10	230
Motorways: M6: Junction 9, southbound entry slip road	230
Motorways: M6: Junction 10 - 10A	233
Motorways: M6: Junction 10, entry slip roads	230
Motorways: M6: Junction 10, northbound entry slip road	230
Motorways: M6: Junction 10, southbound entry slip road	230
Motorways: M6: Junction 10A - 13	230
Motorways: M6: Junction 11 - 13, Staffordshire	233
Motorways: M6: Junction 11, southbound entry slip road	230
Motorways: M6: Junction 11A - 13	233
Motorways: M6: Junction 12	230
Motorways: M6: Junction 12, north of junction 13	230
Motorways: M6: Junction 13, slip roads	230
Motorways: M6: Junction 14 - 15	233
Motorways: M6: Junction 14 - 15, Staffordshire	233
Motorways: M6: Junction 14, northbound exit slip road	230
Motorways: M6: Junction 14, Stafford	231
Motorways: M6: Junction 15 - 16	233
Motorways: M6: Junction 16 - 15, Staffordshire	233
Motorways: M6: Junction 16, Staffordshire	231
Motorways: M6: Junction 17 - 19, northbound carriageway	233
Motorways: M6: Junction 17, northbound entry slip road	231
Motorways: M6: Junction 17, southbound entry slip road, junctions 16-17 northbound & southbound carriageways	231
Motorways: M6: Junction 19: Northbound exit slip road	231
Motorways: M6: Junction 20, northbound entry slip road	231
Motorways: M6: Junction 20, northbound exit slip road	231
Motorways: M6: Junction 20, southbound link roads to M56 westbound & eastbound	231
Motorways: M6: Junction 21, northbound & southbound entry slip roads	231
Motorways: M6: Junction 21A, northbound link road to M62 eastbound	231
Motorways: M6: Junction 21A, northbound link road to M62, westbound	231
Motorways: M6: Junction 21A, northbound link road to the M62 eastbound	231
Motorways: M6: Junction 22, northbound & southbound entry & exit slip roads	231
Motorways: M6: Junction 22, southbound entry slip road	231
Motorways: M6: Junction 24 - 25, northbound & southbound carriageways & junction 25 southbound entry slip road	233
Motorways: M6: Junction 26, eastern roundabout, southbound exit slip road & link roads to the A577	231
Motorways: M6: Junction 27, northbound & southbound carriageway & slip roads	231
Motorways: M6: Junction 27, northbound exit slip road	231
Motorways: M6: Junction 27, southbound entry slip road	231
Motorways: M6: Junction 27-28 Charnock Richard Services, northbound & southbound carriageways	233
Motorways: M6: Junction 28, northbound main carriageway	232
Motorways: M6: Junction 29, northbound entry & southbound exit slip roads	232
Motorways: M6: Junction 29, northbound link road to the junction 29A	232
Motorways: M6: Junction 29, southbound entry slip road	232
Motorways: M6: Junction 30 - 31a, southbound carriageway: Cuerdale Lane Bridge	233
Motorways: M6: Junction 30 to 44	233
Motorways: M6: Junction 30, 31, & 31A northbound main carriageway & exit slip roads	233
Motorways: M6: Junction 31-30, southbound main carriageway	232
Motorways: M6: Junction 31A: Southbound main carriageway & entry slip road	232
Motorways: M6: Junction 32 - 33, Keepers & Woodacre Great Wood footbridges	233
Motorways: M6: Junction 32 - 33, Keepers & Woodacre Great Wood footbridges and Woodacre Lane Bridge	233
Motorways: M6: Junction 32 - 33, northbound & southbound carriageway & slip roads	245
Motorways: M6: Junction 32 - 33, northbound carriageway, Matshead Bridge	233
Motorways: M6: Junction 32, southbound main carriageway	246
Motorways: M6: Junction 33 northbound & southbound main carriageways, northbound entry & exit slip roads	232
Motorways: M6: Junction 33 southbound exit slip road	232
Motorways: M6: Junction 34, northbound entry & exit slip roads	232
Motorways: M6: Junction 34, southbound exit & entry slip roads	232
Motorways: M6: Junction 34: Northbound main carriageway & entry slip road	232

Motorways: M6: Junction 36, Town Head Bridge Parapet Upgrade	232
Motorways: M6: Junction 40: Castletown Bridge, northbound & southbound carriageways	232
Motorways: M6: Junction 42 to 41, Southwaite Services	232
Motorways: M6: Junction 44, Greymoorhill	232
Motorways: M6: Junction 44, Greymoorhill interchange, southbound carriageway	229
Motorways: M6: Low Hurst Bank southbound	233
Motorways: M6: M1 Junction 29, slip roads	234
Motorways: M6: North of junction 4	234
Motorways: M6: Ray Hall interchange	229
Motorways: M6: Shap Fell northbound resurfacing	234
Motorways: M6: South of junction 6	234
Motorways: M6: South of junction 14	234
Motorways: M6: South of junction 16	234
Motorways: M6: South of Walsall	226
Motorways: M6: Speed Limits: Toll	253
Motorways: M6: Toll motorway	243
Motorways: M6: Weedford Park & Great Wyrley Toll Plazas	234
Motorways: M6: Yarnfield Lane, nr Stone, Staffordshire	234
Motorways: M60: Junction 1, anticlockwise slip road	247
Motorways: M60: Junction 3 - 27, clockwise & anticlockwise main carriageways & slip roads	248
Motorways: M60: Junction 3, anticlockwise entry slip road from A34	247
Motorways: M60: Junction 3: Anti-clockwise entry slip road from A34	247
Motorways: M60: Junction 4, clockwise entry slip road from A34	247
Motorways: M60: Junction 11, anticlockwise exit slip	247
Motorways: M60: Junction 12 anticlockwise, link roads from M602 westbound and M62 eastbound	247
Motorways: M60: Junction 13, clockwise & anticlockwise entry slip roads	247
Motorways: M60: Junction 16 clockwise entry slip road	247
Motorways: M60: Junction 19 to 20: Clockwise & anticlockwise carriageway hardshoulder running	248
Motorways: M60: Junction 19: Anticlockwise entry slip road & clockwise exit slip road	247
Motorways: M60: Junction 20 anticlockwise entry slip roads	247
Motorways: M60: Junction 21, anticlockwise entry slip road & main carriageway	247
Motorways: M60: Junction 21, anticlockwise entry slip road from A663	247
Motorways: M60: Junction 22 to 24: Anticlockwise main carriageway	248
Motorways: M60: Junction 22 to 24: Clockwise & anticlockwise main carriageways & slip roads	248
Motorways: M60: Junction 23, clockwise & anticlockwise main carriageways & slip roads	247
Motorways: M60: Junction 24 - 25, clockwise main carriageway	248
Motorways: M60: Junction 25, anticlockwise entry & exit slip roads	248
Motorways: M60: Junction 27, clockwise entry slip road	248
Motorways: M602: Junction 1, westbound exit slip road	252
Motorways: M602: Westbound link road to the M60, clockwise at junction 12	252
Motorways: M61: Junction 1, southbound link road to the anticlockwise M60 junction 15	248
Motorways: M61: Junction 2, southbound link road to A580 eastbound	248
Motorways: M61: Junction 3, southbound exit slip road	248
Motorways: M61: Junction 5-6, northbound carriageway	249
Motorways: M61: Junction 6, Bolton West Services, southbound carriageway	248
Motorways: M61: Junction 6, northbound carriageway	248
Motorways: M61: Junction 6, northbound entry slip road	248
Motorways: M61: Junction 6, northbound exit slip road	248
Motorways: M61: Junction 9, link road to & from Walton Summit Industrial Park	248
Motorways: M61: Junction 9, northbound exit slip road to M65 eastbound	248
Motorways: M61: Junction 9, southbound entry slip road	249
Motorways: M61: Junction 9, southbound exit slip road	249
Motorways: M61: Kearsley Spur	249
Motorways: M61: Northbound carriageway	233
Motorways: M61: Northbound entry slip road from westbound A580	249
Motorways: M61: Northbound link road from the A580 at junction 14 of the M60	249
Motorways: M62	252
Motorways: M62/M1: Lofthouse interchange	219
Motorways: M62: Junction 7, eastbound & westbound exit & entry slip roads	249
Motorways: M62: Junction 7, eastbound exit slip road	249
Motorways: M62: Junction 8, westbound entry slip road	249
Motorways: M62: Junction 9, eastbound entry slip road	249
Motorways: M62: Junction 9, westbound entry slip road	249
Motorways: M62: Junction 11, eastbound access & westbound exit slip roads	249
Motorways: M62: Junction 11, eastbound entry slip road	249

Motorways: M62: Junction 18, eastbound entry slip road. 251
Motorways: M62: Junction 20 to 21, eastbound & westbound carriageways & entry & exit slip roads 250
Motorways: M62: Junction 20: Circulatory carriageway & slip roads 249
Motorways: M62: Junction 21, eastbound & westbound entry & exit slip roads 249
Motorways: M62: Junction 24. 250
Motorways: M62: Junction 24, Ainley Top 249
Motorways: M62: Junction 25 - 26 250
Motorways: M62: Junction 25 & 26 250
Motorways: M62: Junction 28, Tingley 250
Motorways: M62: Junction 29, Lofthouse interchange 250
Motorways: M62: Junction 30 to 31. 250
Motorways: M62: Junction 31 to 32 250
Motorways: M62: Junction 32 250
Motorways: M62: Junction 33, Ferrybridge 250
Motorways: M62: Junction 33, westbound exit slip road 250
Motorways: M62: Junction 34 250
Motorways: M62: Junction 34 & 35 250
Motorways: M62: Junction 36, Airmyn 250
Motorways: M62: Junction 37, Howden. 250
Motorways: M62: Lofthouse interchange 219, 249
Motorways: M621: Gildersome interchange. 252
Motorways: M621: Junction 1, Islington 252
Motorways: M621: Junction 3 to 7 252
Motorways: M621: Junction 4, Hunslet 252
Motorways: M621: Junction 6 to 7 252
Motorways: M621: M62 Motorway to Junction 1. 253
Motorways: M65: Junction 1, eastbound entry slip road 250
Motorways: M65: Junction 1, westbound entry slip road 251
Motorways: M65: Junction 2, eastbound entry slip road 251
Motorways: M65: Junction 2, eastbound exit slip road & circulatory carriageway 251
Motorways: M65: Junction 2, eastbound link road from the A6 251
Motorways: M65: Junction 2, link road to & from Walton Summit Industrial Park 248
Motorways: M65: Junction 2, westbound entry slip road 251
Motorways: M65: Junction 3, eastbound entry slip road 251
Motorways: M65: Junction 3, westbound entry slip road 251
Motorways: M65: Junction 4, eastbound entry slip road 251
Motorways: M65: Junction 4, westbound entry slip road 251
Motorways: M65: Junction 5, eastbound entry slip road 251
Motorways: M65: Junction 5, westbound entry slip road 251
Motorways: M65: Junction 5, westbound exit slip road. 251
Motorways: M65: Junction 6, eastbound exit slip road 251
Motorways: M66: Junction 0 to 2, southbound carriageway & junction 1, southbound entry slip road 252
Motorways: M66: Junction 2, southbound entry slip road. 251
Motorways: M66: Junction 4, northbound entry slip road. 251
Motorways: M66: Junction 4, southbound entry slip road to M60/M62, Simester roundabout. 252
Motorways: M66: M62 junction 18, eastbound entry slip road 251
Motorways: M66: Northbound carriageway & slip roads 251
Motorways: M67: Junction 2, eastbound entry slip road 252
Motorways: M69. 219
Motorways: M69/M1: M1 Junction 21, Leicestershire 219
Motorways: M69: Junction 1 . . . . 180, 252
Motorways: M69: Junction with A46 Coventry 252
Motorways: M69: M1 junction 21, Leicestershire. 219
Motorways: M69: M6 junction 2 229
Motorways: M74: Junction 12, Millbank: Scotland 382
Motorways: M74: Junction 12, northbound: Scotland. 383
Motorways: M74: Junction 13, northbound off slip at Abington: Scotland 383
Motorways: M74: Junction 14, Elvanfoot: Scotland 383
Motorways: M74: Junction 19, northbound on slip at Ecclefechan: Scotland. 383
Motorways: M74: Junction 22, southbound off slip at Gretna Green: Scotland. 383
Motorways: M90/A90: Glendoick, near Perth: Scotland 383
Motorways: M90/A90: Hilton Dr. & Manor Ave. junctions, Aberdeen: Scotland 383
Motorways: M90: Gairneybridge to Milnathort: Scotland. 380
Motorways: Road traffic: Northern Ireland: Northern Ireland 436, 437
Museums & galleries: Natural History Museum: Authorised repositories 131
Mutual assistance provisions: Taxes 84, 116, 162, 276

N

Na h-Eileanan an Iar: Electoral arrangements: Scotland. 362
National Assembly for Wales: Disqualifications 43
National Assembly for Wales: Paying Agency 18
National Assembly for Wales: Representation of the people 43, 59, 165
National Assembly for Wales: Returning officers: Charges. 165
National Assembly for Wales: Transfer of functions 43, 59, 60
National assistance services: Personal requirements: Sums: England. 131
National assistance services: Personal requirements: Sums: Scotland 364
National assistance services: Personal requirements: Sums: Wales. 131
National assistance services: Resources: Assessment: England 131
National assistance services: Resources: Assessment: Scotland. 364
National assistance services: Resources: Assessment: Wales 131
National Bus Travel Concession Scheme for Older & Disabled Persons: Eligible persons & services: Scotland 392
National Bus Travel Concession Scheme for Older & Disabled Persons: Scotland. 392
National Care Standards Commission: Fees. 31, 265
National Crime Squad: Abolition 154
National Criminal Intelligence Service: Abolition. 154
National curriculum: Key stage 4: Exceptions: England 65
National curriculum: Science: Key stage 4: Disapplication: Wales. 72
National election expenditure: Electoral Administration Act 2006: Commencements 74, 131, 156, 162, 163
National election expenditure: Political Parties, Elections & Referendums Act 2000: Commencements 131, 156, 163
National Endowment for Science, Technology & the Arts: Increase of endowment 140
National Health Service & Social Care Partnership Trusts: East Kent 133
National Health Service & Social Care Partnership Trusts: Kent & Medway. 133
National Health Service & Social Care Partnership Trusts: West Kent 133
National Health Service (Scotland) Act 1978: Modifications: Scotland 367
National Health Service Central Register: Scotland 374
National Health Service Logistics Authority: Abolition. 138
National Health Service primary care trusts: City & Hackney 132
National Health Service primary care trusts: Isle of Wight 132
National Health Service primary care trusts: Medway 133
National Health Service primary care trusts: Middlesbrough 133
National Health Service primary care trusts: Solihull 135
National Health Service Trusts: Avon Ambulance Service 132
National Health Service Trusts: Birmingham Children's Hospital 131
National Health Service Trusts: Buckinghamshire Mental Health 131
National Health Service Trusts: County Durham & Darlington Priority Services 136
National Health Service Trusts: Coventry and Warwickshire Partnership 132
National Health Service Trusts: Dissolution. 134
National Health Service Trusts: Doncaster & South Humberside Healthcare. 132
National Health Service Trusts: East Midlands Ambulance Service 132
National Health Service Trusts: East of England Ambulance Service 132
National Health Service Trusts: East Sussex County Healthcare 136
National Health Service Trusts: Gloucestershire Ambulance Service. 132
National Health Service Trusts: Great Western Ambulance Service 132
National Health Service Trusts: Isle of Wight Healthcare. 132
National Health Service Trusts: London Ambulance Service 133
National Health Service Trusts: Newcastle, North Tyneside & Northumberland Mental Health. 135
National Health Service Trusts: North East Ambulance Service 135
National Health Service Trusts: North West Ambulance Service 135
National Health Service Trusts: Northgate & Prudhoe 135
National Health Service Trusts: Northumberland, Tyne & Wear 135
National Health Service Trusts: Nottingham City Hospital 135
National Health Service Trusts: Nottingham University Hospitals 135
National Health Service Trusts: Nottingham University Hospitals: Queen's Medical Centre: Special trustees 136
National Health Service Trusts: Nottingham University Hospitals: Trust funds: Trustees appointment 135
National Health Service Trusts: Oxfordshire Mental Healthcare 135
National Health Service Trusts: Queen's Medical Centre, Nottingham, University Hospital. 135
National Health Service Trusts: South Central Ambulance Service. 135
National Health Service Trusts: South East Coast Ambulance Service 135
National Health Service Trusts: South of Tyne & Wearside Mental Health 135
National Health Service Trusts: South Western Ambulance Service 135
National Health Service Trusts: Surrey & Borders Partnership: Originating Capital 136

National Health Service Trusts: Sussex Partnership. 136
National Health Service Trusts: Tees & North East Yorkshire 136
National Health Service Trusts: Tees, Esk & Wear Valleys. 136
National Health Service Trusts: West Midlands Ambulance Service 136
National Health Service Trusts: West Sussex Health & Social Care 136
National Health Service Trusts: Wiltshire Ambulance Service 132
National Health Service Trusts: Yorkshire Ambulance Service. 136
National Health Service: Acts 6, 7
National Health Service: Acts: Explanatory notes 10
National Health Service: Appointments Commission. 131, 159, 265
National Health Service: Clinical negligence scheme: England. 133
National Health Service: Commission for Patient & Public Involvement in Health: Membership & procedure: England. 132
National Health Service: Common Services Agency: Functions: Scotland 364
National Health Service: Community Health Councils: Carmarthenshire: Wales. 138
National Health Service: Complaints: England 133
National Health Service: Dental charges: England 133
National Health Service: Dental charges: Scotland 364
National Health Service: Dental charges: Wales 139
National Health Service: Discipline committees: Scotland 364
National Health Service: Drugs & appliances: Charges: England. 133
National Health Service: Drugs & appliances: Charges: Scotland 364
National Health Service: Drugs & appliances: Charges: Wales 139
National Health Service: Education: Scotland. 366
National Health Service: General dental services: Contracts & personal dental services agreements: England 134
National Health Service: General dental services: Contracts: Wales 139
National Health Service: General dental services: England & Wales 136
National Health Service: General dental services: Scotland 364, 365
National Health Service: General dental services: Transitional & consequential provisions: Wales. 138
National Health Service: General dental services: Wales 139
National Health Service: General medical services: Contracts: Scotland 365
National Health Service: General medical services: Wales 139
National Health Service: General ophthalmic services 134
National Health Service: General ophthalmic services: Scotland 365
National Health Service: General ophthalmic services: Supplementary list: Wales. 140
National Health Service: Greater Glasgow & Highland Health Boards: Areas: Variation: Scotland 366
National Health Service: Health & Social Care (Community Health & Standards) Act 2003: Commencements. 91, 137, 265
National Health Service: Health & Social Care (Community Health & Standards) Act 2003: Commencements: Wales 139
National Health Service: Health & Social Care Act 2001: Commencements 132
National Health Service: Health Act 2006: Commencements. 56, 97, 136, 137, 159, 266
National Health Service: Health authorities: Membership & procedure: England 132
National Health Service: Health Boards: Constitution: Scotland 364
National Health Service: Health Boards: Functions: Scotland 364
National Health Service: Health Service Commissioner for England: Special health authorities 132, 137
National Health Service: Health start scheme: Healthy start food: Description: Wales. 139
National Health Service: Independent prescribing: Amendments 134
National Health Service: Local health boards: Establishment: Wales. 139
National Health Service: Local health boards: Functions: Dental public health: Wales 138
National Health Service: Local health boards: Functions: Primary dental services: Wales. 138
National Health Service: Local pharmaceutical services 134
National Health Service: National Waiting Times Centre Board: Scotland. 366
National Health Service: NHS Blood & Transplant: Membership & procedures 137
National Health Service: NHS Business Services Authority: Establishment & constitution: Amendments 137
National Health Service: NHS Business Services Authority: Functions: Primary dental services: Wales 138
National Health Service: NHS Pensions Agency: Abolition 138
National Health Service: Optical charges & payments 134
National Health Service: Optical charges & payments: England 134
National Health Service: Optical charges & payments: Scotland 365
National Health Service: Optical charges & payments: Wales 140
National Health Service: Overseas visitors: Charges 133
National Health Service: Overseas visitors: Charges: Scotland. 364
National Health Service: Pension scheme, injury benefits & additional voluntary contributions. 137
National Health Service: Performers lists: England 134
National Health Service: Performers lists: Wales 140
National Health Service: Personal dental services: Agreements: Wales. 139, 140
National Health Service: Personal dental services: England & Wales 136
National Health Service: Personal dental services: Transitional & consequential provisions: Wales. 138

National Health Service: Personal dental services: Wales. 139
National Health Service: Personal injuries: Charges: Amounts: Scotland. 366
National Health Service: Personal injuries: Charges: General: Scotland 366
National Health Service: Personal injuries: Charges: Reviews & appeals: Scotland 367
National Health Service: Personal injury: NHS charges: General: Amendments: England & Wales 138, 255
National Health Service: Personal injury: NHS charges: Reviews & appeals: Amendments: England & Wales 138, 255
National Health Service: Pharmaceutical services. 134
National Health Service: Pharmaceutical services: Scotland 365
National Health Service: Pharmaceutical services: Wales. 140
National Health Service: Pre-consolidation amendments: England & Wales 137
National Health Service: Premature retirement: Pension scheme & compensation: England & Wales. 137
National Health Service: Primary care trusts, strategic health authorities & NHS Business Services Authority: Dental services: Functions
. . . . 132
National Health Service: Primary care trusts: Establishment & dissolution: England 135
National Health Service: Primary care trusts: Establishment orders: Amendments. 135
National Health Service: Primary care trusts: Functions: Dental public health: England 132
National Health Service: Primary medical services & Pharmaceutical services 134
National Health Service: Primary medical services: Performers lists: Scotland. 365
National Health Service: Primary medical services: Section 17C agreements: Scotland 365
National Health Service: Primary medical services: Wales 140
National Health Service: Public Benefit Corporation: Register of members: England & Wales 138
National Health Service: Redress: Tort liability: Acts 7
National Health Service: Redress: Tort liability: Acts: Explanatory notes 10
National Health Service: Road traffic: NHS charges: England & Wales 138, 255
National Health Service: Road traffic: NHS charges: Reviews & appeals: Amendments: England & Wales. 138, 255
National Health Service: Road traffic: NHS charges: Scotland 367, 377
National Health Service: Scotland Act 1998: Agency arrangements: Specifications 43, 58, 131
National Health Service: Service Committees & Tribunal: Scotland 365
National Health Service: Smoking, Health & Social Care (Scotland) Act 2005: Commencements: Scotland 367
National Health Service: Smoking, Health & Social Care (Scotland) Act 2005: Consequential amendments 44, 59, 138
National Health Service: Special health authorities: Abolition 138
National Health Service: Special health authorities: Audit 93
National Health Service: Special health authorities: Summarised accounts 93
National Health Service: Strategic health authorities & primary care trusts: Functions: England 134
National Health Service: Strategic health authorities: Establishment & abolition 136
National Health Service: Superannuation scheme & additional voluntary contributions: Scotland. 366
National Health Service: Superannuation scheme & compensation for premature retirement: Scotland 366
National Health Service: Travel expenses & remission of charges: England 133, 134
National Health Service: Travel expenses & remission of charges: Scotland. 366
National Health Service: Travel expenses & remission of charges: Wales 140
National Health Service: Tribunal: Scotland. 366
National Health Service: Wales: Acts 7
National identity register: Identity cards: Acts 6
National identity register: Identity cards: Acts: Explanatory notes 10
National insurance contributions: Acts. 7
National insurance numbers: Social security 272
National insurance numbers: Social security: Northern Ireland 442
National Lotteries Charities Board: Dissolution. 141
National Lottery Act 1993: Section 23: Amendment 141
National Lottery Act 2006: Commencements 141
National Lottery: Acts 7
National Lottery: Acts: Explanatory notes 10
National lottery: Awards for All (England) Joint Scheme: Authorisation. 141
National lottery: Big lottery fund: Prescribed expenditure 140
National lottery: Distributors: Dissolution. 141
National lottery: National Endowment for Science, Technology & the Arts: Increase of endowment 140
National lottery: Transformational Grants Joint Scheme: Revocation 141
National Park Authorities: England 51
National Savings Bank. 262
National security directions & appointed representatives: Planning: England 279
National security directions & appointed representatives: Planning: Northern Ireland 432
National security directions & appointed representatives: Planning: Scotland 392
National security directions & appointed representatives: Planning: Wales 281
National Waiting Times Centre Board: National Health Service: Scotland. 366
Nationality, Immigration & Asylum Act 2002: Commencements. 109

Nationality, Immigration & Asylum Act 2002: Juxtaposed controls 109
Nationality, Immigration and Asylum Act 2002: Commencements. 109
Nationality: Acts 6
Nationality: Acts: Explanatory notes 10
Nationality: Immigration, Asylum & Nationality Act 2006: Commencements 108
Natural Environment & Rural Communities Act 2006: Commencements 13, 141, 142, 165, 166, 261
Natural environment: Rural communities: Acts 7
Natural environment: Rural communities: Acts: Explanatory notes 10
Natural History Museum: Authorised repositories 131
Nature conservation: Natural Environment & Rural Communities Act 2006: Commencements 13, 141, 142, 261
Naval Discipline Act 1957: Continuation. 56
Navy: Disablement & death: Service pensions 147
Navy: Service pensions 147
Negligence: Clinical negligence scheme: National Health Service: England 133
Negligence: Compensation claims: Acts 5
Negligence: Compensation claims: Acts: Explanatory notes. 9
Network Rail: Thameslink 2000: England 284, 285
Network Rail: West Coast Main Line: Stowe Hill: England 284, 285
New Opportunities Fund: Dissolution 141
Newark & Sherwood College: Dissolution 67
Newcastle, North Tyneside & Northumberland Mental Health: National Health Service Trust 135
Newfield School: Change to school session times 67
NHS Blood & Transplant: Membership & procedures 137
NHS Business Services Authority: Dental services: Functions 132
NHS Business Services Authority: Establishment & constitution: Amendments 137
NHS Business Services Authority: Functions: Primary dental services: Wales. 138
NHS Business Services Authority: Membership & procedure 137
NHS Pensions Agency: Abolition 138
Nitrate pollution: Agricultural: Water: Protection 289
Nitrates Action Programme: Environmental protection: Northern Ireland 414
Nobel School: School session times: Changes 67
Noise: At work: Control: Northern Ireland 421
Noise: Environmental: England. 79
Non-domestic rates: Levying: Scotland 373
Non-domestic rates: Scotland 373
Non-domestic rating: Amendments: England 50, 161
Non-domestic rating: Chargeable amounts: England 161
Non-domestic rating: Contributions: England 161
Non-domestic rating: Contributions: Wales 161
Non-domestic rating: Demand notices & discretionary relief: Wales 161
Non-domestic rating: Demand notices: England. 161
Non-domestic rating: Electronic communications: England. 51, 161
Non-domestic rating: Electronic communications: Scotland. 362, 373
Non-domestic rating: Lists & appeals: Alteration: England. 161
Non-domestic rating: Lists & appeals: Alteration: Wales 161
Non-domestic rating: Rate relief: Small businesses: England 161
Non-domestic rating: Rural areas & rateable value limits: Scotland 374
Non-domestic rating: Small business relief: Wales 162
Non-domestic rating: Telecommunications & canals: Scotland. 374
Non-fossil fuels: Sources: Arrangements: England & Wales 74
Non-prescribed instruments: Weights & measures 292
North Ayrshire: Electoral arrangements: Scotland 362
North East Ambulance Service: National Health Service Trust 135
North Hertfordshire (District): Electoral changes 122
North Kesteven (District): Electoral changes 122
North Korea: United Nations: Measures. 287
North Korea: United Nations: Measures: Overseas territories. 287
North Lanarkshire: Electoral arrangements: Scotland 362
North Shropshire (District): Electoral changes 122
North West Ambulance Service: National Health Service Trust 135
North West Regional Flood Defence Committee 119
North Wiltshire (District): Wiltshire (County): Permitted & special parking areas 254
Northamptonshire: South Northamptonshire (District): Electoral changes 122
Northern Health & Social Services Trust: Northern Ireland. 419
Northern Ireland (Miscellaneous Provisions) Act 2006: Commencements. 54, 143, 164, 276
Northern Ireland Act 1998: Modifications 143, 268

Northern Ireland Act 2000: Modifications. 43, 143
Northern Ireland Arms Decommissioning Act 1997: Amnesty period 143
Northern Ireland Social Care Council: Social care workers: Description: Northern Ireland 420
Northern Ireland Social Care Council: Social care workers: Northern Ireland 420
Northern Ireland: Fire & rescue services 142
Northern Ireland: Government: Restoration preparations: Acts 8
Northern Ireland: Government: Restoration preparations: Acts: Explanatory notes 10
Northern Ireland: Local government: Boundaries 143
Northern Ireland: Miscellaneous provisions: Acts 8
Northern Ireland: Miscellaneous provisions: Acts: Explanatory notes 10
Northern Ireland: Planning: Reform 143
Northern Ireland: Police & Criminal Evidence (Northern Ireland) Order 1989: Code of Practice: Code D: Modifications 143, 156
Northern Ireland: Private tenancies 143
Northern Ireland: Rates 143
Northern Ireland: Rates: Capital values 144
Northern Ireland: St Andrews Agreement: Acts 8
Northern Ireland: St Andrews Agreement: Acts: Explanatory notes 10
Northern Ireland: Statutes 404
Northern Ireland: Statutory rules: Annual volumes 404
Northern Ireland: Statutory rules: Chronological tables 404
Northern Ireland: Terrorism Act 2000: Revised Code of Practice for the Identification of Persons by Police Officers. 144, 157
Northern salmon fishery district: Designation: Scotland 375
Northgate & Prudhoe: National Health Service Trust 135
Northumberland, Tyne & Wear: National Health Service Trust. 135
Nottingham City Hospital: National Health Service Trust 135
Nottingham University Hospitals: National Health Service Trust. 135
Nottingham University Hospitals: National Health Service Trust: Trust funds: Trustees appointment. 135
Nottingham University Hospitals: Queen's Medical Centre: National Health Service Trust: Special trustees 136
Nuclear industries: Security 25
Nuclear reactors: Decommissioning: Environmental impact assessment. 82
Nuisances: Statutory nuisances: Appeals 80
Nuisances: Statutory nuisances: Insects. 80
Nurses & midwives: Medical Act 1983: Amendment 96
Nurses & midwives: Nursing & Midwifery Order 2001: Transitional provisions 96
Nurses & midwives: Parts of & entries in the register. 95, 144
Nursing & Midwifery Council: Practice committees: Constitution 95, 144
Nursing & Midwifery Order 2001: Transitional provisions 96
Nutrition: Food: Addition of substances: England 90
Nutrition: Food: Addition of substances: Northern Ireland 418
Nutrition: Food: Addition of substances: Scotland 355
Nutrition: Standards: School lunches: England 65

O

Occupational & personal pension schemes: Amendments 147, 278
Occupational & personal pension schemes: Consultation by employers & amendments 147, 278
Occupational & personal pension schemes: Taxes: Consequential amendments 277
Occupational pension schemes: Amendments: Northern Ireland 429, 444
Occupational pension schemes: Coal staff & mineworkers' schemes: Transfer values etc. 148
Occupational pension schemes: Consultation by employers: Multi-employer schemes: Modification 147
Occupational pension schemes: Consultation by employers: Multi-employer schemes: Modification: Northern Ireland 429
Occupational pension schemes: Consultation by employers: Northern Ireland 429, 444
Occupational pension schemes: Contracting-out 147
Occupational pension schemes: Contracting-out: Northern Ireland 429
Occupational pension schemes: Cross-border activities 147
Occupational pension schemes: Cross-border activities: Northern Ireland 429
Occupational pension schemes: Early leavers: Cash transfer sums & contribution refunds 147
Occupational pension schemes: Early leavers: Cash transfer sums & contribution refunds: Northern Ireland 429
Occupational pension schemes: Employers: Payments: Northern Ireland. 429
Occupational pension schemes: Fraud compensation levies: Northern Ireland 429
Occupational pension schemes: Fraud compensation levy 148
Occupational pension schemes: Investment: Northern Ireland 429
Occupational pension schemes: Levies 148
Occupational pension schemes: Levies: Northern Ireland 429
Occupational pension schemes: Levy ceiling 148

Occupational pension schemes: Levy ceiling: Earnings percentage increase 148
Occupational pension schemes: Levy ceilings: Northern Ireland 429
Occupational pension schemes: Member-nominated trustees & directors 148
Occupational pension schemes: Member-nominated trustees & directors: Northern Ireland 429
Occupational pension schemes: Modification of schemes. 148
Occupational pension schemes: Payments to employer 148
Occupational pension schemes: Pension protection levies 148
Occupational pension schemes: Pension protection levies: Multi-employer schemes: Transitional period & modification: Northern Ireland 429
Occupational pension schemes: Republic of Ireland schemes exemption: Revocation 148
Occupational pension schemes: Republic of Ireland schemes exemption: Revocation: Northern Ireland 430
Occupational pension schemes: Tax exempt schemes: Amendments 148
Occupational pension schemes: Trustees' knowledge & understanding 148
Occupational pension schemes: Trustees' knowledge & understanding: Northern Ireland 430
Occupational pension schemes: Winding up procedure: Requirements 149
Occupational pension schemes: Winding up procedure: Requirements: Northern Ireland 430
Occupational pensions: Revaluation 149
Occupational pensions: Revaluation: Northern Ireland 430
Offenders: Management of Offenders etc. (Scotland) Act 2005: Supplementary provisions: Scotland 349
Offenders: Rehabilitation of Offenders Act 1974: Exclusions & exceptions: Scotland 375
Offenders: Risk assessment & minimisation: Accreditation schemes: Scotland 349
Office for Standards in Education, Children's Services & Skills: Acts 5
Office for Standards in Education, Children's Services & Skills: Acts: Explanatory notes 10
Office of Her Majesty's Paymaster General: Transfer of functions 130
Official food & feed controls: Wales 18, 92
Offshore funds: Non-qualifying investments tests. 50, 114
Offshore installations: Safety zones 145
Oil pollution: Prevention: Merchant shipping: Bunkers Convention 129
Oil pollution: Supplementary fund protocol: Merchant shipping 129
Oil: Storage: Environmental protection: Scotland 353, 393
Oil: Taxation: Market value 49, 152
Older people: Buses: Travel concession scheme: Eligible persons & services: Scotland 392
Older people: Commissioner: Wales: Acts 4
Older people: Commissioner: Wales: Acts: Explanatory notes 9
Olive oil: Marketing standards 89
Olympic Delivery Authority: Planning functions 287
Olympic games & paralympic games: London Olympic Games & Paralympic Games Act 2006: Commencements: Scotland . . 367, 391
Olympic Games: London: Acts. 7
Olympic Games: London: Acts: Explanatory notes. 10
Olympic lotteries: Payments out of fund 27
Olympics: Association rights: Appointment of proprietors 41, 282
Olympics: London Olympic Games & Paralympic Games Act 2006: Commencements 145, 273
Ombudsman: Public services ombudsman: Standards: Investigations: Wales 125
Ophthalmic services: General: National Health Service: Scotland 365
Ophthalmic services: National Health Service: Scotland 365
Optical charges & payments: National Health Service: England 134
Optical charges & payments: National Health Service: Scotland 365
Optical charges & payments: National Health Service: Wales 140
Optical charges & payments: Northern Ireland 420
Opticians: General Optical Council: Continuing education & training 95, 145
Opticians: Medical Act 1983: Amendment 96
Opticians: Sight testing: Examination & prescription: Scotland. 367
Orchard Primary School: Religious character: Designation 67
Ordinary cause rules: Sheriff Court: Act of Sederunt: Scotland. 389
Ordinary cause rules: Sheriff Court: Family Law (Scotland) Act 2006: Act of Sederunt: Scotland 389
Ordinary cause, summary application, summary cause & small claim rules: Amendments: Act of Sederunt: Scotland 389
Ordnance Survey Trading Fund: Maximum borrowing. 94
Organic farming: Animal housing: Conversion: Northern Ireland 406
Organic products 13, 51
Organs: Research approval: Specified persons: Scotland 358
Orkney Islands: Electoral arrangements: Scotland 362
Osteopaths: General Osteopathic Council: Continuing professional development: Rules 96
Our Lady of Walsingham Catholic Primary School: Religious character: Designation 67
Outer Space Act 1986: Extension: Bermuda. 145
Overseas life insurance companies: Income tax. 49
Overseas territories: Adoption: Children: Hague Convention: Amendments: Northern Ireland 426

Overseas territories: Belarus: Restrictive measures: Funds, financial assets or economic resources 145
Overseas territories: Ivory Coast: Restrictive measures: Arms 145
Overseas territories: Uzbekistan: Restrictive measures: Arms & military activities 146
Oxfordshire Mental Healthcare: National Health Service Trust 135
Ozone depleting substances: Qualifications: Environmental protection 78
Ozone-depleting substances: Qualifications: Environmental protection: Northern Ireland 414

P

Packaged goods: Weights & measures. 292
Packaging waste: Producer responsibility obligations: Northern Ireland 434
Packaging: Essential requirements 78
Pancreatic necrosis: Infectious: Infected waters: Northern Ireland 417
Paralympic Games: London: Acts 7
Paralympic Games: London: Acts: Explanatory notes 10
Paralympics: Association rights: Appointment of proprietors 41, 282
Paralympics: Association rights: Paralympic symbol 41, 282
Paralympics: London Olympic Games & Paralympic Games Act 2006: Commencements 145, 273
Paralytic shellfish poisoning: Food protection: Orkney: Scotland. 373
Parental & maternity leave: Northern Ireland 414
Parental involvement: Schools: Acts: Explanatory notes: Scotland 340
Parental involvement: Schools: Acts: Scotland 339
Parental Responsibilities & Parental Rights Agreement: Scotland 347
Parental separation: Contact disputes: Acts 4
Parental separation: Contact disputes: Acts: Explanatory notes 9
Parenting orders: Anti-social behaviour: Wales. 72
Parish electoral arrangements: Bradford 121
Parish electoral arrangements: East Lindsey 122
Parish electoral arrangements: Isle of Wight 123
Parish electoral arrangements: Uttlesford 123
Parishes: Bradford 121
Parishes: Castle Point 122
Parishes: Gateshead 122
Parishes: Hinckley & Bosworth 122
Parishes: Isle of Wight 123
Parishes: Kettering 123
Parishes: King's Lynn & West Norfolk 123
Parishes: Rugby 123
Parishes: Stratford-on-Avon 123
Parishes: Tandridge 123
Parishes: Torbay 123
Parishes: Wealden 124
Parishes: Wear Valley 124
Parking: Off-street: Northern Ireland 438
Parking: On-street: Northern Ireland 438
Parliament: Parliamentary pensions 149
Parliamentary Commissioner 146
Parliamentary constituencies & Assembly electoral regions: Wales 165
Parliamentary corporate bodies: Crown immunities 146
Parliamentary costs: Acts 8
Parliamentary pensions 149
Parochial fees 61
Partnerships & unlimited companies: Accounts: Northern Ireland 409
Partnerships: Contributions to a trade: Restrictions 111
Partnerships: Insolvent: Amendments: Northern Ireland 426
Partnerships: Limited liability partnerships: Northern Ireland. 428
Passenger & goods vehicles: Recording equipment: Northern Ireland. 415, 438
Passenger vehicles: Recording equipment 168
Passenger vehicles: Recording equipment: Fitting dates 168
Passenger vehicles: Recording equipment: Tachograph cards 168
Patents Act 1977: Amendment: Electronic communications 116
Patents: Convention countries 146
Patents: Trade marks & designs: Service & time limits 116
Paternity & adoption leave 277
Paternity & adoption leave: Northern Ireland 414

Paternity pay: Statutory 278
Paternity, maternity & adoption leave: Employment: Acts 9
Paternity, maternity & adoption leave: Employment: Acts: Explanatory notes 11
Pathogens: Animal: Specified: England. 21
Patient & Public Involvement in Health, Commission: Membership & procedure: England 132
Pay as you earn: Income tax 110
Paying Agency: National Assembly for Wales 18
Pedestrian crossings: Zebra, pelican & puffin: Northern Ireland 439
Pelican crossings: Northern Ireland 439
Penalty charges: Road traffic & vehicles: Criminal proceedings: Exemption: Northern Ireland 438
Pension benefits: Scheme administrator: Insurance company liability 111
Pension Protection Fund: Amendments 149
Pension Protection Fund: Amendments: Northern Ireland 430
Pension Protection Fund: Assets & liabilities: Valuation 149
Pension Protection Fund: Civil partnerships: Dissolution: Northern Ireland 409, 416, 428
Pension Protection Fund: Divorce: Northern Ireland. 416, 428
Pension Protection Fund: Information provision: Northern Ireland 430
Pension Protection Fund: Information: Provision 149
Pension Protection Fund: Insolvent partnerships: Insolvency events: Amendments: Northern Ireland 430
Pension Protection Fund: Levy ceiling 149
Pension Protection Fund: Levy ceiling: Northern Ireland 430
Pension Protection Fund: Payments: Pensions Act 2004. . . . . 150, 269
Pension Protection Fund: Payments: Pensions Act 2004 & 2005 Orders: Northern Ireland. 430, 439
Pension Protection Fund: Pension compensation cap 149
Pension Protection Fund: Pension compensation cap: Northern Ireland 430
Pension Protection Fund: Pension sharing. 149
Pension Protection Fund: Pension sharing: Northern Ireland 430
Pension Protection Fund: PPF payments & FAS payments: Northern Ireland 442
Pension Protection Fund: Review & consideration of reviewable matters: Northern Ireland 430
Pension Protection Fund: Reviewable matters 149
Pension Protection Fund: Risk based levy 149
Pension Protection Fund: Risk-based pension protection levy: Northern Ireland 430
Pension Protection Fund: Tax 29, 49, 111, 115, 274
Pensions Act 2004: Codes of practice: Early leavers, late payments & trustee knowledge & understanding: Appointed day 149
Pensions Act 2004: Codes of practice: Member-nominated trustees & directors: Internal controls: Appointed day 150
Pensions Act 2004: Commencements 150
Pensions Act 2004: Funding defined benefits: Appointed day 150
Pensions Act 2004: PPF payments: FAS payments 150, 269
Pensions Act 2004: Restricted information: Disclosure: Specified persons: Amendment 150
Pensions Appeal Tribunals: Armed Forces & Reserve Forces: Compensation scheme: Rights of appeal 150
Pensions Appeal Tribunals: Rights of appeal 150
Pensions *see also* Pension Protection Fund
Pensions: 2004 Act & 2005 Orders: PPF payments & FAS payments: Northern Ireland 430, 439
Pensions: 2005 Order: Codes of practice: Appointed days: Northern Ireland. 430
Pensions: 2005 Order: Commencements: Northern Ireland 431
Pensions: 2005 Order: Member-nominated trustees & directors & internal controls: Code of practice: Northern Ireland 431
Pensions: 2005 Order: Restricted information: Disclosure: Specified persons: Amendment: Northern Ireland 431Pensions: Armed Forces
& Reserve Forces: Compensation scheme 146
Pensions: Armed Forces: Pension schemes: Amendment 146
Pensions: Armed Forces: Redundancy schemes 146
Pensions: Civil partnership: Dissolution 40, 85, 151
Pensions: Deferral: Shared additional pension & graduated retirement benefit: Northern Ireland 423, 435, 440
Pensions: Divorce 85, 151
Pensions: Divorce & dissolution: Pension Protection Fund: Scotland. 353
Pensions: Employment: Age discrimination: Northern Ireland 404, 428
Pensions: European Parliament: UK representatives 146
Pensions: Financial assistance scheme: Amendments 146
Pensions: Firefighters' compensation schemes: England 88, 151
Pensions: Firefighters' compensation schemes: Scotland 354, 367
Pensions: Firefighters' pension schemes: England 88, 151
Pensions: Firefighters' pension schemes: Northern Ireland 416
Pensions: Firefighters' pension schemes: Scotland. 354, 367
Pensions: Firefighters' pension schemes: Wales. 88, 152
Pensions: Guaranteed minimum increase 146
Pensions: Income tax: Pension funds pooling schemes 111
Pensions: Increase: Armed Forces: Pension schemes & Conservation Board. 150

Pensions: Increase: Guaranteed minimum: Northern Ireland 428
Pensions: Increase review 150
Pensions: Increase review: Northern Ireland. 431
Pensions: Judicial Pensions & Retirement Act 1993: Qualifying judicial offices: Addition 147
Pensions: Judicial pensions: Additional voluntary contributions 146
Pensions: Judicial pensions: Additional voluntary contributions: Northern Ireland. 428
Pensions: Judicial pensions: Contributions 147
Pensions: Judicial pensions: Income tax 114
Pensions: Judicial pensions: Spouses' & children's benefits: Northern Ireland. 428
Pensions: Judicial pensions: Widows' & children's benefits: Northern Ireland. 428
Pensions: Local government schemes: Scotland. 367
Pensions: Local government: Employment: Early termination: Discretionary compensation: England & Wales 151
Pensions: Local government: Pension schemes: Amendments 151
Pensions: Local government: Pension schemes: Civil partnership: Northern Ireland. 427
Pensions: Local government: Pension schemes: Funds: Management & investment: Northern Ireland 427
Pensions: Local government: Pension schemes: Northern Ireland 427
Pensions: Low earnings threshold 272
Pensions: Low earnings threshold: Social security: Northern Ireland 442
Pensions: National Health Service: Pension scheme, injury benefits & additional voluntary contributions 137
Pensions: Naval, military & air forces etc.: Disablement & death. 147
Pensions: Navy, army & air force: Disablement & death: Service pensions 147
Pensions: Occupational & personal pension schemes: Amendments 147, 278
Pensions: Occupational & personal pension schemes: Amendments: Northern Ireland 429, 444
Pensions: Occupational & personal pension schemes: Consultation by employers 147, 278
Pensions: Occupational & personal pension schemes: Consultation by employers: Northern Ireland. 429, 444
Pensions: Occupational pension schemes: Coal staff & mineworkers' schemes: Transfer values etc. 148
Pensions: Occupational pension schemes: Consultation by employers: Multi-employer schemes: Modification 147
Pensions: Occupational pension schemes: Consultation by employers: Multi-employer schemes: Modification: Northern Ireland . . . 429
Pensions: Occupational pension schemes: Contracting-out 147
Pensions: Occupational pension schemes: Contracting-out: Northern Ireland 429
Pensions: Occupational pension schemes: Cross-border activities 147
Pensions: Occupational pension schemes: Cross-border activities: Northern Ireland. 429
Pensions: Occupational pension schemes: Early leavers: Cash transfer sums & contribution refunds 147
Pensions: Occupational pension schemes: Early leavers: Cash transfer sums & contribution refunds: Northern Ireland 429
Pensions: Occupational pension schemes: Employers: Payments: Northern Ireland 429
Pensions: Occupational pension schemes: Fraud compensation levies: Northern Ireland 429
Pensions: Occupational pension schemes: Fraud compensation levy 148
Pensions: Occupational pension schemes: Investment: Northern Ireland 429
Pensions: Occupational pension schemes: Levies 148
Pensions: Occupational pension schemes: Levies: Northern Ireland 429
Pensions: Occupational pension schemes: Levy ceiling 148
Pensions: Occupational pension schemes: Levy ceiling: Earnings percentage increase 148
Pensions: Occupational pension schemes: Levy ceilings: Northern Ireland. 429
Pensions: Occupational pension schemes: Member-nominated trustees & directors 148
Pensions: Occupational pension schemes: Member-nominated trustees & directors: Northern Ireland 429
Pensions: Occupational pension schemes: Modification of schemes 148
Pensions: Occupational pension schemes: Payments to employer 148
Pensions: Occupational pension schemes: Pension protection levies 148
Pensions: Occupational pension schemes: Pension protection levies: Multi-employer schemes: Transitional period & modification: Northern Ireland 429
Pensions: Occupational pension schemes: Republic of Ireland schemes exemption: Revocation 148
Pensions: Occupational pension schemes: Republic of Ireland schemes exemption: Revocation: Northern Ireland 430
Pensions: Occupational pension schemes: Tax exempt schemes: Amendments 148
Pensions: Occupational pension schemes: Trustees' knowledge & understanding 148
Pensions: Occupational pension schemes: Trustees' knowledge & understanding: Northern Ireland 430
Pensions: Occupational pension schemes: Winding up procedure: Requirements 149
Pensions: Occupational pension schemes: Winding up procedure: Requirements: Northern Ireland. 430
Pensions: Occupational pensions: Revaluation 149
Pensions: Occupational pensions: Revaluation: Northern Ireland. 430
Pensions: Parliamentary pensions 149
Pensions: Pension schemes: Categories of country & requirements for overseas & recognised overseas schemes 111
Pensions: Pension schemes: Income tax: Transitional provisions 114
Pensions: Pension schemes: Investment-regulated: Exception of tangible moveable property 111
Pensions: Pension schemes: Local government 151
Pensions: Pension schemes: Local government: Public Services Ombudsman (Wales) Act 2005: Wales 292

Pensions: Pension schemes: Pension rates: Reduction. 111
Pensions: Pension schemes: Qualifying & qualifying recognised overseas schemes & corresponding relief: Information requirements 111
Pensions: Pension schemes: Registered: Up-rating percentages: Defined benefits arrangements & enhanced protection limits. 113
Pensions: Pension schemes: Relevant migrant members 111
Pensions: Pension schemes: Relevant non-UK schemes: Application of UK provisions 112
Pensions: Pension schemes: Taxable property provisions 112
Pensions: Pension schemes: Taxation 114
Pensions: Pension schemes: Taxation: Application of UK provisions to relevant non-UK schemes 112
Pensions: Pension sharing: Police Service: Northern Ireland 434
Pensions: Personal injuries: Civilians 150
Pensions: Personal pension schemes: Appropriate schemes 150
Pensions: Personal pension schemes: Appropriate schemes: Northern Ireland 431
Pensions: Police. 151, 155
Pensions: Police Service: Northern Ireland. 433, 434
Pensions: Police: Scotland 367, 369
Pensions: Registered & overseas pension schemes: Returns & information: Electronic communication. 112
Pensions: Registered pension schemes: Annuities: Determining amount: Prescribed manner 113
Pensions: Registered pension schemes: Authorised arrears payments 112
Pensions: Registered pension schemes: Authorised member payments 112
Pensions: Registered pension schemes: Authorised member payments 112
Pensions: Registered pension schemes: Authorised payments 112
Pensions: Registered pension schemes: Authorised payments: Transfer to Pension Protection Fund 112
Pensions: Registered pension schemes: Authorised reductions 112
Pensions: Registered pension schemes: Authorised surplus payments 112
Pensions: Registered pension schemes: Block transfers: Permitted membership period 112
Pensions: Registered pension schemes: Commencement lump sum: Meaning 113
Pensions: Registered pension schemes: Enhanced lifetime allowances 112, 113
Pensions: Registered pension schemes: Extension of Migrant Member Relief 113
Pensions: Registered pension schemes: Information: Provision. 113
Pensions: Registered pension schemes: Information: Provision. 113
Pensions: Registered pension schemes: Living accommodation: Co-ownership 112
Pensions: Registered pension schemes: Relevant annuities 113
Pensions: Registered pension schemes: Relevant excess: Surrender 113
Pensions: Registered pension schemes: Rules: Modification 113
Pensions: Registered pension schemes: Rules: Unauthorised payments 113
Pensions: Registered pension schemes: Splitting of schemes 113
Pensions: Registered pension schemes: Transfer of sums & assets 113
Pensions: Retirement pensions: Deferral: Social security 270
Pensions: Retirement: Deferral: Northern Ireland 440
Pensions: Service pensions. 147
Pensions: Social security: Class 1 contributions, rebates & minimum contributions: Reduced rates 150
Pensions: Superannuation Act 1972: Admission to Schedule 1 150
Pensions: Superannuation: Agri-food & Biosciences Institute: Northern Ireland 431
Pensions: Superannuation: Chief Electoral Officer for Northern Ireland: Northern Ireland 431
Pensions: Superannuation: Teachers: Scotland. 367, 368
Pensions: Taxes: Consequential amendments 277
Pensions: Teachers' pensions: Amendments 70
Pensions: Teachers' pensions: Reform amendments 70
Pensions: Transfers, reorganisations & winding up 111
Pensions: War Pensions Committees 151
People's College, Nottingham: Dissolution. 67
Perry: Excise. 83
Personal dental services: National Health Service: Agreements: Wales. 139, 140
Personal dental services: National Health Service: England & Wales 136
Personal dental services: National Health Service: Transitional & consequential provisions: Wales 138
Personal dental services: National Health Service: Wales. 139
Personal injuries: Civilians. 150
Personal injuries: National Health Service: Charges: Amounts: Scotland. 366
Personal injuries: National Health Service: Charges: General: Scotland 366
Personal injuries: National Health Service: Charges: Reviews & appeals: Scotland 367
Personal injury: NHS charges: General: Amendments: England & Wales. 138, 255
Personal injury: NHS charges: Reviews & appeals: Amendments: England & Wales 138, 255
Personal pension schemes: Amendments: Northern Ireland 429, 444
Personal pension schemes: Appropriate schemes: Northern Ireland 431
Personal pension schemes: Consultation by employers: Northern Ireland. 429, 444
Perth & Kinross Council: Road traffic: Permitted & special parking area: Scotland 377

Perth & Kinross: Electoral arrangements: Scotland 362
Perth: Pilotage powers: Scotland. 368
Pesticides: Maximum residue levels: Crops, food & feeding stuffs: England & Wales. 16, 152
Pesticides: Maximum residue levels: Crops, food & feeding stuffs: Northern Ireland 406, 407, 431
Pesticides: Maximum residue levels: Crops, food & feeding stuffs: Scotland 342, 368
Pesticides: Plant protection products. 152
Pesticides: Plant protection products: England & Wales 152
Pesticides: Plant protection products: Northern Ireland 431
Pesticides: Plant protection products: Scotland 368
Petroleum revenue tax: Blended crude oil: Attribution 152
Petroleum revenue tax: Disposals & appropriations: Nomination scheme 49, 152
Petroleum revenue tax: Oil: Market value 49, 152
Petroleum: Licensing: Exploration & production: Seaward & landward areas 152
Pharmaceutical services: National Health Service. 134
Pharmaceutical services: National Health Service: Scotland 365
Pharmaceutical services: National Health Service: Wales. 140
Pharmaceutical Society of Northern Ireland: General: Amendments: Northern Ireland 431
Pharmacies: Applications for registration & fees 128
Phosphorus: Agriculture: Use: Northern Ireland. 414
Phytophthora ramorum: Plant health: Wales. 154
Pig carcases: Grading: England 15
Pig carcases: Grading: Northern Ireland 407
Pig carcases: Grading: Scotland 342
Pigs: Slaughter pigs: Salmonella: Survey powers: England 21
Pigs: Slaughter pigs: Salmonella: Survey powers: Northern Ireland 408, 415
Pilotage: Perth: Pilotage powers: Scotland 368
Pipelines: Gas: Designation: Northern Ireland. 419
Planning & Compulsory Purchase Act 2004: Commencements 279, 281
Planning & Compulsory Purchase Act 2004: Commencements: Scotland 391
Planning & Compulsory Purchase Act 2004: Commencements: Wales. 280
Planning & Compulsory Purchase Act 2004: Transitional provisions: Scotland 391
Planning Appeals Commission: Procedures: Appeals & making of reports: Decisions: Northern Ireland 432
Planning permission, listed buildings & conservation areas: Applications 279
Planning: Acts: Explanatory notes: Scotland 340
Planning: Acts: Scotland 339
Planning: Application to the Houses of Parliament 279
Planning: Appointed persons: Determination of appeals: Prescribed classes: England 280
Planning: Certificates: Issue: Northern Ireland 432
Planning: Compensation: Claims: Northern Ireland 432
Planning: Conservation areas: Consultation: Northern Ireland 432
Planning: Development plans: Northern Ireland. 432
Planning: Electricity consents: Northern Ireland 142
Planning: Electronic communication: Northern Ireland 432
Planning: General development: Amendments: Northern Ireland 432
Planning: General development: Northern Ireland 432
Planning: Inquiry procedure: Northern Ireland 432
Planning: Listed buildings & buildings in conservation areas: Scotland 392
Planning: Listed buildings & conservation areas: Wales 281
Planning: Listed buildings, conservation areas & hazardous substances: Crown land: Amendments: Wales . . . 281
Planning: Listed buildings, conservation areas & hazardous substances: England 279
Planning: National security directions & appointed representatives: England 279
Planning: National security directions & appointed representatives: Northern Ireland 432
Planning: National security directions & appointed representatives: Scotland 392
Planning: National security directions & appointed representatives: Wales 281
Planning: Reform: 2006 Order: Commencements: Northern Ireland 432
Planning: Reform: Northern Ireland 143
Planning: Regional transport planning: Wales. 286
Planning: Subordinate legislation: Application to the Crown 280
Planning: Subordinate legislation: Application to the Crown: Inquiries procedure: Scotland 392
Planning: Subordinate legislation: Application to the Crown: Northern Ireland 432
Planning: Town & country planning: Applications & deemed applications: Fees 280
Planning: Town & country planning: Environmental impact assessment 279
Planning: Town & country planning: General development procedure 280
Planning: Town & country planning: General development procedure: Wales 282
Planning: Town & country planning: Subordinate legislation: Application to the Crown: Scotland 392

Planning: Town & country: Applications & deemed applications: Fees: Wales 281
Planning: Town & country: Crown land: Miscellaneous amendments & modifications: Wales 282
Planning: Town & country: Environmental impact assessment: Wales. 281
Planning: Town & country: General permitted development: Wales 282
Plant breeders' rights: Naming & fees 153
Plant breeders' rights: Prior use exemption: Discontinuation: Wales 153
Plant health: England. 153
Plant health: Export certification: Wales. 153
Plant health: Fees: Forestry 153
Plant health: Forestry. 153
Plant health: Forestry: Wood: Packaging material marking 153
Plant health: Import inspection fees 153, 154
Plant health: Import inspection fees: England 153
Plant health: Northern Ireland 433
Plant health: Phytophthora ramorum: Wales. 154
Plant health: Potatoes: Originating in Egypt: Northern Ireland 433
Plant health: Potatoes: Originating in Egypt: Scotland 369
Plant health: Potatoes: Scotland 368
Plant health: Scotland 368
Plant health: Wales. 154
Plant health: Wood & bark: Northern Ireland 433
Plant protection products. 152
Plant protection products: England & Wales 152
Plant protection products: Pesticides: Northern Ireland 431
Plant protection products: Pesticides: Scotland 368
Plastic materials & articles: Food: Contact: England 90, 91
Plastic materials & articles: Food: Contact: Northern Ireland 418
Plastic materials & articles: Food: Contact: Scotland 356
Plastic materials & articles: Food: Contact: Wales 93
Pneumoconiosis etc.: Workers' compensation: Claims: Payment 269
Pneumoconiosis etc.: Workers' compensation: Claims: Payment: Northern Ireland 439
Pneumoconiosis: Byssinosis: Miscellaneous disease benefit 269
Poland: Double taxation: Relief 29, 47, 110
Police & Criminal Evidence (Northern Ireland) Order 1989: Code of Practice: Code D: Modifications 143, 156
Police & Criminal Evidence Act 1984: Armed Forces: Application to 57
Police & Criminal Evidence Act 1984: Code of Practice A: Revisions 155
Police & Criminal Evidence Act 1984: Codes of Practice C & H 154
Police & Justice Act 2006: Commencements 53, 85, 155
Police & Justice Act 2006: Supplementary & transitional provisions 155
Police & justice: Acts 8
Police & justice: Acts: Explanatory notes 10
Police Act 1996: Local policing summaries 154
Police Act 1997: Amendments: Scotland 369
Police Act 1997: Criminal records 154
Police Act 1997: Criminal records: Registration 154
Police Act 1997: Criminal records: Registration: Scotland 369
Police Act 1997: Criminal records: Scotland 369
Police authorities: Best value: Performance indicators: England & Wales 155
Police Service & Police Service & Reserve: Injury benefit: Northern Ireland 433
Police Service & Police Service Reserve (Full-time): Severance: Northern Ireland 433
Police Service Reserve (Full-time): Severance: Northern Ireland 434
Police Service: Pension sharing : Northern Ireland 434
Police Service: Pensions: Northern Ireland. 433, 434
Police, Public Order & Criminal Justice (Scotland) Act 2006: Commencements: Scotland. 349, 369
Police: Acts: Explanatory notes: Scotland 340
Police: Acts: Scotland 339
Police: Antisocial Behaviour etc. (Scotland) Act 2004: Commencements: Scotland 348, 352, 360, 369
Police: Appointment: Minimum age: England & Wales. 155
Police: Appointment: Minimum age: Scotland 369
Police: Complaints & misconduct: England & Wales 155
Police: Criminal Justice Act 2003: Commencements 53, 54, 154
Police: England & Wales 154
Police: Grants: Scotland 369
Police: Injury benefit 155
Police: Injury benefit: Scotland 369
Police: National Criminal Intelligence Service: Abolition. 154

Police: Pensions. 151, 155
Police: Pensions: Scotland 367, 369
Police: Promotion: England & Wales 155
Police: Recruitment: Northern Ireland: Northern Ireland 433
Police: Serious Organised Crime & Police Act 2005: Commencements 53, 54, 155, 157, 265
Police: Serious Organised Crime & Police Act 2005: Commencements: Scotland 349, 370
Police: Serious Organised Crime & Police Act 2005: Consequential & supplementary amendments. 154, 265
Political donations & regulated transactions: Anonymous electors: England & Wales 156
Political Parties, Elections & Referendums Act 2000: Commencements. 131, 156, 163
Political parties: Donations & regulated transactions: Anonymous electors: England & Wales 156
Political parties: Electoral Administration Act 2006: Commencements. 74, 131, 156, 162, 163
Political parties: Political Parties, Elections & Referendums Act 2000: Commencements. 131, 156, 163
Political parties: Registration: Prohibited words & expressions. 162
Polling districts & places: Review: Parliamentary elections. 163
Pollution: Air pollution: Ships: Prevention 127
Pollution: Marine: Prevention: Merchant shipping: Sewage & garbage. 127
Pollution: Merchant shipping: Acts. 7
Pollution: Merchant shipping: Acts: Explanatory notes. 10
Pollution: Nitrates Action Programme: Northern Ireland 414
Pollution: Oil pollution: Supplementary fund protocol: Merchant shipping 129
Pollution: Oil: Prevention: Merchant shipping: Bunkers Convention 129
Pollution: Prevention & control 82
Pollution: Prevention & control: England. 80
Pollution: Prevention & control: Environmental protection: Northern Ireland 414
Pontypool & Blaenavon Railway: Phase I 285, 286
Poole harbour: Opening bridges 284, 285
Port of Blyth: Battleship Wharf railway 284, 285
Port of Ipswich: Harbour revision. 94
Post office: Postal services: Jersey. 156
Postgraduate Medical Education & Training Board: Fees: Rules. 96
Potatoes: Originating in Egypt: Northern Ireland 433
Potatoes: Originating in Egypt: Scotland 369
Potatoes: Plant health: Scotland 368
Potatoes: Seed potatoes: England 264
Potatoes: Seed potatoes: Fees: England 264
Potatoes: Seed potatoes: Fees: Scotland 388
Potatoes: Seed potatoes: Fees: Wales 264
Potatoes: Seed potatoes: Tuber inspection fees: Northern Ireland. 407
Potatoes: Seed potatoes: Wales 264
Poultry: Avian influenza: England 20
Poultry: Avian influenza: Wales 23
PPF *see* Pension Protection Fund
Precept calculations: Grants: Allocation: Greater London Authority 125
Prescription Pricing Authority: Abolition 138
Prescriptions: Independent prescribing: National Health Service: Amendments 134
Pressure equipment: Transportable: Use: Northern Ireland 420, 421
Prevention & suppression of terrorism: Proscribed organisations: Deproscription: Applications 156
Prevention & suppression of terrorism: Terrorism Act 2000: Proscribed organisations 157
Prevention & suppression of terrorism: Terrorism Act 2000: Proscribed organisations: Name changes 156
Prevention & suppression of terrorism: Terrorism Act 2000: Regulated sector: Business 156
Prevention & suppression of terrorism: Terrorism Act 2000: Revised Code of Practice for the Identification of Persons by Police Officers: Northern Ireland 144, 157
Prevention & suppression of terrorism: Terrorism Act 2006: Commencements 157
Prevention of Terrorism Act 2005: Continuance in force of sections 1 to 9. 156
Price indications: Traders: Code of practice: Approval: Northern Ireland 409
Primary care trusts & strategic health authorities: Functions: National Health Service. 134
Primary care trusts: Dental services: Functions 132
Primary care trusts: Establishment & dissolution: England 135
Primary care trusts: Establishment orders: Amendments 135
Primary care trusts: Functions: Dental public health: England 132
Primary Medical Services (Scotland) Act 2004: National Health Service (Scotland) Act 1978: Modifications: Scotland 367
Primary medical services: Amendments: Northern Ireland 419
Primary medical services: National Health Service 134
Primary medical services: National Health Service: Wales 140
Primary medical services: Performers lists: Scotland 365

Primary medical services: Section 17c agreements: National Health Service: Scotland 365
Prisons: Scotland 370, 395
Prisons: Young offender institutions: Scotland. 370, 395
Private & voluntary health care: England 159
Private & voluntary health care: Wales 159
Private hire vehicles: Carriage of guide dogs, etc.: Disability Discrimination Act 1995: England & Wales 61, 285
Private hire vehicles: London 130
Private Security Industry Act 2001: Approved contractor scheme 263
Private Security Industry Act 2001: Aviation security: Exemption 263
Private Security Industry Act 2001: Commencement 263
Private Security Industry Act 2001: Commencements: Scotland 388
Private Security Industry Act 2001: Designated activities. 263
Private Security Industry Act 2001: Licences 263
Private Security Industry Act 2001: Licences: Duration. 263
Private Security Industry Act 2001: Schedule 2: Amendments 263
Private tenancies: 2006 Order: Commencements: Northern Ireland. 426
Private tenancies: Northern Ireland 143
Probation: Local probation boards: Appointments & miscellaneous provisions 157
Proceeds of Crime Act 2002: Amendment. 86, 157
Proceeds of Crime Act 2002: Financial investigators: References 157
Proceeds of Crime Act 2002: Money laundering 157
Proceeds of Crime Act 2002: Regulated sector: Business. 157
Proceeds of Crime Act 2002: Summary proceedings: Cash: Recovery of: Minimum amount 157
Proceeds of crime: Serious Organised Crime & Police Act 2005: Commencements 155, 157
Producer responsibility obligations: Packaging waste: Northern Ireland 434
Products of animal origin: Third country imports: England 15
Products of animal origin: Third country imports: Northern Ireland 407
Products of animal origin: Third country imports: Scotland. 342
Products of animal origin: Third country imports: Wales. 18
Professional qualifications: European Communities: Recognition: Second general system 158
Professional qualifications: Qualifications & experience: Recognition: Third general system: European Communities. 158
Property: Residential Property Tribunal: Fees: England. 103
Property: Residential Property Tribunal: Procedure: England. 103
Proscribed Organisations Appeal Commission: Human Rights Act 1998: Proceedings 106
Proscribed organisations: Deproscription: Applications: Prevention & suppression of terrorism 156
Protection of Military Remains Act 1986: Vessels & controlled sites: Designations. 57
Protection of wrecks: Designation: England. 158
Public Angling Estate: Byelaws: Northern Ireland 417
Public Appointments & Public Bodies etc. (Scotland) Act 2003: Office or body as specified authority: Treatment: Scotland 370
Public Appointments & Public Bodies etc. (Scotland) Act 2003: Scottish Legal Complaints Commission: Treatment as specified
authority: Scotland. 370
Public Appointments & Public Bodies etc. (Scotland) Act 2003: Specified authorities: Amendment: Scotland 370
Public authorities: Statutory duties: Sex Discrimination Act 1975 265
Public Benefit Corporation: Register of members: England & Wales. 138
Public bodies: Ancient Monuments Board for Wales: Abolition 158
Public bodies: Historic Buildings Council for Wales: Abolition 158
Public bodies: Public Appointments & Public Bodies etc. (Scotland) Act 2003: Office or body as specified authority: Treatment:
Scotland 370
Public bodies: Public Appointments & Public Bodies etc. (Scotland) Act 2003: Scottish Legal Complaints Commission: Treatment as
specified authority: Scotland. 370
Public contracts: Public procurement 160
Public contracts: Scotland 373
Public finance & accountability: Budget (Scotland) Act 2005: Amendments: Scotland 370
Public finance & accountability: Budget (Scotland) Act 2006: Amendments: Scotland 370
Public general acts: Bound volumes 12
Public general acts: Tables & index 12
Public health: Appointments Commission 131, 159, 265
Public health: Care services: Fees: Abolition: Wales 31, 159, 266
Public health: Contamination of food: Scotland 371, 372, 373
Public health: Health Act 2006: Commencements 97, 136, 159, 266
Public health: Health Protection Agency: Scottish health functions: Scotland 371
Public health: Private & voluntary health care: England 159
Public health: Private & voluntary health care: Wales. 159
Public health: Producer responsibility obligations: Packaging waste: Northern Ireland 434
Public health: Skin piercing & tattooing: Licensing: Scotland. 360, 370
Public health: Skin piercing & tattooing: Scotland. 360, 371

Public health: Smoke free premises & enforcement 159
Public health: Smoking, Health & Social Care (Scotland) Act 2005: Commencements: Scotland 371
Public health: Smoking, Health & Social Care (Scotland) Act 2005: Consequential amendments: Scotland 371
Public health: Smoking: Prohibition: Enclosed premises: Scotland 371
Public health: Vaccine damage payments: Specified disease 159
Public interest disclosure: Prescribed persons: Northern Ireland 413
Public Lending Right Scheme 1982: Variation: Commencement 121
Public order: Acts: Explanatory notes: Scotland 340
Public order: Acts: Scotland 339
Public passenger transport: Public service vehicles: Drivers, inspectors, conductors & passengers: Conduct: Scotland 373
Public passenger transport: Transport Act 2000: Commencement 159
Public procurement: Public contracts 160
Public procurement: Public contracts: Scotland 373
Public procurement: Utilities contracts 160
Public procurement: Utilities contracts: Scotland 373
Public rights of way: Registers: Wales 101
Public service vehicles: Accessibility: Northern Ireland 438
Public service vehicles: Conditions of fitness, equipment & use: Northern Ireland 438
Public service vehicles: Drivers, inspectors, conductors & passengers: Conduct: Scotland 373
Public service vehicles: Fitness, equipment & use: Conditions: Northern Ireland 438
Public service vehicles: Northern Ireland 438
Public Services Ombudsman (Wales) Act 2005: Commencement: Wales 292
Public Services Ombudsman (Wales) Act 2005: Local government: Pension schemes: Wales 292
Public services ombudsman: Standards: Investigations: Wales 125
Public Transport Users' Committee for Scotland: Establishment: Scotland 392
Public Transport Users' Committee for Scotland: Treatment: As specified authority: Scotland 370
Public transport: Edinburgh: Trams: Acts: Scotland 338
Puffin crossings: Northern Ireland 439
Pupil referral units: Application of enactments: England 65
Pupil registration: England 65
Pupils: Individual pupils: Information: Prescribed persons: England 64
Pupils: Individual: Information: England 64
Pupils: Individual: Information: Wales 72

Q

Quarries: Explosives: Health & safety: Northern Ireland 421
Quarries: Health & safety: Northern Ireland 422
Queen's Medical Centre, Nottingham, University Hospital: National Health Service Trust 135
Queen's Medical Centre: Nottingham University Hospitals: National Health Service Trust: Special trustees 136
Quiet lanes & home zones: Road traffic: England 253

R

Raasay: Highland Council: Harbour revision: Scotland 356
Race Relations Act 1976: General statutory duty 160
Race Relations Act 1976: Statutory duties 160
Race Relations Act 1976: Statutory duties: Scotland 373
Race Relations: Employment: Code of Practice: Appointed day 160
Race Relations: Housing: Code of Practice: Appointed day 160
Racial discrimination: Acts 6
Racial discrimination: Acts: Explanatory notes 10
Racial hatred: Acts 8
Racial hatred: Acts: Explanatory notes 11
Radio: Multiplex services: Digital capacity: Required percentage 28
Radioactive contaminated land: Enactments: Modification: England 80
Radioactive contaminated land: Enactments: Modification: Wales 82
Radioactive substances: Administration: Medicines 127
Radioactive substances: Emergency exemption: England & Wales 25
Radioactive substances: Radioactive contaminated land: Northern Ireland 415, 434
Radioactive substances: Testing instruments: Exemptions: England & Wales 25
Rail transport: Explosives: Carriage: Health & safety: Northern Ireland 421
Rail vehicles: Gatwick Express class 458 vehicles: Accessibility: Exemptions 61, 283
Railway services: Closures guidance: England & Scotland 283
Railways & other guided transport: Health & safety 95

Railways Act 2005: Amendments 283
Railways Act 2005: Commencements 284
Railways: Battleship Wharf railway: Port of Blyth. 284, 285
Railways: Channel Tunnel: International arrangements 29
Railways: Channel Tunnel: Miscellaneous provisions 29
Railways: Docklands Light Railway: Silvertown & London City Airport Extension: Exemptions. 283
Railways: Docklands Light Railway: Stratford International Extension. 284, 285
Railways: Health & safety: Enforcing authorities. 94
Railways: Interoperability 284
Railways: Model clauses 285, 286
Railways: Network Rail: Thameslink 2000: England 284, 285
Railways: Network Rail: West Coast Main Line: Stowe Hill: England 284, 285
Railways: Safety levies 95
Railways: Safety management: Northern Ireland 422
Railways: Services: Closures guidance: England & Wales 283
Railways: Strategic Rail Authority: Abolition 284
Railways: Substitute road services: Exemptions. 283
Railways: Training services: Access. 283
Rates (Amendment): 2006 Order: Commencements: Northern Ireland 435
Rates (Capital Values, etc.): 2006 Order: Commencements: Northern Ireland 435
Rates: Automatic telling machines: Rural areas: Designation: Northern Ireland 435
Rates: Bulgaria & Romania: Northern Ireland 423, 435, 440
Rates: Capital values: Northern Ireland 144
Rates: Children & young persons: Social security: Amendments: Northern Ireland 424, 436, 442
Rates: Housing benefit: Consequential provisions: Northern Ireland. 422, 434, 439
Rates: Housing benefit: Electronic communications: Northern Ireland 422, 434
Rates: Housing benefit: Northern Ireland 422, 423, 434, 435
Rates: Housing benefit: Pension credit: Qualifying age: Northern Ireland. 423, 434
Rates: Making & levying: Different rates: Northern Ireland 435
Rates: Northern Ireland 143
Rates: Regional rates: Northern Ireland 435
Rates: Retirement pensions: Deferral: Shared additional pension & graduated retirement benefit: Northern Ireland 423, 435, 440
Rates: Social security: Amendments: Northern Ireland 423, 424, 436, 441, 442
Rates: Social security: Benefits up-rating: Northern Ireland 413, 423, 435, 440, 443
Rates: Social security: Lebanon: Northern Ireland 423, 435, 441
Rates: Social security: Persons from abroad: Northern Ireland 424, 436, 442
Rates: Students & income-related benefits: Northern Ireland. 424, 436, 442
Rates: Transitional provisions: Northern Ireland 435
Rating & valuation: Central rating list: England. 160
Rating & valuation: Council tax: Electronic communications: Scotland 347, 361, 373
Rating & valuation: Council tax: Non-domestic rating: Amendments: England 50, 161
Rating & valuation: Exempted classes: Scotland 374
Rating & valuation: Licensing Act 2003: Public houses: Non-domestic rating: Consequential amendments: England. 121, 161
Rating & valuation: Non-domestic rates: Levying: Scotland 373
Rating & valuation: Non-domestic rates: Scotland 373
Rating & valuation: Non-domestic rating: Chargeable amounts: England 161
Rating & valuation: Non-domestic rating: Contributions: England 161
Rating & valuation: Non-domestic rating: Contributions: Wales 161
Rating & valuation: Non-domestic rating: Demand notices & discretionary relief: Wales 161
Rating & valuation: Non-domestic rating: Demand notices: England. 161
Rating & valuation: Non-domestic rating: Electronic communications: England. 51, 161
Rating & valuation: Non-domestic rating: Electronic communications: Scotland 362, 373
Rating & valuation: Non-domestic rating: Lists & appeals: Alteration: England 161
Rating & valuation: Non-domestic rating: Lists & appeals: Alteration: Wales 161
Rating & valuation: Non-domestic rating: Rate relief: Small businesses: England 161
Rating & valuation: Non-domestic rating: Rural areas & rateable value limits: Scotland 374
Rating & valuation: Non-domestic rating: Small business relief: Wales 162
Rating & valuation: Non-domestic rating: Telecommunications & canals: Scotland 374
Real estate investment trusts: Breach of conditions. 50
Real estate investment trusts: Group trusts: Financial statements 50
Real estate investment trusts: Joint ventures 50
Real estate investment trusts: Taxes: Assessment & recovery 49
Recreation grounds: Wormley Recreation Ground: Parish Council byelaws: Revocation: England 124
Redundancies: Collective: Northern Ireland 413
Redundancy & premature retirement: Compensation: Teachers 70
Referendums: Conduct: Acts 5

Referendums: Conduct: Acts: Explanatory notes 10
Referendums: Electoral Administration Act 2006: Commencements 74, 131, 156, 162, 163
Refugees: In need of international protection: Qualification: Immigration 109
Regional spatial strategies: Town & country planning: Public examinations: Allowances: England 280
Regional transport planning: Wales 286
Register of Sasines: Application procedure: Scotland 374
Register of Sasines: Methods of operation: Scotland 374
Registered Designs Act 1949: Amendment: Electronic communications 116
Registered pension schemes: Information: Provision 113
Registers & records: Register of Sasines: Application procedure: Scotland 374
Registers & records: Register of Sasines: Methods of operation: Scotland 374
Registers of Scotland: Fees: Scotland 374
Registration of births & deaths: Amendments: England & Wales 162
Registration of births & deaths: Electronic communications & electronic storage 162
Registration of births, deaths, marriages, etc.: Local electoral administration & registration services: Acts: Commencements: Scotland 374
Registration of births, deaths, marriages, etc.: National Health Service Central Register: Scotland 374
Registration of births, deaths, marriages, etc.: Prescription of forms & errors: Scotland 374
Registration of births, deaths, marriages, etc.: Registration services: Attestation & authentication: Scotland 374
Registration of births, deaths, marriages, etc.: Registration services: Fees: Scotland 347, 363, 375
Registration of births, deaths, marriages, etc.: Registration services: Scotland 374
Registration of political parties: Electoral Administration Act 2006: Commencements 74, 131, 156, 162, 163
Registration of political parties: Prohibited words & expressions 162
Registration services: Registration of births, deaths, marriages, etc.: Attestation & authentication: Scotland 374
Registration services: Registration of births, deaths, marriages, etc.: Scotland 374
Regulation & Improvement Authority: Inspections: Fees & frequency: Northern Ireland 420
Regulation of Care (Scotland) Act 2001: Commencements: Scotland 390
Regulation of care: Applications & provision of advice: Scotland 390
Regulation of care: Fees: Scotland 390
Regulation of care: Requirements as to care services: Scotland 390
Regulation of investigatory powers: Prescription of offices, ranks & positions: Scotland 358
Regulatory reform: Acts 7
Regulatory reform: Acts: Explanatory notes 10
Regulatory reform: Agricultural tenancies: England & Wales 119, 163
Regulatory reform: Fire safety: England & Wales 163
Regulatory reform: Forestry 93, 162
Regulatory reform: Registered designs 58, 162
Rehabilitation of Offenders Act 1974: Exceptions: England & Wales 163
Rehabilitation of Offenders Act 1974: Exclusions & exceptions: Scotland 375
Relevant authorities: Local government: Standards Committee 124
Religious hatred: Acts 8
Religious hatred: Acts: Explanatory notes 11
Religious schools: Archbishop Courtenay Primary School: Religious character: Designation 62
Religious schools: Trinity CoE VC Primary School: Religious character: Designation 68
Religious schools: Unity College: Religious character: Designation 69
Religious schools: Westminster Church of England Primary School: Religious character: Designation 69
Renewables obligation: Electricity: England & Wales 74
Renewables obligation: Electricity: Scotland 351
Renfrewshire: East Renfrewshire: Electoral arrangements: Scotland 361
Renfrewshire: Electoral arrangements: Scotland 362
Rents: Registered rents: Increase: Northern Ireland 426
Representation of the people: Amendments: Scotland 165
Representation of the people: Combination of polls: England & Wales 164
Representation of the people: Elections: Absent voting: Transitional provisions: England & Wales 164
Representation of the people: Elections: Policy development grants scheme 163
Representation of the people: Electoral Administration Act 2006: Commencements 74, 131, 156, 162, 163
Representation of the people: Electoral participation: Encouragement: Expenses: Reimbursement: England & Wales 164
Representation of the people: England & Wales 124, 164
Representation of the people: Form of canvass: England & Wales 164
Representation of the people: Form of canvass: Scotland 165
Representation of the people: Local elections: Parishes & communities: England & Wales 164
Representation of the people: Local elections: Principal areas & parishes & communities: England & Wales .. 164
Representation of the people: Local elections: Principal areas: England & Wales 164
Representation of the people: National Assembly for Wales 43, 59, 165
Representation of the people: National Assembly for Wales: Returning officers: Charges 165
Representation of the people: Northern Ireland (Miscellaneous Provisions) Act 2006: Commencements ... 143, 164

Representation of the people: Political Parties, Elections & Referendums Act 2000: Commencements. 131, 156, 163
Representation of the people: Polling districts & places: Review: Parliamentary elections. 163
Representation of the people: Redistribution of seats: Parliamentary constituencies & Assembly electoral regions: Wales. 165
Representation of the people: Service voters: Registration period 163
Reserve Forces: Compensation schemes. 146
Reserve Forces: Compensation schemes: Excluded benefits: Tax purposes 109
Residential Property Tribunal: Fees: England 103
Residential Property Tribunal: Fees: Wales 105
Residential Property Tribunal: Procedure: England 103
Residential Property Tribunal: Procedure: Wales 105
Residential property: Management practice: Approval of codes 104
Retirement benefit: Graduated: Consequential provisions. 270
Retirement benefits: Employer-financed: Excluded benefits: Tax purposes 110
Retirement pensions: Deferral: Northern Ireland 440
Retirement pensions: Deferral: Shared additional pension & graduated retirement benefit: Northern Ireland. 423, 435, 440
Retirement: Premature & redundancy: Compensation: Teachers. 70
Revenue & customs: Complaints & misconduct. 165
Revenue support grant: Specified bodies: Wales 125
Rice products: Marketing: Restrictions: England 15, 91, 93
Rice products: Marketing: Restrictions: Northern Ireland 407, 418
Rice products: Marketing: Restrictions: Scotland 356
Rice products: Marketing: Restrictions: Wales 93
Richmond The American International University in London: Recognised awards 65
Rights in performances: Copyright & performances: Application to other countries 46, 165
Rights in performances: Moral rights 47, 165
Rights of way: Countryside & Rights of Way Act 2000: Commencements: Wales. 51, 166
Rights of way: Natural Environment & Rural Communities Act 2006: Commencements. 141, 165, 166
Rights of way: Public: Registers: Wales. 101
Risk assessment & minimisation: Offenders: Accreditation schemes: Scotland 349
Risk assessment Orders: Orders for lifelong restriction: Criminal procedure: Rules: Act of Adjournal: Scotland 357
River Lagan: Tidal navigation & general byelaws: Northern Ireland 426
River Tweed 44, 59, 166
River Tyne Tunnels: Tolls: Revision 101
River: Salmon & freshwater fisheries: Assynt-Coigach area: Protection: Scotland. 375
River: Salmon & freshwater fisheries: Conservation: Statistics: Collection: Scotland 375
River: Salmon & freshwater fisheries: Northern salmon fishery district: Designation: Scotland. 375
Road fuel gas: Excise: Reliefs. 83
Road safety: Acts 8
Road safety: Acts: Explanatory notes 11
Road traffic & vehicles: Goods vehicles: Testing: Northern Ireland 437
Road traffic & vehicles: Motor hackney carriages: Belfast: Byelaws: Amendments: Northern Ireland 437
Road traffic & vehicles: Motor hackney carriages: By-laws: Belfast: Northern Ireland 437
Road traffic & vehicles: Motor vehicles: Approval: Northern Ireland 437
Road traffic & vehicles: Motor vehicles: Construction & use: Northern Ireland 437
Road traffic & vehicles: Motor vehicles: Immobilisation & release: Prescribed charges: Northern Ireland 437
Road traffic & vehicles: Motor vehicles: Immobilisation & removal: Prescribed conditions: Northern Ireland 437
Road traffic & vehicles: Motor vehicles: Removal, storage & disposal: Prescribed charges: Northern Ireland 438
Road traffic & vehicles: Motor vehicles: Taxi Drivers' licences: Fees: Amendments: Northern Ireland. 437
Road traffic & vehicles: Motor vehicles: Testing: Northern Ireland 437
Road traffic & vehicles: Motorways: Northern Ireland 436, 437
Road traffic & vehicles: Off-street parking: Northern Ireland. 438
Road traffic & vehicles: On-street parking: Northern Ireland. 438
Road traffic & vehicles: Passenger & goods vehicles: Recording equipment: Northern Ireland 415, 438
Road traffic & vehicles: Penalty charges: Criminal proceedings: Exemption: Northern Ireland 438
Road traffic & vehicles: Public service vehicles: Accessibility: Northern Ireland 438
Road traffic & vehicles: Public service vehicles: Conditions of fitness, equipment & use: Northern Ireland 438
Road traffic & vehicles: Public service vehicles: Fitness, equipment & use: Conditions: Northern Ireland 438
Road traffic & vehicles: Public service vehicles: Northern Ireland 438
Road traffic & vehicles: Taxis: Enniskillen: Bye-laws: Northern Ireland. 438
Road traffic & vehicles: Traffic Management 2005 Order: Commencements: Northern Ireland 438
Road traffic & vehicles: Traffic management: Adjudicators: Proceedings: Northern Ireland. 438
Road traffic & vehicles: Traffic management: Penalty charges: Exemption from criminal proceedings: Northern Ireland 438
Road traffic & vehicles: Traffic management: Penalty charges: Prescribed amounts: Northern Ireland 438
Road traffic & vehicles: Traffic signs: Northern Ireland 439
Road traffic: A404: Maidenhead Thicket to Handy Cross: Closure of Layby. 253
Road traffic: A80: Mollinsburn to Auchenkilns, prohibition of specified turns: Scotland 377

Road traffic: Bus lane contraventions: Approved local authorities 121, 122, 253
Road traffic: Community drivers' hours & working time: Road tankers 166
Road traffic: Conwy: Permitted parking area: Wales 255
Road traffic: Health services: Charges: Northern Ireland 437
Road traffic: M53: Bidston Moss viaduct 253
Road traffic: M6: Speed Limits: Toll 253
Road traffic: Motor cars: Driving instruction 166
Road traffic: Motor cycles: EC type approval 167
Road traffic: Motor vehicles: Driving licences 167
Road traffic: Motor vehicles: EC type approval 167
Road traffic: Motor vehicles: Goods vehicles: Type approval 168
Road traffic: Motor vehicles: Seat belts: Wearing of 167
Road traffic: Motor vehicles: Seat belts: Wearing of: Children 167
Road traffic: Motor vehicles: Tests 167
Road traffic: Motor vehicles: Type approval & approval marks: Fees 167
Road traffic: NHS charges: England & Wales 138, 255
Road traffic: NHS charges: Reviews & appeals: Amendments: England & Wales 138, 255
Road traffic: NHS charges: Scotland 367, 377
Road traffic: Passenger & goods vehicles: Recording equipment 168
Road traffic: Passenger & goods vehicles: Recording equipment: Fitting dates 168
Road traffic: Permitted & special parking areas: Aberdeen City Council: Scotland 377
Road traffic: Permitted & special parking areas: Bracknell Forest (Borough) 253
Road traffic: Permitted & special parking areas: Calderdale (Metropolitan Borough) 254
Road traffic: Permitted & special parking areas: City of Glasgow: Scotland 377
Road traffic: Permitted & special parking areas: Derby (City) 254
Road traffic: Permitted & special parking areas: Dundee City Council: Scotland 377
Road traffic: Permitted & special parking areas: Kingston upon Hull (City) 254
Road traffic: Permitted & special parking areas: Kirklees (Metropolitan Borough) 254
Road traffic: Permitted & special parking areas: Leicester (City) 254
Road traffic: Permitted & special parking areas: Perth & Kinross Council: Scotland 377
Road traffic: Permitted & special parking areas: Shropshire (County) 254
Road traffic: Permitted & special parking areas: South Lanarkshire Council: Scotland 377
Road traffic: Permitted & special parking areas: South Tyneside (Metropolitan Borough) 255
Road traffic: Permitted & special parking areas: Surrey (County): Tandridge (District) 254
Road traffic: Permitted & special parking areas: Surrey Heath (Borough) 254
Road traffic: Permitted & special parking areas: Warrington (Borough) 254
Road traffic: Permitted & special parking areas: Warwickshire (County): Rugby (Borough) 254
Road traffic: Permitted & special parking areas: Wiltshire (County): Kennet & North Wiltshire (Districts) 254
Road traffic: Permitted & special parking areas: Wolverhampton (City) 254
Road traffic: Quiet lanes & home zones: England 253
Road traffic: Road vehicles: Construction & use 168
Road traffic: Road vehicles: Registration & licensing: Amendments 168
Road traffic: School crossing patrol: England & Wales 255
Road traffic: Speed limits 169, 170
Road traffic: Speed limits: Scotland 377, 378, 379, 380
Road traffic: Speed limits: Wales 255, 256
Road traffic: Tractors: EC type-approval 168
Road traffic: Traffic regulation . . . . 170 - 255
Road traffic: Traffic regulation: Scotland 380, 381, 382, 383, 384, 385, 386
Road traffic: Traffic regulation: Wales 256, 257, 258, 259, 260, 261
Road traffic: Traffic signs: Amendments 168
Road traffic: Zebra, pelican & puffin pedestrian crossings: Northern Ireland 439
Road transport: Explosives: Carriage: Health & safety: Northern Ireland 421
Road vehicles: Construction & use 168
Road vehicles: Registration & licensing: Amendments 168
Roads & bridges: A8: East Hamilton St., Greenock: Scotland 375
Roads & bridges: A80/M73: Moodiesburn bypass, side roads: Scotland 376, 390
Roads & bridges: A80/M73: Moodiesburn bypass: Scotland 376, 390
Roads & bridges: A80/M80: Stepps to Moodiesburn, detrunking: Scotland 377
Roads & bridges: A80: Auchenkilns to Haggs, appropriation: Scotland 376
Roads & bridges: A80: Auchenkilns to Haggs, scheme: Scotland 376, 390
Roads & bridges: A80: Auchenkilns to Haggs, side roads: Scotland 376
Roads & bridges: A80: Mollinsburn to Auchenkilns, appropriation: Scotland 376
Roads & bridges: A80: Mollinsburn to Auchenkilns, side roads: Scotland 376
Roads & bridges: A830: Arisaig - Loch nan Uamh, side roads: Scotland 376

Roads & bridges: A830: Arisaig - Loch nan Uamh, variation: Scotland 376
Roads & bridges: Aonachan lay-by, Spean Bridge: Scotland 376
Roads & bridges: Balloch to Tarbet Cycle Routes: Scotland 376
Roads & bridges: Environmental impact assessment: Scotland 341, 354, 356, 359, 376, 391
Roads & bridges: Erskine Bridge: Tolls: Temporary suspension: Scotland. 376
Roads & bridges: M73/A80: Moodiesburn bypass, side roads: Scotland 376, 390
Roads & bridges: M73/A80: Moodiesburn bypass: Scotland 376, 390
Roads & bridges: M77: Fenwick to Malletsheugh & Glasgow Southern Orbital: Scotland 377, 391
Roads & bridges: M8/A8: Greenock Rd./Port Glasgow Rd. junction, Greenock: Scotland. 376
Roads & bridges: M8/A8: Rue End St./Dellington St. junction, Greenock: Scotland. 376
Roads & bridges: M80/M73: Mollinsburn to Auchenkilns: Scotland 377
Roads & bridges: M80: Stepps bypass, connecting roads: Scotland 377
Roads & bridges: M80: Stepps bypass, variation: Scotland 377
Roads & bridges: Scotland 375, 376
Roads traffic: Passenger & goods vehicles: Recording equipment: Tachograph cards 168
Roads: Street works: Reinstatement: Northern Ireland 437
Roads: User charging: Schemes: Keeping of accounts & relevant expenses: Scotland 392
Robert Gordon University: Academic awards & distinctions: Scotland. 350
Robert Gordon University: Establishment: Scotland 351
Robert Gordon University: Order of Council: Amendment: Scotland. 351
Robert Gordon University: Transfer & closure: Scotland 351
Romania: Social security. 269
Romania: Social security: Northern Ireland. 423, 435, 440
Royal Marines: Terms of service 57
Royal Navy: Ratings: Terms of service 57
Royalty payments: Exemptions: Income Tax (Trading & Other Income) Act 2005: Section 757 (2): Amendments. 110
Rugby (Borough): Warwickshire (County): Permitted & special parking areas 254
Rugby: Parishes: Local government 123
Rural affairs: Natural Environment & Rural Communities Act 2006: Commencements 13, 141, 261
Rural communities: Natural environment: Acts 7
Rural communities: Natural environment: Acts: Explanatory notes 10
Rural development programmes: Wales 18
Rwanda: International tribunals: United Nations 287

S

Sacred Heart RC Primary School: Religious character: Designation. 67
Saint Cecilia's, Wandsworth Church of England School: Religious character: Designation. 67
Salaries: Assembly Ombudsman & Commissioner for Complaints: Northern Ireland 439
Salaries: Comptroller & Auditor General: Salaries: Northern Ireland. 439
Salaries: Lands Tribunal: Northern Ireland 426
Salmon & freshwater fisheries: Assynt-Coigach area: Protection: Scotland 375
Salmon & freshwater fisheries: Conservation: Statistics: Collection: Scotland 375
Salmon & freshwater fisheries: Northern salmon fishery district: Designation: Scotland 375
Salmonella: Broiler flocks: Survey powers: Wales 24
Salmonella: Laying flocks: Survey powers: England. 21
Salmonella: Turkey flocks & slaughter pigs: Survey powers: England. 21
Salmonella: Turkey flocks & slaughter pigs: Survey powers: Northern Ireland. 408, 415
Sasines: Register: Methods of operation: Scotland 374
Savings banks: National Savings Bank 262
Savings income: Information: Reporting 29, 50, 114
Scallop dredges: Regulation: Scotland. 387
School crossing patrol: England & Wales. 255
School day & school year: Wales. 72
School inspection: Wales 72
School lunches: Nutritional standards: England 65
School performance & absence targets: Wales 72
School teachers: Pay & conditions 69
Schools: Admission: Children: Looked after: England 63
Schools: Chief Inspector: England 64
Schools: Disability discrimination: Codes of practice: Appointed days: Northern Ireland 412
Schools: Finance: England 67
Schools: Independent schools: Registration: Scotland. 351
Schools: Inspectors: England 64
Schools: Maintained schools: Change of category: England 64
Schools: Maintained schools: Staffing: Wales 73

Schools: New school: Admissions 73
Schools: Parental involvement: Acts: Explanatory notes: Scotland. 340
Schools: Parental involvement: Acts: Scotland 339
Schools: Performance information: England 65
Schools: Performance targets: England 65
Schools: Primary to secondary: Transition: Wales 73
Schools: Religious character: Designation: Independent schools: England 63
Schools: Secondary schools: New: Proposals. 65
Schools: Staffing: England 68
Schools: Teachers: Performance management: England 65
Science: National curriculum: Key stage 4: Disapplication: Wales. 72
Scotland Act 1998: Agency arrangements 43, 59, 87
Scotland Act 1998: Agency arrangements: Specifications 43, 58, 89, 131
Scotland Act 1998: River Tweed 44, 59, 166
Scotland Act 1998: Schedule 5: Modifications 43, 59
Scotland Act 1998: Transfer of functions to the Scottish Ministers etc. 44, 59
Scottish Borders: Electoral arrangements: Scotland 363
Scottish Charity Appeals Panel: Rules: Scotland 346
Scottish Charity Register: Transitional arrangements: Scotland. 346
Scottish Commission for Human Rights: Acts: Explanatory notes: Scotland 340
Scottish Commission for Human Rights: Acts: Scotland 339
Scottish Legal Complaints Commission: Public Appointments & Public Bodies etc. (Scotland) Act 2003: Treatment as specified
authority: Scotland 370
Scottish Parliament: Acts: Bound volumes 338
Scottish Parliament: Members: Interests: Acts: Explanatory notes: Scotland 340
Scottish Parliament: Members' interests: Acts: Scotland 339
Scottish Schools (Parental Involvement) Act 2006: Commencements: Scotland 351
Scottish statutory instruments: Annual volumes. 338
Scottish Water: Allt an Lagain: Scotland 394
Scottish Water: Loch Braigh Horrisdale: Scotland 394
Scottish Water: Tomich boreholes: Scotland 394
Scottish Water: Unapool Burn: Scotland 394
Sea fish: Fishing: Prohibited methods: Firth of Clyde: Scotland 387
Sea fisheries: Annual community & third country fishing measures: Enforcement: England 262
Sea fisheries: Community monitoring measures: Satellites: Enforcement: Wales 262
Sea fisheries: Community quota & third country fishing measures: Enforcement: Scotland 387
Sea fisheries: Days at sea: Restriction: Scotland. 387
Sea fisheries: Fish Auction Sites: Designation: Wales 262
Sea fisheries: Fish buyers & sellers: Registration: Wales 262
Sea fisheries: Fishing boats: Satellite-tracking devices: Wales 262
Sea fisheries: Fishing gear & beam trawls: Passive: Marking & identification: England 262
Sea fisheries: Inshore fishing: Cockles: Prohibition: Scotland. 386, 387
Sea fisheries: Lobsters: Goat Is.: Scotland. 387
Sea fisheries: Multiple trawls: Prohibition: Scotland 387
Sea fisheries: Northern hake stock: Scotland 387
Sea fisheries: Northern hake stock: Wales. 262
Sea fisheries: Scallop dredges: Regulation: Scotland 387
Sea fisheries: Solway Firth regulated fishery: Scotland 388
Sea fishing: Community monitoring measures: Satellites: Enforcement: Wales 262
Sea fishing: Days at sea: Restriction: Monitoring, inspection & surveillance. 262
Sea fishing: Days at sea: Restriction: Monitoring, inspection & surveillance: Northern Ireland 407
Sea fishing: Passive fishing gear & beam trawls: Marking & identification: Scotland 387
Secretary of State for Communities & Local Government 130
Secure training centres: Criminal Justice & Public Order Act 1994: Custody Officer Certificate: Suspension 263
Securitisation companies: Taxation 50
Security industry: Private Security Industry Act 2001: Approved contractor scheme 263
Security industry: Private Security Industry Act 2001: Aviation security: Exemption 263
Security industry: Private Security Industry Act 2001: Commencement 263
Security industry: Private Security Industry Act 2001: Commencements: Scotland 388
Security industry: Private Security Industry Act 2001: Designated activities 263
Security industry: Private Security Industry Act 2001: Licences 263
Security industry: Private Security Industry Act 2001: Licences: Duration 263
Security industry: Private Security Industry Act 2001: Schedule 2: Amendments 263
Security industry: Serious Organised Crime & Police Act 2005: Commencements: Scotland 388
Seed potatoes: Crop fees: Northern Ireland 439

Seed potatoes: England ... 264
Seed potatoes: Fees: England ... 264
Seed potatoes: Fees: Scotland ... 388
Seed potatoes: Fees: Wales ... 264
Seed potatoes: Tuber inspection fees: Northern Ireland ... 407
Seed potatoes: Wales ... 264
Seeds: Cereal & fodder plant seeds: England ... 264
Seeds: Cereal & fodder plant seeds: Scotland ... 388
Seeds: Cereal: Wales ... 264
Seeds: Fees: Scotland ... 388
Seeds: Fodder plants: Wales ... 264
Seeds: Forests: Reproductive material: Great Britain ... 264
Seeds: Registration, licensing & enforcement: Scotland ... 388
Seeds: Tests & trials: Amendments: England ... 264
Semiconductor topographies: Design right ... 58
Serious Organised Crime & Police Act 2005: Appeals under s. 74 ... 53, 54
Serious Organised Crime & Police Act 2005: Application & modification of certain enactments to designated staff ... 265
Serious Organised Crime & Police Act 2005: Application & modification of enactments: England & Wales ... 53
Serious Organised Crime & Police Act 2005: Commencements ... 53, 54, 155, 157, 265
Serious Organised Crime & Police Act 2005: Commencements: Scotland ... 349, 370, 388
Serious Organised Crime & Police Act 2005: Consequential & supplementary amendments ... 154, 265
Serious Organised Crime & Police Act 2005: Consequential & supplementary amendments: Scotland ... 370, 388
Serious Organised Crime & Police Act 2005: Financial reporting orders: Specified persons: Scotland ... 349
Serious Organised Crime & Police Act 2005: Section 43: Delegation ... 265
Serious Organised Crime Agency: Deputy Director: Prescribed grade ... 265
Serious Organised Crime Agency: Serious Organised Crime & Police Act 2005: Commencements ... 53, 54, 155, 265
Serious Organised Crime Agency: Serious Organised Crime & Police Act 2005: Consequential & supplementary amendments . 154, 265
Service provision change: Employment protection: Northern Ireland ... 413
Service voters: Registration period ... 163
Severance payments: Local Governance (Scotland) Act 2004: Scotland ... 362
Severn Bridges: Tolls ... 101
Severn-Trent Regional Flood Defence Committee ... 119
Sewerage & water services: Licences: Scotland ... 393
Sewerage nuisance: Code of practice: Scotland ... 393
Sewerage: Charges: Exemptions & reductions: Scotland ... 395
Sewerage: Services cost: Scotland ... 394
Sewerage: Water & sewerage services: Northern Ireland ... 144
Sex Discrimination Act 1975: Public authorities: Statutory duties ... 265
Sex discrimination: Acts ... 6
Sex discrimination: Acts: Explanatory notes ... 10
Sexual orientation discrimination: Equality: Northern Ireland ... 439
Sheep & goats: Records, identification & movement: Wales ... 24, 25
Sheep & goats: Transmissible spongiform encephalopathies: Compensation: Wales ... 25
Sheep: Identification & traceability: Scotland ... 344
Sheep: Radioactivity: Food protection: Scotland ... 373
Sheep: Records, identification & movement: England ... 21
Sheep: Records, identification & movement: Northern Ireland ... 407
Shellfish: Solway Firth: Regulated fishery: Scotland ... 388
Sheriff Court: Caveat Rules: Act of Sederunt: Scotland ... 390
Sheriff Court: Criminal procedure: Rules: Amendments: Act of Adjournal: Scotland ... 350, 357, 389
Sheriff Court: Criminal procedure: Rules: Financial reporting orders: Act of Adjournal: Scotland ... 357, 388
Sheriff Court: Criminal procedure: Rules: Vulnerable Witnesses (Scotland) Act 2004: Act of Adjournal: Scotland ... 357, 389
Sheriff Court: Chancery procedure: Rules: Act of Sederunt: Scotland ... 389
Sheriff Court: Child care & maintenance rules: Act of Sederunt: Scotland ... 389
Sheriff Court: Child care & maintenance rules: Vulnerable Witnesses (Scotland) Act 2004: Act of Sederunt: Scotland ... 389
Sheriff Court: Companies: Insolvency rules: Act of Sederunt: Scotland ... 390
Sheriff Court: Matrimonial & parental responsibility matters: Jurisdiction, recognition & enforcement of judgments: Act of Sederunt: Scotland ... 389
Sheriff Court: Ordinary cause & summary application rules: Act of Sederunt: Scotland ... 389
Sheriff Court: Ordinary cause rules: Causes relating to articles 81 & 82 of the Treaty Establishing the European Community: Act of Sederunt: Scotland ... 389
Sheriff Court: Ordinary cause rules: Family Law (Scotland) Act 2006: Act of Sederunt: Scotland ... 389
Sheriff Court: Ordinary cause, summary application, summary cause & small claim rules: Amendments: Act of Sederunt: Scotland . 389
Sheriff Court: Part-time sheriffs: Maximum number: Scotland ... 390
Sheriff Court: Sheriff officers: Fees: Act of Sederunt: Scotland ... 389
Sheriff Court: Shorthand writers: Fees: Act of Sederunt: Scotland ... 389

Sheriff Court: Solicitor's fees: Act of Sederunt: Scotland 389
Sheriff Court: Summary applications, statutory applications & appeals: Rules: Act of Sederunt: Scotland 390
Sheriff Court: Vulnerable Witnesses (Scotland) Act 2004: Commencements: Scotland 357, 390
Shetland Islands: Electoral arrangements: Scotland 363
Shetland Transport Partnership: Transfer of functions: Scotland 392
Shipping: Merchant shipping: Fees 129
Shipping: Merchant: Pollution: Acts 7
Shipping: Merchant: Pollution: Acts: Explanatory notes 10
Ships: Air pollution: Prevention 127
Shire Oak CofE Primary School: Religious character: Designation 68
Shorthand writers: Fees: Court of Session: Act of Sederunt: Scotland 347
Shorthand writers: Fees: Sheriff Court: Act of Sederunt: Scotland 389
Shropshire (County): Permitted & special parking areas 254
Shropshire: North Shropshire (District): Electoral changes 122
Sight testing: Examination & prescription: Scotland 367
Single European sky: National supervisory authority: Functions 40
Skin piercing: Licensing: Scotland 360, 370, 371
Sloane Square House: Transport for London 121, 283
Small businesses: Non-domestic rating: Rate relief: England 161
Smoke control areas: Authorised fuels: England 40
Smoke control areas: Authorised fuels: Wales 40
Smoke control areas: Exempted fireplaces: England 40
Smoke control areas: Exempted fireplaces: Wales 40
Smoke free premises & enforcement 159
Smoking, Health & Social Care (Scotland) Act 2005: Commencements: Scotland 367, 371
Smoking, Health & Social Care (Scotland) Act 2005: Consequential amendments 44, 59, 138
Smoking, Health & Social Care (Scotland) Act 2005: Consequential amendments: Scotland 371
Smoking, Health & Social Care (Scotland) Act 2005: Prohibition of Smoking in Certain Premises (Scotland) Regulations 2006:
Consequential provisions 44, 59, 94
Smoking: Northern Ireland 144
Smoking: Prohibition: Enclosed premises: Scotland 371
Smoking: Public places: Health: Acts 6
Smoking: Public places: Health: Acts: Explanatory notes 10
Smoking: Smoke free premises & enforcement 159
Social care: Adoption agencies, adoption support agencies & local authority fostering functions: Inspection: Fees 31, 265
Social care: Adoption: Independent Review of Determinations: Wales 32, 266
Social care: Appointments Commission 131, 159, 265
Social care: Care services: Fees: Abolition: Wales 31, 159, 266
Social care: Care Standards Act 2000 & Children Act 1989: Regulatory reform & complaints: Wales 31, 266
Social care: Care Standards Act 2000: Establishments & agencies 265
Social care: Children & young persons: Secure accommodation: Wales 266
Social care: Commission for Social Care Inspection: Fees & frequency of inspections 30, 265
Social care: Fostering services: Private arrangements: Wales 32, 266
Social care: Health Act 2006: Commencements 97, 136, 159, 266
Social care: Local authority social services: Complaints: England 265
Social care: Regulation of Care (Scotland) Act 2001: Commencements: Scotland 390
Social care: Regulation: Applications & provision of advice: Scotland 390
Social care: Regulation: Fees: Scotland 390
Social care: Regulation: Requirements as to care services: Scotland 390
Social care: Social service workers: Scotland 390
Social care: Social work: Inspections: Scotland 390
Social Fund: Applications for review 269
Social Fund: Applications for review: Northern Ireland 439
Social Fund: Cold weather payments 269
Social housing: Grants to bodies other than registered social landlords: Additional purposes: England 104
Social landlords: Caravans: Definitions: England 279
Social landlords: Permissible additional purposes: England 104
Social landlords: Registered: Purposes or objects: Scotland 357
Social Security Act 1998: Commencements 269
Social Security Act 1998: Commencements: Amendments 269
Social Security Act 1998: Prescribed benefits 269
Social security: Electronic communications: Northern Ireland 440
Social security: 1998 Order: Commencement: Northern Ireland 439, 440
Social security: 1998 Order: Prescribed benefits: Northern Ireland 440
Social security: Adult learning option 269

Social security: Amendments... 271, 272
Social security: Amendments: Northern Ireland 423, 424, 436, 441, 442
Social security: Benefits up-rating.. 269
Social security: Benefits up-rating: Northern Ireland 413, 423, 435, 440, 443
Social security: Benefits up-rating: Terms & conditions of employment 269, 278
Social security: Bulgaria & Romania 269
Social security: Bulgaria & Romania: Northern Ireland 423, 435, 440
Social security: Categorisation of earners 269
Social security: Categorisation of earners: Northern Ireland 273
Social security: Child benefit & guardian's allowance 266
Social security: Child benefit: General 267
Social security: Child benefit: Rates.. 267
Social security: Children & young persons: Amendments: Northern Ireland. 424, 436, 442
Social security: Claims & payments 270
Social security: Claims & payments: Northern Ireland 440
Social security: Class 1 contributions, rebates & minimum contributions: Reduced rates ... 150
Social security: Contributions 270
Social security: Contributions: Re-rating & national insurance funds payments 270
Social security: Council benefit: Amendments 268
Social security: Council tax benefit.. 267, 268
Social security: Council tax benefit: State pension credit: Qualifying age 267
Social security: Earnings factors: Revaluation.. 272
Social security: Earnings factors: Revaluation: Northern Ireland 442
Social security: Employment programme: Preparation: Northern Ireland. 442
Social security: Employment zones 267
Social security: Employment zones: Allocation to contractors: Pilot 267
Social security: FAS payments: Consequential amendments 272
Social security: Graduated retirement benefit: Consequential provisions 270
Social security: Guardian's allowance: General 267
Social security: Guardian's allowance: Up-rating 267, 268
Social security: Guardian's allowance: Up-rating: Northern Ireland 273
Social security: Housing benefit... 268
Social security: Housing benefit & council tax benefit 268
Social security: Housing benefit: Amendments 268
Social security: Housing benefit: Consequential provisions: Northern Ireland....... 422, 434, 439
Social security: Housing benefit: State pension credit: Qualifying age ... 268
Social security: Incapacity benefit: Work-focused interviews 270, 271
Social security: Incapacity benefit: Work-focused interviews: Northern Ireland 440
Social security: Incapacity for work 271
Social security: Incapacity for work: Northern Ireland 441
Social security: Income support: Northern Ireland 441
Social security: Income-related benefits: Subsidy to authorities 268
Social security: Income support 271
Social security: Industrial injuries: Dependency: Permitted earnings limits 271
Social security: Industrial injuries: Dependency: Permitted earnings limits: Northern Ireland ... 441
Social security: Industrial injuries: Prescribed diseases 271
Social security: Industrial injuries: Prescribed diseases: Northern Ireland 441
Social security: Jobseeker's allowance 271
Social security: Jobseeker's allowance: Northern Ireland 441
Social security: Lebanon.. 271
Social security: Lebanon: Northern Ireland.. 423, 435, 441
Social security: Maternity allowance & overlapping benefits: Northern Ireland 443
Social security: National Insurance numbers 272
Social security: National Insurance numbers: Northern Ireland.............. 442
Social security: Northern Ireland Act 1998: Modifications 143, 268
Social security: Pensions Act 2004: PPF payments: FAS payments....... 150, 269
Social security: Pensions: 2004 Act & 2005 Order: PPF payments & FAS payments: Northern Ireland ... 430, 439
Social security: Pensions: Low earnings threshold 272
Social security: Pensions: Low earnings threshold: Northern Ireland..... 442
Social security: Persons from abroad 272
Social security: Persons from abroad: Northern Ireland 424, 436, 442
Social security: Pneumoconiosis: Byssinosis: Miscellaneous disease benefit......... 269
Social security: PPF payments & FAS payments: Consequential amendments: Northern Ireland ... 442
Social security: PPF payments: Consequential amendments 272
Social security: Provisions relating to Qualifying Young Persons 272
Social security: Retirement pensions: Deferral 270

Social security: Retirement pensions: Deferral: Northern Ireland.. 440
Social security: Retirement pensions: Deferral: Shared additional pension & graduated retirement benefit: Northern Ireland .. 423, 435, 440
Social security: Social Fund: Applications for review... 269
Social security: Social Fund: Applications for review: Northern Ireland.. 439
Social security: Social Fund: Cold weather payments.. 269
Social security: Statutory maternity pay, maternity allowance & overlapping benefits.................................. 273, 278
Social security: Statutory sick pay: General.. 273, 278
Social security: Students & income-related benefits.. 272
Social security: Students & income-related benefits: Northern Ireland... 424, 436, 442
Social security: Tax credits: Claims & notifications... 276
Social security: Workers' compensation: Pneumoconiosis etc.: Claims: Payment.. 269
Social security: Workers' compensation: Pneumoconiosis etc.: Claims: Payment: Northern Ireland........................ 439
Social security: Workers' compensation: Supplementation.. 273
Social security: Workers' compensation: Supplementation: Northern Ireland.. 443
Social security: Working neighbourhoods.. 273
Social security: Young persons... 273
Social security: Young persons: Provisions relating to qualifying: Northern Ireland.................................. 442
Social services: Local authorities: Complaints: England.. 265
Social work services: Inspection: Acts: Explanatory notes: Scotland.. 340
Social work services: Inspection: Acts: Scotland... 339
Social work: Inspections: Scotland... 390
Solihull: National Health Service primary care trust... 135
Solway Firth: Regulated fishery: Scotland.. 388
Somerset: Devon & Somerset Fire & Rescue Authority: Combination scheme... 87
South Ayrshire: Electoral arrangements: Scotland... 363
South Central Ambulance Service: National Health Service Trust... 135
South East Coast Ambulance Service: National Health Service Trust.. 135
South Eastern Health & Social Services Trust: Establishment: Northern Ireland.. 420
South Humberside: Doncaster & South Humberside Healthcare: National Health Service Trust............................. 132
South Lanarkshire Council: Road traffic: Permitted & special parking area: Scotland.................................. 377
South Larnarkshire: Electoral arrangements: Scotland... 363
South Northamptonshire (District): Electoral changes... 122
South of Tyne & Wearside Mental Health: National Health Service Trust.. 135
South Tyneside (Metropolitan Borough: Permitted & special parking areas.. 255
South Western Ambulance Service: National Health Service Trust... 135
Southern Health & Social Services Trust: Establishment: Northern Ireland... 420
Southern Water Services: Kent Medway, Kent Thanet & Sussex Hastings: Water: Non-essential use: Drought order......... 289
Southern Water Services: Sussex North & Sussex Coast: Water: Non-essential use: Drought order........................ 289
South-West of Scotland Transport Partnership: Transfer of functions to: Scotland..................................... 393
Special educational needs: Further & higher education: Disabled persons: Northern Ireland............................ 411
Special health authorities: Abolition.. 138
Special health authorities: Audit.. 93
Special health authorities: Health Service Commissioner for England.. 137
Special roads: A80/M73: Moodiesburn bypass, side roads: Scotland.. 376, 390
Special roads: A80/M73: Moodiesburn bypass: Scotland.. 376, 390
Special roads: A80: Auchenkilns to Haggs, appropriation: Scotland.. 376
Special roads: A80: Auchenkilns to Haggs, scheme: Scotland... 376, 390
Special roads: A80: Mollinsburn to Auchenkilns, appropriation: Scotland.. 376
Special roads: Edgware Bury-Aldenham special roads scheme: Variation... 101
Special roads: M73/A80: Moodiesburn bypass, side roads: Scotland.. 376, 390
Special roads: M73/A80: Moodiesburn bypass: Scotland.. 376, 390
Special roads: M77: Fenwick to Malletsheugh & Glasgow Southern Orbital: Scotland................................. 377, 391
Special roads: M80/M73: Mollinsburn to Auchenkilns: Scotland... 377
Special roads: M80: Stepps bypass, connecting roads: Scotland.. 377
Special roads: M80: Stepps bypass, variation: Scotland... 377
Spirits: Excise.. 83
Sport: Olympic & paralympic games: London: Acts.. 7
Sport: Olympic & paralympic games: London: Acts: Explanatory notes... 10
Sports grounds & sporting events: Football Spectators: 2006 World Cup: Control period................................ 274
Sports grounds & sporting events: Football spectators: Seating... 274
Sports grounds & sporting events: Football: Spectators: Prescription: England & Wales................................ 274
Sports grounds & sporting events: London Olympic Games & Paralympic Games Act 2006: Commencements: Scotland 367, 391
Sports grounds & sporting events: Sports grounds: Safety: Designation.. 274
Sports grounds: Safety: Designation.. 274

Sports grounds: Safety: Northern Ireland 144
St Anne's RC Primary School: Religious character: Designation 68
St Benedict's Catholic Primary School: Religious character: Designation 68
St Georges VA Church Primary School: Religious character: Designation 68
St John the Baptist Roman Catholic Primary School: Religious character: Designation. 68
St Mary's Music School: Aided places: Scotland 351
St Peter's Church of England Junior & Infant School: Religious character: Designation 68
St Teresa of Lisieux Catholic Infant School: Religious character: Designation 68
Stamp duty & stamp duty reserve tax: Definition of unit trust scheme & open-ended investment company 274, 275
Stamp duty & stamp duty reserve tax: Extension of exceptions relating to recognised exchanges 274, 275
Stamp duty land tax: Administration. 274
Stamp duty land tax: Electronic communications 274
Stamp duty land tax: Finance Act 2003: Amendment 274, 275, 276
Stamp duty land tax: Pension Protection Fund 29, 49, 111, 115, 274
Standards Committees: Wales 125
Standards in Scotland's Schools etc. Act 2000: Commencements: Scotland 351
Standing Civilian courts: Evidence: Rules 57
Statistics of trade: Customs & excise 275
Statutes: Chronological tables. 12
Statutes: Northern Ireland 404
Statutes: Northern Ireland: Title page, index & tables. 404
Statutory instruments: Annual volumes. 12
Statutory instruments: National Assembly for Wales: Annual volumes 12
Statutory instruments: Transfer of functions. 130
Statutory maternity pay: Northern Ireland 443
Statutory maternity pay: Social security: Benefits up-rating: Northern Ireland 413, 423, 435, 440, 443
Statutory maternity, paternity & adoption pay. 278
Statutory nuisances: Artificial lighting: Relevant sports: Designations. 80
Statutory paternity & adoption pay: Northern Ireland 414
Statutory rules (Northern Ireland): Annual volumes. 404
Statutory rules (Northern Ireland): Chronological tables 404
Statutory sick pay: General 273, 278
Statutory sick pay: Northern Ireland 443
Statutory sick pay: Social security: Benefits up-rating: Northern Ireland 413, 423, 435, 440, 443
Stirling: Electoral arrangements: Scotland. 363
Stockton-on-Tees Borough Council: North Shore development: North Shore footbridge scheme 101
Stormont Estate: Northern Ireland 144
Strategic health authorities & primary care trusts: Functions: National Health Service. 134
Strategic health authorities: Dental services: Functions 132
Strategic health authorities: Establishment & abolition 136
Strategic Rail Authority: Abolition 284
Stratford International Extension: Docklands Light Railway 284, 285
Stratford-on-Avon: Parishes: Local government 123
Strathclyde Passenger Transport Area: Variation: Scotland. 392
Strathclyde Passenger Transport Authority & Executive: Functions: Transfer: West of Scotland Transport Partnership: Scotland . . . 392
Strathclyde Passenger Transport Authority & Executive: Property rights & liabilities: Transfer: West of Scotland Transport Partnership: Scotland 393
Street works: Inspection fees: Wales. 101
Street works: Reinstatement: Northern Ireland 437
Street works: Reinstatement: Wales 102
Structural Funds: National Assembly for Wales 83
Student accommodation: Codes of management practice: Approval 103
Student accommodation: Codes of management practice: Approval: Wales 104
Student fees: Amounts: England 68
Student fees: Amounts: Northern Ireland 412
Student fees: Inflation index. 68
Student fees: Qualifying courses & persons. 68
Student fees: Qualifying courses & persons: Northern Ireland 412
Student fees: Specification: Scotland 351
Student loans: Education: Scotland 350
Student loans: England & Wales 70
Student loans: Northern Ireland 412
Student loans: Repayment. 70
Student loans: Repayments: Northern Ireland 412
Student loans: Tuition fees: Repayment & allowances: Scotland 350
Student loans: Tuition fees: Scotland 350

Student support 66
Student support: Cross-border eligibility: Further education: Northern Ireland. 412
Student support: Education: Northern Ireland 412
Student support: England & Wales 70
Student support: England, Wales & Northern Ireland 70
Student support: European institutions 66
Student support: European Institutions 66
Student support: Information: Governing bodies: Northern Ireland. 412
Student support: Information: Supply to governing bodies 62
Student support: Information: Supply to governing bodies: Wales 73
Student support: Northern Ireland 412
Students: Awards: Northern Ireland 412
Students: Income-related benefits 272
Students: Income-related benefits: Northern Ireland 424, 436, 442
Students: Support: Northern Ireland 412
Sudan: United Nations: Measures 287
Suffolk: Coroners' districts 47
Summary application rules: Sheriff Court: Act of Sederunt: Scotland 389
Summary proceedings: Cash: Recovery of: Minimum amount: Proceeds of Crime Act 2002 157
Superannuation Act 1972: Admission to Schedule 1 150
Superannuation scheme & additional voluntary contributions: National Health Service: Scotland. 366
Superannuation: Agri-food & Biosciences Institute: Northern Ireland 431
Superannuation: Chief Electoral Officer for Northern Ireland: Northern Ireland 431
Superannuation: Health & personal social services: Northern Ireland 419
Superannuation: Lands Tribunal: Northern Ireland 426
Superannuation: Teachers: Northern Ireland 412, 413
Superannuation: Teachers: Scotland 367, 368
Supreme Court of England & Wales: Civil Procedure Act 1997: Amendment: England & Wales 51, 275
Supreme Court of England & Wales: Civil procedure: Rules 51, 52, 275
Supreme Court of England & Wales: Civil proceedings: Fees 52, 275
Supreme Court of England & Wales: Constitutional Reform Act 2005: Commencements 275
Supreme Court of England & Wales: Constitutional Reform Act 2005: Temporary modifications 275
Supreme Court of England & Wales: Courts Act 2003: Consequential amendment. 52, 126, 275
Supreme Court of England & Wales: Criminal procedure: Rules 126, 276
Supreme Court of England & Wales: Criminal procedure: Rules: Amendments 126, 276
Supreme Court of England & Wales: Family proceedings 52, 85, 276
Supreme Court of England & Wales: Family proceedings: Fees 52, 85, 276
Supreme Court of England & Wales: Family proceedings: Rules. 52, 85, 276
Supreme Court, Northern Ireland: Criminal appeals: Jury trials: Northern Ireland 443
Supreme Court, Northern Ireland: Criminal appeals: Prosecution appeals: Northern Ireland. 443
Supreme Court, Northern Ireland: Criminal appeals: Serious offences: Retrial: Northern Ireland 443
Supreme Court, Northern Ireland: Family proceedings: Rules: Northern Ireland 410, 416, 443
Supreme Court, Northern Ireland: Procedure: Crown Court: Rules: Amendments: Northern Ireland 444
Supreme Court, Northern Ireland: Rules: Northern Ireland 443, 444
Surrey & Borders Partnership: National Health Service Trust: Originating Capital 136
Surrey (County): Tandridge (District): Permitted & special parking areas 254
Surrey Heath (Borough): Permitted & special parking areas 254
Surveillance: Directed surveillance & covert human intelligence sources: Regulation 118
Sussex North & Sussex Coast: Water: Southern Water Services: Non-essential use: Drought order 289
Sussex Partnership: National Health Service Trust 136
Sussex: East Sussex County Healthcare: National Health Service Trust 136
Sussex: West Sussex Health & Social Care: National Health Service Trust 136
Sustainable & Secure Buildings Act 2004: Commencement 28
Sustainable development: Northern Ireland (Miscellaneous Provisions) Act 2006: Commencements 54, 276
Sustainable energy: Climate change: Acts 4
Sustainable energy: Climate change: Acts: Explanatory notes 9
Sutton & East Surrey Water plc: Non-essential use: Drought order 289
Syria: United Nations: Measures. 287
Syria: United Nations: Measures: Channel Islands 286
Syria: United Nations: Measures: Isle of Man 286

T

Tachograph cards: Passenger & goods vehicles 168
Tachographs: Digital: Passenger & goods vehicles: Fitting dates 168

Takeover bids: Directives: Implementation 42
Taliban & Al-Qaida: United Nations: Measures. 286
Tandridge (District): Surrey (County): Permitted & special parking areas 254
Tandridge: Parishes: Local government 123
Tattooing: Licensing: Scotland 360, 370, 371
Tauheedul Islam Girls High School: Religious character: Designation. 68
Tax Credits Act 2002: Commencements & transitional provisions 276
Tax credits: Amendments 276
Tax credits: Child care providers: Approval: Northern Ireland 444
Tax credits: Child tax credits. 276
Tax credits: Claims & notifications 276
Tax credits: Up-rating 276
Tax exempt schemes: Pensions: Amendments: Northern Ireland 430
Taxes *see also* Capital gains tax
Taxes *see also* Income tax
Taxes *see also* Value added tax
Taxes: Armed Forces & Reserve Forces: Compensation schemes: Excluded benefits 109
Taxes: Authorised investment funds. 28, 47, 109
Taxes: Avoidance schemes: Arrangements: Prescribed descriptions 29, 50, 114
Taxes: Avoidance schemes: Information 29, 50, 114
Taxes: Capital allowances: Energy-saving plant & machinery 47, 109
Taxes: Capital allowances: Environmentally beneficial plant & machinery 47, 109
Taxes: Chargeable gains: Gilt-edged securities. 29, 50
Taxes: Corporation tax: Insurance companies: Amendments. 48
Taxes: Corporation tax: Lloyd's underwriters: Double taxation relief: Corporate members 49
Taxes: Double taxation: Relief: Botswana. 29, 47, 110
Taxes: Double taxation: Relief: Japan 29, 47, 110
Taxes: Double taxation: Relief: Poland 29, 47, 110
Taxes: Energy-saving items 110
Taxes: Finance Act 2002: Schedule 26, parts 2 & 9 48
Taxes: Finance Act 2006: Section 18: Appointed day. 288
Taxes: Finance Act 2006: Section 53 (1): Films & sound recordings: Appointed day 48, 110
Taxes: Finance Act 2006: Section 53 (2): Films & sound recordings: Power to alter dates. 48, 110
Taxes: Gilt-edged securities. 29, 50
Taxes: Individual savings accounts 111
Taxes: Inheritance tax: Accounts: Delivery: Excepted estates 115
Taxes: Insurance companies: Corporation tax acts: Amendments 48
Taxes: Insurance premium tax 116
Taxes: Investment trusts & venture capital trusts: Definition of capital profits, gains or losses 48
Taxes: Landfill tax 119
Taxes: Lloyd's sourcebook: Finance Act 1993 & Finance Act 1994: Amendment 48
Taxes: Lloyd's Underwriters: Limited liability underwriting: Conversion to 48, 111
Taxes: Lloyd's Underwriters: Scottish Limited Partnerships 49, 111
Taxes: Loan relationships & derivative contracts: Accounting practice: Change 49
Taxes: Loan relationships & derivative contracts: Disregard & bringing into account of profits & losses 49
Taxes: Loan relationships & derivative contracts: Profits & losses: Disregard & bringing into account 49
Taxes: Mutual assistance provisions 84, 116, 162, 276
Taxes: Non-resident insurance companies: Overseas losses: Group relief: Corporation Tax Acts: Modification 48
Taxes: Oil: Market value. 49, 152
Taxes: Partnerships: Contributions to a trade: Restrictions 111
Taxes: Pension Protection Fund. 29, 49, 111, 115, 274
Taxes: Pension schemes 114
Taxes: Pension schemes: Application of UK provisions to relevant non-UK schemes 112
Taxes: Pension schemes: Consequential amendments. 277
Taxes: Pension schemes: Investment-regulated: Exception of tangible moveable property 111
Taxes: Pension schemes: Registered: Extension of Migrant Member Relief 113
Taxes: Pension schemes: Registered: Provision of information 113
Taxes: Pension schemes: Taxable property provisions 112
Taxes: Pension schemes: Transitional provisions 114
Taxes: Petroleum revenue tax: Blended crude oil: Attribution 152
Taxes: Petroleum revenue tax: Disposals & appropriations: Nomination scheme 49, 152
Taxes: Savings income: Information: Reporting. 29, 50, 114
Taxes: Stamp duty & stamp duty reserve tax: Definition of unit trust scheme & open-ended investment company 274, 275
Taxes: Stamp duty land tax: Administration. 274
Taxes: Stamp duty land tax: Finance Act 2003: Amendment. 274, 275, 276
Taxes: Stamp duty land tax: Finance Act 2003: Amendments 275

Taxes: Tax credits: Claims & notifications 276
Taxes: Tax information exchange agreements: Gibraltar 114
Taxes: Tonnage tax: Financial year 2006: Exception 50
Taxes: Tonnage tax: Training requirements 277
Taxes: Unit trust schemes & offshore funds: Non-qualifying investments test 50, 114
Taximeters: Measuring instruments: Weights & measures 292
Taxis: Carriage of guide dogs, etc.: Disability Discrimination Act 1995: England & Wales 61, 286
Taxis: Enniskillen: Bye-laws: Northern Ireland 438
TB *see* Tuberculosis
Teachers: Eligibility: Northern Ireland 412
Teachers: General Teaching Council for Scotland: Legal assessor: Rules: Scotland 351
Teachers: Pensions: Reform amendments 70
Teachers: Performance management: Schools: England 65
Teachers: Redundancy & premature retirement: Compensation 70
Teachers: Superannuation: Northern Ireland 412, 413
Teachers: Superannuation: Scotland 367, 368
Teachers' pensions: Amendments 70
Technical assistance: Control: Customs 55
Tees & North East Yorkshire: National Health Service Trust 136
Tees, Esk & Wear Valleys: National Health Service Trust 136
Telecommunications & canals: Non-domestic rating: Scotland 374
Telegraphy: Wireless: Consolidation: Acts 9
Television: Licensable content services 28, 75
Tenancies: Introductory: Review of decisions to extend a trial period: England 103
Tenancies: Private: 2006 Order: Commencements: Northern Ireland 426
Terms & conditions of employment: Adoption & Children Act 2002: Statutory adoption pay: Consequential amendment 277
Terms & conditions of employment: Agricultural wages: Permits: Infirm & incapacitated persons: Abolition: Northern Ireland . 405, 444
Terms & conditions of employment: Collective redundancies 277
Terms & conditions of employment: Employees: Information & consultation 277
Terms & conditions of employment: Employment protection: Transfer of undertakings 278
Terms & conditions of employment: Employment rights: Limits: Increase 277
Terms & conditions of employment: European Cooperative Society: Employees: Involvement 277
Terms & conditions of employment: Flexible working: Eligibility, complaints & remedies 277
Terms & conditions of employment: Maternity, parental, paternity & adoption leave 277
Terms & conditions of employment: National minimum wage 277
Terms & conditions of employment: Occupational & personal pension schemes: Amendments 147, 278
Terms & conditions of employment: Occupational & personal pension schemes: Amendments: Northern Ireland 429, 444
Terms & conditions of employment: Occupational & personal pension schemes: Consultation by employers & amendments . . 147, 278
Terms & conditions of employment: Occupational & personal pension schemes: Consultation by employers: Northern Ireland . 429, 444
Terms & conditions of employment: Statutory maternity pay, maternity allowance & overlapping benefits 273, 278
Terms & conditions of employment: Statutory maternity, paternity & adoption pay 278
Terms & conditions of employment: Statutory sick pay: General 273, 278
Terms & conditions of employment: Transfer of undertakings: Protection of employment 278
Terms & conditions of employment: Work & Families Act 2006: Commencements 273, 278
Terms & conditions of employment: Working time 278, 279
Terrorism Act 2000: Proscribed organisations 157
Terrorism Act 2000: Proscribed organisations: Name changes 156
Terrorism Act 2000: Regulated sector: Business 156
Terrorism Act 2000: Revised Code of Practice for the Identification of Persons by Police Officers: Northern Ireland 144, 157
Terrorism Act 2006: Commencements 157
Terrorism: Acts 8
Terrorism: Acts: Explanatory notes 11
Terrorism: Northern Ireland: Acts 9
Terrorism: Northern Ireland: Acts: Explanatory notes 11
Terrorism: Prevention of Terrorism Act 2005: Continuance in force of sections 1 to 9 156
Terrorism: Proscribed organisations: Deproscription: Applications 156
Terrorism: United Nations: Measures 287
Textile products: Composition: Determination 282
Textile products: Fibre content: Indications: Textile names & allowances 282
Thameslink 2000: Network Rail: England 284, 285
Third countries: Legacies imported from: Relief: Application 55, 84, 288
Tir Cynnal: Wales 18
Tir Gofal: Wales 18
Title Conditions (Scotland) Act 2003: Conservation bodies: Amendments: Scotland 391
Title Conditions (Scotland) Act 2003: Conservation bodies: Scotland 391

Title Conditions (Scotland) Act 2003: Rural housing bodies: Amendments: Scotland 391
Tobacco Advertising & Promotion Act 2002: Amendments 45, 75
Tobacco Advertising & Promotion Act 2002: Commencements 46
Tobacco Advertising & Promotion Act 2002: Commencements: Scotland 347
Tobacco products: Duty 84
Tobacco products: Duty: Evasion: Finance Act 2006: Appointed day 84
Tobacco products: Excise 84
Tolls: Severn Bridges 101
Tomich boreholes: Scottish Water: Scotland 394
Tonnage tax: Financial year 2006: Exception 50
Tonnage tax: Training requirements 277
Torbay: Parishes: Local government 123
Tort liability: National Health Service: Redress: Acts 7
Tort liability: National Health Service: Redress: Acts: Explanatory notes 10
Totalisers: Automatic discontinuous: Weights & measures 290
Tourism: Boards: Acts: Explanatory notes: Scotland 340
Tourism: Boards: Acts: Scotland 339
Town & country planning: Acts: Explanatory notes: Scotland 340
Town & country planning: Acts: Scotland 339
Town & country planning: Application to the Houses of Parliament 279
Town & country planning: Applications & deemed applications: Fees 280
Town & country planning: Applications & deemed applications: Fees: Wales 281
Town & country planning: Appointed persons: Determination of appeals: Prescribed classes: England 280
Town & country planning: Caravans Definitions: England 279
Town & country planning: Conygar Quarry: Mineral planning permissions: Periodic review 279
Town & country planning: Crown land: Miscellaneous amendments & modifications: Wales 282
Town & country planning: Environmental impact assessment 279
Town & country planning: Environmental impact assessment: Scotland 341, 354, 356, 359, 376, 391
Town & country planning: Environmental impact assessment: Wales 281
Town & country planning: General development procedure 280
Town & country planning: General development procedure: Wales 282
Town & country planning: General permitted development: England 280
Town & country planning: General permitted development: Wales 282
Town & country planning: Independent examinations: Costs: Standard daily amount: England 279, 286
Town & country planning: Listed buildings & buildings in conservation areas: Scotland 392
Town & country planning: Listed buildings & conservation areas: Wales 281
Town & country planning: Listed buildings, conservation areas & hazardous substances: Crown land: Amendments: Wales 281
Town & country planning: Listed buildings, conservation areas & hazardous substances: England 279
Town & country planning: National security directions & appointed representatives: England 279
Town & country planning: National security directions & appointed representatives: Northern Ireland 432
Town & country planning: National security directions & appointed representatives: Scotland 392
Town & country planning: National security directions & appointed representatives: Wales 281
Town & country planning: Planning & Compulsory Purchase Act 2004: Commencements 279, 281
Town & country planning: Planning & Compulsory Purchase Act 2004: Commencements: Scotland 391
Town & country planning: Planning & Compulsory Purchase Act 2004: Commencements: Wales 280
Town & country planning: Planning & Compulsory Purchase Act 2004: Transitional provisions: Scotland 391
Town & country planning: Planning permission, listed buildings & conservation areas: Applications 279
Town & country planning: Regional spatial strategies: Public examinations: Allowances: England 280
Town & country planning: Subordinate legislation: Application to the Crown 280
Town & country planning: Subordinate legislation: Application to the Crown: Inquiries procedure: Scotland . . . 392
Town & country planning: Subordinate legislation: Application to the Crown: Scotland 392
Town & country planning: Use classes: England 280
Town & village greens: Common land: Registration, management & protection: Acts 5
Town & village greens: Common land: Registration, management & protection: Acts: Explanatory notes 9
Tractors: Agricultural & forestry: Emission of gaseous & particulate pollutants 78
Tractors: EC type-approval 168
Trade descriptions: Textile products: Composition: Determination 282
Trade descriptions: Textile products: Fibre content: Textile names & allowances 282
Trade marks & designs: Address for service 116
Trade marks & designs: Service & time limits 116
Trade marks: Amendments 282
Trade marks: British Paralympic Association: Association rights: Paralympic symbol 41, 282
Trade marks: European Communities 282
Trade marks: International registration 282
Trade marks: London Olympic & Paralympic Games 2012: Association rights: Appointment of proprietors 41, 282
Trade: Statistics: Customs & excise 275

Traffic Management 2005 Order: Commencements: Northern Ireland 438
Traffic Management Act 2004: Commencements 101, 286
Traffic management: Adjudicators: Proceedings: Northern Ireland 438
Traffic management: Penalty charges: Exemption from criminal proceedings: Northern Ireland 438
Traffic management: Penalty charges: Prescribed amounts: Northern Ireland 438
Traffic signs: Amendments 168
Traffic signs: Northern Ireland 439
Training: Education: Inspectors: Wales 72
Training: Youth & community work: Inspection: Wales 73
Trams: Public transport: Edinburgh: Acts: Scotland 338
Tramways: Luton Dunstable Translink: England 284, 285
Tramways: Model clauses 285, 286
Trans-European Rail System: Interoperability 284
Transfer of functions: Lord Chancellor 125, 126, 283
Transfer of functions: Lord Chief Justice: Lord Chancellor: Consequential provisions: Northern Ireland 428, 444
Transformational Grants Joint Scheme: Revocation 141
Transmissible spongiform encephalopathies: England 21
Transmissible spongiform encephalopathies: Northern Ireland 407, 416
Transmissible spongiform encephalopathies: Scotland 345
Transmissible spongiform encephalopathies: Wales 22, 25
Transplants: Human organs & tissue: Acts: Explanatory notes: Scotland 340
Transplants: Human organs & tissue: Acts: Scotland 339
Transplants: Human tissue: Persons who lack capacity to consent 106
Transplants: Organ & tissue live transplants: Scotland 358
Transplants: Organ transplants: Scotland 358
Transport & works: Applications & objections: Procedure: England & Wales 28, 285, 286
Transport & works: Environmental effects: Assessment 285
Transport & works: Light rapid transit systems: Greater Manchester 284, 285
Transport & works: Luton Dunstable Translink: England 284, 285
Transport & works: Network Rail: Thameslink 2000: England 284, 285
Transport & works: Network Rail: West Coast Main Line: Stowe Hill: England 284, 285
Transport & works: Poole harbour: Opening bridges 284, 285
Transport & works: Railways & tramways: Model clauses 285, 286
Transport & works: Wales 285, 286
Transport (Wales) Act 2006: Commencements 286
Transport Act 2000: Commencement 159
Transport Act 2000: Consequential amendments: Scotland 40
Transport for London: Investment & highway functions: Contracting out: Best value 46, 125
Transport for London: Sloane Square House 121, 283
Transport: Bus User Complaints Tribunal: Scotland 392
Transport: Buses: Travel concession scheme: Older & disabled persons: Eligible persons & services: Scotland 392
Transport: Buses: Travel concession scheme: Older & disabled persons: Scotland 392
Transport: Civil aviation: Acts 4
Transport: Civil aviation: Acts: Explanatory notes 9
Transport: Disability Discrimination Act 1995: Private hire vehicles: Carriage of guide dogs, etc.: England & Wales 61, 285
Transport: Disability Discrimination Act 1995: Taxis: Carriage of guide dogs, etc.: England & Wales 61, 286
Transport: Disability discrimination: Code of practice: Supplement to Part 3: Transport Vehicles: Provision & use: Appointed day . . 60
Transport: Edinburgh: Trams: Acts: Scotland 338
Transport: Public service vehicles: Drivers, inspectors, conductors & passengers: Conduct: Scotland 373
Transport: Public Transport Users' Committee for Scotland: Establishment: Scotland 392
Transport: Rail vehicles: Gatwick Express class 458 vehicles: Accessibility: Exemptions 61, 283
Transport: Railway services: Closures guidance: England & Scotland 283
Transport: Railway services: Closures guidance: England & Wales 283
Transport: Railways & other guided transport: Health & safety 95
Transport: Railways Act 2005: Amendment 283
Transport: Railways Act 2005: Commencements 284
Transport: Railways: Docklands Light Railway: Silvertown & London City Airport Extension: Exemptions 283
Transport: Railways: Docklands Light Railway: Stratford International Extension 284, 285
Transport: Railways: Interoperability 284
Transport: Railways: Network Rail: Thameslink 2000: England 284, 285
Transport: Railways: Network Rail: West Coast Main Line: Stowe Hill: England 284, 285
Transport: Railways: Safety management: Northern Ireland 422
Transport: Railways: Strategic Rail Authority: Abolition 284
Transport: Railways: Substitute road services: Exemptions 283
Transport: Railways: Training services: Access 283

Transport: Regional strategies: Health boards: Scotland 392
Transport: Regional transport planning: Wales 286
Transport: Roads: User charging: Schemes: Keeping of accounts & relevant expenses: Scotland 392
Transport: Security: Electronic communications 283
Transport: Shetland Transport Partnership: Transfer of functions: Scotland 392
Transport: South-West of Scotland Transport Partnership: Transfer of functions to: Scotland 393
Transport: Strathclyde Passenger Transport Area: Variation: Scotland 392
Transport: Strathclyde Passenger Transport Authority & Executive: Functions: Transfer: West of Scotland Transport Partnership: Scotland 392
Transport: Strathclyde Passenger Transport Authority & Executive: Property rights & liabilities: Transfer: West of Scotland Transport Partnership: Scotland. 393
Transport: Tramways: Luton Dunstable Translink: England. 284, 285
Transport: Tyne & Wear Passenger Transport Authority: Members: Increase in number 286
Transport: Wales: Acts 9
Transport: Wales: Acts: Explanatory notes 11
Transportable pressure equipment: Use: Northern Ireland 420, 421
Travel expenses & remission of charges: Health & personal social services: Northern Ireland 420
Travel expenses & remission of charges: National Health Service: England 133, 134
Travel expenses & remission of charges: National Health Service: Scotland 366
Travel expenses & remission of charges: National Health Service: Wales 140
Trawls: Multiple trawls: Prohibition: Sea fisheries: Scotland 387
Tribunals & inquiries: Independent examinations: Costs: Standard daily amount: England. 279, 286
Trinity CoE VC Primary School: Religious character: Designation 68
Trunk roads: A1. . . . . 172, 173
Trunk roads: A1/A1(M): Redhouse interchange to Holmfield interchange & A162 173
Trunk roads: A1: A1(M) junction 46 173
Trunk roads: A1: A5135 junction, northbound entry slip road 173
Trunk roads: A1: A57 & A614: Apleyhead. 98
Trunk roads: A1: A57, A638, B1174 junction improvement: Markham Moor. 98
Trunk roads: A1: Alnwick bypass 173
Trunk roads: A1: Alnwick South junction 173
Trunk roads: A1: Apley Head to South of Elkesley, Nottinghamshire 174
Trunk roads: A1: B1081 junction improvement: Carpenter's Lodge 98
Trunk roads: A1: B1174 junction improvement: Gonerby Moor 98
Trunk roads: A1: B6267, Sinderby junction 174
Trunk roads: A1: Belford 174
Trunk roads: A1: Belford bypass 174
Trunk roads: A1: Biggleswade north roundabout, Bedfordshire 171
Trunk roads: A1: Black Cat roundabout to Tempsford Bridge, Bedfordshire. 174
Trunk roads: A1: Blaydon Interchange to Kenton Bar Interchange 174
Trunk roads: A1: Blyth, Nottinghamshire 171
Trunk roads: A1: Bramham Crossroads 174
Trunk roads: A1: Bramham to Wetherby upgrading: Detrunking 98
Trunk roads: A1: Bramham to Wetherby upgrading: River Wharfe bridge 98
Trunk roads: A1: Brampton Hut & Alconbury interchanges, Cambridgeshire 174
Trunk roads: A1: Brampton Hut interchange, Cambridgeshire 169
Trunk roads: A1: Brampton Hut interchange, Huntingdon, Cambridgeshire 170
Trunk roads: A1: Bridge Mill to Cheswick 174
Trunk roads: A1: Carlton-on-Trent 174
Trunk roads: A1: Carpenters Lodge roundabout, Peterborough 174
Trunk roads: A1: Cawledge layby, Heckley House layby & Browneside layby 174
Trunk roads: A1: Chesterton, Cambridgeshire. 171
Trunk roads: A1: Clow Beck accommodation to the A1231 overbridge 171
Trunk roads: A1: Colsterworth - Great Ponton, Lincolnshire 174
Trunk roads: A1: Cromwell, Nottinghamshire. 174
Trunk roads: A1: Denwick interchange 174
Trunk roads: A1: Dishforth interchange to Baldersby interchange 173
Trunk roads: A1: Elkesley, Nottinghamshire 174
Trunk roads: A1: Fenwick Stead to Fenwick Granary junction 175
Trunk roads: A1: Fenwick Stead to Fenwick Granary Junction 175
Trunk roads: A1: Five Lanes End to Ranby, Nottinghamshire 175
Trunk roads: A1: Gonerby Moor to Long Bennington 175
Trunk roads: A1: Grantham to Stretton 175
Trunk roads: A1: Great North Rd., Bedfordshire to Cambridgeshire 169, 175
Trunk roads: A1: Haggerston 175
Trunk roads: A1: Haggerston to West Mains junction. 175

Trunk roads: A1: Hollinside interchange 175
Trunk roads: A1: Holtby Grange to Leases Hall Bridge. 175
Trunk roads: A1: Junction 1, northbound exit slip road 175
Trunk roads: A1: Kenton Bar interchange. 173
Trunk roads: A1: Ladywood Lane overbridge, Nottinghamshire 175
Trunk roads: A1: Long Bennington southbound access slip road: Detrunking. 98
Trunk roads: A1: Markham Moor to Carlton on Trent, Nottinghamshire 175
Trunk roads: A1: Morpeth bypass 175
Trunk roads: A1: Near Barrowby, Lincolnshire 173
Trunk roads: A1: Newark on Trent to Grantham 175
Trunk roads: A1: Newark-on-Trent, Nottinghamshire. 170
Trunk roads: A1: Newton on the Moor layby 176
Trunk roads: A1: Newton on the Moor South Junction 176
Trunk roads: A1: Ranby, Nottinghamshire, slip roads. 176
Trunk roads: A1: Sandy roundabout, Bedfordshire 176
Trunk roads: A1: Scotch Corner interchange 173, 176, 206
Trunk roads: A1: Scotswood interchange 176
Trunk roads: A1: Scottish Border Layby 176
Trunk roads: A1: Scremerston roundabout to East Ord roundabout. 176
Trunk roads: A1: Seaton Burn to Stannington. 176
Trunk roads: A1: South of Grantham, Lincolnshire 176
Trunk roads: A1: Southoe Bends to Buckden roundabout, Huntingdon, Cambrdigeshire 176
Trunk roads: A1: Stamford to Long Bennington 176
Trunk roads: A1: Stamford to Peterborough. 171
Trunk roads: A1: Stamford to South Witham 176
Trunk roads: A1: Stannington 176
Trunk roads: A1: Tuxford to Markham Moor 176
Trunk roads: A1: Tweed Bridge to Duns Rd junction 176
Trunk roads: A1: Wansford, Peterborough 171, 176
Trunk roads: A1: Winthorpe to Barrowby. 177
Trunk roads: A1: Winthorpe to Dry Doddington 177
Trunk roads: A1: Winthorpe to south of Balderton, Nottinghamshire. 177
Trunk roads: A1: Winthorpe, Newark-on-Trent, Nottinghamshire 177
Trunk roads: A1: Winthorpe, Nottinghamshire 177
Trunk roads: A1: Wothorpe to Wittering 177
Trunk roads: A10: Cheshunt, Hertfordshire 181
Trunk roads: A10: Chipping, Hertfordshire 181
Trunk roads: A10: Gt Cambridge Rd., Cheshunt, Hertfordshire 181
Trunk roads: A10: Half Hide Lane, Turnford, Hertfordshire 181
Trunk roads: A10: Hoddesdon & Ware, Hertfordshire 181
Trunk roads: A10: Hoddesdon interchange, Broxbourne, Hertfordshire 181
Trunk roads: A10: Rush Green interchange, Hertfordshire 181
Trunk roads: A10: Turnford Interchange, Broxbourne, Hertfordshire 181
Trunk roads: A10: Turnford interchange, Hertfordshire. 181
Trunk roads: A1089: ASDA roundabout - Tilbury Docks. 218
Trunk roads: A1089: Marchfoot interchange 218
Trunk roads: A1089: Near Grays 184
Trunk roads: A1089: Orsett Heath, southbound carriageway 218
Trunk roads: A11: A505, Icknield Bridge, Cambridgeshire. 181
Trunk roads: A11: Attleborough, Norfolk 181
Trunk roads: A11: Barton Mills, Suffolk 181
Trunk roads: A11: Bridgham Heath, Breckland, Norfolk 182
Trunk roads: A11: Chalk Hill layby, Barton Mills, Suffolk 182
Trunk roads: A11: Cringleford/Thickthorn interchange, Norfolk 169
Trunk roads: A11: London Road roundabout to Brandon Road roundabout, Thetford, Norfolk 182
Trunk roads: A11: Near Newmarket, Suffolk. 182
Trunk roads: A11: Nine Mile Hill Interchange, Cambridgeshire & Suffolk 181
Trunk roads: A11: Northbound exit slip road, Chippenham, Cambridgeshire 182
Trunk roads: A11: Red Lodge interchange, Forest Heath, Suffolk 182
Trunk roads: A11: Six Mile Bottom - Swaffham Heath, Cambridgeshire. 182
Trunk roads: A11: Six Mile Bottom, Cambridgeshire. 182
Trunk roads: A11: Waterhall Bridge, Cambridgeshire 182
Trunk roads: A11: Wymondham bypass, Norfolk 182
Trunk roads: A12. 237
Trunk roads: A12/A120: Birchwood interchange to Marks Tey interchange, Colchester, Essex 182

Trunk roads: A12/A120: Colchestser bypass 182
Trunk roads: A12/A120: Marks Tey interchange - Ardleigh Crown interchange, Essex 182
Trunk roads: A12/A120: Marks Tey roundabout, Colchester, Essex 182
Trunk roads: A12/A14: Copdock interchange, Babergh, Suffolk 182
Trunk roads: A12: A1117 Bentley Drive roundabout - St Peters Street/Jubilee Way roundabout, Oulton, Suffolk 182
Trunk roads: A12: Bascule Bridge, Lowestoft, Suffolk 183
Trunk roads: A12: Braintree - Marks Tey, Essex 208
Trunk roads: A12: Braiswick, Colchester, Essex 182
Trunk roads: A12: Brentwood, Essex 183
Trunk roads: A12: Breydon Bridge, Great Yarmouth, North Norfolk 183
Trunk roads: A12: Chelmsford bypass, junction 18 - 19 & Howe Green interchange, junction 17, Chelmsford, Essex 183
Trunk roads: A12: Corton Lane, Suffolk 183
Trunk roads: A12: Denmark Road, Lowestoft, Suffolk 183
Trunk roads: A12: Eight Ash Green interchange to Marks Tey, Colchester, Essex 183
Trunk roads: A12: Harfrey's roundabout, Great Yarmouth, Norfolk 183
Trunk roads: A12: Hopton to Gorleston, Norfolk 183
Trunk roads: A12: Ingatestone bypass 169
Trunk roads: A12: Kelvedon bypass, Braintree, Essex 183
Trunk roads: A12: Kelvedon bypass, Essex 183
Trunk roads: A12: M25 Brook Street interchange, junction 11, Brentwood bypass, Essex 183
Trunk roads: A12: Marks Tey interchange, Essex 183
Trunk roads: A12: Marks Tey, Colchester, Essex 183
Trunk roads: A12: Spring Lane interchange, Colchester, Essex 183
Trunk roads: A12: Stanway to Spring Lane, Essex 169
Trunk roads: A12: Webbs Farm interchange, Essex 183
Trunk roads: A120/A12: Birchwood interchange to Marks Tey interchange, Colchester, Essex 182
Trunk roads: A120/A12: Colchestser bypass 182
Trunk roads: A120/A12: Marks Tey interchange - Ardleigh Crown interchange, Essex 182
Trunk roads: A120/A12: Marks Tey roundabout, Colchester, Essex 182
Trunk roads: A120: Ardleigh - Hare Green, Colchester, Essex 208
Trunk roads: A120: Braintree - Marks Tey, Essex 208
Trunk roads: A120: Braintree to Marks Tey, Essex 208
Trunk roads: A120: Braiswick, Colchester, Essex 182
Trunk roads: A120: Coggeshall bypass, Braintree, Essex 208
Trunk roads: A120: Colchester to Stansted, Braintree, Essex 209
Trunk roads: A120: Great Notley, Braintree, Essex 209
Trunk roads: A120: Junction 6, eastbound entry slip road: Stansted Airport, Essex 209
Trunk roads: A1246: Ferrybridge to Boot & Shoe Roundabout 209
Trunk roads: A13/A282: Wennington - A1089 184
Trunk roads: A13: A1012 & A1089 junctions, slip roads 184
Trunk roads: A13: A1012 junction, slip roads 184
Trunk roads: A13: Mardyke interchange - Marshfoot interchange 184
Trunk roads: A13: Near Grays 184
Trunk roads: A133: Ardleigh - Hare Green, Colchester, Essex 208
Trunk roads: A14/A12: Copdock interchange, Babergh, Suffolk 182
Trunk roads: A14: Bar Hill eastbound exit slip road 184
Trunk roads: A14: Barham - Levington, Suffolk 184
Trunk roads: A14: Beacon Hill Interchange to Cedars Interchange, Suffolk 184
Trunk roads: A14: Beacon Hill interchange, Suffolk 184
Trunk roads: A14: Beyton, Suffolk 184
Trunk roads: A14: Blackbridge Footbridge, Barton, Seagrave, Northamptonshire 184
Trunk roads: A14: Brampton Hut interchange, Cambridgeshire 169
Trunk roads: A14: Bury St Edmunds, Suffolk 184
Trunk roads: A14: Cambridge northern bypass, Milton, Cambridgeshire 184
Trunk roads: A14: Cambridgeshire - Northamptonshire 169
Trunk roads: A14: Cambridgeshire - Suffolk 169
Trunk roads: A14: Cambridgeshire & Northamptonshire 184
Trunk roads: A14: Claydon interchange, Suffolk 184
Trunk roads: A14: Copdock Interchange to Felixstowe Dock Gate No. 1 Roundabout, Suffolk 169
Trunk roads: A14: Copdock Mill interchange - Sproughton interchange, Suffolk 184
Trunk roads: A14: Exning bypass, Newmarket, Suffolk 184
Trunk roads: A14: Four Mile Stable to Girton Interchange, Cambridgeshire 185
Trunk roads: A14: Galley Hill interchange, St. Ives, Cambridgeshire 185
Trunk roads: A14: Girton interchange, Cambridgeshire 185
Trunk roads: A14: Girton interchange, Cambridgeshire - Felixstowe, Suffolk 185
Trunk roads: A14: Godmanchester to Bar Hill, Cambridgeshire 185

Trunk roads: A14: Godmanchester, Cambrdigeshire 185
Trunk roads: A14: Hardwick-Girton, Cambridgeshire 212
Trunk roads: A14: Haughley - Beyton, Suffolk 185
Trunk roads: A14: Haughley, Suffolk 185
Trunk roads: A14: Higham, Suffolk 185
Trunk roads: A14: Junction 32, westbound slip road, Histon interchange, Cambridgeshire 185
Trunk roads: A14: Kelmarsh to Orton, Daventry, Northamptonshire 185
Trunk roads: A14: Kentford interchange to Waterhall interchange, Suffolk 185
Trunk roads: A14: Kettering southern bypass, Northamptonshire 185
Trunk roads: A14: Lindale bypass 217
Trunk roads: A14: M1 Junction 19 185
Trunk roads: A14: Milton interchange - Girton interchange 185
Trunk roads: A14: Milton interchange to Fen Ditton interchange, Cambridgeshire 185
Trunk roads: A14: Milton layby - near Millness 217
Trunk roads: A14: Nacton interchange, Suffolk 185
Trunk roads: A14: Nene Viaduct, Thrapston 186
Trunk roads: A14: Nine Mile Hill Interchange, Cambridgeshire & Suffolk 181
Trunk roads: A14: Port of Felixstowe Rd., Suffolk 186
Trunk roads: A14: Risby - Higham interchange, Suffolk 186
Trunk roads: A14: Risby - Trimley St Martin, Suffolk 186
Trunk roads: A14: Risby interchange to Westley interchange, Bury St Edmunds, Suffolk 186
Trunk roads: A14: Risby, Suffolk 186
Trunk roads: A14: Seven Hills interchange, Suffolk 186
Trunk roads: A14: Snailwell, Cambridgeshire 186
Trunk roads: A14: Spittals interchange to Girton interchange 184
Trunk roads: A14: Spittals interchange to Swavesey, Cambridgeshire 186
Trunk roads: A14: Spittals interchange, Huntingdon, Cambridgeshire 169
Trunk roads: A14: St Saviours interchange, Bury St Edmunds, Suffolk 186
Trunk roads: A14: Stow-Cum-Quy, Cambridgeshire 186
Trunk roads: A14: Stowmarket, Suffolk 186
Trunk roads: A14: Thrapston - Catworth, Northamptonshire & Cambridgeshire 186
Trunk roads: A14: Trimley St. Mary, Suffolk 186
Trunk roads: A14: Two Mile Spinney, Bury St Edmunds, Suffolk 186
Trunk roads: A160: Brocklesby interchange 209
Trunk roads: A160: Ulceby Rd. to Top Rd. roundabout 209
Trunk roads: A162: A1/A1(M), Redhouse interchange to Holmfield interchange 173
Trunk roads: A162: Darrington Overbridge to the A645, Knottingley Road 209
Trunk roads: A162: Ferrybridge interchange & A645, Knottingley Road/Pontefract Road junction 209
Trunk roads: A162: Ferrybridge to Boot & Shoe Roundabout 209
Trunk roads: A167: Blind Lane interchange roundabout 170
Trunk roads: A168/A19: Thirsk bypass 187
Trunk roads: A168: Dishforth 173
Trunk roads: A174: Parkway interchange to Blue Bell interchange 187
Trunk roads: A180: Barnetby interchange to Brocklesby interchange 209
Trunk roads: A180: Brocklesby interchange 209
Trunk roads: A19/A168: Thirsk bypass 187
Trunk roads: A19/A66: Stockton Rd interchange 186, 187
Trunk roads: A19/A66: Stockton Rd interchange to Portrack interchange 187
Trunk roads: A19: Borrowby to Over Silton 187
Trunk roads: A19: Chester Road & Herrington interchanges 187
Trunk roads: A19: Chester Road interchange 187
Trunk roads: A19: Cold Hesledon 187
Trunk roads: A19: Crathorne interchange to Tontine interchange 187
Trunk roads: A19: Damsdykes Accommodation Bridge to Moor Farm roundabout 187
Trunk roads: A19: Hangman's Lane overbridge 187
Trunk roads: A19: Howdon interchange to Silverlink interchange 187
Trunk roads: A19: Hylton Bridge to Hylton Grange Interchange 187
Trunk roads: A19: Hylton Grange to Chester Road 187
Trunk roads: A19: Killingworth interchange to Moor Farm roundabout 187
Trunk roads: A19: Parkway interchange to Portrack interchange 187
Trunk roads: A19: Parkway Interchange to Stockton Road Interchange 187
Trunk roads: A19: Seaton Burn 176
Trunk roads: A19: Sheraton Interchange 187
Trunk roads: A19: Three Tuns Overbridge, Knayton 188
Trunk roads: A2/A282/M25: Dartford 177

Trunk roads: A2/M2: Junction 7, Brenley Corner 223
Trunk roads: A2: A2018 junction - Bexley Brough boundary 177
Trunk roads: A2: A2050 junction, near Bridge 177
Trunk roads: A2: A2050, near Bridge 177
Trunk roads: A2: Bean - Cobham 177
Trunk roads: A2: Canterbury bypass 177
Trunk roads: A2: Dunkirk, Londonbound exit slip road 177
Trunk roads: A2: Jubilee Way, coastbound carriageway 177
Trunk roads: A2: Lydden 177
Trunk roads: A2: M25 junction 2 - A227 junction 177
Trunk roads: A2: M25 junction 2, entry slip roads 178
Trunk roads: A2: Pepper Hill - Singlewell 178
Trunk roads: A2: Upper Harbledown - Bridge 178
Trunk roads: A2: Upper Harbledown, coastbound 178
Trunk roads: A20/A2070/A292: M20 junction 9 - east of junction 10 236
Trunk roads: A20: Cheriton interchange - Western Heights roundabout 236
Trunk roads: A20: Court Wood junction 188
Trunk roads: A20: Folkestone - Dover 188
Trunk roads: A20: Junctions 1 - 2, westbound entry slip roads 236
Trunk roads: A20: Limekiln roundabout & the Viaduct 188
Trunk roads: A20: M20, junction 1 - 2, coastbound 236
Trunk roads: A20: Roundhill tunnels 236
Trunk roads: A20: Swanley interchange 188
Trunk roads: A20: Western Heights roundabout - Prince of Wales roundabout 188
Trunk roads: A2070/A20/A292: M20 junction 9 - east of junction 10 236
Trunk roads: A2070: A2042 junction - Brenzett 218
Trunk roads: A2070: Bad Munstereifel Road, Sevington 218
Trunk roads: A2070: Badmunstereifel Road, near Ashford 218
Trunk roads: A2070: Brenzett roundabout 209
Trunk roads: A21: A268 junction, Flimwell 188
Trunk roads: A21: A268/B2087 junctions, Flimwell 188
Trunk roads: A21: Beech House Lane - Northbridge Street 188
Trunk roads: A21: Northbridge Street roundabout 188
Trunk roads: A21: Pierce Barn overbridge - Rosemary Lane 188
Trunk roads: A21: Pierce Barn overbridge to Rosemary Lane & Cuckoo Lane to Forstal Farm roundabout 188
Trunk roads: A21: Robertsbridge/Vinehall St. 188
Trunk roads: A21: Sevenoaks bypass 188
Trunk roads: A21: Tonbridge bypass 188
Trunk roads: A21: Tonbridge bypass, Londonbound exit slip road 188
Trunk roads: A23/M23: Junction 11, Pease Pottage 237
Trunk roads: A249: B2005 junction - Kingsferry roundabout 209
Trunk roads: A249: Brielle Way, Sheerness 209
Trunk roads: A249: Iwade bypass: Queenborough 255
Trunk roads: A249: Iwade bypass: Queenborough improvement 255
Trunk roads: A249: Iwade bypass: Queenborough improvement: Left & right hand turns: Prohibition 255
Trunk roads: A249: Iwade bypass: Queenborough improvement: Speed limits 255
Trunk roads: A249: Iwade bypass: Queenborough improvement: Traffic & pedestrians: Prohibition 255
Trunk roads: A249: Kingsferry roundabout - Cowstead Corner roundabout 209
Trunk roads: A249: Sheppey crossing 209
Trunk roads: A259: Belle Hill/King Offa Way, Bexhill 209
Trunk roads: A259: Brenzett roundabout 209
Trunk roads: A259: East Guldeford - Brookland 210
Trunk roads: A259: Little Common Road, Bexhill 210
Trunk roads: A259: Pevensey - Winchelsea 210
Trunk roads: A259: Royal Military Road 210
Trunk roads: A259: Various roads, Rye 210
Trunk roads: A259: Winchelsea Road, Guestling Green 210
Trunk roads: A26: Itford Farm 188
Trunk roads: A26: Southerham - Beddingham 189
Trunk roads: A26: Three Ponds Caravan Park 189
Trunk roads: A27: A280 junction near Selden & Mill Road junction near Slindon 189
Trunk roads: A27: Beddingham - Polegate 189
Trunk roads: A27: Beddingham roundabout - Southerham roundabout 189
Trunk roads: A27: Busticle Lane - Lancing Manor roundabout 189
Trunk roads: A27: Causeway roundabout - Binsted Lane 189
Trunk roads: A27: Causeway roundabout, Arundel 189

Trunk roads: A27: Drusilla's roundabout, near Berwick	189
Trunk roads: A27: Hammerpot, Westbound	189
Trunk roads: A27: Harts Farm interchange	189
Trunk roads: A27: Havant/Portsmouth	178
Trunk roads: A27: Hilsea, eastbound entry slip road	189
Trunk roads: A27: Holmbush Interchange to Hangleton	189
Trunk roads: A27: New Barn Road - Mill Hill	189
Trunk roads: A27: Old Shoreham Road & Shoreham bypass	189
Trunk roads: A27: Patcham	189
Trunk roads: A27: Patcham, westbound exit slip road	189
Trunk roads: A27: Pook Lane footbridge	189
Trunk roads: A27: Selmeston - Alciston	190
Trunk roads: A27: Southerham - Beddingham	189
Trunk roads: A27: Southerham Railway Bridge	190
Trunk roads: A27: Southerham to Beddingham improvements	99
Trunk roads: A27: Tangmere roundabout	190
Trunk roads: A27: West Firle - Alciston	190
Trunk roads: A282	237
Trunk roads: A282/A13: Wennington - A1089	184
Trunk roads: A282/A2/M25: Dartford	177
Trunk roads: A282: Junction 1A	210
Trunk roads: A282: Junction 1A, northbound entry slip road	210
Trunk roads: A282: Junction 1B, southbound entry slip road	210
Trunk roads: A282: M25 junction 2 - Dartford Tunnels	210
Trunk roads: A282: M25 junction 29, 30 & 31: Slip roads	237
Trunk roads: A292/A2070/A20: M20 junction 9 - east of junction 10	236
Trunk roads: A3/A3(M): Junction 2 - 1, northbound	178
Trunk roads: A3: A31 Hogs Back interchange	178
Trunk roads: A3: Bramshott Chase - Hindhead	178
Trunk roads: A3: Clanfield, slip roads	178
Trunk roads: A3: Esher bypass	178
Trunk roads: A3: Esher bypass, northbound carriageway	169
Trunk roads: A3: Gravel Hill, near Clanfield	178
Trunk roads: A3: Guildford bypass	178
Trunk roads: A3: Havant/Portsmouth	178
Trunk roads: A3: Hindhead	99
Trunk roads: A3: Hindhead - Liphook	178
Trunk roads: A3: Hindhead, slip roads	99
Trunk roads: A3: Hindhead: Detrunking	99
Trunk roads: A3: Hog's Bank junction - Compton	178
Trunk roads: A3: Hurtmore interchange	179
Trunk roads: A3: Ladymead Bridges	179
Trunk roads: A3: Longmoor - Flexcombe	179
Trunk roads: A3: M25 junction 10, Hook	179
Trunk roads: A3: M25 junction 10, Wisley interchange	179
Trunk roads: A3: Milford interchange - Compton interchange	179
Trunk roads: A3: Ockham, Northbound entry slip road	179
Trunk roads: A3: Wisley Interchange at junction 10 & Ockham junction	237
Trunk roads: A3: Wisley Lane & Wisley Lay-by	179
Trunk roads: A30: Alphington interchange to Pearces Hill interchange, Exeter	190
Trunk roads: A30: Alphington interchange to Pearces Hill interchange, south of Exeter	190
Trunk roads: A30: Alphington interchange, near Exeter	190
Trunk roads: A30: Blowing House Viaduct, Redruth	190
Trunk roads: A30: Callestick Crossroads, nr Zelah	190
Trunk roads: A30: Dunheved Bridge, Launceston	190
Trunk roads: A30: Dunheved to Bulsworthy, Launceston	190
Trunk roads: A30: Gilberts Coombe Viaduct, Redruth	190
Trunk roads: A30: Highgate Interchange, Indian Queens, Cornwall	190
Trunk roads: A30: Indian Queens contraflow	190
Trunk roads: A30: Indian Queens to Lanivet	190
Trunk roads: A30: Innis Downs junction, near Bodmin	190
Trunk roads: A30: Innis Downs roundabout	190
Trunk roads: A30: Loggans Moor roundabout to Treswithian interchange, Cornwall	191
Trunk roads: A30: Menacrin Downs, near Bodmin	191
Trunk roads: A30: Merrymeet junction	191

Trunk roads: A30: Merrymeet roundabout	191
Trunk roads: A30: Merrymeet roundabout to Coombe Head, Devon	191
Trunk roads: A30: Pounds Conce to Temple Fishery junction, nr Bodmin	191
Trunk roads: A30: Tavistock Rd to Liftondown, Dunheved Bridge, Launceston	191
Trunk roads: A303: A343 Salisbury Rd. junction	210
Trunk roads: A303: Amesbury to Berwick Down	210
Trunk roads: A303: Bishopswood junction to A30	210
Trunk roads: A303: Bullington Cross, eastbound slip road	210
Trunk roads: A303: Hundred Acre roundabout, eastbound entry slip road	210
Trunk roads: A303: Mere to the junction with A350	210
Trunk roads: A303: Micheldever junction, eastbound	211
Trunk roads: A303: Picket Twenty interchange	211
Trunk roads: A303: Podimore roundabout to Hazelgrove roundabout	211
Trunk roads: A303: Podimore roundabout to South Petherton	211
Trunk roads: A303: Slip Road to A350, west of Chicklade	211
Trunk roads: A303: Thruxton Circuit interchange, eastbound entry slip road	211
Trunk roads: A303: Thruxton Hill, eastbound carriageway	211
Trunk roads: A303: Tinkers Lane, Wincanton to Hazlegrove roundabout, Sparkford	211
Trunk roads: A303: Tintinhull	211
Trunk roads: A303: Winchester Rd interchange, eastbound carriageway	211
Trunk roads: A3038: Mardyke interchange - Marshfoot interchange	184
Trunk roads: A31: Ashley Heath junction, westbound exit slip/link road	191
Trunk roads: A31: Ashley Heath roundabout, eastbound exit slip road	191
Trunk roads: A31: Canford Bottom Roundabout	191
Trunk roads: A31: Merley roundabout - Ameysford roundabout	191
Trunk roads: A31: Ringwood - Ashley Heath	191
Trunk roads: A31: Ringwood - Verwood interchange	191
Trunk roads: A31: Sturminster Marshall	191
Trunk roads: A31: Woolsbridge roundabout - Boundary Lane roundabout	191
Trunk roads: A3113: M25 junction 14 - A3044	218
Trunk roads: A34/A500: Talke, Staffordshire	191
Trunk roads: A34: A33 junction - Bullington Cross	191
Trunk roads: A34: A420 Botley interchange, southbound	192
Trunk roads: A34: B4027 junction, northbound slip roads	192
Trunk roads: A34: Beedon - Speen	192
Trunk roads: A34: Bullington Cross - Whitchurch	192
Trunk roads: A34: Litchfield, northbound carriageway	192
Trunk roads: A34: M4 junction 13	192
Trunk roads: A34: Marcham interchange	192
Trunk roads: A34: Milton interchange - Marcham interchange	192
Trunk roads: A34: Near Didcot	192
Trunk roads: A34: Speen, northbound exit slip road	192
Trunk roads: A34: Speen, southbound exit slip road	192
Trunk roads: A34: Sutton, Scotney - M3 junction 9	192
Trunk roads: A34: Sutton, Scotney - South Wonston	192
Trunk roads: A34: Whitchurch interchange, southbound	192
Trunk roads: A35: Melplash Show, Bridport, Dorset	192
Trunk roads: A35: Sea Rd. South Bridport, Dorset	192
Trunk roads: A36: Churchill Way North, Salisbury	192
Trunk roads: A36: Claverton, Bath	192
Trunk roads: A36: Heytesbury to Stockton Bend, Wiltshire	193
Trunk roads: A36: Landford to Holwell Green, near Salisbury	193
Trunk roads: A36: Monkton Combe to Limpley Stoke near Bath	193
Trunk roads: A36: Wilton to Salisbury	169
Trunk roads: A38	221
Trunk roads: A38: A50 to A61, Derbyshire	169
Trunk roads: A38: A50/A38 interchange, Derbyshire	170
Trunk roads: A38: Alfreton, Derbyshire	193
Trunk roads: A38: Allestree, Derby	193
Trunk roads: A38: Alrewas to Barton-under-Needwood, Staffordshire	193
Trunk roads: A38: Bassett's Pole roundabout, Staffordshire	193
Trunk roads: A38: Belper, Derbyshire	193
Trunk roads: A38: Between A50, Derby southern bypass & M1 junction 28, Derbyshire	193
Trunk roads: A38: Boley Park, Lichfield, Staffordshire	193
Trunk roads: A38: Branston, Staffordshire	193
Trunk roads: A38: Burton on Trent, Staffordshire	193

Trunk roads: A38: Chudleigh Station Bridge to Clay Lane junction at Chudleigh Knighton, near Newton Abbot. 193
Trunk roads: A38: Clay Mills to Willington. 194
Trunk roads: A38: Clay Mills, Burton-on-Trent, Staffordshire 193
Trunk roads: A38: Clay Mills, Staffordshire. 194
Trunk roads: A38: Darnford, Near Lichfield, Staffordshire 194
Trunk roads: A38: Dobwalls bypass 99
Trunk roads: A38: Dobwalls bypass: Detrunking. 99
Trunk roads: A38: Drumbridges interchange to Goodstone interchange, near Newton Abbot 194
Trunk roads: A38: Eggington, Derbyshire. 194
Trunk roads: A38: Egginton Brook Bridge, Derbyshire 194
Trunk roads: A38: Findern Interchange to Markeaton roundabout, Derby & A516 194
Trunk roads: A38: Fradley to Hilliards Cross, Staffordshire 194
Trunk roads: A38: Glynn Valley. 194
Trunk roads: A38: Glynn Valley, Bodmin. 194
Trunk roads: A38: Haldon Hill, south of Exeter. 194
Trunk roads: A38: Holbrook, Derbyshire, link roads 169
Trunk roads: A38: Junction 15 - 16 194
Trunk roads: A38: Junction with A6 to junction with A61, Derbyshire. 194
Trunk roads: A38: Kingsway, Derby 194
Trunk roads: A38: Lichfield to Barton Under Needwood, Staffordshire 194
Trunk roads: A38: Liskeard to North Treviddo, Cornwall 194
Trunk roads: A38: Lower Clicker, near Liskeard, Cornwall 194
Trunk roads: A38: Manadon interchange to Forder Valley interchange, Plymouth. 194
Trunk roads: A38: Minworth roundabout, Sutton Coldfield. 195
Trunk roads: A38: Notterbridge junction, nr Saltash 195
Trunk roads: A38: Pearces Hill interchange, Exeter. 195
Trunk roads: A38: River Derwent Bridge, Derbyshire 195
Trunk roads: A38: Smithaleigh Overbridge, near Ivybridge, Devon 195
Trunk roads: A38: South of Derby. 193
Trunk roads: A38: South of Weeford, Staffordshire. 195
Trunk roads: A38: Splatford interchange, Kennford. 195
Trunk roads: A38: Streethay to Alrewas, Staffordshire 195
Trunk roads: A38: Swinfen roundabout, Staffordshire 195
Trunk roads: A38: Tinkers Lane to Trerulefoot, nr Liskeard 195
Trunk roads: A38: Torhill Underbridge, Bittaford, Devon 195
Trunk roads: A38: Toyota interchange to Kingsway roundabout, Derbyshire 195
Trunk roads: A38: Toyota interchange to Mickleover, Derbyshire 195
Trunk roads: A38: Toyota intersection, Derbyshire 193
Trunk roads: A38: Turfdown Crossroads, Bodmin 195
Trunk roads: A38: West coast railway bridge, Lichfield, Staffordshire 195
Trunk roads: A4: Bailbrook underpass, Bath 179
Trunk roads: A4: Batheaston, Bath 192
Trunk roads: A4: Globe roundabout, Bath. 192
Trunk roads: A4: Saltford, between Bristol & Bath 179
Trunk roads: A40/A48: West of Meifrim junction to south of Llangunnor roundabout & east of Pensarn roundabout, Carmarthenshire
. . . . 257
Trunk roads: A40: Denham roundabout, eastbound slip road 196
Trunk roads: A40: Gibraltar Tunnels to County Boundary, Monmouthshire 257
Trunk roads: A40: High St., Fishguard, Monmouthshire 257
Trunk roads: A40: Huntley to Churcham, Gloucestershire 196
Trunk roads: A40: Llansantffraed, Talybont-on-Usk junction improvement side roads 260
Trunk roads: A40: Llansantffraed, Talybont-on-Usk, Powys 257
Trunk roads: A40: London to Fishguard, Llansantffraed, Talybont-on-Usk junction improvement: Compulsory purchase order . . 13, 101
Trunk roads: A40: Longford layby, Gloucester northern bypass 196
Trunk roads: A40: Mitchel Troy picnic site, southwest of Monmouth, Monmouthshire 257
Trunk roads: A40: Over roundabout to Elmbridge roundabout, Gloucester. 196
Trunk roads: A40: Raglan Interchange to Monmouth, Monmouthshire. 257
Trunk roads: A40: Ross-on-Wye, Herefordshire 195
Trunk roads: A40: Tangiers lay-by, Haverfordwest, Pembrokeshire 257
Trunk roads: A40: Wilton roundabout to Overross roundabout, Herefordshire. 196
Trunk roads: A40: Withybush, Haverfordwest, Pembrokeshire. 255
Trunk roads: A404/A404(M): Western Region Railway Bridge 211
Trunk roads: A404/M40: Handy Cross 211
Trunk roads: A404: Handy Cross - A4155 junction 211
Trunk roads: A404: Maidenhead Thicket to Handy Cross: Closure of Layby 253

Trunk roads: A4042: Little Mill junction, Monmouthshire	260
Trunk roads: A405: M1 junction 6	211
Trunk roads: A405: M1 junction 6 - M25 junction 21A	211
Trunk roads: A405: M25 junction 21A - M1 junction 6	237
Trunk roads: A4060: Triangle Business Park roundabout to Mountain Hare roundabout, Merthyr Tydfil	260
Trunk roads: A4076: Johnston, Haverfordwest, Pembrokeshire	256
Trunk roads: A4123: Oldbury	218
Trunk roads: A4123: Wolverhampton Road	218
Trunk roads: A414	219, 220
Trunk roads: A417: Blakey Lane	99
Trunk roads: A417: Cowley roundabout to Churn Valley viaduct, Cirencester	211
Trunk roads: A417: Cricklade, Wiltshire to Cirencester, Gloucestershire	212
Trunk roads: A417: Shurdington Rd., junction to Air Balloon roundabout, Crickley Hill, Cheltenham	211
Trunk roads: A417: Zoons Court roundabout to Business Park roundabout, Gloucester	212
Trunk roads: A419: A420 junction to A361 Rat Trap junction, Swindon	212
Trunk roads: A419: A420 junction to Commonhead roundabout, Swindon	212
Trunk roads: A419: Blunsdon bypass & slip roads	99
Trunk roads: A419: Blunsdon bypass & slip roads: Detrunking	99
Trunk roads: A419: Castle Eaton & Kingshill Junctions, near Cricklade	212
Trunk roads: A419: Castle Eaton junction to Calcutt overbridge near Swindon	212
Trunk roads: A419: Commonhead roundabout, Swindon	212
Trunk roads: A419: Cricklade, Wiltshire to Cirencester, Gloucestershire	212
Trunk roads: A42: Ashby-de-la-Zouch	196
Trunk roads: A42: Leicestershire	243
Trunk roads: A42: M42 junction 11 to M1 junction 23A, Leicestershire	219
Trunk roads: A421: Bedfordshire	212
Trunk roads: A421: Bedordshire	170
Trunk roads: A421: Great Barford bypass, Bedfordshire	212
Trunk roads: A421: Great Barford bypass, Bedfordshire: Derestriction	170
Trunk roads: A421: Kempston Retail Park, Bedfordshire	212
Trunk roads: A421: Marsh Leys Roundabout, Kempstonbrogborough, Bedfordshire	212
Trunk roads: A423: South of Coventry	197
Trunk roads: A428: Cambourne junction, Cambridgeshire	212
Trunk roads: A428: Cambourne to Hardwick improvement	212
Trunk roads: A428: Cambridgeshire & Bedfordshire	170, 212
Trunk roads: A428: Caxton Common to Hardwick, Cambridgeshire	213
Trunk roads: A428: Hardwick-Girton, Cambridgeshire	212
Trunk roads: A43: Bandbrook, nr Whittlebury, Northamptonshire	196
Trunk roads: A43: Brackley & Evenley, Northamptonshire	196
Trunk roads: A43: Brackley Hatch, Northamptonshire	196
Trunk roads: A43: Buckingham Road roundabout - Whitfield Turn, Northamptonshire	196
Trunk roads: A43: Buckingham Road roundabout, Brackley, Northamptonshire	196
Trunk roads: A43: Evenley roundabout, Brackley, Northamptonshire	196
Trunk roads: A43: Hazelborough, Northamptonshire	196
Trunk roads: A43: M1 Motorway - Tove roundabout, Northamptonshire	196
Trunk roads: A43: Northamptonshire - Oxfordshire	170
Trunk roads: A43: Silverstone British Grand Prix, Brackley to Towcester, Northamptonshire	196
Trunk roads: A43: Swan Valley roundabout & Rothersthorpe service area, Northamptonshire	196
Trunk roads: A43: Tiffield and Blisworth junctions, Northamptonshire	196
Trunk roads: A43: Towcester bypass, Northamptonshire	197
Trunk roads: A43: Whitefield Layby, Northamptonshire	197
Trunk roads: A43: Whitfield Turn, Northamptonshire	197
Trunk roads: A43: Whittlewood Bridge to Brackley Road roundabout, Northamptonshire	197
Trunk roads: A435: Alcester to M42 junction 3	213
Trunk roads: A435: Branson's Cross, Worcestershire	213
Trunk roads: A435: Coughton, North of Alcester, Warwickshire	213
Trunk roads: A435: Gorcott Hill to Kings Coughton	213
Trunk roads: A435: Gorcott Hill, Warwickshire	213
Trunk roads: A435: Mappleborough Green to Studley, Warwickshire	213
Trunk roads: A44: Primrose Hill junction, Llanbadarn Fawr, Aberystwyth, Ceredigion	257
Trunk roads: A446: Coleshill to Hams Hall roundabout, Warwickshire	213
Trunk roads: A446: Little Packington	213
Trunk roads: A446: M6 junction 4 slip roads	230
Trunk roads: A449 & A456: Kidderminster, Blakedown & Hagley bypass & slip roads: Revocation	99
Trunk roads: A449: Beggars Bush Lane, Wombourne, Staffordshire	213
Trunk roads: A449: Caunsell, Worcestershire	213

Trunk roads: A449: Chester Road North, Kidderminster, Worcestershire 213
Trunk roads: A449: Claines to Ombersley, Worcestershire 213
Trunk roads: A449: Crossway Green, Worcestershire. 213
Trunk roads: A449: Gilbert Lane, Wombourne, Staffordshire 213
Trunk roads: A449: Himley to Wombourne, Staffordshire 214
Trunk roads: A449: Himley, Staffordshire. 213
Trunk roads: A449: Hoobrook to Summerfield, Kidderminster 214
Trunk roads: A449: Kingswinford to Prestwood 214
Trunk roads: A449: Lloyd Hill, Wolverhampton 214
Trunk roads: A449: M5 junction 6 to Ombersley, Worcestershire 214
Trunk roads: A449: Mitre Oak roundabout to Ombersley, Worcestershire 214
Trunk roads: A449: North of Hartlebury, Worcestershire 214
Trunk roads: A449: Ross-on-Wye, Herefordshire 195, 244
Trunk roads: A449: Stourbridge Rd., Wombourne 214
Trunk roads: A449: Wall Heath 170, 214
Trunk roads: A449: Warndon to Claines, Worcestershire 214
Trunk roads: A449: Wombourne to Lloyd Hill 214
Trunk roads: A45/M42: Slip roads, Warwickshire 243
Trunk roads: A45: Aggate Way Bridge, Earls Barton, Northamptonshire 197
Trunk roads: A45: Barnes Meadow interchange, Northamptonshire, eastbound entry slip road 197
Trunk roads: A45: Brackmills interchange to Queen Eleanor interchange, Northamptonshire 197
Trunk roads: A45: Brackmills to Queen Eleanor, Northamptonshire 197
Trunk roads: A45: Ditchford Lane Bridge, Rushden, Northamptonshire 197
Trunk roads: A45: Festival Is. to Tollbar End, Coventry 197
Trunk roads: A45: Festival Island to Tollbar End, Coventry 197
Trunk roads: A45: Festival Island, Coventry 197
Trunk roads: A45: Junction with A452, Stonebridge 197
Trunk roads: A45: Lumbertubs interchange - Barnes Meadow interchange, Northamptonshire 197
Trunk roads: A45: M1 junction 15 to Earls Barton, Northamptonshire 197
Trunk roads: A45: M42 junction 6, slip road 197
Trunk roads: A45: Northamptonshire 170, 198, 214
Trunk roads: A45: Queen Eleanor interchange, Northamptonshire 198
Trunk roads: A45: Raunds Roundabout to Stanwick Roundabout, Northamptonshire 198
Trunk roads: A45: Ryton-on-Dunsmore, Warwickshire 170, 198
Trunk roads: A45: South of Coventry 197
Trunk roads: A45: Stretton-on-Dunsmore, Warwickshire 198
Trunk roads: A453: Clifton Bridge, Nottingham 214
Trunk roads: A453: Clifton Lane, Nottingham, side roads 203
Trunk roads: A453: M1 junction 24 to Barton in Fabis 214
Trunk roads: A453: M1 junctions 23A - 24, Kegworth 214
Trunk roads: A453: Nottingham 170, 214
Trunk roads: A453: Silverdale roundabout, Nottinghamshire 203
Trunk roads: A456: Hagley Causeway, Worcestershire 214
Trunk roads: A456: Hagley, Worcestershire 214
Trunk roads: A456: Hayley Green, Dudley 215
Trunk roads: A456: Near Hagley, Worcestershire 215
Trunk roads: A456: West Hagley, Worcestershire 215
Trunk roads: A458/A5: Montford Bridge to Woodcote, Shropshire 179
Trunk roads: A458: Cardeston, Shropshire 215
Trunk roads: A46: A46/A607 junction, Leicestershire 198
Trunk roads: A46: Anstey to M1 junction 21A, Leicestershire 198
Trunk roads: A46: Anstey, Leicestershire, slip road 198, 204
Trunk roads: A46: Bailbrook underpass, Bath. 179
Trunk roads: A46: Between Broughton Lodge & Six Hills 198
Trunk roads: A46: Car Colston, Nottinghamshire 198
Trunk roads: A46: Carholme roundabout, Lincolnshire 198
Trunk roads: A46: Cold Ashton roundabout, near Bath 198
Trunk roads: A46: Evesham bypass, Worcestershire 198
Trunk roads: A46: Leicester western bypass 198
Trunk roads: A46: M5, junction 9, slip roads 227
Trunk roads: A46: M6 junction 2 229
Trunk roads: A46: Marraway roundabout, northeast of Snitterfield, Warwickshire 198
Trunk roads: A46: Near Swinderby, Lincolnshire 198
Trunk roads: A46: Near Widmerpool, Nottinghamshire 198
Trunk roads: A46: Newark-on-Trent, Nottinghamshire 170, 199

Trunk roads: A46: Pennsylvania . . . 199
Trunk roads: A46: Pennsylvania to Nimlet, near Cold Ashton . . . 199
Trunk roads: A46: Ratcliffe on the Wreake, Leicestershire, slip road . . . 199
Trunk roads: A46: Ratcliffe on the Wreake, Leicestershire . . . 199
Trunk roads: A46: Saxondale roundabout to Widmerpool roundabout, Nottinghamshire . . . 199
Trunk roads: A46: Saxondale to Newark on Trent, Nottinghamshire . . . 199
Trunk roads: A46: Saxondale to Widmerpool, Nottinghamshire . . . 199
Trunk roads: A46: Six Hills to Widmerpool . . . 199
Trunk roads: A46: Six Hills, Charnwood, Leicestershire . . . 199
Trunk roads: A46: South west of Lincoln, Lincolnshire . . . 199
Trunk roads: A46: Stratford-upon-Avon northern bypass, Warwickshire . . . 199
Trunk roads: A46: Temple Grafton, Warwickshire . . . 199
Trunk roads: A46: Upper Swainswick, Bath . . . 192
Trunk roads: A46: Warwick bypass, slip road . . . 199
Trunk roads: A46: Warwick bypass, Warwickshire . . . 199
Trunk roads: A46: Willoughby-Widmerpool, Nottinghamshire . . . 199
Trunk roads: A465: Allensmore, Herefordshire . . . 215
Trunk roads: A465: Belmond Road, Herefordshire . . . 215
Trunk roads: A465: Cefn Coed to Dowlais . . . 258
Trunk roads: A465: Didley, Herefordshire . . . 215
Trunk roads: A465: Galon Uchaf, Merthyr Tydfil . . . 258
Trunk roads: A465: Garnlydan, Brynmawr, Blaenau Gwent . . . 258
Trunk roads: A465: Gilwern to Abergavenny, Monmouthshire . . . 259
Trunk roads: A465: Govilon, Monmouthshire . . . 259
Trunk roads: A465: Hereford, footway . . . 215
Trunk roads: A465: Nant Ffrwd Viaduct, nr Merthyr Tydfil . . . 259
Trunk roads: A465: Nantybwch, Tredegar, Blaenau Gwent . . . 259
Trunk roads: A465: Neath interchange, Saltings Viaduct, Neath Port Talbot . . . 259
Trunk roads: A465: Pont Neath Vaughan Viaduct, Rhondda Cynon Taff . . . 259
Trunk roads: A47: Acle Straight, Norfolk . . . 199
Trunk roads: A47: Brampton Hut interchange, Huntingdon, Cambridgeshire . . . 170
Trunk roads: A47: Bretton Way interchange - Paston interchange, Soke Parkway, Peterborough . . . 199
Trunk roads: A47: City of Peterborough . . . 200
Trunk roads: A47: Cringleford/Thickthorn interchange, Norfolk . . . 169
Trunk roads: A47: Elm, Wisbech, Cambridgeshire . . . 200
Trunk roads: A47: Fulbridge Interchange to Dogsthorpe Interchange, Cambridge . . . 200
Trunk roads: A47: Hardwick roundabout, Kings Lynn bypass, Norfolk . . . 200
Trunk roads: A47: Little Fransham, Norfolk . . . 170
Trunk roads: A47: Middleton Village, Kings Lynn, Norfolk . . . 200
Trunk roads: A47: North Pickenham, Norfolk . . . 200
Trunk roads: A47: Norwich southern bypass, Norfolk . . . 200
Trunk roads: A47: Peterborough, Cambridgeshire . . . 200
Trunk roads: A47: Saddlebow interchange to Pullover interchange, Kings Lynn, Norfolk . . . 200
Trunk roads: A47: Swaffham, Norfolk . . . 200
Trunk roads: A47: Thorney Toll to Guyhirn, Cambridgeshire . . . 200
Trunk roads: A47: Wansford, City of Peterborough . . . 200
Trunk roads: A47: Wansford, Peterborough . . . 171
Trunk roads: A47: Wisbech Level Crossing, Cambridgeshire . . . 200
Trunk roads: A470: Abercynon Roundabout, Rhondda Cynon Taf . . . 256
Trunk roads: A470: Coryton, Cardiff . . . 259
Trunk roads: A470: Coryton, Cardiff to Nantgarw Junction, Rhondda Cynon Taf . . . 259
Trunk roads: A470: Coryton, Cardiff to Taff's Well, Rhondda Cynon Taf . . . 256
Trunk roads: A470: Glan y Mor to Pentrefelin, Conwy . . . 259
Trunk roads: A470: Llan Ffestiniog, Blaenau Ffestiniog, Gwynedd . . . 256
Trunk roads: A470: Nantgarw interchange to Bridge Street interchange, Rhondda Cynon Taf . . . 259
Trunk roads: A470: Nantgarw interchange, Rhondda Cynon Taf . . . 259
Trunk roads: A477: Backe Rd junction, west of St. Clears, Carmarthenshire . . . 259
Trunk roads: A48/A40: West of Meifrim junction to south of Llangunnor roundabout & east of Pensarn roundabout, Carmarthenshire 257
Trunk roads: A48/A483/M4: North of Cross Hands to south of Pont Abraham, Camarthenshire . . . 257
Trunk roads: A48: Pontardulais Rd. junction, Cross Hands, Camarthenshire . . . 258
Trunk roads: A483/A48/M4: North of Cross Hands to south of Pont Abraham, Camarthenshires . . . 257
Trunk roads: A483: Crossgates, near Llandrindod Wells, Powys . . . 256
Trunk roads: A483: Garth Road, Builth Wells, Powys . . . 256
Trunk roads: A483: Gresford, Wrexham . . . 259
Trunk roads: A483: Llynclys, Shropshire . . . 215
Trunk roads: A483: Mile End roundabout, Shropshire . . . 179

Trunk roads: A483: Rhosmaen St., Llandeilo, Carmarthenshire 260
Trunk roads: A483: Rhosmaen/Bridge St., Llandeilo, Carmarthenshire 259
Trunk roads: A487: Caernarfon, Gwynedd 256
Trunk roads: A487: Mill Street, Aberystwyth, Ceredigion 260
Trunk roads: A487: Tremadog, Gwynedd 256
Trunk roads: A487: Vergam Terr., Fishguard, Pembrokeshire 260
Trunk roads: A487: West Street, Fishguard, Pembrokeshire 260
Trunk roads: A49: Brimfield, Herefordshire. 200
Trunk roads: A49: Bromfield to Craven Arms, Shropshire 200
Trunk roads: A49: Greyfriars Bridge, Hereford 200
Trunk roads: A49: Harewood End to Much Birch, Herefordshire. 200
Trunk roads: A49: Hereford 200
Trunk roads: A49: Hope under Dinmore to Hereford 201
Trunk roads: A49: Kings Thorn, Herefordshire 201
Trunk roads: A49: Leominster, Herefordshire. 201
Trunk roads: A49: Longnor, Shropshire 201
Trunk roads: A49: North of Ludlow, Shropshire 201
Trunk roads: A49: Onibury Bridge, Shropshire 201
Trunk roads: A49: Poolmill - Bridstow, Herefordshire 201
Trunk roads: A49: Strefford, Shropshire. 201
Trunk roads: A49: Wellington to Moreton on Lugg, Herefordshire. 201
Trunk roads: A49: Wistanstow, Shropshire 201
Trunk roads: A49: Woofferton, Shropshire 201
Trunk roads: A494/A5: Druids junction, west of Corwen, Denbighshire 256
Trunk roads: A494/A550: Deeside Park interchange, Queensferry 260
Trunk roads: A494/A550: Deeside, Flintshire 260
Trunk roads: A494: Ruthin, Denbighshire. 260
Trunk roads: A5 243
Trunk roads: A5/A458: Montford Bridge to Woodcote, Shropshire 179
Trunk roads: A5/A494: Druids junction, west of Corwen, Denbighshire 256
Trunk roads: A5/M54: Telford to Shrewsbury, Shropshire 245
Trunk roads: A5: Atherstone, Warwickshire 179
Trunk roads: A5: Bethesda, Bangor, Gwynedd 256
Trunk roads: A5: Carrog, Llidiart Y Parc, Corwen, Denbighshire 256
Trunk roads: A5: Cuttle Mill, Northamptonshire 179
Trunk roads: A5: Dordon, Warwickshire 179
Trunk roads: A5: Gailey to Brownhills 230
Trunk roads: A5: Gibbet Hill to Catthorpe, Warwickshire 179
Trunk roads: A5: Halfway Bridge, Bethesda, Gwynedd. 256
Trunk roads: A5: High Cross to Gibbet Hill 179
Trunk roads: A5: Hinckley, Leicestershire 180
Trunk roads: A5: Little Brickhill roundabout, Milton Keynes 180
Trunk roads: A5: Llyn Ogwen to Pont Rhyd Goch, nr Capel Curig, Gwynedd 256
Trunk roads: A5: Llyn Ogwen, north of Capel Curig, Conwy County Borough 256
Trunk roads: A5: London Road, Dunstable, Bedfordshire 180
Trunk roads: A5: M1, junction 9, Hertfordshire 180
Trunk roads: A5: M42 junction 10 to Dordon, Warwickshire 242
Trunk roads: A5: Mile End roundabout, Shropshire 179
Trunk roads: A5: Milton Keynes. 180
Trunk roads: A5: Milton Keynes bypass, Buckinghamshire 180
Trunk roads: A5: Near Higham on the Hill, Warwickshire 180
Trunk roads: A5: Near Hinckley 252
Trunk roads: A5: Old Stratford roundabout, Northamptonshire 180
Trunk roads: A5: Pentrefoelas, Conwy 257
Trunk roads: A5: Pont Melin Rug improvement 260
Trunk roads: A5: Portway interchange, Milton Keynes 180
Trunk roads: A5: Portway, Milton Keynes 180
Trunk roads: A5: Redmoor roundabout, Milton Keynes 180
Trunk roads: A5: Shrewsbury bypass, Shropshire 180
Trunk roads: A5: Tamworth bypass, Staffordshire 180
Trunk roads: A5: Tamworth, Staffordshire 180
Trunk roads: A5: Tamworth, Staffordshire, slip roads 180
Trunk roads: A5: Thorn, south Bedfordshire 180
Trunk roads: A5: Ty Nant to Dinmael (Glyn Bends), east of Cerrigydrudion, Conwy 257
Trunk roads: A5: Wall, Staffordshire 180

Trunk roads: A5: Watford Locks Underbridge, Northamptonshire 181
Trunk roads: A5: Weedon, Northamptonshire. 181
Trunk roads: A5: Weeford to Gailey, Staffordshire 181
Trunk roads: A5: Wolfshead roundabout to Shotatton, Shropshire 181
Trunk roads: A50: A50/A38 interchange, Derbyshire. 170
Trunk roads: A50: A6 Spur, Derbyshire: Slip roads 201
Trunk roads: A50: Blythe Bridge to Uttoxeter, Staffordshire 201
Trunk roads: A50: Chellaston, Derbyshire, slip road 201
Trunk roads: A50: Church Street, Lockington, Leicestershire 202
Trunk roads: A50: Derbyshire 202
Trunk roads: A50: Doveridge bypass 202
Trunk roads: A50: Doveridge, Derbyshire. 202
Trunk roads: A50: Etwall, Derbyshire 202
Trunk roads: A50: Findern, Derbyshire 202
Trunk roads: A50: Foston, Derbyshire. 202
Trunk roads: A50: Grindley Lane interchange, Staffordshire 202
Trunk roads: A50: Junction with A6, Aston-on-Trent. 202
Trunk roads: A50: Junction with A6, near Chellaston 202
Trunk roads: A50: Junction with Blurton Road, Stoke on Trent 202
Trunk roads: A50: Lockington 220
Trunk roads: A50: Lockington roundabout, Leicestershire 202
Trunk roads: A50: Meir Tunnel, Stoke-on-Trent 202
Trunk roads: A50: Meir, Stoke-on-Trent, footway 202
Trunk roads: A50: Nr Chellaston, Derbyshire 202
Trunk roads: A50: Sideway to Heron Cross, Stoke-on-Trent 202
Trunk roads: A50: Stoke on Trent 202
Trunk roads: A50: Toyota intersection, Derbyshire 193
Trunk roads: A50: Uttoxeter to Stoke-on-Trent, Staffordshire 203
Trunk roads: A50: West Broughton, Derbyshire 203
Trunk roads: A500/A34: Talke, Staffordshire 191
Trunk roads: A500: Audley, Staffordshire 215
Trunk roads: A500: East of Barthomley roundabout, Staffordshire 215
Trunk roads: A500: Hanford to Sideway, Stoke-on-Trent 215
Trunk roads: A500: M6 junction 16 215
Trunk roads: A500: Near Bignall End, Staffordshire 215
Trunk roads: A500: Porthill to Wolstanton, Newcastle-under-Lyme, Stoke-on-Trent 215
Trunk roads: A500: Porthill interchange, Stoke-on-Trent 215
Trunk roads: A500: Sideway, Stoke-on-Trent 215
Trunk roads: A500: Southbound exit slip road to Whieldon Road 216
Trunk roads: A500: Stoke Pathfinder Project 216
Trunk roads: A500: Talke Pits, Staffordshire 216
Trunk roads: A500: Talke, Staffordshire 216
Trunk roads: A500: Wolstanton, Staffordshire 216
Trunk roads: A5036: Church Road 218
Trunk roads: A5036: Princess Way, eastbound carriageway between A567 (Bridge Road) roundabout & A5090 (Hawthorne Road) . 218
Trunk roads: A5036: Switch Island 204
Trunk roads: A5036: Westbound between St Mathew's Avenue & Orrell Road 218
Trunk roads: A5092: Between A595 & A590: Detrunking 100
Trunk roads: A5103: Southbound, exit slip road to the A560 Altrincham Road 218
Trunk roads: A5103: Southbound, exit slip road to the B5167 Palatine Road 219
Trunk roads: A5111: Link road, Raynesway, Derby 219
Trunk roads: A5111: Raynesway, Derby, Link roads 219
Trunk roads: A5117: Deeside junction improvement 219
Trunk roads: A516 193
Trunk roads: A516: South of Derby 193
Trunk roads: A52: Bardills roundabout, Stapleford, Nottinghamshire 203
Trunk roads: A52: Beeston, Nottinghamshire 203
Trunk roads: A52: Bingham, Nottinghamshire 203
Trunk roads: A52: Borrowash bypass, Derbyshire 203
Trunk roads: A52: Bottesford bypass 203
Trunk roads: A52: Bottesford to Sedgebrook 203
Trunk roads: A52: Bramcote Is., Nottinghamshire 203
Trunk roads: A52: Clifton Bridge, Nottingham 214
Trunk roads: A52: Clifton Lane, Nottingham, side roads 203
Trunk roads: A52: Derby Road, Nottingham: Bus/cycle lane 203
Trunk roads: A52: Muston, Leicestershire 203

Trunk roads: A52: Near Barrowby, Lincolnshire	173
Trunk roads: A52: Near Radcliffe-on-Trent, Nottinghamshire	203
Trunk roads: A52: Nottingham	170, 214
Trunk roads: A52: Nottingham Knight roundabout to Wheatcroft roundabout, Nottinghamshire	203
Trunk roads: A52: Queens Medical Centre roundabout, Nottingham	203
Trunk roads: A52: Risley, Derbyshire	203
Trunk roads: A52: Saxondale, Nottinghamshire	204
Trunk roads: A52: Silverdale roundabout, Nottinghamshire	203
Trunk roads: A52: Stapleford	204
Trunk roads: A52: Stapleford, Nottinghamshire	204
Trunk roads: A55: Abergele, Conwy to St Asaph, Denbighshire	258
Trunk roads: A55: Bangor, Gwynedd	258
Trunk roads: A55: Britannia Bridge, Gwynedd & Anglesey	258
Trunk roads: A55: Conwy Tunnel, Conwy	258
Trunk roads: A55: Holywell bypass, Flintshire	258
Trunk roads: A55: Junction 1, Kingsland roundabout, Holyhead - junction 6, Nant Turnpike Interchange, Llangefni, Isle of Anglesey	258
Trunk roads: A55: Junction 33, Northop interchange, Flintshire	258
Trunk roads: A55: Junctions with A51 & A56 & access slip road from A51	204
Trunk roads: A55: Northbound entry slip road from the A51 at Vicars Cross	204
Trunk roads: A55: Pen-y-clip Tunnel, Conwy	258
Trunk roads: A55: Southbound entry slip road at junction 12, M53	204
Trunk roads: A55: Tal-y-bont, Bangor, Gwynedd	258
Trunk roads: A55: Westbound carriageway, junction 24 to 27, Asaph, Denbighshire	258
Trunk roads: A550 Deeside Park to Ledsham: Improvement: Detrunking: Revocation	100
Trunk roads: A550/A494: Deeside Park interchange, Queensferry	260
Trunk roads: A550/A5117: M56 & A548 improvement: Connecting roads	100
Trunk roads: A556: M6 junction 19 to Bucklow Hill	216
Trunk roads: A556: M6 junction 19, Tabley roundabout	216
Trunk roads: A556: RHS Flower Show	216
Trunk roads: A56: Northbound carriageway & slip roads	251
Trunk roads: A56: Southbound carriageway & entry slip road from the A680	204
Trunk roads: A57: Market Street junction, Mottram	204
Trunk roads: A570: Scarth Hill to Stanley Gate	216
Trunk roads: A585: Dock St., Fleetwood	216
Trunk roads: A585: Fleetwood Rd., Greenhalgh	216
Trunk roads: A585: Singleton crossroads	216
Trunk roads: A59: Switch Island	204
Trunk roads: A590: A5092 Greenodd junction	216
Trunk roads: A590: Ayside, High & Low Newton bypass	216
Trunk roads: A590: Brettargh Holt Entry Slip Road	216
Trunk roads: A590: Green Lane	217
Trunk roads: A590: Haverthwaite	217
Trunk roads: A590: High Newton to Ayside	217
Trunk roads: A590: M6 junction 36, Farleton interchange	206
Trunk roads: A590: Meathop roundabout to Catcragg	217
Trunk roads: A590: Milton	217
Trunk roads: A590: Newby Bridge Surfacing Scheme	217
Trunk roads: A590: Witherslack to Meathop	217
Trunk roads: A595 Grizebeck to Chapel Brow: Parton to Lillyhall improvement	100
Trunk roads: A595: Broadgate resurfacing scheme	217
Trunk roads: A595: Calder Bridge to A5092 at Grizebeck: Detrunking	100
Trunk roads: A595: Gosforth drainage renewal scheme	217
Trunk roads: A595: Lillyhall	217
Trunk roads: A595: Lillyhall to Distington	217
Trunk roads: A595: Saltcoats to Thornflatt	217
Trunk roads: A6/A50/A453/M1: Junction 24	221
Trunk roads: A61: A614 & B6045: Blyth	98
Trunk roads: A61: A614 & B6045: Blyth: Detrunking	98
Trunk roads: A61: M1 Motorway to Westwood roundabout	204
Trunk roads: A616: Westwood Roundabout to Newton Chambers Roundabout	217
Trunk roads: A616: Wortley junction to Westwood roundabout	217
Trunk roads: A627: Southbound & northbound main carriageways	249
Trunk roads: A628: Crowden to Tintwistle	217
Trunk roads: A628: Crowden Youth Hostel	217
Trunk roads: A628: Five Arches Bridge to Salter's Brook Bridge	218

Trunk roads: A628: Five Arches Bridge, Woodhead Pass. 218
Trunk roads: A628: Woolley Lane (West) junction to Hollingworth Brook Bridge 218
Trunk roads: A629: Cononley crossroads 218
Trunk roads: A63: Austhorpe interchange roundabout 204
Trunk roads: A63: Cliffe & Hemingbrough 170
Trunk roads: A63: Daltry Street interchange to Mytongate rondabout 204
Trunk roads: A63: East of Peckfield Bar to Boot & Shoe: Detrunking. 99
Trunk roads: A63: Ferrybridge to Boot & Shoe Roundabout 209
Trunk roads: A63: Lowfield Lane junction, Welton. 204
Trunk roads: A63: Lowfield Lane, Welton 204
Trunk roads: A63: Melton 204
Trunk roads: A63: Melton to North Ferriby 204
Trunk roads: A63: Myton Bridge 204
Trunk roads: A63: North Cave interchange, westbound exit slip road 205
Trunk roads: A63: Priory Way junction 205
Trunk roads: A63: Queen St./Market Place junction, Hull 205
Trunk roads: A63: Selby bypass. 205
Trunk roads: A63: Selby bypass: A1041 to A19 205
Trunk roads: A64: Askham Bryan to Bilbrough. 205
Trunk roads: A64: Bilbrough to Copmanthorpe. 205
Trunk roads: A64: Bond Hill Ash Junction 205
Trunk roads: A64: Calcaria (RIver Wharf) Bridge 205
Trunk roads: A64: Chapel Close junction, Staxton to Seamer roundabout 205
Trunk roads: A64: Chestnut Avenue, Welburn 205
Trunk roads: A64: Chestnut Avenue, Welburn to Malton. 205
Trunk roads: A64: Ganton to Staxton 205
Trunk roads: A64: Jinnah Restaurant to Chestnut Ave., Welburn. 205
Trunk roads: A64: River Ouse Bridge. 205
Trunk roads: A64: Seamer roundabout to Eastfield roundabout. 205
Trunk roads: A64: Tadcaster Bar to Bilbrough 205
Trunk roads: A65: Austwick. 206
Trunk roads: A65: Boothes roundabout 206
Trunk roads: A65: Far west houses patching scheme 206
Trunk roads: A65: Gargrave Bypass: 1990 & 1993 Orders. 99
Trunk roads: A65: Hellifield & Long Preston: Bypass & slip roads 99
Trunk roads: A65: Hornsbarrow Farm patching scheme 206
Trunk roads: A65: Ingleton 170
Trunk roads: A65: Kirkby Lonsdale 170
Trunk roads: A65: Long Preston renewal scheme 206
Trunk roads: A65: M6 junction 36, Farleton interchange 206
Trunk roads: A65: New Rd., Ingleton 206
Trunk roads: A65: Rathmell 206
Trunk roads: A65: Thorlby. 206
Trunk roads: A650: Crossflatts roundabout 218
Trunk roads: A66/A19: Stockton Rd interchange 186, 187
Trunk roads: A66/A19: Stockton Rd interchange to Portrack interchange 187
Trunk roads: A66: Blackhill Farm, Winston Crossings 206
Trunk roads: A66: Bowes. 175, 206
Trunk roads: A66: Briery interchange 206
Trunk roads: A66: Cocker Bridge, Cockermouth 206
Trunk roads: A66: Coltsford Bridge, Brough 206
Trunk roads: A66: Eaglescliffe interchange to Little Burdon roundabout. 206
Trunk roads: A66: Flitholme Junction. 206
Trunk roads: A66: Greta Bridge to Threlkeld 207
Trunk roads: A66: Haverthwaite. 207
Trunk roads: A66: Kemplay Bank to Brougham 207
Trunk roads: A66: Kentigern Bridge, Keswick 207
Trunk roads: A66: Little Burdon roundabout to Elton interchange 207
Trunk roads: A66: Morton Palms roundabout. 207
Trunk roads: A66: Morton Palms roundabout to Yarm Road interchange 207
Trunk roads: A66: Penrith to Workington. 207
Trunk roads: A66: Rokeby Junction to Thorpe Grange Junction 207
Trunk roads: A66: Scotch Corner interchange 173, 206
Trunk roads: A66: Scotch Corner to Greta Bridge. 207
Trunk roads: A66: Smallways Beck New Bridge 207
Trunk roads: A66: Stockton & Thornaby bypass 207

Trunk roads: A66: Stockton Road Interchange 187
Trunk roads: A66: Temple Sowerby bypass. 207
Trunk roads: A66: Westray Farm to Embleton 207
Trunk roads: A66: Whinfell Park Resurfacing Scheme 207
Trunk roads: A68: Bongate, Jedburgh: Scotland 380
Trunk roads: A68: Dalkeith & St David's Primary School: Scotland 377
Trunk roads: A68: Pathhead & Pathhead Primary School: Scotland 378
Trunk roads: A69: Denton Burn roundabout to West Denton Interchange 208
Trunk roads: A69: Denton Burn to Hexham. 208
Trunk roads: A69: Haydon Bridge bypass 99
Trunk roads: A69: Marsh Lane overbridge to Throckley interchange. 208
Trunk roads: A69: Rosehill roundabout to Aglionby 208
Trunk roads: A69: Scarrow Hill to Low Row and Haltwhistle to Melkridge 208
Trunk roads: A69: Warwick Bridge. 208
Trunk roads: A696: Kenton Bar interchange 173
Trunk roads: A7: Auchenrivock improvement, side roads: Scotland 375
Trunk roads: A7: Auchenrivock improvement: Scotland 375
Trunk roads: A7: Circulatory carriageway. 232
Trunk roads: A7: Hawick High School & Wilton Primary School: Scotland 377
Trunk roads: A7: Selkirk & Selkirk High School & St Joseph's Primary School: Scotland 377
Trunk roads: A702: Biggar High St., special event: Scotland 381
Trunk roads: A702: Biggar Road, Edinburgh: Scotland 379
Trunk roads: A702: Hillend: Scotland 379, 382
Trunk roads: A702: Kilwinning: Scotland 379
Trunk roads: A702: West Linton: Scotland 379
Trunk roads: A720: Calder junction to Baberton junction: Scotland 382
Trunk roads: A725/A726: Carmunnock bypass, Kingsway: Scotland. 382
Trunk roads: A725/A726: Queensway: Scotland 382
Trunk roads: A725/A726: Righead roundabout: Scotland. 382
Trunk roads: A726: Paisley to East Kilbride, central reserve: Scotland 382
Trunk roads: A726: Paisley to East Kilbride: Scotland 382
Trunk roads: A737: Roadhead roundabout improvement, side roads: Scotland. 376
Trunk roads: A737: Roadhead roundabout improvement: Scotland. 376
Trunk roads: A74 . . . . 232, 233
Trunk roads: A74/M6: Harker Bridge 208
Trunk roads: A74: Carlisle to Guards Mill section: Detrunking 99
Trunk roads: A74: Guardmill to Mossband resurfacing 208
Trunk roads: A74: M6 extension project 208
Trunk roads: A74: M6 extension project: Carlisle to Guardsmill 208
Trunk roads: A74: M6, junction 44: Greymoorhill interchange, southbound carriageway 229
Trunk roads: A74: Swaffham, Norfolk 208
Trunk roads: A74: Todhills to Mossband, layby closures 208
Trunk roads: A76: Cumnock & Castle Primary School: Scotland. 378
Trunk roads: A76: Glenairlie improvement: Scotland. 375
Trunk roads: A77: British Seniors Open Golf Championship, Turnberry: Scotland 378
Trunk roads: A77: Central reserve: Scotland 380
Trunk roads: A77: Dalrymple Street, Girvan: Scotland 380
Trunk roads: A77: Girvan & Sacred Heart & Invergarven Primary Schools: Scotland 378
Trunk roads: A77: Haggstone Climbing Lane, side roads: Scotland 376
Trunk roads: A77: Lendalfoot picnic area, special event: Scotland 380
Trunk roads: A77: Maybole: Scotland. 380
Trunk roads: A77: Whitletts roundabout to Dutchhouse roundabout, Ayr bypass: Scotland 383
Trunk roads: A77: Whitletts roundabout: Scotland 378, 380
Trunk roads: A78: Eglinton interchange to Pennyburn roundabout: Scotland 380
Trunk roads: A78: Greenock Schools: Scotland. 378
Trunk roads: A78: Inverkip St., Greenock: Scotland. 380, 381
Trunk roads: A78: Longhill, Skelmorlie: Scotland 381
Trunk roads: A78: Pennyburn roundabout to Longford Ave., Kilwinning: Scotland 381
Trunk roads: A8: East Hamilton St., Greenock: Scotland 375
Trunk roads: A8: Ratho St., Greenock: Scotland 380
Trunk roads: A80/M80: Stepps to Moodiesburn, detrunking: Scotland 377
Trunk roads: A80: Auchenkilns junction: Scotland 378
Trunk roads: A80: Auchenkilns to Haggs, side roads: Scotland. 376
Trunk roads: A80: Mollinsburn to Auchenkilns, prohibition of specified turns: Scotland 377
Trunk roads: A80: Mollinsburn to Auchenkilns, side roads: Scotland 376

Trunk roads: A82: Aonachan lay-by, Spean Bridge: Scotland 376
Trunk roads: A82: Balloch to Tarbet Cycle Routes: Scotland. 376
Trunk roads: A82: Drumnadrochit & Lewiston: Scotland. 378
Trunk roads: A82: Fort William & Fort William Primary School: Scotland 378
Trunk roads: A82: Lairig Eilde Bridge, Glencoe: Scotland 381
Trunk roads: A82: Scottish Open Golf Tournament, Loch Lomond: Scotland 378
Trunk roads: A82: Stoneymollan roundabout, Balloch: Scotland. 381
Trunk roads: A83: Tarbert: Special event: Scotland. 375
Trunk roads: A830: Arisaig - Loch nan Uamh, side roads: Scotland 376
Trunk roads: A830: Arisaig - Loch nan Uamh, variation: Scotland 376
Trunk roads: A830: Corpach (speed limit) & Banavie Primary School: Scotland 379
Trunk roads: A830: Lochybridge & Lochaber High School: Scotland 379
Trunk roads: A85: Lochawe: Scotland. 386
Trunk roads: A86: Dalwhinnie junction to Creag Meagaidh: Scotland 381
Trunk roads: A86: Newtownmore Bridge & Newtownmore Primary School: Scotland 378
Trunk roads: A86: Roybridge & Roybridge Primary School: Scotland 378
Trunk roads: A86: Spean Bridge & Spean Bridge Primary School: Scotland 378
Trunk roads: A87: Invergarry & Invergarry Primary School: Scotland 378
Trunk roads: A87: Inverinate & Loch Duich Primary School: Scotland 378
Trunk roads: A87: Uig, Isle of Skye & Uig Primary School: Scotland 378
Trunk roads: A876: Upper Forth Crossing at Kincardine: Scotland. 382
Trunk roads: A9: Auchterarder, Perthshire: Scotland 380
Trunk roads: A9: Ballinluig junction improvement, side roads: Scotland. 375
Trunk roads: A9: Ballinluig junction improvement, slip roads: Scotland 375
Trunk roads: A9: Ballinluig junction improvement: Scotland 380
Trunk roads: A9: Golspie & Golspie High School: Scotland 377
Trunk roads: A9: Greenloaning, Perthshire: Scotland 380
Trunk roads: A9: Helmsdale to Ord of Caithness improvements, side roads: Scotland. 375
Trunk roads: A9: Portree & Portree High School: Scotland. 377
Trunk roads: A9: Schoolhill Development: Scotland 380
Trunk roads: A9: Tore: Scotland. 380
Trunk roads: A90/M90: Glendoick, near Perth: Scotland 383
Trunk roads: A90: Ellon Rd., Aberdeen: Scotland 379
Trunk roads: A90: Hilton Dr. & Manor Ave. junctions, Aberdeen: Scotland. 381
Trunk roads: A90: Kingsway, Dundee: Scotland 379
Trunk roads: A90: Mill of Marcus, Angus: Scotland 381
Trunk roads: A90: Nether Careston, Angus: Scotland. 381
Trunk roads: A90: Perth to Dundee: Scotland 381
Trunk roads: A90: Petterden, Angus: Scotland 381
Trunk roads: A90: Schoolhill Development: Scotland 379, 381
Trunk roads: A90: The Parkway, Bridge of Don, Aberdeen: Scotland 379
Trunk roads: A92/A972: Kingsway, Dundee: Scotland. 381
Trunk roads: A92: Forgan roundabout, Fife: Scotland 381
Trunk roads: A92: Freuchie: Scotland 379
Trunk roads: A95: Cromdale Village: Scotland 379
Trunk roads: A96: Fochabers & Milnes Primary School: Scotland 379
Trunk roads: A96: Ladyhill Rd. Car Park, Elgin: Scotland 381
Trunk roads: A96: Nairn & Rosebank Primary School: Scotland 379
Trunk roads: A977: Kincardine Toll Road: Scotland 379
Trunk roads: A977: Upper Forth Crossing at Kincardine: Scotland. 382
Trunk roads: B6353, Fenwick Junction 174
Trunk roads: Doncaster by-pass: Special road schemes 100
Trunk roads: M6: Extension project: Carlisle to Guardsmill 208
Trunk roads: M77/A77: Bogend Toll: Scotland 383
Trunk roads: M77/A77: Junction 5 (Maidenhill) to Junction 2 (Barrhead Rd.): Scotland 383
Trunk roads: M8/A8: Bogston Lane to Mackenzie St., Greenock: Scotland 382
Trunk roads: M8/A8: Chapleton St. to Anderson St., Port Glasgow: Scotland 379
Trunk roads: M8/A8: Greenock Rd./Port Glasgow Rd. junction, Greenock: Scotland 376
Trunk roads: M8/A8: Port Glasgow: Scotland. 382
Trunk roads: M8/A8: Rue End St./Dellington St. junction, Greenock: Scotland 376
Trunk roads: M8/A8: William St., Port Glasgow Rd., Belhaven St.& Anderson St., Port Glasgow: Scotland . . . 382
Trunk roads: M80/A80: Junction 5 - 9: Scotland 383
Trunk roads: M9/A9: Artafallie junction: Scotland 382
Trunk roads: M9/A9: Between junction 5 & junction 6: Scotland 382
Trunk roads: M9: Junction 1A, Kirkliston: Scotland 382
Trunk roads: M90/A90: Persley Bridge, Aberdeen: Scotland. 380

Trunk roads: North east unit trunk roads area: Scotland 383, 384
Trunk roads: North west unit trunk roads area: Scotland. 384, 385
Trunk roads: South east unit trunk roads area: Scotland 385, 386
Trunk roads: South west unit trunk roads area: Scotland 386
TSE *see* Transmissible spongiform encephalopathies21, 25
Tuberculosis: Animal health: England 21
Tuberculosis: Animal health: Wales 25
Tuition: Fees: Student loans: Scotland. 350
Tunbridge Wells (Borough): Electoral changes 121
Turkey flocks: Salmonella: Survey powers: England 21
Turkey flocks: Salmonella: Survey powers: Northern Ireland 408, 415
Turks & Caicos Islands: Constitution 29
Tyne & Wear Passenger Transport Authority: Members: Increase in number 286
Tyneside: South Tyneside (Metropolitan Borough: Permitted & special parking areas 255

U

Unapool Burn: Scottish Water: Scotland 394
Unauthorised encampments: 2005 Order: Commencements: Northern Ireland. 444
Unauthorised encampments: Vehicles: Retention & disposal: Northern Ireland 444
Unit trust schemes: Non-qualifying investments tests 50, 114
United Nations: Al-Qaida & Taliban: Measures. 286
United Nations: International tribunals: Former Yugoslavia & Rwanda 287
United Nations: Measures: Lebanon & Syria 287
United Nations: Measures: Lebanon & Syria: Channel Islands 286
United Nations: Measures: Lebanon & Syria: Isle of Man 286
United Nations: North Korea: Measures. 287
United Nations: North Korea: Measures: Overseas territories. 287
United Nations: Sudan: Measures 287
United Nations: Terrorism: Measures 287
Unity College: Religious character: Designation 69
Urban development: London Thames Gateway Development Corporation: Planning functions 287
Urban development: Olympic Delivery Authority: Planning functions 287
Utilities contracts: Public procurement 160
Utilities contracts: Scotland 373
Uttlesford: Parish electoral arrangements: Local government. 123
Uzbekistan: Restrictive measures: Arms & military activities: Overseas territories 146

V

Vaccine damage payments: Specified disease. 159
Valuation & rating: Exempted classes: Scotland 374
Valuation lists: Council tax: Acts: England 5
Valuation lists: Council tax: Acts: Explanatory notes: England 10
Value added tax see *also* Taxes
Value added tax 288
Value added tax: Betting, gaming & lotteries 288
Value added tax: Cars 288
Value added tax: Customs & excise duties: Travellers' allowances & personal reliefs: New member states 54, 83, 287, 288
Value added tax: Finance Act 2006: Section 18: Appointed day 288
Value added tax: Fuel: Private use: Consideration 288
Value added tax: Gaming machines 288
Value added tax: Lifeboats. 288
Value added tax: Reduced rate 288
Value added tax: Refund 289
Value added tax: Registration limits: Increase 288
Value added tax: Special provisions 289
Value added tax: Supply of services 288
Value added tax: Third countries: Legacies imported from: Relief: Application 55, 84, 288
Value added tax: Transactions & special provisions: Treatment 289
Vehicles: Goods vehicles: Testing: Northern Ireland 437
Vehicles: Motor cars: Driving instruction 166
Vehicles: Motor vehicles: Construction & use: Northern Ireland 437
Vehicles: Motor vehicles: Driving licences 167
Vehicles: Motor vehicles: EC type approval. 167

Vehicles: Motor vehicles: Immobilisation & release: Prescribed charges: Northern Ireland 437
Vehicles: Motor vehicles: Immobilisation & removal: Prescribed conditions: Northern Ireland 437
Vehicles: Motor vehicles: Removal, storage & disposal: Prescribed charges: Northern Ireland 438
Vehicles: Motor vehicles: Taxi Drivers' licences: Fees: Amendments: Northern Ireland 437
Vehicles: Motor vehicles: Type approval & approval marks: Fees 167
Vehicles: Passenger & goods vehicles: Recording equipment 168
Vehicles: Passenger & goods vehicles: Recording equipment: Fitting dates 168
Vehicles: Passenger & goods vehicles: Recording equipment: Tachograph cards 168
Vehicles: Private hire: Carriage of guide dogs, etc.: Disability Discrimination Act 1995: England & Wales 61, 285
Vehicles: Public service vehicles: Accessibility: Northern Ireland 438
Vehicles: Public service vehicles: Conditions of fitness, equipment & use: Northern Ireland 438
Vehicles: Public service vehicles: Northern Ireland 438
Vehicles: Public service: Fitness, equipment & use: Conditions: Northern Ireland 438
Veterinary medicines 128
Veterinary surgeons & practitioners: Registration 289
Victims & survivors: Commissioner: Northern Ireland 144
Violent crime: Reduction: Acts 9
Violent crime: Reduction: Acts: Explanatory notes 11
Visas: Passenger transit: Immigration 109
Voting: Absent: Transitional provisions: England & Wales 164
Vulnerable adults: Care Standards Tribunal: Disqualification orders: Review: England & Wales 31
Vulnerable adults: Care Standards Tribunal: England & Wales 31, 266
Vulnerable groups: Children & adults: Safeguarding: Acts 8
Vulnerable groups: Children & adults: Safeguarding: Acts: Explanatory notes 11
Vulnerable Witnesses (Scotland) Act 2004: Commencements: Scotland 357, 390

W

Wages: National minimum wage 277
Wales: National Assembly for Wales: Disqualifications 43
Wales: National Health Service: Community Health Councils: Carmarthenshire 138
War Pensions Committees 151
Warehousekeepers & owners of warehoused goods: Excise 84
Warrington (Borough): Permitted & special parking areas 254
Warwickshire (County): Rugby (Borough): Permitted & special parking areas 254
Warwickshire: Coventry & Warwickshire Partnership: National Health Service Trust 132
Waste electrical & electronic equipment 79
Waste electrical & electronic equipment: Waste management licensing: England & Wales 81
Waste management: England & Wales 81
Waste management: Household waste: Duty of care: Wales 82
Waste management: Licensing: Scotland 352
Waste management: Licensing: Water environment: Scotland 352
Waste management: Northern Ireland 415
Waste recycling payments: England 80
Waste: Electrical & electronic equipment: Charges: Northern Ireland 415
Waste: Electrical & electronic equipment: Waste management licensing: Northern Ireland 415
Waste: Joint waste disposal authorities: Levies: England 124
Waste: Joint Waste Disposal Authorities: Recycling payments: Disapplication: England 80
Waste: Landfill tax 119
Water & sewerage services: Licences: Scotland 393
Water & sewerage services: Northern Ireland 144
Water Act 2003: Commencement, transitional provisions & savings 289
Water Act 2003: Transitional provisions: Consumer protection 46, 289
Water Environment & Water Services (Scotland) Act 2003: Commencements: Scotland 393
Water Environment & Water Services (Scotland) Act 2003: Consequential provisions & modifications 44, 59, 290
Water Environment & Water Services (Scotland) Act 2003: Designation of responsible authorities & functions: Scotland . . . 352, 393
Water environment: Consequential & savings provisions: Scotland 353, 393
Water environment: Consequential provisions: Scotland 353, 393
Water environment: Waste management: Licensing: Scotland 352
Water industry: Sewerage nuisance: Code of practice: Scotland 393
Water industry: Water & sewerage services: Licences: Scotland 393
Water industry: Water Services etc. (Scotland) Act 2005: Commencements: Scotland 394
Water resources: Abstraction & impounding 290
Water resources: Environmental impact assessment: England & Wales 290
Water resources: Environmental impact assessment: Northern Ireland 416, 445
Water resources: Mid Kent Water: Non-essential use: Drought order 289

Water resources: Southern Water Services: Kent Medway, Kent Thanet & Sussex Hastings: Non-essential use: Drought order 289
Water resources: Southern Water Services: Sussex North & Sussex Coast: Non-essential use: Drought order 289
Water resources: Sutton & East Surrey Water plc: Non-essential use: Drought order 289
Water Services etc. (Scotland) Act 2005: Commencements: Scotland 394
Water supply: Abhainn Dhubh: Scottish Water: Scotland. 394
Water supply: Allt an Lagain: Scottish Water: Scotland 394
Water supply: Loch Braigh Horrisdale: Scottish Water: Scotland. 394
Water supply: Private supplies: Grants: Scotland 394
Water supply: Private supplies: Notices: Scotland. 394
Water supply: Private supplies: Scotland 394
Water supply: Services: Charges: Billing & collection: Scotland 395
Water supply: Tomich boreholes: Scottish Water: Scotland. 394
Water supply: Unapool Burn: Scottish Water: Scotland. 394
Water supply: Water & sewerage: Charges: Exemptions & reductions: Scotland 395
Water supply: Water & sewerage: Services cost: Scotland 394
Water: Abstraction & impoundment: Licensing: Northern Ireland 415
Water: Agricultural nitrate pollution: Protection 289
Water: Charges: Exemptions & reductions: Scotland 395
Water: Environmental protection: Oil: Storage: Scotland 353, 393
Water: Services cost: Scotland. 394
Water: Services: Charges: Billing & collection: Scotland 395
Water: Water Environment (Controlled Activities) (Scotland) Regulations 2005: Notices in the interests of national security . 44, 59, 81, 290
Water: Water environment: Controlled activities: Relevant enactments: Scotland 353, 393
Water: Water environment: Controlled activities: Third party representations, etc.: Scotland 353, 393
Waveney, Lower Yare, & Lothingland Internal Drainage Board 119
Waverley (Borough): Electoral changes 121
Waverley Railway: Acts: Scotland. 340
Wealden: Parishes: Local government. 124
Wear Valley: Parishes: Local government. 124
Weighbridges: Rail: Automatic: Weights & measures 291
Weighing equipment: Automatic catchweighing instruments: Northern Ireland 445
Weighing equipment: Beltweighters: Northern Ireland 445
Weighing machines: Non-automatic: Northern Ireland 445
Weights & measures: Active electrical energy meters. 290
Weights & measures: Measuring instruments: Amendments 290
Weights & measures: Measuring instruments: Automatic catchweighers. 290
Weights & measures: Measuring instruments: Automatic discontinuous totalisers 290
Weights & measures: Measuring instruments: Automatic gravimetric filling instruments 290
Weights & measures: Measuring instruments: Automatic rail-weighbridges 291
Weights & measures: Measuring instruments: Beltweighers 291
Weights & measures: Measuring instruments: Capacity serving measures 291
Weights & measures: Measuring instruments: Cold-water meters 291
Weights & measures: Measuring instruments: Exhaust gas analysers. 291
Weights & measures: Measuring instruments: Gas meters 291
Weights & measures: Measuring instruments: Liquid fuel & lubricants 291
Weights & measures: Measuring instruments: Liquid fuel delivered from road tankers 291
Weights & measures: Measuring instruments: Material measures of length 292
Weights & measures: Measuring instruments: Non-prescribed instruments 292
Weights & measures: Measuring instruments: Taximeters 292
Weights & measures: Non-automatic weighing machines: Northern Ireland 445
Weights & measures: Packaged goods. 292
Weights & measures: Passing as fit for use for trade & adjustment: Fees: Northern Ireland 445
Weights & measures: Weighing equipment: Automatic catchweighing instruments: Northern Ireland 445
Weights & measures: Weighing equipment: Beltweighters: Northern Ireland 445
Welfare food. 89
Welfare food: Northern Ireland 445
Welsh Regional Flood Defence Committee: Composition 119
Welsh Statutory instruments: National Assembly for Wales: Annual volumes 12
West Coast Main Line: Stowe Hill: Network Rail: England 284, 285
West Dunbartonshire: Electoral arrangements: Scotland 363
West Kent: National Health Service & Social Care Partnership Trust 133
West Lothian: Electoral arrangements: Scotland 363
West Midlands Ambulance Service: National Health Service Trust 136
West Norfolk: Parishes: Local government 123

West Northamptonshire Development Corporation: Planning functions 287
West of Scotland Transport Partnership: Functions: Transfer: Strathclyde Passenger Transport Authority & Executive: Scotland . . . 392
West of Scotland Transport Partnership: Property rights & liabilities: Strathclyde Passenger Transport Authority & Executive: Scotland
. . . . 393
West Sussex Health & Social Care: National Health Service Trust 136
Western Health & Social Services Trust: Establishment: Northern Ireland. 420
Westminster Church of England Primary School: Religious character: Designation. 69
Widnes & Runcorn Sixth Form College: Dissolution. 69
Wild birds: Avian influenza *see* Avian influenza
Wiltshire (County): Kennet & North Wiltshire (Districts): Permitted & special parking areas 254
Wiltshire Ambulance Service: National Health Service Trust. 132
Wimbledon School of Art Higher Education Corporation: Dissolution 69
Wine & made-wine: Excise 83
Wine: Common Agricultural Policy: England & Northern Ireland. 14, 16
Wine: Common Agricultural Policy: Scotland 341
Wine: Common Agricultural Policy: Wales 17
Wireless telegraphy: Consolidation: Acts 9
Wireless telegraphy: Exemption 75
Wireless telegraphy: Guernsey. 28, 75, 292
Wireless telegraphy: Jersey 28, 75, 293
Wireless telegraphy: Licence award. 75, 76
Wireless telegraphy: Licence charges. 76
Wireless telegraphy: Licences: Number of: Limitation 76
Wireless telegraphy: Licensing procedures 76
Wireless telegraphy: Pre-consolidation amendments 76
Wireless telegraphy: Register 76
Wireless telegraphy: Spectrum access licences: Concurrent: Limitation 76
Wireless telegraphy: Spectrum access licences: Limitation of number. 76
Wireless telegraphy: Spectrum trading 76
Witham Third District Internal Drainage District 119
Wolverhampton (City): Permitted & special parking areas 254
Wood: Packaging material marking 153
Wood: Plant health: Northern Ireland 433
Work & Families Act 2006: Commencements 273, 278
Work & families: 2006 Order: Commencements: Northern Ireland. 414
Work & families: Maternity & parental leave: Northern Ireland 414
Work & families: Northern Ireland 144
Work & families: Paternity & adoption leave: Northern Ireland 414
Work & families: Statutory paternity & adoption pay: Northern Ireland 414
Work/life balance: Families: Employment: Acts. 9
Work/life balance: Families: Employment: Acts: Explanatory notes. 11
Workers' compensation: Pneumoconiosis etc.: Claims: Payment. 269
Workers' compensation: Pneumoconiosis etc.: Claims: Payment: Northern Ireland 439
Workers' compensation: Supplementation 273
Workers' compensation: Supplementation: Northern Ireland 443
Workers' Educational Association: Further education: Designated institutions 69
Work-focused interviews: Incapacity benefit. 270, 271
Working time. 279
Working time: Northern Ireland 414
Working time: Terms & conditions of employment 278
Wrecks: Protection: Designation: England 158

Y

Yorkshire Ambulance Service: National Health Service Trust 136
Young offender institutions: Prisons: Scotland. 370, 395
Young offender institutions: Scotland 370, 395
Young persons: Provisions relating to qualifying: Social security: Northern Ireland 442
Young persons: Social security 273
Youth & community work: Education & training: Inspection: Wales 73
Youth Justice & Criminal Evidence Act 1999: Application: Courts-martial 57
Youth Justice & Criminal Evidence Act 1999: Application: Courts-Martial Appeal Court 57
Youth Justice & Criminal Evidence Act 1999: Application: Standing civilian courts 57
Youth Justice & Criminal Evidence Act 1999: Commencements 57
Yugoslavia, Former: International tribunals: United Nations 287

Z

Zebra crossings: Northern Ireland 439
Zootechnical standards: Horses: England 19